The Rough Guide to

The Czech &
Slovak Republics

D0498994

There are more than one hundred and fifty Rough Guide titles
covering destinations from Amsterdam to Zimbabwe

Forthcoming titles include
Argentina • Croatia • Ecuador • Southeast Asia

Rough Guide Reference Series
Classical Music • Country Music • Drum 'n' Bass • English Football
European Football • House • The Internet • Jazz • Music USA • Opera
Reggae • Rock Music • Techno • Unexplained Phenomena • World Music

Rough Guide Phrasebooks
Czech • Dutch • Egyptian Arabic • European Languages • French • German
Greek • Hindi & Urdu • Hungarian • Indonesian • Italian • Japanese
Mandarin Chinese • Mexican Spanish • Polish • Portuguese • Russian
Spanish • Swahili • Thai • Turkish • Vietnamese

Rough Guides on the Internet
www.roughguides.com

ROUGH GUIDE CREDITS

Text editor: Sophie Martin
Series editor: Mark Ellingham
Editorial: Martin Dunford, Jonathan Buckley, Jo Mead, Kate Berens, Amanda Tomlin, Ann-Marie Shaw, Paul Gray, Helena Smith, Judith Bamber, Orla Duane, Olivia Eccleshall, Ruth Blackmore, Geoff Howard, Claire Saunders, Gavin Thomas, Alexander Mark Rogers, Polly Thomas, Joe Staines, Lisa Nellis, Andrew Tomičić, Claire Fogg, Richard Lim, Duncan Clark, Peter Buckley (UK); Andrew Rosenberg, Mary Beth Maioli, Don Bapst, Stephen Timblin (US)
Cartography: Melissa Baker, Maxine Repath, Nichola Goodliffe, Ed Wright

Production: Susanne Hillen, Andy Hilliard, Link Hall, Helen Ostick, Julia Bovis, Michelle Draycott, Katie Pringle, Robert Evers, Niamh Hatton, Mike Hancock
Picture research: Louise Boulton, Sharon Martins
Online editors: Kelly Cross (US)
Finance: John Fisher, Gary Singh, Edward Downey, Mark Hall, Tim Bill
Marketing & Publicity: Richard Trillo, Niki Smith, David Wearn, Jemima Broadbridge (UK); Jean-Marie Kelly, Myra Campolo, Simon Carloss (US)
Administration: Tania Hummel, Charlotte Marriott, Demelza Dallow

ACKNOWLEDGEMENTS

Big thanks go to Sophie for making the work enjoyable, to Gordon for coming on a lightning tour of the Czech Lands, to Tim for his enthusiasm, to Val for the biblio, and to Petr for a warm welcome. Thanks, too, to Kingston Presentation Graphics for cartography, David Price for proofreading and Link Hall for typesetting.

The Author

Rob Humphreys joined Rough Guides in 1989, having worked as a failed actor, taxi driver and male model. He has travelled extensively in central and eastern Europe, writing guides to Prague, the Czech and Slovak Republics, St Petersburg, and the Scottish Highlands and Islands, as well as London. He has lived in London since 1988.

Readers' letters

Thanks to the following people, whose letters and comments contributed to this edition: Dave Barber & Clare Pennock, Rev. & Mrs R. J. Blakeway-Phillips, Bob Cann, M. Chambers, Mark Foreman, Mr & Mrs E. T. Hancock, Alex Hetwer, Richard Johnson, Michael Leahy, Adrian Marsden, Dr & Mrs M. H. Milnes, Tom Kinsey, Norbert Kopco, Jill Lambert, Joseph Lawton, Geoff Piper, J. W. van Sandick, Alan Wilkins.

PUBLISHING INFORMATION

This fifth edition published May 2000 by Rough Guides Ltd, 62–70 Shorts Gardens, London, WC2H 9AB.
Distributed by the Penguin Group:
Penguin Books Ltd, 27 Wrights Lane, London W8 5TZ
Penguin Books USA Inc., 375 Hudson Street, New York 10014, USA
Penguin Books Australia Ltd, 487 Maroondah Highway, PO Box 257, Ringwood, Victoria 3134, Australia
Penguin Books Canada Ltd, 10 Alcorn Avenue, Toronto, Ontario, Canada M4V 1E4
Penguin Books (NZ) Ltd, 182–190 Wairau Road, Auckland 10, New Zealand
Typeset in Linotron Univers and Century Old Style to an original design by Andrew Oliver.
Printed in England by Clays Ltd, St Ives PLC
Illustrations in Part One and Part Three by Edward Briant.
Illustrations: p.1 by Tommy Yamaha & p.481 by Sally Davies
© Rob Humphreys 2000
No part of this book may be reproduced in any form without permission from the publisher except for the quotation of brief passages in reviews.
544pp – Includes index
A catalogue record for this book is available from the British Library
ISBN 1-85828-529-1

The publishers and authors have done their best to ensure the accuracy and currency of all the information in *The Rough Guide to the Czech and Slovak Republics*, however, they can accept no responsibility for any loss, injury, or inconvenience sustained by any traveller as a result of information or advice contained in the guide.

The Rough Guide to

The Czech & Slovak Republics

written and researched by

Rob Humphreys

with additional accounts by

Tim Nollen

ROUGH GUIDES

THE ROUGH GUIDES

TRAVEL GUIDES • PHRASEBOOKS • MUSIC AND REFERENCE GUIDES

 We set out to do something different when the first Rough Guide was published in 1982. Mark Ellingham, just out of university, was travelling in Greece. He brought along the popular guides of the day, but found they were all lacking in some way. They were either strong on ruins and museums but went on for pages without mentioning a beach or taverna. Or they were so conscious of the need to save money that they lost sight of Greece's cultural and historical significance. Also, none of the books told him anything about Greece's contemporary life – its politics, its culture, its people, and how they lived.

So with no job in prospect, Mark decided to write his own guidebook, one which aimed to provide practical information that was second to none, detailing the best beaches and the hottest clubs and restaurants, while also giving hard-hitting accounts of every sight, both famous and obscure, and providing up-to-the-minute information on contemporary culture. It was a guide that encouraged independent travellers to find the best of Greece, and was a great success, getting shortlisted for the Thomas Cook travel guide award,

and encouraging Mark, along with three friends, to expand the series.

The Rough Guide list grew rapidly and the letters flooded in, indicating a much broader readership than had been anticipated, but one which uniformly appreciated the Rough Guide mix of practical detail and humour, irreverence and enthusiasm. Things haven't changed. The same four friends who began the series are still the caretakers of the Rough Guide mission today: to provide the most reliable, up-to-date and entertaining information to independent-minded travellers of all ages, on all budgets.

We now publish more than 150 titles and have offices in London and New York. The travel guides are written and researched by a dedicated team of more than 100 authors, based in Britain, Europe, the USA and Australia. We have also created a unique series of phrasebooks to accompany the travel series, along with an acclaimed series of music guides, and a best-selling pocket guide to the Internet and World Wide Web. We also publish comprehensive travel information on our Web site:

www.roughguides.com

HELP US UPDATE

We've gone to a lot of effort to ensure that the fifth edition of *The Rough Guide to the Czech and Slovak Republics* is accurate and up to date. However, things change – places get "discovered", opening hours are notoriously fickle, restaurants and rooms raise prices or lower standards. If you feel we've got it wrong or left something out, we'd like to know, and if you can remember the address, the price, the time, the phone number, so much the better.

We'll credit all contributions, and send a copy of the next edition (or any other Rough Guide if you prefer) for the best letters. Please mark letters: "Rough Guide Czech and Slovak Republics Update" and send to:
Rough Guides, 62–70 Shorts Gardens, London WC2H 9AB, or Rough Guides, 375 Hudson St, New York NY 10014.
Or send email to: mail@roughguides.co.uk
Online updates about this book can be found on Rough Guides' Web site at www.roughguides.com

CONTENTS

- ## CHAPTER 9: THE MOUNTAIN REGIONS 406

- ## CHAPTER 10: EAST SLOVAKIA 447

PART FOUR CONTEXTS 481

LIST OF MAPS

MAP SYMBOLS

▬▬	Railway	⌒	Cave
▬▬	Motorway	▲	Peak
═══	Main road	✄	Battle site
──	Road	✗	Airport
▬▬	Pedestrianised road	Ⓜ	Underground station
┄┄┄	Passageway	🅿	Parking
----	Path	ⓘ	Tourist office
▥▥▥	Steps	⊠	Post office
─ ─ ─	Ferry route	☝	Swimming pool
──	Waterway	ⓒ	Telephone
▬ ▬ ▬	Chapter division boundary	▮	Building
▬·▬·▬	International borders	⊞	Church
♦	Points of interest	✡	Synagogue
⚠	Campsite	₊⁺₊	Christian Cemetery
♀	Public gardens	❖	Jewish Cemetery
♛	Castle	▒	Park
◣	Ruined castle		

INTRODUCTION

The **Czechs and Slovaks** have rarely been in full control of their historical destiny. The Nazis carved up their country in 1938, only twenty years after its foundation; the Iron Curtain descended just ten years later; and in 1968, Warsaw Pact tanks trampled on the country's dreams of "socialism with a human face". Even the break-up of the country was cooked up by the intransigent leaders of the two main political parties, and went ahead against the will of the majority of the population, and without even a proper referendum.

Yet the events of November 1989 – the **Velvet Revolution** – were probably the most unequivocally positive of all the anticommunist upheavals in Eastern Europe. True to their pacifist past, the Czechs and Slovaks shrugged off 41 years of Communist rule without so much as a shot being fired. In the parliamentary elections the following summer, the Communists were roundly defeated, and Václav Havel, a playwright of international renown with an impeccable record of resistance against the previous regime, was chosen as president. The euphoria and unity of those first few months evaporated more quickly than anyone could have imagined, and just three years after the revolution, against most people's predictions, the country split into two separate republics.

In contrast to the political upheavals that have plagued the region, the Czech and Slovak republics have suffered very little physical damage over the last few centuries. Gothic castles and Baroque chateaux have been preserved in abundance, town after town in Bohemia and Moravia has retained its old medieval quarter, and even the wooden architecture of Slovakia has survived beyond all expectations. Geographically speaking, the two republics are the most diverse of all the former Eastern Bloc states. Together they span the full range of central European cultures, from the old German towns of the west to the Hungarian and Rusyn villages in East Slovakia. In physical terms, too, there's enormous variety: Bohemia's rolling hills, lush and relentless, couldn't be more different from the flat Danube basin, or the granite alpine peaks of the High Tatras, the beech forests of the far east, or the coal basins of the Moravian north.

More accessible today than at any time since the 1930s, the major **cities** are now buzzing with a cultural and commercial diversity, and fail to conform to most people's idea of Eastern Europe. At the same time, the remoter regions are more reminiscent of the early twentieth century than the twenty-first. Prague has withstood a whole decade of Western-style tourism, and now has the facilities to cope. In the remoter regions, however, facilities are only slowly being upgraded. Inevitably, the continuing **pace of change** in both republics means that certain sections of this book are going to be out of date even as you read them, such is the volatility and speed of the current transformation.

The break-up of Czechoslovakia

The sharpest division in the country before 1989 was between Party member and non-Party member; nowadays, the most acute problems are between **ethnic groups** – Czech and Slovak, Slovak and Hungarian, Slav and Romany. The Czechs who inhabit the western provinces of Bohemia and Moravia are among the most Westernized Slavs in Europe: urbane, agnostic, liberal and traditionally quite well-off. By contrast, the Slovaks are, for the most part, more devoutly Catholic and socially conservative. Though their peasant way of life is slowly dying out, the traditional, agrarian codes of conduct remain embedded in the Slovak culture.

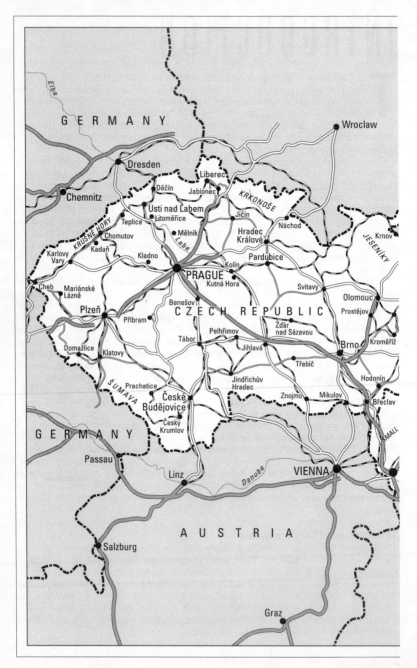

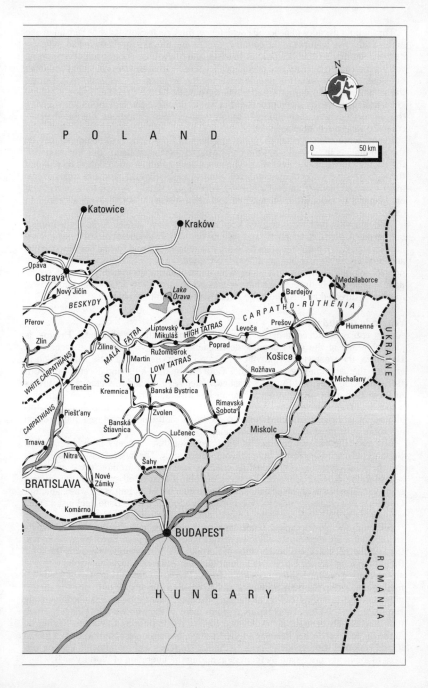

Throughout decades of peaceful coexistence, the Czech–Slovak divide remained one of the distinctive features of the country: Czechs and Slovaks rarely mixed socially, visited one another's republics only as tourists, and knew little about each other's ways, relying instead on hearsay and prejudice. Yet despite this, and the constant rumblings of discontent in Slovakia, few people predicted the break-up of Czechoslovakia. During the summer of 1992, numerous attempts were made by the Czech and Slovak federal governments to reach a compromise that would preserve the federation while giving the Slovaks a degree of autonomy to satisfy their national aspirations, but for whatever reasons, no agreement emerged.

Events were soon overtaken by the elections of June 1992. A sweeping victory by the nationalists in Slovakia and the right wing in the Czech Lands quickly propelled the country towards disintegration. The new Czech administration, intent on pushing through free-market economic policies inimical to the Slovaks, and a Slovak government that had pledged to declare Slovak sovereignty, finally agreed to disagree, and on January 1, 1993, after 74 years of turbulent history, Czechoslovakia ceased to exist.

To begin with, both sides seemed keen to help preserve at least some of the numerous personal, political, economic and cultural ties of the old federation. In the end, very little has survived: both countries have separate currencies and formal border controls, and dual citizenship is not permitted. Predictions of a post-Yugoslav scenario have proved unfounded, though the issue of Slovakia's Hungarian minority remains potentially volatile, and both republics have witnessed an upsurge in nationalism and racism, much of it directed against the large Romany population they share.

Where to go and when

Almost entirely untouched by the wars of this century, the Czech capital, **Prague**, is justifiably one of the most popular destinations in Europe. Poised at the centre of **Bohemia**, the westernmost province, Prague is also the perfect base from which to explore the surrounding countryside. Both the gentle hills and forests of **South Bohemia**, one of central Europe's least-populated regions, and the famous **spa towns of West Bohemia** – Karlovy Vary, Mariánské Lázně and Františkovy Lázně – are only a couple of hours' drive from Prague. Pine-covered **mountains** form Bohemia's natural borders, and the weird **sandstone "rock cities"** in the north and east of the region are some of its most memorable landscapes.

Moravia, the eastern province of the Czech Republic, is every bit as beautiful as Bohemia, though the crowds here thin out significantly. The largest city, **Brno**, has its own peculiar pleasures – not least its interwar functionalist architecture – and gives access to the popular Moravian karst region, plus a host of other nearby castles and chateaux. The north of the province is often written off as an industrial wasteland, but **Olomouc** is a charming city, more immediately appealing than Brno, and just a short step away from the region's highest mountains, the **Jeseníky** and **Beskydy**.

Although the Slovak capital, **Bratislava**, can't compare with Prague, it does have its virtues, not least its compact old town and its position on one of Europe's great rivers, the Danube. Slovakia also boasts some of Europe's highest mountains outside the Alps: these have long formed barriers to industrialization and modernization, preserving and strengthening regional differences in the face of Prague's centralizing efforts. Medieval mining towns like **Banská Štiavnica** and **Kremnica** still smack of their German origins, and the cathedral capital of the east, **Košice**, was for centuries predominantly Hungarian. In the **Orava** and **Liptov** regions, many of the wooden-built villages, which have traditionally been the focus of Slovak life, survive to this day. **Carpatho-Ruthenia**, in the far east bordering Poland and the Ukraine, has a timeless, impoverished feel to it, and is dotted with wooden Greek Orthodox churches and monuments bearing witness to the heavy price paid by the region during the liberation of World War II.

In general, the **climate** is continental, with short, hot summers and bitterly cold winters. Spring and autumn are often both pleasantly warm and miserably wet, all in the same week. Winter can be a good time to come to Prague: the city looks beautiful under snow and there are fewer tourists to compete with. Other parts of the country have little to offer during winter (aside from skiing), and most sights stay firmly closed between November and March.

Taking all this into account, the **best months to come** are May, June and September, thereby avoiding the congestion that plagues the major cities and resorts in July and August. Prague in particular suffers from crowds all year round, though steering clear of this high season will make a big difference. In other areas, you may find yourself the only visitor whatever time of year you choose to go, such is the continuing isolation of the former Eastern Bloc countries' nether regions.

AVERAGE TEMPERATURES (°C)											
	Jan	Feb	March	April	May	June	July	Aug	Sept	Oct	Nov	Dec
Prague	-1	0	4	9	14	17	19	18	14	9	4	0
Brno	-2	-1	3	8	13	16	18	17	14	8	3	-1
Bratislava	-1	0	5	10	15	18	20	19	16	10	4	0
Banská Štiavnica	-3	-2	2	7	12	15	18	17	13	8	2	-1
Košice	-3	-2	3	9	14	17	19	18	14	9	3	-1

Note that these are **average daily temperatures**. At midday in summer, Bratislava can be blisteringly hot. Equally, in most mountainous regions it can get extremely cold and wet at any time of the year.

PART ONE

THE

BASICS

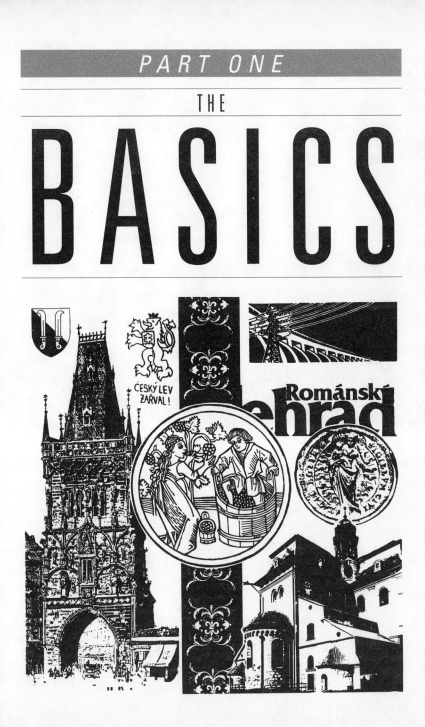

GETTING THERE FROM BRITAIN AND IRELAND

By far the most convenient way to get to either the Czech or the Slovak republic is by plane. It takes just under two hours to reach Prague (compared with around 19 hours by train), and there are at least four direct flights from London daily throughout the year. There are no direct flights from Britain to Bratislava, but Vienna airport is only a brief bus journey from the Slovak capital (or from Brno, the Moravian capital for that matter), and daily flights take just over two hours.

BY PLANE

Both British Airways (BA) and Czech Airlines (ČSA) run two daily **scheduled flights** from London Heathrow to **Prague**. British Airways fly from Terminal 1, while ČSA fly out of Terminal 2, and less frequently from Stansted. BA's low-cost airline, Go, also fly daily from Stansted, while British Midland fly daily out of Heathrow (Terminal 1). Currently, ČSA run the only direct service from Manchester.

Both Austrian Airlines and British Airways run three or more daily scheduled flights from London to **Vienna**. Austrian Airlines flies out of Heathrow, while British Airways flies from Heathrow and Gatwick. Lauda Air flies four times a week from Gatwick (North Terminal); it's also the only carrier flying directly from Manchester to Vienna. Buzz, KLM's cut-price airline, flies up to three times daily from Stansted to Vienna.

Go and Buzz tend to offer the cheapest fares, although you'll have to book well in advance to

get their very lowest fares of £100 return (including tax). You've more chance of catching one of their £130 return fares, and, for a fully flexible ticket, you're looking at £260 return. Low-cost airlines are deliberately no frills: they don't tend to give out free meals and drinks, though you can buy sandwiches and coffee on board, or pay extra beforehand.

The other airlines can't really compete with Go and Buzz on price, but they have been in the business longer. Their budget tickets usually require you to stay at least one Saturday night, and don't allow for change or cancellation. However, to get the cheapest fares, you usually have to fly out midweek, as well. Booking tickets direct through the airlines themselves is rarely the cheapest option, though prices are usually fairly competitive: from as little as £160 return from London (£200 from Manchester). Fares vary according to season – they tend to be highest from April to October and in the two weeks around Christmas – though some kind of economy fare is usually available all year round. Be sure to enquire whether the fare you are being quoted includes tax (currently around £20–25 per person).

Discounted flights to Prague and Vienna feature in most of the "bucket shop" adverts of the various London freebie magazines, *Time Out*, *The Evening Standard* and the quality Sunday papers.

USEFUL INTERNET SITES FOR TRAVELLERS

British Foreign and Commonwealth Office
www.fco.gov.uk
Constantly updated advice for travellers on circumstances affecting your safety in over 130 countries.

UK Meteorological Office
www.met-office.gov.uk
Weather forecasts and links to other sites.

Online Tourist Information
www.travel.yahoo.com incorporates a lot of Rough Guide material in its coverage of destination countries and cities across the world, with information about places to eat and sleep etc.

AIRLINES IN BRITAIN

Austrian Airlines ☎020/7434 7350
British Airways ☎0345/222111;
www.british-airways.com
British Midland ☎0870/607 0555;
www.britishmidland.com
Buzz ☎0870/240 7070; *www.buzzaway.com*

Czech Airlines (ČSA)
London ☎0207/255 1898
Manchester ☎0161/489 0241
www.csa.cz
Go ☎0845/605 4321; *www.go-fly.com*
Lauda Air ☎020/7630 5924; *www.laudaair.com*

AGENTS AND OPERATORS IN BRITAIN

Bohemian Promotions, 61 Mere Rd, Erdington, Birmingham B23 7LL (☎0121/373 9107). Offers a full range of accommodation in Prague, Bohemia and parts of Moravia.

Bridgewater Travel, P.O Box 2333, Kidderminster DY14 0YT (☎01299/271717; *www.bridgewater-travel.co.uk*). Accommodation and package deals to Bohemia.

ČEDOK, 4th Floor, 53–54 Haymarket, London SW1 (☎0207/378 6009). Former state-owned tourist board offering flights, accommodation and package deals.

Czech & Slovak Tourist Centre, 16 Frognal Parade, Finchley Rd, London NW3 (☎0207/794 3263; *www.czech-slovak-tourist.co.uk*). Information, accommodation, bus tickets, flights and lots more for both republics.

Czech Travel Ltd, Trinity House, 1 Trinity Square, South Woodham Ferrers, Essex CM3 5JX (☎01245/328647; *www.czechtravel.freeuk.com*).

Rooms and flats for rent all over the Czech and Slovak republics.

Czechbook Agency, Jopes Mill, Trebrownbridge, Near Liskeard, Cornwall PL14 3PX (☎01503/240629). Cheap private and self-catering accommodation all over the Czech and Slovak republics.

Czechdays, 89 Valence Road, Lewes BN7 1SJ (☎01273/474738). Cheap rooms in Prague suburbs; self-catering apartments in Bohemia and Slovakia.

Czechscene, 1 Thon Lea, Evesham, Worcestershire WR11 6TN (☎01386/442782). B&B and self-catering flats available in Prague and Bohemia.

Explore Worldwide, 1 Frederick St, Aldershot, Hants GU11 1LQ (☎01252/760 000; *www.explore.co.uk*). Tailor-made trips for wildlife and wilderness enthusiasts.

Return fares to Prague can be bought for as little as £130, occasionally even less to Vienna. You might also try specialist agents, such as Campus Travel or STA (see box above for details), or one of the following Web sites: *www.cheapflights.co.uk*, *www.lastminute.co.uk*, or Bob Geldof's *www.deckchair.com*. Note, however, that in peak season discount flights are often booked up weeks in advance. For Prague, it might also be worth considering flying to a neighbouring European city like Berlin or Leipzig, for which return fares can be as little as £100 – again, you'll find the cheapest fares in the sources quoted above.

PACKAGE DEALS

Several tour operators offer simple flight-and-accommodation **package deals** to the Czech and Slovak republics, which, for a short trip, can often be better value than travelling independently. Most of the companies listed below will put together some kind of package for you. Package tour operators like Travelscene offer a two-night city break including flights and accommodation for around £300. Even with these packages, there's no compulsion to go on any organized tours once you're there. If you're flying with Go, you can claim a discount if you book your accommodation through Hotel Connect. Similar deals crop up from time to time so it's worth enquiring; a list of the main agents can be found in the box above.

FLIGHTS FROM IRELAND

There are **no direct flights** from anywhere in Ireland to Prague, Bratislava or Vienna. The

Hotel Connect, Berkeley House, 18–24 High Street, Edgware HA8 7RP (☎0208/731 5005; *www.hotelconnect.co.uk*).

Martin Randall Travel, 10 Barley Mow Passage, London W4 4PH (☎0208/742 3355). Pricey, specialist cultural guided tours of the Czech Republic.

New Millennium, Greville Court, 1665 High Street, Solihull, West Midlands B93 0LL (☎01564/770750). Cheap packages to the Czech Republic.

North South Travel, Moulsham Mill Centre, Parkway, Chelmsford, Essex CM2 7PX (☎01245/492882). Friendly, competitive travel agency offering discounted fares worldwide – profits are used to support projects in the developing world.

STA Travel, *www.statravel.co.uk*
86 Old Brompton Rd, London SW7 3LH
117 Euston Rd, London NW1 2SX
38 Store St, London WC1E 7BZ
(all ☎0207/361 6161)
25 Queen's Rd, Bristol BS8 1QE (☎0117/929 3399)
38 Sidney St, Cambridge CB2 3HX (☎01223/366966)
27 Forest Rd, Edinburgh (☎0131/226 7747)
88 Vicar Lane, Leeds LS1 7JH (☎0113/244 9212)
75 Deansgate, Manchester M3 2BW (☎0161/834 0668)
36 George St, Oxford OX1 2OJ (☎01865/792800).

Independent travel and discount flight specialists; offices also in Aberdeen, Glasgow, Liverpool, Newcastle, and on university campuses in Birmingham, Bristol, Canterbury, Cardiff, Coventry, Durham, Glasgow, Leeds, London, Loughborough, Nottingham, Sheffield and Warwick.

Travelscene, 11–15 St Ann's Rd, Harrow, Middlesex HA1 (☎0208/427 4445; *www.travelscene.co.uk*). Two-night breaks and upwards in Prague.

USIT Campus Travel, *www.campustravel.co.uk*
52 Grosvenor Gardens, London SW1W 0AG (☎0207/730 3402).
541 Bristol Rd, Selly Oak, Birmingham B29 6AU (☎0121/414 1848).
61 Ditchling Rd, Brighton BN1 4SD (☎01273/570226).
39 Queen's Rd, Clifton, Bristol BS8 1QE (☎0117/929 2494).
5 Emmanuel St, Cambridge CB1 1NE (☎01223/324283).
53 Forest Rd, Edinburgh EH1 2QP (☎0131/668 3303)
166 Deansgate, Manchester M3 3FE (☎0161/833 2046).
105–106 St Aldates, Oxford OX1 1DD (☎01865/242067).
Student/youth travel specialists; branches also in YHA shops and universities around Britain.

cheapest way of getting there is usually to fly to London, then pick up a connecting flight or package from there (see above). Discount travel agents, such as USIT, may be able to organize both flights. As usual, the cheapest tickets are only available if you make sure you stay away over a Saturday night, and fly midweek (Mon–Thurs).

Most airlines can offer budget return tickets **from Dublin** to London from IR£60 and under. Ryanair fly to Gatwick, Stansted and Luton from Dublin (as well as Cork, Derry, Kerry and Knock) and tend to be the cheapest – their best deals are on flights into Stansted – although Aer Lingus, who fly out of Dublin, Shannon and Cork into Heathrow and from Dublin into Stansted, offer similar budget fares, as do British Airways, who

fly into Gatwick from Dublin, and CityJet, who fly from Dublin to London City Airport.

Flying **from Belfast**, however, your best bet is British Midland, who fly into Heathrow from Belfast International for around £70 return; BA cover the same route, but are usually a little more expensive. It's also worth checking with Jersey European, who fly from Belfast City airport to Gatwick and Stansted, and can usually match – and often undercut – the prices of their competitors.

All the above prices are for economy tickets, which are usually non-changeable, non-refundable, and assume you're prepared to travel midweek and stay over a Saturday night. Note that **airport tax** out of Dublin is IR£5, and can be as much as a further IR£20 into London.

AIRLINES IN IRELAND

Aer Lingus Dublin ☎01/705 3333;
www.aerlingus.ie

British Airways
Belfast ☎0345/222111
Dublin ☎01800/626747
www.british-airways.com

British Midland Belfast ☎0870/607 0555;
www.iflybritishmidland.com

CityJet Dublin ☎01/844 5566; *www.cityjet.com*

Jersey European Belfast ☎0990/676676;
www.jersey-european.co.uk

Ryanair Dublin ☎01/677 4422; *www.ryanair.com*

AGENTS AND OPERATORS IN IRELAND

Aran Travel, Granary House, 58 Dominick St,
Galway (☎091/562595; *arantvl@iol.com*).

Joe Walsh Tours
34 Grafton St, Dublin 2 (☎01/671 8751).
69 Upper O'Connell St, Dublin 2 (☎01/676 3053)
8–11 Baggot St, Dublin 2 (☎01/676 8915)
117 St Patrick St, Cork ☎021/277959)
General budget fares agent.

Student & Group Travel
1st Floor, 71 Dame St, Dublin 2 (☎01/677 7834).
Student and group specialists.

Thomas Cook
www.tch.thomascook.com
11 Donegal Place, Belfast (☎01232/242341).
118 Grafton St, Dublin (☎01/677 1721).
Package holiday and flight agent with occasional
discount offers.

Trailfinders
4–5 Dawson St, Dublin 2 (☎01/677 7888;
www.trailfinders.com). General discount agent.

USIT
www.usitcampus.com
Fountain Centre, College St, Belfast BT1
(☎01849/324073).
10–11 Market Parade, Patrick Street, Cork
(☎021/270900).
33 Ferryquay St, Derry (☎01504/371888).
Aston Quay, Dublin 2 (☎01/602 1600).
Victoria Place, Eyre Square, Galway
(☎091/565177).
Central Buildings, O'Connell St, Waterford
☎051/872601.
Student/youth specialists for flights and trains.

BY TRAIN

Thanks to the Eurostar service through the Channel Tunnel, you can travel from London to Prague in around nineteen hours by **train**. The train journey from London to Bratislava takes just over twenty hours if you go via Vienna; five or six hours longer if you go via Prague.

THE ROUTES

The quickest way to get from London to Prague by train is on the **Eurostar via Brussels**. By catching the train at around noon from London Waterloo International, you arrive at Brussels Midi with around forty minutes to change onto the Brussels–Cologne service. From Cologne, there's an overnight service to Prague, which gets into the Czech capital just after 8am the following morning. If you're heading straight for Bratislava, there's a direct overnight service from Brussels to Vienna. Arriving at Vienna's Westbahnhof, you must make your way to the

city's Südbahnhof and catch one of the four daily trains to Bratislava.

Travelling to Prague with **Eurostar via Paris** is more expensive and more hassle. For a start, you have to cross Paris, and, as there is no direct overnight service to Prague, either stay the night in Paris and catch the daytime train, or change at Frankfurt in order to join up with the overnight service.

Travelling **via the ferry to Ostend** is more difficult to organize than it used to be, as it can only be booked separately through Hoverspeed. Trains leave London Charing Cross, and use the Dover to Ostend crossing; the journey taking roughly eight hours. The return fare from London to Brussels is £49 for a five-day return, or £65 for a ticket valid for one year.

Although you can simply crash out on the seats on the overnight service from Cologne to Prague or from Brussels to Vienna, you won't get much sleep as the border guards and ticket inspectors wake you up at regular intervals. To travel in more comfort, it makes sense to book a **couchette** which costs around £10 one-way in a six-berth compartment, rising to £13.50 in a four-berth compartment. Couchettes are mixed sex and allow little privacy; for a bit more comfort, you can book a bed in a single sex two-berth **sleeper** for around £35 one-way. However you decide to sleep on the Cologne to Prague service, you'll be woken up anyway in the early hours of the morning when the train crosses the Czech border.

TICKETS AND PASSES

Fares for continental rail travel are much more flexible than they used to be, so it's worth shopping around for the best deal rather than taking the first offer you get. The cheapest deals for a return ticket London–Prague or London–Vienna tend to hover around £200 return. To qualify for the most heavily discounted fares, however, there are usually various restrictions: you may have to stay over a Saturday night, and your ticket may well be non-exchangeable and non-refundable. If you're travelling with one or more companions, you may well be eligible for a further discount, which can bring the fare down as low as £160 return. You should also be able to get through-ticketing, including the tube journey to Waterloo International, from mainline train stations in Britain, when you buy your ticket.

Those under 26 can purchase a discounted **BIJ** ticket, available from Rail Europe, USIT Campus or Wasteels, thus saving around £30 on the return fare. USIT Campus also offers a range of **Eurotrain Explorer** passes, which allow unlimited travel within the Czech Republic (£16 for seven consecutive days, or for five days in a month). Travellers over 60 can get a thirty-percent discount on rail travel between, but not within, European countries by purchasing a **RES Card** (Rail Europe Senior Card) at a cost of £5. However, before you can buy this card, you must already possess a British Senior Card (£18); both are valid for a year.

Eurotrain also offers a range of **Explorer** tickets, which allow you to go and come back a different route: for example, the "Eastern Explorer", currently £256, covers London–Amsterdam–Hanover–Berlin–Prague–Budapest–Vienna–Salzburg–Basel–Luxembourg–Brussels–London. These are valid for two months, and you can stop off freely at each place.

If you're planning to visit the Czech and Slovak republics as part of a more extensive trip round Europe, it may be worth purchasing an **InterRail pass**, which gives you unlimited rail travel within certain countries; you must, however, have been resident in Europe for at least six months. InterRail tickets are currently zonal: to travel to the Czech & Slovak republics and back, you'll

---

TRAIN, BUS AND CROSS-CHANNEL INFORMATION

TRAIN INFORMATION

European Rail
☎0207/387 0444

Eurostar
☎0990/186186; *www.eurostar.com*

USIT Campus
☎0207/730 3402; *www.campustravel.co.uk*

German Railways
☎0207/317 0919; *www.bahn.de*

Rail Europe
☎0990/848848; *www.sncf.fr*

Wasteels
☎0207/834 7066; *www.wasteels.dk*

BUS INFORMATION

Capital Express
☎0207/243 0488;
www.capitalexpress.demon.co.uk

Eurolines
☎0990/808080; *www.eurolines.co.uk*

Kingscourt Express
☎0208/673 7500; *www.kce.cz*

CROSS-CHANNEL INFORMATION

Eurotunnel
☎0990/353535; *www.eurotunnel.com*
Folkstone–Calais through the tunnel.

Hoverspeed
☎0990/240241; *www.hoverspeed.co.uk*
Dover–Calais, Folkstone–Boulogne and Dover–Ostend.

P&O Stena Line
☎0870/600 0600; *www.posl.com*
Dover–Calais

need at least a three-zone pass, costing £229 for one month for those under 26, and £309 a month for those aged 26 and over. Passes are not valid in the UK, though you're entitled to discounts in Britain and on Eurostar and cross-Channel ferries. Either way, though, you're only really going to get your money back if you do a lot of travelling. For the latest information, visit British Rail's **home page** at *www.britrail.com*.

BY BUS

The cheapest way to get to Prague, Brno or Bratislava is by **bus**. There are direct services from London's Victoria Station more or less daily throughout the year, all of which take around 24 hours to reach Prague's main bus terminal, Florenc. Some bus companies continue their journeys via Brno and Bratislava, though it's easy enough to use domestic services, too. Prices between companies vary only slightly, so it's hardly worth ringing round to find the best deal; a return ticket currently costs around £80 return for those under 26, around £90 for those over 26. Addresses and telephone numbers for all current operators are in the box above.

The journey is long but just about bearable – make sure you bring along enough to eat, drink and read, and a small amount of Belgian and German currency for coffee and any spending en route. There are stops for around half an hour every four hours or so, and the routine is broken by the Channel crossing (included in the cost of the ticket).

For those keen on bus travel, and intent on visiting other parts of Europe, there's a **Eurolines Pass**, allowing free travel between 48 cities (including London and Prague) in 21 countries. Between June and September, the month-long pass costs £199 for under-26s, and £229 for those aged 26 and over; the rest of the year, the passes cost £159 and £199 respectively. A two-month-long pass is also available.

BY CAR – THE FERRIES AND THE TUNNEL

Driving to the Czech or the Slovak republic is not the most relaxing option – even if you're into driving virtually non-stop, it'll take between fifteen and twenty hours or, with an overnight stop, the best part of two days – but with two or more passengers it can work out relatively inexpensive. The quickest way of taking your car over to the conti-

nent is to drive to the **Channel Tunnel** near Folkstone, where Eurotunnel operates a 24-hour service carrying cars, motorcycles, buses and their passengers to Calais. At peak times, services run every fifteen minutes, making advance bookings for the 35-minute journey unnecessary. However, if you simply turn up unannounced, you'll have to pay from £169 return per carload, whereas if you give fixed dates for your travel, you can bring the price down to between £80 and £110 return.

The alternative cross-Channel options for most travellers are the conventional **ferry**, **catamaran** or **hovercraft** links between Dover and Calais or Ostend, Folkstone and Calais or Boulogne. Fares vary enormously with the time of year, month and even day that you travel, and the size of your car. If you book in advance, the cheapest standard fare on the Dover–Calais run, for example, can be as little as £100 return per carload.

The most direct route from northern France to Prague is via Brussels, Liège (Luik), Cologne (Köln), Frankfurt, Würzburg and Nuremberg (Nürnberg), entering the Czech Republic at the **Waidhaus–Rozvadov** border crossing. Another possibility is to head east from Cologne through Hessen via Erfurt and Chemnitz, and enter at the **Reitzenhain–Pohraniční** border crossing. If you're heading straight for Slovakia, continue along the autobahns from Nuremberg (Nürnberg) in a southeasterly direction via Regensburg, Passau, Linz and Vienna, entering Slovakia at the Berg–Bratislava border crossing. Note that if you want to travel on any motorway within Austria, Slovakia or the Czech Republic, you'll need to buy the relevant **tax disc** in each of those countries, available from all border crossings and most post offices and petrol stations.

INSURANCE

Though not compulsory, **travel insurance**, including medical cover, is a good idea. Check before shelling out, however, that you are not already covered: many credit cards (particularly American Express) often have certain levels of medical or other insurance included, especially if you use them to pay for your trip; in addition, if you have a good "all risks" home insurance policy it may well cover your possessions against loss or theft even when overseas, and many private medical schemes also cover you while abroad.

Most travel agents and tour operators will offer you travel insurance – those policies offered by Campus Travel or STA in the UK, and USIT in

Ireland, are usually reasonable value. If you feel the cover is inadequate, or you want to compare prices, any insurance broker, bank or specialist travel insurance company should be able to help: try Columbus Travel Insurance (☎0207/375 0011; *www.columbusdirect.co.uk*). Two weeks' cover for a trip to Prague should cost around £20 in both

Britain and Ireland. If you do have to pay for any medical treatment or drugs when abroad, keep the receipts for claiming on your insurance once you're home. If you have anything stolen (including money) register the loss immediately with the local police – without their report you won't be able to claim.

GETTING THERE FROM THE US AND CANADA

The quickest and easiest way to reach Prague from the US or Canada is **to fly**. Czech Airlines (ČSA) offers one of the most convenient options, with direct flights from New York, Chicago, Toronto and Montreal. In addition, the major carriers offer dozens of one- and two-stop flights from any number of North American gateways via major European cities. However, peak season flights from North America to Prague are still comparatively expensive, so it may be worth your while flying to Munich, Berlin or Leipzig and making your way overland from there. If you plan on travelling overland, it is worth noting that Eurail passes are not valid in the Czech Republic. While the Europe East Railpass includes the Czech Republic, along with Austria, Hungary and Slovakia, at $205 for five days' travel its cost-effectiveness is debatable. The New York–Prague **flying time** is about eight and a half hours. Toronto–Prague is around ten hours.

SHOPPING FOR TICKETS

Outside of frequent special offers, the cheapest of the airlines' published fares is usually an **Apex** ticket, although this will carry certain restrictions:

you have to book – and pay – at least 21 days before departure (and in some cases 90 days), spend at least seven days abroad (maximum stay three months), and you tend to get penalized if you change your schedule. On transatlantic routes, there are also winter **Super Apex** tickets, sometimes known as "Eurosavers" – slightly cheaper than an ordinary Apex, but limiting your stay to between 7 and 21 days. Some airlines also issue **Special Apex** tickets to people younger than 24, often extending the maximum stay to a year. Many airlines offer youth or student fares to **under 26s**; a passport or driving licence is sufficient proof of age, though these tickets are subject to availability and can have eccentric booking conditions.

You can normally cut costs further by going through a **specialist flight agent** – either a **consolidator**, who buys up blocks of tickets from the airlines and sells them at a discount, or a **discount agent**, who in addition to dealing with discounted flights may also offer special student and youth fares and a range of other travel-related services such as travel insurance, rail passes, car rentals, tours and the like. Bear in mind, though, that penalties for changing your plans can be stiff. Some agents specialize in **charter flights**, which may be cheaper than anything available on a scheduled flight, but again departure dates are fixed and withdrawal penalties are high (check the refund policy). If you travel a lot, **discount travel clubs** are another option – the annual membership fee may be worth it for benefits such as cut-price air tickets and car rental.

Don't automatically assume that tickets purchased through a travel specialist will be cheapest – once you get a quote, check with the airlines and you may turn up an even better deal. Be advised also that the pool of travel companies is swimming with sharks – exercise caution and never deal with a company that demands

AIRLINES IN THE US AND CANADA

Air Canada
US ☎1-800/776-3000, Canada ☎1-800/555-1212
for local toll-free number; *www.aircanada.ca*

Air France
US ☎1-800/237-2747, Canada ☎1-800/667-2747;
www.airfrance.fr

American
US ☎1-800/433-7300; *www.aa.com*

Austrian Airlines
US ☎1-800/843-0002; *www.austrianair.com*

British Airways
US ☎1-800/247-9297, Canada ☎1-800/668-1059;
www.british-airways.com

CSA Czech Airlines
US ☎1-212-765-6022 or 1-800/223-2365, Canada
☎1-800/555-1212; *www.csa.cz*

Delta
US ☎1-800/241-4141, Canada ☎1-800/ 555-
1212; *www.delta-air.com*

Finnair
US ☎1-800/950-5000; *www.finnair.com*

KLM
US ☎1-800/777-5553, Canada ☎1-800/361-5073;
www.klm.com or *www.nwa.com*

Lufthansa
US ☎1-800/645-3880, Canada ☎1-800/563-5954;
www.lufhansa.com

SAS
US & Canada ☎1-800/221-2350; *www.sas.se*

Swissair
US ☎1-800/221-4750, Canada ☎1-800/267-9477;
www.swissair.com

United
US ☎1-800/538-2929; *www.ual.com*

DISCOUNT AGENTS, CONSOLIDATORS AND TRAVEL CLUBS

Airhitch
2641 Broadway, 3rd Fl #100, New York NY 10025
(☎800/326-2009; *www.airhitch.org*). Stand-by
tickets at reduced prices; offices in the US and
Europe.

Council Travel
205 E 42nd St, New York, NY 10017 (☎212/822-
2700 or 1-800/226-8624; *www.counciltravel.
com*). Nationwide US organization, with
branches in many US cities. Specializes in student travel.

Encore Travel Club
4501 Forbes Blvd, Lanham, MD 20706
(☎1-800/444-9800). Discount travel club.

Interworld
800 Douglass Rd, Miami, FL 33134 (☎305/443-
4929 or 1-800/468-3796). Consolidator.

Moment's Notice
7301 New Utrecht Ave, Brooklyn, NY 11204
(☎718/234-6295 or 212/486-0500;
www.moments-notice.com). Discount travel club.

New Frontiers/Nouvelles Frontières
12 E 33rd St, New York, NY 10016 (☎212/779-
0600 or 1-800/366-6387;
www.newfrontiers.com); 1001 Sherbrook East,
Suite 720, Montreal, PQ H2L 1L3 (☎514/526-
8444). Discount travel firm, with other branches
in LA, San Francisco and Quebec City.

STA Travel
10 Downing St, New York, NY 10014 (☎212/627-
3111 or 1-800/777-0112; *www.sta-travel.com*).
Worldwide specialists in independent travel,
with branches in many US cities.

Travac
989 6th Ave, New York, NY 10018 (☎1-800/872-
8800). Consolidator and charter broker; has
another office in Orlando.

Travel Avenue
10 S Riverside, Suite 1404, Chicago, IL 60606
(☎1-800/333-3335; *www.travel-avenue.com*).
Discount travel agent.

Travel Cuts
187 College St, Toronto, ON M5T 1P7 (☎416/979-
2406 or 1-800/667-2887; ☎1-888/238-2887 from
US; *www.travelcuts.com*). Canadian student travel organization, with branches across the country.

Travelers Advantage
3033 S Parker Rd, Suite 900, Aurora, CO 80014
(☎1-800/548-1116). Discount travel club.

Unitravel
11737 Administration Blvd, Ste 120, St Louis, MO
63146 (☎1-800/325-2222; *www.unitravel.com*).
Consolidator.

Worldwide Discount Travel Club
1674 Meridian Ave, Miami Beach, FL 33139
(☎305/534-2082). Discount travel club.

cash up front or refuses to accept payment by credit card.

Regardless of where you buy your ticket, **fares** will depend on the season, and are highest from around mid-June to the end of August, plus a two-week spell up to Christmas, and lowest from November through mid-December, and late December to the end of March; the rest of the year, shoulder fares operate. Note also that the ticket prices quoted below are for midweek travel. Weekend flights cost around $50 extra. All prices are round-trip, exclusive of taxes and subject to availability and change.

FLIGHTS FROM THE US

ČSA is the only airline flying **nonstop** from the US **to Prague**, departing daily from New York and Chicago in the summer and on certain days the rest of the year (check with the airline as their flight days are variable). Various airlines offer **flights to Prague** from US hub cities, with stops in European hubs: Air France (via Paris), Delta (via Frankfurt or Vienna), Finnair (via Helsinki) Lufthansa (via Frankfurt), SAS (via Copenhagen) and KLM (via Amsterdam). Barring sales, which can drop fares by as much as thirty percent, **Apex fares** are pretty much identical whichever airline you choose, with rates from New York starting at around $600 (low season), $1000 (high); from Chicago add on about $100 and from LA $250. However, as airlines often run special limited offers, it's definitely worth shopping around. Also, since direct flights to Prague are usually more expensive than flights to other European cities, it may pay to fly to another country and continue overland from there. Another possible option would be an "open-jaw" fare. These provide more flexibility, enabling you to fly into one city and out of another. Again, Lufthansa is currently offering a limited special fare from New York into Berlin, then out of Prague two weeks later, for around $430 (low season).

Independent travel agencies such as Council Travel, STA and Nouvelles Frontières can often undercut the Apex fares on major carriers like British Airways or Air France, and they are especially useful if you are a full-time student or under 26. Student fares often allow you to stop over en route for little or no extra charge, something you can't do on an Apex ticket. For real bargain basement tickets, try the discount agents, discount travel clubs or seat consolidators, where you may be able to track down non-student, low season, round-trip fares to Prague

for as little as $370 (from New York), $460 (from Chicago) or $600 from LA. Note, however, that these tickets are basically impossible to change once you've paid for them, so be sure about your dates and ask about the routeing of the flight – many involve lengthy stopovers and multiple changes of plane. Finally, hype aside, the **Internet** has become a valuable shopping tool, allowing travellers to compare rates and bid on tickets, the risk being that it is often unclear who exactly you're dealing with; travellers should bear in mind that Internet commerce remains a somewhat risky, unregulated frontier.

If you're visiting Prague as part of a more extensive tour of Europe, it may be worth considering buying a **Eurail Pass**, though travellers should bear in mind that these are not valid in the Czech Republic. The all-country pass, which you must purchase before you leave for Europe, allows unlimited free travel on the railways of seventeen European countries. The **Eurail Youthpass** (for under-26s) costs US$365 for fifteen days, $587 for one month or $832 for two months; if you're 26 or over you'll have to buy a first-class pass, available in fifteen-day ($522), 21-day ($678), one-month ($838), two-month ($1188) and three-month ($1468) increments.

You stand a better chance of getting your money's worth out of a **Eurail Flexipass**, which is good for a certain number of travel days in a two-month period. This, too, comes in under-26/first-class versions: ten days, $431/$616; fifteen days, $568/$812. If you're travelling in a group of two or more, you might also want to consider the **Eurail Saverpass**. This costs $444 for fifteen consecutive days, $576 for 21; $712 for a month; $1010 for two months or $1248 for three. There's also a **Flexi Saverpass** at $524 for ten days or $690 for fifteen.

Another possibility is the **European East pass**, valid for travel in Hungary, Austria, Poland, Slovakia and the Czech Republic. Any five days in one month costs $195; and you can add on a maximum of five extra days for $21 per day. Finally, there's a **Czech Flexipass** which is valid for travel within the Czech Republic for five days out of fifteen and costs around $69.

FLIGHTS FROM CANADA

ČSA is the only airline flying nonstop from **Canada to Prague**, departing daily from Montreal and Toronto in the summer and two (variable) days the rest of the year. The lowest scheduled Apex fares from either city are around CDN$1050 (low season)

SPECIALIST AGENTS

American-International Homestays, Inc, PO Box 1754, Nederland, CO 80466 (☎303/642-3088 or 1-800/876-2048). Accommodation with English-speaking families.

Backroads, 801 Cedar St, Berkeley, CA 94710 (☎1-800/462-2848; *www.backroads.com*). Hiking/canoeing/rafting tours starting and finishing in Prague.

Central Europe Holidays, 10 E 40th St, suite 3601 New York, NY 10016 (☎1-800/800-8879, *ceheurope@aol.com*). Tour packages to Prague.

Czech & Slovak Travel Service, 7033 Sunset Blvd, Suite 210, Los Angeles, CA 90028 (☎213/389-2157). Travel agent specializing in Central/Eastern Europe.

Delta Vacations, 53 Summer St, Keene, NH 03431 (☎1-800/872-7786; *www.deltavacations.com*). City breaks to Prague.

Eastern Europe Tours, 600 Stewart St, Suite 524, Seattle, WA 98101 (☎1-800/641-3456). Customized tours to the Czech

Republic, with a "Chateaux, Museums and Spas" set package.

Europe Train Tours, 198 E Boston Post Rd, Mararoneck, NY 10543 (☎1-800/551-2085). Customized tours by rail, with special rates on Swiss Air.

Fugazy International, 770 US-1, North Brunswick, NJ 08902 (☎1-800/828-4488; *www.fugazy.com*). Customized tours and agents for package deals.

La Boheme, 875 N Michigan Ave, Suite 3530, Chicago, IL 60611 (☎312/440-0866 or 1-888/LA BOHEME, *info@la-boheme.com*). Customized tours in the Czech Republic and Central Europe.

Summit International Travel, 789 Springfield Ave, Summit, NJ 07901 (☎1-800/527-8664). Highly regarded specialists in the area. Walking, bicycling and car packages plus customized tours.

Tradesco, 6033 Century Blvd, Suite 670, Los Angeles, CA 90045 (☎1-800/833-3402). Wide variety of packages.

---

or CDN$1500 (high). Outside Montreal, your best bet is Lufthansa, which flies more or less daily from several major Canadian airports (sometimes in conjunction with Air Canada) to Prague via Frankfurt. Fares from Vancouver start at around CDN$1350 (low season) or CDN$1800 (high).

For discounted flights, check out Travel Cuts or Nouvelles Frontières where you may be able to find non-student, low season, round-trip fares to Prague for as little as CDN$729 (from Toronto) or CDN$988 (from Vancouver).

PACKAGE TOURS

Since the situation regarding tourism is still very changeable, along with everything else in the former Eastern bloc, **travel agencies specializing in Eastern Europe**, such as the Czech & Slovak Travel Service, are good sources of up-to-date information, as well as being the best way to find out about any other cheap flight deals. Unfortunately, ČEDOK, the old state tourist monopoly, which once offered the broadest range of all-inclusive tours, no longer has an office in North America, although with US–Czech/Slovak tourism on the rise, they are rumoured to be considering returning. (Currently, an entirely different, American, company operates, from the same

address, under the name ČEDOK.) A list of specialist travel agents is given in the box above.

TRAVEL INSURANCE

Before buying an **insurance policy**, check that you're not already covered. Some homeowners'

TRAVEL INSURANCE SUPPLIERS

Access America ☎1-800/284-8300; *www.accessamerica.com*

Carefree Travel Insurance ☎1-800/323-3149

Council Travel ☎1-800/226-8624; *www.counciltravel.com*

Desjardins Travel Insurance (Canada only) ☎1-800/463-7830

STA Travel ☎1-800/781-4040; *www.sta-travel.com*

Travel Guard ☎1-800/826-1300; *www.travel-guard.com*

Travel Insurance Services ☎1-800/937-1387; *www.travelinsure.com*

Worldwide Assistance ☎1-800/821-2828; *www.worldwideassistance.com*

or renters' policies are valid on vacation, and credit cards such as American Express often include some medical insurance, while most Canadians' provincial health plans typically provide limited overseas medical coverage. If you're not covered or you want to take additional precautions, you might want to contact a specialist travel insurance company; see the box below or ask your travel agent for a recommendation.

The cheapest coverage is currently with STA Travel, whose comprehensive policy for fifteen days in the Czech Republic starts at $55. Rates for a month start at $115.

Note that most North American travel policies apply only to items lost, stolen or damaged while in the custody of an identifiable, responsible third party – hotel porter, airline, luggage consignment, etc. Even in these cases, it will be necessary for you to contact the local police within a certain time limit to have a complete report made out so that your insurer can process the claim.

GETTING THERE FROM AUSTRALIA & NEW ZEALAND

Although there are no direct **flights** to Prague from Australia or New Zealand, several mid-priced airlines, such as Czech Airlines (ČSA), Alitalia, Olympic Airways, Lufthansa and KLM (often in conjunction with Qantas/Air New Zealand), can get you there via Asia or Europe for around A$1760/NZ$2199. And as travelling time between Australasia and the Czech Republic can be twenty hours plus, the chance of a stopover and a good night's sleep can be a positive bonus.

Another alternative is to get a cheap flight to another European city and complete your journey by road or rail. Major carriers such as Qantas and

AIRLINES IN AUSTRALIA AND NEW ZEALAND

Aeroflot Australia ☎02/9262 2233. No NZ office.

Air New Zealand Australia ☎13 2476, New Zealand ☎09/366 2424 or 0800/737 000.

Airtours/Britannia Australia ☎02/9247 4833. No NZ office.

Alitalia Australia ☎1300/653 747, New Zealand ☎09/379 4455.

Ansett Australia Australia ☎13 1414, New Zealand ☎09/9652 9665.

British Airways Australia ☎02/8904 8800, New Zealand ☎09/356 8690.

Czech Airlines Australia ☎02/9247 6196. No NZ office.

Garuda Australia ☎1300/365 330, New Zealand ☎09/366 1855.

Gulf Air Australia ☎02/9244 2199, New Zealand ☎09/9244 2199.

Japan Airlines Australia ☎02/9272 1111, New Zealand ☎09/379 9906.

KLM Australia ☎02/9231 6333 or 1800/505 747. No NZ office.

Korean Airlines Australia ☎02/9262 6000, New Zealand ☎09/307 3687.

Lufthansa Australia ☎02/9367 3888, New Zealand ☎09/303 1529.

Malaysia Airlines Australia ☎13 2627, New Zealand ☎09/373 2741.

Olympic Airlines Australia ☎02/9251 2044. No NZ office.

Qantas Australia ☎13 1313, New Zealand ☎09/357 8900 or 0800/808 767.

Swissair Australia ☎02/9232 1744, New Zealand ☎09/358 3925.

Thai Airways Australia ☎1300/651 960, New Zealand ☎09/377 3886.

AGENTS AND OPERATORS IN AUSTRALIA AND NEW ZEALAND

Anywhere Travel, 345 Anzac Parade, Kingsford, Sydney (☎02/9663 0411; anywhere@ozemail.com.au).

Budget Travel, 16 Fort St, Auckland, plus branches around the city (☎09/366 0061or 0-800/808 040).

Destinations Unlimited, 3 Milford Rd, Auckland (☎09/373 4033).

Flight Centres 82 Elizabeth St, Sydney, plus branches nationwide (☎13 1600); 205 Queen St, Auckland (☎09/309 6171), plus branches nationwide; www.flightcentre.com.au.

Status Travel, 22 Cavenagh St, Darwin (☎08/8941 1843).

STA Travel, 702 Harris St, Ultimo, Sydney, plus branches nationwide. Nearest branch ☎13 1776, fastfare telesales ☎1-300/360 960; 10 High St, Auckland ☎09/309 0458, fastfare telesales ☎09/366 6673, and other offices countrywide; www.statravel.com.au; email:traveller@statravelaus.com.au

Student Uni Travel, 92 Pitt St, Sydney (☎02/9232 8444), plus branches in Brisbane, Cairns, Darwin, Melbourne and Perth.

Thomas Cook, 175 Pitt St, Sydney, plus branches in other state capitals (local branch ☎13 1771, Thomas Cook Direct telesales ☎1-800/063 913); New Zealand: 159 Queen St, Auckland (☎09/359 5200; www.thomascook.com.au).

Trailfinders, 8 Spring St, Sydney (☎02/9247 7666); 80 Clarence St, Sydney (☎02/9290 1500); www.travel.com.au; email consultant@travel.com.au

Usit Beyond, corner of Shortland St and Jean Batten Place, Auckland (☎09/379 4224), plus branches in Christchurch, Hamilton, Palmerston North and Wellington; www.usitbeyond.co.nz

SPECIALIST OPERATORS

Australians Studying Abroad, 1/970 High St, Armadale, Melbourne (☎03/9509 1955 or 1800/645 755). Art and cultural tours drawing on the significance of the Habsburg cities of Budapest, Prague and Vienna.

Contal Travel, 40 Roma St, Brisbane (☎07/3236 2929). Prague accommodation, car rental and day tours.

Eastern Europe Travel Bureau, 75 King St, Sydney (☎02/9262 1144), and branches in Melbourne, Adelaide, Perth and Brisbane. Packages to Prague.

Eastern Eurotours, Level 9, Seabank, 12-14 Marine Parade, Southport, QLD 4215 (☎07/5591 0326 or 1-800 242 353). City and spa town coach tours.

Eurolynx, 3/20 Fort St, Auckland (☎09/379 9716). Sightseeing tours to Prague.

Gateway Travel, 48 The Boulevarde, Strathfield, Sydney (☎02/9745 3333). Accommodation and tours.

British Airways include free return trips to Prague and stopovers en route on their London service, with fares from A$1900–2500/NZ$2475–2775. Cheaper operators include Garuda, Gulf, Japan, Korean and Malaysia airlines, with extra stopovers in Bali/Jakarta, Abu Dhabi, Tokyo, Seoul or Kuala Lumpur respectively, from around A$1350/NZ$2275. Cheapest of the lot are the Airtours/Britannia charter flights to London during their limited charter season from November to March, when you can pick up a fare for A$1100–1760/NZ$1620–2110.

Round the World (RTW) fares, valid for up to a year, are another good option, especially from New Zealand, where airlines offer fewer incentives to fly with them. Qantas, British Airways,

Global Explorer and One World fares, starting at A$2400/NZ$3000, are probably the most versatile, taking in four continents, including Europe (with stops in Prague or Bratislava). The Star Alliance fare (from A$2699/NZ$3299) incorporating Air New Zealand, Ansett, Air Canada, Varig, Thai, United and SAS also includes stops in Europe on a mileage basis.

Fares vary according to the season, loosely defined as high (mid-May to end-Aug & Dec to mid-Jan), shoulder (March to mid-May & Sept) and low (rest of year), with a A$/NZ$500–600 difference between high- and low-season prices.

Tickets purchased direct from the airlines tend to be expensive; you'll get much better deals, as well as the latest information on limited specials and packages from your local travel agent. Some of the best fares are through discount agents like Flight Centres and STA (for students and under-26s), who can also advise on visa regulations. Seat availability on most international flights out of Australia and New Zealand is often limited, so it's best to book at least three weeks ahead.

FLIGHTS FROM AUSTRALIA

Flights from eastern cities are common rated (they all cost the same), so if you're travelling from Perth or Darwin deduct A$200–400.

The nearest to a direct flight to Prague is with Czech Airlines in conjunction with Qantas via Bangkok/Singapore for around A$1760 low season, to A$2100 high season. For a little more (A$1900–2200), Ansett/SAS get there via Copenhagen and Singapore. Additional flights to Prague only are with Olympic Airways via Athens and Lufthansa via Frankfurt starting around A$1700, while KLM's fares via Amsterdam start at A$1650.

FLIGHTS FROM NEW ZEALAND

There are even fewer options from New Zealand, and all involve a combination of airlines that take you via Asia or the US to a European hub city, and thence to Prague. The best deal is with Qantas to Los Angeles, Singapore or Bangkok, where you connect with Alitalia via Rome; and with Air New

Zealand/United Airlines via LA and New York, both for around NZ$2199 in low season and NZ$2899 in high.

Most flights leave from Auckland, so you'll need to add on around NZ$100–300 for Christchurch and Wellington connections.

TRAVEL INSURANCE

Travel insurance is put together by the airlines and specialist groups such as those listed above, in conjunction with insurance companies. Policies are broadly comparable in premium and coverage, though Ready Plan usually give the best value for money. A typical policy for the Czech Republic costs A$110/NZ$140 for two weeks, and A$190/NZ$240 for one month.

TRAVEL INSURANCE COMPANIES IN AUSTRALIA AND NEW ZEALAND

AFTA ☎02/9956 4800

Cover More ☎02/9202 8000 in Sydney; elsewhere ☎1800/251881; New Zealand ☎09/377 5958 or ☎0800/657 744

Ready Plan Australia ☎03/9791 5077 in Melbourne; elsewhere ☎1300/555 017; New Zealand ☎09/300 5333

UTAG ☎02/9744 7833 in Sydney; elsewhere ☎1800/809 462

RED TAPE AND VISAS

British, Irish, US, Canadian and all EU nationals need only a full passport to enter the Czech Republic. New Zealanders need a visa to enter

Slovakia, and at the time of writing Australian citizens need a visa for each of the republics (valid for thirty days and costing $30 for each country), which can be obtained from the relevant embassy/consulate. If you go in person, the process should take no more than three days, or you can apply by post up to six months in advance. Note that entry requirements do change, sometimes at very short notice, so if in doubt, check with your nearest embassy or consulate before you leave, or look on the Czech and Slovak foreign ministry Web sites (*www.czech.cz* or *www.foreign.gov.sk*).

Most nationals are allowed to stay for up to thirty days in either republic, though some nationalities are granted longer stays – check before you leave if you need to know exactly. Those entering on a visa must register with the police within three days of arrival, and if you're staying

CZECH EMBASSIES AND CONSULATES

Australia, 169 Military Rd, Dover Heights, Sydney, NSW 2030 (☎02/9371 0860).

Austria, Penzingerstrasse 11–13, 1140 Vienna (☎0222/894 1200).

Belgium, 555 rue Engeland, 1180 Bruxelles-Uccle (☎02/374 1203).

Canada, 541 Sussex Drive, Ottawa, Ontario K1N 6Z6 (☎613/562 3875); 1305 Avenue des Pins Ouest, Montreal, Quebec H3G 1B2 (☎514/849-4495).

France, 15 avenue Charles Floquet, 75343 Paris (☎44 14 51 20).

Germany, Wilhelmstrasse 44, 10117 Berlin (☎030/226 380).

Ireland, 57 Northumberland Road, Ballsbridge, Dublin 4 (☎01/668 1135).

New Zealand 48 Hair St, Wainviomata Wellington (☎44/564 6001).

UK, 28 Kensington Palace Gdns, London W8 4QY (☎020/7243 1115; Visa hotline ☎0891/171267).

USA, 3900 Spring of Freedom St, NW, Washington DC 20008 (☎202/274 9100); 1109 Madison Ave, New York, NY 10028 (☎212/535-8814); 10990 Wilshire Blvd, Suite 1100, Los Angeles, CA (☎310/473-0889).

SLOVAK EMBASSIES AND CONSULATES

Australia, 47 Culgoa Circuit, O'Malley, Canberra, ACT 2606 (☎06/290 1516).

Austria, Armbrustergasse 24,1190 Vienna (☎0222/318 9055).

Belgium, 195 ave Molière,1050 Bruxelles (☎02/346 4045).

Canada, 50 Rideau Terrace, Ottawa, Ontario K1M 2A1 (☎613/749 4442).

France, 125 rue du Ranelagh, 75016 Paris (☎44 14 56 00).

Germany, Leipzigerstrasse 36, 10117 Berlin (☎030/204 4538).

Ireland, 20 Clyde Rd, Ballsbridge, Dublin 4 (☎01/660 0012).

New Zealand, 48 Hair St, Wainuiomata, Wellington (☎44/564 6001).

UK, 25 Kensington Palace Gardens, London W8 4QY (☎020/7243 0803).

USA, 2201 Wisconsin Ave NW, Suite 250, Washington DC 20007 (☎202/965 5160).

for over a month, you must register with the police before the month is out. If you're staying in a hotel, all this will be done for you. If you need a **visa extension**, you should apply for an extension at the Foreigners' Police headquarters in Prague or Bratislava (addresses are given in the directories of those cities).

Customs allowances into the Czech and Slovak republics are 250 cigarettes or 50 cigars, one litre of spirits and two litres of wine. Allowances when taking goods from either repub-

lic into EU countries are the same. However, these allowances may change in the future, so if in doubt, check with customs before you leave.

Both republics have recently introduced laws allowing border guards to ask visitors to prove they have sufficient funds for their visit. It has to be said that these restrictions are primarily aimed at visitors from the east, but it's as well to be aware of this. The easiest way around the problem is to carry a credit card or at least £20/$32 a day for either republic in travellers' cheques or cash.

COSTS, MONEY AND BUSINESS HOURS

In general terms, the Czech & Slovak republics are still incredibly cheap for Westerners, with the exception of accommodation, which is comparable with many EU countries. That said, price differentiation across the country is now quite marked: costs in the centre of Prague (and, to a lesser extent, Bratislava) creep ever upwards, while in some parts of the countryside, they remain much more static.

At the bottom end of the scale, if you stay in a hostel and stick to pubs and takeaways, you could get by on as little as £10/$16 a day. If you stay in private accommodation or cheapish hotels, and eat in slightly fancier restaurants, then you could easily spend £25/$40 a day. To put things in perspective, however, it's worth bearing in mind that the average monthly salary for Czechs is currently around 6500Kč (£125/$200), and less than that for Slovaks. Most of your daily allowance will go on **accommodation**, with even the cheapest places charging around £10/$16 a night. All other

basic costs, like food, drink and transport, remain very cheap indeed.

Tipping is normal practice in cafés, bars, restaurants and taxis, though this is usually done by simply rounding up the total. For example, if the waiter tots up the bill and asks you for 74 crowns, you should hand him a 100-crown note and say "take 80 crowns".

CURRENCY

The Czech Republic and the Slovak Republic use separate currencies, both known as the crown. The Czech crown is now fully convertible, so it's possible to buy some currency and bring it with you; the Slovak crown is not fully convertible, which theoretically means you can't buy any currency until you arrive in the country.

The currency in the Czech Republic is the **Czech crown** or *koruna česká* (abbreviated to Kč), which is divided into one hundred relatively worthless heller or *halíře* (abbreviated to h). Notes come in 20Kč, 50Kč, 100Kč, 200Kč, 500Kč, 1000Kč (less frequently 2000Kč and 5000Kč) denominations; coins as 1Kč, 2Kč, 5Kč, 10Kč, 20Kč and 50Kč, plus 10h, 20h and 50h. At the time of going to press there were around 60Kč to the pound sterling and around 35Kč to the US dollar. The crown's value is likely to fall further in the future as the political and economic stability of the country is looking uncertain.

The currency in Slovakia is the **Slovak crown** or *Slovenská koruna* (abbreviated to Sk), which is divided into 100 heller or *halér* (abbreviated to h). Coins come in the denominations 1Sk, 2Sk, 5Sk, 10Sk, 20Sk and 50Sk, plus 10h, 20h, 50h; notes in 20Sk, 50Sk, 100Sk, 200Sk, 500Sk and 1000Sk.

The Slovak crown is not yet fully convertible, but is tied to the dollar and Deutschmark, with the **exchange rate** hovering at around 60Sk to the pound sterling and 35Sk to the US dollar. It's still technically illegal to import or export more than a small amount of Slovak currency, though if you keep your exchange receipts, you can convert any surplus crowns back into Western currency, for a small commission, of course. It's best not to buy any Slovak crowns while in the Czech Republic as Czech banks tend to give a much poorer exchange rate than you'll get in Slovakia itself.

TRAVELLERS' CHEQUES AND CREDIT CARDS

Travellers' cheques are the safest and easiest way to carry money. American Express and Thomas Cook are the most widely used – available for a small commission (usually one percent of the amount ordered) from any bank and some building societies, whether or not you have an account, and from branches of American Express and Thomas Cook. The cheques can be exchanged commission-free at their respective branches.

Even if you have travellers' cheques, it's a good idea to take a **credit card** with a PIN as well. You can pay with plastic (Visa, Master Card/Access and Amex are the most acceptable) in most upmarket hotels, restaurants and shops, though it's not as widely used as in the UK or the US. You can also withdraw cash from the automatic teller machines (ATMs) or cashpoints, which are now a feature of most Czech and Slovak towns and cities. It's also a good idea to keep at least some hard currency in **cash** for emergencies, as it will be accepted almost anywhere.

CHANGING MONEY

Most Czech and Slovak **banks** should be prepared to change travellers' cheques, accept Eurocheques and give cash advances on credit cards – look for the window marked *směnárna/zmenáreň*. Commissions at banks are fairly rea-

For details of accommodation, eating and transport in the Czech Republic, see p.32, p.36 and p.28; for Slovakia, see pp.359, 362 and 357.

sonable, but the queues and the bureaucracy can mean a long wait. Quicker, but more of a rip-off in terms of commission (six percent is the norm), are the exchange outlets that crop up here and there in the bigger towns.

Banking hours are Monday to Friday 8am to 5pm, often with a break at lunchtime. Outside these times you may find the odd bank open, but will otherwise have to rely on the exchange outlets and international hotels. The 24-hour exchange desk at Prague airport arrivals, run by *Československá obchodní banka*, is, somewhat surprisingly, an excellent place to change money, regularly charging a mere one- or two-percent commission.

CASH EMERGENCIES

When you buy your travellers' cheques, make a note of the emergency phone number given. On your trip keep a record of all cheques and note which ones you spend – and report any loss or theft immediately. All being well, you should get the missing cheques reissued within a couple of days. Things can get trickier if you lose your credit card: your bank should be able to give you details of the number to call if this happens, but you won't be provided with a replacement card until you get home.

Assuming you know someone who is prepared to send you the money, the quickest and easiest way to have funds sent out to you in an emergency is to do it through **Western Union**, who will wire the money to you in a couple of hours (some banks will also do this via Western Union); get your sponsor to phone ☎0800/833833 in the UK or ☎1-800/325-6000 in North America.

BUSINESS HOURS

Business hours in both republics are generally Monday to Friday 9am to 5pm, though most supermarkets and tourist shops work longer hours. Smaller shops usually close for lunch for an hour sometime between noon and 2pm. Those shops that open on Saturday are generally shut by noon or 1pm, and very few open on Sunday. The majority of pubs and restaurants outside the big cities tend to close between 10pm and 11pm, with food often unavailable after 9pm.

Western Union has numerous branches across both republics: phone ☎02/24 22 85 18 in the Czech Republic to find out the nearest agent; phone ☎07/63 83 07 90 in Slovakia; or visit their Web site (*www.westernunion.com*).

If you have a few days' leeway, you can simply get your bank to wire your money to a Czech bank, a process that shouldn't take more than a couple of working days. If you can last out the week, then an **international money order**, exchangeable at any post office, is by far the cheapest way of sending money. If you're in really dire straits, get in touch with your **consulate** in Prague, who will usually let you make one phone call home free of charge, and will – in worst cases only – repatriate you, but will never, under any circumstances, lend you money.

HEALTH MATTERS

No inoculations are required for the Czech and Slovak republics, and on a short visit you're unlikely to fall victim to anything worse than an upset stomach. However, with both countries blighted by decades of ecological abuse, there is well-founded concern about the quality of the water, milk, meat and vegetables. If you have respiratory problems, avoid Prague, North Bohemia and the industrial regions of North Moravia during the winter months, when sulphur dioxide levels regularly breach World Health Organization safety levels.

Reciprocal arrangements between the Czech and Slovak republics and most EU countries (including Britain and Ireland) mean that you're entitled to free emergency medical care, with a charge only for imported drugs and certain specialized treatments. Citizens of other countries should have their own health insurance, and even EU residents would be well advised to take out their own health policy, as the reciprocal agreement only covers emergency treatment and not a visit to a doctor.

> Further details of **travel insurance** for citizens of the UK and Ireland, the USA and Canada, and Australia and New Zealand appear on pp.8, 12, and 15 respectively.

If you should fall ill, it's easiest to go to a **pharmacy** (*lékárna* in Czech, *lekáreň* in Slovak). Pharmacists are willing to give advice (though language may be a problem) and able to dispense many drugs available only on prescription in other Western countries. They usually keep normal business hours, but at least one in each major town will be open 24 hours for minor emergencies. If it's an emergency, dial ☎155 for an ambulance and you'll be taken to the nearest hospital.

HEALTH INFORMATION AND WEB SITES

The **Department of Health** publishes a free publication *Health Advice for Travellers*, a comprehensive booklet available at the post office (or by calling the Health Literature Line on ☎0800/555777). The content of the booklet, which contains immunization advice, is constantly updated on pages 460–464 of CEEFAX (or you can consult it on *www.open.gov.uk/*)

The **Yahoo! Health Web site** gives information about specific diseases and conditions, drugs and herbal remedies, as well as advice from health experts: *http://health.yahoo.com*

The newly launched **UK Health Net** (*www.ukhealthnet.co.uk/travel/*) outlines health risks in most countries, though for more detailed info a travel clinic is better.

INFORMATION AND MAPS

The collapse of communism and the demise of the ČEDOK state tourist board left the Czech and Slovak national tourist infrastructures in tatters. **Czech Centres** have now been established across the globe in major capital cities and should be able to answer any queries (addresses are given below). The Slovaks have yet to establish tourist board offices abroad, and any enquiries should be addressed to the embassies and consulates listed on p.16. In the UK, folk are directed to the **Czech & Slovak Tourist Centre** (see p.4), while there's a Slovak Information Center at 406E 67th St, NY 10021 (☎212-737 3971).

CZECH TOURIST OFFICES

Once in the Czech Republic, you'll find most large towns and cities now have a **tourist office**, usually known as an *informační centrum*, specifically designed to assist visitors. Most will hand out (or

---

CZECH TOURIST OFFICES

Austria, Herrengasse 17, 1010 Vienna (☎535 2361; *ccwien@czech.cz*).

Belgium, Boulevard Leopold II Laan 262, 1080 Brussels (☎02/644 9527; *ccbrussels@czech.cz*).

Germany, Karl Liebknecht Str. 3, 10178 Berlin (☎030/204 47 70; *ccberlin@czech.cz*).

Slovakia, nám. SNP 12, 812 34 Bratislava (☎07/381 4188; *ccbratislava@czech.cz*).

UK, 95 Great Portland St, London W1 5RA (☎0207/291 9925; *cclondon.czech.cz*).

USA, 1109 Madison Ave, New York, NY 10028 (☎212/288 0830; *nycenter@pop.ne*).

USEFUL WEB SITES

Central Europe On-Line *www.centraleurope.cz*
News and information on the countries of the former Eastern Bloc, including the Czech Republic, with lots of links to other Czech sites.

Do města/Downtown *www.downtown.cz*
Prague's useful fortnightly listings leaflet online in English and Czech.

High Tatras *www.tatry.sk*
An interesting guide to the High Tatras, with plenty of info, travel and accommodation details, and particularly good for walkers, climbers and skiers.

Prague Post *www.praguepost.cz*
A very useful site, not just for getting the latest news, but also for finding out what's on in Prague over the coming week.

Radio Prague *www.radio.cz*
An informative site well worth visiting, with updated news and weather as audio or text.

Spectacular Slovakia *www.travel.sk*
An online travel guide of the country (in English), outlining the major sights, written by Slovak Spectator journalists.

Slovak Spectator *www.slovakspectator.sk*
Online version of the Bratislava based English-language weekly, with news, sport, weather and listings.

Ticketpro *www.ticketpro.cz*
Prague's largest ticket agency is online so you can book concert tickets ahead.

Welcome to the Czech Republic
www.czech.cz
Basic information on the country in English, and on the worldwide network of Czech Centres, run by the Czech Foreign Ministry.

sell for a small fee) basic maps and pamphlets on local sights. They may also be able to assist with finding accommodation, but don't rely on this. Hours vary and are detailed in the text. In those places where there is no information centre, your best bet is probably to try the reception at the nearest large hotel. In Prague itself, simply go to one of the branches of the **PIS** (*Pražská informační služba*), whose staff can book accommodation and theatre and concert tickets, and answer most questions.

SLOVAK TOURIST OFFICES

The **BIS** (*Bratislavská informačná služba*) in Bratislava is a tourist office specifically set up to give information to foreign visitors, selling maps, booking accommodation and helping with general enquiries. Most large towns and cities in Slovakia have followed suit, and now have their own tourist office, or centre for *informácie*. In the High Tatras, for instance, the PIA (*Popradská informačná agentúra*) fulfils much the same role. Otherwise, your best bet for local information and help with accommodation is probably the reception of the nearest hotel.

MAPS

For touring purposes, the best **road map** of the Czech and Slovak republics is the 1:200,000 *Autoatlas* produced by Geocenter, or the 1:300,000 *Euroatlas* published by RV Verlag. For more detailed coverage, there's a 1:100,000 *Autoatlas* of the Czech Republic produced jointly by Geodézie and Freytag & Berndt, and one to the same scale produced by VKU for Slovakia. There's also a series of 1:100,000 **regional maps**, which cover both republics, published by Kartografie Praha for the Czech Republic and Slovenská kartografia for Slovakia, and featuring multilingual legends. These are suitable for cyclists and walkers since they mark all the colour-coded paths which criss-cross the countryside. For more serious walkers, there is also the series of 1:50,000 *turistická mapa* produced by VKU. Town maps should be adequate for sightseeing purposes, but if you crave more detail, local **town plans** (*plán města* or *orientačná mapa*), showing bus, tram and trolleybus routes, should be available from most bookshops and some hotels. Most of these have been redrawn with all the new post-communist street names marked on them – if you're in any doubt, however, check the copyright date and beware of anything pre-1993.

To get hold of one of the above maps of Prague in the UK, try Stanfords, 12–14 Long Acre, London WC2 (☎0171/836 1321; *sales@stanfords.co.uk*). In the US, Rand McNally should be able to help (call ☎1-800/333-0136 ext 2111 for the location of their nearest store and for direct-mail details). In Australasia, Mapland, 372 Little Bourke St, Melbourne (☎03/9670 4383), the Travel Bookshop, Shop 3, 175 Liverpool St, Sydney (☎02/9261 8200) and Worldwide Maps and Guides, 187 George St, Brisbane (☎07/3221 4330), are worth contacting, as are Speciality Maps, 58 Albert St, Auckland (☎09/307 2217). Otherwise, you can wait until you get to either country, where you'll get more choice and it'll cost you a lot less.

ADDRESSES AND TOWN NAMES

The street name is always written before the number in **addresses**. The word for street (*ulice/ulica*) is either abbreviated to *ul.* or simply missed out altogether – Celetná ulice, for instance, is commonly known as Celetná. Other terms often abbreviated are *náměstí/námestie* (square), *třída/trieda* (avenue), and *nábřeží/nábrežie* (embankment), which become *nám.*, *tř.*/*tr* and *nábř*/*nábr* respectively.

Bear in mind when using a Czech or Slovak **index** that "Ch" is considered a separate letter and comes after H in the alphabet. Similarly, "Č", "Ď", "Ľ", "Ř", "Š" and "Ž" are all listed separately, immediately after their non-accented cousins.

Many towns and villages in the Czech and Slovak republics were once (or still are) inhabited by **German** (or **Hungarian**) minorities. In these places we have given the German (or Hungarian) name in brackets after the Czech or Slovak, for example Mariánské Lázně (Marienbad).

TROUBLE AND THE POLICE

Despite their change of name to *Policie* (in Czech) and *Polícia* (in Slovak), the national police are still extremely unpopular. Public confidence in their competence has suffered a severe blow due to the dramatic rise in the level of crime since 1989. However, you shouldn't be unduly paranoid: the crime rate is still very low compared with most European or North American cities.

The **national police**, who wear navy blue, grey and white in the Czech Republic, and khaki-green with red lapels in Slovakia, are under the control of their respective ministries of interior. However, if you do need the police – and above all if you're reporting a serious crime – you should always go to the **municipal police**, run by the local authorities and known as *Městská policie* (in Czech) and *Mestská polícia* (in Slovak); their uniforms differ from region to region.

In addition, there are various **private police forces**, employed mostly by hotels and banks, who dress in black – hence their nickname *Černí šerifové* (Black Sheriffs). They are often officious, incompetent and trigger-happy, though in reality they are little more than glorified security guards. They are allowed to carry guns, but have no powers of arrest, and you are not legally obliged to show them your ID.

AVOIDING TROUBLE

Almost all the problems encountered by tourists in the Czech and Slovak republics are to do with **petty crime** – mostly from cars and hotel rooms – rather than more serious physical confrontations. Sensible precautions include making photocopies of your passport, leaving passport and tickets in the hotel safe, and noting down travellers' cheque and credit card numbers. If you have a car, don't leave anything in view when you park it, and take the radio with you if possible. Vehicles are rarely stolen, but luggage and valuables do make tempting targets, and rental cars are easy to spot.

In theory, you're supposed to carry some form of **identification** at all times, and the police can stop you in the street and demand it. In practice, they're rarely bothered if you're clearly a foreigner (unless you're driving). In any case, the police are now so deferential that they tend to confine themselves to socially acceptable activities like traffic control and harassing Romanies.

If you are unlucky enough to have something stolen, you need to **go to the police** to report it, not least because your insurance company will require a police report. It's unlikely that there'll be anyone there who speaks English, and even less likely that your belongings will be retrieved but, at the very least, you should get a statement detailing what you've lost for your insurance claim. Try the phrase *byl jsem oloupen* or, if you're a woman, *byla jsem oloupena* – "I have been robbed." (NB. The "j" is silent in "jsem").

DISABLED TRAVELLERS

In the past, very little attention was paid to the needs of the disabled in either republic. Attitudes are slowly changing, but there is still a long way to go, and the chronic shortage of funds makes matters worse.

Transport is a major problem, since buses and trams are virtually impossible for wheelchairs and trains are only slightly better (though there are special carriages designed to take wheelchairs on certain trains). At the time of writing, none of the car rental companies could offer vehicles with hand controls anywhere in the Czech or Slovak republics. If you're driving overland, most cross-Channel ferries now have adequate facilities, as do British Airways for those who are flying.

CONTACTS FOR DISABLED TRAVELLERS

AUSTRALIA
ACROD (Australian Council for Rehabilitation of the Disabled), PO Box 60, Curtin, ACT 2605 (☎02/6282 4333); 24 Cabarita Rd, Cabarita (☎02/9743 2699).

BRITAIN
Holiday Care Service, 2nd Floor, Imperial Building, Victoria Rd, Horley, Surrey RH6 7PZ (☎01293/774535). Information on all aspects of travel.
RADAR (The Royal Association for Disability and Rehabilitation), 12 City Forum, 250 City Rd, London EC1V 8AF (☎0207/250 3222; Minicom @0207/250 4119; *www.radar.org.uk*). Information on all aspects of travel.

CZECH REPUBLIC
Prague Wheelchair Association, Pražská organizace vozíčkářů, Benediktská 6, Nové Město, Prague (☎232 58 31, fax 24 81 62 31). Disabled-run organization that can provide limited assistance when you're in Prague, and which also produces the *Accessible Prague* (*Přístupná Praha*) guidebook.

IRELAND
Irish Wheelchair Association, Blackheath Drive, Clontarf, Dublin 3 (☎01/833 8241). National voluntary organization working with people with disabilities, with related services for holidaymakers.

NEW ZEALAND
Disabled Persons Assembly, 173–175 Victoria St, Wellington (☎04/801 9100).

NORTH AMERICA
Directions Unlimited, 720 N Bedford Rd, Bedford Hills, NY 10507 (☎1-800/533-5343). Tour operator specializing in custom tours for people with disabilities.
Mobility International USA, PO Box 10767, Eugene, OR 97440; Voice and TDD (☎541/343-1284; *www.minsa.org*). Information and referral services, access guides, tours and exchange programs. Annual membership $25 (includes quarterly newsletter).
Society for the Advancement of Travel for the Handicapped (SATH), 347 5th Ave, Suite 610, New York, NY 10016 (☎212/447-7284; *www.sittravel.com*). Non-profit-making travel industry referral service that passes queries on to its members as appropriate; allow plenty of time for a response.
Twin Peaks Press, Box 129, Vancouver, WA 98666 (☎206/694-2462 or 1-800/637-2256). Publisher of the *Directory of Travel Agencies for the Disabled*, and a number of other useful publications loaded with personal tips.

DIRECTORY

BOTTLES Neither republic is quite yet a fully paid-up member of the throwaway culture, and many drinks still come in bottles with a deposit that can be reclaimed at most supermarkets. Otherwise, there are now bottle banks scattered around most towns and cities.

CHILDREN The attitude to kids is generally very positive in both republics. That said, you'll see few babies out in the open, unless snuggled up in their prams, and almost no children in pubs, cafés or even most restaurants. Children are generally expected to be unreasonably well behaved and respectful to their elders, and many of the older generation may frown at over-boisterous behaviour. Kids under six go free on public transport; six- to fifteen-year-olds pay half-fare. Disposable nappies are becoming more widely available, but convenience food for babies is thin on the ground.

CONTRACEPTIVES Condoms (*kondom* or *prezervativ*) are now available in most major cities from the machines marked Men's Shop, Easy Shop or some such euphemism. They're also on sale from pharmacies everywhere.

ELECTRICITY This is the standard continental 220 volts AC. Most European appliances should work as long as you have an adaptor for European-style two-pin round plugs. North Americans will need this plus a transformer.

GAY MEN AND LESBIANS Homosexuality is legal in both republics, with the age of consent at fifteen (in the Czech Republic) and sixteen (in Slovakia), whatever your sexuality. That said, attitudes remain conservative. The main gay organization in the Czech Republic is Lambda, Zborovská 22, Prague 5 (☎02/54 91 27); the main one in the Slovak Republic is Ganymede, PO Box 4, Pošta 3, Bratislava (☎07/25 38 88).

LAUNDRY Self-service laundries don't exist, except in Prague, though you can get clothes beautifully service-washed or dry-cleaned for a very reasonable price at a *čistírna* as long as you've got a few days to spare.

LEFT LUGGAGE Most bus and train stations have lockers and/or a 24-hour left-luggage office, which officially only take bags under 15kg. If your bag is very heavy, say *promiňte je těšký*, and offer to carry it yourself – *já to vezmu*. Modern lockers have instructions in English. To work the old-fashioned lockers, put the correct change in the slot on the inside of the door, and set the code (choose and make a note of a number you can easily remember) before shutting it. To open the locker, set the code on the outside and wait a few seconds before trying the door. The lockers are usually checked every night, and the contents of any still occupied are taken to the 24-hour left-luggage office.

TAMPONS Tampons (*tampóny*) and sanitary towels (*dámské vložky*) are cheap and easy to get hold of in department stores and supermarkets.

TIME The Czech and Slovak republics are generally one hour ahead of Britain and six hours ahead of EST, with the clocks going forward as late as May and back again some time in September – the exact date changes from year to year.

TOILETS Public toilets (*toaleta*) can seem few and far between. In some, you still buy toilet paper (by the sheet) from the attendant, whom you usually have to pay as you enter, the amount depending on the purpose of your visit. The word for the gents' toilets is *muži* or *páni*; for ladies, *ženy* or *dámy*. In dire straits you should make use of conveniences in restaurants and pubs, as most Czechs and Slovaks do.

PART TWO

THE
CZECH REPUBLIC

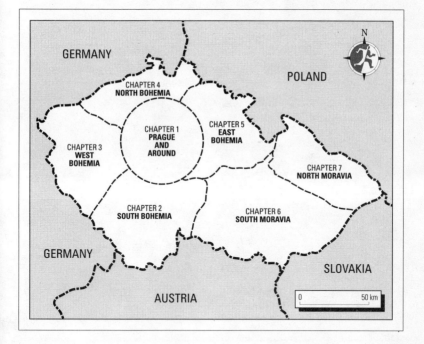

Introduction

With the official break-up of Czechoslovakia on January 1, 1993, the Czech Republic became one of Europe's newest nations, with a population of just over ten million. Compared to their former Slovak compatriots, the Czechs had comparatively few problems in gaining recognition on the international stage, and are due to join both NATO and the EU in the new millennium. The Czechs, after all, still have – in playwright Václav Havel – a president many people have actually heard of; they have a capital city – Prague – that has been one of the most popular tourist destinations of the last decade; and they had, for much of the 1990s, a stable government widely praised at home and abroad for the speed and efficacy of their economic reforms.

Geographically, the Czech Republic lies at the very heart of central Europe and, despite more than forty years' isolation behind the Iron Curtain, its towns and villages still bear the stamp of numerous, much older cultural influences. The millions of Germans who lived here for centuries before their postwar expulsion have left perhaps the most obvious traces: their splendid burgher houses line countless town squares and their timber-framed farmhouses still dot the borderlands. The Habsburg dynasty, which ruled over the Czechs for nearly four hundred years, has left the landscape punctuated by the onion domes of the Counter-Reformation and castellated follies of the old aristocracy. And for much of the modern era, the Czechs themselves have been at the forefront of European culture. Before World War I, Prague boasted a Cubist movement second only to Paris, and, between the wars, a modernist architectural flowering to rival Bauhaus. Even today, its writers, artists and film directors continue to exert a profound influence on European culture, out of all proportion to their numbers.

■ Where to go

Before the fall of communism, a staggering ninety percent of foreign tourists never strayed from the environs of **Prague**. While that no longer quite holds true, Prague is still the main focus for most people's trips to the Czech Republic, certainly for English-speaking tourists, who are still a relatively rare sight even in the beer capitals of Plzeň and České Budějovice, or in the country's number-two city, Brno.

Of course, much of the attention heaped on Prague is perfectly justified. It is one of the most remarkable cities in Europe, having emerged virtually unscathed from two world wars. Baroque palaces and churches shout out from cobbles, Gothic pinnacles spike the skyline, and Art Nouveau edifices line the main boulevards. As if its architectural glory isn't enough, the city has also become something of a mecca for young travellers, making it one of the most vibrant of Europe's emergent capital cities.

The rest of the country divides neatly into two: Bohemia to the west and Moravia to the east. Poised at the geographical centre of **Bohemia**, Prague is the perfect launching pad from which to explore the rolling countryside that characterizes the whole country. The pace of life here – and the pace of change – is much slower than in Prague. It may take just a couple of hours to drive to the pine-covered mountains that form Bohemia's natural borders, but most Czechs don't own a vehicle, and on public transport travelling is a much more time-consuming business.

The most unspoilt of Bohemia's hills and forests are in **South Bohemia**, whose capital is **České Budějovice**, a grid-plan medieval city and home to the original Budweiser beer. The real gem of the region is **Český Krumlov**, arguably the most stunning medieval town in the country, beautifully preserved in a narrow U-bend of the River Vltava. **West Bohemia**'s capital, **Plzeň**, produces the most famous of all the Czech beers, Pilsener Urquell, the original golden nectar from which all other lagers derive. The region's triangle of relaxing spa towns – **Karlovy Vary**, **Mariánské Lázně** and **Františkovy Lázně** – retain an air of their halcyon days in the last years of the Habsburg Empire.

Of all the areas in Bohemia, it's the north that has paid the highest price for the unbridled industrialization of the last hundred years. Yet even here, there are border areas like **České Švýcarsko** – the name means "Bohemian Switzerland", though that's stretching the point – where you can remain in blissful ignorance of such matters. The mountains of **East Bohemia** known as the **Krkonoše** – are the highest in the country, and as such make a prime holiday destination for Czechs and Germans for many years. They remain great hiking and skiing terrain, but the resorts at the foot of the mountains have been somewhat overdeveloped. More memorable landscapes exist to the south and east, where you can explore the weird sandstone "rock cities" of **Český ráj**, **Adršpach** and **Teplice**. To finish off, there are the more urbane pleasures of the region's two rival cities, **Hradec Králové** and **Pardubice**, both of which have preserved their old, medieval quarters intact.

The adventurous few who make it to **Moravia** generally head for the capital, **Brno**. A third of the size of Prague and with none of its vitality or cosmopolitanism, Brno is something of a disappointment to most visitors. That said, it's worth spending a day or two visiting some of its more unusual attractions: the dungeons of the local fortress, the mummified corpses in the Capuchin crypt, or the modernist exhibition halls of the city's trade fair grounds.

The countryside of **South Moravia**, especially around Brno, is much more immediately rewarding; castles guard just about every road out of the city, and to the northeast lies the **Moravský kras**, a karst region of dramatic limestone caves. The southern borders of Moravia comprise the country's main wine region, while in the uplands to the west are two of the most perfectly preserved medieval towns in the entire country, **Telč** and **Slavonice**.

North Moravia is sometimes written off as an industrial wasteland, but **Olomouc**, for many centuries the Moravian capital, is a charming city, more appealing than Brno in many ways and just a short step away from the **Jeseníky** mountains of Moravian Silesia. Lastly, in the far east of the country bordering Poland, the **Beskydy** region has preserved its folk architecture and traditions better than most, and is home to the country's largest open-air folk museum in **Rožnov pod Radhoštěm**.

Getting around

The most relaxing way of travelling around the Czech Republic is by train. The system, bequeathed by the Habsburgs in 1918, is one of the most dense

in Europe, and has changed little since those days, with only five percent of the tracks allowing train speeds of over 120kph. Though often wonderfully scenic, it's also extremely slow, so if you're in a hurry, buses are nearly always faster. Bus and train timetables can be found in the "Travel Details" section at the end of each chapter.

■ Trains

One railway official recently described the country's state-run train system, Czech Railways, České dráhy (ČD), as "the world's largest open-air museum". He's certainly got a point: ČD remains the country's largest employer, largely due to overemployment, and runs at a huge loss. The constant threats to close down up to a third of the railway system – which cast a shadow over much of the last decade – look more likely than ever to become a reality. In the meantime, enjoy the system while you can.

There are two main **types of train** (*vlak*): *rychlík* (express), *expres* or *spěšný* (through) trains are the faster ones, which stop only at major towns; *osobní* or *zastavkový* trains stop at every single station on the line and average about 30kph. Fastest of the lot are the international expresses – InterCity (IC) or EuroCity (EC), plus the first-class-only SuperCity (SC) – all of which require a supplement. Overall, however, fares, which are calculated by the kilometre, remain remarkably low; a second-class single from Prague to Brno still only costs around £5/$8.

Once you've worked out when your train leaves (for which, see opposite), the best thing to do when buying a **ticket** (*lístek*) is to write down all the relevant information (date/time/destination) on a piece of paper and hand it to the ticket clerk. This avoids any linguistic misunderstandings – rectifying any mistakes involves a lengthy bureaucratic process and costs you ten percent of the ticket price.

If you want a return ticket (*zpáteční*) or you're travelling on a *rychlík* train, you must say so when you buy your ticket. First-class carriages (*první třída*) exist on all fast trains; tickets are fifty-percent more expensive, but should guarantee you a seat on a busy train. If you should end up in the wrong carriage, you'll be given an on-the-spot fine.

There are half-price **discount fares** for children aged 6–15, and you can take two under-6s for free, providing they don't take up more than one seat. There are even crèche carriages on some trains – marked with a "D" on the timetable – for the exclusive use of those with children under 16. Czech Railways have also recently introduced a whole series of **rail passes**. These are only really worth considering if you're staying in the country for a long period of time, or are covering a lot of distance. The Junior pass for those under 26 costs just 390Kč for six months (690Kč for a year) and gives thirty-percent reductions on most trains, while the Karta Z, available to anyone of any age, costs 590Kč for a year and gives a twenty-percent discount.

For all international services (and any other trains marked with an "R" on the timetable), you can buy a **seat reservation** (*místenka*). It's advisable to get one if you're travelling at the weekend on one of the main routes and want to be sure of a seat. The *místenka* costs very little, but you must get it at least an hour before your train leaves, and either after or at the same time as you purchase your ticket.

Information and timetables

With very few English-speakers employed on the trains, it can be extremely difficult getting **train information**. The main stations (*nádraží*) have an airport-style arrivals and departures board, with information on delays under the heading *zpoždění*. Other stations have poster displays of arrivals (*příjezd*) and departures (*odjezd*), the former on white paper, the latter on yellow, with fast trains printed in red. The smallest stations list destinations and departures on simple boards under the heading *směr*. In addition to the above, all but the smallest stations have a comprehensive display of **timings and route information**

on rollers. These timetables are undeniably daunting, and unless you're a trainspotter with a gift for languages, you'll find them pretty indecipherable. If you're up for it, though, there's a description of how to read the rollers in the box below.

■ Buses

Price rises on the trains have made travelling by **bus** (*autobus*) even more popular among Czechs, though the price difference is of less significance to foreign travellers. Buses go almost everywhere, and from town to town they're often faster than the train. Bear in mind, though, that in rural areas timetables are often designed with the working and/or school day in mind. During the week this can mean departures at 6am, returning at around 3pm, with completely different (or no) services at weekends. The majority of routes are still run by the state bus company, Česká státní automobilová doprava (ČSAD). Private companies are becoming more prevalent, though their services tend to be confined to the more popular, long-distance routes.

In many towns and villages, the **bus station** (*autobusové nádraží*) is adjacent to the train station, though you may be able to pick up the bus from the centre of town. The bigger terminals, like Prague's Florenc, are run with train-like efficiency, with airport-style departure boards and numerous platforms. Often you can book your ticket in advance, and it's essential to do so if you're travelling at the weekend or early in the morning on one of the main routes. For most minor routes, simply buy your ticket from the driver. Large items of **luggage** (*zavazadla*) go in the boot, and you'll have to pay the driver a couple of crowns for the privilege.

HOW TO READ CZECH TRAIN TIMETABLES

First find the route you need to take on the route map and make a note of the number printed beside it; then follow the timetable rollers through until you come to the appropriate number. The only problem now is the language. Czech timetables are moving increasingly towards symbols, though inevitably the crucial notes and explanations are in Czech. Times given are always for departure unless there's a white circle after the name of the station. Arrivals are *příjezd* (*příj.* in short form) and departures are *odjezd* (*odj.* in short form). A platform or *nástupiště* is usually divided into two *kolej* on either side. Some of the more common notes at the side of the timetable are *jede v* (running on) or *nejede v* (not running on), followed by a date or a number/symbol: 1–6 for Monday–Saturday, two hammers for a weekday and a cross for a Sunday. If you're going to be travelling on the trains a lot, it might be an idea to invest in a ČD **timetable** (*jízdní řád*), which comes out every May (often selling out soon afterwards) and is available from bookshops and tobacconists; ČD also run an online timetable on their Web site (*www.cdrail.cz*), though it's currently only in Czech and German.

HOW TO READ CZECH BUS TIMETABLES

Bus **timetables** are even more difficult to figure out than train ones as there are no route maps at any of the stations. Each route from A to B is listed separately, so you may have to scour several timetables before you discover when the next bus is. Make sure you check on which day the service runs. The following is a brief rundown of the most common symbols: crossed hammers denote a service run only on weekdays; Saturday-only services are marked with a capital "S"; Sunday-only services are marked with a capital "N"; a cross denotes a Sunday or holiday service; Monday to Saturday services are marked with a "b"; Saturday, Sunday and holiday services are marked with an "a"; Monday-only services are marked with a "P"; Friday-only services are marked with a capital "V"; schoolday-only services are marked with a "c"; services running daily except Saturday are marked with a "g"; Monday to Thursday services are marked with a "d"; Tuesday to Friday services are marked with a "y".

Minor bus stops are marked with a rusty metal sign saying *zastávka*. If you want to get off, say *já chci vystoupit*; "the next stop" is *příští zastávka*. It's probably not worth buying any of the hefty *jízdní řád* (regional bus timetables), though you might feel the need to buy the comparatively slim *mezistátní a dálkové linky* volume (international and long-distance services). You can also consult the bus timetables (in Czech, German or English) on the Web site *www.svt.cz*.

■ Urban transport

Urban public transport is generally excellent, with buses (*autobus*), trolleybuses (*trolejbus*) and sometimes also trams (*tramvaj*) running from dawn until around midnight in most major towns (and all night in Prague and Brno). Ticket prices vary from place to place (generally 6–10Kč for an adult; reduced rates for those aged 6–15; under-6s travel free), but are universally cheap. In Prague and Brno, various **passes** are available (see the "Getting Around" sections of the relevant city accounts).

With a few exceptions, you must buy your **ticket** (*lístek*) before getting on board. Tickets, which are standard for all types of transport, are available from newsagents, tobacconists and the yellow machines at major stops, and are validated in the punching machines once you're on board. There are no conductors, only plain-clothes **inspectors**, who will fine anyone without a ticket 200Kč or more.

Taxis

Taxis are cheap and plentiful. Beware, however, that tourists are seen as easy prey by some taxi drivers, especially in Prague; if the meter isn't switched on, ask the driver to do so – *zapněte*

taxametr, prosím; and if you suspect you've been overcharged, asking for a receipt – *prosím, dejte mi povrzení* – should have the desired effect.

■ Driving

Since the majority of Czechs do not own a vehicle, and most of those who do only use them at the weekend, traffic outside the big cities is pretty light. Road conditions are generally not bad, though there's only a very limited motorway system. The only place where you might encounter difficulties is in the bigger cities and towns, where the lane system is confusing, tramlines hazardous and parking a nightmare. You have to be 18 or over to drive in the Czech Republic, and if you want to travel on long-distance motorways within the Czech Republic, you'll need a **motorway tax disc** or *dálniční známka*, which currently costs around 100Kč for ten days, 200Kč for a month, and is available from all border crossings and most post offices and petrol stations. Failing to display the disc will result in a hefty fine of several thousand crowns. If you're using car rental, check that your car will already have a disc.

Most foreign driving licences are honoured in the Czech Republic – including all EU, US and Canadian ones – but an **International Driving Licence** (available from most motoring organizations) might set your mind at rest. If you're bringing your own car, you are legally required to carry the vehicle's registration document; if it's not in your name, carry a letter of permission signed by the owner and authorized by an official motoring organization (this does not apply if you're renting a car). Check with your insurance company before leaving home whether you need a **green card**, as without one you may only get third-party cover. You're also required to carry a red warning triangle, a first-aid kit and a set of replacement bulbs, and to display a national identification sticker.

Rules of the road

Rules and regulations are pretty stringent, and on-the-spot fines, ranging from 40Kč to around 500Kč, are still regularly handed out. If you think you're being overcharged, ask for a receipt (*paragon*). The basic rules are driving on the right; compulsory wearing of seatbelts; and children under 12 must travel in the back. It's against the law to have any alcohol in your blood when you're driving. Also, don't overtake a tram when passengers are getting on and off if there's no safety island for them, and give way to pedestrians crossing at traffic lights if you're turning right or left. As in other continental countries, a yellow diamond sign means you have right of way, a black line through it means you don't; it's important to clock this sign before you reach the junction since the road markings at junctions rarely make priorities very clear.

Speed limits are 130kph on motorways (and if you travel any faster you will be fined), 90kph on other roads and 50kph in all cities, towns and villages – you need to remember these, as there are few signs to remind you. In addition, there's a special speed limit of 30kph for **level crossings** (you'll soon realize why if you try ignoring it). Many level crossings have no barriers, simply a sign saying *pozor* and a series of lights: a single flashing light means that the line is live; two red flashing lights mean there's a train coming.

Fuel and garages

Petrol (*benzín*) comes in three types: super (96 octane), special (90 octane) and **lead-free** petrol (*natural*). Diesel (*nafta*) is also available, but two-stroke fuel (*mix*), which powers the old East German Trabants and Wartburgs, is being phased out. Remember that petrol stations aren't as frequent as in some parts of Western Europe and many are closed at lunchtimes and after 6pm (though 24-hour ones can be found around most cities and along motorways). The price of petrol is cheaper than in much of Western Europe, currently costing around 25Kč a litre (£0.50/$0.80).

If you have **car trouble**, dial ☎154 at the nearest phone and wait for assistance. For peace of mind it might be worth taking out an insurance policy which will pay for any on-the-spot repairs and, if necessary, ship you and your passengers home free of charge.

Car rental

To rent a car, you'll need to be at least 21 years of age and have been driving for at least a year. If you book from abroad, you're looking at a whopping £60/$96 a day, and over £250/$400 a week for a small car. The big companies all have offices in Prague and Brno, but you'll get a far better deal with a local agent, though with very little of the back-up you'd get from an international firm should things go wrong.

Motorcycling

The Czech Republic is a great country for motorcycling and the speed limits for bikes are now the

INTERNATIONAL CAR RENTAL RESERVATIONS

UK		AUSTRALIA	
Avis	☎0990/900500	Avis	☎1800/225 533
Budget	☎0800/181181	Budget	☎1300/362 848
Europcar	☎0345/222 525	Dollar	☎02/9223 1444
National Car Rental	☎0990/365365	Hertz	☎1800/550 067
Hertz	☎0990/996699	National	☎13/1908
Holiday Autos	☎0990/300400	Thrifty	☎1300/367 227
Thrifty	☎0990/168238		
		NEW ZEALAND	
US		Avis	☎09/579 5231, 0800 655 111
Avis	☎1-800/331-1212	Budget	☎0800/ 652 227
Budget	☎1-800/527-070	Dollar	☎0800/486 677
Hertz	☎1-800/654-3131	Hertz	☎09/309 0989, 0800 655 955
Holiday Autos	☎1-800/422-7737	National	☎09/379 5080 or 0800/800 115
Thrifty	☎1-800/367-2277	Thrifty	☎09/275 6666

USEFUL HIKING TERMS

cesta/stezka/pěšina	road/path/trail
bouda	mountain refuge
hranice	border
jeskyně	cave
lanovka/lánova draha	chairlift/cable car
les	wood
lyžařský vlek	ski lift
pramen	spring
rozhled/vyhlídka	viewpoint
skála	rock
údolí	valley
vodopad	waterfall

same as those for cars (see previous page). Unless you ride a Jawa or an MZ, be prepared for curious onlookers in towns and villages, and a lot of hassle finding spare parts should you break down. Helmets are compulsory, as is some form of eye protection (goggles or visor) for the driver, and dipped headlights should be used at all times.

■ Cycling and hiking

Cycling is catching on fast in the Czech Republic, and the rolling countryside, though hard work on the legs, is rewarding. Facilities for **bike rental** are improving, and the increasing number of bike shops makes repairs possible and spare parts slightly easier to obtain. To take your bike (*kolo*) on the train, you must buy a separate ticket before taking it down to the freight section of the station, where, after filling in the mountains of paperwork, your bike should be smoothly sent on to its destination.

Hiking is a very popular pastime with the young and old alike, the most enthusiastic indulging in an activity curiously known as going *na trampu*; dressing up in quasi-military gear, camping in the wilds, playing guitar and singing songs round the campfire. There is a dense network of paths that covers the whole countryside – sometimes reaching even within the city boundaries of Prague. All the trails are colour-coded with clear markers every 200m or so and signs indicating roughly how long it'll take you to reach your destination. Many of the walks are fairly easy-going, but it can be wet and muddy underfoot even in summer, so sturdy boots are a good idea, particularly if you venture into the mountains proper. There are no hiking guides in English, but VKÚ produces 1:50,000 maps which cover the

whole country and detail all the marked paths in the area (see "Information and Maps", p.20).

■ Planes and boats

Domestic flights, run by ČSA and a variety of other carriers, link Prague with Brno and Ostrava, and there are regular international flights to the Slovak cities of Bratislava, Poprad and Košice. Though not exactly cheap, particularly when compared with the train or bus, they can prove useful if time is short and you want to get to eastern Slovakia quickly, reducing the travel time from Prague to Košice to two hours from twelve, for example. If you do decide to fly, make sure you book well in advance as demand is high, and flights to places like Poprad in the High Tatras are booked solid in the high season. Further details can be obtained from ČSA offices or agents in most large towns.

The opportunity for travelling by **boat** (*loď*) is pretty limited in the Czech Republic, but there are a few services worth mentioning. From Prague, boats sail all the way down to Orlík, with a change of vessel at each of the dams on the way. There's also a summer service on Lake Lipno in South Bohemia, and down the River Labe (Elbe) between Děčín and Hřensko.

Accommodation

Compared to the rest of life in the Czech Republic, accommodation is by no means cheap, unless you're camping. Standards have improved enormously, however, with privately owned pensions, joint-venture hotels and a whole host of private rooms providing choice and badly needed competition for the old state-owned dinosaurs.

If you're going to one of the big cities from late spring to late summer or over the Christmas holidays, it's as well to arrange accommodation before you arrive. There are now inexpensive

ACCOMMODATION PRICE CODES

After each entry in the **hotel** lists below, you'll find a symbol which corresponds to one of nine **price categories**:

① Under 500kč   ④ 1000–1250kč   ⑦ 1750–2000kč
② 500–750kč   ⑤ 1250–1500kč   ⑧ 2000–2500kč
③ 750–1000kč   ⑥ 1500–1750kč   ⑨ 2500Kčand upwards

All prices are for the cheapest **double room** available during high season, which usually means without private bath or shower in the less expensive places. For a **single room**, expect to pay around two-thirds the price of a double.

accommodation specialists on both sides of the Atlantic who can arrange this for you (see boxes on pp.4 & 12 for a list of current operators). Another alternative is to use the listings in the guide to ring or email a hotel and book yourself in.

■ Hotels, pensions and private rooms

The good news is that most Czech **hotels** have been renovated and reopened under private management, with services vastly improved. The bad news is that there are still some areas where the old state-owned dinosaurs live on. On the whole, though, the country has witnessed a great leap forwards from the bad old days when foreign visitors were shepherded into high-rise monstrosities and charged three times as much as locals for services that were uniformly bad.

Despite government attempts to stop hotels charging foreigners more than locals, many places outside Prague continue the practice. All hotels now operate a star system, though it's self-regulatory and therefore none too reliable. Prices vary wildly and, unsurprisingly, tend to be much higher in those areas which receive the most tourists. Continental breakfast is normally included in the price of the room, and you'll find a restaurant and/or bar in almost every hotel.

Some of the new privately owned guest houses bill themselves as **pensions**. Though, again, prices and standards can vary widely, a good pension can often be cheaper, friendlier and better equipped than many hotels. **Private rooms**, too, are a case of pot luck. You can be sure that they will be clean and tidy, but in what proximity you'll be to your hosts is difficult to predict. So, before agreeing to part with any money, try to figure whether you'll be sharing bathroom, cooking facilities, etc, with the family – Czech hospitality can be somewhat overwhelming, although meals other than breakfast are

not generally included in the price. In some parts of the countryside you'll see plenty of signs saying either *ubytování* ("accommodation" in Czech) or, more frequently, *Zimmer Frei* ("rooms to rent" in German). In some towns and cities, you may be able to book rooms through the local tourist office (details are listed in the main text).

■ Youth hostels and student rooms

A smattering of **hostels** are now affiliated to Hostelling International, but these are few and far between, vary wildly in size and quality, and are often in very out-of-the-way places. The Czech hostel organization is KMC (Club of Young Travellers), based in Prague at Karolíny Světlé 30 (☎ & fax 02/24 23 06 33). There are, of course, lots of other unofficial hostels – especially in Prague – where you can pay very little and usually get very little in return, beyond a place to lay your sleeping bag.

A more reliable alternative to youth hostels in the big university towns is **student accommodation** – known as *kolej* – which is let out cheap to travellers from June to August. Though heavily booked up in advance by groups, they'll try their best to squeeze you in. Curfews operate in some hostels and can be as early as 10 or 11pm, so check before you book in. Addresses can change from year to year, so to find out the most recent, go to the local tourist office or the youth organization, CKM, which has offices in most major towns.

Other dormitories, which go by the catch-all term of *ubytovna*, can be anything from sports halls to dorms used to house immigrant workers or workers on vacation. They are uniformly cheap and basic with few facilities beyond a bunk bed, toilet and cold shower, though they may remain unconvinced that a Western tourist should demean themselves by staying there.

■ Camping and other options

Campsites are plentiful all over the Czech Republic. Some are huge, ostentatious affairs, known as *autokemping*, with shops, swimming pools, draught beer and so on; others, known often as *tábořiště*, are just a simple stretch of grass with loos and cold showers. Many sites feature **bungalows** (*chaty*), sometimes reserved for groups but often for rent for around £10/$16 for two people. The flashiest bungalows are really small chalets, while the most primitive are little more than rabbit hutches.

The most basic campsites are only marked on the 1:50,000 hiking maps. Most are open only from May until September and provide just ad hoc toilets and a little running water. Very few are open all year round. Even though prices are inflated for foreigners, costs are still reasonable; two people plus car and tent weigh in at around £5/$8. Campfires, though officially banned, are tolerated at many campsites, and the guitar-playing barbecues go on until well into the night.

Mountain Huts

In the mountains of the Krkonoše, there are a fair number of **mountain huts** (*bouda* or *chata*) scattered about the hillsides. Some are little less than hotels and charge similar prices, but the more isolated ones are simple wooden shelters costing around £5/$8 per person. Few are accessible by road, but many are only a few miles from civilization. Ideally, these should be booked in advance through the various accommodation agencies in the nearest settlements. The more isolated ones work on a first-come, first-served basis, but if you turn up before 6pm, you're unlikely to be turned away.

Communications

SOME FOREIGN COUNTRIES IN CZECH

Australia	*Austrálie*
Austria	*Rakousko*
Canada	*Kanada*
Germany	*Německo*
Great Britain	*Velká Británie*
Hungary	*Maďarsko*
Ireland	*Írsko*
Netherlands	*Nizozemí*
New Zealand	*Nový Zéland*
Poland	*Polsko*
Slovakia	*Slovenkso*
USA	*Spojené státy americké*

■ Post

Most **post offices** (*pošta*) are open from 8am to 5pm Monday to Friday, and Saturdays until noon. They're pretty baffling institutions with separate windows for just about every service. Look out for the right sign to avoid queueing unnecessarily: *známky* (stamps), *dopisy* (letters) or *balky* (parcels).

Outbound mail is reasonably reliable, with letters or postcards taking around four to five working days to reach Britain, a week to ten days to reach North America. You can also buy **stamps** from newsagents and kiosks as well as post offices, though often only for domestic mail.

Poste restante (pronounced as five syllables in Czech) services are available in major towns, but remember to write Pošta 1 (the main office), followed by the name of the town. Get the sender to write their name and address on the back so that mail can at least be returned if something goes wrong. If you're passing through the capital at some point, it might be safer to have mail sent to your embassy, but write and tell them beforehand that you intend to do this.

The Czechs are keen users of **electronic mail** and the **Internet**, and you'll find an Internet café in most major cities (we've listed the better ones in the text), where you can send and receive mail and do a bit of surfing.

■ Phones

The **phone** system in the Czech Republic is gradually being overhauled, but often the system simply can't cope. Things are improving in the larger towns and cities where new touch-tone phones are being introduced. Public phones are, for the most part, **card phones**, which take only phonecards (*telefonní karty*), currently available in 50, 100 and 150 units, from post offices, tobacconists and some shops (prices vary). You can make international calls from all card phones (calls cost over 20Kč a minute to Britain and Ireland, over 30–40Kč to North America and a whopping 40–60Kč to Australasia). There are instructions in English, and if you press the appropriate button the language on the digital read-out will change to English. If you have any problems, ring ☎0149 and ask for an English-speaking operator.

In the grey, **coin-operated phones**, you need to insert a minimum of 3Kč to make a local call, 5Kč for long-distance. The **dialling tone** is a short followed by a long pulse; the **ringing tone** is long and regular; **engaged** is short and rapid (not to be confused with the connecting tone, which is very short and rapid). The standard Czech response is *prosím*; and the word for extension is *linka*.

You can also make phone calls from the local **telephone exchanges** situated in Prague, Brno and a few other cities. Write down the town and number you want, leave a deposit of around 200Kč and wait for your name to be called out. Keep a close watch on the time unless you've unlimited funds. You can also make calls from most hotels, although their surcharge is usually pretty hefty. To make a **collect call** – which will probably cost the recipient less than it would cost you – you need to get through to the international operator in the country you're phoning: ring ☎00 420 00 44 01 for Britain; ☎ 00 420 001 01 for the US; and ☎00 420 001 51 for Canada; these calls are not free.

DIALLING CODES

To the Czech Republic
From Britain ☎00 420
From the USA ☎011 420 and Canada
From Australia ☎0011 420 and New Zealand

From the Czech Republic
UK ☎0044
Eire ☎00353
Australia ☎0061
New Zealand ☎0064
US and Canada ☎001

Leave the first zero off the area code when phoning.

■ Media

In Prague and Brno, it's possible to get day-old copies of most of the broadsheet British papers, though one that you can buy on the day of issue is the European edition of *The Guardian*, printed in Frankfurt (it arrives on the streets of Prague and Brno around mid-morning). As far as **American newspapers** are concerned, there's just the reliable old *International Herald Tribune*. In addition, there's the weekly English-language *Prague Post*, a broadsheet with strong business coverage and a useful pull-out listings section.

It's a sign of the times that the most famous **Czech newspaper**, *Lidové noviny* (the best-known *samizdat* under the Communists), is now owned by a Swiss company, Ringier. In fact, over half the Czech press is now foreign-owned, including the country's most popular daily, *Blesk*, a sensationalist tabloid with lurid colour pictures, naked women and reactionary politics. The most popular quality paper nowadays is *Mladá fronta dnes*, former mouthpiece of the Communist youth movement, now a centrist daily with solid coverage of local and international news. Next in the popularity stakes is *Právo* (formerly the official mouthpiece of the Communist Party *Rudé právo* or "Red Justice"), a surprisingly successful "left-wing daily". The other positive independent political voice is the weekly *Respekt*, which prides itself on its investigative journalism. If all you want, however, is yesterday's (or, more often than not, the day before yesterday's) international football results, pick up a copy of the daily *Sport*.

As for **television**, Česká televize's two state-owned channels, ČT1 and ČT2 have both been eclipsed as far as ratings go by the runaway success of the commercial channel, Nova. The latter features lots of American sitcoms dubbed into Czech, plenty of game shows and the most comprehensive coverage of Czech football. Prima, the other commercial channel, has yet to make any significant inroads into Nova's audience monopoly. ČT2 is your best bet for foreign films with subtitles; it also shows news in English from the BBC on Monday to Friday at 8am, and on Saturday and Sunday at 7am.

On the **radio**, the BBC World Service broadcasts loud and clear on various FM wavelengths from the major cities, mostly in English, with occasional Czech news summaries; you can also get the regular all-English European version on shortwave. The most popular domestic station is still, as in communist days, the state-run Český rozhlas (92.6/102.7FM), on which Havel broadcasts his presidential Sunday evening chat; an English-language news summary goes out Monday to Friday at 5.30pm. The three top FM music channels are Evropa 2 (88.2FM), Radio Bonton (99.7FM) and Kiss FM (98FM), which dish out bland Euro-pop. More interesting is Radio 1 (91.9FM), which plays a wide range of indie rock from East and West, and broadcasts a brief news summary at 7am Monday to Friday.

Eating and drinking

The good news is that you can eat and drink very cheaply in the Czech Republic: the food is filling and the beer is divine. The bad news is that the kindest thing you can say about Czech food is that it is hearty. Forty years of culinary isolation under the Communists introduced few innovations to Czech cuisine, with its predilection for big slabs of meat served with dumplings and pickled cabbage. Fresh vegetables (other than potatoes) remain a rare sight on traditional Czech menus, and salads are still waiting for their day.

■ Food

There are several ways of eating out in the Czech Republic: you can go to a *restaurace* or *vinárna* and have a full meal; you can have something cheaper, more basic (though equally filling) and in less formal surroundings at a *pivnice*, *hostinec* or *hospoda*; or, at the budget end of the scale, you can eat very cheaply indeed at a stand-up *bufet* or self-service joint.

Breakfast, snacks and bufets

Most Czechs get up so early in the morning (often around 5 or 6am) that they don't have time to start the day with anything more than a quick cup of coffee. As a result, the whole concept of **breakfast** as such is alien to the Czechs. If your hotel or pension is offering breakfast, then the best advice is to grab it, because hunting for your own out on the streets is a thankless task. Bear in mind, though, that if you get up much past 10am, you'll have missed it and may as well join the country's working population for lunch.

Pastries (*pečivo*) are available from most bakeries (*pekařství*), but rarely in bars and cafés, so you'll probably have to eat them on the go. The traditional pastry (*koláč*) is more like sweet bread; dry and fairly dense with only a little flavouring in the form of hazelnuts (*oříškový*), poppy-seed jam (*makový*), prune jam (*povidlový*) or a kind of sour-sweet curd cheese (*tvarohový*). Recently, French- and Viennese-style bakeries have started to appear in the big cities, selling croissants (*loupáky*) and lighter cream cakes.

Czech **bread** (*chléb*) is some of the tastiest around when fresh. The standard loaf is *Šumava*, a dense mixture of wheat and rye, which you can buy whole, in halves (*půl*) or quarters (*čtvrtina*). *Česky chléb* is a mixture of rye, wheat and whey, with distinctive slashes across the top; *kmínový chléb* is the same loaf packed full of caraway seeds. Rolls come in two varieties: *rohlík*, a plain white finger roll, and *houska*, a rougher, tastier round bun.

The ubiquitous street **takeaway** is the hot dog or *párek*, a dubious-looking frankfurter (traditionally two – *párek* means a pair), dipped in mustard and served with a white roll (*v rohlíku*). A Czech speciality all year round is *smažený sýr* – a slab of melted cheese (and, more often than not, ham) fried in breadcrumbs and served with a roll (*v housce*). If it's *plněný* or *se šunkou*, then you can be certain it's got ham in it, and it generally comes with a large dose of the local tartare sauce – a lot less piquant than its Western counterpart. The greasiest option of the lot is *bramborák*, a thin potato pancake with little flecks of bacon or salami in it.

Stand-up **bufets** often open from as early as 6am and offer everything from light snacks to full meals. They're usually self-service (*samoobsluha*) and non-smoking, and occasionally have rudimentary seats. The cheapest of the wide range of meat sausages on offer is *sekaná*, bits of old meat and bread squashed together to form a meat loaf – for connoisseurs only. *Guláš* is popular, though it may bear little relation to the original of that name – usually *Szegedinský* (pork with sauerkraut) but sometimes *special* (with better meat and a creamier sauce). Less substantial fare boils down to *chlebíčky* – artistically presented **open sandwiches** with differing combinations of gherkins, cheese, salami, ham and aspic – and great mountains of mayonnaise-based **salad** (*salát*), bought by weight (200g is a medium-sized portion).

As for **fast food**, pizza places abound, though they can vary from vague approximations to quality imitations. Other staple Czech fast-food snacks include *hranolky* (chips/French fries) or *krokety* (croquettes) served with tartare sauce. Czech crisps (*chips*) have struggled to compete with foreign imports, but a few new brands are holding their own. Finally, it should also be noted that *McDonald's* now has a prime slice of real estate in almost every major Czech city.

Coffee, tea and cakes

Like the Austrians who once ruled over them, the Czechs have a grotesquely sweet tooth, and the coffee-and-cake hit is part of the daily ritual. **Coffee** is drunk black and described rather hopefully as *turecká* (Turkish) – it's really just hot water poured over coffee grains. Downmarket bufets sell *ledová káva*, a weak, cold black coffee, while at the other end of the scale *Vídeňská káva* (Viennese coffee) is a favourite with the older generation. Though not quite as refined as the Austrian original, it's still served with an adequate dollop of whipped cream. Espresso coffee (*presso*) is usually available in the bigger towns and hotels, and though it varies in quality, it's generally the best you'll get.

Tea is drunk weak and without milk, although you'll usually be given a glass of hot water and a tea bag so you can do your own thing. **Milk** itself is rarely drunk on its own, though it can be bought in supermarkets. The country used to produce vast quantities of delicious **yoghurts** and sour milks, which, if you can still find them, you should buy in preference to the sugary imported stuff that dominates the market; *bílý jogurt* is natural yoghurt, but look out for *kefír*, deliciously thick sour milk, or *acidofilní mléko*, its slightly thinner counterpart.

The **cukrárna** is the place to go for cake-eating. There are two main types of cake: *dort*, like the German *Tort*, consist of a series of custard cream, chocolate and sponge layers, while *řez* are lighter square cakes, usually containing a bit of fruit. A *věneček*, filled with "cream", is the nearest you'll get to an eclair; a *větrník* is simply a larger version with a bit of fresh cream added. One speciality to look out for is *rakvička*, which literally means "little coffin", an extended piece of sugar with cream, moulded vaguely into the shape of a coffin. Whatever the season, Czechs have to have their daily fix of **ice cream** (*zmrzlina*), available in soft form from machines or scooped, either dispensed from little window kiosks in the sides of buildings, or dished out from within a *cukrárna*.

■ Full meals

For a **full meal**, you can go anywhere from a local *pivnice* to a regular *restaurace* or late-night *vinárna*. It's as well to remember that Czechs eat their main meal of the day at lunchtime, between noon and 2pm. Traditionally, they only have cold meats and bread later on, but obviously the posher restaurants make more of the evening. If your main concern is price, the local beer-swilling *pivnice*, *hospoda* or *hostinec* are the ones to go for. Nearly all of them will serve hot meals from mid-morning until 2 or 3pm, and some continue serving until 8 or 9pm. A *vinárna* (wine bar) – though not necessarily its kitchen – will sometimes stay open after 11pm.

Away from the big hotels, the **menu** (*jídelní lístek*), which should be displayed outside, is often in Czech only, and deciphering it without a grounding in the language can be quite a feat. Just bear in mind that the right-hand column lists the prices, while the far left column usually gives you the estimated weight of every dish in grams; if what you get weighs more or less, the price will alter accordingly (this applies in particular to fish).

Most menus start with the **soups** (*polévky*), one of the region's culinary strong points and mainly served at lunchtimes. Posher restaurants will have a serious selection of starters, such as *uzený jazyk* (smoked tongue), *tresčí játra* (cod's liver) or perhaps *kaviárové vejce* (a hard-boiled egg with caviar on top). *Šunková rolka* is another favourite, consisting of ham topped with whipped cream and horseradish. You're more likely, though, to find yourself skipping the starters,

FOOD AND DRINK GLOSSARY

BASICS

chléb	bread	moučník	dessert	rýže	rice
chlebíček	(open) sandwich	nápoje	drinks	sklenice	glass
cukr	sugar	nůž	knife	snídaně	breakfast
hořčice	mustard	oběd	lunch	sůl	salt
houska	round roll	obloha	garnish	šálek	cup
jídla na	main dishes	ocet	vinegar	talíř	plate
objednávku	to order	ovoce	fruit	tartarská	tartare sauce
knedlíky	dumplings	pečivo	pastry	omáčka	
křen	horseradish	pepř	pepper	těstoviny	noodles, pasta
lžíce	spoon	polévka	soup	večeře	supper/dinner
maso	meat	předkrmy	starters	vejce	eggs
máslo	butter	přílohy	side dishes	vidlička	fork
med	honey	rohlík	finger roll	volské oko	fried egg
mléko	milk	ryby	fish	zeleniny	vegetables

SOUPS

boršč	beetroot soup	hovězí vývar	beef broth	kuřecí	thin chicken soup
bramborová	potato soup	hrachová	pea soup	rajská	tomato soup
čočková	lentil soup	zelná	sauerkraut and	zeleninová	vegetable soup
fazolová	bean soup		meat soup		

FISH

kapr	carp	pstruh	trout	treska	cod
losos	salmon	rybí filé	fillet of fish	úhoř	eel
makrela	mackerel	sardinka	sardine	zavináč	herring/rollmop
platýs	flounder	stika	pike		

MEAT DISHES

bažant	pheasant	karbanátky	minced meat	skopové maso	mutton
biftek	beef steak		rissoles	slanina	bacon
čevapčiči	spicy meatballs	klobásy	sausages	svíčková	fillet of beef
dršťky	tripe	kotleta	cutlet	šunka	ham
drůbež	poultry	kuře	chicken	telecí	veal
guláš	goulash	kýta	leg	vepřový	pork
hovězí	beef	ledvinky	kidneys	vepřové řízek	breaded pork
husa	goose	řízek	steak		cutlet or
játra	liver	roštěná	sirloin		schnitzel
jazyk	tongue	salám	salami	žebírko	ribs
kachna	duck	sekaná	meat loaf		

which are usually little more than a selection of cold meats.

Main courses tend to be divided into several separate sections. *Hotová jídla* (ready-made meals) and *jídla na objednávku* (meals made to order) or *minutky*. In either case, dishes are overwhelmingly based on **meat** (*maso*), usually pork, sometimes beef. The Czechs are experts on these meats, and

VEGETABLES

brambory	potatoes	hranolky	chips, French fries	okurka	cucumber
brokolice	broccoli			pórek	leek
celer	celery	hrášek	peas	rajče	tomato
cibule	onion	karotka	carrot	ředkev	radish
česnek	garlic	květák	cauliflower	řepná bulva	beetroot
chřest	asparagus	kyselá okurka	pickled gherkin	špenát	spinach
čočka	lentils	kyselé zelí	sauerkraut	zelí	cabbage
fazole	beans	lečo	ratatouille	žampiony	mushroom
houby	mushrooms	lilek	aubergine		

FRUIT, CHEESE AND NUTS

banán	banana	maliny	raspberries	pivní sýr	cheese flavoured with beer
borůvky	blueberries	mandle	almonds		
broskev	peach	měkký sýr	soft cheese	pomeranč	orange
bryndza	goat's cheese in brine	meruňka	apricot	rozinky	raisins
		niva	semi-soft, crumbly, blue cheese	švestky	plums
citrón	lemon			třešně	cherries
grep	grapefruit	oříšky	peanuts	tvaroh	fresh curd cheese
hermelín	Czech brie	ostružiny	blackberries	urda	soft, fresh, whey cheese
hrozny	grapes	oštěpek	heavily smoked curd cheese		
hruška	pear			uzený sýr	smoked cheese
jablko	apple	parenica	rolled strips of lightly smoked curd cheese	vlašské ořechy	walnuts
jahody	strawberries				
kompot	stewed fruit				

COMMON TERMS

čerstvý	fresh	na zdraví	cheers!	smažený	fried in bread-crumbs
domácí	home-made	nadívaný	stuffed		
duzený	stew/casserole	nakládaný	pickled	studený	cold
grilovaný	roast on the spit	(za)pebený	baked/roast	syrový	raw
		plněný	stuffed	sýrový	cheesy
kyselý	sour	m.m. (maštěny máslem)	with melted butter	teplý	hot
na kmíně	with caraway seeds			uzený	smoked
		sladký	sweet	vavený	boiled
na roztu	grilled	slaný	salted	znojemský	with gherkins
na smetaně	in cream sauce				

DRINKS

burčá	young wine	koňak	brandy	suché víno	dry wine
bílé víno	white wine	láhev	bottle	svařené víno	mulled wine
čaj	tea	led	ice	vinný střik	white wine with soda
červené víno	red wine	minerálka	mineral water		
destiláty	spirits	mléko	milk	víno	wine
káva	coffcc	pivo	beer		

although the quality could often be better, the variety of sauces and preparative techniques is usually good. The difficulty lies in decoding names such as *klašterny tajemství* ("mystery of the monastery")

or even a common dish like *Moravský vrabec* (literally "Moravian sparrow", but actually roast pork).

Fish (*ryby*), along with chicken and other fowl like duck, are generally listed under a separate

VEGETARIANS

Czech meat consumption has dropped dramatically since 1989, but it remains one of the highest in the world. It's hardly suprisingly then that **vegetarianism** is still a minority sport. Nevertheless, you're better off in Prague than anywhere else in the country. For a start, places which cater mostly for ex-pats usually have one or two veggie options, and there are plenty of pizzerias.

Even in traditional Czech places, most menus have a section called *bezmasa* (literally "without meat") – don't take this too literally, though, for it simply means the main ingredient is not dead animal; dishes like *omeleta se šunkou* (ham omelette) regularly appear under these headings, so always check first. Emergency standbys which most Czech pubs will knock up for you without too much fuss include *knedlíky s vejci* (dumplings and egg), *omeleta s hráškem* (pea omelette), or *smažený sýr*, a slab of melted cheese (and, more often than not, ham) deep-fried in breadcrumbs. Other common deep-fried dishes include *smažené žampiony* (mushrooms) and *smažený květák* (cauliflower).

The phrases to remember are *jsem vegeterián/vegeteriánka. Máte něco bez masa?* ("I'm a vegetarian. Is there anything without meat?"); and for emphasis, you could add *nejím ani maso ani ryby* ("I don't eat meat or fish").

heading. River trout and carp (the traditional dish at Christmas) are cheaply and widely available, and although their freshness may be questionable, they are usually served grilled or roasted in delicious buttery sauces.

Dumplings (*knedlíky*), though German in origin and name, are now the mainstay of Bohemian cooking. The term itself is misleading for English-speakers, since they resemble nothing like the English dumpling – more like a heavy white bread. *Houskové knedlíky* come in large flour-based slices (four or five to a dish), while *bramborové knedlíky* are smaller and made from potato and flour. Occasionally, you may be treated to *ovocné knedlíky* (fruit dumplings), the king of Czech dumplings. **Fresh salads** rarely rise above tomato, cucumber or cabbage (*zelí*), often swimming in a slightly sweet, watery dressing.

With the exception of *palačinky* (pancakes) filled with chocolate or fruit and cream, **desserts**

(*moučníky*), where they exist at all, can be pretty uninspiring. Often the ice cream and cakes on offer in restaurants aren't really up to the standards of the stuff sold on the street, so go to a *cukrárna* if you want a dose of sugar.

■ Drinking

Traditional Czech pubs (*pivnice* or *hospoda*) are smoky, male-dominated places, where 99 percent of the customers are drinking copious quantities of Czech beer by the half-litre. If you want a more mixed environment, you're better off heading for a wine cellar (*vinárna*) or café (*kavárna*), where you'll get a better selection of wine and spirits, but probably only bottled beer.

Beer

Alcohol consumption among Czechs has always been high, and in the decade following the events

---

CZECH BEERS

The most famous Czech beer is **Pilsner Urquell**, known to the Czechs as Plzeňský Prazdroj, the original bottom-fermented Pils from Plzeň (Pilsen), a city 80km southwest of Prague. Plzeň also boasts the **Gambrinus** brewery, whose domestic sales currently exceed those of Pilsner Urquell. The other big Bohemian brewing town is České Budějovice (Budweis), home to the country's biggest-selling export beer, **Budvar**, a comparatively mild brew but still leagues ahead of Budweiser, the German name for Budvar that was adopted by American brewers, Anheuser-Busch, in 1876 (and a cause of litigious grief ever since, for more on which, see p.168).

The biggest brewery in the country is, in fact, in the Smíchov suburb of Prague where **Staropramen** (meaning "ancient spring") is produced, a typical Bohemian brew with a mild hoppy flavour. Some Staropramen is also produced at Prague's Holešovice brewery, better known for its popular, dark **Měšťan**. It's difficult to avoid **Radegast**, a very popular drinkable brew from North Moravia, and the German-owned **Krušovice** beer, but one beer worth seeking out is the award-winning, hoppy and slightly bitter **Velkopopovický kozel**. There are also numerous small breweries across the country, many of which only distribute locally, and which consequently struggle to survive, but are well worth the effort of tracking down.

of 1968 it doubled. A whole generation found solace in drinking, mostly beer, whose world league table of consumption the Czechs topped some time ago. However, it's a problem which seldom spills out onto the streets; violence in pubs is uncommon and you won't see that many drunks in public.

Czech **beer** ranks among the best in the world, and the country remains the true home of most of the lager drunk around the world today. It was in the Bohemian city of Plzeň (Pilsen) that the first **bottom-fermented** beer was introduced in 1842, after complaints from the citizens about the quality of its top-fermented predecessor. The new brewing style quickly spread to Germany, and is now blamed for the bland rubbish served up in the English-speaking world as lager or Pils.

The distinctive flavour of Czech beer comes from the famous Bohemian hops, Žatec (Saaz) Red, still hand-picked and then combined with the soft local water and served with a high content of absorbed carbon dioxide – hence the thick, creamy head. Under the Communists, brewing methods in the Czech Republic remained stuck in the old ways, but the 1990s have seen many breweries opt for modernization: pasteurization, de-oxidization, rapid maturation and carbon dioxide injections – all of which mean less taste, more fizz. It's a development against which the Czech Beer Party and Britain's Campaign for Real Ale (CAMRA) are fighting hard.

CZECH ETIQUETTE

It's common practice to share a table with other eaters or drinkers; *je tu volno?* ("Is this seat free?") is the standard question. Waiter-service is the norm, even in pubs, so sit tight and a beer should come your way. You may have to ask to see the menu (*jídelní lístek*) in pubs and some cafés to indicate that you wish to eat. When food arrives for your neighbours, it's common courtesy to wish them bon appetit (*dobrou chuť*). When you want to leave, simply say *zaplatím, prosím* (literally "I'll pay, please"), and your tab will be totted up. A modest form of tipping exists in all establishments, generally done by rounding up the bill to the nearest few crowns, though beware that the waiters haven't already done this for you. On leaving, bid your neighbours farewell (*na shledanou*).

Beer (*pivo*) is served by the half-litre; if you want anything smaller, you must specifically ask for a *malé pivo* (0.3 litres). The average jar is medium strength, usually about 1050 specific gravity or 4.2 percent alcohol. Somewhat confusingly, the Czechs class their beers using the Balling scale, which measures the original gravity, calculated according to the amount of malt and dissolved sugar present before fermentation. The most common varieties are 10° (*desítka*), which are generally slightly weaker than 12° (*dvanáctka*). Light beer (*světlé*) is the norm, but many pubs also serve a slightly sweeter dark variety (*černé*) – or, if you prefer, you can have a mixture of the two (*řezané*).

Wine and spirits

Czech **wine** will never win over as many people as has Czech beer, but since the import of French and German vines in the fourteenth century, it has produced a modest selection of medium-quality wines. The main wine region is South Moravia, though a little is produced around the town of Mělník (see p.133). Suffice to say that most domestic wine is pretty drinkable – Frankovka is a perfectly respectable, though slightly sweet, red; Veltlínské zelené a good, dry white – and rarely much more than £1/$1.60 a bottle in shops, while the best stuff can only be had from the private wine cellars (*sklepy*), hundreds of which still exist out in the regions. A Czech speciality to look out for is *burčák*, a very young, misty wine of varying (and often very strong) alcoholic content, which appears on the streets in the vine harvest season in September.

All the usual **spirits** are on sale and known by their generic names, with rum and vodka dominating the market. The home production of brandies is a national pastime, which results in some almost terminally strong liquors. The most renowned of the lot is *slivovice*, a plum brandy originally from the border hills between Moravia and Slovakia. You'll probably also come across *borovička*, a popular Slovak firewater, made from pine trees; *myslivec* is a rough brandy with a firm following. There's also a fair selection of intoxicating **herbal concoctions**: *fernet* is a dark-brown bitter drink, known as *bavorák* (Bavarian beer) when it's mixed with tonic, while *becherovka* is a supposedly healthy herbal spirit from the Bohemian spa town of Karlovy Vary, with a very unusual, almost medicinal taste.

The Czech Republic is also one of the few countries in the world where **absinthe** is still legal. The preferred poison of Parisian painters and poets in the nineteenth century, absinthe is a nasty green spirit made from fermented wormwood – it even gets a biblical mention in Revelation: "and the name of the star is called Wormwood: and the third part of the waters became wormwood; and many men died of the waters, because they were made bitter". St John wasn't wrong: at 170 degrees proof, it's dangerous stuff and virtually undrinkable neat. To make it vaguely palatable, you need to set light to an absinthe-soaked spoonful of sugar, and then mix the caramelized mess with the absinthe.

There's not much to say about Czech **soft drinks**, with the exception of the high-energy drink Semtex, a can of which will amuse friends back home. Last of all, if you're looking for a decent **mineral water** (*minerální voda*), ask for the ubiquitous Mattoni, a mild and not too fizzy option.

Castles, churches and museums

The Czech Republic boasts well over a thousand castles, many of which have been converted for modern use, while others have been returned to their former owners. The country's churches and monasteries are similarly blighted by years of structural neglect and, more recently, by art thefts; most now lock their doors outside worshipping hours. Museums and galleries, by contrast, thrived under the Communists, filled to the gunnels with dull propaganda. Many have bitten the dust, others have changed out of all recognition, but most are now much more interesting to visit.

■ Castles and guided tours

Czech castles divide into two categories: a **hrad** is a defensive castle, usually medieval in origin and character, while a **zámek** is more of a chateau, built for comfort rather than for military purposes. The basic **opening hours** for both are the same: Tuesday to Sunday 8 or 9am to noon, then 1 to 4pm or later. From the end of October to the beginning of April, most castles are closed. In April and October, opening hours are often restricted to weekends and holidays only.

Whatever the time of year, if you want to see the interior of the building, nine times out of ten you'll be compelled to go on a **guided tour** that usually lasts for an hour. More and more places are now offering a choice of tours, of varying length, and some places insist on a minimum number of people before they begin a tour. Since most tours are in Czech (occasionally German) ask for an *anglický text*, an often unintentionally hilarious English resumé of the castle's history. You may also be asked to wear special furry overshoes (*papučky*), which protect and polish the floors at the same time. Tours almost invariably set off on the hour, and the last one leaves an hour before the lunchtime break (in other words, 11am) and an hour before the final closing time. Entrance charges are still comparatively low, rarely exceeding 100Kč – hence no prices are quoted in the text – and students and children usually get in for half-price.

■ Churches and monasteries

Getting into **churches** can present something of a problem. While the really important churches operate in much the same way as museums, occasionally charging an entry fee, particularly for their crypts or cloisters, the hundreds of more minor Baroque churches that litter the countryside – a legacy of the Counter-Reformation – are usually kept locked due to the enormous number of art thefts that have taken place. Usually, you can at least have a peek inside through the railings, but the only time you can guarantee the church is open is just before and after services in the early morning (around 7 or 8am) and/or evening (around 6 or 7pm); times are posted outside the main doors. Otherwise, it's worth asking around for the local *kněz* (priest) or *kaplan*, who's usually only too happy to oblige with the key (*klíč*).

In the Czech Lands, widespread agnosticism and the punitive policies of the last regime (self-confessed believers were not allowed to join the Party or take up teaching posts) have left many churches in a terrible state of disrepair. A similar fate has befallen many of the country's **monasteries**, some of which were closed down by the Emperor Joseph II in the late eighteenth century, while the remainder fell prey to the Communists. Nowadays, many of the buildings have become schools, factories and prisons, or been returned to their former orders, but a few remain as museums, which keep similar opening hours to the country's castles.

The country's once considerable Jewish population has been whittled down to an official figure of around 2000, over half of whom live in Prague, one of only a handful of places where regular worship still takes place. A few **synagogues** and graveyards have been saved from neglect, and some are well worth visiting, such as those in Plzeň, Děčín, Kolín and Mikulov.

■ Museums and galleries

Czech **museums** have tended to be stronger on quantity than quality, with exclusively Czech labelling designed to baffle any passing foreigner. This is changing slowly as tourism becomes more important, and many places do have an *anglický text* on offer. There are two main types of museum outside Prague: a **krajské, okresní** or **oblastní muzeum** or district museum traces the local history through arts, crafts and old photos, while a **městské muzeum** or town museum is more provincial still, with stuffed animals and displays of mushrooms the only diversion. Occasionally you'll come across a real gem, but many of the local museums are far from riveting, and school groups are often the only visitors. However, their temporary exhibitions can be worth seeing as they often cover previously taboo subjects, such as the events of 1968, the history of the First Republic and so forth.

The big cities boast the best **art galleries**, though even the collections of Prague's Národní galerie (National Gallery) pale in comparison with those of most major Western European cities. The impact of Socialist Realism was as heavy here as elsewhere in the Soviet empire, and the repercussions can still be seen in the country's provincial art galleries. In addition, many of the country's best artists – like Kupka and Mucha – worked abroad for much of their careers, and their works now grace the galleries of Paris and New York. However, previously unshown work from the 1950s and 60s is now beginning to find its way onto gallery walls, alongside exhibitions of new contemporary artists.

Opening hours for museums and galleries tend to be from 9am or 10am to 4pm or later, usually without a break at lunch. Most stay open all year round and some switch from a Tuesday–Sunday summer routine to Monday–Friday during the winter. Full opening hours are detailed in the guide. Ticket prices are still negligible, and students usually go for half-price.

Public holidays and festivals

There are remarkably few large-scale national events. Aside from the usual religious-oriented celebrations, most annual shindigs are arts- and music-based festivals, confined to a particular town or city. In addition, there are also folkloric events in the nether regions, which take place in the summer only, the Strážnice folk festival in Moravia being by far the most famous.

■ Public holidays

National holidays were always a potential source of contention with the old regime, and they remain controversial even today. **May Day**, once a nationwide compulsory march under dull commie slogans, remains a public holiday in the Czech Republic, though only a few skinheads and anarchists bother to slug it out on the streets of Prague now. Of the other *slavné májové dny* (Glorious May Days), as they used to be known, May 5, the beginning of the 1945 Prague Uprising, has been binned, and VE Day is now celebrated

---

CLOSED FOR TECHNICAL REASONS

A regular feature of the region is for museums, galleries and chateaux to be temporarily "closed for technical reasons", or, more permanently, "closed for reconstruction". Notices are rarely more specific than that, but the widespread shortage of staff and funds is often the reason. It's impossible to predict what will be closed when, but it's as well to make alternative plans when visiting galleries, museums and castles, just in case.

on **May 8** (not on May 9 as it was under the Communists, and still is in Russia). To scupper any celebration of the founding of the First Republic on **October 28**, the Communists hijacked the date for their very own Nationalization Day. Some Czechs nowadays argue that this Czechoslovak/Communist holiday, should be ditched in favour of September 28, the feast day of St Wenceslas.

■ Festivals and annual events

At **Easter** (*Velikonoce*), the age-old sexist ritual persists of whipping girls' calves with braided birch twigs tied with ribbons (*pomlázky*) – objects you'll see being furiously bought and sold from markets in the run-up to Easter Sunday. To prevent such a fate, the girls are supposed to offer the boys a coloured easter egg and pour a bucket of cold

---

PUBLIC HOLIDAYS

January 1
Easter Monday
May 1
May 8 (VE Day)
July 5 (Introduction of Christianity)
July 6 (Death of Jan Hus)
October 28 (Foundation of Czechoslovakia)
December 24
December 25
December 26

---

water over them. What may once have been an innocent bucolic frolic has now become another excuse for Czech men to harass any woman who dares to venture onto the street during this period.

FESTIVALS DIARY

APRIL
Late April–early May Brno: International Trade Fair.
Late April–early May Šumperk: home-grown Jazz Festival.

MAY
Early May Prague: Czech-Moravian soccer cup final at the Strahov stadium.
May Karlovy Vary: Beer Festival.
May 12–June 2 Prague Spring International Music Festival.
Mid-May Olomouc: Flower Festival.
Mid-May Zlín: International Childrens' Film Festival.
Late May Vlčnov: Folk Festival.
Late May–early June Ostrava: Janáček International Music Festival.

JUNE
June Olomouc: Spring Music Festival.
Mid-June Český Krumlov: Five-Petalled Rose Festival.
Mid-June Litomyšl: National Opera Festival.
Mid-June Mariánské Lázně: International Festival of Mime.
Mid-June Pelhřimov: Festival of Records and Curious Performances.
Late June–early July Strážnice: International Folk Festival.

JULY
July Karlovy Vary: International Film Festival.
Early July Chrudim: Puppet Festival.
Late July Uherské Hradiště: Czech/Slovak Film Festival.
Late July/early Aug Telč: International Folk Festival.

AUGUST
August Prague: Czech Open Tennis Championships.
Early Aug Valtice: Baroque Music Festival.
Mid-Aug Domažlice: Chodové Folk Festival.
Late Aug Brno: International Grand Prix motor-cycling event.
Late Aug Strakonice: Biennial International Bagpipers' Festival.

SEPTEMBER
Early Sept Kroměříž: Chamber Music Festival.
Early Sept Žatec: Hop (and beer) Festival.
Mid-September Tábor: Setkání Festival
Late Sept–early Oct Brno: International Music Festival.
Late Sept–early Oct Teplice: Beethoven Music Festival.

OCTOBER
Early Oct Pardubice: Velká Pardubická steeple-chase.
Early Oct Plzeň: Beer Festival.

Two ancient rituals which herald the end of winter continue in some parts of the country. The "**Slaughter of the Pig**", known as *zabíjačka*, takes place in rural parts towards the end of January, traditionally a time when all other winter provisions are exhausted. Every single bit of the animal is prepared as food for the feast that accompanies the event. Halloween comes early to the Czech Republic on April 30, when the "**Burning of the Witches**", known as *pálení Čarodějnic*, takes place. It's an old pagan ritual, during which huge bonfires are lit across the country and old brooms are thrown out and burned to ward off evil spirits.

As in the rest of the Christian world, **Christmas** (*Vánoce*) is a time for over-consumption and family gatherings, and is therefore a fairly private occasion. On December 4, the feast day of St Barbara, cherry tree branches are bought as decorations, the aim being to get them to blossom before Christmas. On the eve of December 5, numerous trios, dressed up as St Nicholas (*svatý Mikuláš*), an angel and a devil, tour round the neighbourhoods, the angel handing out sweets and fruit to children who've been good, while the devil dishes out coal and potatoes to those who've been naughty. The Czech St Nicholas has white hair and a beard, and dresses not in red but in a white priest's outfit with a bishop's mitre.

With a week or so to go, large barrels are set up in the streets from which huge quantities of live *kapr* (carp), the traditional Christmas dish, are sold. Christmas Eve (*Štědrý večer*) is traditionally a day of fasting, broken only when the evening star appears, signalling the beginning of the Christmas feast of carp, potato salad, schnitzel and sweet breads. Only after the meal are the children allowed to open their presents, which miraculously appear beneath the tree thanks not to Santa Claus but to *Ježíšek* (Baby Jesus).

Birthdays are much less important in the Czech Republic than in English-speaking countries. Even their Czech equivalent, saints' name days, which fall on the same day each year, are a fading tradition. Saints' days for popular names like Jan or Anna were once practically national celebrations since everyone was bound to know at least one person with those names.

Popular culture

Popular culture has diversified considerably in the last decade; theatre, jazz and rock, in particular, are enjoying something of a renaissance. Even sport and classical music, both actively encouraged and heavily subsidized by the old regime, have recovered from the upheavals of the 1990s, and are looking relatively healthy in the new millennium.

■ Music

Folk songs lie at the heart of all Czech music; people strike up traditional songs and contemporary folk tunes at the slightest excuse, especially in the countryside. A living tradition only really exists in the Chodsko region of Bohemia, and the Slovácko region of Moravia, but there are numerous professional and amateur groups across the country – for more on Czech (and Slovak) folk music.

The nation's great wealth of folk tunes has found its way into much of the country's **classical** music, of which the Czechs are justifiably proud, having produced four composers of considerable stature – Smetana, Dvořák, Janáček and Martinů – and the more liberal can even claim Mahler as a fifth. The Czechs have also produced a host of singers, from Ema Destinnová (see p.165) to Eva Urbanová, virtuoso violinists, such as those who play with the prestigious Suk Quartet, and conductors like Jiří Bělohlávek.

All the major cities have **music festivals**, which give much of their space over to Czech composers. Smaller towns have annual festivals often dedicated to composers: for instance Smetana (Litomyšl), Beethoven (Teplice) and Chopin (Mariánské Lázně). Throughout the year it's easy to catch works by Czech composers, since the repertoires of most regional companies are ardently nationalistic. Most opera houses and concert halls are closed for much of July and August; as compensation, watch out for the summer concerts held in many of the country's castles and churches.

Jazz (or *džez* as it's sometimes written) has an established tradition, particularly in the Czech Republic, despite the best efforts of the Nazis and the Communists to suppress it. Except for occasional one-off gigs in the other big cities, however, venues are almost entirely confined to Prague. The traditional big band sound is by far the most popular, but there are one or two venues that put on more varied fare (see p.126).

As for Czech **rock and pop** music, the scene has diversified enormously in the last decade. Bland Western pop, heavy metal and country and western have an alarmingly large following nationwide, though nowadays you can also sample such delights as Czech (mostly white) reggae or skinhead punk. The wild experimental folk guru Iva Bittová is a woman worth catching if you can, as is Věra Bílá, the gargantuan Gypsy singer, and her band, Kale. Lastly, a word of warning: Support Lesbians, while an admirable name for a band, are a thrash outfit emphatically not made up of women, gay or heterosexual.

■ Cinema

Though attendances have dipped dramatically over the last few years (with the advent of video machines, more TV stations and steadily increasing ticket prices), the **cinema** (*kino*) remains a cheap and popular form of entertainment. Hollywood blockbusters form a large part of the weekly fare, but the Czech film industry has enjoyed something of a renaissance in the late 1990s, with Jan Svěrák collecting an Oscar in 1997 for his film *Kolja*. Hollywood films tend to be shown dubbed, while more obscure art films are usually shown in their original language with subtitles (*titulky*). The month's film listings are usually fly-posted up around town or outside each cinema. Film titles are nearly always translated into Czech, so you'll need to have your wits about you to identify films such as *Královna Alžběta* as Brit blockbuster *Elizabeth*.

Prague's Barrandov Studios produced a string of innovative films in the 1960s, known collectively as the **Czech New Wave**, in which Miloš Forman, perhaps the country's best-known director, played a part. The industry's strength has always been in comedy, satire, and history as farce, as seen in Jiří Menzel's film *Ostře sledované vlaky* (*Closely Observed Trains*), which is set in the final stages of World War II and provides an antidote to the endless, overblown stories of heroism.

One of the fields in which the Czechs have long excelled is **animation**, with Jan Švankmajer establishing a considerable international following with his disturbing version of *Alice in Wonderland* and, most recently, *Conspirators of Pleasure*.

The **International Film Festival** held in Karlovy Vary every July has established a good reputation.

■ Theatre and opera

Theatre (*divadlo*) has always had a special place in Czech culture, one which the events of 1989 only strengthened. Not only did the country end up with a playwright as president, but it was the capital's theatres that served as information centres during those first few crucial weeks. After the revolution, however, the whole theatre scene, for so long heavily subsidized – and censored – by the authorities, went through a difficult patch. More recently, audiences at the opulent theatres, built by the Habsburgs in all major Czech towns and cities, have picked up considerably; in Prague, tourists are also a lucrative source of income and there are several English-language theatre companies now based there.

Outside of Prague there's obviously precious little in English, although ticket prices are cheap, and the venue and the event itself are often interesting enough to sustain you – older-generation Czechs go as much for the interval promenade as for the show itself. There's less of a linguistic problem with **opera**, of course, and Dvořák, Janáček and Smetana's works in particular are regularly performed.

With numerous permanent puppet theatres across the country, Czech **puppetry** is still very popular. Sadly, few traditional marionette or puppet-only theatres survive; the rest have introduced live actors into their repertoire, making the shows less accessible if you don't speak the language. However, this trend has produced innovative and highly professional companies like Hradec Králové's Drak, which has toured extensively throughout Europe and now only occasionally uses puppets in its shows. If you want to see a performance, look out for the words *loutkové divadlo*.

■ Sport

The Czech Republic is equally famous for its world-class tennis players, its national football squad and its ice hockey players; however, the sport which pulls the biggest crowds, by far, is soccer. Getting tickets to watch a particular sport is easy (and cheap) enough on the day – even big soccer matches rarely sell out. Taking part is more difficult – Czechs who do so belong to local clubs, and there are still relatively few facilities for the general public outside of Prague.

Soccer

The Czech national **soccer** (*fotbal*) team have enjoyed mixed fortunes since splitting from the Slovaks in 1993. After losing the Euro 96 final in extra time, they failed even to qualify for the 1998

World Cup. On the domestic front, however, things have been much worse. As with most former Eastern Bloc countries, the best home-grown players have, almost without exception, chosen to seek fame and fortune abroad. As a result, domestic teams have underperformed in all European competitions, and four-figure crowds remain the norm.

Big money was pumped into certain clubs by local entrepreneurs, but a combination of mismanagement and corruption has spelled disaster for several of the big clubs. Despite a decade of turmoil, however, the most consistent teams in the *Českomoravského liga*, are still arch rivals Sparta Praha and Slavia Praha. The season runs from August to late November and late February to early June, and matches are usually held on Sundays. And the best thing, of course, is that, somewhat unbelievably, you can still drink inexpensive and delicious beer on the terraces.

Ice hockey

Ice hockey (*lední hokej*) runs soccer a close second as the country's most popular sport. It's not unusual to see kids in the street playing their own form of the game, rather than kicking a ball around. As with soccer, the fall of communism prompted an exodus by the country's best players who left to seek fame and fortune in North America's National Hockey League (NHL). One of the NHL's top scorers, Jaromír Jágr, who currently plays for the Pittsburgh Penguins, is by far the most famous Czech player. Even without Jágr, the Czech national team succeeded in winning the World Championships in 1996, and in 1998, the Czechs surprised everyone by taking the gold medal in the Winter Olympics.

Unlike in soccer, there are several teams usually in close contention for the *Extraliga* title, though Sparta Praha are usually among them. Games are fast and physical, cold but compelling, and can take anything up to three hours. They are held in the local *zimní stadión* (winter stadium) on Saturday afternoons. The season starts at the end of September and culminates in the annual World Championships, when the fortunes of the national side are subject to close scrutiny, especially if pitched against the Slovaks or the Russians. A double victory against the latter in 1969 precipitated riots in towns across the country, culminating in the torching of the Aeroflot (Soviet airlines) offices in Prague.

Tennis

Tennis has been one of the country's most successful exports, with the likes of Martina Navrátilová and Ivan Lendl among the game's all-time greats. The glory days of Czech tennis may well be over, though the country still provides a smattering of world-class players each year. (Contrary to what you might read in the Western press, however, the Swiss player and top seed Martina Hingis is of Slovak, not Czech, descent). Any home-grown talent there is will be on domestic display only in the Škoda Czech Open, the country's only ATP event, held every August on Prague's Štvanice island.

Skiing and rock climbing

The Czechs may not produce any world-class skiers, but with much of the country covered in a thick blanket of snow for three months of the year, **skiing** is a popular and necessary skill which most children learn at school. One or two companies can put together skiing packages, but more and more people are going independently and simply renting self-catering flats. If you do go it alone, it's worth considering taking your own equipment, even though rental facilities have improved greatly over the last few years. Prices for ski passes are very low when compared with the West, but fewer facilities and long queues are often the payback.

There are some great opportunities for **rock climbing**, particularly in Bohemia. North and east of Prague there are concentrated areas of limestone and basalt rocks: the most popular is the Český ráj, just 80km northeast of the Czech capital; equally good is the České Švýcarsko region, which borders with Saxony. In Teplice, the main base for the Adršpach rocks near the Polish border, there's even an annual climbers' convention which takes place in early September. You'll need to take your own equipment wherever you go, and take the usual precautions on all climbs.

CHAPTER ONE

PRAGUE AND AROUND

Prague (Praha to the Czechs) is one of the least "Eastern" European cities you could imagine. Architecturally, and in terms of city sights, it is a revelation: with some six hundred years of architecture virtually untouched by natural disaster or war, few other cities, anywhere in Europe, look so good. Four decades of Soviet-imposed isolation obscured the fact that Prague has always been, geographically and culturally, much closer to the West than it is to Moscow. For over three centuries, it was firmly under the sway of the Habsburg dynasty, while between the two world wars, during the country's brief period of independence, Prague was second only to Paris as a centre of Cubist painting and the only place in the world where Cubist architecture was attempted.

The best way to appreciate the city's artistic treasures is simply to stroll through the cobbled streets and squares and soak in the scene. Its town planning took place in medieval times, the palaces and churches were decorated with a rich mantle of Baroque, and the whole lot has escaped the vanities and excesses of postwar redevelopment. Prague's unique compactness allows you to walk from the grandeur of the city's castle district, via a series of intimate Baroque lanes, across a medieval stone bridge, through one of the most alluring central squares on the continent, and end up sipping coffee on Wenceslas Square, the modern hub of the city, in under half an hour.

That's not to say that Prague doesn't have more than its fair share of problems. The city's mini-boom during the 1990s brought crowds of tourists, gave the city a very low unemployment rate, and increased wages significantly, but prices rose even faster. The Westernized shops and restaurants in the centre and the products advertised on the hoardings remain out of reach for the vast majority of Praguers. Racial tensions, suppressed under the Communists, have surfaced once more, with continuing violent attacks on the city's considerable Romany community that the police and politicians are powerless or unwilling to prevent.

The city's outer suburbs, where most of the population live, are typical of Eastern Europe – half-built, high-rise housing estates, known locally as *paneláky*, swimming in a sea of mud – but once you're clear of them, the area **around Prague** shifts gear straight into the somnolent villages and softly rolling hills of Bohemia. Many Praguers own a *chata*, or country cottage, somewhere in these rural backwaters, and every weekend the roads are jammed with weekenders. Few places are more than an hour from the centre by public transport, making most an easy day-trip for visitors.

The most popular destinations for foreign day-trippers are the castles of **Karlštejn** and **Konopště**, both of which suffer from a daily swarm of coach parties. You're better rewarded by heading north, away from the hills and the crowds, to the chateau of **Veltrusy** near Dvořák's birthplace of Nelahozeves, or to the wine town of **Mělník**. The wooded hills around **Křivoklát** in the northeast or **Kokořín** in the southwest, both around 40km from Prague, are also good places to lose the crowds. Even further afield is the undisputed gem of the region, the medieval silver-mining town of **Kutná Hora**, 60km east of Prague, with a glorious Gothic cathedral.

A brief history

The Czechs have a **legend** for every occasion, and the founding of Prague is no exception. Sometime in the seventh or eighth century AD, the Czech prince Krok (aka Pace)

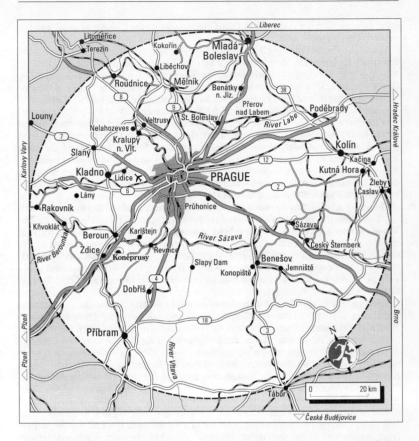

moved his people south from the plains of the River Labe (Elbe) to the rocky knoll that is now Vyšehrad (literally "high castle"). His youngest daughter, **Libuše**, who was to become the country's first and last female leader, was endowed with the gift of prophecy. Falling into a trance one day, she pronounced that they should build a city "whose glory will touch the stars", at the point in the forest where they would find an old man constructing the threshold of his house. He was duly discovered on the Hradčany hill overlooking the Vltava, and the city was named **Praha**, meaning "threshold". Subsequently, Libuše was compelled to take a husband and again fell into a trance, this time pronouncing that they should follow her horse to a ploughman, whose descendants would rule over them. Sure enough, a man called **Přemysl** (meaning "ploughman") was discovered and became the mythical founder of the Přemyslid dynasty, which ruled Bohemia until the fourteenth century.

So much for the legend. **Historically**, Hradčany and not Vyšehrad was the site of the first Slav settlement. The Vltava was relatively shallow at this point, and it probably seemed a safer bet than the plains of the Labe. The earliest recorded **Přemyslid** was Prince Bořivoj, the first Christian ruler of Prague, baptized in the ninth century by the Byzantine missionaries to the Slavs, Cyril and Methodius (for more on whom, see p.317). However, it was his grandson, Prince Václav, who was to become the dynasty's most famous member – the Good "King" Wenceslas of the Christmas carol and the modern Czech patron saint.

Under the Přemyslids the city prospered, benefiting from its position on the central European trade routes. Merchants from all over Europe came to settle here, and in 1234 the first of Prague's historic towns, the **Staré Město**, was founded to accommodate them. In 1257, King Otakar II founded the **Malá Strana** on the slopes of the castle as a separate quarter for Prague's German merchants, but he failed in his attempt to become Holy Roman Emperor, and the Přemyslid dynasty died out in 1306. The crown was handed over by the Czech nobles to the Luxembourgs, and it was under **Charles IV** (1346–78), who succeeded in being elected emperor, that Prague enjoyed its **first golden age**. In just thirty years, Charles transformed Prague into one of the most important cities in fourteenth-century Europe, establishing institutions and buildings that survive today – the Charles University, St Vitus Cathedral, the Charles Bridge, a host of monasteries and churches – and founding an entire new town, **Nové Město**, to accommodate the influx of students and clergy.

His son, Václav IV, was no match for such an inheritance, and the city was soon in crisis. Following the execution of the radical reformist preacher Jan Hus in 1415, the whole country became engulfed in **religious wars**, with Prague experiencing some of the most bitter struggles. Not until the Polish Jagiellonian dynasty succeeded to the throne later that century was a degree of prosperity and religious tolerance restored. Surprisingly enough, it was a Habsburg, **Rudolf II**, who gave the city its **second golden age**, inviting artists, scientists (and quacks) from all over Europe, and filling the castle galleries with the finest art.

However, trouble broke out again between the Protestant nobles and the Catholic Habsburgs in 1618, this time culminating in a decisive defeat of the Protestants at the **Battle of Bílá hora** (White Mountain) on the outskirts of the city. Then followed the period the Czechs refer to as the **dark ages**, when the full force of the Counter-Reformation was brought to bear on the city's people: all forms of Protestantism were outlawed and the education system handed over to the Jesuits, while Germanization continued apace. Paradoxically, though, the spurt of Baroque rebuilding during the Counter-Reformation lent Prague its most striking architectural aspect, and from this period date the majority of the city's impressive palaces.

The next two centuries saw Prague's importance gradually whittled away within the Habsburg Empire. Two things dragged it out of the doldrums. The first was the **industrial revolution** of the mid-nineteenth century, which brought large numbers of Czechs in from the countryside to work in the factories, and led the city to expand beyond its medieval boundaries for the first time. The second was the contemporaneous **Czech national revival** or *národní obrození*, which gave Prague a number of symbolic monuments, such as its Národní divadlo (National Theatre), the Národní muzeum (National Museum), the Rudolfinum and the Obecní dům. More importantly, the national revival led eventually to the foundation of Czechoslovakia in 1918, which once again put Prague at the centre of the country's political events and marked the beginning of the city's third golden age, the **First Republic**. Architecturally, the first three decades of this century left Prague with a unique legacy of Art Nouveau, Cubist, Rondo-Cubist and Functionalist buildings.

The virtual annihilation of the city's Jews and the expulsion of the German-speaking community changed Prague forever, though the city itself survived World War II physically more or less unscathed and industrially intact, before disappearing completely behind the Iron Curtain. Internal centralization only increased the city's importance – it hosted the country's macabre show trials, and at one time boasted the largest statue of Stalin in the world. The city briefly re-emerged onto the world stage during the cultural blossoming of the **1968 Prague Spring**, but following the Soviet invasion in August of that year, Prague vanished from view once more. Just over twenty years later, the **1989 Velvet Revolution** finally toppled the Communist government without so much as a shot being fired. The exhilarating popular unity of that period is now history, but there is still a great sense of new-found potential in the capital. Paranoia and fear, at least, are things of the past, and there's a sense of openness and opportunity here which makes any visit rewarding.

PRAGUE PRACTICALITIES

With a population of just one and a quarter million, **Prague** is one of Europe's smaller capital cities. It originally developed as four separate, self-governing towns and a Jewish ghetto, whose individual identities and medieval street plans have been preserved, more or less intact, to this day. Almost everything of any historical interest lies within these central districts, the majority of which are easy to master quickly on foot. Only in the last hundred years has Prague spread beyond its ancient perimeter, and its suburbs now stretch for miles on every side. There's a cheap and efficient transport system, so even from the furthest edges of the capital, you should be able to get into town within half an hour.

Arrival

If you fly into Prague, you'll find yourself just over 10km northwest of the city centre, with only a bus link to get you into town. By contrast, both the international train stations and the main bus terminal are linked to the centre by the fast and efficient metro system. Driving into Prague is easy enough, though the city authorities, quite rightly, make it very awkward for drivers to enter the old town, and finding a parking space is also extremely difficult. A sensible option is to make use of one of the park-and-ride car parks situated close to the Dejvická, Hradčanská, Nové Butovice, Opatov, Radlická, Skalka and Strašnická metro stations.

By air

Prague's airport, **Ruzyně**, has been thoroughly revamped over the last decade and now has most of the facilities you'd expect of a European capital city airport, with shops, cafés, 24-hour exchange facilities and a variety of accommodation agencies (see p.58) and car rental outlets (see p.57).

The cheapest way to get into town is to take the **local bus** #119 (daily: 5am–8pm every 10–15min, 8pm–5am every 30min), which stops frequently and ends its journey outside Dejvická metro station; you must buy your ticket from the orange ticket machines or the newsagents in the airport. More convenient if you've a lot of luggage is to take the **express minibus service** (daily 5.30am–9.30pm; every 30min), which stops first at Dejvická metro station, at the end of metro line A (journey time 20min) and ends up at náměstí Republiky (journey time 30min); the full journey currently costs 90Kč. Express minibuses will also take you straight to your hotel for around 350Kč per drop-off – a bargain if there's a few of you. If you arrive after midnight, you can catch a night bus #510 to Divoká šárka, the terminus for night tram #51, which will take you to Národní in the centre of town; again, you'll need to buy a ticket in the airport.

Of course, it's easy enough to take a **taxi** from the airport into the centre. However, Prague taxi drivers have such a deservedly bad reputation that you're unlikely to be charged the correct fare, which should be around 350Kč to the centre. If you do end up taking a taxi, make sure the driver turns on the meter, or, if in doubt, agree on a price before getting in.

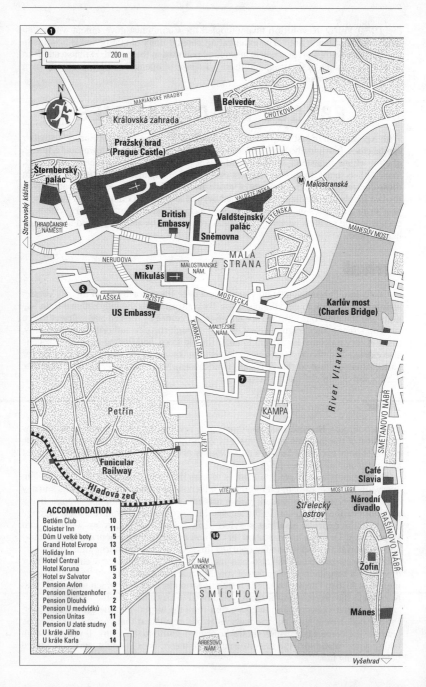

0   200 m

N

MARIÁNSKÉ HRADBY

Belvedér

CHOTKOVA

Královská zahrada

**Pražský hrad
(Prague Castle)**

**Šternberský
palác**

Strahovský klášter

M *Malostranská*

VALDŠTEJNSKÁ

HRADČANSKÉ
NÁMĚSTÍ

LETENSKÁ

MÁNESŮV MOST

**British
Embassy**

**Valdštejnský
palác**

Sněmovna

**MALÁ
STRANA**

NERUDOVA

**sv
Mikuláš**

MALOSTRANSKÉ
NÁM.

⑤

VLAŠSKÁ

TRŽIŠTĚ

MOSTECKÁ

**Karlův most
(Charles Bridge)**

US Embassy

KARMELITSKÁ

MALTÉZSKÉ
NÁM.

⑦

River Vltava

Petřín

KAMPA

SMETANOVO NÁBŘ

ÚJEZD

**Funicular
Railway**

Hladová zeď

VÍTĚZNÁ

MOST LEGIÍ

**Café
Slavia**

Střelecký
ostrov

**Národní
divadlo**

RAŠÍNOVO NÁBŘ

ACCOMMODATION	
Betlém Club	10
Cloister Inn	11
Dům U velké boty	5
Grand Hotel Evropa	13
Holiday Inn	1
Hotel Central	4
Hotel Koruna	15
Hotel sv Salvator	3
Pension Avlon	9
Pension Dientzenhofer	7
Pension Dlouhá	2
Pension U medvídků	12
Pension Unitas	11
Pension U zlaté studny	6
U krále Jiřího	8
U krále Karla	14

⑭

NÁM
KINSKÝCH

SMÍCHOV

Žofín

Mánes

ARBESOVO
NÁM.

Vyšehrad

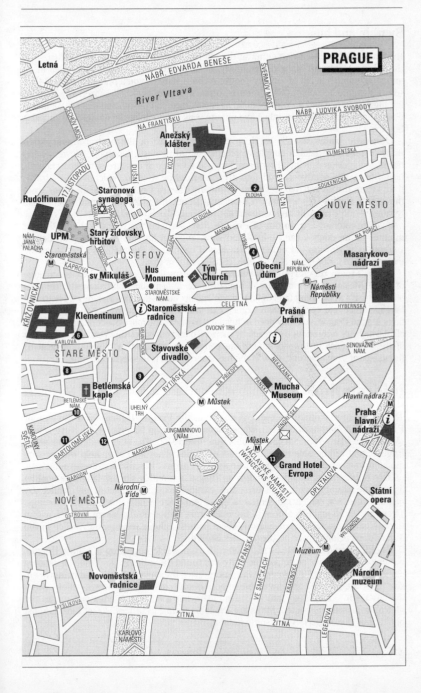

By train and bus

International trains arrive either at the old Art Nouveau **Praha hlavní nádraží**, on the edge of Nové Město and Vinohrady, or at **Praha-Holešovice**, which lies in an industrial suburb north of the city centre. At both stations you'll find exchange outlets (there's even a branch of the PIS tourist office at Hlavní nádraží), as well as a 24-hour left-luggage office and accommodation agencies (see p.58). Both stations are on metro lines, and Hlavní nádraží is only a five-minute walk from Václavské náměstí (Wenceslas Square).

Domestic trains usually wind up at Hlavní nádraží or the central **Masarykovo nádraží** on Hybernská, a couple of blocks east of náměstí Republiky. Slower *osobní* trains and various provincial services arrive at a variety of obscure suburban stations: trains from the southwest pull into **Praha-Smíchov** (metro Smíchovské nádraží); trains from the east arrive at **Praha-Vysočany** (metro Českomoravská); trains from the west at **Praha-Dejvice** (metro Hradčanská); and trains from the south occasionally rumble into **Praha-Vršovice** (tram #24 to Wenceslas Square).

If you're catching a **train out of Prague**, don't leave buying your ticket until the last minute, as the queues can be long and slow. You can buy international train tickets (*mezinárodní jízdenky)* at either Praha hlavní nádraží or Praha-Holešovice, or at the main office of ČEDOK on Na příkopě, in the centre of town.

Prague's **main bus terminal** is **Praha-Florenc** (metro Florenc), on the eastern edge of Nové Město, where virtually all long-distance international and domestic services terminate. It's a confusing (and ugly) place to end up, but its facilities include a 24-hour left-luggage office and you can make a quick exit to the adjacent metro station. For destinations around Prague, you may need to head out to one of the more obscure bus terminals, all of which are easy enough to reach by metro. To find out which one you want, ask at any of the PIS offices in town or check the comprehensive (and extremely complicated) timetables at Praha-Florenc: *stání* is the bus stand; *odjezd* is the departure time.

Information

The official tourist office in Prague is known as the **Prague Information Service** or **PIS** (*Pražská informační služba*), whose main branch is at Na příkopě 20, Nové Město (Mon–Fri 8.30am–7pm, Sat & Sun 9am–5pm; ☎26 40 22). The staff usually speak some English, and will be able to answer most enquiries. They also offer help with accommodation, sell maps and guides, and act as ticket agents. PIS also distributes some useful free publications, including *Culture in Prague*, a monthly English-language booklet listing the major events, concerts and exhibitions, and a fortnightly leaflet *Do města/Downtown*, which concentrates on cinema, art exhibitions and club listings. There are additional PIS offices in the main train station, Praha hlavní nádraží, within the Staroměstská radnice on Staroměstské náměstí, plus a summer-only office in the Malá Strana bridge tower on the Charles Bridge.

The PIS should be able to furnish you with a quick reference **map** of central Prague, but to locate a specific street, or find your way round the suburbs, you'll need a detailed city map (*plán města*). *Kartografie Praha* produces the cheapest and most comprehensive ones: the 1:20,000 map (available in both booklet and fold-out form), which covers the city centre as well as many of the suburbs, has a full street index and marks the metro, tram and bus routes. Maps are available from PIS offices, street kiosks, most bookshops (*knihkupectví*) and some hotels.

The phone code for Prague is ☎02.

Another good source of information is the weekly **English-language paper**, *Prague Post*, which carries **listings** on the latest exhibitions, shows, gigs and events around the capital. Another useful listings magazine is *Přehled*, a monthly publication in Czech (but easy enough to decipher), which lists all the city's museums, exhibitions, concerts, gigs, films and events.

Getting around

The centre of Prague, where most of the city's sights are concentrated, is reasonably small and best explored on foot. At some point, however, in order to cross the city quickly or reach some of the more widely dispersed attractions, you'll need to use the city's cheap and efficient public transport system, which comprises the metro and a network of trams and buses. To get a clearer picture, it's essential to invest in a **city map** (see above), which marks all the tram, bus and metro lines.

Public transport

Prague's **public transport system** (*dopravní podnik* or *DP*), used to have a simple ticketing system – not any more. Most Praguers simply buy monthly passes, and to avoid having to understand the complexities of the system, you too are best off buying a travel pass (for more on which, see below).

Probably the single most daunting aspect of buying a ticket is the new machines found inside all metro stations and at some bus and tram stops. The machines are covered in buttons, but only two are really relevant, since for a single **ticket** (*lístek* or *jízdenka*) in the two central zones (*2 pásma*), there are just two basic choices. The 8Kč version (*zlevněná*) allows you to travel for up to fifteen minutes on the trams or buses, or up to four stops on the metro; it's known as a *nepřestupní jízdenka*, or "no change ticket", although you can in fact change metro lines (but not buses or trams). The 12Kč version (*plnocenná*) is valid for one hour at peak times (an hour and a half off-peak), during which you may change trams, buses or metro lines as many times as you like, hence its name, *přestupní jízdenka*, or "changing ticket". Half-price tickets are available for those aged 6 to 15, bikes and other large objects; under-6s travel free.

If you're buying a ticket from one of the new machines, you must press the appropriate button – press it once for one ticket, twice for two and so on – followed by the *výdej/enter* button, after which you put your money in. The machines do give change, but if you don't have enough coins, the person on duty in the metro office by the barriers will usually be able to give you change or sell you a ticket. Tickets can also be bought, en masse, and rather more easily, from a tobacconist (*tabák*), street kiosk, newsagents, PIS office or any place that displays the yellow DP sticker. When you enter the metro, or board a tram or bus, you must validate your ticket by placing it in one of the electronic machines to hand.

To save hassle, it's best to buy a **travel pass** (*denní jízdenka*). These are available for 24 hours (70Kč), three days (180Kč), seven days (250Kč) and fifteen days (280Kč); no photos or ID are needed, though you must write your name and date of birth on the reverse of the ticket, and punch it to validate when you first use it. All the passes are available from *DP* outlets, and the 24-hour pass is also available from ticket machines. Most Praguers buy a monthly, quarterly or yearly pass (*průkaz*), which is why you see so few of them punching tickets. To obtain one, simply present your ID and a passport-sized photo to the windows marked *DP* at major metro stations and ask for a *měsíční jízdenka*. Monthly passes currently cost around 380Kč. There's nothing to stop people from freeloading on the system, of course, since there are no barriers. However, plain-clothes **inspectors** (*revizoři*) make spot checks and will issue an on-the-spot fine of 200Kč to anyone caught without a valid ticket or pass; controllers should show you their ID (a small metal disc), and give you a receipt (*paragon*).

Metro

The futuristic Soviet-built **metro** is fast, smooth and ultra-clean, running daily from just before 5am to midnight, with trains every two minutes during peak hours, slowing down to every four to ten minutes by late in the evening. Its three lines (with a fourth planned) intersect at various points in the city centre, and the route maps are easy to follow (see overleaf). The stations are discreetly marked above ground with the logo shown on the map overleaf, in green (line A), yellow (line B) or red (line C). The constant bleeping at metro entrances is to enable blind people to locate the escalators. Once inside the metro, it's worth knowing that *výstup* means exit and *přestup* will lead you to one of the connecting lines at an interchange. The digital clock at the end of the platform tells you not only what time it is, but also how long it's been since the last train.

Trams and buses

The electric **tram** (*tramvaj*) system, in operation since 1891, negotiates Prague's hills and cobbles with remarkable dexterity. After the metro, trams are the fastest and most efficient way of getting around, running every six to eight minutes at peak times, and every five to fifteen minutes at other times – check the timetables posted at every stop (*zastávka*), which list the departure times from that specific stop.

Tram #22, which runs from Vinohrady to Hradčany via the centre of town and Malá Strana, is a good way to get to grips with the lie of the land, and a cheap method of sightseeing. From Easter to October, an interwar tram (#91) runs from Výstaviště to náměstí Republiky via Malá Strana (Sat & Sun hourly 1–7pm) and back again; the ride takes forty minutes and costs 15Kč. **Night trams** (*noční tramvaje*; #51–58) run roughly every thirty to forty minutes from around midnight to 5am, and all of them pass by Lazarská and Spálená in Nové Město.

Unless you're intent on staying in the more obscure suburbs, you'll rarely need to use Prague's **buses** (*autobusy*), which, for the most part, keep well out of the centre of town; they operate similar (though generally less frequent) hours to the trams, and route numbers are given in the text where appropriate. **Night buses** run just once an hour between midnight and 5am.

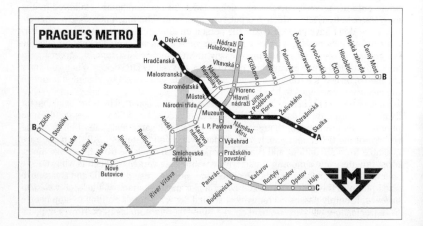

PRAGUE ADDRESSES, HOUSE SIGNS AND NUMBERS

In order to help locate **addresses** more easily, we have used the names of the city districts as they appear on street signs, for example Hradčany, Staré Město, etc. Prague's **postal districts**, which also appear on street signs, are too large to be of much help in orientation, since the city centre lies almost entirely within Prague 1.

In the older districts, many houses have retained their original medieval **house signs**, a system that is still used today, though predominantly by pubs, restaurants and wine bars, for example *U zeleného hroznu* (The Green Grape). In the 1770s, the Habsburgs, in their rationalizing fashion, introduced a numerical system, with each house in the city entered onto a register according to a strict chronology. Later, the conventional system of progressive **street numbering** was introduced; so don't be surprised if seventeenth-century pubs like *U medvídků* (The Little Bears) have, in addition to a house sign, two numbers: in this case 345 and 7; the former Habsburg number written on a red background, the latter modern number on blue.

Taxis, cars and bikes

Taxis come in all shapes and sizes, and, theoretically at least, are extremely cheap. However, Prague taxi drivers have a terrible reputation, and many will almost certainly attempt to rip you off if they think they can. Needless to say, the drivers with the worst reputations hang out at the ranks closest to the tourist sights. Officially, the initial fare on the meter should be 25Kč, plus 17kč per kilometre within Prague. The best advice is to hail a cab, rather than pick one up at the taxi ranks; if the meter isn't switched on, ask the driver to do so – *zapněte taxametr, prosím* – and, if you suspect you've been overcharged, asking for a receipt – *prosím, dejte mi potrzení* – should have the desired effect. The following cab companies have fairly good reputations: Profitaxi ☎2213 5551; AAA taxi ☎312 2112.

You really don't need a **car** in Prague, since much of the city centre is pedestrianized and the public transport system is so cheap and efficient. Should you want to drive out of Prague, however, **car rental** is easy to arrange, with all the major companies operating out of Ruzyně airport. If you book in advance with an international outfit you're looking at a whopping £60/$96 per day for a small car. You'll get a much cheaper deal, however, if you book your car through a local agent such as Car Lend, Hovorčovice (☎687 0519 or ☎0602 229 155); prices can be as low as £10/$16 a day. In order to rent a car, you'll need to be at least 21 and have been driving for at least a year.

Cycling as a leisure activity is beginning to catch on in the Czech Republic, but only the brave (or foolish) use it as a form of transport in Prague. The combination of cobbled streets, tram lines and sulphurous air is enough to put most people off. Facilities for **bike rental** are still not that widespread, but if you're determined to give cycling a go, head for Landa, Šumavská 33, Vinohrady (Mon–Fri 9am–6pm; ☎2425 6121; metro náměstí Míru), which rents out mountain bikes all year round.

Accommodation

Finding a place to stay in Prague is no longer the nightmare it was back in the early 1990s when the city simply couldn't cope with the influx of new visitors. That said, accommodation is twice as expensive in Prague as anywhere else in the country, and is still likely to be by far the largest chunk of your daily expenditure, with most private rooms starting at around 500Kč per person. At the extreme ends of the spectrum, you can spend as little as 200Kč per person for the cheapest hostel bed, or 5000Kč and upwards in the more salubrious hotels. If you're going to Prague during high season (from Easter to September, or over the Christmas holidays), it's sensible to arrange accommodation before you arrive either directly with the hotels or through one of the specialist agencies listed on pp.8, 12 & 15. As for camping, the main sites are a fair trek from the centre of town and have only basic facilities, but cheapness is their virtue: for two people and a tent pitch, prices start at around 300Kč.

Private rooms

Renting a **private room** remains by far the most popular way to stay in Prague. Most Czechs keep their places very tidy and clean, but before agreeing to part with any money, be sure you know exactly where you're staying and check about transport to the centre – some places can be a long way out of town. The abundance of private accommodation in Prague means it's not really necessary to book in advance – although it can be worth doing to save time queueing and for peace of mind, especially in high season or if you're arriving late in the evening. If you arrive without a room reservation, the easiest thing is to head for one of the **accommodation agencies** at the airport or main train station. If the queues are horrendous, or it's not too late in the evening, then try one of the other agencies in town (see below for a list). Alternatively, you're almost certain to be approached by a tout at the station, airport or sometimes outside the agencies themselves. Most offers are genuine, but make sure you ask for a receipt before you pass over any money. Again, check exactly how far out of the centre you're going to be (and preferably see the room) before committing yourself.

Accommodation agencies

AVE (☎24 22 35 21; *avetours@avetours.anet.cz*; daily 6am–11pm). AVE is the largest agency in Prague, with offices at the airport and both international train stations, and is therefore an excellent last-minute fall-back.

City of Prague Accommodation Service Haštalská 7, Staré Město; metro náměstí Republiky (☎231 02 02, fax 231 66 40; daily 9am–1pm, 2–6pm). More upmarket outfit with a good selection of centrally located private rooms.

Pragotur, Za Poříčskou bránou 7, Karlín; metro Florenc (☎231 11 16; Mon–Fri 9am–6pm; Sat & Sun 8.30am–4pm). The main office is situated just across the road from Florenc bus station, but it also operates through the various PIS offices. Can book anything from private rooms to hotels and hostels.

Tom's Travel, Ostrovní 7, Nové Město; metro Národní třída (☎29 39 72; *toms@travel.cz*; daily 8am–8pm; June–Aug daily 8am–10pm). Upmarket travel agency that can book you into hotels, pensions and apartments in Prague, and help with accommodation outside Prague, too.

Hotels and pensions

Pre-1989, Prague's **hotels** were much of a muchness: 1950s decor, a radio permanently tuned to the state channel (very *1984*) and sporadically hot showers. Matters have

---

ACCOMMODATION PRICE CODES

After each entry in the **hotel** lists below, you'll find a symbol which corresponds to one of nine **price categories**:

① Under 500Kč	④ 1000–1250Kč	⑦ 1750–2000Kč
② 500–750Kč	⑤ 1250–1500Kč	⑧ 2000–2500Kč
③ 750–1000Kč	⑥ 1500–1750Kč	⑨ 2500Kč and upwards

All prices are for the cheapest **double room** available during high season, which usually means without private bath or shower in the less expensive places. For a **single room**, expect to pay around two-thirds the price of a double.

improved enormously since then, with almost all hotels now modernized to some degree, and more and more guaranteeing en-suite bathrooms, TVs and breakfast. The latter is usually included in the price of your room and, though more often than not little more than coffee and rolls, it's worth grabbing given the lack of any great alternatives out on the streets of Prague. **Pensions** are a new phenomenon and, though they tend to be smaller and less expensive, this can't be guaranteed. Over all, standards still vary wildly, and don't always keep up with prices.

Since demand still exceeds supply, there's really no point in trekking around any of the hotels listed below on the off chance that they will have vacancies. Besides, Prague's cheaper hotels and pensions are scattered throughout the city, with few in the older quarters of Hradčany, Malá Strana and Staré Město. The best policy is to contact the hotel by email or phone before you arrive in Prague and attempt to make a reservation that way, or use one of the agencies listed on p.58.

Most of the places listed below are marked on the map on p.52; others appear on area maps as detailed.

Inexpensive

Hotel Balkán, Svornosti 28, Smíchov; metro Anděl (☎57 32 71 80, fax 57 32 55 83). One of the cheapest hotels in Prague; like Smíchov itself, no frills, but clean and comfortable. See map on p.98. ⑤.

Hotel Kafka, Cimburkova 24, Žižkov; tram #5, #9 or #26 from metro Hlavní nádraží (☎24 61 71 18, fax 24 22 57 69); see map on p.98. TVs, en-suite shower and toilet, but only sporadic hot water – still better than what the residents on the other side of the courtyard can expect. ⑤.

Pension Avalon, Havelská 15, Staré Město; metro Můstek (☎26 36 43; fax 26 36 42). Perfect location right over the market on Havelská, with seven small, plainly furnished, but clean rooms, with or without en-suite facilities. ⑤.

Pension Unitas, Bartolomějská 9; metro Národní třída (☎232 12 89, *unitas@cloisterinn.cz*). Run by the *Cloister Inn* (see p.60), with hostel rooms, plus bargain rooms in converted secret police prison cells (Havel stayed in P6), now owned by Franciscan nuns. No smoking, and no drinking, but unbelievably cheap. ④.

Moderate

Dům U velké boty (The Big Shoe), Vlašská 30, Malá Strana; metro Malostranská (☎57 31 11 07, fax 53 35 46). The sheer anonymity of this pension, in a lovely old building in the quiet backstreets, is one of its main draws. A series of characterful, tastefully modernized rooms – some without en-suite, some with – run by a very friendly, English-speaking couple. Breakfast is extra, but worth it. ⑧.

Gay Penzion David, Holubova 5, Smíchov; tram #14 from metro Anděl (☎90 01 12 93, fax 54 98 20). Friendly gay/lesbian pension (complete with sauna) in the hills above Smíchov, with its own restaurant; advance booking essential. See map on p.98. ⑧.

Grand Hotel Evropa, Václavské náměstí 25, Nové Město; metro Můstek/Muzeum (☎24 22 81 17, fax 24 22 45 44). Without doubt, the most beautiful hotel in Prague, built in the 1900s and sumptuously decorated in Art Nouveau style. The rooms are furnished in repro Louis XIV, and there are still some cheaper ones without en-suite facilities. Despite its prime location and its incredible decor, this place is run like an old communist hotel – a blast from the past in every sense. ⑨.

Hotel Hlávkova kolej, Jenštejnská 1, Nové Město; metro Karlovo náměstí (☎ & fax 29 00 98); see map on p.98. Ornate late-nineteenth-century hotel on the outside; former student hostel on the inside, with spartan but clean en-suite doubles. ⑥.

Hotel Legie, Sokolská 33, Nové Město; metro I. P. Pavlova (☎24 92 02 54, fax 24 91 44 41). Former military R&R centre on a busy road, just one stop or a short stroll from Wenceslas Square. It looks bad from the outside, but the rooms are fine inside and are all en-suite. See map on p.98. ⑧.

Hotel sv Salvator, Truhlářská 10, Nové Město; metro náměstí Republiky (☎231 22 34, fax 231 63 55). Very good location, just a minute's walk from náměstí Republiky, with small, but clean rooms (the cheaper ones without en-suite facilities), and a bar/breakfast/pool room. ⑥.

Pension City, Belgická 10, Vinohrady; metro náměstí Míru (☎691 13 34, fax 691 09 77). Quiet locale, cheap, clean en-suite rooms with TVs and within walking distance of Wenceslas Square. See map on p.98. ⑥.

Pension Dientzenhofer, Nosticova 2, Malá Strana; metro Malostranská (☎53 16 72, fax 57 32 08 88). Birthplace of its namesake, and a very popular pension due to its price and the fact that it's one of the few reasonably priced places (anywhere in Prague) to have wheelchair access. Just seven rooms on offer. ⑧.

Pension U medvídků (The Little Bears), Na Perštýně 7, Staré Město; metro Národní třída (☎24 21 19 16, fax 24 22 09 30). Eight plainly furnished rooms (doubles and triples only) above a famous Prague pub; booking ahead essential. ⑥–⑨.

Expensive

Betlém Club, Betlémské náměstí 9, Staré Město; metro Národní třída (☎24 21 68 72, fax 24 21 80 54). Small rooms, at just over 3000Kč a double, with slightly tacky decor, but a perfect location and a Gothic cellar for breakfast. ⑨.

Cloister Inn, Bartolomějská 9, Staré Město; metro Národní třída (☎232 77 00, *cloister@cloisterinn.cz*). Pleasant well-equipped hotel housed in a nunnery in one of the backstreets. There are cheaper rooms and a hostel below in *Pension Unitas* (see previous page). ⑥.

U krále Jiřího, Liliová 10, Staré Město; metro Staroměstská(☎24 22 20 13, fax 24 22 19 83). Eight cosy attic rooms (at under 3000Kč a double) above an "Irish" pub, hidden in the network of lanes which characterize this part of Staré Město. ⑨.

Holiday Inn, Koulova 15, Dejvice; tram #20 or #25 from metro Dejvická (☎24 39 31 11, fax 24 31 06 16). Prague's classic 1950s Stalinist *International Hotel*, with its dour Socialist Realist friezes and large helpings of marble, is now somewhat unbelievably a bona fide *Holiday Inn*, with double rooms going for around 5000Kč. ⑨.

Hotel U krále Karla, Úvoz 4, Malá Strana; metro Malostranská (☎53 88 05, fax 53 88 11). Possibly the most tasteful and exquisite of all the small luxury hotels in Malá Strana, with beautiful antique furnishings and stained-glass windows. ⑨.

Hotel U raka, Černínská 10, Malá Strana; tram #22 from metro Malostranská (☎20 51 11 00; *uraka@login.cz*); see map on p.62. The perfect hideaway, six rooms (6000Kč a double) in a little half-timbered eighteenth-century cottage in Nový Svět. No children under 12 or dogs. ⑨.

Penzion U zlaté studny (The Golden Well), Karlova 3, Staré Město; metro Staroměstská (☎ & fax 24 21 05 39). Three apartments for 3500Kč and upwards, overlooking the tourist thoroughfare of Karlova, and decked out in High Baroque style. ⑨.

Budget hotels and hostels

There are a fair few **hostels** in Prague, catering for the large number of backpackers who hit the city all year round – and these are further supplemented by a whole host of more transient, high-season-only hostels. **Prices** range from 200Kč to 400Kč for a bed, usually in a dormitory. Some hostels operate **curfews** – it's worth asking before you commit yourself – and, although some rent out blankets and sheets, it's as well to bring your own sleeping bag. Note that some of the accommodation agencies in Prague also deal with hostels (see p.58 for details).

Most Prague hostels are not affiliated to Hostelling International; the one Czech organization that is affiliated is KMC, Karolíny Světlé 30, Staré Město (☎ & fax 24 23 06 33). Prague's university, the Karolinum, rents out over a thousand **student rooms** from June to mid-September, starting at 200Kč for a bed. Go to the head booking office at Terronská 28, Dejvice (☎24 31 11 05, fax 24 31 11 07; metro Dejvická; daily 9am–7pm). Another organization specializing in summer-only dorms is *Traveller's Hostels*, a chain of centrally located youth hostels which are very popular with US students. Their main booking office is round the corner at Dlouhá 33, Staré Město (☎231 13 18; *hostel@terminal.cz*), where there is a hostel (see below); dorm beds go for 350Kč and upwards per person.

Clown and Bard, Bořivojova 102, Žižkov; tram #5, #9 or #26 from metro Hlavní nádraží (☎27 24 36). So laid-back it's horizontal, and not a place to go if you don't like hippies, but it's clean, undeniably cheap, and rents out cheap doubles (①) as well as dorm beds for under 200Kč per person.

Club Habitat, Na Zbořenci 10, Nové Město; metro Karlovo náměstí (☎29 03 15, fax 29 31 01). The best of Prague's official HI hostels, located a short walk from Karlovo náměstí. Dorm beds for 350Kč per person.

ESTEC Hostel, Vaníčkova 5, Strahov; bus #217, #149 or #143 to the Strahov stadium from metro Dejvická (☎57 21 04 10; *estec@jrc.cz*). This is a chaotic but cheap hostel in the midst of student-land, but only a fifteen-minute walk from Hradčany through Petřín. To find the hostel, head for block 5, opposite the east stand of the Strahov stadium. Dorms 160Kč for a bed; doubles 290Kč per person; singles 400Kč plus.

Libra Q, Senovážné náměstí 21; metro Hlavní nádraží (☎24 10 55 36, fax 24 22 15 79). Friendly, centrally located, inexpensive hostel with dorm beds from 350Kč per person, and cheap doubles (③).

Kolej Komenského, Parléřova 6, Břevnov; tram #8 or #22 (☎35 03 37, fax 35 20 10). You can turn up on spec, but it's best to book through Universitas Tour, Opletalova 38, Nové Město (☎26 04 26, fax 24 21 22 90). Good location, just ten minutes' walk from the Hrad; dorm beds as well as doubles for around 500Kč per person.

Pension Dlouhá, Dlouhá 33, Staré Město; metro náměstí Republiky (☎57 21 04 10; *estec@jrc.cz*). Very centrally located hostel and booking office, so if there's not enough room here, they'll find you a bed somewhere for around 350Kč per person.

Campsites

Prague abounds in **campsites** – there's a whole rash of them in Troja (see below) – and most are relatively easy to get to on public transport. Facilities, on the whole, are rudimentary and poorly maintained, but the prices reflect this, starting at around 300Kč for a tent and two people.

Autocamp Trojská, Trojská 375, Troja; bus #112 from metro Nádraží Holešovice (☎ & fax 854 29 45). Good location, in someone's large back garden, 3km north of the centre, on the road to the Troja chateau. Open all year.

Kemp Džbán, Nad lávkou 5, Vokovice; tram #20 or #26 from metro Dejvická (☎36 90 06, fax 36 13 65). Large field with tent pitches, bungalows and basic facilities, 4km west of the centre, near the Šárka valley. Open all year.

THE CITY

The city's most obvious orientational axis is the **River Vltava** (known as the Moldau in German), which divides the capital into two unequal halves. The steeply inclined left bank is dominated by the castle district of **Hradčany**, which contains the most obvious sights – Prague Castle (known simply as the Hrad in Czech), the city's cathedral, and the old royal palace and gardens, as well as a host of museums and galleries. The rest of Hradčany lies to the west of the castle: a sleepy district ranging in scale from the miniature cottages of Nový Svět to the gargantuan facade of the Černínský palác. Squeezed between the castle hill and the river are the picturesque Baroque palaces and houses of the "Little Quarter" or **Malá Strana** – around 150 acres of twisting cobbled streets and secret walled gardens – home to the Czech parliament and most of the city's embassies, and dominated by one of the landmarks of the left bank, the green dome and tower of the church of sv Mikuláš.

The city's twisting matrix of streets is at its most confusing in the original medieval hub of the city, **Staré Město** – literally, the "Old Town" – on the right bank of the Vltava. The Karlův most, or **Charles Bridge**, its main link with the opposite bank, is easily the city's most popular historical monument, and one of the most beautiful places from which to view Prague Castle. Staré Město's other great showpiece is its main square, Staroměstské náměstí, where you can view Prague's famous astronomical clock, the Hus monument and the spiky towers of the Týn Church.

Enclosed within the boundaries of Staré Město, to the northwest of the main square, is the former Jewish quarter, or **Josefov**. The ghetto walls have long since gone and the whole area was remodelled at the turn of the century, but six synagogues, a medieval cemetery and a town hall survive as powerful reminders of a community that has existed here for over a millennium. South and east of the old town is the large sprawling district of **Nové Město**, whose main arteries make up the city's commercial and business centre. The nexus of Nové Město is Wenceslas Square (Václavské náměstí), focus of the political upheavals of the modern-day republic. Further afield lie various **suburbs**, most of which were developed only in the last hundred years or so. The single exception is **Vyšehrad**, one of the original fortress settlements of the newly arrived Slavs in the last millennium, now the final resting-place of leading Czech artists of the modern age, including the composers Smetana and Dvořák.

Hradčany

HRADČANY's *raison d'être* is its castle, or **Hrad**, built on the site of one of the original hill settlements of the Slav tribes who migrated to the area in the seventh or eighth century AD. The Přemyslid prince, Bořivoj I, erected the first castle here sometime in the late ninth century, and, since then, whoever has had control of the Hrad has exercised authority over the Czech Lands. Consequently, unlike the city's other districts, Hradčany has never had a real identity of its own – it became a royal town only in 1598

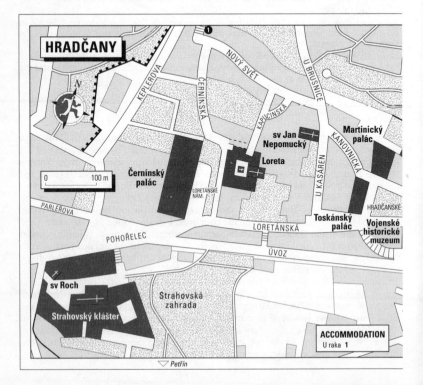

– existing instead as a mere appendage, its inhabitants serving and working for their masters in the Hrad. The same is still true now. For although the odd café or *pivnice* (pub) survives in amongst the palaces (and even in the Hrad itself), there's very little real life here beyond the stream of tourists who trek through the castle and the civil servants who work either for the president or the government, whose departmental tentacles spread right across Hradčany and down into Malá Strana.

Stretched out along a high spur above the River Vltava, Hradčany shows a suitable disdain for the public transport system. There's a choice of **approaches** from Malá Strana, all of which involve at least some walking. From Malostranská metro station, most people take the steep short cut up the Staré zámecké schody, which brings you into the castle from its rear end. A better approach is up the stately Zámecké schody, where you can stop and admire the view, before entering the castle via the main gates. The alternative to all this climbing is to take tram #22 from Malostranská metro, which tackles the hairpin bends of Chotkova with ease, and deposits you either outside the Královská zahrada (Royal Gardens) to the north of the Hrad, or, if you prefer, outside the gates of the Strahovský klášter (monastery), at the far western edge of Hradčany.

Pražský hrad (Prague Castle)

The castle grounds are open daily: April–Oct 5am–midnight; Nov–March 6am–11pm. Unless otherwise stated, the sights within the castle are open daily: April–Oct 9am–5pm; Nov–March 9am–4pm. A single ticket, costing 100kč and valid for three

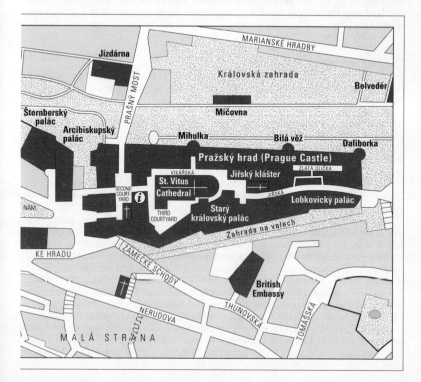

days, will give you entry to four sights within the castle: the choir, crypt and tower of the cathedral; the Starý královský palác (Old Royal Palace); the Basilica of sv Jiří and the Prašná věž (Powder Tower). Tickets are available from the main information centre in the third courtyard, opposite the cathedral, where you can also pick up an audio-guide (in English) for another 100Kč.

Viewed from the Charles Bridge, **Pražský hrad** (Prague Castle) stands aloof from the rest of the city, protected, not by bastions and castellated towers, but by its palatial Neoclassical facade – an "immense unbroken sheer blank wall", as Hilaire Belloc described it – breached only by the great Gothic mass of St Vitus Cathedral. It's *the* picture-postcard image of Prague, though for the Czechs the castle has been an object of disdain as much as admiration, its alternating fortunes mirroring the shifts in the nation's history. The golden age and the dark ages, interwar democracy and Stalinist terror – all have emanated from the Hrad. When the first posters appeared in December 1989 demanding "*HAVEL NA HRAD*" (Havel to the Castle), they weren't asking for his reincarceration. Havel's occupancy of the Hrad was the sign that the reins of government had finally been wrested from the Communist regime.

The site has been successively built on since the first castle was erected here in the ninth century, but two **architects** in particular bear responsibility for the present outward appearance of the Hrad. The first is **Nicolo Pacassi**, court architect to Empress Maria Theresa, whose austere restorations went hand in hand with the deliberate rundown of the Hrad until it was little more than an administrative barracks. For the Czechs, his grey-green eighteenth-century cover-up, which hides a variety of much older buildings, is unforgivable. Less apparent, though no less controversial, is the hand of **Josip Plečnik**, the Slovene architect who was commissioned by T.G. Masaryk, president of the newly founded Czechoslovak Republic, to restore and modernize the castle in the 1920s.

The first and second courtyards

The **first courtyard** (první nádvoří), which opens on to Hradčanské náměstí, is guarded by Ignaz Platzer's blood-curdling *Battling Titans* – two gargantuan figures, one on each of the gate piers, wielding club and dagger and about to inflict fatal blows on their respective victims. Below them stand a couple of impassive presidential sentries, sporting blue uniforms that deliberately recall those of the First Republic. The hourly **Changing of the Guard** is a fairly subdued affair, but every day at noon there's a much more elaborate parade, accompanied by a brass ensemble which appears at the first-floor windows to play local rock star Michal Kocáb's gentle, slightly comical, modern fanfare.

To reach the **second courtyard** (druhé nádvoří), you must pass through the early Baroque Matyášova brána (Matthias Gate), originally a freestanding triumphal arch in the middle of the long since defunct moat, now set into one of Pacassi's blank walls. Grand stairways on either side lead to the presidential apartments in the south wing, and to the **Španělský sál** (Spanish Hall) and **Rudofova galerie** (Rudolf Gallery) in the north wing – two of the most stunning rooms in the entire complex. Sadly, both are generally out of bounds, though concerts are occasionally held in the Španělský sál. Surrounded by monotonous Pacassi plasterwork, the courtyard itself is really just a through-route to the cathedral, with an early Baroque stone fountain, the **Kohlova kašna**, and a wrought-iron well grille the only distractions. The most visible intrusion is Anselmo Lurago's **chapel of sv Kříž**, which cowers in one corner. Its richly painted interior, dating mostly from the mid-nineteenth century, used to house the cathedral treasury, a macabre selection of medieval reliquaries. In the north wing of the courtyard are the former **Císařská konírna** (Imperial Stables), which still boast their original, magnificent Renaissance vaulting dating from the reign of Rudolf II, and are now used to house temporary exhibitions (Tues–Sun 10am–6pm).

Obrazárna Pražského hradu (Prague Castle Picture Gallery)

The remnants of the imperial collection, begun by the Habsburg Emperor Rudolf II, are housed in the **Obrazárna Pražského hradu** (daily 10am–6pm), opposite the old imperial stables. The surviving collection is definitely patchy, and the lighting in the newly revamped gallery could be better, but it still contains one or two masterpieces. One of the collection's finest paintings is **Rubens'** richly coloured *Assembly of the Gods at Olympus*, featuring a typically voluptuous Venus and a slightly phased Jupiter. The illusionist triple portrait of Rudolf (when viewed from the left), and his Habsburg predecessors (when viewed from the right), by Paulus Roy, is typical of the sort of tricksy work that appealed to the emperor. Elsewhere, there's an early, very beautiful *Young Woman at her Toilet* by **Titian**, and a superbly observed *Portrait of a Musician* by one of his pupils, Bordone. **Veronese's** best offering is his portrait of his friend Jakob König, a German art dealer in Venice, who worked for, among others, Rudolf II. Look out, too, for **Tintoretto's** *Flagellation of Christ*, a late work in which the artist makes very effective and dramatic use of light.

St Vitus Cathedral

St Vitus Cathedral (chram sv Víta) takes up so much of the third courtyard that it's difficult to get an overall impression of this chaotic Gothic edifice. Its asymmetrical appearance is the product of a long and chequered history, for although the foundation stone was laid in 1344, the cathedral was not completed until 1929 – exactly 1000 years after the death of Bohemia's most famous patron saint, Wenceslas.

The inspiration for the medieval cathedral came from Emperor Charles IV, who, while still only heir to the throne, had not only wangled an independent archbishopric for Prague, but had also managed to gather together the relics of Saint Vitus. Inspired by the cathedral at Narbonne, Charles commissioned the Frenchman **Matthias of Arras** to start work on a similar structure. Matthias died eight years into the job in 1352, with the cathedral barely started, so Charles summoned **Peter Parler**, a precocious 23-year-old from a family of great German masons, to continue the work. For the next 46 years, Parler imprinted his slightly flashier, more inventive *Sonder Gotik* ("Unusual Gothic") style on the city, but the cathedral got no further than the construction of the choir and the south transept before his death in 1399.

Little significant work was carried out during the next four centuries, and the half-built cathedral became a symbol of the Czechs' frustrated aspirations of nationhood. Not until the Czech national revival or *národní obrození* of the nineteenth century did building begin again in earnest, with the foundation, in 1859, of the **Union for the Completion of the Cathedral**. A succession of architects, including Josef Mocker and Kamil Hilbert, oversaw the completion of the entire west end, and with the help of countless other Czech artists and sculptors, the building was transformed into a treasure-house of Czech art. The cathedral was finally given an official opening ceremony in 1929, though in fact work continued right up to and beyond World War II.

The sooty Prague air has made it hard now to differentiate between the two building periods. Close inspection, however, reveals that the **western facade**, including the twin spires, sports the rigorous if unimaginative work of the neo-Gothic restorers (their besuited portraits can be found below the rose window), while the **eastern section** – best viewed from the Belvedér – shows the building's authentic Gothic roots. The south door (see Zlatá brána, below) is also pure Parler. Oddly then, it's above the south door that the cathedral's tallest steeple reveals the most conspicuous stylistic join: Pacassi's Baroque topping resting absurdly on a Renaissance parapet of light stone, which is itself glued onto the blackened body of the original Gothic tower.

THE NAVE

The cathedral is the country's largest, and once inside, it's difficult not to be impressed by the sheer height of the **nave**. This is the newest part of the building, and, consequently, is decorated mostly with twentieth-century furnishings. The most arresting of these is the cathedral's modern **stained-glass** windows, which on sunny days send shafts of rainbow light into the nave. The effect is stunning, though entirely out of keeping with Parler's original concept, which was to have almost exclusively clear-glass windows. The most unusual windows are those by František Kysela, which look as though they have been shattered into hundreds of tiny pieces, a technique used to greatest effect in the rose window over the west door with its kaleidoscopic *Creation of the World* (1921). In keeping with its secular nature, two of the works from the time of the First Republic were paid for by financial institutions: the *Cyril and Methodius* window, in the third chapel in the north wall, was commissioned from Art Nouveau artist Alfons Mucha by the Banka Slavie; while on the opposite side of the nave, the window on the theme *Those Who Sow in Tears Shall Reap in Joy* was sponsored by a Prague insurance company.

Of the cathedral's 22 side chapels, the grand **Chapel of sv Václav**, by the south door, is easily the main attraction. Although officially dedicated to St Vitus, spiritually the cathedral belongs as much to the Přemyslid prince, Václav (Wenceslas, of "Good King" fame; see box opposite), the country's patron saint, who was killed by his pagan brother, Boleslav the Cruel. Ten years later, in 939, Boleslav repented, converted, and apparently transferred his brother's remains to this very spot. Charles, who was keen to promote the cult of Wenceslas in order to cement his own Luxembourgeois dynasty's rather tenuous claim to the Bohemian throne, had Peter Parler build the present chapel on top of the original grave; the lion's head **door-ring** set into the north door is said to be the one to which Václav clung before being killed. The chapel's rich, almost Byzantine decoration is like the inside of a jewel casket: the gilded walls are inlaid with approximately 1372 semiprecious Bohemian stones (corresponding to the year of its creation and symbolizing the New Jerusalem from Revelation), set around ethereal fourteenth-century frescoes of the Passion; meanwhile the tragedy of Wenceslas unfolds above the cornice in the later paintings of the Litoměřice school.

Though a dazzling testament to the golden age of Charles IV's reign, it's not just the chapel's artistic merit which draws visitors. A door in the south wall gives access to a staircase leading to the coronation chamber (rarely open to the public) which houses the **Bohemian crown jewels**, including the gold crown of Saint Wenceslas, studded with some of the largest sapphires in the world. Closed to the public since 1867, the door is secured by seven different locks, the keys kept by seven different people, starting with the president himself – like the seven seals of the holy scroll from Revelation. Replicas of the crown jewels can be seen in the Lobkovický palác (see p.70).

THE CHANCEL AND CRYPT

Having sated yourself on the Chapel of sv Václav, buy a ticket from the nearby box office and head off to the north choir aisle – the only place where you can currently enter the **chancel**. Slap bang in the middle of the ambulatory, close to the Saxon Chapel, is the perfect Baroque answer to the medieval Chapel of sv Václav, the **Tomb of St John of Nepomuk**, plonked here in 1736. It's a work of grotesque excess, designed by Johann Bernhard Fischer von Erlach's son, Johann Michael, and sculpted in solid silver with free-flying angels holding up the heavy drapery of the baldachin. Where Charles sought to promote Wenceslas as the nation's preferred saint, the Jesuits, with Habsburg backing, replaced him with another Czech martyr, John of Nepomuk (Jan Nepomucký), who had been arrested, tortured, and then thrown – bound and gagged – off the Charles Bridge in 1393 on the orders of Václav IV, allegedly for refusing to divulge the secrets of the queen's confession. A cluster of stars was

GOOD KING WENCESLAS

As it turns out, there's very little substance to the story related in the nineteenth-century Christmas carol, *Good King Wenceslas*, by J.M. Neale, itself a reworking of the medieval carol *Tempus adest floridum*. For a start, **Václav** was only a duke and never a king (though he did become a saint); he wasn't even that "good", except in comparison with the rest of his family; the St Agnes fountain, by which "yonder peasant dwelt", wasn't built until the thirteenth century; and he was killed a full three months before the Feast of Stephen.

Born in 907, Václav inherited his title at the tender age of thirteen. His Christian grandmother, Ludmila, was appointed regent in preference to Drahomíra, his pagan mother, who had Ludmila murdered in a fit of jealousy the following year. On coming of age in 925, Václav became duke in his own right and took a vow of celibacy, intent on promoting Christianity throughout the dukedom. Even so, the local Christians didn't take to him, and when he began making conciliatory overtures to the neighbouring Germans, they persuaded his pagan younger brother, Boleslav the Cruel, to do away with him. On September 20, 929, Václav was stabbed to death by Boleslav at the entrance to a church just outside Prague.

said to have appeared over the spot where he drowned, hence the halo of stars on every subsequent portrayal of the saint.

The Jesuits, in their efforts to get him canonized, exhumed his corpse and produced what they claimed to be his tongue – alive and licking, so to speak (it was in fact his very dead brain). In 1729, he duly became a saint, and, on the lid of the tomb, back-to-back with the martyr himself, a cherub points to his severed tongue, sadly no longer the "real" thing. The more prosaic reason for John of Nepomuk's death was simply that he was caught up in a dispute between the archbishop and the king over the appointment of the abbot of Kladruby, and backed the wrong side. John was tortured on the rack along with two other priests, who were then made to sign a document denying that they had been maltreated; John, however, died before he could sign, and his dead body was secretly dumped in the river. The Vatican finally admitted this in 1961, some 232 years after his canonization.

Before you leave the chancel, check out the sixteenth-century marble **Imperial Mausoleum**, situated in the centre of the choir, and surrounded by a fine Renaissance grille, on which numerous cherubs are irreverently larking about. It was commissioned by Rudolf II and contains the remains of his grandfather Ferdinand I, his Polish grandmother, and his father Maximilian II, the first Habsburgs to wear the Bohemian crown. Rudolf himself rests beneath them, in one of the two pewter coffins in the somewhat cramped **Royal Crypt** (Královská hrobka), whose entrance is beside the Royal Oratory. Rudolf's coffin (at the back, in the centre) features yet more cherubs, brandishing quills, while the one to the right contains the remains of Maria Amelia, daughter of the Empress Maria Theresa. A good number of other Czech kings and queens are buried here, too, reinterred this century in incongruously modern 1930s sarcophagi, among them the Hussite King George of Poděbrady, Charles IV and, sharing a single sarcophagus, all four of his wives. The exit from the crypt brings you out in the centre of the nave.

Starý královský palác (Old Royal Palace)

Across the courtyard from the Zlatá brána, the **Starý královský palác** (Old Royal Palace) was home to the princes and kings of Bohemia from the eleventh to the sixteenth centuries. It's a sandwich of royal apartments, built one on top of the other by successive generations, but left largely unfurnished and unused for the last three hundred years. The original Romanesque palace of Soběslav I now forms the cellars of the present building, above which Charles IV built his own Gothic chambers; these days you enter at the third and top floor, built at the end of the fifteenth century.

Immediately past the antechamber is the bare expanse of the massive **Vladislavský sál** (Vladislav Hall), the work of Benedikt Ried, the German mason appointed by Vladislav Jagiello as his court architect. It displays some remarkable, sweeping rib-vaulting which forms floral patterns on the ceiling, the petals reaching almost to the floor. It was here that the early Bohemian kings were elected, and since 1918 every president from Masaryk to Havel has been sworn into office in the hall. In medieval times, the hall was also used for banquets and jousting tournaments, which explains the ramp-like **Riders' Staircase** in the north wing (now the exit). At the far end of the hall, to the right, there's an outdoor **viewing platform**, from which you can enjoy a magnificent view of Prague (at its best in the late afternoon).

From a staircase in the southwest corner of the hall, you can gain access to the Ludvík Wing. The rooms themselves are pretty uninspiring, but the furthest one, the **Bohemian Chancellery**, was the scene of Prague's **second defenestration** (see p.105 for details of the first). After almost two centuries of uneasy coexistence between Catholics and Protestants, matters came to a head over the succession to the throne of the Habsburg Archduke Ferdinand, a notoriously intolerant Catholic. On May 23, 1618, a posse of more than one hundred Protestant nobles, led by Count Thurn, marched to the chancellery for a showdown with Jaroslav Bořita z Martinic and Vilém Slavata, the two Catholic governors appointed by Ferdinand. After a "stormy discussion", the two councillors (and their personal secretary, Filip Fabricius) were thrown out of the window. As a contemporary historian recounted: "No mercy was granted them and they were both thrown dressed in their cloaks with their rapiers and decoration head-first out of the western window into a moat beneath the palace. They loudly screamed *ach, ach, oweh!* and attempted to hold on to the narrow window-ledge, but Thurn beat their knuckles with the hilt of his sword until they were both obliged to let go." There's some controversy about the exact window from which they were ejected, although it's generally agreed that they survived to tell the tale, landing in a medieval dung heap below, and – so the story goes – precipitating the Thirty Years' War.

Back down in the Vladislavský sál, there are more rooms to explore through the doorways on either side of the Riders' Staircase, but you're better off heading down the ramp to the **Gothic and Romanesque chambers** of the palace. Although equally bare, they contain a couple of interesting models showing the castle at various stages in its development, plus copies of the busts by Peter Parler's workshop, including the architect's remarkable self-portrait; the originals are hidden from view in the triforium of the cathedral.

The Basilica and Convent of sv Jiří

The only exit from the Old Royal Palace is via the Riders' Staircase, which deposits you in Jiřské náměstí. Don't be fooled by the russet red Baroque facade of the **Basilica of sv Jiří** (St George) which dominates the square; inside is Prague's most beautiful Romanesque building, meticulously scrubbed clean and restored to re-create something like the honey-coloured stone basilica that replaced the original tenth-century church in 1173. The double staircase to the chancel is a remarkably harmonious late-Baroque addition and now provides a perfect stage for chamber music concerts. The choir vault contains a rare early thirteenth-century painting of the New Jerusalem from Revelation – not to be confused with the very patchy sixteenth-century painting on the apse – while to the right of the chancel, only partially visible, are sixteenth-century frescoes of the **burial chapel of sv Ludmila**, grandmother of St Wenceslas, who was strangled by her own daughter-in-law in 921 (see box on p.67), thus becoming Bohemia's first Christian martyr and saint. There's a replica of the recumbent Ludmila, which you can inspect at close quarters, in the south aisle. Also worth a quick peek is the Romanesque crypt, situated beneath the choir, which contains a macabre sixteenth-century statue of Vanity, whose shrouded, skeletal body is crawling with snakes and lizards.

THE OLD BOHEMIAN ART COLLECTION

Next door is Bohemia's first monastery, the **Jiřský klášter** (St George's Convent) founded in 973 by Mlada, sister of the Přemyslid prince Boleslav the Pious, who became its first abbess. Like most of the country's religious institutions, it was closed down and turned into a barracks by Joseph II in 1782, and now houses the Národní galerie's **old Bohemian art collection** (Tues–Sun 10am–6pm). The exhibition is arranged chronologically, starting in the crypt with a remarkable collection of Gothic art, which first flourished here under the patronage of Charles IV.

The **earliest works** are almost exclusively symbolic depictions of the Madonna and Child, the artists known only by their works and locations, not by name. The first named artist is **Master Theodoric**, who painted over one hundred panels for Charles IV's castle at Karlštejn (see p.146); just six are on display here, their larger-than-life portraits overflowing onto the edges of the panels. On the next floor, are paintings by the **Master of Třeboň**, whose work shows even greater variety of balance and depth, moving ever closer to realistic portraiture. The following room contains the stone-carved tympanum from the Týn church (see p.85) – originally coloured and gilded – with high-relief figures by Peter Parler's workshop, whose mastery of composition and depth heralded a new stage in the development of Bohemian art. The last room on this floor is devoted to a series of superb sixteenth-century woodcuts by **Master I.P.**, including the incredibly detailed *Christ the Redeemer before Death*, depicting a skeleton whose entrails are in the process of being devoured by a frog.

The transition from this to the next floor, where you are immediately thrown into a small sample of overtly sensual and erotic **Mannerist paintings** of Rudolf II's reign, is something of a shock. However, the majority of the works that survive from Rudolf's superlative collection are now displayed in the Obrazárna Pražského hradu (see p.65). The rest of the gallery is given over to Czech **Baroque art**, as pursued by the likes of Bohemia's Karel Škréta and Petr Brandl, whose paintings and sculptures fill chapels and churches across the Czech Lands. Willmann's portrait of St Bartholomew being skinned alive is disturbingly gruesome, but aside from the works of Jan Kupecký and the statues of Matthias Bernhard Braun and Ferdinand Maximilian Brokof, this section is unlikely to hold most people's attention for long.

Zlatá ulička and the castle towers

Around the corner from the convent is the **Zlatá ulička** (Golden Lane), a seemingly blind alley of miniature sixteenth-century cottages in dolly-mixture colours, built for the 24 members of Rudolf II's castle guard. The lane takes its name from the goldsmiths who followed (and modified the buildings) a century later. By the nineteenth century, it had become a kind of palace slum, attracting artists and craftsmen, its two most famous inhabitants being Jaroslav Seifert, the Nobel prize-winning Czech poet, and Franz Kafka. Kafka's youngest sister, Ottla, rented no. 22, and during a creative period in the winter of 1916, he came here in the evenings to write short stories. Finally, in 1951, the Communists kicked out the remaining residents and turned most of the houses into souvenir shops for tourists.

At no. 12, at the eastern end of Zlatá ulička, is a throughway to the **Černá věž** (Black Tower), standing at the top of the Staré zamecké schody, which leads down to Malostranská metro. There's no access to the Černá věž, but at the other end of the lane, at no. 24, you can climb a flight of stairs to the **Obranná chodba** (defence corridor), which is lined with wooden shields, suits of armour and period costumes. The

Bílá věž (White Tower), at the western end of the corridor, was the city's main prison from Rudolf's reign onwards. There's a reconstructed torture chamber on the first floor, and in the shop on the floor above you can kit yourself out as a medieval knight with replica swords and maces, not to mention chastity belts and various torture instruments. In the opposite direction, the corridor leads to a shooting range, where you can practise firing off a crossbow. Beyond lies **Daliborka**, the castle tower dedicated to its first prisoner, the young Czech noble Dalibor, accused of supporting a peasants' revolt at the beginning of the fifteenth century, who was finally executed in 1498. According to Prague legend, he learnt to play the violin while imprisoned here, and his playing could be heard all over the castle – a tale that provided material for Smetana's opera, *Dalibor*.

To get inside the castle's other tower, the **Prašná věž** (Powder Tower) or Mihulka, which once served as the workshop of gunsmith and bell-founder Tomáš Jaroš, you'll have to backtrack to Vikářská, the street which runs along the north side of the cathedral. The Powder Tower's name comes from the lamprey (*mihule*), an eel-like fish supposedly bred here for royal consumption, though it's actually more noteworthy as the place where Rudolf's team of alchemists (including Kelley) were put to work trying to discover the philosopher's stone. Despite its colourful history, the exhibition currently on display within the tower is dull, with just a pair of furry slippers and hat belonging to Ferdinand I to get excited about.

Muzeum hraček (Toy Museum) and the Lobkovický palác

If you continue east down Jiřská, which runs parallel with Zlatá ulička, you'll come to the courtyard of the former Purkrabství (Burgrave's House) on the left, which hides a café, exhibition space and **Muzeum hraček** (daily 9.30am–5.30pm). With brief, Czech-only captions and unimaginative displays, this is a disappointing new venture, which fails to live up to its potential. The succession of glass cabinets contains an impressive array of toy cars, robots and even Barbie dolls, but there are only a few buttons for younger kids to press, and unless you're really lost for something to do, you could happily skip the whole enterprise.

The hotchpotch historical collection in the **Lobkovický palác** (Tues–Sun 9am–5pm), on the opposite side of Jiřská, is marginally more rewarding, despite the ropey English text. The exhibition actually begins on the top floor, but by no means all the objects on display deserve attention. The prize exhibits are replicas of the Bohemian crown jewels, an interesting sixteenth-century carving of *The Last Supper*, originally an altarpiece from the Bethlehem Chapel, and the sword (and invoice) of the famous Prague executioner Jan Mydlář, who could lop a man's head off with just one chop, as he demonstrated on 24 Protestant Czechs in 1621 (see p.84).

The Castle Gardens

For recuperation and a superlative view over the rest of Prague – not to mention a chance to inspect some of Plečnik's quirky additions to the castle – head for the **Jižní zahrady** (South Gardens), accessible via Plečnik's copper-canopied Bull Staircase on the south side of the third courtyard. Alternatively, make a short detour beyond the official limits of the castle walls from the second courtyard, by crossing the **Prašný most** (Powder Bridge), erected in the sixteenth century to connect the newly established royal gardens with the Hrad. Beyond the bridge, opposite Jean-Baptiste Mathey's plain French Baroque Jízdárna (Riding School), now an art gallery, is the entrance to the Royal Gardens or **Královská zahrada** (May–Oct Tues–Sun 10am–5.45pm), founded by Emperor Ferdinand I on the site of a former vineyard. Today, this is one of the best-kept gardens in the capital, with fully functioning fountains and immaculately cropped lawns. Consequently, it's a very popular spot, though more a place for admiring the azaleas and almond trees than lounging around on the grass. It was here that tulips brought from Turkey were first acclimatized to Europe before being exported to the Netherlands, and every spring there's an impressive, disciplined crop.

Built into the gardens' south terrace is Rudolf's distinctive Renaissance ball-game court, known as the **Míčovna** (occasionally open to the public for concerts and exhibitions) and tattooed with sgraffito. At the far end of the gardens is Prague's most celebrated Renaissance legacy, the Letohrádek královny Anny (Queen Anne's Summer Palace) or **Belvedér**, a delicately arcaded summerhouse topped by an inverted copper ship's hull, built by Ferdinand I for his wife, Anne. Unlike the gardens, the Belvedér is open most of the year and is now used for exhibitions of contemporary artists. At the centre of the palace's miniature formal garden is the **Zpívající fontána** (Singing Fountain), built shortly after the palace and so named from the musical sound of the drops of water falling in the metal bowls below. From the garden terrace you can enjoy an unrivalled view of the castle's finest treasure – the cathedral.

From Hradčanské náměstí to Strahovský klášter

The monumental scale and appearance of the rest of Hradčany, outside the castle, is a direct result of the **great fire of 1541**, which swept up from Malá Strana and wiped out most of the old dwelling places belonging to the serfs, tradesmen, clergy and masons who had settled here in the Middle Ages. With the Turks at the gates of Vienna, the Habsburg nobility were more inclined to pursue their major building projects in Prague instead, and, following the Battle of Bílá hora in 1620, the palaces of the exiled (or executed) Protestant nobility were up for grabs too. The newly ensconced Catholic aristocrats were keen to spend some of their expropriated wealth, and over the next two centuries they turned Hradčany into a grand architectural showpiece. As the Turkish threat subsided, the political focus of the empire gradually shifted back to Vienna and the building spree stopped. For the last two hundred years, Hradčany has been frozen in time.

Hradčanské náměstí
Hradčanské náměstí fans out from the castle gates, surrounded by the oversized palaces of the old Catholic nobility. For the most part, it's a tranquil space that's overlooked by the tour groups marching through, intent on the Hrad. The one spot everyone heads for is the ramparts in the southeastern corner, by the top of the Zámecké schody, which allow an unrivalled view over the red rooftops of Malá Strana, past the famous green dome and tower of the church of sv Mikuláš and beyond, to the spires of Staré Město.

Until the great fire of 1541, the square was the hub of Hradčany, lined with medieval shops and stalls but with no real market as such. After the fire, the developers moved in; the powerful Lobkowicz family replaced seven houses on the south side of the square with the over-the-top sgraffitoed pile at no. 2, now known as the **Schwarzenberský palác** after its last aristocratic owners (the present-day count, Karl, is one of the republic's leading capitalists). The palace now houses the **Vojenské historické muzeum** (Museum of Military History; May–Oct Tues–Sun 10am–5.30pm). Predictably enough, it was the Nazis who founded the museum, though the Czechs themselves have a long history of manufacturing top-class weaponry to world powers (Semtex is probably their best-known export), so it's no coincidence that one of the two Czech words to have made it into the English language is pistol (*pistole* in Czech) – the other is *robot*, in case you're wondering. Among the endless Habsburg uniforms and instruments of death – all of which are pre-1918 – you'll find the first Colt 45 produced outside the USA, manufactured in 1849 for the Austrian Navy.

Šternberský palác – the Old European Art Collection

A passage down the side of the Arcibiskupský palác leads to the early-eighteenth-century Šternberský palác (Tues–Sun 10am–6pm), which houses the Národní's galerie's old European art collection mostly ranging from the fourteenth to the eighteenth century, but excluding works by Czech artists of the period (you'll find them in the Jiřský klášter in the Hrad). It would be fair to say that the collection is relatively modest, in comparison with those of other major European capitals, though the handful of masterpieces makes a visit here worthwhile. To see the late-nineteenth- and twentieth-century European art which used to be housed here, you need to pay a visit to the Národní galerie's modern and contemporary art collection in the Veletržní palác (see p.114).

The **first floor** kicks off with Florentine religious art, most notably a series of exquisite miniature triptychs by Bernardo Daddi, plus several gilded polyptychs by the Venetian artist Antonio Vivarini. Moving swiftly into the gallery's large Flemish contingent, it's worth checking out Dieric Bouts' *Lamentation*, a complex composition crowded with figures in medieval garb, and the bizarre *Well of Life*, painted around 1500 by an unknown artist. The latter features a squatting Christ depicted as a Gothic fountain issuing forth blood which angels in turn serve in goblets to passing punters. One of the most eye-catching works is Jan Gossaert's *St Luke Drawing the Virgin*, an exercise in architectural geometry and perspective which used to hang in the cathedral. The section ends with a series of canvases by the least famous members of the Brueghel family; before you head upstairs, though, don't miss the side rooms containing Orthodox icons from Venice and the Balkans to Russia.

The **second floor** contains one of the most prized paintings in the whole collection, the *Feast of the Rosary* by Albrecht Dürer, depicting, among others, the Virgin Mary, the Pope, the Holy Roman Emperor, and even a self-portrait of Dürer himself (top right). This was one of Rudolf's most prized acquisitions (he was an avid Dürer fan), transported on foot across the Alps to Prague (he didn't trust wheeled transport with such a precious object). There are other outstanding works here, too: two richly coloured Bronzino portraits, a Rembrandt, a Canaletto of the Thames, a whole series by the Saxon master, Lucas Cranach, and a mesmerizing *Praying Christ* by El Greco. Rubens' colossal *Murder of St Thomas* is difficult to miss, with its pink-buttocked cherubs hovering over the bloody scene. Nearby, in the hugely expanded (and uneven) Dutch section, there's a wonderful portrait of an arrogant "young gun" named Jasper by Frans Hals. A few of the rooms in the gallery have preserved their original decor, the best of which is the Chinoiserie of the Čínský kabinet.

From Nový Svět to Loreta

At the other end of Hradčanské náměstí, Kanovnická heads off towards the northwest corner of Hradčany. Nestling in this shallow dip, **Nový Svět** (meaning "New World", though not Dvořák's) provides a glimpse of life on a totally different scale from Hradčanské náměstí. Similar in many ways to the Zlatá ulička in the Hrad, this cluster of brightly coloured cottages, which curls around the corner into Černínská, is all that's left of Hradčany's medieval slums, painted up and sanitized in the eighteenth and nineteenth centuries. Despite having all the same ingredients for mass tourist appeal as Zlatá ulička, it remains remarkably undisturbed, save for a few swish wine bars, and Gambra, a surrealist art gallery at Černínská 5 (Wed–Sun noon–6pm), which sells works by, among others, the renowned Czech animator, Jan Švankmajer, and his wife Eva, who live nearby.

Up the hill from Nový Svět, Loretánské náměstí is dominated by the phenomenal 135-metre-long facade of the **Černínský palác** (Černín Palace), decorated with thirty Palladian half-pillars and supported by a swathe of diamond-pointed rustication. For all its grandeur, it's a miserable, brutal building, whose construction nearly bankrupted future generations of Černíns, who were forced to sell the palace in 1851 to the Austrian state. Since the First Republic, the palace has housed the Foreign Ministry, and during the war it was the Nazi *Reichsprotektor*'s residence. On March 10, 1948, it was the scene of Prague's third – and most widely mourned – defenestration. Only days after the Communist coup, **Jan Masaryk**, only son of the founder of Czechoslovakia and the last non-Communist in the cabinet, plunged 45 feet to his death from a top-floor bathroom window. Whether it was suicide (he had been suffering from bouts of depression, partly induced by the country's political path) or murder will probably never be satisfactorily resolved, but for most people Masaryk's death cast a dark shadow over the newly established regime.

The façade of the **Loreta** (Tues–Sun 9am–12.15pm & 1–4.30pm), immediately opposite the Černínský palác, was built by the Dientzenhofers, a Bavarian family of architects, in the early part of the eighteenth century, and is the perfect antidote to the Černíns' humourless monster. It's all hot flourishes and twirls, topped by a tower which lights up like a Chinese lantern at night, and by day clanks out the hymn *We Greet Thee a Thousand Times* on its 27 Dutch bells (it does special performances of other tunes from time to time, too).

The façade and the cloisters are, in fact, just the outer casing for the focus of the complex, the **Santa Casa**, founded in 1626 and smothered in a mantle of stucco depicting the building's miraculous transportation from the Holy Land. Legend has it that the Santa Casa (Mary's home in Nazareth), under threat from the heathen Turks, was transported by a host of angels to a small village in Dalmatia and from there, via a number of brief stopoffs, to a small laurel grove (*lauretum* in Latin, hence Loreta) in northern Italy. News of the miracle spread across the Catholic lands, prompting a spate of copycat shrines. During the Counter-Reformation, the cult was actively encouraged in an attempt to broaden the popular appeal of Catholicism. The Prague Loreta is one of fifty to be built in the Czech Lands, each of the shrines following an identical design, with pride of place given to a limewood statue of the *Black Madonna and Child*, encased in silver.

Behind the Santa Casa, the Dientzenhofers built the much larger **Church of Narození Páně** (Church of the Nativity), which is like a mini-version of sv Mikuláš, down in Malá Strana. The Santa Casa's serious financial backing is evident in the **treasury** on the first floor of the west wing, much ransacked over the years but still stuffed full of gold. The padded ceilings and low lighting create a kind of giant jewellery box for the master exhibit, a tasteless Viennese silver monstrance designed by Fischer von Erlach in 1699, and studded with diamonds, taken from the wedding dress of Countess Kolovrat, who had made the Loreto sole heir to her fortune.

Strahovský klášter

Continuing westwards from Loretánské náměstí, Pohořelec, an arcaded street-cum-square, leads to the chunky remnants of the zigzag eighteenth-century fortifications that mark the edge of the old city, as defined by Charles IV back in the fourteenth century. Close by, to the left, is the **Strahovský klášter** (Strahov Monastery), founded in 1140 by the Premonstratensian order. Having managed to evade Joseph II's 1783 dissolution of the monasteries, it continued to function until shortly after the Communists took power, when, along with all other religious establishments, it was closed down and most of its inmates thrown into prison; following the events of 1989, the monks have returned.

The first library you come to is the later and larger of the two, the **Filosofický sál** (Philosophical Hall), built in some haste in the 1780s, in order to accommodate the books and bookcases from Louka, a Premonstratensian monastery in Moravia (see p.306) that failed to escape Joseph's decree. The walnut bookcases are so tall they touch the library's lofty ceiling, which is busily decorated with frescoes by the

Viennese painter Franz Maulbertsch on the theme of the search for truth. Don't, whatever you do, miss the collection of curios exhibited in the glass cabinets outside the library, which features shells, turtles, crabs, lobsters, dried-up sea monsters, butterflies, beetles, plastic fruit and moths. There's even a pair of whale's penises set amidst a narwhal horn, several harpoons and a model ship. The other main room is the low-ceilinged **Teologický sál** (Theological Hall), studded with ancient globes, its wedding-cake stucco framing frescoes on a similar theme, executed by one of the monks seventy years earlier. Outside the hall the library's oldest book, the ninth-century gem-studded Strahov Gospel, is displayed – look out, too, for the cabinet of books documenting Czech trees, each of which has the bark of the tree on its spine.

If you leave the monastery through the narrow doorway in the eastern wall, you enter the gardens and orchards of the **Strahovská zahrada**, from where you can see the whole city in perspective. The gardens form part of wooded hill known as Petřín, and the path to the right contours round to the Stations of the Cross that lead up to the miniature Eiffel Tower known as the Rozhledna (see p.79). Alternatively, you can catch tram #22 from outside Strahov's main entrance to Malostranská metro or the centre of town.

Malá Strana

More than anywhere else, **MALÁ STRANA**, the "Little Quarter", conforms to the image of Prague as the ultimate Baroque city. It was here that film director Miloš Forman chose to shoot many of the street scenes in *Amadeus*, judging that its picturesque alleyways resembled Mozart's Vienna more than Vienna itself. And it's true;

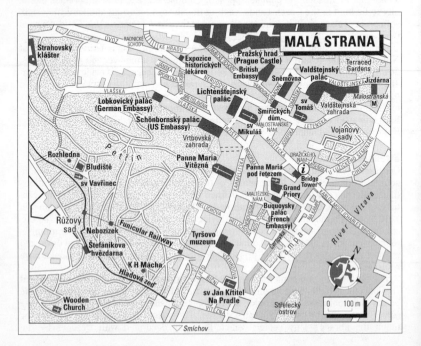

the streets have changed very little since Mozart walked them, as he often did on his frequent visits to Prague between 1787 and 1791. Unlike Hradčany, its main square is filled with city life during the day; while around practically every corner, narrow cobbled streets lead to some quiet walled garden, the perfect inner-city escape.

Foolishly, many visitors never stray from the well-trodden paths that link the Charles Bridge with Hradčany, thus bypassing most of Malá Strana. This is easy to do given that the whole town takes up a mere 600 square metres of land squeezed in between the river and the Hrad, but it means missing out on one of the greatest pleasures of Malá Strana – casually exploring its hilly eighteenth-century backstreets.

Malostranské náměstí and around

The main focus of Malá Strana has always been the sloping, cobbled **Malostranské náměstí**, which is dominated and divided into two by the church of sv Mikuláš (see below). Trams and cars hurtle across it, regularly dodged by a procession of people – some heading up the hill to the Hrad, others pausing for coffee and cakes at the numerous bars and restaurants hidden in the square's arcades and Gothic vaults.

Towering above the square, and the whole of Malá Strana, is the church of **sv Mikuláš** (St Nicholas), easily the most magnificent Baroque building in the city, and one of the last great structures to be built on the left bank, begun in 1702. For Christoph Dientzenhofer, a German immigrant from a dynasty of Bavarian architects, this was his most prestigious commission and is, without doubt, his finest work. For the Jesuits, who were already ensconced in the adjoining college, it was their most ambitious project yet in Bohemia, and the ultimate symbol of their stranglehold on the country. When Christoph died in 1722, it was left to his son Kilian Ignaz Dientzenhofer, along with Kilian's son-in-law, Anselmo Lurago, to finish the project, which they did with a masterful flourish, adding the giant green dome and tower – now among the most characteristic landmarks on Prague's left bank. Sadly for the Jesuits, they were able to enjoy the finished product for just twenty years, before they were banished from the Habsburg Empire in 1773.

Nothing about the relatively plain west facade prepares you for the overwhelming High Baroque **interior**. The vast fresco in the nave, by Johann Lukas Kracker, portrays

---

MOZART IN PRAGUE

Mozart made the first of several visits to Prague with his wife Constanze in 1787, staying with his friend and patron Count Thun in what is now the British Embassy (Thunovská 14). A year earlier, his opera *The Marriage of Figaro*, which had failed to please the opera snobs in Vienna, had been given a rapturous reception at Prague's Nostitz Theater (now the Stavovské divadlo; see p.75) and on his arrival in 1787, Mozart was already flavour of the month, as he wrote in his diary: "Here they talk about nothing but *Figaro*. Nothing is played, sung or whistled but *Figaro*. Nothing, nothing but *Figaro*. Certainly a great honour for me!" Encouraged by this, he chose to premiere his next opera, *Don Giovanni*, later that year, in Prague rather than Vienna. He arrived with an incomplete score in hand, and wrote the overture at the Dušeks' Bertramka villa in Smíchov (see p.117), dedicating it to the "good people of Prague". Apart from a brief sojourn while on a concert tour, Mozart's fourth and final visit to Prague took place in 1791, the year of his death. The climax of the stay was the première of Mozart's final opera, *La Clemenza di Tito*, commissioned for the coronation of Leopold II as King of Bohemia (and according to tradition written on the coach from Vienna to Prague). The opera didn't go down quite as well as previous ones – according to tradition it sent the queen to sleep. Nevertheless, four thousand people turned out for his memorial service, held in Malá Strana's church of sv Mikuláš to the strains of his *Requiem Mass*.

some of the more fanciful miraculous feats of Saint Nicholas. Apart from his role as Santa Claus, he is depicted here rescuing sailors in distress, saving women from prostitution by throwing them bags of gold, and reprieving from death three unjustly condemned men. Even given the overwhelming proportions of the nave, the dome at the far end of the church, built by the younger Dientzenhofer, remains impressive, thanks, more than anything, to its sheer height. Leering over you as you gaze up at the dome are Ignaz Platzer's four terrifyingly oversized and stern Church Fathers, one of whom brandishes a gilded thunderbolt, leaving no doubt as to the gravity of the Jesuit message. Before you leave, check out the church's superb organ, its white case and gilded musical cherubs nicely offsetting the grey pipes.

Nerudova, Tržiště and Vlašská

The most important of the various streets leading up to the Hrad from Malostranské náměstí is **Nerudova**, named after the Czech journalist and writer Jan Neruda (1834–91), who was born at *U dvou slunců* (The Two Suns), at no. 47, an inn at the top of the street. His tales of Malá Strana immortalized bohemian life on Prague's left bank, though he's perhaps best known in the West via the Chilean Nobel prize-winner, Pablo Neruda, who took his pen name from the lesser-known Czech. Historically, this is Prague's **artists' quarter**, and although few of the present inhabitants are names to conjure with, the various private galleries and craft shops that have sprouted up over the last few years continue the tradition.

The houses that line the steep climb to the Hrad are typically restrained, many retaining their medieval barn doors and most adorned with their own peculiar house signs (see p.57). Halfway up the hill, Nerudova halts at a crossroads where it meets the cobbled hairpin of Ke Hradu, which the royal coronation procession used to ascend; continuing west along **Úvoz** (The Cutting) takes you to the Strahovský klášter (see p.73). On the south side of Úvoz, the houses come to an end, and a view opens up over the picturesque jumble of Malá Strana's red-tiled roofs, while to the north, narrow stairways squeeze between the towering buildings of Hradčany, emerging on the path to the Loreta.

Running (very) roughly parallel to Nerudova – and linked to it by several side streets and steps – is **Tržiště**, which sets off from the south side of Malostranské náměstí. Halfway up on the left is the **Schönbornský palác**, now the US Embassy. The entrance, and the renowned gardens, are nowadays watched over by closed-circuit TV and twitchy Czech policemen – a far cry from the dilapidated palace in which Kafka rented an apartment in March 1917, and where he suffered his first bout of tuberculosis.

As Tržiště swings to the right, bear left up **Vlašská**, home to yet another **Lobkovický palác**, now the German Embassy. In the summer of 1989, several thousand East Germans climbed over the garden wall and entered the embassy compound to demand West German citizenship, which had been every German's right since partition. The neighbouring streets were soon jam-packed with abandoned Trabants, as the beautiful palace gardens became a muddy home to the refugees. Finally, the Czechoslovak government gave in and organized special trains to take the East Germans over the federal border, cheered on their way by thousands of Praguers, and thus prompted the exodus that eventually brought the Berlin Wall down.

Valdštejnský palác and around

To the north of Malostranské náměstí, up Tomášská, lies the **Valdštejnský palác**, which takes up the whole of the eastern side of **Valdštejnské náměstí** and Valdštejnská. As early as 1621, Albrecht von Waldstein started to build a palace which would reflect his status as commander of the Imperial Catholic armies of the Thirty Years' War. By buying, confiscating, and then destroying 26 houses, three gardens and a brick factory, he succeeded in ripping apart a densely populated area of Malá Strana to make way for one of the first, largest and, quite frankly, most unappealing Baroque palaces in the city – at least from the outside.

The Czech parliament's upper house, or Senát, is now housed in the palace, and only the former stables, housing the **Pedagogické muzeum** (Museum of Education; Tues–Sun 10am–12.30pm & 1–5pm), are accessible to the public. This is a small and none too exciting exhibition on Czech education and, in particular, the influential teachings of Jan Amos Komenský (1592–1670) – often anglicized to John Comenius – who was forced to leave his homeland after the victory of Waldstein's Catholic armies, eventually settling in Protestant England. To get to the exhibition, go through the main gateway and continue straight across the first courtyard; the museum is on your right. The only way to get to see the palace's magnificent main hall – used in the filming of *Amadeus* – is to go to one of the concerts occasionally held there.

If you've no interest in pedagogical matters, the palace's formal gardens, the **Valdštejnská zahrada** – accessible only from a doorway in the palace walls along Letenská – are a good place to take a breather from the city streets. The focus of the gardens is the gigantic Italianate *sala terrena*, a monumental loggia decorated with frescoes of the Trojan Wars, which stands at the end of an avenue of sculptures by Adriaen de Vries. The originals, which were intended to form a fountain, were taken off as booty by the Swedes in 1648 and now adorn the royal gardens in Drottningholm. In addition, there's a café, a pseudo-grotto along the south wall, with quasi-stalactites, a door that once led to Waldstein's observatory, and a small aviary, home to the gardens' peacock population.

There are a number of other Baroque palace **gardens** (May–Sept daily 10am–6pm) worth exploring on the slopes below the castle where the royal vineyards used to be. Alternatively, head for the **Vojanovy sady** (May–Sept daily 9am–7pm), securely concealed behind a ring of high walls off U lužického semináře. It's a public park rather than a palace garden, with sleeping babies, weeping willows and the occasional open-air performance or art exhibition.

Southern Malá Strana

Karmelitská is the busy cobbled street that runs south from Malostranské náměstí along the base of Petřín towards the industrial suburb of Smíchov, becoming Újezd at roughly its halfway point. Between here and the River Vltava are some of Malá Strana's most picturesque and secluded streets. Although there are no major sights around here, the island of **Kampa**, in particular, makes up one of the most peaceful stretches of riverfront in Prague.

Maltézské náměstí and around

From the trams and traffic fumes of Karmelitská, it's a relief to cut across to the calm restraint of **Maltézské náměstí**, one of a number of delightful little squares between here and the river. It takes its name from the Order of the Knights of St John of Jerusalem (better known by their later title, the Maltese Knights), who in 1160 founded the nearby church of **Panna Maria pod řetězem** (Saint Mary below-the-chain), so called because it was the knights' job to guard the Judith Bridge. The original Romanesque church was pulled down by the knights themselves in the fourteenth century, but only the chancel and towers were successfully rebuilt by the time of the Hussite Wars. The two bulky Gothic towers are still standing and the apse is now thoroughly Baroque, but the nave remains unfinished and open to the elements.

The knights have now reclaimed (and restored) the church and the adjacent Grand Priory, which backs onto **Velkopřevorské náměstí**, another pretty little square to the south, which echoes to the sound of music from the nearby Prague conservatoire. Following the violent death of John Lennon in 1980, Prague's youth established an ad hoc shrine smothered in graffiti tributes to the ex-Beatle along the Grand Priory's garden wall. The running battle between police and graffiti artists continued well into the Nineties, with the Maltese Knights taking an equally dim view of the mural, but a compromise has now been reached and the wall's scribblings legalized. On the opposite side of the square from the wall, sitting pretty in pink behind a row of chestnut trees, is the Rococo **Buquoyský palác**, built for a French family and appropriately enough now the French Embassy.

Kampa

The two or three streets that make up **Kampa**, the largest of the Vltava's islands, contain no notable palaces or museums; just a couple of old mills, an exquisite main square, and a serene riverside park – in other words, plenty enough diversion for a lazy summer afternoon. The island is separated from the left bank by Prague's "Little Venice", a thin strip of water called **Čertovka** (Devil's Stream), which used to power several millwheels until the last one ceased to function in 1936. In contrast to the rest of the left bank, the fire of 1541 had a positive effect on Kampa, since the flotsam from the blaze effectively stabilized the island's shifting shoreline. Nevertheless, Kampa was still subject to frequent flooding right up until the Vltava was dammed in the 1950s.

For much of its history, the island was the city's main wash house, and it wasn't until the sixteenth and seventeenth centuries that the Nostitz family, who owned Kampa, began to develop the northern half of the island; the southern half was left untouched and is today laid out as a public park, with riverside views across to Staré Město. To the north, the oval main square, **Na Kampě**, once a pottery market, is studded with slender acacia trees and cut through by the Charles Bridge, to which it is connected by a double flight of steps.

Panna Maria Vítězná

Halfway down busy Karmelitská is the rather plain church of **Panna Maria Vítězná**, which was begun in early Baroque style by German Lutherans in 1611, and later handed over to the Carmelites after the Battle of Bílá hora. The main reason for coming here is to see the **Pražské Jezulátko** or *Bambino di Praga*, a high-kitsch wax effigy of the infant Jesus as a precocious three-year-old, enthroned in a glass case illuminated with strip-lights, donated by one of the Lobkowicz family's Spanish brides in 1628. Attributed with miraculous powers, the *pražské Jezulátko* became an object of international pilgrimage equal in stature to the Santa Casa in Loreta, similarly inspiring a whole series of replicas. It continues to attract visitors (as the multilingual prayer cards attest) and boasts a vast personal wardrobe of expensive swaddling clothes – approaching a hundred separate outfits at the last count – regularly changed by the Carmelite nuns. If you're keen to see some of the infant's outfits, there's a small museum, up the spiral staircase in the south aisle. Here, you get to see his lacy camisoles, as well as a selection of his velvet and satin overgarments sent from all over the world. There are also chalices, monstrances and a Rococo crown studded with diamonds and pearls to admire.

Petřín

The scaled-down version of the Eiffel Tower is the most obvious landmark on the wooded hill of **Petřín**, the largest green space in the city centre. The tower is just one of the exhibits built for the 1891 Prague Exhibition, whose modest legacy includes the **funicular railway** (lanová dráha; daily 9.15am–8.45pm), which climbs up from a station just off Újezd. The original funicular was powered by a simple but ingenious system whereby two carriages, one at either end of the steep track, were fitted with large watertanks that were alternately filled at the top and emptied at the bottom; it was replaced in the 1960s by the current electric system. As the carriages pass each other at the halfway station of Nebozízek, you can get out and soak in the view from the restaurant of the same name.

At the top of the hill, it's possible to trace the southernmost perimeter wall of the old city – popularly known as the **Hladová zeď** (Hunger Wall) – as it creeps eastwards back down to Újezd, and northwestwards to the Strahovský klášter. Instigated in the 1460s by Charles IV, it was much lauded at the time (and later by the Communists) as a great public work which provided employment for the burgeoning ranks of the city's destitute (hence its name); in fact, much of the wall's construction was paid for by the expropriation of Jewish property.

Follow the wall southeast and you come to the aromatic **Růžový sad** (Rose Garden), whose colour-co-ordinated rose beds are laid out in front of Petřín's observatory, the **Štefánikova hvězdárna** (April–Aug Tues–Fri 2–7pm & 9–11pm, Sat & Sun 10am–noon, 2–7pm & 9–11pm; shorter hours in winter), run by star-gazing enthusiasts. The small astrological exhibition inside is hardly worth bothering with, but if it's a clear night, a quick peek through the observatory's two powerful telescopes is a treat. Follow the wall northwest and you'll come to Palliardi's twin-towered church of **sv Vavřinec** (St Lawrence), from which derives the German name for Petřín – Laurenziberg. Dotted along the path that leads to Strahov are the Stations of the Cross, culminating in the sgraffitoed Calvary Chapel, just beyond the church.

Opposite the church are a series of buildings from the 1891 Exhibition, starting with the diminutive **Rozhledna** (April–Oct daily 9.30am–7pm; Nov–March Sat & Sun 9.30am–5pm), an octagonal interpretation – though a mere fifth of the size – of the Eiffel Tower which shocked Paris in 1889, and a tribute to the city's strong cultural and political links with Paris at the time; naturally, the view from the public gallery is terrific in fine weather. The next building along is the **Bludiště** (April–Oct daily 10am–7pm; Nov–March Sat & Sun 10am–5pm), a mini neo-Gothic castle complete with mock drawbridge. The first section of the interior features a **mirror maze**, followed by an action-packed, life-sized diorama of the Prague students' and Jews' victory over the Swedes on the Charles Bridge in 1648. The humour of the convex and concave mirrors that lie beyond the diorama is so simple, it has both adults and kids giggling away. From the tower and maze, the path with the Stations of the Cross will eventually lead you to the perimeter wall of the Strahovský klášter (see p.73), giving great views over Petřín's palatial orchards and the sea of red tiles below.

Staré Město

STARÉ MĚSTO, literally the "Old Town", is Prague's most central, vital ingredient. It's where you'll find the capital's busiest markets, shops, restaurants and pubs, and during the day a gaggle of shoppers and tourists fills its narrow streets. The district is bounded on one side by the river, on the other by the arc of Národní, Na příkopě and Revoluční, and at its heart is **Staroměstské náměstí**, Prague's showpiece main square, easily the most magnificent in central Europe.

Merchants and craftsmen began settling in what is now Staré Město as early as the tenth century, and in the mid-thirteenth century it was granted town status, with jurisdiction over its own affairs. The fire of 1541, which ripped through the quarters on the other side of the river, never reached Staré Město, though the 1689 conflagration made up for it. Nevertheless, the victorious Catholic nobles built fewer large palaces here than on the left bank, leaving the medieval street plan intact with the exception of the Klementinum (the Jesuits' powerhouse) and the Jewish Quarter, Josefov, which was largely reconstructed in the late nineteenth century (see p.90). Like so much of Prague,

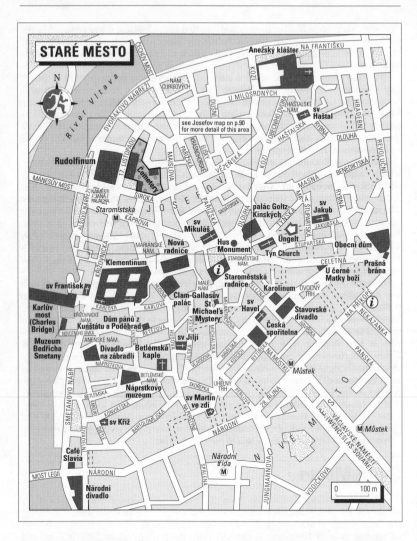

however, Staré Město is still, on the surface, overwhelmingly Baroque, built literally on top of its Gothic predecessor to guard against the floods which plagued the town.

In their explorations of Staré Město, most people unknowingly retrace the **králová cesta**, the traditional route of the coronation procession from the medieval gateway, the Prašná brána (see p.86), to the Hrad. Established by the Přemyslids, the route was followed, with a few minor variations, by every king until the Emperor Ferdinand IV in 1836, the last of the Habsburgs to bother having himself crowned in Prague. It's also the most direct route from the Charles Bridge to Prague's main square, Staroměstské náměstí, and therefore a natural choice. However, many of the real treasures of Staré Město lie away from the *králová cesta*, so if you want to escape the crowds, it's worth heading off into the quarter's silent, twisted matrix of streets, then simply following your nose – for details of specific sights to the south of Karlova, see p.87.

Karlův most (Charles Bridge)

The **Karlův most**, or Charles Bridge – which for over four hundred years was the only link between the two halves of Prague – is by far the city's most familiar monument. It's an impressive piece of medieval engineering, aligned slightly askew between two mighty Gothic gateways, but its fame is due almost entirely to the magnificent, mostly Baroque statues, additions to the original structure, that punctuate its length. Individually, only a few of the works are outstanding, but taken collectively, set against the backdrop of the Hrad, the effect is breathtaking.

The bridge was begun in 1357 to replace an earlier structure that was swept away in 1342 by one of the Vltava's frequent floods. Charles IV commissioned his young German court architect, Peter Parler, to carry out the work, which was finally completed in the early fifteenth century. For the first four hundred years it was known simply as the Prague or Stone Bridge – only in 1870 was it officially named after its patron. Since 1950, the bridge has been closed to vehicles, and is now one of the most popular places to hang out, day and night; apart from the steady stream of sightseers, the niches created by the bridge-piers are keenly fought over by souvenir hawkers and buskers.

A bronze **crucifix** has stood on the bridge since its construction, but its gold-leaf Hebrew inscription, "Holy, Holy, Holy Lord", was added in 1696, paid for by a Prague Jew who was ordered to do so by the city court, having been found guilty of blasphemy before the cross. The first of the sculptures wasn't added until 1683, when a bronze statue of **St John of Nepomuk** appeared as part of the Jesuits' persistent campaign to have him canonized (see p.66); this later inspired hundreds of copies, which adorn bridges throughout central Europe. On the base, there's a bronze relief depicting his martyrdom, the figure of John now extremely worn through years of being touched for good luck. The statue was such a propaganda success with the Catholic Church authorities that another 21 were added between 1706 and 1714. These included works by Prague's leading Baroque sculptors, including Matthias Bernhard Braun and Ferdinand Maximilian Brokof; the remaining piers (and a few swept away in the 1890 flood) were filled in with unimaginative nineteenth-century sculptures. The originals, mostly crafted in sandstone, have weathered badly over the years and have now been replaced by copies and put into storage in the Lapidárium (see p.116).

The **bridge towers** (April–Oct daily 9am–5.30pm) at each end of the bridge, can be climbed for a bird's eye view of the masses pouring across. On the Malá Strana side, two unequal towers, connected by a castellated arch, form the entrance to the bridge. The smaller, stumpy tower was once part of the original Judith Bridge (named after the wife of Vladislav I, who built the twelfth-century original); the taller tower is crowned by one of the pinnacled wedge-spires more commonly associated with Prague's right bank. On the Staré Město side is arguably the finest bridge tower of the lot, its eastern facade still encrusted in Gothic cake-like decorations from Peter Parler's workshop. The severed heads of twelve of the Protestant leaders were displayed here for ten years, following their executions on Staroměstské náměstí in 1621 (see p.84). In 1648, it was the site of the last battle of the Thirty Years' War, fought between the besieging Swedes and an ad hoc army of Prague's students and Jews, which trashed the western facade of the bridge tower.

Křižovnické náměstí to Malé náměstí

Pass under the Staré Město bridge tower and you're in **Křižovnické náměstí**, an awkward space hemmed in by its constituent buildings and, with traffic hurtling across the square, a dangerous spot for unwary pedestrians.

The two churches facing onto the square are both quite striking and definitely worth exploring. The half-brick church of **sv František z Assisi** (St Francis of Assisi) was built in the 1680s to a design by Jean-Baptiste Mathey for the Czech Order of Knights of the Cross with a Red Star, the original gatekeepers of the old Judith Bridge. The design of the church's interior, dominated by its huge dome, decorated with a fresco of *The Last Judgement* by Václav Vavřinec Reiner, and rich marble furnishings, served as a blueprint for numerous subsequent Baroque churches in Prague. The **Galerie Křižovníků** (Tues–Sun: May–Oct 10am–5pm; Nov–April 10am–5pm; closed Jan; 40Kč), next door, houses a stunning collection of silver and gold chalices, monstrances and reliquaries. Don't miss the subterranean chapel on your way out, whose unusual stalactite decor was completed in 1683.

Over the road is the church of **sv Salvátor**, its facade prickling with saintly statues which are lit up enticingly at night. Founded in 1593, but not completed until 1714, sv Salvátor marks the beginning of the Jesuits' rise to power and, like many of their churches, its design copies that of the Gesù church in Rome. It's worth a quick look, if only for the frothy stucco plasterwork and delicate ironwork in its triple-naved interior.

Along Karlova

Running from Křižovnické náměstí all the way to Malé náměstí is the narrow street of **Karlova**, packed with people winding their way towards Staroměstské náměstí, their attention divided between checking out the souvenir shops and not losing their way. With Europop blaring out from several shops, jester's hats and puppets in overabundance and a strip club for good measure, the whole atmosphere can be oppressive in the height of summer, and is, in many ways, better savoured at night. While much of what's on offer in Karlova is eminently missable, there is one sight worth seeking out, and that's the **Muzeum loutkářkých kultur** (Puppet Museum; summer daily 9am–8pm; winter Sat & Sun only), in the cool Gothic cellars of Karlova 12. Despite the appalling lack of information in either Czech or English, the museum boasts a highly impressive display of historic Czech puppets, both string and rod, mostly dating from the late nineteenth and the early twentieth centuries.

As they stroll down Karlova, few people notice the **Klementinum**, the former Jesuit College on the north side of the street, which covers an area second in size only to the Hrad. In 1556, Ferdinand I summoned the Jesuits to Prague to help bolster the Catholic cause in Bohemia, giving them the church of sv Kliment, which Dientzenhofer later rebuilt for them. Initially, the Jesuits proceeded with caution, but once the Counter-Reformation set in, they were put in control of the entire university and provincial education system. From their secure base at sv Kliment, they began to establish space for a great Catholic seat of learning in the city by buying up the surrounding land, demolishing more than thirty old town houses, and, over the next two hundred years, gradually building themselves a palatial headquarters. In 1773, soon after the Klementinum was completed, the Jesuits were turfed out of the country and the building handed over to the university authorities.

Nowadays the Klementinum houses the National Library's collection of over five million volumes, but much of the original building has been left intact. The **entrance**, inconspicuously placed just past the church of sv Kliment, lets you into a series of rather plain courtyards. The entrance to the **Zrcadlová kaple** (Mirrored Chapel) is immediately to the left after passing through the archway on the far side of the first courtyard; its interior of fake marble, gilded stucco and mirror panels boasts fine acoustics and is regularly used for concerts. At roughly the centre of the Klementinum complex is the Jesuits' **observatory tower**, which is the only place in the world that has being monitoring and recording meteorological data since 1775 – too late, though, for Prague's most illustrious visiting scientist, Johannes Kepler, who did his planet-gazing in the Belvedér. A religious exile from his native Germany, Kepler succeeded Tycho Brahe as court astronomer to Rudolf II, and lived at no. 4 Karlova for a number of years, during which time he drew up the first heliocentric laws on the movement of the planets.

Malé náměstí

After a couple more shops, boutiques, hole-in-the-wall bars and a final twist in Karlova, you emerge onto **Malé náměstí**, a square originally settled by French merchants in the twelfth century. The square was also home to the first apothecary in Prague, opened by a Florentine in 1353, and the tradition is continued today by the pharmacy **U zlaté koruny** (The Golden Crown) at no. 13, which boasts chandeliers and a restored Baroque interior. The square's best-known building, though, is the russet-red, neo-Renaissance **Rott Haus**, originally an ironmongers' shop founded by V. J. Rott in 1840, whose facade is smothered in agricultural scenes and motifs inspired by the Czech artist Mikuláš Aleš. The building is currently home to Prague's largest delicatessen, Dům lahůdek (see p.118). At the centre of the square is a (non-functioning) fountain from 1560, which retains its beautiful, original wrought-iron canopy.

Staroměstské náměstí

East of Malé náměstí is **Staroměstské náměstí** (Old Town Square), easily the most spectacular square in Prague, and the traditional heart of the city. Most of the brightly coloured houses look solidly eighteenth-century, but their Baroque facades hide considerably older buildings. From the eleventh century onwards, this was the city's main marketplace, known simply as Velké náměstí (Great Square), to which all roads in Bohemia led, and where merchants from all over Europe gathered. When the five towns that made up Prague were united in 1784, it was the Old Town Square's town hall that was made the seat of the new city council, and for the next two hundred years the square was the scene of the country's most violent demonstrations and battles. For a long time now, the whole place has been closed to traffic, and the cafés spread out their tables in summer, while tourists pour in to watch the town hall clock chime, to sit on the steps of the Hus Monument, and to drink in this historic showpiece.

The most recent arrival in the square is the colossal **Jan Hus Monument**, a turbulent sea of blackened bodies – the oppressed to the right, the defiant to the left – out of which rises the majestic moral authority of Hus himself, gazing into the horizon. For the sculptor Ladislav Šaloun, a maverick who received no formal training, the monument was his life's work. Commissioned in 1900 when the Art Nouveau style Viennese Secession was at its peak, but strangely old-fashioned by the time it was completed in 1915, it would be difficult to claim that it blends in with its Baroque surroundings, yet this has never mattered to the Czechs, for whom its significance goes far beyond aesthetic merit. The Austrians refused to hold an official unveiling; in protest, on July 6, 1915, the 500th anniversary of the death of Hus, Praguers smothered the monument in flowers. Since then it has been a powerful symbol of Czech nationalism: in March 1939, it was draped in swastikas by the invading Nazis, and in August 1968, it was shrouded in funereal black by Praguers, protesting at the Soviet invasion. The inscription along the base is a quote from the will of Comenius, one of Hus's later followers, and includes Hus's most famous dictum, *Pravda vitězí* (Truth Prevails), which has been the motto of just about every Czech revolution since then.

Staroměstská radnice

It wasn't until the reign of King John of Luxembourg (1310–46) that Staré Město was allowed to build its own town hall, the **Staroměstská radnice**. Short of funds, the citizens decided against an entirely new structure, buying a corner house on the square instead and simply adding an extra floor; later on, they added the east wing, with its graceful Gothic oriel and obligatory wedge-tower. Gradually, over the centuries, the neighbouring merchants' houses to the west were incorporated into the building, so that now it stretches all the way across to the richly sgraffitoed **Dům U minuty**, which juts out into the square.

On May 8, 1945, on the final day of the Prague Uprising, the Nazis still held on to Staroměstské náměstí, and in a last desperate act set fire to the town hall – one of the few buildings to be irrevocably damaged in the old town in World War II. The tower was rebuilt immediately, but only a crumbling fragment remains of the neo-Gothic **east wing**, which once stretched almost as far as the church of sv Mikuláš. Set into the paving nearby are 27 **white crosses** commemorating the Protestant leaders who were condemned to death on the orders of the emperor Ferdinand II, following the Battle of Bílá hora. They were publicly executed in the square on June 21, 1621: 24 enjoyed the nobleman's privilege and had their heads lopped off; the three remaining commoners were hung, drawn and quartered.

Today, the town hall's most popular feature is its *orloj* or **Astronomical Clock** – on the hour (daily 8am–8pm), a crowd of tourists and Praguers gather in front of the tower to watch a mechanical dumbshow by the clock's assorted figures. The Apostles shuffle past the top two windows, bowing to the audience, while perched on pinnacles below are the four threats to the city as perceived by the medieval mind: Death carrying his hourglass and tolling his bell, the Jew with his moneybags (since 1945 minus his stereotypical beard), Vanity admiring his reflection, and a turbaned Turk shaking his head. Beneath the moving figures, four characters representing Philosophy, Religion, Astronomy and History stand motionless throughout the performance. Finally, a cockerel pops out and flaps its wings to signal that the show's over; the clock then chimes the hour.

The powder-pink facade on the south side of the town hall now forms the **entrance** to the whole complex (Mon 11am–5pm, Tues–Sun 9am–5pm). A twenty-minute guided tour of the four rooms that survived World War II sets off every hour when the clock has finished striking (more frequently in summer). Despite being steeped in history, there's not much of interest here, apart from a few decorated ceilings with chunky beams and a couple of Renaissance portals. You'll probably get more enjoyment from climbing the tower – with access for the disabled – for the panoramic sweep across Prague's spires. You can also visit the chapel, designed by Peter Parler, which has patches of medieval wall painting, and wonderful grimacing corbels at the foot of the ribbed vaulting. If you get there just before the clock strikes the hour, you can watch the apostles going out on their parade; the figures all had to be re-carved by a local puppeteer after the war.

The church of sv Mikuláš and palác Goltz-Kinských

The destruction of the east wing of the town hall in 1945 rudely exposed Kilian Ignaz Dientzenhofer's church of **sv Mikuláš**, built in just three years between 1732 and 1735 for the Benedictines. Dientzenhofer's hand is obvious: the south front is decidedly luscious – painted creamy white, with Braun's blackened statuary popping up at every cornice – promising an interior to surpass even its sister church of sv Mikuláš in Malá Strana, which Dientzenhofer built with his father immediately afterwards (see p.75). Inside, however, is a curious mixture. Although caked in the usual mixture of stucco and fresco and boasting an impressive dome, the church has been stripped over the years of much of its ornament and lacks the sumptuousness of its namesake on the left bank. This is partly due to the fact that Joseph II closed down the monastery and turned the church into a storehouse, and partly because it's now owned by the very "low", modern, Czech Hussite Church.

The largest secular building on the square is the Rococo **palác Goltz-Kinských**, designed by Kilian Ignaz Dientzenhofer and built by his son-in-law Anselmo Lurago. In the nineteenth century it became a German *Gymnasium*, which was attended by, among others, Franz Kafka (whose father ran a haberdashery shop on the ground floor). The palace is perhaps most notorious, however, as the venue for the fateful speech by the Communist prime minister, Klement Gottwald, who walked out on to the grey stone balcony one snowy February morning in 1948, flanked by his Party henchmen, to address the thousands of enthusiastic supporters who packed the square below. It was the beginning of *Vitězná února* (Victorious February), the bloodless coup which brought the Communists to power and sealed the fate of the country for the next 41 years. The top floor now hosts top-flight exhibitions of graphic art put on by the Národní galerie.

The Týn church and Ungelt

Staré Město's most impressive Gothic structure, the mighty **Týn church** (Matka boží před Týnem), whose two irregular towers, bristling with baubles, spires and pinnacles, rise like giant antennae above the arcaded houses which otherwise obscure its facade, is a far more imposing building than sv Mikuláš. Like the nearby Hus monument, the Týn church, begun in the fourteenth century, is a source of Czech national pride. In an act of defiance, George of Poděbrady, the last Czech and the only Hussite King of Bohemia, adorned the high stone gable with a statue of himself and a giant gilded *kalich* (chalice), the mascot of all Hussite sects. The church remained a hotbed of Hussitism until the Protestants' crushing defeat at the Battle of Bílá hora, after which the chalice was melted down to provide the newly ensconced statue of the Virgin Mary with a golden halo, sceptre and crown.

Despite being one of the main landmarks of Staré Město, it's well-nigh impossible to appreciate the church from anything but a considerable distance, since it's boxed in by the houses around it, some of which are actually built right against the walls. The church's **interior** has been undergoing a very lengthy, thorough restoration and should once more be open to the public. The rather appealing gloom of the place has been swept away by the repainting, leaving a lofty, thin nave, dominated at ground level by the dark morass of black and gold Baroque altarpieces. The pillar on the right of the chancel steps contains the marble **tomb of Tycho Brahe**, the famous Danish astronomer, who arrived in Prague wearing a silver and gold false nose, having lost his own in a duel in Rostock. Court astronomer to Rudolf II for just two years, Brahe laid much of the groundwork for Johannes Kepler's later discoveries – Kepler getting his chance of employment when Brahe died of a burst bladder in 1601 after joining Petr Vok in one of his notorious binges.

Behind the Týn Church lies the Týn courtyard, better known by its German name, **Ungelt** (meaning "No Money", a pseudonym used to deter marauding invaders), which, as the trading base of German merchants, was one of the first settlements on the Vltava. A hospice, church and hostel were built for the use of the merchants, and by the fourteenth century the area had become an extremely successful international marketplace; soon afterwards the traders moved up to the Hrad, and the court was transformed into a palace. The whole complex has now been restored, and the Dominicans have reclaimed one section, while the rest houses various shops, restaurants, and a luxury hotel.

Dům U zlatého prstenu

Back on Týnská, the City of Prague Gallery has renovated the handsome Gothic townhouse of **Dům U zlatého prstenu** (House of the Golden Key; daily 10am–6pm), and converted it into a fascinating new art gallery, dedicated to twentieth-century Czech art. The permanent collection is spread out over three floors, and arranged thematically rather than chronologically, while the cellar provides space for installations by up-and-coming contemporary artists; there's also a nice café across the courtyard.

On the first floor, symbolism looms large, with *Destitute Land*, Max Švabinský's none-too-subtle view of life under the Habsburg yoke, and works by two of Bohemia's best-loved eccentrics, Josef Váchal and František Bílek. There's a decent selection of grim 1920s paintings, too, typified by *Slagheaps in the Evening* by Jan Zrzavý, plus the usual Czech Surrealist suspects. More refreshing is the sight of Eduard Stavinoha's *Striking Demonstrator*, an ideological painting from 1948 that appears almost like Pop Art. Antonín Slavíček's easy-on-the-eye Impressionist views of Prague kick off proceedings on the second floor, along with works by Cubist Emil Filla, and abstract artist Mikuláš Medek. Also on this floor, there's the chance to see a lot of 1980s works that don't often see the light of day nowadays, such as Michael Rittstein's political allegory *Slumber beneath a Large Hand*. Highlights on the third floor include an excellent collection of mad collages by Jiří Kolář, abstract Vorticist works by Zdeněk Sýkora, and studies for kinetic-light sculptures by Zdeněk Pešanek .

From Celetná to Anežský klášter

Celetná, whose name comes from the bakers who used to bake a particular type of small loaf (*calty*) here in the Middle Ages, leads east from Staroměstské náměstí direct to the Prašná brána, one of the original gateways of the old town. It's one of the oldest streets in Prague, lying along the former trade route from the old town market square, as well as on the *králová cesta*. Its buildings were smartly refaced in the Baroque period, and their pastel shades are now crisply maintained. Most of Celetná's shops veer towards the chic end of the Czech market, making it a popular place for a bit of window-shopping. Dive down one of the covered passages to the left and into the backstreets, however, and you'll soon lose the crowds, and eventually end up at the atmospheric ruins of Anežský klášter, now home to the National Gallery's nineteenth-century Czech art collection.

Two-thirds of the way along Celetná, at the junction with Ovocný trh, is the **Dům U černé Matky boží** (House of the Black Madonna), built as a department store in 1911–12 by Josef Gočár and one of the best examples of Czech Cubist architecture in Prague (see p.110 for more). The building now houses, among other things, a small, but excellent permanent exhibition of **Český Kubismus** (Czech Cubism) on the top two floors. There's a little bit of everything, from sofas and sideboards by Gočár himself to porcelain and paintings, plus some wonderful sculptures by Otto Gutfreund. To whet your appetite further, there are photographs of the Cubist villas in Vyšehrad (covered on p.110). The first, second and third floors are currently given over to temporary exhibitions of twentieth-century art.

Celetná ends at the fourteenth-century Prašná brána (see p.104), beyond which is náměstí Republiky, at which point, strictly speaking, you've left Staré Město behind. Back in the old town, head north from Celetná into the backstreets which conceal the Franciscan church of **sv Jakub** (Mon–Fri 9am–1pm & 2.30–4pm, Sat 9.30am–12.30pm & 2–4pm, Sun 2–4pm), with its distinctive bubbling, stucco portal on Malá Štupartská. The church's massive Gothic proportions – it has the longest nave in Prague after the cathedral – make it a favourite venue for organ recitals, Mozart masses and other concerts. After the great fire of 1689, Prague's Baroque artists remodelled the entire interior, adding huge pillasters, a series of colourful frescoes and over twenty side altars. The most famous of these is the tomb of the Count of Mitrovice, in the northern aisle, designed by Fischer von Erlach and Prague's own Maximilian Brokof.

Anežský klášter

Further north through the backstreets, the **Anežský klášter** (Convent of St Agnes), Prague's oldest surviving Gothic building, stands within a stone's throw of the river as it loops around to the east. It was founded in 1233 as a Franciscan convent for the Order of the Poor Clares, and takes its name from Agnes (Anežka), youngest daughter of

Přemysl Otakar I, who left her life of regal privilege to become the convent's first abbess. Agnes herself was beatified in 1874 to try to combat the spread of Hussitism amongst the Czechs, and there was much speculation about the wonders that would occur when she was officially canonized. This event finally took place on November 12, 1989, when Czech Catholics were invited to a special mass at St Peter's in Rome. Four days later the revolution began: a happy coincidence, even for agnostic Czechs.

The convent itself was closed down in 1782 and fell into rack and ruin. It was squatted for most of the next century, and although saved from demolition by the Czech nationalist lobby, its restoration only took place in the 1980s. The convent now houses the Národní galerie's **nineteenth-century Czech art collection**, and if the art inside is not always of the highest quality, it has at least been attractively rehung, with fulsome descriptions in Czech and English, and is at least interesting in terms of the Czech national revival. The building itself is also worth inspecting, and the gallery's temporary exhibitions are now among the best in the capital.

The well-preserved cloisters and the three remaining chapels on the ground floor are used for special exhibitions; for the permanent collection, you need to go up to the first floor. The collection kicks off in room 1 with Ludvík Kohl's fantasy paintings: the one of Vienna's Stephansdom shows the cathedral with two complete towers (instead of one); his imaginary completion of Prague's St Vitus Cathedral was eventually fulfilled more or less to the letter by nineteenth-century architects. Rooms 2 and 3 focus on the work of the **Mánes family**: father Antonín gave birth to romantic Czech landscape painting, and three of his offspring – Quido, Josef and Amálie – took up the brush. Josef Mánes was the most successful of the trio, much in demand as a portrait artist among the newly emerging Czech bourgeoisie, and one of the leading exponents of patriotically uplifting depictions of events of national significance (Mánes himself took part in the 1848 disturbances in Prague). Favourite themes – on display in several works in rooms 3 and 5 – range from legendary figures such as Břetislav and Jitka to the real-life tragedy of the Battle of Bílá hora.

The first six rooms can be taken at a steady canter, for the cream of the collection's late-nineteenth-century works are reserved for the gallery's final double room (7 & 8). Some of the most eye-catching works are **Jaroslav Čermák**'s paintings of Yugoslavia, where he was decorated for his bravery by the Montenegrin prince Nicholas I. With a dark, treacle-brown palette and an eye for drama, Čermák displays an unhealthy obsession with the depiction of white Slav women being captured by swarthy Ottoman Turks. **Antonín Chittussi**'s Corot-esque landscapes proved very popular in the Parisian salons of the 1880s, not so his most influential and uncharacteristic work, *Paris seen from Montmartre*, whose flat colours and precise lines were deemed beyond the pale.

Mikuláš Aleš, whose designs can be seen in the sgraffito on many of the city's nineteenth-century buildings, provides a few wonderfully decorative historical moments, such as the meeting between George of Poděbrady and Matthias Corvinus. Prize for most striking portrait goes to Václav Brožík's portrayal of his wife, the daughter of a wealthy Parisian art dealer. There are several other crowd pleasers, including Josef Schusser's *Lady with a Red Parasol* and G.C. Max's *Saint Julia*, which features a woman being crucified. And the collection ends with a bevy of decadent Art Nouveau nudes by Maximilián Pirner, and several of Jakub Schikaneder's misty, moody streetscapes.

Southern Staré Město

The southern half of Staré Město is bounded by the *králová cesta* (the coronation route; see p.80) to the north, and the curve of Národní and Na příkopě, which follow the course of the old fortifications, to the south. There are no showpiece squares like Staroměstské náměstí here, but the complex web of narrow lanes and hidden passageways, many of which have changed little since medieval times, make this an intriguing quarter to explore, and one where it's easy to lose the worst of the crowds.

From Ovocný trh to Uhelný trh

Heading southwest from the Dům U černé Matky boží (see above), you enter **Ovocný trh**, site of the old fruit market, its cobbles fanning out towards the back of the lime-green and white **Stavovské divadlo** (Estates Theatre). Built in the early 1780s by Count Nostitz (after whom the theatre was originally named) for the entertainment of Prague's large and powerful German community, the theatre is one of the finest Neoclassical buildings in Prague, reflecting the enormous self-confidence of its patrons. The Stavovské divadlo has a place in Czech history too, for it was here that the Czech national anthem, *Kde domov můj* (Where is My Home), was first performed, as part of the comic opera *Fidlovačka*, by J.K. Tyl. It is also something of a mecca for Mozart fans, since it was here, rather than in the hostile climate of Vienna, that the composer chose to première both *Don Giovanni* and *La Clemenza di Tito*. This is, in fact, one of the few opera houses in Europe which remains intact from Mozart's time, though it underwent major refurbishment during the nineteenth century – it was here that Miloš Forman filmed the concert scenes for his Oscar-laden *Amadeus*.

On the north side of the Stavovské divadlo is the home base of the **Karolinum** or Charles University, named after its founder Charles IV, who established it in 1348 as the first university in this part of Europe. To begin with, the university had no fixed abode; it wasn't until 1383 that Václav IV bought the present site. All that's left of the original fourteenth-century building is the Gothic oriel window which emerges from the south wall; the rest was trashed by the Nazis in 1945. The new main entrance is a peculiarly ugly red-brick curtain wall building by Jaroslav Fragner, set back from the street and inscribed with the original Latin name *Universitas Karolina*. Only a couple of small departments and the chancellor's office and administration are now housed here, with the rest spread over the length and breadth of the city. The heavily restored Gothic vaults, on the ground floor of the south wing, are now used as a contemporary **art gallery**.

The junction of Melantrichova and Rytířská is always teeming with people pouring out of Staroměstské náměstí and heading for Wenceslas Square. Clearly visible from Melantrichova is Prague's last surviving **open-air market** – a poor relation of its Germanic predecessor, which stretched all the way from Ovocný trh to Uhelný trh. Traditionally a flower and vegetable market, it runs the full length of the arcaded Havelská, and sells everything from celery to CDs, with plenty of souvenirs and wooden toys in between. The market runs west into **Uhelný trh**, which gets its name from the *uhlí* (coal) that was sold here in medieval times. Nowadays, however, it's Prague's red-light district – particularly Perlová and Na Perštýně – and although you'll see little evidence during the day, it can get busy at night, as a result of which the local authorities are constantly drawing up plans to move the trade elsewhere.

Sv Martin ve zdi and Bartolomějská

South of Uhelný trh, down Martinská, the street miraculously opens out to make room for the twelfth-century church of **sv Martin ve zdi** (St Martin-in-the-Walls), originally built to serve the Czech community of the village of sv Martin, until it found itself the wrong side of the Gothic fortifications. It's still essentially a Romanesque structure, adapted to suit Gothic tastes a century later; it was, however, closed down in 1784 by Joseph II and turned into a warehouse, shops and flats. The city bought the church in 1904 and thoroughly restored it, adding the creamy neo-Renaissance tower, and eventually handing it over to the Czech Brethren. For them, it has a special significance as the place where communion "in both kinds" (ie bread and wine), one of the fundamental demands of the Hussites, was first administered to the whole congregation, in

1414. To be honest, there's very little to see inside, which is just as well as it's only open for concerts nowadays.

Around the corner from sv Martin ve zdi is the gloomy, lifeless street of **Bartolomějská**, dominated by a tall, grim-looking building on its south side, which served as the main interrogation centre of the universally detested Communist secret police, the *Statní bezpečnost*, or *StB*. The building is now back in the hands of the Franciscan nuns who occupied the place prior to 1948; the former police cells – where Havel himself was once incarcerated – today serve as rooms for a small pension (see p.59).

Betlémské náměstí

After leaving the dark shadows of Bartolomějská, the brighter aspect of **Betlémské náměstí** comes as a welcome relief. The square is named after the **Betlémská kaple** (Bethlehem Chapel; daily 9am–6pm), whose high wooden gables face on to the square. This was founded in 1391 by religious reformists, who, denied the right to build a church, proceeded instead to build the largest chapel in Bohemia, with a total capacity of 3000. Sermons were delivered not in the customary Latin, but in the language of the masses – Czech. From 1402 to 1413, **Jan Hus** preached here (see box on p.180), regularly pulling in more than enough commoners to fill the chapel. Hus was eventually excommunicated for his outspokenness, found guilty of heresy and burnt at the stake at the Council of Constance in 1415.

The chapel continued to attract reformists from all over Europe for another two centuries – the leader of the German Peasants' Revolt, **Thomas Müntzer**, preached here in the sixteenth century – until the advent of the Counter-Reformation in Bohemia. Inevitably, the chapel was handed over to the Jesuits, who completely altered the original building, only for it to be demolished after they were expelled by the Habsburgs in 1773. Of the original building, only the three outer walls remain, with patches of their original decoration – biblical scenes which were used to get the message across to the illiterate congregation. The rest is a scrupulous reconstruction of the fourteenth-century building by Jaroslav Fragner, using the original plans and a fair amount of imaginative guesswork. The initial reconstruction work was carried out after the war by the Communists, who were keen to portray Hus as a Czech nationalist and social critic as much as a religious reformer, and, of course, to dwell on the revolutionary Müntzer's later appearances here.

At the western end of the square stands the **Náprstkovo muzeum** (Tues–Sun 9am–noon & 12.45–5.30pm), whose founder, Czech nationalist Vojta Náprstek, was inspired by the great Victorian museums of London while in exile following the 1848 revolution. Despite the fact that the museum could clearly do with an injection of cash, it still manages to put on some really excellent temporary ethnographic exhibitions on the ground floor, and does a useful job of promoting tolerance of different cultures. The permanent collection of Náprstek's American, Australasian and Oceanic collections occupies the top two floors. Náprstek's technological exhibits now form part of the collections of the Národné technické muzeum (see p.113), while his Asian and Oriental collections are housed in the chateau at Liběchov (see p.134).

St Michael's Mystery and Muzeum Bedřicha Smetany

Prague's most crude, out-and-out tourist trap is **St Michael's Mystery** (Tajemství u sv. Michala), which occupies the Baroque church of sv Michal, tucked away down a passageway connecting Melantrichova with Michalská. Impressionistic is probably the kindest term you could use to describe this very expensive multimedia assault on the senses. Led round by folk dressed as monks, you walk through a labyrinth of wacky stage sets inspired in the vaguest possible way by Prague's history, and interspersed by random quotes from Kafka. The special effects reach a crescendo as you eventually make your way into the main body of the church, where you get to sit in a pew and watch a multimedia film lasting twenty minutes or so, and surprisingly – given the average clientele – in Czech.

More in the traditional museum mould is the newly revamped **Muzeum Bedřicha Smetany** (daily except Tues 10am–5pm), on the first floor of the gaily decorated neo-Renaissance building, on the riverfront itself, situated a couple of blocks west of Betlémské náměstí. Despite having German as his mother tongue, Bedřich Smetana (1824–84) was without doubt the most nationalistic of all the great Czech composers, taking an active part in the 1848 revolution and the later national revival movement. He enjoyed his greatest success as a composer with *The Bartered Bride*, which marked the birth of Czech opera. Sadly, he was forced to give up conducting in 1874 with the onset of deafness, and eventually died of syphilis in a mental asylum. Sadly, the museum fails to capture much of the spirit of the man, though you get to see his spectacles, and the garnet jewellery of his first wife. Still, the views across to the castle are good, and you get to wave a laser baton around in order to listen to his music.

Josefov

> *It is crowded with horses; traversed by narrow streets not remarkable for cleanliness, and has altogether an uninviting aspect. Your sanitary reformer would here find a strong case of overcrowding.*
>
> Walter White, "A July Holiday in Saxony, Bohemia and Silesia" (1857)

Less than half a century after Walter White's comments, all that was left of the former ghetto of **JOSEFOV** were six synagogues, the town hall and the medieval cemetery. At

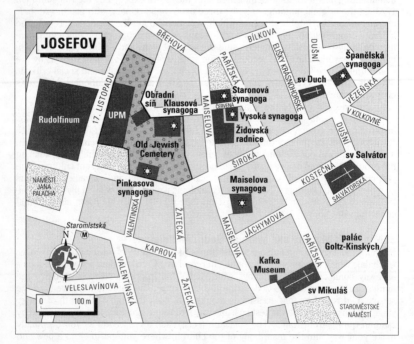

the end of the nineteenth century, a period of great economic growth for the Habsburg Empire, it was decided that Prague should be turned into a beautiful bourgeois city, modelled on Paris. The key to this transformation was the "sanitization" of the ghetto, a process, begun in 1893, which reduced the notorious malodorous backstreets and alleyways of Josefov to rubble and replaced them with block after block of luxurious five-storey mansions. The Jews, the poor, the gypsies and the prostitutes were cleared out so that the area could become a desirable residential quarter, rich in Art Nouveau buildings festooned with decorative murals, doorways and sculpturing. This building frenzy marked the beginning of the end for a community which had existed in Prague for almost a millennium.

In any other European city occupied by the Nazis in World War II, what little was left of the old ghetto would have been demolished. But although Prague's Jews were transported to the new ghetto in Terezín, by a grotesque twist of fate the ghetto itself was preserved by Hitler himself in order to provide a site for his planned "Exotic Museum of an Extinct Race". With this in mind, Jewish artefacts from all over central Europe were gathered here, and now make up one of the richest collections of Judaica in Europe, and one of the most fascinating sights in Prague.

A history of Jewish settlement in Prague

Jews probably arrived in Prague as early as the tenth century and, initially at least, are thought to have settled on both sides of the river. In 1096, at the time of the first crusade, the earliest recorded **pogrom** took place, which may have hastened the formation of a much more closely-knit "Jewish town" within Staré Město during the twelfth century. However, it wasn't until much later that Jews were actually herded into a **walled ghetto** (and several centuries before the word "ghetto" was actually first coined in Venice), sealed off from the rest of the town and subject to a curfew. From the beginning, though, they were subject to laws restricting their choice of profession to usury and the rag trade; in addition, some form of visible identification, a cap or badge (notably the Star of David), remained a more or less constant feature of Jewish life until the Enlightenment.

In 1262, Přemysl King Otakar II issued a *Statuta Judaeorum*, which granted the Jews their own religious and civil self-administration. In effect, however, the Jews were little more than the personal property of the king, and though Otakar himself appears to have been genuine in his motives, later rulers used the *Statuta* as a form of blackmail, extorting money whenever they saw fit. During the **1389 pogrom**, 3000 Jews were massacred over Easter, some while sheltering in the Old-New Synagogue – an event commemorated every year thereafter on Yom Kippur.

The reign of Rudolf II (1576–1612) was a time of economic and cultural prosperity for the Prague Jewish community. The Jewish mayor, **Mordecai Maisel**, Rudolf's minister of finance, became one of the richest men in Bohemia and the success symbol of a generation; his money bought the Jewish quarter a town hall, a bath house, pavements and several synagogues. This was the "golden age" of the ghetto: the time of **Rabbi Löw**, the severe and conservative chief rabbi of Prague, who is now best known as the legendary creator of the Jewish Frankenstein or "golem" (a precursor of Frankenstein's monster).

It was the enlightened **Emperor Joseph II** (1780–90) who did most to lift the restrictions on Jews. His 1781 Toleration Edict ended the dress codes, opened up education to all non-Catholics, and removed the gates from the ghetto. The community paid him homage in the following century by officially naming the ghetto Josefov, or Josefstadt. It was not until the **1848 revolution**, however, that Jews were granted equal status as citizens and permitted to settle outside the ghetto. Gradually, the more prosperous Jewish families began to move to other districts of Prague, leaving behind only the poorest Jews and strictly Orthodox families, who were rapidly joined by the underprivileged ranks of Prague society: gypsies, beggars, prostitutes and alcoholics. By 1890, only twenty percent of Josefov's population was Jewish, yet it was still the most densely populated area in Prague.

The ending of restrictions, and the destruction of most of the old ghetto, increased the pressure on Jews to assimilate, a process which brought its own set of problems. Prague's Jews were split roughly half and half between predominantly German- or Yiddish-speakers and Czech-speakers. Yet since some two-thirds of Prague's German population was Jewish, and all Jews had been forced to take German names by Josef II, all Jews were seen by Czech nationalists as a Germanizing influence. Tensions between the country's German-speaking minority and the Czechs grew steadily worse in the run-up to World War I, and the Jews found themselves caught in the firing line "like powerless stowaways attempting to steer a course through the storms of embattled nationalities", as one Prague Jew put it.

After the **Nazi occupation** of Prague on March 15, 1939, the city's Jews were subject to an increasingly harsh set of regulations, which saw them again barred from most professions, placed under curfew, and compelled once more to wear the yellow Star of David. In November 1941, the first transport of Prague Jews set off for the new ghetto in Terezín, 60km northwest of Prague. Of the estimated 55,000 Jews in Prague at the time of the Nazi invasion, over 36,000 died in the camps. Many survivors emigrated to Israel and the USA. Of the 8000 who registered as Jewish in the Prague census of 1947, a significant number joined the Communist Party, only to find themselves victims of Stalinist anti-Semitic wrath during the 1950s.

It's difficult to calculate exactly how many Jews now live in Prague – around a thousand were officially registered as such prior to 1989 – though their numbers have undoubtedly been bolstered by a new generation of Czech Jews who have rediscovered their roots, and by the new influx of Jewish Americans and Israelis. The controversy over Jewish property – most of which was seized by the Nazis, and therefore not covered by the original restitution law – has finally been resolved, allowing the community to reclaim at least some of its buildings, most importantly the six synagogues, town hall and cemetery of Josefov itself.

The former ghetto

Geographically, Josefov lies to the northwest of Staroměstské náměstí, between the church of sv Mikuláš and the Vltava river. The warren-like street plan of Josefov disappeared during the sanitization, and through the heart of the old ghetto runs the ultimate bourgeois avenue, **Pařížská**, a riot of turn-of-the-century sculpturing, spikes and turrets, home to a parade of international airline offices and boutiques. If Josefov can still be said to have a main street, though, it is really the parallel street of **Maiselova**, named after the community's sixteenth-century leader. The sheer volume of tourists – over a million a year – that visit Josefov has brought with it the inevitable rash of souvenir stalls flogging dubious "Jewish" souvenirs, and the whole area is now something of a tourist trap. Yet to skip this part of the old town is to miss out on an entire slice of the city's cultural history.

All the "sights" of Josefov, bar the Staronová synagóga, are covered by an all-in-one 450Kč ticket, available from any of the quarter's ticket offices. Opening hours vary but are basically daily except Sat: April–Oct 9.30am–6pm; Nov–March 9.30am–4.30pm. In order to try and regulate the flow of visitors, the authorities have introduced a timed entry system, giving you around twenty minutes at each sight, though don't worry if you don't adhere rigidly to your timetable.

Staronová synagóga and Židovská radnice

Walking down Maiselova, it's impossible to miss the steep sawtooth brick gables of the **Staronová synagóga** or Altneuschul (Old-New Synagogue), so called because when it was built it was indeed very new, though as time went on, it became anything but. Begun in the second half of the thirteenth century, it is, in fact, the oldest functioning synagogue in Europe, one of the earliest Gothic buildings in Prague and still the religious centre for Prague's Orthodox Jews. Since Jews were prevented by law from becoming architects, the synagogue was probably constructed by the Franciscan builders working on the convent of sv Anežka. Its five-ribbed vaulting is unique in Bohemia; the extra, purely decorative rib was added to avoid any hint of a cross.

To enter the synagogue (April–Oct Mon–Thurs & Sun 9am–6pm, Fri 9am–5pm; Nov–March Mon–Thurs & Sun 9am–5pm, Fri 9am–2pm), you must buy a separate ticket (200Kč) from the ticket office opposite the synagogue's entrance on Červená (or from one of the other ticket offices in Josefov). Men are asked to cover their heads out of respect – paper *kippahs* are available at the ticket office. To get to the **main hall**, you must pass through one of the two low vestibules from which women are allowed to watch the proceedings. Above the entrance is an elaborate tympanum covered in the twisting branches of a vine tree, its twelve bunches of grapes representing the tribes of Israel. The low glow from the chandeliers is the only light in the hall, which is mostly taken up with the elaborate wrought-iron cage enclosing the *bimah* in the centre. In 1357, Charles IV allowed the Jews to fly their own municipal standard, a moth-eaten remnant of which is still on show. The other flag – a tattered red banner – was a gift to the community from Emperor Ferdinand III for helping fend off the Swedes in 1648. On the west wall is a glass cabinet, shaped like Moses' two tablets of stone and filled with tiny personalized light bulbs, which are paid for by grieving relatives or friends and light up on the anniversary of the person's death (there's even one for Kafka).

Just south of the synagogue is the **Židovská radnice** (Jewish Town Hall), one of the few such buildings to survive the Holocaust. Founded and funded by Maisel in the sixteenth century, it was later rebuilt as the creamy-pink Baroque house you see now, housing an overpriced kosher restaurant. The belfry, permission for which was granted by Ferdinand III, has a clock on each of its four sides, plus a Hebrew one stuck on the north gable which, like the Hebrew script, goes "backwards".

Pinkasova synagóga

Jutting out at an angle on the south side of the Old Jewish Cemetery (see next page), with its entrance on Široká, the **Pinkasova synagóga** was built in the 1530s for the powerful Pinkas family, and has undergone countless restorations over the centuries. In 1958, the synagogue was transformed into a chilling memorial to the 77,297 Czech Jews killed during the Holocaust. The memorial was closed shortly after the 1967 Six Days' War – due to damp, according to the Communists – and remained so, allegedly due to problems with the masonry, until it was finally, painstakingly restored in the 1990s.

Of all the sights of the Jewish quarter, the **Holocaust memorial** is perhaps the most moving, with every bit of wall space taken up with the carved stone list of victims, stating simply their names, dates of birth and dates of transportation to the camps. It is the longest epitaph in the world, yet it represents only the merest fraction of those who died in the Nazi concentration camps. All that remains of the synagogue's original decor is the ornate *bimah* surrounded by a beautiful wrought-iron grille, supported by barleysugar columns. Upstairs in a room beside the women's gallery, there's now a harrowing exhibition of naive drawings by children from the Jewish ghetto in Terezín (see p.224), most of whom later perished in the camps.

Starý Židovský hřbitov (Old Jewish Cemetery)

At the heart of Josefov is the **Starý židovský hřbitov** (Old Jewish Cemetery), called *Bet Hayyim* in Hebrew, meaning "House of Life". Established in the fifteenth century, it was in use until 1787, by which time there were an estimated 100,000 buried here, one on top of the other, as many as twelve layers deep. The enormous number of visitors has meant that the graves themselves have been roped off to protect them, and a one-way system introduced: you enter from the Pinkasova synagóga, on Široká, and leave by the Klausová synagóga (see below). The oldest grave, dating from 1439, belongs to the poet Avigdor Karo, who lived to tell the tale of the 1389 pogrom. Get there before the crowds – a difficult task at most times of the year – and you'll find the cemetery a poignant reminder of the ghetto, its inhabitants subjected to inhuman overcrowding even in death. The rest of Prague recedes beyond the sombre lime trees and cramped perimeter walls, the haphazard headstones and Hebrew inscriptions casting a powerful spell.

Obřadní síň and the other synagogues

Immediately on your left as you leave the cemetery is the **Obřadní síň**, a lugubrious neo-Renaissance house built in 1906 as a ceremonial hall by the Jewish Burial Society. Appropriately enough, it's now devoted to an exhibition on Jewish traditions of burial and death, good to peruse before you head off into the cemetery.

Close to the entrance to the cemetery is the **Klausová synagóga**, a late seventeenth-century building, founded in the 1690s by Mordecai Maisel on the site of several

---

ON KAFKA'S TRAIL

Franz Kafka was born on July 3, 1883, above the *Batalion* Schnapps bar on the corner of Maiselova and Kaprova (the original building has long since been torn down, but a gaunt-looking modern bust now commemorates the site). He spent most of his life in and around Josefov. His father was an upwardly mobile small businessman from a Czech-Jewish family of kosher butchers (Kafka himself was a vegetarian), his mother from a wealthy German-Jewish family of merchants. The family owned a haberdashery shop, located at various premises on or near Staroměstské náměstí. In 1889, they moved out of Josefov and lived for the next seven years in the beautiful Renaissance Dům U minuty, next door to the Staroměstská radnice, during which time Kafka attended the *Volksschule* on Masná (now a Czech primary school), followed by a spell at an exceptionally strict German *Gymnasium*, located on the third floor of the palác Goltz-Kinských.

At eighteen, he began a law degree at the German half of the Karolinum, which was where he met his lifelong friend and posthumous biographer and editor, Max Brod. Kafka spent most of his working life as an accident insurance clerk, until he was forced to retire through ill health in 1922. Illness plagued him throughout his life and he spent many months as a patient at the innumerable spas in *Mitteleuropa*. He was engaged three times, twice to the same woman, but never married, finally leaving home at the age of 31 for bachelor digs on the corner of Dlouhá and Masná, where he wrote the bulk of his most famous work, *The Trial*. He died of tuberculosis at the age of 40 in a sanatorium just outside Vienna, on June 3, 1924, and is buried in the Nový židovský hřbitov in Žižkov.

Nowadays, thanks to his popularity with Western tourists, Kafka has become an extremely marketable commodity, with his image plastered across T-shirts, mugs and postcards all over the city centre. A small museum, Expozice Franza Kafky (Tues–Fri 10am–6pm, Sat 10am–5pm), next door to the church of sv Mikuláš, retells his life simply but effectively with pictures and quotes (in Czech, German and English). It's run by the Kafka Society, as is the Franz Kafka bookshop and *Café Milena* (named after one of his lovers), situated opposite the town hall on Staroměstské náměstí.

medieval prayer halls (*klausen*), in what was then a notorious red-light district of Josefov. The ornate Baroque interior contains a rich display of religious objects from embroidered *kippah* to *Kiddush* cups, and explains the very basics of Jewish religious practice.

Founded and paid for entirely by Mordecai Maisel, the neo-Gothic **Maiselova synagóga**, set back from the neighbouring houses on Maiselova, was, in its day, one of the most ornate synagogues in Josefov. Nowadays, its whitewashed interior is almost entirely bare apart from the rich offerings of its glass cabinets, which contain gold and silverwork, *hanukkah* candlesticks, *torah* scrolls and other religious artefacts.

East of Pařížská, up Široká, stands the **Španělská synagóga** (Spanish Synagogue), built in 1868. By far the most ornate synagogue in Josefov, every available surface of its stunning, gilded Moorish interior is smothered with a profusion of floral motifs and geometric patterns, in vibrant reds, greens and blues, which are repeated in the synagogue's huge stained-glass windows. The synagogue now houses an interesting exhibition on the history of Prague's Jews, from the time of the 1848 emancipation. Lovely, slender, painted cast-iron columns hold up the women's gallery, where the displays contain a fascinating set of photos depicting the old ghetto at the time of its demolition. There's a section on Prague's German-Jewish writers, including Kafka, and information on the planned Nazi museum and the Holocaust.

Around náměstí Jana Palacha

As Kaprova and Široká emerge from Josefov, they meet at the newly christened **náměstí Jana Palacha**, previously called náměstí Krasnoarmejců (Red Army Square) and embellished with a flowerbed in the shape of a red star (now replaced by the circular vent of an underground car park), in memory of the Soviet dead who were temporarily buried here in May 1945 (see p.100). It was probably this, as much as the fact that the building on the east side of the square is the Faculty of Philosophy where Palach was a student, that prompted the new authorities to make the first of the street name changes here in 1989 (there's a bust of Palach on the corner of the building). By a happy coincidence, the road which intersects the square from the north is called 17 listopadu (17 November), originally commemorating the students' anti-Nazi demonstration of 1939, but now equally good for the 1989 march (see p.102).

The north side of the square is taken up by the **Rudolfinum** or Dům umělců (House of Artists), designed by Josef Zítek and Josef Schulz. One of the proud civic buildings of the nineteenth-century national revival, it was originally built to house an art gallery, museum and concert hall for the Czech-speaking community. In 1918, however, it became the seat of the new Czechoslovak parliament, only returning to its original artistic purpose in 1946. In the last couple of years it's been sandblasted back to its original woody-brown hue, and is now one of the capital's main exhibition and concert venues (it's home to the Czech Philharmonic), with a wonderfully grand café on the first floor (see p.120).

UPM – the Decorative Arts Museum

A short way down 17 listopadu from the square is the **UPM**, or Umělecko-průmyslové muzeum (Tues–Sun 10am–6pm), installed in another of Schulz's worthy nineteenth-century creations, richly decorated in mosaics, stained glass and sculptures. Literally translated, this is a "Museum of Decorative Arts", though the translation hardly does justice to what is one of the most fascinating museums in the capital. From its foundation in 1885 through to the end of the First Republic, the UPM received the best that the Czech modern movement had to offer – from Art Nouveau to the avant-garde – and judging from previous catalogues and the various short-term exhibitions mounted in the past, its collection is unrivalled.

Unfortunately, the permanent exhibition consists of just a sample from each of the main artistic periods from the Renaissance to the 1930s, giving only the vaguest hints at the wealth of exhibits stored away in the museum's vaults. Worse still, the top floor, which covers the period from the 1880s to the 1930s, has been closed for a number of years. As a consolation, the museum's ground and first floors are used for some of the best temporary exhibitions in Prague, mostly taken from its twentieth-century collections. There's also a **public library** in the building (Mon noon–6pm, Tues–Fri 10am–6pm; closed July & Aug), specializing in catalogues and material from previous exhibitions, and an excellent café on the ground floor (see p.120).

Nové Město

Although it comes over as a sprawling, late-nineteenth-century bourgeois quarter, **NOVÉ MĚSTO** was actually founded in 1348 by Charles IV as an entirely new town – three times as large as Staré Město – intended to link the southern fortress of Vyšehrad with Staré Město to the north. Large market squares, wide streets, and a level of town-planning far ahead of its time were employed to transform Prague into the new capital city of the Holy Roman Empire. However, this quickly became the city's poorest quarter after Josefov, renowned as a hotbed of Hussitism and radicalism throughout the centuries. In the second half of the nineteenth century, the authorities set about a campaign of slum clearance similar to that inflicted on the Jewish quarter; only the churches and a few important historical buildings were left standing, though Charles' street layout survived pretty much intact. The leading architects of the day began to line the wide boulevards with ostentatious examples of their work, which were eagerly snapped up by the new class of status-conscious businessmen – a process that has continued well into this century, making Nové Město the most architecturally varied part of Prague.

Today, Nové Město remains the city's main commercial and business district, housing most of its hotels, nightclubs, cafés, fast-food outlets and department stores. The obvious starting point, and probably the only place in Prague most visitors can put a name to, is **Wenceslas Square**, known to the Czechs as **Václavské náměstí**, hub of the modern city and somewhere you'll find yourself passing through again and again. The two principal, partially pedestrianized, streets which lead off it are **Národní třída** and **Na příkopě**, which together form the *zlatý kříž* or golden cross, for over a century the most expensive slice of real estate in the capital. The *zlatý kříž*, and the surrounding streets, also contain some of Prague's finest late-nineteenth-century, Art-Nouveau and twentieth-century architecture.

The rest of Nové Město, which spreads out northeast and southwest of the square, is much less explored and, for the most part, solidly residential; unusually for Prague, using the tram and metro systems to get around here will save some unnecessary legwork.

Václavské náměstí (Wenceslas Square)

The natural pivot around which modern Prague revolves, and the focus of the events of November 1989, **Václavské náměstí** (Wenceslas Square) is more of a wide, gently sloping boulevard than a square as such. It's scarcely a conventional – or even convenient – space in which to hold mass demonstrations, yet night after night in November 1989, more than 250,000 people crammed into the square, often enduring subzero temperatures to call for the resignation of the Party leaders and demand free elections. On November 27, the whole of Prague came to a standstill, a bigger crowd than ever converging on the square to show their support for the two-hour nationwide general strike called by the opposition umbrella group, Občanské fórum (Civic Forum), who led the revolution. It was this last mass mobilization that proved decisive – by noon the next day, the Communist old guard had thrown in the towel.

The square's **history of protest** goes back to the 1848 revolution, whose violent denouement began here on June 12 with a peaceful open-air mass organized by the Prague students. On the crest of the nationalist disturbances, the square – which had been known as Komský trh (Horse Market) since medieval times – was given its present name. Naturally enough, it was one of the natural rallying points for the jubilant milling crowds on October 28, 1918, when Czechoslovakia's independence was declared. Thirty years later, in 1948, the square was filled to capacity once more, this time with Communist demonstrators enthusiastically supporting the February coup. Then in August 1968, it was the scene of some of the most violent confrontations between the Soviet invaders and the local Czechs. And, of course, it was at the top of the square, on January 16, 1969, that Jan Palach set fire to himself in protest at the continuing occupation of the country by Warsaw Pact troops.

Despite the square's medieval origins, its oldest building dates only from the eighteenth century, and the vast majority are much younger. As the city's money moved south of Staré Město during the industrial revolution, so the square became the architectural showpiece of the nation, and it is now lined with self-important six- or seven-storey buildings, representing every artistic trend of the last hundred years, from neo-Renaissance to Socialist Realism. Even if you've no interest in modern architecture, there's plenty to keep you occupied in the swanky shops, time-piece arcades or *pasáže*, cinemas, theatres and general hubbub of the square.

Up the square

The busiest part of Wenceslas Square and a popular place to meet up before hitting town is around **Můstek**, the city's most central metro station, at the northern end of the square. The area is dominated by the **Palác Koruna**, a hulking wedge of sculptured concrete and gold, built for an insurance company in 1914 by Antonín Pfeiffer, one of Jan Kotěra's many pupils. The building is a rare mixture of heavy constructivism and gilded Secession-style ornamentation, but the *pièce de résistance* is the palace's bejewelled crown which lights up at night.

On the opposite side of the square, adjacent to one another, are two functionalist buildings designed by Ludvík Kysela in the late 1920s, billed at the time as the first glass curtain-wall buildings. Along with the *Hotel Juliš* (see below), they represent the perfect expression of the optimistic mood of progress and modernism that permeated the interwar republic. The building on the right, as you face them, was erected by the chocolate firm Lindt; the **Baťa** store, on the left, followed a few years later. The latter was built for the Czech shoe magnate Tomáš Baťa, one of the greatest patrons of avant-garde Czech art, who fled the country in 1948, when the Communists nationalized the shoe industry; the store was returned to the family, along with a number of their shoe factories, after 1989.

Twenty-five years earlier, Czech architecture was in the throes of its own version of Art Nouveau, one of whose earliest practitioners was Jan Kotěra. The **Peterkův dům**, a slender essay in the new style, was his first work, undertaken at the age of 28. Kotěra, a pupil of the great architect of the Viennese Secession, Otto Wagner, eventually moved on to a much more brutal constructivism. Another supreme example of Czech functionalism, a few doors further up at no. 22, is the former **Hotel Juliš**, designed by Pavel Janák, who had already made his name as one of the leading lights of the short-lived Czech Cubist (and later Rondo-Cubist) movement (see p.110).

Further up on the same side of the square is the **Melantrich** publishing house, whose first floor is occupied by the offices of the Socialist Party newspaper, *Svobodné slovo* (The Free Word). For forty years the Socialist Party was a loyal puppet of the Communist government, but on the second night of the demonstrations in November

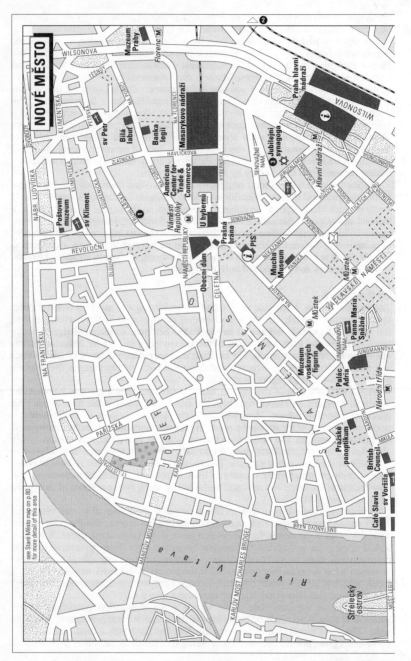

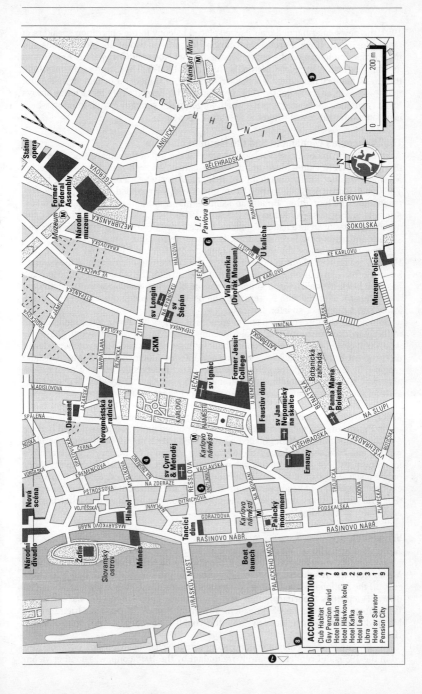

ACCOMMODATION
Club Habitat 4
Gay Penzion David 7
Hotel Balkán 8
Hotel Hlávkova kolej 5
Hotel Kafka 2
Hotel Legie 6
Libra 3
Hotel sv Salvator 1
Pension City 9

1989, the newspaper handed over its well-placed balcony to the opposition speakers of Občanské fórum (Civic Forum). Melantrich House faces two of the most famous and most ornate buildings on the entire square, the Art Nouveau *Grand Hotel Evropa* and its slim neighbour, the *Hotel Meran*, both built in 1903–5. They represent everything the Czech modern movement stood against, chiefly, ornament for ornament's sake, not that this has in any way dented their popularity. The *Evropa's* café terrace has always had a reputation for posing, but it's worth forgoing the sunlight for the interior, which is as sumptuous as it was when the hotel first opened.

The Wenceslas Monument and the Národní muzeum

A statue of St Wenceslas (sv Václav) has stood at the top of the square since 1680, but the present **Wenceslas Monument**, by the father of Czech sculpture, Josef Václav Myslbek, was not finally unveiled until 1912, after thirty years on the drawing board. The Czech patron saint sits astride his mighty steed, surrounded by smaller-scale representations of four other Bohemian saints – his grandmother Ludmila, Procopius, Adalbert and Agnes – added in the 1920s. In 1918, 1948, 1968, and again in 1989, the monument was used as a national political notice board, festooned in posters, flags and slogans and, even now, it remains the city's favourite soapbox venue.

A few metres below the statue, on January 16, 1969, a 21-year-old student, **Jan Palach**, set himself alight in protest against the continuing occupation of his country by the Soviets. An impromptu martyrs' shrine, set up after the fall of the regime in 1989, has now been formalized as a simple memorial of *obětem komunismu* (the victims of communism), adorned with flowers and photos of Palach and another student who followed suit a month or so later, Jan Zajíc.

Dominating the top, southern end of Wenceslas Square sits the broad, brooding hulk of the **Národní muzeum** (National Museum; daily: May–Sept 10am–6pm; Oct–April 9am–5pm; closed first Tues of month), built by Josef Schulz and deliberately modelled on the great European museums of Paris and Vienna. Along with the Národní divadlo (see p.103), this is one of the great landmarks of the nineteenth-century Czech national revival, sporting a monumental gilt-framed glass cupola, worthy clumps of sculptural decoration and narrative frescoes depicting scenes from Czech history.

The museum is old-fashioned and underfunded, but it's worth taking at least a quick look at the ornate marble entrance hall and the splendid monumental staircase leading to the **Pantheon** of Czech notables at the top. Arranged under the glass-domed hall are 48 busts and statues of distinguished bewhiskered Czech men (plus a couple of token women and Slovaks), including the universally adored T.G. Masaryk, the country's founding president, whose statue was removed by the Communists from every other public place. The rest of the museum is dowdy and badly labelled, though those with children might like to head upstairs for the fossils and stuffed animals. The museum's temporary exhibitions, displayed on the ground floor, can be very good indeed, so it's always worth checking to see what's on.

Wilsonova

At the southern end of Wenceslas Square is some of the worst blight that Communist planners inflicted on Prague – above all, the six-lane highway that now separates Nové Město from the residential suburb of Vinohrady to the east and south and effectively cuts off the National Museum from Wenceslas Square. Previously known as Vítězného února (Victorious February) after the Communist coup, the road was renamed **Wilsonova** in honour of US President Woodrow Wilson (a personal friend of the Masaryk family), who effectively gave the country its independence from Austria-Hungary in 1918.

The Prague stock exchange building alongside the National Museum, only completed in the 1930s but rendered entirely redundant by the 1948 coup, was another victim of postwar "reconstruction". The architect Karel Prager was given the task of designing a new "socialist" **Federal Assembly** building on the same site, without destroying the old bourse. He opted for a supremely unappealing, bronze-tinted, plate-glass structure, supported by concrete stilts and sitting uncomfortably on top of its diminutive predecessor. Since the break-up of the country, the building has lost its *raison d'être* once more, and now provides a home for, among other things, Radio Free Europe's headquarters.

Next to the old parliament building, the grandiose **Státní opera** (State Opera), built by the Viennese duo Helmer and Fellner, looks stunted and deeply affronted by the traffic which now tears past its front entrance. It was opened in 1888 as the *Neues Deutsches Theater*, shortly after the Czechs had built their own National Theatre on the waterfront. Always second fiddle to the Stavovské divadlo, though equally ornate inside, it was one of the last great building projects of Prague's once all-powerful German minority. The velvet and gold interior is still as fresh as it was when the Bohemian-born composer Gustav Mahler brought the traffic to a standstill, conducting the premiere of his *Seventh Symphony*.

The last building on this deafening freeway is **Praha hlavní nádraží**, Prague's main railway station. One of the final glories of the dying empire, it was designed by Josef Fanta and officially opened in 1909 as the *Franz-Josefs Bahnhof*. Trapped in the overpolished subterranean modern section, it's easy to miss the station's surviving Art Nouveau parts. The original entrance on Wilsonova still exudes imperial confidence, with its wrought-iron canopy and naked figurines clinging to the sides of the towers; on the other side of the road, two great glass protrusions signal the new entrance that opens out into the seedy green space of the Vrchlického sady.

Národní and Na příkopě

Národní and **Na příkopě** trace the course of the old moat, which was finally filled in in 1760. Their boomerang curve marks the border between Staré Město and Nové Město (strictly speaking, the dividing line runs down the middle of the street). Ranged around here are a variety of stylish edifices, including some of the city's most flamboyant Art Nouveau buildings.

Jungmannovo náměstí and around

Before you hit Národní proper, you must pass through **Jungmannovo náměstí**, which takes its name from Josef Jungmann (1772–1847), a prolific writer, translator and leading light of the Czech national revival, whose pensive, seated statue was erected here in 1878. This small, ill-proportioned square boasts one of Prague's most endearing architectural curiosities, Emil Králíček and Matěj Blecha's unique **Cubist streetlamp** (and seat) from 1912, which is currently crumbling away beyond the Jungmann statue in the far eastern corner of the square.

On the south side stands the square's most imposing building, the chunky, vigorously sculptured **Palác Adria**, on the south side of the square. It was designed in the early 1920s by Pavel Janák and Josef Zasche, with sculptural extras by Otto Gutfreund and a central *Seafaring* group by Jan Štursa. Janák was a pioneering figure in the short-lived, prewar Czech Cubist movement; after the war, he and Josef Gočár attempted to create a national style of architecture appropriate for the newly founded republic. The style was dubbed "Rondo-Cubism" – semi-circular motifs are a recurrent theme – though the Palác Adria owes as much to the Italian Renaissance as it does to the new national style.

Originally constructed for the Italian insurance company *Reunione Adriatica di Sicurità* – hence its current name – the building's *pasáž* still retains its wonderful original portal featuring sculptures by Bohumil Kafka, depicting the twelve signs of the zodiac. The theatre in the basement of the building was once a studio for the multimedia **Laterna magika** (Magic Lantern) company. In 1989, it became the underground nerve centre of the Velvet Revolution, when Civic Forum found temporary shelter here shortly after their inaugural meeting on the Sunday following the November 17 demonstration. Against a stage backdrop for Dürenmatt's *Minotaurus*, the Forum thrashed out tactics in the dressing rooms and gave daily press conferences in the auditorium during the crucial fortnight before the Communists relinquished power.

Through the unpromising courtyard back near the Jungmann statue, you can gain access to the church of **Panna Maria Sněžná** (St Mary-of-the-Snows). Once one of the great landmarks of Wenceslas Square, towering over the backs of the old two-storey houses that lined the square, it's now barely visible from any of the surrounding streets. Charles IV, who founded the church, envisaged a vast coronation church on a scale comparable with St Vitus Cathedral, on which work had just begun. Unfortunately, the money ran out shortly after completion of the chancel; the result is curious – a church that is short in length, but equal to the cathedral in height. The hundred-foot-high vaulting – which collapsed on the Franciscans who inherited the half-completed building in the seventeenth century – is awesome, as is the gold and black Baroque altar which touches the ceiling. To get an idea of the intended scale of the finished structure, take a stroll through the **Františkanská zahrada**, to the south of the church, which links up with one of the arcades off Wenceslas Square.

Prague's wax museums

A short walk down ulica 28 pijna, which connects Jungmannovo náměstí with the bottom end of Wenceslas Square, is one of Prague's new commercial museums, the **Muzeum voskových figurín** (Wax Museum; daily 10am–8pm; 120Kč), laid out on the ground floor of the Art Nouveau palác Rapid at no. 13. The current entrance fee is steep for most Czechs, yet the museum is aimed primarily at a domestic audience. For anyone familiar with London's Madame Tussaud's, the formula is predictable enough, but unless your grasp of Czech history, past and present, is pretty good, many of the wax tableaux will remain slightly baffling. The most popular section with the locals is the podium of commie stooges ranging from Lenin to the Czechs' home-grown Stalinist, Klement Gottwald, followed by today's generation of Czech politicians dressed in bad suits, sat amidst naff office furniture.

Within a few months of the Muzeum voskových figurín opening, a second wax museum, the **Pražské panoptikum** (daily 10am–8pm; 99Kč), opened up just down the street at Národní 25 in the *pasáž* of the palác Metro. It's equally professional and slick, with similar ticket prices, and follows pretty much the same formula, with many of the same historical characters, from Hus to Havel, appearing again. If anything, you'll need

---

THE MASAKR - NOVEMBER 17, 1989

On the night of Friday, November 17, 1989, a 50,000-strong, officially sanctioned student demo, organized by the students' union, *SSM* (League of Young Socialists), worked its way down Národní with the intention of reaching Wenceslas Square. Halfway down the street they were confronted by the *bílé přílby* (white helmets) and *červené barety* (red berets) of the hated riot police. For what must have seemed like hours, there was a stalemate as the students sat down and refused to disperse, some of them handing out flowers to the police. Suddenly, without any warning, the police attacked, and what became known as the **masakr** (massacre) began. No one was actually killed, though it wasn't for want of trying by the police. Under the arches of Národní 16, there's a small symbolic bronze relief of eight hands reaching out for help, a permanent shrine in memory of the hundreds who were hospitalized in the violence.

an even better knowledge of Czech history and culture to enjoy the *panoptikum*, though you do get the added extra of a short miniature dance show cleverly projected onto a three-dimensional stage.

Národní třída

The eastern end of **Národní** is taken up with shops, galleries and clubs, which begin to peter out as you near the river. Three-quarters of the way down on the north side is an eye-catching duo of Art Nouveau buildings designed by Osvald Polívka in 1907–8. The first, at no. 7, was built for the **pojišťovna Praha** (Prague Savings Bank), hence the beautiful mosaic lettering above the windows, advertising *život* (life insurance) and *kapital* (loans), as well as help with your *důchod* (pension) and *věno* (dowry). Next door, the slightly more ostentatious **Topičův dům**, built for a publishing house, provides the perfect accompaniment, with a similarly ornate wrought-iron and glass canopy.

At the western end of Národní, overlooking the Vltava, is the gold-crested **Národní divadlo** (National Theatre), proud symbol of the Czech nation. Refused money by the Habsburg state, Czechs of all classes dug deep into their pockets to raise funds for the venture themselves. The foundation stones, gathered from various historically significant sites in Bohemia and Moravia, were laid in 1868 by the historian and politician Frantisek Palacký and the composer Bedřich Smetana; the architect, Josef Zítek, spent the next thirteen years on the project. In June 1881, the theatre opened with a première of Smetana's opera *Libuše*. In August of the same year, fire ripped through the building, destroying everything except the outer walls. Within two years the whole thing was rebuilt – even the emperor contributed this time – under the supervision of Josef Schulz (who went on to design the Národní muzeum), opening once more to the strains of *Libuše*. The grand portal on the north side of the theatre is embellished with suitably triumphant allegorical figures, and inside, every square inch is taken up with paintings and sculptures by leading artists of the Czech national revival.

Standing behind and in dramatic contrast to the National Theatre is its state-of-the-art extension, the ultra-modern glass box of the **Nová scéna** (New Stage), designed by Karel Prager, the leading architect of the communist era, and completed in 1983. It's one of those buildings most Praguers love to hate – it has been memorably described as looking like "frozen piss" – though compared to much of Prague's communist-era architecture, it's not that bad.

The **Café Slavia**, opposite the theatre, has been a favourite haunt of the city's writers, dissidents and artists (and, inevitably, actors) since the days of the First Republic. The Czech avant-garde movement, *Devětsil*, led by Karel Teige, used to hold its meetings here in the 1920s; the meetings are recorded for posterity by another of its members, the Nobel prize-winner Jaroslav Seifert, in his *Slavia Poems*. The café has been carelessly modernized since those arcadian days, and was closed for over five years in the 1990s much to the annoyance of its regulars, but it still has a great riverside view and the famous *Absinthe Drinker* canvas on the wall.

Na příkopě

Heading northeast from Můstek, at the bottom end of Wenceslas Square, you can join the crush of bodies ambling down **Na příkopě** (literally "on the moat"). The big multinational franchises have staked their claim on this stretch of Prague, with the **Pasáž Myslbek**, fronted by Marks & Spencer, one of the few contemporary works of architecture in central Prague. The street has, of course, been an architectural showcase for more than a century. The street was once lined on both sides with grandiose Habsburg-era buildings; the Art Nouveau **U Dörflerů**, at no. 7, is one of the few survivors along this stretch, its gilded floral curlicues gleaming in the midday sun.

There are another couple of interesting buildings at nos. 18 and 20, designed by Polívka over a twenty-year period for the **Zemská banka** and connected by a kind of

Bridge of Sighs suspended over Nekázanka. The style veers between 1890s neo-Renaissance and later Art Nouveau elements, such as Jan Preisler's gilded mosaics and Ladislav Saloun's attic sculptures. It's worth nipping upstairs to the main banking hall of the **Živnostenka banka**, at no. 20, to appreciate the financial might of Czech capital in the last decades of the Austro-Hungarian Empire. Further financial institutions, this time from the dour 1930s, line the far end of Na příkopě, as it opens up into náměstí Republiky, including the palatial Národní banka (National Bank), which has recently undergone a controversial and very expensive makeover.

Mucha Museum

Alfons Mucha (1860–1939) is probably the most famous of all Czech artists in the West, and since the **Mucha Museum** opened in 1998, in the Kaunicky palác on Panská, south off Na příkopě, it's proved very popular indeed. Mucha made his name in fin-de-siècle Paris, where he shot to fame after designing the Art Nouveau poster *Gismonda* for the actress Sarah Bernhardt. "Le Style Mucha" became all the rage, but the artist himself came to despise this "commercial" period of his work, and in 1910, Mucha moved back to his homeland and threw himself into the national cause, designing patriotic stamps, banknotes and posters for the new republic.

The whole of Mucha's career is covered in the permanent exhibition, and there's a good selection of informal photos, taken by the artist himself, of his models, and Paul Gauguin (with whom he shared a studio), playing the harmonium with his trousers down. The only work not represented here is his massive *Slav Epic*, but the excellent video (in English) covers the decade of his life he devoted to this cycle of nationalist paintings. In the end, Mucha paid for his Czech nationalism with his life; dragged in for questioning by the Gestapo after the 1939 Nazi invasion, he died shortly after being released.

Náměstí Republiky

The oldest structure on **náměstí Republiky** is the **Prašná brána** (Powder Tower; daily 10am–6pm), one of the eight medieval gate-towers that once guarded Staré Město. The present tower was begun by Vladislav Jagiello in 1475, shortly after he had moved into the royal court, which was situated next door at the time. A small historical exhibition inside traces the tower's architectural metamorphosis up to its present remodelling by the nineteenth-century restorer Josef Mocker. Most people, though, ignore the displays and climb straight up for the modest view from the top.

Attached to the tower, and built on the ruins of the old royal court, the **Obecní dům** (Municipal House) is by far the city's most exciting Art Nouveau building, one of the few places that still manages to conjure up the atmosphere of Prague's turn-of-the-century café society. Conceived as a cultural centre for the Czech community, it's probably the finest architectural achievement of the Czech national revival, designed by Osvald Polívka and Antonín Balšánek, and extravagantly decorated inside and out with the help of almost every artist connected with the Czech Secession. From the lifts to the cloakrooms, just about all the furnishings remain as they were when the building was completed in 1911, and every square inch of the interior and exterior has recently been lovingly renovated.

The simplest way of soaking up the interior – peppered with mosaics and pendulous brass chandeliers – is to have a drink in the cavernous café, or a meal in the equally spacious *Francouská restaurace* or the *Plzeňská restaurace* in the basement. For a more detailed inspection of the building's spectacular interior (which includes paintings by Alfons Mucha, Jan Preisler and Max Svabinský, among others), you can sign up for a **guided tour**; tickets are available from the new information and ticket centre (daily 10am–6pm) on the ground floor, beyond the main foyer. Several rooms on the second floor are given over to temporary art exhibitions, while the building's **Smetanova síň**, Prague's largest concert hall, stages numerous concerts, including the opening salvo of the *Pražské jaro* (Prague Spring Festival) – traditionally a rendition of Smetana's *Má vlast* (My Country) – which takes place in the presence of the president.

Around Karlovo náměstí

The streets south of Národní and Wenceslas Square still run along the medieval lines of Charles IV's town plan, though they're now lined with grand nineteenth- and twentieth-century buildings. Of the many roads which head down towards Karlovo náměstí, **Vodičkova** is probably the most impressive, running southwest for half a kilometre from Wenceslas Square. You can catch several trams (#3, #14 or #24) along this route, though there are a handful of buildings worth checking out on the way. The first, U **Nováků**, is impossible to miss, thanks to Jan Preisler's mosaic of bucolic frolicking (its actual subject, *Trade and Industry*, is confined to the edges of the picture) and Polívka's curvilinear window frames and delicate, ivy-like ironwork – look out for the frog-prince holding up a window sill. Originally built for the Novák department store in the early 1900s, for the last sixty years it has been a cabaret hall, restaurant and café all rolled into one, and the original fittings have long since gone.

A little further down the street stands the imposing neo-Renaissance **Minerva** girls' school, covered in bright-red sgraffito. Founded in 1866, it was the first such institution in Prague and later became notorious for the antics of its pupils, the "Minervans" – most famously Milená Jesenská, the epistolary lover of Franz Kafka – who shocked bourgeois Czech society with their experimentations with fashion, drugs and sexual freedom.

Karlovo náměstí

Vodičkova eventually curves left into Prague's biggest square, **Karlovo náměstí**, created by Charles IV as Nové Město's cattle market (Dobytčí trh). Unfortunately, its once impressive proportions are no longer so easy to appreciate, obscured by a tree-planted public garden and cut in two by the busy thoroughfare of Ječná. The Gothic **Novoměstská radnice**, at the northern end of the square, sports three steep, triangular gables embellished with intricate tracery. Once a town hall to rival that of Staré Město, it remains one of the finest Gothic buildings in the city. After the amalgamation of Prague's separate towns in 1784, however, it was used solely as a criminal court and prison; public access is limited to the building's art gallery (Tues–Sun 10am–6pm), which puts on temporary exhibitions. It was here that Prague's **first defenestration** took place on July 30, 1419, when the radical Hussite preacher Jan Želivský and his penniless religious followers stormed the building, mobbed the councillors and burghers, and threw twelve or thirteen of them out of the town hall windows onto the pikes of the Hussite mob below. Václav IV, on hearing the news, suffered a stroke and died just two weeks later. So began the long and bloody Hussite Wars.

The crypt of sv Cyril and Metoděj

West off Karlovo náměstí, down Resslova, the noisy extension of Ječná, is the Orthodox cathedral of **sv Cyril and Metoděj**, originally constructed for the Roman Catholics by Bayer and Dientzenhofer in the eighteenth century, but since the 1930s the main base of the Orthodox church in the Czech Republic. Amid all the traffic, it's extremely difficult to imagine the scene here on June 18, 1942, when seven of the Czechoslovak secret agents involved in the most dramatic assassination of World War II (see box on next page) were besieged in the church by over 700 members of the Waffen SS. Acting on a

THE ASSASSINATION OF REINHARD HEYDRICH

The assassination of Reinhard Heydrich in 1942 was the only attempt the Allies ever made on the life of a leading Nazi. It's an incident which the Allies have always billed as a great success in the otherwise rather dismal seven-year history of the Czech resistance. But, as with all acts of brave resistance during the war, there was a price to be paid. Given that the reprisals meted out on the Czech population were entirely predictable, it remains a controversial, if not suicidal, decision to have made.

The target, **Reinhard Tristan Eugen Heydrich**, was a talented and upwardly mobile anti-Semite (despite rumours that he was partly Jewish himself), a great organizer and a skilful concert violinist. He was a late recruit to the Nazi Party, signing up in 1931 after his dismissal from the German Navy for dishonourable conduct towards a woman. However, he swiftly rose through the ranks of the SS to become second in command to Himmler and, in the autumn of 1941, *Reichsprotektor* of the puppet state of *Böhmen und Mähren* – effectively, the most powerful man in the Czech Lands. Although his rule began with brutality, it soon settled into the tried-and-tested policy which Heydrich liked to call *Peitsche und Zucker* (literally, "whip and sugar").

On the morning of May 27, 1942, as Heydrich was being driven by his personal bodyguard, *Oberscharführer* Klein, in his open-top Mercedes from his house north of Prague to his office in Hradčany, three Czechoslovak agents (parachuted in from England) were taking up positions in the northern suburb of Libeň. As the car pulled into Kirchmayer Boulevard (now V Holešovičkách), one of them, a Slovak called Gabčík, pulled out a gun and tried to shoot. The gun jammed, at which Heydrich, rather than driving out of the situation, ordered Klein to stop the car and attempted to shoot back. At this point, another agent, Kubiš, threw a bomb at the car. The blast injured Kubiš and Heydrich, who immediately leapt out and began firing at Kubiš. Kubiš, with blood pouring down his face, jumped on his bicycle and fled downhill. Gabčík meanwhile pulled out a second gun and exchanged shots with Heydrich, until the latter collapsed from his wounds. Gabčík fled into a butcher's, shot Klein – who was in hot pursuit – in the legs and escaped down the backstreets.

Meanwhile back at the Mercedes, a baker's van was flagged down by a passer-by, but the driver refused to get involved. Eventually, a small truck carrying floor polish was commandeered and Heydrich taken to the Bulovka hospital. Heydrich died eight days later from shrapnel wounds and was given full Nazi honours at his Prague funeral; the cortège passed down Wenceslas Square, in front of a crowd of thousands. As the home resistance had forewarned, revenge was quick to follow. The day after Heydrich's funeral service in Berlin, the village of **Lidice** (see p.148) was burnt to the ground and its male inhabitants murdered; two weeks later the village of **Ležáky** (see p.275) suffered a similar fate.

The plan to assassinate Heydrich had been formulated in the early months of 1942 by the Czechoslovak government-in-exile in London, without consultation with the Czech Communist leadership in Moscow, and despite fierce opposition from the resistance within Czechoslovakia. Since it was clear that the reprisals would be horrific, the only logical explanation for the plan is that this was precisely the aim of the government-in-exile's operation – to forge a solid wedge of resentment between the Germans and Czechs. In this respect, if in no other, the operation was ultimately successful.

tip-off by one of the Czech resistance who turned himself in, the Nazis surrounded the building just after 4am and fought a pitched battle, trying explosives, flooding and any other method they could think of to drive the men out of their stronghold in the crypt. Eventually, all seven agents committed suicide rather than give themselves up. There's a plaque at street level on the south wall commemorating those who died, and an exhibition on the whole affair in the **crypt** (Tues–Sun 10am–4pm) itself, which has been left pretty much as it was; the entrance is underneath the church steps on Na Zderaze.

The islands and the embankments

Magnificent turn-of-the-century mansions line the Vltava's right bank, almost without interruption, for some two kilometres from the Charles Bridge south to the rocky outcrop of Vyšehrad. It's a long walk, even just along the length of **Masarykovo** and **Rašínovo nábřeží**, though there's no need to do the whole lot in one go; you can hop on a tram (#17 or #21) at various points, drop down from the embankments to the waterfront itself, or escape to one of the two islands connected to them, Střelecký ostrov and Slovanský ostrov, better known as Žofín.

The islands

Access to either of the two islands in the central section of the Vltava is from close to the Národní divadlo. The first, **Střelecký ostrov**, or Shooters' Island, is where the army held their shooting practice, on and off, from the fifteenth until the nineteenth century. Closer to the other bank and accessible via the most Legií (Legion's Bridge), it became a favourite spot for a Sunday promenade and is still popular, especially in summer. The first *Sokol* festival took place here in 1882; the first May Day demonstrations were in 1890.

The second island, Slovanský ostrov, more commonly known as **Žofín** (after the island's concert hall, itself named after Sophie, the mother of the Emperor Franz-Josef I), came about as a result of the natural silting of the river in the eighteenth century. By the late nineteenth century it had become one of the city's foremost pleasure gardens, where, as the composer Berlioz remarked, "bad musicians shamelessly make abominable music in the open air and immodest young males and females indulge in brazen dancing, while idlers and wasters . . . lounge about smoking foul tobacco and drinking beer." On a good day, things seem pretty much unchanged from those heady times; concerts, balls, and other social gatherings take place here, and there are rowing boats for hire from May to October.

Along the embankment

Most of the buildings along the waterfront are private apartments and therefore inaccessible. One exception to this, and architecturally atypical of this part of Prague, is the striking white functionalist mass of the **Mánes** art gallery (Tues–Sun 10am–6pm), halfway down Masarykovo nábřeží. Designed in open-plan style by Otakar Novotný in 1930, it spans the narrow channel between Slovanský ostrov and the waterfront, close to the onion-domed Šítek watertower. The gallery is named after Josef Mánes, a traditional nineteenth-century landscape painter and Czech nationalist, and houses consistently interesting exhibitions, as well as two cafés and an upstairs restaurant suspended above the channel. Clearly visible from Mánes is the **Tančící dům** (Dancing House) also known as "Fred and Ginger" after the shape of building's two towers, which look vaguely like a couple ballroom dancing. It was designed in the 1990s by the Canadian-born Frank O. Gehry and the Yugoslav-born Vlado Milunič, and stands next door to the block of flats where Havel lived before becoming president (when he wasn't in prison).

Further along the embankment, at **Palackého náměstí**, the buildings retreat for a moment to reveal an Art Nouveau sculpture to rival Šaloun's monument in Staroměstské náměstí (see p.83): Stanislav Sucharda's **Monument to František Palacký**, the great nineteenth-century Czech historian, politician and nationalist. Like the Hus Monument, which was unveiled three years later, this mammoth project – fifteen years in the making – had missed its moment by the time it was completed in 1912, and found universal disfavour. The critics have mellowed over the years, and nowadays it's appreciated for what it is – an energetic and inspirational piece of work. Ethereal bronze bodies, representing the world of the imagination, shoot out at all angles, contrasting sharply with the plain stone mass of the plinth and, below, the giant seated figure of Palacký himself, representing the real world.

Vyšehradská and Ke Karlovu

Behind Palackého náměstí, off **Vyšehradská**, the twisted concrete spires of the **Emauzy** monastery are an unusual modern addition to the Prague skyline. The monastery was one of the few important historical buildings to be damaged in the last war, in this case by a stray Anglo-American bomb. The cloisters contain some extremely valuable Gothic frescoes, but since the return of the monks from their forty-year exile, access has become unpredictable. Heading south from here, Vyšehradská descends to a junction, where you'll find the entrance to the university's **Botanická zahrada** (Botanical Gardens; daily: April–Oct 10am–6pm; Nov–March 10am–4pm), laid out in 1897 on a series of terraces up the other side of the hill; though far from spectacular – the 1930s greenhouses are a bit sad – they're one of the few patches of green in this part of town.

On the far side of the gardens, Apolinářská runs along the south wall and past a grimly Gothic red-brick maternity hospital with steep, stepped gables, before joining up with **Ke Karlovu**. Head north up here and the first street off to the right is Na bojisti, usually packed with tour coaches. The reason for this is the **U kalicha** pub, on the right, which was immortalized in the opening passages of the consistently popular comic novel *The Good Soldier Švejk*, by Jaroslav Hašek. In the story, on the eve of the Great War, Švejk (*Schweik* to the Germans) walks into *U kalicha*, where a plain-clothes officer of the Austrian constabulary is sitting drinking and, after a brief conversation, finds himself arrested in connection with the assassination of Archduke Ferdinand. Whatever the pub may have been like in Hašek's day (and even then, it wasn't his local), it's now unashamedly orientated towards reaping in the Deutschmarks, and about the only authentic thing you'll find inside – albeit at a price – is the beer.

Further north along Ke Karlovu, set back from the road behind wrought-iron gates, is a more rewarding place of pilgrimage, the russet-coloured **Vila Amerika** (Tues–Sun 10am–5pm), now a museum devoted to the Czech composer **Antonín Dvořák**, who lived for a time on nearby Žitná. Even if you've no interest in Dvořák, the house itself is a delight, built as a Baroque summer palace around 1720 and one of Kilian Ignaz Dientzenhofer's most successful secular works. Dvořák, easily the most famous of all Czech composers, for many years had to play second fiddle to Smetana in the orchestra at the Národní divadlo, where Smetana was the conductor. In his forties, Dvořák received an honorary degree from Cambridge before leaving for the "New World", and his gown is one of the very few items of memorabilia to have found its way into the museum's collection, along with the programme of a concert given at London's Guildhall in 1891. However, the tasteful period rooms echoing with the composer's music and the tiny garden dotted with Baroque sculptures compensate for what the display cabinets may lack.

Vyšehrad

At the southern tip of Nové Město, around 3km south of the city centre, the rocky red-brick fortress of **VYŠEHRAD** (literally "High Castle") has more myths attached to it per square inch than any other place in Bohemia. According to Czech legend, this is the place where the Slav tribes first settled in Prague, where the "wise and tireless chieftain" Krok built a castle, and whence his youngest daughter Libuše went on to found Praha itself (see p.49). Alas, the archeological evidence doesn't bear this claim out, but it's clear that Vratislav II (1061–92), the first Bohemian ruler to bear the title "king", built a royal palace here, to get away from his younger brother who was lording it in the Hrad. Within half a century the royals had moved back to Hradčany and into a new palace, and from then on Vyšehrad began to lose its political significance.

Keen to associate himself with the early Přemyslids, Emperor Charles IV had a system of walls built to link Vyšehrad to the newly founded Nové Město, and decreed that the *králová cesta* (coronation route) begin from here. These fortifications were destroyed by the Hussites in 1420, but over the next two hundred years the hill was settled again, until the Habsburgs turfed everyone out in the mid-seventeenth century and rebuilt the place as a fortified barracks, only to tear it down in 1866 to create a public park. When only the red-brick fortifications were left, a reminder of Vyšehrad's former strategic importance, the Czech national revival movement became interested in it, rediscovering the history and legends and gradually transforming it into a symbol of Czech nationhood. Today, Vyšehrad is a perfect place from which to escape the human congestion of the city and watch the evening sun set behind the Hrad.

The fortress

There are several approaches to the **fortress**, depending on where you arrive in Vyšehrad. From the Vyšehrad metro station, walk west, past the modern Palác kultury, and enter through the Leopoldová brána; if you've come by tram #3, #7, #17 or #21, all of which pass along the waterfront, you can either wind your way up Vratislavova and enter through the Cihelná brána, or take the steep stairway from Rašínovo nábřeží that leads up through the trees to a small side entrance in the west wall.

The last approach brings you out right in front of the blackened sandstone church of **sv Petr and Pavel**, rebuilt in the 1880s by Josef Mocker in neo-Gothic style (with further, even more ruthless additions in the 1900s) on the site of an eleventh-century basilica; the twin openwork spires are the fortress's most familiar landmark. The church's polychrome interior is often closed to the public to protect against vandalism and allow archeologists to search for the remains of the eleventh-century royal palace discovered here some years ago.

Vyšehradský hřbitov (Vyšehrad Cemetery)

One of the first initiatives of the national revival movement was to establish the **Vyšehradský hřbitov** (daily May–Sept 8am–7pm; March, April & Oct 8am–6pm; Nov–Feb 9am–4pm), which spreads out to the north and east of the church. It's a measure of the part that artists and intellectuals played in the foundation of the nation, and the regard in which they are still held, that the most prestigious graveyard in the city is given over to them: no soldiers, no politicians, not even the Communists managed to muscle their way in here (except on artistic merit).

The place is alive with great Czech names, and there's a useful plan of the most notable graves at the entrance nearest the church. **Dvořák**'s grave, under the arches, is one of the more showy ones, with a mosaic inscription, studded with gold stones, glistening behind wrought-iron railings. **Smetana**, who died twenty years earlier, is buried in comparatively modest surroundings near the Slavín monument. The Spring Music Festival begins on the anniversary of his death (May 12) with a procession from his grave to the Obecní dům.

The focus of the cemetery, though, is the **Slavín monument**, a bulky stele, covered in commemorative plaques and topped by a sarcophagus and a statue representing Genius. It's the communal resting place of over fifty Czech artists, including the painter Alfons Mucha, the sculptors Josef Václav Myslbek and Ladislav Šaloun, the architect Josef Gočár and the opera singer Ema Destinová.

The rest of the fortress

The next best thing to do after a stroll around the cemetery is to head off and explore the **Kasematy** (dungeons), which you enter via the Cihelná brána . After a short guided tour of a section of the underground passageways underneath the ramparts, you enter a vast storage hall, which shelters several of the original statues from the Charles Bridge, and, when the lights are switched off, reveals a camera obscura image of a tree.

The rest of the deserted fortress makes for a pleasant afternoon stroll; you can walk almost the entire length of the ramparts, which give some superb views out across the city. The **rotunda of sv Martin** – one of a number of Romanesque rotundas scattered across Prague – is the sole survivor of the medieval fortress, originally built by Vratislav II in the eleventh century but heavily restored by the nineteenth-century nationalists; it's only open for services. Time is probably better spent lounging on the grass to the south of the church, where you'll come across the gargantuan legendary statues by Myslbek that used to grace the city's Palackého most.

Czech Cubism in Vyšehrad

Even if you harbour only a passing interest in modern architecture, it's worth seeking out the cluster of **Cubist villas** below the fortress in Vyšehrad. Whereas Czech Art Nouveau was heavily influenced by the Viennese Secession, it was Paris rather than the imperial capital that provided the stimulus for the short-lived but extremely productive Czech Cubist movement. In 1911, the *Skupina výtvarných umělců* or *SVU* (Group of Fine Artists) was founded in Prague and quickly became the movement's organizing force. **Pavel Janák** was the *SVU*'s chief theorist, **Josef Gočár** its most illustrious exponent, but **Josef Chochol** was the most successful practitioner of the style in Prague.

Cubism is associated mostly with painting, and the unique contribution of its Czech offshoot was to apply the theory to furniture (some of which is now on permanent display at the Dům U černé Matky boží, see p.86) and **architecture**. In Vyšehrad alone, Chochol completed three buildings, close to one another below the fortress, using prismatic shapes and angular lines to produce the sharp geometric contrasts of light and dark shadows characteristic of Cubist painting.

The most impressive example of Czech Cubist architecture, brilliantly exploiting its angular location, is Chochol's apartment block **nájemný obytný dům** at Neklanova 30; begun in 1913 for František Hodek, it now houses a restaurant on the ground floor. Further along Neklanova, at no. 2, there's Antonín Belada's Cubist street facade, and around the corner is the largest project of the lot – Chochol's **Kovařovicova vila**, which backs onto Libušina. The front, on Rašínovo nábřeží, is presently concealed behind some over-enthusiastic shrubs, but it's still possible to appreciate the clever, slightly askew layout of the garden, designed right down to its zigzag garden railings. Further along the embankment is Chochol's largest commission, the **rodinný trojdům**, a large building complex with a heavy mansard roof, a central "Baroque" gable with a pedimental frieze, and room enough for three families.

The suburbs

By the end of his reign in 1378, Charles IV had laid out his city on such a grand scale that it wasn't until the industrial revolution hit Bohemia in the mid-nineteenth century that the first **suburbs** began to sprout up around its boundaries. A few were rigidly planned, with public parks and grid street plans; most grew with less grace, trailing their tenements across the hills and swallowing up existing villages on the way. The majority still retain a distinctive individual identity, and are free from the crowds in the centre, all of which makes them worth checking out on even a short visit to the city.

Vinohrady

Southeast of Nové Město is the well-to-do late-nineteenth-century suburb of **VINOHRADY**, home over the years to many of the country's most notable personages. In one of its two main squares, **náměstí Jiřího z Poděbrad** (metro Jiřího z Poděbrad), stands Prague's most celebrated modern church, **Nejsvětější Srdce Páně** (Most Sacred Heart of Our Lord), built in 1928 by Josip Plečník, the Slovene architect responsible for much of the remodelling of the Hrad. It's a marvellously eclectic and individualistic work, employing a sophisticated potpourri of architectural styles: a Neoclassical pediment and a great slab of a tower with a giant transparent face in imitation of a Gothic rose window. Plečník also had a sharp eye for detail; look out for the little gold crosses set into the brickwork both inside and out, and for the celestial orbs of light suspended above the heads of the congregation.

Žižkov

Though they share much the same architectural heritage, **ŽIŽKOV**, unlike Vinohrady, is a traditionally working-class area, and was a Communist Party stronghold even before the war, earning it the nickname "Red Žižkov". Nowadays it's home to a large proportion of Prague's Romany community and other less privileged sections of Czech society. The main reason for venturing into Žižkov is to visit the ancient landmark of Žižkov hill and the city's main Olšany cemeteries, at the eastern end of Vyšehradská.

Žižkov TV tower

At over 100m in height, the **Žižkov TV tower** (Televizní vysílač), is the tallest building in Prague – and the most unpopular. Close up, though, it's difficult not to be impressed by this truly intimidating piece of futuristic architecture, its smooth grey exterior giving no hint of humanity. Begun in the 1970s in a desperate bid to jam West German television transmission, the tower only became fully operational in the 1990s. In the course of its construction, however, the Communists saw fit to demolish part of a nearby Jewish cemetery, that had served the community between 1787 and 1891; a small section survives to the northwest of the tower. From the fifth-floor café or the viewing platform on the eighth floor (daily 10am–11pm), you can enjoy a spectacular view across Prague. To get to the tower, take the metro to Jiřího z Poděbrad and walk northeast a couple of blocks – it's difficult to miss.

The cemeteries

Approaching from the west, the first and the largest of the **Olšanské hřbitovy** (Olšany cemeteries; metro Flora) – each of which is bigger than the entire Jewish quarter – was originally created for the victims of the great plague epidemic of 1680. The perimeter walls are lined with glass cabinets, stacked like shoe-boxes, containing funereal urns and mementoes, while the graves themselves are a mixed bag of artistic achievement, reflecting funereal fashions of the day as much as the character of the deceased. The cemetery's two most famous incumbents are an ill-fitting couple: Klement Gottwald, the country's first Communist president, whose ashes were removed from the mausoleum on Žižkov hill after 1989 and reinterred here; and the martyr Jan Palach, the philosophy student who set himself alight in protest at the continuing Soviet occupation in January 1969.

Immediately east of Olšany is the **Nový židovský hřbitov** (New Jewish Cemetery; daily except Sat: April–Aug 8am–5pm; Sept–March 8am–4pm), founded in the 1890s when the one by the Žižkov TV tower was full. It's a melancholy spot, particularly in the east of the cemetery, where large, empty allotments wait in vain to be filled by the generation who perished in the Holocaust. In fact, the community is now so small that it's unlikely the graveyard will ever be full. Most people come here to visit **Franz Kafka**'s grave, 400m east along the south wall and signposted from the entrance (for more on Kafka, see p.94). He is buried, along with his mother and father (both of whom outlived him), beneath a plain headstone; the plaque below commemorates his three sisters who died in the camps.

Žižkov hill

Žižkov hill (also known as Vítkov) is the thin green wedge of land that separates Žižkov from Karlín, a grid-plan industrial district to the north. From its westernmost point, which juts out almost to the edge of Nové Město, is probably the definitive panoramic view over the city centre. It was here, on July 14, 1420, that the Hussites enjoyed their first and finest victory at the **Battle of Vítkov**, under the inspired leadership of the one-eyed general, Jan Žižka (hence the name of the district). Ludicrously outnumbered by more than ten to one, Žižka and his fanatically motivated troops thoroughly trounced Emperor Sigismund and his papal forces.

Despite its overblown totalitarian aesthetics, the giant concrete **Žižkov monument** which graces the crest of the hill, was actually built between the wars as a memorial to the Czechoslovak Legion who fought against the Habsburgs – the gargantuan equestrian statue of the mace-wielding Žižka, which fronts the monument, is reputedly the world's largest. The building was later used by the Nazis as an arsenal, and eventually became a Communist hacks' mausoleum. In 1990, however, the bodies were cremated and quietly reinterred in Olšany, and at present there's an ongoing legal battle over what should happen next with the monument.

To get to the monument, take the metro to Florenc, walk under the railway lines and then up the steep lane U památníku. On the right as you climb the hill is the **Armádní muzeum** (Army Museum; Tues–Sun 10am–6pm), guarded by a handful of unmanned tanks, howitzers and armoured vehicles. Before 1989, this museum was a glorification of the Warsaw Pact, pure and simple; its recent overhaul has produced a much more evenly balanced account of both world wars, particularly in its treatment of the previously controversial subjects of the Czechoslovak Legion, the Heydrich assassination (see p.106) and the Prague Uprising.

Holešovice and Bubeneč

The late-nineteenth-century districts of **HOLEŠOVICE** and **BUBENEČ**, tucked into a huge U-bend in the Vltava, have little in the way of magnificent architecture, but they make up for it with two huge areas of green: to the south, **Letná**, where Prague's greatest gatherings occur, and to the north, the **Stromovka park**, bordering the Výstaviště funfair and international trade fair grounds. In addition, Holešovice boasts a couple of excellent museums: the city's **Národní technické muzeum**, which shows off the Czechs' past scientific and industrial achievements, and the **Veletržní palác**, home of Prague's impressive modern art museum.

Chotkovy sady and the Bílkova vila

This first sight is, strictly speaking, a part of the Hradčany that lies to the northeast of the castle, but it makes a convenient starting point for this account. The easiest way to this part of town is to take tram #22 one stop from Malostranská metro to the Belvedér, to the east of which lies the **Chotkovy sady**, Prague's first public park, founded in 1833. You can enjoy an unrivalled view of the bridges and islands of the Vltava from its south wall, or check out the elaborate, grotto-like memorial to the nineteenth-century Romantic poet Julius Zeyer, from whose blackened rocks emerge life-sized, marble characters from his works.

THE STALIN MONUMENT

Letná's – indeed Prague's – most famous monument is one which no longer exists. The **Stalin monument**, the largest in the world, was once visible from almost every part of the city: a thirty-metre-high granite sculpture portraying a procession of people being led to communism by the Pied Piper figure of Stalin, popularly dubbed *tlačenice* (the crush) because of its resemblance to a communist-era bread queue. Designed by Jiří Štursa and Otakar Švec, it took 600 workers 500 days to erect the 14,200-ton monster. Švec, the sculptor, committed suicide shortly before it was unveiled, as his wife had done three years previously, leaving all his money to a school for blind children, since they at least would not have to see his creation. It was eventually revealed to the cheering masses on May 1, 1955 – the first and last popular celebration to take place at the monument. Within a year, Khrushchev had denounced his predecessor and, after pressure from Moscow, the monument was blown to smithereens by a series of explosions spread over a fortnight in 1962.

Across the road from the park and hidden behind its overgrown garden, the **Bílkova vila** (mid-May to mid-Oct Tues–Sun 10am–6pm; mid-Oct to mid-May Sat & Sun 10am–5pm), at Mieckiewiczova 1, honours one of the most unusual Czech sculptors, František Bílek (1872–1941). Born in Chýnov (see p.160), in a part of South Bohemia steeped in Hussite tradition, Bílek lived a monkish life, spending years in spiritual contemplation, reading the works of Hus and other Czech reformers. The villa was built in 1911 to Bílek's own design, intended as both a "cathedral of art" and the family home. At first sight, it appears a strangely mute red-brick building, out of keeping with the extravagant Symbolist style of Bílek's sculptures: from the outside, only the front porch, supported by giant sheaves of corn, and the sculptural group, the fleeing Comenius and his followers, in the garden, give a clue as to what lies within.

Inside, the brickwork gives way to bare stone walls lined with Bílek's religious sculptures, giving the impression that you've walked into a chapel rather than an artist's studio: "a workshop and temple", in Bílek's own words. In addition to his sculptural and relief work in wood and stone, often wildly expressive and anguished, there are also ceramics, graphics and a few mementoes of Bílek's life. His work is little known outside his native country, but his contemporary admirers included Franz Kafka, Julius Zeyer, and Otakar Březina, whose poems and novels provided the inspiration for much of Bílek's art. Bílek's living quarters have also now been restored and opened to the public, with much of the original wooden furniture, designed and carved by Bílek himself, still in place: check out the dressing table for his wife, shaped like some giant church lectern, and the wardrobe decorated with a border of hearts, a penis, a nose, an ear and an eye, plus the sun, stars and moon.

Letná

Cross over the bridge at the eastern end of the Chotkovy sady and you'll find yourself on the flat green expanse of the **Letná plain**, traditional assembly point for invading and besieging armies. It was laid out as a public park in the mid-nineteenth century, but its main post-1948 function was as the site of the May Day parades. For these, thousands of citizens were dragooned into marching past the south side of the city's main football ground, the Sparta stadium, where the old Communist cronies would take the salute from a giant red podium. The post-Communist Party parades still take place here, but are a shadow of their former selves.

Národní technické muzeum (National Technical Museum)

Despite its dull title, the **Národní technické muzeum** (Tues–Sun 9am–5pm) on Kostelní is a surprisingly interesting museum. Its showpiece hanger-like main hall contains an impressive gallery of motorbikes, Czech and foreign, and a wonderful collection of old planes, trains and automobiles, from Czechoslovakia's industrial heyday between the wars, when the country's Škoda cars and Tatra soft-top stretch limos were really something to brag about. The oldest car in the collection is Laurin & Klement's 1898 *Präsident*, more of a motorized carriage than a car; the museum also boasts the world's oldest Bugatti. Upstairs, there are interactive displays (a rarity in a Czech museum) tracing the development of early photography, and a collection of some of Kepler's and Tycho Brahe's astrological instruments. Below ground, a mock-up of a coal mine offers guided tours every other hour, kicking off at 11am, 1 & 3pm.

Veletržní palác

Situated at the corner of Dukelských hrdinů and Veletržní, some distance from the nearest metro station (tram #5, #12 or #17 from Nádraží Holešovice), the **Veletržní palác** (Tues–Sun 10am–6pm, Thurs until 9pm), or Trade Fair Palace, gets nothing like the number of visitors it should. Prague's most ambitious museum to date, it houses the Národní galerie's vast collection of twentieth-century Czech art, plus a fine selection of European art from the late nineteenth and early twentieth centuries. Last but not least, there's the building itself, Prague's ultimate functionalist masterpiece, a seven-storey building constructed in 1928 by Oldřich Tyl and Josef Fuchs; it doesn't look much from the outside, but inside, its gleaming white vastness is suitably awesome.

Despite the fact that the Národní galerie doesn't even use the main exhibition hall, but confines itself to the north wing of the building, the museum is both big and bewildering. Special exhibitions occupy the ground, first and fourth floors; from the ground floor you can stare up at the glass-roofed atrium, a glorious space for wacky modern pieces of art, overlooked by six floors of balconies. The permanent collection occupies the second and third floors, but there is no easy way to follow it chronologically. The best approach is to take the lift to the third floor and start with the Czech art from 1900 to 1960 (as the account below does), since this was the museum's original *raison d'être*.

CZECH MODERN ART 1900–1960

The collection of **Czech modern art from 1900 to 1960**, on the third floor, begins with a smattering of works by two of the most successful Czech exponents of moody post-Impressionism: **Antonín Slavíček**, whose landscapes range from the Klimt-like *Birch Mood* to paintings full of foreboding, like *In the Rain*; and **Antonín Hudeček**, whose canvases, such as *Moon Landscape,* are even more dreamlike and ethereal.

Nearby are a whole series of works by **František Kupka**, a Czech by birth, though he lived and worked in Paris from 1896. In international terms, Kupka is by far the most important Czech painter of this century, having secured his place in the history of art by being (possibly) the first artist in the Western world to exhibit abstract paintings. *Fugue in Two Colours (Amorpha)*, one of the two abstract paintings Kupka exhibited at the Salon d'Automne in 1912, is displayed here. First, though, before you reach this seminal work are earlier, pre-abstract paintings such as *Money*, which formed part of a satirical cycle; a Munch-like portrait of a Parisian cabaret actress; and *Piano Keys – Lake*, a strange, abstracted, though by no means abstract, work from 1909. You'll come across more of Kupka's later abstract and cosmic works elsewhere in the collection.

While Kupka is thought of by many as a French artist, **Jan Preisler** couldn't be more thoroughly Czech. His mosaics and murals, which can be found on Art Nouveau buildings all over Prague, tend to be ethereal and slightly detached, whereas his oil paintings, like the cycle of *Black Lake* paintings displayed here, are more typically melancholic. Several wood sculptures by **František Bílek**, one of the country's finest sculptors, offer a taste of his anguished style, but for a more comprehensive insight into his art, you should visit the Bílkova vila (see p.113).

The Edvard Munch retrospective held in Prague in 1905 prompted the formation in 1907 of the first Czech modern art movement, Osma (The Eight), three of whose members feature in **Bohumil Kubišta**'s defiant *Triple Portrait* from the same year. Works like Kubišta's *Card Players*, and **Emil Filla**'s *Ace of Hearts* and *Reader of Dostoyevsky* – in which the subject appears to have fallen asleep, though, in fact, he's mind-blown – are both firmly within the Expressionist genre. However, it wasn't long before several of the Osma group were beginning to experiment with Cubism. Filla eventually adopted the style wholesale, helping found the Cubist SVU in 1911; Kubišta refused to follow suit, instead pursuing his own unique blend of Cubo-Expressionism, typified by the wonderful self-portrait, *The Smoker*.

Look out, too, for the sculptures of SVU member **Otto Gutfreund**, whose works range from his Cubo-Expressionist *Anxiety* to the more purely Cubist *Sitting Woman* (1915). After World War I, during which he joined the advance guard of Impressionism: interned for three years for insubordination, Gutfreund switched to depicting everyday folk in technicolor, as in his self-portrait bust and *Business*, in a style that prefigures Socialist Realism. His life was cut short in 1927, when he drowned while swimming in the Vltava.

Devětsil, founded in 1920 and the driving force of the Czech avant-garde between the wars, is represented here by the movement's two leading artists: **Toyen** (Marie Cermínová) and her life-long companion **Jindřich Štyrský**, whose abstract works – they dubbed them "Artificialism" – are clearly influenced by the French Surrealists. One Czech artist who had already enthusiastically embraced Surrealism was **Josef Šíma**, who settled permanently in Paris in the 1920s; several of his trademark floating torsoes and cosmic eggs can be seen here. Lastly, be sure to check out the wild kinetic-light sculpture (1936) by **Zdeněk Pešánek**, a world pioneer in the use of neon in art, who created a stir the following year at the Paris Expo with a neon fountain.

NINETEENTH- AND TWENTIETH-CENTURY FRENCH ART

By far the most popular section of the gallery is the **nineteenth- and twentieth-century French art section**, on the second floor, featuring everyone of note who hovered around Paris in the fifty years from 1880 onwards. There are few well-known masterpieces here, but it's all high-quality stuff.

The collection kicks off with several works by **Auguste Rodin**, particularly appropriate given the ecstatic reception given to the Prague exhibition of his work in 1902. Rodin's sculptures are surrounded by works from the advance guard of Impressionism: Courbet, Delacroix, Corot and early Monet and Pissarro. Beyond, the loose brushwork, cool turquoise and emerald colours of **Auguste Renoir**'s *Lovers* are typical of the period of so-called High Impressionism. There's also a surprisingly good collection of works by **Pablo Picasso**, including several paintings and sculptures from his crucial early Cubist period (1907–08); his *Landscape with Bridge* from 1909 uses precisely the kind of prisms and geometric blocks of shading that influenced the Czech Cubist architects (see p.110).

Among the other works here, there's a characteristically sunny, Provençal *Green Wheat* by **Vincent van Gogh**, a couple by Paul Cézanne and Georges Seurat, and the only known self-portrait by **Henri Rousseau**, at once both confident and comical, the artist depicting himself, palette in hand, against a boat decked with bunting and the recently erected Eiffel Tower. *Bonjour Monsieur Gauguin* is a tongue-in-cheek tribute to Courbet's painting of similar name, with Gauguin donning a suitably bohemian beret and overcoat. Another first-rate portrait is *Joaquina*, painted in 1910–11 by **Henri Matisse**, in which both Fauvist and Oriental influences are evident.

TWENTIETH-CENTURY EUROPEAN ART

If the French art section is modest, the collection of **twentieth-century European art** is minuscule. It does, however, contain a couple of minor gems, beginning with **Gustav Klimt**'s mischievous *Virgins*, a mass of naked bodies and tangled limbs painted in psychedelic colours. Although none of the artists here is Czech, many of them had close connections with Bohemia: the handful of typically vigorous landscapes by **Oskar Kokoschka** date from his brief stay here in the 1930s, when the political temperature got too hot in Vienna, while **Egon Schiele**'s mother came from Český Krumlov, the subject of a gloomy autumnal canvas, *Dead City*. The gallery also owns one of Schiele's most popular female portraits, wrongly entitled *The Artist's Wife*, an unusually graceful and gentle watercolour of a seated woman in green top and black leggings. Perhaps the most influential artist on show is **Edvard Munch**, whose one canvas, *Dance at the Seaside*, hardly does justice to the considerable effect he had on a generation of Czech artists after his celebrated 1905 Prague exhibition.

CZECH ART 1960–95

The collection of **Czech art from 1960 to 1995** sits rather uncomfortably on the same floor as the French and European art. Coming from the latter, Ivan Kafka's *On Potent Impotence* installation should raise a smile, whereas Jiří Sozanský's photos and videos of the destruction of the town of Most to make way for an open-cast lignite mine is chilling (metaphorically and literally). Surprisingly there's very little overtly political art here, with the exception of Květa Válová's *Recognition and Amazement*, featuring a pair of Big Brother eyes, and *Great Dialogue* by Karel Nepraš, in which two red figures lambaste each other at close quarters with loudspeakers.

As with the 1900–1960 gallery, there is a total absence of Socialist Realist works. Instead, the gallery concentrates on artists like **Mikuláš Medek**, whose Surrealist and abstract works were more or less banned from public galleries throughout the communist period. Still, you do get a rare chance to see a couple of pieces by **Jiří Kolář** (pronounced "collage") who, coincidentally, specializes in collages of random words and reproductions of other people's paintings. The collection of post-1989 works spills over onto the balcony, and includes an entire, hermetically sealed office, by Milan Knížák, that you can peek into.

Výstaviště and Stromovka

Five minutes' walk north up Dukelských hrdinů takes you right to the front gates of the **Výstaviště** (Tues–Fri 2–10pm, Sat & Sun 10am–10pm), a motley assortment of buildings, originally created for the 1891 Prague Exhibition, that have served as the city's main trade fair arena and funfair ever since. The Communist Party held its rubber-stamp congresses in the flamboyant glass and iron **Průmyslový palác** at the centre of the complex, from 1948 until the late 1970s, and more recently several brand new permanent structures were built for the 1991 Prague Exhibition, including a circular theatre, **Divadlo Spirála**.

The grounds are at their busiest on summer weekends, when hordes of Prague families descend on the place to down hot dogs, drink beer and listen to traditional brass-band music. Apart from the annual fairs and lavish special exhibitions, there are a few permanent attractions, such as the city's **Planetárium** (Mon–Thurs 8am–noon & 1–9pm, Sat & Sun 9.30am–noon & 1–5pm), the **Maroldovo panorama** (Tues–Fri 1–5pm, Sat & Sun 11am–5pm), a giant diorama of the 1434 Battle of Lipany (see p.486); and the **Dětský svět**, a run-down funfair and playground for kids.

In the long summer evenings, there's also an open-air **cinema** (*letní kino*), and regular performances by the **Křižíkova fontána**, dancing fountains devised for the 1891 Exhibition by the Czech inventor František Křižík, which perform a music and light show to packed audiences; ask at the tourist office, or check the listings magazines, for the current schedule. Lastly, to the right as you enter the fairgrounds, there's the much overlooked **Lapidarium** (Tues–Fri noon–6pm, Sat & Sun 10am–6pm), official depository for the city's monumental sculptures that are under threat from demolition or the weather.

To the west is the *královská obora* or royal enclosure, more commonly known as **Stromovka**. Originally a game park for the noble occupants of the Hrad, it's now

Prague's largest and leafiest public park. From here, you can wander northwards to Troja and the city's zoo (see below), following a path that leads under the railway, over the canal, and on to the Císařský ostrov (Emperor's Island) – and from there to the right bank of the Vltava. Bus #112, which runs every fifteen minutes, will take you back to metro Nádraží Holešovice.

Troja

Though still well within the municipal boundaries, the suburb of **TROJA**, across the river to the north of Holešovice and Bubeneč, has a distinctly provincial air. Its most celebrated sight is Prague's only genuine chateau, the late-seventeenth-century **Trojský zámek** (April–Sept Tues–Sun 10am–6pm; Nov–March Sat & Sun 10am–5pm; bus #112 from metro Nádraží Holešovice), perfectly situated against a hilly backdrop of vines. Despite a recent renovation and rusty red repaint, its plain early Baroque facade is no match for the action-packed, blackened figures of giants and titans who battle it out on the chateau's monumental balustrades. To visit the **interior**, you'll have to join one of the guided tours. The star exhibits are the gushing frescoes depicting the victories of the Habsburg Emperor Leopold I (who reigned from 1657 to 1705) over the Turks, which cover every inch of the walls and ceilings of the grand hall; ask for the *anglický text* when you enter. You also get to wander through the chateau's pristine trend-setting French-style formal **gardens**, the first of their kind in Bohemia.

On the other side of U trojského zámku, which runs along the west wall of the chateau, is the city's capacious but underfunded **zoo** (zoologická zahrada; daily: March & April 9am–5pm; May 9am–6pm; June–Sept 9am–7pm; Oct–Feb 9am–4pm), founded in 1931 on the site of one of Troja's numerous hillside vineyards. Despite its rather weary appearance, all the usual animals are on show here, and kids, at least, have few problems enjoying themselves. Thankfully, a programme of modernization is currently under way, though some cramped cages still remain. In the summer, you can take a "ski-lift" (*lanová dráha*) from the duck pond to the top of the hill, where the prize exhibits – a rare breed of miniature horse known as Przewalski – hang out.

Hvězda and Bertramka

Spread across the hills to the northwest of the city centre are the leafy, garden suburbs of **Dejvice** and **Střešovice**, peppered with fashionable villas built between the wars for the upwardly mobile Prague bourgeoisie and commanding magnificent views across the north of the city.

A couple of kilometres southwest of Dejvice, trams #1, #2 and #18 terminate close to the hunting park of **Hvězda**, one of Prague's most beautiful and peaceful parks. Wide, green avenues of trees radiate from a bizarre star-shaped building (*hvězda* means "star" in Czech) designed by the Archduke Ferdinand of Tyrol for his wife in 1555. Recently restored, it houses a worthy but dull **museum** (Tues–Sat 9am–4pm, Sun 10am–5pm) devoted to the reactionary writer Alois Jirásek (1851–1930), who popularized old Czech legends during the national revival, and to the artist Mikuláš Aleš (1852–1913), whose drawings were likewise inspired by Czech history. On the top floor there's a small exhibition on the **Battle of Bílá hora** (White Mountain), the first battle of the Thirty Years' War, which took place in 1620 a short distance southwest of Hvězda. However, it's the building itself – decorated with delicate stucco work and frescoes – that's the greatest attraction; it makes a perfect setting for the chamber music concerts occasionally staged here.

Bertramka (Mozart Museum)

In the hills above the late-nineteenth-century suburb of Smíchov is the Dušeks' **Bertramka** villa (daily: April–Oct 9.30am–6pm; Nov–April 9.30am–5pm), where, so the story goes, Mozart put the finishing touches to his *Don Giovanni* overture, the night before the première at the Stavovské divadlo (see p.75). As long ago as 1838, the villa was turned into a shrine to Mozart, though very little survives of the house he knew, thanks to a fire on New Year's Day 1871 – not that this has deterred generations of Mozart-lovers from flocking here. These days, what the museum lacks in memorabilia, it makes up for with its Rococo ambience, lovely garden and regular Mozart recitals. To get to Bertramka, take the metro to Anděl, walk a couple of blocks west up Plzeňská, then left up Mozartova.

Eating and drinking

The good news is that you can eat and drink for very little in Prague: the food is filling and the beer divine. The bad news is that the locals still have little concern for cholesterol levels, and almost no interest in fresh vegetables or side salads. But while traditional Czech food still predominates in the city's pubs, Prague has a much wider choice of restaurants than anywhere else in the country: nowadays, you have a worldwide choice of cuisines, and a whole range of new, slightly more expensive restaurants aimed at the palates (and wallets) of the passing tourist, the expat community, wealthy Czechs and the diplomatic crowd.

The biggest mistake most first-time visitors make is to confine their eating and drinking to obvious sightseeing areas, where prices are generally much higher, quality lower and, in summer, spare tables a rarity. It's worth venturing instead into the backstreets of Staré Město and Nové Město, where many of the better-value restaurants tend to hide.

Breakfast, snacks and fast food

Unless a continental **breakfast** is included in the price of your accommodation, you'll find it difficult to know what to eat for breakfast and where to get it. The Czechs start their day so early that they rarely bother with more than a gulp of grainy black coffee with perhaps a slice of bread and salami. Only a few, newer **bakeries** offer croissants, sundry pastries and coffee all under the same roof, however, there are various **fast-food places** to try out (not all of them *McDonald's*), and a few of the **self-service bufets** that used to be ubiquitous during the communist period.

Adonis, Jungmannova 21, Nové Město; metro Národní třída. Cheap Middle Eastern fare – stuffed vine leaves, *felafel*, *taboule* and a salad bar – sit-in or takeaway, a stone's throw from Wenceslas Square and Národní třída. Daily 11am–7pm.

Bohemia Bagel, Újezd 16, Malá Strana; tram#12 or #22 from metro Malostranská. Takeaway bagels at the side, but with a sit-down café too, where you can have an all-day breakfast or sandwiches as well as bagels. Daily 8am–midnight.

Country Life, Melantrichova 15, Staré Město; metro Můstek. Health-food shop up front, and large sit-down self-service buffet, serving veggie slop and salads in the courtyard behind. Mon–Fri 9am–9.30pm, Sun 11am–9.30pm.

Dům lahůdek, Malé náměstí; metro Staroměstská. Prague's largest and best delicatessen, on several levels, with great picnic fodder plus traditional *chlebíčky*, salads, coffee and cakes. Mon–Sat 9.30am–7pm, Sun noon–7pm.

Le Gourmand, Václavské náměstí 18, Nové Město; metro Můstek. Neither French nor gourmet, but a large, cheap, convenient self-service salad bar with a few standard hot Czech dishes on offer, too. Daily 8am–2am.

Pekařství v Karmelitské, Karmelitská 20, Malá Strana; tram #12 or #22 from metro Malostranská. Nice new bakery, just south of Malostranské náměstí, with a café attached where you can wash down your cakes and pastries with coffee. Bakery: Mon–Fri 7am–7pm, Sun noon–6pm. Café: Mon–Fri 10am–8pm, Sat & Sun 10am–8pm.

Safir, Havelská 12, Staré Město; metro Můstek. Inexpensive centrally located Middle Eastern kebab and *felafel* outlet. Mon–Sat 10am–8pm.

U Bakaláře, Celetná 13, Staré Město; metro Staroměstská/náměstí Republiky. Self-service veggie hole-filler, serving typical Czech fry-up food to hungry tourists. Mon–Fri 9am–9pm, Sat & Sun 10am–9pm.

Cafés

With only a handful of classic haunts surviving, Prague can no longer boast a **café society** to rival that of Vienna or Paris, as it could at the beginning of this century and between the wars. Nevertheless, many Praguers still spend a large part of the day smoking and drinking in the city's cafés, particularly in the summer, when the tables spill out onto the streets and squares. The cafés listed below are a mixed bunch. The majority serve just coffee, cakes and, more often than not, alcohol; others also serve up cheap and filling (though by no means gourmet) meals.

Malá Strana

Malostranská kavárna, Malostranské náměstí 28; metro Malostranská. A time-honoured café founded in 1874 in a late-eighteenth-century palace, and despite its prime location still a very pleasant place inside. Daily 9am–11pm.

Savoy, Vítězná 5; tram #12 or #22 from metro Malostranská. Renovated nineteenth-century café with high, gilded ceilings but rather unfortunate modern fittings and little atmosphere. Daily 9am–midnight.

U zavěšenýho kafe, Radnické schody 7. A "hanging coffee" is one that has been paid for by the haves for the have-nots who drop in. That apart, this place is a pleasant smoky crossover café/pub, serving cheap Měšťan beer and traditional Czech food in a handy spot on the steps down from the Hrad. Daily 11am–midnight.

Staré Město

Barock, Pařížská 24; metro Staroměstská. Deeply fashionable, and popular, French-style candlelit café with framed photos of supermodels on the walls. The Thai, Japanese and Chinese is good but pricey. Mon–Fri 8.30am–1am, Sat & Sun 10am–2am.

Blatouch, Vězenská 7; metro Staroměstská. Smoky, literary café, frequented mostly by Czech students rather than expats. Olives, snacks, jazz and alcoholic/non-alcoholic cocktails available. Mon–Fri 11am–midnight, Sat 2pm–1am, Sun 2pm–midnight.

Café Milena, Staroměstské náměstí 22; metro Staroměstská. Nice attempt at a 1920s-style café – by far the best in this part of town – opposite the astronomical clock. Daily 10am–10pm.

Chez Marcel, Haštalská 12; metro náměstí Republiky. Effortlessly chic French café. A good place to grab a coffee, flick through a magazine and eat some moderately priced bistro-style food. Mon–Fri 8am–1am, Sat & Sun 9am–1am.

Gulu Gulu, Betlémské náměstí 8; metro Národní třída. Popular café/pub with beaten bare boards, Miró-style murals, newspapers, friendly bar staff and Radegast beer. Daily 10am–midnight.

INTERNET CAFES

Pl@neta, Vinohradská 102, Vinohrady; metro Jiřího z Poděbrad. A businesslike place that's not somewhere to linger, but the English-speaking staff will help you pick up and write email happily enough. Daily 8am–10pm.

Terminal Bar, Soukenická 6, Nové Město; metro náměstí Republiky. Definitely the number one choice in terms of atmosphere, this is a funky, loud bar, with a groovy chill-out basement littered with kitsch sofas and weird lighting. English-speakers can help with any technical problems. Daily 10am–2am.

Hogo Fogo, Salvátorská 4; metro Staroměstská. Modish, monochrome café in backstreets off Pařížská, serving cheap, filling Czech pasta and meat dishes. Mon–Thurs & Sun noon–midnight, Fri & Sat noon–2am.

Reno, UPM, 17 listopadu; metro Staroměstská. Great place to relax after surveying the treasures of the Decorative Arts Museum (see p.95). Mon–Fri 10am–6pm, Sat & Sun 11am–6pm.

Rudolfinum, Alšovo nábřeží 12; metro Staroměstská. Gloriously ornate nineteenth-century café on the first floor of the old parliament building – only open when there's an exhibition on. Tues–Sun 10am–6pm.

Nové Město

Grand Hotel Evropa, Václavské náměstí 25; metro Můstek/Muzeum. To truly appreciate the sumptuous Art Nouveau decor, you'll have to forsake the terrace and step inside – worth it even if the music, coffee and staff are below par, and they slap a surcharge on for the music. Daily 10am–midnight.

Louvre, Národní 20; metro Národní třída. High ceiling, mirrors, daily papers, billiard hall and window seats overlooking Národní make this a popular refuelling spot for tourists and shoppers. Daily 8am–11pm.

Obecní dům, náměstí Republiky; metro náměstí Republiky. The *kavárna*, with its famous fountain, is in the more restrained south hall of this wonderful huge Art Nouveau complex, and has recently been glitteringly restored – an absolute aesthetic treat. Daily 7.30am–11pm.

Slavia, Národní 1; metro Národní třída. An enduring and endearing Prague institution (see p.103) that still pulls in a mixed crowd from shoppers and tourists to older folk and the pre- and post-theatre mob. Mon–Fri 8am–midnight, Sat & Sun 9am–midnight.

Velryba (The Whale), Opatovická 24; metro Národní třída. One of the most determinedly cool cafés in Prague, serving cheap, post-revolutionary Czech food. Daily 11am–2am.

Further afield

The Globe, Janovského 14, Holešovice; metro Vltavská. This laid-back café – like the adjoining bookshop of the same name – is one big expat hang-out, but enjoyable nevertheless. Daily 10am–midnight.

PRAGUE TEAHOUSES

Prague's **teahouses** are a 1990s phenomenon, though they have their historical roots in the First Republic. Partly a reaction to the smoke-filled, alcohol-driven atmosphere of the ubiquitous Czech pub, and partly a reaction against the multinational, fast-food culture that has recently arrived in Prague, teahouses are non-smoking, slightly hippified places to enjoy a quiet cuppa or chill out. The tea drinking is taken very seriously, and several of the places listed below stock a staggering array of leaves.

Dobrá čajovna, Boršov 6, Staré Město; metro Staroměstská. Probably the most successful of all the teahouses at re-creating a distinctively mellow, rarified atmosphere, with hookah smoking permitted. An astonishing variety of teas (and a few Middle Eastern snacks) are served by young male proto-Buddhist waiters who slip silently by in their sandals. This place is very difficult to find (it's off Karoliny Světlé) and the door is frequently locked, so you'll need to ring the bell to find out if there's any space available (or if they like the look of you). Daily 8am–noon & 4–10pm.

Dobrá čajovna, Václavské náměstí 14, Nové Město; metro Můstek/Muzeum. Prague's first teahouse with a slightly less rarified but equally relaxing ambience. It's set back from the square, has world music wafting through it, floor seating and a vast range of teas. Mon–Sat 10am–9pm, Sun 3–9pm.

Malý Buddha, Úvoz 44, Malá Strana; tram #12 or #22 from metro Malostranská. Typical Prague teahouse decor, with a Buddhist altar in one corner, and a very useful haven just down from the Hrad. Tues–Sun 11am–10pm.

U zeleného čaje, Nerudova 19, Malá Strana; tram #12 or #22 from metro Malostranská. The "green tea" is a great little stop-off for a pot of tea or a veggie snack en route to or from the Hrad. The only problem is getting a place at one of the four tables. Daily 11am–9.30pm.

U knihomola (The Bookworm), Mánesova 79, Vinohrady; metro Jiřího z Poděbrad. Basement café in one of Prague's main expat bookstores, with foreign papers to browse and art exhibitions to admire. Mon–Thurs 10am–11pm, Fri & Sat 10am–midnight, Sun 11am–8pm.

Pubs and bars

Traditional Czech **pubs** (*pivnice*) are smoky, male-dominated, hard-drinking establishments and they're a dying breed in the capital; those with a more youthful or expat clientele tend to be a bit more mixed, but if you're not interested in drinking (and preferably smoking), you'll find it hard to have a good time. Still, as with British pubs, whatever their faults, they remain deeply embedded in the local culture, and to sample that, you'll need to sample the amber nectar. Food is almost always of the traditional Czech variety: cheap, filling but ultimately capable of shortening your life by a couple of years.

Hradčany and Malá Strana

Baráčnická rychta, Na tržiště 22 (a narrow passageway leading south off Nerudova), Malá Strana; metro Malostranská. A real survivor – a small backstreet *pivnice* squeezed in between the embassies, with cheap, filling menu. Daily 11am–11pm.

Jo's Bar, Malostranské náměstí 7; metro Malostranská. A narrow bar that's a perennially popular expat/backpacker hang-out. Tex-Mex food served all day, bottled beer only and a heaving crowd guaranteed most evenings. Daily 11am–2am.

Na Kampě, Na Kampě, 15, Malá Strana; metro Malostranská. Friendly wood-panelled pub on the lovely Kampa Island with all the classic Czech pub snacks on offer. Daily noon–midnight.

U černého orla (The Black Eagle), Újezd 33, Malá Strana; tram #12 or #22 from metro Malostranská. Popular student pub with cheap food and Staropramen 10° beer, across the bridge from the Národní divadlo. Mon–Fri 10am–10pm, Sat & Sun 11am–10pm.

U černého vola (The Black Ox), Loretánské náměstí 1, Hradčany. Does brisk business providing thirsty local workers with huge quantities of the popular light beer Velkopopovický kozel. Daily 11am–11pm.

U hrocha (The Hippo), Thunovská 10, Malá Strana; metro Malostranská. A genuine Czech pub in the heart of Malá Strana, difficult to believe but true; cheap grub and beer. Daily noon–11pm.

U kocoura (The Cat), Nerudova 2, Malá Strana; metro Malostranská. One of the few surviving pubs on Nerudova, owned by the Beer Party, but, for the most part, abandoned by its old clientele. Some of the best Budvar in town, plus the obvious Czech stomach fillers. Daily 11.30am–midnight.

U malého Glena, Karmelitská 23, Malá Strana; metro Malostranská. Smart-looking pub/jazz bar that attracts a fair mixture of Czechs and expats thanks to its better-than-average food and live music in the basement. Daily 10am–2am.

Staré Město

Chapeau Rouge, Malá Štupartská; metro náměstí Republiky. Loud, posey boozer with wooden floorboards and red hat on door in the heart of the so-called French Quarter or "Bermuda Triangle", absolutely packed out with non-Czechs. Daily 4pm–4am.

Konvikt, Bartolomějská 11; metro Národní třída. New, but very normal, smoky *pivnice* in the back-streets of the old town, serving Pilsner and Czech food. Mon–Fri 9am–11pm, Sat & Sun 11am–11pm.

Marquis de Sade, Templová 8; metro náměstí Republiky. Great space: huge high ceiling, big comfy sofas, and a mostly expat crowd. Crap beer and limited snacks, but a good place to start an evening, before the live band kicks in. Daily 4pm–2am.

Molly Malone's, U obecního dvora 4; metro Staroměstská. Real Irish pub with real Irish staff (who don't speak much Czech), an open fire and draught Kilkenny and Guinness (neither of them very cheap). Daily 11am–1am.

Na Ovocném trhu, Ovocný trh 17; metro náměstí Republiky. New pub behind the Stavovské divadlo – perfect for a pre-theatre bite and a jar of Velkopopovický kozel. Mon–Sat 10am–10pm, Sun 11am–10pm.

Radegast, Templová 2; metro náměstí Republiky. Typically boozy pub divided into booths, serving its namesake plus decent Czech food, and attracting a mix of locals and expats. Daily 11am–midnight.

U krále Jiřího (The King George), Liliová 10; metro Staroměstská. Forget the more visible *James Joyce* nearby, and head down the steps to this nice Czech pub serving Gambrinus beer instead. Mon–Fri 11am–midnight, Sat & Sun noon–midnight.

U medvídků (The Little Bears), Na Perstýně 7; metro Národní třída. Another Prague institution going back to the thirteenth century. Nowadays, the food isn't great, and the beer, Budvar, not always what it should be, but it is central, unpretentious and roomy. Mon–Sat 11.30am–11pm, Sun 11.30am–10pm.

U milosrdných, Kozí 21; metro Staroměstská. Refurbished pub far enough away from the tourist crowds, serving typical Czech food and Plzeň beers. Daily 10am–10pm.

Nové Město

Jáma (The Hollow), V jámě 7; metro Můstek/Muzeum. Loud expat pub with lots of cocktails and a range of passable attempts at Tex-Mex dishes. Daily 11am–1am.

Novoměstský pivovar, Vodičkova 20; metro Můstek. Micro-brewery serving up its own misty home brew, plus solid Czech food, in a series of bright, sprawling, modern beer halls. Mon–Sat 11.30am–11.30pm, Sun noon–10pm.

Pivovarský dům, corner of Lipová/Ječná; metro Karlovo náměstí. Busy micro-brewery dominated by its big shiny copper vats, serving light, mixed and dark unfiltered beer (plus banana, coffee and wheat varieties), and all the standard Czech pub dishes (including *pivný sýr*). Daily 11am–11.30pm.

U Fleků, Křemencova 11; metro Karlovo náměstí. Famous *pivnice* where the dark, 13° beer, Flek, has been exclusively brewed and consumed since 1499. Seats over 500 German tourists at a go, serves short measures (0.4l) for high prices, slaps on an extra charge for bad music, and still you have to queue to get in. This is a tourist trap and the only reason to visit is to sample the beer, which you're best off doing during the day. Daily 9am–11pm.

U havrana (The Crow), Hálkova 8; metro I. P. Pavlova. Surprisingly unseedy pub serving food and Měšťan and Kozel beer throughout the night. Mon–Fri 24hr, Sat & Sun 6pm–6am.

Zlatá Hvězda (Golden Star), Ve Smečkách 12; metro Muzeum. The main reason to hit this big, loud pub is to watch the match you want on the numerous satellite TV screens. Mon–Wed 11am–midnight, Thurs 11am–1am, Fri 11am–2.30am, Sat noon–1am, Sun noon–midnight.

Further afield

Akropolis, Kubelíkova 27, Žižkov; metro Jiřího z Poděbrad. Funkily decked out and very popular smoke-filled pub that plays half-decent music and serves cheap Czech food, Kozel beer. Mon–Fri 10am–1am, Sat & Sun 4pm–1am.

Na staré kovárně v Braníku (The Old Blacksmith's in Braník), Kamenická 17, Holešovice; tram #26 from metro náměstí Republiky. Nicely refurbished pub that's popular with the locals and a crowd of young Czechs. Small menu of meaty daily dishes, Radegast beer and good music. Mon–Sat 11.30am–1am, Sun 11.30am–11.30pm.

U vystřeleného oka (The Shot-Out Eye), U božích bojovníků, Žižkov; metro Florenc. Big smoky pub just south of the Žižkov hill, with (unusually) good music and lashings of Radegast beer, and absinthe chasers. Daily 3.30pm–1am.

Restaurants and wine bars

Prague's **restaurant** scene has greatly improved in the last few years in terms of both choice and quality. The influx of tourists has, of course, pushed the prices out of the reach of many Czechs, who tend more than ever to stick to pubs when eating out. However, even in the city's top restaurants, you can't guarantee faultless food and service, so keep an open mind. Service is gradually becoming more sophisticated, though surly staff are still no rarity, nor are unscrupulous waiters who exercise dubious arithmetic when totting up the bill. Beware of extras in the pricier restaurants, where you will be charged for everything you touch, including the almonds you thought were courtesy of the house.

As prices continue to rise, we have classified the following listings in comparative terms. Expect to pay no more than 250Kč a head for a full meal with drinks in an **inexpensive** place; between 250Kč and 500Kč per head in a **moderate** restaurant; and upwards of 400Kč in an **expensive** one. While 500Kč for a meal is hardly expensive to a Westerner, it still is for most Czechs, so it's unlikely you'll be sharing your table with locals. Note that at restaurants where we have included phone numbers, it is advisable to book beforehand.

Hradčany and Malá Strana

Avalon, Malostranské náměstí 12, Malá Strana; metro Malostranská. American-style brasserie upstairs from *Circle Line* (see below) offering a California-inspired menu with everything from burgers to fresh salads, but particularly strong on shellfish and the finned variety; tables outside in the summer. Daily 11am–1am. Moderate.

Bar Bar, Všehrdova 17, Malá Strana; tram #12 or #22 from metro Malostranská. Arty creperie with big cheap salads, savoury and sweet crepes and Jamaican *palačinky* on offer. Mon–Fri 11am–11pm, Sat & Sun noon–11pm. Inexpensive.

Bazaar, Nerudova 40, Malá Strana; metro Malostranská. Big labyrinthine candlelit complex on several levels, with bare brick vaults and an al fresco rooftop section. The Med food usually hits the spot. Daily noon–11pm. Moderate.

Circle Line, Malostranské náměstí 12 (☎57 53 00 23). The fresh seafood and sumptuous salads are the main draw, though the meat and veggie courses are equally good. Approaching 1000Kč a head and situated below the less expensive *Avalon* (see above). Mon–Sat 6–11pm. Expensive.

Faros, Šporkova 5, Malá Strana; metro Malostranská (☎53 34 82). Cosy little Greek restaurant in the backstreets of Malá Strana; a nice change and fairly veggie-friendly. Daily noon–11pm. Moderate.

Kampa Park, Na Kampě 8b, Malá Strana (☎53 48 00). Pink house exquisitely located right by the Vltava on Kampa Island with a superb international menu and tables outside in summer. Daily noon–midnight. Expensive.

Nebozízek (Little Auger), Petřínské sady 411, Malá Strana (☎53 79 05). Situated at the halfway stop on the funicular up Petřín. The view is superb, and the traditional Czech menu heavy with game dishes. Daily 11am–11pm. Moderate.

Saté Grill, Pohořelec 3, Hradčany; tram #22 from metro Malostranská. One of the few places in the vicinity of the Hrad where you can fill your belly for very little. Simple veggie and non-veggie noodle dishes prepared, all with a vaguely Indonesian bent. Daily 11am–10pm. Inexpensive.

U maltézských rytířů, Prokopská 10, Malá Strana; metro Malostranská (☎53 63 57). One of the best Gothic cellars in Prague to sample faultless local cuisine (particularly game) and excellent apple strudel. Daily 11am–11pm. Moderate.

U modré kachničky (The Blue Duck), Nebovidská 6, Malá Strana; metro Malostranská (☎57 32 03 08). Cosy little restaurant, decorated with murals and antiques, and offering a mouth-watering selection of dishes, including many Czech favourites, given the gourmet treatment. Daily noon–4pm & 6.30–11.30pm. Moderate.

U patrona, Dražického náměstí 4, Malá Strana; metro Malostranská. An excellent restaurant very close to the Charles Bridge, offering beautifully prepared local dishes. Daily 11.30am–2.30pm & 5.30–11.30pm. Moderate.

Staré Město and Josefov

Bellevue, Smetanovo nábřeží 18 (☎24 22 76 14); metro Národní třída. The view of the Charles Bridge and the Hrad is outstanding and they serve imaginative Czech-centred cuisine – hardly surprising then that it's around 1000Kč a head and you need to book ahead to eat here. Mon–Sat noon–3pm & 7–11.30pm, Sun 11am–3.30pm & 5.30–11pm. Expensive.

Le Café Colonial, Široká 6; metro Staroměstská. Situated right opposite the Klausová synagoga, this café/restaurant is a successfully classy place. The colonial theme isn't overplayed, though the menu has a touch of Chinese and Indian. Mon–Sat 7.30am–1am, Sun 8.30am–5pm. Expensive.

Le Saint-Jacques, Jakubská 4; metro náměstí Republiky. Excellent French brasserie cuisine on offer here in the heart of the so-called "French quarter". Daily noon–3pm & 6pm–midnight. Moderate.

Lotos, Platnéřská 13; metro Staroměstská. Decor's an odd mixture of tie-dye and ultra-tidy sterility. Food's bizarre too: banana ragout but also veggie wholefood versions of Czech cuisine – this is your chance to have a meat-free pork and dumplings. No smoking but there is alcohol. Daily 11am–10pm. Inexpensive.

Maestro, Křižovnická 10; metro Staroměstská. Very good pizza place close to the metro (and to Charles Bridge); the chicken dishes are also worth sampling, as are the profiteroles. Daily 11am–11pm. Inexpensive.

Massada, Michalská 16; metro Můstek. Smart kosher restaurant, offering some unusual dishes such as latkes, aubergines and fruit dumplings, though I'm not sure what the Talmud says about microwaves. Flesh-based dishes upstairs; dairy and veggie dishes downstairs. Daily except Fri & Sat 8am–midnight. Moderate.

Pizzeria Rugantino, Dušní 4; metro Staroměstská. This is the real thing – an oak-fired oven, gargantuan thin bases, nineteen toppings to choose from and Bernard beer on tap. Mon–Sat 11am–11pm, Sun 4–11pm. Inexpensive.

Reykjavik, Karlova 20; metro Staroměstská. Prime tourist location and pleasant decor and service make this Icelandic-owned restaurant a very popular place. The best feature is the wonderful variety of fresh fish, flown in from you know where. Daily 11am–midnight. Expensive.

U zátiší (Still Life), Liliová 1 (☎24 22 89 77); metro Národní třída. Exquisitely prepared international cuisine with fresh vegetables, fresh pasta, and regular non-meat dishes, all served in *nouvelle cuisine* sized portions by professional waiters. Daily noon–3pm & 5.30–11pm. Expensive.

Nové Město

Casablanca, Na příkopě 10; metro Můstek (☎24 21 05 19). The full Moroccan monty, both in terms of decor, belly dancing and food (at around 750Kč a head). Daily 6–10pm. Expensive.

Cicala, Žitná 43; metro I.P. Pavlova. Very good little Italian basement restaurant that does a good range of pasta and pizza, has an appetizing *antipasti* selection, and specializes (midweek) in fresh seafood. Mon–Sat 11.30am–10.30pm. Moderate.

Francouzská restaurace, Obecní dům, náměstí Republiky; metro náměstí Republiky. The Art Nouveau decor in this cavernous hall is absolutely stunning; the setting is formal and therefore puts a lot of tourists off, though the food's actually not that expensive (nor that French). Daily noon–3pm & 6–11pm. Expensive.

Góvinda, Soukenická 27; metro náměstí Republiky. Hare Krishna (*Haré Kršna* in Czech) restaurant serving organic Indian veggie slop for knock-down prices. Mon–Sat 11am–5pm. Inexpensive.

Ostroff, Střelecký ostrov; tram #6, #9 or #22. Top-notch Italian restaurant in a great location on one of the islands in the Vltava (over 1000Kč a head); this place also has a great riverside bar that stays open until 3am. Daily noon–2pm & 7pm–midnight. Expensive.

Pizzeria Coloseum, Vodičkova 32; metro Můstek. Basement pizzeria in the passage beside *Kentucky Fried Chicken*, dishing up big pizzas and pasta dishes, washed down with *Krušovice* beer and Moravian wine – good for a pre-cinema filler. Daily noon–11.30pm. Inexpensive.

Pizzeria Kmotra, (Godmother), V jirchářích 12; metro Národní třída (☎24 91 58 09). This sweaty basement pizza place is one of Prague's most popular, justifiably so – if possible book a table in advance. Daily 11am–1am. Inexpensive.

Further afield

Kongzi, Seifertova 18, Žižkov; tram #5, #9 or #26 from metro Hlavní nádraží. Very reasonable, very hot Chinese food in deepest Žižkov. Daily 11am–3pm & 6–11pm. Moderate.

Il Ritrovo, Lublaňská 11, Vinohrady; metro I.P. Pavlova. Italian-run outfit with a wide range of pasta dishes and salads, a great *antipasta* bar in the centre of the restaurant and good *tiramisu* for dessert. Mon–Sat noon–3pm & 6pm–midnight. Moderate.

La Creperie, Janovského 4, Holešovice; tram #5, #12 or #17. Stylish French-run creperie serving sweet and savoury pancakes, French liqueurs and even the rare Nová Paka beer. Mon–Sat noon–11pm.

Myslivna (The Hunting Lodge), Jagellonská 21, Žižkov; metro Flora. One of Prague's best game restaurants, serving up excellent venison and quail. Daily 11.30am–3.30pm & 6–11pm. Inexpensive.

Na rybárně, Gorazdova 17; metro Karlovo náměstí. Dependable Czech fish restaurant near the river, that's cosy, unpretentious and, depending on the fish you choose, pretty cheap. Mon–Sat noon–midnight, Sun 5pm–midnight. Inexpensive.

Radost FX Café, Bělehradská 120, Vinohrady; metro I.P. Pavlova. Without doubt the best choice of vegetarian dishes in town (okay, so there's not much competition), that draw in a large expat posse, particularly for the Sunday brunch. Daily 11.30am–4am. Moderate.

Shalimar, Balbínova 10, Vinohrady; metro Muzeum. Prague's best-value curry restaurant, situated behind the Národní muzeum, serving the real thing: poppadums, bhajees, samosas and an excellent chicken kerahi. Mon–Thurs & Sun 5pm–midnight, Fri & Sat noon–midnight. Moderate.

Thajský restaurant, V Holešovičkách 22a, Troja; bus #102, #156 or #175 from metro Nádraží Holešovice. A bit of a trek, unless you're camping at Troja, but inexpensive authentic Thai food is the reward. Mon–Sat 11am–3pm & 6–10.30pm. Moderate.

Entertainment

For many Praguers, **entertainment** is confined to an evening's drinking in one of the city's beer-swilling *pivnice*. But if you're looking for a bit more action, there's plenty to keep you from night-time frustration. To find out **what's on**, check out the listings sections of the English-language weekly, *Prague Post*, or the monthly English-language bulletin, *Culture in Prague*. Other sources are the bilingual *Do města/Downtown*, or the Czech monthly *Přehled*, which both give a full rundown of films, concerts, gigs and events.

Clubs and live venues

The great thing about going out for the night in Prague is that the beer flows cheaply, entry to most late-night places is pretty negligible, and there are one or two venues open until 5 or 6am. That said, Prague has nothing like the number of **clubs** you'd expect from a European capital. The dance craze has a small, but dedicated following, and there are a few good one-off raves over the summer (a case of scouring the fly

---

GAY AND LESBIAN NIGHTLIFE

Prague Post does the occasional update on **gay and lesbian nightlife** in Prague, otherwise you'll need to get hold of the monthly gay magazine *SOHO Revue*, which has an English summary, *Amigo*, another bimonthly listings mag, or the lesbian monthly, *ProFem*. You'll also find useful flyers at the places listed below (for more on gay life, see p.130).

"A" Klub, Milíčova 32, Žižkov; tram #5, #9 or #26. The city's premier lesbian bar with women-only Friday nights. It's small but stylish and definitely worth checking out. Mon–Sat 6pm–6am, Sun 3pm–midnight.

Drake's, Petřínská 5, Smíchov; tram #6 or #9 from metro Národní třída. Expensive, almost exclusively male hang-out, which bills itself as a "really big cruise facility"; the private video booths are the biggest draw. Open 24 hours a day, seven days a week.

L Club, Lublaňská 48, Vinohrady; metro I.P. Pavlova. Mixed lesbian/gay crowd at this restaurant, which turns into a disco after 10pm. Daily 8pm–4am.

Medúza, Belgická 17, Vinohrady; metro náměstí Míru. Laid-back café run by women for women, the best gyno-centric spot in Prague. Mon–Fri 11am–1am, Sat & Sun noon–1am.

Mascot Club, Kolínská 11, Žižkov; metro Flora. A mixed gay/lesbian crowd enjoys this camp but classy place where you can eat, dance and watch strip shows and drag at the weekend. Entrance on Slezská. Daily 9pm–6am.

Stella, Lužická 10, Vinohrady; metro náměstí Míru. Currently one of the most popular mixed gay/lesbian hot spots in the capital. Daily 8pm–5am.

U střelce, Karoliny Světlé 12, Staré Město; metro Národní třída. Sweaty cellar club whose drag shows pull in a mixed straight/gay crowd. Wed–Sat 9.30pm–late.

posters around), but pure dance clubs are the exception. The continuing survival of timeless tacky discos around Wenceslas Square, is remarkable; less so, the more recent arrival of a bevy of thriving strip clubs. Many nightclubs double as live music venues, with lots of world music bands finding their way to Prague in recent years, along with Czech bands that span the entire range of musical tastes from (mostly white) reggae to thrash.

Rock, pop and dance music

Major Western bands usually include Prague in their European tours and, to be sure of a full house, many offer tickets at a fraction of their usual price. There are also gigs by Czech bands almost every night in the city's clubs and discos – a selection of the better ones is listed below, but bear in mind that many clubs in Prague appear to be under constant threat of closure, so always check in the local listings before setting out.

Akropolis, Kubelíkova 27, Žižkov; tram #5, #9 or #26. Decent live venue space adjacent to the café/bar of the same name in Žižkov, that attracts some very good bands – everything from world music to avant-garde Czech stuff – and a discerning, mostly Czech crowd. Doors open 7pm.

Jo's Garáž, Malostranské náměstí 7; tram #12 or #22 from metro Malostranská. Loud, sweaty, packed backpacker- and expat-free disco in the cellar next door to *Jo's Bar*. Daily 9pm–late.

Lucerna music bar, Vodičkova 36, Nové Město; metro Můstek/Muzeum. Without doubt the best gig venue in Prague, a gilded turn-of-the-century hall with balcony, situated underneath the Lucerna *pasáž*. Gigs start at 9pm.

Radost FX, Bělehradská 120, Vinohrady; metro I.P. Pavlova. Still by far the slickest (and longest-running) dance club in Prague, attracting a mix of clubbers and despots; good veggie café upstairs (see p.125). Daily 10pm–5am.

Rock Café, Národní 22, Nové Město; metro Národní třída. The *Rock Café* has had its day. It made its name in the early 1990s, but is now considered passé. Still, its frequent "revival" bands continue to pull in plenty of tourists and out-of-town Czechs, and it shows rockumentaries all afternoon in the bar. Daily 4pm–3am.

Roxy, Dlouhá 33, Staré Město; metro náměstí Republiky. The *Roxy* is a great little venue: a rambling old theatre with an interesting programme of events from arty films and exhibitions to live acts and dance nights. Tues–Sun 8pm–late.

Subway, Na příkopě 22, Nové Město; metro náměstí Republiky. DJs, jazz and good old r 'n' r entertain a mixed bunch of tourists and locals, but the biggest draw is the outdoor beer courtyard. Situated on the ground floor of the Slovanský dům. Daily 9pm–5am.

Újezd, Újezd 18, Malá Strana; tram #12 or #22 from metro Malostranská. Like *Rock Café*, this place has a long pedigree, but unlike *Rock Café* it still hosts real low-tech Czech bands – the only problem is they're usually grim. Daily 7pm–3am.

Jazz

Prague has a surprisingly long indigenous tradition, and is home to a handful of good jazz clubs. With little money to attract acts from abroad, the artists are almost exclusively Czech and do the entire round of venues each month. The one exception is *AghaRTA* (see below) who usually get a few international jazz musicians to drop in on Prague during their summer and autumn festival. More often than not, it's a good idea to book a table at the jazz clubs listed below – this is particularly true of *AghaRTA* and *Reduta*.

AghaRTA Jazz Centrum, Krakovská 5, Nové Město (☎24 21 29 14); metro Muzeum. Probably the best jazz club in Prague, with a good mix of Czechs and foreigners and a consistently good programme of gigs; in a side street off the top end of Wenceslas Square. Daily 7pm–1am.

Malostranská beseda, Malostranské náměstí 21, Malá Strana (☎53 90 24); metro Malostranská. Ramshackle venue, by no means exclusively jazz, but worth checking out nevertheless. Daily until 1am; gigs start at 8pm.

Metropolitan Jazz Club, Jungmannova 14, Nové Město (☎24 21 60 25); metro Můstek. Small jazz restaurant that tends to stick to a traditional menu on stage and in the kitchen. Daily until 1am; gigs start at 9pm.

Reduta, Národní 20, Nové Město (☎24 91 22 46); metro Národní třída. Prague's best-known jazz club – Bill Clinton played his sax here in front of Havel. Live jazz daily from 9pm.

U malého Glena, Karmelitská 23, Malá Strana; tram #12 or #22 from metro Malostranská (☎535 81 15). Tiny downstairs stage is worth checking out for its eclectic mix of bluegrass, acid jazz, bebop and blues. Sunday jam sessions start at 6pm; all other gigs begin at 9pm. Daily 10am–2am.

U staré paní, Michalská 9, Staré Město; metro Můstek (☎26 49 20). Decent jazz restaurant that really gets going when the live music kicks in from 9pm onwards. Daily 7pm–4am.

Železná, Železná 16, Staré Město; metro Můstek (☎24 21 25 41). Inexpensive, centrally located cellar venue that puts on a regular live programme of mostly trad jazz bands. Daily from 5pm.

The arts

Alongside the city's numerous cafés, pubs and clubs, there's a rich **cultural life** in Prague. Music is everywhere, especially in the summer, when the streets, churches, palaces, opera houses, concert halls and gardens are filled with the strains of classical music. True, there are too many Mozart concerts pandering to the tourist trade, but equally there are some very high-quality chamber concerts. Czech theatre and film has recovered significantly since the early 1990s, when subsidies and censorship both disappeared more or less overnight. Even if you don't understand Czech, there are theatre performances worth catching – Prague has a strong tradition of mime, "black theatre" and puppetry, and many cinemas show films in their original language.

You can obtain **tickets** from the box office (*pokladna*) of the venue concerned, but you might find it easier to go to one of the city's numerous **ticket agencies** – it will cost you more, but might save you a lot of hassle. Ticketpro has branches all over the city, with its main branch at Salvátorská 10, Staré Město (☎24 81 40 20; Mon–Fri 8am–6pm). Another option is Bohemia Ticket International which has several offices, including one at Na příkopě 16, Nové Město (☎24 21 50 31; Mon–Fri 9am–6pm, Sat 9am–4pm, Sun 10am–3pm). Ticket **prices**, with a few notable exceptions, are still extremely cheap, ranging from 250–500Kč. Lastly, don't despair if everything is officially sold out (*vyprodáno*), as stand-by tickets are often available at the venue's box office on the night.

By far the biggest annual event is the *Pražské jaro* (Prague Spring), the country's most prestigious **international music festival**. It traditionally begins on May 12, the anniversary of Smetana's death, with a performance of *Má vlast*, and finishes on June 2 with a rendition of Beethoven's *Ninth Symphony*. Tickets for the festival sell out fast – try your luck by writing, a month before the festival begins, to the Prague Spring Festival box office at Hellichova 18, Malá Strana; *festival@login.cz*. The main venues are listed below, but keep an eye out for concerts in the city's churches and palaces, gardens and courtyards; note that evening performances tend to start fairly early, either at 5 or 7pm.

The main opera houses and concert halls

Národní divadlo (National Theatre), Národní 2, Nové Město (☎24 91 34 37); metro Národní třída. Prague's grandest nineteenth-century theatre is the living embodiment of the Czech national revival movement, and continues to put on a wide variety of mostly, though by no means exclusively, Czech plays, opera and ballet. Worth visiting for the decor alone. Box office Mon–Fri 10am–6pm, Sat & Sun 10am–12.30pm & 3–6pm.

Rudolfinum, Alšovo nábřeží 12, Staré Město (☎24 89 31 11); metro Staroměstská. A truly stunning neo-Renaissance concert hall from the late nineteenth century, and home base for the Czech Philharmonic. The Dvořákova síň is the large hall; the Sukova síň is the chamber concert hall. Box office open Mon–Fri 10am–12.30pm & 1.30–6pm, plus an hour before the preformance

Smetanova síň, Obecní dům, náměstí Republiky 5, Nové Město; metro náměstí Republiky. Fantastically ornate and recently renovated Art Nouveau concert hall which usually kicks off the Prague Spring festival, and is home to the excellent Prague Symphony Orchestra. Box office open Mon–Fri 10am–12.30pm & 1.30–6pm.

Státní opera (State Opera), Wilsonova 4, Nové Město (☎24 22 76 93); metro Muzeum. A sumptuous nineteenth-century opera house built by the city's German community, and now the number-two venue for opera, with a repertoire that tends to rely on the Italian classics. Box office Mon–Fri 10am–5.30pm, Sat & Sun 10am–noon & 1–5.30pm.

Stavovské divadlo (Estates Theatre), Ovocný trh 1, Staré Město (☎24 21 50 01); metro Můstek. Prague's oldest opera house, which witnessed the premiere of *Don Giovanni*, puts on a mixture of opera, ballet and straight theatre (with simultaneous headphone translation available). Box office Mon–Fri 10am–6pm, Sat & Sun 10am–12.30pm & 3–6pm.

Other concert venues

Anežký klášter (Convent of sv Anežka), U milosrdných 17, Staré Město; ☎24 81 08 35; metro náměstí Republiky. Regular Czech chamber concerts, often of the big four Czech composers, are given in the convent's atmospheric Gothic chapel (see p.86).

Basilika sv Jakuba, Malá Štupartská, Staré Město; metro náměstí Republiky. Choral church music, sung Mass and Prague's finest organ used for regular recitals (see p.86).

Bertramka, Mozartova 169, Smíchov; ☎54 38 93; metro Anděl. Occasional concerts given at the Mozart Museum, mostly though not entirely of the composer's own music.

Dům U kamenného zvonu (House at the Stone Bell), Staroměstské náměstí 13, Staré Město (☎24 81 00 36); metro Staroměstská. An adventurous programme of modern and classical concerts is staged in this contemporary art gallery, housed in an old building on Old Town Square (see p.83).

Lichtenštejnský palác (Liechtenstein Palace), Malostranské náměstí, Malá Strana; metro Malostranská. The university music department lives here and puts on mostly Baroque music by chamber orchestras and string quartets.

Nostický palác (Nostitz Palace), Maltézské náměstí 1, Malá Strana; metro Malostranská. Chamber concerts here start at the civilized hour of 8pm, and include a glass of wine as part of the ticket price

Zrcadlová kaple, Klemintinum, Mariánské náměstí, Staré Město; metro Staroměstská. Regular chamber concerts held in the ornate, pink Baroque Mirrored Chapel.

Theatres

Archa, Na poříčí 26, Nové Město (☎232 88 00); metro Florenc. By far the most innovative venue in Prague, with two very versatile spaces, an art gallery and a café. The programming includes music, dance and theatre with an emphasis on the avant-garde. Box office Mon–Fri 10am–6pm.

Divadlo Alfred ve dvoře, Fr. Křížka 36, Holešovice; ☎20 57 15 84; metro Vltavská. Experimental theatre run by mime theatre guru, Ctibor Turba, and an occasional student drama venue. Box office open from 5pm on the day of performance.

Divadlo minor, Senovážné náměstí 28, Nové Město (☎24 21 96 75); metro náměstí Republiky. The former state puppet theatre puts on children's puppet shows most days, plus adult shows on occasional evenings – sometimes with English subtitles. Box office open Mon–Fri 2–5pm and one hour before performance.

Divadlo na Klárově, nábřeží Edvarda Beneša 3, Malá Strana; ☎53 98 37; metro Malostranská. This is a good place to catch traditional Czech folk songs and dancing. Shows begin at 7.30pm.

Divadlo v Celetné, Celetná 17, Staré Město (☎232 68 43); metro náměstí Republiky. Home of several fringe companies (including an English-language one), and a student drama venue, which puts on tourist-friendly productions (occasionally puppetry and černé divadlo). Box office daily 9am–midnight.

Duncan Centre, Branická 41, Braník; ☎44 46 18 10; tram #3, #16, #17 or #21, stop Přístaviště. Interesting dance pieces by resident and visiting artists at this dance theatre based in a school for contemporary dance in the southern suburb of Braník. Tickets from Ticketpro.

Laterna magika (Magic Lantern), Nová scéna, Národní 4, Nové Město (☎24 91 41 29); metro Národní třída. The National Theatre's *Nová scéna*, one of Prague's most modern and versatile stages, is now the main base for Laterna magika, founders of multimedia theatre way back in 1958, now content just to pull in crowds of tourists. Box office Mon–Fri 10am–8pm, Sat & Sun 3–8pm.

Ta Fantastika, Karlova 8, Staré Město (☎24 22 90 78); metro Staroměstská. Probably the best of the "black theatre" venues, albeit strategically located close to the Charles Bridge, offering dialogue-free shows specifically aimed at tourists. Box office daily 11am–9pm.

Film

Cinema Broadway, Na příkopě 31, Nové Město; ☎21 61 32 78; metro náměstí Republiky. The second largest screen in the city, and the best sound system, Broadway is the most central of Prague's newly refurbished cinemas and shows mainstream films.

Dlabačov, Bělohorská 24, Břevnov (☎33 35 90 58); tram #22 from metro Malostranská. Excellent film club (membership 20Kč) on the ground floor of the *Hotel Pyramid*, showing a discerning selection of new releases and plenty of other art-house classics.

Jalta, Václavské náměstí 43, Nové Město (☎24 22 88 14); metro Můstek. Two screens here, including one of the few *kinokavárna* left in Prague, where you can have a drink and a smoke while you watch the film.

Lucerna, Vodičkova, Nové Město (☎24 21 69 72); metro Můstek/Muzeum. Without doubt the most ornate film theatre in Prague, decked out in Moorish style by Havel's grandfather.

MAT, Karlovo náměstí 19, Nové Město (☎24 91 57 65); metro Karlovo náměstí. Café and cinema popular with the film crowd, with an eclectic programme of shorts, documentaries and full-length features.

Ponrepo – Bio Konvikt, Bartolomějská 11, Staré Město; metro Národní třída. Really old classics from the black-and-white era, dug out from the National Film Archives. Membership cards (150Kč) can only be bought Mon–Fri 2–5pm.

Sport

Prague is a great place to catch live **sports** action, especially soccer and ice hockey. The quality is not always the highest, but, somewhat unbelievably, you can still drink inexpensive and delicious beer on the terraces.

Soccer

The most successful club in the country is **Sparta Praha**, who won eight league titles in the 1990s, and look set to maintain their hold over Czech football for some time to come. That said, in 1996, they had to endure the embarassment of being saved from bankruptcy by the Slovak steelworks VSŽ Košice, and are currently owned by a German publishing group. They play at the country's finest, and newly renovated, Sparta stadium, by the Letná plain (five minutes' walk from metro Hradčanská); international matches are also regularly played there. Sparta's closest rivals, **Slavia Praha**, majority-owned by a British investment firm, won the league title in 1996 for the first time in nearly fifty years. It has not, however, heralded a new dawn for Slavia, who remain second best to Sparta. Their ground, optimistically called Eden, is on Vladivostocká in Vršovice, just off U Slavie (tram #4 or #22 from metro náměstí Míru). **Viktoria Žižkov**, based in the traditionally working-class district of Prague 3, enjoyed a brief period of glory when they won the Czech cup in 1994. Sadly, the man who helped get them there, Vratislav Čekan, was forced to pull out in 1996 after a financial scandal. Viktoria's ground is on Seifertova (tram #5, #9 or #26 from metro Hlavní nádraží). **Tickets** for all matches are extremely cheap and can be bought at the ground on match day (even Sparta have only sold out twice in the last twenty-odd years). The season runs from August to late November and from late February to early June, and matches are usually held on a Sunday.

Ice hockey

Ice hockey runs a close second as the nation's most popular sport. Unlike in football, **Sparta Praha** are only one of a number of successful teams, and the *Extraliga* is usually hotly contested. Sparta's *zimní stadión* (winter stadium) is next door to the Výstaviště exhibition grounds in Holešovice (metro nádraží Holešovice). Prague's only other first division team are **Slavia Praha**, who play at the *zimní stadión* to the south of the Havlíčkovy sady in Vršovice (tram #4 or #22 from metro náměstí Míru). **Tickets** can be bought from the stadium on match day and, again, cost very little. Matches are fast and physical, and can last anything up to three hours; they take place at the weekend.

Horse racing

Prague's main racecourse is at **Velká Chuchle**, 5km or so south of the city centre; bus #129, #172, #241, #244, or *osobní* train from metro Smíchovské nádraží. Steeplechases and hurdles take place on Tuesday and Sunday afternoons from May to October. There are also less frequent races at a smaller trot course on **Cisářský ostrov** (May–Oct only); walk through the Stromovka park and across the river to the island from metro Nádraží Holešovice.

Listings

Airlines Austrian Airlines, Revoluční 15, Nové Město; ☎231 18 72 British Airways, Ovocný trh 8, Staré Město; ☎22 11 44 44; metro Můstek. British Midland, Washingtonova 17, Nové Město; ☎24 23 92 80; metro Muzeum. Czech Airlines (ČSA), V celnici 5, Nové Město; ☎20 10 43 10; metro náměstí Republiky. Delta, Národní 32, Nové Město; ☎24 23 22 58; metro Národní třída. KLM, Na příkopě 13 37, Nové Město; ☎24 21 69 50; metro Můstek. Lufthansa, Pařížská 28, Staré Město; ☎24 81 10 07; metro Staroměstská.

American Express, Amex, Václavské náměstí 56, Nové Město; ☎24 22 98 83; metro Muzeum. May–Sept Mon–Fri 9am–6pm, Sat 9am–2pm; Oct–April Mon–Fri 9am–5pm, Sat 9am–noon; exchange office daily 9am–7pm.

Books The Globe, Janovského 14, Holešovice (daily 10am–midnight); tram #5 or #26 from metro náměstí Republiky: superbly well-stocked, ramshackle expat bookstore cum social centre, with adjacent café and friendly staff.

Cultural centres Austrian Cultural Institute, Jungmannovo náměstí 18, Nové Město; British Council, Národní 10, Nové Město; Goethe Institut, Masarykovo nábřeží 32, Nové Město; Hungarian Cultural Centre, Rytířská 25, Staré Město; Institut Français, Štěpánská 35, Nové Město; Polish Institute, Václavské náměstí 51, Nové Město.

Dentists Vladislavova 22, Nové Město (☎24 22 76 63; Mon–Thurs 7pm–7am; Fri–Sun 24hr).

Department stores Bílá labuť, Na poříčí 23, Nové Město; Kotva, náměstí Republiky 8, Nové Město; Tesco, Národní 26, Nové Město.

Embassies/consulates Australia, Na Ořechovce 38, Břevnov; (☎24 31 07 43); Britain, Thunovská 14, Malá Strana (☎57 32 03 55); Canada, Mickiewiczova 6, Hradčany (☎24 31 11 08); France, Velkopřevorské náměstí 2, Malá Strana (☎57 32 03 52); Germany, Vlašská 19 (☎57 32 01 90); Ireland, Tržiště 13, Malá Strana; (☎53 09 11); Poland, Valdštejnská 8, Malá Strana (☎57 32 06 78); Slovakia, Pod hradbami 1, Dejvice (☎32 05 21); USA, Tržiště 15, Malá Strana (☎57 32 06 63).

Exchange offices 24hr service at 28 píjna 13, Nové Město; metro Můstek.

Gay & Lesbian There is no great "scene" in Prague as such, but there are a few bars and clubs that have become an established part of Prague nightlife (see p.125) and even a gay-friendly hotel (see p.59). A good source of information is the *SOHO revue*, a monthly Czech gay magazine, with a brief section in English and some useful listings. Lambda, the first organization for Czech gays and lesbians which started up in 1989, is based at Krakovská 2, Nové Město; ☎73 92 76; metro Muzeum.

Health food Country Life, Melantrichova 15, Staré Město (Mon–Thurs 8am–7pm, Fri 8.30am–3pm, Sun 11am–6pm).

Hospitals For an English-speaking doctor, you should go to the private Nemocnice na Homolce, Roentgenova 2, Motol (☎52 92 11 11; bus #167 from metro Anděl). If it's an emergency, dial ☎155 for an ambulance and you'll be taken to the nearest hospital.

Laundries Laundry Kings, Dejvická 16, Dejvice (☎312 37 43); Laundryland, Londýnská 71, Vinohrady (☎25 11 24); both open daily 8am–10pm.

Markets Flea market at Pražská tržnice, Bubenské nábřeží, Holešovice (Mon–Fri 8am–6pm, Sat 8am–2pm; metro Vltava); food, flowers and sundry goods at Havelská, Staré Město (Mon–Fri 8am–6pm, Sat & Sun 9am–6pm; metro Můstek).

Pharmacies 24hr chemists at Belgická 37, Vinohrady; metro náměstí Míru (☎24 23 72 07).

Police Benediktská 6, Staré Město.

Post office Main office/poste restante at Jindřišská 14, Nové Město (limited 24hr service); parcels over 1kg at Plzeňská 139, Smíchov.

Records Bontonland Megastore, palác Koruna, Václavské náměstí 1; metro Můstek. Prague's biggest record store in the newly renovated *pasáž* at the bottom of Wenceslas Square, with rock, folk, jazz and classical, and headphones for pre-listening to boot. Mon–Sat 9am–8pm, Sun 10am–7pm.

Swimming Divoká Šárka, Vokovice; tram #20 or #26 from metro Dejvická. Idyllically located in a craggy valley to the northwest of Prague, with two small oudoor pools filled with cold but fresh and clean water – great for a full, hot day out. Food and drink and plenty of shade available, too. May–Oct daily 9am–7pm.

Thomas Cook Staroměstské náměstí 5, Staré Město; metro Staroměstská (☎24 81 71 73; Mon–Fri 9am–9pm, Sat 9am–4pm, Sun 10am–2pm).

AROUND PRAGUE

Few capital cities can boast such extensive unspoilt tracts of woodland so near at hand as Prague. Once you leave the half-built high-rise estates of the outer suburbs behind, the traditional, provincial feel of **Bohemia** (Čechy) immediately makes itself felt. Many towns and villages still huddle below the grand residences of their former lords, their street layouts little changed since medieval times.

To the north, several such chateaux grace the banks of the Vltava, including that of the wine-producing town of **Mělník**, on the Labe (Elbe) plain. Beyond Mělník lie the wooded gorges of the **Kokořínsko** region, too far for a day-trip unless you've your own transport, but perfect for a weekend in the country. One of the most obvious day-trip destinations is to the east of Prague: **Kutná Hora**, a medieval silver-mining town with one of the most beautiful Gothic cathedrals in the country and a macabre gallery of bones in the suburb of **Sedlec**.

Further south, there are a couple of chateaux worth visiting along the **Sázava valley**; while nearby, two more, **Průhonice** and **Konopiště**, are set in exceptionally beautiful and expansive grounds – with a car, you could take in several in a day. Southwest of Prague, a similar mix of woods and rolling hills surrounds the popular castle of **Karlštejn**, a gem of Gothic architecture, dramatically situated above the River Berounka. There are numerous possibilities for walking in the region around Karlštejn and, further upstream, in the forests of **Křivoklátsko**. West of Prague, near Kladno, there are two places of pilgrimage: **Lány** is the resting place of the founder of the modern Czechoslovak state and summer residence of the president; and **Lidice**, razed to the ground by the SS, recalls the horror of Nazi occupation.

Transport throughout Bohemia is fairly straightforward, thanks to a comprehensive network of railway lines and regional bus services, though connections can be less than smooth and journeys slow. However, if you're planning to see a few places outside Prague, or one of the destinations more difficult to reach, it might be worth hiring a car.

North along the Vltava

One of the quickest and most rewarding trips out of the capital is to follow the Vltava as it twists northwards across the plain towards the River Labe at Mělník. This is the beginning of the so-called **záhrada Čech** (Garden of Bohemia), a flat and fertile region whose cherry blossoms are always the first to herald the Bohemian spring and whose roads in summer are lined with stalls overflowing with fruit and vegetables. But the real reason to venture into this relatively flat landscape is to visit the **chateaux** that lie along the banks of the river, all easily reached by train from Prague's Masarykovo nádraží (with a possible change at Kralupy).

Beyond Kralupy

The Nobel prize-winning poet Jaroslav Seifert didn't beat around the bush when he wrote that **KRALUPY NAD VLTAVOU** "is not a beautiful town and never was". Seifert had happy childhood memories of the place, but it was heavily bombed in World War II, and postwar industrial development left it with "smokestacks . . . like phantom trees, without branches, without leaves, without blossoms, without bees". Now, Kralupy's oil refineries and chemical plants have spread across both sides of the river, but it's still worth making the thirty-minute train journey from Prague, as just a few kilometres to the north, on either side of the Vltava, are two fine chateaux: Nelahozeves on the left bank and Veltrusy on the right – again, both accessible by train.

Nelahozeves

Shortly after pulling out of Kralupy, the train passes through a short tunnel and comes to rest at Nelahozeves zastávka, the first of two stations in the village of **NELA-HOZEVES**. Above the railway sits the village's monumentally large **zámek** (Tues–Sun 9am–6pm), built in the 1550s by Italian builders for one of the lackeys of the Habsburg Ferdinand I, and totally smothered in sgraffito. In the early 1990s, the chateau was returned to the Lobkowicz family, who bought the place way back in 1623, and it's now enjoying a new lease of life.

The interior is well worth a visit, having been restored and replenished with paintings given back to the family since 1989. There's a choice of tours, and often the possibility of paying extra for an English-speaking guide, but since the family's vast **art collection** is one of the highlights, there seems little point in opting for the half-hour tour (trasa 2), which skips the European masters, rather than the hour-long tour (trasa 1). Only the most exceptional works are on display, among them, Pieter Bruegel the Elder's sublime *Haymaking* from the artist's famous cycle of seasons, a view of St Paul's Cathedral across the Thames by Canaletto, and a portrait of the Infanta Margarita Teresa (possibly by Velázquez), who was betrothed to her uncle the emperor Leopold I from the age of three. The family also has a long history of musical patronage (most notably Beethoven) and the musical scores on show are pretty impressive, while the family library's prize possession is a Gutenberg Bible.

The other reason for stopping at Nelahozeves is that **Antonín Dvořák** (1841–1904) was born and bred under the shadow of the chateau, at the house (no. 12) next door to the post office. Dvořák was originally apprenticed to a butcher but, on the recommendation of his schoolmaster, was sent to the Prague Organ School instead. He went on to become director of the Prague conservatoire and by far the country's most famous composer. If there's someone around at the house (Tues–Thurs, Sat & Sun 9am–noon & 2–5pm, Fri 9am–noon), you can have a quick look at the great man's rocking chair and various other personal effects.

Veltrusy

The industrial suburbs of Kralupy stop just short of the gardens of the zámek of **Veltrusy** (May–Sept Tues–Sun 8am–noon & 1–5pm). The classic Baroque symmetry of the chateau is altogether more hospitable than the one at Nelahozeves, its green shutters and four hennaed wings pivoting round a bulbous, green-domed building that recalls earlier country houses in France or Italy. It was built in the early eighteenth century as a plaything for the upwardly mobile Chotek family, its 290 acres of surrounding woodland perfect for a little light hunting. It was also the unlikely venue for the world's first trade fair, which took place in 1754 under the title "The Veltrusy Large Trade Fair of Products of the Czech Kingdom", and drew a distinguished audience including the empress Maria Theresa.

Once again, there's a choice of **guided tours**, both lasting half an hour: Trasa 1 concentrates almost exclusively on the period furniture, while trasa 2 intersperses period interiors with a lot of porcelain and a peek at the library. Don't whatever you do, miss out on the **Zámecký park**, as the Choteks were keen gardeners, and the grounds are liberally dotted with fallow deer and follies. To get to the chateau from the train station at Nelahozeves (one stop on from Nelahozeves zastávka), it's a 1.5km walk across the busy road bridge, or the smaller bridge further south. There are also regular buses to Veltrusy from Prague's Florenc bus station.

Practicalities

If you fancy staying, there are several houses also offering inexpensive **private rooms** on the road to Veltrusy, and just outside the chateau grounds, there's a very good **campsite**, *ATC Obora* (Feb–Dec). It's a great spot for watching the barges on the Vltava, but, given the pollutants that pour into the river further upstream, no place for a dip. There are a couple of pubs in Nelahozeves, but the nicest place to **eat** is the *Zámecký restaurace* in the courtyard of Nelahozeves zámek, where you can quaff Lobkowicz wine or beer with your meal.

Mělník

Occupying a spectacular, commanding site at the confluence of the Vltava and Labe rivers, **MĚLNÍK**, 33km north of Prague on route 9, lies at the heart of Bohemia's tiny wine-growing region. The town's history goes back to the ninth century, when it was handed over to the Přemyslids as part of Ludmila's dowry on her marriage to Prince Bořivoj (see p.484). And it was here, too, that she introduced her heathen grandson, Václav (later to become Saint Wenceslas, aka "Good King"; see p.67), to the joys of Christianity. Viticulture became the town's economic mainstay only after Charles IV, aching for a little of the French wine of his youth, introduced grapes from Burgundy (over which he also ruled).

The old town

Mělník's greatest monument is its Renaissance **zámek** (daily March–Dec 10am–5pm), perched high above the flat plains and visible for miles around. The present building, its courtyard covered in familiar sgraffito patterns, is back in the hands of its last aristocratic owners, the Lobkowicz family, who have restored the chateau's magnificently proportioned rooms, which also provide great views out over the plain. Visits are by guided tour only, and you've a choice between a half-hour trawl round seven beautifully painted rooms of the castle interior, filled with artefacts and Old Masters returned to the family since 1989, or touring the wine museum in the cellars, finishing up with free samples of plonk; alternatively you can do both tours. In addition, there's a museum of prams, strollers and baby carriages which forms part of the local museum (April–Oct Tues–Sun 9am–5pm) on the first floor of the chateau.

Below the chateau, vines cling to the south-facing terraces, as the land plunges into the river below. From beneath the great tower of Mělník's onion-domed church of **sv Petr and Pavel**, next door to the chateau, there's an even better view of the rivers' confluence and the subsidiary canal, once so congested with vessels that traffic lights had to be introduced. The church itself contains a compellingly macabre **ossuary** or *kostnice* (Tues–Sun 10.30am–4pm), filled with over 10,000 bones of medieval plague victims, fashioned into weird and wonderful shapes by students around a hundred years ago.

The rest of the old town is pleasant enough for a casual stroll. One half of the main square, **náměstí Míru**, is lined with Baroque arcades typical of the region, and there's an old medieval gateway nearby, the **Pražská brána**, which has been converted into an art gallery.

Practicalities

The main line from Prague veers northwest beyond Nelahozeves, which means there are only one or two (very) slow, stopping direct **trains** to Mělník. It's easy enough, however, to take a fast train from Prague's Hlavní nádraží to Všetaty, and change, getting you to Mělník in around an hour. There's a regular **bus** service from Prague, too, which takes around fifty minutes. To reach the older part of town from the **bus station**, simply head up Krombholcova in the direction of the big church tower. If your next destination is Liběchov or Litoměřice, you have the choice of either the bus or the train; the **train station** is further still from the old town, a couple of blocks northeast of the bus station, down Jiřího z Poděbrad.

The tourist office is on náměstí Míru, and can help with accommodation, if you're hoping to stay over. There are **private rooms** available on Legionářů, to the north of the old town, and on Palackého náměstí, off the main square, and the relatively plush *Hotel Jaro*, 17 listopadu 174 (☎0206/62 68 52; ⑥), or the *Penzion V podzámčí*, J. Seiferta 167 (☎0206/62 28 89; ③), both situated in the shadow of the chateau to the south. The nearest **campsite** (open all year except Christmas & New Year) is around 750m north of the old town, on Klášterní (a continuation of Fügnerova).

As for **food and drink**, the *Zámecká restaurace* is as good (and cheap) a place as any to sample some of the local wine (and enjoy the view): the red Ludmila is the most famous of Mělník's wines, and there's even a rare Czech rosé produced by the castle vineyards, but if you prefer white, try a bottle of Tramín. Equally good views can be had from *Stará škola* restaurant, behind the church; otherwise, you could try *Na hradbách*, on náměstí Míru, which serves up big portions and local wines, plus Guinness and Kilkenny, in a cosy brick and wood-panelled interior.

Liběchov

Seven kilometres north and ten minutes by train from Mělník – just out of sight of the giant coal-fired power station that provides most of Prague's electricity – is the rhubarb-and-custard-coloured **zámek** (Tues–Sun 9am–5pm) at **LIBĚCHOV** (Liboch). Even without the sickly colour scheme, it's a bizarre place: formal and two-dimensional when viewed from the French gardens at the front, but bulging like an amphitheatre around the back by the entrance. Inside is another surprise, a **Museum of Asian and Oriental Cultures**, based around the collections of Czech explorer Vojta Náprstek and featuring endless Buddhas, Mongolian printing equipment, Balinese monster gear and Javanese puppets – all of which make for a fascinating half-hour tour. The main dining hall, now full of Asian musical instruments, is curious, too, smothered in its original barley-sugar decor with little sculpted jesters crouching mischievously in the corners of the ceiling.

For all the chateau's excesses, the **village** itself is little more than a *hostinec* (pub) and a bend in the road, but straggling up the valley are the remains of what was once an attractive spa resort for ailing Praguers. Many of the old *Gasthäuser* are still standing, including the *Pension Stüdl* where **Franz Kafka** spent the winter of 1918. It was here that he met and became engaged to Julie Wohryzek, daughter of a Jewish shoemaker from Prague – a match vigorously opposed by his father. Kafka was prompted to write his vitriolic *Letter to His Father*, which he passed on to his mother, who wisely made sure it never got any further. On the other side of the trickling River Liběchovka, there's a **campsite** (mid-May to mid-Sept), a possible starting point for hikes into the Kokořín region (see opposite).

Kokořínsko

Northeast of Mělník, you leave the low plains of the Labe for a plateau region known as **Kokořínsko**, a hidden pocket of wooded hills which takes its name from the Gothic castle rising through the treetops at its centre. The sandstone plateau has weathered over the millennia to form sunken valleys and bizarre rocky outcrops, providing great scope for some gentle hiking. With picturesque valleys, such as the Kokořínský důl, dotted with well-preserved, half-timbered villages and riddled with marked paths, it comes as a surprise that the whole area isn't buzzing all summer.

At the centre of the region is the village of **KOKOŘÍN**, whose dramatic setting and spectacular fourteenth-century **hrad** (April & Oct Sat & Sun 9am–4pm; May–Sept Tues–Sun 9am–5pm) greatly inspired the Czech nineteenth-century Romantics. The castle is a perfect hideaway, ideal for the robbers who used it as a base after it fell into disrepair in the sixteenth century. Not until the end of the nineteenth century did it get a new lease of life, from a jumped-up local landowner, Václav Špaček, who bought himself a title and refurbished the place as a family memorial. There's precious little inside and no incentive to endure the guided tour, as you can explore the ramparts and climb the tallest tower on your own.

If you've got your own transport, Kokořínsko makes a pleasant day-trip from Prague. For those using public transport, there's one direct **bus** a week from Prague's Praha-Holešovice bus station (leaving at around 4.20pm on a Friday); otherwise, take the regular buses to Mělník and change there. Alternatively, you could catch the local train from Mělník to Mšeno, from where it's a three-kilometre walk west to Kokořín on the green-marked path. Finding **accommodation** shouldn't be too much of a problem, with plenty of private rooms available in Kokořín, and Kanina 2km further east, plus a decent pension *Myslivna* (☎0206/69 50 36; ④), and a cluster of **campsites** (May–Oct) at Kokořínský důl, a couple of kilometres down the valley.

East of Prague

The scenery **east of Prague** is as flat as it is around Mělník, a rich blanket of fields spreading over the plain as far as the eye can see. Two places you might consider heading for are **Mladá Boleslav**, where Škoda cars are produced, and **Přerov nad Labem**, an open-air museum of the kind of folk architecture that was common in Bohemia less than a century ago. **Poděbrady** and **Kolín** are not likely to be high on most people's itineraries, but make convenient stop-off points when heading east.

Přerov nad Labem

The **open-air museum** (April–Oct & Dec Tues–Sun 9am–5pm) of folk architecture at the village of **PŘEROV NAD LABEM** was the first of its kind in central Europe when it was founded in 1895 (it is called a *skansen*, after the first such museum founded in a Stockholm suburb in 1891). Later, in the 1950s and 1960s, skansens became quite a fad, as collectivization and urbanization wiped out traditional rural communities, along with their distinctive folk culture and wooden architecture. During the summer, Přerov's skansen is busy with tour groups from Prague, wandering through the various half-timbered and stone buildings, some brought here plank by plank from nearby villages, some from Přerov itself. Particularly evocative is the reconstructed eighteenth-century village school, with a portrait of the Austrian emperor taking pride of place amid the Catholic icons, and a delicate paper theatre that was used in drama lessons.

To get to the village, you can take a **train** from Praha hlavní nádraží to Čelákovice, and transfer to a bus. Alternatively, take one of the slow **buses** from Prague's Palmovka bus station to Poděbrady and get off at the crossroads just after the turn-off to Mochov

– the village of Přerov is a kilometre's walk north. If you're driving, the village is around 25km east of Prague (take exit 18 off the E67 at Bříství and follow the signs).

Mladá Boleslav

Fast trains from Praha hlavní nádraží take an hour to reach **MLADÁ BOLESLAV** (Jungblunzau), 30km or so northeast of Prague on the E65, where Václav Laurin and Václav Klement set up a bicycle factory in the mid-nineteenth century. They went on to produce the country's first car in 1905, and in the 1920s merged with the Škoda industrial empire. Škoda Auto, as the company is now known, is now the largest employer in the republic, and is entirely separate from the heavy engineering arm of the Škoda empire, which is based in Plzeň (see p.188).

The main reason for coming here is to visit the **Škoda Museum** (daily 9am–5pm), which exhibits over 25 old Škodas and Laurin & Klements in its showroom. The exhibition starts off, as the factory itself did, with an L & K bicycle and a couple of motorbikes. There are also several vintage vehicles and a 1917 fire engine, but the vast majority of the cars date from the 1920s and 1930s – big, mostly black, gangster-style motors. The museum is on třída Václava Klementa, northeast of the town centre and badly signposted. Diagonally opposite the museum, and handy for orientation, is a park with a palatial neo-Baroque *Gymnasium* at the far end. Close by, there's a wonderfully provincial Art Nouveau theatre from 1912, brightly painted in white, gold and blue.

The **staré město** lies to the east of the River Jizera, in a tight bend of one of its tributaries, the Klenice. It has little going for it besides its pristinely painted Renaissance **radnice** and the Gothic **hrad** tucked into the southernmost part of town, used as a barracks by the Habsburgs and now home to the local museum (Tues–Sun: May–Sept 9am–noon & 1–5pm; Oct, Nov & Jan–April closes 4pm). However, if you're looking for somewhere to **eat**, the *Jihočeská hostinec*, beside the castle entrance, has a big fish restaurant adjacent to it, called the *Rybářská restaurace* (closed Sat), with an amazing menu that includes pike, eel and plaice. Your best bet for **accommodation** is the pension *Zlatý kohout* (☎0326/72 19 37; ⑦) opposite the radnice. The nearest **campsite**, *Škoda* (May–Sept), is 2km north of town in the suburb of Kosmonosy.

Poděbrady

If spa towns evoke turn-of-the-century hotels, then **PODĚBRADY** will come as something of a disappointment. The spa waters were actually only discovered this century,

---

THE STORY OF ŠKODA

For Czechs, the **Škoda industrial empire** is a great Czech achievement and a source of national pride. It's therefore doubly ironic that the word *škoda* means "shame" or "pity" in Czech – a marketing own-goal were it not the name of the founding father of the Czech car industry, **Emil Škoda**. The last Škoda model produced under the Communists was very favourably received, even in the West (whence a large proportion of its components derived). In 1989, there was a three-year waiting list for the car, despite a retail price equivalent to over twice the average yearly salary. Then in 1991, in one of the many controversial deals in the country's privatization programme, the German company Volkswagen bought a majority stake in Škoda for a song. The Czechs may not feel quite the same way about the company since the VW takeover, but the new models brought out under VW guidance have vastly improved the international image of Škoda Auto. The company has gone from strength to strength, and is currently building a huge new car plant in Mladá Boleslav itself.

with the town's previous existence simply due to its strategic position on the east–west trade routes. However, the **spa** itself is pleasant enough, attracting thousands of patients every year, most of whom can be seen promenading through the town's park around teatime, admiring the fully functioning floral clock. For a glimpse of the town's halcyon days in the last years of the Empire, check out the local **Polabské muzeum** at Palackého 68 (Tues–Sun 9am–5pm).

Facing onto the main square, **Jiřího náměstí**, is the **zámek** (May–Oct Tues–Sun 9am–5pm), birthplace of the town's most famous son, **George of Poděbrady** (Jiří z Poděbrad to the Czechs), the only Hussite (and last Czech) king of Bohemia. The present structure was actually built a hundred years after his death and houses only the minutest of historical exhibitions. The only other trace of George is the green copper equestrian statue in the main square.

Poděbrady does provide a convenient stop on the road heading east from Prague, and is less than an hour by train from the city. To get to the main square and castle from the train station, simply walk south through the park of náměstí T.G. Masaryka. Furthermore, Poděbrady has a wide choice of **hotels**: the *G-Rex* (☎0324/43 30; *lazne@podebrady.cz*; ⑦), situated between the main square and the park on Divadelní, looks tackily modern from the outside, but is pleasant enough inside; another option is the *Bellevue – Tlapák*, overlooking the park on náměstí T.G. Masaryka (☎0324/734 83; *hotel@bellevue.cz*; ⑧), or the *Soudek* on Palackého (☎0324/31 91; ⑤). Alternatively, there's a **campsite**, *Golf* (April–Oct), a little further upstream from the castle.

With visitors of one kind or another all summer, there's a fair selection of films and classical concerts on offer, as well as some rather exotic **eating** options: the *Klub Netopýr* in the castle courtyard, for inexpensive Czech food; *Bašta U krále Jiřího*, on the main square, for Radegast beer; or, for something different, try the Chinese food at the nearby *Savoy*, or dinner aboard the *Král Jiří*, moored by the castle.

Kolín

In addition to its railway sidings and industrial plants, **KOLÍN** – 16km south of Poděbrady along the Labe – has actually managed to preserve its central medieval core. One of numerous towns in Bohemia founded by German colonists in the thirteenth century, its streets are laid out in chessboard fashion, so finding the cobbled main square, Karlovo náměstí, should present few problems. There's a wonderfully imposing Renaissance **radnice**, covered in sgraffito and decorated with four rose-coloured panels from the last century, and four unusual Baroque gables on the west side, but the rest of the square is unspectacular.

Kolín's most significant monument is actually tucked away in the southeast corner of the old town. On raised ground at the end of Karlova, on a rather cramped site, stands the Gothic church of **sv Bartoloměj** (St Bartholomew), begun in 1261. The church's fairly gloomy nave is suffused with an unusually intense blue light from the modern stained-glass windows, which disturbs the otherwise resolutely medieval ambience. But it's the choir, rebuilt and extended in the fourteenth century by Peter Parler, which provides the highlight, taking up almost half the church with its seven chapels, intricate tracery and spectacular ribbed vaulting.

Like many towns in Bohemia and Moravia, Kolín had a significant **Jewish community**, which was subsequently all but wiped out in the Holocaust. The ghetto was situated in the southwest corner of the old town, in what is now Na Hradbach and Karoliny Světlé, and is now slowly being restored. There's a plaque commemorating the 2200 Jews deported during the Holocaust at Na Hradbach 157. If the door is open, you can walk through to the seventeenth-century **synagogue**, hidden in the rear courtyard. The delicate stuccoed interior has been restored for use as a concert hall; to gain entry, ask at the **tourist office** (Mon–Fri 10am–noon & 1–3pm, Sat 10am–3pm), which is situated in the adjacent building.

Fans of the turn-of-the-century sculpture of František Bílek should check out his **statue of Jan Hus**, which is hidden behind the Hussite church in the town park. Though slightly weathered, it's an impressive, and typically expressive, piece of work, rising a good three metres off the ground. To get there, head west down Kutnohorská, turn right into Smetanova, then right again for the park.

If you need **to stay overnight**, there's the *Hotel Theresia*, Na Petříně (☎0321/71 11 17; ⑦), on a busy road west of the old town, or two excellent pensions in the old town itself, both with equally commendable restaurants: *Pension pod věží*, Parléřova 40 (☎0321/72 38 77; ⑤), or *U rabína*, on Karoliny Světlé (☎0321/72 44 63; ⑤). Kolín also happens to be closely associated with **František Kmoch** (1848–1912), king of Bohemian oom-pah-pah music, and every year, on the last weekend of June, a brass band festival is held in the town in his honour, featuring a wide range of music from Kmoch to Dvořák and a huge parade of bands from all over the country.

Kutná Hora

For 250 years or so, **KUTNÁ HORA** (Kuttenberg) was one of the most important towns in Bohemia, second only to Prague. At the end of the fourteenth century its population was equal to that of London, its shantytown suburbs straggled across what are now green fields, and its ambitious building projects set out to rival those of the capital itself. Today, Kutná Hora is a small provincial town with a population of just over 20,000, but the monuments dotted around it, the superb Gothic cathedral, and the remarkable monastery and ossuary in the suburb of **Sedlec**, make it one of the most enjoyable of all possible day-trips from Prague. In addition to the new influx of tourists, Kutná Hora has also benefited from a large injection of cash from the American tobacco giants Phillip Morris, who now run the local tobacco factory as a joint venture.

A brief history

Kutná Hora's road to prosperity began in the late thirteenth century with the discovery of **silver deposits** in the surrounding area. German miners were invited to settle and work the seams, and around 1300 Václav II founded the royal mint here, importing Italian craftsmen to run it. Much of the town's wealth was used to fund the beautification of Prague, but it also allowed for the construction of one of the most magnificent churches in central Europe and a number of other prestigious Gothic monuments in Kutná Hora itself.

At the time of the Hussite Wars, the town was mostly German-speaking and staunchly Catholic; local miners used to throw captured Hussites into the deep mine shafts and leave them to die of starvation. Word got out, and the town was besieged and eventually taken by Žižka's fanatical Táborites in 1421, only to be recaptured by Emperor Sigismund and his papal forces shortly afterwards, and again by Žižka the following year.

While the silver stocks remained high, the town was able to recover some of its former prosperity, but cheap imports of Spanish silver from South America caused a collapse in the price of silver during the sixteenth century. By the end of the century the mines had dried up, and Kutná Hora's wealth and importance came to an abrupt end – when the Swedes marched on the town during the Thirty Years' War, they had to be bought off with beer rather than silver. The town never fully recovered, shrivelling to less than a third of its former size, its fate emphatically sealed by a devastating fire in 1770.

Sedlec & Main Train Station (2 km)

Kutná Hora město station (200 m)

The Town

The small, unassuming houses that line the town's medieval lanes and main square, **Palackého náměstí**, give little idea of its former glories. A narrow alleyway on the south side of the square, however, leads to the leafy Havličkovo náměstí, on which lies the **Vlašský dvůr** (Italian Court), originally conceived as a palace by Václav II, and for three centuries the town's bottomless purse. It was here that Florentine minters produced the Prague Groschen (*pražské groše*), a silver coin widely used throughout central Europe until the nineteenth century. The building itself has been mucked about with over the years, most recently – and most brutally – by nineteenth-century restorers, who left only the chestnut trees, a fourteenth-century oriel window (capped by an unlikely looking wooden onion dome) and the miner's fountain unmolested. The original workshops of the minters have been bricked in, but the outlines of their little doors and windows are still visible in the courtyard. The short **guided tour** (daily: April & Oct 10am–5pm; May–Sept 9am–6pm; Nov–April 10am–4pm) of the old chapel, treasury and royal palace gives you a fair idea of the building's former importance.

Outside the court is a statue of the country's founder and first president, **T.G. Masaryk**; twice removed – once by the Nazis and once by the Communists – it has now been returned to its pride of place. Before you leave, take a quick look in the court gardens, which descend in steps to the Vrchlice Valley. This is undoubtedly Kutná Hora's best profile, with a splendid view over to the Cathedral of sv Barbora (see below).

Behind the Vlašský dvůr is **sv Jakub** (St James), the town's oldest church, begun a generation or so after the discovery of the silver deposits. Its grand scale is a clear indication of the town's quite considerable wealth by the time of the fourteenth century, though in terms of artistry it pales in comparison with Kutná Hora's other ecclesiastical buildings. The leaning tower is a reminder of the precarious position of the town, the church's foundations prone to subsidence from the disused mines below. If you want to see some of these, head for the **Hrádek**, an old fort which was used as a second mint and now serves as a **Mining Museum** (Muzeum a středověké důlní dílo; April–Oct Tues–Sun 9am–5pm; Nov–March Tues–Fri 9am–4pm). Here you can pick up a white coat, miner's helmet and torch, and visit some of the medieval mines that were discovered beneath the fort in the 1960s.

The Cathedral of sv Barbora

Kutná Hora's **Cathedral of sv Barbora** (Tues–Sun: April & Oct 9–11.30am & 1–3.30pm; May–Sept 9am–5.30pm; Nov–March 9–11.30am & 2–3.30pm) is arguably the most spectacular and moving ecclesiastical building in central Europe. Not to be outdone by the great monastery at Sedlec (see below) or the St Vitus Cathedral in Prague, the miners of Kutná Hora began financing the construction of a great Gothic cathedral of their own, dedicated to St Barbara, the patron saint of miners and gunners. The foundations were probably laid by Parler in the 1380s, but work was interrupted by the Hussite wars, and the church remained unfinished until the late nineteenth century, despite being worked on in the intervening centuries by numerous architects, including Master Hanuš, Matouš Rejsek and Benedikt Ried.

The approach road to the cathedral, Barborská, is lined with a parade of gesticulating Baroque saints and cherubs that rival the sculptures on the Charles Bridge; and on the right-hand side is the palatial seventeenth-century former **Jesuit College**. The cathedral itself bristles with pinnacles, finials and flying buttresses which support its most striking feature, a roof of three tent-like towers added in the sixteenth century, culminating in unequal, needle-sharp spires. Inside, cold light streams through the plain glass windows, illuminating Ried's playful vaulted nave, whose ribs form branches and petals stamped with coats of arms belonging to Václav II and the local miners' guilds. The wide spread of the five-aisled nave is remarkably uncluttered: a Gothic pulpit – half wood, half stone – creeps tastefully up a central pillar, and black and gold Renaissance confessionals lie discreetly in the north aisle. On the south wall is the Minters' Chapel, its walls decorated with fifteenth-century frescoes showing the Florentines at work, while in the ambulatory chapels are some fascinating paintings – unique for their period – of local miners at work.

The rest of the town

There are a few minor sights worth seeking out in the rest of the town. On Rejskovo náměstí, the squat, polygonal **Kašna** (fountain), built by Rejsek in 1495, strikes a very odd pose – peppered with finials and replete with blind arcading, anything less like a fountain would be hard to imagine. At the bottom of the sloping Šultyskovo náměstí is a particularly fine **Morový sloup** (Plague Column), giving thanks for the end of the plague of 1713; while just around the corner from the top of the square is one of the few Gothic buildings to survive the 1770 fire, the **Kamenný dům**, built around 1480, with an oriel and a steep gable, covered in an ornate sculptural icing. This used to contain an unexceptional local museum, which has now been moved a couple of blocks down Poděbradova to Kilian Ignaz Dientzenhofer's unfinished **Voršilský klášter** (Ursuline Convent; April & Oct Sat & Sun 9am–4pm; May–Sept Tues–Sun 9am–5pm). Only three sides of the convent's ambitious pentagonal plan were actually finished, its neo-

Baroque church (now derelict) being added in the late nineteenth century while sv Barbora was being restored.

Sedlec

Buses #1 and #4 run 3km northeast to **SEDLEC**, once a separate village but now a suburb of Kutná Hora. Adjoining Sedlec's defunct eighteenth-century Cistercian monastery (now the largest tobacco factory in Europe, owned by Phillip Morris) is the fourteenth-century church of **Panna Maria** (Virgin Mary; Tues–Sat 9am–noon & 1–5pm) imaginatively redesigned in the eighteenth century by Giovanni Santini, who specialized in melding Gothic with Baroque. Here, given a plain French Gothic church gutted during the Hussite wars, Santini set to work on the vaulting, adding his characteristic sweeping stucco rib patterns, relieved only by the occasional Baroque splash of colour above the chancel steps.

Cross the main road, following the signs, and you'll come to the monks' graveyard, where an ancient Gothic chapel leans heavily over the entrance to the macabre subterranean **kostnice** or ossuary (daily: March 8am–5pm; April–Sept 8am–6pm; Nov 8am–4pm; Dec–Feb 9am–noon & 1–4pm), full to overflowing with human bones. When holy earth from Golgotha was scattered over the graveyard in the twelfth century, all of Bohemia's nobility wanted to be buried here, and the bones mounted up until there were over 40,000 complete sets. In 1870, worried about the ever-growing piles, the authorities commissioned František Rint to do something creative with them. He rose to the challenge and moulded out of bones four giant bells, one in each corner of the crypt, designed wall-to-ceiling skeletal decorations, including the Schwarzenberg coat of arms, and, as the centrepiece, put together a chandelier made out of every bone in the human body. Rint's signature (in bones) is at the bottom of the steps.

Kačina and Žleby

Nothing quite so ghoulish confronts you at the early-nineteenth-century zámek of **Kačina**, 5km northeast of Kutná Hora hlavní nádraží along route 2 to Přelouč (or a much shorter walk if you catch one of the buses heading out to the satellite village of Nový Dvory). It's a colossal Neoclassical summer residence, the semicircular wings of the building stretching for over 200m across the lawn. For the owners, the up-and-coming Chotek family (who also owned Veltrusy), the chateau grounds came first, with planting begun a full fifteen years before a stone was laid. The Choteks forfeited their properties after collaborating with the Nazis, and the chateau now houses a **Zemědělské muzeum** (agriculture museum; April–Oct daily 8am–5pm). You can skip the museum entirely, but to view the chateau's surviving period interiors, you must sign up for an hour-long guided tour; however, it's the wide informal expanse of the "English Park" that draws carloads of Czechs here throughout the summer.

For those who prefer more exotic castles, there's a more flamboyant aristocratic haunt at **Žleby** (Schleb), 20km southeast of Kutná Hora, beyond Čáslav (where you must change trains; buses from Kutná Hora are direct but much less frequent). Here, in the mid-nineteenth century, Franz Schmoranz created a pseudo-Gothic extravaganza out of the original medieval **hrad** (April, Oct & Nov Sat & Sun 9am–noon & 1–4pm; May–Sept Tues–Sun 9am–noon & 1–5pm) for the Auersperg family. For once, the family failed to take the necessary precautions at the end of the war, and were forced to leave behind virtually all the castle's contents. The result is a full-blown neo-Gothic interior filled with lots of weaponry and heavy Baroque and quasi-medieval furnishings. There are two **guided tours** to choose from: trasa 1 (1hr) includes pretty much everything except the Velká věž, the castle's look-out tower, which you only get to see on trasa 2 (1hr 45min).

Practicalities

The simplest way to get to Kutná Hora is to take a **bus** from outside metro Želivského (1hr 15min). Fast **trains** from Prague's Masarykovo nádraží take around an hour (there's only one in the morning); slow ones take two hours; trains from Praha hlavní nádraží involve a change at Kolín. The main **train station** (Kutná Hora hlavní nádraží) is a long way out of town, near Sedlec; bus #1 or #4 will take you into town, or there's usually a shuttle train service ready to leave for Kutná Hora město train station, near the centre of town.

The town has a highly efficient system of orientation signs and, at almost every street corner, a pictorial list of the chief places of interest (beware, though, that the train station signposted is not the main one). The town's **tourist office** at Palackého náměstí 5 (May–Sept daily 9am–5.30pm; shorter hours in winter) can arrange reasonably priced private rooms or other **accommodation**. *U rytířů*, on Rejskovo náměstí (✆0327/51 22 56; ①) is a simple inexpensive pension, while *Hotel Anna*, Vladislavova (✆ & fax 0327/51 63 15; ④) is more upmarket, as is *U vlašského dvora*, on Havlíčkovo náměstí (✆0327/51 46 18; ⑤), which has a decent restaurant and a sauna, and *Zlatá stoupa*, on Tylova (✆0327/51 15 40; *zlatastoupa@iol.cz*; ⑦). The nearest **campsite** is the unlikely sounding *Santa Barbara*, northwest of the town centre on Česká (April–Oct).

On the **eating and drinking** front, you're spoilt for choice: *U Bakaláře*, at the junction of Husova and Šultysova, is one of the best restaurants in town, with a wide choice for vegetarians; *U Jakuba*, near the church of the same name, has an outdoor patio and a good fish menu, while *Piazza Navona*, on Palackého náměstí, is an excellent pizzeria. There are plenty of good pubs, too, where you can get more simple fare: try *U havířů* on Šultysova (closed Mon), which offers a variety of brews including the local Dačický beer.

Průhonice and the Sázava Valley

A short train ride **southeast** of Prague is enough to transport you from the urban sprawl of the capital into one of the prettiest regions of central Bohemia, starting with the park at **Průhonice**. Until the motorway to Brno and Bratislava ripped through the area in the 1970s, the roads and railways linking the three big cities followed the longer, flatter option, further north along the Labe Valley. As a result, commerce and tourism passed the **Sázava Valley** by, and, with the notable exception of **Konopiště**, it remains relatively undeveloped, unspoilt and out of the way.

Průhonice

Barely outside Prague's city limits, and just off the country's chief motorway, **PRŮHONICE** is a popular weekend destination in the summer. A whole series of new buildings, including a large conference centre, have been erected over the last decade, and have somewhat spoilt the character of the original village. Nevertheless, it's still worth a visit, not for the newly restored neo-Renaissance **zámek**, which as a botanical and horticultural research centre is out of bounds, but for the 625-acre **park** (daily: April–Oct 7am–7pm; Nov–March 8am–dusk), which boasts an unusually fine array of flora.

Another good reason for coming to Průhonice is to have a beer at the family-run micro-brewery *U Bezoušků* on the main square, which serves up its very own Bernard brew. There are also two well-equipped **campsites** a couple of kilometres west of the park: *Apple Garden* (April–Oct) to the north of Šeberov, and *Prager* (mid-May to Sept), to the south. To get to Průhonice, you can either catch the half-hourly *ČSAD* **bus** service from metro Opatov, or else you can walk the 4km along the red-marked route, via the Hostivař lake (a good place for a dip in summer), starting from the penultimate tram stop on the #22 or #26 routes.

Sázava and Český Šternberk

Rising majestically above the slow-moving River Sázava, is the **Sázava klášter** and **zámek** (April & Sept Sat & Sun 9am–4pm; May & Sept Tues–Sun 9am–5pm; June–Aug Tues–Sun 9am–6pm). The monastery was founded by the eleventh-century Prince Oldřich, on the instigation of a passing hermit called **Prokop** (St Procopius), whom he met by chance in the forest. Prokop became the first abbot of what was initially a Slavonic Basilian monastery, and, for a while, Sázava became an important centre for the dissemination of Slavonic texts. Later, a large Gothic church was planned, and this now bares its red sandstone nave to the world, incomplete but intact. The chancel was converted into a Baroque church, later bought by the Tiegel family, who started to build themselves a modest chateau. Of this architectural miscellany, only the surviving Gothic frescoes – in the popular "Beautiful Style", but of a sophistication unmatched in Bohemian art at the time – are truly memorable. The village itself thrived on the glass trade, and the rest of the monastery's hour-long guided tour concentrates on the local glassware.

Without your own transport, it'll take a good hour and a half by bus or train to cover the 55km from Prague to Sázava. Of the two, the **train** ride (change at Čerčany) is the more visually absorbing, at least by the time you join the branch line that meanders down the Sázava Valley; the train station is a fifteen-minute walk across the river from the monastery.

Český Šternberk
Several bends later in the Sázava river, the village of **ČESKÝ ŠTERNBERK** is overlooked by the great castellated mass of its **hrad** (April & Oct Sat & Sun 9am–4pm; May–Sept Tues–Sun 9am–5pm), strung out along a knife's edge above the river. It's a breathtaking sight, but unfortunately that's all it is, since apart from its fiercely defensive position, not much remains of the original Gothic castle, headquarters of the powerful Šternberk family (who still own it now). The highlight of the 45-minute guided tour is the Italian stucco work that survives from the seventeenth century, but you wouldn't be missing much if you skipped the tour altogether. If you have a car, however, it's worth driving past for the view – though there's an even better one from the lookout tower (*rozhledna*), a fifteen-minute walk through the woods behind the castle. If you're coming by train, you'll need to change trains at Čerčany and get out at Český Šternberk zastávka, one stop past Český Šternberk's main station. If you need to stay, ask for a room at the *Parkhotel* (☎0303/85 51 68; ④), with a view overlooking the castle.

Konopiště

The popularity of **Konopiště** (Tues–Sun: April & Oct 9am–3pm; May–Aug 9am–5pm; Sept 9am–4pm), with a quarter of a million visitors passing through its portcullis every year, is surpassed only by the likes of Karlštejn (see p.146). Of the two, Konopiště is the most interesting, though Karlštejn looks better from the outside. Coach parties from all over the world home in on this Gothic castle, which is stuffed with dead animals, weaponry and hunting trophies. Most interesting are its historical associations: King Václav IV was imprisoned for a while by his own nobles in the castle's distinctive round tower, and the Archduke Franz Ferdinand, heir to the Habsburg throne, lived here with his wife, Sophie Chotek, until their assassination in Sarajevo in 1914. The archduke shared his generation's voracious appetite for hunting, eliminating all living creatures foolish enough to venture into the grounds. However, he surpassed all his contemporaries by recording, stuffing and displaying a significant number of the 171,537 birds and animals he shot between the years 1880 and 1906, the details of which are recorded in his *Schuss Liste* displayed inside.

There's a choice of **guided tours**. The *I okruh* explores the period interiors, which contain some splendid Renaissance cabinets and lots of Meissen porcelain, while the *II okruh* takes you through the chapel, past the stuffed bears and deer teeth, to the assorted lethal weapons of one of the finest armouries in Europe. Both the above tours take 45 minutes, and, you'll be relieved to know, include the hunting trophies. The *III okruh* takes an hour, costs twice as much, is restricted to just eight people per tour, and concentrates on the personal apartments of the archduke and his wife. The couple hid themselves away in Konopiště, as they were shunned by the Habsburg court in Vienna, due to the fact that Sophie was a mere countess, and not an archduchess. Occasionally there are tours in English, French and German, too, so ask at the box office before you sign up.

Even if you don't fancy a guided tour, there are plenty of other things to do in Konopiště. In the main courtyard of the chateau, you can pop into the purpose-built **Střelnice** (Shooting Range; times as above), where the archduke used to hone his skills as a marksmen against moving mechanical targets, all of which have recently been lovingly restored. Tucked underneath the south terrace is the **Galerie sv Jiří** (Tues–Sun: April, May, Sept & Oct 9am–1pm & 2–3pm; June–Aug 9am–1pm & 2–5pm), which is stuffed to the gunnels with artefacts from paintings to statuettes and trinkets relating to St George, the fictional father of medieval chivalry, with whom the archduke was obsessed. Much the best reason to come to Konopiště, though, is to explore its 555-acre **park**, which boasts several lakes, sundry statuary, an unrivalled rose garden and a deer park. There are also regular displays of **falconry** in the chateau's grounds (April & Oct Sat & Sun 10am, noon, 2 & 4pm; May–Sept Tues–Sun same times).

Practicalities

To get to Konopiště take a fast (50min) or slow (1hr 5min) **train** from Praha hlavní nádraží to **Benešov** u Prahy, 45km southeast of Prague, on the main line to České Budějovice; the castle is a pleasant two-kilometre walk west of the railway station along the red- or yellow-marked path (buses are relatively infrequent). Since train connections are good from Prague, you don't need to **stay** the night, but if you do, the *Nová Myslivna* (☎0301/230 17; ②) is a modern hotel right by the main car park. If that's full, there's a **campsite** (May–Sept), to the southeast of the castle, near the ugly *Motel Konopiště* (☎0301/227 32; ⑦), which has a good restaurant. If the weather's fine, though, you might as well come equipped with a picnic; otherwise, there are numerous food stalls by the main car park, and decent Czech fare available in the nineteenth-century *Stará Myslivna*, on the path to the castle.

Příbram

PŘÍBRAM (Pibrans), like Kutná Hora, was once a royal silver-mining town, though it contains nothing like the same treasures. Among older Czechs, however, the town is better known for its notorious uranium mines, where thousands of political prisoners worked and died in appalling conditions in the 1950s. Since 1989, all mining operations have ceased here, and there's now a museum to those terrible years called **Muzeum třetího odboje** (Tues–Sun 10am–4pm), housed in an unprepossessing block at Mariánská 260. Bus #15 from the train station passes close by every half hour, or you can walk in ten minutes by crossing over the tracks, heading west up Anenská, and then first left down Aloise Jiráska to the crossroads with Mariánská.

In the southwestern suburb of Březové Hory, there's also an extensive **Hornické muzeum** (Mining Museum; hourly guided tours April–Oct Tues–Sun 9am–3pm; Nov–March Tues–Fri 9am–3pm), accessible via bus #1 or #14 from the train station. The museum is divided between five separate buildings, the most impressive of which is the splendidly ornate pit head of the UNESCO-protected Ševčínský důl (Ševčín Shaft), which was built in 1813. The other buildings, which include a traditional miner's cottage, contain displays on mineralogy, and numerous Bethlehem folk scenes filled with wooden figurines. You can also don a hard hat and take a trip down one of the old mine shafts, in the company of a retired miner, after which you're encouraged to pay a visit to the nearby miners' pub *Na vrších* (see below).

The real reason most people trek out to Příbram, however, is to see the beautiful Marian shrine of **Svatá hora** (Holy Mountain; daily 8.30am–5pm), whose pepperpot domes rise up above the town on a wooded hill to the east of the main square. According to legend, the first shrine was built here in the thirteenth century, but was transformed out of all recognition by the Jesuits, who in 1658 employed Carlo Lurago to produce the striking set-piece of Italianate Baroque you now see. The best way to reach the shrine is via the Svatohorské schody or covered stairway off Dlouhá, built by Kilian Ignaz Dientzenhofer in 1728. From the stairs, you enter the arcaded ambulatory which surrounds the main church, whose newly restored frescoes, dating from the late nineteenth century, recount the history of Svatá hora. Thick stucco work surrounds the hell, fire and damnation ceiling paintings, with cherubs fighting and hugging skulls surrounded by swags made from bones and egg-timers on more skulls. At the centre of the complex is the pilgrim church or basilica, its balustrade dotted with saintly statuary; inside, pride of place goes to a kitsch Gothic statue of the Madonna and Child, whose clothes are regularly changed.

Practicalities

Příbram itself is around 50km southwest of Prague along the motorway of route 4. The easiest way to get there on **public transport** is by bus from Prague's Na Knížecí bus station, next to metro Anděl; the train from Prague's Smíchovské nádraží takes longer and often involves a change at Zdice, on the main line to Plzeň. Příbram is not a great place to stay the night, though the *Modrý hrozen* (☎0306/289 01; hotel@modryhrozen.cz; ⑨), on the main square, is a pleasant and comfortable enough **hotel**, and boasts a restaurant with an original seventeenth-century ceiling. For cheaper food and drink, undoubtedly the best **pub** around is the aforementioned *Na vrších* close to the mining museum; back in the town centre, there's *U havlínů*, on Václavské náměstí.

Since 1997, Příbram has also been the home town of the old army football team, **Dukla Praha** – immortalized in the pop song *All I Want for Christmas is a Dukla Prague Away-Kit* by British band Half Man Half Biscuit – after they were forced to leave the capital due to financial difficulties, and merge with the town's local team. Dukla have since bounced back into the first division, and now play rent-free in Příbram's Na Litavce stadium, which is situated a couple of kilometres south of the town centre.

Along the Berounka river

The green belt area to the **west of Prague** is easily the most varied of the regions around the city, and consequently one of the most popular escapes for citizens of the Czech capital. The **River Berounka** carves itself an enticingly craggy valley up to Charles IV's magnificent country castle at **Karlštejn**, the busiest destination of all, and further upstream is the more isolated stronghold of **Křivoklát**.

Karlštejn and around

KARLŠTEJN (Karlstein) is a small ribbon of a village, strung out along one of the tributaries of the Berounka – no doubt once pretty, it's now jam-packed with tacky souvenir stands and tourists visiting its **hrad** (Tues–Sun: April & Oct 9am–noon & 1–5pm; May, June & Sept 9am–noon & 1–6pm; July & Aug 9am–7pm; mid-Feb to March & early Nov 9am–noon & 1–4pm), which occupies a spectacular, defiantly unassailable position above the village. Designed in the fourteenth century by Matthias of Arras for Emperor Charles IV as a giant safe-box for the imperial crown jewels and his large personal collection of precious relics, it quickly became Charles' favourite retreat from the vast city he himself had masterminded. Women were strictly forbidden to enter the castle, and the story of his third wife Anna's successful break-in (in drag) became one of the most popular Czech comedies of the nineteenth century.

Ruthlessly returned to a kind of replica of its original Gothic style in the late nineteenth century by Josef Mocker, the hrad now looks much better from a distance, with its giant wedge towers rising above a series of castellated walls. Most of the rooms visited on the overpriced half-hour guided tour contain only the barest of furnishings, the empty spaces taken up by uninspiring displays on the history of the castle. Theoretically, the top two chambers would make the whole trip worthwhile: unfortunately, you can only look into (but not enter) the emperor's residential **Mariánská věž**, where Charles shut himself off from the rest of the world, with any urgent business passed to him through a hole in the wall of the tiny ornate chapel of **sv Kateřina**.

As for the castle's finest treasure, the **Holy Rood Chapel** (Kaple svatého kříže), connected by a wooden bridge that leads onto the highest point of the castle, the **Velká věž**, this has been closed since 1980 and it looks like it will remain so, as the sheer number of visitors would damage the decor irrevocably. Traditionally, only the emperor, the archbishop and the electoral princes could enter this gilded treasure-house, whose six-metre-thick walls contain 2200 semiprecious stones and 128 painted panels, the work of Master Theodoric, Bohemia's greatest fourteenth-century painter (a small selection of his panels are exhibited in Prague's Jiřský klášter, see p.69). The imperial crown jewels, once secured here behind nineteen separate locks, were removed to Hungary after an abortive attack by the Hussites, while the Bohemian jewels are now stashed away in the cathedral in Prague.

Elsewhere in the village – transformed over the last decade, with every other house offering rooms to rent or selling souvenirs – most of what you see is eminently missable, with the exception of the **Muzeum Betlémů** (times as for the castle, but without a lunch break), which occupies the ground floor of a house towards the top of the village. For a modest entrance fee, you can admire an impressive array of nativity scenes dating back to the early nineteenth century. They range in size from complex mechanical set-ups to miniature affairs that can fit into small sea shells – there's even one in gingerbread.

Practicalities

Trains for Karlštejn leave Prague's Smíchovské nádraží roughly every hour, and take about 35 minutes to cover the 28km. The village is ten minutes' walk across the river from the station, and it's a further fifteen- to twenty-minute climb up to the castle entrance. If you're looking for somewhere to grab a beer and a bite to **eat**, try *U Janů* which has an outdoor terrace, or the *Koruna*, both on the main street. Alternatively, bring a picnic with you and eat by the banks of the river.

There are loads of **accommodation** options in Karlštejn, but since prices are something like fifty percent higher than in most places in the country, only a masochist would choose to stay here. If you are stuck here for some reason, your best bet is the *Hotel Mlýn* (☎0311/68 11 94; ⑥), an unpretentious, but well-run converted fishing lodge, on the same side of the river as the train station, ten minutes' walk downstream. Karlštejn's **campsite** (open all year) is on the opposite bank, upstream from the village, and allows fires, but there's a nicer site at **Řevnice** (April–Sept), two stops on the train before Karlštejn (and, incidentally, the village in which Martina Navrátilová spent her tennis-playing childhood), with a small pool, restaurant, draught beer, and good train links with Prague.

Walks around Karlštejn and the Český kras

There are some great possibilities for **hiking** in the countryside around Karlštejn. Several marked paths cover the stiff climb through the forests of the Hřebeny ridge. If you're armed with a *Praha okolí* map, these are easy enough to follow; you can pick up a bus back to Prague from Mníšek on the other side of the hills.

If you're feeling energetic, you could go for a swim at the popular flooded quarry, **Malá Amerika**. You'll need your own wheels, though, as getting there is tricky: either take the red-marked path from near the castle at Karlštejn, and head off northwest through the woods at U dubu (you may need to ask a Czech to point you in the right direction), or head west down the track, which comes off the road between Mořina and Bubovice.

From **SRBSKO** (one stop on from Karlštejn), a red-marked path winds its way through the woods to **sv Jan pod Skalou** (St John Under the Rock), whose monastery is strikingly situated, as the name suggests, underneath a steep bluff in a landscape full of dramatic craggy flourishes. Designed by Christoph Dientzenhofer, the monastery was used as a training camp for the Communist secret police, but is now an ecological research centre. This is also the place where the country's remaining aristocrats were imprisoned following the 1948 coup. Again, you can catch a bus back to Prague easily enough from Vráž, a kilometre or so to the north.

Another option from Srbsko is to take the yellow-marked path west into the **Český kras** (Bohemian Karst). The geology of this region has fascinated scientists since the early nineteenth century, but the one set of caves open to the public, the **Koněpruské jeskyně** (April–Oct daily 8am–4pm), 3km west of Srbsko, lay undiscovered until 1950. Nowadays it's not so easy to miss, thanks to the Hollywood-style giant white lettering on the hillside above. Much more fascinating than the dripstone decorations, however, was the simultaneous discovery of an illegal mint in the upper level of the caves. A full set of weights, miners' lamps and even the remains of food were found here, dating back to the second half of the fifteenth century. To reach the caves other than by foot, you'll need to catch one of the infrequent **buses** from the nearby soap-producing town of **Beroun** (50min by train from Praha hlavní nádraží). Finally, just for the record, Czech film buffs may like to know that the station at **Loděnice**, two stops up the line from Beroun, was used as the location for Jiří Menzel's classic, Oscar-winning, 1960s film, *Closely Observed Trains*, based on the novel by Bohumil Hrabal.

Křivoklátsko

Further up the Berounka is the beautiful, mixed woodland of the UNESCO nature reserve, **Křivoklátsko**. Just out of reach of day-trippers, it's an altogether sleepier place than the area around Karlštejn. The agonized twists (*křivky*) of the river cast up the highest crags of the region, which cluster round the lofty castle of **Křivoklát** (Pürglitz; March, April & Oct–Dec Tues–Sun 9am–4pm; May & Sept Tues–Sun 9am–5pm; June 9am–6pm; July & Aug daily 9am–6pm). With such a perfect location in the heart of the best hunting ground in Bohemia, Křivoklát naturally enjoyed the royal patronage of the Přemyslids, whose hunting parties were legendary. Charles IV also spent the early part of his childhood here before being sent off to Burgundy. From the outside, it's a scruffy but impressive stronghold, dominated by the round tower in which English alchemist Edward Kelley was incarcerated for two and a half years for failing to reveal the secret of the philosopher's stone to Rudolf II. Kelley was, by all accounts, a slippery character, a swindler and a seducer, with a hooked nose and no ears (they were cut off by the Lancastrians as a punishment for forgery). In an attempt to escape, he jumped out of the window, only to break his leg so badly it had to be amputated.

There are now two tours to choose from, with the hour-long guided tour (trasa 1) round the interior taking in most of the castle's good points, including the Great Hall and the Chapel, which date back to the thirteenth century. Both have kept their original late-Gothic vaulting, studded with corbels carved with colourful figureheads, and retain an austere beauty quite at odds with the castle's reputation as a venue for bacchanalian goings-on. An appealing alternative for those with kids (or an aversion to guided tours) is the half-hour scramble around the fortifications (trasa 2). In the high season, you can watch traditional woodcarving demonstrations, and visit the hunting exhibition in the castle's outbuildings, too.

Practicalities

Virtually all journeys by **train** from Prague to Křivoklát require a change at Beroun. **Buses** from the Praha-Dejvice terminal run frequently only at weekends, less regularly during the week, and take around an hour and a half. Křivoklát is just one of several castles in the region, and you could happily spend days exploring the surrounding countryside on the network of well-marked footpaths. There's an **information centre** (June & Sept Sat & Sun 10am–6pm; July & Aug Tues–Sun 10am–6pm) right in the centre of the village, which can advise on walks, and also book private **accommodation**. If the office is closed, try the nearby *Sýkora* (☎0313/55 81 14; ④), which could do with a lick of paint on the outside but is fine inside, or one of the many **campsites** in the vicinity, such as *Višňová II* (June–Aug) by the river. Be warned that Křivoklát hosts an annual **film festival** at the end of August, during which it will be all but impossible to find anywhere to stay.

Around Kladno

No Czech would seriously suggest you should visit **KLADNO**, just under 30km west of Prague, but if you're heading for Lány by bus, you may need to change here. As you approach the town, nicknamed "Black Kladno", it's difficult to miss the low, blue barracks of the giant Poldi Kladno steelworks, insensitively built on a section of the old town in the heyday of central planning in 1975. Founded way back in 1855, the steelworks were one of the first foundries in the world to produce stainless steel in 1910. It was here, too, that the Czech Communist Party was founded in 1921, and Kladno's workers were rewarded with some of the best wages in the country after the 1948 coup.

Poldi's problems began in earnest in 1992 when the factory, which once employed a majority of the town's 70,000 inhabitants, was forced to shut down for eight months due to a lack of orders. Then, two years later, it was sold to the fiery entrepreneur Vladimír Stehlík, who was known to fire his pistol in the air on the shop floor in order to gain the attention of his employees. During the 1996 elections, he gave his entire workforce the day off so that they could march in Prague against prime minister Václav Klaus's government. The following year, having failed to pay their workers for several months, Stehlík and his son Marko were behind bars, awaiting trial for defaulting on bank loans. They were released, after four months inside, only on condition that they sell the steelworks, which they duly did to a Liechtenstein-based company. However, the factory remains firmly shut, and the citizens of Kladno have now more or less got used to commuting to Prague for their work.

Lidice

The small mining village of **LIDICE**, 18km northwest of Prague, hit the world headlines on June 10, 1942, at the moment when it ceased to exist. On the flimsiest pretext, it was chosen as the scapegoat for the assassination of the Nazi leader Reinhard Heydrich (see p.106). All 173 men from the village were rounded up and shot by the SS, the 198 women were sent off to Ravensbrück concentration camp, and the 89 children either went to the camps or, if they were considered Aryan enough, were packed off to "good" German homes, while the village itself was burnt to the ground.

Knowing all this as you approach Lidice makes the modern village seem almost perversely unexceptional. At the end of the straight, tree-lined main street, 10 června 1942 (June 10, 1942), there's a dour concrete memorial with a small but horrific **museum** (daily: April–Oct 8am–5pm; Nov–March 8am–4pm) where you can watch a short film about Lidice, including footage shot by the SS themselves as the village was burning. The spot where the old village used to lie is just south of the memorial, now merely smooth green pasture punctuated with a few simple symbolic reminders and a new bronze memorial to the 82 local children who were gassed in the camps.

After the massacre, the "Lidice shall live" campaign was launched and villages all over the world began to change their name to Lidice. The first was Stern Park Gardens, Illinois, soon followed by villages in Mexico and other Latin American countries. From Coventry to Montevideo, towns twinned themselves with Lidice, so that rather than "wiping a Czech village off the face of the earth", as Hitler had hoped, the Nazis inadvertently created a symbol of anti-fascist resistance.

There's no place nor reason to stay, and most people come here as a day-trip from Prague on one of the regular buses from Praha Florenc, getting off at the turn-off to the village on the main road.

Lány

On summer weekends, Škoda-loads of Czech families, pensioners and assorted pilgrims make their way to **LÁNY**, a plain, grey village on a hill by the edge of the Křivoklát forest, 12km beyond Kladno. They congregate in the town's pristine cemetery to pay their respects to one of the country's most important historical figures,

---

TGM

Tomáš Garrigue Masaryk – known affectionately as TGM – was born in 1850 in Hodonín, a town in a part of Moravia where Slovaks and Czechs lived harmoniously together. His father was an illiterate Slovak peasant who worked for the local bigwig, his mother a German. Tomáš himself trained as a blacksmith. From such humble beginnings, he rose to become professor of philosophy at the Charles University, a Social Democrat MP in the Viennese *Reichsrat*, and finally the country's first, and longest-serving, president. A liberal humanist through and through, Masaryk created what was, at the time, probably the most progressive democracy in central Europe, featuring universal suffrage, an enviable social security system and a strong social democratic thrust. The whole country went into mourning when he died in 1937, leaving Czechoslovakia one of the few remaining democracies in central Europe, "a lighthouse high on a cliff with the waves crashing on it on all sides", as Masaryk's less fortunate successor, Edvard Beneš, put it. A year later the Nazis marched into Sudetenland.

After the 1948 coup, the Communists began to dismantle the myth of Masaryk, whose name was synonymous with the "bourgeois" First Republic. All mention of him was removed from textbooks, street names were changed, and his statue was taken down from almost every town and village in the country. However, during liberalization in 1968, his bespectacled face and goatee beard popped up again in shop windows, and his image returned once more in 1989 to haunt the beleaguered Communists.

Tomáš Garrigue Masaryk, the founding father and president of Czechoslovakia from 1918 to 1935.

The Masaryk plot is separated from the rest of the cemetery (*hřbitov*) by a little wooden fence and flanked by two bushy trees. Tomás is buried alongside his American wife, Charlotte Garrigue Masaryková, who died some fifteen years earlier, and their son Jan, who became Foreign Minister in the post-1945 government, only to die in mysterious circumstances shortly after the Communist coup (see p.73). The Masaryks have since been joined by their daughter, Alice, who founded the Czechoslovak Red Cross and died in exile in 1966.

After laying their wreaths, the crowds generally wander over to the presidential summer **zámek**, with its blue-liveried guards, on the other side of the village. The chateau still serves as the president's out-of-town retreat, and its rooms are strictly out of bounds, but the large English gardens, orangerie and deer park, which were landscaped by Josip Plečnik, are open to the public (April–Oct Wed & Thurs 2–6pm, Sat & Sun 10am–6pm). To get to Lány, either change buses at Kladno, or take the slow train to Chomutov from Prague's Masarykovo nádraží, getting out at Stochov – the nearest station to Lány, 3km away to the southwest – which boasts a presidential waiting room.

travel details

Trains
Beroun to: Křivoklát (11–12 daily; 40–50min); Prague (5–9 daily; 50min–1hr);

Čerčany to: Český Šternberk (7–8 daily; 1 hr); Sázava (7–8 daily; 30min).

Mělník to: Liběchov (7 daily; 8min); Litoměřice město (7–9 daily; 35min).

Prague (Praha hlavní nádraží) to: Benešov (hourly; 40min–1hr 5min); Čerčany (hourly; 55min); Kolín (1–2 hourly; 45min); Kutná Hora (4 daily; 55min–1hr); Mělník (2–3 daily; 1hr 30min); Mladá Boleslav (7–8 daily; 1hr 10min–1hr 50min); Poděbrady (hourly; 50min–1hr).

Prague (Praha Masarykovo nádraží) to: Kladno (hourly; 40–55min); Kolín (hourly; 1hr 10min); Nelahozeves (3 daily; 30min–55min); Stochov (hourly; 1hr–1hr 15min).

Prague (Praha–Holešovice) to: Kolín (5 daily; 40min).

Prague (Praha–Smíchov) to: Beroun (5–9 daily; 50min–1hr); Karlštejn (1–2 hourly; 30min); Příbram (2–4 daily; 1hr 15min); Řevnice (1–2 hourly; 25min).

Buses
Prague (Praha, Dejvická) to: Lidice (1–2 hourly; 25–35min); Kladno (1–2 hourly; 45–50min).

Prague (Praha, Florenc) to: Konopiště (up to every 45min; 1hr); Kutná Hora (Mon–Fri 1 daily; 1hr 15min); Mělník (up to 10 daily; 50min); Mladá Boleslav (frequently; 1hr 15min).

Prague (Praha, Na Knížecí) to: Příbram (10 daily; 1hr).

Prague (Praha, Opatov) to: Průhonice (every 30min–1hr; 15min).

Prague (Praha, Želivského) to: Kutná Hora (up to 5 daily; 1hr 15min); Sázava (5–12 daily; 1hr 10min).

CHAPTER TWO

SOUTH BOHEMIA

South Bohemia (Jižní Čechy), more than any other region, conforms to the popular myth of Bohemia as a bucolic backwater of rolling hills and endless forests. A century of conspicuous industrialization and destruction from two world wars have pretty much passed it by. The only city to speak of is the regional capital, **České Budějovice**, which makes up for its urban sprawl with a good-looking old town (and a beer of no less standing). The rest of the countryside is dotted with a series of exceptionally beautiful medieval walled towns, known collectively as the **"Rose Towns"** after the emblems of the two most powerful families: the red rose of the Rožmberks and the black rose of the lords of Hradec. Both dynasties died out at the beginning of the seventeenth century, and their prize possessions have been in almost terminal decline ever since, despite the subsequent rise of the Bavarian-based Schwarzenbergs.

Český Krumlov is by far the most popular of the Rose Towns; others, like **Pelhřimov** and **Třeboň**, are equally well preserved, if not quite as picturesquely located. The latter lies in an uncharacteristically flat part of the country, known as **Třeboňsko**, a unique ecosystem of medieval fishponds that still supply much of the country's Christmas carp. Bohemia's chief river, the **Vltava**, runs through South Bohemia and provides the setting for the region's most popular **castles**, some, like **Zvíkov**, almost monastic in their simplicity, and others, such as **Orlík**, **Hluboká** and **Rožmberk**, marvels of aristocratic decadence.

To the south, the **Šumava**, which forms the natural border with Austria and Germany, is one of the most unspoiled mountain ranges in the country. The German-speaking foresters and traders who settled on the northern slopes have left their mark on the architecture of the Bohemian towns and villages in that area. Following the postwar expulsions, however, the local population is now greatly reduced, their number augmented only by a seasonal influx of walkers, fishermen, canoeists and inland beachniks, drawn by the natural beauty of the region, which is probably the least affected by acid rain in the Czech Republic.

Regional **transport** in South Bohemia isn't as bad as might be expected, given the overwhelmingly hilly, rural nature of the terrain. Travelling by train allows you to experience more of the countryside, and even parts of the Šumava are served by a scenic single-track railway that winds its way from České Budějovice to Český Krumlov, along

---

ACCOMMODATION PRICE CODES

After each entry in the **hotel** lists below, you'll find a symbol which corresponds to one of nine **price categories**:

① Under 500Kč	④ 1000–1250Kč	⑦ 1750–2000Kč
② 500–750Kč	⑤ 1250–1500Kč	⑧ 2000–2500Kč
③ 750–1000Kč	⑥ 1500–1750Kč	⑨ 2500Kč and upwards

All prices are for the cheapest **double room** available during high season, which usually means without private bath or shower in the less expensive places. For a **single room**, expect to pay around two-thirds the price of a double.

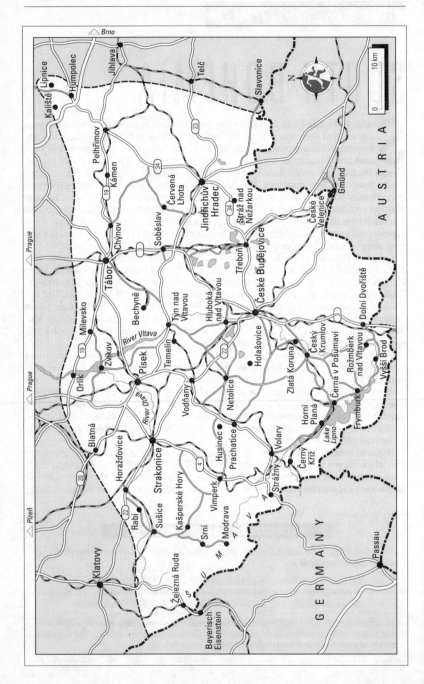

BOATS ON THE VLTAVA

There are **boat services** three times a day from Orlík to Zvíkov (June & early Sept Sat & Sun; July & Aug Tues–Sun; 45min), which also head north to the Orlík dam, via the Trhovky, Podskalá, Radava and Velký Vír campsites. Another less frequent service plies between Zvíkov and Podolsko (July & Aug Tues & Wed; 1hr 45min; 1 daily), to the south, which lies close to Cervená nad Vltavou train station. In addition, there are round-trip boat excursions, both short and long, on offer from the pier below Orlík castle. For more information on the timetable, call ☎0362/84 13 33.

the shores of Lake Lipno and then north to Prachatice. While they can be less frequent than trains, buses go virtually everywhere and are almost invariably faster.

Up the Vltava

South of Prague and the Slapy dam, the **River Vltava** has been transformed into a series of long, winding lakes, which remain a favourite destination for Czechs in the summer. The campsites, many of them fairly ad hoc affairs, are full to capacity, and campfires burn into the night every night. There are also two **castles** worth visiting: **Orlík** and **Zvíkov**, both of which overlook the Vltava and are difficult to reach without your own vehicle. A possible base from which to see them is the nearby town of **Písek**, which has recently been prettily spruced up, and is easily accessible by bus or train.

Orlík nad Vltavou

With its vanilla-coloured rendering and mock castellations, you're unlikely to be disappointed by your first impressions of **Orlík** (which means literally "eagle's nest"), a creamy nineteenth-century castle which juts out into this wide stretch of the Vltava. No doubt the view was a great deal more spectacular before the valley was dammed in the 1960s; nowadays the water laps rather tamely at the foot of the castle, and concrete has been injected into its foundations to prevent it from being swept away.

As some of the region's greatest self-propagandists, the Schwarzenbergs turned this old Gothic **hrad** (Tues–Sun: April, Sept & Oct 9am–4pm; May–Aug 9am–5pm) into a pseudo-Gothic money-waster in the second half of the nineteenth century. There's

ROMANY MEMORIAL AT LETY

It has taken fifty years, but there is now a memorial at **Lety**, 7km west of Orlík, to the Czech Romanies who died here during World War II. Between 1942 and 1943, some 1300 Romanies passed through the transit camp in Lety, amidst what is now a pig farm, en route to Auschwitz; thousands more were interned in Hodonín, in Moravia. About a quarter of those interned at Lety died in the camp – in the end around ninety percent of the prewar Czech Romany population was killed. Touching the raw nerve of Czech-gypsy relations, it is inevitable that the memorial has provoked controversy, not least because of the accusation that the camp was staffed not by Germans, nor even Sudeten Germans, but by Czechs. The memorial is made up of a series of slabs of rock, already overgrown, with an information panel in Czech, Roma and English. To get there, take the road from Lety to Kožlí u Orlíka, and follow the inconspicuous sign *památník* into the woods, a fifteen-minute walk.

nothing among the faïence, weaponry and Schwarzenberg military memorabilia on the hour-long guided tour to hint at its 700-year history, and even the gardens were only laid out last century, but if you're interested in the Schwarzenbergs, this is one of the best places to find out about them.

For moderately priced **food**, head for the restaurant *U Toryka* (named after the current count's pet fox terrier); for cheaper fare, try the café in the orangery, or go off into the castle grounds for a picnic. In the high season, there are also falcons and other birds of prey on display in the grounds. Of the many **campsites** in the area, the nearest to the castle is 2km downriver at Velký Vír (June–Sept; 0362/84 11 61). En route, there's a nice **pension**, *U Nováku* (☎0602/46 78 86; ②), with a friendly pub downstairs serving cheap food and Gambrinus and Purkmistr beers.

Zvíkov

Fourteen kilometres upstream, hidden amid the woods of an isolated rocky promontory at the confluence of the Vltava and the Otava, is the bare medieval husk of **Zvíkov** (April & Oct Sat & Sun 9.30am–noon & 1–4pm; May & Sept Tues–Sun 9.30am–noon & 1–4.30pm; June–Aug Tues–Sun 9am–5.30pm), its simplicity a welcome relief after the "romantic interiors" of Orlík. You can wander at will among the light honey-coloured stone buildings, left to rack and ruin by the Rožmberks as long ago as the 1500s, then further destroyed by imperial troops during the Thirty Years' War. A small dusty track passes under three gatehouses before leading to the central courtyard, which boasts a simple, early Gothic, two-storey arcade, reconstructed in the nineteenth century from the few bays that still stood. Even the meagre offerings in the museum are more than compensated for by the absence of tour groups, the cool stone floors and the wonderful views over the water. A further incentive to visit are the chapel's faded fifteenth-century frescoes, featuring a particularly memorable scene "where nimbed souls in underpants float uncomfortably through a forest", as one critic aptly described it.

Buses from Písek (which run on weekdays only) generally only go as far as the village of **ZVÍKOVSKÉ PODHRADÍ**, 1km south of the castle, from where the castle is signposted. Here you'll find private **rooms**, as well as plusher accommodation at the *Hotel Zvíkov* (☎0362/89 96 59; ⑦).

TEMELÍN

The cooling towers of **Temelín**, which rise up beside the main road from Písek to České Budějovice, are a chastening sight. Built to a Soviet design similar to the one used at Chernobyl, Temelín was designed to be the largest nuclear power station in the world – reason enough to give the place a wide berth. A long campaign of protest by local and international groups persuaded the first post-Communist government to postpone the opening of the power station, which is situated on a tectonic fault line. However, in 1992, the US energy giant Westinghouse was commissioned to complete at least two of the four reactor units. With so much of the countryside devastated by the effects of coal-produced energy, however, the majority of Czechs think the plant should be completed, while top politicians such as Václav Klaus and Václav Havel have taken vociferous stands, the former in favour and the latter against it; Austria, meanwhile, has said that it will block Czech entry into the EU if the government goes ahead with the reactor. The latest completion date is set for 2001 – more than ten years' late and more than 60 billion Kč ($1.7 billion) over budget. Once on-line, Temelín will provide twenty percent of the nation's electricity, as does the republic's only other (much older) nuclear reactor in the southern Moravian town of Dukovany.

Písek

Twenty kilometres south of Zvíkov is the pretty little town of **PÍSEK**, which gets its name from the gold-producing sand (*písek*) of the Otava. Gold fever has waxed and waned in the town over the centuries (an annual gold-panning championship is now held every August on the river around Slaník). At present commercial exploration, mostly around the nearby village of Mokrsko, has been suspended, and the likelihood of any company getting the go-ahead to mine looks very slim indeed. The problem is that the gold is dispersed in microscopic particles, which means for every tonne of gold, the mining companies would have to shift half a million tonnes of rock, crush it into powder and then leach the gold out in pools of cyanide. Obviously, the environmental consequences would be disastrous, and so far the locals (and even the government) are against any mining.

The Town

Písek experienced its last gold rush in the thirteenth century, but its prosperity was later demolished by the Thirty Years' War. The chief reminder of those days is the town's wonderful **medieval stone bridge** (Kamenný most), which predates even the Charles Bridge in Prague and which likewise accrued a fine selection of beatific Baroque statuary during the Counter-Reformation. Located in the westernmost edge of the staré město, it is now closed to traffic, and has recently been lovingly restored.

From the bridge, it's a short hop to the main square, **Velké náměstí**, overlooked by the magnificent golden yellow Baroque **radnice**. Behind the town hall, at the far end of the courtyard, you'll find the entrance to the **Prácheňské muzeum** (Tues–Sun 9am–6pm), which occupies the only surviving wing of the medieval riverside castle, built by Přemysl King Otakar II in the thirteenth century and destroyed by fire in 1532. The highlight of this newly refurbished and vast museum is the Gothic Knights' Hall, which has retained its original black floor tiles, and contains a model of how the castle once looked. The rest of the museum is also worth a quick canter for its unusually frank account of the area's history, including a section on the gypsy concentration camp of Lety (see p.153), and the more recent events of 1968 and 1989; and before you leave, don't miss the gold exhibits in the basement.

A few doors down the main square from the radnice is the pretty little former monastery church of **sv Kříž**, with its gabled sgraffitoed facade. Inside, it has a superbly kitsch Baroque main altar, sporting a golden sunburst in the shape of a love heart and a backdrop of blue, ruched curtains dotted with gold stars. There are several other buildings around the town which boast more recent sgraffito decoration, mostly the work of the late-nineteenth-century artist (and local student) Mikuláš Aleš. A short walk up Fráni Šrámka brings you to the **Putimská brána**, the only remaining bastion, adjoined by a number of quiet backstreets heading east. These lead to a small market which takes place under the aegis of the 74-metre-high, onion-domed *hláska* (watchtower) of the Dominican church.

Finally, the technically turned-on might consider paying a visit to Písek's latest attraction, the **Městská elektrárna** (power station; Tues–Sun 9am–noon & 1–4pm), a short walk upstream from the Kamenný most. It became operational in 1887, thus making Písek the first Czech town to have electric lighting supplied by its very own power station.

Practicalities

Písek has a useful **information centre** (Mon–Fri 10am–5pm; July & Aug also Sat & Sun), a stone's throw from the Kamenný most, on Fügnerovo náměstí. For traditional Czech **food** and beer, head for *U Reinerů*, whose outdoor terrace backs onto the town's lovely, leafy Palackého sady, behind Heydukova; the nearby *Pizzeria Venezia* does reasonable Czech-style pizzas. The *City Hotel* (☎0362/21 51 92; ⑤) is a pleasant new **hotel** in the old town at Alšovo náměstí 35; a cheaper alternative is *U Kloudů* (☎0362/21 50 18; ③), a **pension** on Nerudova with a café/bar downstairs – follow Heydukova through Havlíčkovo náměstí. The two **campsites** nearest Písek are a long way out of town and a couple of kilometres from the nearest train stations: *Soutok* (May–Oct) is to the south, nearest Rutim station, while the *Vrcovice* site (open all year) is north of town, nearest Vrcovice station. In the novel by Jaroslav Hašek, the Good Soldier Švejk makes his fictional appearance at Písek in a blizzard, handcuffed to a lance-corporal in the Austrian constabulary "for comfort", before moving on to Tábor on the next train. Should you wish to do the same, the main **bus** and **train stations** are both a kilometre or so south of town, at the end of Nádražní (bus #1).

Tábor

Founded in 1420 by religious exiles from Prague, 88km away to the north, **TÁBOR** – named after the mountain where the transfiguration of Christ took place – was the spiritual and strategic centre of the social and religious revolution which swept through Bohemia in the first half of the fifteenth century. It gave its name to the radical wing of the reformist Hussite movement, the **Táborites**, whose philosophy – that all people should be equal on earth as in heaven – found few friends among the church hierarchy and feudal-minded nobility of the time, Hussite or Catholic. Under constant threat of physical attack, they developed into a formidable fighting force, declaring war on the established Church and remaining undefeated until 1452, when the town was taken by a force led by the moderate Hussite King George of Poděbrady.

Anti-authoritarianism persists here, and despite the efforts of the Jesuits and others over the centuries, Tábor still boasts the smallest percentage of Catholics in the country. Considering its pugnacious history, though, and despite being a major bus and rail

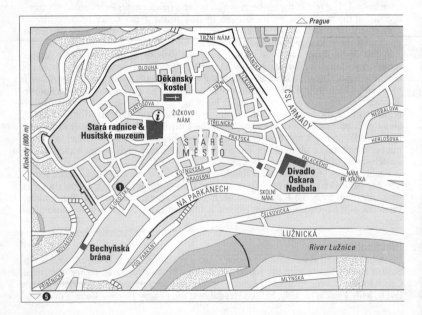

junction, Tábor is a relatively quiet little town nowadays, especially in the beautifully preserved old quarter, which is virtually devoid of traffic and has kept its labyrinthine street plan. In the staré město's back alleys, many houses have retained their rich sgraffito decoration and pretty Renaissance gables, while the main square boasts the country's premier museum devoted to the Hussite movement.

The Town

To reach the staré město from the new town or **nové město**, walk west from the train or bus station through the Husův park, making sure you take note of the unusual and passionate **statue of Jan Hus** by local turn-of-the-century sculptor František Bílek (you can see more of his work at the nearby village of Chýnov: see p.160). Continue past the statue down třída 9 května until you reach the busy square, náměstí Fr. Křižíka, which straddles the ridge between the new and old towns, then head up Palackého into the old town.

The street plan of the **staré město**, with its vast maze of narrow medieval streets designed to confuse the enemy, has changed very little since its foundation back in the fifteenth century. No fewer than twelve streets lead onto the central square, **Žižkovo náměstí**, with its brightly coloured houses and stunning variety of gables and gargoyles, all of which had to be rebuilt after fires in the fifteenth and sixteenth centuries. The square is dominated by the **Děkanský kostel**, with its unusual triple gable; for a bird's-eye view of Tábor's weblike street layout, climb the 199 steps of the church's extremely tall **belltower** (summer daily 9.30am–6pm), and try to time your climb between the hourly tolling, since you have to pass within inches of the bell to reach the top.

It was on Tábor's main square in 1420 that the Táborites threw theological caution to the wind and set up a religious commune under the principle of *není nic mé a nic tvé, než všecko v obec rovně mají* ("nothing is mine, nothing is yours, everything is common to all"). Large urns were set up in the square and anyone – male or female – wishing to

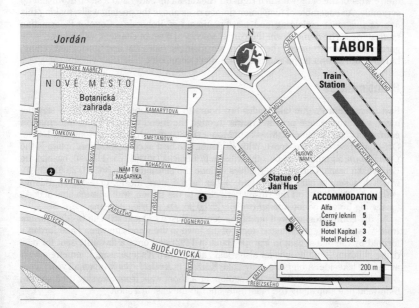

live in the commune had first to place all their possessions in them, after which they were given work on a daily rota. Men and women were granted equal rights, there was a complete ban on alcohol, and from the stone table which still stands outside the stará radnice, communion was given to the people "in both kinds" – as opposed to the established practice of reserving the wine (the blood of Christ) for the priesthood. The Hussites had this last symbolic act emblazoned on their flag – a red chalice on a black background – which, like the rousing religious war songs they sang before going into battle, struck fear into the crusaders from thirty nations who came against them.

Matching the church's triple gable on the west side of the square are the three steeply stepped neo-Gothic gables of the **stará radnice**, which now houses the **Husitské muzeum** (Hussite Museum; June–Aug daily 8.30am–5pm, rest of year Tues–Sun only). Inside, in amongst the nasty-looking pikes, there's a model of medieval Tábor, and several versions of Myslbek's late-nineteenth-century statue of **Jan Žižka**, the Táborites' brilliant, blind military leader (traditionally depicted with one eye still functioning), which stands on the square in front of the church. You also get the chance to peek inside the Gothic hall, with its diamond rib-vaulting and irreverent medieval corbels. The museum also runs hourly guided tours of a small section of the huge network of **underground passages** (*podzemí*); originally used to store beer barrels, they also served as a refuge from fire and siege, and as the town prison.

As for the rest of the town, its hotchpotch of backstreets, enlivened by the occasional sgraffito flourish, are perfect for a spot of aimless wandering – there's a great view of the surrounding countryside from the town's southern walls along Na parkánech. To give direction to your strolling, head down Klokotská to the **Bechyňská brána**, the town's only remaining gateway; its adjoining tower, now housing the Muzeum života a práce středověké společnosti (Museum of Life and Work in Medieval Society; May–Oct Tues–Sun 9.30am–5pm), has display cases full of farm tools and dioramas of house-building, and shows a video in English on life in Bohemia in medieval times.

Another place to aim for is the pilgrimage church and monastery of **Klokoty**, a kilometre west of the old town (turn right off Klokotská up Sady) and a steep down-and-up scramble. An ensemble of nine onion domes rises above the peeling walls, making this one of the most endearing and least pompous of Bohemia's Counter-Reformation monasteries. The domes form the corner towers of a set of cloisters with a lovely rose garden as its centrepiece. The church, surprisingly, has a flat and unadorned ceiling, but the putti-strewn pulpit and main altar don't disappoint.

Practicalities

Fast trains from Prague take under two hours to reach Tábor. If you wish to stay the night, you can arrange **private rooms** through the friendly and efficient **information centre** on Žižkovo náměstí (May–Sept Mon–Fri 8.30am–7pm, Sat 9am–1pm, Sun 1–5pm; Oct–April Tues–Fri 9am–4pm). Without doubt, the best **accommodation** option is the *Černý leknín*, a grandiose neo-Gothic villa on Příběnická (☎0361/25 64 05; ⑥), beyond the Bechyňská brána. Cheaper alternatives include the pensions *Alfa* (☎0361/25 61 65; ②), which has simple attic rooms above a bar in the staré město, or *Dáša* on Bílková (☎0361/25 62 53; ③), off the Husův park close to the station, with a sauna attached. As for the big **hotels**, go for *Kapital* (☎0361/25 60 96; ④), on třída 9 května.

All the **campsites** are well out of the centre. Buses #20 and #21 run to *Malý Jordán* (mid-May to mid-Sept), situated north of the town in the woods between Lake Jordán – formed by the oldest dam in Europe (built in 1492) and once a favourite spot for baptizing children – and its smaller sister lake, after which it's a pleasant kilometre's walk along the lakeside. A bigger site by Lake Knížecí is *Knížecí rybník* (open all year), connected by bus #30 from Tábor bus station, or a short walk from Smyslov train station, 6km (and one stop along the Pelhřimov line) to the east of Tábor.

If it's **food** you want, there's traditional Czech fare and Budvar and Bernard beers at *Beseda* (closed Sun eve), the popular pub at the top of the main square in the old town, whose patio spills out onto the square itself. More pleasant is *U dvou koček*, on Svatošova, to the west of the Děkanský kostel, which offers dark Purkmistr beer and light Pilsner to go with good solid cooking, and stays open late to serve a youthful clientele who go there to play pool and table football. For your afternoon coffee break, there's a good *cukrárna* on the main square, or for pizza, try *Pizza Napoli* on Husovo náměstí near the stations. As for **nightlife**, Tábor has its very own theatre, Divadlo Oskara Nedbala, on Palackého, though the plays are all in Czech, and a rock club, *Orion*, on náměstí Fr. Křižíka, featuring the occasional live band. If you're in town around the middle of September, be prepared for a lot of medieval fooling around as part of Tábor's annual **festival**, *Setkání*.

West of Tábor

Tábor's old town will keep you occupied for the best part of a day. However, if you've an afternoon to spare, a couple of side-trips are possible west of Tábor, both of them just a short train journey from the town.

Milevsko

Halfway along the branch line from Tábor to Písek, **MILEVSKO** has a couple of interesting sights besides its impressive array of late-nineteenth-century buildings. The most unusual is the former **synagogue**, on Sokolovská, designed by Oldřich Tyl and completed in 1919, which has been used by the local Hussite congregation since 1965. Its Neoclassical facade is disrupted by a double staircase that leads to the women's gallery, and by the distinctive Cubist prisms in the tympanum. There's a memorial to the town's hundred-strong Jewish community, which was wiped out in the Holocaust. The town's sturdy, twelfth-century **Basilica of sv Jiljí**, just off the main Tábor–Plzeň road, used to attract a stream of royal and ecclesiastical admirers until the Hussites wrecked it; despite repairs and later additions, it's currently in a desperate state. The nearby Premonstratensian monastery houses the small **Milevské muzeum** (Tues–Fri 9am–5pm, Sat & Sun 9am–4pm) charting the history of the town, with details as fascinating as the price of a fifteenth-century chicken.

Bechyně

Every hour and a half, a dinky electric train covers the 24-kilometre journey from Tábor to the small soporific spa and pottery-producing town of **BECHYNĚ**. The line from Tábor to Bechyně was the empire's first electrified line when it was opened in 1903, and on Saturdays in July and August, you can travel there and back on the original train. As you enter the town, both rail and road cross a spectacular viaduct over the Lužnice gorge, known locally as the "Rainbow". The old town teeters on the edge of the gorge, ten minutes' walk southwest of the station down Libušina.

At the far side of the leafy main square, which has long since lost its function as a marketplace, is the **Alšova jihočeská galerie** (May–Oct Tues–Sun 9am–noon & 12.30–5pm), housed in the old town castle brewery, which has an impressive collection of locally produced ceramics and hosts regular international exhibitions. Opposite is the medieval **Zámecká sýpka** (Tues–Sun 11am–6pm), now home to local history and temporary art exhibitions. Just beyond lies the Rožmberks' Renaissance **zámek**, whose treasures, unfortunately, are off-limits to the public. The Franciscan **monastery** nearby is now a school, but the church is open on Sundays for mass, and the gardens host summer concerts and afford excellent views of the gorge. Also worth exploring before you leave town is the **Hasičské muzeum** (Firefighting Museum; May–Oct Tues–Sun 9am–1pm & 1–5pm) in Široká, to the north of the main square, interesting less for its old fire engines than for the fact that it occupies the town's former **synagogue**. There's also a well-kept **Jewish cemetery** just beyond the old town walls on Michalská; ask at the museum.

The **last train back to Tábor** leaves at around 7.45pm; the last bus much earlier. If you wish to **stay the night**, head for the *Pichlův dům* (☎0361/81 10 75; ④), a lovely little Baroque cottage on the main square, with a bar and ceramics shop downstairs; alternatively, there's the *Hotel Jupiter*, a newly renovated late-nineteenth-century villa on Libušina (☎0361/96 21 31; ④), which has a good restaurant and also offers spa treatment. For **beer and food**, try the *Hospoda u města Bechyně*, a popular pub on the main square, or the *Hostinec pod skálou*, by the riverside at the bottom of the steps leading down from the corner of the square.

East of Tábor

East of Tábor, there are several more possible day-trips: to the village of **Chýnov**, where the turn-of-the-century sculptor František Bílek built his own house, now a museum to his exceptional talents; and, for those with an interest in the country's motorcycling history, to **Kámen**. Even **Pelhřimov** is possible as a day-trip by train or bus, though you're more likely to pass through en route to Moravia. Only devotees of Jaroslav Hašek will journey even further east beyond Humpolec to the village of **Lipnice**, to pay their respects to the last resting place of the creator of the *Good Soldier Švejk*. Likewise, admirers of Gustav Mahler might want to make the trip to **Kaliště**, northwest of Humpolec, to visit his birthplace, though unfortunately there's no dedicated museum there.

Chýnov

The little village of **CHÝNOV**, three stations east of Tábor, is the birthplace of the sculptor **František Bílek** (1872–1941), whose former home (though not his birthplace), the **Bílkův dům** at Údolní 133 (June–Sept Tues–Sun 10am–5pm), has recently been restored, and is an absolute must if you're in the area. Far from being a simple house-museum, this is a remarkable piece of architecture, designed by Bílek himself in 1897. Built in red bricks, with a large overhanging wooden roof and balcony, it stands out, above all, thanks to Bílek's biblical plaster relief on the south facade, and the miniature wooden chapel on the north side of the house. A large part of the interior is taken up with Bílek's studio, which is suffused with natural light and filled with studies for his large-scale works, but there is no attempt to re-create Bílek's home as it would have been in his day; instead, the building simply serves as a gallery for his works. Trained in Paris, Bílek was clearly influenced stylistically by Art Nouveau, though the tortured gestures and expressions of his subjects are derived more from the religious fervour that imbues all his work, which he himself described as "a sacrifice for the recovery of the brethren".

The Bílkův dům is situated on the south side of the river, across from the main part of town, signposted off the road to Tábor, and is a good 1.5km from Chýnov train station. While you're in the vicinity, you might consider paying a visit to the **Chýnovská jeskyně** (April–Oct Tues–Fri 10am–4pm, Sat & Sun 9am–4pm), a three-kilometre walk northeast across the fields from the train station on the blue-marked path. Amid gentle meadows and orchards, the entrance to the caves consists of a fifty-metre plunge down narrow, precipitous steps, to the sounds of Bach's *Toccata and Fugue in D minor*. What's fun about the thirty-minute guided tour is that it's a lot more like real potholing than the larger caves in Moravia or Slovakia, and there are even some stalactites and stalagmites to admire when you reach the bottom.

Kámen

There's a sporadic branch-line service between Tábor and Pelhřimov, but you'll have to take the bus along route 19 to reach the one-street village of **KÁMEN** (meaning "Rock"), whose castle was once a fortified staging-post between these two strongly pro-Hussite walled towns. It's worth a detour, since in 1974, after centuries of neglect, the castle was reopened – somewhat incongruously – as a **Motorcycle Museum** (April & Oct Sat & Sun 9am–noon & 1–4pm; May–Sept Tues–Sun 9am–noon & 1–5pm). Some wonderful old Czech bikes are on display, from the very first Laurin & Klement Model TB from 1899 – not much more than a bicycle with a petrol tank tacked on – to stylish examples from the heyday of Czech biking between the wars. Other machines include ČZs and Jawas, which may have cut some ice back in the 1940s when they were designed, but now only exacerbate the country's environmental problems. To trace the sad demise of the Czech motorcycle industry, you have to join the short guided tour of the castle before reaching the machines.

Pelhřimov

If you're heading east into Moravia and need a place to stay, make for the tiny medieval town of **PELHŘIMOV**, only 16km further east along route 19. Barely 200m across, the walled town still retains two sixteenth-century tower gates, on one of which, the **Rynárecká brána**, two rams tirelessly butt each other on the hour. In one corner of the very pretty, cobbled main square stands the very beautiful Renaissance **Šrejnarovský dům**, and the Venetian-red sixteenth-century **zámek Říčanských**, both now part of the local **museum** (Tues–Fri 9–11am & 1–4pm, Sat & Sun 10am–noon). On the main square itself, it's surprisingly easy to miss a minor work of Cubist architecture by Pavel Janák, who in 1913 adapted the Baroque **Fárovy dům** at no. 13, without forsaking the intentions of the original. You can get a good feel for the angled interior by stopping for a drink at the *Denní* bar upstairs. If you're on the Cubist trail, head through the chateau's archway and a short distance north up Strachovská to check out Janák's **Drechselův dům** at no. 331, right by the town brewery. The maroon and mustard colour scheme looks snazzy, especially on the stripy columns of the garden canopy, but it's not on the quietest of roads.

On one weekend in the middle of June the rather unlikely spectacle of Pelhřimov's **Festival of Records and Curious Performances** takes place, during which Czech eccentrics attempt to enter the *Guinness Book of World Records*, by whatever means necessary: recent new records include 157 people on one tractor, and a man with 82 socks on one foot, while "Železný Zekon" allowed seven cars to roll over him whilst lying on a bed of 970 nails. A museum cataloguing these great feats, the **Muzeum rekord a kuriozit** (nominally June–Aug Tues–Sat 9am–4.30pm, though hours are unpredictable), is now open in the Dolní (Jihlavská) brána, to the east of the main square. Inside, you can see the world's longest paper chain, the largest picture made from pasta, a giant toothbrush and pyjamas, the smallest paper boat (2 x 5mm) and a bicycle made entirely of wood. There's also photographic evidence of one-off achievements, and various rather tedious displays of strength. All in all, it's a fun museum, which the local children love.

The **train** station is, unfortunately, a good 2km south of the town centre; the **bus** station is about halfway along the road into town. Pelhřimov still brews its own **beer**, which you can sup to your heart's content at *U Vlasáků*, right next to the brewery, beyond the chateau; they also do passable Czech **food**, though the atmosphere is decidedly grungy. The social scene in town is looking up with the recent restoration of the Secessionist-era *Hotel Slavia* (☎0366/32 15 40; ③) on the main square, which, in addition to housing the best restaurant in town, is also the nicest place **to stay**. The other option is the unlovely communist-era *Rekrea* (☎0366/35 01 11; ④), just outside the historical centre, though its rooms are fine, with en-suite facilities and TVs.

Kaliště

Devotees of composer Gustav Mahler might want to make a detour to his birthplace in **KALIŠTĚ**, a tiny village 24km northeast of Pelhřimov. Several years of fundraising have finally resulted in the renovation of the building in which the great symphonist was born, in an apartment above the former town pub. The pub is now operating again (although the thoroughly modern decor lends little character), but the upstairs is, frustratingly, still used as an apartment and is firmly closed to the public. If you still want to make the trip, you can catch the rare bus from Humpolec, 16km northeast of Pelhřimov and linked by regular buses, and look for the white house opposite the church with "Mahler" painted across one side. While you're in Humpolec, you might want to visit the **Muzeum Dr Alše Hrdličký** (April–Oct Tues & Thurs–Sat 8–11am & 1–4pm, Wed 8–11am & 1–6pm, Sun 9–11am), which has a room full of photos and newspaper clippings of Mahler, with extensive captions in Czech only.

Lipnice nad Sázavou

Around 20km northeast of Pelhřimov, just beyond Humpolec and the Prague–Brno motorway, in the midst of some glorious Bohemian countryside, is the village of **LIP-NICE NAD SÁZAVOU**. Here, Bohemia's ultimate bohemian, the writer **Jaroslav Hašek**, died on January 3, 1923, his most famous work still unfinished. The village has changed little over the intervening years; the pub he lived, drank and died in is still going strong, and the castle, ruined even in Hašek's day, is still mostly rubble. A flattering bust of the author has been erected on the way up to the castle, and his gravestone is a little less ignominious these days. Beside the castle, in the house where he died, the **Memorial to Jaroslav Hašek** (May–Sept Tues–Sun 9am–noon

---

JAROSLAV HAŠEK

Stories about Hašek's life – many propagated by the author himself – have always been a mixture of fact and fiction, but at one time or another he was an anarchist, dog-breeder, lab assistant, bigamist, cabaret artist and people's commissar in the Red Army. He alternately shocked and delighted both close friends and the public at large with his drunken antics and occasional acts of political extremism. When, towards the end of his life, he made his home in the *Česká koruna* pub in Lipnice, he wrote happily, "Now I live bang in the middle of a *pivnice*. Nothing better could have happened to me." Few friends attended his funeral, and none of his family, with the exception of his eleven-year-old son, who had met his father only two or three times. In a final act of contempt, the local priest would only allow his body to be buried alongside the cemetery wall, among the unbaptized and suicide victims. Before long, however, the protagonist in Hašek's *The Good Soldier Švejk* had become the most famous (fictional) Czech of all time, culminating in Hašek's "canonization" by the Communist regime – his works even being published by the military publishing house.

& 1–4pm) is respectfully vague about the many contradictions in Hašek's life, not least the alcoholism which eventually cost him his life. If you want to pay homage to Hašek at Lipnice, roughly five buses a day make the ten-kilometre trip from Humpolec.

Třeboňsko

The **Třeboňsko** region, with the picturesque town of **Třeboň** at its heart, is unlike the rest of South Bohemia – characterized not by rolling hills but by peat bogs, flatlands and fishponds. This monotonous marshland, broken only by the occasional Gothic fortress, was moulded into an intricate system of canal-linked **ponds** (totalling over 6000) as early as the fifteenth century, ushering in profitable times for the nobles who owned the land. The fish industry still dominates the region, and around September the ponds are drained to allow the fish to be "harvested". Larger ponds, like the Rožmberk, are drained only every other year, and for three days people from the surrounding district gather to feast, sing and participate in a great local event that's worth seeking out if you're in the vicinity. Wildlife also thrives on the soggy plains, and in 1977 UNESCO declared a large area – from Soběslav south as far as the Austrian border – a **nature reserve**.

Jindřichův Hradec

JINDŘICHŮV HRADEC (Neuhaus) is the largest of the towns set amongst Třeboňsko's fish ponds. Hemmed in by walls and water, it's typical of the region – blessed with a glorious medieval past and, structurally at least, untouched by modern conflicts. Although the staré město was robbed of much of its rich medieval dressing by a fire in 1801, the main square, **náměstí Míru**, still displays an attractive array of wealthy merchants' houses, sporting brightly coloured early-nineteenth-century facades, and an exceptionally fine Baroque Trinity column. Only one house, the **Langrův dům** from 1579, hints at the Renaissance riches that were once the norm here. The diamond vaulting in the arcaded ground floor, and the sgraffito biblical scenes that cover the facade bear closer inspection, especially the depiction of Jonah being swallowed by what looks like a giant crocodile, on the side of the oriel window.

Rybniční leads down from the main square to a bridge that bisects the Vaygar fish pond, creating a small harbour. From here, the town's thirteenth-century **zámek** (Tues–Sun: April & Oct 9am–noon & 1–3.15pm; May & Sept 9am–noon & 1–4.15pm; June–Aug 9am–noon & 1–5pm) – chief residence of the lords of Hradec, and later the Černíns – is picturesquely mirrored in the water, its forbidding exterior giving no hint of the exuberant interior renovations by Italian architects in the sixteenth century, nor the recent extensive restoration – all of which make a visit here an absolute must.

To get to the chateau's main entrance, head down Dobrovského. You currently have a choice of three different forty-minute **guided tours** (only occasionally in English), which set off from the second courtyard. Tour A, the Adamovo stavení, leads you through the Neoclassical and Baroque "Green Rooms", and past Petr Brandel's painting of St Joseph curing the lepers; tour B, the Středověký hrad, explores the Gothic interiors, and features the starkly beautiful thirteenth-century chapel, fourteenth-century frescoes and the black kitchen; tour C, the Procházka staletími, takes you round the slender, triple-tiered, Renaissance loggia (which you can view without a guide) and the Černíns' bizarre collection of dog portraits, as well as gaining you entrance to the chateau's pride and joy, the striking bubble-gum pink garden rotunda, known as the "Rondel", with its incredible gilded stucco work. The Spanish Wing, which was designed as a Communist conference centre, complete with lift and cinema, is likely to be under restoration for some time to come. The chateau's Černá věž (Black Tower), accessible from the second courtyard, is open to the public without a guided tour, and you can peek through the windows into the Rondel anytime.

With most tour groups visiting only the chateau, there's hardly anyone exploring the cobbled alleyways to the north of the old town at the top of Komenského. You can climb the tall **tower** (daily 10am–noon & 1–4pm) of the Gothic church of Nanebevzetí Panny Marie, which doubled as the town's watchtower, and pay a visit to the former Jesuit seminary on Balbínovo náměstí, founded by Adam II of Hradec and Catherine de Montfort in 1604, and now home to the local **museum** (daily 8.30am–noon & 12.30–5pm). One room is devoted to Ferenc Rákóczi II, leading light of the Hungarian War of Independence (1703–11), who studied here, while another honours the composer Bedřich Smetana, who seems to have moved from one brewery to another; born in one in Litomyšl (see p.275), he lived in another here, below the castle, from 1831 to 1835. Still another room features folk costumes from the vicinity, plus the reconstructed parlour of opera singer Ema Destinnová, who lived nearby in Stráž nad Nežárkou (see box opposite). However, the museum's chief exhibit is its eighteenth-century 3-D Bethlehem Nativity scene, allegedly the largest in the world, with fully mechanized figures.

Practicalities

To get to the staré město from the **bus and train stations** to the north, it's a fifteen-minute walk along Nádražní, then left down Klášterská. This brings you to the edge of the old town, where the walls have long since been replaced by a park, the Husovy sady; the old town lies beyond. There's a **tourist office** on Panská (Mon–Fri 8am–5pm, Sat & Sun 8am–noon; 0331/36 35 46), just off the main square, and plenty of places to **stay** close by. On the main square alone, there's the flashy *Hotel Concertino* (☎0331/36 23 20; ⑧), the unremarkable *Grand Hotel Schneider* (☎0331/36 12 52; ⑤), and the better-value *Vajgar* (☎0331/36 12 71; ②), which has clean, modern doubles with shared facilities and more expensive rooms with TV and en-suite bathroom. The *Bílá paní* (☎0331/36 26 60; ③), above a restaurant right by the chateau, is also good value. The **restaurants** in the *Grand* and the *Vajgar* are both reasonable places to eat, but the locals seem to prefer *U Kateřina*, on Panská. There's also a pleasant café in the zámek courtyard.

THE WHITE LADY

If you're in the castle in Jindřichův Hradec and you hear a clinking of keys or a door unexpectedly slamming, or notice a figure in white floating about in the evening, it could be the *Bílá paní* or **White Lady**, the most famous ghost in the Czech Republic, whose favourite haunt is the castle. According to legend, she is the spirit of Perchta Rožmberková, born in 1430, who fell in love with the young Count Šternberk but was married against her wishes to Count Liechtenstein of Styria. On her wedding night, she secretly met Šternberk to bid him farewell, but was caught *in flagrante* by her husband, who thenceforth mistreated his wife. Many years later, Perchta returned to Jindřichův Hradec as a widow and used to hand out porridge, warm beer and honey to the poor. Since her husband never pardoned her, she was condemned to roam the castle as a ghost, though a benevolent one, prophesying births and deaths in the Rožmberk family by wearing white gloves for the former and black for the latter, and pointing out hidden treasure in the various family properties throughout Bohemia. Evenings in August are her favourite spooking time, when she is regularly spotted handing out porridge along the approach to the castle, outside the restaurant that bears her name.

EMA DESTINNOVÁ

Halfway between Jindřichův Hradec and Třeboň lies the town of Stráž nad Nežárkou, whose chateau was once the estate of Czech diva **Ema Destinnová** – her initials "ED" are emblazoned on the gates. The world's premier soprano of the early twentieth century, she won huge critical acclaim in Berlin and as the *prima donna* at New York's Metropolitan Opera. However, she also had strong ties to the Czech independence movement, and in 1916, during the height of World War I, she decided to return to Stráž for a visit, where she was arrested for smuggling revolutionary plans over the border. She was sentenced to confinement at her estate – though given that the penalty for espionage was, in fact, death without trial, Destinnová got off relatively lightly. Sadly, however, when the war ended, the singer was unable to re-establish her presence on the world's stages, and was even inexplicably shunned in Prague. With no financial resources, she spent her last twelve years living off the fish she caught from the Nežárka river, before dying of a stroke at the age of 52. Upon her death in 1930 the Czech public recognized the great figure it had lost, and Destinnová was given a lavish burial at Prague's Vyšehrad cemetery, as if to make up for past injustices. Then, in 1996, the Czech treasury placed Ema Destinnová on its new 2000Kč note. Her chateau, however, is closed to the public, pending sale.

Červená Lhota

In the middle of nowhere, off the main road between Jindřichův Hradec and Soběslav, the red sugar-lump castle of **Červená Lhota** (April & Oct Sat & Sun 9am–noon & 1–3.45pm; May, June & Sept Tues–Thurs, Sat & Sun 9am–noon & 1–3.45pm, Fri 1–3.45pm; July & Aug closes 4.45pm) is reflected perfectly in the still waters that surround it. This breathtaking sight – a Gothic waterfort converted into a Renaissance retreat for the rich in 1551 – appears on almost every regional tourist handout, but its isolated location makes it a nightmare to reach on public transport. Given this, and the unremarkable nature of the chateau's interior, it's really only for dedicated fans of Karl Ditters von Dittersdorf, Mozart's composing chum who died here in 1799. That said, the lakeside grounds around the chateau are perfect for a picnic, and in high season there's a horse and carriage available in which to take a turn.

Třeboň

Right in the midst of some of the region's largest fishponds, the spa town of **TŘEBOŇ** (Wittingau) is as medieval and minute as they come. The houses lining the long, thin main square, Masarykovo náměstí, make an attractive parade, but the *Bílý koníček* (*White Horse*) – now a hotel – built in 1544, steals the show with a stepped gable of miniature turrets. The entire **staré město** is made up of just three more streets, a fourteenth-century monastery and a chateau. Three gateways (including the impressive double south gate, next to the local brewery) and the entire ring of walls have survived from the sixteenth century, though many houses suffered badly during the last great fire in 1781.

Out of all proportion to the rest of the town is the huge Renaissance **zámek** (April–Oct Tues–Sun 9am–noon & 1–4pm; June–Aug closes 5pm), built by Petr Vok, a colourful character, notoriously fond of sex, drugs and alchemy, friend of the mad Emperor Rudolf II, legendary thrower of parties, and the last heir of the Rožmberk family. The chateau, daubed in blinding white sgraffito and taking up almost a fifth of the town, is a pretty clumsy affair, but the interior is definitely worth visiting. There's a choice of two 45-minute guided tours: trasa A is the one to go for as it concentrates on Petr Vok and the chateau's Renaissance legacy; the Baroque and nineteenth-century period furniture imported by the later owners, the Schwarzenbergs, forms the bedrock of trasa B. Adjacent to the chateau and equal in size to the old town is a very pleasant "English park", where the town's spa patients can take a stroll.

South of the town is the Svět pond, beside which stands the local **fishery** on Novohradská, which handles the region's huge fish harvest and, most importantly, its *kapr* (carp) culling. **Carp**, not turkey, is the centrepiece of the Christmas meal in the Czech Lands, traditionally sold live and wriggling from town squares across the country, then transferred to the family bathtub until the big day.

The Schwarzenberg mausoleum

Head south out of Třeboň in the direction of Borovany along the lake, and you'll pick up signs to the **Schwarzenberg mausoleum** (Schwarzenberská hrobka; April & Oct Sat & Sun 9am–4pm; May & Sept Tues–Sun 9am–4pm; June–Aug Tues–Sun 9am–5pm), twenty minutes' walk from the town centre. Hidden among the silver birch trees south of the Svět pond, it's a rather subdued, out-of-the-way site for a family so fond of ostentatious displays of wealth. The building itself is equally strange: a seemingly brand-new neo-Gothic building, with a bare chapel above and a dark crypt below (guided tours only). Třeboň was the first Bohemian town to be bought up by the Bavarian-based Schwarzenberg family in 1660 who, having sided with the Habsburgs in the Counter-Reformation, became the unofficial heirs of ousted or defunct Czech aristocrats like the Vítkovci and Rožmberks. By 1875, the family owned more estates in Bohemia than anyone else and decided to "honour" Třeboň by establishing the family mausoleum in the town. After 1945, the family's possessions were expropriated and, along with all their fellow German-speakers, they were thrown out of the country. Today, the most famous descendant is probably Count Karl von Schwarzenberg, a former emigré and today one of Havel's closest advisers.

Practicalities

The local **tourist office** (Mon–Fri 7.30am–5pm) can book **private rooms**. It's situated on the main square in the old town, where you'll also find two **hotels**: the aforementioned *Bílý koníček* (☎0333/72 12 13; ③) is not as pretty inside, but offers cheap en-suite rooms; the *Zlatá hvězda* (☎0333/75 72 00; ⑧), opposite, has much more comfortable en-suite rooms with TV for more than twice the price. For **camping** (and swimming), head for the *Domanín* campsite (May–Sept), south of the fishpond, near the mausoleum. The local fish **restaurant** is the *Šupina*, opposite the town's Regent brewery and signposted from the main square; otherwise you could try your luck at one of the hotels or, better still, if you're camping and cooking your own food, buy fresh fish from the *rybárna* (fishmonger) right by the carp pools, to the south of town. If you fancy a game of pool with the locals, head for *U zámku*, near the town gate by the brewery, though the town's most lively spot is *Torpedo*, by the main gates to the chateau.

It's possible to **cross into Austria** by catching one of the three daily expresses from Prague to Gmünd which pass through Třeboň, one of which continues to Vienna. The main train station, called simply Třeboň, is 2km north of the old town, off the road to Tábor; Třeboň lázně station is only five minutes' walk east of the old town, but only slow local trains stop there. Alternatively, there are frequent **bus** services west to České Budějovice or east to Jindřichův Hradec from the bus station, a five-minute walk west of the old town.

České Budějovice and around

The flat, urban sprawl of **ČESKÉ BUDĚJOVICE** (Budweis) comes as something of a surprise after the small-town mentality of the rest of South Bohemia. But first impres-

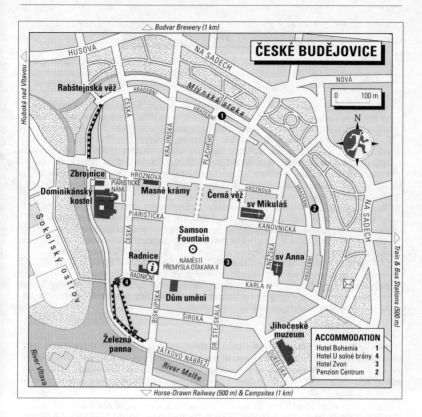

sions are deceptive, for at its heart it's a laid-back city, no more cosmopolitan than any-where else in the region, with a perfectly preserved staré město that attracts a good number of Bavarian and Austrian tourists. Founded by King Otakar II in 1265 as a German merchants' colony, the town's wealth was based on medieval silver mines and its position on the old salt route from Linz to Prague. All this was wiped out in the seventeenth century by the twin ravages of war and fire. But perhaps because it remained a loyal Catholic town in a hotbed of Hussitism, the Habsburgs lavishly reconstructed most of České Budějovice in the eighteenth century. Miraculously, in the face of two centuries of rapid industrial growth, the city's staré město has been carefully preserved. Besides, its renown nowadays is due to its local brew Budvar, better known abroad under its original German name, Budweiser (see box on next page).

The Town

České Budějovice's medieval grid plan leads inevitably to the town's showpiece, the magnificent **náměstí Přemysla Otakara II**, one of Europe's largest squares. The buildings are supremely elegant, testifying to the last three centuries of German burgher power (it wasn't until the 1890s that the first Czech was able to buy one of the houses here), but it's the square's arcades, its Baroque radnice, and the octagonal **Samson's Fountain** – once the only tap in town – that make the greatest impression.

BUDVAR V BUDWEISER

As far as taste goes, Czech Budvar bears little resemblance to the bland American Budweiser or Bud as it's universally known – it wins hands-down. However, the fact that two of the world's beers are sold under the same name has caused over a century of problems.

The story begins in 1857 when a German brewer named Adolphus Busch moved to the US. German beer names sold well in the States, so in 1876, Busch adopted the name Budweiser. At that time, the only beer brewed in what is now České Budějovice (but at the time was better known as Budweis) was Samson – another excellent brand which is still brewed today. It was only in 1882, that local Czech brewers registered the name Budweiser for one of their beers. As early as 1911, the Czechs and the American brewers, now known as Anheuser-Busch, came to an agreement, allowing the Czechs to call their beer "Original Budweiser"; in return, the Americans could market their "Budweiser" anywhere in the world, except Europe.

More negotiations followed over the course of the century, until the issue was forgotten behind the Iron Curtain. Then in the 1990s, the two breweries came together for talks once more, with the scales tipped heavily in Anheuser-Busch's favour. Not only were the American brewers now the largest brewing company in the world, the Czechs were desperate for cash to try and modernize their operation. A takeover seemed the most obvious solution. However, thanks to Britain's Campaign for Real Ale (CAMRA), worried that Czech Budvar would not be safe in Anheuser-Busch's hands, the issue became widely publicized. Sporadic litigious skirmishes take place across the globe, but for the moment České Budějovice's Budvar brewery is safely protected, as it remains the only one in the country to still be state-owned.

It was German merchants, too, who paid in silver and salt for the 72-metre status symbol, the **Černá věž** (Black Tower), one of the few survivors of the 1641 fire, which leans gently to one side of the square; its roof gallery (March–June Tues–Sun 10am–6pm; July & Aug daily until 7pm; Sept–Nov Tues–Sun 9am–5pm) provides a superb view of the staré město.

The streets immediately off the square – Krajinská, Česká and Kněžská – are worth wandering down, and if the weather's fine, folk promenade by the banks of the Malše, where parts of the original town walls have survived along with some of České Budějovice's oldest buildings, like the fifteenth-century prison tower, named after its most infamous torture instrument, **Železná panna** (literally "Iron Maiden"). All that is left of the bishop's palace is his serene **garden**, occasionally accessible in summer through a small gateway in the walls a little further on. At the second bridge, a right turn down Hroznová will lead you round into Piaristické náměstí, where the rough-looking, thoroughly medieval **zbrojnice** (originally the town's arsenal) stands, its stepped gables proof of its former importance as centre of the town's salt trade. The nearby church retains some of its Gothic cloisters, and patches of medieval fresco, too.

Two possible refuges in wet weather are the grandiose **Jihočeské muzeum** (Tues–Sun 9am–5.30pm), southeast of the old town on Dukelská, which contains all the usual thrills of a regional museum (stuffed birds, mushrooms, armoury, coins, etc), but occasionally puts on an interesting exhibition. Further south, at the bottom of F.A. Gerstnera, beyond the pencil factory, there's a meagre museum dedicated to the **Horse-Drawn Train Station** (Nádraží koněspřežská; May–Sept Tues–Sun 9am–noon & 12.30–5pm), which tells the history of continental Europe's first horse-drawn railway link, constructed between Linz and České Budějovice in 1827. With only a few photos and maps to accompany the video presentation, it's really only for aficionados – and only those who understand Czech or German. En route to the museum, you pass a vacant lot where the city's main **synagogue** stood until it was destroyed by the Nazis in

July 1942, a few months after the city's 909 Jews had been deported to Terezín – thirty returned after the war.

The **Budvar brewery** is off the road to Prague, on U Trojice (bus #2, #4, or #8), and has a newly refurbished *pivnice* (daily 10am–10pm) inside the nasty titanium-blue head-quarters; despite appearances, the beer and food are both inexpensive. Those who wish to make a pilgrimage should phone (☎038/770 53 40) to find out if they can join up with one of the guided tours; the tours need a minimum of five people, and have a maximum limit of fifty.

Practicalities

Ten minutes' walk from the **train and bus stations** down Lannova třída will bring you to Na sadech, the busy ring road flanked by small parks that encloses the staré město in place of the greater part of the old town walls.

Given České Budějovice's popularity with neighbouring Austrians and Germans, **hotels**, like the luxurious *Zvon* (☎038/731 13 83; ⑧) on the main square, tend to charge over the odds. There are, however, a few exceptions in the old town: *Penzión Centrum* (☎038/635 20 30; ③), just off Kanovnická at Na mlýnské stoce 6, offers small, clean rooms, while *Bohemia*, Hradební 20 (☎038/731 13 81; ⑤), and *U solné brány*, Radniční 11 (☎038/635 41 21; ⑥), are both good-value new hotels. The cheapest option of the lot is to go for a private room; the **tourist office** at no. 2 on the main square (Mon–Fri 9am–5pm, Sat 9am–2pm, Sun 9am–noon; ☎038/635 94 80) can help. CKM, at Lannova 63 near the train station (☎038/635 12 70), has information on **student rooms** avail-able in July and August; if they say they're full, go to the hostels themselves and beg. The only guaranteed cheap sleep is to **camp** in your own tent or rent a **bungalow** at the *Dlouhá louka* site (open all year), southwest of the centre on Litvínovská silnice; it's a half-hour walk, or else you can take red bus #6 from the museum or #16 from the sta-tion (both stop running around 7pm). The *Stromovka* site (mid-April to mid-Oct), a lit-tle further along the same road, is even cheaper and also has bungalows.

Drinking is obviously an important activity in České Budějovice, and without doubt the most atmospheric place to quaff Budvar is at the *Masné krámy*, on Krajinská, for-merly a sixteenth-century covered meat market, which also serves typical Czech food. For more sophisticated **eating**, the fish restaurant *Rossini,* on Biskupská, serves carp and trout fresh from the ponds northwest of town, and the *Bohemia* has a very nice brick-vaulted restaurant serving typical Czech food. If drinking's not your bag, then make for the *Dobrá Čajovna*, on Hroznová right behind the Černá Věž; this branch of the country's only teashop chain is typically relaxing. There's also an **Internet café** called *X-Files*, at the corner of Žižkova and Na Sadech. Nightlife is still thin on the ground, though *Legend Pub*, at Radniční 9, is a Harley-Davidson-inspired bar that thumps away until late.

Across the Českobudějovická pánev

To the northwest of České Budějovice lies the flat basin of soggy land known as the **Českobudějovická pánev**. Most people head for **Hluboká**, whose chateau receives an incredible number of tourists each year. Its neo-Gothic pastiche is not to everyone's taste – in many ways, you'd be better off seeking out the more elusive gems of Holašovice's folk-Baroque architecture or Kratochvíle's simple Renaissance beauty.

Hluboká nad Vltavou

Eight kilometres northwest of České Budějovice is the village of **HLUBOKÁ NAD VLTAVOU** (Frauenberg), from whose main square it's a stiff climb up to the **zámek**

(April, Sept & Oct Tues–Sun 9am–noon & 12.30–4.30pm; May–June Tues–Sun 9am–noon & 12.30–5pm; July & Aug daily 9am–noon & 12.30–5pm), originally founded as a Přemyslid stronghold as early as the thirteenth century. Sequestered from its Protestant Czech owners in 1622 for their part in the anti-Habsburg rebellion, it was then given to the arriviste Schwarzenberg family, who, during the course of the nineteenth century, spent some of their considerable fortune turning it into its present mock-Gothic incarnation. In 1945, when all the German estates were nationalized, the Schwarzenbergs decamped with most of the loot, but they've since returned and filled the interior with the odds and ends they left behind at their numerous other castles. The results are impressive, both inside and out, and pull in a quarter of a million visitors every year. You have a choice of guided tours: the main one (*hlavní okruh*) covers everything, or else you can simply visit the armoury (*zámecká zbrojnice*); guided tours are available in Czech or English.

If the surrounding mock-Tudor fails to move you, it's possible to seek sanctuary in the former riding school (*jízdárna*), which now houses the **Alšova jihočeské galerie** (Tues–Sun 9am–6pm), a permanent collection of Gothic religious art, Dutch and Flemish seventeenth-century masters and a large hall filled with a superb collection of twentieth-century Czech art, including Art Nouveau works by Bílek and Jan Preisler, a smattering of Cubist canvases by Čapek, Kubišta and Filla, a good selection of Surrealist paintings by the likes of Toyen and Štyrský, through to 1960s Pop Art. Alternatively, you can head off into the chateau's very beautiful English-style grounds, where South Bohemia's wild boars are reputed to roam; other distractions include occasional displays of falconry and hot-air balloon flights (ask at the tourist office for details).

There are plenty of places to **stay** in Hluboká, but prices are no cheaper than in České Budějovice; ask at the **tourist office** in the village about private rooms. There's also a **campsite** (mid-May to Sept) in Křivonoska, 3km north along route 105. **Eating** options are good: *Na Růžku*, on the corner of the main street serves Samson beer and reasonably priced food, and there's an excellent fish restaurant, *Rybí restaurace*, further down the road. Regular **buses** run from České Budějovice, dropping passengers off in the main square. If you're arriving by **train**, two out-of-the-way stations (nominally) serve the village: Hluboká nad Vltavou station, 3km southwest on the Plzeň line; and Hluboká nad Vltavou-Zámostí station, 2km east on the main line to Prague. There's also a new **cycling path** from České Budějovice to Hluboká along the Vltava; ask the tourist office for a leaflet.

Holašovice

If you have the time (and preferably your own car or bike), it's worth making a quick detour to the village of **HOLAŠOVICE**, 15km west of České Budějovice off the road to Lhenice, where you can see some of the finest examples of **Baroque folk architecture** unique to this part of Bohemia. The stone farmhouses (including the one and only pub) date from the first six decades of the nineteenth century, and face onto the original green. Every house on the square follows the same basic design, though the decorative details on barn doors and gables are unique to each. There are other nearby villages displaying similar architectural treats – like Záboří, 2km north, and Dobčice, another 2km west – but none can compete with the consummate effect of Holašovice.

Kratochvíle

Further west along route 145, and 2km beyond Netolice, lies **Kratochvíle** (Kurzweil), without doubt the most charming Renaissance chateau in Bohemia. It stands unaltered since its rapid six-year construction by Italian architects between 1583 and 1589, commissioned by the last generation of Rožmberks to while away the time – the literal meaning of *kratochvíle*. The attention to detail is still clearly visible in the exquisite stucco work and painted vaults, but the rest of the place is now given over to the **Museum of Animated Film** (April & Oct Sat & Sun 9am–noon & 1–4pm; May–Sept Tues–Sun 9am–noon & 1–5.15pm), which is aimed primarily at a young, domestic audience, with original puppet "actors" and drawings from well-known Czech kids' cartoons like *Boris* and *Mach a Šebestová*. However, the thoughtfully laid out exhibition, demonstrating all the painstaking processes involved in animation, should interest anyone, particularly with Josef Lada's amusing drawings of the Good Soldier Švejk and two typically disturbing new sculptures by Jan Švankmajer: a weird bird skeleton with butterfly wings and crab claws, and a human face formed of seashells. Kratochvíle is served by several daily buses plying the České Budějovice–Prachatice route, though as usual service is cut short at weekends.

The foothills of the Šumava

An alternative to heading up the Českobudějovická pánev is to aim for the large bulge of forest, known as the **Blanský les**, to the southwest of České Budějovice. Its highest point is **Mount Kleť** (1083m), which stands slightly apart from the rest of the Šumava range and looks all the more impressive for it, towering above the Vltava basin to the north. From the summit on a clear day, aside from the obligatory TV tower, you can see the undulating forested peaks of the Šumava laid out before you. To reach the top, either hop into one of the single-seat chairlifts (Tues–Sun hourly) or opt for the stiff but enchanting four-kilometre hike through the woods. To reach Mount Kleť from České Budějovice or Český Krumlov, catch a train to the idyllic rural station at Holubov and walk the last 2km to Krasetín, where the chairlift starts.

There's little **accommodation** in this neck of the woods, aside from a few private rooms and a basic **campsite** (May–Sept) in **ZLATÁ KORUNA** (Goldenkron), a tiny village on the Vltava, 6km along the line from Holubov. Here you can visit the strongly fortified **Cistercian monastery** (Tues–Sun: April, May, Sept & Oct 9am–noon & 1–4pm; June–Aug 9am–noon & 1–5pm), founded in the thirteenth century by King Otakar II. As a wealthy bastion of Catholicism, it suffered badly at the hands of the Hussites, but parts of the original medieval structures survive. In one building there's a worthy museum on Czech literature, but the main focus of interest is the vaulted chapterhouse dating from 1280 and the Gothic church, built in part by Peter Parler's masons and one of the first to employ ribbed vaulting without any accompanying capitols.

Český Krumlov

Squeezed into a tight S-bend of the Vltava, in the foothills of the Šumava, **ČESKÝ KRUMLOV** (Krumau) is undoubtedly one of the most exquisite towns in the Czech Republic. Rose-brown houses tumble down steep slopes to the blue-green river below, creating a magical effect whose beauty has barely changed in the last three hundred years. Under the Communists, few foreign tourists made it here, but nowadays the huge rise in tourism has made this the one place outside Prague where the warren of narrow streets can get uncomfortably crowded with day-trippers, including a new wave of young backpackers. The whole town is a UNESCO-designated site, but with rich pickings now on offer, many of its residents are renovating their properties, causing great concern among conservationists, who foresee overdevelopment and insensitive restoration – not to mention the loss of character that occurs when virtually every building is turned over to pensions and restaurants. For all that, it's a place that never fails to impress.

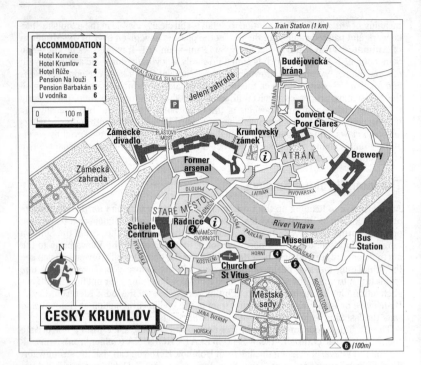

Train Station (1 km)

ACCOMMODATION
Hotel Konvice	3
Hotel Krumlov	2
Hotel Růže	4
Pension Na louži	1
Pension Barbakán	5
U vodníka	6

0   100 m

Budějovická brána

Jelení zahrada

Convent of Poor Clares

Zámecké divadlo

PLÁŠŤOVÝ MOST

Krumlovský zámek

LATRÁN

Brewery

Former arsenal

Zámecká zahrada

DLOUHÁ

LATRÁN   PIVOVARSKÁ

STARÉ MĚSTO

RADNIČNÍ

River Vltava

Schiele Centrum

Radnice

NÁMĚSTÍ SVORNOSTI

MASNÁ   PARKÁN

Museum

Bus Station

RYBÁŘSKÁ

KOSTELNÍ

HORNÍ

KAPLICKÁ

N

Church of St Vitus

Městské sady

ROOSEVELTOVA

ČESKÝ KRUMLOV

JANA ŠVERMY

HORSKÁ

(100m)

The Town

Český Krumlov's **history** is dominated by those great seigneurs of the region, the Rožmberks and the Schwarzenbergs. Thanks to special privileges won after the Battle of Leipzig in 1813, the Schwarzenbergs were permitted to keep a private army of twelve soldiers dressed in Napoleonic uniform (who also doubled as the castle's private orchestra), one of whom would sound the bugle at 9am every morning from the thirteenth-century round tower. In 1945, Krumau awoke abruptly from this semifeudal coma when the Schwarzenbergs and the majority of the town's inhabitants, who were also German-speaking, were booted out; three years later, the town went back into aspic as the Iron Curtain descended. Now a thoroughly Czech town, its economy relies increasingly heavily on the steady flow of German and Austrian tourists.

The town is divided into two separate quarters by the twisting snake of the River Vltava: the circular staré město on the right bank and the Latrán quarter on the hillier left bank.

The zámek

For centuries, the focal point of the town has been its chateau, **Krumlovský zámek** in the **Latrán quarter**, as good a place as any to begin a tour. Once you've passed through the first gateway, you enter the sprawling first courtyard, which belongs to the older, lower castle; from here you can climb the beautifully restored **castle tower** (daily: April & Oct 9.30am–5pm; May–Sept 9am–6pm), for a superb view over the town. To reach the ticket office, cross the medvědí příkop (bear moat), where the latest batch of unfortunate bears are incarcerated; it's located between the two smaller prettily painted courtyards of the upper castle, added in the fifteenth century. There are currently two **guided tours** (April & Oct Tues–Sun 9am–noon & 1–3pm; May & Sept 9am–noon & 1–4pm; June–Aug 9am–noon & 1–5pm) to choose between: the first takes you through the Rococo excesses of the blue and pink marble chapel, followed by the **Maškarní sál**, a ballroom exquisitely decorated with trompe l'oeil murals of *commedia dell'arte* scenes; the second concentrates on portraits of the Schwarzenbergs and doles out rich helpings of feudal opulence.

The castle's unique gem, however, is its ornate eighteenth-century Rococo **Zámecké divadlo**, on the other side of the covered Plášťový most, a many-tiered viaduct with a superb view over the town. This is one of the few Rococo theatres in the world to retain so much of its original scenery and wardrobe. An ingenious system of flies and flats meant that a typical comic opera of the kind the theatre specialized in could have more than forty scene changes without interrupting the action. Unfortunately, the theatre's fragility means that it is unlikely to reopen to the public on anything like a regular basis, so your only hope is that one of the rare performances is taking place.

Another covered walkway takes you high above the town into the unexpectedly expansive and formal **terraced gardens** (daily: April & Oct 8am–5pm; May–Sept 8am–7pm), whose tranquillity is disturbed only by the operas and ballets performed in the gardens' modern, revolving, **open-air theatre**, Otáčivé hlediště, during July and August; details from the tourist office.

The staré město

Latrán, lined with shabby, overhanging houses, leads to a wooden, ramp-like bridge that connects with the **staré město**. There's a compelling beauty in the old town, whose precarious existence is best viewed from the circling River Vltava. Turning right down Dlouhá, where the houses glow red at dusk, will bring you to the site of the town's former arsenal. From here, if the river's not swollen, you can walk across the gangplanks of the footbridge to Rybářská, which then follows the left bank to the south-ernmost bridge, taking you back into the old town.

Heading straight up the soft incline of Radniční brings you to the main square, **náměstí Svornosti** – look back for a great view of the castle. On one side of the

---

SCHIELE IN KRUMAU

In the spring of 1911, the Austrian painter **Egon Schiele** decided to leave Vienna and spend some time in Krumau, his mother's home town. During his brief sojourn here, Schiele painted a number of intense townscapes of Krumau, like *Houses and Roofs near Krumau* and *Dead City*, in which he managed to make even the buildings look sexually anguished. At the time, he was not making much money from his art, and was forced to shuffle from rooming house to rooming house with his 17-year-old lover, Wally Neuzil, a model handed down to him by Gustav Klimt.

Finally he succeeded in buying a studio, a crumbling Baroque cottage by the river in Plešivec, south of the old town. Schiele and his bohemian companions, Erwin Osen and Moa Mandu, caused more than a little controversy in this resolutely petit-bourgeois town – hiring young local girls for nude modelling and painting Wally naked in the orchard were among his more famous *faux pas*. Forced to leave before the year was out, he vowed never to return.

Under the Communists, the town made no attempt to advertise Schiele's brief but productive stay; now, however, he looks like being for Krumlov what Kafka is for Prague. Fans of the artist should head for the **Schiele Centrum** (daily 10am–6pm), a vast, rambling art complex housed in a fifteenth-century former brewery on Široká, which has a permanent collection of his works as well as shows by contemporary artists.

square, a long, white, Renaissance entablature combines two and a half Gothic houses to create the former **radnice**, while on the other, the high lancet windows of Sv Vít rise vertically above the ramshackle rooftops. If you continue east off the square, down Horní, you'll meet the beautiful sgraffitoed sixteenth-century Jesuit college, which now houses the *Hotel Růže*, among other things.

Opposite the *Růže*, the local **museum** (Okresní vlastivědné muzeum; May–Sept daily 10am–12.30pm & 1–5pm; Oct–April Tues–Fri 9am–noon & 12.30–5pm, Sat & Sun 1–4pm) puts on small, temporary exhibitions relating to the history of the town. Also on display are a reconstructed seventeenth-century shop interior and models of the town and the 2000-seater theatre at nearby Hořice, where the Passion Plays were staged until the tradition was stamped out by the Communists.

Practicalities

The **train station** is twenty minutes' walk north of the old town up a precipitous set of steps, while the main **bus station** is closer to the heart of town, on the right bank – either way, the best method of exploring Český Krumlov is on foot. There are two main **tourist offices**, one on náměstí Svornosti (daily 9am–6pm; ☎0337/711183), and one opposite the police station within the castle (daily 10am–4pm); the Agatha agency, Latrán 44, can also provide information and book private rooms.

Before losing yourself in the town's maze of streets, it's best to find some **accommodation**. The *Hotel Růže*, on Horní (☎0337/77 21 00; ⑧), originally built by the Rožmberks to house their guests, is right in the heart of the staré město, and has retained some of its original features – while it's undeniably superior, you do pay for the pleasure. The nearby *Konvice* (☎0337/71 16 11; ⑤), also on Horní, has none of the history, but is a good option – and cheaper. *Pension Barbakán*, Horní 26 and 27 (☎0337/71 70 17; ④), is a wonderfully refurbished place with tastefully decorated rooms and terrace dining. Another excellent pension is *Na louži*, Kájovská 66 (☎0337/54 95 or 71 54 95; ③), above a great pub by the Schiele Centrum. If and when it reopens, you shouldn't have trouble finding a room at the *Krumlov* on the main square (☎0337/71 15 65; ③). This hotel looks great from the outside, but is much plainer inside, and the cheaper rooms have shared facilities. There are also numerous small pensions and **private rooms** in town: Parkán, a little street along the river, is literally heaving with them and most come with views over to the zámek and riverside terraces. Even cheaper is the friendly English-speaking *U vodníka* **hostel** (☎0337/71 19 35; ①), just outside the old town and very popular with summer backpackers (the same people run the nearby *Krumlov House* hostel); to get there, follow Horní out of the old town, turn right into Rooseveltova and follow the signs. If they're full, there are a few other summertime hostels scattered about the town. There's also a primitive **campsite** (May–Sept) 2km south on route 160 to Nové Spolí, though it's aimed at summer canoers. More and better campsites lie several kilometres further south along the road to Rožmberk nad Vltavou.

As far as **eating** goes, there's plenty of choice. *Cikánská jizba* on Dlouhá is a nifty, cheap little place with a country theme and all the usual Czech and Slovak specialities. Also good is the fish restaurant *Rybářská bašta*, in the Krčinův dům off Široká, while *Na louži*, by the Schiele Centrum, is one of the town's best pubs, with fine food to boot. *Vegetarian*, on Parkán, has a surprisingly long, all-vegetarian menu and great riverside seating. Of the new pizzerias in town, *Pizzeria Nonnagina*, up Latrán near the zámek entrance, has the best reputation. For teas from around the world, slip into the *Dobrá čajovna*, also on Latrán, and if you need to check email, there's an **Internet café** just inside the zámek gates. There's no shortage of **drinking** spots either, and if it's late-night action you're after, *U Hada*, across the river from the old town on Rybářská, rocks on into the wee hours.

In summer, you can **rent canoes** from outfits at the ends of both Parkán and Kajovská and float downstream (with a shuttle minibus bringing you back). If you arrive in town at the weekend nearest the summer solstice, you'll witness the **Five-Petalled Rose Festival** (Slavnosti pětilisté růže), an excuse for the townsfolk to don medieval dress worn in the days of the Rožmberks, as well as let off fireworks, sing, dance and generally make merry. The town also hosts two **music festivals**: one dedicated to ancient music, held in late July, and an international one which takes place mid-August.

The Šumava

The dense pine forests and peat bogs of the **Šumava** region stretch for miles along the Austrian and German borders southwest of Český Krumlov, part of a much larger whole spreading across into Bavaria to form one of the last wildernesses in central Europe. The original inhabitants of this sparsely populated region were German foresters, who called the area Böhmerwald and scraped a living from its meagre soil – their Austrian lilt and agricultural poverty separating them from their "civilized" Sudetenland brothers in western and northern Bohemia. Up to the declaration of the First Republic in 1918, the economic armlock of the all-powerful Schwarzenberg and Buquoy dynasties kept the region in a permanent semifeudal state. Even in the nineteenth century, peasants had to have permission from their landlords to marry, and their customary greeting to the local squire was *Brotvater* (literally "Breadfather").

Following the expulsion of the German-speakers in 1945, all links with the past were severed, and despite financial incentives for Czechs to move here the Šumava has remained underpopulated. Poor, provincial and out of the way compared to the rest of the former Sudetenland, it had the added misfortune of lying alongside one of the most sensitive stretches of the East–West border during the Cold War – in the 1970s, large areas of forest along the south shore of Lake Lipno were closed off by the military. Much of this land has now been relinquished, the border dismantled, and contact between the two areas re-established, all of which are beginning to revive the area considerably. Ironically, while the Iron Curtain was there, the area was safely protected from overdevelopment, and local campaigners are now fighting hard to try and keep it that way. As a consequence, most of the roads to the south of Lake Lipno are closed to vehicles except bicycles. For more on the region's border crossings, see p.177.

Aside from the region's one truly medieval town, **Prachatice**, the majority of visitors come here for the scenery, which is among the most unspoilt in the country, thanks to the lack of heavy industry and, compared to the rest of Bohemia, minimal acid rain. Most tourists crowd round the northern shore of the artificial **Lake Lipno**, creating their own peculiar brand of beach culture, while others head for the hills, which rise up more gently than those on the Austrian and German side. The deepest part of the forest, hugging the German and Austrian borders between Lake Lipno and Železná Ruda, is preserved as the **Šumava National Park** (Národní park Šumava), where tiny villages blend into the silent hills, meadows and peat bogs. If you're considering **hiking**, two maps, available at most bookshops, cover the area from southeast to northwest: *Šumava–Prachaticko* and *Šumava–Klatovsko*; a third map, *Národní park Šumava*, covers the Šumava Park region. The most scenic way of **getting around**, apart from walking, is the regular České Budějovice–Volary branch train line. Much more convenient, though, are the local buses – though at weekends services begin to peter out. Two special **summer bus** lines, meant to keep the traffic light, run three to four times daily through the heart of the Šumava National Park: one traverses the park east–west from Lenora to Železná Ruda via Borová Lada, Kvilda, Modrava and Srní; the second cuts a north–south path from Sušice to Kvilda via Kašperský Kory, Srní and Modrava. Due to its gently hilly landscape, the park is also great **cycling** territory, although bike rental outlets are few and far between. In the summer, Czechs often float down the Vltava in **canoes**, which can be rented from the odd town along the river.

Rožmberk nad Vltavou

Buses from Český Krumlov follow the Vltava valley to the pretty village of **ROŽMBERK NAD VLTAVOU** (Rosenberg), which is tucked into a U-bend of the river, and overlooked by a sgraffitoed **fortress** towering above it. As the name suggests, its *raison d'être* was as the headquarters of the powerful and single-minded Rožmberk family, regional supremos from the thirteenth century until their extinction in 1611. Only one round tower remains from the Rožmberk era, though the highlight of the guided tour, the castle's sixteenth-century Italian frescoes, is also a Rožmberk legacy. The rest of the interior speaks little of that family, but volumes of its later French owners, the Buquoys, who stuffed the dull, mannerless rooms with heavy neo-Gothic furnishings and instruments of torture, the latter being displayed in the Katovna, separate from the tour. In summer, Czech tour groups fall over one another for a place on the 45-minute **guided tours** (April & Oct Sat & Sun 9am–3.15pm; May & Sept Tues–Sun same hours; June–Aug closes 4.15pm), which are occasionally given in English.

Finding **accommodation** in this small village is relatively easy at any of the many private rooms on offer. Otherwise, the *Hotel Růže* (☎0337/74 97 15; ⑤) has well-appointed rooms and a restaurant, while the *Hotel Studenec* (☎0337/74 98 88; ③), north of the village off route 160 to Český Krumlov, rents out canoes and bikes. Nearby is the *U lipse* **campsite** (mid-June to mid-Sept); you can get there by climbing up to the castle and back down the other side of the bluff, or along the road.

Vyšší Brod

Upriver from Rožmberk, just fifteen minutes south by bus, is **VYŠŠÍ BROD** (Hohenfurth), notable for its white Cistercian monastery on the western edge of town, founded in the thirteenth century in response to the Přemyslids' founding of nearby Zlatá Koruna (see p.171). Its proximity to the border and its extreme wealth gave rise to a set of immodest fortifications that withstood two sieges by the Hussites. Despite its pews, the essentially Gothic **monastery church** (July & Aug daily 9am–noon & 1–5pm; April–June & Sept–Oct Tues–Sat 9am–noon & 1–5pm, Sun 1–5pm) was for the exclusive use of the monks, who sat in the fancy gilded stalls that take up almost half the church – only on religious holidays were the locals allowed in at the back. In the blue side chapel rests Petr Vok, the last of the Rožmberks, who died of drink and drugs but was nonetheless given pride of place as the monastery's rich patron. Monks still inhabit the complex to this day.

The only way to see the church's interior properly is by **guided tour** (at 9, 10 & 11am, 1, 3 & 4pm), which also takes you through the beautiful Gothic chapterhouse and ends with the star attraction, a Rococo library decorated with 24-carat gold, accessible only via a secret door in one of the bookcases. The monastery's outer buildings house a mildly diverting **Postal Museum** (Poštovní muzeum; April–Oct Tues–Sun 9am–5pm), charting the history of the republic's postal system since the late medieval period, with displays of period uniforms, old phones and typewriters, new stamps and old stage and post coaches.

If you need a place **to stay**, there's the *Hotel Panský dům* (☎0337/74 66 69; ①), which has unfortunate decor throughout, but very cheap rooms with or without en-suite shower. There are also several private rooms and pensions, including *Pension Inge* (☎0337/74 64 82; ①), right by the monastery, which also rents out canoes; you can even stay in the monastery itself (☎0337/74 64 57; ①). The *Pod hrází* **campsite** (mid-May to Sept) is a short walk along route 163 towards Lipno nad Vltavou.

There are **buses** from Rožmberk to Vyšší Brod, or else you can catch a train from Rybník, 10km east on the Prague–Linz main line (get out at Vyšší Brod klášter, not Vyšší Brod, for the monastery). Local buses and trains continue 10km to Lipno nad Vltavou, at the eastern edge of Lake Lipno, where a host of other facilities are available (see below). If you are walking from Vyšší Brod, be sure to take the red route to the viewpoint at **Čertova stěna** (Devil's Walls), a giant scree of granite slabs that tumble into the river below.

Lake Lipno

Beyond the giant paper mill on the Vltava, a dam marks the southeastern end of **Lake Lipno**. The barrage turns the turbines of a huge underground hydroelectric power station, and on the face of it, there's not much to get excited about. The northern shore is punctuated by small beach resorts, which have developed rapidly over the last twenty years, mostly created to give workers some well-needed fresh air. The area is popular with Czechs, Germans and Austrians, so the **hotels** are often full in July and August, but you're rarely far from **private rooms** – look for the *unterkunft/ubytování* signs dotted about – or a **campsite**, often with cheap bungalows for rent. **Buses** link most places, supplemented by trains from Černá v Pošumaví westwards. If you're planning to spend some time walking here it might be worth buying the very detailed *Lipenská přehrada* map.

About the only reason to come to **LIPNO NAD VLTAVOU** is to take the one- or two-hour **cruise** on the lake. From May to October there are three boats leaving daily from the small pier in town. The town has a couple of run-down hotels, though you're almost certainly better off trying any of the numerous pensions signposted off the road to Frymburk, or one of the campsites by the lake. Note that the train station at Lipno is situated below the dam, a couple of kilometres east of the town itself. The lake's south-easternmost villages are the least developed, and of these, **FRYMBURK** (Friedberg), with its delicate white, octagonal spire, is arguably the best place to head for. First choice for accommodation is the family-run *Hotel Maxant* (☎0337/73 52 29; ②), situated on the leafy main square, followed by *Pension Markus* (☎0337/73 54 18; ③), opposite, and there are two low-key campsites just south of the village.

NEW BORDER CROSSINGS

Before 1989, the main road from Horní Planá northwest to Volary was punctuated at regular intervals by little red signs warning about the impending Iron Curtain; all villages west of the Vltava were closed to road vehicles, with trains the only legal means of transport. The military have now given up their patch, and there are now several new **border crossings** into Austria and Germany. From west to east, these are: Strážný/Philippsreut (open to all vehicles; daily 24hr); Stožec/Haidmühle (pedestrians and cyclists only; daily: April–Sept 7am–9pm; Oct–March 7am–7pm); Plešné Jezero/Halzschlag (pedestrians and cyclists only; daily: April–Sept 7am–9pm; Oct–March 7am–7pm); Zadní Zvonková/Schöneben (pedestrians and cyclists only; daily: April–Sept 7am–9pm; Oct–March 7am–7pm); Ježová/Iglbach (pedestrians and cyclists only; daily: April–Sept 7am–9pm; Oct–March 7am–7pm); and Přední Výtoň/Guglwald (open to all vehicles; mid-March to Oct 6am–10pm), on the opposite side of the lake from Frymburk. With the exception of infrequent local buses, all other vehicles are still forbidden to enter the area through most of the crossings, partly due to the state of the roads and partly to the recent decision to turn the whole area into a nature reserve.

There are plenty more accommodation options 10km down the road in **ČERNÁ V POŠUMAVÍ** (Schwarzbach), a village divided into two by the lake: on the eastern shore is the village proper and the road junction; on the western shore, across the road bridge, is the train station. In addition to the regular service between České Budějovice and Volary, a **historic steam train** plies the rails at weekends in July and August from here to Nové Údoli, hard up against the German border to the west. Czechs in search of a beach head off to nearby **DOLNÍ VLTAVICE**, 6km south on a secluded thumb of land, where a small crowd enjoys the grassy "beach" with a view over to the short stretch of hillside on the opposite, Austrian shore.

HORNÍ PLANÁ (Oberplan), 7km west of Černá, is the lake's chief resort, and has a useful **tourist office** (Mon–Sat 9am–4pm; July–Aug daily 9am–6pm) in the Česká spořitelna building on the leafy main square, which can help you fix up some accommodation and also rents out **mountain bikes**. There is a cheap hotel on the square as well, the *Smrčina* (☎0337/73 82 28; ②), with a decent restaurant, and the town has several new pensions, plus a concrete-surfaced campsite (June–Sept). The locals happily soak up the sun, cheek-by-jowl on the almost sandy beach, surrounded by a dubious combination of crazy golf, candy floss and beer. A little cultural distraction can be experienced at the birthplace of the German-speaking writer and painter **Adalbert Stifter**, who cut short his life in 1868 by slashing his throat to escape cancer of the liver. The house (mid-Jan to March & Nov to mid-Dec Wed–Sun 9am–noon & 12.30–4pm; April–June & Sept Tues–Sun 10am–noon & 1–6pm; July & Aug daily 10am–noon & 1–6pm), on the road into town from the east, is now a small memorial to his life and work; his statue stands behind the church, and there's another memorial to him overlooking the waters of the Plešné jezero, which sits below Plechy at the meeting of the German, Austrian and Czech borders.

Hiking west of the Vltava

One of the most interesting **hikes** in the border region to the west of the Vltava sets off from Ovesná station, at the top of Lake Lipno, following the yellow-marked route northwest through gigantic boulders and thick forest to Perník (1049m), before dropping down to Jelení, where the **Schwarzenberg Canal** (Švarcenberský kanál) emerges from a tunnel. Built at the turn of the eighteenth century to transport the Šumava's valuable timber straight to the Danube (less than 40km due south), the canal was abandoned as a waterway in 1962. A little further on you reach the **Medvědí kámen** (Bären Stein), marking the spot where the last bear in the Šumava was shot in 1856. The only threat now is 25 lynx, which were resettled hereabouts in 1985.

Moving on, you should reach the village station at **ČERNÝ KŘÍŽ** in around six hours from Ovesná. Here, the railway divides: the main branch heading north to Volary (see p.181), while a short spur heads southwest to Nové Údoli station, just 300m from the German border (the historic steam trains run along this line as well). From here, you can take the red-marked trail south 5km to the peak of Třístoličník (1302m), where it's another 5km to Trojmezí, the meeting-point of the German, Austrian and the Czech Republic borders, and 1km further to the summit of Šumava's highest peak, Plechý or Plöckenstein (1378m), on the Austrian border. Another option is the red-marked path northwest, passing through Krásná Hora (Schönberg), one of the numerous "dead" Sudeten villages in the region. Heading north by train from Černý Kříž brings you to **VOLARY** (Wallern), founded by colonists from the Tyrol and now a sizeable town for these parts, with a few traditional wooden Šumava cottages, a handsome Baroque church and a fair amount of industry. You may have to change trains here for Vimperk or Prachatice.

Accommodation in the area is improving: there's a simple pension, *Černý Kříž* (☎0338/33 51 08; ①), in the village of the same name, or the more plush *U Mauritzů* (☎0338/33 51 66; ③) in Stožec, the railway stop between Černý Kříž and Nové Údolí,

PETER WILSON

Malá Strana backstreets, Prague

SEAN GALLUP

Fred and Ginger building, Prague

SEAN GALLUP

Bridges over the Vltava, Prague

Fruit and vegetable stall, Hradec Králové   The Cathedral of sv Barbora, Kutná Hora

Grand Hotel Pupp, Karlovy Vary

The main square in Telč, South Moravia

Prachovské skály, Český ráj

Backstreet in Pardubice

HANS-HORST SKUPY

MIREK FRANK

Sgraffito decoration in Slavonice   Pernštejn, South Moravia

MIREK FRANK

Velké Losiny, North Moravia

where you'll also find the excellent restaurant *Rosenaurova chalupa*. There's more choice in Volary: two drab hotels, the *Bobík* (☎0338/33 53 51; ③) and the *Chata* (☎0338/33 52 60; ②), and a pension, *Kukačka* (☎0338/33 52 32; ①). The nearest **campsite** is *Soumarský Most* (April–Oct), 4km west along the road to Lenora.

Prachatice and around

The slopes of Libín (1096m) merge into the Otava and Vltava plain by the amiable little market town of **PRACHATICE** (Prachatitz), known as the "Gateway to the Šumava". Most people do come here en route to the Šumava, but it's a beautiful medieval town in its own right, as well as being a useful base for visiting **Husinec**, birthplace of Jan Hus (see p.180). Founded in 1325, Prachatice flourished in the following century, when it controlled the all-important salt trade route into Bohemia. A fire in 1507 is responsible for the uniformly sixteenth-century appearance of the town and its famous collection of sgraffito facades.

The Town

A short walk uphill from the bus and train stations brings you to Malé náměstí, the main square-cum-crossroads of the nondescript new part of town. Everything of interest is contained within the walls of the tiny circular **staré město**, reached through the bulky fifteenth-century **Písecká brána**, a gateway with a faded mural showing Vílem of Rožmberk on horseback and, above it, in among the battlements, the red rose symbol of his family, who acquired the town briefly in 1501.

The gate's double arches open out on the small Kostelní náměstí, where old women sell spices and vegetables in the shade of the trees. The Gothic church of **sv Jakub**, with its steeply pitched, rather peculiar red-ribbed roof, is the oldest building and most obvious landmark in town. Prachatice is best known, however, for the exquisitely decorative **Heydlův dům** to the left, which sports bizarre depictions of men clubbing each other to death, unintentionally apposite given its present incumbents, a family butcher's. Next door is the Latin school or **Literátská škola**, also crowned with miniature Renaissance battlements, and which local heroes Hus and Žižka are said to have attended in their youth.

At this point the cobbles open out into the old town square, **Velké náměstí**, which has a thoroughly Germanic air. Its most striking aspect is the riot of **sgraffito** on the facades of many of the buildings; if you haven't already come across the style, Prachatice is as good a place as any to get to grips with it. The technique – extremely popular in the sixteenth century and revived in the nineteenth – involves scraping away painted plaster to form geometric, monochrome patterns or even whole pictorial friezes, producing a distinctive lace-work effect. The most lavish example of this style is the arcaded **Rumpálův dům**, at no. 41 on the east side of the square, which depicts a ferociously confused battle scene. At no. 45 is another arcaded building, the former **solnice** or salt house (also known as the Bozovského dům), through which the town accrued its enormous wealth in the Middle Ages and which features Vílem of Rožmberk once more on horseback.

On the north side of the square, the sixteenth-century **stará radnice**, decorated with copies of Hans Holbein's disturbing, apocalyptic parables, employing a much more sophisticated use of perspective, stands just a few doors down from the **nová radnice**, whose sgraffito dates from the late nineteenth century. One of the fanciest houses on the square is the **Sittrův dům**, now the local museum (Tues–Fri 9am–4pm, Sat & Sun 10am–4pm), on the east side of the square, distinguished not by its sgraffito, but by its colourful painted facade and ornate Renaissance gable. Four doors down at no. 9 is the **Knížecí dům**, which hides its sgraffito round the side, on which you'll find, among other things, a stag hunt, several devils and an elephant mermaid with two tails.

Practicalities

Hotel Parkán (☎0338/31 18 68; ④), on Věžní, is probably the nicest **place to stay**, with en-suite facilities and TVs in all its rooms, and a solid Czech restaurant; to get there head up Křišťanova by sv Jakub and take the first left. Alternatively, you can ask at the **tourist office** (Mon–Fri 9am–noon & 1–4pm, Sat 9am–noon), in the Písecká brána, or the one between the two town halls (Mon–Fri 7.30am–4pm), about the availability of the various private rooms advertised in the backstreets of the old town. To get to the primitive **campsite**, 10km south by the lake at Křišťanovice (July & Aug only), infrequent buses drop you on the main road, from where it's a 1500m walk.

Husinec

"You may burn the goose [hus]*,*
but one day there will come a swan,
and him you will not burn."
                    Martin Luther

Six kilometres north of Prachatice is the unassuming village of **HUSINEC**, birthplace of **Jan Hus** (see box below), the man whose death in 1415 triggered off the Hussite revolution. In the nineteenth century, when interest in Hus began to emerge after the dark years of the Counter-Reformation, the poet Jan Neruda visited Husinec and was horrified to find Hus' former home shabby and neglected. No expense has been spared since, with the family house at nos. 36 & 37 converted into a **museum** (Památník M.J. Husa; Tues–Sun 9am–noon & 1–4pm) and many of Hus' old haunts in the surrounding region turned into points of pilgrimage over the last century. That said, there are few visitors nowadays to the museum's small exhibition and only one original room, a tiny garret on the top floor. To give you an idea of Hus' place in the Czech nationalist canon, take a look at the stirring multicoloured sgraffito illustration on no. 42. Getting to Husinec is easiest on one of the regular **buses** from Prachatice; the train station is 3km east of the village.

JAN HUS

The legendary preacher – and Czech national hero – **Jan Hus** (often anglicized to John Huss) was born in the small village of Husinec around 1372. From a childhood of poverty, he enjoyed a steady rise through the Czech education system, taking his degree at Prague's Karolinum in the 1390s, and eventually being ordained as a deacon and priest around 1400. Although without doubt an admirer of the English religious reformer, John Wycliffe, Hus was by no means as radical as many of his colleagues who preached at the Betlémská kaple. Nor did he actually advocate many of the more famous tenets of the heretical religious movement that took his name: Hussitism. In particular, he never advocated giving communion "in both kinds" (bread and wine) to the general congregation.

In the end, it wasn't the disputes over Wycliffe, whose books were burned on the orders of the archbishop in 1414, that proved Hus' downfall, but an argument over the sale of indulgences to fund the papal wars that prompted his unofficial trial at the Council of Constance in 1415. Having been guaranteed safe conduct by Emperor Sigismund himself, Hus naively went to Constance to defend his views, and was burnt at the stake as a heretic. The Czechs were outraged, and Hus became a national hero overnight, inspiring thousands to rebel against the authorities of the day. In 1965, the Vatican finally overturned the sentence, and the anniversary of his death (July 6) is now a national holiday.

Volary to Vimperk

The scenic train ride from Volary, 18km south of Prachatice, to Vimperk takes you deep into the Šumava forest, and it's worth breaking the journey at some point to delve further into the woods. At **LENORA**, there's a glass factory, several old, wooden, Šumava cottages and a picturesque covered wooden bridge over the river. One stop further on, at Zátoň station, a green-marked path skirts the primeval **Forest of Boubín**, and just 1500m from the station are the primitive *Boubín* campsite (open all year) and *Penzión Ida* (☎0339/43 62 14; ④), a charming little country house by the railway, whose price includes dinner and breakfast. The park's summer bus from Lenora (see p.175) also pulls in here.

It's forbidden to walk among the pines and firs of Boubín, some of which are over 400 years old, but the green markers take you 4km around the perimeter and on to a small **deer park**; from here you can get back to the rail line without retracing your steps by following the blue-marked path 6km to the station at **KUBOVÁ HUŤ**, where there are several hotels and pensions to choose from, including the comfortable *Arnika* (☎0339/43 63 26; ⑤). From May to September, trains skirting the south slope of Boubín also stop at the station high above the village of **HORNÍ VLTAVICE**. The two-kilometre scramble down through the forest is worth it for the justly popular riverside **campsite** (May–Sept) and *hostinec* below.

Vimperk

From Horní Vltavice, a few local buses cover the 13km to the 24-hour Strážný–Kleinphilippsreuth German border crossing; trains continue for 13km to **VIMPERK** (Winterberg), where the first printing press in Bohemia was established in 1484 – a few decades after Gutenberg's invention. The business of the day goes on in the lower part of town, leaving the steep narrow streets of the **staré město** virtually deserted. The leafy main square, náměstí Svobody, is overlooked by the town's **hrad**, originally built in the thirteenth century by Otakar II, and last owned by the Schwarzenbergs. The castle, a stiff fifteen-minute hike up from the square, has been knocked about a bit over the centuries, and now houses the local museum (May–Oct Tues–Sun 9am–noon & 1–4pm), with little of interest beyond a selective display of local glassware, though you're rewarded with great views over the old town.

Despite its relative lack of local attractions, Vimperk is another possible base for exploring this part of the Šumava. There are a couple of **hotels** by the train station, but that leaves you a good 1500m from the town centre down Nádražní. A better idea is to head for the *Hotel Anna*, right in the centre (☎0339/41 20 50; ⑤), a lovely old building that's been rather brutally modernized, but a very comfortable place to stay all the same. The hotel also conveniently houses the **tourist office** (Mon–Fri 9.30am–12.30pm & 1–5pm), which can point you in the right direction if you want a private room. The nearest **campsite** is *Vodník* (mid-May to Sept), at Hájna Hora, a kilometre or so up the hill to the south of town. For a cheap Platán **beer** and some traditional **food**, head for the *Hospoda na náměstí* on náměstí Svobody.

Strakonice

The rest of the Šumava lies, strictly speaking, in West Bohemia: the mountainous part is only accessible from the east by an infrequent bus service. Sticking with the railway, another 30km takes you to **STRAKONICE** (Strakonitz), which qualifies as a large industrial town in these parts. It grew up as a textile town in the nineteenth century, and its factories now produce an unusual trio of products: Turkish fez hats, ČZ motorcycles, and *dudy*, the Bohemian equivalent of bagpipes.

There's a **museum** (Muzeum středního pootaví; Tues–Sun: May, Sept & Oct 8am–4pm; July & Aug 9am–5pm) on these very subjects in the town's extremely large thirteenth-century **hrad**, at the confluence of the Volyňka and the Otava, on the south bank of the latter. It's a fun place to explore: there are plenty of old motorbikes to admire, an international selection of *dudy* in everything from velvet to sheepskin, and a fez-making machine. Ironically enough, the fez-making venture was established back in the nineteenth century by some enterprising local Jewish textile merchants. You also get to climb the castle watchtower, Rumpál. If you're really into *dudy*, there's an **International Bagpipe Festival** held in the castle courtyard every year in the middle of August, which attracts a regular contingent from Scotland and elsewhere.

The rest of the town, on the other side of the river, can't quite match the eclectic attractions of the castle, though **Velké náměstí** boasts two very attractive late-nine-teenth-century buildings – one a savings bank, the other the old radnice – facing each other across the square. Both are designed in florid neo-Renaissance style, and deco-rated with pretty folk-inspired and floral murals and friezes.

From the **train** and **bus stations**, it's a five-minute walk to the castle – west down Alfonse Šťástného, then right down Bezděkovská. If you're **staying the night**, head for the excellent **information centre** (Mon–Fri 9am–noon & 1–5pm) in the Mapové cen-trum, located in the main gateway of the castle, where you can book private rooms. Alternatively, try the *Fontána* (☎0342/32 14 40; ④), northeast of the main square on Lidická, the *Švanda dudák* (☎0342/32 13 05; ②), which is near the junction of Alfonse Šťástného and Bezděkovská and has rooms without facilities for about half the price of those with en-suite, or the tasteless, communist-style high-rise *Hotel Bavor*, across from the castle (☎0342/32 13 00; ⑤). There's a **campsite**, *Podskalí* (June to mid-Sept), by the banks of the Otava, fifteen minutes' walk west along Pod Hradem, which runs south of the castle. Strakonice brews its own **beer**, across the river from the castle, and you can sup the local Nektar nearby at *U zborova*, at Bavorova 20, which heads off north from the western end of the main square.

Rabí and Sušice

There are several ruined castles along the banks of the River Otava beyond Strakonice, but by far the most impressive – and the largest in Bohemia – are the vast and crum-bling fortifications of **Rabí**, 25km away by train (change at Horažďovice). A key fortress in the Hussite Wars, and allegedly the place where the Hussite general Jan Žižka lost his second eye, it was deliberately allowed to fall into rack and ruin in the eighteenth century for fear of its strategic value should it fall into the wrong hands. The village sold the castle to the state for one crown in 1920, and recent renovation work, aimed at sta-bilizing some of the more dangerously disintegrating bits, has now allowed the public access to most of the site (April & Oct Sat & Sun 9am–noon & 1–3pm; May & Sept Tues–Sun 9am–noon & 1–4pm; June–Aug Tues–Sun 9am–noon & 1–5pm) – however, you must endure an hour-long guided tour in English to explore it. The castle also hosts regular falconry displays in the high season (Tues–Sun 11am, 2 & 4.30pm).

A few stops on from Rabí is **SUŠICE** (Schüttenhofen), which means just one thing to the Czechs – matches. The local SOLO match factory is one of the largest in Europe, and dominates the domestic market. Aside from that, there's little evidence of the town's wealthy medieval past, which, like Prachatice's, was based on the salt trade. The exception is the main square, náměstí Svobody, which boasts a handful of striking Renaissance houses; the most arresting are the **Rozacínovský dům** at no. 48, with a fantastic sgraffitoed gable sporting several tiers of mini-pilasters, and the **Voprchovský dům** at no. 40, featuring a similarly eye-catching gable with a triple tier of blind arcad-ing. The latter now houses the **muzeum Šumavy** (May–Oct Tues–Sat 9am–noon & 12.45–5pm, Sun 9am–noon), established as far back as 1880, with exhibits ranging from local glassware to fifteenth-century woodcarvings and, of course, the match-making industry, though it's the carefully restored interior that makes it worth a visit.

Sušice's **train station** is a regrettable 2.5km northeast of the town centre, with only infrequent bus connections; if you arrive by bus, make sure to get off at the town centre and not at the train and bus station, if you have the option. The only **hotel** in town is the *Gabreta*, just off the main square at Americké armády 73 (☎0187/52 80 16; ③), a bit of a bargain given that all its rooms have en-suite shower, toilet and TV; otherwise, there's a nice little pension *Milli* (☎0187/52 65 98; ②), with its own restaurant, down Kostelní, by the side of the old *Hotel Fialka*, or, as a last resort, rooms with shower only (①) above the *Granát* restaurant on the main square. The *Granát* has a characterful pub as well. There's a good regional **tourist office** next to the museum on the square (Mon–Fri 9am–noon & 1–5pm, Sat 9am–noon). If you're looking to camp, you're best off heading up the Otava to one of the riverside **campsites** like *Annín* (May–Oct), 7.5km south of Sušice, and a favourite spot for canoeists.

Kašperské Hory and around

Twice daily from Vimperk, more frequently from Sušice, a local bus heads for **KAŠPERSKÉ HORY** (Bergreichenstein), an old German mining village on the River Otava, positioned below the ruined castle of Kašperk that was built by Charles IV to guard over the local gold mines. The town's smartest building is its pristine Renaissance **radnice** with its three perfect eighteenth-century gables, featuring – from left to right – a Czech lion, a clock and the town's mining emblem.

In addition, the town's **muzeum Šumavy** (Tues–Sat 9am–5pm, Sun 9am–noon), on the main square, displays some wonderful local glassware on its top floor, ranging from fourteenth-century to turn-of-the-century gear, with pieces by local firms such as Lötz, Schmid and Kralik, from the neighbouring town of Klášterský Mlýn (Klöstermühle). In the late nineteenth century, Lötz in particular won many prizes in Brussels and Paris for its Tiffany-style iridescent glass vases and weird vegetal shapes, many of which inexplicably escaped the auctioneer's hammer and ended up here. There's yet more glassware on display in the next-door building, where the museum stages temporary exhibitions (Tues–Sun 9.30am–5pm).

Also on the main square is the newly opened **Moto muzeum** (May Sat & Sun 9am–noon & 12.30–5.30pm; June–Aug daily 9am–noon & 12.30–5.30pm), containing one of the finest collections of old motorbikes in the country, displayed rather surprisingly in the building's attic. More than forty bikes line the eaves, all in pristine condition, and ranging from interwar BMW boxers to domestic trials bikes; pride of place, though, goes to a beautiful red 1928 Indian. The exhibition of Czech toys (České hračky) in an adjacent attic, is more of a blatant moneymaker than a labour of love, and only really worth visiting if you want to buy something.

Accommodation boils down to the top-class *Park Hotel Tosch* (☎0187/92 25 92; ⑧), built with German capital to cater for the German tourists who pass through, and a smattering of private rooms in the outskirts of the town. You can get a decent bite to eat and a glass of Radegast beer at the *Pod věží* restaurant near the museum.

Srní and around

The heart of the Šumava National Park lies south of Kašperské Hory, and while there are few attractions in the way of museums or churches, it's the unblemished mountains that people come to see. The first stop of note south of Kašperské Hory is **ČEŇKOVA PILA**, a spot made up of little more than the *Hotel Bystřina* (☎0187/59 92 21; ③), and a bridge across the Vydra stream, where composer Bedřich Smetana is said to have been inspired to write the swirling flute introduction to his symphonic poem "Vltava" from *Má Vlast*.

A few kilometres further on, the cute village of **SRNÍ** has a wooden-shingled church and a few hotels and pensions, such as *Hotel Srní* (☎0187/59 92 12; ③) – surprisingly good value with indoor pool, sauna, weight room and bowling; and *Penzión Liška* (☎0187/59 93 86; ②), a pretty little house with inexpensive rooms along the road to Modrava. A few kilometres deeper into the forest, **ANTÝGL** is nothing more than a few wooden houses that make up a picturesquely situated **campsite** (often full in summer) and basic lodging (☎0187/59 93 31; ①); right nearby is the *Hotel Antýgl* (☎0187/59 93 28; ①), a cheap but clean place with a very good, if smoky, restaurant. Srní and Antýgl both make fine bases for hikes in the area. One popular walk from Antýgl takes you 6km along the boulder-strewn Vydra stream (which was the setting for a scene from the film *Kolya*) back down to Čeňkova pila, and you can make a longer day of it by returning via roundabout paths such as the blue-marked trail to Srní and Modrava, or the yellow-marked trail that descends from Srní back down to the Vydra.

Pushing on, the quiet settlements of **MODRAVA**, 3km south of Antýgl, and **KVILDA**, another 4km further east, are both surrounded by peat bogs. These were restricted areas when the Iron Curtain was draped just a few km beyond; because of this, the landscape is refreshingly underdeveloped, but there are just enough pensions and simple restaurants today to keep visitors happy. Buses from Sušice wind their way all the way up here at fairly regular intervals.

Železná Ruda and Špičák

The northwestern tip of the Šumava centres on the town of **ŽELEZNÁ RUDA** (Eisenstein), 2km from the German border and best approached on the scenic railway line from Klatovy or by bus from Klatovy (see p.193). In its triple role as a border town, ski resort and summer hiking base, the place has certainly lost much of its original charm. Souvenir shops filled with "traditional" Czech art and garden gnomes, plus the odd strip club, attempt to coax every last Deutschmark out of the Germans who come here. In many ways, you're better off using quieter neighbouring resorts like Špičák as a base. Local sights are confined to the ludicrously oversized wooden onion dome over the nave of the village church, and the small **muzeum Šumavy** (Tues–Sat 9am–noon & 12.45–5pm, Sun 9am–noon), local repository for glassware and folk art.

Still, if you need to stock up on provisions or draw some cash, then Železná Ruda is a good place to come. The *Šumava* restaurant, opposite the Spar supermarket, is reasonably priced, and, as far as **accommodation** goes, you're spoilt for choice: try the *Bultas* (☎0187/69 71 23; ④), which has its own restaurant, or its cheaper cousin, *Richard* (☎0187/69 74 58; ②). An electronic board on the main road at the centre of town shows availability of many hotels and pensions, and provides a free phone from which you can call them; there's also a **tourist office** (daily 8am–6pm) further down the main road. Finally, the town's **campsite**, *U mlýna* (June–Sept), lies a kilometre or so out of town up route 27. The **rail link with Germany**, which was severed during the Cold War, has now been re-established, and six trains a day now run on to the *Bahnhof* in Bayerische Eisenstein, terminating 70km southwest of Železná Ruda at Plattling.

From **ŠPIČÁK**, one stop back along the railway from Železná Ruda, a two-stage chairlift can take you to the top of **Pancíř** (1214m) all year round. The first stage takes you as far as Hofmanky, and the comfortable *Hotel Horizont* (☎0186/69 72 19; ⑤); more modest (and with just as good a view) is *Hotel Piák* (☎0186/69 72 53; ④), a few hundred metres back down the road. Towards the German border, there are two idyllically situated glacial lakes – Černé jezero and Čertovo jezero – surrounded by forests, which you can reach via the yellow-marked path from Špičák station.

travel details

Trains

Prague to: České Budějovice (11 daily; 2hr 30min–4hr 20min); Písek (2 daily; 2hr 30min); Strakonice (1 daily; 3hr); Sušice (1 daily; 3hr 45min); Tábor (every 1–2hr; 1hr 30min–2hr 20min).

České Budějovice to: Brno (1 daily; 4hr 30min); Český Krumlov (8 daily; 1hr); Horní Planá/Černý Špíš (4 daily; 2hr 15min/2hr 30min); Linz (2 daily; 2hr 30min); Plzeň (10 daily; 1hr 45min–3hr); Strakonice (12 daily; 50min–1hr 20min); Tábor (13 daily; 1hr–2hr 15min); Volary (3 daily; 3hr).

Tábor to: Bechyně (9–10 daily; 50min); České Budějovice (12 daily; 1hr–1hr 40min); Jihlava/Brno (1 daily; 1hr 50min/4hr); Milevsko/Písek (9 daily; 40min/1hr 30min); Pelhřimov (8 daily; 55min–1hr 20min); Třeboň/Gmünd (3–4 daily; 30min/1hr 30min).

Volary to: Prachatice (8 daily; 40min); Vimperk/Strakonice (6 daily; 1hr/2hr).

Buses

Prague to: České Budějovice (up to 6 daily; 2hr 25min–3hr); Český Krumlov (up to 3 daily; 3hr 20min); Orlík/Písek (up to 6 daily; 1hr 30min/2hr 10min); Pelhřimov (up to 10 daily; 2hr 15min); Rabí/Sušice (2–3 daily; 2hr 30min/2hr 45min); Strakonice/Prachatice (up to 4 daily; 2hr/3hr); Tábor (up to 10 daily; 1hr 30min–2hr); Volary (up to 2 daily; 3hr 30min).

České Budějovice to: Český Krumlov (up to 15 daily; 45min-1hr); Hluboká nad Vltavou (1–2 hourly; 20min); Holašovice (2–5 daily; 40min); Kratochvíle/Prachatice (up to 10 daily; 30min/1hr 15min); Tábor (4–10 daily; 1hr 10min); Třeboň/Jindřichův Hradec (10–12 daily; 30min/1hr 10min).

Český Krumlov to: Rožmberk/Vyšší Brod (3–9 daily; 30/40min); Lipno nad Vltavou (1–4 daily; 1hr 15min); Horní Planá (up to 7 daily; 45min-1hr).

Jindřichův Hradec to: České Budějovice (10–12 daily; 1hr 10min); Pelhřimov (3 daily; 45 min); Slavonice (up to 8 daily; 1hr 30min).

Pelhřimov to: Humpolec (up to 10 daily; 30min); Jihlava (up to 8 daily; 45min); Kámen (up to 7 daily; 30min).

Tábor to: Bechyně (up to 14 daily; 40min–1hr 15min); Kámen (up to 6 daily; 30min).

Sušice to: Srní/Modrava (up to 5 daily; 45min/1hr).

CHAPTER THREE

WEST BOHEMIA

For centuries, the rolling hills of **West Bohemia** (Západní Čechy) have been a buffer zone between the Slav world and the German-speaking lands. Encouraged by the Czech Přemyslid rulers, the border regions were heavily colonized by neighbouring Germans from the twelfth century onwards. The German settlers provided urgently needed skilled craftsmen and miners for the Bohemian economy, and for much of their history vast swathes of the region were almost exclusively German-speaking.

With the emergence of nationalism, and the subsequent rise of the pro-Nazi Sudeten German Party in the 1930s, the region became deeply divided along ethnic lines. The violent expulsions of the entire German-speaking population after World War II left vast areas of the countryside and several large towns virtually empty of people. Czechs and Slovaks were encouraged to resettle the area after the war, yet the countryside, particularly close to the border, remains eerily underpopulated even today.

The economic mainstay of the region for the last century has been the big industrial city of **Plzeň**, home of the Škoda engineering works, centre of the country's beer industry, and capital of the region. It's by no means the most picturesque of cities, but it does have a certain nineteenth-century grandeur, and remains a magnet for anyone who admires Czech beer. Within easy reach of Plzeň are the monasteries of **Kladruby** and **Plasy**, monuments to the outstanding architectural genius of Giovanni Santini, the master of "Baroque-Gothic". Further south, the historic border town of **Domažlice** is one of the best-preserved towns in the region, and a jumping-off point to the neighbouring Šumava (see p.175).

West Bohemia's busiest tourist region, however, is the famous triangle of spas: **Mariánské Lázně**, **Františkovy Lázně** and **Karlovy Vary**. Conveniently scattered along the German border, these three Bohemian spa resorts were the Côte d'Azur of Habsburg Europe, attracting the European elite of the nineteenth century. Following the wholesale nationalization of the spa industry, every factory and trade union received an annual three weeks' holiday at a *lázně dům* (spa pension): a perk aimed at proving the success of socialism. Taking "the cure" remains very popular with Czechs, but also with Russia's nouveaux riches, and, of course, with the neighbouring Germans. All three spa towns are very attractive visually, but they do tend to be full of the plethor-

---

ACCOMMODATION PRICE CODES

After each entry in the **hotel** lists below, you'll find a symbol which corresponds to one of nine **price categories**:

① Under 500Kč	④ 1000–1250Kč	⑦ 1750–2000Kč
② 500–750Kč	⑤ 1250–1500Kč	⑧ 2000–2500Kč
③ 750–1000Kč	⑥ 1500–1750Kč	⑨ 2500Kč and upwards

All prices are for the cheapest **double room** available during high season, which usually means without private bath or shower in the less expensive places. For a **single room**, expect to pay around two-thirds the price of a double.

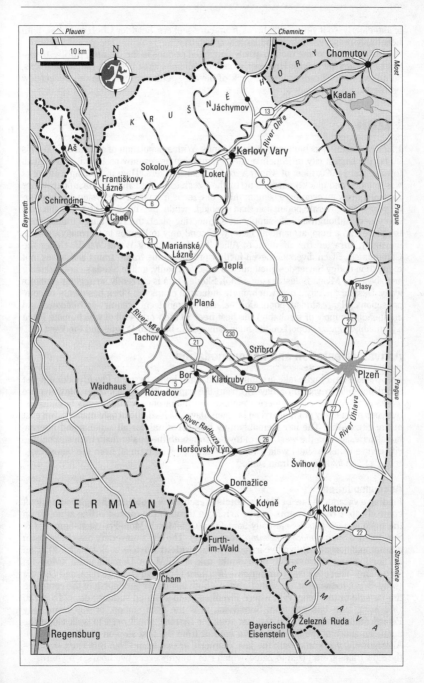

ic and elderly, so if you need a break from cure-seekers, head for **Cheb** or **Loket**, both beautifully preserved towns and largely crowd-free.

This being one of the most sparsely populated regions in the country, **public transport** is somewhat patchy. However, excellent rail links exist between the major towns, so unless you're heading for the back of beyond, getting around should present few problems.

Plzeň

PLZEŇ (Pilsen) was built on beer and bombs. With a population of around 175,000, it's by far the largest city in Bohemia after Prague, but as recently as 1850 it was a small town of just 14,000, most of whom were German-speakers. Then in 1859 an ironworks was founded and quickly snapped up by the Czech capitalist **Emil Škoda**, under whose control it drew an ever-increasing number of Czechs from the countryside. Within thirty years, the overall population had trebled, while the number of Germans had decreased. Although initially simply an engineering plant, the Habsburgs transformed the place into a huge armaments factory (second only to Krupps in Germany), which, inevitably, attracted the attention of Allied bombers during World War II. Under the Communists, Plzeň diversified even further producing the trams, trains and buses, not to mention dodgy Soviet-designed nuclear reactors. Sadly, unlike Škoda's car-producing arm, based in Mladá Boleslav (see p.136), Škoda Plzeň is currently struggling economically. Despite the city's overwhelmingly industrial character, Plzeň has plenty of compensations: a large student population, eclectic late-nineteenth-century architecture, and an unending supply of (probably) the best **beer** in the world – all of which make Plzeň a justifiably popular stopoff on the main railway line between Prague and the West.

Arrival, orientation and accommodation

Fast trains from Prague take around one and a half hours to reach Plzeň, making it just about possible to visit on a day-trip from the capital. The town's **train stations** are works of art in themselves: there are numerous minor ones within the city boundaries, but your most likely point of arrival is Plzeň hlavní nádraží, the ornate main station east of the city centre. The irredeemably ugly **bus terminal**, for all national and international arrivals, is on the west side of town. From both the bus or main train station, the city centre is just a short walk away – or a few stops on tram #2 from the bus station, trams #1 and #2 from the train station.

Accommodation
Finding a vacancy in one of Plzeň's **hotels** presents few problems, though rooms don't come cheap. **Private rooms** can be arranged through the **tourist office** at no. 41 on the main square (April–Sept daily 9am–6pm; Oct–March Mon–Fri 10am–5pm, Sat & Sun 10am–3.30pm; *infocenter@mmp.plzen-city.cz*). The city's university has cheap dorm accommodation available all year round at its **student hostels** at Bolevecká 30; tram #4 north along Karlovarská; if in doubt ask at CKM on Dominikánská (Mon–Fri 9am–5pm). There are two **campsites** – *Bílá hora* (April–Sept), on 28 října, and *Ostende* (May–Sept), to the west, on Malý Bolevec – both just under 5km north of the centre on the far side of the Velký rýb, where Plzeňites go to swim on summer days. To get to *Bílá hora*, take bus #20 from Šumavská, near the train station, or #39 from Sady Pětatřicátníků and get off at the last stop; for *Ostende*, you'll need to walk along the northern shore of the lake from *Bílá hora* or from the first stop on Plaská (tram #1). Alternatively, you could walk the last kilometre or two from Plzeň-Bílá Hora station – the slow trains from Plzeň to Žatec, which run roughly every two hours, stop here.

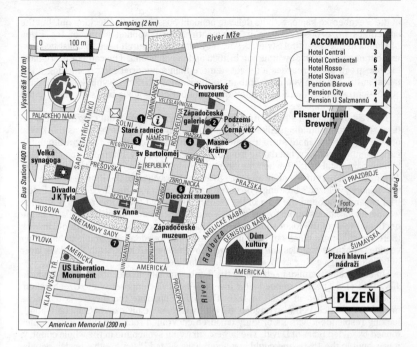

Hotel Central, náměstí Republiky 33 (☎019/722 67 57; _pech@top.cz_). Communist-era eyesore, which enjoys the best possible position, with en-suite rooms looking out onto náměstí Republiky itself. ⑨.

Hotel Continental, Zbrojnická 8 (☎019/723 64 79; _continental@plz.pvtnet.cz_). Painstakingly restored to something like its former glory by its original First Republic owners; the cheapest rooms here have en-suite shower, but no toilet. ⑤.

Hotel Rosso, Pallova 12 (☎019/722 64 73). Large, new hotel on the edge of the old town, with comfortable, fully en-suite rooms. ⑦.

Hotel Slovan, Smetanovy sady 1 (☎019/722 72 56; _hotelslovan@iol.cz_). Once splendid, with a wonderfully ornate stairwell, but otherwise a pretty unreconstructed communist-style hotel. ③.

Pension Bárová, Solní 8 (☎019/723 66 52). Best-value rooms in town are the three at this small pension, just off the main square. ③.

Pension City, sady 5. května 52 (☎019/22 60 69). Small, very central pension on the northeastern edge of the old town, with plainly furnished rooms with TV, and optional en-suite bathroom. ⑤.

U Salzmannů, Pražská 8 (☎019/723 58 55). Double rooms are available at Plzeň's renowned, recently refurbished pub. ⑤.

The City

Stepping out of the main station onto Americká, you're confronted with a variety of bad-taste communist-era buildings. Close by, the River Radbuza – one of four rivers running through Plzeň – doesn't bear close inspection, but the historical core of the city beyond it certainly does.

Laid out in chessboard fashion by Václav II in 1295, the old town is still dominated by the exalted heights of the Gothic cathedral of **sv Bartoloměj** (St Bartholomew), stranded awkwardly in the middle of the main square. Inside, the late-Gothic vaulting of the Šternberská kaple, with its delicate pendant boss, is worth checking out, but the cathedral's prize possession is its thirteenth-century wooden statue of the Plzeň Madonna in the "Beautiful Style", on the high altar. The church used to boast two towers, but one was struck by lightning in 1525 and never rebuilt. The cathedral's remaining bile-green **spire** reaches a height of more than a hundred metres, making it the tallest in the country; you can climb up to the viewing platform (vyhlídková věž; daily 10am–6pm) – which doubled as the town's lookout post – for a bird's-eye view of the local industrial complexes.

The rest of the main square, **náměstí Republiky**, presents a full range of architectural styles: some buildings, like the squat, grey *Hotel Central*, as recent as the 1960s; others, like the Italianate **stará radnice** (old town hall), smothered in sgraffito in the early twentieth century, but dating from the sixteenth century. Plzeň became an unlikely imperial capital in 1599, when the Emperor Rudolf II based himself next door at no. 41 for the best part of a year, in an effort to avoid the ravages of the Prague plague. The vast majority of Plzeň's buildings, however, hail from the city's heyday during the industrial expansion around the turn of the century. In the old town, this resulted in some wonderful variations on historical themes and Art Nouveau motifs, particularly to the north and west of the main square. West of Sady Pětatřicátníků, and south of Husova, there are still more blocks of late-nineteenth-century residential apartments, boasting vestiges of ornate mosaics and sculpturing, now barely visible beneath the black layer of pollution that's eating away at their fanciful facades.

On Sady Pětatřicátníků itself stands the flamboyant late-nineteenth-century **Divadlo J.K. Tyla** (Tyl Theatre), named after Josef Kajétan Tyl, composer of the Czech national anthem, who died in Plzeň in 1856. Diagonally opposite the theatre is the city's imposing red-brick **Velká synagóga** (Great Synagogue; daily except Sat 11am–5pm), looking resplendent with its brightly coloured chevroned roof, and twin onion domes topped by gilded Stars of David. The largest surviving synagogue in the whole country, it was built in the 1890s and could just about have seated Plzeň's entire Jewish population of nearly 3500. The city's few remaining Jews use a small prayer room at the back of the building, while the partially restored main hall now serves as a concert venue and exhibition space. The ornate interior, which boasts an organ at the east end, also contains a permanent exhibition on the history of the local Jewish community.

Beer and the brewery

Whatever its other attractions, the real reason most people come to Plzeň is to sample its famous beer, *Plzeňský Prazdroj* or **Pilsner Urquell** (its more familiar Germanized export name). Beer has been brewed in the town since its foundation in 1295, but it wasn't until 1842 that the famous *Bürgerliches Brauhaus* was built by the German banker Bleichröder, after a near-riot by the townsfolk over the declining quality of their beer. The new brew was a bottom-fermented beer which quickly became popular across central Europe, spawning thousands of paler imitations under the generic name of *Pilsner* – hence the brewers' addition of the suffix *Prazdroj* or *Urquell* (meaning "original"), to show just who thought of it first. The superiority of Plzeň's beer is allegedly due to a combination of the soft local water and world-renowned Žatec hops.

For a **guided tour** of the **brewery**, you need to ring or fax in advance between Monday and Friday (weekend tours are usually reserved for tour groups); ☎019/706 28 88, fax 706 27 15. There are a range of tours lasting up to two hours, but you have to pay extra for a tasting, after which you get to keep the glass. If the technological details of brewing don't appeal, you could just settle for the real thing at the vast *Na spílce* pub (daily from 11am), beyond the brewery's triumphal arch – avoid the much less interesting *Pilsner Urquell Original* restaurant, which you come to before passing through the archway. The arch itself, built in 1892 to commemorate the beer's fiftieth birthday, has been depicted on every authentic bottle of *Pilsner Urquell* ever since. Alternatively, you could try the historical angle at the Pivovarské muzeum (see below), or time your visit with Plzeň's annual **beer festival**, held early in October, as a preamble to the Munich Bierfest.

Plzeň's museums

Plzeň has a fair few museums, the biggest being the copper-topped **Západočeské muzeum** (West Bohemian Museum; Tues–Sun 10am–5pm), a neo-Baroque extravaganza, built in the nineteenth century to help educate the peasants who were flocking to the city. It's recently reopened, after more than a decade of restoration, and is worth a visit, if only for its ornate interior. The museum stages temporary exhibitions on the upper floor, and houses the impressive town armoury (Plzeňská městská zbrojnice) – established by Charles IV – on the ground floor.

More interesting than the city's big museum is the **Západočeské galerie** (Tues–Fri 10am–6pm, Sat 10am–1pm, Sun 9am–5pm), which puts on temporary exhibitions in a newly renovated Gothic building at Pražská 13, and is due to house its impressive permanent collection in the distinctive elongated vaults of the town's Gothic butchers' stalls or **Masné krámy** (times as above), which stand opposite the city's sixteenth-century water tower or Černá věž (now a commercial art gallery).

At the end of Veleslavínova is the most popular of Plzeň's museums, the **Pivovarské muzeum** (Brewery Museum; June to mid-Oct daily 10am–6pm; mid-Oct to May Tues–Sun 9am–5pm). Housed in what was originally a Gothic malthouse and later a pub, this is a more-than-sufficient consolation for those who fail to get into the brewery itself; ask the curator to get the old *Würlitzer* organ going while you check out the numerous exhibits, including the smallest beer barrel in the world (a mere one-centimetre cube) and case after case of kitsch Baroque beer mugs.

Also worth a quick once over is the little-visited **Diecézní muzeum** (April, May, Oct & Nov Wed–Sun 9am–5pm; June–Sept Tues–Sun 9am–5pm), housed in the cloisters of the former Franciscan monastery on Františkánská. The highlight of the museum is the Gothic chapel of sv Barbora (Saint Barbara) in the presbytery, on whose walls beautiful rose-coloured frescoes survive from the 1460s. The frescoes depict Barbara's martyrdom, which was gruesome even by biblical standards. Condemned to death by her father for converting to Christianity, she was racked, birched, carded with a metal comb, forced to lie on a bed of shards, slashed with red-hot blades, paraded naked, dragged up a mountain and finally beheaded, upon which her father was struck down by lightning.

THE AMERICAN LIBERATION OF PLZEŇ

By May 6, 1945, General Patton's US Third Army had liberated much of West Bohemia, including Plzeň. Less than 100km of virtually open road lay between the Americans and Prague, by then into the second day of its costly uprising against the Nazis. However, the agreement between the big three Allies at Yalta was that Prague should be liberated by the Soviets, who at the time were still 200km from Prague, en route from Berlin. Patton offered to march on Prague, and in fact, on May 7, three US armoured cars reached the outskirts of the city, but the order was to stay put.

Following the 1948 coup, the Communists took down all the monuments and deleted all references in history books to the American liberation of Plzeň. They even went so far as to say that the Americans had deliberately hung back from Prague, allowing thousands to die in the uprising. However, in May 1990, the city was able once again to celebrate the liberation, and in the presence of large numbers of US army veterans, a new memorial was erected on Chodské náměstí, just off Klatovská třída. In 1995, the granite memorial planned after the war but never built was finally erected at the top of Americká, saying simply "Thank You America".

Of minor interest only are the **Plzeňské historické podzemí** or underground tunnels (April, May, Oct & Nov Wed–Sun 9am–5pm; June–Sept Tues–Sun 9am–5pm), accessible from Perlova 4, built as a defensive ploy in the fourteenth century, but also very useful for storing beer. The guided tours are in Czech only, but there's a fairly lucid English written commentary available on request.

Eating, drinking and entertainment

All the hotels in town have **restaurants** attached to them, but most Czechs prefer to head for the city's pubs or pizzerias. Apart from the aforementioned *Na spílce* **pub** (see opposite), you can get *Pilsner Urquell* (and cheap grub) at *U Salzmannů*, the town's famous wood-panelled pub on Pražská. Gambrinus and the dark Purkmistr, Plzeň's other beers, are best drunk at *Žumbera* on Bezručova. The city boasts several decent **pizzerias**: try the stylish *Ranugo*, Pražská 10, or the cave-like *Paganini*, Rooseveltova 12, south of the old town. Plzeň's very own *McDonald's* opened in 1994, a happy homecoming for the junk-food chain founder, Ray Krok, whose family originally hailed from the nearby village of Stupno.

Plzeň's wonderful Beaux-Arts Divadlo J.K. Tyla (Tyl Theatre) is the city's main venue for opera and ballet. Most other concerts and cultural events take place at the Dům kultury on Americká, though the **Festival of Folk Songs** (known as *Porta* and held over the first weekend in July) is held in the Výstavistě, on Radčická, off Palackého náměstí. Výstavistě is also home to the city's summer-only open-air **cinema** (*letní kino*), and there's an arthouse cinema complex called *Elektra*, at Americká 24, which also has a restaurant and occasional live music. The main **rock/DJ venue** is *C Music Club*, Americká 18, but check the flyposters for the latest.

Around Plzeň

Within easy reach of Plzeň are two monasteries that bear the hallmark of Giovanni Santini, arguably the most original Baroque architect to work in the Czech Lands. Of the two, **Plasy** – 18km north of Plzeň – is the easiest to get to (by train or bus), though **Kladruby** – over 30km west – is without doubt a more rewarding day-trip.

Plasy

The **Cistercian monastery** at **PLASY** (Plass) is submerged in a green valley around 25km north of Plzeň. Originally founded in 1144 by Vladislav II, the present muddle of flaking Baroque outbuildings is the work of two of Prague's leading architects, Jean-Baptiste Mathey and Giovanni Santini-Aichl. Of the two, **Santini** (1667–1723), the Prague-born son of north Italian immigrants, is the more interesting: a popular architect whose personal, slightly ironic Baroque-Gothic style produced some of the most original works in the country. The brilliant white cloisters harbour palatial side chapels, while the rest of the monastery (April & Oct Sat & Sun 9am–3pm; May & Sept Tues–Sun 9am–4pm; June–Aug Tues–Sun 9am–5pm) is now an art gallery; the highlight of the 45-minute guided tour is a look at the tall side chapels off the cloisters, whose frescoes create an incredible splash of colour on the ceiling. The best time to visit the monastery is during the annual **Hermit Festival** of contemporary art and music in late June/early July, which draws avant-garde artists from all over Europe.

Shortly after its Baroque redevelopment, the monastery was dissolved and in 1826 fell into the hands of **Prince Clemenz von Metternich**, the arch-conservative Habsburg chancellor and political architect of the post-Napoleonic European order. Over the road, obscured by willow trees, the cemetery church was transformed by the prince into the family mausoleum. In tune with his politics, its oppressively Neoclassical forms dwarf the commoners' graveyard behind it.

Kladruby

If Plasy fails to move you, the **Benedictine monastery** (Tues–Sun: May & June 10am–3pm; July & Aug 9am–5pm; Sept 9am–4pm) at **KLADRUBY** (Kladrau), 35km west of Plzeň, should do the trick. It's an altogether less gloomy affair, founded by Vladislav I in 1115 (he's buried here, too) and once the richest monastery in Bohemia. Gutted by the Hussites and again during the Thirty Years' War, the whole place was transformed under Santini's supervision once the Counter-Reformation had set in. The main attraction is the huge monastery church, where the original Romanesque and Gothic elements blend imperceptibly with Santini's idiosyncratic additions. The original lantern tower has been converted into an extravagant Baroque cupola, which filters a faded pink light into the transepts, themselves covered in stars and zigzags mirrored on the cold stone paving below. It's the perfect expression of Santini's style, and a work of consummate skill.

The easiest way to get from Plzeň to Kladruby on public transport is to go as far as **STŘÍBRO** (Mies) by train, and then change on to one of the fairly frequent local buses that cover the last 6km to Kladruby. Dramatically poised over the Mže (Mies) river, Stříbro itself was previously the vague frontier post between the German- and Czech-speaking districts, its tidy square sporting arguably the most beautiful Renaissance **radnice** in Bohemia, paid for by the town's long-extinct silver mines (*stříbro* means silver).

Klatovy and around

Tightly walled in and nervously perched on high ground, **KLATOVY** (Klattau) warns of the approaching border with Germany. Founded by Přemyslid King Otakar II in 1260, the medieval prosperity of the town is still visible in the main square, but it can't compete with the Rose Towns further east. Still, there's enough to keep you occupied for at least a couple of hours, and with Plzeň only an hour away by train it's another possible day-trip; or a potential base for exploring the northwest tip of the nearby Šumava region (see p.175).

The Town

Klatovy's best feature is undoubtedly the cluster of tall buildings jostling for position in the southwest corner of the cramped town square, **náměstí Míru**. The façade of the Renaissance radnice is decorated with 1920s sgraffito and features two liberation plaques: one to the Russians (who liberated the country), and one to the Americans (who liberated the town). Tucked in beside the town hall is the sixteenth-century **Černá věž** (April & Oct Sat & Sun 9am–noon & 1–4pm; May–Sept Tues–Sun 9am–noon & 1–5pm), the clearest evidence of the town's bygone prosperity. Its pinnacled parapet, once a lookout post to protect the town, offers views of the forests at the Bavarian border and, closer at hand, across the rooftops to the smaller and later **Bílá věž** (see below).

Next to the Černá věž, Dientzenhofer's white **Jezuitský kostel** exudes incense and cooled air from its curvaceous interior emblazoned with frescoes, including a spectacularly theatrical trompe l'oeil main altar and backdrop. More fascinating, though, are the church's musty **katakomby** (catacombs; May–Sept Tues–Sun 9am–noon & 1–5pm; Oct–April Tues–Fri 9am–noon & 1–4pm), where Jesuits and other wealthy locals are preserved in varying stages of decomposition; the entrance is round the side of the church. Next door is **U bílého jednorožce** (The White Unicorn), a seventeenth-century *lékárna* or apothecary (April–Oct Tues–Sun 9am–noon & 1–5pm), which functioned until 1964 and has since become a UNESCO registered monument. The bottles and pots are all labelled in Latin, with swirling wooden pillars flanking the shelves, and a unicorn's horn (strictly speaking it's a tusk from an arctic narwhal), the pharmacists' mascot, jutting out into the centre. The back room, where the drugs were mixed, comes complete with horror-movie flasks of dried goat's blood and pickled children's intestines. Adjacent to the pharmacy is the town's **art gallery**, Galerie U bílého jednorožce (daily 9am–noon & 1–5pm), a pristine vaulted white room used for temporary exhibitions.

Before you give up on sightseeing, it's worth strolling over to the **Bílá věž** (White Tower), built during the Renaissance period, but later Baroquified. Next door to the tower stands the Gothic church, **Arciděkanský chrám**, whose spires sport charming gilded crowns slipped on like rings on fingers. Inside, the church retains its medieval stellar vaulting, and features a fetching shell-shaped baldachin, held up by barleysugar columns. Beyond the church and Bílá věž are the impressive remains of the town's medieval walls, which, if followed south, will bring you to the **local museum** (Okresní muzeum; Tues–Sun 9am–noon & 1–5pm), on Hostašova, more interesting for its salmon-pink Austro-Hungarian architecture than for its humdrum exhibits.

Practicalities

Klatovy's main **train and bus stations** are situated over a kilometre northwest of the old town (bus #1 or #2 to the main square); Klatovy-město station, just under a kilometre south of the old town, is only served by slow trains to and from Sušice. **Accommodation**, including private rooms, can be organized through the *Pergolia* **tourist office** by the Černá věž on the main square (Mon–Sat 9am–noon & 1–5pm, Sat 10am–noon; *pergolia@investtel.cz*); they also offer bike rental.

There are a few decent pensions in the old town, such as *U Hejtmana* on ul. kpt. Jaroše (☎0186/279 18; ②), just off the main square, plus the modern *Hotel Ennius*, Randova 111 (☎0186/32 05 64; ⑤), also in the old town, and owned by the same outfit who run the *Hotel Centrál*, on Masarykova (☎0186/245 71; ⑤), which isn't really that central, but is at least conveniently situated between the old town and the train and bus stations. Another option is the *Klatovský dvůr* (☎ & fax 0186/32 15 17; ③), out on the road to Domažlice. Alternatively, there's an excellent **campsite**, *Sluneční mlýn* (May–Sept) by an old water mill on the River Úhlava; it's signposted a couple of kilometres along the Domažlice, has a swimming pool, bungalows and tent space.

Back in Klatovy, you can admire the main square best from the tables outside the *Beseda* restaurant. The *Stará rychta*, on Denisova, west of the main square, is the town's liveliest **pub**, and serves Gambrinus, while the best **restaurant** is the *Zlatý drak*, Viděnská 32, on the corner of Podbranská, which dishes up good Chinese-Czech food along with views of the town's towers.

Švihov

Ruined castles are ten-a-penny in these border regions; the virtue of the one at **ŠVIHOV**, 11km north of Klatovy, is that it still looks like a proper castle – and it's easy to reach by train, from either Plzeň or Klatovy. It was begun in 1480 by the Rožmberks as a vast concentric structure, with traditional double fortifications creating an inner and outer castle surrounded by a moat. Suspicious of such an unusually well-fortified stronghold, the Habsburgs ordered the owners to tear down the eastern section, and what remains today is a kind of cross-section of a castle, partially surrounded by its original moat. The highlights of the fifty-minute guided tour (April & Oct Sat & Sun 9–11am & 1–3pm; May & Sept Tues–Sun 9–11am & 1–4pm; June–Aug closes 5pm) are the late-Gothic chapel by Benedikt Ried, and a very fine Renaissance strapwork ceiling.

Domažlice

Fifteen kilometres from the German border, **DOMAŽLICE** (Taus) is an attractive little town, situated in one of the few border areas that has always been predominantly Czech-speaking. For centuries the town was the local customs house, and the Chodové (see box) as the folk round here are known, were given the task of guarding the border with Bavaria, but in 1707 the town lost much of its former importance when the border was fixed. The town's biggest bash is the annual Chod folk festival, **Chodské slavnosti**, held in the middle of August.

The town

Like many small Bohemian towns, Domažlice starts and ends at its main square, **náměstí Míru**, a long, thin affair, positioned along a perfect east-west axis. Flanked by uninterrupted arcades under every possible style of colourful gable, the pretty, elongated cobbled square seems like a perfect setting for a Bohemian-Bavarian skirmish. Halfway down one side, the thirteenth-century **church tower** or *věž* (April–Sept daily 9am–noon & 1–5pm), now leaning to one side quite noticeably, used to double as a look-out post for the vulnerable town, and ascending its 196 steps provides a bird's-eye view of the whole area. The **Děkanský kostel** itself, whose entrance is round the corner in Kostelní, has a wonderful series of Baroque frescoes, colourful furnishings and a particularly fine trompe l'oeil scenic backdrop for the gilded main altar.

The town's other remaining thirteenth-century round tower lies to the southwest, down Chodská, and belongs to the **Chodský hrad**, seat of the Chodové self-government until it fell into the hands of Wilhelm Lamminger von Albreneuth. The castle has

---

THE CHODOVÉ

"The spearhead of the Slavic march into central Europe", as writer Josef Skvorecký described them, the **Chodové** are one of the few Czech peoples to have kept their identity. Very little is certain about their origin, but their name comes from *chodit* (to walk about), and undoubtedly refers to their traditional occupation as guardians of the frontier. Since the earliest times, their proud independence was exploited by a succession of Bohemian kings, who employed them as border guards in return for granting them freedom from serfdom, plus various other feudal privileges.

However, after the Battle of Bílá hora, the Habsburgs were keen to curb the power of the Chodové, and the whole region was handed over lock, stock and barrel to one of the victorious generals, Wilhelm Lamminger von Albenreuth (also known as Lomikar). At first the Chodové tried to reaffirm their ancient privileges by legal means, but when this proved fruitless, with the encouragement of one Jan Sladký – better known as Kozina – they simply refused to acknowledge their new despot. Seventy of the rebels were thrown into the prison in Prague, while Kozina was singled out to be publicly hanged in Plzeň on November 28, 1695, as an example to the rest of the Chodové. From the gallows, Kozina prophesied the death of Lomikar "within a year and a day" – the general died as Kozina foresaw, from a stroke following a banquet held to celebrate Kozina's demise.

Although the empire prevailed, the Chodové never allowed the loss of their freedom to quash their ebullience or their peculiar local dialect, which still survives in the villages. Stubbornly resistant to Germanization, they carried the banner of Czech national defiance through the Dark Ages. Even now, of all the regions of Bohemia, Chodsko is closest to its cultural roots, known above all for its rich local costumes, still worn on Sundays and religious holidays, and for its *dudy* (bagpipes), now played only in folk ensembles and at festivals.

recently been renovated and now houses the **Muzeum Chodska** (mid-April to mid-Oct Tues–Sun 9am–noon & 1–5pm; mid-Oct to mid-April Mon–Fri 10am–noon & 1–3pm), which worthily traces the town's colourful history.

More fascinating by half, though, is the **Muzeum Jindřicha Jindřicha**, east of the old town just beyond the medieval gateway (Mon–Fri: mid-April to mid-Oct 8am–noon & 1–3pm; mid-Oct to mid-April 8am–noon), and founded by local composer Jindřich Jindřich. His extensive collection of Chod folk costumes, ceramics and other regional items, all displayed in a mock-up cottage interior, are ample compensation if you fail to catch the annual festival.

Practicalities

The town's **main train station**, called simply Domažlice, is 1km east of town; the Domažlice město station, five minutes' walk south of the old town down Jiráskova, is served only by slow trains to Bor and Tachov. The main **bus terminal** lies just north of the main square, on Poděbradova. The town's **tourist office** (Mon–Fri 7.30am–5pm; June–Aug also Sat 9am–noon) is situated in the nineteenth-century radnice on the main square; nearby there's a cashpoint, useful if you've just crossed over from Germany.

As for **accommodation**, there are plenty of simple family-run pensions in the old town: try *Café-Pension Tiffany* (☎0189/72 55 91; ②), beside the church on Kostelní. Alternatively, check for vacancies at *Pension Viola* (☎0189/72 24 35; ③), an interwar villa north of the old town up Thomayerova (off the road to Luženice), with its own restaurant and garden, or *Hotel Koruna* (☎0189/22 79; ②), west of the main square on M.B. Staška, which has plain, cheap rooms. For those with a tent, there's a choice between the riverside *Babylon* **campsite** (mid-May to Oct), 6km south by bus or train, or the *Hájovna* site (May–Sept), a kilometre or so north of Kdyně (20min by train from Domažlice). As for **food**, the *Ural*, on the north side of the main square is a regular Czech pub-restaurant; *Dalibor Kubů*, south off the main square on Branská, is slightly pricier and more used to tourists, or else there's *Chodská rychta*, a pleasant new restaurant on M.B. Staška, opposite the town's art gallery. Domažlice has its own **brewery**, by the bus station, though no brewery tap; instead, head for the *Štika*, a real drinkers' pub serving the local brew, on the road out to Plzeň.

If you're heading for Germany, there are now three trains a day from Domažlice to the Bavarian town of **Furth-im-Wald**, whose *Drachenstich* festival – during which the townsfolk fight a gory battle with a giant dragon – takes place shortly after the Chod Folk Festival on the second and third Sundays in August.

Horšovský Týn

A lazy afternoon could happily be spent at **HORŠOVSKÝ TÝN** (Bischofteinitz), just 10km north of Domažlice. Its main square, **náměstí Republiky**, is a picturesque grassy, sloping affair centred on the church of sv Petr and Pavel, and lined with Gothic houses sporting brightly coloured Baroque facades. At the top end, surrounded by a bear- and raccoon-inhabited moat, is the quadrilateral sgraffitoed **zámek** (April & Oct Sat & Sun 9am–noon & 1–3pm; May & Sept Tues–Sun 9am–noon & 1–4pm; June–Aug closes 5pm), transformed by the Lobkowicz family into a rich Renaissance pile. There's a rather complicated choice of **guided tours**: the Hrad tour (trasa 1; 50min) takes you through the Gothic chapel, the Renaissance-era rooms and the armoury, and is probably the one to go for; the Zámek tour (trasa 2; 1hr) is for period furniture freaks only; and the Kuchyně tour (45min) features a trawl round the kitchens, tacky china chandeliers equipped with their original Edison bulbs and other delights. Behind the chateau, the vast **Zámecký park** stretches northwards, complete with hidden chapels, a large lake and hosts of peacocks. It's a ten-minute walk to the centre from the train station: head east up Nádražní to the main crossroads, then north over the river, and the main square will appear on your right. If you haven't brought your own picnic, the *Hotel Šumava* restaurant, along from the chateau entrance (closed Mon), offers some fairly imaginative dishes.

Mariánské Lázně

At the end of the eighteenth century, what is now **MARIÁNSKÉ LÁZNĚ** (Marienbad) was unadulterated woodland. It was not until the 1790s that the local abbot, Karel Reitenberger, and a German doctor, Josef Nehr, took the initiative and established a spa here. Within a hundred years, Marienbad (as it was known in its heyday) had joined the clique of world-famous European spas, boasting a clientele that ranged from writers to royalty. That inveterate spa-man Goethe was among the earliest of the VIPs to popularize the place, and a few generations later it became the favourite holiday spot of King Edward VII, a passion he shared with his pal, the Emperor Franz-Josef I. During

World War I, even the incorrigibly infirm Franz Kafka spent a brief, happy spell here with Felice Bauer, writing "things are different now and good, we are engaged to be married right after the war", though in fact they never were.

Today, Mariánské Lázně is much less exclusive, though no less attractive – what was a fat-farm for the rich and famous only two generations ago is now eminently accessible to all and sundry. Over the last decade, the riotous, late-nineteenth-century architecture has been restored to its former flamboyance, and the whole place has been successfully brought back to life. Above all, though, it's the spa's beautiful setting, amidst thickly forested hills, that remains its most beguiling asset. The air around town is cool and refreshing and the centre of the spa is more or less free of cars, all of which comes something of a relief after the usual traffic-choked streets.

The spa

Mariánské Lázně was the last of Bohemia's famous triangle of spas to be built, and as such is the most consistently flamboyant in its architecture. As far as the eye can see, sumptuously regal buildings rise up from the pine-clad surrounds, most dating from the second half of the nineteenth century. For all their sculptural theatricality and invention, there's an intriguing homogeneity in the fin-de-siècle opulence, with each building dressed up, almost without exception, in buttery *Kaisergelb* (imperial yellow) and white plasterwork.

Hlavní třída
Hlavní třída, the spa's main thoroughfare, is several kilometres long, and forms an almost uninterrupted parade of luxury, four-storey mansions. The vast majority are thoroughly in keeping with the fin-de-siècle ambience of the place. There are, however, one or two hideous modern hotels built over the last decade, though even these have failed to impinge on the most impressive final section of the street, where layer upon layer of shapely balconies overlook the spa gardens. Several of the shops here sell tins of *oplatky*, the ubiquitous sugar- or chocolate-filled wafers which make the waters you are about to taste infinitely more palatable. At no. 47 is the *Bílá labuť* (The White Swan), a modest three-storey building where Frédéric Chopin stayed in 1836 on his way from Paris to Warsaw. Known as the **dům Chopin**, it serves as the spa's tourist office, and has a tiny museum to the composer on the first floor (Tues, Thurs & Sun 2–5pm).

The spa's **synagogue**, which stood on Hlavní třída itself, was burnt down in 1938 on *Kristallnacht*, and no trace now remains. By contrast, the spa's small, red-brick **Anglikánský kostel** (Anglican church; Tues–Sun 9am–noon & 12.30–4pm), survives, hidden in the trees behind the *Hotel Bohemia*. Abandoned by its royal patrons and neglected under the Communists, the church has recently been restored, and is now used as an exhibition space. All that remains of the interior, however, is the pulpit, a rose window and a plaque to its most famous patron, King Edward VII. Better preserved is the nearby neo-Byzantine **Pravoslavný kostel** (Russian Orthodox church; May–Oct Mon–Fri 8.30am–noon & 1–4.30pm, Sat 8.30am–4.30pm; Nov–April daily 9.30–11.30am & 2–4pm) on Ruská, the road running parallel to Hlavní třída. Dating from 1902, the rather plain interior is made remarkable by the spectacular iconostasis that won the Grand Prix de France at the 1900 Paris World Exhibition. Designed in the shape of a miniature Orthodox church, and made from enamel and porcelain, it is coated in over nine kilograms of gold and cobalt, and is reputedly the largest piece of porcelain in the world. Mass is still held in the church every Sunday.

Around the Kolonáda
The focal point of the spa, overlooking the town, is the gently curving **Kolonáda**. Easily the most beautiful wrought-iron colonnade in Bohemia, it's rather like a whale-ribbed

---

THE SPA TRADITION

Following the Habsburg tradition, **spa holidays** remain extremely popular in the Czech and Slovak republics, which boast over a hundred spa resorts (*lázně* in Czech, *kúpele* in Slovak) between them. One of the chief perks of the Communist system, they were a form of recreation open to all and usually paid for by one's employers (ie the state). Nowadays, the spas attract an increasing number of Germans, Austrians and wealthy Russians, for whom the holidays are still relatively inexpensive. At a few resorts, you can book in for one or two days' "treatment", but most are intended for longer stays (three weeks is the norm), and you don't actually have to be ill to be treated. Some people find spa resorts rather like open hospitals, but many are beautifully situated deep in the countryside, with fresh air and constitutionals very much part of the cure.

The basic treatment involves drinking the mineral waters from the spa's natural springs, for which many guests use their own ornate drinking vessels called *becher*. These curious miniature teapots each have a spout through which you sip the waters, thus preventing coloration of the teeth. The waters come in an amazing variety: alkaline, chlorinated, carbogaseous and even radioactive, though they usually share one common characteristic, in that they are all pretty foul, or at least an acquired taste. In addition – and this is the more appealing bit – you can bathe in hot springs or sapropelic muds, breathe in pungent fumes or indulge in a new generation of complementary therapies, such as ultrasound and aerosol treatment, ultraviolet light baths, acupuncture and electrotherapy. Each spa resort tends to specialize in "curing" a particular ailment. For example, Františkovy Lázněis the best place for gynaecological problems; Luhačovice for respiratory diseases; Karlovy Vary for digestive complaints; and Trenčianske Teplice for motor problems. The most famous (and most oversubscribed) of the spa resorts are Karlovy Vary and Mariánské Lázněin Bohemia, Luhačovice in Moravia and Piešťany in Slovakia.

---

nineteenth-century railway station without the trains, and despite the lurid 1970s ceiling frescoes, the atmosphere is genteel and sober. In summer, there are daily concerts by Bohemian bands, and occasional performances by the local symphony orchestra. Adjoining the northern tip of the colonnade is the spa's first and foremost spring, the **Křížový pramen**, housed in its very own Neoclassical colonnade, and there are further springs in the main Kolonáda; however, access to the life-giving faucets is restricted (daily 6am–noon & 4–6pm).

Beyond the southern end of the Kolonáda stands the **zpívající fontána**, a computer-controlled dancing fountain, no great beauty, which does its thing to a popular piece of classical music, roughly every two hours until 10pm (the last two shows are accompanied by a light display – see the nearby poster for the latest programme). Beyond and, more importantly, out of earshot of the fountain, is the elegant Neoclassical colonnade of the **Karolinin pramen**, whose springs spurt forth water round the clock. The town was once patrolled by special spa police, who imposed strict fines on those discovered smoking or committing other crimes against health – it's still forbidden to smoke in this part of the spa.

Behind and above the colonnades lies **Goethovo náměstí**, which boasts a new aluminium, seated statue of Goethe; the original was carried off by the retreating Nazis, leaving just the granite plinth, to which the Czechs added a commemorative postwar plaque in Czech, Latin and French (but, significantly, not German). On his last visit in 1823, Goethe stayed at the house on the corner that now houses the **Městské muzeum** (Wed–Sun 9am–noon & 1–4pm). On the ground floor, the displays trace the history of the spa's development; upstairs, along with period furnishings from Goethe's time, there are new historical sections that are more frank about the spa's German roots (and about the American liberation), but still silent on the postwar expulsions that more or less cleared the spa of its remaining inhabitants.

The square is overlooked by yet more giant, ochre spa buildings, including the **Hotel Weimar**, at no. 9, in which King Edward VII preferred to stay (above the central portico there's a well-concealed German Gothic plaque commemorating his visit). Below, at the centre of the square, is the unusual octagonal church of **Nanebevzetí Panna Maria** (Assumption of the Virgin Mary), decorated inside in rich neo-Byzantine style. Still further down the hill are two buildings definitely worth checking out. The first is the old **Casino** building, now the spa's main social centre, with an old faded dance hall (bands and discos on most nights) of fin-de-siècle marbled elegance; the other is the equally ornate **Nové lázně**, which accepts "out-patients" for a sauna and massage (at a price) – ask for *kabina* 1 or 2, which were fitted out for visiting royalty – and where you can also now stay.

Walks around the spa

Even if you're not booked in for treatment, you should participate in the other spa rituals – drinking the water, wolfing down the wafers and taking the obligatory constitutional. Mariánské Lázně's altitude lends an almost subalpine freshness to the air, even at the height of summer, and **walking** is as important to "the cure" as are the various specialized treatments. To this end, the expert nineteenth-century landscape gardener Václav Skalník was employed to transform the valley into an open park, providing an intricate network of paths leading to the many springs dotted around the surrounding countryside.

There are several maps posted up by the Kolonáda which show the various marked walks around the spa; armed with a *plán města* (available from most hotels, bookshops and newsagents) you can head off on your own. Goethe's favourite walk, up to the *Miramonte* for morning coffee, is retraced by most visitors, though the café has since been converted into a *lázně dům* (spa home) for kids; head north to the *Café Panoráma* for refreshment, instead. The energetic can continue to the lower town of **Úšovice** whence you can return to town via the Rudolfův and Ferdinandův springs, where, according to one tourist brochure, you can experience "hypotonic calcareous magnesium hydrogen carbonate ferrugineous acidulous waters".

There are several vantage points to head for in order to enjoy a **panoramic view** of the spa: Na Polomu (805m) or the Podhorn (847m), north along the strenuous red-marked paths; or, with considerably less exertion, the old **Kaiserturm** or *rozhledna* (723m), on the hillside southeast of the spa. Another option is to take the **chairlift** (*lánová draha*; daily: May–Sept 9.30am–5pm; Oct–April 9.30am–4.30pm) from the *Koliba* up Dusíkova, which will transport you to the *Hotel Krakanoš*. Those with small kids, might want to take a peek at the nearby **Miniaturpark**, a low-key, fairly risible stab at a miniature world.

Practicalities

Passengers arriving by train or bus are unloaded at a suitably discreet distance from the spa, some 3km south of the centre; trolleybus #4 or #5 covers the 3km up the former Kaiserstrasse, now Hlavní třída. The main **tourist office** (daily 10am–6pm) is in the dům Chopin at Hlavní 47, has lots of information, and can help with accommodation (see below).

Accommodation

The tourist office can book **private rooms**, or, if you have your own transport, you can search for yourself in the suburbs of Úšovice, where they predominate. There's a vast choice of **hotels**, including the *Hotel Krakanoš* (see below), an expensive, modern triangular-shaped hotel, whose late-nineteenth-century annexe still functions as an official HI **hostel**.

There are also two **campsites** to choose from: the *Luxor* (May–Sept), which is awkwardly located several kilometres to the west of the train station along the road to Cheb (bus #6 to Velká Hleďsebe, then walk 1km south down the Plzeň road); and *Start*, on Plzeňská (open all year), a small campsite with motel and cheap bungalows, walking distance from the train station, but a touch noisy.

Hotel Bohemia, Hlavní třída 100 (☎0165/62 32 51). Late-nineteenth-century hotel, somewhat brutally modernized, but still fairly classy and very comfortable: all rooms come with en-suite facilities and satellite TV. ⑧.

Hotel Evropa, Třebízkého 2 (☎0165/62 20 63). Unreconstructed communist-style hotel at the top of Hlavní třída; some rooms have shared facilities. ⑤.

Hotel Helga, Třebízkého 10 (☎0165/62 04 33). Friendly, fairly swish, family-run hotel with a decent restaurant, just beyond the top of Hlavní třída. ⑦.

Hotel Kossuth/Suvurov, Ruská 77 (☎0165/62 28 61). Two cheap hotels, a few doors down from each other that have joined forces. Quiet location, good views but absolutely no frills. ④.

Hotel Krakanoš (☎0165/62 26 24). This hotel consists of two buildings: a dilapidated late-nineteenth-century hotel, which still functions as an official HI hostel, and an expensive, modern triangular-shaped hotel of the same name opposite. You can reach it either via the chairlift or bus #12, which runs hourly from Hlavní třída. ②–⑨.

Nové Lázně, Reitenbergerova 53 (☎0165/64 41 11). If you're staying for the cure, this is the place to stay, with its full-blown 1890s opulence – at around 5000Kč a double. ⑨.

Hotel Polonia, Hlavní třída 50 (☎0165/24 52). Simply modernized, but dripping with original fin-de-siècle features in the foyer and the café; ask for a room overlooking the spa gardens. ⑤.

Zlatý zámek, Klíčová 4 (☎0165/62 39 24). Clean to the point of sterility, but good value for its central locale. ④.

Eating, drinking and entertainment

Café Polonia, at Hlavní třída 50, is probably Mariánské Lázně's most opulent surviving **café** offering stucco decoration as rich as its cakes. The choice of **restaurants** has improved over the last few years, with the moderately expensive *U zlaté koule*, Nehrova 3, currently the most stylish of the lot. The *Classic* restaurant, just down from the *Excelsior* at Hlavní třída 50, has fewer pretensions, and is especially recommended for vegetarians. Lastly, if you're staying at or near the *Start* campsite, *Pizzeria U Müllerů*, Na průhonu 24, does decent pizzas and pasta.

There's usually a fair bit of high-brow **entertainment** on offer, including an international music festival in early summer, a week-long Chopin festival in mid-August and a mini-Mozart festival in early October. For **late-night spots**, there's plenty of opportunities for ballroom dancing in the hotels or in the more splendid surroundings of the old casino. Mariánské Lázně also boasts the best **golf course** in the former Eastern bloc, the first to hold a PGA Tour event in the 1990s; to get there, take bus #12 to the *Hotel Golf*.

Lázně Kynžvart and Teplá

If you're looking for a longer excursion out of Mariánské Lázně, you could spend the afternoon walking over to **LÁZNĚ KYNŽVART** (Königswart), 8km northwest of town. Now a spa for children, it was founded in the 1820s by the Metternich family as their own private spa, where they entertained Goethe, Beethoven and Dumas (among others) at their Neoclassical **zámek** (April & Oct Sat & Sun 9am–4pm; May & Sept Tues–Sun 9am–4pm; June–Aug closes 5pm), built in the following decade by Pietro Nobile. Now open after more than a decade of renovation work, the chateau contains lots of period furniture, Metternich mementoes and a large English park. If your legs aren't up to the return journey, the nearest train station is 2km southeast of the chateau.

A longer day-trip is to the monastery at **TEPLÁ** (Tepl), 15km to the east off route 24, whose abbots used to own the springs at Mariánské Lázně. The **Klášter premon-strátů** (daily: May–Oct 9am–4.30pm; Feb–April, Nov & Dec 9am–3pm) – until recently used as an army barracks – is 1km east of the village along the Toužim road. It's easy enough to spot thanks to the plain stone towers of the original twelfth-century monastery church, though the rest of the monastery carries the universal stamp of the Baroque Counter-Reformation, courtesy of the Dientzenhofer duo. However, the real reason for coming here is to see the Neo-Baroque library (*nová knihovna*); built in the 1900s, it boasts almost edible stucco decoration, triple-decker bookshelves and swirling black iron balconies framed by white pilasters.

If your next stop is Karlovy Vary, be sure to take the train, which winds its way slowly but picturesquely, via Teplá, through the **Slavkovský les**, the thick forest that lies between the two spas.

Cheb

CHEB (Eger), 10km from the German border, is a typical Czech frontier town, with prostitutes lining the main roads, and Vietnamese stall-holders occupying the centre of town. For many Western visitors it's their first taste of the Czech Republic, and for most, it's a slightly bewildering introduction. Cheb is a beautiful historic town, but it is also primarily a German one, and postwar expulsion of the German-speaking popula-

EGERLAND

Most Germans still refer to Cheb as **Eger**, the name given to the town by the German colonists who settled here from the eleventh century onwards. The settlers were typically hard-working and proud of their folk traditions and peculiar dialect. Aided by its status as a Free Imperial City of the Holy Roman Empire, the town soon came to dominate trade between Bavaria and Bohemia. Shunted around between Babenbergs, Swabians and Přemyslids, Egerland finally accepted the suzerainty of King John of Luxembourg in 1322, in return for certain privileges, and in fact the *Egerländer* remained self-governing until well into the nineteenth century.

Hardly surprising, then, that the town was at the centre of the (anti-Semitic) **Pan-German Schönerer movement** of the late nineteenth century, which fought desperately against the advance of Czech nationalism, aided and abetted (as they saw it) by the weak and liberal Habsburg state. Here, too, was the most vociferous protest against the 1897 Badeni Decrees, which granted the Czech language equal status with German throughout the Czech Lands. The establishment of Czechoslovakia in 1918 was seen as a serious setback by most *Egerländer*, who made no bones about where their real sympathies lay; Eger remained the only town to successfully rebuff all attempts at putting up street names in Czech as well as German.

Thus, in the 1930s, the pro-Nazi **Sudeten German Party** (SdP) found Egerland receptive to its anti-Semitism as much as to its irredentism. Although it's estimated that a quarter of the German-speaking voters stubbornly refused to vote for the SdP, the majority of *Egerländer* welcomed their incorporation into the Third Reich, completed in 1938. At the end of World War II, only those Germans who could prove themselves to have been actively antifascist (Czechs were luckily exempted from this acid test) were permitted to remain on Czechoslovak soil; the others were bodily kicked out, reducing the population of Cheb to 27 percent of its prewar level. The mass expulsions were accompanied by numerous acts of vengeance, and the issue remains a delicate one. Havel's suggestion in his first presidential address that an apology to the Germans was in order remains one of the most unpopular statements of his entire presidency.

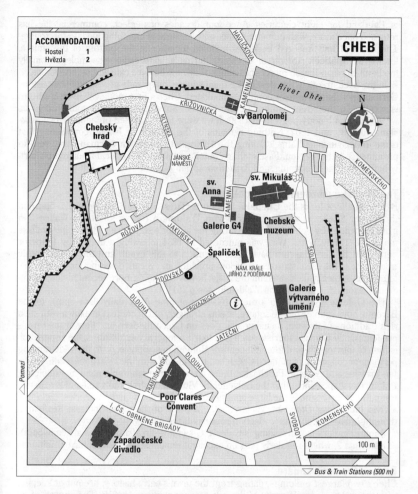

▽ Bus & Train Stations (500 m)

tion left it with less than a third of its prewar population, and an identity crisis of mammoth proportions. Money was poured into the town, but Czechs were reluctant to move here (not so Romanies and Slovaks). The root of the malaise lay in the authorities' ambivalence to Cheb, simultaneously encouraging its future and denying its past. Nevertheless, the town's historic centre is worth an afternoon stopoff – even if it is overrun by German day-trippers for much of the summer.

The Town

Cheb's showpiece main square, **náměstí krále Jiřího z Poděbrad**, is named after one of the few Czech leaders the *Egerländer* ever willingly supported. Established in the twelfth century, but today lined with handsome, mostly seventeenth-century houses, with steeply pitched red roofs, this was the old *Marktplatz*, the commercial and political heart of Egerland for eight centuries. After four decades of neglect, commercial life has returned once more, with numerous cafés and restaurants breathing life into the square. The batch of half-timbered buildings huddled together at the bottom of the square, known as **Špalíček** (*Stöckl* in German), forms a picturesque ensemble; originally medieval German-Jewish merchant houses, they now house a café and several shops.

In the backstreets to the west of the main square, the parade of seventeenth-century German merchants' houses continues unabated. Cheb's first medieval **Jewish ghetto** is recalled in the street name, Židovská (Jewish Street), though the community was wiped out in a bloody pogrom in 1350; Jews were later expelled on another two occasions, in 1430 and 1502. Nothing remains of the 500-strong Jewish community that came under sustained attack during the 1930s as the Sudeten German Party rose to prominence in the region. Fascist thugs butchered a pig in the local synagogue shortly before its official opening, and *Kristallnacht* demolished what was left.

The Chebské muzeum and art gallery

Behind Spalíček lurks the **Chebské muzeum** (Tues–Sun 9am–12.30pm & 1–5pm), in the former *Stadthaus* where **Albrecht von Waldstein** (better known as Wallenstein from the trilogy by Schiller, written during the author's stay here in 1791), generalissimo of the Thirty Years' War, was murdered in 1634 following a decree by Emperor Ferdinand II. The museum pays great attention to this event, and the heavy Gothic woodwork of his reconstructed bedroom provides an evocative setting for Waldstein's murder, graphically illustrated on the walls; however, Cheb's more recent history is studiously avoided. (For more on Waldstein, see p.251.)

The **Galerie výtvarného umění** (Gallery of Fine Arts; daily 9am–5pm), in the Baroque nová radnice on the square, seems strangely out of context in a town with such rich traditions of its own, focusing as it does on Czech modern art. Few of the town's predominantly German tourists pay a visit to the temporary exhibitions, the superb collection of fourteenth- and fifteenth-century Bohemian sculpture, or to the wide-ranging permanent collection of modern Czech art. Kicking off with the 1890 generation, led by Jan Preisler and Antonín Procházka, there are several memorable paintings depicting Prague cityscapes, including the Belvedér, St Vitus Cathedral, and a red-and-cream city tram. More surprising is the large contingent of Cubist and Fauvist canvases, including a vivid blue *River Otava* by Václav Špála. In place of the usual Socialist Realism, a thought-provoking postwar collection rounds off the gallery.

Another gallery worth visiting is **Galerie G4** (Tues–Fri 10am–6pm, Sat 10am–5pm), at Kamenná 2, which regularly puts on excellent temporary photographic exhibitions.

Beyond the main square

Cheb's two largest buildings, dating from the town's early history, are out of keeping with the red-roofed uniformity of the seventeenth-century *Altstadt*. The church of **sv Mikuláš** has a bizarre multifaceted roof, like the scales of a dinosaur, though since the renowned local-born architect Balthasar Neumann restored the interior in the eighteenth century, only the bulky towers remain from the original thirteenth-century building, conceived as a monumental Romanesque basilica. Very few of the original furnishings survive, and most of what you see is neo-Gothic infill, but there are two very fine Renaissance tombs worth inspecting inside the porch of the south door.

In the northwestern corner of the town walls, by the River Ohpe (Eger), is the **Chebský hrad** (Tues–Sun April & Oct 9am–noon & 1–4pm; May & Sept until 5pm; June–Aug until 6pm), or Kaiserburg as it used to be known; the sprawl of ruins built on and with volcanic rock is all that remains of the twelfth-century castle bequeathed by that obsessive crusader, the Holy Roman emperor Frederick Barbarossa. In among the Baroque fortifications, the Gothic Černá věž (Black Tower) presents an impressive front and offers peeks at Cheb's chimneys and roof-tiles through its tiny windows. In the northeastern corner, the lower storey of the ruined chapel with its beautifully carved Romanesque capitals will give you an idea of the castle of Barbarossa's time.

Practicalities

Had you arrived at Cheb's **train station** before 1945, you'd have had the impression of never having left Germany: by a quirk of railway history, the Deutsche Bundesbahn built and ran all the lines heading west out of Eger. It's a none too pleasant ten-minute walk from the ugly postwar station, north along **Svobody**, to the old town.

The **tourist office** is at no. 33 on the main square (Mon–Fri 9am–5pm, Sat 10am–2pm, Sun 10am–1.30pm; *cheb.infocentrum@post.cz*), and can sell you a Chebcard, giving discounted entry into the town's three main sights. They can also help with **accommodation**, though the choice is fairly limited, and, in many ways, you'd be better off staying the night in nearby Františkový Lázně (see below). There's basically one half-decent **hotel** in Cheb, the *Hvězda*, on the main square (☎0166/42 25 49; ③), plus a number of small pensions, and a **hostel** at Židovská 7 (☎0166/42 34 01). Otherwise, there's a **campsite**, *Camp Karel* (mid-May to mid-Sept) 5km away at Dřenice by the artificial lake, Jesenickypřehrada (plus the *Amerika* site in Františkovy Lázně).

There are several **places to eat** on the main square, which basically cater for German tourists – they're not bad for a drink and to soak in the square, but for something more traditional try *U koček*, at the beginning of Kamenná. The Cheb youth play billiards and drink beer at *U kata*, an otherwise typical Czech *pivnice* on Židovská; *Rock Café Elektra*, opposite the train station on Žižkova, is the town's alternative nightspot, with regular gigs; *Kino Art*, Kamenná 5, puts on some interesting art-house films.

Františkovy Lázně

"The present Františkovy Lázně has nothing of historic interest", wrote Nagel's Guide in the 1960s, casually dismissing a town hailed by Goethe as "paradise on earth". Yet while **FRANTIŠKOVY LÁZNĚ** (Franzensbad), 5km north of Cheb and linked by regular trains, may not boast any individual architectural gems, it is, in many ways, *the* archetypal spa town. Originally known as Egerbrunnen, the spa was founded in 1793 and named Franzensbad after the then Habsburg emperor Franz I. Laid out in the early nineteenth century, the Neoclassical architecture of the period finds its way into every building – even the cinema has Doric pillars – and virtually every conceivable building has been daubed in the soft ochre colour of *Kaisergelb*. The centre of the spa is barely five streets across, and surrounded on all sides by a backdrop of luscious greenery. The virtual absence of vehicles and rowdy nightlife makes it the most peaceful of the spas, though as patients stagger about and people in white coats run between buildings, it can resemble a large, open-plan hospital.

The town

From the ochre-coloured train station, the road opens out onto the former *Kurpark* or **Městské sady**, whose principal path leads diagonally to a white, wooden bandstand at the head of pedestrianized **Národní**, the spa's modestly elegant main boulevard, lined with potted palms and diminutive lime trees. Beethoven stayed at no. 7 in 1812, as the German plaque by the entrance recalls; while *U tří lilie*, the eponymous garden café further down, features in a poem by the Czech surrealist Vítězslav Nezval. You can sit outside and take in the scene from *Café Corso* or one of the street's other cafés with al fresco tables.

At the bottom of Národní, a plain Neoclassical rotunda shelters the **Františkův pramen** (Franzensquelle; daily 8–11.30am & 12.30–4.30pm). While the faithful queue to

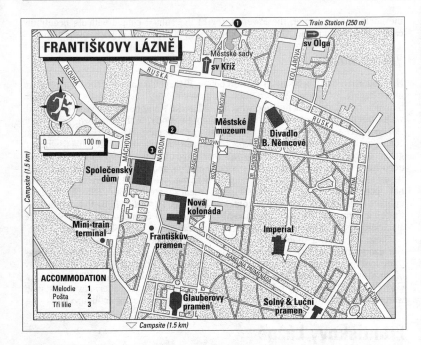

have their receptacles filled from the dazzling brass pipes, the real spa snobs retire to drink from their beakers by the fruit-encrusted sphinxes or under the nearby modern colonnade. Don't worry if you've come unprepared, as you can buy a plastic cupful, though like most spa water, it's pretty unpalatable, on this occasion due to its high sulphur content. You've an even greater choice of tipple at the **Glauberovy pramen** (daily 7–11.30am & 1–5pm), to the south: more or less salty, and hot or cold. A different kind of faith drives women to touch the feet (and other more specific parts) of a repulsive bronze cherub who sits holding a phallic fish, not far from the spring: Františkovy Lázně specializes in the treatment of gynaecological problems, and popular myth has it that doing so will ensure fertility.

The Neoclassical church of **sv Kříž**, dating from 1820, strikes an appropriately imperial pose at one end of Jiráskova, another riot of princely mansions with wrought-iron balconies. A more intriguing church is that of **sv Olga**, a richly decorated Russian Orthodox church on Kollárova. Set apart from the other spa buildings, and a favourite with visiting Germans, is Františkovy Lázně's finest spa villa, the **Imperial**, its corner balconies held up by caryatids. In the **Městské muzeum**, dr. Pohořeckého 8 (Tues–Fri 10am–noon & 1–5pm, Sat & Sun 10am–4pm), you can see previous generations of Teutonic guests being subjected to gruesome nineteenth-century cures; don't miss the man with a leech on each buttock, held in place by two jam jars.

Walks and excursions

As with all the Bohemian spas, the formal parks quickly give way to untamed woodland, the difference being that in Františkovy Lázně the landscape is almost entirely flat, which is easier on the legs but shorter on views. A two-kilometre **walk** through the silver birches will take you to Lake Amerika (in dry weather a **mini-train**, or *mikrovláček*, runs every

30min), though swimming is not advisable. On the other side of town, a path marked by red hearts leads to the popular *Zámeček Café*, hidden away amidst the acacia.

A **longer walk** will take you to Cheb itself, just over 5km south; follow the red markers down Klostermannova. Alternatively, it's 8km northeast to **Soos**, a small area of peatland pockmarked with **hot gaseous springs**. As you approach the place in summer, the smell of salt emanating from the mini-geysers wafts across from the marsh. A nature trail raised above the bogland allows closer inspection of the springs that gurgle and bubble just above the surface, staining the land with a brown-yellow crust. A unique phenomenon in mainland Europe, the area attracts rare species of flora and fauna – not to mention insects, which make it no place to linger in the height of summer. Soos is also accessible by train from Cheb: three stops to Nový Drahov on the Luby u Chebu line.

Practicalities

Františkovy Lázně may not be the busiest spot in Bohemia, but with patients and tourists vying for **beds**, it can sometimes be difficult to find a place. Probably the nicest place to stay is the *Tři lilie*, Národní 3 (☎ & fax 0166/54 24 15; ③), which has been sensitively modernized. Cheaper options include the *Květen/Pošta* (☎0166/54 20 25; ④), the spa hotel opposite, and the *Melodie* on Francouská (☎0166/54 35 77; ④), whose green shutters overlook the Městské sady. The *Amerika* **campsite** (April–Oct) with **bungalows** is 1.5km southwest of the town by the lake; you can get there on the mini-train. All the above-mentioned hotels have reasonable **restaurants**, with the *Tři lilie* far and away the best (and most expensive). The *Café Milano*, next to the departure point of the *mikrovláček* on Máchova, is a popular outdoor place.

Karlovy Vary

KARLOVY VARY (Karlsbad) is the undisputed king of the famous triangle of Bohemian spas, with by far the most illustrious guest list of European notables. What makes it so special is its wonderful hilly setting – *Belle Époque* mansions pile on top of one another along the steeply wooded banks of the endlessly twisting River Teplá. It is best known throughout the world by its German name, **Karlsbad** (Carlsbad in its anglicized form), and it was German-speakers who made up the vast majority of the town's population until their forced expulsion in 1945. Despite this violent uprooting, the spa has survived and continues to attract an international clientele – particularly Russians – which annually doubles the local population, further supplemented in the summer by thousands of able-bodied tourists, the greatest number of whom are, naturally, German.

Tradition grants the Emperor Charles IV (or rather one of his hunting dogs) with discovery of the springs (hence Karlsbad); in actual fact, the village of Vary (which means "boiling" in Czech) had existed for centuries before Charles' trip, though he did found a German town here in around 1350 and set a precedent for subsequent Bohemian rulers by granting Karlsbad various privileges. By the nineteenth century its position at the meeting point of two great German-speaking empires, and the much heralded efficacy of its waters, ensured the most impressive visitors' book in Europe. In addition, a lot of money has been spent over the last decade to ensure that Karlovy Vary returns to something like its former glory.

Arrival, information and accommodation

The main train station or **horní nádraží** is to the north of the River Ohře, while the **dolní nádraží** (where trains from Mariánské Lázně arrive), off Západní, and the **bus**

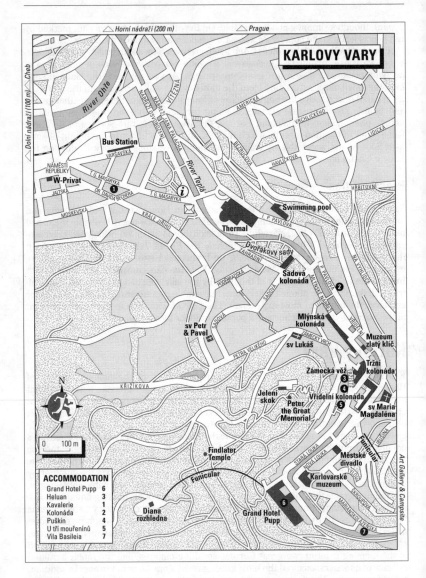

△ Horní nádraží (200 m)   △ Prague

KARLOVY VARY

Cheb

Dolní nádraží (100 m)

River Ohře

NÁBŘEŽÍ JANA PALACHA

VÍTĚZNÁ

AMERICKÁ

VRCHLICKÉHO

LIDICKÁ

Bus Station

VARŠAVSKÁ

NÁMĚSTÍ
REPUBLIKY

W-Privat

JALTSKÁ

T. G. MASARYKA

❶

DR. DAVIDA BECHERA

MOSKEVSKÁ

KRÁLE JIŘÍHO

T. G. MASARYKA

River Teplá

BERBIOVA

HAVLÍČKOVA

HÁBITOVNÍ

i

I. P. PAVLOVA

Swimming pool

Thermal

Dvořákovy sady

ZAHRADNÍ

P. PAVLOVA

NA VYHLÍDCE

**Sadová
kolonáda**

❷

PODĚBRADSKÁ

SADOVÁ

MLÝNSKÉ NÁBŘEŽÍ

**sv Petr
& Pavel**

SADOVÁ

**Mlýnská
kolonáda**

ZÁMECKÝ VRCH

sv Lukáš

**Muzeum
zlatý klíč**

PETRA VELIKÉHO

Zámecká věž

ZÁMECKÝ VRCH

**Tržní
kolonáda**

❸
❹

Vřídelní kolonáda

❺

**sv Maria
Magdaléna**

KŘIŽÍKOVA

N

**Jelení
skok**

**Peter
the Great
Memorial**

STARÁ LOUKA

DIVADELNÍ

Funicular

0   100 m

**Findlater
Temple**

Funicular

NOVÁ LOUKA

**Městské
divadlo**

**Karlovarské
muzeum**

TYLOVA

ZÁHRADNÍ

SADROVOVA

Art Gallery & Campsite

ACCOMMODATION

Grand Hotel Pupp	6
Heluan	3
Kavalerie	1
Kolonáda	2
Puškin	4
U tří mouřenínů	5
Vila Basileia	7

**Diana
rozhledna**

❻

**Grand Hotel
Pupp**

MARIÁNSKÁ

MARIÁNSKOLÁZEŇSKÁ

❼

station, on Varšavská, are both south of the river. Whichever one you arrive at, you're basically in the unattractive, northern part of town, where the otherwise invisible local residents live and shop. The spa proper stretches south along the winding Teplá Valley and, in fact, the best way to approach Karlovy Vary is from the south. However, to do that you need your own transport, in which case you'll have the devil of a job finding somewhere safe to park it, as parking and traffic in the centre of the spa are strictly controlled.

For general **information** (and help with accommodation), there's basically just a small kiosk called *City-Info*, opposite the post office on T.G. Masaryka (Mon–Fri 9am–5pm, Sat 8am–5pm, Sun 10am–4pm). For information on **spa treatment**, go to the Kur-Info office in the Vřídelní kolonáda (Mon–Fri 7am–5pm, Sat 9am–4pm).

Accommodation

Karlovy Vary can get pretty busy in the summer, especially in July during the film festival (see p.212), so it's best to start looking for **accommodation** early in the day. *W Privat*, an office on náměstí Republiky (Mon–Fri 8.30am–5pm, Sat & Sun 9am–1pm), can organize **private rooms**. If you're **camping**, head for the site with bungalows near the *Motel Gejzír* (April–Oct) on Slovenská, south and upstream from the *Grand Hotel Pupp*; take bus #7 from the local bus station.

Grand Hotel Pupp, Mírové náměstí 2 (☎017/310 91 11; *sales@pupp.kpgroup.cz*). They don't come better (nor more expensive) than this outside Prague – 6000Kč a double and upwards – and though the decor is pretty stunning, the service is not as good as it should be for the price. ⑨.

Heluan, Tržiště 41 (☎017/257 56). Peaceful hotel, with spacious, tastefully uncluttered en-suite rooms. ⑦.

Kavalerie, T.G. Masaryka 43 (☎017/322 96 13). Relatively cheap, but at the wrong end of town really, near the bus station and not in the spa proper. ⑤.

Kolonáda, I.P. Pavlova 8 (☎017/313 11 11; *reservation@kolonadahotel.cz*). Very plush and efficient place; rooms have all mod cons, and there's even a sauna, and an acceptable cellar restaurant. ⑧.

Puškin, Tržiště 37 (☎017/322 26 46). Decent doubles with breakfast, in the central section of the spa. ⑧.

U tří mouřenínů, Stará louka 2 (☎017/323 50 53; *penkucera@plz.pvtnet.cz*). Pension occupying two adjacent buildings; clean and reasonably priced for its prime central location. ⑤.

Vila Basileia, Mariánskolázeňská 2 (☎017/322 41 32). Secluded late-nineteenth-century villa at the quiet, southern end of the spa, close to the *Pupp*, with just six large en-suite rooms on offer. ⑤.

The spa

Unfortunately, many visitors' first impressions of Karlovy Vary are marred by the unavoidable sight of the **Thermal** sanatorium, an inexcusable concrete scab built in the 1970s, for whose sake a large slice of the old town bit the dust. It's serves as home base for the annual film festival, and there's a certain perverse appeal to the faded 1970s' kitsch interior decor, but the most useful aspect of the *Thermal* is its open-air *bazén*, a spring-water **swimming pool** set high up above the river. The poolside view over the town is wonderful, but don't be taken in by the clouds of steam – the water is only tepid.

On the other side of the River Teplá from the *Thermal*, the late-nineteenth-century grandeur of Karlovy Vary begins to unfold along the river banks. The first of a series of colonnades designed by the Viennese duo Helmer and Fellner is the **Sadová kolonáda**, a delicate white-and-grey colonnade made of wrought iron. As the valley narrows, the river disappears under a wide terrace in front of Josef Zítek's graceful **Mlýnská kolonáda** (Mühlbrunnen Colonnade), whose forest of columns shelter four separate springs, each one more scalding than the last. At the next bend in the river, stands the **Tržní kolonáda**, designed by Helmer and Fellner as a temporary structure, but one whose intricate whitewashed woodwork has lasted for over a century. Directly opposite is the **dům Zawojski** (now the Živnostenska banka), one of the best Art Nouveau houses in the spa, with its green wrought-iron and gilded detailing. Rising above the colonnade is the **Zámecká věž** (Schlossberg), the only link with the spa's founder, Charles IV, built on the site of his original hunting lodge.

Most powerful of the twelve springs is the **Vřídlo** or Sprudel, which belches out over 2500 gallons of water every hour. The old wrought-iron **Vřídelní kolonáda** (daily 6am–6.30pm) was melted down for armaments by the Nazis, and only finally replaced in the 1970s by a rather uninspiring modern building, which the Communists liked to call the Yuri Gagarin Colonnade (his statue once stood outside, but now resides at the airport). The smooth marble floor allows patients to shuffle up and down contentedly, while inside the glass rotunda the geyser pops and splutters, shooting hot water forty feet upwards. Ensuing clouds of steam obscure what would otherwise be a perfect view of Kilian Ignaz Dientzenhofer's Baroque masterpiece, the church of **sv Maria Magdaléna**, pitched nearby on a precipitous site. The light, pink interior, full of playful oval shapes, is a striking contrast with the relentlessly nineteenth-century air of the rest of the town.

If you've forgotten your cure cup, you can buy the faintly ridiculous *becher* vessels from one of the many souvenir shops. The purpose behind these is to avoid colouring your teeth with the water, though plenty of people cut costs and buy a plastic cup. Popular wisdom has it that "when the disorder becomes a disease, doctors prescribe the hot waters of Carlsbad" – in other words, it's strong stuff. In the eighteenth century, the poor were advised to drink up to five hundred cups of the salty waters to cure the disease of poverty. The German playwright Schiller (who came here on his honeymoon in 1791) drank eighteen cups and lived to tell the tale, but generally no more than five to seven cups a day are recommended.

Stará and Nová louka

South of the Sprudel is Karlovy Vary's most famous shopping street, the **Stará louka** (Alte Wiese), described rather mystifyingly by Le Corbusier as "a set of *Torten* (cakes) all the same style and the same elegance". Its shops, which once rivalled Vienna's Kärntnerstrasse, are beginning once more to exude the snobbery of former days – there's even a branch of *Versace* at the far end of the street. Don't miss the Moser shop (everyone who's anyone, from Stalin to the Shah, has had a Moser glass made for them) where you can buy some of the local glassware, made in the factory in the suburb of Dvory, just off the Cheb road.

At the end of Stará louka is the **Grand Hotel Pupp**, named after its founder, the eighteenth-century confectioner Johann Georg Pupp. Rebuilt at the late-nineteenth-century by the ubiquitous Helmer and Fellner, *Pupp*'s was *the* place to be seen, a meeting place for Europe's elite. Despite the odd spot of careless modernization, it boasts an interior that can't fail to impress, and the cakes are allegedly still made to Mr Pupp's own recipe. On the opposite bank, the former Kaiserbad – now known rather more prosaically as Lázně I – is another sumptuous edifice, designed like a theatre by Helmer and Fellner, with a luscious velvet and marble interior.

Back round the corner in Nová louka, the spa's richly decorated, creamy white **Městské divadlo** is another Helmer and Fellner construction, where Dvořák gave the première of his *New World Symphony* in 1893. What makes this place special, though, is that the frescoes and main curtain were executed by a group of painters that included a young **Gustav Klimt**, later to become one of the most famous figures in the Viennese Secession. If you ask at the box office, you should be able to get a glimpse of the auditorium, though the curtain – by far the most interesting work – is rarely fully exposed to the audience. Nevertheless, you can spot Klimt's self-portrait in the bottom right-hand corner, playing the flute and looking at the audience.

A short distance beyond the casino is the spa's main **Galerie umění** (Tues–Sun 10am–noon & 1–6pm), on Goethova stezka, which contains a small but interesting cross-section of twentieth-century Czech canvases, and a disappointingly limited selection of glassware. Neither of Karlovy Vary's two museums are really worth bothering with: the **Karlovarské muzeum** (Wed–Sun 9am–noon & 1–5pm), on Nová louka, plods through the spa's history, glossing over the controversial (and interesting) bits, while the **Muzeum zlatý klíč**, Lázeňská 3 (same times), contains a fairly mediocre series of soft-focus oil paintings of the spa at its pre-World War I zenith, by Wilhelm Gause.

Walking in the hills

Of all the spas, Karlovy Vary's constitutional **walks** are the most physically taxing and visually rewarding. You can let the **funicular** (*lanová draha*) take the strain by hopping aboard one of the trains (9am–7pm; every 15min) from behind the *Grand Hotel Pupp* up to a café and viewpoint. Alternatively, you can climb up through the beech and oak trees to the wooden crucifix above Stará louka, and then on to the spectacular panorama where the **Peter the Great Memorial** commemorates the visiting Russian tsar and his dozen or so royal hangers-on. In season, you can enjoy the (not so perfect) view northwards from the **Jelení skok** restaurant (Tues–Sun 10am–6pm).

The road below *Jelení skok* slopes down to **Zámecký vrch**, where Turgenev stayed at no. 22 in 1874–75 and which the English aristocracy used to ascend in order to absolve their sins at the red-brick Anglican church of **sv Lukáš** (Evangelical and Methodist services are still held here). Clearly visible from here, high on the opposite bank, is the *Imperial* sanatorium, a huge fortress hotel built in 1912 to rival *Pupp*'s and flying in the face of the popular Art Nouveau architecture of the spa; it was converted into a hospital during World War II, handed over to the Soviets during the communist period, and has only recently been turned back into a hotel (it even has its own funicular to transport guests to and from the spa below).

An alternative route back down to the Sadová kolonáda is the street of **Sadová** itself, which is lined with some of the most gloriously flamboyant mansions in the whole spa. Topping the lot, though, is the fabulous white Russian Orthodox church of **sv Petr and Pavel** (daily 10am–5pm), built to serve the visiting Russian aristocracy and now equally popular with the spa's current crop of Russian visitors. It's the church's stunning exterior, crowned by a series of gilded onion domes, that steals the show, so don't worry if the janitor is out to lunch, thus preventing you from visiting the icon-filled interior.

Eating, drinking and entertainment

What I indulged in, what I enjoyed
What I conceived there
What joy, what knowledge
But it would be too long a confession
I hope all will enjoy it that way
Those with experience and the uninitiated.

Needless to say, Goethe had a good time here. His coy innuendos are a reference to the enduring reputation of spas like Karlovy Vary for providing extramarital romance.

MARX IN KARLSBAD

A certain Mr Charles Marx from London (as he signed himself in the visitors' book) visited the spa several times towards the end of his life, staying at the former *Hotel Germania*, at Zámecký vrch 41, above the Mühlbrunnen Colonnade. He was under police surveillance each time, but neither his daughter Eleanor's letters (she was with him on both trips) nor the police reports have much to say about the old revolutionary, except that he took the waters at 6am (as was the custom) and went on long walks. The Communists couldn't resist the excuse to set up a Karl Marx Museum, just down from the Mühlbrunnen Colonnade, at the house where Marx used to visit his doctor. Somewhat unbelievably, it was the only one of its kind in the entire communist world, Lenin being the orthodox choice. Needless to say, it has long since been dismantled, and is now the even duller Muzeum zlatý klíč.

Dancing, after all, was encouraged by the spa doctors as a means of losing weight. These days, it's all a bit less racy. Nevertheless, if you're looking to indulge yourself, you might as well head for the *Grand Hotel Pupp*, whose bar and restaurant boast unrivalled decor. Otherwise, there's the *Zámecký vrch*, a more intimate restaurant up the street of the same name, or the *Colonáda* restaurant, a typical Bohemian beer restaurant, with the occasional oom-pah-pah band.

Karlovy Vary is, of course, the home of one of the country's most peculiar drinks, **becherovka**, a liqueur made from nineteen different herbs, which is supposed to ease digestion and is fondly referred to as Karlovy Vary's "thirteenth spring". It was actually invented by the unlikely sounding Brit, Dr Frobig, in 1805, but only launched commercially two years later by the enterprising Dr Jan Becher. It's available in bars and restaurants all over town (and just about anywhere else in the republic), though the company's factory shop is on T. G. Masaryka, near náměstí Republiky – be warned: it's an acquired taste, not unlike cough medicine. Not so good for you, but all part of the spa ritual, are coffee and cakes: the *Elefant Café* on Stará louka is the nearest Karlovy Vary comes to an elegant Habsburg-style café, and as a result is very popular.

Karlovy Vary's **cultural life** is pretty varied, from classical concerts at the former *Kurhaus* (Lázně III) and occasionally at *Pupp's*, to the rock club *Propaganda*, Jaltská 7. The town also plays host to an **International Film Festival** in July, which attracts at least a handful of big names. All showings are open to the public. For details on these and the town's other events, ask at City-Info or Kur-Info (see p.209).

Loket

The tiny hill-top town of **LOKET** (Elbogan) is an exquisite, virtually undiscovered, miniature gem, just 12km west of the crowds of Karlovy Vary. It takes its name from the sharp bend in the River Ohře – *loket* means elbow – that provides the town with its dramatic setting. The fourteenth-century **hrad** (Tues–Sun: April–Oct 9am–noon & 1–5pm; Nov–March 9am–4pm), which slots into the precipitous fortifications, displays porcelain manufactured in the town over the last couple of centuries; you can also explore the castle's former prison, and climb the lookout tower. Loket's beautifully picturesque streets form a garland around the base of the castle, sheltering half-timbered houses and secluded courtyards like Sklenařská, where the redundant German sign *Glaser Gasse* remains unmolested since the forced expulsions of 1945 stripped the town of its German-speaking inhabitants.

Accommodation is available at various pensions, including the friendly *Goethe* (☎0168/68 41 84; ⑤) or the *Actus* (☎0168/68 41 03; *actus@mbox.cz*; ⑤), both on the main square and both with restaurants. It was at *Zum weissen Ross* – now the vanilla and pistachio coloured, neo-Gothic *Bílý kůň* – on the main square, that Goethe met his last love, Ulrike von Lewetzow, he in his seventies, she a mere seventeen. Hardly surprisingly, she refused his marriage proposal – his *Marienbader Elegie* describes the event – though she remained unmarried throughout her long life.

Loket is easily accessible by bus from Karlovy Vary, but by far the most inspiring way of getting there is to take the beautiful, blue-marked track from Karlovy Vary, which crosses over to the left bank of the River Ohře at the halfway point and passes the giant pillar-like rocks of the **Svatošské skály** (Hans Heiling Felsen), which have inspired writers from Goethe to the Brothers Grimm.

Jáchymov

JÁCHYMOV (Joachimsthal), 20km northeast of Karlovy Vary and only 5km from the German border, is haunted by its past. In the early 1950s, literally thousands of citizens (many of them former Communist Party members) were rounded up during the country's Stalinist terror and sentenced to hard labour in the **uranium mines** to the north of the town. Underfed and subject to harsh treatment by their jailers, untold numbers died of exhaustion, starvation and leukaemia.

Joachimsthal was founded in the sixteenth century when silver deposits were discovered. The royal mint established here struck the famous *Joachimsthaler* (eventually giving rise to the dollar, a corrupt form of the abbreviation *Thaler*). In 1896 the Frenchman Henri Bequerel discovered uranium, and it was from Joachimsthal uranium that Marie and Pierre Curie discovered radium earlier this century. The experiment proved as fatal to them as it did to the generations of German miners who worked the pits: even under the First Republic their average life expectancy was 42 years. Although the mine was closed down in 1964, some 300 houses are now thought to be so contaminated by radon that they represent a serious health risk to the occupants. Despite this, the citizens of Jáchymov continue to work in the local tobacco factory and the *Radiumpalác* and *Curie* spa facilities still draws in thousands of patients annually, to be "cured" by treatment involving the town's radioactive springs.

travel details

Trains

Connections with Prague: Domažlice (2 daily; 2hr 40min); Františkovy Lázně (3 daily; 3hr 45min); Karlovy Vary (3 daily; 3hr 20min–4hr); Mariánské Lázně/Cheb (every 2hr; 2hr/3hr 30min); Plzeň (hourly; 1hr 40min–2hr 15min).

Cheb to: Františkovy Lázně (10–14 daily; 10min); Karlovy Vary (15 daily; 50min–1hr 10min); Mariánské Lázně (11–13 daily; 30min); Nürnberg (5–6 daily; 2hr); Plzeň (10–12 daily; 1hr 35min–2hr 15min)

Domažlice to: Klatovy (5–6 daily; 1hr).

Karlovy Vary to: Kadaň (8–9 daily; 50min–1hr 15min); Leipzig (1 daily; 4hr 30min); Teplice (5 daily; 2hr).

Klatovy to: Železná Ruda (6–8 daily; 1hr 10min).

Mariánské Lázně to: Teplá (6–7 daily; 30min); Karlovy Vary (6–7 daily; 1hr 40min).

Plzeň to: Domažlice (10–12 daily; 50min–1hr 25min); Furth-im-Wald (2 daily; 1hr 20min); Klatovy (8–12 daily; 45min–1hr); Munich (3 daily; 4hr 20min–7hr); Plasy (8–12 daily; 30–45min); Stříbro (12–14 daily; 25–45min); Železná Ruda (4 daily; 2hr 10min–2hr 40min).

Buses

Connections with Prague: Jáchymov (2 daily; 3hr); Karlovy Vary (hourly; 2hr 30min); Plzeň (hourly; 1hr 30min).

Karlovy Vary to: Františkovy Lázně (5 daily; 30min); Jáchymov (up to 18 daily; 50min); Loket (5–7 daily; 25min).

Plzeň to: Horšovský Týn (7 daily; 1hr); Karlovy Vary (7 daily; 1hr 30min).

CHAPTER FOUR

NORTH BOHEMIA

North Bohemia (Severní Čechy) has become a byword for the ecological disaster facing the country in the postcommunist era. Its forests have all but disappeared, weakened by acid rain and finished off by parasites, its villages have been bull-dozed to make way for open-cast mines, and its citizens are literally choking to death – all due to the brown-coal-burning power stations that have provided the region with employment for the last hundred years. Despite this grim reality, parts of North Bohemia remain popular with Czech and German tourists, in particular the eastern half of the region, where the industrial landscape gives way to areas of outstanding natural beauty like **České Švýcarsko**, and towns of architectural finesse, like **Litoměřice**.

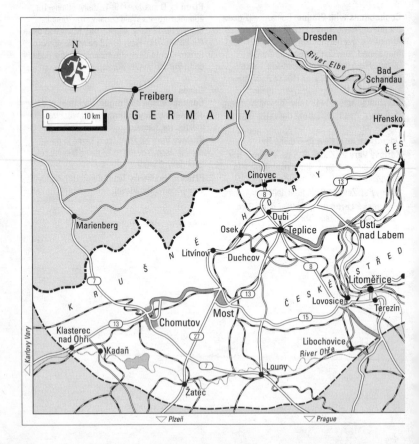

ACCOMMODATION PRICE CODES

After each entry in the **hotel** lists below, you'll find a symbol which corresponds to one of nine **price categories**:

① Under 500Kč   ④ 1000–1250Kč   ⑦ 1750–2000Kč
② 500–750Kč   ⑤ 1250–1500Kč   ⑧ 2000–2500Kč
③ 750–1000Kč   ⑥ 1500–1750Kč   ⑨ 2500Kč and upwards

All prices are for the cheapest **double room** available during high season, which usually means without private bath or shower in the less expensive places. For a **single room**, expect to pay around two-thirds the price of a double.

Geographically, the region is divided by the River Labe (Elbe) into two roughly equal halves. To the east, where the frontier mountains are slightly less pronounced, two rich German-speaking cities developed: **Liberec** (Reichenberg), built on the cloth industry, and **Jablonec** (Gablonz), famed for its jewellery. In addition, much of Bohemia's world-

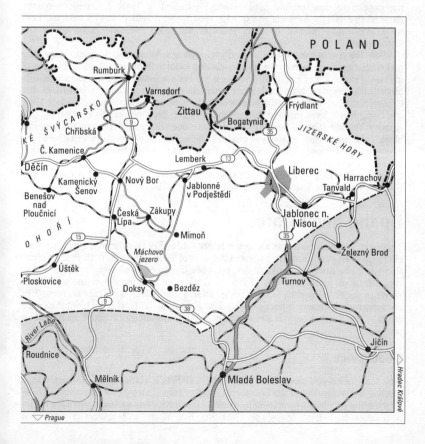

famous crystal and glass is still based in the smaller settlements located in the very north of the region. To the west of the Labe lie the **Krušné hory** (Erzegebirge or Ore Mountains), which, as their name suggests, were once a valuable source of iron ore and other minerals. Nowadays, however, the mountains are best known for their depleted forests, and for their brown coal deposits.

Historically, the region has been part of Bohemia since the first Přemyslid princes, but from very early on, large numbers of Germans from neighbouring Saxony drifted over the ill-defined border, some taking up their traditional wood-based crafts, others working in the mines that sprang up along the base of the mountains. By the end of the nineteenth century, **factories** and **mines** had become as much a part of the landscape of North Bohemia as mountains and chateaux. Then, with the collapse of the empire, the new-born Czechoslovak state inherited three-quarters of the Habsburg Empire's industry, and at a stroke became the world's tenth most industrialized country.

German and Czech miners remained loyal to the Left until the disastrous slump of the 1930s, when the majority of North Bohemia's German-speakers put their trust in the pro-Nazi Sudeten German Party or SdP, with disastrous consequences for the country – and for Europe. Allied bombings took their toll during the war, and with the backing of the Big Three (Churchill, Roosevelt and Stalin) at Potsdam, the German-speaking population was forcibly (and bloodily) expelled in 1945. Economic necessity ensured that North Bohemia was quickly rebuilt and resettled, but its land and lives were irrevocably marred by forty years of unbridled industrialization under the Communists.

While the rest of Europe was belatedly tempering sulphur emissions and increasing fuel efficiency, the Czechs were steadily sinking to fortieth place in the world league of industrial powers and rising to first place for male mortality rates, cancer and stillbirths. It's easy to blame all these calamities on the factory fetishism of the Communists, but damage to the forests of the Krušné hory was noted well before 1948, and smog levels have irritated the citizens of North Bohemia for the best part of this century. Yet now that the voices of dissent have been unleashed, the outlook is not all bleak – the brown-coal industry is gradually being wound down and alternative forms of energy being sought. The downside to this is that these measures are likely to leave the region with one of the highest unemployment rates in the Czech Republic, something that can only exacerbate the smouldering tensions between the Czechs and Romanies who have shared this polluted home since 1945.

Up the River Ohře

There are five historic towns along the **River Ohře** (Eger), overlooked by most travellers eager to reach Karlovy Vary and the spas of West Bohemia. With your own car, they can all be easily covered in a day; by public transport (preferably bus), it's best to concentrate on just one or two. If you are driving, be sure to take in one of the best **views** in the entire region, from the ridge shortly after Panenský Týnec on route 7: in the foreground, bizarre hillocks rise up like giant mole hills, while behind, the entire range of the Krušné hory is stretched out in all its distant glory (close up it's not so pretty).

Libochovice

First place of interest along the Ohře is **LIBOCHOVICE** (Libokowitz), a sleepy village nestling in the shadow of the Rožmberks' mighty ruined fortress of Hazmburk, whose Dracula-like profile is a prominent landmark. Libochovice has a **zámek** (April Sat & Sun 9am–noon & 1–4pm; May–Sept Tues–Sun 8am–noon & 1–5pm; Oct Tues–Sun

9am–noon & 1–4pm) of its own, given a Baroque cladding by the Lobkowicz family when they took it over in the seventeenth century, but with many of its original Gothic features intact. The entrance is presided over by a brooding bust of one of the heroes of the Czech national revival movement, Jan Evangelista Purkyně, father of Czech medicine, who was born in the chateau in 1787. Two lasting Lobkowicz additions provide the highlight of the chateau tour: the rather splendid *sala terrena* featuring trompe l'oeil frescoes by Italian artists, and the grandiose Saturn Hall. You could picnic with the noisy peacocks that stalk the carefully manicured French gardens, have a snack at the café in the courtyard of the chateau, or enjoy good Czech food at the *Zámecký šenk* next door.

Louny

LOUNY (Laun) is the first of the medieval fortified towns on route 7 (the road from Prague to Chomutov), its perfect Gothic appearance all but entirely destroyed by fire in 1517 – all, that is, except the strikingly beautiful church of **sv Mikuláš** (Tues–Sun 12.30–4pm), whose spiky, tent-like triple roof, the town's most famous landmark, is thought to have been rebuilt by the German mason Benedikt Ried (he used a similar design to great effect on the cathedral in Kutná Hora; see p.138), who died here in 1534. Even if the church is closed, you can peek in at his skilful ribbed vaulting through the glass in the entrance lobby. If you do get inside, be sure to check out the intricately carved limewood altars, barleysugar pillars and remarkable knobbly filigree work; when the church is open you can also climb the tower.

A couple of other isolated buildings in Louny are worth inspecting: round the back of the church in Pivovarská, the local museum occupies the **Dům rytířů z Mor** (Tues–Fri 10am–5pm, Sat & Sun 10am–noon & 1–5pm), with its distinctive Gothic stone oriel window and wedge-shaped roof, while the town's nineteenth-century **synagogue**, on Hilbertova, has now been restored and houses the district archives. The **Žatecká brána**, Louny's only remaining medieval gateway, is extremely impressive, and marks the beginning of a pleasant walk along the town's surviving ramparts, by the river on the northern edge of the old town.

Louny is less than an hour's drive from Prague airport. There are a few direct **trains** from Prague's Masarykovo nádraží, but for most you have to change at Kralupy nad Vltavou; the main train station is a kilometre or so east of the old town, while Louny předměstí, a short walk south of the old town, is only good for trains to Rakovník, and the once daily České Budějovice–Most express. If you need a place **to stay**, by far the best deal is the *Hotel Union* (☎0395/65 33 30; ③), literally in the shadow of sv Mikuláš on Beneše z Loun, with its own half-decent restaurant serving the local **beer**. There are good pizzas (and great views over the ramparts to be had at *Vivaldi*, or the usual Czech staples (plus the odd surprise, like eel in mustard sauce) at *U Daliborky* (closed Sun), both east of the main square on Hilbertova.

Žatec

ŽATEC (Saaz), 24km up the Ohře from Louny, is the centre of the hop-growing region that supports the famous Czech beer industry. In summer, from here as far south as Rakovník (Rakonitz), the roads are hemmed in by endless tall, green groves of hop vines. No one quite knows why Czech hops are the best in the world for brewing beer, but everyone accepts the fact, and even Belgian beer giants like Stella Artois import them in preference to their own. Since as long ago as the twelfth century, Bohemia's *Red Saaz* hops have been sent down the Elbe to the Hamburg hop market, and Žatec's biggest annual binge is still the September hop festival held in the town square.

The **old town** itself, on the hilltop opposite the train station, is a substantial, though scruffy, medieval affair, with two of its fifteenth-century western gates still intact. In those days the town was predominantly Czech, but during the next three centuries, wave upon wave of German immigrants gradually reversed the balance. The central square, headed by the plain, grey Renaissance **radnice**, is pleasant enough, with arcades down one side and a very busy plague column in the middle. To the right of the radnice there's a small garden of hops – the perfect advertisement for the town's wares – beyond which lies the town's ruined synagogue. Behind the radnice, the town's Jesuitized church is guarded by a wonderful gallery of beatific sculptures, while the town **brewery** (no admission) occupies pride of place in the thirteenth-century castle.

Life is beginning to return to the main square after decades of inactivity – you can sit outside and have a coffee beside the Baroque statuary, or browse among the market stalls that have begun to appear in between the arcades. As for **hotels**, the *Motes* (0397/71 11 69; ④), on Chelčického náměstí, is hidden in the scruffy backstreets east of the main square, and has great views; it's better value than the pricier *U hada* on the main square (☎0397/71 10 00; ⑤). The **restaurant** in the *Motes* is fine, as is the *Na baště*, near the theatre on Dvořákova, while the *Kapitán Drake*ˌ behind the hop garden, offers delicious seafood dishes and has an outdoor terrace. *Čajovna Altán* is a hippy **tearoom** with lots of drapes, situated opposite *U hada*.

Kadaň

Very much in the same mould as Louny and Žatec, **KADAŇ** (Kaaden), 22km west, is an altogether more picturesque halt on the Ohře. From the train station, you enter the old town through the round, whitewashed barbican of the **Žatecká brána**. The town suffered badly during the Thirty Years' War, the population was driven out in 1945, and the whole place lived under a dusty air of neglect for the following fifty years. Now the town's handsome eighteenth-century buildings have all been more or less restored to their former glory, and the place has really come alive once more. The most striking sights on the partially arcaded town square are the prickly white conical octagonal spire of the **radnice** and the twin red onion domes of the imposing **Děkanský kostel**, which contains some good Baroque furnishings. Directly opposite the radnice, you'll find **Katová ulička** ("Hangman's Lane" – his house is below the gate at the end), Bohemia's narrowest street, which is barely more than a passage, the light straining to make its way past the maze of buttresses. From the end of Katová ulička, you can gain access to the best-preserved part of the town walls or **hradby**, which lead round to the southern tip of town, where Kadaň's partially renovated **hrad**, a modest provincial seat, sits overlooking the Ohře; it's currently undergoing restoration and looks set to remain closed for some time to come.

Accommodation shouldn't be a problem, with the lovely pension *Horoskop* (☎0398/46 11; ④), across from the hrad, easily the best place to stay. There are several **campsites** in the vicinity, with the *Hradec* site (mid-April to Sept) 3km southeast of the town, enjoying the nicest position on the banks of the Ohře, not far from Hradec train station. A good place to grab a bite **to eat** in Kadaň is the excellent *Slunce* restaurant on the main square, next door to the radnice; for serious drinking, you can quaff beer from Úštěk at the pub on Tyršova.

Klášterec nad Ohří

Also worth a visit is **KLÁŠTEREC NAD OHŘÍ** (Klösterle-an-der-Eger), 5km west of Kadaň, the pretty quadrilateral seat of one of the many branches of the Thun family. Although, as the name suggests, the town was originally centred on a Benedictine monastery, it was the Thuns who really determined its present appearance, commissioning the two colourful Baroque churches and establishing the porcelain factory and spa facilities that made the town wealthy in the previous two centuries.

The Thuns' **zámek**, built up the hill from the village in 1646, today houses a **Muzeum porcelánu** (April–Oct Tues–Sun 10am–noon & 1–5pm), containing over 6000 pieces of local and imported china from the vast collection belonging to Prague's UPM (Decorative Arts Museum); visits are by guided tour only on the hour, and replicas can be purchased in the museum shop. More accessible are the wonderful **zámecká zahrada** sloping down to the river, filled with 46 varieties of rare trees – there's a map to show where each one stands – dotted with Baroque sculptures by Brokoff and boasting a *sala terrena*, whose gaudy red and cream colour scheme matches the church across the road. To get inside the family vault or **Thunská hrobka**, you need to ask at the museum, though it offers little of interest besides the odd quadruple-barrelled name – viz. Josef Oswald II Thun-Hohenstein-Salm-Reifferscheid, who has barely enough room on his coffin to fit his aristocratic credentials. The guide disappointedly concedes that all that remains of the first Thun of Klášterec is "a skull and a few bones" – rather impressive considering that he died some 300 years ago and when all that's left of another, eighteenth-century, Thun is a shoe.

The chateau is a 1.5km trek from the main bus or train station. There are plenty of places **to stay** in Klášterec, of which the most convenient is probably the very reasonable *Hotel Slavie* (☎0396/37 52 11; ①), just down the hill from the chateau on Tyršova, with its own restaurant. Alternatively, the *U Jezu* **campsite** (mid-April to Oct), is not far away on the banks of the Ohře.

The North Bohemian brown-coal basin

The **North Bohemian brown-coal basin** contrives to be even less enticing than it sounds. Stretching the sixty kilometres from Kadaň to Ústí nad Labem, it comprises an almost continuous rash of open-cast mines, factories and prefabricated towns, earning it the nickname *černý trojúhelník* or "black triangle". The majority of the country's brown coal (lignite) is mined here, most of it from just ten metres below the surface. As a result, huge tracts of land at the foot of the **Krušné hory** have been transformed by giant diggers that crawl across fields of brown sludge like the last surviving cockroaches in a post-nuclear desert. Around one hundred villages have been bulldozed, rail and road links shifted, and the entire town of Most flattened to make way for the ever-expanding mines.

Not only is the stuff extracted here, but much of it is burnt locally, and brown coal is by far the filthiest and most harmful of all fossil fuels. Lethal yellowish clouds billow out of the power stations at Tušimice and Prunéřov, situated less than 5km to the north and east of Kadaň. Both have now been fitted with filters, and Tušimice is due to be closed down soon. In the meantime, filter masks have to be distributed every winter to local schoolchildren as the whole valley slowly suffocates in a thick, 24-hour smog of noxious gases.

Chomutov

CHOMUTOV (Komotau), a major road and rail junction that's difficult to avoid if you're passing through the area, has a history more notable for its repeated destruction than for anything else. Three devastating fires, sackings by the Hussites and Swedes, outbreaks of the plague, World War II bombs, the violent postwar expulsion of most of the German-speaking townsfolk, and finally the legacy of the communist period – an ironworks, a meat-processing factory and vast swathes of high-rise *paneláky* – have all taken a heavy toll on the town. If, for some unfortunate set of circumstances, you should find yourself here, you can survey the entire scene best from the top of the Renaissance **tower** (May–Oct Tues–Sun 9am–5pm), which dominates the main square;

STATISTICS FROM THE BLACK TRIANGLE

- A total of 240 square kilometres of countryside have been destroyed since 1950.
- Four square metres of earth have to be removed to extract one tonne of coal.
- The region's annual coal output peaked at 75 million tonnes in 1984.
- Every year four percent of the country's coal deposits are mined.
- Air pollution exceeds government safety regulations for 120 days a year.
- Life expectancy in the region is seven years lower than the European average.
- Twenty percent of the power generated by coal is consumed by the mining industry.

---

the landings on the way up trace the town's history. You can fritter still more time away at the local **museum** in the town's radnice/zámek (Tues–Fri 9am–4pm, Sat 9am–2pm, Sun 2–5pm), opposite.

All Czech towns close to the German and Austrian borders suffer from a high level of **prostitution**, but the 17km along route 7 between Chomutov and the German border is one of the worst-affected areas. Sparsely populated since the expulsion of the German-speaking inhabitants in 1945, many of the derelict buildings have been turned into brothels, with women sitting bored in the doorways, or dancing half-heartedly in the windows. There have been several highly publicized police raids in the area, highlighting the fact that many of the women are brought here against their will from other former Eastern Bloc countries, but the authorities seem uncertain as to how to proceed: whether to legitimize the industry, which would be unpopular with the locals but safer for the women, or crack down on it. The whole scene is made all the more surreal by the fact that the brothels share roadside space with countless Vietnamese traders, whose stalls are lined with technicolour **garden gnomes** (a particular favourite of the neighbouring Germans).

Most, Litvínov and Libkovice

MOST (Brüx) is like a sort of architectural paean to the *panelák*, the prefabricated high-rise blocks that are perhaps the Communists' most obvious visual legacy. The only historic building to survive the town's demolition in the 1960s was the late-Gothic church of **Nanebevzetí Panna Maria** (Tues–Sun: May–Sept 9am–6pm; Oct–April 9am–4pm), which was transported in one piece on a specially built railway to the edge of the mine, 841 metres away (the move took 28 days). Designed by Jakob Heilmann of Schweinfurt, a pupil of Benedikt Ried, in the early sixteenth century, it's now something of a lonesome sight, stranded between a motorway and the edge of the mining area, a short walk upriver from the train station. Ask to see the video in the crypt which lauds the state's wonderful achievement in shifting the church – a hollow feat given that they relocated it above a polluted underground lake, whose sulphurous liquid has to be drained off to prevent the site from flooding. If your morbid fascination is captured, head for the vast **local museum** (Tues–Fri 9am–5pm, Sat & Sun 1–5pm), visible to the west beneath the hilltop castle of Hněvín; outside the museum is a new memorial to František Niedermertl, who was shot in 1952 for insubordination in one of the local forced labour camps.

Trams connect Most with **LITVÍNOV** (Leutensdorf), 6km north. En route, they pass a huge Chemopetrol plant just south of the town, which, coupled with the constant sulphur emissions from a neighbouring power station, creates a bank of cloud that regularly blots out the sun and reduces all light to a grey haze. At the side of the road, special red lights illuminate the simple command (in Czech) "STOP! DON'T SMOKE! SWITCH OFF YOUR ENGINE!" when the authorities deem the chemical levels to be too dangerous. Amazingly, Litvínov still has the leftovers of its nineteenth-century *Ringstrasse*, now boarded up and long since overtaken by the town's new constructions.

With any luck, the village of **LIBKOVICE**, 5km southeast of Litvínov, will be the last settlement in the "black triangle" to be bulldozed to make way for open-cast mining. In 1994, on the eve of the village's demise, Czech environmentalists managed to pressurize the local mining company into preserving the village's Baroque church as a kind of monument to the postwar destruction that has marred the region. It remains to be seen whether the public will be granted access to the building in the future, or whether, as some fear, the whole structure will simply sink into the ground.

Duchcov

At first, **DUCHCOV** (Dux), 8km east of Litvínov, appears no different, encircled as it is by coal mines. But in this unlikely town, there's a grandly conceived Baroque **zámek** (April & Oct Wed–Sun 9am–4pm; May–Sept Tues–Sun 9am–6pm), designed by Jean-Baptiste Mathey, which once hosted emperors and kings, as well as artistic luminaries such as Schiller, Goethe and Beethoven. The chateau's former librarian was none other than **Giacomo Casanova** (1725–98), who took refuge here at the invitation of Count Waldstein. Broke, almost impotent and painfully aware of his age, Casanova whiled away his final, fairly miserable thirteen years writing his steamy memoirs, the twelve-volume *Histoire de ma vie*. He took a vow of celibacy on entering Duchcov, though rumours continued to link him with various women, including the leading lady at the première of Mozart's *Don Giovanni* in Prague. The Venetians would like Casanova's remains, but no one is sure where they lie now, and the likelihood is that they have disappeared under the open-cast mines.

The tour guides are well aware that today's trickle of visitors are more concerned with Casanova than with the chateau's period furniture, and so save the exhibition dedicated to the world's most famous bounder till last. Duchcov also boasts a vast collection of Czech Baroque art, including sculptures by Brokoff and Braun, and a series of obsequious portraits of the Waldstein family, mostly by Václav Vavřinec Reiner, who is also responsible for the fresco in the Great Hall. Much of the chateau park, along with the Baroque hospital designed by Octavio Broggio, was bulldozed in the 1950s by the Communists, who (wrongly) suspected that large coal deposits lay beneath the gardens. The priceless frescoes were shifted to a purpose-built concrete pavilion, where – forlorn, badly lit and brutally restored – they remain today; to see the frescoes, you must endure a thirty-minute guided tour.

If you need a bite **to eat**, the *Zámecká bašta* on Masarykova, just by the chateau, serves up the usual with dumplings. The hotel opposite the chateau is currently being restored; until then, the only **accommodation** is the *Pension ráj*, Havířská 58 (☎0417/93 58 90; ①).

Osek

Another monument worth visiting, just out of earshot of the region's mines, is **OSEK** (Ossegg), 7km northeast of Litvínov, whose twelfth-century **Cistercian abbey** (April, May, Sept & Oct Tues–Sat 10am–noon & 1–4pm, Sun 1–4pm; June–Aug closes 5pm) is a reminder of the wealth of the area before the dawn of industrialization. After the destruction of the Thirty Years' War, some of the country's leading Baroque artists – painter Václav Vavřinec Reiner, architects Broggio and Santini, and the sculptor Corbellini, whose vigorous stucco drapery upstages the lot – set to work restoring the place. The abbey's real artistic treasure, however, is the thirteenth-century chapel off the cloisters, where light filters through to illuminate a central altar and an elegant stone pulpit with a rotating lectern. Under the Communists, the abbey was used as an internment camp for monks and nuns who refused to abandon their religious calling; now, happily, the Cistercians are back, putting the place to use as a refuge for the homeless and a religious education centre for a new generation of Czech monks. There's a **campsite** (May–Sept) and an inexpensive pension just west of the monastery, by the lake.

Teplice

In the midst of this polluted region lies the traumatized town of **TEPLICE-ŠANOV** (Teplitz-Schönau), the forgotten fourth spa of the once celebrated quartet of Bohemian resorts that included Mariánské Lázně, Františkovy Lázně and Karlovy Vary (see previous chapter). In the early nineteenth century it became "the drawing room of Europe", prompting the likes of Beethoven, Liszt and Wagner to appear on its *Kurliste*. By the 1880s, however, the adjacent mining industry had already inflicted its first blow on Teplice's idyllic way of life: the nearby Döllinger mine breached an underwater lake, flooding the natural springs, which subsequently had to be artificially pumped to the surface. The lingering smell of lignite was a characteristic of the town even then, and is now complemented by several additional chemical vapours.

The accumulative cost of this assault on the environment is extremely serious, but it has been compounded by the fact that, following the expulsion of the spa's German-speaking inhabitants, the Communists proceeded to wreck the place aesthetically too, dismembering much of the old town and erecting tasteless edifices. In addition, Teplice

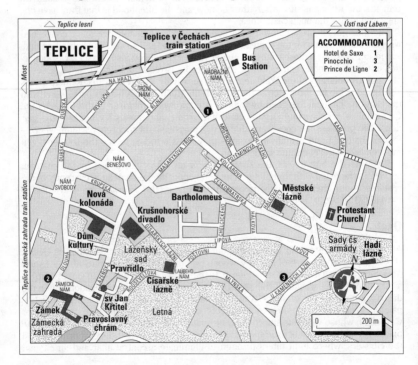

now has more than its fair share of social problems: there's a large and vocal skinhead movement here, which has come to blows with the town's Vietnamese and Romany communities on several occasions over the last decade; meanwhile, as at Chomutov, prostitution is endemic along route 8 to Dresden. All this doesn't make for a great introduction to the town, but elements of the old spa have survived, and if you're in the area, Teplice merits at least an afternoon's halt.

The Town

Arriving at the main train station, **Teplice v Čechách**, with its rich neo-Renaissance frescoes adorning the vaulted ceiling, injects a sense of hope in innocent minds, though this is soon dispelled by block after block of silent and peeling late-nineteenth-century houses as you head for the centre via 28 října or the main street, Masarykova třída, one block south.

At the end of Masarykova, behind the rather brutal Krušnohorské divadlo (an uncharacteristic, late work by Helmer and Fellner), the spa proper begins. Even the old *Kur Garten* – now the **Lázeňský sad** – has a somewhat diseased air about it, despite the lively sounds of birdlife. Nowadays, the communist-era white concrete **Dům kultury** is the dominant feature of the park, fronted by the **Nová kolonáda**, a glorified greenhouse made from some of Bohemia's great glass surplus.

Only when you cross the valley to the brightly coloured Neoclassical houses on **Lázeňská** is it possible to make the imaginative leap into Teplice's arcadian past. Beethoven once stayed in a house on Lázeňská, and it was in Teplice that he wrote his famous love letter to a woman he called his "Immortal Beloved", but whose identity still remains a mystery. Beyond Lázeňská lies the town's monumental **zámek**, seat of the Clary-Aldringen family until 1945, when they and most other *Teplitzer* took flight from the approaching Red Army. It was here, in 1813, that Tsar Alexander I, the Emperor Franz I and Kaiser Friedrich Wilhelm of Prussia concluded the "Holy Alliance" against Napoleon. The countless rooms of the chateau are now part of the local museum (Tues–Sun 10am–noon & 1–5pm), with memorials to Beethoven, Pushkin, and (of course) Goethe, wall-to-wall *Biedermeyer* and much else besides.

Outside the main gates of the chateau is the cobbled expanse of **Zámecké náměstí** centred on Matthias Bernhard Braun's flamboyant charcoaled plague column. To the east, there are two churches: the first is the **Pravoslavný chrám**, a neo-Gothic Orthodox church; the second is the more handsome Baroque church of **sv Jan Křtitel**, whose richly painted interior is worth a quick peek. Hot water dribbles through a sculpted boar's mouth into the occasional tourist's palms from the original spring, known as the **Pravřídlo** (Urquelle), which is set into the wall opposite the northeast corner of the church. Further east still, a splendid staircase, the Ptačí schody (Birds' Staircase), takes you past the twin turrets of the *U Petra* restaurant to the blissful **zámecká zahrada**, which spreads itself around two lakes still "enlivened with swans", just as Baedeker noted approvingly back in 1905.

Šanov

The rest of the spa lies in the eastern part of town, once the separate village of **Šanov** (Schönau) linked to Teplice by Lipová (Lindenstrasse), which still clings to its lime trees despite the acid onslaught. Like the bark on the trees, the paint is slowly dropping off the grandiose private villas and spa pensions that characterize this part of the spa. Lipová culminates in the sady Československé armády, overlooked by a large, run-down, red-brick Protestant church and peppered with yellowing Neoclassical spa buildings. If you haven't prebooked into a spa hotel, you can get non-prescribed treatment at *Hadí lázně*, on the south side of the sady Československé armády. Unfortunately, the sky-blue Art Nouveau *Termalní lázně*, just off Lipová on Hálkova, is currently not functioning. However, you could improve your health by climbing the 230 steps to the summit of Letná (accessible from Laubeho náměstí, at the eastern corner of the Lázeňský sad) for a great **view** over the spa.

Practicalities

By far Teplice's nicest (and most expensive) place to stay is the *Hotel Prince de Ligne* (☎0417/247 55; ⑨), a pristinely renovated late-nineteenth-century hotel overlooking Zámecké náměstí. Cheaper alternatives include the *Hotel de Saxe* (☎0417/438 43; *desaxe@mbox.vol.cz*; ⑤), on the corner of Masarykova and Husitská, near the main train station, or the rooms above the *Pinocchio* ice cream parlour on U kamenných lázní (☎0417/279 06; ③). Avoid *U Petra* when looking for somewhere **to eat**; head instead for the *Beethoven*, the nearby daytime-only eatery, or the *Cedr*, round the corner on Lázeňská, which does Middle Eastern dishes as well as Czech ones (you can also buy warm *oplatky* in the same building). There's a pleasant café on the first floor of the smart nineteenth-century Císařské lázně; the *U palmy* pub in a converted eighteenth-century villa on the opposite side of Laubeho náměstí is also recommended.

Moving on from Teplice, the main **bus terminal** and **train station** (Teplice v Čechách) are next to one another just off Masarykova; Teplice zámecká zahrada train station, to the west of the chateau garden, is served only by slow trains to Lovosice. Slow, scenic trains to Děčín leave from Teplice lesní brána, 1km northwest of the centre – a fifteen-minute walk down Dubská from the town hall and across the motorway, or bus #20 from the main train station, or buses #16 and #23 from Benešovo náměstí.

Terezín

The old road from Prague to Berlin passes through the fortress town of **TEREZÍN** (Theresienstadt), just over 60km northwest of the capital. Purpose-built in the 1780s by the Habsburgs to defend the northern border against Prussia, it was capable of accommodating 14,500 soldiers and hundreds of prisoners. In 1941, the population was ejected and the whole town turned into a **Jewish ghetto**, and used as a transit camp for Jews whose final destination was Auschwitz.

Hlavná pevnost (Main Fortress)

Although the **Hlavná pevnost** (Main Fortress) has never been put to the test in battle, Terezín remains intact as a garrison town. Today, it's an eerie, soulless place, built to a dour eighteenth-century grid plan, its bare streets empty apart from the residual civilian population and visitors making their way between the various museums and memorials. As you enter, the red-brick zigzag fortifications are still an awesome sight, though the huge moat has been put to good use by local gardening enthusiasts.

The first place to head for is the **Muzeum Ghetta** (Ghetto Museum; daily: April–Sept 9am–6pm; Oct–March 9am–5.30pm), which was finally opened in 1991, on the fiftieth anniversary of the arrival of the first transports in Terezín. After the war, the Communists had followed the consistent Soviet line by deliberately underplaying the Jewish perspective on Terezín. Instead, the emphasis was on the Malá pevnost (see below), where the majority of victims were not Jewish, and on the war as an antifascist struggle, in which good (communism and the Soviet Union) had triumphed over evil (fascism and Nazi Germany). It wasn't until the Prague Spring of 1968 that the idea of a museum dedicated specifically to the history of the Jewish ghetto first

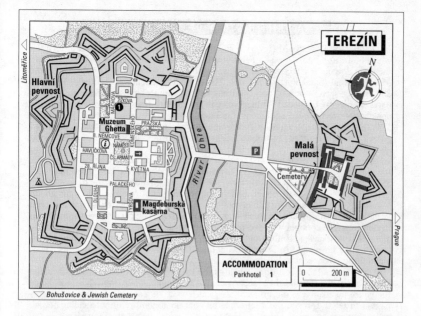

△ Litoměřice

TEREZÍN

Hlavní pevnost

Muzeum Ghetta (i)

Malá pevnost

Cemetery

Magdeburská kasárna

ACCOMMODATION
Parkhotel **1**

0   200 m

△ Prague

▽ Bohušovice & Jewish Cemetery

emerged. In the 1970s, however, the intended building was turned into a Museum of the Ministry of the Interior instead. Now that it's finally open, this extremely informative and well-laid-out exhibition at last attempts to do some justice to the extraordinary and tragic events which took place here between 1941 and 1945, including background displays on the measures which led inexorably to the *Endlösung*. There's also a fascinating video (with English subtitles) showing clips of the Nazi propaganda film shot in Terezín – *Hitler Gives the Jews a Town* – intercut with harrowing interviews with survivors.

The **Magdeburská kasárna** (Magdeburg Barracks), former seat of the Jewish self-governing council or *Freizeitgestaltung*, in the south of the ghetto, has recently been turned into a fascinating museum concentrating on the remarkable artistic life of Terezín. First off, however, there's a reconstructed women's dormitory, with three-tier bunks and all the luggage and belongings in place to give some kind of idea as to the cramped living conditions endured by the ghetto inhabitants. The first exhibition room has displays on the various Jewish musicians who passed through Terezín, including Pavel Haas, a pupil of Janáček, Hans Krása, a pupil of Zemlinsky, who wrote the score for *Brundibár*, and Karel Ančerl, who survived the Holocaust to become conductor of the Czech Philharmonic. The final exhibition room concentrates on the writers who contributed to the ghetto's underground magazines, but the greatest space is given over to the work of Terezín's numerous artists. Many were put to work by the SS, who set up a graphics department headed by cartoonist Bedřich Fritta, producing visual propaganda, showing how smoothly the ghetto ran. In addition, there are many clandestine works, ranging from portraits of inmates, to harrowing depictions of the cramped dormitories, and the transports. These provide some of the most vivid and deeply affecting insights into the reality of ghetto life in the whole of Terezín, and it was for this "propaganda of horror" that several artists, including Fritta, were eventually deported to Auschwitz

A BRIEF HISTORY OF THE GHETTO

In October 1941, Reinhard Heydrich and the Nazi high command decided to turn the whole of Terezín into a Jewish ghetto. It was an obvious choice: fully fortified, close to the main Prague–Dresden railway line, and with an SS prison already established in the **Malá pevnost** (Small Fortress) nearby. The original inhabitants of the town – less than 3500 people – were moved out, and transports began arriving at Terezín from many parts of central Europe. Within a year, nearly 60,000 Jews were interned here in appallingly overcrowded conditions; the monthly death rate rose to 4000. In October 1942, the first transport left for Auschwitz. By the end of the war, 140,000 Jews had passed through Terezín; fewer than 17,500 remained when the ghetto was finally liberated on May 8, 1945.

One of the perverse ironies of Terezín is that it was used by the Nazis as a cover for the real purpose of the *Endlösung* or "final solution", devised at the Wannsee conference in January 1942 (at which Heydrich was present). The ghetto was made to appear self-governing, with its own council or *Freizeitgestaltung*, its own bank printing ghetto money, its own shops selling goods confiscated from the internees on arrival, and even a café on the main square. For a while, a special "Terezín family camp" was even set up in Auschwitz, to continue the deception. The deportees were kept in mixed barracks, allowed to wear civilian clothes and – the main purpose of the whole thing – send letters back to their loved ones in Terezín telling them they were OK. After six months' "quarantine", they were sent to the gas chambers.

Despite the fact that Terezín was being used by the Nazis as cynical propaganda, the ghetto population turned their unprecedented freedom to their own advantage. Since the entire population of the Protectorate (and Jews from many other parts of Europe) passed through Terezín, the ghetto had an enormous number of outstanding Jewish artists, musicians, scholars and writers (many of whom subsequently perished in the camps). Thus, in addition to the officially sponsored activities, countless clandestine cultural events were organized in the cellars and attics of the barracks: teachers gave lessons to children, puppet-theatre productions were held, and literary evenings were put on.

Towards the end of 1943, the so-called *Verschönerung* or "beautification" of the ghetto was implemented, in preparation for the arrival of the International Red Cross inspectors. Streets were given names instead of numbers, and the whole place was decked out as if it were a spa town. When the International Red Cross asked to inspect one of the Nazi camps, they were brought here and treated to a week of Jewish cultural events. A circus tent was set up in the main square; a children's pavilion erected in the park; numerous performances of Hans Krása's children's opera, *Brundibár* (Bumble Bee), staged; and a jazz band, called the Ghetto Swingers, performed in the bandstand on the main square. The Red Cross visited Terezín twice, once in June 1944, and again in April 1945; both times the delegates filed positive reports.

Malá pevnost (Small Fortress)

On the other side of the River Ohře, east down Pražská, lies the **Malá pevnost** (Small Fortress; daily: April–Sept 8am–6.30pm; Oct–March 8am–4.30pm), built as a military prison in the 1780s, at the same time as the main fortress. The prison's most famous inmate was the young Bosnian Serb, Gavrilo Princip, who succeeded in assassinating Archduke Ferdinand in Sarajevo in 1914, and was interned and died here during World War I. In 1940 it was turned into an SS prison by Heydrich and, after the war, it became the official memorial and museum of Terezín. The majority of the 32,000 inmates who passed through the prison were active in the resistance (and, more often than not, Communists). Some 2500 inmates perished in the prison, while another

8000 died subsequently in the concentration camps. The vast cemetery laid out by the entrance contains the graves of over 2300 individuals, plus numerous other corpses, and is rather insensitively dominated by a large Christian cross, plus a smaller Star of David.

There are guides available (occasionally survivors of Terezín), or else you can simply use the brief guide to the prison in English, and walk around yourself. The infamous Nazi refrain *Arbeit Macht Frei* (Work Brings Freedom) is daubed across the entrance on the left, which leads to the exemplary washrooms, still as they were when built for the Red Cross tour of inspection. The rest of the camp has been left empty but intact, and graphically evokes the cramped conditions under which the prisoners were kept half-starved and badly clothed, subject to indiscriminate cruelty and execution. The prison's main **exhibition** is housed in the SS barracks opposite the luxurious home of the camp *Kommandant* and his family. A short documentary, intelligible in any language, is regularly shown in the cinema that was set up in 1942 to entertain the SS guards.

Practicalities

Terezín is about an hour's **bus** ride from Prague's Florenc bus terminal, or a short hop from Litoměřice, just 3km to the north. The nearest train station to Terezín (from which the transports used to leave) is at Bohušovice, on the main Prague–Dresden line; occasional buses run to and from Terezín, or else it's a two-kilometre walk southwest of the main fortress. **Foodwise**, you're best off either bringing a picnic or heading for *U hojtašů*, on Komenského, just north of the museum. It's difficult to imagine a less appealing place **to stay**, but stay you may, at the very basic *Parkhotel*, on Máchova (☎0416/78 22 60; ②), or at the **campsite** *Kréta* (April–Sept) just west of town. Alternatively, the **tourist office** (daily 9am–4pm) on the main square can advise you on the many accommodation possibilities in Litoměřice (see below).

Litoměřice

If the idea of lingering in Terezín is unappealing, you can walk or catch the bus 3km north to **LITOMĚŘICE** (Leitmeritz), at the confluence of the Ohře and the Labe rivers. The town has been an ecclesiastical centre since the Přemyslid Spytihněv II founded a collegiate chapter here in 1057. From the eleventh century onwards, German craftsmen flooded into Litoměřice, thanks to its strategic trading position on the Labe, and it soon became the third or fourth city of Bohemia. Having survived the Hussite Wars by the skin of its teeth, it was devastated in the Thirty Years' War, but its most recent upheaval came in 1945, when virtually the entire population (which was predominantly German-speaking) was forcibly expelled. Since 1989, the town has begun to pick up the pieces after forty years of neglect. Restoration work is continuing apace, and the re-establishment here of a Catholic seminary has brought some pride back to the town.

The main reason people come here now is to pay their respects at Terezín, just south of the town (see above); however, Litoměřice is of more than passing interest, since the entire town is a virtual museum to **Octavio Broggio**. Broggio was born here in 1668 and, along with his father Giulio, redesigned the town's many churches following the arrival of the Jesuits and the establishment of a Catholic bishopric here in the mid-seventeenth century. The reason for this zealous re-Catholicization was Litoměřice's rather too eager conversion to the heretical beliefs of the Hussites and its disastrous allegiance to the Protestants in the Thirty Years' War.

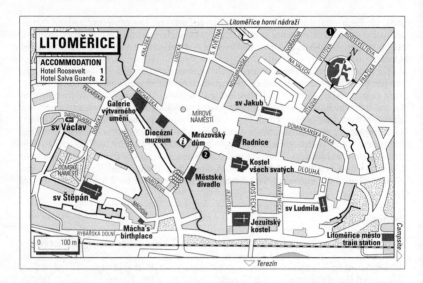

The Town

Stepping out of the train station, you're greeted by the last remaining bastion of the old town walls across the road; behind it lies the historical quarter, entered via the wide boulevard of Dlouhá. The first church you come to is the hybrid church of **Kostel všech svatých** (All Saints) at the top of the street, which started life as a Romanesque church, and now boasts the only Gothic spires left on the skyline, a beautiful wedge-shaped affair reminiscent of Prague's right bank, plus three smaller spikier ones behind. Its present Baroque facade was designed by Broggio, but the oppressively low ceiling and dusty furnishings are disappointing, with the notable exception of the fifteenth-century panel painting by the Master of Litoměřice. More impressive is the light-infused interior of the nearby **Jezuitský kostel** (Jesuit Church), another work by Broggio, whose ceiling is adorned with colourful frescoes. While you're in the vicinity, check out the bizarre modern driftwood installation occupying the nearby flight of steps.

The town's vast cobbled marketplace, **Mírové náměstí**, once one of the most important in Bohemia, now boasts only a couple of buildings from before the Thirty Years' War. The best known is the **Mrázovský dům**, at no. 15 on the south side of the square, whose owner at the time, a devout Hussite, had a huge wooden *kalich* (chalice) – the symbol of all Hussites – plonked on the roof in 1537. The other building that stands out is the arcaded fourteenth-century **radnice**, at the eastern end of the square, topped by a shapely Renaissance gable. It now serves as the town museum (Tues–Sun 10am–5pm), worth a quick spin round, if only for the coffered sixteenth-century ceiling of the council hall; there's still precious little mention in the exhibition of the 1945 expulsions, however.

The town's art galleries

In the western corner of the square is the town's excellent **Diecézní muzeum** (Tues–Sun: April–Sept 9am–noon & 1–6pm; Oct–March 9am–noon & 1–5pm). As befits a rich ecclesiastical region, there are a lot of very fine religious paintings here beginning with the serene *Madonna with Child in an Enclosed Garden*, an early oil painting from 1494. In the gruesome *Donor, Christ and Death*, Christ's flesh appears almost translucent, while Death appears as a skeleton tightly wrapped in skin. Among the museum's most valuable paintings is Lucas Cranach the Elder's *St Anthony the Hermit*, which depicts the saint being tempted heavenwards by a grisly collection of devilish animals. The most remarkable and unusual section of the gallery, however, is the timber-built building at the back of the museum, which contains a vast collection of "naive art": works from the last century by local amateur artists on a variety of themes from the religious to the political, from landscapes to portraits.

A few doors up nearby Michalská, the town's **Galerie výtvarného umění** (Gallery of Fine Art; Tues–Sun: April–Sept 9am–noon & 1–6pm; Oct–April closes 5pm) occupies a wonderfully rambling sixteenth-century building, whose inner courtyard is draped in ivy and echoing to the trickle of a modern fountain. Exhibitions doing the Bohemian circuit stop off here, supplementing the small permanent collection of late-nineteenth- and early-twentieth-century Czech canvases, including Impressionist work by Jan Preisler, Antonín Hudeček and Antonín Slavíček, plus a few pieces of Baroque art, and a bizarre Gothic statue of Mary Magdalene, depicted with her hair covering her entire body, except her knees. There's more Gothic art on the ground floor, in particular the surviving panels of the early-sixteenth-century winged altar by the Master of Litoměřice, whose paintings are peopled by folk with expressive, almost grotesque faces, whose poses and gestures are remarkably sophisticated for the period. Baroque dwarfs and other more modern sculptures pepper the gallery's terrace overlooking the ramparts.

Around sv Štěpán

On a promontory 500m southwest of the town centre, the **Dómský pahorek** (Cathedral Hill), where the bishop and his entourage once held residence, was originally entirely separate from the town, with its own fortifications. The small Orthodox chapel of **sv Václav** (St Wenceslas) on the northern slope is perhaps the younger Broggio's finest work, grand despite its cramped proportions and location, though suffering a little from a rather gaudy salmon-pink and silver-grey facelift. But the real reason to come out here is to wonder at the former cathedral of **sv Štěpán** (St Stephen), which looks out onto the quiet, grassy enclosure of Dómské náměstí. Redesigned by Giulio Broggio (among others) in the seventeenth century, sv Štěpán marked the start of the extensive rebuilding of Litoměřice. The cathedral's ceiling is disappointing, but the dark wood and the gloomy altar paintings from the school of Cranach the Elder add a bit of atmosphere. Outside, the freestanding Italianate campanile, designed by the Viennese architect Heinrich Ferstel in the 1880s, adds a peculiarly Tuscan touch.

A path along the north side of sv Štěpán leads down the cobbled lane of Máchova, where the Czech poet **Karel Hynek Mácha** died in 1836; there's a commemoration plaque at no. 3. In true Romantic style, Mácha died of consumption at the age of 26. His most famous poem, *Máj* (May), was hijacked by the Communists as their May Day anthem, but remains a popular love poem. He used to be buried in the local cemetery, but when the Nazis drew up the Sudetenland borders, Litoměřice lay inside the Greater German Reich, so the Czechs dug up the poet and reinterred him in the Vyšehrad cemetery in Prague (see p.109). Once you've reached the bottom of the cathedral hill, the stairway of the Máchovy schody will take you back up into town.

Practicalities

All **buses** terminate at the Litoměřice město **train station**, at the southeast corner of the old town, terminus for trains to Mělník and Ústí nad Labem; trains to Lovosice, Úštěk and Česká Lípa depart from Litoměřice horní nádraží, to the north of the old town. The town's **tourist office** (May–Sept Mon–Sat 8am–6pm, Sun 9.30am–4pm; Oct–April Mon–Fri 8am–4pm, Sat 8–11am) is in the Mrázovský dům on Mírové náměstí, and can arrange **private rooms**. If you want to treat yourself, stay at the friendly *Hotel Salva Guarda* (☎0416/73 25 06; ⑤), located in a lovely sgraffitoed building on Mírové náměstí and named after the house's sixteenth-century owner, who was an imperial bodyguard. Otherwise, try the *Roosevelt*, on Rooseveltova (☎0416/73 35 95; ④), or the simple pension *U Pavouka*, Pekářská 7 (☎0416/73 44 09; ②). There's also the *Slavoj* **campsite** (May–Sept) with bungalows, near the open-air cinema (*letní kino*) on Střelecký ostrov, the woody island on the river. The **restaurant** in the *Salva Guarda* is the best choice in town; in warm weather, the locals congregate at the *Zahradní restaurace* on Zítkova, though don't be fooled by the name, as in fact there's no food on offer.

Ploskovice and Úštěk

An easy day-trip from Litoměřice, the village of **PLOSKOVICE**, 6km to the northeast, off route 15, hides one of Octavio Broggio's few secular works, a crisp, light summer **zámek** (April & Oct Sat & Sun 9am–4pm; May–Sept Tues–Sun 8am–5pm). After his abdication in 1848, this became a favourite summer watering hole for the Habsburg emperor Ferdinand I, who commissioned the exuberant Rococo plasterwork – sometimes frivolous, sometimes tasteless, always fun. The whole place has recently undergone a lengthy restoration: the beautiful walled grounds (daily dawn–dusk) are beginning to flourish and the fountains are issuing forth once more. To reach the chateau from the train station, follow the little stream north for 1km.

Bypassed by the main road – and, it seems, by the entire last three centuries – **ÚŠTĚK** (Auscha) originally grew up around a now-ruined medieval fortress. On one side of the main square there's a line of fourteenth-century burgher houses, which, unusually for Bohemia, still retain their original triangular gables of wood or slate. The **Jezuitský kostel**, built after the devastating fire of 1765, occupies centre stage in the square, and features a trompe l'oeil main altar, a Karel Škréta altarpiece and several fine wooden sculptures. Down by the waters of the Úštěcký potok to the southwest of the town, in among the geese and hens, there are some fascinating wooden shacks known as **ptačí domky** (birds' houses). Perched on top of each other on the highest ledge of the steeply terraced banks, they provided ad hoc accommodation for Jewish families who were forced to live in ghettos until at least 1848, and for the Italian workers who built the town's railway link in the late nineteenth century.

It's fifty minutes by train from Litoměřice and about another half a kilometre's walk from the train station east to the old town. If you're **camping**, there's a site (mid-June to mid-Sept) by the pleasant sandy shores of Chmelař lake (boat rental available in season), behind the train station. You'll find alternative accommodation in the form of several modest pensions, and there are a couple of good restaurants: *Restaurace na růžku*, in a pink building off the square, and *Restaurace pod loubím*, behind the church on the main square.

Ústí nad Labem

Twenty kilometres north, on the other side of the České středohoří (Central Bohemian Hills), which part only to allow the River Labe to slither through, lies the vast metropolis of **ÚSTÍ NAD LABEM** (Aussig). From a small town, Aussig grew very rapidly into the second largest port on the Labe (Elbe) after Hamburg, and the busiest in the Habsburg Empire. Solidly German-speaking and heavily industrialized, Aussig suffered terrible bomb damage during World War II. Worse was to follow. On July 30, 1945, a devastating terrorist attack took place when Ústí's sugar refinery, being used to store ammunition confiscated from the Germans, was blown up, killing fourteen Czechs and triggering a riot. The attack was blamed on die-hard Nazis, and enraged Czechs stormed through the town, dragging off any German they could find, and lynching hundreds before throwing them into the Labe. The incident is thought to have been instrumental in persuading President Beneš to declare the three million ethnic Germans living in Czechoslovakia enemies of the state and call for their forceful expulsion from the country.

Ústí was resettled after the war, its industries further expanded, and it now has a population of 110,000, making it the third largest city in Bohemia. However, the city has lost almost all of its charm – even the tram system (once second only to Prague's) was wound up in 1970. More recently, it has hit the headlines across the world as the place where the local council tried to build a wall to divide some of the city's Romany residents from their white Czech neighbours (for more on which, see box on next page). Given the city's aesthetic limitations, and its almost unbearable historical baggage, most people give the place a wide berth. If, however, for whatever reason, you find yourself here, there are a couple of sights of minor interest, where you can while away an hour or so.

The town

Trains usually stop at Ústí for only four or five minutes, which is long enough for most people – one whiff of the air, one look at the discoloured river, tells you that this is yet another chemical town. For those venturing into town, it's just a couple of blocks west from the main train station to Ústí's chief sights, the Dominican church of **sv Vojtěch**, given a Baroque facelift by Ottavio Broggio in the 1730s, and the fourteenth-century cathedral of **Nanebevzetí Panny Maria**. Destroyed by the Hussites during their bloody occupation of the town in 1426, the cathedral was rebuilt in late-Gothic style, and has recently been nicely restored. The building's outrageously leaning steeple is the result of bomb damage in World War II. From behind the churches you can view the 1930s road bridge over the Labe, opened in 1936 by President Beneš and somewhat optimistically named the "Bridge of Brotherhood" (between the Czech- and German-speakers).

The main square, **Mírové náměstí**, has had its entire northern side ripped out, and is now only really remarkable for the surviving Socialist Realist mosaic, depicting the inevitable road from the workers' revolution to world peace, which adorns the headquarters of the local council. One final building worthy of mention is the town's theatre or **Městské divadlo**, built in 1909 in the style of the Viennese Secession, and situated to the west of the main square, overlooking the concrete paving stones of Lidické náměstí.

On the opposite side of the Labe from the city centre is the suburb of **Střekov** (Schreckenstein), dominated by its ruined **hrad** (Tues–Sun: April & Sept–Dec 9am–4pm; May–Aug 9am–5pm), a dramatic nightmare fairy-tale pile built into a bleak, black rocky outcrop high above the river. Like the Lorelei on the Rhine, it was much loved by the nineteenth-century Romantics, and provided inspiration for one of Wagner's operas (in this case, *Tannhäuser*). Now back in the hands of the Lobkowicz family, you're free to explore the ruins, and revel in the utterly incredible views up the Labe valley and over to Ústí's grim smokestacks and awesome *paneláky*. The castle kitchen is now the *Wágnerka* café and restaurant, with a shady terrace from which you can watch the barges negotiating the lock below.

Practicalities

Ústí's **bus station** is just south of Lidické náměstí, a couple of blocks west of the main square. Travelling by fast train from Prague, Dresden or Berlin, you're most likely to arrive at Ústí's main **train station**, hlavní nádraží, at the southeast corner of the old town by the river; trains from Most, Litoměřice and Mělník pass through Střekov station, on the other side of the river, and terminate at Ústí nad Labem západ, which is another couple of blocks west of the bus station, down Revoluční.

THE WALL IN ÚSTÍ

Ústí nad Labem leapt into the media spotlight in 1998 when the municipal authorities decided to erect a 2.65m high "sound barrier" in Matiční, a street in the city's industrial eastern suburb of Krásné Březno. White Czech residents on one side of the street had complained about "antisocial and unhygienic behaviour" by the Romanies who lived in the housing block across the street. Ultimately, however, the plan was to subject the Romanies to a 10pm curfew, by locking them inside the compound. The decision was criticized by the EU, and by the Czech parliament, though few people actually believed the city council in Ústí – where fifteen percent of the population are Romany – would go ahead with the project. Then early one morning in October 1999, the council suddenly began construction. Human rights groups protested, the Romanies attempted to tear the wall down, and the Czech parliament declared the wall illegal. After several weeks of bad international publicity, and stalemate between the central government and the municipal authorities, the council was finally forced to back down. However, the gesture was not one of peace and reconciliation. The state has offered to buy up the houses of the non-Romany residents and pay for them to be rehoused. As one Czech government minister put it "there are many streets like Matiční in our country" – in other words, this is not an issue that's going to go away overnight.

The **tourist office** (Mon–Fri 8am–5pm, Sat 8am–3pm; *info.ul@mbox.vol.cz*) is on Hrnčířská 1, at the eastern edge of the main square, and can hand out a basic town map. If you do need to **stay the night** in Ústí, you might as well enjoy the communist-era luxury of the *Hotel Bohemia*, the high-rise monstrosity on the main square, Mírové náměstí (047/522 08 43; *bohemia@unl.pvtnet.cz*; ④).

České Švýcarsko

The area of sandstone rocks around Děčín is popularly known as **České Švýcarsko** (Bohemian Switzerland), a nickname coined by artists of the Romantic movement, though the landscape is in fact far from alpine. The River Labe drives a deep wedge into the geographical defences of Bohemia, forging a grand valley through the dense forests, interrupted by outcrops of sandstone rock welded into truly fantastic shapes.

Like the other *skaní město*, or "rock-cities", in the Český ráj (see p.246) and the Broumov region (see p.260), the whole area was formed when volcanic rock thrust its way to the surface, causing fissures and cracks that later widened. The result is probably the most impressive geological amusement park in the country, a dense network of mini-canyons and bluffs all covered in a blanket of woodland – spectacular stuff, and a favourite with rock climbers, but also fairly easy **hiking** country.

Transport throughout the region is not great – just infrequent rural bus services to most places – though the distances are small enough to make hiking an attractive proposition. In season, there's plenty of inexpensive **private accommodation** throughout the region, making it possible for non-campers to spend more than just a day in the countryside.

Děčín

Despite being German-speaking for most of the last thousand years, **DĚČÍN** has long been the geographical gateway to Bohemia, its castle rising up to the east as you enter the country from Dresden. Modern Děčín is really two towns – **Děčín** (Tetschen) itself and

Podmokly (Bodenbach) – amalgamated in 1942 but still divided by the River Labe, which has always been the driving force behind the town's economy. As a busy industrial port, its attractions are limited, but its position on the river is quite dramatic, and, lying at the heart of České Švýcarsko, it does serve as a convenient base for exploring the region.

Podmokly

The main point of **arrival** is Děčín's grubby hlavní nádraží in **Podmokly**, which looks out onto a mass of grey concrete and an unsightly supermarket. It's not a great start, but then Podmokly was a late developer, only coming into existence in 1850 through the amalgamation of three villages on the left bank. Sixty years of furious building followed, funded by the town's flourishing shipping industry, the results of which are still visible in the four or five blocks west of the station, where the locals go shopping and wolf down ice cream.

With time to kill and an interest in stuffed birds, medieval Madonnas or seamanship and navigation, you can spend a happy hour in the **Okresní muzeum** (Tues–Sun 9am–noon & 1–5pm), situated in a former hunting lodge on Zbrojnická. There's even a hands-on knots section, and a bit of the chain from the 720m-long cable that was cooked up in the nineteenth century to help ships get upstream. A more miraculous sight is the Moorish Art Nouveau **synagogue**, round the corner on Žižkova, dating from 1907, which was saved from being torched on *Kristallnacht* by a local German, and is one of

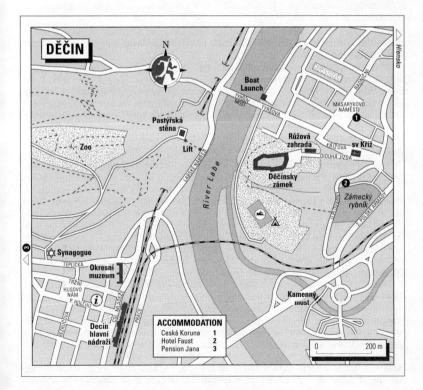

the few to survive in what was Sudetenland. Recently given a slightly injudicious lick of garish yellow and blue paint, it is now back in use by the local Jewish community for exhibitions (and services).

Afterwards, head for the meringue-coloured mansion (ultraviolet lighting at night) atop the precipitous **Pastýřská stěna** (Hirtenfelswände or Shepherd's Wall); head down Mládeže and under the railway, then take the lift (*výtah*) cut into the rock halfway along Labské nábřeží. At the top there's a small **café** with an incredible view over Děčín, and, a little further back from the cliff, a small **zoo** (daily April–Sept 8am–6pm; Oct–March 8am–4pm).

Děčín

To cross the river to **Děčín** from Podmokly, take any of the buses from outside the station, or continue downstream from the above-mentioned lift until you reach the Tyršův most. Děčín itself is much older than Podmokly, as witnessed by the austerely impressive **Děčínský zámek** (Schloss Tetschen-Bodenbach) at its centre, elevated above the town and river on an isolated lump of rock. The chateau's current mostly Baroque appearance dates from the time of the Thun-Hohensteins, but it has been much abused since the family sold it to the state in the 1930s. Used as a barracks by the Germans, Czechs and lastly Russians, there's not much left of the original interior. Part of the newly restored interior has now been given over to a **Muzeum loutek** (Puppet Museum; Wed–Sun 10am–noon & 1–4pm), based on the private collection of Milan Knížák.

The chief attraction of the chateau, however, is the **Růžová zahrada** (May–Oct Tues–Sun 10am–5pm), a truly wonderful Baroque rose garden, laid out on a terrace cut into the north face of the rock high above the town. At one end is a befrescoed *sala terrena*, while at the far end is an ornate Baroque belvedere peppered with statuary. To gain access to the garden (and the chateau), you must walk up the sloping **Dlouhá jízda**, a gloomy 300-metre-long drive cut into the rock. Directly below the garden are the distinctive black dome and twin tower lanterns of the salmon-pink Baroque church of **sv Kříž**, which has a richly painted and furnished interior. Two other sights worth noting are the striking 1906 Art Nouveau **fountain** on Děčín's main square, Masarykovo náměstí, and to the south of the castle, the slowly disintegrating stone bridge or **Kamenný most**, over the River Ploučnice, punctuated by Brokoff's Baroque statuary.

Practicalities

Most **trains** end up at Děčín hlavní nádraží in Podmokly, where you'll find the town's **tourist office** (Mon–Fri 9am–5pm, Sat 9am–noon). There are regular trains north from Děčín, but they travel along the west bank of the Labe, as far as Dolní Žleb, before crossing over into Germany. To get to Hřensko, you'll either have to take the **bus** or, on summer weekends, catch the **boat** (May–Oct Sat & Sun 9am & 12.30pm).

For **accommodation**, walk over or catch any bus over to Děčín proper, where your best bet is probably the comfortable *Česká koruna* (☎0412/51 61 04; ⑤), on Masarykovo náměstí, or the slightly seedy *Hotel Faust*, on U plovárny (☎0412/51 88 59; *p.vitek@telecom.cz*; ③), just south of the zámek. With your own transport, you might also consider the *Pension Jana* (☎0412/54 45 71; ③), a couple of kilometres out of town on route 13 to Teplice. There's also a small **campsite** (April–Oct) on the south side of the zámek, with an open-air swimming pool nearby, and some equally well-equipped sites in the České Švýcarsko itself (see below). The restaurant at the *Česká koruna* features fish from Třeboň, while the nearby *Pošta* is good for a beer.

Exploring the České Švýcarsko

The České Švýcarsko splits neatly in half, with Děčín as the meeting point. Whichever part you're heading for, it's a good idea to get hold of a proper walking **map**, which marks all campsites and footpaths in the area, including those on the German side. The popular **Jetřichovické stěny**, to the northeast of Děčín, is topographically more interesting and covers a much greater area than its western counterpart. At its base runs the Kamenice river, accessible in parts only by boat (for boat trips, see next page). The smaller range to the west, the **Děčínské stěny**, is less spectacular but doesn't suffer the same human congestion and can easily be reached on a day's hike from Děčín itself.

Děčínské stěny

If your sole aim is to see the rocks, it's simplest to catch one of the few buses a day from Děčín to Tisá, or to take the train to Libouchec station and walk the 2.5km north to Tisá. If, however, you're intent on a day's walking, follow the red-marked path from the Tyršův most in Děčín for 10km to **Děčínský Sněžník** (723m), a giant table mountain thrust up above the decaying tree line, on top of which stands a handsome sandstone look-out tower (*rozhledna*), erected in 1864 by Count Thun-Hohenstein. The red-marked path eschews the direct route to Tisá and instead heads north to Ostrov, the last village before the border, where there's a simple **campsite** (April to mid-Nov) by a pretty lake, overlooked by the cliffs of the Ostrovské skály. (The nearest border crossing is the 24-hour one at Petrovice, northwest of Tisá.)

From the village of **TISÁ** itself, the **Tiské stěny** are hidden from view, but climb the hill and the whole "sandstone city" opens up before you. Sandy trails crisscross this secret gully, and it's fairly simple to get to the top of one or two of the gigantic boulders without any specialist equipment. You could spend hours here, exploring, picnicking and taking in the panoramic views. Via Děčínský Sněžník, it's a full day's walk from Děčín, but it's easy enough to hole up for the night, as there's plenty of private accommodation in the village, and a **campsite** (mid-April to mid-Oct).

Hřensko

Despite its dramatic mountainous setting, **HŘENSKO** (Herrnskretchen), at 116m above sea level, is in fact the lowest point in Bohemia. It's a pretty village on the right bank of the Labe, dotted with half-timbered houses and redolent of Saxony on the oppo-site bank. However, Hřensko currently makes its living out of the German day-trippers flocking to the nearby rocks, and with their former East German neighbours now flush with Deutschmarks, business is booming. Prostitutes line the road coming into Hřensko, and the village itself is barely visible under the sheer number of shops and stalls, the majority run by the republic's Vietnamese minority. It's unlikely you'll want to stay here, though there are several hotels to choose from; try the rather splendid *Hotel Labe* (☎0412/55 40 95; ④), right by the river front.

Jetřichovické stěny

The only way to get to the Jetřichovické stěny and the Kamenice gorge is by bus, with three or four **buses** a day making the roundabout journey to Jetřichovice, via Hřensko, Tři prameny, Mezní Louka and Mezná; car drivers should note that there is no parking between Hřensko and Mezní Louka.

By far the most popular destination is the **Pravčická brána**, at 30m long and 21m high the largest natural stone bridge in Europe. It's a truly breathtaking sight, though not one you're likely to enjoy alone unless you get there very early or out of season. It's a two-kilometre hike up from Tři prameny, a clearing (and bus stop) 3km up the road from Hřensko, and you'll have to pay an admission fee to get up close. The German bor-der is less than 1km away, but the red-marked path that appears to head towards it actu-ally rejoins the road 4.5km further east at **MEZNÍ LOUKA**, whose **hotel** (☎0412/55 40 84; ③) of the same name stands opposite a **campsite** (May–Sept) with bungalows for rent.

From Mezní Louka, the red-marked path continues another 14km to Jetřichovice, meandering through the southern part of the complex of mini-canyons, taking in the **Malá Pravčická brána**, a smaller version of the bridge, and a couple of very ruined border castles. **JETŘICHOVICE** itself is a lovely old Saxon hamlet made up of huge wooden farmsteads typical of the region. Several, such as as *Dřevák* (☎0412/ 55 50 15; ④), in the centre of the village, now serve as pensions, and, 1.5km to the south, across a ford, there's the *U Ferdinanda* **campsite** and swimming pool (April–Oct).

The Kamenice gorge

Another option from Mezní Louka is to walk the 2km southwest to **MEZNÁ**, an unas-suming little village that basks in a sunny meadow above the River Kamenice. From the village green, a green-marked path plunges a hundred feet into the cool, dank shade of the river, traversed by the wooden bridge Mezní můstek. Here you have a choice of heading up or down the **Kamenice gorge** to landing stages, where boatmen take you on a short but dramatic boat trip down (or up) the river. The trips (April, Sept & Oct Sat & Sun 9am–6pm; May–Aug daily 8am–6pm) are justifiably popular, so be prepared to wait a couple of hours in high season. The downstream trip, along the **Tichá soutěska**, drops you at the edge of Hřensko (see above), while the upstream one unloads its passengers just 500m further up the **Divoká soutěska**. With the lat-ter trip, you can either return to Mezní Louka via the blue-marked path, or continue along first the blue- then the yellow-marked path up a shallower gorge to Jetřichovice, about 5km east.

Česká Kamenice and Benešov nad Ploučnicí

With your own transport, **ČESKÁ KAMENICE** (Böhmisch Kamnitz), 18km east of Děčín on route 13 (or forty minutes by train), would make a great alternative base for exploring the České Švýcarsko. For a start, it's a lot more pleasant to rest up in than Děčín, with its interesting blend of nineteenth-century Habsburg edifices, the odd wooden folk building and a splendid Baroque pilgrimage chapel. Unfortunately, there's a serious lack of accommodation, though this may change in the future; in the meantime, there's a nice pub, the *Hvězda* on Dvořákova, just off the main square, serving simple food and Břežňák beer from Ústěk.

Five kilometres east of Česká Kamenice, on the other side of Kamenický Šenov, is another, much rarer geological phenomenon: the **Panská skála** (Herrnhausfelsen), a series of polygonal basalt columns like a miniature Giant's Causeway minus the sea. These are the result of a massive subterranean explosion millions of years ago, during which molten basalt was spewed out onto the surface and cooled into what are, essentially, crystals. They make a strange, supernatural sight in this unassuming rolling countryside, but are too small to be really awe-inspiring. Unlike Northern Ireland's major tourist attraction, the Panská skála are easily missed, even though they're only 500m south of route 13; ask the bus driver to tell you when to get out.

Halfway between Děčín and Česká Kamenice, and easily reached from either by train, is **BENEŠOV NAD PLOUČNICÍ**, a pretty little town characterized by its two connected **zámky** (April & Oct Wed–Sun 9am–4pm; May–Sept Tues–Sun 9am–6pm). The lower one is a neo-Gothic hunting lodge with meticulously restored interiors (restored after a fire in 1968); the upper one boasts Renaissance ceilings and an offbeat collection of Japanese and Chinese art. With several **accommodation** options, the town makes another possible base for exploring the region: try and find somewhere better before resorting to the rather dour *Jelen* (☎0412/58 62 23; ①), on the attractive main square.

The Česká Lípa region

The eastern border of České Švýcarsko marks the beginning of Bohemia's vast glass-making industry, stretching far into the east of the region. Bohemian glass and crystal has always been considered among the world's finest, though the industry suffered badly as a consequence of the postwar expulsions of the majority German-speaking population. If you're heading east towards Liberec (see p.239) or the Krkonoše (see p.253), there are several sights worth checking out for those interested in Bohemian glass, as well as a handful of chateaux en route.

Česká Lípa and Nový Bor

ČESKÁ LÍPA (Böhmisch Leipa) gets its name from the Czech national tree, the linden (*lípa*). The town itself has precious few trees now, thanks to the uranium boom of the 1970s that trebled the town's population, most of whom now live in endless highrise estates around the town. There are, however, a few minor distractions: a small sgraffitoed Renaissance hunting lodge, known as the Červený dům, an extraordinary tent-roofed chapel of sv Kříž and a former Augustinian monastery. However, the town's main virtue is its location at the meeting point of five railway lines, making it a good base for exploring the area; the main **train station** is around 2km south of the old town. For the most central **accommodation**, try *Penzion Monika*, on Jiráskova (☎0425/246 47; ①). There's also the lakeside *Neptun* **campsite** (June–Sept), 3km southwest of the station beyond Dubice.

NOVÝ BOR (Haida) is 8km north of Česká Lípa, on route 9, and best approached by train. Its **Sklářské muzeum** (Glass Museum; Tues–Sun 9am–noon & 1–4pm) was founded over one hundred years ago and boasts a particularly rich collection of glassware, including a functionalist tea set by Adolf Loos and a great Art Deco *vitraille*. The museum is on the main square, itself a typical mixture of folk cottages and late nineteenth-century industrial wealth. Nearby stands the *Parkhotel* (☎0424/72 31 57; *agdpark@clnet.cz*; ⑨), a newly converted, very comfortable place to stay.

Máchovo jezero and Bezděz

Trains from Česká Lípa take less than half an hour to reach **DOKSY** on the southernmost sandy shores of the **Máchovo jezero**, 15km southeast on route 9. The lake, created in medieval times, has been a popular recreational spot since nineteenth-century Romantics like Karel Hynek Mácha (after whom the lake is named) used to trek out here. Nowadays it's surrounded by hotels, bungalows and campsites: the lakeside *Klůček* **campsite** (May–Sept) is the nearest to Doksy train station. There's a mercifully small museum dedicated to Mácha in Doksy itself, though you're infinitely better off going on the poet's favourite walk: the eight-kilometre hike southeast along the red-marked Máchova cesta up to the ruined hilltop castle of **Bezděz** (Bösig; April & Oct Sat & Sun 9am–4pm; May–Sept Tues–Sun 9am–5pm), clearly visible for miles around. It was one of the most important castles in Bohemia until its destruction in the Thirty Years' War, but there's not much to see now aside from a Gothic chapel and, of course, the unbeatable view from the top of the hill (604m) – still, at least you can get to explore it without taking a guided tour. You can take the train another two stops to Bezděz to cut the walking distance down to just 2km.

East of Česká Lípa

Fifteen minutes by train east of Česká Lípa is the village of **ZÁKUPY** (Reichstadt), which boasts a rather fancy radnice and two prickly church towers – signs of the wealth that arrived when the Habsburg Emperor Ferdinand I chose it as one of his retirement homes after his abdication in 1848. The local **zámek** (April & Oct Sat & Sun 9am–4pm; May–Sept Tues–Sun 9am–5pm) was also lavishly renovated for him in neo-Renaissance style and adorned with a giant snooker table and Rococo paintings by, among others, Josef Navrátil. Outside in the moat, the brown bears pace up and down, but there's little life in the crumbling aviary or the formal terraced gardens with their mermaid fountains.

To the southeast of Zákupy is the strangely uninhabited tract of land known as **Ralsko**, after its highest peak. When the region's German-speaking population was expelled after the war, the Soviets took the opportunity to create a vast army base for their war games. When the troops finally withdrew in 1990, they left an estimated 3000 tonnes of pollutants, antitank mines and countless unexploded bombs. A ten-year clean-up operation is under way, as planners argue whether to build a giant international cargo airport here or turn the place into a safari park for the white rhino, which has been successfully bred at Dvůr Králové zoo (see p.270) for a number of years.

Fourteen kilometres northeast of Zákupy, the village of **JABLONNÉ V PODJEŠTĚDÍ** (Gabel) is dwarfed by the huge dome of the local Dominican church, an early work by the great Austrian Baroque architect Johann Lukas von Hildebrandt, dating from 1699. The inspiration for the church was the thirteenth-century wonder-worker Zdislava, wife of the lord of Lemberk (see below), who was beatified in 1907 and canonized in 1995, and whose remains (along with several mummified cadavers) lie in the crypt. Just over two kilometres northeast of the village is the military stronghold of **Lemberk** (April & Oct Sat & Sun 9am–4pm; May–Sept Tues–Sun 9am–5pm), a thirteenth-century zámek which owes its Baroque outer coating to one of Waldstein's Dutch generals, who held on to the place after Waldstein's murder (see box on p.251). The overlong guided tour (trasa 1) is probably worth skipping in favour of a stroll round the castle's displays about Zdislava and temporary exhibitions of local and international glassware (trasa 2).

Liberec and around

Lying comfortably in the broad east–west sweep of the Nisa Valley, framed by the Jizera Mountains to the north and the isolated peak of Ještěd to the south, **LIBEREC** (Reichenberg) couldn't hope for a grander location. The city itself, made prosperous and enormous by its famous textile industry, can't quite live up to its setting, but it's lively and bustling, with a smattering of interesting buildings and a couple of fairly good museums, all of which could keep you happily amused for the best part of a day. For further entertainment, you can while away a few hours in the glass and jewellery museum in the neighbouring town of Jablonec nad Nisou.

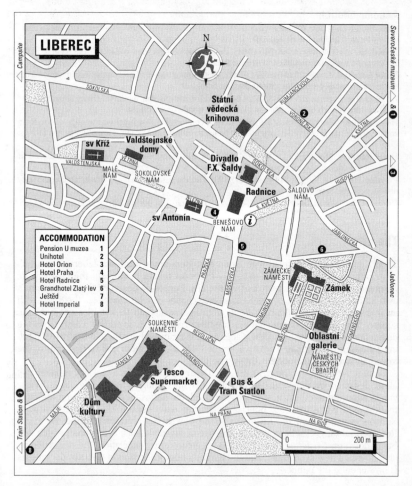

Arrival, information and accommodation

From the main **train and bus station** in Liberec, simply walk or jump on one of the trams heading down 1 máje to Soukenné náměstí, which is overlooked on one side by the city's eyesore Tesco superstore, and on the other by one of the functionalist Baťa shops designed by Vladimír Karfík in the 1930s. From here, it's a short steep walk up Pražská to the main square, náměstí dr E. Beneše, where you'll find the **tourist office** (Mon–Fri 9am–5pm, Sat 9am–1pm; *mic@infolbc.cz*), who can arrange very reasonable private accommodation. If you're scouting about yourself, you'll find that Liberec's hotels tend to be rather pricey, relying as they do on German tourists and business travellers. The nearest **campsite** is at the well-equipped site with a swimming pool at the *Stadión Pavlovice*, Letná (May to mid-Oct), in the midst of a housing estate (bus #13, #24 or #26 to Letná stop).

Accommodation

Grandhotel Zlatý lev, Gutenbergova 3 (☎048/271 02 70). Vast, turn-of-the-century hotel, conveniently located behind the chateau. ⑥.

Ještěd, Horní Hanychov (☎048/510 42 91). Unbeatable location, view and kitsch 1960s decor in the TV tower on top of the mountain of the same name. ⑦.

Hotel Imperial, 1. máje 29 (☎048/271 07 42). Giant communist-era hotel on the way into town from the stations that undercuts the city's other big hotels. ⑤.

Hotel Orion, Jizerská 250 (☎048/46 20 64). Modernized monster mountain chalet situated in the northeastern suburb of Starý Harcov, close to the woods (bus #19). ④.

Hotel Praha, Železná 2 (☎048/510 26 55). Very comfortable new hotel on the edge of the main square, which has preserved its original Art Nouveau entrance foyer, and a few other period fittings. ⑦.

Hotel Radnice, Moskevská 11 (☎048/510 03 62; *hotelradnicelb@mbox.vol.cz*). Luxurious three-star hotel, on the edge of the main square, that's probably worth the extra money. ⑧.

Pension U muzea, Vítězná 24 (☎048/510 26 93). Large nineteenth-century villa located in the leafy district near the Severočeské muzeum. ③.

Unihotel, Voroněžská 13 (☎048/535 24 62). A real cheapie, just north of the main square, in a high-rise university complex. ③.

The city

Totally dominating the small main square of **Benešovo náměstí**, Liberec's magnificent, cathedral-like **radnice** is probably the most telling monument the chauvinistic *Reichenberger* could have bestowed on the city. Purposely designed to recall Vienna's own Rathaus, its lofty trio of neo-Renaissance copper cupolas completes the effect with an impressive Flemish flourish. Several cafés now spread their tables out onto the square, from which you can contemplate this great Germanic edifice. Liberec has the distinction of being one of the few places outside Prague where there was any real fighting following the Warsaw Pact invasion of 1968; a small memorial to the right of the town hall steps commemorates those who died.

Behind the radnice is the city's theatre, **Divadlo F.X. Šaldy**, a typically solid, showy affair designed by the Viennese architects Helmer and Fellner in the 1880s. While you're admiring the theatre, you can also check the atmospheric pressure on the nineteenth-century weather machine opposite the main façade. At the beginning of Rumjancevova, behind the theatre, a brand new **Státní vědecká knihovna** (State Research Library) has been built on the site of the city's main synagogue, which was burnt down on *Kristallnacht* in 1938. As a gesture of reconciliation, the new building also houses a new synagogue, and the library's huge collection of German documents is now open to the public.

A couple of blocks west of the main square, on the far side of Sokolovské náměstí, the narrow sidestreet of Větrná hides the town's most unusual treasure, the **Valdštejnské domky**, a terrace of four crisscross timber-framed houses dating from the early seventeenth century. To the east of the main square is the town's rouge-and-cream sixteenth-century **zámek**, previously owned by the Clam-Gallas family. It has recently been converted into a vast exhibition centre for the local glass giants Glassexport, and has been remarketed as the Skleněný zámeček. There's another, more historical, exhibition of glassmaking at the Severočeské muzeum (see below).

Oblastní galerie

Across the newly replanted formal gardens from the chateau is the **Oblastní galerie** (Tues–Sun 10am–6pm), a white nineteenth-century building off 8 března that has been an art gallery since 1873. Its unusually large collection includes a series of nineteenth-century French landscapes and some much earlier Dutch and Flemish masters, all of which were bequeathed to the gallery by the local German textile king, Johann Liebig.

The excellent collection of modern Czech paintings and sculptures includes two striking female portraits by the Impressionists Jiránek and Hudeček, a characteristic canvas by super-weird Symbolist Josef Váchal, and a lovely swaggering sculpture of a woman by Šaloun. The room of Cubist and Fauvist canvases includes Josef Čapek's much reproduced *Woman Over the City*, Kubišta's grim *Kiss of Death*, and one of the few extant sculptures by Otakar Švec, the man who gave Prague the Stalin Monument. In the new postwar section there's a bevy of Surrealist paintings, Abstract Expressionist works by the likes of Mikuláš Medek, and even a smattering of pieces from the 1980s.

Severočeské muzeum and beyond

Liberec's grandest museum is without doubt the **Severočeské muzeum** (Tues–Sun 9am–5pm), a wonderful period piece from the 1890s built in a theatrical neo-Renaissance style. The museum is a couple of tram stops up 5. Května, which turns into Masarykova, a long, leafy avenue flanked by decadent turn-of-the-century mansions, once the property of a wealthy *Reichenberger*, now converted into pensions, flats, clinics and the like. Inside the museum, the old communist-era displays on local and natural history are eminently skippable, but the glassware, jewellery and bronzework upstairs make a visit worthwhile. In addition to the locally produced stuff, there's an Art Nouveau lamp and vase by Lötz and another by Gallé, plus a Cubist tea set by Janák, some Wiener Werkstätte silverwork and some wacky shaggy tapestries from the 1970s.

KONRAD HENLEIN IN REICHENBERG

Sited just the wrong side of the historical borders of Germany, the *Reichenberger* made up for this geographical oversight with their ardent pan-Germanism. It was the home town of the First Republic's ultimate fifth columnist, **Konrad Henlein**, born in the nearby village of Reichenau (Rychnov) in 1898 and destined to become the leader of the pro-Nazi Sudeten German Party (SdP). Henlein played an unheroic role in World War I, and after a spell as a bank clerk in Reichenau he became a gym teacher in the pure-German-speaking town of Asch (Aš) in West Bohemia. The combined effects of the slump and the events in the neighbouring German Reich excited the Sudeten Germans, who proclaimed Henlein their *Führer* at a huge rally outside Saaz (Žatec) in 1933. When the newly formed SdP won roughly two-thirds of the Sudeten German vote in the 1935 elections (thus becoming the largest single party in the country), Reichenberg became a centre of pro-Nazi sentiment. However, few of the German-speakers survived the postwar expulsions, and Liberec (unlike Cheb) was swiftly repopulated and successfully Czechified after the war.

At the top of the road is the city's chief park, and the popular **Botanical Gardens** (Botanická zahrada: daily 8am–6pm), famous for their orchids. Here, too, you'll find the oldest **Zoo** (zoologická zahrada: same hours as above) in Bohemia, which boasts seven giraffes, two white tigers and a free-roaming peacock.

Ještěd

Liberec's top hotel – in every sense – sits on the summit of **Ještěd** (1012m) or Jeschken, from which you can look over into Poland and Germany on a clear day. Even if you don't stay the night, be sure to check out the bar-cum-diner and the restaurant with its crazy mirrors, either of which wouldn't look out of place in an episode of a 1960s sci-fi series. To get there from the centre of town, take tram #3 to the end of the line and then follow the signs to the **cable car** (*lanovka dráha*), which runs to the summit and hotel hourly 8am to 7pm all year (Mon from 2pm only).

Eating and drinking

As for **restaurants**, the *Radniční sklípek* occupies the impressive vaults underneath the radnice and serves up typical Czech meals and *Krušovice*. For something a bit more special, head for the restaurant at the *Hotel Radnice*, whose food is a cut above the average (as are the prices). Whatever you do, you must check out the *Pošta* **café**, across the road from the theatre, on the corner of Mariánská. Decorated inside in white and gold Neoclassical style, with dazzling chandeliers, it conjures up late-nineteenth-century Reichenberg beautifully. *U salamandra*, the big modern **pub** halfway down Pražská, doles out heaps of Czech food and mugs of Gambrinus; *Fortuna* on the parallel street of Moskevská, is the place to go to watch sport on the box. Late-night drinking can be happily continued until the early hours at the *Rockový club* (aka *Golet*), at Tržní náměstí 11, which has live bands most nights. Alternatively, you can combine drinking with playing pool at *Edward's Billiards* on Sokolovské náměstí.

Jablonec nad Nisou

JABLONEC NAD NISOU (Gablonz) starts where the southwestern suburbs of Liberec end. It began life as a small Czech village, but was cut short in its prime by the Hussite Wars, when the whole area was laid waste by the neighbouring Catholic Lusatians. Apocryphally, the only survivor was the large apple tree (*jabloň*) that stood on the village green and gave the subsequent town its name. From the sixteenth century onwards, it was better known as Gablonz, the name used by the Saxon glassmakers who began to settle in the area, but it wasn't until the late nineteenth century that the town's **jewellery trade** really took off.

By the turn of the century Gablonz was exporting its produce to all corners of the globe, and its burghers grew very rich indeed, erecting private mansions fit for millionaires and lavish public buildings. Everything changed in 1945, when almost the entire German-speaking population of 100,000 was expelled, throwing the local glass industry into crisis (the Communists solved the problem by using forced labour in the factories). Meanwhile, uniquely for German refugees from Eastern Europe, nearly a fifth of the exiled townsfolk stayed together and resettled in a suburb of Kaufbeuren, in Bavarian Swabia, which they named Neugablonz after their Bohemian hometown.

The town

The main reason for venturing into Jablonec is to visit the engaging **Muzeum skla a bižuterie** (Glass and Jewellery Museum; Tues–Sun 9am–4pm), downhill from the town hall, in the palatial turn-of-the-century Zimmer & Schmidt building on U muzea, east off Dolní náměstí. The museum suffers from a lack of labelling but makes up for it with a ten-foot tower of bangles set against a backdrop of hundreds of ear-rings, and – on the stairs – the longest necklace in the world, 220m long and made in just four hours by local art students (it shows). Among the best items are the Lötz and Moser glass, the works by Adolf Loos, the Secession and Art Deco hatpins and the incredible collection of turn-of-the-century jet jewellery.

The rest of the town centre boasts a number of dour, though impressive, 1930s structures, most notably the **Nová radnice**, whose slimline clock tower dominates the skyline. Up the hill from the town hall, the gargantuan brick-built church, **Nejsvětější Srdce Páně** (Most Sacred Heart of Our Lord), towers over Horní náměstí; local boy Josef Zasche was the architect responsible. The former wealth of the town is obvious from the leafy suburbs, though many of the buildings have not been well looked after. One that has recently been beautifully restored is the town theatre or **Městské divadlo**, designed by the ubiquitous Helmer and Fellner in 1907 and located west down Protofašistických bojovníků. Another that is finally receiving long overdue attention is the graceful **Starokatolický kostel** (open for services only), an earlier minimalist Art Nouveau church designed by Josef Zasche in 1900, situated 500m or so east of the centre, just off route 4 to Tanvald.

Practicalities

You can reach Jablonec on **tram** #11 from Liberec, which winds its way scenically and slowly up the Nisa Valley and deposits you close to the main **train station** to the southwest of the town centre. The choice of accommodation in Jablonec is more limited, though the town's **tourist office** (Mon–Fri 8am–5pm, Sat 8am–noon; *icjablonec@jablonec.cz*), on the main square, should be able to help. The best **hotel** is the fairly brutally modernized late-nineteenth-century *Rehavital* on Jugoslavská (☎0428/31 75 91; ⑤), which boasts a pool, sauna, gym and excellent restaurant; alternatively, there's the totally modern *Hotel na baště* opposite Zasche's church on Horní náměstí (☎0428/263 67; ④). For decent pizzas, head for *Pizzeria Franco,* just down from the radnice at Lidická 15; close by at no. 1 is *Balada,* a funky new place that has a stab at some unusual dishes. On warm summer days, locals head out to the nearby **Mšeno lake**, north of the town centre, for a spot of sunbathing and swimming; to join them, take bus #1 or #10 from the centre.

Jizerské hory

Northeast of Liberec, the **Jizerské hory** (Isergebirge) form the western edge of the Krkonoše mountain range, which, in turn, makes up the northern border of Bohemia. Like their eastern neighbours, they have been very badly affected by acid rain, though extensive replanting has softened the impact visually. In fact, on first sight the mountains are undeniably dramatic, rising suddenly from Liberec's northern suburbs to heights over 1000m. Large numbers of Czech and German tourists flock here in summer and winter – and you can follow suit by taking tram #3 from Liberec, or bus #1 from Jablonec to Janov or Bedřichov.

Frýdlant

It was neither an old stronghold nor a new mansion, but a rambling pile consisting of innumerable small buildings closely packed together and of one or two storeys; if K had not known that it was a castle he might have taken it for a little town.

Franz Kafka, *The Castle*

No one is quite sure which castle Kafka had in mind when he wrote his novel, but a strong candidate is surely the hybrid sprawling castle at **FRÝDLANT** (Friedland), a town on the north side of the frontier mountains, forty minutes by train from Liberec.

Like his fictional character K, Kafka himself came here on business, though not as a land surveyor but as an accident insurance clerk, a job he did for most of his brief life. In Kafka's time the **hrad** and **zámek**(Tues–Sun: April & Oct 9am–3.30pm; May, June & Sept 9am–4pm; July & Aug 9am–4.30pm) was still owned by the Clam-Gallas clan, but its most famous proprietor was Albrecht von Waldstein, Duke of Friedland, whose statue stands within the castle precincts. Such was the fame of Waldstein that the Clam-Gallas family opened the castle to the public as early as 1801. The guided tour (1hr 40min) might be a bit too much for some people, but the interior is, for once, richly furnished and in good condition, having been a museum now for almost two hundred years. The castle is ensconced on a rock over the river, a short walk southeast of the train station and town centre along a pretty, tree-lined avenue.

If you want to stay in the area, try the large, friendly *Frýdlant* **campsite** (May to mid-Sept) by a bend in the river beyond the castle, or the campsite (May–Sept) in **HEJNICE**, 10km southeast (30min by train; change at Raspenava), a village dominated by its towering pilgrimage church, with an attractive frescoed interior. Hejnice also has a good choice of hotels and pensions; try the *Hotel Zvon* on Jizerská (☎0427/32 28 40; ②). In nearby **LÁZNĚ LIBVERDA**, 1km north of Hejnice, there's also the *Chata Jizerka* (☎0427/933 52; ③), which has a pool and sauna and offers various spa treatments. You can cross the border into Poland just 13km north of Frýdlant at Habartice-Zawidów, on the road to Zgorzelec/Görlitz.

travel details

Trains

Prague to: Bohušovice (5–7 daily; 1hr); Chomutov (2–3 daily; 2hr 30min); Děčín (9–12 daily; 1hr 50min); Kadaň (2 daily; 2hr 50min); Liberec (1 daily; 2hr 45min); Louny (2–3 daily; 1hr 50min); Most (2–3 daily; 2hr 30min); Teplice (2–3 daily; 2hr); Ústí nad Labem (12–16 daily; 1hr 30min); Žatec (3–4 daily; 2hr).

Česká Lípa to: Benešov nad Ploučnicí (8–10 daily; 20–30min); Děčín (7–8 daily; 35–50min); Liberec (11–12 daily; 1hr 5min–1hr 30min); Litoměřice (every 2–3hr; 1hr 10min); Jablonné v Podještědí (11–12 daily; 35–50min); Mimoň (11–12 daily; 20–30min); Zákupy (8–9 daily; 12min).

Chomutov to: Karlovy Vary (13–14 daily; 1hr–1hr 15min); Kadaň (hourly; 10–15min); Klášterec nad Ohři (15–17 daily; 20min); Most (16–18 daily; 25–30min); Plzeň (4 daily; 2hr 30min); Ústí nad Labem (hourly; 1hr 15min); Žatec (11–13 daily; 20–30min).

Děčín to: Benešov nad Ploučnicí (every 1–2hr; 15–20min); Česká Kamenice (10–12 daily; 35–40min); Liberec (5–6 daily; 2hr–2hr 30min); Teplice lesní brána (7 daily; 1hr 30min); Ústí nad Labem (every 1–2hr; 20–30min).

Liberec to: Frýdlant (7–11 daily; 35min); Jablonec nad Nisou (every 1–2hr; 30min); Turnov (16 daily; 50min).

Litoměřice to: Mělník (10 daily; 30–45min); Ploskovice (every 2–3hr; 12min); Úštěk (every 2–3hr; 35min); Ústí nad Labem (7–10 daily; 25min).

Louny to: Libochovice (6–8 daily; 45min); Most (13–15 daily; 30–45min); Žatec (5 daily; 35min).

Most to: Děčín (4 daily; 1hr 15min–1hr 40min); Duchcov (every 1–2hr; 15–25min); Teplice (every 1–2hr; 30–40min); Ústí nad Labem (every 1–2hr; 45min–1hr).

Teplice to: Litvínov (4–6 daily; 35min); Osek (7–10 daily; 20min).

Buses

Prague to: Chomutov (up to 7 daily; 2hr 30min); Liberec (hourly; 1hr 40min); Litoměřice (hourly; 1hr 15min); Terezín (hourly; 1hr 10min).

Česká Kamenice to: Jetřichovice (Mon–Fri 4 daily; 25min).

Děčín to: Hřensko (6 daily; 20min); Mezná (up to 4 daily; 35min).

Jablonec to Harrachov (6 or more daily; 1hr 15min).

CHAPTER FIVE

EAST BOHEMIA

East Bohemia (Východní Čechy) is probably the most difficult Czech region to categorize. It has none of the polluting industry of its immediate neighbours, though it has suffered indirectly from their excesses; it contains some of the flattest landscape in Bohemia, but also its highest peaks; historically it has been pre-

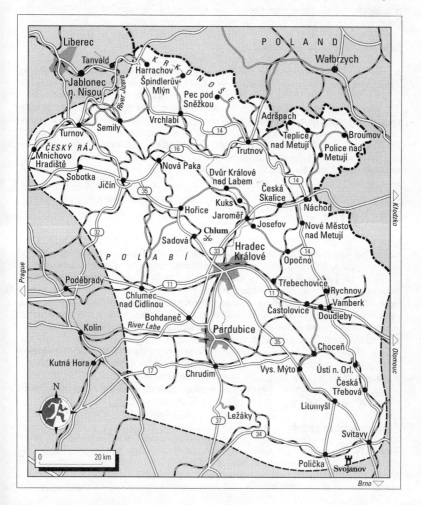

ACCOMMODATION PRICE CODES

All accommodation in this guide is graded according to the price bands listed below. Prices are for the cheapest **double room** available during high season, which usually means without private bath or shower in the less expensive places. For a **single room**, expect to pay around two-thirds the price of a double.

① Under 500Kč	④ 1000–1250Kč	⑦ 1750–2000Kč
② 500–750Kč	⑤ 1250–1500Kč	⑧ 2000–2500Kč
③ 750–1000Kč	⑥ 1500–1750Kč	⑨ 2500Kč and upwards

dominantly Czech, though pockets of German settlement have left their mark in the culture and architecture. Lastly, the region has never really enjoyed fixed borders, a confusion compounded by the administrative borders currently in operation, which have arbitrarily added on parts of Moravia.

For variety of scenery, however, East Bohemia is hard to beat. Along the northern border with Poland, the peaks of the **Krkonoše** and the **Orlické hory** form an almost continuous mountain range. The havoc wreaked by acid rain is depressing and unavoidable on the summits, but in the valleys and foothills its effects are hardly noticeable. The lower-lying **Český ráj**, to the south, and the area around **Broumov** to the east have escaped the worst of the damage – both are typical Bohemian landscapes, rocky sandstone regions covered in thick forest. Further south still, the terrain on either side of the River Labe – the *Polabí,* as it is known – is flat, fertile and, for the most part, fairly dull. But the towns of the river basin do much to make up for it – **Hradec Králové**, the regional capital, and its historic rival, **Pardubice**, both boast handsomely preserved historic centres.

Český ráj

Less than 100km from Prague, the sandstone rocks and densely wooded hills of the Český ráj (Bohemian Paradise) have been a popular spot for weekending Praguers for over a century. Although the Český ráj is officially limited to a small nature reserve southeast of Turnov, the term is loosely applied to the entire swathe of hills from Mnichovo Hradiště to Jičín. **Turnov** is the most convenient base for exploring the region, though **Jičín** is infinitely more appealing, with its seventeenth-century old town preserved intact. But more interesting than either of the towns is the surrounding **countryside**: ruined fortresses, bizarre rock formations and traditional folk architecture, all smothered in a blanket of pine forests.

From Turnov, local **trains** run roughly every two hours to Jičín, and local **buses** from both towns infrequently wind their way through the otherwise inaccessible villages nearby. Generally, though, the distances are so small – Turnov to Jičín, for example, is just 24km – that you'd be better off buying a map and **walking** along the network of marked-out footpaths.

Turnov and around

TURNOV (Turnau), as the name suggests, can be less than stimulating, though it's undoubtedly the most convenient base in the region. The town's chief attraction is the **Český ráj museum**, on Skálova, containing an interminable collection of semiprecious stones dug out of a nearby hillside, and temporary exhibitions of nature photography

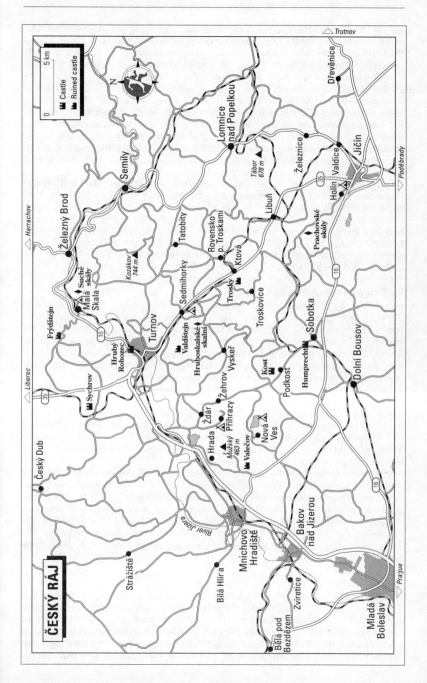

ČESKÝ RÁJ

0   5 km

■ Castle
▲ Ruined castle

N

△ Trutnov
△ Harrachov
△ Liberec
▽ Podĕbrady
▽ Prague

Dřevĕnice
Jičín
Valdice
Holín
Železnice
Lomnice nad Popelkou
Tábor 678 m
Libuň
Prachovské skály
Semily
Ktová
Rovensko p. Troskami
Železný Brod
Tatobity
Kozákov 744 m
Sedmihorky
Trosky
Troskovice
Sobotka
Dolní Bousov
Suché skály
Malá Skala
Frýdštejn
Turnov
Valdštejn
Hruboskalské skály
Vyskeř
Kost
Humprecht
Podkost
Hrubý Rohozec
Sychrov
Žehrov
Ždár
Příhrazy
Mužský 453 m
Valečov
Nová Ves
Český Dub
Hrada
Strážiště
Bílá Hlína
River Jizera
Mnichovo Hradiště
Bakov nad Jizerou
Zvíretice
Bĕla pod Bezdĕzem
Mladá Boleslav

and the like. None of this matters, of course, if you're spending your days walking. The best **hotels** in town are the late-nineteenth-century *Korunní Princ* on the main square (☎0436/242 12; ④), which also boasts the best restaurant in town, and the newly remodelled *Cleopatra* (☎0436/224 17; ④), just up from the main square on 5 května. Cheapest beds are found at the simple *Karel IV* at Žižkova 501 (☎0436/ 238 55; ②); to get there, head left up Husova from 5 května, which then becomes Žižkova. The pick of the pensions is the *Alfa* (☎0436/213 38; ③), off the square down Palackého. In addition to the **restaurants** at the *Korunní Princ* and *Cleopatra* hotels, the smoky red *Pizzeria K* on the square does mini-pizzas from 30Kč. The town's **tourist office** (Mon 10am–5pm, Tues–Fri 8am–5pm, Sat 9am–12pm; *turnov@mail.firstnet.cz*), also on the main square, can book all kinds of accommodation, including private rooms, as can Čechotour, located on Nádražní near the train station, a ten-minute walk away west of the old town on the other side of the river.

One place worth visiting, on the outskirts of Turnov, is the chateau of **Hrubý Rohozec** (Tues–Sun: April, Sept & Oct 9am–noon & 1–4pm; May–Aug 8am–noon & 1–5pm), high up on the left bank of the Jizera river, just off route 10 to Železný Brod. A Gothic castle redesigned in the Renaissance, it's a welcome contrast to the rest of the town, and its hour-long guided tour gives you access to some great views and a series of handsome Renaissance chambers. Check before heading out here, however, as the chateau's future is uncertain, with the family of former leading Sudeten German Party member Karel des Fours Walderode currently hoping to regain its former ancestral home.

Valdštejn and Hruboskalské skalní

A beautiful two-kilometre walk through the woods along either the red- or green-marked path from the Turnov-město train station (one stop down the Jičín line) brings you to the former Gothic stronghold of **Valdštejn** (April & Oct Sat & Sun 9am–4pm, May–Sept Tues–Sun 9am–4pm), ancestral seat of the Waldsteins for many years. Already in ruins by the late sixteenth century, it was occupied by vagrants, and later attempts to restore it never came to fruition, though its position remains impressive – as does the eighteenth-century stone bridge, flanked by Baroque statues.

Another 2km southeast, the first (and arguably the best) of Český ráj's skalní města or "sandstone cities", **Hruboskalské skalní**, unfolds amidst the trees. It's easy to spend hours clambering up and down the bluffs and dodging the crevices, whose names – Myší díra (Mouse Hole), Dračí věž (Dragon's Tower) and Sahara – give some idea of the variety of rock formations. Various viewpoints, like Zamecká vyhlídka or Mariánská vyhlídka, range high above the tree line, with the protruding stone slabs emerging from the pine trees like ossified giants.

The nearby castle of **Hrubá skála** is a colossal nineteenth-century reconstruction of the original Gothic castle. It's very popular with Czech film crews, and is now a wonderful and very reasonably priced hotel, *Zámek Hrubá Skála* (☎0436/91 62 81; ④), with a baronial restaurant open to non-guests. From here, a green-marked path descends through the Myší díra and the Dračí skály, zigzagging down to the large lakeside **campsite**, *Sedmihorky* (April–Oct), near the Karlovice-Sedmihorky station on the Turnov–Jičín line. Also down here is a lovely, if faded, spa hotel, *Lázně Sedmihorky* (☎0436/91 61 12; ③).

Trosky

The spectacular ruined castle of **Trosky** (April & Oct Sat & Sun 9am–4pm; May–Aug Tues–Sun 8am–6pm; Sept Tues–Sun 9am–4pm), which means literally "rubble", 5km southeast of Hrubá skála, is the Český ráj's number-one landmark. Its twin Gothic towers, Bába (Grandmother) and Panna (Virgin), were built on volcanic basalt rocks which burst through the sandstone strata millions of years ago. You can climb the ridge between Bába and Panna (the higher of the two) for a far-reaching view of the Jizera basin. The flash new **hotel** and restaurant complex, *Trosky* (☎0436/912 90; ③), by the castle car park, offers cheap doubles, and there are two very basic **campsites**, the *Svitacka* site (May–Sept), a short distance to the south, and the *Vidlák* site (June–Aug), 2km northwest along the red-marked path, by the lake of the same name, with a cheap but decent *hospoda* across the road. Three or four **buses** a day run to Trosky from Turnov; trains are slower but more frequent and deliver you at Ktová station on the Jičín line, whence it's a two-kilometre walk uphill.

Sobotka and around

Compared to Turnov or Jičín, **SOBOTKA** is off the beaten track: 13km from either place, with only limited accommodation, and only accessible by train from Jičín (50min; change at Libuň). Unless you're camping (and hiking) or staying in one of the handful of pensions, it's no good as a base for exploring the region, though it does harbour some good examples of the local brightly painted half-timbered architecture and – just northwest of the town, on a strange conical hill – the striking seventeenth-century **Humprecht** hunting lodge (April & Oct Sat & Sun 9am–noon & 1–3.30pm; May–Aug Tues–Sun 8am–noon & 1–4.30pm; Sept 9am–noon & 1–3.30pm), named after its eccentric aristocratic instigator, Jan Humprecht Černín. It's a bizarre building, worth a peek inside if only for the central trompe l'oeil dining room, a windowless sixteen-metre-high oval cylinder with the acoustics of a cathedral. On the other side of the hill from Sobotka is a rudimentary **campsite** (mid-June to Sept) and a swimming pool. The best **pension** in the immediate vicinity is the *Ort* (☎0433/57 11 37; ③), 4km to the northeast in Mladějov.

Podkost

One bus daily (at around 1pm) covers the 3km northwest from Sobotka to **PODKOST**, a small settlement by a pond at the edge of the Žehrov forest. The village is dominated in every way by **Kost** castle (April & Oct Sat & Sun 9am–noon & 1–4pm; May–Aug Tues–Sun 8am–noon & 1–5pm; Sept Tues–Sun 9am–noon & 1–5pm), which sits on top of a gigantic sandstone pedestal and sports a characteristic rectangular keep. Thanks to a fire in 1635, after which it was used as a granary, Kost was spared the attentions of later architectural trends and retains the full flavour of its fourteenth-century origins, making it the best-preserved castle in the Český ráj. The late-Gothic art exhibition is well worth seeing, too, though it's only open to tours, which can be very popular at the height of summer. Down in the village, there's one cheap **hotel**, the *Helikar* (☎0433/57 11 27; ③), good for a bed or a beer.

Around Mužský

You're more likely to find suitable accommodation at **NOVÁ VES**, another 4km northwest along the scenic red-marked path through the woods of the Žehrovský les. This tiny village by the **Komárovský lake** has three campsites and plenty of pensions along its shore. North of the lake lies a matrix of paths that crisscross the complex rock systems within the forest, emerging 3km later at the hotel (☎0329/78 90 07; ②) and **campsite** (May–Sept) in **PŘÍHRAZY**. Paths spread out west from here and back into the woods until they reach **Mužský** (463m), from where it's another 2km uphill to the prehistoric burial ground of Hrada and the rocky viewpoint at Drábské světničky. The truly amazing sight of **Valečov**, a ruined fort cut into the rock, lies another 2km to the south at the southwestern edge of the woodland. On a day's hike, you could easily do a round trip from Nová Ves or Příhrazy by heading east from Valečov, or else continuing another 3km west on the red-marked path to the station at Mnichovo Hradiště (see nest page), on the main railway line to Prague.

Mnichovo Hradiště

If you're thinking of exploring the area around Mužský, you could use the small industrial town of **MNICHOVO HRADIŠTĚ** (Münchengrätz), at the southwest corner of the Český ráj, as a base. The main square has a very handsome neo-Renaissance radnice smothered in sgraffito, as well as one of the region's better **hotels**, *U hroznu* (☎0329/77 16 17; ⑤), with its own *vinárna*. If you arrive by bus, you'll be deposited right on the main square; the **train station** is about five blocks to the southeast.

The town itself has an attractive Renaissance **zámek** (April & Oct Sat & Sun 9am–noon & 12.45–3pm; May–Sept Tues–Sun 9am–noon & 12.45–4pm), 1km north of the main square, that was owned by the Waldstein family right up to 1945. Interesting enough in itself, with lots of period furniture, a fine library, Chinese porcelain and attractive English-style grounds, the chateau is also the final resting place of **Albrecht von Waldstein**, who was murdered in Cheb (Eger) in 1634 (see opposite). Initially buried in Valdice, outside Jičín, the general's body wasn't brought to Mnichovo Hradiště until the eighteenth century, by which time the family couldn't afford the lavish mausoleum Albrecht himself had hoped for – instead, all you see is a modest plaque, which wasn't erected until 1934. Despite this, the Baroque chapel of **sv Anna**, in which Waldstein is buried, still merits a visit if only for its impressive stucco ceilings and lapidarium; the chapel is northeast of the chateau, accessible from the road to Podolí.

Jičín and around

At the southeastern tip of the Český ráj, where the fertile plain of the River Labe touches the foothills of the Krkonoše, **JIČÍN** (Gitschin), an hour by train from Turnov, is easily the most rewarding stop in the region. Its location, close to some of the Český ráj's most dramatic scenery, makes it a convenient base for some easy hiking, while its Renaissance zámek and arcaded main square make it by far the most attractive town in which to stay.

The Town

The town is closely associated with the infamous **Albrecht von Waldstein**, who, during his brief and meteoric rise to eminence (see opposite), owned almost every chateau in the region. Waldstein confiscated Jičín early on in the Thirty Years' War, and chose this rather unlikely town as the capital of his new personal empire, the Duchy of Friedland. He established a hospital to ensure his workers were not incapacitated for long, insisted everyone attend the Jesuit college he founded, and established a mint here; but for his murder, he would no doubt have fulfilled his plans for a bishopric and a university.

In the 1620s he rebuilt the main square – now named **Valdštejnovo náměstí** after him – in stone, in a late-Renaissance style, full of light touches. Waldstein even lent the local burghers money to adapt their houses to suit his plans for the square. One side is still dominated by Waldstein's **zámek** (Tues–Sun 9am–5pm), which now contains a dull local museum and, in the converted riding school, an art gallery, as well as the great conference hall in which the leaders of the three great European powers, Russia, Austria and Prussia, formed the Holy Alliance against Napoleon in 1813. A covered passage connects the chateau's eastern wing with the **Jesuit church** next door, allowing the nobility to avoid their unsavoury subjects while en route to mass. But this steepleless Baroque church is eclipsed by the mighty sixteenth-century **Valdická brána** (Tues–Sun 9am–5pm) close by, whose newly restored tower gallery offers a panorama over the town.

One of Waldstein's more endearing additions to the town is the **lipová alej** (now known as Revoluční), an avenue of 1200 lime trees, planted simultaneously in two dead

WALDSTEIN

Albrecht von Waldstein (known to the Czechs as Albrecht z Valdštejna, and to the English as Wallenstein – the name given to him by the German playwright Schiller in his tragic trilogy) was the most notorious warlord of the Thirty Years' War. If the imperial astrologer Johannes Kepler is to be believed, this is all because he was born at four in the afternoon on September 14, 1583. According to Kepler's horoscope, Waldstein was destined to be greedy, deceitful, unloved and unloving. Sure enough, at an early age he tried to kill a servant, for which he was expelled from his Lutheran school. Recuperating in Italy, he converted to Catholicism (an astute career move) and married a wealthy widow who conveniently died shortly after the marriage. Waldstein used his new fortune to cultivate a friendship with Prince Ferdinand, heir to the Habsburg Empire, who in turn thought that a tame Bohemian noble could come in handy.

Within five years of the Battle of Bílá hora in 1620, Waldstein owned a quarter of Bohemia, either by compulsory purchase or in return for money or troops loaned to Ferdinand. It was a good time to go into property: Ferdinand's imperial armies, who were busy restoring Catholicism throughout Europe, provided a ready-made market for agricultural produce. And as a rising general, Waldstein could get away with a certain amount of insider trading, marching armies with as many as 125,000 men over enemy territory or land owned by rivals, laying waste to fields and then selling his troops supplies from his own pristine Bohemian estates.

As Waldstein ranged further afield in Germany, conquering Jutland, Pomerania, Alsace and most of Brandenburg on Ferdinand's behalf, his demands for reward grew ever more outrageous. Already duke of Friedland and governor of Prague, Waldstein was appointed duke of Mecklenburg in 1628. This upset not only the existing duke, who had backed Ferdinand's opponents, but even the emperor's loyalist supporters. If Ferdinand thought fit to hand one of the greatest German titles to this Czech upstart, was any family's inheritance secure? By 1630, Waldstein had earned himself the right to keep his hat on in the imperial presence as well as the dubious honour of handing the emperor a napkin after he had used his fingerbowl. However, at this point Waldstein's services became too expensive for Ferdinand, so the duke was relieved of his command.

The following year the Saxons occupied Prague, and the emperor was forced to reinstate Waldstein. Ferdinand couldn't afford to do without the supplies from Waldstein's estates, but knew he was mortgaging large chunks of the empire to pay for his services. More alarmingly, there were persistent rumours that Waldstein was about to declare himself king of Bohemia and defect to the French enemy. In 1634, Waldstein openly rebelled against Ferdinand, who immediately hatched a plot to murder Waldstein, sending a motley posse including English, Irish and Scottish mercenaries to the border town of Cheb, where they cut the general down in his nightshirt as he tried to rise from his sickbed. Some see Waldstein as the first man to unify Germany since Charlemagne, others see him as a wily Czech hero. In reality, he was probably just an ambitious, violent man, as his stars had predicted.

straight lines, 2km long, by Waldstein's soldiers. At the far end is the once princely garden of **Libosad**, now an overgrown spinney but still worth a wander. The melancholy of its Renaissance loggia, last repaired at the end of the First Republic, is matched by the nearby Jewish cemetery, which boasts some finely carved tombstones and is overshadowed by the horror of one of the country's most brutal Communist prisons in nearby **VALDICE**. Originally a seventeenth-century Carthusian monastery, it was converted into a prison by the Habsburgs, and used after 1948 to keep the regime's political prisoners in a suitably medieval state of deprivation. It still functions as a prison today, housing some of the country's most hardened criminals.

Practicalities

The **tourist office** (Mon–Fri 9am–5.30pm, Sat 9am–2pm), on the main square, is very helpful with finding **accommodation**, including private rooms in and around town. The most central accommodation is the pleasant pension *U České koruny* (☎0433/212 41; ③), on the main square, though the friendly pension *Albrecht*, 1km down the lime-tree avenue that leads to Valdice at Revoluční 712 (☎0433/225 44; ②), and the *Sportcentrum Brada*, 4km north of Jičín, off route 35 to Turnov, are both cheaper. You can also fall back on the poorly kept *Hotel Paříž* (☎0433/22750; ③), just outside the Valdická brana on Žižkovo náměstí, if need be. Two kilometres down route 16 to Mladá Boleslav there's a **motel**, *Rumcajs* (☎0433/210 78; ①), with a **campsite** and wooden **chalets** (May–Sept).

There are plenty of new **restaurants** to choose from in the old town: *U rynečku*, behind the run-down church of sv Ignác down Chelčického does the usual meat-and-dumplings, while *U Matěje*, on Nerudova just off the main square, offers a more off-beat menu, including venison and Chinese dishes. Highly imaginative and filling pizzas, as well as what the menu describes as "food for those who say meat is meat", can be had in the little patio at *Pizzerie U Henryho*, just behind the pension on the main square. Given the dearth of public transport in the region, you might want to enquire about **bike rental** at either the tourist office, or at *Sportcentrum*, on the other side of the square.

Prachovské skály

Despite the very real attractions of the town, the reason most people come to Jičín is to see the **Prachovské skály**, a series of sandstone and basalt rocks hidden in woods 8km to the northwest. To get there, it's a gentle walk along the yellow-marked path, via the *Rumcajs* campsite, though there are local buses too. The rocks lack the subtlety of the Hruboskalské skalní, but make up for it in sheer size and area; their name derives from the dust (*prach*) that covers the forest floor, forming a carpet of sand. In high season, swarms of climbers cling to the silent, grey rocks like a plague of locusts, but out of season it's possible to find a tranquil spot; try the green-marked path. There are dorm beds available in the *ubytovna* right by the rocks, but these are usually booked solid in summer; try instead a private room, or the *Hotel Skalní město* (☎0433/52 50 11; ⑤), a nice place back down the road to Jičín.

Železný Brod and around

Heading northeast from Turnov, the railway follows the course of the Jizera river to **ŽELEZNÝ BROD** (Eisenbrod), one of the many centres of Bohemia's world-famous glassmaking industry. It's a town of contradictions, its factories and high-rises spread along the banks of the river, while half-timbered cottages in the traditional Český ráj colours cover the hillside. The tiny main square is a typical mix of styles: one side is taken up by two wholly uninspiring 1950s buildings – the glass and crystal factory and the now-abandoned *Hotel Cristal* – while the other side shelters the nineteenth-century town hall and the timber-framed **museum** (May–Sept Tues–Sun 8.30am–noon & 1–4pm; Oct–April Sat & Sun only) of local arts and crafts. Up the hillside by the town church, which sports a nifty little wooden belfry, are some outstanding examples of **folk architecture**, usually confined to more inaccessible villages. **Accommodation** in Železný Brod is limited to two pensions, both off the main square on Štefánikova: the *Starý Mlýn* (☎0428/39 05 08; ③) at no. 89, and the *Veselý* (☎0428/38 93 23; ①) at no. 416.

Six kilometres back down the valley towards Turnov (and also accessible by train) is the wonderful little village of **MALÁ SKÁLA**. Nothing much ever really happens here, but it's a supremely pretty place to be based for hikes into the surrounding hills. A steep red-marked path leads from behind the train station to the **Suché skály** (Dry Rocks) and a number of rock caves, used during the Counter-Reformation as safe houses for persecuted Protestants. A green-marked path then leads to the hamlet of Prosička, after which the blue-marked path heads back to Malá Skála; the whole route takes two to three hours. Another red-marked path from Malá Skala follows a ridge on the other side of the river, from where the view across the valley to the ruined castle of **Frýdštejn** is the reward for your pains. You could extend the day by dropping into the castle, then continuing on up the blue-marked path to the viewpoint atop Kopanina, and returning to Malá Skála via the green-marked path. Should you wish to stay the night, there's a **campsite** on the right bank of the river, and a delightful little **pension** with a very good restaurant, *Teta Marta* (☎0428/39 21 40 or 39 20 76; ②), 1km up the road to Frýdštejn. Right near the train station is the large wooden *Hotel Skála* (☎0428/34 22 99; ③), which also serves up steaks and chops from its outdoor grill.

Six kilometres northwest of Turnov, off route 35, **Sychrov** (Tues–Sun: April, Sept & Oct 9am–noon & 1–3.30pm; May 9am–noon & 1–4.30pm; June–Aug 8am–noon & 1–4.30pm) is a relatively recent aristocratic pile, romantically remodelled in neo-Gothic style by the Rohans, who bought the estate in 1820 having been forced into exile by the French Revolution. Apart from the pseudo-medieval craftsmanship of its interior, the castle is famed for its long-standing connections with Dvořák, who enjoyed the family's patronage and visited often. This partly explains the excellent season of concerts that take place here each year. The castle is only about ten minutes by train from Turnov on the railway line to Liberec.

The Krkonoše

The **Krkonoše** (Giant Mountains) are the highest mountains in Bohemia and formed part of the historical northeastern border of its ancient kingdom. They were uninhabited until the sixteenth and seventeenth centuries, when glassmaking and ore-mining brought the first German and Italian settlers to the Riesengebirge, as they were then known. The mountains' undoubted beauty ensured an early tourist following, and, for resorts like Špindlerův Mlýn, it's now the sole industry. Despite being one of the few protected national parks in the country, since the war thousands upon thousands of trees have become fatally weakened by **acid rain** (the annual level of rainfall here is among the highest in the country). Once the trees are badly affected, insects do the rest, transforming them into grey husks, devoid of foliage. Extensive felling has taken place aimed at stopping the spread of the destructive insects – but it's a bit like a smoker removing their lungs to prevent cancer.

For many, the fate of Bohemia's ancient forests is the most damning indictment of the Communists' forty years of mismanagement, and as if to rub it in, the focus during the 1980s was on new hotels and chairlifts rather than environmental measures. Since 1989, the government has paid lip service to the importance of environmental issues, but the reality is that the country cannot afford the luxury of (expensive) green policies without outside assistance.

Czechs will reassure you that things here are nowhere near as bad as in the Krušné hory (see p.219), and it's true: if you stay in the largely unspoiled valley, or come here in winter when the snow obscures much of the damage, it's possible to remain oblivious. In summer, though, when walking is the main mode of transport, it's well-nigh impossible to ignore the rain's effects the higher up you go.

Some practicalities

These grim realities fail to deter the coachloads, which means **accommodation** can be difficult to obtain at the height of the winter ski season, and in July and August. That said, the entire mountain range is teeming with cheap **private rooms**, which can be booked through the numerous accommodation agencies in the resorts. Theoretically,

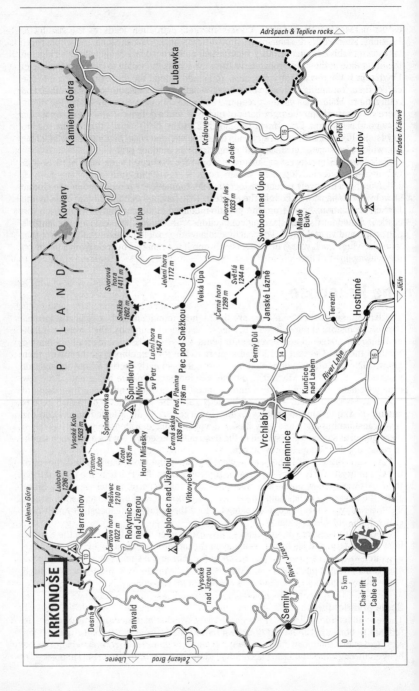

KRKONOŠE

Adršpach & Teplice rocks

Kamienna Góra

Lubawka

Kowary

Králevec

Žacléř

Trutnov

Poříčí

Hradec Králové

Malá Úpa

Dvorský les 1033 m

Svoboda nad Úpou

Mladé Buky

Svorová hora 1411 m

Jelení hora 1172 m

Velká Úpa

Světlá 1244 m

Janské Lázně

Hostinné

Sněžka 1602 m

Černá hora 1299 m

Terezín

Jičín

Vysoké Kolo 1503 m

Luční hora 1547 m

Pec pod Sněžkou

Černý Důl

Špindlerův Mlýn

sv Petr

Spindlerovka

Přéd. Planina 1196 m

Kunčice nad Labem

River Labe

Jelenia Góra

Luboch 1296 m

Pramen Labe

Vysoké Kolo 1503 m

Černá skála 1038 m

Vrchlabí

Kotel 1435 m

Horní Mišečky

Jilemnice

P O L A N D

Plešivec 1210 m

Vítkovice

Jablonec nad Jizerou

Čertova hora 1022 m

Harrachov

Rokytnice nad Jizerou

N

Desná

Tanvald

Vysoké nad Jizerou

River Jizera

Semily

Železný Brod

Liberec

Zelezný Brod

5 km

------- Chair lift

— · — Cable car

0

you can also stay at one of the **bouda** (chalets) dotted across the mountains, originally hideouts for the fleeing Protestants of the seventeenth century, but in practice it's often difficult to find a vacancy. **Camping** is one way of ensuring a place for the night, although facilities are restricted, with just two sites within the strict boundaries of the national park.

As for transport, **trains** can get you as far as Harrachov, Vrchlabí and Trutnov; **buses** occasionally run right the way to *Špindlerova bouda*, on the Polish border; and there are numerous **chairlifts** that operate even in summer. There are now three 24-hour **border crossings into Poland**: Harrachov-Jakuszyce, Královec-Lubawka and Pomezní Boudy-Przelecz Okraj. However, **hiking** is undoubtedly the best way of getting around, since each valley is basically a long, winding dead end for motor vehicles, with pretty hefty car parking fees (and often queues) aimed at dissuading drivers from bringing their vehicles into the park.

For those intent on serious hiking, a detailed **map** of the mountains, showing the network of colour-coded marked paths, is essential. **Warm clothing** is also important, no matter what the season – the summits are battered by wind almost every day, and have an average annual temperature of around freezing point. Persistent **mist** – around for about 300 days in the year – makes sticking to the marked paths a must. In winter, most of the high-level paths are closed, and recently, even in summer, several have been closed to give the mountains a rest. To find out the latest details, head for the tourist information offices in any of the resorts.

The Krkonoše is also one of the most popular regions in the Czech Republic for **skiing**, since it receives by far the longest and most reliable snowfall in the country. Queues for lifts can be long and slow, but are more than compensated for by the cheapness of the ski passes and accommodation – although these have also risen to levels formidable to the average Czech. Lift tickets in Pec pod Sněžkou cost upwards of 350Kč per day, less in the other resorts, and **ski rental** is easily had for around 250Kč per day. In summer, numerous outlets in each resort offer **bike rental**, and in Špindlerův Mlýn you can even go **hang gliding**.

Vrchlabí

VRCHLABÍ (Hohenelbe) is the hub of the Krkonoše for transport and supplies, but not as well situated for skiing or hiking as the other main towns. Reservations are essential for the direct **buses** from Prague, some of which continue on to Špindlerův Mlýn (see p.256); if you're travelling by **train**, you'll need to change at Kunčice nad Labem, 4km south. Hotel **accommodation** boils down to the newly renovated *Labuť* (☎0438/42 19 64; ④) and the *Wirth* (☎0438/223 51; ⑤), both on the main street, though there are many small pensions to choose from, too. The lakeside *Výsplachy* **campsite** (June to mid-Sept) is just south of route 14. Locals tend to head to the **restaurant** at the *Wirth*, because of the generous portions of meat and dumplings served. You can also indulge in pizzas or steaks in the new *Klasika*, a little further down, or sit at the outdoor grill of the *Krušovická Restaurace* on the main square.

Vrchlabí's long main street stretches for 3km along the banks of the Labe, taking you past the gardens and zoo of the sixteenth-century chateau and a number of traditional wooden arcaded folk buildings around the centre. A trio of folk houses at the far end of the street – one in stone flanked by two timber-framed neighbours – have been converted into the small **Krkonošské muzeum** (Tues–Sun 9am–noon & 1–4pm), containing folk art, sundry stones and displays on regional life through the ages. The town's most important asset, however, is its IT Centrum near the chateau, which has a good supermarket and a travel agency, ING Tours (Mon–Fri 8am–6pm, Sat 9am–noon; ☎0438/29 86 23), which can arrange accommodation in private rooms, pensions and hotels right across the Krkonoše. Vrchlabí's official **tourist office** (Mon–Fri 9am–5pm,

Sat 9am–noon) is in the sgraffitoed radnice on the main square, náměstí T.G. Masaryka.

Špindlerův Mlýn and around

No doubt **ŠPINDLERŮV MLÝN** (Spindlermühle), 15km north up the Labe Valley and accessible by bus from Vrchlabí, was once an idyllic, isolated mountain hamlet. Successive generations, however, have found it difficult to resist exploiting a town where seven valleys meet, and the town is now a major ski resort with countless private pensions and ugly hotels lying scattered across the hillside. Still, the place retains a cosy feel, and makes a fine base for a few days of outdoor activity. The river Labe, here still a stream, flows through its tiny centre, which is just a convergence of a few roads.

It's all but essential to book **accommodation** in advance during high season, and the booking office of the tourist shop in the pavilion (☎0438/933 64), right in the centre, can help. The official **tourist office** (daily 9–11.30am & 12.30–5pm) is hidden beyond the post office on the other side of the stream, and posts a complete list of accommodation possibilities in the vicinity. Recommendable hotels include the lovely wood-panelled mountain lodge *Start Hotel* (☎0438/933 05 or 49 33 05; ⑨), which stands on a slope above the equally sylvan *Hotel Nechanický* (☎0438/932 63 or 49 31 63; ⑦). Lower-end rooms can be found in the rustic *Pension Jaro* (☎0438/933 64; ③) or the very pretty *Pension U Čeňků* (☎0438/937 00; ③), across the road from each other near the tourist office, while up the hill to the east in Svatý Petr is the modernized chalet *Pension Stráž* (☎0438/933 50; ③). There are two fairly pricey **campsites** a couple of kilometres north of the central area, both open all year. The best place to grab a bite **to eat** is the terrace pizzeria in the Pavilion, by the edge of the stream. The aforementioned *Hotel Nechanický* and *Pension U Čeňků* both have cute terrace restaurants, and the *Nechanický* has a cellar *vinárna* as well. You could otherwise sample one of the many beers on offer at the *hospoda* connected to the *Hotel Central*, just across the stream from the Pavilion. If you're driving, keep in mind that **parking** is severely restricted in town, and unless your hotel has reserved space you'll have to leave your vehicle at the car park just to the south, and pay a high fee for the privilege.

It's possible to see huge tracts of mostly dead forest from Špindlerův Mlýn itself, but should you want a closer look, head north from the centre en route to the campsite, then cross to the left bank where a chairlift will take you to just below the summit of **Medvědín** (1235m). The **River Labe**, which flows into the North Sea (as the Elbe) near Hamburg, has its source in the Krkonoše. It takes about three hours to reach the source (*pramen Labe*): a long, boulder-strewn walk along the valley, followed by a short, sharp climb out of the forest to the modern *Labská bouda* (☎0438/42 17 54; ②), which is actually more of a **hotel**. Characteristically for the Krkonoše, the summit is disappointingly flat and boggy, and the source itself (500m from the Polish border) no great sight. If you're carrying your pack with you, continue for three hours along the blue-marked track to Harrachov (see below). Otherwise, it's around two hours back to Špindlerův Mlýn, via Horní Misečky and Medvědín. For a **glimpse of Poland**, you should catch a bus from Špindlerův Mlýn to *Špindlerova bouda*, where dead trees, Polish border guards and the odd grazing sheep provide the entertainment.

Harrachov

Five buses and one train a day (change at nearby Tanvald) make the journey from Prague to the westernmost resort in the Krkonoše, **HARRACHOV** (Harrachsdorf), whose cottages are scattered about the Mumlava Valley. A glassworks was established here in 1712, and the **Muzeum skla** (Glass Museum; Mon–Fri 9am–5pm, Sat 9am–1pm) has a small sample of glassware throughout the ages. There's also a new **Lyžařské muzeum** (Ski Museum; daily 9am–3pm), further up the road, which traces the history of skiing, and celebrates Harrachov's most recent claim to fame, when it hosted a round of the world ski-jump championships in 1997. Otherwise, your time is best spent in the surrounding mountains.

Accommodation in Harrachov can be significantly cheaper than in the neighbouring resorts, but it can still take some effort to secure a room in high season. The official **tourist office**, HIC (☎0432/52 96 00; daily 8am–8pm), can book hotels, pensions and private rooms in the area; there's even a free phone outside the office so you can ring round yourself after hours. Otherwise you can try the neighbouring *Pension Jitka* (☎0432/52 81 88; ①), *Pension Eliška* (☎0432/52 93 32; ①), and the *Chata Kamenice* (☎0432/52 92 87; ②), all of which cater for summer hikers and winter skiers. Or you could splurge away at the aptly named *Hotel Fit & Fun* (☎0432/52 81 17; ⑨), a big modern place complete with indoor swimming pool, weight room, sauna and tennis courts; longer stays are rewarded with significant discounts. Alternatively, there's a **campsite** up the road towards the Polish border. To the west in Nový Svět, the *Hotel Diana* (☎0432/52 90 04; ②) also has a decent **restaurant**, or you can fill your stomach at the *Pánský dům*, in the Glass Museum. Those seeking a view with their meal would do well at the *Myslivna*, halfway up the **chairlift** to Čertova hora. For cheap thrills, continue on up above the dry tobogganing course to the top of the mountain, which at 1022m is high enough to view the pollution damage all around.

Pec pod Sněžkou and Janské Lázně

The sole attribute of **PEC POD SNĚŽKOU** (Petzer) is its proximity to the mountains. In winter it becomes the Czech Republic's chief ski centre, strung along a long winding road. In summer it is the main hiking base for climbing **Sněžka** (Schneekoppe or Snow Peak), at 1602m the highest mountain in Bohemia and the most impressive in the entire range. Its bleak, grey summit rises above the tree line, relieving walkers of the painful sight of gently expiring pines, and making for a fine panorama. If you don't fancy the six-kilometre ascent, take the **chairlift** from the village, which will take you right to the top. The border, signified by discreet white-and-red stone markers, divides the rounded summit; on the Czech side there's a restaurant (of sorts), while Polish border guards patrol with Kalashnikovs swinging nonchalantly at their sides, though they're unlikely to use them unless Czech–Polish relations take a dramatic turn for the worse.

Many Czechs use the chairlift as a launching pad for further **hiking**. To the east of the summit, a path follows the narrow mountain ridge (which also marks the border) for 2.5km to another peak, Svorová hora (Czarna Kopa to the Poles). To the west, there's a steep drop, again along the ridge, to *Slezská bouda* (on the Polish side). To reach Špindlerův Mlýn from here (3hr 30min), follow the blue markers (via *Luční bouda*), and not the red and blue ones, that veer into Polish territory. The Krkonoše National Park **information centre**, on the main road up from the bus station, has good maps and can provide hiking and skiing information. Ski rental is available from dozens of shops around town.

There are regular **buses from Prague** to Pec pod Sněžkou, plus several to Trutnov and the occasional one to Janské Lázně (see below). As for **accommodation**, Pec has no campsite and its hotels are generally overpriced and booked-up, though the concentration of private rooms strewn across the hills is even denser here than in other Krkonoše resorts. The Turista information and travel agency (daily in winter 9am–7pm, shorter hours out of ski season; ☎0439/79 62 80) in the centre of town handles the whole range of accommodation. There is also an information stand near the bus station with an electronic board posting hotel and pension vacancies, and you can call from the free telephone provided. Best bets for cheaper beds include the *Pension Bohumír Berger* (☎0439/96 24 93; ②) and *Pension U Bláhu* (☎0439/96 23 13 or 79 62 13; ③), both near the centre of things. A bit up the price scale is the amiable *Pension Nikola*

(☎0439/96 20 51 or 79 61 51; ⑤), near the park information centre, or *Pension Výsok Straž*, (☎0439/96 22 29; ⑤), which is up the hill beyond the eyesore (and expensive) *Hotel Horizont*. Many hotels and pensions have their own **restaurants**, or try the *Hospoda na Peci* across from the Turista office, which provides a smoky mountain-lodge atmosphere to go with your cheap beer and *guláš*. Up the road towards the *Pension Nikola*, *Enzian Gril* is a tasty little pub and grill with a few roadside tables, and the *Hotel Hořec* close by has an upscale café and restaurant.

Janské Lázně

JANSKÉ LÁZNĚ (Johannisbad), hidden away in a sheltered, fertile valley on the southern edge of the national park, has a different atmosphere from the other resorts, and as such is probably the nicest (and certainly the cheapest) place to base yourself in the entire Krkonoše. Visitors tend to come here to take the cure rather than climb the surrounding peaks (although even the lazy can reach the top of Černá hora by the hourly cable car). On a hot summer's day all the classic images of spa life converge on the central stretch of lawn: a brass band plays "oom-pah-pah" tunes in slightly lack-adaisical fashion, while the elderly and disabled spill from the tearoom onto the bench-es outside. The best place to stay is the friendly, cosy *Villa Ludmila* (☎0439/87 52 60; ③), followed by the *Lesní dům* (☎0439/87 51 67; ②).

Trutnov

The modern factories and housing complexes that ring Bohemia's easternmost textile town, **TRUTNOV** (Trautenau), signal the end of the national park, though the town is a useful fall-back for the Krkonoše in the height of summer and an equally good base for exploring the Adršpach and Teplice rocks (see opposite).

The busy arcaded main square, **Krakonošovo náměstí**, downstream and uphill from the train station, has been beautifully restored. Alongside its plague column stands a fountain depicting Krakonoš (Rübezahl to the Germans), the sylvan spirit who guards the Giant Mountains and gave them their Czech name, both best appreciated from one of the cafés under the arcades of the main square. If you have time to kill, there's the odd exhibition at the **museum** (Tues–Sun 9am–5pm) in the former *stará škola*, just off the old town square. Trutnov's most recent claim to fame is that in the early 1970s, **Václav Havel** used to work in the local brewery, which produces a very good beer called, predictably enough, Krakonoš. His experiences later provided material for *Audience*, one of three plays centred around the character Vaněk (a lightly disguised version of himself).

The **tourist office** (Mon–Fri 8–11.45am & 12.30–5.30pm, Sat 8am–12.30pm) in the radnice can point you towards some **private rooms**, or else you could try one of Trutnov's **hotels**: the *Grand* (☎0439/81 19 01; ④) on the main square, or the *Bohemia* (☎0439/81 19 51; ④), just off the square on Palackého. The *Dolce Vita* **campsite** (open all year) is by a small lake, 4km southwest of Trutnov – take the blue-marked path from the centre of town. The *Grand* has a good, jungle-themed **restaurant**, called *Palmovka*, and there are several cafés on the main square to choose from. The town's annual August rock festival is the largest in the country, featuring mostly Czech bands, plus the odd headline Western band.

East to Broumov

Between Trutnov and Broumov, some 30km east, lie two seemingly innocuous hilly strips smothered in trees, which only on much closer inspection reveal themselves to be riddled with sandstone protrusions and weird rock formations on the same lines as those in Český ráj (see p.246). Distances here are small and the gradients gentle, making it ideal for a bit of none-too-strenuous – but no less spectacular – **hiking**. If you're thinking of exploring the rocks, get hold of the extremely detailed *Teplicko-Adršpašské skály/Broumovské stěny* map before you get there, which shows all the colour-coded footpaths and the campsites. The local **buses** do serve the more out-of-the-way places like Broumov, but it's worth taking advantage of the slow but scenic **train** service from Trutnov to Teplice nad Metují, via Adršpach.

The Adršpach and Teplice rocks

The **Adršpach and Teplice rocks** (Teplicko-Adršpašské skály), 15km east of Trutnov, rise up out of the pine forest like petrified phalluses. Some even take trees with them as they launch themselves hundreds of feet into the air. German tourists have flocked here since the nineteenth century, though nowadays they are outnumbered by Czech rock-climbers and ramblers. The rocks are concentrated in two separate *skalní města*, or "rock cities": the Adršpach rocks, just south of the village of the same name, and the Teplice rocks, 2km south through the woods. The latter can also be approached from the villages of Janovice or Teplice.

Adršpach
ADRŠPACH (Adersbach) train station (one stop on from Horní Adršpach) lies at the northern extremity of the rock system, though you can't really miss it, since some of the rocks have crept right up to the station itself. In high season, there's a small entrance fee to enter the **Adršpašské skalní město** (your ticket includes a boat ride, see below). Once through the perimeter fence, the outside world recedes and you're surrounded by new sensations – sand underfoot, the scent of pine, boulders and shady trees. Most of the sandstone rocks are dangerous to climb without the correct equipment and experience, so you'll probably have to content yourself with strolling and gawping at the formations, best described by their nicknames: Babiččina lenoška (Grandmother's Armchair), Španělská stěna (Spanish Wall) and the ironic Trpaslík (Dwarf).

The green-marked path winds its way along and over a stream, through narrow clefts between the rocks, eventually bringing you to a couple of waterfalls (*vodopády*). From here, steps hewn out of the rock, lead up to the Adršpašské jezírko, a lake trapped above ground level between the rocks, where jovial boatmen pole you along in rafts a short distance to the other side. From here, the yellow-marked path continues through the woods for 2km to the entrance to the Teplice rocks (see below). If you fancy a swim or a spot of nude bathing, head for the Pískovna lake to the east of the Adršpach entrance, with its dramatic backdrop of craggy rocks and pine trees. The *Lesní zátiší* (☎0447/58 60 18; ④), right by the entrance to the rocks, offers simple **rooms** and **food**.

Teplice nad Metují
The easiest approach for the **Teplické skalní město** is from Teplice nad Metují-skály station, just across the river from the entrance to the rocks. A blue-marked path heads west for 1km, after which you need to switch to the green-marked path, which threads its way through the Anenské údolí, the main valley of the *skalní město* – another theatrical burst of geological abnormalities that form a narrow valley of rocks. Right by the woods' edge you can also explore the rock fortress of **Střmen**, which once served as a Hussite hide-out. The *Hotel Orlík* (☎0447/58 10 25; ②) and *Penzión pod Ozvěnou* (☎0447/58 10 69; ③) are both situated right by the entrance to the rocks.

Alternatively, **TEPLICE NAD METUJÍ** (Wekelsdorf) itself, 2km east, is a functional base, with a supermarket, a cinema, several pensions and a couple of hotels. There's also the *Bučnice* **campsite** (May–Sept), 1km up the road from Teplice nad Metují-skály station. If you're a keen rock-climber, then the annual **festival of mountaineering films,** held here in late August/early September may be of interest. It's basically an excuse for a lot of boozing and boasting, though it attracts people from all over Europe, who come to share their experiences, many demonstrating their skills on the local formations.

The Broumov walls

The **Broumov walls** (Broumovské stěny) make up a thin sandstone ridge that almost cuts Broumov off from the rest of the country. From the west, there's no indication of the approaching precipice, from which a wonderful vista sweeps out over to Broumov and beyond into Poland, but from the east, the ridge is clearly spread out before you. The best place to appreciate the view is from Dientzenhofer's chapel of **Panna Maria Sněžná,** situated in among the boulders at the edge of the big drop. The best rock formations are 9km south of here, close by the highest point of the wall, **Božanovský Špičák** (733m), only a few hundred metres from the Polish border. You can approach the Dientzenhofer chapel from either Police nad Metují, 5km to the southwest, or Broumov (see below), 6km to the east. To get to the rocks around Božanovský Špičák, take the bus from Police to Machov, and walk the final 3.5km; alternatively, there's the train from Broumov to Božanov, followed by a walk of 3.5km.

Broumov

BROUMOV (Braunau), a predominantly German-speaking town before the war, 30km due east of Trutnov, is probably the best place to base yourself if you're thinking of exploring the Broumov walls. The town is particularly impressive from a distance, with its colossal Dientzenhofer-designed Baroque **Benediktinský klášter** (Tues–Sat 9–11am & 1–4pm, Sun 10–11am & 2–4pm), perched on a sandstone pedestal above the River Stěnava. The monastery was used by the Communists to incarcerate much of the country's priesthood after 1948, and a small section of the museum inside describes their treatment. The complex also contains an enchanting Gothic courtyard. In addition, Broumov has a compact old town, with a handsome cobbled main square, Mírové náměstí, lined with lime trees and pastel-coloured houses, and centred on a fine barleysugar Marian column.

As for **accommodation,** the *Hotel Veba* (☎0447/52 36 33; ⑤) is the town's best, set in its own grounds and with a fine restaurant, to the southwest of the centre off Šalounova. Other options in the old town include the newly refurbished *Winterswijk* (☎0447/214 80; ⑤), tucked in beside the town brewery on Pivovarská, and the communist-era *Hotel Praha* (☎0447/52 37 86; ④) on the main square. The **train** and **bus stations** are both close to one another, five to ten minutes' walk southeast of the old town.

One attraction you shouldn't overlook is the unusual Silesian **wooden church** on the Křivinice road out of town. With a car and a passion for Baroque churches, you could also happily spend a morning exploring the local Stěnava valley. In the eighteenth century, Kilian Ignaz Dientzenhofer, Bohemia's foremost ecclesiastical architect, was chosen by the local abbot to redesign the Broumov monastery. He was also commissioned to build numerous **Baroque churches** in the area (and in the Klodzko region, over the border in Poland), in an attempt to Catholicize the staunchly Protestant Silesian Germans who used to live here. For each church, he experimented with a different design – a simple oval plan at Verneřovice (Wernersdorf), an elongated octagon at Ruprechtice (Rupperdorf), a crushed oval at Vižňov (Wiesen). Most are now down to their bricks and mortar and firmly closed, but the key is usually easily traceable, and the effort well rewarded.

Náchod and around

Cowering at the base of its large, lordly seat, built to guard the gateway to Bohemia from Silesia, **NÁCHOD** is one of the few Czech border towns that has been predominantly Czech for most of its life. Even the Nazis stopped short of annexing it when they marched into the Sudetenland in 1938, since at the time there were only four German-speaking families in the whole town. Nowadays, most people just stop off in order to break the journey and spend their last remaining crowns en route to Poland, whose border is a couple of kilometres east of the town centre, though Náchod actually makes a useful base for exploring the surrounding area, including the two exceptional **chateaux** at Nové Město nad Metují and Opočno.

The Town

Náchod is a lot better-looking than your average border town: the main square, **náměstí T.G. Masaryka**, in particular, has had a new lease of life following its recent restoration. Its two most winsome buildings are the fourteenth-century church of **sv Vavřinec** (St Lawrence) at the centre of the square, its entrance flanked by two fat square towers sporting comically large wooden onion domes, and the Art Nouveau *Hotel U beránka*, with sinewy lines and marvellously detailed mosaic lettering and interior light fittings.

Peeking out of the foliage, high above the town, and a very stiff climb from the main square, is Náchod's sprawling, unassailable, sgraffitoed **zámek** (April & Oct Sat & Sun 9am–noon & 1–4pm; May–Sept Tues–Sun 9am–noon & 1–5pm). The original Gothic structure survives only in the pretty little round tower in the centre of the complex; everything else is the result of successive building projects spanning the Renaissance and Baroque periods. There's a choice of two tours: the *malý okruh* (short tour), which allows access to the tower, the dungeons and the viewing terrace, and the *velký okruh* (long tour), which guides you through the interior. Inside, you get to see the castle art collection courtesy of the exiled Duke of Kurland, and an interesting hotchpotch of furnishings and exhibits accrued over the centuries by descendents of the Italian Ottavio Piccolomini-Pieri, Waldstein's bodyguard, who was given the castle by Ferdinand II after informing the emperor of Waldstein's secret plans (see p.251). If you've children in tow, you might also like to peruse the phantasmagoric figures in **Strašidla** (May–Sept Tues–Sun 9am–5pm), in the bastions of the castle's fourth courtyard. The dimly lit tableaux of mythological creatures from Czech legends are guaranteed to keep the kids amused and the adults bemused.

THE COWARDS IN NÁCHOD

The exiled writer **Josef Škvorecký** was born and bred in Náchod – a "narrow cleavage between the mountains", as he characteristically dubbed it. During his wartime adolescence he was joined by film-director-to-be Miloš Forman, then only a young boy, who came to stay with his uncle when his parents were sent to a concentration camp from which they never returned. Later, in the cultural thaw of the 1960s, before they were both forced to emigrate, the two men planned (unsuccessfully) to make a film based on *The Cowards*, Škvorecký's most famous novel. Set in "a small Bohemian town" (ie Náchod) in the last few days of the war, the book caused a sensation when it was published (briefly) in 1958 because of its bawdy treatment of Czech resistance to the Nazis. Škvorecký also set the action of a later novel, *The Miracle Game*, in the nearby village of Hronov. In both novels, and in *The Engineer of Human Souls*, the name of the main character is Danny Smiřický, after Náchod's local aristos.

The former riding school, or **jízdárna** (Tues–Sun 9am–noon & 1–5pm), situated beyond the bear-inhabited moat by the car park, houses a surprisingly healthy permanent collection of **Russian paintings**. The highlights include two finely studied female portraits by Ilya Repin, the most famous of the "Wanderers", who broke away from the official Russian academy of art, better known for his epic works filled with fiery bearded figures like the *Trial of Christ*. The leader of the Wanderers, Ivan Kramskoy, is responsible for the superbly aloof portrait of an aristocratic lady in a carriage, with a St Petersburg palace as a backdrop. Also on display are works by Serov and Makovsky, but best of all by far are the wildly colourful depictions of peasant women by late-nineteenth-century artist Filip Malyavin, who was a lay brother on Mount Athos in Greece before he took up painting full-time.

Practicalities

The town's **train** and **bus stations** are both five minutes' walk east of the centre, at the end of Kamenice. The **tourist office** (Mon–Fri 8am–5pm, Sat 8–11.30am), in a travel agency off the square at Kamenice 144, should be able to help with **accommodation**. You can stay the night in the zámek – enquire at the ticket office (☎0441/212 01; ②) – though the aforementioned *U beránka* (☎0441/43 31 18; ④) is a more comfortable option and probably the town's greatest institution – a hotel, café, theatre and restaurant (serving the local Primátor beer as well as traditional Czech food) in one. An alternative, also on the main square, is the small hotel-restaurant *U města Prahy* (☎0441/42 18 17; ②). The town's pretty riverside **campsite** (mid-May to mid-Sept), is by the woods 1.5km east of the centre, signposted down Běloveská.

Nové Město nad Metují

NOVÉ MĚSTO NAD METUJÍ, 9km south of Náchod, boasts a stunningly beautiful old town square, with one of the country's most interesting chateaux crouched in one corner. While the town's modern quarter sprawls unattractively over the lower ground, the staré město sits quietly (and extremely prettily) on a high spur hemmed in by the River Metuje, a tributary of the River Labe. Restored sixteenth-century houses line each side of the rectangular arcaded main square, **Husovo náměstí**, though the most photographed set of gables are the identical cream-coloured ones that parade along the north side.

What makes Nové Město's old town extra special is its remarkable seventeenth-century **zámek** (May, June & Sept Tues–Sun 9am–4pm; July & Aug daily 9am–5pm), which looks out across the Labe basin (known as the Polabí) from the northeast corner of the square. After piecemeal alterations, it fell into disrepair in the nineteenth century, until the industrialist Josef Bartoň bought the place in 1908 and commissioned the quirky Slovak architect **Dušan Jurkovič** to entirely redesign it – which he did, most notably with the timber-framed structures, redolent of his native land, in the terraced gardens, and the bizarre wall-to-wall leather vaulting of the Žebrový sál (Ribbed Hall). The other rooms are lavishly furnished in every period from the original Renaissance to Cubism, including highly unusual works by Czech Cubists like **Pavel Janák**. Bartoň eventually died here in 1951, at the ripe old age of 98. In an uncharacteristically magnanimous gesture, the Communists had allowed him and his wife (and their cook) to live out their last days in three rooms at the top of the chateau. The place is now back in the hands of the Bartoň family, who actually live here and run it with great efficiency. Before you buy your ticket, be sure to check out the set of dwarfs by the Baroque sculptor Braun, which stand along the terrace and bridge across the moat.

An extra treat is on hand in the outlying village of **Slavoňov** in the form of a precious little wooden church dating from 1533. The wood-panelled interior is exquisite, almost entirely covered with simple yet rich paintings of local people and scenes. The flat ceiling panels each show a different scene, while the almost cartoon-like paintings on the choir depict local scenes and nobility. Be sure to ask the tourist office in Nové Město to call ahead to the friar's office next door, so that someone will be on hand to let you in. To get to Slavoňov, follow the yellow-marked path 4km through the woods from Nové Město's main square, or catch the occasional bus from the square, marked Slavoňov.

Practicalities

Nové Město nad Metují itself is a beautiful eight-kilometre **walk** from Náchod down the winding River Metuje (yellow-marked path, followed by red). If you arrive here by **train**, you'll end up 2km northwest of the chateau, in Nové Město's new town; infrequent local buses link the old town square with the station or you can follow the blue markers. If you arrive by **bus** from Náchod or Hradec Králové, you can get off at Husovo náměstí itself. If you want to **stay the night**, the *Hotel U Broučka*, on Husovo náměstí (☎0441/725 71; ③) offers simple rooms with en-suite facilities. The **tourist office** (May–Sept Mon–Fri 8am–noon & 1–5pm; Oct–April Mon–Fri 9am–noon & 1–4pm), just off the main square, can set you up in a private room or nearby pension. One good **restaurant** on the square is, surprisingly, the rather grubby *Restaurace U Paďourů*, where the standard Czech fare is cheap and tasty. Better yet, the chateau has its very own *Pivní sklep*, a nice cellar pub with an outside terrace, serving pub snacks and Náchod's excellent Primátor beer.

Opočno

Ten kilometres south of Nové Město nad Metují is the town of **OPOČNO**, whose **zámek** (April & Oct Sat & Sun 9–11.30am & 12.30–5pm; May–Aug Tues–Sun 9–11.30am & 12.30–6pm; Sept Tues–Sun 9–11.30am & 12.30–5pm) is spectacularly poised on a knife's edge above the Polabí plain. The main attraction here is the tripledecker loggia, built in the sixteenth-century by Italian architects around the chateau's three-sided courtyard. Clinging to the chateau's foundations are the lovely wooded grounds (daily April–Sept 7am–8pm; Oct–March 8am–3pm) with a summer palace or *letohrádek*, now used for temporary exhibitions. All these treats, and the view, can be appreciated without having to sign up for either of the two guided tours: trasa 1 (*velký*) takes 1hr 15min and trasa 2 (*zkřceň*) takes 50min. Opočno is famous for its armoury, which includes a priceless collection of rifles, swords, a Roman helmet, and even a well-worn chastity belt. The rest of the chateau consists of beautifully restored rooms in which are contained sundry possessions of the Colloredo family, who owned the place until 1945; the last remaining family member is in the process of reacquiring it. Highlights include hunting trophies, ivory-inlaid furniture, thirteenth-century crystal and numerous portraits, many of which hang underneath extravagant stucco ceilings that practically sag with the extra weight.

   Buses are the most direct means of getting to Opočno; several connect with Hradec Králové daily. The train station (Opočno pod Orlicki horami) is a good 2km below the town to the west. You can eat or shoot pool in the very Sixties, but good, *Zámecká restaurace* next to the castle gates on Trčkovo náměstí.

The Babiččino údolí

Ten kilometres west of Náchod by train, the town of **ČESKÁ SKALICE** marks the beginning of the Úpa Valley, better known as the **Babiččino údolí** after the novel that has made it famous, *Babička* (Grandmother) by **Božena Němcová** (1820–62). A very precise, and realistic, portrait of Czech peasant life in the mid-nineteenth century, dominated by the kindly wisdom of the story's grandmother figure, the tale is still required reading for Czechs of all ages. Němcová's tragic life is almost as well known as the tale itself: forced to marry at seventeen to a man more than twice her age, Němcová wrote, "The years of my childhood were the most beautiful of my life. When I married I wept over my lost liberty, over the dreams and ideals forever ruined." Moving in Czech republican and literary circles in the 1840s, she caused considerable outrage with her numerous passionate and very public affairs. Her independent spirit, her championing of women's education, and her involvement in the 1848 revolution have endeared her to many Czech women. Nowadays, she is still very much a household name, and one of the few Czech women to have entered the country's literary canon.

There are now several **museums** dedicated to Němcová in the area, two in Česká Skalice itself. The first is in her old schoolhouse, the timber-framed Barunčina škola (Tues–Sun: May–Aug 8am–noon & 1–5pm; Sept 9am–noon & 1–4pm), northwest off the main square up B. Němcové; the second is in the former pub, *U bílého českého lva*, in which she got married, now part of the town's Textilní muzeum (Tues–Sun: April, Sept & Oct 9am–4pm; May–Aug 8am–5pm), further up B. Němcové and across the river. Her birthplace in Červený Kostelec, 8km north of Česká Skalice, is also now a museum (times as for the škola). Perhaps the most rewarding of the lot, though, for the non-Czech-speaker is **Ratibořice**, 2.5km north of Česká Skalice, (April & Oct Sat & Sun 9am–noon & 1–4pm; May & Sept Tues–Sun 9am–noon & 1–5pm; June–Aug closes 6pm), the pretty little pink chateau with green shutters where Němcová's father was equerry, and her mother laundress.

An alternative to visiting one of the above is to explore the gentle valley, which was her childhood haunt and the main inspiration for the book – a very beautiful place in its own right. Be sure not to miss the modern statue group by Otto Gutfreund, north of the chateau; walk through the chateau's lovely English gardens (daily: May–Oct 8am–8pm; Nov–April 9am–5pm) and upstream through the fields.

Hradec Králové

Capital of East Bohemia and the largest city on the fertile plain known as the Polabí, **HRADEC KRÁLOVÉ** (Königgrätz) has a typically handsome historical quarter, paid for by the rich trade that used to pass through en route to Silesia. But there's another side to the town, too. To the west of the medieval centre is one of the great urban projects of the interwar Republic, built by the leading modern Czech architects of the day. The two towns don't really blend in with one another – in fact, they barely communicate – and these days, the staré město is still more like a museum piece. Even if you don't particularly take to the new town, it's a fascinating testimony to the early optimism of the First Republic, and gives the whole of Hradec Králové a unique, expansive and prosperous atmosphere.

Hradec Králové spreads itself out on both banks of the Labe: on the left bank, the **staré město** (old town) sits on an oval rock between the Labe and the Orlice rivers; the **nové město** (new town) begins as soon as you leave the old town, straddling the river and then composing itself in fairly logical fashion between the river and the station to the west.

The staré město

In the eighteenth century, the **staré město** was entirely surrounded by zigzag redbrick fortifications (those at nearby Jaroměř can still be seen), though they've now been replaced by a modern ring road that keeps most of the traffic out of the old quarter. With most daily business being conducted over in the new town, a few shops and restaurants are all that remain to disturb Hradec Králové's two adjoining medieval

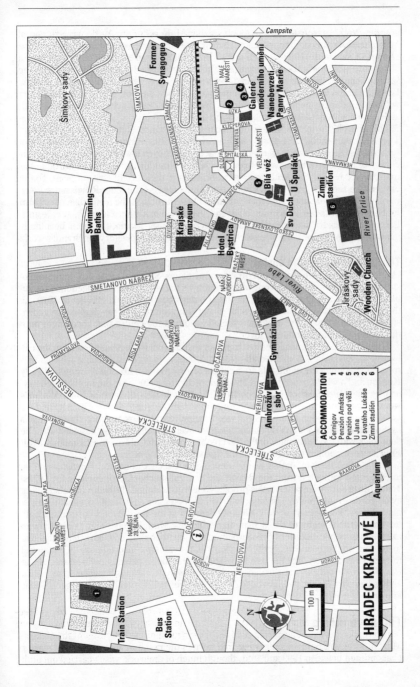

△ Campsite

Former Synagogue

Šimkovy sady

ŠIMKOVA

ČESKOSLOVENSKÉ ARMÁDY

DLOUHA

MALÉ NAMĚSTÍ

UZKÁ

Galerie moderního umění

Nanebevzetí Panny Marie

KLICPEROVA

TOMKOVA

VELKÉ NAMĚSTÍ

DLOUHA

ŠPITÁLSKÁ

Bilá věž

U Špuláků

KOMENSKÉHO

JANA

HRADEBNÍ

RADNICE

HERMANNA

River Orlice

sv Duch

Zimní stadión

Swimming Baths

Krajské muzeum

DUKSOVA

PALACKÉHO

Hotel Bystrica

PRAŽSKÝ MOST

ČESKOSLOVENSKÉ ARMÁDY

V KOPEČKU

River Labe

SMETANOVO NÁBŘEŽÍ

NAM. SVOBODY

TŘÍDA NÁBŘEŽÍ

Wooden Church

Jiráskovy sady

ŠKROUPOVA

PRŮMYSLOVÁ

ŠKROUPOVA

TŘÍDA KARLA IV

MASARYKOVO NAMĚSTÍ

GOČÁROVA

V LIPKÁCH

Gymnázium

WONKOVA

RESSLOVA

MÁNESOVA

ŠTROSSMAYEROVA

DIVÍŠKOVO NÁM.

NERUDOVA

Ambrožův sbor

STŘELECKÁ

DUKELSKÁ

STŘELECKÁ

BAAROVA

KARLA ČAPKA

HOŘICKÁ

BLAŽKOVO NAMĚSTÍ

NAMĚSTÍ 28. ŘÍJNA

GOČÁROVA

NERUDOVA

HOROVA

V LIPKÁCH

Aquarium

HRADEC KRÁLOVÉ

Train Station

Bus Station

N

0   100 m

squares, **Velké náměstí** and the much smaller **Malé náměstí**. At the western end of Velké náměstí, the skyline is punctuated by five towers. Two of them belong to the church of **sv Duch** (Holy Ghost), one of Bohemia's few great brick-built churches, a style more commonly associated with neighbouring Silesia. Jan Žižka, the blind Hussite warrior, died of the plague here in 1424, and was for a while buried in this church. Given its grand Gothic scale, though, the whitewashed interior, filled for the most part with neo-Gothic furnishings, is a letdown, despite Petr Brandl's *St Anthony* in the north aisle, and a superb stone tabernacle dating from 1497.

The church's twin towers are outreached by the once-white **Bílá věž** (April–Oct Tues–Sun 9am–noon & 1–5pm), built in the sixteenth century from the profits of Bohemian–Silesian trade, and *the* place to get a bird's-eye view of the town. Also in this corner of the square is the town **brewery**, invisible but for the terrace of Baroque former canons' houses that leads to its gate, bristling in their bright coats of paint. To the east, where the two sides of the square begin to converge, the older Renaissance houses on the north side have kept their arcades. Opposite stands the distinctive pink **Dům U Špuláků**, with its projecting oriel and copper dome, and, close by, the Jesuits' Baroque "barracks" and church of **Nanebevzetí Panny Marie**, the latter beautifully maintained, its trompe l'oeil altarpiece providing a suitable repository for Brandl's work.

The Galerie moderního umění

Hradec Králové's **Galerie moderního umění** (Tues–Sun 9am–noon & 1–6pm), opposite the Jesuit church, houses one of the country's finest permanent collections of twentieth-century Czech art. The building itself – designed by Osvald Polívka in 1910–12, the genius behind much of Prague's finest Art Nouveau structures – is also a treat: five storeys high, with a large oval glass-roofed atrium at the centre that sheds light onto the corridors and ground-level foyer.

The ground floor is given over to temporary exhibitions, while on the first floor, the collection of works by late-nineteenth-century artists is entirely in keeping with its surroundings. Among the highlights are a couple of lesser-known **Mucha** drawings, an early **Kupka**, and a whole series by **Jan Preisler**, including a study for the mural which now adorns the *Hotel Bystrica* (see opposite). The unexpected pleasure is **Josef Váchal's** work, in particular the mysterious *Satanic Invocation* (*Vzývaci ďabla*), which spills over onto its carved wooden frame. Several wood sculptures by **Bílek** and three bronze reliefs by **Sucharda** make for a fairly comprehensive overview of Czech Secessionist art. The floor ends with the beginnings of the Czech obsession with Cubism, most famously **Emil Filla's** own version of *Les Demoiselles d'Avignon*, *Salome's Dance*.

The second floor is almost wholly devoted to Czech Cubist and Fauvist painters, interspersed with a few from the Realist and Surrealist school, prominent in the 1920s. **Josef Šíma's** semi-surreal work is probably the most original (he was a member of the avant-garde group *Devětsil*), though only two canvases and a pen-and-ink sketch are displayed here. Postwar art up to 1968 is the subject of the third floor, interesting if only for the fact that many of the artists, like **Mikuláš Medek**, have only recently been exhibited in public galleries. The views from the top floor should be sufficient incentive to get you up there, and again there's plenty of previously censored post-1968 material to feast your eyes on, like the psychedelic *Přátelé*, though patently political works like *Red Wall* (*Červená zeď*) are the exception. Surrealism was always frowned upon, hence artists like **Jiří Kolář**, two of whose classic collages are shown here, are much better known in the West.

The nové město

Most of what you now see outside the old town is the result of an architectural master plan outlined between 1909 and 1911, though much of the work wasn't carried out until the 1920s. Building began on a grand scale with the **Krajské muzeum** (Tues–Sun 9am–noon & 1–5pm) on the leafy waterfront, designed by the father of the Czech modern movement, **Jan Kotěra**. With the rest of central Europe still under the hold of the Viennese Secession, Kotěra's museum, crowned with one of his characteristic domes, represents a shot across the bows of contemporary taste, finished in what was at the time an unconventional mixture of red-brick and concrete rendering. The entrance is guarded by two colossal sphynx-like janitors, but otherwise the ornamentation is low-key – as is the exhibition inside, a straightforward though attractive display of nineteenth- and twentieth-century arts and crafts, books and posters, plus a model of the town from 1865, showing the fortifications intact. The museum was closed for repairs at the time of writing, but should be reopened by the time you read this.

Close by, on the inner ring road, is another work by Kotěra, the *Hotel Bystrica* (originally called, simply, the *Grand Hotel*), built immediately after the museum. It's currently in such a desperate state it's difficult to see beyond the pollutant-caked rendering to appreciate the subtleties of the facade. If and when it ever reopens, head for the Art Nouveau restaurant – the fruit of an earlier work by Kotěra – adorned with murals by Jan Preisler and František Kysela's graceful stained-glass cranes. Kotěra is also responsible for the distinctive **Pražský most**, with its squat kiosks at either end and wrought-iron arch decorated with fairy lights.

Before crossing the river into Gočár's new town, there are a couple of minor attractions around the inner ring road. To the northeast is the town's **former synagogue** (now a library), a very handsome Art Nouveau edifice with an oddly oriental flavour to the lantern above the dome and the adjacent pagoda-style tower. To the southwest, the **Jiráskovy sady** occupy the slip of land at the confluence of the rivers Labe and Orlice and boast a colourful rose garden and a sixteenth-century **wooden Greek-Catholic church** (invariably closed) in the Lemk style, transported here from Sub-Carpathian Ruthenia in 1935. At the opposite end of the Labe embankment are some **swimming baths**, designed in the 1920s, with an artificial wave machine.

Gočár's new town

Kotěra died shortly after World War I, and it was left to one of his pupils, **Josef Gočár**, to complete the construction of the new town. Gočár had been among the foremost exponents of Czech Cubist architecture before the war, but, along with Pavel Janák, he changed tack in the 1920s and attempted to establish a specifically Czechoslovak style of architecture, which incorporated prewar Cubism. It was dubbed "Rondo-Cubism" because of its recurrent semicircular motifs, and though few projects got off the ground, elements of the style are reflected in the appealing homogeneity of the new town. On a sunny day, the light pastel shades of the buildings provide a cool and refreshing backdrop; bad weather brings out the brutalism that underlies much of Gočár's work.

This brutalism is most evident in his largest commission, the **Státní gymnázium** on the right bank, a sprawling series of buildings with an L-shaped, four-storey, red-brick structure, fronted by an atypically slender bronze nude by Jan Štursa. Up the side of the school, on V lipkách, is a later, still more uncompromising work, the Protestant **Ambrožův sbor**, built in functionalist style on a striking angular site. But by far Gočár's most successful set-piece is **Masarykovo náměstí**, which basks in the sun at the heart of the new town, shaped like a big slice of lemon sponge, with a pivotal statue of Masaryk back in its rightful place after a forty-year absence. Lastly, if you're travelling by train, be sure to admire the **train station**'s splendidly modernist design, again by Gočár, in particular the wonderfully slimline 1930s clock tower.

A short walk south of the new town lies Hradec Králové's newest attraction, its **aquarium** (*akvárium*; Tues–Sun 9am–6pm), at Baarova 10. Its centrepiece is a glass tunnel through which you can walk and view Amazonian fish, while a small reconstruction of a rainforest helps you forget briefly that you're in central Europe.

Practicalities

By **train** or **bus**, you arrive in the nové město; to reach the staré město, either take bus #5, #6, #11, #15 or #17, all of which plough down Gočárova, or take trolleybus #2, #3 or #7 and get off by the Krajské muzeum. Hradec Králové's **tourist office** (Jun–Aug Mon–Fri 8am–6pm, Sat & Sun 10am–5pm; Sept–April weekdays only), located near the stations at Gočarova 1225, provides maps and books. **Accommodation** can be hard to find, but there are four pensions on or about the two old town squares. On Velké náměstí, there's *U Jana* (☎049/25 25 28 61 or 551 23 55; ⑤) at no. 137, and *Penzión pod věži* (☎049/551 49 32; ⑤), right under the tower as its name states; both are acceptable, but a tad pricey for what you get. A touch better is *U svatého Lukáše*, just off the main square on Úzká (☎049/521 06 16; ⑥), or you can save your crowns at the more basic *Penzión Amátka* (☎049/551 49 35; ②), on Malé náměstí. Just outside the staré město, the *Hotel Stadión* (☎049/551 46 64; ③), by the ice hockey stadium on Komenského, is better than it looks from the outside. Otherwise, you can plump for the *Hotel Černigov* (☎049/581 41 11; ⑦), opposite the train station, a perfectly comfortable communist-era high-rise hotel. The *Stříbrný rybník* **campsite** (mid-June to Sept) is very popular in the height of summer, due to the adjacent lake; you can even rent **bicycles**. To get there, take bus #17.

A good number of **restaurants** in town dish up the usual plain but filling fare. Apart from those in the above pensions, of which *U svatého Lukáše* is the best, the *Černý kůň*, on Malé náměstí, has tables outside underneath the arcades and serves traditional food and Gambrinus beer. You can down beers and sausages for breakfast at *Na hradě* on Špitálská, which opens at 9am, or spend late nights at the Irish pub, *Buvol*, on V Kopečku, which serves up grilled meats and turns into a rock club after hours with live music. Finally, the *vinárna* at the *Hotel Černigov* (accessed down the broad steps along the side of the hotel) does surprising twists on the old theme, such as curried chicken, and is also surprisingly good value.

Around Hradec Králové

The flat expanse around Hradec Králové, known as the **Polabí**, is a fertile region whose hedgeless cornfields stretch for miles on end. It's pretty dreary to look at, baking hot in summer and covered in a misty drizzle most of the winter, but there are several places worth a day-trip or overnight stop within easy reaching distance of Hradec Králové by bus or train.

Třebechovice, Častolovice and Doudleby

TŘEBECHOVICE POD OREBEM, 11km east of Hradec Králové along route 11, is a nondescript town, famous only for its wood-carved Nativity scene or *Betlém*, housed in a purpose-built **museum** (Tues–Sun: May–Sept 9am–noon & 1–5pm; Oct–April closes 4pm). It all began in 1871, when local joiner Josef Probošt and his wood-carving friend, Josef Kapucián, set out to create the largest Nativity scene in the world. Only the death of Kapucián forty years later brought the project to an end, by which time the two men had carved 400 moving figures, many of them modelled on their friends and neighbours. And if you think that's kitsch, take a look at the museum's other room, which displays *Betlém* scenes in glass, pottery and paper.

Eighteen kilometres on is the Renaissance chateau of **Častolovice** (April–Oct Tues–Sun 9am–6pm), recently returned to the Šternberk family, who acquired it back in 1694. It's a pretty hybrid pile, right by route 11, with a huge English-style park stretching away to the north. The inner courtyard is particularly beautiful, and the tour takes you through the glorious Rytířský sál (Knights' Hall), with a Renaissance painted panel ceiling and portraits of various regional noblemen. If you're heading in this direction, you could continue another 6km to **Doudleby** (April–Oct Tues–Fri 8am–5pm, Sat & Sun 9am–5pm), a lovely little chateau, again right by route 11, but this time covered in intricate swirling sgraffito, not unlike the locally made lace displayed inside. Tours lead through predictably elaborate Baroque rooms, many with frescoes and paintings, including a satirical *Devil's Wedding*.

Jaroměř and Josefov

JAROMĚŘ, 36km northeast of Hradec Králové and accessible by train, is a pleasant town with a curving cobbled square, arcaded on one side and with one of its medieval gateways intact. The main attraction, though, is one of Gočár's early works, the **Wenke department store**, situated on route 33, the busy main road from Hradec Králové to the Polish border. In this exceedingly unpromising street (now called Husova), Gočár undertook one of the first self-conscious experiments in Cubist architecture in 1911. It's an imaginative, eclectic work, quite unlike the much plainer Cubism of Prague's Vyšehrad villas or the nearby spa of Bohdaneč, the plate-glass facade topped by a Neoclassical top floor and the monochrome, geometric interior still intact. Instead of selling goods, it now serves as the **Městské muzeum a galerie** (Mon–Fri 9am–4pm, Sat & Sun 9am–noon), its tiny art gallery upstairs displaying works by all three of Jaroměř's home-grown artists: the sculptors Otakar Španiel and Josef Wagner, and the *Devětsil* painter Josef Šíma, whose wilfully optimistic painting of Jaroměř is just one of a number of his works on show.

One kilometre south of Jaroměř, where the Labe and the Metuje rivers converge, is the fortress town of **JOSEFOV** (Josefstadt). In the 1780s the Habsburgs created three fortified towns along the northern border with their new enemy, Prussia: Hradec Králové (which has since lost its walls), Terezín and Josefov – the last two purpose-built from scratch and preserved as they were. Terezín was put to terrible use by the Nazis during World War II (see p.226), but Josefov remains the great white elephant of the empire, never having witnessed a single battle. Their mutual designs are unerringly similar: two fortresses (one large, one small), identikit eighteenth-century streets, and a grid plan whose monotony is broken only by the imposing **Empire Church** on the main square. Again like Terezín, Josefov is still a garrison town, though there aren't many soldiers left; the empty buildings have mostly been taken over by Romany families. Though not a great day out, it's worth taking a stroll along the thick zigzag trail of red-brick fortifications, now topped by beautiful tree-lined paths, with views across the wheat fields of the Polabí. If you're really keen, you can even visit the town's underground tunnel system; follow the signs to the **Podzemí** (April & Oct Sat & Sun 9am–noon & 1–4pm; May–Sept Tues–Sun 9am–noon & 1–5pm).

Kuks and around

Magnificently poised above a rustic village of timber-framed cottages, the great complex of Baroque spa buildings at **KUKS**, just 5km north of Jaroměř, on the banks of the Labe, was the creation of the enlightened Bohemian dilettante Count Franz Anton Graf von Sporck (Špork in Czech). Work began, largely according to Sporck's own designs, in the 1690s, after the discovery of a nearby mineral spring with healing properties. By 1730 he had created his own private **spa resort**, with a garden maze, a hospital, a concert hall (complete with its own orchestra) and a racecourse (surrounded by statues of dwarfs). For a while, Kuks' social life was on a par with the likes of Karlsbad; then, in 1738, the impresario died, and two years later, on December 22, 1740, disaster struck when the river broke its banks, destroying all the buildings on the left bank and, worse still, the springs themselves.

All that remains of the original spa is an overgrown monumental stairway leading nowhere, and, on the right bank, the hospital building fronted by **Matthias Bernhard Braun**'s famous terrace, now the chief reason for visiting Kuks. Sporck became the Tyrolean sculptor's chief patron in Bohemia, commissioning from him a series of **allegorical statues** intended to elevate the minds of his spa guests: to the west, the twelve *Vices* culminate in the grim *Angel of Grievous Death*; to the east, the twelve *Virtues* end with the *Angel of Blessed Death*. Over the years the elements have not been too kind to Braun's work, whose originals, including a few surviving dwarfs, have retreated inside the hospital building and now provide the highlight of the 45-minute guided tour (April & Oct Sat & Sun 9am–noon & 1–4pm; May–Aug Tues–Sun until 6pm; Sept Tues–Sun until 5pm). Also in the tour is the beautifully restored eighteenth-century pharmacy and Baroque chapel, though Sporck's subterranean mausoleum is no longer on show.

There's a good **restaurant** next to the zámek, ladling out big portions of meat and gravy, but there's nowhere to stay. **Buses** will either drop you at the main road, a short walk north of the village, or in the village itself; the train station lies to the south of the hospital building and formal gardens (follow the blue-marked path).

Betlém

One stop along the tracks, or a steep 5km walk along the blue-marked path, upriver from Kuks, is **Betlém** (Bethlehem), Braun's outdoor Nativity sculpture park, again sponsored by Sporck. It's an unlikely, ingenious location, deep in the midst of a silver birch wood, and used to include several working springs, including one that shot water high up into the foliage. However, centuries of neglect, pilfering and weathering have taken their toll, and what you see now are the few survivors of what would once have been a remarkable open-air *atelier* – exclusively the ones that Braun hacked out of various boulders he found strewn about the wood. In contrast to Kuks, the theme here is more explicitly religious, with the best-preserved sculptural groups depicting *The Journey of the Magi* and the *Nativity*. The dishevelled man crawling out of his cave, and looking very much like a 3-D representation of William Blake's *Fall of Man*, is in fact an obscure Egyptian hermit called Garinus.

The zoo at Dvůr Králové nad Labem

DVŮR KRÁLOVÉ NAD LABEM, 8km northwest of Kuks, is familiar to postwar generations of Czech kids as the site of the country's largest **zoo** (daily 9am–6pm or dusk). As underfunded Eastern European zoos go, Dvůr Králové has tried harder than most to make the animals' lives bearable, but a "safari park" it is not. The section of the zoo nearest the entrance is full of caged animals like any other zoo; all the usual beasts are here – lions, elephants, monkeys and so on – and there's a *dětský koutek* (kids' corner), where children can stroke the more domesticated animals. The "safari" bit consists of a free bus ride through a series of open enclosures, where there's a serious surfeit of antelopes. The safari bus sets off from the far side of the zoo – a long way to walk for smaller kids, so it's best to take the horse and cart or mini-train there.

Dvůr Králové **bus station** is on 17 listopadu; to get to the main square, walk north two blocks, then left down Švehlova. The **train station** is 2km southwest of the centre; a bus meets all trains and drops passengers in the centre, or you can walk down 5 května, which becomes 28 října before crossing the river, after which it's due north up Riegrova and Revoluční to the main square. The zoo is 1km west of the town, on Štefánikova, and is well signposted. The town itself has an arcaded main square, with a basic **pension** (☎0437/45 16; ①) and the excellent *Country Saloon* **restaurant**, whose name gives you an idea of the decor and occasional live music within.

Hořice

Just about every Czech sculptor over the last hundred years was trained at the School of Masonry and Sculpture founded in 1884 at **HOŘICE V PODKRKONOŠÍ**, 23km northwest of Hradec Králové. As a result, the town now boasts one of the country's richest collections of sculpture and plays host to an annual **international symposium of contemporary sculpture** in July and August.

There are sculptures all over town and exhibitions of contemporary works in the town museum (Tues–Sun 9am–noon & 1–5pm) on the main square, but the largest collection is in the **Galerie plastik** (Tues–Sun 9am–noon & 1–4pm), halfway up the sv Gothard hill to the east of town (five minutes' walk down Janderova). Half the gallery is given over to temporary exhibitions, but the permanent collection is still impressive. All the leading lights of Czech sculpture are represented here, even Šaloun, famous for his Jan Hus Monument in Prague, and Bílek, neither of whom actually studied here, as well as one of the few extant works by Otakar Švec, the man responsible for Prague's since-dynamited Stalin Monument. In the meadows and orchards to the north of the gallery is the **symposium area**, with previous years' exhibits out on show. To the east is the local **cemetery** (*hřbitov*), which has a wonderful triumphal arch over the entrance and a scattering of well-sculpted headstones. To the west, the **Smetanovy sady** are dotted with mostly nineteenth-century sculptures of leading figures of the Czech national revival.

Despite the town's enormous artistic treasures, it sees very few visitors, which means there's little in the way of **accommodation** beyond the run-down *Hotel Beránek* (☎0435/25 98; ①), just south of the main square on Husova. There are, however, no fewer than three **campsites** in the area – the nearest being the *U věže* site (mid-May to mid-Sept), 1km north of town on the road to Dvůr Králové. The **train station** (Hořice v Podkrkonoší) is 1km south of town down Husova (there's an occasional connecting bus).

Chlum

Nine kilometres northwest of Hradec Králové, the flat fields around **CHLUM** make an ideal **battleground**. And in 1866, the forces of the Prussian and Austro-Hungarian armies clashed here as part of a long-running disagreement over how to divide central Europe. Following the 1848 revolts against the Habsburgs, the Austro-Hungarian Empire found itself in a precarious position, with the Prussians gaining increasing power over Germanic matters. Both sides flexed their muscles in the spring and summer of 1866, with several skirmishes taking place across what is now eastern Bohemia. By late June, the Austrians had established a tenuous position around the tiny village of Chlum, but early in the morning of July 3, the Prussians attacked on the northern and western flanks, and by early afternoon had clearly gained the upper hand. At day's end, over 5500 Austrian soldiers and some 2100 Prussians lay dead, and what remained of the Habsburg army had begun its retreat. This marked a decisive defeat for Austria, as it lost yet more control over its German-speaking constituency. Its weakened status had no benefits for the Czechs either, as they remained second-class citizens to the Germans in an increasingly unstable Habsburg Empire.

Despite its rather important role in the downfall of the Habsburgs, Chlum is really only appealing for war buffs. The site of the battle is marked with a monument, a mass grave, a viewing tower over the fields and a small **museum** (April–Oct Tues–Sun 9am–noon & 1–5pm), which displays uniforms worn by some of the fallen as well as a thorough description, with dioramas, of the battle – but only in Czech and German. Two or three midday buses run to Chlum from Hradec Králové (the stop is marked Všestary, Chlum), but service is curtailed at weekends.

Chlumec nad Cidlinou

CHLUMEC NAD CIDLINOU, 29km west of Hradec Králové, in the middle of the featureless, dusty Polabí, was the scene of one of the largest peasant uprisings in the country in 1775, after which 3000 of those who had taken part were burned to death in a nearby farm. Just over fifty years before that bloody incident, Count Kinský built himself one of Bohemia's most exquisite provincial chateaux, **Karlova Koruna** (April & Oct Sat & Sun 9am–noon & 1–4pm; May–Aug Tues–Sun 8am–noon & 1–5pm; Sept Tues–Sun 9am–noon & 1–5pm). Begun in 1721 by Giovanni Santini, it stands on a rare patch of raised ground to the northwest of the town, south of the train station. Santini's ground plan is a simple but intriguing triple-winged affair, dominated by a central circular hall, with a two-storey-high pink-and-grey marble dome and a grand staircase leading to the upper balcony. Following the return of the property to the Kinskýs, the gardens have been tidied up and the hotel renovated, while the modest Baroque pleasure house displays copies of Braun's statuary.

Pardubice

There's always been a certain amount of rivalry between the two big cities of the Polabí, Hradec Králové and **PARDUBICE**, just under 20km to the south. On balance, Pardubice's historical core is probably more immediately appealing than Hradec Králové's, with a lovely newly renovated chateau, but its new town lacks the logic and cohesion of its neighbour, which makes the whole place feel a lot smaller. Throughout the horse-racing world, Pardubice is best known for its **steeplechase course** (second only to Liverpool's Aintree course for difficulty), where the *Velká Pardubická* (first run in 1874) takes place in early October, usually accompanied by protests by Czech animal rights activists.

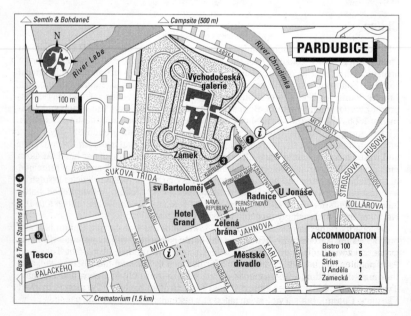

SEMTEX

Pardubice is the home of the most famous Czech export, **Semtex**. This plastic explosive became a firm favourite with the world's terrorists during the 1980s because of its ability to avoid electronic detection in customs halls and withstand rough handling. Approximately 1000 tonnes of the explosive is reckoned to have gone to Libya alone (and from there – it seems – into the hands of the IRA). It's still produced at the huge chemical complex in the village of Semtín (from which it gets its name), a few kilometres northwest of Pardubice – until recently the village was etched out of all maps due to the sensitive nature of its operations. Selling arms and explosives is not at all new to the Czechs, but it sits ill with the republic's new squeaky-clean image, and the company has pledged to tag all future exports of the explosive so that it can be easily spotted by airport x-ray machines. A local firm has since cashed in on the name by producing a high-energy soft drink.

The Town

The **train** and **bus stations** lie at the end of Palackého in the new town, a busy thoroughfare and the beginning of Pardubice's long parade of shops. It's a good ten-minute walk from here (or a short ride on trolleybus #2) northeast to the old town, much of it along **Míru**, a busy commercial street that contains an arresting threesome of late Secession buildings on the left-hand side, with U lva at the centre, distinguished by the two tiny lion heads on its gable.

Míru comes to an end at **náměstí Republiky**, which marks the transition from the new town to the old. At one end, the seriously striking Art Nouveau **Městské divadlo** (Town Theatre) is a deliberately Czech structure, designed by Antonín Balšánek (who collaborated with Polívka on Prague's Obecní dům), its magnificent facade flanked by multicoloured mosaics: Libuše founding Prague on one side and a blind Žižka leading the Hussites into battle on the other. The other truly arresting building on the square is the church of **sv Bartoloměj**, originally Gothic but more memorable for the Renaissance additions to its exterior – courtesy of local bigwigs, the Pernštejns – which makes up for its lack of a tower with a syringe-like central spike. Josef Gočár worked in Pardubice, as well as in Hradec Králové: the squat, grey Komerční banka and the *Hotel Grand* (currently undergoing complete restoration), opposite, are both his.

The soaring Gothic gateway, **Zelená brána** (May–Sept Tues–Sun 9am–noon & 1–5pm), with its twisted uppermost tower and wonderful baubled spikes, makes for a memorable entrance to the old town, and a good place from which to survey it. The main square, **Pernštýnovo náměstí**, is an intimate affair, an effect made all the more pronounced by the tall three-storey buildings on each side, handsome gabled sixteenth- and eighteenth-century houses for the most part, with the exception of the flamboyant neo-Renaissance **radnice**. The sculptural decoration throughout the old town is remarkable and at its most striking on U Jonáše, whose plasterwork includes an exuberant depiction of Jonah at the moment of digestion by the whale. A handful of picturesque backstreets spread north from here, with the buttressed beauty of Bartolomějská or the crumbling facades of Pernštýnská, both leading eventually to the romantic embankment, Wernerovo nábřeží, whose drooping willow trees provide a perfect spot of shade in summer.

At this point, you should head up Zámecká, and cross the vast dry moat to the newly restored **zámek** (Tues–Sun 10am–6pm), which is protected by an impressive series of walls, gates and barbicans, and occupies more space than the entire staré město. The chateau's sgraffitoed appearance and its beautiful loggia in the main courtyard date from the sixteenth century when it became the chief seat of the powerful Pernštejn family. The latter were also responsible for the chateau's precious Renaissance wall paintings, which have been partially preserved in the **Rytířské sály** on the first floor. There are trompe l'oeil doorframes and decorative motifs, plus two very large pictures: the first is of Moses being given the Ten Commandments, while the second (and best preserved) one features Delilah cutting the hair of the sleeping Samson, while a phalanx of Philistines arrives hotfoot. You can see the frescoes – as well as the tiny arms collection and the local museum, which are also housed in the chateau – without a guided tour; just make sure you buy the useful English information leaflets when you purchase your ticket.

On the other side of the outer courtyard is the **Východočeské galerie** (Tues–Sun 10am–5pm), which puts on temporary exhibitions on the ground floor, and contains a small collection of modern Czech art on the first floor. The gallery owns works by all the major Czech artists of the last century, from Čapek to Medek, but only a few pieces stick out: in particular Kamil Lhoták's realist canvases from the 1940s and 1950s, the giant (cracked) *Human Egg* by Eva Kmentová, and a great little pair of papier-mâché wellingtons called *Homage to Jules Verne* by Jiří Kolář.

Practicalities

You could easily come to Pardubice on a day-trip from Hradec Králové (it's only 30min away by train), though there are at least a pair of reasonable **hotels** in the old town. *Bistro 100* (☎040/51 11 79; ④) has a fine location on Kostelní, while the *Hotel U anděla* (☎040/51 40 28; ④) on Zámecká is similarly well kept. You could also splash out in the apartments at the very plush *Zámecká* opposite (☎040/51 81 11; ⑨). These are recommended over the communist-era *Labe* (☎040/51 81 11; ⑦), by the Tesco department store, despite its good location. At the other end, both geographically and aesthetically, the *Sirius* (☎040/51 15 48; ②) rises above the train station and is only recommended if you're pinching pennies. Otherwise, the town's *Cihelna* **campsite** (June to mid-Oct) is just north of the river up K cihelně.

There's a very pleasant chilled-out *čajovna* on Wernerovo nábřeží, and a good little *vinárna* named *Bazalka,* across the way, which does great salads. You'll also find several **restaurants** on the old town square: *U bílého koníčka* (closed Sun), which boasts a garden out the back and a *vinárna* (closed Mon) and disco that stays open until late; *U černého orla*, which serves up the local brew; and *Pizzeria U dušičků*. Note that accommodation is impossible to find over the weekend of the *Velká Pardubická* in early October. Less prestigious **horse races** take place every other weekend at Pardubice's **steeplechase course** (*závodiště*), which is 2km out of town; take bus #4 or #14. Pardubice's **tourist office** (Mon–Fri 9am–7pm) is located at Míru 60.

Chrudim and Ležáky

Twelve kilometres south of Pardubice, the pretty little town of **CHRUDIM** springs into life in early July for its annual **Puppet Festival**. At other times of the year, it's still

---

JANÁK'S CREMATORIUM AND GOČÁR'S SPA

A traditional handicraft and metal-working town, at the turn of this century Nancy became a centre of **Art Nouveau** to rival Paris, the most illustrious exponent of the "School of Nancy" being the manufacturer of glass and ceramics, Émile Gallé. The town's moment of glory was short-lived, however, and all that now remains are a handful of buildings and, best of all, the Musée de l'École de Nancy, housed in a turn-of-the-century villa. For a post-museum coffee in the same kind of atmosphere, try the Art Nouveau café-restaurant of the former hotel *L'Excelsior*, opposite the train station, built in 1910 and preserved virtually intact to this day.

worth the short train ride to visit the marvellous **Puppet Museum** (Muzeum loutkář ských kultur; April–Sept daily 9–11am & 1–5pm; Oct–March Mon–Fri 9am–noon & 1–5pm, Sat & Sun 1–5pm), housed in the splendid sixteenth-century Mydlářovský dům on Břetislavova, just off the main square. The Czech Lands have a long tradition of pup- petry, going back to the country's peasant roots, and the museum acts as a repository for marionettes and puppets donated from all over the world.

Southeast of Chrudim off route 37, in a quiet, shady glen, is a memorial to the village of **Ležáky**. On June 24, 1942, the village was destroyed by Nazi SS soldiers, who round- ed up all the village's men from their jobs in surrounding rock quarries, forced the women and children from their homes, and then shot everyone. The motive for Ležáky's destruction was the same as for Lidice's (see p.148): Hitler wanted revenge for the assassination of Reinhard Heydrich, Nazi leader of the Protectorate of Bohemia and Moravia. Exactly two weeks after Lidice was wiped out, Ležáky suffered the same fate. Today the foundation stones of the houses, which were all burned down, are all that remain of the village, and these have been carefully rearranged and topped with memo- rial stones. The main difference between Ležáky and Lidice, though, is that no new town was built here: the road simply passes through, with signs to mark the bound- aries. A **museum** (May–Sept Tues–Sun 9am–5pm) displays photographs of the town after the destruction, as well as of each of the 56 victims. There are no buses to Ležáky, only a few daily ones from Chrudim to Miřetice, 2km to the west.

Litomyšl and around

For a small town in the northern reaches of the Bohemian-Moravian Uplands, **LITO- MYŠL** (Leitomischl) has big ideas. In 1992, a School for Restoration and Conservation was founded here and immediately set to work restoring the Portmoneum, a house dec- orated with fantastical murals and furniture by Josef Váchal, which opened the follow- ing year. Soon after the town pulled off an even more amazing coup by getting seven presidents of central Europe – including Václav Havel, Lech Walesa and Richard von Weizsäcker – to meet here for a summit. The prime mover behind these dramatic devel- opments is the town's mayor, Miroslav Brýdl, who, along with his brothers, Jiří (mayor of neighbouring Svitavy) and Tomáš (who runs a local advertising agency), is deter- mined to put Litomyšl on the map.

The Town

The town's picturesque main square, **Smetanovo náměstí**, is strung out like a juicy fat Czech sausage and lined with almost uninterrupted arcades, a pastel parade of Baroque and Neoclassical facades, all pristinely repainted in preparation for the presidents' visit. The sixteenth-century **U rytířů**, at no. 110 (Tues–Sun 10am–noon & 1–5pm), is the finest of the lot, decorated with medieval knights and merchants holding bags of money, clinging mischievously to their carved columns; the building now hosts art exhibitions, worth checking out if only to admire the coffered Renaissance ceiling inside. The town's most famous son is the composer **Bedřich Smetana**, who was born here in 1824, hence Jan Štursa's effete statue of the composer at the northwest corner of the main square. Every year in his honour, the town puts on a ten-day **internation- al opera festival**, *Smetanova Litomyšl*, towards the end of June. Smetana is not the only Czech aesthete to stroll the streets of Lytomyšl, though: nationalist writers Božena Němcová and Alois Jirásek also lived here for short times, as plaques on their homes on the square recall.

To the northeast of the main square, a knot of ramshackle backstreets, punctuated by churches, leads up to the town's most celebrated monument, the Pernštejns' **zámek**

(April & Oct Sat & Sun 9am–noon & 1–4pm; May–Aug Tues–Sun 8am–noon & 1–5pm; Sept Tues–Sun 9am–noon & 1–4pm), a smart, sgraffitoed affair that bursts into frivolous gables and finials on its roof and which boasts one of Bohemia's finest triple-decker loggias inside. It used to house a fascinating exhibition of old musical instruments, now replaced by porcelain and period furniture, but it retains its remarkable late-eighteenth-century theatre (where the young Smetana made his debut as a pianist), along with much of the original scenery painted by Josef Platzer. If you don't fancy a guided tour, head instead for the former riding school, which now houses the **Muzeum antického sochařství a architecktury** (May–Oct Tues–Sun 9am–noon & 1–5pm), a bizarre collection of plaster and bronze casts of Greek and Roman classical statues from museums around the world.

The inspiration for the chateau's original musical exhibition came from the adjacent brewery, where Smetana, one of eighteen children of an upwardly mobile brewery manager, was born. The building now houses the **Rodný byt Smetany** (times as for zámek), a modest memorial museum to the composer. Smetana was a veritable *Wunderkind*, playing in a string quartet at the age of five and composing his first symphony at eight, but a year before that, the family moved to Jindřichův Hradec. Catalysed by the events of 1848, Smetana became a leading figure in the Czech national revival (despite German being his mother tongue), helping to found Prague's Národní divadlo. In 1874, he had to resign as the theatre's chief conductor after becoming deaf through a syphilitic infection. He went on to promote the nationalist cause through works like *Má vlast* ("My Country"), a symphonic poem inspired by Czech legends, but sadly ended his days in a mental asylum.

A short walk southeast of the chateau, at Terézy Novákové 75, is without doubt Litomyšl's most extraordinary and unique artistic treasure, the **Portmoneum** (May–Sept Tues–Sun 9am–noon & 1–5pm), painstakingly restored and opened in 1993. From the outside, it looks like any other provincial town house, but inside, the walls, ceilings and furniture of two rooms are decorated with the strange and wonderful work of the self-taught artist **Josef Váchal** (1884–1969), from the early 1920s. Váchal's ghoulish art is difficult to categorize (though "weird" would be the simplest shorthand): the ceiling in one room is a whirlwind of devils, spirits and sinful creatures; elsewhere there are cherubs, Kupkaesque celestial orbs of light, quotations from Hindu religious poems and a Crucifixion, while Váchal himself appears at one point as a rat-catcher. The man who wanted his house decorated with such disturbing murals was **Josef Portman** (after whom the house is named), a civil servant, amateur printer and lifelong collector of Váchal's art, who died here in 1968.

Practicalities

Buses are probably the easiest way to get to Litomyšl, since the town lies on a little-used branch line from Chocheň. The **bus station** is on Mařákova, five minutes' walk southeast of the centre, a pleasant stroll along (and across) the River Loučná; the **train station** is five minutes' walk west of the old town, again along (and across) the river. As befits a town with ambition, there's an efficient **tourist office** (Mon–Fri 9am–7pm, Sat 9am–4pm, Sun 10am–3pm) on the south side of the main square at no. 72, which can help with **accommodation**. The upmarket *Zlatá hvězda* on the main square (☎0464/23 38; ⑤), where Havel stayed, is the town's finest hotel, or there's the clean modern pension *Petra* on B. Němcové (☎0464/20 95; ③). The *Primátor* **campsite** (May–Sept) is 2km northeast of the town centre on route 358 to Ústí nad Orlicí. For **food**, *Pod klážterem*, on the quiet square by the Piarist church, serves traditional fare and Kozel beer, either in its ancient cellar, or, in fine weather, on tables outside, and the *Hotel Zlatá Hvězda* also has an excellent restaurant.

SCHINDLER'S SVITAVY

When Spielberg's Holocaust film, *Schindler's List*, reached the Czech Republic in 1994, it was premièred in **Svitavy** (Zwittau), a small Moravian town 20km southeast of Litomyšl. The simple reason for this was that the "hero" of the film, Nazi industrialist **Oskar Schindler**, was born here in 1908, son of an insurance salesman, at Iglauerstrasse (now Poličská) 24. In Svitavy, he was known as a hard-drinking womanizer who was expelled from school for falsifying his school report and some years later arrested in the *Hotel Ungar*, on the town's main square, for supplying the German *Abwehr* with information.

Schindler became a member of the Nazi Party early on and, during the war, he used his Party contacts to establish a kitchenware factory in Kraków, using Jewish slave labour. It was here that Schindler began to shelter Jews, hiring them even though they were too sick or weak to work, in order to save them from certain death in the nearby camps. In 1943, he took 900 Jewish workers with him and set up an armaments factory in Brněnec, a town 15km south of Svitavy. In fact, Schindler made sure that not a single weapon was actually produced at the factory and by the end of the war he had saved 1200 Jews from deportation. He died in 1974 in Hildesheim in Germany, though his remains were transferred to Israel as a mark of gratitude.

The majority of Svitavy's population (most of whom were German-speaking) were expelled after the war, and only a few of the older inhabitants can remember Schindler from his Svitavy days. The film therefore came as something of a revelation to many of Svitavy's residents, who had previously been told only the Communists' postwar version of events: ie that Schindler was simply the Nazi chief of the local concentration camp. Despite the release of the film, the town council still had to overcome fierce local opposition in order to erect a memorial plaque – in Czech and German – in the park opposite Schindler's birthplace. The plaque was eventually unveiled by the republic's chief rabbi shortly after the film's première.

Polička

The Bohemian-Moravian Uplands are clearly a musically fertile region: Mahler spent his childhood in Jihlava (see p.310), while the town of **POLIČKA**, 18km south of Litomyšl, produced **Bohuslav Martinů**, who was born in 1890 at the top of the 75-metre-tall fairy-tale neo-Gothic tower of the church of **sv Jakub**, just west of the main square. The composer's father – a cobbler by trade – was also the local watchman, and the single room, in which the family of five lived until 1902, has to be one of the most memorable memorials to any composer. To climb the tower, you must first buy a ticket from the local **museum** (Tues–Sun 9am–5pm), on Tylova, north off the main square, where you can see an exhibition and watch a video on Martinů's life. Despite spending much of his life in exile, Martinů always carried a postcard of the view from the tower, and twenty years after his death in a Swiss hospital in 1959, he was finally buried in the town cemetery, within sight of the tower.

Apart from the composer, there's little other reason for coming to Polička, which lost its aesthetic charms in a devastating fire in 1845, though the town's beautifully preserved fortifications are pretty impressive (and clearly visible from the tower). If you need to while away an hour, the radnice on the main square has a good exhibition on the history of art in Polička. The **train station** is north of the town, off route 359 to Litomyšl, but only connects with Svitavy and Česká Třebová, not Litomyšl. The best place to stay in town is the pretty blue *Penzion U purkmistra* (☎0463/72 23 10; ③), on Riegrova near the church of sv Jakub; alternatively there's a **campsite** (May–Sept), 1.5km south of the town off route 360 to Nové Město na Moravě.

Svojanov

In addition to being one of the prettiest castles in the charming Bohemian-Moravian Uplands, **SVOJANOV** (April & Oct Sat & Sun 9am–noon & 1–4pm; May–Sept Tues–Sun 9am–5pm), 15km southeast of Polička, has an impressive position atop a granite protuberance. It's a small place, and each stage of its many constructions is clearly visible, from a thirteenth-century guard tower through to the Empire-style ornamentation of the interior halls. A guided tour takes you through the usual collection of paintings and glassware, along with an exceptional array of old clocks. If you're here in mid-July, you can also go to the annual **puppet festival** , where some of the country's leading artisans put on displays and shows of the craft particular to this region. There's a hostel right in the castle (☎0463/918 24; ①), and the *Penzión Pála* (☎0463/918 27; ①), down at the base of the rock, which also has a nice **restaurant**. Svojanov is served by fairly regular buses from Polička on weekdays, though at the weekend there's only one a day, which continues on to Brno.

travel details

Trains

Prague to: Jičín (2 daily; 1hr 50min); Pardubice (1–2 hourly; 1hr 10min–2hr 20min); Trutnov (1 daily; 4hr); Turnov (11 daily; 2hr–2hr 40min).

Hradec Králové to: Častolovice/Doudleby nad Orlicí (5–6 daily; 50min/1hr 10min); Chlum (up to 5 daily; 20–30min); Chlumec nad Cidlinou (13 daily; 20–40min); Dvůr Králové (9 daily; 40min–1hr); Hořice (12 daily; 30–50min); Jaroměř (hourly; 20–30min); Kuks (6 daily; 40min); Pardubice (1–2 hourly; 30min); Třebechovice pod Orebem (10–15 daily; 15min).

Náchod to: Nové Město nad Metují/Opočno (10–14 daily; 15min/20–30min); Teplice nad Metují (9–12 daily; 40min).

Trutnov to: Adršpach/Teplice nad Metují (7–8 daily; 1hr/1hr 15min); Česká Skalice/Jaroměř (10–14 daily; 1hr/1hr 15min); Kunčice nad Labem (10–12 daily; 30min); Chlumec nad Cidlinou (6–8 daily; 1hr–2hr 40min).

Turnov to: Hradec Králové (12 daily; 1hr 50min–3hr); Jičín (10 daily; 50min–1hr 10min); Železný Brod (8 daily; 20min).

Buses

Connections with Prague: Harrachov (up to 5 daily; 3hr); Jičín (up to 12 daily; 2hr); Litomyšl (up to 6 daily; 3hr 30min); Náchod (up to 6 daily; 3hr); Pec pod Sněžkou (up to 9 daily; 3hr); Trutnov (up to 15 daily; 2hr 45min); Vrchlabí (up to 8 daily; 2hr 30min).

Hradec Králové to: Jaroměř (hourly; 25min); Kuks (up to 10 daily; 30–40min); Litomyšl (5 or more daily; 1hr 10min); Náchod (up to 6 daily; 1hr); Nové Město nad Metují (up to 4 daily; 1hr 20min); Pec pod Sněžkou (up to 4 daily; 2hr); Trutnov (up to 9 daily; 1hr 10min).

CHAPTER SIX

SOUTH MORAVIA

At first sight, the landscape of **South Moravia** (Jižní Morava) appears little different from that of much of Bohemia, with rolling hills, dense forests and cultivation. Only as you move south towards Vienna does the land become noticeably more plump and fertile, with the orchards and vineyards continuing into Austria itself. **Brno** is the most obvious starting point: an engaging city, whose attractions are often underrated due to its heavy industrial base and conspicuous peripheral housing estates. Brno is also within easy reaching distance of a host of sights, most notably Moravia's karst region, the Moravský kras, which boasts the country's most spectacular **limestone caves**. South of Brno a whole string of pretty villages, towns and chateaux punctuate the **River Dyje** as it meanders along the Austrian border.

By contrast, the **Bohemian-Moravian Uplands** or Vysočina, which separate Bohemia and Moravia, are poor and sparsely populated, viewed by most travellers only from the window of their bus, train or car en route to Brno. If you do stop off in the Vysočina – and parts of it are definitely worth visiting – make sure you go further than **Jihlava**, the area's most convenient starting point. To the south, **Telč** and **Slavonice** are arguably the country's most perfect architectural set-pieces, and even if you're not a devotee of Santini's Baroque-Gothic confections, the pilgrimage church at **Žďár nad Sázavou** is something special.

To the east of Brno, the landscape around the River Morava is visually pretty uninspiring, but the wine and rich rural heritage are good reasons for stopping here. To the south, the area known as **Slovácko** hosts the country's two largest **folk festivals**, in Vlčnov and Strážnice. Further north, the provincial treasure house and graceful gardens of **Kroměříž** provide a fascinating contrast with the modernist aesthetics of **Zlín**, where the multinational Baťa shoe empire has its roots.

Transport is fairly good throughout Moravia, though the **train system** is not quite as comprehensive as that of Bohemia, petering out in the Vysočina and degenerating into a series of overcomplex branch lines along the more industrialized River Morava. In such instances, **buses** are invariably quicker and more direct.

ACCOMMODATION PRICE CODES

All accommodation in this guide is graded according to the price bands listed below. Prices are for the cheapest **double room** available during high season, which usually means without private bath or shower in the less expensive places. For a **single room**, cxpcct to pay around two thirds the price of a double.

① Under 500Kč   ④ 1000–1250Kč   ⑦ 1750–2000Kč
② 500–750Kč   ⑤ 1250–1500Kč   ⑧ 2000–2500Kč
③ 750–1000Kč   ⑥ 1500–1750Kč   ⑨ 2500Kč and upwards

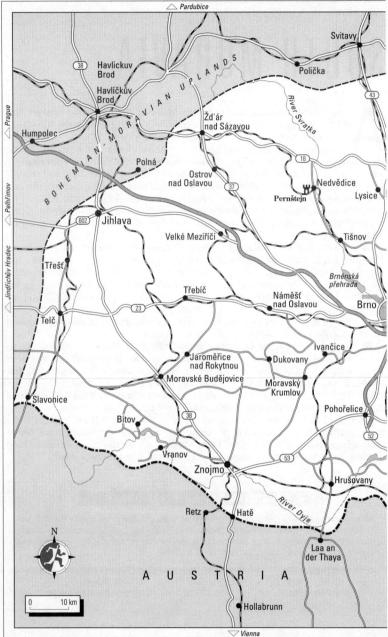

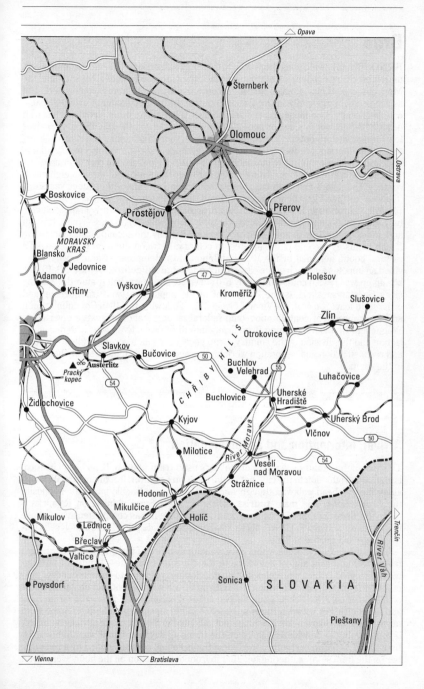

△ Opava

Šternbek

Olomouc

△ Ostrava

Boskovice

Prostějov

Přerov

Sloup
MORAVSKÝ
KRAS

Blansko
Jedovnice

Adamov
Křtiny

Vyškov

47

Holešov

Kroměříž

Slušovice

Zlín

49

Otrokovice

Slavkov
Bučovice

50

CHŘIBY HILLS

Buchlov
Velehrad

55

Luhačovice

▲ Austerlitz
*Pracký
kopec*

54

Buchlovice

Uherské
Hradiště

Židlochovice

Uherský Brod

50

Kyjov

Vlčnov

River Moravou

Milotice

Veselí
nad Moravou

54

Hodonín

Strážnice

△ Trenčín

Mikulov

Mikulčice

Holíč

River Váh

Lednice

Břeclav

Valtice

Poysdorf

Sonica

S L O V A K I A

Piešťany

▽ Vienna   ▽ Bratislava

Brno

BRNO (Brünn) "welcomes the visitor with new constructions", as one communist-era tourist brochure euphemistically put it. In fact, the high-rise *paneláky* that surround the Moravian capital play a major part in discouraging travellers from stopping here. But as the second largest city in the Czech Republic, with a population of over 400,000, a couple of really good museums and art galleries, a handful of other sights and a fair bit of nightlife, it's worth a day or two of anyone's time. As yet, though, the city receives few foreign visitors outside the annual trade fairs, though of course this has its advantages, too: tourists are welcomed here with genuine interest, and the pace of life is endearingly (some might say infuriatingly) provincial, compared to that of Prague.

Brno was a late developer, being no bigger than Olomouc until the late eighteenth century. The town's first cloth factory was founded in 1766, and within fifteen years was followed by another twenty, earning Brno the nickname of *rakouský Manchestr* (Austrian Manchester). With the building of an engineering plant early in the next century, the city began to attract Czech workers, along with Austrian, German, English and, in particular, Jewish entrepreneurs, making it easily the second largest city in the Czech Lands by the end of the nineteenth century. Between the wars Brno enjoyed a cultural boom, heralded by the 1928 Exhibition of Contemporary Culture, which provided an impetus for much of the city's **functionalist architecture**. Of the city's 10,000-strong prewar Jewish community, only 670 survived, and immediately after the war, the city's German-speakers (some 25 percent of the population) were rounded up and ordered to leave, on foot, for Vienna (see p.301). Following the 1948 Communist coup and the subsequent centralization (and federalization), state funds were diverted to Prague and Bratislava, pushing Brno firmly into third place. Even now, with decentralization and the division of the country, Brno plays very much second fiddle to Prague, and reconstruction and restoration work have progressed much more slowly here than in the capital.

> The Brno area telephone code is ☎05

Arrival, information and accommodation

The turn-of-the-century splendour of the city's main **train station**, Brno hlavní nádraží, is a great introduction to the city; not so the main **bus station**, five minutes' walk south along the overhead walkway, though some buses arrive at the old bus station opposite the *Grand Hotel*. The main **tourist office** is in the Stará radnice, on Radnická 8 (Mon–Fri 8am–6pm, Sat & Sun 9am–5pm), though it's not as comprehensive as those in Prague or Bratislava. There's also a smaller office inside the station, which sells various maps and guides to Brno.

Most of Brno's sights are within easy walking distance of the train station, although **trams** will take you almost anywhere in the city within minutes. Brno has, unfortunately, adopted Prague's complex system of ticketing: you need to buy either a 5Kč ticket for two zones (2 *pásma*), which will last you fifteen minutes without changing trams or buses, or an 11Kč ticket, again for two zones (2 *pásma*), which is valid for an hour and allow changes between trams or buses. Tickets must be bought beforehand from news kiosks or yellow ticket machines and validated in the electronic devices on board; if you're going to be whizzing about on the trams all day, you might want to buy a 24-hour *denní jízdenka*, currently 50Kč. Some trams run all night (signified by a red number on the tram stop), gathering together in front of the station on the hour, every hour.

The same tickets are valid for the city's **buses** and **trolleybuses**, which congregate at Moravské náměstí and Mendlovo náměstí, though you're unlikely to need to use them unless you're staying right out in suburbia.

Accommodation

Finding **accommodation** in Brno is relatively easy, though prices are fairly high thanks to the expense-account business people who come here for the various trade fairs (when prices can double). Taxatour Brno, the 24-hour agency in the train station, can arrange cheap **private rooms**, as can the tourist office in Radnická (see opposite); the latter also books hotels, though most of the ones on their books are out of the centre.

There are several **campsites** along the shores of the Brněnská přehrada (Brno Dam), 10km northwest of the city centre; the nearest one is *Radka* (June–Aug), on the east bank by the Sokolské swimming pool, and also near the HI-affiliated hostel, *Hotel Přehrada* (☎46 21 01 67). To get to the dam, take tram #1, #3 or #11. Alternatively, there's the *Bobrava* site, by the motorway 10km south of Brno at Modřice (open all year), which is a 1.5km walk from Popovice train station.

HOTELS AND PENSIONS

Amphone, třída kpt. Jaroše 29 (☎45 21 17 83; *amphone@brn.czn.cz*). A really good choice: clean, plain and positioned on a lovely tree-lined boulevard, just ten minutes' walk from the city centre. ⑤.

Avion, Česká 20 (☎42 21 50 16). Bohuslav Fuchs' slimline functionalist hotel, minus the original fittings; central location and some cheap doubles without showers. ④.

Grand Hotel, Benešova 18–20 (☎42 32 12 87). The Art Nouveau mural on the facade is sadly no indication of the interior, which retains no original features whatsoever. Nevertheless, this is the best of the city's luxury hotels, with doubles from 3600Kč upwards. ⑨.

Pegas, Jakubská 4 (☎42 21 01 04). Small but nicely decorated rooms located right in the old town above the micro-brewery/pub of the same name. ⑥.

Pyramida, Zahradnická 19 (☎43 23 23 47). Plainly modernized hotel a couple of tram stops southwest of the old town. ⑤.

Slavia, Solniční 15–17 (☎42 32 12 49). Communist-era hotel that's actually pretty comfortable, very central and competitively priced. ⑦.

Slovan, Lidická 23 (☎41 32 12 07; *slovan@brno.elnet.cz*). Another comfortable and unpretentious communist-era hotel, just a step away from the Janáčkovo divadlo. ⑥.

U Jakuba, Jakubské náměstí 6 (☎42 21 07 95). Unmodernized for the most part, but right in the heart of the old town. Not a good choice for insomniacs, however, with the incessant church bells and nearby disco at weekends; ask for a room at the back. ⑥.

U královny Elišky, Mendlovo náměstí 1a (☎43 21 68 98). Small vaulted rooms in a cosy pension tucked behind the church in the grounds of the Augustinian monastery, slightly out of the centre. ③.

The City

One of the nicest things about Brno is that its historical centre is compact and almost entirely traffic-free. The city's main action goes on within the small egg-shaped old town, pedestrianized for the most part and encircled by a swathe of parks and the inner ring road. Around **Zelný trh** and **náměstí Svobody** you'll find most of the city's shops and markets. In the southwestern corner raised above the old town are the quieter streets around Petrov, the lesser of Brno's two hills, topped by the **katedrála**. Further west, the squat fortress of **Špilberk** looks down on the old town to the east and Staré Brno to the south, site of the original early medieval settlement. Worth a visit, but still further from the centre, are Brno's modern architectural sights: the exhibition grounds of **Výstaviště** and – on the opposite side of town – Mies van der Rohe's **Vila Tugendhat**.

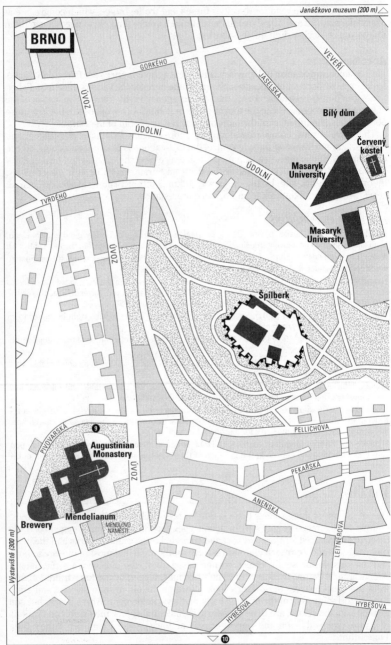

BRNO

Janáčkovo muzeum (200 m)

VEVEŘÍ

GORKÉHO

JASELSKÁ

ÚVOZ

ÚDOLNÍ

ÚDOLNÍ

Bílý dům

Červený kostel

Masaryk University

TVRDÉHO

ÚVOZ

Masaryk University

Špilberk

PELLICHOVA

PIVOVARSKÁ

9

Augustinian Monastery

ÚVOZ

PEKAŘSKÁ

ANENSKÁ

Mendelianum

MENDLOVO NÁMĚSTÍ

Brewery

LEITNEROVA

Výstaviště (300 m)

HYBEŠOVA

HYBEŠOVA

10

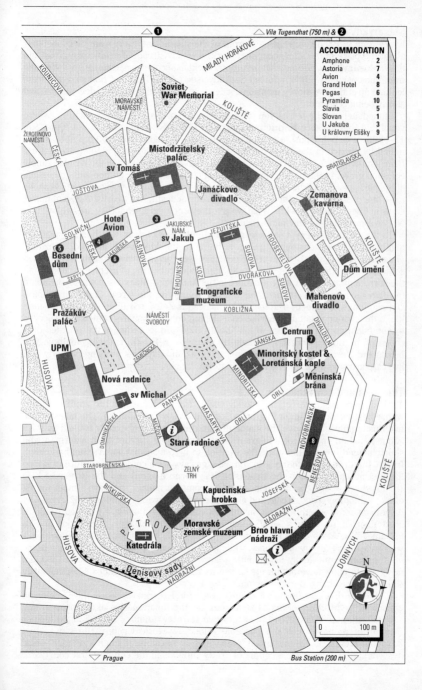

① △ Vila Tugendhat (750 m) & ②

MILADY HORÁKOVÉ

KOUNICOVA

MORAVSKÉ
NÁMĚSTÍ

Soviet
War Memorial

KOLIŠTĚ

ŽEROTÍNOVO
NÁMĚSTÍ

ČESKÁ

BRATISLAVSKÁ

ACCOMMODATION

Amphone	2
Astoria	7
Avion	4
Grand Hotel	8
Pegas	6
Pyramida	10
Slavia	5
Slovan	1
U Jakuba	3
U královny Elišky	9

Místodržitelský
palác

sv Tomáš

JOŠTOVA

Janáčkovo
divadlo

Zemanova
kavárna

Hotel
Avion

③ JAKUBSKÉ
NÁM.

sv Jakub

JEZUITSKÁ

SOLNIČNÍ

ČESKÁ

RAŠÍNOVA

SUKOVA

ROOSEVELTOVA

KOLIŠTĚ

⑤
Besedni
dům

LAKUBSKÁ

④

⑥

SKRYTÁ

BĚHOUNSKÁ

KOZÍ

DVOŘÁKOVA

SUKOVA

Dům umění

Etnografické
muzeum

Mahenovo
divadlo

KOBLIŽNÁ

Pražákův
palác

NÁMĚSTÍ
SVOBODY

Centrum
⑦

DIVADELNÍ

JÁNSKÁ

UPM

ZÁMEČNICKÁ

Minoritský kostel &
Loretánská kaple

MINORITSKÁ

Měnínská
brána

HUSOVA

Nová radnice

sv Michal

PANSKÁ

MASARYKOVA

ORLÍ

ORLÍ

NOVOBRANSKÁ

DOMINIKÁNSKÁ

MEČOVÁ

ⓘ
Stará radnice

STAROBRNĚNSKÁ

ZELNÝ
TRH

⑧

KOLIŠTĚ

BISKUPSKÁ

Kapucínská
hrobka

JOSEFSKÁ

BENEŠOVA

P E T R O V

Moravské
zemské muzeum

NÁDRAŽNÍ

Brno hlavní
nádraží

DORNYCH

HUSOVA

Katedrála

Denisovy sady

NÁDRAŽNÍ

✉
ⓘ

N

0   100 m

▽ Prague

Bus Station (200 m) ▽

Masarykova and Zelný trh

Every tram in Brno congregates in front of the station, and there's an infectious buzz about the place in the afternoon, after work. A steady stream of people plough up and down **Masarykova**, a somewhat hazardous cocktail of cobbles, steaming manholes and tram lines, which leads to náměstí Svobody (see p.288). Don't let that stop you from looking up at the five-storey mansions, laden with a fantastic mantle of decorations, and slowly being restored.

Immediately to the left as you head up Masarykova is Kapucínské náměstí, where you'll find the macabre **Kapucínská hrobka** (Tues–Sat 9am–noon & 2–4.30pm, Sun 11–11.45am & 2–4.30pm), a gruesome collection of dead monks and top nobs, mummified by chance in the crypt of the Capuchin church. Until the eighteenth century, Brno's moneyed classes forked out large sums to be buried here in the monks' simple common grave, in the hope of finding a short cut to heaven – righteousness by association, perhaps. The bodies lie fully clothed, some with the hollow expressions of skeletons, others still frozen in the last painful grimace of death. Just to drive the point home, signs in Czech chime in with "What we are, they once were, what they are, we will be." Not an experience for the faint-hearted.

To the west of the crypt steps lead up to the Biskupský dvůr, which, along with the neighbouring Dietrichsteinský palác, is home to the **Moravské zemské muzeum** (Tues–Sat 9am–5pm). Brno is at the centre of quite an extensive area of early human settlement, and the museum contains an impressive collection of prehistoric finds from the surrounding region (there are more in the Anthropos annexe, see p.292), including the famous *Venus of Věstonice*, plus a large section on the Great Moravian Empire. Opening out to the north of Kapucínské náměstí is **Zelný trh** (literally "cabbage market"), the chaotic vegetable market on a sloping cobbled square, somewhat ill-served by the mishmash of buildings which line its edges. At its centre is the petrified diarrhoea of the huge *Parnassus* fountain by Fischer von Erlach, featuring mythological beasts and Hercules himself: now, as in the good old days, it's working properly, and live carp are sold from its waters at Christmas.

The stará and nová radnice

Tucked down a side street, but clearly visible from Zelný trh, is the **stará radnice**, whose best feature is Anton Pilgram's Gothic doorway on Radnická. The tallest of the five thistly pinnacles above the statue of Blind Justice is deliberately twisted as if it's about to fall on your head – Pilgram's testament to the corrupt town aldermen who shortchanged him for his work (he went on to help furnish Vienna's Stephansdom). Inside, the town hall's courtyards and passageways are a confusing mixture of styles, the first of which contain the Brněnský drak (Brno dragon) and the Brněnské kolo (Brno wheel) – see the box opposite. The complex houses the town's main tourist office, exhibition space, a café and an **observation tower** (vyhlídková věž; April–Oct daily 9am–5pm), worth a climb for the panorama across the city's red-tiled rooftops. Next door at no. 6 is a small **akvárium** (Tues–Fri 9.30am–5.30pm, Sat & Sun 9.30am–4pm). At no. 5, **U zlaté koruny** (Mon–Fri 8.30am–6pm, Sat 8am–noon) is a well-preserved Baroque pharmacy, while no. 10 currently provides a temporary home for the **Panorama** (daily 9am–5pm), a large wooden stereoscope built in 1890 and designed to allow several viewers to see its three-dimensional slides simultaneously (the slides are changed every fortnight or so).

Round the back of the stará radnice, the cobbled square below the Dominican church of **sv Michal** serves as a car park for the functionaries of the present city council who hold office at the adjacent **nová radnice**, founded in 1935 in the former Dominican monastery. It's a passable effort by Mořic Grimm, the city's chief Baroque architect, "a provincial talent but a sound craftsman", as one critic described him. There are a couple of pretty sundials in the echoing first courtyard,

THE BRNO MASCOTS

Countless local legends surround the **Brněnský drak** (literally "Brno dragon", though in fact it's a stuffed alligator), which hangs from the ceiling of the town hall entrance. The standard version is that the marauding beast was tricked into eating a carcass stuffed full of lime, upon which it rushed down to the River Svratka and drank so much it burst. The most likely origin of the creature is that it was a gift from the Turkish sultan to Archduke Matthias, who in turn bequeathed it to Brno in an attempt to ingratiate himself with the local aristocrats.

The other town mascot displayed here is the **Brněnské kolo** (Brno wheel), made in 1636 by a cartwright from Lednice, who bet a friend that he could fell a tree, make a wheel and roll it to Brno (some 50km away), all before sunset. He won the bet and the wheel has been given pride of place in the stará radnice ever since, though the story goes that following his great feat people began to suspect that the cartwright was in league with the devil: his business fell off and he died in poverty.

and a modern fountain from the 1928 Exhibition in the second courtyard, but otherwise nothing much to get too excited about unless someone's getting married. The handful of cobbled streets that lead south from here to Petrov hill are the nearest Brno gets to a secluded, intimate spot: walk up Dominikanská from the cobbled square, and take a quick look inside the **Dům pánů z Kunštátu**, one of Brno's few Renaissance buildings.

Petrov

Continue up Biskupská to **Petrov**, the smaller of the city's two central hills and one of the best places in which to make a quick escape from the choked streets below. At the top of the hill stands the **Katedrála** of sv Petr and Pavel, whose needle-sharp Gothic spires dominate the skyline for miles around. Close up, the crude nineteenth-century rebuilding has made it a lukewarm affair, but it holds a special place in Brno's history for having been instrumental in saving the town from the Swedes during the Thirty Years' War. After months besieging the town during the course of 1645, the Swedish general Tortennson decided to make one last attempt at taking the place, declaring he would give up at midday if the town hadn't surrendered. In a fit of inspiration, the bell-ringer, seeing that the town was on the brink of defeat, decided to ring the midday bells an hour early. The Swedes gave up their attack, the city was saved, and as a reward the Habsburg emperor switched the Moravian capital from Olomouc to Brno (well, so the story goes). The clock strikes twelve at 11am to this day. Inside the lofty nave, there's a valuable fourteenth-century *Madonna and Child*, but the most intriguing art treasures are the aluminium *Stations of the Cross*, by Jiří Marek. Constructed in the early 1960s, these get progressively more outrageous and abstract as the story unfolds, until the final relief is no more than flailing limbs and anguished metal.

The cathedral is not the only reason to climb Petrov: from the nearby **Denisovy sady**, tucked into the city ramparts, there's a far-reaching view over the great plain south to Vienna, and an interesting angle on the cathedral itself. In among the trees, a slender white obelisk commemorates the end of the Napoleonic Wars (the Battle of Austerlitz took place just outside Brno – see p.299), lining up perfectly with the avenue of Husova which leads to the red-brick Protestant church, known as the **Červený kostel** (Red Church), and, beyond it, the bright white former Party headquarters, known affectionately as the **Bílý dům** (White House). When this was at the planning stages in the 1950s, the more committed cadres wanted to remove the offending Protestant church, which blocked the view up Husova. Fortunately, aestheticism triumphed over atheism and the plan was somehow foiled.

PLAGUE COLUMNS

The **plague column** (*morový sloup*) is a frequent feature of Catholic towns and cities across Central Europe. When the plague struck a city, as it did frequently right up until the eighteenth century, the locals would gather at the column and pray for deliverance. The plague columns you see today date from the Baroque period, when the columns took on an extra religious and political significance. The image of the Virgin Mary praying for the sins of the world, surrounded by twelve stars, became a popular and distinctively Catholic image. Many columns, like the one in Brno, were in fact erected in 1648, in thanks for the town's liberation from the Protestant "plague", in this case the unsuccessful Swedish (Protestant) siege of the city. In the Czech Lands, the columns came to be regarded by Czech nationalists as symbols of the Austro-Hungarian hegemony, and a number were torn down during the celebrations following the foundation of the Czechoslovak Republic in 1918, including the one which used to grace Prague's old town square.

Náměstí Svobody

Back down on Masarykova, follow the flow north and you'll end up at **náměstí Svobody**, the city's main square and focus of the November 1989 demonstrations for Brno's citizens. Compared with other squares across the country, Brno's is a second-division affair; nonetheless it's the place where most of Brno comes to meet up, chat and shop. In summer, you can sit and drink coffee in the shadow of the square's gilded plague column (see box above) and admire the square's finer buildings, which together span almost four centuries. The earliest is the **Schwarzův palác** (just out of view if you're actually sitting by the plague column), with an ornate Renaissance facade decorated with late-nineteenth-century sgraffito, all in desparate need of renovation. A few doors along, at no. 15, the **Kleinův palác** was designed around 1848 in neo-

JANÁČEK IN BRNO

Although he was born in Hukvaldy, in northern Moravia, **Leoš Janáček** moved to Brno at the age of eleven and spent most of his life here, first as a chorister and then teacher and choirmaster at the local Augustinian monastery. Battling against the prejudices of the German-speaking town administration, he managed to drag Czech music out of the pubs and into the concert hall, eventually founding the Brno Conservatoire and Organ School in 1882. All but one of his operas were premièred in Brno, and as a composer he remained virtually unknown outside Moravia until well into his sixties, when he began the last and most prolific creative period of his life (for more on his life and works, see p.349). For much of this century, Janáček has been overshadowed by his compatriots, Smetana (whom the Communists were particularly keen on) and Dvořák (whom the Western world has always revered), but recently his music has become increasingly popular, with works such as *The Cunning Little Vixen* enjoying international acclaim.

Across the park from the opera house named after him, at the junction of Kounicova and Smetanova, there's the fairly dull **Janáčkovo muzeum** (Mon–Fri 8am–noon & 1–4pm) in the cottage where he lived at the back of the Organ School. Unlike his predecessors, Smetana and Dvořák, Janáček chose not to be buried in Prague's illustrious Vyšehrad cemetery, opting instead for Brno's municipal one. If you're on the Janáček trail, bus #62 from the train station terminates at the main entrance off Jihlavská; or else tram #2, #5, #6 or #8 will take you to within walking distance – the cemetery is easy enough to spot thanks to the bright white pinnacles of Arnošt Wiesner's strikingly modern crematorium, designed in 1930.

Renaissance style by Theophil Hansen, the Danish architect responsible for some of the finest buildings on Vienna's Ringstrasse; the Klein family owned a nearby ironworks, hence the elegant wrought-iron oriel windows held up with miniature Atlantes. Opposite, and totally lacking in such subtlety, is **Dům u čtyř mamlasů**, belonging to another of Brno's richest nineteenth-century Jewish industrialists, whose four muscle-bound employees (nicknamed the "four stupid boys") struggle to hold up both his building and their loincloths. And in the northwest corner of the square, Bohuslav Fuchs' functionalist **Moravská banka** (now simply the Komerční banka) has turned a rather nasty green since its inception in the 1930s.

Heading north from náměstí Svobody, a steady stream of people flows past the concentration of book and record shops, pubs and cafés on **Česká**, wolfing down takeaways and *zmrzlina* on the way and, at the top, waiting for the trams and buses that congregate on Joštova, which marks the end of the old town. On the northeast corner of the square is the **Etnografické muzeum** (Tues–Sat 9am–5pm), which contains a large permanent collection of Moravian folk costumes, ceramics, painted Easter eggs and an album of old photos, as well as occasionally hosting exhibitions on ethnographic themes from other countries.

East of náměstí Svobody

The finest architectural work in Brno by the Grimm brothers (there really were two of them) is the **Minoritský kostel** on the corner of Minoritská and Jánská, whose vivacious frontage makes the most of its cramped site. The right-hand portal leads to the main gilded nave, whose renovated interior is much the best Baroque in town, high to the point of giddiness, an effect that's intensified by the false perspectives of the frescoes. Linked to the church next door by double doors in the north aisle is an equally stunning chapel, with a steep altar staircase that must be ascended on bended knee, and full-size colour terracotta statues of Jesus and the two robbers looking down from the gallery above. The greater part of the church is taken up with a **Loretanská kaple** (Loreto Chapel), its outer walls smothered in grisaille depictions of the miracle; the atmospheric red-brick interior holds the standard *Black Madonna and Child* set against a rich marble backdrop.

At the bottom of Jánská, the department store **Centrum**, built in 1928 by the shoe magnate Tomás Baťa, still cuts a bold figure. It was originally intended to be 28 storeys high (rather than its current seven), which would have made it the tallest building in Europe at the time, but not surprisingly the local council refused planning permission. Beyond lies one of Brno's finest late-nineteenth-century buildings, the **Mahenovo divadlo**, a forthright structure exuding the municipal confidence of its original German patrons with its Corinthian columns and pediment. Its insides are smothered in gold sculpturing and glittering chandeliers, and it had the distinction of being the first theatre in the Austro-Hungarian Empire to be fitted with electric light bulbs. In total contrast to the flamboyant Mahenovo is Bohuslav Fuchs' squat functionalist **Dům umění** (art gallery; Tues–Sun 10am–6pm), which puts on some of the city's most innovative art exhibitions, theatre performances, and even the occasional gig. A little further up Rooseveltova from the Mahenovo is the grey and fairly unappealing **Janáčkovo divadlo**, built in the 1960s as the city's – indeed the country's – largest opera house.

Moravská galerie: UPM, Pražákův palác and Místodržitelský palác

On Husova, which forms the western limit of the old town, you'll find the **UPM** (closed for reconstruction), one of the best collections of modern applied art in the country, which forms part of the Moravská galerie. The building itself is a neo-Renaissance pile built as a museum in the 1880s by one of Brno's many wealthy Jewish industrialists. The richly decorated ground and first floors (and the garden) are used for consistently good temporary exhibitions of anything from avant-garde photomontages to the work of the local art school. The gallery's permanent applied arts collection is located on the top floor, and ranges from the Gothic period to the present day. German and Austrian craftsmanship predominates, as it did for much of Brno's history, but there are works from all over Europe. The section from the Art Nouveau period onwards is particularly interesting in terms of the development of Czech applied arts. A curving Gaillard sideboard stands alongside a standing *bufet* by Brno's own Jan Kotěra, and Pavel Janák's Cubist ceramics and Josef Gočár's angular furniture are just some of the specifically Czech highlights. Also on display are the few surviving pieces of original furniture from Mies van der Rohe's Vila Tugendhat (see p.292). Finally, there is a whole room of 1960s and 1970s gear, which will appeal to lovers of kitsch.

Further up Husova is the **Pražákův palác** (Wed & Fri–Sun 10am–6pm, Thurs 10am–7pm), another sturdy nineteenth-century edifice, designed by Theophil Hansen and now housing the Moravská galerie's excellent permanent collection of twentieth-century Czech art on its first and second floors. To go through the collection chronologically, you need to start on the second floor with the sculptures by Bílek, Štursa and Gutfreund, some early Cubist works by Kubišta and Procházka, plus later pieces by Josef Čapek and Šíma. The first floor features postwar Czech art, which until recently was gathering dust in the gallery vaults: Surrealist artists like Janousek and Matal, and the likes of Mikuláš Medek, were considered ideologically unsound by the Communists.

The third building belonging to the Moravská galerie is the **Místodržitelský palác** (times as above), the former residence of the governor of Moravia, originally built as an Augustinian monastery at the eastern end of Joštova. Under the Communists it served as the old museum of the working class, but it now hosts temporary exhibitions put on by the Moravská galerie, plus a small permanent collection that includes a smattering of Gothic works, a few minor Baroque works by fresco specialists Kremser Schmidt, Maultbertsch and Daniel Gran, and some sentimental Biedermeier paintings. The final room contains the palace's only truly memorable works: a portrait of a woman by Hans Makart, painted with his characteristically dark, chocolate-brown palette, and Max Švabinský's striking *Red Sunshade*.

Špilberk

Skulking on a thickly wooded hill to the west of Husova and barely visible through the trees, the ugly, squat fortress of **Špilberk** (Spielberg) acquired a reputation as one of the most god-awful prisons in the Habsburg Empire. As you walk up through the castle grounds, a monument featuring a wolf suckling Romulus and Remus commemorates the many Italians who died here, having been incarcerated fighting for their country's freedom in the northern regions – then under Austrian rule – of what is now Italy. The testimony of one Italian inmate, the poet Count Silvio Pellico, so shocked the empire's middle classes that the prison was closed down in 1855. In 1880, it was opened up to the public as a tourist attraction by the local military commander, Costa-Rosetti, who installed a model torture chamber and wrote the guide himself, recounting and embellishing myths and legends associated with the place. Sixty years later, it was put back into use by the Nazis who confined, tortured and killed countless prisoners during the war.

There are now two entrances to the fortress, the first of which, on the east side, leads to the atmospheric **kasematy** or dungeons (Tues–Sun 9am–5pm). The most chilling section is the reconstructions of the so-called "dark cells" in the north wing, installed by the great reforming emperor Josef II, who first turned the barracks into a prison. In these, prisoners were chained by the neck and hands in complete darkness and given only bread and water – a practice eventually stopped by Josef II's successor, Leopold II. Silvio Pellico and his contemporaries were actually incarcerated in the upper storey of the fortress, in – as it were – the best cells. Before you set off round the dungeons, make sure you pick up a leaflet with a plan, since the place is a veritable labyrinth.

The entrance on the far, west side of the fortress leads to the exhibition rooms of the **Muzeum města Brna** (Museum of the City of Brno), which is best taken at a canter. Temporary exhibitions take place on the ground floor, along with a permanent display on the history of the prison (plus a few torture instruments and diagrams for good luck), and an *anglický text* in each room to help you decipher the exhibits. Unfortunately, non-Czech speakers get no such help upstairs in the section on the general history of Brno. On the second floor, Baroque statues and sixteenth-century votive paintings from the church of sv Jakub, paid for by rich local burghers and painted by Dutch masters, hang alongside a decent collection of eighteenth- and nineteenth-century portraits of rich local townsfolk. There's also a modest selection of works from the first half of the last century, including a good spread of works by Antonín Procházka, from his Cubist *Girl with Garland* to the loose brushwork of *Bathing Horses* from the 1940s. Also worthy of note are Jaroslav Král's Cubist paintings, such as his portrait of Cubist architect Emil Králík; František Foltýn's pastel-shaded abstract works; and the minimalist egg cups and glasses designed by Bohuslav Fuchs.

But by far the most interesting part of the museum is the section on Brno's **interwar architecture**, a long overdue tribute to the city's modern golden age. The work of Bohuslav Fuchs occupies centre stage and rightly so as he was without doubt the most successful of the city's functionalist architects (see next page). There's a good section on the Nový dům colony (see next page), and the original plans for the (unrealized) Centrum skyscraper. For the most part, it's an exhibition of photos and architectural drawings, but there are a couple of pieces of original furniture by the likes of Adolf Loos, Alvar Aalto and Mies van der Rohe.

Mendlovo náměstí and Výstaviště

The area south of the Špilberk hill, where the first settlements sprang up in the early Middle Ages, is known as Staré Brno. Few traces of these survive and nowadays there's nothing particularly old or interesting about this part of town, with the exception of the fourteenth-century **Augustinian monastery** on **Mendlovo náměstí**. Despite its unpromising locale – the square is little more than a glorified bus terminal – the monastery church is one of Brno's finest Gothic buildings, its pillars and walls smothered in delicate geometric patterning; sadly, though, it's only usually open for services. If you do get inside, be sure to take a look at the church's *Black Madonna* icon at the high altar, which dates from the thirteenth century and which, it was believed, protected the city from foreign troops.

The monastery is best known for one of its monks, **Gregor Mendel** (1822–84), whose experiments in the abbey gardens with peas and bees eventually led to the discovery of the principles of heredity and, subsequently, genetics. Despite the publication of several seminal papers outlining his discoveries, his work was ignored by the scientific establishment and in 1868 he gave up his research to become the monastery's abbot. Only after his death was he acknowledged as one of the greats of modern biology, and now several rooms in the western wing of the monastery have been given over to the **Mendelianum** (Mon–Fri 8am–5pm). In addition, the Augustinian library, Mendel's beehives and the garden he used for his experiments are all now open to the public.

To the southwest of the city centre, where the River Svratka opens up to the plain (tram #1 or #18 from the station), is the **Výstaviště** (exhibition ground). The main buildings were laid out in 1928 for the city's Exhibition of Contemporary Culture, and most of the leading Czech architects of the day were involved in the scheme, which prompted a flurry of functionalist building projects across the city's burgeoning suburbs. The most arresting (and largest) building on the site, the circular crystal-and-con-

FUCHS AND FUNCTIONALISM

Although Brno produced two great modern architects in Adolf Loos and Jan Kotěra, they spent most of their time in Vienna and Prague respectively, and it was left to another Moravian, **Bohuslav Fuchs**, who began working here in 1923, to shape the face of modern Brno. Fuchs and his functionalist cohorts turned their hand to everything from the town's crematorium to the Protestant church on Botanická, its interior decoration as "low-church" and prosaic as you can get. Fuchs' own hand is everywhere in the city, in the low-slung post office extension to the main train station, in the now gloomy arcade off Jánská, in the slimline *Hotel Avion*, and in Výstaviště itself. His most famous works are the open-plan boarding school and Vesna girls' school (on Lipová, just north of Výstaviště), two simple four-storey functionalist buildings, way ahead of their time at the time, but already gone to seed in the intervening years. Perhaps the best way to appreciate Fuchs' work is to head out to the outdoor swimming pool he built in the city's eastern suburbs, just off Zábrdovická (tram #2 or #7 down Cejl), where you can laze by the pool and take in the culture at the same time.

crete **Z pavilion**, is actually one of the postwar additions, but one which kept to the spirit of the original concept. The only building which predates the complex is the **Zámeček**, which features an interior by Brno-born arch-minimalist Adolf Loos. Even if you've no interest in modern architecture, the various fairs and exhibitions staged here between March and November are the largest in the country, and often interesting in their own right. Once the showpieces of socialism, they're now more an opportunity for foreign companies to tout their wares.

The part of the 1928 exhibition which really caused a sensation was the **Nový dům** settlement, worth a look if you're keen on Bauhaus-style architecture. Inspired by the *Weissenhofsiedlung* built a year earlier in Stuttgart, Bohuslav Fuchs and various others designed a series of boxy, white, concrete villas by the woods of the Wilsonův les, north of Výstaviště, up Kamenomlýnská (tram #18 from Výstaviště), in the streets of Drnovická and Petřvaldská. The brief for each architect was to create modest two-storey houses for middle-income families, using standard fittings and ordinary materials to keep the unit cost down. They are now grey, peeling and overrun by vegetation, and it takes a leap of imagination to appreciate the shock of the new that these buildings must have aroused at the time.

There are two other sights worth visiting, close, but entirely unrelated, to Výstaviště. The first, visible from the main trade ground entrance, is a Louis XIV summer palace, **Letohrádek Mitrovských**, an unusual sight in this part of the world. Napoleon stayed here the night before the Battle of Austerlitz (see p.299), while his opposite number, the Russian general Kutuzov, stayed in the Dietrichsteinský palác on Zelný trh. Nowadays, the palace serves as a temporary exhibition space. On the opposite side of Výstaviště, over the River Svitava, is **Anthropos** (April–Nov Tues–Sun 8.30am–5pm), an annexe of the Moravian Museum, which concentrates on Ice Age geology and fauna, including remains of mammoths, Neanderthals and early *Homo sapiens*. As well as fossil bones and replicas of prehistoric cave paintings, the museum contains numerous paintings by Zdeněk Burian, a Czech painter who specializes in scientifically authentic illustrations of Stone Age life.

Vila Tugendhat

On the opposite side of town, in the northeastern suburb of Černá Pole, modernist guru Mies van der Rohe built the **Vila Tugendhat** (Wed–Sun 10am–6pm) in the same functionalist style as the above-mentioned Nový dům settlement, but to a very different brief: the Tugendhats, an exceptionally rich Jewish family who ran a number of the city's textile factories, wanted a state-of-the-art house kitted out in the most expensive gear money could buy. It was completed in 1930, but the family had barely eight years to enjoy the luxury of the place before fleeing to South America (with most of the period furniture) in the wake of the Nazi invasion. For the next fifty years it was put to many uses – both the Nazis and Communists were particularly partial to it for exclusive social functions – but it is now possible again for the public to gain access to the place. Access is still unpredictable, so it's worth checking at the tourist office in the stará radnice before setting out. You enter through the top floor, but the main living space is actually downstairs, open-plan for the most part and originally decked out in minimalist monochrome furnishings (a few surviving pieces are on show in the UPM) offset by colourful Persian carpets. The Communists' "modernization" after the war was depressingly thorough, and the huge unbroken front window, which looked out over the garden and the whole cityscape beyond it, has been replaced by a series of much smaller panes, being all the Communists' glassworks could muster. The house is at Černopolní 45, off Merhautova, itself a continuation of M. Horákové; take tram #3, #5 or #11 three stops east from Joštova, and then walk north three blocks up Černopolní.

Eating, drinking and entertainment

There's no shortage of good places **to eat and drink** in Brno, but equally, there's nothing like the choice of cuisines available now in Prague. Brno also has nowhere near the same volume of American expats, so prices are uniformly low, and the clientele predominantly Czech. As for **nightlife**, lovers of classical music and opera are well catered for, with two big opera houses/theatres, a philharmonic orchestra, and numerous smaller venues. With a large contingent of students, the city usually has something a bit less formal going on, particularly during term time. One word of warning, however: Brno (including most of its shops, and even some of its pubs and restaurants) tends to close down for the weekend at around noon Saturday, so if you want to experience city life to the full, come on a weekday.

Eating and drinking

For **Vietnamese fast food** head for one of the branches of the *Asijské bistro*, such as the one by the staré radnice. If you need provisions, the daily **vegetable market** in Zelný trh is worth a visit. The Terra Nostra bakery and *cukrárna* on Česká is also excellent, and there's another branch on Květinářská. The choice of sit-down **restaurants** has improved in the last year or so. For simple, traditional **Czech food**, the pubs listed below are likely to be the cheapest; the restaurants, while offering much the same food, are likely to be a bit pricier and a lot more formal. And before you leave the city, be sure to check out the decor of the late-nineteenth-century *restaurace* at the station (not the station's snack bar).

Hotel Slavia, Solniční 15–17. Experience Czech cuisine as it was under the Communists in the excellent hotel restaurant. Daily noon–11pm.

El Greco, Merhautova 98; tram #3, #5 or #11. An excellent Greek restaurant run by a guy called Kostas, who doesn't hold back on the garlic, does a great Greek salad and serves real retsina. Daily noon–midnight.

Haribol, Lužánecká 4. Sit-down Hare Krishna restaurant, off Lidická, with a cheap fixed menu of veggie slop. Mon–Fri 10.30am–5pm.

Italia bar, Zamečnická. Cake-and-coffee place which also serves excellent thin-base Italian pizzas, *gelati* and real cappuccino. Daily 8.30am–11pm.

Spirala, Lidická. Clean, bright and pleasant veggie restaurant just beyond Lužánky, that serves some very unusual and interesting dishes (take a dictionary). Daily 11am–11pm.

U starého Billa, náměstí 28 října. Friendly basement Czech-Mex place off M. Horákové, which serves up serious steaks. Mon–Thurs 11am–11pm, Fri 11am–midnight, Sat noon–midnight & Sun noon–11pm.

U **královny Elišky**, Mendlovo náměstí 1a. A good cellar *vinárna* tucked into the hillside behind the Augustinian monastery, with live music and the whole Moravian caboodle. Tues–Sat 7pm–3am.

Cafés

Brno is better for pubs than **cafés**, though of course you can get a coffee in either. During the summer, outdoor tables abound at the various cafés around náměstí Svobody and Zelný trh.

Adria, Josefská. A wood-panelled, high-ceilinged café with coffee, cakes and pizzas, run by Yugoslavs but very much in the Viennese tradition. Daily 7am–midnight.

Café Blau, Jakubské náměstí. Designer café, decked out in (you guessed it) blue, and something of a media hang-out due to its location in the same building as Czech TV's Brno studios. Mon–Fri 8am–10pm, Sat 11am–10pm, Sun 2–10pm.

Fischer Café, Masarykova. Continuing the city's tradition for minimalism, this is a stylish designer café in a prime location. Daily 10am–11pm.

Kabinet múz, Sukova 4–6. Closed during theatre performances, but a nice place to hang out for a before- or after-show drink.

Poslední leč, Jakubské náměstí 5. The ultimate late-night drinking hole, attached to the Divadlo Bolka Polívky. Open until 3am.

Zemanova kavárna, off Jezuitská. Brno's newest café is an exact replica of Fuchs' functionalist café of 1923, which was torn down by the Communists in order to build the Janáčkovo divadlo; now pristine white with red trimmings, it stands in the park to the southeast of the theatre. Mon–Fri & Sun 9am–11pm, Sat 9am–midnight.

Pubs and bars

Starobrno is the local brew, though according to many the best pubs are those that don't serve it. Brno has its fair share of traditional old boozers, now joined by numerous trendy pubs for the city's young urban professionals.

Mescalito, Starobrněnská 3. Grotto-like basement bar that packs in a posey crowd, who like to shout over the loud house/dance or live music. Mon–Thurs noon–3am, Fri & Sat until 4am.

Pegas, Jakubská 4. If there are any foreigners in town, guaranteed they'll be drinking here – and fair enough, for this is a large and very pleasant pub which brews its own light and dark beer on the premises. Daily 9am–midnight.

Pivovarská, Mendlovo náměstí. The true Starobrno experience: a rough-and-ready drinkers' pub right by the brewery itself. Daily 8am–10pm.

Skleněná louka, Kounicova 23. Great barrel-vaulted cellar bar by Brno's *Moulin Rouge*, that has occasional live music, and, above it, the city's best Internet café. Mon–Fri 11am–1am, Sat & Sun 4pm–1am.

Špalíček, Zelný trh. Overlooking the vegetable market, with tables outside in summer and lashings of Starobrno. Daily 11am–11pm.

Traubova, Traubova. Dark, Gothic den, off M. Horákové, thick with smoke and filled to the cobwebs with the free-thinking youth of Brno.

U Ječmínka, Kapucinské náměstí 8. Huge city-centre cellar beer hall located south of Zelný trh, serving traditional Czech food and beer. Mon–Sat 11am–11pm.

U dvou kozlů, Jostova 1. New decor and a youngish crowd hang out at this big, smoky, beery pub serving *Velkopopovický kozel* in the pea-green building opposite the church of sv Tomáš. Mon–Sat 9am–6am, Sun 9am–midnight.

U tří knížat, Minoritská 2. Unpretentious central drinking hole serving the local brew underneath renovated Gothic vaults. Daily 10am–10pm.

Entertainment and nightlife

Ballet, opera and orchestral concerts are the most accessible of the **classical arts** for those without any Czech, and the Mahenovo and Janáčkovo divadlo, both off Rooseveltova, along with the Besední dům, share the load. It's true that the best Moravian singers are eventually lost to Prague, but they make their reputations here as much as anywhere, and productions are usually competent, if a little conservative. There's a lively fringe theatre scene, but unless you understand Czech or chance upon a particularly physical, visual show, the language is going to be an insurmountable barrier. Two places that are worth checking out are Kabinet múz, Sukova 4–6, home base for the fringe company HaDivadlo, and CED, the centre for experimental theatre group Divadlo na provázku, in Dům pánů z Fanalu on Zelný trh, both of which put on a variety of events and gigs. Divaldo Bolka Polívky, Jakubské náměstí 5, features mainly kids' shows, mime and "black theatre". Tickets for most shows can be bought in advance from the **box office** at Dvořákova 11 (Mon–Fri 9am–5.30pm, Sat 9am–noon), or from the venue itself, half an hour before the performance starts. A good listings pamphlet for the city is the monthly *Kam v Brně*.

There aren't that many **clubs** in Brno, so check out the monthly posters dotted round town. One of the most reliable **live venues** is *Mersey*, Minská 15 (tram #3, #11, #12, #13 from Joštova up Veveří), with gigs more or less every night beginning at around 9pm; another less frequent venue is *Semilasso*, Palackého 126 (tram #1, #6 or #7 from Moravské náměstí up Lidická). Other possibilities include *Klub alterna*, in the ground floor of a grim student hostel at Kounicova 48 (term-time only), and *Studio Boleslava Polívky*, a new jazz club on Šelepova; for either, take tram #12 or #13 from Joštova, Klusáčkova stop.

There's an excellent **art-house cinema**, Kino Art, at Cihlářská 19; walk a short distance up Lidická from Moravské náměstí. The city hosts its own small-scale European film festival in April, while in late September/early October, there's a three-week-long **international classical music festival**, known as **Moravský podzim** (Moravian Autumn). Finally, in the first week of December, *Klub alterna* organizes a week of gigs featuring bands from all over Europe.

Listings

Currency exchange Komerční banka, náměstí Svobody 21. 24-hour exchange at the main train station.

Hospital Bratislavská 2; emergency medical attention ☎155.

Laundrette Mýdlo, Traubova. A pub/café and laundrette rolled into one, situated opposite the *Traubova* pub (see opposite), from which you can order food.

Motorcycle Grand Prix Brno hosts the grand prix at the end of August at the Masarykův okruh. Special buses are laid on during the competition; otherwise take bus #52 or #54 and walk westwards for five minutes.

Newspapers The tourist office in the main train station stocks most foreign dailies.

Pharmacy All-night service at Kobližná 7 (☎42 21 02 22).

Police The main police station is at Kounicova 46.

Post office The most convenient post office is next door to the train station. It runs a 24-hour telephone exchange.

Taxis The main taxi ranks are outside the station and on Solniční, or dial ☎42 32 13 21 for City Taxi.

Around Brno

Brno has plenty to keep you occupied, but if you're staying any amount of time, follow the advice of the health authorities (and the example of most of its citizens) and get out of the city at the weekend. One of the few good things about living in Brno's drab concrete suburbs is that you can walk straight out into the woods and bump into a deer. If that doesn't take your fancy, the most popular day-trip is to the limestone caves of the **Moravský kras**, closely followed by the castle of **Pernštejn** and the battlefield at **Slavkov** (Austerlitz). Potentially more interesting than any of those, however, is the

KARST TOPOGRAPHY

Named after the Karst, the barren limestone plateau around Trieste, **karst** landscapes
are formed by the action of rainwater on limestone. Rain picks up small amounts of carbon dioxide from the atmosphere, which, when it falls on limestone rock, slowly dis-
solves it. Gradually, over millions of years, the action of rain attacking the rock causes
hairline cracks in the limestone, which are steadily enlarged by running water. In its
early stages, karst scenery is characterized by narrow ridges and fissures; as these grow
and deepen, the dry limestone is raked into wild, sharp-edged fragments – practically
bare of vegetation since any topsoil is blown away – and bleached bright white, like
shards of bone. Karst scenery is found throughout the Czech and Slovak republics, particularly in southern **Moravia** and central and eastern **Slovakia**.

Rivers do odd things in karst landscapes: they disappear down holes where the limestone is weakest, and flow for miles underground, suddenly bursting from rocks when
the geology changes. When an underground river widens and forms a cavern, the drips
of rainwater percolating through the soil deposit minuscule amounts of the calcium
bicarbonate that it has dissolved from the limestone above. Over millions of years these
deposits form stalactites hanging from the roof of the cavern; the drips on the floor form
columns called stalagmites. Traces of other minerals such as iron and copper colour the
stalactites and stalagmites, and the whole process forms cave systems like the
Punkevní jeskyně.

Renaissance chateau at **Moravský Krumlov**, which houses a museum dedicated to the
work of the Art Nouveau painter Alfons Mucha.

The Moravský kras

Well worth a visit is Moravia's number-one tourist attraction: the limestone **karst
region** of the **Moravský kras**, just over 25km northeast of Brno. However, unless
you have your own transport, or you're part of a coach tour (enquire about these at
the tourist office in Brno), it's not that easy to reach the caves. The best thing to do
is to catch an early morning train from Brno out to **Blansko-Macocha** station, and
walk 200m southwards to the bus station. From here, buses depart for **Skalní Mlýn**,
location of the main ticket office and information centre for the caves. All visitors for
the Punkevní jeskyně must either walk the 1.5km from Skalní Mlýn or catch the regular Eko-Train service; there are also bikes for hire. Alternatively, it's a very nice five-
kilometre walk through the woods all the way from Blansko along the green-marked
path.

The caves

The most popular tour target is the **Punkevní jeskyně**, the largest cave system and the
deepest part of the gorge – get there early as tickets can sell out for the whole day in
high season. Daily tours run every fifteen minutes (May–Sept 8.20am–3.50pm;
Oct–April 8.20am–2pm; closed Dec) and take around fifty minutes. The fantastic array
of stalactites and stalagmites justifies the hassle of getting here. After a series of five
chambers, you come to the bottom of the **Propast Macocha** (Macocha Abyss), a
gigantic 138-metre mossy chasm created when the roof of one of the caves collapsed.
The first man to descend into the abyss and return alive was Father "Lazerus" Erker in
1728, almost two hundred years before the caves themselves were properly explored.
From the abyss, you're punted 500m along the slimy underground Punkva river, which
gives the cave its name. Just beyond the entrance to the caves, there's a very steep
cable car (*lanová dráha*), which can whisk you swiftly to the top of the abyss, so you

can look down on where you've just been. If you're going to take the Eko-Train and the cable car, be sure to buy a *Kombi-Karte* when you first set out.

The two other caves open to the public are only slightly less spectacular, with the added advantage that the queues are correspondingly smaller. The **Kateřinská jeskyně** (30min tour; May–Sept 8.20am–4pm; Oct–April 8.20am–2pm), one and a half kilometres before the Punkevní jeskyně at the point where the Punkva river re-emerges, is basically one huge "cathedral" of rock formations, a hundred metres long and twenty high. The smallest of the lot is the **Balcarka jeskyně** (50min tour; May–Sept Mon–Fri 7.30am–3.30pm, Sat & Sun 8.30am–3.15pm; Oct–April Mon–Fri 7.30am–1.15pm, Sat & Sun 8.30am–2.30pm; closed Dec), which lies 2km east of the Propast Macocha. A fourth cave system called Sloupsko-Šošůvské jeskyně sits on the southern edge of the village of Sloup, but is really only worth visiting for the occasional concerts that take place there.

Křtiny, Jedovnice and Senetářov

The whole karst region boasts some dramatic and varied scenery, all smothered in a thick coating of coniferous forest and riddled with marked paths, providing great **walking country**. If you're not in a hurry, three churches deserve a visit, providing a more relaxed alternative to the crush of tourists along the Punkva river.

You can avoid the crowds by getting off the Blansko train one stop after Adamov and walking east up the **Josefovské údolí** (the blue-marked path follows the road), a steep craggy valley with remnants of the original primeval forest cover and open-air stalagmites. After 3km, at the top of the valley, there's a special nature trail round a mini-karst region of around five caves, none of which is actually accessible. Another 3km further east along the blue path, and out of the woods, leaps the enormous dome and tower of the pilgrimage church of **KŘTINY**, designed by the Baroque genius Giovanni Santini. One door is usually open to let you inside, where the nave has been handed over to a series of interlinking frescoed domes that fuse into one, giving the church a Byzantine feel. The interior decor is gaudy High Baroque, especially the main altar, sheltering under its marble baldachin, with technicolor cherubs and saints strewn about the place, but the overall effect is satisfyingly impressive and unified. Only one set of curvaceous cloisters was completed, now filled with the gifts of paintings from previous pilgrims.

Taking the yellow-marked path, skirt the edge of the woods to the northeast, which rise gently past the understated peak of Proklest (574m). Six kilometres on from Křtiny, you emerge from the trees at the small lake by the village of **JEDOVNICE**, no beauty itself thanks to a fire in 1822, which also torched the late-eighteenth-century village church. From the outside the latter looks hurriedly restored; the interior, however, redesigned in the 1960s, contains symbolic art, stained glass and, as the centrepiece, a striking **altar** painting by Mikuláš Medek, *persona non grata* in Czechoslovakia in the 1950s for his penchant for Surrealism and social comment. His choice of colours is didactic: a blue cross for hope, and red for the chaos of the world. Unless it's a Sunday, you'll have to get the key from the *kaplan* who lives opposite the church and who can also furnish you with an *anglický text*.

There's no escaping the modernity of Ludvík Kolek's concrete church at **SENETÁŘOV**, completed in 1971, 4km down the road to Vyškov; it's built in the shape of a ship, its "mast" visible as you approach from the plateau – though as a concept, its symbolism is reminiscent of the work of Santini. It's an uncompromising building, with huge plate-glass panels at the west end, through which you can clearly see the main altarpiece, an abstract version of the *Last Supper* against a vivid blue background. But it's Medek's *Stations of the Cross*, on the north wall and difficult to see without getting inside, that are the church's masterpiece. Starting with a deep red crown of thorns, the pictures progress in bold simple colours and symbols, fusing into one long fourteen-piece canvas and signalling an original working of an otherwise hackneyed theme.

On a completely different note, there's a minute **folk museum** (expozice tradičního bydlení a perleťářství; April–Oct Sat & Sun 8am–6pm) in a thatched house opposite the church, with displays on the region's mother-of-pearl button cottage industry, introduced in the 1880s that flourished until World War I. It was all over by the 1930s, though there is a still a button-making factory in the area; ask for an *anglický text* to find out more.

Practicalities

A regular **bus** service runs from Brno and Blansko to Jedovnice, passing through Křtiny and occasionally continuing to Senetářov, making all the above places relatively easy to visit on a day-trip from Brno. The best base is Křtiny, where **accommodation** choices include several new pensions such as the *Santini* (☎0506/944 23; ②). The *Hotel Skální Mlýn* (☎0506/41 81 13; ③), in Skální Mlýn itself, is busy with tourists, but the perfect base if you're keen to visit several of the caves. The nicest of the region's campsites is the *Relaxa* **campsite** (May–Sept) in Sloup, to the north of the caves, though you'll have to walk or cycle to the caves from it, if you've no transport of your own.

Brněnská přehrada and Pernštejn

Just as Brno's housing estates peter out to the northwest, you come to the long, snakelike **Brněnská přehrada** (Brno Dam), a favourite with Brno's inhabitants on a sunny weekend (tram #3, #10, #14, #18, #20 or #21). The further you get from the lake's bulbous southern end, the thinner the crowds and the thicker the woods along the shoreline. In the summer, boats zigzag their way to Veverská Bítýška, passing the thirteenth-century cliff-top fortress of **Veveří**, currently undergoing a lengthy restoration. There's a pretty path through the spruce on the left bank, should you miss the boat back.

Pernštejn

The Gothic stronghold of **Pernštejn** is many people's idea of what a medieval castle should look like, and is consequently one of the most popular targets around Brno. The nearest station to Pernštejn is at the village of Nedvědice – from the platform, the castle is immediately visible to the west; to get there follow the yellow-marked track. After a series of outer defences, the **hrad** (April & Oct Sat & Sun 9am–noon & 1–4pm; May, June & Sept Tues–Sun 9am–noon & 1–5pm; July & Aug closes 6pm) proper is a truly dramatic sight, with kestrels circling the dizzying sheer walls. It was originally built in the thirteenth century, and various reconstructions have left it a jumble of unpredictable angles and extras, including a death-defying covered wooden bridge that spans the castle's main keeps. The hour-long guided tour is highly atmospheric, giving out spectacular views across the mixed woodland of the nearby hills.

The picturesque train journey up the Svratka Valley to Nedvědice takes just over an hour from Brno, making this one of the easiest and most rewarding day-trips. If you have to change at **TIŠNOV**, be sure to check out the remarkable Romanesque portal, *Porta Coeli*, at the entrance to the church of the former Cistercian nunnery, 2km west of the train station along the blue-marked path in the neighbouring settlement of Předklášteří.

Moravský Krumlov

Squeezed into a tight bend of the Rokytná river, southwest of Brno, is **MORAVSKÝ KRUMLOV**, whose **zámek**, to the west of town, boasts a delicate arcaded loggia from 1557, and an **art gallery** (April–Oct Tues–Sun 9am–noon & 1–4pm), housed in one of the outbuildings, containing paintings and drawings by one of the better-known Czech artists, **Alfons Mucha** (1860–1939). Mucha was actually born in the mining town of Ivančice, a few kilometres to the north, an odd starting point for an artist who is best known for his graceful Art Nouveau posters. In the West he is known solely for the work he did while in Paris – particularly his Sarah Bernhardt posters – where he shared a studio with Gauguin (there's a photo of the latter playing the piano with his trousers down just to prove it). In fact, Mucha came to despise this "commercial" period of his work, and when the First Republic was declared in 1918, he threw himself into the national cause, designing its stamps, banknotes and numerous posters.

However, it was left to an American millionaire to commission him to do what he saw as his life's work: a cycle of twenty monumental canvases called the *Slovanská epopej* (Slav Epic), which constitute the bulk of the work on display here. In Czech terms they're well-worn themes – Komenský fleeing the "fatherland", the Battle of Vítkov and so on – but they were obviously heartfelt for Mucha. In the end he paid for his nationalism with his life: dragged in for questioning by the Gestapo after the 1939 Nazi invasion, he died shortly after being released. In this forlorn chateau, Mucha's gloomy, melodramatic paintings take on a fascination all of their own, though there are moves afoot to transport the whole lot to Prague.

Trains from Brno are fairly frequent and direct (those from Znojmo or Mikulov require you to change at Hrušovany nad Jevišovkou), but the station is a good 2km east of the town; **buses** will drop you in the centre, but timings are only really any good from Znojmo.

Slavkov

Twenty kilometres by train across the flat plain east of Brno, **SLAVKOV** (Austerlitz) would be just another humble ribbon village were it not for the great mass of Martinelli's late Baroque **zámek** (Tues–Sun: April, May, Oct & Nov 9am–noon & 1–4pm; June–Aug 9am–5pm) and accompanying Neoclassical church. Like so many chateaux close to the Austrian border, its contents were quickly and judiciously removed by their owners before the arrival of the Red Army in 1945, but the 45-minute guided tour is still worth it for the incredible acoustics of the central concave hall. Every whisper of sound in the giant dome echoes for a full ten seconds, while outside not one word can be heard.

On December 2, 1805, in the fields between Slavkov and Brno, the Austrians and Russians received a decisive drubbing at the hands of the numerically inferior Napoleonic troops in the **Battle of Austerlitz** (also known as the "Battle of the Three Emperors"). The Austrians and Russians committed themselves early, charging into the morning fog to attack the French on both flanks. From his vantage point on the Žuráň hill to the north, Napoleon, confident of victory, held back until the enemy had established its position, and then attacked at their weakest point, the central commanding heights of the Pratzen hill (Pracký kopec), splitting their forces and throwing them into disarray. It was all over by lunchtime, with over 24,000 troops dead. After the battle, all three emperors signed a peace treaty, marking an end to Napoleon's eastern campaign until the fateful march on Moscow in 1812. There's a graphic description of the battle in Tolstoy's epic novel *War and Peace*.

Just over one hundred years later, on the strategic Pratzen hill, 8km southwest of Slavkov, the **Mohyla míru** (Monument of Peace) was erected on the instigation of a local pacifist priest, and paid for by the governments of France, Austria and Russia, who within three years of pledging the money were once again at war with one another. There's a superb view of the surrounding killing fields, now just a series of ploughed fields peppered with crosses and dotted with the odd little Calvary. The tent-like stone monument, designed by the Art Nouveau architect Josef Fanta, contains a small chapel, and nearby there's a **museum** (April–Sept daily 8am–noon & 1–5pm; Oct–March Tues–Sun 9am–noon & 1–3.30pm), including the obligatory toy soldier mock-up of the battle. Military enthusiasts without their own transport have a choice of uphill walks: 2km from Ponětovice train station, 3km from Sokolnice train station, or 1km from the bus stop in Prace. If you happen to be here on the anniversary of the battle, the Friends of the French Revolution treat onlookers to a chilly re-enactment.

Bučovice

Ten kilometres further east, and accessible by train from Brno, the **zámek** (April & Oct Sat & Sun 9am–noon & 1–4pm; May–Sept Tues–Sun 9am–noon & 1–5pm) at **BUČOVICE**, circled by kestrels, gets a fraction of the visitors of Slavkov, partly perhaps because of its unpromising exterior: a dull grey fortress with four ugly squat towers. None of it prepares you for the subtle, slender Italianate arcading of the courtyard's loggia, with each set of supporting columns topped by a different carved motif. At the centre of the courtyard a stone fountain was added a few generations later – "a little too robust", as the guide puts it, and out of keeping with the rest of the masonry. The towers, the gardens and countless rooms once matched the charm and elegance of the courtyard, but the Liechtensteins, who obtained the chateau through marriage in 1597, soon turned it into little more than a storage house for the family records, scattering its original furnishings among their many other Moravian residences.

The only things they couldn't remove were the original sixteenth-century **ceiling decorations**, a fantastical mantle of sculpture and paint, coating just five or so rooms, none more than twenty feet across. The first few are just a warm-up for the thick stucco of the **císařský sál**, with the bejewelled relief figures of Mars, Diana, a half-naked Europa and, most magnificent of all, the emperor Charles V trampling a turbaned Turk into the paintwork. But the decoration of the **zaječí sál** (The Hall of Hares) is the real star turn, an anthropomorphic work reckoned to be one of the few of that period still in existence. It's a comical scene, with the hares exacting their revenge on the world of man and his closest ally, the dog. The aftermath of the hares' revolution sees them sitting in judgement (wigs and all) over their defeated enemies, as well as indulging in more highbrow activities – hare as Rembrandt, hare as scholar and so on.

Along the Austrian border

Historically, the land on either side of the River Dyje (Thaya), which either forms, or runs parallel with, the border between Moravia and Austria, has for centuries been German-speaking, its buildings designed by Austrian architects and its sights set firmly on Vienna, just 60km to the south. However, as in the rest of the country, the ethnic German population was forcibly removed from South Moravia after 1945 and their private vineyards and orchards handed out to the demobilized Czech heroes of the liberation. The region's viticulture was one of the few industries that kept going on private plots even after nationalization in 1948, but in every other way the last half century has driven a great wedge between two previously identical regions on either side of the river: the neat, prim and wealthy Austrian Weinviertel to the south now seems worlds apart from the shabbier Moravian side of the Dyje. Nevertheless, there are one or two real high spots that make this a region worth exploring. The reopening of the border in 1990 has been a mixed blessing, boosting the local economy with Schillings thanks to Austrians popping over to do their shopping, and locals working in Austria. With it, however, have come the sex industry, out-of-town shopping complexes and an air of tackiness that has done little to improve the area's aesthetics.

THE BRNO DEATH MARCH

On May 30, 1945, an estimated 23,000 German-speaking Czechs from Brno and its environs were rounded up and forced to walk the 60km from Brno into Austria. Deportees
were allowed to take only what they could carry (and no money or jewels). The following
night, the refugees reached the village of **Pohořelice**, just over halfway from Brno to the
border. Those who were too weak or ill with dysentery to continue were housed in a local
brick factory. The Czechs maintain that their doctors treated the sick and that all those
who died were victims of dysentery. Sudeten Germans argue that acts of brutality and
mass murder were committed, while others died of starvation. No one knows quite how
many Germans were buried in Pohořelice, but after years of official silence on the matter
during the Communist period, a memorial to 890 known victims was finally erected in 1992
by the farm field in which the victims were buried, on route 52, just south of Pohořelice.

Mikulov and around

Clinging on to the southern tip of the Pavlovské vrchy, the last hills before the Austrian
plain, **MIKULOV** (Nikolsburg) is one of South Moravia's minor gems. Slap bang in the
middle of the wine-producing region, it's been a border post for centuries – hence the
narrow streets and siege mentality of much of the architecture. The town still functions
as a busy crossing point between the two countries; if you're driving from Vienna, it's a
great introduction to the country and, given its strategic locale, surprisingly tourist-free.

Raised above the jumble of red rooftops is the **zámek** (April & Oct Sat & Sun
9am–4pm; May–Sept Tues–Sun 8am–5pm), an imposing complex built right into the
rocky hill on the west side of town. Close up, it's a plain, rather characterless building;
used by the Gestapo to hoard confiscated art objects, it was then blown to smithereens
by them in the last days of the war in a final nihilistic gesture. It was rebuilt in the 1950s
to house a museum, which covers the town's history (minus the controversial
episodes) and viticulture and dishes out amazing views over into Austria.

In 1575, castle and town fell into the hands of the fervently Catholic Dietrichsteins,
who established various religious edifices and institutions here. They're also responsible for the hint of Renaissance in the town – the occasional arcade or pictorial sgraffito
– and the main square itself, which is called simply "náměstí", appealingly misshapen
and huddled below the castle. Later, behind the oversized plague column, they built the
church of **sv Anna**, now a strange, monstrous building undergoing restoration. The
main body of the church has no roof after a fire in 1784, and was only partially rebuilt
in 1845 when the Dietrichsteins intended to turn it into a family mausoleum. At least it
retains its imposing west front of smooth classical columns flanked by stumpy Baroque
towers, designed by Fischer von Erlach. The family was also responsible for the series
of chapels to the east of the town on the bleak, exposed limestone hill, well worth the
climb for the view across the vineyards to Vienna.

Mikulov boasted a thriving **Jewish community** until the advent of the Nazis: in the
mid-nineteenth century, it was the second largest in the Czech Lands and was the seat
of the chief rabbi (Landesrabbiner) of Moravia from the sixteenth century until 1851.
The old Jewish ghetto lies to the west of the castle, where the town's seventeenth-century **synagogue** (May–Sept Tues–Sun 1–5pm), on Husova, has recently been renovated and should theoretically be open at the times advertised. Uniquely for a Czech synagogue, the interior is in the Lvov style, with four central columns supporting the dome
and bimah, and now houses an exhibition on the Jewish history of the town. Round the
corner in Brněnská, a rugged path leads to the overgrown medieval **Jewish cemetery**
(Židovský hřbitov), with finely carved marble tombstones dating back to 1618; to get
into it, you'll need to pick up the key from Brněnská 28, though it's closed on Saturdays.

The town is rarely busy, except during the wine festival, the majority of visitors pausing for a couple of hours at the most before moving on. There's a **tourist office** on the main square (May–Sept daily 8am–6pm; Oct–April 9am–5pm), which can help with **accommodation**, and any other queries. The best choice of hotels is between the *Rohatý krokodýl*, in the former Jewish quarter at Husova 8 (☎0625/26 92; ③), and the *Réva*, Česká 2 (☎0625/39 01; ②). Alternatively, you can enquire about a cheap hostel bed at the *Národní dům* on the main square. Being in the wine region, the best time to come here is after the grape harvest in late September, when the first bouquet of the year is being tried and tested in vast quantities at the local *sklepy* (wine caves) on the edge of town. Apart from the *Rohatý krokodýl's* restaurant, and the traditional fare on offer at the *Národní dům*, there's a good pizzeria, *Ronrico*, on A. Muchy, and another excellent restaurant, *U nás doma*, at the far end of 1 květná, ten minutes' walk northeast of the town centre.

Pálava

Mikulov is the starting point for hiking and exploring the **Pavlovské vrchy**, a big, bulging ridge of rugged and treeless limestone hills, and the surrounding region, known as the **Pálava**. Since the damming of the Dyje and the creation of the artificial Nový mlýn lake, the rare plant life on the Pavlovské vrchy has suffered badly. In a rather belated and empty gesture, the authorities declared this a protected region. With or without its original vegetation, though, it's good, gentle **hiking country**, with wide-angle views on both sides and a couple of picturesque ruined castles along the ten-kilometre red-marked path to Dolní Věstonice.

Archeological research has been going on here since 1924, when an early Stone Age settlement was discovered. Brno's Moravské zemské muzeum (see p.286) displays the best findings, which include wolves' teeth jewellery and clay figurines such as the voluptuous *Venus of Věstonice*, a tiny female fertility figure with swollen belly and breasts. However, there is a small **Archaeologická expozice** (Tues–Sun 8am–noon & 1–5pm) in Dolní Věstonice, which, despite the lack of information in English, exhibits some interesting finds: skulls, a woolly mammoth's tooth, several animal and fertility statues, including, inevitably, a copy of the aforementioned Venus. From Dolní Věstonice you can either walk another 4km to the station at Popice or catch one of the hourly buses back to Mikulov.

Lednicko-Valtický areál

To the southeast of Mikulov, nose to nose with the Austrian border, is the UNESCO-protected **Lednicko-Valtický areál**, a landscape dominated by the twin residences of the Liechtensteins, one of the most powerful landowning families in the country until 1945 (see box opposite). The chateaux lie 7km apart at either end of the dead-straight *lipova alej* (lime-tree avenue), in a vast, magnificent stately park, dotted with follies and fish ponds and surrounded by acres of woodland, and in many ways, it's this delightful setting that is the best feature of the whole area.

Lednice

The most popular of the two chateaux is undoubtedly the family's summer residence at **LEDNICE** (Eisgrub). Part of the Liechtenstein estate since 1243, the **zámek** (April & Oct Sat & Sun 9am–noon & 1–4pm; May–Aug Tues–Sun 9am–noon & 1–6pm; Sept closes 5pm) was subjected to a lavish rebuild job in the 1840s, which turned it into a neo-Gothic extravaganza. Part of the chateau is occupied by an exhibition devoted to agri-culture, but there's plenty to look at on the main guided tour, with vivid, over-the-top Romantic interiors crowding each of its wood-panelled rooms.

If fake medievalism doesn't turn you on, however, there are several other attractions to sample, such as the chateau's vast wrought-iron and glass palm house or **skleník**

(April & Oct Sat & Sun 9am–4pm; May–Aug daily 9am–5pm; Sept closes 4pm), and the expansive, watery **zámecký park**, home to numerous herons and laughing gulls, as well as regular falconry displays in summer. Piqued by local objections to their plan for a colossal church, the Liechtensteins decided to further alienate the village by building the largest **minaret** outside the Islamic world, which dominates the view of the park from the chateau; further east is the **Janův hrad** (April & Oct Sat & Sun 9am–4.30pm; May–Sept Tues–Sun 9am–4.30pm), a ruined "Gothick" castle. Those with kids in tow might want to seek out the new **Akvárium Malawi** (April–Oct daily 9am–5pm), in a wing of the old stables. It's something of an ad hoc installation, and there's very little information on offer, but you're guaranteed to see piranhas, alligators, terrapins and countless colourful tropical fish.

Valtice

At **VALTICE** (Feldsberg), once the family's foremost residence, the Baroque **zámek** (Tues–Sun: April, Sept & Oct 9am–noon & 1–4pm; May–Aug 8am–noon & 1–5pm) was cleaned out just before the end of the war, leaving its beautifully restored rooms relentlessly bare. The east wing has recently been converted into a budget hotel and restaurant which does a brisk trade with holidaying Austrians. Valtice only became part of the Czech Lands during a minor border adjustment dictated by the 1920 Treaty of St Germain, and from the end of the garden you used to be able see the watchtowers of the Iron Curtain in amongst the chateau's vineyards, which produce a good Moravian red.

From the train station, a scenic red-marked path leads you through the woods of the **Bořì les**, via a series of follies erected around the 1820s: a triumphal arch called Rendezvous; *U tří grácií*, a copy of the *Three Graces*; and the Apollonův chrám, a Neoclassical pavilion overlooking one of the two fifteenth-century fish ponds, now a popular summer swimming spot. The blue-marked path from Valtice takes you past the Hraniční zámeček, whose current incarnation dates from the 1920s (and is now a restaurant), and once marked the historical Austrian-Moravian border.

Practicalities

Valtice is just twenty minutes by **train** from Mikulov and twenty-five from Břeclav, while Lednice is served only by a little branch line from Břeclav; between Valtice and

---

THE LIECHTENSTEINS

The **Liechtensteins** (of Grand Duchy fame) were for many centuries one of the most powerful families in the Czech Lands, particularly in Moravia. At their peak they owned no fewer than 99 estates – one more and they would have had to maintain a standing army in the service of the emperor. The one who made the most of all this wealth was Prince-Bishop Karl Eusebius von Liechtenstein-Kastelcorn, who came into the family fortune in 1627 and whose motto – "Money exists only that one may leave beautiful monuments to eternal and undying remembrance" – can be seen in practice all over Moravia.

Like nearly all the ethnic Germans who lived in Czechoslovakia, the Liechtensteins were forced to leave in 1945. For the last 45 years, it looked like the long history of the Liechtensteins in the Czech Lands had come to an end. Then in 1990, the new government passed a law of *restituce* (restitution), which meant that all property confiscated by the Communists from 1948 onwards was to be handed back to its original owners. Despite having had their property taken from them in the earlier appropriations of 1918 and 1945, the Liechtensteins continue to request compensation from the Czech government for the seizure of their former residences, which comprise something like 1600 square kilometres of land – ten times the area of present-day Liechtenstein.

Lednice, however, there are just a couple of buses a day. The most convenient place to stay if you're travelling by train might well be the rather drab town of Břeclav (Lundenberg), 8km east of the two chateaux, on the main line from Prague to Bratislava, but you'll have a much better time in either Lednice or Valtice.

At either place, there's plenty of **accommodation**. In Lednice, the *Mario* (☎0627/34 01 52; ⑤), opposite the chateau, has some dubious modern decor, but is probably the most comfortable option; while the large *Hotel Harlekin* (☎0627/34 01 35; *harlekin@bva.czn.cz*; ⑥), up the road to Podivín, is slightly more tasteful and has good disabled access. Alternatively, there are numerous private rooms and pensions such as the *Jordán* (☎0627/34 02 85; ②), further up the road to Podivín, which has clean, brightly painted en-suite rooms. The *U radnice*, just outside the chateau gates in Lednice, will furnish you with inexpensive Czech food and beer.

Accommodation in Valtice tends to be better value, particularly the *Hubertus* (☎0627/35 25 37; ③) in the chateau itself, and the *Apollon* (☎0627/35 26 25; ②), set in its own gardens up the *lipovej alej* at P. Bezruče 720. All accommmodation in the area tends to be fully booked in the middle of August when there's a Baroque Music Festival in Valtice, in which case, you'll probably have to fall back on the *Apollo* **campsite** (May–Sept) by the Lednice fish pond.

Znojmo

ZNOJMO (Znaim), further up the Dyje, approximately 45km west of Mikulov, is not as immediately appealing as the latter, despite a spectacular hill-top location and an old town blessed with an unrivalled set of Romanesque frescoes. What puts many first-time visitors off is that this is a town whose industry and suburbs have spread out in unsight-

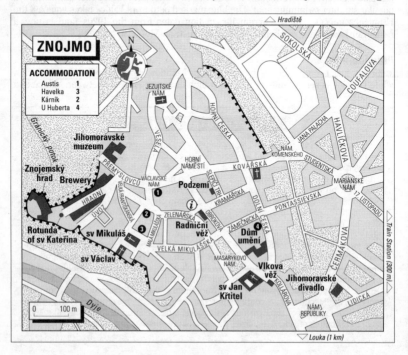

ly fashion to the north and east over the last hundred years. It's also something of a classic Czech border town, long blighted by the Iron Curtain, and now plagued by brothels and other institutions making a quick Schilling or two out of day-tripping Austrians.

The Town

Unfortunately, the town's main square, **Masarykovo náměstí**, was badly damaged in World War II, and the Capuchin buildings at the bottom of the square are as uninspiring as the concrete supermarket that squats at the opposite end. Only the central Marian column and a couple of attractive surviving buildings on the east side of the square deserve attention: the **Měšťanský dům**, which has a very fine sixteenth-century stone portal and matching pilasters, and the **Dům umění** (Tues–Sat 10am–6pm), a beautiful Renaissance building, two doors down. The latter has an arcaded courtyard out back, and diamond vaulting on the first floor, where temporary exhibitions are held. On the second floor there's a room devoted to local artist, Jan Tomáš Fisher, a pupil of Otakar Španiel, who, like his master, specialized in designing reliefs on medals. There's also a small collection of Gothic and Baroque art, particularly strong on sculpture, and a genial English-speaking curator to show you round.

Hope rears up at the top of the square, in the shape of the late-Gothic pinnacled **radniční věž** (April & Oct Mon–Sat 9am–4pm; May–Sept daily 9am–5pm; Nov–March Mon–Fri 9am–4pm), all that's left of the old town hall, burnt down by the Nazis in the closing stages of the war. From this soaring romantic affair, its uppermost gallery twisting at an angle to the main body, the view through its wooden hatches is little short of spectacular – a good way to get your bearings and a feel for this decidedly neglected town. One block east on Slepičí trh (Chicken Market) is the entrance to the town's underground tunnels or **podzemí** (April Mon–Sat 10am–4pm; May–Sept daily 9am–4pm; Oct Sat 9am–4pm) that run for miles under the old town; originally built for defensive purposes, they were later used for storing wine.

At this point you can head off in a number of directions, but the most interesting is the narrow lane of Velká Mikulášská, which leads to the oldest part of Znojmo – a tight web of alleyways woven round the cathedral of **sv Mikuláš**, a plain Gothic hall church sporting an unusual gable embellished with blind arcading. Inside, it has retained its elegant Gothic net vaulting and slender round pillars, but the most amazing thing about the church is its Baroque pulpit – a giant globe, with its top sliced off, crowned by a sounding-board of free-flying clouds, sunbursts, cherubs and saints. Also worth inspecting is the glass coffin underneath the organ loft, containing the macabre clothed skeleton of a Christian martyr.

Set at a right angle to the cathedral is the much smaller **chapel of sv Václav**, tucked into the town walls, from which you get a commanding view up and down the Dyje valley as it blends into the Austrian plain. The chapel itself is a curious building, built literally on top of its Gothic predecessor in the sixteenth century, when the town's fortifications against the Turks were erected (and smothered the old building). The church now belongs to the local Orthodox community, and the priest will happily show you round the chapel and the bare Gothic original.

"Better a living brewery than a dead castle", goes one of the more obscure Czech proverbs, and as far as **Znojmský hrad** (May Sat & Sun 9am 5pm; June–Sept Tues–Sun 9am–5pm) goes it's hard to disagree. The parts that didn't become a brewery have since been turned into a deceptively large local **museum** distinguished, for the most part, by its trompe l'oeil Baroque fresco in the oval entrance hall, glorifying the Deblín family, who rebuilt the chateau in 1720 only to run out of male heirs in 1784. During the week, you must approach the castle via the path that clings to the outside of the town walls from the end of Přemyslovců, entering via a secret door in the fortifications; at the weekend, you can walk straight through the brewery along Hradní.

Unfortunately, access to the castle's most precious relic, the **rotunda of sv Kateřina** (times as above), home to the best-preserved twelfth-century frescoes in the country, including contemporary portraits of the Přemyslid princes, is often restricted in an attempt to keep the temperature inside the rotunda constant; ask at the museum for the latest.

Znojmo's old town is perched high above the deep gorge of the Podyjí national park, to the southwest, so that on leaving the safety of the town walls at the end of Přemyslovců, you plunge straight into thickly wooded countryside. It's a gentle wander round the foot of the castle to the chapel of sv Václav, but for a longer **walk** and an unbeatable vista of Znojmo and the Dyje, take the blue-marked path down to the stream and continue past the Stations of the Cross, up to the village and nunnery of Hradiště; bus #1 will run you back into town.

Architecture buffs may want to take a look at the huge yellow colossus of the **Premonstratensian convent** at **Louka** (Klosterbruck), now a suburb of Znojmo (10min walk or bus #4 down Vídeňská třída). It was begun but never finished by, among others, the Baroque architect Johann Lukas von Hildebrandt, and soon afterwards was turned into a barracks, its precious library carried off to Prague's Strahov monastery. From a distance it still manages to make an impression, and the main basilica has recently been restored, but renovation work will take some years to bring the rest of the complex up to scratch.

Practicalities

Trains run fairly frequently from Mikulov to Znojmo, taking around an hour; trains from Brno take around two hours, often with a change (but no wait) at Hrušovany nad Jevišovkou. The old town is a stiff hike from the station: up 17 listopadu to Marianské náměstí, then west along Pontassievská and Zámečnická. If you're heading into Austria, there's a 24-hour **border crossing** at Hatě, 12km southeast on route 38 (the occasional bus goes there), and a railway border crossing at nearby Satov; note, however, that the Hnanice-Mitterretzbach border crossing to the west is for Austrian and Czech passport holders only.

The **tourist office** (April & Oct Mon–Sat 9am–4pm, May–Sept daily 9am–5pm; Nov–March Mon–Fri 9am–4pm), at Obroková 12, can help with **accommodation**. Your best bet is to try one of the town's small pensions, such as the excellent *Havelka* (☎0624/22 01 38; ③), right by the church of sv Mikuláš, or the *Austis*, Václavské náměstí 5 (☎0624/24 19 49; ③). If the above are full, you can fall back on the *Kárník*, Zelenářská 25 (☎0624/22 68 26; ④), a new hotel in the old town, or the rooms above *U Huberta*, a pub on Dolní Česká (☎0624/22 11 02; ②). Znojmo has a surprisingly large choice of **restaurants**, catering for day-tripping Austrians, but in many ways you're better off eating at one of the pensions mentioned above, all of which have their own restaurants. If you need to get on-line, there's an Internet café called *U legionáře* at Dolní Česká 44 (closed Sun). Znojmo stages its own **wine festival**, *Znojemské vinobraní*, in the middle of September. Aside from booze, **pickled gherkins** (*kyselá okurka*) flavoured with paprika are another Znojmo speciality to look out for.

Podyjí

The meandering River Dyje, and the artifical lake, to the west of Znojmo are now part of the heavily forested and very pretty **Podyjí** national park, that provides a summer playground for large numbers of holidaying Czechs. There are plenty of opportunities for swimming and lazing around, plus a couple of interesting chateaux and lots of hiking possibilities. Without your own transport, getting about can be time-consuming, so you might want to plan to spend at least one or two days in the area.

Vranov

VRANOV NAD DYJÍ (Frain) itself is a regular South Moravian village, entirely dominated by its cliff-top **zámek** (April & Oct Sat & Sun 9am–noon & 1–4pm; May, June &
Sept Tues–Sun 9am–noon & 1–5pm; July & Aug 9am–noon & 1–6pm), magnificently
poised on a knife's edge above the Dyje. Originally a medieval stronghold, it was converted into a beautiful Baroque chateau by the Viennese genius Johann Bernhard
Fischer von Erlach after a fire in 1665. Nothing else on the guided tour of the sprawling complex (not even the medieval sauna) can quite compare to Fischer's trump card
at the far end – the cavernous dome of the **Sál předků** (Ancestors' Hall), whose truly
awesome overall effect is as much due to Rottmayr's wild frescoes as to Fischer's great
oval skylights: its frenzied, over-the-top paintings depict the (fictitious) achievements of
the Althan family who commissioned the work. One other piece of Fischer von Erlach
genius worth inspecting is the palace's tiny **chapel** (June Sun 9am–5pm; July & Aug
Tues–Sun 9am–6pm), a visit to which is not included in the chateau tour. Again, it's the
frescoes, executed by a pupil of Rottmayr, that make the place so special. The main fresco features the archangel Michael smiting Satan's followers who tumble over the cornice itself, while in the side chapels skeletons frolic and angels pray.

At the weekend **buses** run regularly from Znojmo to Vranov, less often during the
week. Alternatively, you could take the more frequent **train** to Sumná station and walk
the 4km to Vranov. In Vranov, you can **stay** above the *Country Saloon* courtyard pub
(☎0624/972 38; ②) or in the en-suite rooms of the *Pension Herold* (☎0624/29 60 70; ③).
From the village, it's a fifteen-minute walk to the dam (*přehrada*) and the sandy **beach**
known as Vranovská pláž, accessible via the new footbridge across the lake. From May
to September there's a fair bit of life here: **camping**, chalets, boat rental, a couple of
shops and an occasional **boat service** up the lake to Bítov and beyond. The sun-wor-
shippers are shoulder to shoulder on the beach in the high season, but it's easy to lose
the crowd by picking a rocky spot further upstream.

One of the most interesting **walks** in the area is to take the red-marked path from
Vranov village along the Dyje, then up into the woods and hills until you reach the road
from Cízov to the Austrian border (6km). From here, it's just 2km by either the blue-
marked path by the road, or the green-marked path through the woods via the
Hardeggská vyhlídka, a look-out post from which you can view the picturesque
Austrian border village of Hardegg, accessible via a small footbridge. The round trip is
about 16km and will take all day, so carry a picnic or some Austrian Schillings (and
your passport, of course) in order to grab a bite to eat in Hardegg.

Bítov

The village of **BÍTOV**, 8km west up the lake, is more geared to vacationing Czechs than
is Vranov. Perched high above the lake, it has two decent **places to stay**: the popular
café/pension *U Tesařů* on the main square (☎0624/29 46 16; ②), and the comfortable,
friendly *Hotel Bítov* (☎0624/963 97; ④), a communist-era place on the road north out of
the village, which has its own outdoor swimming pool. The nearby Bítov-Horka **campsite** (June–Sept) is situated down by the lakeside. The only way to get from Vranov to
Bítov – apart from hitching or walking – is to take the boat. There are just one or two
buses from Znojmo to Bítov; connections with Jihlava (see next page) are much the
same.

The ruined castle that can be seen from the lake is a fourteenth-century defence fort
of Cornštejn, and is unsafe to explore. Bítov's own **hrad** (April & Oct Sat & Sun
9am–noon & 1–4pm; May, June & Sept Tues–Sun 9am–noon & 1–5pm; July & Aug closes 6pm) has weathered slightly better and is located 2.5km to the west of the village,
along the red-marked path. Like Vranov, it boasts a classic defensive location on a spit
of grey rock high above the river, which the flooding of the valley has diminished only
slightly, and for this reason alone it's worth clambering up to enjoy the view. In the cas-

tle's courtyard, there's a lovely, cool thirteenth-century **wine cellar** where you can taste and purchase the local wine, and an *občerstvení* where you can get a snack and a glass of beer, but inside, lacking Fischer's ingenious touch, the castle's not a patch on Vranov. The **guided tour** (1. trasa) through the contrived neo-Gothic decor and soulless, unlived-in rooms is enlivened only by a pack of stuffed dogs. A better bet is take the short unguided tour (2. trasa) of the castle's pink and white **chapel** in the main courtyard (July & Aug only).

Jaroměřice nad Rokytnou

One hour northwest by train from Znojmo, and a convenient place to break the journey to Jihlava, the village of **JAROMĚŘICE NAD ROKYTNOU** is completely overwhelmed by its gargantuan russet-and-cream Baroque **zámek** (April & Oct Sat & Sun 9am–noon & 1–4pm; May, June & Sept Tues–Sun 9am–noon & 1–5pm; July & Aug closes 6pm), built over the course of 37 years by the wealthy and extravagant Johann Adam von Questenberg. For the most part it's the work of Dominico d'Angeli, but the two Austrian architects Jakob Prandtauer and Johann Lukas von Hildebrandt also appear to have been involved at various stages. The highlights of the chateau are the elegant Rococo halls, the hlavní sál and the táneční sál, where Questenberg used to put on lavish classical concerts. To see these you must join the longer tour (1. trasa); the shorter tour (2. trasa) only takes you round the later interiors and the porcelain collection. Alternatively, you could skip both tours and spend the morning exploring the great domed chapel or pottering around the formal gardens. Even better, come during July and August, when the chateau stages a festival of classical music.

Jihlava

When silver deposits were discovered in the nearby hills in the 1240s, **JIHLAVA** (Iglau) was transformed overnight from a tiny Moravian village into one of the biggest mining towns in central Europe. Scores of German miners came and settled here, and by the end of the century Jihlava could boast two hospitals, two monasteries and, most importantly, the royal mint. The veins of silver ran out in the fourteenth century, but the town continued to flourish thanks to the cloth trade, reaching its zenith around the latter half of the sixteenth century when over 700 master spinners worked in the town.

Jihlava retains a surprisingly attractive staré město, which has been painstakingly renovated over the last decade. That the town isn't quite as lovely as it should be is partly down to a fire in 1523 and the ravages of the Thirty Years' War, which drastically reduced Jihlava's population. Most of all, however, it was the expulsion of ethnic Germans from this "language-island" after 1945 that changed the face of the town for ever, or, as the Communist guidebooks used to put it, "marked the beginning of a new stage in the development of Jihlava". In reality, the town immediately went into decline, plagued by an ignorant Communist council which, in its comparatively brief forty-year rule, left the most indelible mark on the town: the mud-brown, multistorey car park/supermarket complex plonked in the middle of Jihlava's huge main square in place of a block of medieval houses.

The Town

If you can look beyond Jihlava's most glaring addition, the cobbled main square, **Masarykovo náměstí**, is actually a wonderfully expansive space. Sloping steeply to the south and lined with restrained Baroque and Rococo houses, it sports two fountains, and a Marian column, beside which is a plaque to Evžen Plocek the 41-year-old

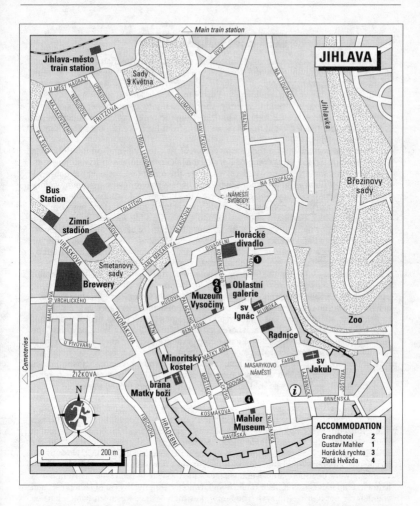

who set himself alight on April 4, 1969 in protest against the Soviet invasion. At the top of the square, in no. 58, is the **muzeum Vysočiny** (Tues–Sun 9am–noon & 12.30–5pm), worth a visit for the interior alone, being one of the few Renaissance houses to survive the 1523 fire. Its covered inner courtyard, with an arcaded gallery, patchy murals and diamond vaulting, is perfectly preserved. The museum's collections of stuffed animals and mushrooms, are less remarkable, though there is a well-preserved eighteenth-century pharmacy from nearby Polná.

You can see different kinds of interior design in the **oblastní galerie Vysočiny** (Tues–Fri 9am–noon & 12.30–5pm, Sat & Sun 10am–noon & 12.30–4pm), round the corner at Komenského 10, north off the main square, which houses a small but excellent collection of nineteenth- and twentieth-century art. You can also take a trip down into the town's extensive catacombs, known as **katakomby** (daily: April & Oct–Dec 10am–noon & 2–4pm; May, June & Sept 10am–noon & 2–4pm; July & Aug 9am–noon & 2–5pm) or

MAHLER IN IGLAU

"I am thrice homeless, as a native of Bohemia in Austria, as an Austrian among Germans and as a Jew throughout the world. Everywhere an intruder, never welcomed." **Gustav Mahler**'s predicament was typical of the Jews of *Mitteleuropa*, and it only exacerbated his already highly strung personality. Prone to Wagnerian excesses and bouts of extreme pessimism, he would frequently work himself into a state of nervous collapse when composing or conducting. It was this Teutonic temperament as much as his German-speaking background that separated him from his more laid-back Czech musical contemporaries.

Mahler was born in 1860 in the nearby village of Kaliště (Kalischt) on the Bohemian side of the border, the second son of Bernhard Mahler, an ambitious Jewish businessman. The very same year, the Mahlers, who were the only non-Czechs in the entire village, moved to Jihlava (Iglau), where there had been a strong Jewish community since the mid-fourteenth century. The family moved to Znojemská 4, where Mahler's father opened a pub, a drunken dive by all accounts and certainly too much for a sensitive vegetarian like Mahler. Bernhard's business ventures proved a big success, and he eventually opened his own distillery, but at home there was little to rejoice about. Judging by his frequent court appearances, Bernhard was a bad-tempered, violent man, while his wife, Marie, was a frail woman, whose minor heart condition was only exacerbated by her fourteen pregnancies (only six children survived to adulthood).

Mahler went to school at the German *Gymnasium* on Hluboká (some fifty years after Smetana), but showed more musical than academic promise. At the age of just ten, he made his first public appearance as a pianist at the town's municipal theatre, then in a converted church on Komenského. A local farmer persuaded Bernhard to send his boy to Prague to study music, but Mahler returned homesick after less than a year. After completing his studies in Jihlava, where he later claimed "I didn't learn anything", he was accepted as a student at the Vienna conservatoire. Mahler then enjoyed a fairly stormy career as a conductor that included stints at, among other places, Olomouc and Prague, before finally settling in Vienna, the place with which he is most closely associated. His links with Jihlava were permanently severed in 1889, when both his parents died, the family property was sold, and his remaining siblings moved away.

Under the Communists there was little mention of the town's greatest son – now, predictably enough, all that has changed. The house in which Mahler grew up is under restoration and set to become a kind of cultural centre, while round the corner a branch of the muzeum Vysočiny (see overleaf) contains a permanent exhibition on him – and of course, there's the *Gustav Mahler* hotel. Mahler's parents' grave still stands in the Jewish cemetery, 1km west of the town centre on U cvičiště, off Žižkova, close to the municipal cemetery. Dedicated fans who wish to track down the village of Mahler's birth should beware that there are several villages called Kaliště in Bohemia: the right one is listed in map indexes as Kaliště (Pelhřimov), roughly 7km northwest of Humpolec, and confusingly not Kaliště (Jihlava). The house, in which Mahler was born (which burned down in 1937 and had to be rebuilt), is due to open as a museum in 2000.

historické podzemí. The entrance to the tunnels is beside the imposing early Baroque facade of the Jesuit church of **sv Ignác**, built at the top of the square in the 1680s. Unfortunately, the church is usually closed, so to see the ceiling fresco and the stupendous trompe l'oeil main altar, you'll need to get there before one of the services.

Apart from the Jesuit church, all the town's other churches comply with medieval requirements and are set back from the square. The most obvious of these is the church of **sv Jakub** (St James), east of the square down Farní, whose two plain stone towers and steeply pitched, chevroned roof rise majestically above the surrounding burgher houses. The church is best admired from afar, though it's also possible to climb the church's northern **tower** (May–Sept Tues–Sun 10am–noon & 2–6pm) for a panoramic view over the town. You can peek at the spectacular gilded Baroque altar-pieces, but if you want a closer look you'll have to ask round for the key or wait for one of the church services. The town walls run round the back of the church, and in the leafy gorge below are the woods of the Březinovy sady and the town's **zoo** (daily: April & Oct 9am–5pm; May–Sept 8am–6pm; Nov–March 9am–4pm), where tigers, zebras, kangaroos, monkeys, hippos and snakes share cramped quarters.

For a town originally built on silver, Jihlava lacks the vestiges of prosperity that grace, for example, Kutná Hora. A few finely carved portals and the remnants of fif-teenth-century frescoes survive here and there, but just one gateway, **brána Matky boží** (May–Sept Tues–Sun 9am–noon & 12.30–5pm), guarding the road from the west, is all that's left of the town's five gates. Next door to the gateway is the beautifully restored **Minoritský kostel**, a remarkable little church that dates back to around 1250. The building's antiquity – it's the oldest stone building in the town – is evident in the thick Romanesque pillars and fragments of medieval frescoes in the nave. However, the Baroque fittings are no less interesting, particularly the technicolor Crucifixion scene opposite the pulpit, which is played out in front of a ruched silver drape. Make sure you venture into the choir to admire the mural depicting the medieval town, located above the sedilia, which harbours three finely sculpted female saints.

There is, however, just one more sight worth mentioning, the branch of the **muzeum Vysočiny** (mid-April to Sept Tues–Fri 9am–noon & 1–5pm, Sat & Sun 1–5pm), at Kosmákova 9, off the southwest corner of the square, which houses a per-manent exhibition on Gustav Mahler's childhood in Jihlava (expozice mladý Gustav Mahler a Jihlava). The captions for the black-and-white photos are in Czech and German only, so you'll need to buy the English catalogue to get anything out of the museum. That said, there's not a lot to get excited about: no original artefacts and little imagination to the displays.

Practicalities

The **main train station** – simply called Jihlava – is a good 2km northeast of the town centre, so hop on trolleybus #A or #B; slow trains to or from Tábor, Jindřichův Hradec or České Budějovice also stop at **Jihlava-město**, 1km north of the old town – there are no trolleybuses, but it's an easy walk to the staré město along třída Legionářů. From the **bus station**, northwest of the old town, it's a five-minute walk to the main square. Jihlava's **tourist office** (Mon–Fri 9am–5pm, Sat 9am–noon), is at no. 18 on the main square, and can organize **private rooms**.

Jihlava sees relatively few tourists, other than passing business folk, Austrians and homesick Sudeten Germans, so **accommodation** is limited to a few choices. Perhaps the most reliable place to stay is the *Hotel Gustav Mahler*, Křížová 4 (☎066/732 05 01; *gustavmahler@aol.cz*; ⑤), which has taken over the former Dominican monastery north of the main square; the hotel is wonderfully spacious, though there's little original decor left – ask for a room with shared facilities if you want to save money. The sgraf-fitoed *Hotel Zlatá Hvězda* (☎066/294 21; ⑤) is slightly cheaper and enjoys a good posi-tion on the main square, though it has a seedy non-stop bar in the basement. Other fall-backs include the rooms above the *Horácká rychta* restaurant (☎066/227 21; ⑤), on Komenského, which are okay despite the dodgy lilac touches, and the Art Nouveau *Hotel Grand* (☎066/235 41; ⑥), which has a few cheap rooms with shared facilities, and is situated further down Komenského at the junction with Husova. If you're camping, take a local bus to the lakeside *Pávov* **campsite** (open all year) situated 4km north of Jihlava, not far from the motorway.

All the above accommodation choices will happily serve you food and drink, but Jihlava's most aesthetically pleasing **restaurant** is *U vévody Albrechta*, which occupies a banquet room decorated with Renaissance frescoes, on the first floor at no. 41 on the west side of the main square. If you want to sample Jihlava's local *Ježek* (hedgehog or *Iglau* in German) **beer**, head for the self-service *Tři knížata* (closed Sun), at no. 44 on the west side of the main square, or the brewery tap on Vrchlického, to the west of the old town, off Jiráskova. A more mellow place to spend the evening is the *Kuba a Pařízek čajovna*, at the back of the bookshop on Brněnská.

Žďár nad Sázavou

The highest point in the Bohemian-Moravian Uplands, or Vysočina, is around 40km northeast of Jihlava, though the whole range is actually more like a high rolling plateau. This has always been a poor region, but one really good reason for venturing into the hinterland is to visit **ŽĎÁR NAD SÁZAVOU**, established in the thirteenth century as a small settlement pitched near its Cistercian monastery. Since the war the population has increased tenfold, making it one of the largest towns in the region, producing, among other things, ice skates. The only thing worth seeing, however, is the **monastery** complex, a three-kilometre walk (or short bus ride) north through the grey new town of Žďár – instructive if nothing else. As you approach the woods and fish ponds, there's a small bridge decorated with the familiar figures of eighteenth-century saints, on the other side of which is the monastery now back in the hands of the Kinskýs.

The whole complex is the work of **Giovanni Santini** (who also had a hand in the monasteries of Plasy and Kladruby near Plzeň), perhaps the most gifted architect of the Czech Counter-Reformation. His two great talents were marrying Gothic and Baroque forms in a new and creative way, and producing buildings with a humour and irony often lacking in eighteenth-century architecture. The monastery church isn't a particularly good example, but keys from the monastic office (daily: April–June, Sept & Oct 8am–4pm; July & Aug 9am–5pm), to the right of it, will allow you access to one that is: the UNESCO-protected **Zelená hora** (Green Hill) pilgrimage church, up through the wooded hill to the south of the monastery. It's a unique and intriguing structure, with zigzag cemetery walls forming a decagon of cloisters around the central star-shaped church, a giant mushroom sprouting a half-formed, almost Byzantine dome, dedicated to sv Jan Nepomucký (St John of Nepomuk). The interior is filled with details of his

---

MORE SANTINI

For further exposure to Santini's work, a number of his more lighthearted minor buildings are dotted about the Žďár region. The first, a couple of hundred yards further north of the Cistercian monastery in Žďár, is the eerie **dolní hřbitov** (lower cemetery), whose three simple chapels symbolize the Trinity. Built to accommodate plague victims who never materialized, the graveless space is empty but for a lonesome angel calling the tune for Judgement Day, and is enclosed by the gentle ripples of the cemetery walls.

Down the road at **OSTROV NAD OSLAVOU** (7min by train), using a similar design to the one he employed in the chateau at Chlumec nad Cidlinou, Santini built a *hostinec* in the shape of a "W" in memory of his local patron, the Abbot of Žďár, Václav Vejmluva (the initials W.W. in German). It has seen a lot of use and abuse over the years, but is still the local boozer: buy a pint and appreciate the architecture at leisure.

Just 2km northeast of Ostrov and within easy walking distance, the local church at **OBYČTOV** is another Santini design, built in the shape of a turtle, one of the Virgin Mary's more obscure symbols. Four chapels mark each leg, a presbytery the neck, and the west onion-domed tower the distorted head. Ask around for the key to the whitewashed interior, which features more turtle symbolism.

martyrdom (for which see p.66), along with symbolic and numerical references to the saint and the Cistercians. On the pulpit, a gilded relief depicts his being thrown off the Charles Bridge in Prague by the king's men, while everywhere in macabre repetition are the saint's severed tongue and the stars that appeared above his head: above the pulpit, on the ceiling, in the shapes of the windows, and in the five side chapels.

Back in the main part of the monastery there's a **Muzeum knihy** (Book Museum), and a small exhibition dedicated to Santini (April & Oct Sat & Sun 8am–4pm; May, June & Sept Tues–Sun 8am–4pm; July & Aug Tues–Sun 9am–5pm), housed in the stables he himself designed, with swirling zigzag patterning on the ceiling. Packed with plans and photos of his other works in the Czech Lands, the exhibition traces Santini's influences and places him in the wider context of European architecture of the time.

Practicalities

Žďár is only an hour's fast train ride from Brno; the town centre is 1km north of the train station, and another 2km from the monastery. It's easy to get a room in the town, whose **hotels** include the *U labutě* (☎0616/229 49; ②), on the main square, and the high-rise *Hotelový dům* (☎0616/241 46; ③), just below the square. There's a decent *hostinec* called *Teferna*, serving Starobrno, by the monastery, and, a little further up the road, the *Pilská nádrž* lakeside **campsite** (May–Sept).

Telč and Slavonice

Telč and Slavonice are two of the most beautiful Renaissance towns anywhere in Europe. Yet while Telč is a popular stopoff on whirlwind tours of the country, Slavonice – every bit as perfect – sees many fewer visitors. Both are feasible day-trips from Jihlava, even on the ridiculously slow **trains**, which take up to an hour and a half to reach Telč and slightly over two hours to get to Slavonice (change at Kostelec u Jihlavy for both). On the other hand, **buses** to Telč take just 45 minutes (there's even a direct service from Brno), though there's no direct service to Slavonice from Jihlava.

Telč

It's hardly an exaggeration to say that the last momentous event in **TELČ** (Teltsch) was the great fire of 1530, which wiped out all the town's wooden Gothic houses and forced it to start afresh. It is this fortuitous disaster that has made Telč what it is: a perfect museum-piece sixteenth-century provincial town. Squeezed between two fish ponds, the Štěpnický to the east and the Ulický to the west, the **staré město** is little more than two medieval gate towers, one huge wedge-shaped square and a chateau. Renaissance arcades extend the length of the main square, **náměstí Zachariáše z Hradce**, lined with pastel-coloured houses (including the town's fire station) that display a breathtaking variety of gables and pediments, none less than two hundred and fifty years old. At the eastern end of the square, you can climb the **věž sv Ducha** (June–Sept daily noon–5pm) for an overview of the ensemble.

At the narrow western end of the square, the **zámek** (Tues–Sun: April & Oct 9am–noon & 1–4pm; May–Sept until 5pm) in no way disturbs the sixteenth-century atmosphere of the town; it too was badly damaged in the fire and had to be rebuilt in similar fashion. Like the chateau at the nearby Bohemian town of Jindřichův Hradec (see p.163), it was the inspiration of Zachariáš of Hradec, whose passion for all things Italian is again strongly in evidence. Of the two guided tours on offer, the hour-long tour (trasa A) is the one to go for, as it concentrates on the Renaissance-era rooms, which boast a truly exceptional array of period ceilings. The shorter tour (trasa B) features living spaces from later periods, but even this can be fun as the whole place is refreshingly intimate and low-key after the intimidating pomposity of the Baroque chateaux of the region.

Even if you don't fancy going on a guided tour, you should take a look inside the chateau's exquisite All Saints' **chapel**, opposite the ticket office. The chapel was built in 1580 as the last resting place of Zachariáš of Hradec and his wife Kateřina of Valdštejn, who lie, arms outstretched in prayer, surrounded by a beautiful, multi-coloured wrought-iron grille. For a funereal chapel, the decor is surprisingly bright and upbeat, and the stuccowork is absolutely outstanding, with gilded trumpets erupting from a farrago of figs, olives, pomegranates and other fruit. In the central relief on the ceiling of the nave, a whole host of skeletons are being restored to life on the Day of Judgement, as prophesized by Ezekiel: "there was a noise, and behold a shaking, and the bones came together, bone to his bone".

You can also stroll through the cloistered formal garden at leisure, and pay a visit to the **Galerie Jana Zrzavého** (April–Oct Tues–Sun 9am–5pm; Nov–March Tues–Fri & Sun 9am–4pm, Sat 9am–1pm) in the east wing, dedicated to the Surrealist painter Jan Zrzavý, whose career spanned the first three quarters of the twentieth century. Born in nearby Havlíčkův Brod in 1890, Zrzavý's early works were Post-Impressionist, but he quickly adopted his own peculiar dreamlike, slightly surreal style. His paintings are definitely an acquired taste, though they are by no means monotonous; particularly striking are his pallid, grey, virtually uninhabited Breton landscapes painted between the wars.

The local branch of the **muzeum Vysočiny** (times as for the zámek) is housed in the chateau, too, with a model of the town, a miniature Bethlehem scene and displays on local history. More intriguing, though, is the exquisite World War I memorial, made from ceramic tiles, at the end of the covered passageway that leads to the town's church. Although the adjacent World War II memorial doesn't explicitly say so, it's clear that the majority of the town's victims in the last war were from the local Jewish community.

The **train station** is a ten-minute walk east of the old town along Masarykova. The **tourist office** (Mon–Fri 8am–5pm, Sat & Sun 10am–5pm; winter Mon–Fri only), at no. 10 on the main square, is very helpful and friendly and can book **private rooms**. Most tour groups come here only for a couple of hours, so **accommodation** shouldn't be too much of a problem. The *Hotel Celerin* (☎066/96 24 77; *celerin@dnd.cz*; ④), enjoys the best location, right on the main square, but the *Telč* on Na Můstku (☎066/96 21 09; ⑤) is more stylish. The *Na hrázi* (☎066/721 31 50; ④) is a pleasant new pub hotel overlooking the fish ponds to the south of the old town on Na hrázi, and there are numerous other smaller pensions to choose from in the old town. The nearest **campsite** is the *Velkopařezitý* lakeside site (open all year), 7km northwest of Telč. **Bike rental** is available from an outlet next door to *Celerin,* and there's a **cashpoint** at the wide end of the square. *U Marušky,* by the tower, at the opposite end of the square from the chateau, and *Na kopečku,* a short walk north of the old town up Jihlavská, are both perfectly decent Czech **pubs**. Telč can get busy in the summer, but it gets even busier for two weeks at the turn of July and August when the town hosts a non-traditional folk music festival.

Slavonice

SLAVONICE (Zlabings), 25km south of Telč and a stone's throw from the Austrian border, is in many ways even more remarkable. It's a monument to a prosperity that lasted for just one hundred years, shattered by the Thirty Years' War which halved the population, then dealt its deathblow in the 1730s when the post road from Prague to Vienna was rerouted via Jihlava. In 1945, the forced removal of the local German-speaking inhabitants emptied Slavonice, and matters deteriorated when the Iron Curtain wrapped itself around the village, severing road and rail links with the West.

Even now, the **staré město** – not much larger than the one at Telč – still has a strange and haunting beauty. The impression is further enhanced by the bizarre biblical and apocalyptic sixteenth-century "strip cartoons" played out on the houses in monochrome sgraffito, many of which have been restored to their former glory. Life has returned to Slavonice since the border crossing reopened (daily 6am–10pm), the Cold War paranoia has gone, the whole town has been spruced up considerably, and Austrians, at least, have rediscovered the town in large numbers.

The best way to start a tour of the town is to pick up an ice cream at the local *cukrárna*, on **náměstí Míru**, the larger of the town's two squares, if only for a closer look at the stunning diamond vaulting in the building's entrance hall. Next, you should pay a visit to the former **Lutheran prayer room** (daily 9am–7pm or dusk) at house no. 517 on Horní náměstí. Here, on the first floor, the very friendly Italian owner will show you the exceptional wall paintings of the Apocalypse, which miraculously survived the Counter-Reformation: look out, in particular, for the mischievous depiction of the Devil as a crocodile wearing the papal crown, not to mention the horse-riding Whore of Babylon. Last of all, you can now climb the **Městská věž** (April, May & Sept Sat & Sun 8am–noon & 1–5pm; June–Aug daily), which is attached to the town's central church.

Most people come to Slavonice on a day-trip, but you can **stay the night** at the *Hotel Alfa* (☎0332/49 32 61; ①) on the main square, which is basically a pub with simple rooms upstairs, or above the *Besídka* bar and gallery (☎0332/49 32 93; ①), on Horní náměstí, which runs arty workshops over the summer. For **food**, you can also try *Apetito*, on the main square, with its own courtyard out back, which serves traditional Czech food. If you don't fancy the slow train journey northwards, Slavonice is connected by the occasional bus to Jindřichův Hradec and points to the west. You can also enjoy a quick day-trip into Austria, by walking or driving across the former Iron Curtain, a few hundred metres south of the station, to the Austrian hamlet of Fratres.

The Slovácko region

What the Labe basin is to the Bohemians, the **Slovácko region**, around the plains of the River Morava 50km east of Brno, is to the Moravians. They settled in this fertile land around the late eighth century, taking their name from the river and eventually lending it to the short-lived Great Moravian Empire, the first coherent political unit in the region to be ruled by Slavs and the subject of intense archeological research (and controversy) over the last forty years. Geographically the River Morava (along with the River Odra further north) forms a natural corridor between east and west, difficult to defend against intruders and consequently trashed by numerous armies marching their way across Europe, from the Turks to the Tatars. Nowadays, at various different points, the Morava forms the border between Slovakia and Austria, then, moving north, Moravia and Slovakia.

Ethnically, it's a grey area where Moravians and Slovaks happily coexist – the local dialect and customs virtually indistinguishable from West Slovakia – despite the new cross-border restrictions now in place. Tomáš Garrigue Masaryk, the country's founder and first president, hailed from here, and his mixed parentage – his mother was German-speaking, his father a Slovak peasant – was typical of the region in the nineteenth century. For the visitor, though, it's a dour, mostly undistinguished landscape – flat, low farming country, with just the occasional factory or ribbon village to break the monotony – and most people pass through en route to more established sights. In summer this can be a great mistake, for almost every village in the area has its own folk festival, and in early autumn the local wine caves are bursting with life and ready to demonstrate the region's legendary and lavish hospitality.

Uherské Hradiště and around

The industrial town of **UHERSKÉ HRADIŠTĚ** (Ungarisch-Hradisch), like many towns on the Morava, has made a remarkable recovery after the devastating floods of 1997. The town sees few visitors at the best of times, and the only reason travellers stray into its shapeless centre is in their search for the **Pamatník Velké Moravy** (April–Oct Tues–Fri 8.30am–4.30pm, Sat & Sun 8.30am–noon & 1–5pm), suspected site of the capital of the Great Moravian Empire, which is actually north of the centre, across the Morava, on Jezuitská in a part of town known confusingly as Staré Město (10min by foot, or bus #4 to the second stop after the bridge). The archeological remains, housed in what looks like a concrete bunker from the last war, include the foundations of a ninth-century church, discovered in 1949, and a lot of bones and broken crockery – a specialist's paradise, but less gripping for the rest of us.

A more accessible load of old rocks, along with a good selection of folk costumes and suchlike, is on display at the **Slovácké muzeum** (daily 9am–noon & 12.30–5pm) in the Smetanovy sady, to the east of town. The obligatory Jesuit church aside, the town's only other sight as such is the late Baroque **apothecary U zlaté koruny** on the main square; it's still functioning as a *lékárna* (pharmacy), and you can peep through into the frescoed back room.

Arriving at Uherské Hradiště by **bus**, simply walk west along Velehradská třída to the centre; arriving by train is more complicated – **trains** travelling north or south tend to arrive at Staré Město u Uherského Hradiště on the north bank of the river (bus #4 into town), while trains from the east or west arrive in the southern suburb of Kunovice (bus #2 into town). The more central Uherské Hradiště station, southwest of the main square, is only served by the occasional shuttle service between the two (or bus #1). When choosing a **hotel**, you might as well stay at the *Grand* (☎0632/55 15 11; ④) on Palackého náměstí, the best the town has to offer; the same management team runs the *Morava* on Šafaříkova (☎0632/55 15 08; ④). The *Fojta* (☎0632/55 12 37; ③), on the main square, is a last resort. Uherské Hradiště's **cinema**, Kino Hvězda, on náměstí Míru, puts on a good range of mainstream and art house movies, stages exhibitions, and puts on a low-key film festival in April. It's also worth checking out what's on at *Klub Mír*, on náměstí Míru, which puts on a surprisingly good mix of gigs.

Velehrad

The **Cistercian monastery** at **VELEHRAD**, just 9km across the fields from Uherské Hradiště, is one of the most important pilgrimage sites in the Czech Republic. It's an impressive sight, too, with the twin ochre towers of its **church** (daily 9am–5pm) set

---

VELKÁ MORAVA – THE GREAT MORAVIAN EMPIRE

The Moravians took their name from the **River Morava** when they settled here around the late eighth century; their Great Moravian Empire was the first coherent political unit in the region to be ruled by Slavs. At its peak under the Slav prince Svätopluk (870–894), the territories of **Velká Morava** (the Great Moravian Empire) extended well into Slovakia, Bohemia, and parts of western Hungary and southern Poland, and arguments over the whereabouts of its legendary capital, Veligrad, have been puzzling scholars for many years. At first, the most obvious choice seemed to be Velehrad in Moravia, but excavations there have proved fruitless. Opinion is nowadays divided among Nitra, in West Slovakia, Mikulčice, right on the Slovak border southeast of Hodonín, and Staré Město, now part of Uherské Hradiště. Whatever the truth, the whole lot had been laid waste by the Magyar hordes by 906, not long after the death of Svätopluk, and Slovakia remained under Hungarian rule for the next millennium.

THE APOSTLES OF THE SLAVS

The significance of saints **Cyril** (827–69) and **Methodius** (815–85) goes far beyond their mere canonization. Brothers from a wealthy family in Constantinople, they were sent as missionaries to the Great Moravian Empire in 863 at the invitation of its ruler, Rastislav, less for reasons of piety than to assert his independence from his German neighbours. Thrust headlong into a political minefield, they were given a hard time by the local German clergy, and had to retreat to Rome, where Cyril became a monk and died. Methodius, meanwhile, insisted on returning to Moravia, only to be imprisoned for two years at the instigation of the German bishops. The pope eventually got him released, but dragged him back to Rome to answer charges of heterodoxy. He was cleared of all charges, consecrated bishop of Pannonia and Moravia, and continued to teach in the vernacular until his death in 885.

More important than their achievements in converting the local populace was the fact that they preached in the tongue of the common people. Cyril in particular is regarded as the founder of Slavonic literature, having been accredited with single-handedly inventing the Glagolitic script, still used in the Eastern Church and the basis of the modern Cyrillic alphabet that takes his name, while Methodius is venerated by both Western and Eastern Christians as a pioneer of the vernacular liturgy and a man dedicated to ecumenism. After Methodius' death, his followers were duly chased out and forced to take refuge in Bulgaria. The Czech Lands and most of Slovakia came under Rome's sway once and for all, and had to wait until the end of the fourteenth century before they once more heard their own language used to preach the gospel.

against the backdrop of the Chřiby hills, a low beech-covered ridge that separates Brno from the Morava basin.

The monastery's importance as an object of pilgrimage derives from the belief (now proved to be false) that it was the seat of St Methodius' archbishopric, the first in the Slav Lands, and the place where he died on July 5, 885 (see box above). The 1100th anniversary of this last fact attracted over 150,000 pilgrims from across Czechoslovakia in 1985, the largest single, unofficial gathering in the country since the first anniversary of the Soviet invasion in August 1969 (July 5 is now a national holiday). Five years later, Velehrad entertained Pope John Paul II, and half a million people turned up.

There's certainly something about the place that sets it apart, whether it's the historical associations, the sheer magnificence of its High Baroque, or its strange limitless emptiness outside of the annual pilgrimage. The church owes its gigantic scale to the foundations of the original Romanesque church on which it's built. This burned down in 1681 after being sacked several times by marauding Protestants, but you can visit its remains in the crypt's **lapidárium** (April–Sept daily 9am–noon & 1–4pm; Oct & Nov Tues–Sun only). Inside the church itself, the finer points of the artistry may be lacking in finesse, but the faded glory of the frescoed nave, suffused with a pink-grey light and empty but for the bent old women who come here for their daily prayers, is bewilderingly powerful.

There's a new **hotel**, *Hotel Mlýn Velehrad* (☎0632/714 60; *hotel-mlyn@hitech.cz*; ⑤), and a **campsite** (April–Oct) 1.5km up the road to Šalas, and the village is served by regular buses from Uherské Hradiště.

Buchlovice and Buchlov

Four kilometres west of Velehrad, still just out of reach of the Chřiby hills, is the village of **BUCHLOVICE** (Buchlowitz), easily accessible by bus from Uherské Hradiště. The reason for being here is to see the Berchtolds' pretty little eighteenth-century **zámek** (April & Oct Tues–Sun 9am–noon & 1–4pm; May, June & Sept Tues–Sun 9am–noon &

1–5pm; July & Aug daily 9am–noon & 1–6pm), a warm and hospitable country house with a lovely arboretum bursting with rhododendrons, fuschias and peacocks. The house, composed of two symmetrically opposed semicircles around a central octagon, has been recently renovated, and the smallish suite of rooms still contains most of its original Rococo furniture, left behind by the family when they fled to Austria in 1945. Another prize exhibit abandoned in haste was a leaf from the tree beneath which Mary Queen of Scots was executed.

A stiff three-and-a-half-kilometre climb up into the forest of the Chřiby hills will take you to the Gothic hrad of **Buchlov** (May & June Tues–Sun 8am–5pm; July & Aug daily 9am–6pm; Sept Tues–Sun 9am–4pm), which couldn't be more dissimilar. In bad weather, as the mist whips round the bastions, it's hard to imagine a more forbidding place, but in summer the view over the treetops is terrific and the whole place has a cool, breezy feel to it. Founded as a royal seat by the Přemyslids in the thirteenth century, it has suffered none of the painful neo-Gothicizing of other medieval castles – in fact the Berchtolds had turned it into a museum as early as the late nineteenth century. Heavy, rusty keys open up a series of sparsely furnished rooms lit only by thin slit windows, and dungeons in which the Habsburgs used to confine the odd rebellious Hungarian. If you're on for a bit of hiking, the stillness and extraordinary beauty of the surrounding beech forests are difficult to match, but make sure you stock up with provisions as there are few shops in the area. There's a restaurant in the castle, and the *Smraďavka* **campsite** (April–Oct) is 2km southeast of Buchlovice.

Strážnice and around

For most of the year **STRÁŽNICE** (Strassnitz), 20km or so southwest of Uherské Hradiště, sees perhaps a handful of visitors, but on the last weekend of June, thousands converge on this unexceptional town for the annual **International Folk Festival** – the largest in the country – held in three purpose-built stadiums in the grounds of the local chateau. During the festival, hotels are booked solid for miles around, and the only thing to do is to bring your own tent and try to squeeze onto the castle campsite (April–Oct) or just crash out somewhere in your sleeping bag.

If you're here at any other time of the year, there's only enough to keep you occupied for an hour or two. Though no work of art itself, the **zámek**, ten minutes' walk north of the centre, off the road to Bzeneč, contains an exceptionally good **folk museum** (May–Oct Tues–Sun 8am–5pm), part of the Institute of Folk Art. En route to the chateau, you'll pass the town's excellent **skanzen** (times as above), called variously Muzeum v přírodě or Muzeum vesnice jihovýchodní Moravy, with numerous restored thatched, timber-built cottages and peasant gear from the outlying villages.

The **train station** is five minutes' walk south of the town centre. Outside of the festival, it should be easy enough **to stay** at the *Strážnice Flag Hotel* (☎0631/33 20 59; ⑤), which has comfortable en-suite rooms. The best place for a **meal** and to sample local wines is *Zámecká vinárna* in the chateau, with live music at weekends; the *Na rynku*, on the main square, is a decent pub serving Starobrno.

Wine caves and festivals around Strážnice

Strážnice makes a good base for visiting the private *sklepy* or **wine caves** that provide the focus of village life in the summer months before and after the grape harvest. Perhaps the easiest *sklepy* to visit for those without their own transport are the Plže caves at **PETROV**, a thin settlement strung out along the main road from Hodonín, one stop down the railway line from Strážnice. Hidden from sight, on the other side of the railway track, are around twenty whitewashed stone caves over two hundred years old, some beautifully decorated with intricate floral designs, others with just a simple deep-blue stripe. Around late September there are usually one or two locals overseeing their new harvest who'll be happy to show you around and no doubt invite you to sample (and of course buy) some of their wine. During the rest of the summer, merrymaking goes on in the evenings at weekends. Those with their own transport and a taste for the stuff could check out Polesovice, 12km north, or Mutěnice, 15km west, or better still the thatched *sklepy* at Prušánky.

There are countless other festivals in the area, such as the Dolmácké festival, held every four years in Hluk (next one in 2001), and pilgrimages to places like Blatnice, held in September. The most famous festival of the lot after Strážnice is the annual *Jízda králů* or "Ride of the Kings" held over the weekend of Whitsuntide (the last Sunday in May) in **VLČNOV**, which lies south of route 50 between Uherské Hradiště and the pistol-producing town of Uherský Brod. Young villagers in traditional folk costumes ride through the town on horseback, and folk concerts and dances are staged all weekend.

Luhačovice

Twenty-seven kilometres east of Uherské Hradiště is the genteel spa town of **LUHA-ČOVICE**, decidedly lush after the rather demure Morava valley but without the pomp and majesty of the west Bohemian spas. Although its springs are mentioned as far back as the twelfth century, nothing much was done about developing the place until it was bought up in 1902 and building began on the first of Slovak Dušan Jurkovič's quirky, folksy, half-timbered villas, which have become the spa's hallmark.

The largest of these buildings, the **Dům Dušana Jurkoviče**, dominates the central spa gardens spreading northeast from the train station. The beams are purely decorative, occasionally breaking out into a swirling flourish, and the roof is a playful pagoda-type affair, creating a uniquely Slovak folk version of Art Nouveau. The blot on Luhačovice's copybook is the new **Kolonáda**, a graceless curving concrete colonnade that's nevertheless a good place to sit and watch the patients pass by as they sip the waters from their grotesquely decorated mugs. The rest of the spa forms a snake-like promenade boxed in by shrubs and trees, with folksy bridges spanning the gently trickling river. Soon enough you hit another cluster of Jurkovič buildings, one of which is the open-air natural spring **swimming pool**, good for a cheap unchlorinated dip. The villas continue into the leafy suburbs, but unless you fancy a hike into the surrounding woods or are staying at the lakeside **campsite** 1km up the main road (mid-April to Sept), there's no reason to continue walking. If you're interested in finding out more about the folk traditions of the area, and the history of the spa, hop across to the west bank of the stream to the museum in the **Vila Lipová** (Tues–Sun 9am–noon & 1–5pm).

To get to Luhačovice by train from Uherské Hradiště, you need to change at Uherský Brod; buses run direct, but less frequently. The **bus** and **train stations** are at the southwestern end of the spa. Good-value **accommodation** can be found all over the spa; try the *Hotel Lužná* (☎067/713 11 12; ⑤), to the south on Solné. Although buses from all over the country run regular services to Luhačovice, it's still a bit out on a limb, stuck halfway up the Šťávnice Valley. If you're planning to continue into Slovakia, however, the scenic train journey from Uherský Brod through the White Carpathians to Trenčianska Teplá is as good a way as any to get there.

Zlín

Hidden in a gentle green valley east of the Morava, **ZLÍN** is one of the most fascinating Moravian towns. Despite appearances, it's not just another factory town, it is *the* factory town – a museum of functionalist architecture and the inspiration of one man,

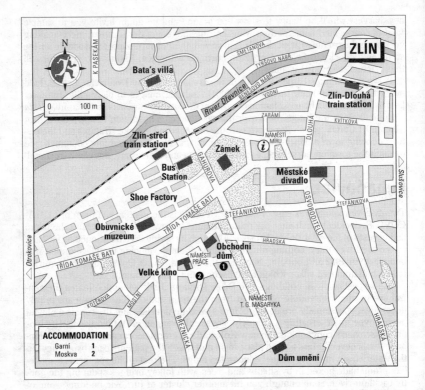

Tomáš Baťa (pronounced "Batya"). When Baťa founded his company in 1894 with his brother and sister, Zlín's population was less than 3000. Now, with suburbs trailing for miles along the River Dřevnice, it's approaching 90,000. The town's heyday was during the First Republic, when Baťa planned and started to build the ultimate production-line city, a place where workers would be provided with good housing, schooling, leisure facilities and a fair wage. "Work collectively, live individually", was one of Baťa's favourite aphorisms, and all along the approach roads to the town centre you can see the red-brick shoe-box houses that Baťa constructed for his workers as "temporary accommodation" – houses which have lasted better than anything built after 1948. The combined effects of Allied bombing, nationalization and economic stagnation have left only a hint of the model garden city Baťa had in mind. Zlín can't hope to appeal to everyone's aesthetic tastes, but it does present an entirely different side of the country from the usual provincial medieval staré město.

A little history

Son of a local cobbler, Tomáš Baťa worked his way up from nothing to become the First Republic's most famous millionaire. He grew rich supplying the Austro-Hungarian army with its boots during World War I, and between the wars quickly became the larges manufacturer of shoes in the world, producing over 50 million pairs annually. Baťa became the town's mayor in 1923, but died in a plane crash in 1932 at the peak of his power, and although his work was continued by his son (also called Tomáš), the family and firm were forced to leave the country in 1938. Tomáš Junior elected to go to Canada, taking his own management team (100 families) and shoemaking machinery with him. There, he quickly set about building another model factory town, known as Bataville, just outside Ottawa, and the company continued to expand into the vast multinational it is today.

Nationalization in 1945 robbed Baťa of the company's spiritual home, and in 1949, zealous Party hacks added insult to injury by renaming the town Gottwaldov after the country's notorious first Communist president, Klement Gottwald, also known as the "Stalinist butcher". It was no doubt seen as a just revenge on Baťa, who rid his shop floor of Communists by decree in the 1920s. When the Communists fell from power in November 1989, Tomáš Junior paid his first visit to Zlín for over forty years, and the whole town turned out to greet him, draping banners out of their windows proclaiming "ať žije Zlín" ("Long live Zlín"). In 1990, the town once more became officially known as Zlín, but due to alleged Nazi collaboration by members of his family, Baťa was unable to reclaim the factory through restitution. Nevertheless, Baťa now has a significant stake in the shoe market, with numerous outlets across the country, including the flagship modernist store on Wenceslas Square in Prague.

The Town

Baťa was a longstanding patron of modern art that he felt would reflect the thrust and modernity of his own business. In 1911 he had his own **villa** built on the north side of the river by the leading Czech architect of the time, Jan Kotěra; it's a very understated affair, virtually devoid of ornamentation, and now institutionalized. In the late 1920s, Le Corbusier was called in to design the town, but after an abortive sketch of the place, this chance of a lifetime fell to local-born architect **František Gahura**, who had studied under Kotěra.

Unlike any other town in the country, Zlín does not revolve around the local chateau or marketplace but around the **shoe factory** itself, its sixteen-storey administrative offices designed by one of Gahura's assistants, the Slovene Vladimír Karfík. The style – concrete frame, red-brick infill and plate-glass windows – was intended to be "the leitmotif of Zlín's architecture", as Gahura put it, and is indeed typical of all the town's original 1930s buildings, later copied and barbarized by undistinguished postwar architects. Baťa's own office was a huge, air-conditioned, glass-encased lift capable of visiting every floor. Nowadays, as well as serving as the corporation's administration office, it houses Zlín's main "sight", the Shoe Museum or **Obuvnické muzeum** (Tues–Sun 10am–noon & 1–5pm). Even if you're not a foot fetishist, it's a wonderful 1930s-style museum, with shoes from all over the world from medieval *boty* to the sad attempts of the Communist Zlín factory (renamed Svit after nationalization in 1945), plus a "revised" final section on Baťa himself, and, tucked away in one corner, the old man's fantastic lift/office. It's also worth asking if you can see the museum's video on the architectural development of the town.

From out of the factory grounds rises the obligatory red-and-white-striped chimney, industriously spewing black smoke over the town – in its own way a reassuring guarantee of further employment (half the local workforce are employed by the company). When the siren goes at 2pm for the end of the day shift, workers pour out of the factory gates and onto the trolleybuses, as if part of some strange Orwellian dumb show. Directly opposite the main entrance, across třída Tomáše Bati, is Karfík's plate-glass department store, **Obchodní dům**, which naturally includes a shoe shop (the country still led the world in one respect in 1989 – in shoe consumption, which stood at an annual rate of 4.2 pairs per capita). Beyond here, on náměstí Práce (literally "Work Square"), lies Gahura's faded white 1931 **Velké kino**, which holds 2000 movie-goers, and the eleven-storey Společenský dům, built by Karfík and Lorenz in 1932–33 and now occupied by the **Hotel Moskva**.

Gahura's master plan was never fully realized, and much of the town is accidental and ill-conceived. Only the sloping green of the **Masarykovo náměstí**, flanked by more boxy buildings, gives some idea of the trajectory of Gahura's ideas. The first block on the left is Gahura's Masarykovy školy, where Baťa pursued his revolutionary teaching methods still admired today. At the top of this leafy space is the **Dům umění** (Tues–Sun 9am–5pm), designed by Gahura in 1932 as a memorial to Baťa, where his (recently re-erected) statue, some memorabilia, and the wreckage of the biplane in which he crashed, used to stand. It now serves as the concert hall for the town's orchestra and for exhibitions of contemporary art – appropriate enough given Baťa's tireless patronage of the **avant-garde**, which he not only utilized in his photographic advertising but also produced in the film studios that were built here between the wars, where many of the country's renowned animation films are still made.

The only other place of interest is the modest country **zámek** (Tues–Sun 9am–noon & 1–5pm) in the park opposite the factory, which houses the town's **Muzeum jihovýchodní Moravy** (South Moravian Museum) boasting a small, but excellent collection of **twentieth-century Czech art**, ranging from the Cubists Kubišta, Filla, Čapek and Procházka to wacky Pop Art sculptures from the 1960s and more contemporary works. In a separate part of the chateau there's an obscure **Orienteering Museum** (Historie orientačního běhu; Tues–Sun 10am–noon & 1–5pm), with compasses, maps, photos and, of course, Zlín-made orienteering shoes dating back to the 1950s, when the sport was introduced into the country.

Lastly, Zlín is the birthplace of two unlikely bedfellows: the not so avant-garde playwright **Tom Stoppard** and the New York magnate's ex-wife, Ivana Trump. Stoppard's father was a Czech doctor by the name of Eugene Straussler, who fled with his wife and two-year-old son to Singapore to escape the Nazis. After his father's death, Tom's mother married a major in the British army (named Stoppard) and settled in England. These two snippets explain two otherwise puzzling points: why Stoppard has a slight foreign accent and why the Tom Stoppard Prize is given to Czech or Slovak authors in translation. **Ivana Trump** (Trumpová to the Czechs) was born here as Ivana Zelníčková, and rose to fame in her home country in the 1972 Olympic ski team. Her shocking blonde hair and formidable physique allowed her to pursue a modelling career in Canada before making the headlines as wife (and now ex-wife) of the New York tycoon Donald Trump.

Practicalities

Arriving at Zlín's **train station** (Zlín-střed) or **bus terminal**, you're just a few minutes' walk from the centre and everything there is to see. The **tourist office** (Mon–Fri 8am–5pm, Sat 8am–noon), in the radnice on náměstí Míru, should be able to help with any enquiries. **Accommodation** is uniformly overpriced, catering mostly for business clientele. *The* hotel to stay at is Gahura's high-rise *Hotel Moskva* (☎067/836 11 11; ⑥), on náměstí Práce, though it's also the centre of the town's fairly dubious nightlife. Next door, you can enjoy the gleaming white decor of the *Hotel Garní* (☎067/721 19 41; ⑤) for slightly less.

The *Záložna* (closed Sat & Sun), on náměstí Míru, is the local dive, serving Zubr beer; *Café Corso* (closed Sun), above the *Česká spořitelna* on nearby třída Tomáše Bati, has a good vegetarian selection and the usual Czech staples. More pleasant than both, though, is the **pizzeria** *U čápa*, by the river on Benešovo nábřeží, east of Dlouhá. Avoiding the casino and disco in the *Moskva*, and the tacky *Flip* disco in the Dům kultury, your choices for **nightlife** boil down to watching a film in the cavernous *Velké kino*, listening to the local philharmonic orchestra in the Dům uměni, and catching a band or playing ten-pin bowling at the *Golem* on náměstí Práce.

Otrokovice

An alternative Baťa experience can be had in neighbouring **OTROKOVICE**, 11km west of Zlín, by the River Morava. As is evident from the architecture, this is another Baťa town, built as an extension of Zlín in the 1930s – in fact the town was originally named Baťov, and was only renamed Otrokovice (after *otrok*, meaning "slave") by the Communists. Despite the overwhelming presence of the local factory (in this case Barum), Otrokovice works better than Zlín as a planned "garden city". At its centre is the Constructivist *Společenský dům*, Karfík's three-winged radial building in reinforced concrete, shaped rather like the sails of a windmill.

The nearest **campsite** to Zlín is the *Pahrbek* site (open all year), 7km south of (and one stop down the line from) Otrokovice in **NAPAJEDLA**, on the River Morava.

Kroměříž and around

KROMĚŘÍŽ (Kremsier), 30km or so up the Morava from Uherské Hradiště and seat of the bishops of Olomouc from the Middle Ages to the nineteenth century, is one of Moravia's most graceful towns. Its once-powerful German-speaking population has long since gone, and nowadays the town feels pleasantly provincial, famous only for its Moravian male-voice choir and folk music tradition. Though quiet, Kroměříž is definitely worth a day-trip, if only for the chateau's rich collections and the town's very beautiful and extensive gardens.

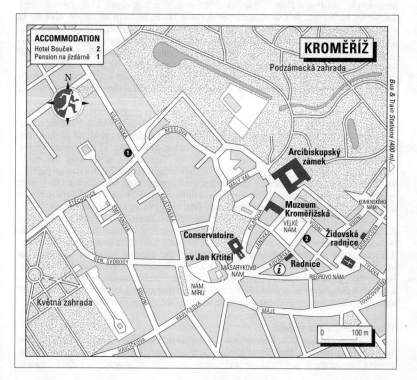

Savagely set upon by the Swedish army in the Thirty Years' War, Kroměříž was rebuilt by order of **Prince-Bishop Karl Eusebius von Liechtenstein-Kastelcorn**, a pathological builder (see p.303) and a member of the richest dynasty in Moravia at the time. Vast sums of money were spent not only on hiring Italian architects, but also on enriching the chateau's art collection and establishing a musical life to rival Vienna. Liechtenstein founded a college for choristers, maintained a thirty-piece court orchestra and employed a series of prestigious *Kapellmeister*, though nowadays, aside from the chateau's extensive archives, there's little evidence of the courtly life.

The old town

Standing on the southwest side of the River Morava, the centre of the staré město is the former marketplace of **Velké náměstí**. A broad, gracious square, its sea of cobblestones is interrupted only by the lime trees that surround a plague column and fountain (there's an even better column and fountain ensemble on Riegrovo náměstí). Arcades have survived here and there round the square, the radnice has a fine white Renaissance tower, and the houses themselves, though they have suffered over the years, are now prettily painted up. Jánská, just off the square, hides the town's finest ensemble: a flourish of terraced canons' houses with bright Empire frontages in primary colours.

Arcibiskupský zámek

The houses at the northern corner of Velké náměstí part to reveal the **Arcibiskupský zámek** (Archbishop's Palace; April & Oct Sat & Sun 9am–5pm; May, June & Sept Tues–Sun 9am–5pm; July & Aug closes 6pm), a Baroque fortress whose severity is relieved only by the fifteenth-century lanterned tower, sole survivor of the Swedes' rampage in the Thirty Years' War. Inside, the chateau is a more gentle Rococo than its uncompromising exterior might suggest. The dark wood and marble decor of the small **manský sál**, where the bishops held court, is overwhelmed by Maulbertsch's celebratory frescoes, which bear down on guests from the unusually low ceiling. The archbishop's bedroom rather alarmingly contains a double bed – the official story being that it was for his parents when they came to visit.

The showpiece of the palace is the fiddly white-and-gold excess of the **sněmovní sál**, as high and mighty as anything in Prague, and featured in Miloš Forman's film *Amadeus*. In the first three months of 1849, Reichstag delegates from all parts of the empire met to thrash out a new liberal constitution in the face of the revolutionary events of the previous year. In the end, though, the "Kremsier Constitution" that came out of these brainstorming sessions and acknowledged "equality of national rights", was unceremoniously ditched by the new imperial government, who drew up their own version. Police were sent to Kremsier to close down the Reichstag, with orders to arrest the most radical delegates. The Habsburgs' final bout of absolutism had begun.

You can skip the main tour (trasa 1) and just visit the **Zámecká obrazárna** (Chateau Gallery), which contains what's left of the Liechtensteins' vast art collection, still the best selection of sixteenth- and seventeenth-century European paintings in Moravia. There's plenty of bucolic frolicking supplied by the Flemish masters, including an earthy Breughel and a more sober portrait of Charles I of England and his wife Henrietta by Van Dyck. Others worth noting are Veronese's awestruck *Apostles*, Cranach's *Beheading of St John the Baptist* (with a mangy dog lapping up the spillage) and, the gallery's prize possession, Titian's gruesome *Apollo Punishing Marsyas*.

The rest of the old town

Like Olomouc (see p.327), Kroměříž is a place as rich in gardens as in buildings. The watery **Podzámecká zahrada** (daily dawn–dusk), established by one of the green-fingered Chotek family who held the archbishopric in the 1830s, stretches right down to the Morava, covering an area twice the size of the old town. Having long since lost its formality, it's now a pleasantly unruly park, reeking of wild garlic and hiding an aviary and menagerie, harbouring raccoons, baboons and parrots, plus a deer park and a few stalking peacocks.

Ten minutes' walk west of the chateau is the **Květná zahrada** (daily 7am–7pm), more formal but also more beautiful and generally in a better state of repair. The garden was laid out by the Liechtensteins in the 1670s, "ten years and no expense spared" as the Latin inscription reminds you. Its finest vista is the Neoclassical colonnade along the gardens' north side, with each of the 46 columns topped by a Roman bust. There are chestnut and lime hedges and tall avenues of trees, plus two waist-high mazes and a huge domed **rotunda** at the centre, thickly stuccoed and gaudily frescoed by Italian artists, and featuring mini-grottoes stuffed with satyrs and strange wild creatures. Equally remarkable is the **Foucault pendulum**, suspended from the ceiling, which, as the guide proudly tells you, is one of only four in the world.

The **Muzeum Kroměřížska** (Tues–Sun 9am–noon & 1–5pm), on the main square, contains a large collection of work by Max Švabinský, a late-nineteenth-century artist and graphicist who was born here in 1872. There's no denying his skill nor his prolific output, but he's a mite too gushy and romantic for some people's tastes, and the drawings of nudes and tigers, not to mention his collection of exotic butterflies and stuffed birds, displayed here are unlikely to make many new converts. Of the town's churches, the Gothic sv Mořič is the oldest, but its innards were ripped out by fire in 1836 and rebuilt without much feeling. A better bet is the Baroque church of **sv Jan Křtitel** at the top of Jánská, whose sensuous lines and frescoed oval dome combine to form one of the showpieces of Moravian Baroque.

Lastly, it's worth wandering round to Moravcova in the easternmost corner of the old town, which was formerly the Jewish ghetto. Jewish communities in places like Kroměříž, Uherské Hradiště and Prostějov were among the largest in the Czech Lands before World War II, and since they provided many essential services the local bigwigs left them alone. The **Židovská radnice** (Jewish Town Hall) in Moravcova – the only one outside Prague – is remarkable not for its architectural beauty but for its mere existence, the result of a magnanimous gesture by the prince-bishop for services rendered in the Thirty Years' War; today it serves as a local cultural centre and gives little hint of its previous life.

Practicalities

The **train station** is on the north bank of the River Morava from the chateau gardens; head down Vejvanovského to reach the old town. The local **tourist office** (Mon–Fri 8am–6pm, Sat 9am–1pm, Sun 9am–noon) is at Kovářská 1 and can arrange private rooms. The **accommodation** scene in Kroměříž is pretty limited, with a choice between the *Hotel Bouček* (☎0634/257 77; ④), on the main square, and the *Pension na jízdárně*, on Štěchovice (☎0634/251 75; ②), which offers rooms above a pizzeria near the Květná zahrada. A good place to **eat** is the *Radniční sklípek*, Kovářská 20 (closed Sun), a wine restaurant in the cellars of the town hall, serving delicious food and a good range of wines from Valtice. The *Central* on the main square is back in business with a very pleasant restaurant on the ground floor and weekend dances in the café upstairs. There's also a decent pizzeria beside the *Bouček*, and a nice pub, *U Nohejlů*, on Vodní. You can buy the local wine and have a tour of the cellars at the *Arcibiskupské vinné sklepy*, behind the archway beside the chateau.

Holešov

HOLEŠOV (Holleschau), 15km northeast on route 432 (and just fifteen minutes by train) makes an interesting day-trip from Kroměříž. The town had one of the largest

Jewish communities in Moravia, peaking at around 1700 in the mid-nineteenth century. It also has the dubious distinction of being a victim of the last Jewish pogrom on Czech soil in December 1918, during which two Jews were killed. The old ghetto lies to the northwest of the town square, náměstí dr. E. Beneše, centred on the bulky, rough-hewn **Šachova synagoga** (April–Sept Tues–Sun 9am–noon & 1–5pm), on Příční. Built in 1560, the synagogue retains its remarkable decorated interior from the eighteenth century, and now houses an exhibition on the town's Jewish history. Further north, in a kink of the River Rusava, lies the Jewish cemetery or **Židovský hřbitov**, with graves dating back to 1647, including – enclosed within a protective glass case – the tomb of Rabbi Shabtai ben Meir Kohen, known as Shakh (after whom the synagogue is named). The town's seventeenth-century, dry-moated **zámek**, off the main square, is closed to the public, but its lovely formal French gardens are open daily dawn to dusk.

travel details

Trains

Connections with Prague: Brno (hourly; 3hr–4hr 30min); Žďár nad Sázavou (7 daily; 2hr 30min–3hr 30min).

Brno to: Blansko (hourly; 20–30min); Bratislava (8 daily; 2hr); Bučovice (every 2hr; 40min); České Budějovice (4 daily; 4hr 30min); Jihlava (6 or more daily; 2hr–2hr 40min); Kroměříž (2–3 daily; 1hr 20min); Liberec (1 daily; 6hr); Moravský Krumlov (every 2hr; 45min–1hr); Olomouc (up to 6 daily; 1hr 40min); Pardubice (2 daily; 2hr 20min); Slavkov (every 2hr; 25min); Vienna (3 daily; 1hr 45min); Žďár nad Sázavou (every 1–2hr; 1hr–1hr 40min); Znojmo (up to 8 daily; 1hr 50min).

Znojmo to: Jaroměřice nad Rokytnou (up to every 2hr; 50min–1hr 15min); Jihlava (up to 8 daily; 1hr 45min); Mikulov (every 2hr; 45min–1hr 10min); Šatov (4–10 daily; 10–20min); Retz (3–5 daily; 30min); Valtice (every 2hr; 1hr–1hr 20min).

Buses

Connections with Prague: Brno (hourly; 2hr); Znojmo (up to 3 daily; 3hr).

Brno to: Buchlovice (up to 10 daily; 1hr 10min); Jaroměřice nad Rokytnou (up to 6 daily; 1hr 30min); Jedovnice (up to 10 daily; 1hr); Kroměříž (up to 14 daily; 1hr 30min); Křtiny (up to 10 daily; 45min); Luhačovice (up to 4 daily; 2hr 10min); Mikulov (up to 10 daily; 1hr 20min); Zlín (up to 10 daily; 2hr–2hr 40min); Moravský Krumlov (3–5 daily; 1hr); Telč (up to 5 daily; 2hr); Uherské Hradiště (up to 10 daily; 1hr 20min); Znojmo (up to 8 daily; 1hr 10min).

Uherské Hradiště to: Buchlovice (up to 10 daily; 20min); Kroměříž (up to 6 daily; 1hr); Luhačovice (up to 5 daily; 40min); Strážnice (up to 4 daily; 45min/1hr); Trenčín (up to 6 daily; 1hr 15min); Velehrad (up to 8 daily; 25min); Zlín (up to 10 daily; 40min–1hr).

CHAPTER SEVEN

NORTH MORAVIA

North Moravia (Severní Morava) is not the never-ending conglomeration of factories that its critics would have you believe, though it certainly has more than
its fair share of ecological disaster zones, in particular the industrial belt in the
Odra (Oder) basin, now in the grip of an economic depression. At the same
time, the north also boasts some of Moravia's wildest and most varied countryside,
including the **Jeseníky**, the region's highest peaks, which form part of what is still –
nominally at least – known as Czech Silesia. As with the Sudetenland regions of
Bohemia, Silesia's long-standing German community was forcibly expelled after World
War II, leaving many villages and towns visibly underpopulated even today.

To the east, near the border with Slovakia, the traditional communities in the nether
reaches of the **Beskydy** hills have fared much better. Wooden houses and churches are
dotted along the valley, and a whole range of folk buildings have been gathered together and restored in the republic's largest open-air museum in **Rožnov pod Radhoštěm**.
In addition to its folk culture and hiking potential, the Beskydy is endowed with some
intriguing museums: a large car collection at the Tatra plant in **Kopřivnice**, a hat museum in **Nový Jičín**, and two memorials to famous local boys – Sigmund Freud, who was
born in **Příbor**, and Leoš Janáček, who lived and worked in **Hukvaldy**.

The region's two largest cities typify North Moravia's contradictions: **Ostrava**, the
country's largest mining and steel town, is a place no Moravian would ever recommend
you visit (with some justification); **Olomouc**, on the other hand, the old medieval capital on the banks of the River Morava, is probably Moravia's most attractive and vibrant
city after Brno, and a must on anyone's itinerary.

Olomouc

OLOMOUC (pronounced "Olla-moats" and known to the city's sizeable prewar
German-speaking community as Olmütz) is easily the most immediately satisfying of
Moravia's three big cities, thanks to its well-preserved staré město, sloping cobbled
squares, Baroque fountains, and healthy quota of university students. Occupying the
crucial Morava crossing point on the road to Kraków, Olomouc was actually the capital
of Moravia from 1187 to 1641 and the seat of a bishopric (later archbishopric) for even

---

ACCOMMODATION PRICE CODES

All accommodation in this guide is graded according to the price bands listed below.
Prices are for the cheapest **double room** available during high season, which usually
means without private bath or shower in the less expensive places. For a **single room**,
expect to pay around two-thirds the price of a double.

① Under 500Kč	④ 1000–1250Kč	⑦ 1750–2000Kč
② 500–750Kč	⑤ 1250–1500Kč	⑧ 2000–2500Kč
③ 750–1000Kč	⑥ 1500–1750Kč	⑨ 2500Kč and upwards

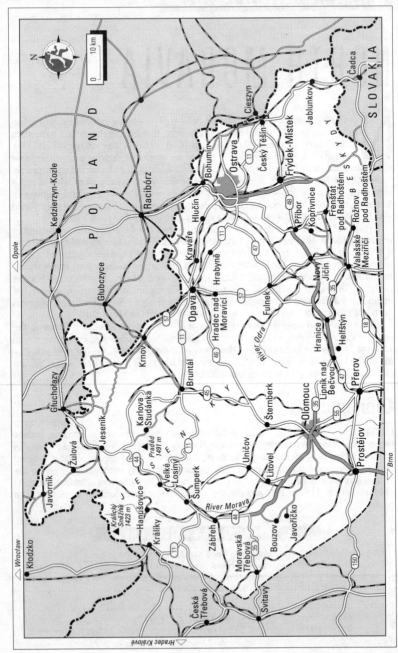

longer. All this attracted the destructive attention of Swedish troops in the Thirty Years' War, and their occupation in the 1640s left the town for dead. During this period, Brno took over as capital, in reward for its heroic stand against the Swedes; only the wealth of the church and its strategic trading position kept Olomouc alive. Meanwhile, the military threat from Prussia confined the town to within its eighteenth-century red-brick fortifications, and only after these were finally torn down in 1888 did the city begin to evolve into the industrial centre it is today.

Arrival, information and accommodation

The **train** and **bus terminals** are 1.5km east of the old town – on arrival, walk or take **tram** #2, #4 or #6 heading west up Masarykova and get off after three or four stops. The city is divided into two zones: to go to the centre of town you need only an inner zone ticket (*vnitřní jizdenka*). Tickets should be bought beforehand from machines or news kiosks, and there is also a one-day ticket (*jednodenní lístek*), available from the main bus station. The **tourist office** in the arcades on the north side of the radnice (daily: March–Nov 9am–7pm; Dec–Feb 9am–5pm April–Oct 8.30am–5pm; *infocentrum@olomoucko.cz*) provides information as well as booking private rooms.

Accommodation

Hotel **accommodation** is uniformly pricey as the city receives mostly tour groups and flush business folk. For real budget accommodation head down Ztracená to CKM (Mon–Fri 9am–5pm) at Denisova 4; if you want to **camp**, the nearest site is in Šternberk (see p.337). A word of warning: rooms can be hard to come by in May when the Spring Music Festival (Olomoucké hudební jaro) follows the Flower Festival (Flora Olomouc).

Gemo, Pavelčákova 22 (☎068/522 21 15; *gemo@hotel-gemo.cz*). Something of a modern eyesore from the outside, but an efficiently run, centrally located place nevertheless, with all mod cons. ⑨.

Lafayette, Alšova 8 (☎068/543 66 00). Late-nineteenth-century hotel that's been fairly tastefully renovated, but a good ten minutes' walk from the old town. ⑦.

Na hradbách, Hrnčířská 14 (☎068/523 32 43). Small, inexpensive, four-bed pension hidden away in one of the city's prettiest, quietest backstreets; if it's full try U anděla a few doors down. ②.

Národní dům, 8 května 21 (☎068/522 48 08). No doubt this late-nineteenth-century hotel was once a glorious place to stay, but, despite vestiges of its original decor, it's now overpriced. ⑥.

Palác, 1 máje 27 (☎068/522 40 96). A communist-era hotel that needs a thorough going over, but remains one of the least expensive central options in the city. ④.

Sigma, Jeremenkova 36 (☎068/523 20 76). This is the city's only bargain hotel, located directly opposite the train station. ④.

U dómu, Dómská 4 (☎068/522 05 02). Small, centrally located pension near the cathedral with six plain en-suite doubles. ④.

The city

Despite being a quarter the size of Brno, Olomouc has the same exciting buzz, with its main arteries clogged with shoppers in the afternoon rush. The **staré město** is a strange contorted shape, squeezed in the middle by an arm of the Morava.

Horní and Dolní náměstí

In the western half of the staré město, all roads lead to the city's two central cobbled main squares, which are hinged to one another at right angles. The lower of the two, Dolní náměstí, is more or less triangular, but the upper one, **Horní náměstí**, is thoroughly irregular. At its centre is the **radnice**, a cream-coloured amalgamation of buildings and styles with the occasional late-Gothic or Renaissance gesture – a freestanding

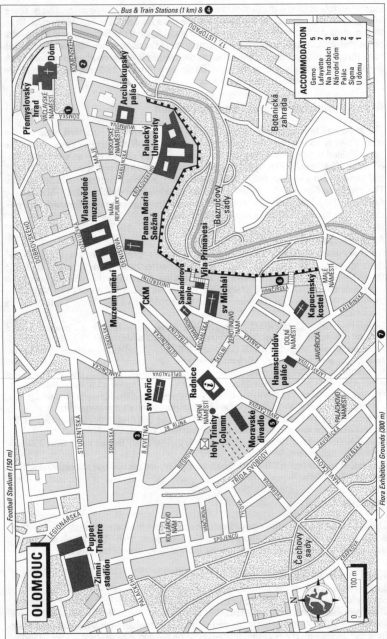

OLOMOUC

ACCOMMODATION
Gemo 5
Lafayette 7
Na hradbách 3
Národní dům 6
Palác 2
Sigma 4
U dómu 1

Přemyslovský hrad
Dóm
Arcibiskupský palác
Palacký University
Vlastivědné muzeum
Panna Maria Sněžná
Vila Primavesi
Muzeum umění
CKM
Sarkandrova kaple
sv Michal
Kapucinský kostel
Haunschildův palác
Radnice
sv Mořic
Moravské divadlo
Holy Trinity Column
Puppet Theatre
Zimní stadión
Botanická zahrada
Bezručovy sady

△ Football Stadium (150 m)
▷ Flora Exhibition Grounds (300 m)

N

0   100 m

flight of steps, the handsome lanterned tower soaring up to its conclusion of baubles and pinnacles, and, tucked round the back, a lonely oriel above a self-portrait of the mason holding out his hand for more money from the miserly town council. But it's the north side that draws the crowds, with its crude arcade of shops and **astronomical clock**, which was originally built by Master Hanuš, like its more famous successor in Prague, but destroyed in World War II. The rather soulless workerist remake chimes all right, but the hourly mechanical show of proletarians is disappointing.

Far more action-packed is the monumental, polygonal **Holy Trinity Column** (Sousoší největší Trojice), erected in the first half of the eighteenth century to the west of the radnice, its ornamental urns sprouting dramatic gilded flames. It's big enough to be a chapel and is easily the largest plague column in either republic. It's also a favourite place for meeting up, eating your lunch, or just sitting and soaking it all in. Set into the west facade of the square is the **Moravské divadlo**, a Neoclassical theatre designed by Josef Kornhäusel in 1830, and previously known as the *Olmützer Stadttheater*, where the young Gustav Mahler arrived as the newly appointed *Kapellmeister* in 1883. The local press took an instant dislike to him: according to his own words, "from the moment I crossed the threshold . . . I felt like a man who is awaiting the judgement of God". No doubt there was a strong element of knee-jerk anti-Semitism in his hostile reception, but this was not helped by Mahler's autocratic style, which caused a number of the local prima donnas to live up to their name. He lasted just three months.

Olomouc makes a big fuss of its sculpture, like that adorning the Edelmannův palác, at no. 28, and even more of its **fountains**, which grace each one of Olomouc's six ancient market squares. Horní náměstí boasts two of them: Hercules, looking unusually athletic for his years, and, to the east of the radnice, a vigorous depiction of Julius Caesar – the fabled founder of the city – bucking on a steed which coughs up water from its mouth. Jupiter and Neptune can be found in **Dolní náměstí**, which has a dustier feel to it, sloping down to the characteristically low-key Capuchin church. Of all the square's subdued Baroque facades, it's the **Haunschildův palác**, on the corner with Lafayettova, which stands out, its single Renaissance oriel decorated with scenes from Ovid.

The central sidestreets

From the bile-green late-Secession bank (now the main post office) on Horní náměstí, it's worth taking a quick turn northwest up **Riegrova** to see a cluster of fine Art Nouveau buildings: the first, at no. 10, has a ceramic facade and a delicate wrought-iron canopy, while the second, at no. 18, is decorated with low-relief figures, and the third, at no. 24, sports sapphire ovals. North of Horní náměstí, off Opletalova, is the church of **sv Mořic**, an oddly mutant building from the west at least, and defensive like a Norman fort, but inside overcome by a thick coat of pink paint that makes the original Gothic interior difficult to stomach. It does, however, boast the Engler organ, the largest in either republic; an ugly, dark, wooden affair with over 10,000 dirty grey pipes and a fair few cherubs, it sounds better than it looks (there's an organ festival held here in early September). You can also climb the church **tower** (May–Sept Mon–Fri 9–11.30am & 1–5pm, Sat 9–11.30am, Sun 2–5pm) for an overview of the staré město. Opposite its west door is a typical 1970s supermarket building, which muscled its way into the historic part of town with the connivance of the philistine Communist council.

Two of the city's best-looking backstreets, Školní and Michalská, lead southeast from Horní náměstí up to the long slope of Žerotínovo náměstí, which features an appealing ensemble of lime trees, streetlamps and Baroque statuary at its upper end. Overlooking them all is the Italianate church of **sv Michal**, whose rather plain facade hides a cool, spacious interior clad in the masterly excess of High Baroque. Three octagonal saucer domes rise up in Byzantine fashion atop Roman pilasters with gilded

Corinthian capitals so large their acanthus leaves bear fruit. There's a very high cherub count on the side altars and a wonderful silver relief of sheep on the gilded pulpit; before you leave, look up at the equally exuberant late-nineteenth-century organ loft. Close to sv Michal, on the corner of Univerzitní, the late-nineteenth-century **vila Primavesi** is well hidden behind dense foliage and a coat of blackened pebbledash. It's currently in a parlous state, though you can still make out a blaze of gold-and-blue mosaic on the entrance steps. Fortunately, there are plans to restore the place, which was designed by, among others, the local sculptor Anton Hanak and the Viennese architect Josef Hofmann for the Primavesi family who went on to finance the Wiener Werkstätte in the 1920s.

More accessible is the mini-dome of the neo-Baroque **Sarkandrova kaple**, which replaced the old prison on Mahlerova at the beginning of this century. It's hardly big enough to kneel in, though this is perhaps its main charm. The chapel takes its name from a Catholic priest of Silesian origin, **Jan Sarkander** (1576–1620), who was incarcerated in the aforementioned prison and died after being tortured by local Protestants. In 1995, Pope John Paul II visited Olomouc and officially canonized Sarkander, whose relics now rest in the gilded casket opposite the pulpit in the local cathedral (see below). His canonization angered the local non-Catholic community, who charged that Sarkander was extremely anti-evangelical and a willing instrument of the Counter-Reformation, taking over the parish of Holešov after the local Protestants had been kicked out by the Jesuits, and that he was implicated in a very unsaintly treason plot involving Polish Cossacks.

Muzeum umění to the Dóm

Firmly wedged between the two sections of the staré město is the obligatory Jesuit church of **Panna Maria Sněžná**, deemed to be particularly necessary in a city where Protestantism spread like wildfire among the German community during the sixteenth century. Jutting out into the road, the church marks the former gateway from the old town to the archbishop's territory to the east, where the great mass of the former Jesuit College, now the **Palacký University**, dominates the neighbouring square, náměstí Republiky.

Above the Divadlo hudby, on the opposite side of the square, is the **Muzeum umění** (Tues–Sun 10am–6pm), which has a nice café (open until 10pm) and a permanent collection of fourteenth- to eighteenth-century Italian paintings, including one or two excellent sixteenth-century Venetian works. Best of all, though, is the **twentieth-century gallery** in the attic, which features a model of the town from 1895 with the zigzag fortifications still intact, 1930s photos of the city by, among others, the outstanding Otakar Lenhart (from a local-born family of fine artists), plus models of the city's modernist Konstandt Haus by Adolf Loos and Paul Engelmann and the Vila Primavesi. From the latter have been salvaged an Art Nouveau stained-glass window, table and chair by Anton Hanak, and a model of his strange *Child over an Ordinary Day* (a cherub standing over a four-headed plinth around which four snakes have wrapped themselves), originally positioned under the pergola in the villa's garden. There are lots of other great exhibits here, not least a model of the famous statue of Stalin and Lenin that once graced the city (see below), and you can gain access to the gallery's vyhlídka věž for a rooftop view over Olomouc. Next door is the town's **Vlastivědné muzeum** (May–Sept Tues–Sun 10am–6pm; Oct–April Wed–Sun 10am–4pm), housed in the former Poor Clares' convent and cloisters, with a pretty dull permanent display on the region's natural history.

The trams and cars hurtling across the cobbles make this one of Olomouc's least accommodating squares, so, after admiring the Bernini-esque Triton fountain, you'd be as well to slip down Mariánská to leafy **Biskupské náměstí**, one of the most peaceful spots in town. Among its fine Baroque buildings, erected after the destructive occupation of the Swedes, is the **Arcibiskupský palác** (Archbishop's Palace), financed by the multimillionaire Bishop Liechtenstein in the 1660s; it was here, at a safe distance from Vienna, that the eighteen-year-old Franz-Josef I was proclaimed emperor in 1848. On the south side of the square is the former armoury, placed there by Maria Theresa after a disagreement with the archbishop. A popular spot nearby is the **student centre** (and British Council reading room) in the main university building, up Wurmova, which has a suntrap terrace café.

On the other side of the tramlines, the Cathedral of sv Václav, or **Dóm**, started life as a twelfth-century Romanesque basilica, but, as with Brno and Prague, the current structure is mostly the result of nineteenth-century neo-Gothic restoration, which included the addition of the 100-metre-high eastern spire. However, the nave is bright and airy, its walls and pillars prettily painted in imitation of the great Romanesque churches of the West; the modern, high-relief Stations of the Cross are quite striking, and the **krypta** (Mon–Sat 9am–5pm, Sun 11am–5pm) has a wonderful display of gory reliquaries and priestly sartorial wealth. Even the secluded cathedral close – a less famous Václavské náměstí (Wenceslas Square) – is a cut above its counterparts. Even better, next door in the chapterhouse, you can view the fascinating remains of the original twelfth-century Románský biskupský palác or **Přemyslovský hrad** (April–Sept Tues–Sun 10am–6pm), now believed to have been built as a bishop's (and not a royal) palace. The late Gothic cloister and frescoes and the Romanesque stonework are unrivalled in the Czech Lands, and well worth a look. Right by the entrance is the Baroque chapel of sv Anna and, set back from it, the university deanery where the teenage King Václav III, the last of the Přemyslids, was murdered in mysterious circumstances in 1306, throwing the country into a bloodletting war of succession.

Beyond the staré město

The Habsburg defences to the west of the staré město were completely torn down in the late nineteenth century to make way for what is now a long, busy thoroughfare known as **třída Svobody**. Starting in the north with the former Edison cinema, a late-Secession building from 1913 decorated with caryatids worshipping light bulbs, it continues with the familiar trail of Habsburg bureaucratic architecture. Halfway down on the right, a leftover water tower is the only survivor on a square that contained a synagogue until the Nazis burnt it down in 1939, and where a double statue of Stalin and Lenin subsequently stood. The former (and only the former) was defaced badly towards the end of the 1980s, apparently by an outraged Gorby-supporting Soviet soldier; neither survived the iconoclasm of November 1989, and the square is now named after the 1969 martyr Jan Palach (see p.100).

If you're tired of Olomouc's uneven cobbles, the best places to head for are the **parks**, which practically encircle the town. A couple of blocks of *fin-de-siècle* houses stand between Svobody and the long well-maintained patchwork strip of crisscross paths, flowerbeds and manicured lawns. It's just a small sample of what goes on show at the annual **Flower Festival** (Flora Olomouc), a minor international gathering of florists, held at the end of April or beginning of May in the Flora Výstaviště or exhibition grounds. The grounds also contain the city's **botanical gardens** (botanická zahrada; April–Sept Tues–Sun 10am–5pm), which are worth visiting at any time of the year. Another pleasant walk is out of the southern end of Dolní náměstí and left into the tiny Malé náměstí, which has a flight of steps leading down to the Bezručovy sady, once the city moat, where the local youth like to hang out.

Eating, drinking and nightlife

For a big city, most of Olomouc goes to bed pretty early. As far as **nightlife** goes, there's always a good turnout at the Moravské divadlo, on Horní náměstí, which puts on a good selection of opera as well as regular concerts by the city's philharmonic orchestra. In late May, Olomouc has its own Spring Music Festival (Olomoucké hudební jaro), when concerts are spread evenly around the town's churches, monasteries and other venues. The Divadlo hudby, below the Muzeum umění at Denisova 47, puts on a more adventurous programme of **gigs**, films and videos. Olomouc has its own jazz club, the *Jazz Tibet Club*, Sokolská 48, which features trad and swing bands mostly, with the music kicking off at 8pm. It's also worth checking out what's on at the student clubs: *S-Klub*, třída 17 listopadu 43, just outside the old town, the *U-Klub*, which hosts gigs east of the city centre at the student union, Šmeralova 12, or the late-night *Depo no. 8*, at náměstí Republiky 1. Art-house **films** can be seen on Tuesdays at the Metropol, Sokolská 25, but for a full rundown of the month's events, buy the listings magazine *Kdy, Kde Co v Olomouci* at the tourist office or newsagents around town. And before you leave town be sure to try out the city's famously pungent fat-free local cheese, *Olomoucký sýr.*

Arkáda, Ostružnická 28. The best place to get on-line in Olomouc is this central Internet café. Mon–Fri 11am–7pm, Sat & Sun 2–7pm.

Caesar, Horní náměstí. An excellent, popular pizzeria in the cobbled vaults of the radnice, from which the smell of garlic wafts enticingly across the main square. Mon–Sat 9am–1am, Sun 11am–midnight.

Café Mahler, Horní náměstí 11. Popular place to go for coffee and a cake, with tables outside looking over to the radnice. Mon–Sat 8am–9pm, Sun 10am–9pm.

Kamenný šenk, Žerotínovo náměstí 13. Lively night-time student cellar bar on the corner of Michalská. Mon–Sat 3pm–midnight.

Maruška, 28 října 2. More functional than the *Mahler*, but a decent coffee-and-cake dispenser, with seating upstairs. Mon–Sat 8am–10pm, Sun 10am–10pm.

Moravská restaurace, Horní náměstí 23. Slap bang next to the main theatre on the main square, and a good place for pre- or post-theatre food and drink. Daily 11am–11pm.

U anděla, Hrnčířská 10. Popular little restaurant serving traditional Czech fare in the backstreets behind Dolní náměstí. Daily 11am–10pm.

U bakaláře, Žerotínovo náměstí 3. Nice modern take on the traditional pub, with wooden benches and tables. Mon–Fri 10am–10pm, Sat 10am–3pm.

U bílého slona, Univerzitní 10. The city's very own *čajovna* or teahouse/art gallery is housed in a lovely seventeenth-century building. Mon–Fri 10am–9pm, Sat 2–8pm.

U červeného volka, Dolní náměstí 39. Wide choice of pasta and veggie dishes as well as the usual Czech pub-restaurant food. Daily 10am–11pm.

U Huberta, 1 máje 3. A real drinkers' pub, which serves the local beer unfiltered and unpasteurized. Mon–Sat 10am–10pm.

Around Olomouc

Olomouc sits happily in the wide plain of the **Haná region**, famous for its multifarious folk costumes and for its songs reflecting the fertility of the land. Naturally enough in a strongly agricultural area, the harvest festivals (*Hanácké dožínky* or *dožínkový slavnost*) are the highlight of the year, advertised on posters everywhere in the second half of September. All the places covered below are situated in the Morava plain, and easily reached by bus or train on day-trips from Olomouc, with the exception of Helfštýn and the area round Bouzov, which are really only accessible to those who have their own transport.

Přerov and around

Twenty-three kilometres southeast of Olomouc, and twenty minutes by train, **PŘEROV** (Prerau) is an important rail junction and ungainly town dedicated to the chemical and engineering industries. Apart from a brief jazz festival in late September, its chief redeeming feature is the endearing old town square, **Horní náměstí**, a tight semicircle of colourful houses elevated above the rest of the town. At its centre is a typically anguished statue by František Bílek, depicting the sixteenth-century religious reformer Jan Blahoslav brandishing his Czech translation of the New Testament. The straight side of the square is taken up by the sixteenth-century chateau, whose **Muzeum Komenského** (March, Oct & Nov Wed, Sat & Sun 9am–noon & 1–5pm; April–Sept Tues–Sun 9am–noon & 1–5pm) commemorates Blahoslav's more famous successor in the Protestant Unity of Brethren, Jan Ámos Komenský (aka Comenius; see box on p.336). The **bus** and **train stations** are about 1km southwest of the town centre.

If you're heading east into the Beskydy by rail or road, it's difficult to miss the spectacular ruined castle of **Helfštýn** (March & Nov Sat & Sun 9am–4pm; April, Sept & Oct Tues–Sun 9am–5pm; May–Aug closes 6pm), which looks down from the wooded hills to the south of River Bečva, 15km east of Přerov. Founded sometime in the fourteenth century, it's one of the largest medieval castles in the Czech Republic, and was used by the Hussites as a base from which to attack Olomouc, before being deliberately laid to waste by the Habsburgs following the Thirty Years' War. Sections of the complex have since been restored, but the place is still, for the most part, a ruin and you can wander at will. Concerts, mock battles and various other attractions are staged here over the summer, and there's a permanent display of modern **blacksmith** artistry in one of the castle wings (expozice kovářství; May–Sept Tues–Sun 9am–5pm), plus an annual blacksmiths' convention in late August. To get to the castle, you can either walk the 5km along the red-marked path from the train station at Lipník nad Bečvou, or catch one of the infrequent buses to Týn nad Bečvou, 1.5km below the castle.

Prostějov and around

Twenty kilometres and half an hour by train from Olomouc, the big textile town of **PROSTĚJOV** (Prossnitz) has a more grand and spacious old centre based around a large, well-laid-out main square, Masarykovo náměstí. Dominating this is the **nová radnice**, with its ludicrously large landmark tower built just before World War I and an asymmetrical appearance caused by the council's failure to purchase one of the neighbouring houses. The Renaissance **stará radnice**, in the opposite corner of the square, now houses the local **museum** (Tues–Sun 9am–noon & 1–5pm), with folk artefacts from the Haná region, but very little on the town's brightest star, Edmund Husserl (1859–1938), the founder of phenomenology. A better bet is to pop into the nearby **church**, which has some terrific Baroque furnishings, a technicolor pulpit covered with carved figures and an extravagant crown-shaped baldachin, as well as a set of Stations of the Cross carved by František Bílek.

Just off the main square is the town's prettily sgraffitoed Renaissance **zámek** (times as above), which puts on art exhibitions and contains a permanent collection of graphics by Jan Köhler. The town's real architectural highlight, however, is Jan Kotěra's 1908 **Národní dům**, northeast of the main square near the last remaining bastion of the old town walls and now housing a theatre and restaurant. As in his museum at Hradec Králové (see p.264), Kotěra was moving rapidly away from the "swirl and blob" of the Secession, but here and there the old elements persist in the sweep of the brass door handles and the pattern on the poster frames. Apart from its furniture, the restaurant has been left unmolested, and the bold Klimt-like ceramic relief of the *Three Graces* above the mantlepiece is still as striking as ever.

To reach the old town from the main **bus** and **train stations**, head west down Svatoplukova. Prostějov doesn't get too many visitors, but there are a couple of **places to stay**, ranging from the expensive *Hotel Grand* (☎0508/33 23 11; ⑨), on Palackého, a couple of blocks south of the main square, to the old stalwart *Hotel Avion* (☎0508/245

COMENIUS

Jan Ámos Komenský (John Amos Comenius) was born in 1592 in a village close to Uherský Brod, but his Latin schooling took place at the Unity of Brethren's school in Přerov. He served as a Protestant minister in Fulnek from 1616 to 1621, before being forced to flee the Czech Lands after the victory of the papal forces at the Battle of Bílá hora. Komenský and the Brethren set up an academy in the Polish city of Leszno, until forced to move on once more by the Swedish Wars of the 1650s. Of his many writings, Komenský's graded and pictorial Latin textbooks (the first of their kind) have proved more influential than his religious treatises, and he was called to put his educational theories into practice in Sweden, Hungary, Holland and England. He even received invitations from the Protestant-loathing Cardinal Richelieu in France, and from Harvard University, which wanted him as its president. He is buried in Naarden, Holland. Throughout the eastern part of Moravia, the Brethren rode out the Counter-Reformation to emerge in significant numbers once Austrian liberalism began to take effect in the late eighteenth century. They were later transformed into the Moravian Church, a body which continues to have an influence out of all proportion to its size, particularly in the Czech Lands and the US.

61; ③), east of the main square on náměstí Sv Čecha. Five kilometres west of Prostějov are two good **campsites**, *Přehrada* and *Žralok* (both May–Sept), whose lakeside locations provide plenty of opportunities for swimming. The latter sits below a high mound above the westernmost reservoir, on top of which stands the imposing slab of the chateau of **PLUMLOV** (Plumenau), another of the Liechtensteins' fancies. Designed by Prince-Bishop Karl Eusebius von Liechtenstein-Kastelcorn himself, only one wing of the four planned got off the drawing board. Reconstruction work continues slowly, but in high season you can now wander round the courtyards, and visit a small exhibition on the **zámek** (July & Aug Tues–Sun 10am–4pm), which makes a scenic backdrop if you're swimming.

Bouzov and around

The northernmost tip of the Drahanská vrchovina around **BOUZOV** (Busau) – an extension of the hills of the Moravský kras – has enough to keep you occupied on a lazy weekend. The village itself is nothing but its **hrad** (April & Oct Tues–Sun 9am–noon & 1–4pm; May–Sept Tues–Sun 9am–noon & 1–5pm; Nov–March Sat & Sun 10am–noon & 1–3pm), a Romantic neo-Gothic fortress right on the high point of the vrchovina, and perfectly suited as a base for its former proprietors, the Teutonic Knights. Predictably enough, it also took the fancy of the Nazi SS, who used it as a base during World War II. The pompous pseudo-medievalism of the interior decor is not to everyone's taste, and the place is absolutely huge, so there's a choice of guide tours: trasa 1 (klasická) is the regular one that gives you an hour-long whirl around the place; trasa 2 (velká) lasts an extra forty minutes and is for real enthusiasts; trasa 3 takes you up the tower (věž) only.

Four kilometres south at **JAVOŘÍČKO**, the local SS burnt the village to the ground and shot 38 of the inhabitants in the last days of the war. This futile and tragic act aside, the reason for coming here is to visit the **Javoříčské jeskyně** (Tues–Sun: April & Oct 9am–3pm; May–Sept 9am–4pm), limestone karst caves on a par with those near Brno but without the crowds. Five kilometres east of Bouzov, **BÍLÁ LHOTA** has an eighteenth-century chateau worth visiting for its beautiful **arboretum** (April & Oct Sat & Sun 8am–5pm; May–Sept Tues–Sun 8am–6pm). The **Mladečské jeskyně**, a more extensive and popular limestone cave system another couple of kilometres on, is just off the main Olomouc–Prague road, at the end of the most twig-like of branch lines from Litovel.

Svatý Kopeček and Šternberk

If you're heading north from Olomouc on route 46, you can't fail to spot the twin clock towers of the gleaming yellow-and-white Baroque pilgrimage church on the nearby hill of **Svatý Kopeček** (Heiligberg), just 8km northeast of the city. Perched 200m above the plain and flanked by its vast convent wings, the site and scale are truly spectacular. Close up, though, it doesn't live up to expectations, and is really only worth visiting for its adjoining **zoo** (daily 8am–7pm or dusk); bus #11 from Olomouc train station will take you there.

Further north on route 46, you hit the ridge of the Jeseníky foothills at **ŠTERN-BERK** (Sternberg), where the annual *Ecce Homo* motor race is held in mid-September over the lethal switchbacks on the road to Opava. The town itself, a long two-kilometre haul north of the train and bus stations, is dominated by its giant Baroque church and **hrad** (April & Oct Sat & Sun 9am–4pm; May–Sept Tues–Sun 8am–5pm), the latter rebuilt in Romantic style in the late nineteenth century and worth a visit for its **Muzeum hodin** (Clock Museum), which houses a fabulous collection of timepieces and watches, from ancient Chinese alarm clocks through to the wild excesses of the Baroque era and examples of the substandard work churned out by the old state watch manufacturers, Prim, who are based in the town.

Šternberk has a **tourist office** (Mon–Fri 9am–5pm; July & Aug daily), at Čs. armády 30, that can help with accommodation, though the *Šternberský dvůr* (☎0643/41 50 42; ④) is a good place to start. Šternberk's two **campsites** (both mid-May to mid-Sept) are the nearest you'll get to Olomouc: the *Šternberk* site is slightly closer to the town than *U zlatého muflona*, in Dolní Žleb, 3km north of Šternberk.

The Jeseníky

Extending east from the Bohemian Krkonoše are the **Jeseníky** (Altvatergebirge), the highest peaks in what is now Moravia. Sparsely populated since the postwar expulsion of its German-speakers, the region is worlds apart from the dense network of industrial centres in the north and east of the province, or even the vine-clad hills of the south. The highest reaches, to the northwest between Šumperk and Jeseník, have been damaged by acid rain, and, of course, the whole region was one of the worst-hit by the devastating floods of 1997. One of the nicest areas to head for is the foothills on either side of the big peaks, which harbour some low-key spa resorts like Lázně Jeseník, Karlova Studánka, and the historical remains of Czech Silesia in Krnov and Opava.

Šumperk

ŠUMPERK (Schönberg) is the gateway to the upper Jeseníky, and has the feel of a mountain town, despite the fact that the shift from plain to hills is much less dramatic here than at Šternberk. For the last two centuries it was a thriving German-speaking textile town, at the vanguard of the language frontier, and though the town's original inhabitants may have been expelled, it still relies on its cloth-making tradition.

Unusually for a provincial town, there's no obvious centre to Šumperk. The main drag is **Hlavní třída**, beyond the park to the north of the train station, and, at the far western end of Hlavní, the tiny old town is easy to miss, its neo-Renaissance radnice standing on the pretty little square of **náměstí Míru**. Unreconstructed street names were a feature of most towns under the Communist regime, but Šumperk topped the lot with a Stalin Square, a Stalingrad Street and a statue of the man himself in a car park by the old town walls – all intact right up to November 1989.

Nowadays, there's not much to see here, but if you end up staying, details of current entertainments are available from the **tourist office** at Hlavní 12 (June–Aug Mon–Fri 8am–6pm, Sat 8am–2pm; Sept–May Mon–Fri 9am–noon & 1–5pm). Finding a **room** should be easy enough; try the *Grand* (☎0649/21 21 41; ③), by the park, or the *Pension U Jirsáka* (☎0649/21 38 49; ⑦), on the road heading northeast to the suburb of Vikýřovice.

Velké Losiny

One good reason for staying in Šumperk is to visit the tiny Moravian spa of **VELKÉ LOSINY** (Gross-Ullersdorf), 9km northeast of Šumperk and one of the last oases of civilization before you hit the deserted heights of the Jeseníky. The town's Renaissance **zámek** (April & Oct Sat & Sun 9am–noon & 1–4pm; May–Aug Tues–Sun 8am–noon & 1–5pm; Sept Tues–Sun 9am–noon & 1–4pm) is set in particularly lush grounds beside a tributary of the River Desná. It's a three-winged, triple-decker structure, opening out into a beautifully restored sixteenth-century arcaded loggia, and for once the guided tour is really worthwhile. The chateau was the northernmost property of the extremely wealthy Žerotín family, but was inhabited for less than a hundred years; its grandest chamber is the Knights' Hall, which has retained its original parquet floor and leather wall hangings. Strong supporters of the Unity of Brethren, the Žerotíns were stripped of their wealth after the Battle of Bílá hora and the chateau was left empty – except as a venue for the region's notorious witch trials during the Counter-Reformation.

Velké Losiny is also home to the country's one remaining **paper mill** or *papírna* (April & Oct Mon–Fri 9am–3pm; May–Sept Tues–Sun 9am–noon & 1–5pm), which still produces handmade paper. Built in the 1590s by the Žerotín family, and still bearing the family's coat of arms on its watermark, the mill is situated between the chateau and the spa and houses a small museum on the history of paper. The **train** and **bus stations** are in the spa itself, from which the chateau is a pleasant one-kilometre walk south through the verdant garden buildings.

Hrubý Jeseník

The River Desná peters out before the real climb into the central mountain range of **Hrubý Jeseník**. A bus from Šumperk runs roughly every two hours via the last train station, Kouty nad Desnou, to the saddle of Červenohorské sedlo (1013m) and beyond. The ascent by route 44 from Kouty is a dramatic series of hairpin bends, but the top of the pass is a disappointment. The tourist board may talk of "mountain meadows and pastures", but the reality is low-lying scrub and moorland: any spruce or pine trees that dare to rise above this are beaten down by acid rain. There's a restaurant by the roadside for beer and food, and an impromptu and very basic **campsite**, 500m away to the northwest. For a better view, it's a 45-minute walk northwest to **Červená hora** (1333m) and another hour and a half to **Šerák** (1351m), which looks down onto the Ramzovské sedlo, the much lower pass to the west that the railway from Šumperk to Jeseník wisely opts for. A chairlift here will take you down to the campsite and train station at Ramzová, or you could walk two hours in the opposite direction to **Praděd** (Altvater), at 1491m, the highest and most barren peak in the range.

Below and to the east of Praděd is the picturesque Silesian spa resort of **KARLOVA STUDÁNKA**, strung out along the valley of the bubbling River Bílá Opava. The spa has a useful **information centre** (daily 9am–5pm), and is dotted with cold fizzy springs (with an extraordinarily high iron content) and attractive dark-brown weatherboarded spa buildings, many with cream shutters and balconies for enjoying the fresh mountain

The Slovenské národné divadlo, Bratislava

The most SNP and Petržalka, Bratislava

Timber-framed house in Čičmany

Renaissance belfry in Kežmarok

A gaggle of Slovak geese

Spišská Sobota, High Tatras

Icon in the Šarišské múzeum, Bardejov

HANS-HORST SKUPY

Bilingual sign, East Slovakia

HANS-HORST SKUPY

Starý hrad, Malá Fatra

MIREK FRANK

Štrbské Pleso, High Tatras

SEAN GALLUP

View over the main square, Bardejov

SEAN GALLUP

Wooden church in Lukov

air. Most of the **accommodation** in the spa is for patients, but you could try the *Hotel Hubertus* (☎0647/75 14 40; ②), right by the waterfall close to the main road above the spa. There's also the *Dolina* **campsite** (mid-May to Sept), 7km northeast of the spa near Vrbno pod Pradědem (Würbenthal).

Another option is to stay in **MALÁ MORÁVKA**, 6km to the south down route 445, which has the advantage of being at the end of an idyllic little branch line from Bruntál (trains don't always run daily on this line so check it's running). M Service acts as a sort of **tourist office** (daily 8am–6pm) and can help with accommodation in the area; you can also hire bikes and skis there, too. There are numerous inexpensive pensions and rooms along the valley between here and Karlova Studánka, so **accommodation** shouldn't be a problem.

BRUNTÁL (Freudenthal) is situated 14km east of Malá Morávka on the scenic railway line between Olomouc and Krnov, and has the dubious distinction of having one of the highest rates of unemployment in the country. It's worth a mention, though, for its Baroque **zámek** (Tues–Sun: April, Sept & Oct 9am–noon & 1–5pm; May–Aug 9am–noon & 1–6pm), another hangout of the Teutonic Knights. After the chateau's solid Baroque exterior, the beautiful sixteenth-century arcaded courtyard with loggia comes as something of a surprise; inside, amidst the lush furnishings, are a series of vast Baroque landscape frescoes.

Jeseník and around

On the other side of the pass, the road plunges down with equal ferocity to **JESENÍK** (Freiwaldau), a fairly nondescript town busy in summer with Polish day-trippers. Over the stream, north of the main square in the Smetanovy sady, there's a wonderful Art Nouveau monument to local farmer Vincent Priessnitz, founder of the nearby spa (see below), presiding godlike over the skinny and ill on his right and the "cured" (or at least plump) on his left. Otherwise, Jeseník is mainly useful as a base for exploring the surrounding area; there are several reasonably priced hotels and pensions, and a **campsite** (open all year) with a swimming pool less than 2km west along the valley en route to another spa resort, Lipová Lázně.

Two kilometres above the town, with fantastic views south to the Jeseníky and north into Poland, is **LÁZNĚ JESENÍK** (Gräfenberg). Here Priessnitz established one of the most famous Silesian spas in the nineteenth century, where the likes of Russian writer Gogol and King Carol I of Romania took the cure. Nowadays, the only grandish spa building is the grey rendered Priessnitz Sanatorium, built in 1910. Scattered about the surrounding countryside, and interspersed with numerous monuments erected by grateful patients, are the natural springs, which provide hot and sulphuric refreshment on the obligatory constitutionals (you can buy a map from the Priessnitz Sanatorium). If you'd prefer to get clean away from people, and particularly sickly spa patients, make your way to the viewpoint from the summit of Zlatý chlum, 2km east of Jeseník.

From Lipová Lázně, a tiny, picturesque branch line heads northeast, eventually terminating at Javorník (see below), in the northernmost Silesian salient. The first stop, though, is Lipová Lázně jeskyně, just over the ridge from the entrance to the **Jeskyně na pomezí** (April–Oct Tues–Sun 9am–4pm), a mini-karst cave system with colourful stalactites and stalagmites in the shape of fruit, vegetables and fungi. Another two stops along the line is **ŽULOVÁ**, whose local fortress, precipitously situated on a moated island of rock, was converted into a church in the nineteenth century, its Gothic round tower now the steeple of an otherwise Baroque building. You only have to look at the names on the World War I memorial in the porch to see that the village was once entirely German-speaking – the old German graves have since been stuck to the church wall to make way for the postwar Czech ones.

Beyond Žulová, the countryside flattens out as it slips into Poland, and the train continues to **JAVORNÍK** (Jauernig), where the local chateau, **Janský vrch** (April & Oct

Sat & Sun 9am–noon & 1–4pm; May–Aug Tues–Sun 8am–noon & 1–5pm; Sept 9am–noon & 1–4pm), perches high above the village. There's a choice of guided tours: the 45-minute tour (trasa 1) takes you round the period interior which features a collection of historical pipes and ornate smoking devices, as well as a small theatre, where the composer Karl Ditters von Dittersdorf used to stage operas (when he wasn't being the local forest warden); the half-hour tour (trasa 2) whisks you round the servants' quarters, the chapel and the look-out tower. If you need a place to stay, head for the *Hotel pod zámkem* (☎0645/95 62 36; ③), down in the village.

Krnov

As if to underline the arbitrary nature of the region's current borders, the railway line from Jeseník passes in and out of Polish territory en route to **KRNOV** (Jägerndorf), famous for its Rieger-Kloss organ factory – the largest in Europe – established here in 1873. The town was flattened in World War II, and lost most of its primarily German-speaking population in the postwar expulsions – the current population of 26,000 is only two-thirds of the town's prewar level – but it's still worth a brief stopover if you're heading for Opava or into Poland just 3km away.

From the town's otherwise nondescript main square, **Hlavní náměstí**, two buildings stand out: the salmon-pink-and-white **radnice** from 1902, topped by an excitable clock tower, modelled on the one in the Viennese suburb of Währing and decorated with patterned tiling; and the late-nineteenth-century **spořitelna**, a savings bank, in two shades of green. Beyond the Atlantes who guard the entrance to the latter, you can see the beautifully restored foyer and staircase, its stained glass, ironwork and plastering smothered in Art Nouveau floral motifs. On the ground floor is the *Městská kavárna*, restored and slightly modernized, but with enough of its original fittings – brass chandeliers, wooden panelling and so forth – to give some idea of its glory days. To the west on Zámecké náměstí, one side of the street features an unusual arcade held up by round, squat pillars, while beyond, to the north, lies the so-called **Švedská zeď** (Swedish Wall), a short, surviving stretch of the town's fortifications with decorative Renaissance battlements, later used in the unsuccessful defence of the town against the Swedes during the Thirty Years' War.

Krnov's main **train station** is 1km west of the centre along Mikulášská, though most trains heading to or from Opava and Ostrava also stop at Krnov-Cvilín, about half the distance northeast of the centre down Hlubčická. The **tourist office**, Štursova 3 (Mon–Fri 9am–6pm, Sat 9am–noon), can help with private accommodation. Opposite is the entrance to the town's most stylish **hotel**, the *Hotel Morava* (☎0652/71 10 03; ③), housed in the former Minorite monastery on Štursova 2; otherwise it's a choice of the overpriced *Hotel Pepa* (☎0652/71 10 05; *pepa@krnov.cesnet.cz*; ⑧), on Zámecké náměstí, or the kitschy but comfortable *Hotel Praha* (☎0652/71 07 41; ③), Revoluční 10.

Opava and around

Right by the Polish border, 24km southeast of Krnov, **OPAVA** (Troppau) is one of the oldest towns in the country, an important trading centre on the Amber Road from the Adriatic to the Baltic Sea, but perhaps better known as **Troppau**, capital of Austrian (and later Czech) Silesia (see box opposite). Badly damaged in the last few weeks of World War II, then depopulated by the expulsion of the town's majority of Germans, it nevertheless retains enough grandiose nineteenth-century buildings to give some idea of how it looked in its heyday. Much has been rebuilt since 1945, and while Opava may not merit a detour, it's a good place to break a journey or do a bit of chateau-seeing.

The most spectacular reminder of the town's former days, the huge church of **Nanebevzetí Panny Marie**, lies in the west of the old town, built in Silesian Gothic style in the late fourteenth century, and sheltering a lovely crown-shaped high altar. East of this giant red-brick church is the town's main square, **Horní náměstí**, above which rises the tall tower of the old *Schmetterhaus*, or **Hláska**, symbol of the town's forgotten prosperity, where foreign merchants were permitted to sell their wares. Opposite this stands another object of civic pride, the neo-Baroque **Slezské divadlo**. Opava's best-looking street is Masarykova třída, lined with noble Baroque palaces that once belonged to the likes of General Blücher and one of Beethoven's chief patrons, Count Razumovský. The **Silesian Diet** used to meet in the Jesuit college at the northern end of the street, while the Minorite monastery, further south, was the venue for the 1820 Troppau Conference, when the "Holy Alliance" of Austria, Russia and Prussia met to thrash out a common policy towards the revolutionary stirrings of post-Napoleonic Europe.

Set in the town's pretty semicircle of parks to the east is the grandiose **Slezské zemské muzeum** (Tues–Sat 9am–noon & 1–4pm, Sun 9am–noon & 2–4pm), built in neo-Renaissance style in 1893. It has been painstakingly restored since the war and houses a large but uninspiring exhibition that manages to avoid all the most controversial aspects of Silesian history. Opava does have one superb piece of twentieth-century architecture worth seeking out, the **church of sv Hedvik**, about 500m up Krnovská, one block to the south. The western facade is truly striking, made from big slabs of rusticated stone with concrete infill, plastered with giant Latin lettering and rising vertically in steps to form a strictly geometric tower. Begun in 1933 by local architect Leopold Bauer, it was used as a storehouse by the Nazis and Communists, and was only finished and opened for religious services in 1992.

Opava has two **train stations**; the main one – and the most central – is Opava východ, at the southeastern corner of the old town. There's just one central **hotel** to speak of at present, the none-too-cheap, dark-red, modern monstrosity known as the *Koruna*, náměstí Republiky 17 (☎0653/62 11 32; ⑨), plus a few pensions in the suburbs. As for **food**: *U bílého koníčka*, on Dolní náměstí, is a vaulted beer hall, serving mugs of Gambrinus and all the usual Czech dishes, or else there's *Pizzeria Uno*, at the corner of Olbrichova and Otická. It only remains to say that lion-lovers all over the world might be interested to know that **Joy Adamson** (of *Born Free* fame) was born Friderika Viktoria Gessner at Na rybníčku 48 in 1910 – and there's a plaque on the house to prove it.

SILESIA

From 1335 onwards, **Silesia** (*Slezsko* in Czech) was an integral part of the Historic Lands of the Bohemian Crown. In the 1740s, the majority of it was carelessly lost to the Prussians by the young Habsburg Empress Maria Theresa. The three remaining Duchies – Troppau (Opava), Jägerndorf (Krnov) and Teschen (Těšín) – became known as Austrian Silesia, with Troppau as their capital, separated from each other by the Moravian salient around Ostrava. The population, though predominantly German, contained large numbers of Czechs and Poles – a mishmash typical of the region and one which caused often violent clashes and interminable territorial disputes. In 1920, after a few bloody skirmishes, the new state of Czechoslovakia lost part of Těšín to Poland and gained part of Hlučín from Germany, and in 1928, Czech Silesia was amalgamated with Moravia. This last act, in particular, annoyed the violently irredentist prewar German population. However, like the majority of the country's German-speaking minority, they were expelled in 1945, making the whole issue of a separate Silesia fairly redundant. Nevertheless, in the early 1990s, the newly formed Moravian nationalists teamed up with their Silesian counterparts (HSD-SMS) and scored some surprise election victories that briefly put the whole issue back on the agenda.

HRABYNĚ

No one driving between Ostrava and Opava on route 11 can fail to notice the ugly great slab of concrete which crowns the strategic heights around the village of **Hrabyně**. In the final few weeks of World War II, the Red Army was forced to engage in a costly pitched battle for the area. As recently as the 1980s, the sycophantic Communist regime decided to erect this bombastic tribute to the fallen, at a cost of millions of crowns, thereby proving the indissoluble friendship between Czechoslovakia and the Soviet Union – "Together with the Soviet Union for ever and ever and never any other way", as the slogans used to say. Army vehicles are scattered about the giant runway, which forms the approach to the monument and which gives out superb views north into Poland. Inside, there's a typically lavish but dull permanent display on the military operation, and rather more enlightening temporary exhibitions upstairs (Tues–Sun 9am–3.30pm).

Hradec nad Moravicí

The castle high above the town of **HRADEC NAD MORAVICÍ**, 8km south on route 57, is a Hammer-horror neo-Gothic castle – or so it appears at first sight. In fact, the red-brick castle's magnificent gateway opens up to reveal another, earlier, Neoclassical zámek covered in smooth white plaster. The **Červený zámek**, or *Rotes Schloss* as the red-brick castle was known, is now home to the local museum, while the **Bílý zámek** or *Weisses Schloss* (April, Oct & Nov Sat & Sun 9am–noon & 1–4pm; May–Sept Tues–Sun 9am–noon & 1–5pm) contains a rather more interesting collection of porcelain and paintings. The latter used to belong to the Lichnovský family, who invited performances from the likes of Beethoven, Liszt and Paganini – in early June there's a Beethoven music festival, *Beethovenův Hradec*, held here. On a clear day it's well worth exploring the lovely grounds that stretch out along the ridge beyond the white castle.

Lying at the end of its very own branch line, and offering a wide range of **accommodation**, Hradec is a suitable base for visiting Opava and even Ostrava. First choice for a bed has to be the *Zámecký hotel* (☎0653/91 12 17; ③), in the neo-Gothic red-brick castle, which also has a restaurant open to non-guests, though there are other options. There's also the *Hradec* **campsite** (May–Sept) a short distance to the south of the town and castles, along route 57.

Ostrava

If you told a Czech you were going to **OSTRAVA** (Ostrau), they'd probably think you were mad. The city is regularly shrouded in a pall of pungent sulphurous smog, and although huge efforts have been made in the last decade to clean up the centre, they can't hide the fact that it's coal and steel that made the town. From a village of less than 2000 inhabitants at the beginning of the nineteenth century, Ostrava has grown into the Czech Republic's third largest city with a population of 330,000, a significant number of whom are Polish due to its position as the main gateway into Poland. Ostrava does, however, have plenty of high culture and a packed sporting calendar, so if you should end up having to stay in the North Moravian coal basin, this is as good a place as any.

Arrival, information and accommodation

Ostrava's main **train station**, Ostrava hlavní nádraží, is 2km north of the city centre (tram #2, #8 or #14). Trains from Krnov and Opava terminate at Ostrava-Svinov (most fast trains also call here), 5km west of the centre (tram #3, #4, #9, or #10). One or two trains an hour from the main train station (including trains to and from Frýdek-Místek and Kroměříž) will take you to the most central of the city terminals, Ostrava střed, next door to the main **bus station** and just ten minutes' walk west of the centre (tram #2, #6, #12 or #13). The **tourist office** (Mon–Fri 8am–6pm, Sat 9am–2pm), on Nádražní, is helpful. Anyone needing a Polish visa can get one quickly and easily at the **Polish consulate** (Mon–Fri 8.30am–noon), at Blahoslavova 4, just north of the Nová radnice.

Accommodation

Despite the lack of tourists, Ostrava's **hotels** can get booked up by a combination of people on business and Polish migrant workers, so it's worth ringing in advance or starting your search early in the day.

Dom Polski, Poděbradova 53 (☎069/612 20 01). A striking Art Nouveau villa dating from 1899, that has been modernized inside, but is probably the place with most character in Ostrava. ⑨.

Imperial, Tyršova 6 (☎069/611 66 21; *hotel-imperial@imperial.cz*). A luxury, four-star hotel that has all the mod cons, but is expensive at nearly 4000Kč a double. ⑨.

Jindřich, Nádražní 66 (☎069/611 29 79). Smart, modern, red-brick hotel with a sauna, situated right by the disused nineteenth-century pithead of the same name. ⑨.

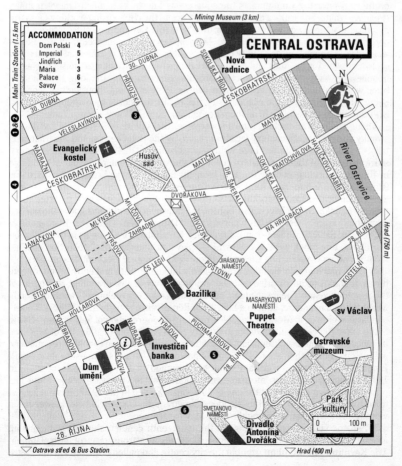

CENTRAL OSTRAVA

ACCOMMODATION
Dom Polski	4
Imperial	5
Jindřich	1
Maria	3
Palace	6
Savoy	2

Maria, Přívozská 23 (☎069/611 06 76). A decent, medium-range hotel, a short walk from the city centre. ⑤.

Palace, 28 října 59 (☎069/615 81 11; *palace@applet.cz*). An old communist-era luxury hotel that can't quite pass muster in that category any more, hence the bargain prices. ④.

Savoy, Macharova 16 (☎069/613 40 90; *reception@hotelsavoy.cz*). Inexpensive, but comfortable, modernized hotel situated within walking distance of the main train station. ③.

The city

Ostrava divides into three distinct districts: **Slezská Ostrava**, on the east bank of the River Ostravice, where the first black-coal deposits were discovered back in the 1760s, **Vítkovice**, south of the centre on the opposite side of the river, where the first foundry was set up in 1828, and **Moravská Ostrava**, the largely pedestrianized downtown district.

It's in Moravská Ostrava that you'll find most of the town's shops and department stores, bunched up around the old marketplace and main square, **Masarykovo náměstí**. Under the Communists the square was known as náměstí Lidových milicí (People's Militia Square) – a once-proud reference to the city's strong working-class traditions and staunch postwar support for the Party (the Communists still capture a high percentage of the vote here). This largely unspoken alliance ensured high wages and well-stocked shops, and for the two decades after 1968, the commercial district was always crowded with Poles and Soviet soldiers gaping in awe at what to them was an unbelievably wide range of products. Hard times have now hit the local heavy industries, with steel production at less than half its 1989 level and thousands of workers being laid off. Similarly, the coal industry has cut its workforce by over forty percent, with the distinct possibility of all its mines closing down in the very near future.

Though hardly an architectural masterpiece, the square still vaunts a handful of swanky late-nineteenth-century facades erected by the rich German and Austrian capitalists who owned the mines here until nationalization in 1945. The sixteenth-century **stará radnice**, in the southeastern corner of the square, is one of the oldest buildings in the city and now houses the less than thrilling **Ostravské muzeum** (Mon–Fri 9am–5pm, Sat & Sun 9am–1pm). Ostrava's most lavish museum, at Nádražní 10, was the one dedicated to the working-class movement, though it has now reverted to its original function as the **Investiční banka**, the muscular proletarians above the portico now simply employees. The city's purpose-built **Dům umění** (Tues–Fri 10am–noon & 12.30–6pm, Sat & Sun 10am–3pm), a red-brick functionalist building from the 1920s, on Jurečkova, one block west of Nádražní, displays an unexceptional collection of nineteenth-century Czech art on the ground floor, with temporary exhibitions upstairs.

With so much money sloshing around in the late nineteenth and early twentieth centuries, it comes as no surprise that Ostrava boasts one or two grandiose reminders of those golden years. The gargantuan salmon-pink-and-cream-coloured **Bazilika**, northwest of the main square, built in a heavy neo-Renaissance style in the 1880s, is the second largest church in Moravia, capable of seating a congregation of four thousand. One of the finest Art Nouveau buildings in the city stands to the north at the top of Miličova, its facade decorated with delicate floral stuccowork – just don't look at the modern extension round the back. Directly opposite is Ostrava's imposing brick-built **Evangelický kostel** (Protestant Church), designed in Dutch Renaissance style in 1907. However, by far the most awesome monument to Ostrava's former municipal pride is the **nová radnice**, at the end of 30 dubna. Erected in the 1920s, it is the largest town hall in the country, and its slender, 72-metre-high, copper-clad clocktower has a viewing platform open to the public from May to October.

When the coal industry took off in the nineteenth century, the city just grew up around the pit heads – a convenient, but ecologically disastrous, piece of town planning. The **Karolina coking plant**, right in the city centre and pulled down only in the 1980s, spewed out lethal carcinogenic filth over the city's main shopping district for over a century, and you can still see the red-brick **Jindřich pithead** (těžní věž), just past 30 dubna on Nádražní. Elsewhere, antiquated derricks, silver snaking pipes and red-and-white-striped chimneys are very much a part of the cityscape: an awesome sight, lit up at night like proverbial satanic mills. Those with a passionate interest in the local mining industry should hop on bus #34, #52 or #56 at the top of Sokolská třída, east of the main train station, which provide a regular service north across the River Odra to the suburb of Petřkovice (get off at the U Jana stop). Here, at the now defunct Anselm mine (once owned by the Rothschilds), there's a **Hornický skanzen** or open-air mining museum (Tues–Sun guided tours at 9am, 11am, 1pm & 3pm), where you can descend into the pit, inspect the seams and take a look at the exhibition in the manager's villa.

The city continues to pay a high price for the mining exploitation of the last two centuries, especially when it comes to subsidence. The local **hrad**, originally built in the thirteenth century to guard the border between Moravia and Silesia, has already sunk fourteen metres and, according to city officials, is now beyond redemption. You can still visit it at any time by crossing one of the bridges over the Ostravice and negotiating the motorway (alternatively take tram #9, #10, #13 or #18 and get off at the first stop across the river). If you're walking, as you cross the bridge, Sýkorův most, you'll pass by one of the few surviving monuments celebrating the city's liberation by the Soviets, which features a tank on a plinth.

Eating, drinking and nightlife

Eating options include thin-base pizzas from the *Domino* pizzeria and steak restaurant, on the east side of the main square – one of the few places open on Sunday. The *Staročeská pivnice* on the ground floor of the *Hotel Palace* is a standard Czech pub where you eat and drink cheaply, while the *Radniční restaurace*, through the arch to the right of the Nová radnice, allows you a glimpse of this magnificent interwar edifice from the inside; it also serves Radegast and even has disabled access. For something completely different, head for the new Spanish-themed restaurant, *España*, at Tyršova 31, decked like a Spanish galleon. The *Kavárna Elektra*, near the tourist office on Nádražní, is the best **café** in town, a smart and spacious place run Viennese-style, with 1920s repro decor. Lastly, if you need to send an email or get online, there's an **Internet café**, on Českobratská, near the town hall (closed Sat & Sun).

Ostrava boasts a good **philharmonic orchestra**, once backed by big state funds, which plays in various venues across the city, while the Divadlo Antonína Dvořáka puts on a range of opera, ballet and theatre. Predictably enough, Janáček, who died in Ostrava, is the subject of the city's May music festival, **Janáčkův máj**. A more eclectic range of **jazz, rock and folk music** is staged upstairs at *Klub Parník*, the city's best alternative venue, housed in a striking late-nineteenth-century villa at the corner of Sokolská and Matiční; the pub downstairs (closed Sat & Sun lunch) is also a popular hangout. The city that produced Ivan Lendl is home to one of the republic's most important sports centres. Predictably enough, as a working-class city *par excellence*, Ostrava's strongest tradition is in **football**, and the city boasts two top-flight teams, Baník Ostrava and Vítkovice. A large number of the country's big sporting events are held here, so ask at the tourist office for the latest fixtures.

The Beskydy

Despite their proximity, the hilly **Beskydy** region and the apocalyptic filth of the Ostrava coal basin are poles apart. In the foothills there's a whole cluster of interesting sights not far from (and including) **Nový Jičín**. Further south and east, into hiking country proper, the old Wallachian traditions have been preserved both *in situ*, in the more inaccessible villages, and at the open-air folk museum or *skansen* at **Rožnov pod Radhoštěm**.

Nový Jičín

NOVÝ JIČÍN (Neu-Titschein) is a typical one-square town on the main road from Olomouc to Ostrava. That said, Masarykovo náměstí is a particularly fine square, with wide whitewashed arcades tunnelling their way under a host of restrained, late-Baroque facades in pastel colours. The **radnice** is an unusual white, boxy affair rebuilt in the 1930s, its wonderfully jagged gable a reminder of its seventeenth-century origins. However, the one building that stands out (literally) from the rest is the **stará pošta**, where Tsar Alexander I and General Suvurov have both stayed the night; its pretty two-storey loggia dates from the town's boom time in the sixteenth century when it bought its independence from the Žerotín family.

Nowadays, the town's chief attraction is its **Kloboučnické muzeum** or Hat Museum (Tues–Fri 8am–noon & 1–4pm, Sat & Sun 9am–3pm), laid out in the Žerotíns' old chateau, accessed through the covered passageway of Lidická underneath the radnice. Thankfully, the present exploits of the old state hat enterprise, Tonak (based in the town), are only lightly touched on, leaving most of the museum to a wonderful variety of hats produced in Nový Jičín since 1799 by the original firms of Hückel, Peschel and Böhm. The bit that gets the Czechs going is the array of hats worn by famous national personages – a bit esoteric for non-Czechs, though some might be stirred by the sight of Masaryk's topper.

Nový Jičín has two **train stations**, both located at the end of obscure and inconvenient branch lines, making the **bus** by far the easiest way to come and go. The **tourist office** (Mon–Fri 9am–noon & 1–4pm, Sat & Sun 9am–noon), in the chateau, can book **private rooms**, or you could try the *Kalač* (☎0656/70 16 12; ⑦), an unprepossessing

---

WOODEN CHURCHES IN THE BESKYDY

If you can't make it out to the Greek-Catholic churches of East Slovakia (see p.471), the next best place for visiting **wooden churches** is the Beskydy region. Although numerous timber-framed houses were torn down during the course of the last century, churches appear to have fared a little better. Below is a selection of the region's best examples.

Bystřice nad Olší, 12km southeast of Český Těšín. Polish/Czech town in the Olše valley, with a wooden neo-Gothic Catholic church, built in 1896 to replace the sixteenth-century stone one.

Guty, 11km south of Český Těšín. Probably the most striking of all the Beskydy's wooden churches, with its bulky Lemk-style western tower erected in 1781 above the narthex or entrance porch.

Hodslavice, 8km south of Nový Jičín. Birthplace of Czech nationalist and historian František Palacký, one of the chief political figures of the nineteenth-century Czech national revival. Hodslavice also boasts the sixteenth-century wooden church of sv Ondřej.

Kunčice pod Ondřejníkem, 4km east of Frenštát pod Radhoštěm. This mountain village was a favourite summer resort of the wealthy steel and coal magnates of Ostrava, one of whom, in 1931, brought an entire Greek-Catholic church over from what is now Ukraine for his wedding.

Radhošť, 6km south of Frenštát pod Radhoštěm. You have to climb a mountain to see the wooden chapel of sv Cyril & Metoděj, built in neo-Byzantine style in 1905, from which there's an unbeatable view across the Beskydy.

Rybí, 4km northwest of Štramberk. Fifteenth-century Gothic church with shingled roof, tower and onion dome steeple, plus a dinky little sundial in its main gable.

and overpriced hotel on Dvořákova, or the *Hotel Praha* (☎0656/70 12 29; ③), at Lidická 6, a late-nineteenth-century building opposite the chateau that looks better outside than in.

Štramberk

Eight kilometres east of Nový Jičín, accessible by the occasional bus or an easy two-hour walk, the smokestack settlement of **ŠTRAMBERK** (Strallenburg) is one of the best places to take your first dip into Wallachian culture. Clumped under the conic Bílá hora (not to be confused with *the* Bílá hora in Prague) like an ancient funeral pyre, Štramberk feels very old indeed, yet many of its wooden cottages were built as recently as the first half of the nineteenth century. Its virtue is in displaying Wallachian architecture *in situ*, the cottages simply constructed out of whole tree trunks, unpainted and free of tourists rather than cooped and mummified in a sanitized *skansen*.

Despite being no more than a village, Štramberk does have a nominal main square. At one end are several stone buildings in "folk Baroque", behind which rises up the galleried wooden *klopačka* (belfry) of the original church. At the other end is an old Jesuit church painted in sherbet orange, next door to a small **Muzeum Štramberk** (April–Oct Tues–Sun 9am–noon & 1–5pm) displaying archeological finds from the nearby Šipka cave (see below). The castle, laid waste by the Tatars and never rebuilt, has just one remaining round tower, **Trúba** (April–Oct daily 9am–5pm), which translates as "The Tube" and is now a lookout post, with a restaurant nearby.

Just below the main square is the newly established **Zdeněk Burian Museum** (Easter to mid-Sept Tues–Sun 8.30am–noon & 12.30–4pm), dedicated to the work of this prolific painter, who was born in nearby Kopřivnice and spent his childhood in Štramberk. Burian (1905–81) was a book illustrator and paleontologist, but is perhaps best known (to Czechs at any rate) for his painstaking representations of the world of prehistoric humans. His inspiration came from the nearby **Šipka cave**, beneath the limestone hill of Kotouč (532m), where remains of Neanderthal man were discovered in the late nineteenth century. The caves are a short walk through the woods of the Národní sad, signposted off the road to Kopřivnice.

Hotel Šipka (☎0656/85 21 81; ①), on the main square, lets out cheap simple **rooms** and serves good Czech food and beer. A more comfortable option is the tastefully timber-clad *Hotel Roubenka* (☎ & fax 00656/85 25 66; ④), which enjoys great views up to the Trúba; to get there follow the signs off the road from Nový Jičín, or head down Dolní from the post office. Another, more expensive option is *Hotel Gong* (☎0656/72 10 36; ⑥), a slightly unsightly modern edifice next door to the post office. At the bakery on the corner of the main square, you can sample the local speciality, *Štramberské uši* (Štramberk Ears), honeyed gingerbread (often filled with cream), which commemo-

---

WALLACHIAN CULTURE

As far as anybody can make out, the **Wallachs** or **Vlachs** were seminomadic sheep and goat farmers who settled the mountainous areas of eastern Moravia and western Slovakia in the fifteenth century. Although their name clearly derives from the Romanian Vlachs, it is believed that they arrived from eastern Poland and the Ukraine, and the name Vlach is simply a generic term for sheep farmer. Whatever their true origins, they were certainly considered a race apart by the surrounding Slav peasants. Successive Habsburg military campaigns against the Vlachs in the seventeenth century destroyed their separate identity, and nowadays Wallachian culture lives on only in the folk customs and distinctive wooden architecture of the region.

rates a particularly gruesome legend: during the Tatar invasion, the local people were saved by a judiciously timed flood which kept the marauders at bay – when the waters subsided, so the story goes, sacks full of the ears of Tatar victims were found.

Kopřivnice

On the other side of Bílá hora from Štramberk (and an easy half-hour walk), **KOPŘIVNICE** (Nesselsdorf) is an ugly, sprawling factory town, but nevertheless worth a quick visit for its **Tatra Museum** (Tues–Sun 9am–4pm), situated in the hangar-like building next door to the train station. Even if spark plugs don't usually fire your imagination, there are some wonderful old cars here. Unlike the popular and ubiquitous Škoda, Tatra cars have always aimed to be exclusive: the first model, which came out in 1897, was called the "President", and from 1948 onwards that's exactly who rode in them. The silent and powerful black Tatra, looking like something out of a gangster B-movie, became the ultimate symbol of Party privilege. Ordinary mortals could buy any colour they liked except black – the colour reserved for Party functionaries. When you've seen the Tatra 87 and the 603, it's a slightly hysterical and somewhat frightening thought to imagine the country's top Stalinists cruising around in these cars, which were succeeded in the 1970s by the Tatra 613. The post-Communist leadership has decided to do away with the stigma of the Tatra, and with the Party no longer in a position to pay for its usual bulk order, the firm has had a hard time trying to modernize its Tonka-tough trucks and continue production of its super-luxury cars.

Příbor

Five kilometres and one train station north of Kopřivnice, **PRÍBOR** (Freiberg) appears at first to be a rerun of Nový Jičín, with a similarly pleasant, arcaded main square. However, as the birthplace of **Sigmund Freud**, Příbor has a much greater claim to fame. Although the family's financial problems forced them to leave for Vienna when Sigmund was only four, it's difficult to resist the chance to visit the place where Freud went through his oral and anal phases: the ten-metre-square room at Freudova 117 (then belonging to Zajík the blacksmith; now, appropriately enough, a therapy centre offering reflexology and herbal remedies), which is now marked by a plaque. The local **Muzeum v Příboře** (Tues & Thurs 8am–noon & 1–4pm, Sun 9am–noon), situated in the former monastery on Lidická, has devoted only one of its four rooms to the man, and sadly there are no pictures of baby Sigi, only dull official photos of learned and

---

FREUD IN FREIBERG

Born in 1856 to a hard-up Jewish wool merchant and his third wife, Freud had no hesitation in ascribing significance to events that took place during the family's brief sojourn here. "Of one thing I am certain," Freud wrote later, "deep within me, although overlaid, there continues to live the happy child from Freiberg [Příbor], the first-born child of a young mother who received from this air, from this soil, the first indelible impressions." Things were not always so idyllic, and Freud later used a number of events from his early childhood to prove psychoanalytical theories. The family maidservant, "my instructress in sexual matters" in Freud's own words, was a local Czech woman who used to drag him off to the nearby Catholic church and in Freud's eyes was responsible for his "Rome neurosis". She was eventually sacked for alleged theft (and for encouraging baby Sigmund to thieve, too) and sent to prison. Things weren't too bad on the Oedipal front either, Freud suspecting his half-brother of being the father of his younger sister, Anna.

bearded men (including Jung) at conferences on psychoanalysis. In the rest of the town, few associations present themselves, apart from Freud's bust, which stands just outside the pretty main square, náměstí S. Freuda.

Hukvaldy

Moravians hold Janáček much dearer to their hearts than Freud, and the village of **HUKVALDY**, 6km east of Příbor, has become a modest shrine to the composer. Born just two years before Freud, **Leoš Janáček** was the fifth of nine children, too many for his impecunious father who taught at the local school. Thus, at the age of eleven, Janáček was sent to Brno to be a chorister, and from then on he made his home in the city, battling against the prejudices of the powerful German elite who ruled over the Moravian classical music scene. When at last he achieved recognition outside Moravia, through the success of the opera *Jenůfa*, he was already in his sixties. Having bought a cottage in Hukvaldy, he spent his last, most fruitful years based here and in Brno, composing such works as *The Glagolitic Mass, The Cunning Little Vixen* and *From the House of the Dead*. The music of this period was fired by his obsessive love for a woman called Kamila Strösslová, wife of a Jewish antique dealer in Písek, who had sent him food parcels throughout World War I. Although he never left his wife, Janáček wrote over 700 letters to Kamila, the most passionate ones written almost daily in the last sixteen months of his life. In August 1928, he caught a chill searching for her son in the nearby woods, and died in a hospital in Ostrava.

Even if you've no interest whatsoever in Janáček, Hukvaldy is a homely little village nestling into a wooded hill on top of which sits a ruined **hrad** (April & Oct Sat & Sun 9am–4pm; May–Aug Tues–Sun 9am–6pm; Sept closes 5pm), complete with deer park – there's a statue of the Cunning Little Vixen in the woods. The composer's **museum**, housed in his sandy yellow cottage, is pleasantly low-key (April & Oct Sat & Sun Tues–Sun 9am–noon & 1–4pm; May–Sept Tues–Sun 9am–noon & 1–4pm), containing just a little modest furniture and his lectern (he always composed standing up). However, it's the gentle pastoral setting, an element underlying all Janáček's music, that provides the most instructive impression of the place. Should you wish to stay, there's a **tourist office** (Mon & Wed 7–11am & noon–5pm, Tues 7–11am & noon–3pm, Fri 7–11am) in the village that can help with **accommodation**, if there's no room at the friendly *Hukvaldský dvůr* (☎0658/69 92 41; ②), opposite.

Into the hills of the Beskydy

Between the sparsely wooded pastureland around Nový Jičín and the Rožnovská Bečva valley to the south are the **hills of the Beskydy**. Starting off in North Moravia and entering Poland, they actually extend right over into Ukraine, shadowing the much higher Carpathian range to the south. Spruce has gradually given way to pine, which, though damaged by acid rain, is as yet not too badly affected by pollutants, and in the westernmost reaches patches of beech forest still exist.

Around Radhošť

During the Cold War, **FRENŠTÁT POD RADHOŠTĚM** (Frankstadt) was dominated by its Red Army barracks, but over the last decade, the town has been spruced up, and the main square, which is peppered with Baroque statuary, is now looking very pretty indeed. Though not exactly in the thick of the Beskydy, it's easily the chief starting point for people heading off into the hills. There's a **tourist office** (Mon–Fri 9am–5pm, Sat 8.30am–noon) in the town hall, and a couple of decent **hotels**: the *Přerov* (☎0656/83 59 91; ②), on the main square, is exceptionally cheap, friendly and has a restaurant on the ground floor, and a cellar **pub** a few doors down, named after Oliver Hardy.

Alternatively, there's the *Vlčina* (☎0656/83 53 51; ⑤), a communist-era hotel southwest of the town with outstanding views over the valley – to get there either take the ski-lift (*lánova draha*) or walk 1.5km up the hill from town on the green-marked path. There's also the *Radhošť* **campsite** (May to mid-Oct), on the north bank of the river, 1km north-west of the town centre.

Radhošť (1129m), which Rožnov (see below) and Frenštát both dub themselves under (*pod*), is the most famous peak – thanks to its legends – though not the tallest. The view from the summit is still pretty good, and there's a fanciful wooden chapel, done out in neo-Byzantine style. Two kilometres east, there's a statue of Radegast, the mountain's legendary pagan god (who lends his name to the famous local beer). Another kilometre east, there's a series of late-nineteenth-century timber-slat buildings designed by Dusan Jurkovič, including the fantastical hotel, the *Tanečnica* (☎0656/83 53 41; ⑤), named after the nearby mountain, as well as a nifty, carefully balanced *zvonička* (belfry). With the help of a chairlift (*lanovka*), the less athletic can reach the *Tanečnica*; the yellow- and/or green-marked path will take you down to the *Kněhyně* **campsite** (open all year) in Prostřední Bečva.

Rožnov pod Radhoštěm

Halfway up the Rožnovská Bečva valley, on the south side of Radhošť, lies the former spa town of **ROŽNOV POD RADHOŠTĚM**, now home of the biggest and most popular **skansen** of folk architecture in the Czech Republic, the main entrance to which lies on the other side of the river from the train station. The open-air museum – officially entitled **Valašské muzeum v přírodě** – is divided into three parts, each with a different opening time; guided tours (in Czech) are compulsory only in the Mlýnská dolina, so ask for the *anglický text*.

The moving force behind the first part, the Wooden Town or **Městečko dřevené** (Tues–Sun: May–Sept 8am–6pm; Oct 9am–5pm), was local artist Bohumír Jaromek, who was inspired by the outdoor folk museum in Stockholm (from which the word *skansen* derives). In 1925, Rožnov's eighteenth-century wooden radnice was moved from the main square to its present site, followed by a number of other superb timber buildings from the town and neighbouring villages like Větřkovice u Příbora, which supplied the beautiful seventeenth-century wooden church (where services are still held). There are Wallachian beehives decorated with grimacing faces, a smithy and even a couple of *hospoda* selling food and warm *slivovice*.

The second part of the museum, the Wallachian Village or **Valašská dědina** (daily: mid-May to Aug 9am–5.30pm; Sept 9am–5pm) was built in the 1970s on a hillside across the road from the Městečko dřevené. It takes a more erudite approach, attempting to re-create a typical highland sheep-farming settlement – the traditional Wallachian community – complete with a variety of farm animals and organic crops, plus a schoolhouse, dairy and blacksmith. Enthusiastic guides take you round the third and newest section, **Mlýnská dolina** (Mill Valley; daily: mid-April to May & Sept to mid-Oct 9am–5pm; July & Aug 8am–6pm), which is centred around an old flour mill and includes a water-powered blacksmith's and sawmill, peopled by period-dressed artisans.

Rožnov attracts a lot of coach parties who tend to book out the cheaper hotels, so you may have to scout around for private **accommodation**. The best hotel in town is currently the *Eroplán* (☎0651/64 80 14; ⑦), situated, like the nearby *Hotel Energetik* (☎0651/65 40 45; ③), up the hill across from the skansen; the real bargain option is the high-rise *Pension Bečva* (☎0651/544 58; ②), opposite the *Billa* supermarket on the road to Valašské Meziříčí. **Campsites** are thick on the ground to the east of the museum, with one on either side of the road to Prostřední Bečva – the *Rožnov* (open all year) and the *Sport* (mid-June to mid-Sept) – and a third, *Pod lipami* (July & Aug), 3km up the road in Dolní Bečva. There's a nice **restaurant** in the *Společenský dům* (closed Sun), in the Městský sad, which also houses its own micro-brewery.

ÓNDRA L'YSOHORSKY

The ninth child of a Frýdek miner, the poet **Óndra L'ysohorsky** (whose real name was Erwin Goy) took his pen-name from the local Robin Hood rebel, Ondrás, who was imprisoned in, and escaped from, Frýdek castle back in the seventeenth century, when it was owned by the wicked Duke Pragma. His surname comes from the highest peak in the Beskydy, Lysa hora (Bare Mountain). L'ysohorsky was brought up speaking German and the local Slav dialect, but, after writing his first verses in German, decided to change to Lachian, a written form of the local dialect which he himself invented, but which never really caught on. The dialect (or language, depending on your point of view), somewhere between Czech and Polish, survives in the towns and villages along the Polish border and was spoken by around a million people (mostly miners) at its peak between the two world wars. L'ysohorsky's obstinacy on this linguistic point eventually brought him into conflict with the postwar Communist authorities, who accused him of supporting the region's Polish irredentists. Apart from a brief reprise in 1958, his verse remained unpublished in Czechoslovakia, despite his being one of the country's better-known poets abroad. L'ysohorsky died shortly after the upheavals of 1989 in Bratislava, and the poet's vast archives are now safely deposited in Frýdek castle.

Frýdek-Místek

Lying halfway between the Beskydy and Ostrava, and accessible by train from either, **FRÝDEK-MÍSTEK** (Friedeck-Friedburg) is a rather rude re-entry into the Ostrava coal basin. Its charms are few – the tourist authorities call it "a city of possibilities" – and its soulless industrial quarter has assumed a much greater importance than its twin old towns straddling the River Ostravice: **Místek**, on the flat left bank, where the business of the town now goes on, and **Frýdek**, the prettiest and quietest part of town on the hill opposite. Frýdek's main square has now been beautifully restored, with a statue of Saint Florian, patron saint of firefighters, superintending the central fountain, and the town's landmark **zámek** (Tues, Wed & Fri 8am–noon & 12.30–4pm, Thurs closes 5pm, Sat & Sun 1–5pm) in one corner. Once the property of the lords of Těšín, it now contains an art gallery, and a small museum with tributes to Janáček, Óndra L'ysohorsky (see box above) and the Silesian poet Petr Bezruč, who stayed in Místek for a while, championing the grievances of the poverty-stricken local miners – unfortunately you have to go round the castle and the museum with a guide.

Český Těšín

If you fancy a quick jaunt into **Poland**, the easiest place is probably **ČESKÝ TĚŠÍN** (Cieszyn), 20km east of dek-Místek, which found itself arbitrarily divided when the borders were drawn up following the collapse of the Habsburg Empire after World War I. The town was claimed by both Poland and Czechoslovakia, and it was finally decided in 1920 to use the fairly insignificant River Olše (Olza) as the frontier. In this instance, the Poles got the best deal, ending up with most of the town, including the staré město and the castle on the right bank. The Czech part is made up of grim, grey housing blocks built between the wars, and the only reason for coming here is to cross over to see the more interesting sights of the Polish side (see *Poland: the Rough Guide* for details).

When **crossing the border** into Poland, you have to use the Střelniční most (most Wolnołci), 400m due east of the train station; when returning to the Czech side, use Hlavní most (most Przyjazni), 700m downstream, at the end of Hlavní třída; both bridges are for pedestrians and cyclists only. Visa regulations and price disparities between the two countries have fluctuated over the years. At the height of Solidarity, during the 1980s, it was almost as difficult for Czechs to get into Poland as to travel to the West. Then the tables were turned and, with the Polish economy in free fall, the Czechs clamped down on Poles entering the country. Nowadays, people on either side of the border can cross using just their ID cards.

travel details

Trains

Connections with Prague: Olomouc (every 1–2hr; 3hr–3hr 30min); Ostrava (every 2–3hr; 3hr 40min–5hr).

Jeseník to: Javorník (3 daily; 1hr 10min); Žulová (8 daily; 35min).

Lipová Lázně to: Javorník (6 or more daily; 50min); Žulová (8 or more daily; 20min).

Olomouc to: Bruntál (10 daily; 1hr 15min–1hr 45min); Jeseník (3 daily; 2hr 15min); Krnov (10 daily; 1hr 45min–2hr 30min); Lipová Lázně (3 daily; 2hr); Opava (4 daily; 2hr 20min–3hr); Ostrava (1–2 hourly; 1hr 30min–2hr 30min); Přerov (1–2 hourly; 20min); Prostějov (every 1–2hr; 15–25min); Šumperk (10 daily; 1hr 5min–1hr 25min).

Opava to: Hradec nad Moravicí (10 or more daily; 15min); Jeseník (4 daily; 2hr 10min); Krnov (every 1–2hr; 30–40min); Ostrava (hourly; 25–40min).

Ostrava to: Český Těšín (1–2 hourly; 50min); Frýdek-Místek (1–2 hourly; 40min/1hr).

Šumperk to: Jeseník (6 daily; 1hr 45min–2hr); Lipová Lázně (6 daily; 1hr 40min).

Buses

Connections with Prague: Nový Jičín (2 daily; 5hr); Olomouc (2 daily; 4hr); Ostrava (2 daily; 6hr).

Olomouc to: Nový Jičín (up to 6 daily; 1hr 15min); Opava (2–4 daily; 2hr); Ostrava (up to 6 daily; 2hr); Příbor (3–10 daily; 1hr 30min); Rožnov pod Radhoštěm (2 daily; 1hr 15min).

Nový Jičín to: Frenštát pod Radhoštěm (hourly; 40min); Frýdek-Místek (up to 8 daily; 45min); Kopřivnice (hourly; 35min); Příbor (hourly; 25min); Štramberk (1–2 hourly; 15–30 min).

PART THREE

SLOVAKIA

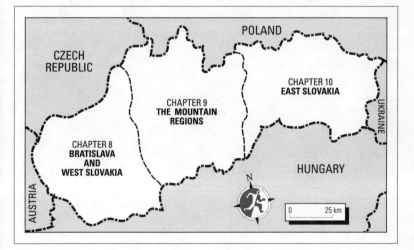

Introduction

After centuries of cultural repression by the Hungarians, followed by 75 years of playing second fiddle to the Czechs within Czechoslovakia, the Slovaks finally gained their independence on January 1, 1993. Since those heady celebratory days, however, life has been much harder for the Slovaks than for the Czechs. With no internationally popular figurehead to act as a public relations officer, the new Slovakia has found it difficult jockeying for a position in the new Europe. Political instability, corruption and slow-moving reforms have deterred overseas investors and drawn criticism from abroad, and as a consequence the country has fallen behind in the queue to join both NATO and the EU.

For the first-time visitor, however, perhaps the most striking difference between the Czechs and the Slovaks is their attitude to religion. **Catholicism** is much stronger in Slovakia and the country's churches are visibly fuller on a Sunday; indeed, it is not uncommon to see people crowded outside the entrance of an overflowing church with a service in progress. The republic also has a much more diverse population, with over half a million **Hungarian**-speakers in the area bordering Hungary, one of the largest **Romany** minorities in Europe and thousands of **Rusyns** in the east of the country bordering Ukraine. Geographically, Slovakia lies between two extremes: the flat, parched plains of the Danube basin in the west, and the granite peaks of the Tatras – some of Europe's highest mountains outside the Alps – in the east. These have long formed barriers to industrialization and modernization, preserving and strengthening regional differences in the face of centralization from Vienna, Budapest, Prague and now Bratislava.

■ The road to Slovak independence

For most of the last thousand years, Slovakia was simply known as northern Hungary. It wasn't until the nineteenth century that there was any kind of **Slovak national revival**, or *národné ubrudenie*. The most popular political philosophy of the day was Pan-Slavism, which viewed all Slavs, be they Slovak, Czech, Polish or Russian, as kin, and usually looked to the Russian tsar for any hope of liberation. Few singled out the Czechs for special attention, and when they did, briefly in 1848 and later in 1918 with the formation of

Czechoslovakia, it was partly on the grounds of expediency, to scupper any of the compromise plans of a federal "Greater Hungary" (which would have included what is now Slovakia) put forward by the Hungarians. When the Czechs began behaving uncannily like their previous Hungarian masters – taking all the top jobs and ruling by decree from Prague – many Slovaks became disillusioned with the First Republic and viewed the Munich Diktat of September 1938 as a blessing in disguise.

In October 1938, the Slovaks set up their own autonomous government, according to the Žilina Accord, which was superseded six months later when the country gained its **independence**, under the leadership of Jozef Tiso, as part of a deal with Hitler. For many this brief period of independence, which lasted from 1939 to 1944, was a genuine expression of Slovak statehood, even if, at the end of the day, the country was little more than a Nazi puppet state, whose Jews shared the fate of their brethren elsewhere in Nazi-occupied Europe. In August 1944, thousands of Slovaks took to the hills to fight in the anti-fascist Slovak National Uprising, which was seen by many as yet another plea for sovereignty, rather than a call for the re-establishment of Czechoslovakia.

Whatever their differences over World War II, few Slovaks were happy with the **post-1945 situation**. Once more, Czech promises of Slovak autonomy, set out in the Košice Programme of April 1945, were reneged upon. Slovak Communists were put into positions of power by their highly placed comrades in Prague despite the fact that the Communists, by far the largest party in the Czech Lands, trailed behind the newly formed Democrats in the Slovak polls. After 1948, Stalinist centralization policies put paid to any hopes Slovak Communists might have had of running their own affairs; and in the 1950s, the victims of the country's show trials and purges were more often than not Slovak and/or Jewish.

In January 1968, Alexander Dubček was elected First Secretary of the Communist Party, the first Slovak to hold such a high position **The events of 1968** were primarily Prague-inspired, and it was the Slovaks who actually benefited most from the Warsaw Pact invasion, the fruits of which included federalization, a bilingual national media, and a large injection of state money to help adjust the economic imbalance between the two republics. It was a sop to the Slovak

Communists – classic divide-and-rule tactics – and one that worked, at least for a while, with the Slovak Gustáv Husák (himself a victim of the show trials) put in charge of the "normalization" policies of the 1970s.

However, from the dissident movement of Charter 77 to the Velvet Revolution of November 1989, events during the last twenty years of Communist rule were focused on Prague, and it wasn't long before old differences began to emerge. These were most evident in the summer of 1990 when it came to deciding on a new name for the country, in what became known as the **great hyphen debate**. The Slovaks' insistence that a hyphen be inserted in "Czechoslovakia" was greeted with ridicule by most Czechs; Havel was one of the few who understood that what was just a hyphen to the Czechs meant a whole lot more to the Slovaks.

The electoral failure of the extremist Slovak Nationalist Party (SNS) lulled the Czechs into thinking that most Slovaks wanted the federation to stay together. This theory was shot to pieces in the **June 1992 elections** by the victory of the Movement for a Democratic Slovakia (HZDS), under the canny leadership of populist politician **Vladimír Mečiar**. Events moved rapidly towards the break-up of the federation, despite the major reservations of the republic's Hungarian minority and many Slovaks. In the end, neither the Czechs nor the Slovaks were given the chance to put the question to the vote in a referendum, before the country became fully independent in 1993.

■ Where to go

Bratislava, the Slovak capital, is potentially disappointing for those expecting a Slovak Prague, though taken on its own terms, it's a rewarding place, with a compact old town and a fairly lively nightlife. The flat plains of the Danube basin are of little visual interest, but there are two historic towns that make worthwhile day-trips from the capital: **Trnava**, the seat of the Hungarian archbishopric for many years, and **Nitra**, a bishopric and the spiritual centre of Slovak Catholicism today.

The central **mountain regions** divide easily into two main valleys: the **Váh**, Slovakia's longest river, which forms the backbone of the country, and the **Hron**, which runs more or less parallel to the south. This is the Slovaks' real homeland; the dialect here was chosen to form the basis of the

written language in the nineteenth century, and it's from here that most of the country's leaders have hailed, from the nationalist figure of Andrej Hlinka to present-day politician Vladimír Mečiar. However, the Slovak influence on the towns themselves is less evident than that of the country's former ruling class, the Hungarian overlords, and of the German workers who came here in medieval times to work in the mines and were expelled after 1945.

At the heart of the mountain regions lies **Banská Bystrica**, an old German mining town perhaps best known as the headquarters of the unsuccessful 1944 antifascist uprising. It's also one of the few central Slovak towns to have any architectural merit, though nearby **Banská Štiavnica** is a gem. Other towns, like Žilina and Liptovský Mikuláš, are mainly of interest as bases for exploring the chief attractions of the region, its mountain ranges – in particular the **Malá Fatra** and the **Low Tatras**. These pine-clad peaks provide great hiking opportunities and skiing terrain. Some of the more isolated corners of the region also remain rich in **folk architecture**, with the timber structures of villages like Čičmany and Vlkolínec forming virtual open-air museums or *skanzen*.

In many ways, **East Slovakia** is the most rewarding part of the country, with the granite peaks of the **High Tatras** including the tallest and most dramatic of all the Slovak mountains. Few tourists venture further, but just a step away from **Poprad**, the High Tatras' transport hub, is the **Slovenský raj**, a thickly wooded region of verdant ravines and rocky outcrops. Also within easy reach is the **Spiš region**, East Slovakia's architectural high point; once predominantly German-speaking, the area is dotted with intriguing medieval towns like **Levoča**, which have been preserved more or less untouched since the sixteenth century.

Further east still is **Prešov**, the cultural centre of Slovak **Carpatho-Ruthenia** (most of which is now in Ukraine), whose villages are inhabited by the country's Rusyn minority. Here you'll find an extraordinary wealth of **wooden churches**, many of them belonging to the Greek-Catholic church. **Medzilaborce**, in the far northeastern corner of the country, is the ultimate destination for the truly adventurous, and the unlikely home of Europe's only **Andy Warhol Museum**. Finally, **Košice**, Slovakia's second largest city, boasts Europe's easternmost Gothic cathedral and has a strongly Hungarian ambience. It's also a good launch pad for the Slovak karst region of **Slovenský kras**.

Getting around

Geographical considerations mean that Slovakia has nothing like the same density of railways as the Czech Republic. Some of the lines, however, are breathtakingly beautiful and serve most places along the chief valleys – after that you'll have to rely on the patchy bus network and, in some places (particularly in the far east of the country), you really need your own transport. Bus and train frequencies can be found in the "Travel Details" section at the end of each chapter.

■ Trains

The **train system** may be less developed than in the Czech Republic, but many journeys are worth making for the scenery alone: try the Banská Bystrica–Diviaky line, the Brezno–Margecany trip in the Low Tatras, or any of the electric trains in the High Tatras. Ticket prices are still remarkably low compared with the West.

The state railways, Železnice Slovenskej republiky (ŽSR), run two main types of service: **rýchlik** trains are the faster, stopping only at major towns, but still costing very little per kilometre; the **osobný vlak**, or local train, is even cheaper, almost half as much, but stops everywhere and averages about 30km an hour. Inter-city (IC) or

Euro-city (EC) trains are the fastest and require a supplement which you should purchase before boarding the train (it costs more otherwise). **Tickets** (*lístok*) for domestic journeys can be bought at the station (*stanica*) before or on the day of departure, and a useful tip is to write down the relevant travel information (date/time/destination) for the ticket clerk to avoid linguistic confusion.

Fares are cheap, with a second-class single from Bratislava to Košice currently costing around £5/$8. First-class carriages (*prvá trieda*) exist on all fast trains, and though tickets are fifty percent more expensive, they should guarantee you a seat on a busy train. There are half-price **discounts** for children under 15, and you can take two under-5s for free. ŽSR also run reasonably priced **sleepers** (*lehátkový vozeň*), which should be booked as far in advance as possible and certainly no later than six hours before departure.

Information and timetables

As in the Czech Republic, obtaining **train information** can be problematic unless you have some knowledge of the language. Most stations have poster-style displays of arrivals (*príchod*) and departures (*odchod*), the former on white paper, the latter on yellow, with fast trains printed in red; timetables in the smaller stations are displayed on simple boards (*smer*). Rollers are an alternative source of information available in most stations. See the box below for advice on how to read them.

■ Buses

Trains will take you most places, but if you have to change a lot, it might be easier to take one of the regional **buses** (*autobus*), run by either the state bus company, Slovenská autobusová doprava (SAD), or one of numerous private operations.

READING SLOVAK TRAIN TIMETABLES

Select your route on the diagrammatic map and make a note of the number printed beside it, then find the appropriate number on the timetable rollers. Crucial notes and explanations are in Slovak: arrivals are often abbreviated to *pr.* or *prích.* and departures to *od.* or *odch.*; a platform or *nástupište* is usually divided into two *koľaj* on either side. At the side of the timetable you'll often find the notes *chodí v* (running on), or *nechodí v* (not running on), followed by a date or a number/symbol: 1–6 for Monday–Saturday, two hammers for a weekday and a cross for a Sunday. The main station in larger towns is known as *hlavná stanica*, while minor stations often have the suffix *mesto* or *zástavka* after the name. If you're planning on using the trains a lot, you could invest in a ŽSR timetable (*cestovný poriadok*), which comes out every May and is available from most bookshops and tobacconists.

Bus stations (*autobusová stanica*) are usually next to the train station, and if there's no separate terminal you'll have to buy your ticket from the driver. It's a good idea to book your ticket in advance if you're travelling at the weekend or early in the morning on one of the main routes.

Tickets can be bought at the station (*autobusová stanica*) before or on the day of departure; for more minor routes, tickets are on sale from the driver. Large items of **luggage** have to go in the boot, for which the driver will charge you an extra 10–15Sk. Minor bus stops are signposted *zastávka*. To get off, say *ja chcem vystúpiť,* "the next stop" is *ďalšia zastávka*.

■ Urban transport

Buses (*autobus*) and trolleybuses (*trolejbus*) – plus trams (*električka*) in Košice and Bratislava – combine to provide a generally excellent urban public transport system that operates from dawn until around 11pm in most major towns (and all night in Bratislava). Ticket prices are currently 10Sk in Bratislava for an adult (less elsewhere); reduced rates for those aged 6–15; under-6s travel free, and though costs can vary, they are universally cheap.

In most cases, you have to buy your **ticket** before travelling; these are available from newsagents, tobacconists and the yellow machines at major stops, and must be validated in the punching machine on board; plain-clothes **inspectors** will impose an on-the-spot fine of 500Sk or more on anyone caught without a ticket.

■ Driving

Driving under your own steam is a viable alternative to public transport in Slovakia. Traffic is light and road conditions usually good. Only in Bratislava might you encounter difficulties, due to the confusing lane system, tramlines and lack of parking facilities. Although there are only a few short stretches of motorway to speak of, you need a **motorway sticker** or *úhrada*, currently costing 200Sk, in order to use them.

Most foreign driving licences are valid – including all EC, US and Canadian ones – but getting an **International Driver's Licence** can set your mind at rest. If you're driving your own car, you are legally required to carry its registration document; if it's not in your name, you must have a letter of permission signed by the owner and authorized by an official motoring organization

(not applicable to a rented car). Other essential items are a red warning triangle, a first-aid kit, a set of replacement bulbs, and a national identification sticker. Your insurance company at home will advise you as to whether you need a green card; without one you may only be able to get third-party insurance.

Rules of the road

The strict **rules and regulations**, a legacy of the old police state, are less strictly adhered to nowadays, though on-the-spot fines are common and range from a paltry 20Sk to 500Sk or more. Basic rules are: drive on the right, always wear your seatbelt, never take the wheel with any alcohol in your bloodstream, and give way to pedestrians on zebra crossings, and those crossing the road at traffic lights if you're turning right or left. Road markings at junctions are sparse, so look out for the yellow diamond sign, which means you have right of way; a black line through it means you haven't.

Speed limits are 130kph on motorways and 90kph on other roads, except in cities, towns and villages where the maximum is 60kph. There's a special speed limit of 30kph at **level crossings**, where instead of a barrier you'll often find simply the sign *pozor* and a series of lights: a single flashing light means the line is live; two red flashing lights mean a train is approaching.

Fuel and garages

Petrol (*benzín*) comes in super (96 octane) and *special* (90 octane); diesel (*nafta*) is also available, but two-stroke fuel (*mix*) is being phased out. You can fill up with **lead-free** petrol (*natural*) at virtually all petrol stations from green-marked pumps. Bear in mind that there are still fewer petrol stations than in Western Europe, and that some close at lunchtimes and after 6pm (though the number of 24-hour ones is increasing steadily). The price of petrol is slightly cheaper than in much of Western Europe. If you have **car trouble**, dial ☎154 and wait for assistance. You might consider an insurance policy that covers on-the-spot repairs, car rental and travel home for you and your passengers in case of an emergency.

Car rental

To rent a car, you have to be at least 21 years of age and to have held a licence for at least a year. Booking from abroad will cost you upwards of $250 a week for a small car, plus insurance and hefty taxes. The big companies have offices in Bratislava, but local agents offer far better deals. Car rental firms at Vienna airport allow customers to take their cars over the border into Slovakia, but do check before you book and inform them of your intention; you will incur an extra daily insurance charge. For details of international car rental reservations, see p.31.

■ Motorcycling

Slovakia is great for **motorcycling**, though there are very few garages that can cope with even the most rudimentary repairs. Speed limits are the same as for cars, except on motorways where the limit is just 90kph. Helmets are compulsory as are goggles or a visor for the driver, and you must use dipped headlights at all times.

■ Cycling and hiking

Cycling is yet to catch on in Slovakia and the few outlets for **bike rental** are mostly in the more touristy areas such as the High Tatras. Spare parts are difficult to obtain, so bring as many with you as you can. On the faster trains you can take your bike (*bicykel*) for a small supplement, and it's easy enough to persuade the guard on the slower trains to let you on, for a small fee.

Walking is a popular pastime, with a dense network of trails covering the entire countryside; each path is colour-coded with clear markers every 100m or so and signs indicate how long it'll take you to reach your destination. The walks are usually fairly easy-going, but if you venture into the mountains proper, you'll need some sturdy boots. In the High Tatras, you must stick to the

paths indicated and should really have some serious walking experience before attempting any ascent; this mountain range is one of the few areas on which hiking guides have been published in English, so you might consider investing in one before you leave home.

Wherever you're going, it's a good idea to get hold of a *turistická mapa*, which details all the marked paths in the area (see p.21).

Accommodation

On the whole, accommodation in Slovakia is still relatively inexpensive. However, improvement in hotel standards is slow, and in terms of quality of service, you'll often be better off staying in the new privately owned pensions, or private rooms in general, than in the old communist-era hotels, even those that have been nominally "modernized". The further east you go, the more difficult it becomes to find accommodation, and service can be quite poor.

■ Hotels, pensions and private rooms

The modernization of Slovakia's hotels is proving a lengthy process, resulting in the temporary closure of large numbers while looking for new owners or undergoing renovation. In some areas, though, you'll still come across the old state-owned behemoths, whose standards are stuck in the communist era. Prices vary enormously – they're at their highest in Bratislava and the High Tatras – but are generally lower than in the Czech Republic, even though many places still charge visitors from abroad roughly twice as much as Slovaks. Most hotels now operate some kind of star system, though it gives only a very vague indication of what to expect.

In many areas, the gap in the market has been filled by newly established **pensions** (often written as *penzión*), which are often excellent value,

USEFUL HIKING TERMS

cesta	path
chata	mountain refuge
dolina	valley
hranica	border
jaskyňa	cave
lanovka	chairlift/cable car
les	forest
lyžiarsky vlek	ski lift
prameň	spring
rozhľadňa/prehliadka	viewpoint
skala	rock
vodopád	waterfall

ACCOMMODATION PRICE CODES

All accommodation in this guide is graded according to the price bands listed below. Prices are for the cheapest **double room** available during high season, which usually means without private bath or shower in the less expensive places. For a **single room**, expect to pay around two-thirds the price of a double.

① Under 500Sk   ④ 1000–1250Sk   ⑦ 1750–2000Sk
② 500–750Sk   ⑤ 1250–1500Sk   ⑧ 2000–2500Sk
③ 750–1000Sk   ⑥ 1500–1750Sk   ⑨ 2500Sk and upwards

---

though not necessarily any less expensive than hotels. **Private rooms** are also available along many of the main roads and in the more tourist-frequented regions. You can be sure that these will be pristine, though how much privacy you'll have and to what extent you'll have to share facilities with the family will vary. Outside the bigger cities and more popular mountain areas, accommodation can be hard to come by and standards low, particularly in the eastern part of the country, so flexibility is a valuable asset.

■ Hostels, student rooms and campsites

There are no HI-affiliated **youth hostels** in Slovakia, such as you would find in Western Europe, though private hostels exist in some cities and in areas of popular outdoor activity. Those hostels that do exist range from places run much like hotels to dormitories primarily used by domestic tour groups or local workers but which may have a spare bed if you're lucky. With relatively few university towns, **student rooms** let out cheap to travellers in July and August are limited to Bratislava.

There are a large number of **campsites** (usually known as *autokemping*) scattered throughout Slovakia, varying enormously in standards and facilities. Many have **bungalows** (*chaty*), which are very cheap to rent but are often block-booked by groups. Most sites are open from April or May until September or October, with a very few open all year round. The more basic campsites (*táborisko*) are marked on the 1:100,000 hiking maps; open only in the height of summer, they provide just ad hoc toilets and a little running water. Prices are inflated for foreigners, but are still reasonable; two people plus car and tent weigh in at around £5/$8, often less.

There are a fair number of **mountain huts** (*chaty*) on the hillsides of the High Tatras; though

few are accessible by road, most are just a few kilometres' walk from civilization. Some cost as much as £10/$16 per person, while the more isolated and basic ones can cost as little as £4/$6 per person. These can really only be booked through local agencies or tourist offices within the republic, though you're unlikely to be turned away if you turn up before 6pm at the more isolated ones.

Communications

■ Post

Post offices (*pošta*) are usually open between 8am and 5pm Monday to Friday, and till noon on Saturdays. Letters or postcards take around five working days to reach the UK, and a week to ten days to North America. **Stamps** (*známky*) are available from newsagents and kiosks as well as post offices, though often only for domestic mail.

Poste restante (pronounced as five syllables in Slovak) is available in major towns. The sender should write Pošta 1 (the main office), followed by the name of the town, and their name and address on the back. It might be safer to have mail sent to your embassy in Bratislava, though you should inform them of this beforehand.

SOME FOREIGN COUNTRIES IN SLOVAK

Australia	*Austrália*
Austria	*Rakúsko*
Canada	*Kanada*
Czech Republic	*Česká republika*
Germany	*Nemecko*
Great Britain	*Veľká Británia*
Hungary	*Maďarsko*
Ireland	*Írsko*
Netherlands	*Nizozemí*
New Zealand	*Nový Zéland*
Poland	*Poľsko*
Ukraine	*Ukrajina*
USA	*Spojené štáty americké*

■ Phones

Slovak public **phones** (*telefón*) themselves are pretty reliable, it's the system that needs overhauling. There are usually instructions in English, but despite the graphic description you may still encounter problems. Theoretically, you simply pick up the receiver, drop in the minimum fee demanded, then dial the number. When you run out of money, you'll hear a recorded message urging you in Slovak to insert more. Fortunately, most coin-operated phones are now being phased out, replaced by more reliable **card phones**, which makes international calls much easier. Phone cards (*telefonní karty*), currently available in 75 and 150 units (and costing 150Sk and 300Sk respectively), can be bought at post offices and most tobacconists and kiosks. Insert the card into the telephone, and the number of units remaining on the card appears on the phone's display.

The **dialling tone** is a short followed by a long pulse; the **ringing tone** is long and regular;

DIALLING CODES

To Slovakia
From Britain ☎00 42 1
From USA and Canada ☎011 42 1
From Australia and New Zealand ☎0011 42 1

From Slovakia
UK ☎0044
Eire ☎00353
Australia ☎0061
New Zealand ☎0064
USA and Canada ☎001

engaged is short and rapid, but shouldn't be confused with the very rapid tone which indicates the line is being connected; the standard Slovak response is *prosím*; and the word for extension is *linka*. If you have any problems, dial ☎0149 and ask for an English-speaking operator.

You may still find it simpler to make **international calls** from one of the telephone exchanges found in the major towns. Write down the town and telephone number, leave a deposit of around 200Sk, then wait for your name to be called out; bear in mind that international calls are extremely expensive at any time. Calls can be made from most hotels, but the surcharge is usually quite heavy. An easier option is a **collect call**, which will cost the recipient less than it would cost you. Dial ☎0149 and ask for an English speaker. Calling cards issued by your home long-distance carrier often have the best rates, but be sure you know the direct number to call in order to place the call from Slovakia.

■ Media

Besides the European edition of *The Guardian*, most of the broadsheet **British papers** on sale in Bratislava are a day old. **American newspapers** are pretty much restricted to *USA Today* and the *International Herald Tribune*. In addition, there's the weekly *Slovak Spectator*, a thin, broadsheet newspaper that concentrates on current affairs and finance, but carries a useful listings section on Bratislava. Unfortunately, it is hard to find anywhere but in Bratislava. Outside the capital, English-speaking newspapers are rare; your best bet are the more expensive hotels. If all you want are the latest soccer results, then the Slovak sports daily *Šport* will do the job.

The **Slovak press** came in for constant criticism when Mečiar and his allies were in power. Shortly after independence in 1993, Mečiar sacked the editor of the government-backed daily, *Smena*, for publishing critical articles. Eighty percent of the staff then left in protest and formed *Sme*, a paper whose readership quickly overtook that of *Smena*. As a further humiliation, *Sme* has now taken over *Smena*. It has a one-page English-language section covering the main news on Tuesdays and Thursdays.

The only good thing to be said about Czechoslovak state **television** under the Communists was that after federalization in 1969 it consistently broadcast in Czech and Slovak. This commitment to bilingual broadcasting was strictly adhered to, so that in the course of an ice hockey match, the first half would be commentated in Czech and the second in Slovak. For twenty years, this helped nurture a generation for whom the differences between the two nations, at least linguistically, were irrelevant. Now the Slovaks and Czechs have gone their different ways, and both have their own commercial channels. The Slovak Republic's Nova now attracts by far the largest slice of the country's audience, pushing the two state-run channels, STV1 and STV2, into second and third place, respectively.

As far as **radio** goes, most cafés and bars tune in to one of the new FM pop/Muzak stations. You can pick up the **BBC World Service** fairly easily now from the two big cities, around the 100MHz mark, and on shortwave; most FM stations give out pretty weak signals, so don't expect much once you leave the suburbs.

Eating and drinking

Seventy-five years of close contact with the Czechs and forty years of Communist rule have left Slovak cuisine with many of the same predilections as the Czechs. The secret ingredient, however, is the Hungarian influence, which left a legacy of marginally spicier cooking.

■ Food

The similarities between Slovak and Czech cuisine mean that much of the information contained in the section on Czech food starting on p.36 is relevant here. The few differences are outlined below.

There are several types of eating establishments: the *reštaurácia* is the most common and varies in formality; a *vináreň* (wine cellar), which often stays open later, will also guarantee a full meal; a *pivnica* or *piváreň* (pub) is based on the Czech version but less commonplace, usually serving filling food at a good price; and, at the budget end of the scale, you can stoke up with the local workers at very cheap self-service *bufet*.

■ Full meals

Most menus start with **soup** (*polievky*), followed by a main course of **meat** (*mäso*) – usually pork or beef – with potatoes, pickled cabbage and/or **dumplings** (*knedle*). *Guláš* is popular, usually *Szegedinský* (pork with sauerkraut) but sometimes *special* (with better meat and a creamier sauce). The Slovak national dish, *bryndzové halušky*, is basically a heavy version of macaroni cheese, but made with sheep's cheese and flaked potato dumplings, and usually topped with specks of fried pork fat (veggies beware).

■ Drinking

The Slovaks make some pretty decent **wine**, though exports are low compared to neighbouring Hungary. The two main wine regions are along the hot southern edge of the republic; the vineyards of the Small Carpathians stretch right down to the suburbs of Bratislava, while those of the

---

VEGETARIANS

Though the Slovaks are a nation of carnivores, the outlook is not all bleak for vegetarians. Many menus have a section called *bezmäsité jedlá*; beware, however, that though this translates literally as "without meat", this can simply mean that meat is included to a lesser degree than usual. The most popular non-meat dish is *vyprážený syr*, a slab of melted cheese fried in breadcrumbs served with potatoes and a large dose of tartare sauce, though watch out – if it's *plnený* or *se šunkou*, then it will certainly include ham. The phrases to remember are *som vegeterián/vegeteriánka*, and for emphasis add *nejem ani mäso ani rybu* (I don't eat meat or fish), at which point your server may shake his or her head in disbelief.

A FOOD AND DRINK GLOSSARY

BASICS

raňajky	breakfast	máslo	butter	cukor	sugar
obed	lunch	rohlík	finger roll	soľ	salt
večera	supper/dinner	chlebíček	open sandwich	čierne korenie	pepper
nôž	knife	med	honey	ocot	vinegar
vidlička	fork	mlieko	milk	horčica	mustard
lyžica	spoon	vajcia	eggs	tartarská omáčka	tartare sauce
tanier	plate	pečivo	pastry	chren	horseradish
šálka	cup	mäso	meat	ryža	rice
pohár	glass	ryba	fish	knedle	dumplings
predkrmy	starters	zeleniny	vegetables	jidla na objednávku	
polievka	soup	rezance	noodles/pasta		main dishes
múčnik	dessert	šalát	salad		to order
chlieb	bread	ovocie	fruit	jedálny lístok	menu

SOUPS

boršč	beetroot soup	kuracia	thin chicken soup
fazuľová	bean soup	paradajková	tomato soup
hovädzia	beef soup	šošovicová	lentil soup
hrachová	pea soup	zeleninová	vegetable soup
kapustnica	sauerkraut and meat soup	zemiaková	potato soup

FISH

losos	salmon	pstruh	trout	treska	cod
kapor	carp	sardinka	sardine	zavináč	herring/rollmop
makrela	mackerel	šťuka	pike		

MEAT DISHES

baranina	mutton	hydina	poultry	pečeň	liver
bravčové	pork	jazyk	tongue	saláma	salami
bravčový rezeň		klobásy	sausages	sekaná	meat loaf
	breaded pork cutlet/schnitzel	kotleta	cutlet	slanina	bacon
		kurča	chicken	sviečková	sirloin
čevabčiče	spicy meatballs	kačica	duck	šunka	ham
dršky	tripe	stehno	thigh	teľacie	veal
hovädzie	beef	obličky	kidneys	rebierko	ribs

VEGETABLES

cibuľa	onion	kapusta	cabbage	rajčina	tomato
cesnak	garlic	karfiol	cauliflower	reďkovka	radish
cukrová repa	beetroot	kyslá okurka	pickled gherkin	žampiony	mushrooms
fazuľa	beans	kyslá kapusta	sauerkraut	šošovica	lentils
hranolky	chips, French fries	liečo	ratatouille (canned)	špargľa	asparagus
				špenát	spinach
hrášky	peas	mrkva	carrots	uhorka	cucumber
huby	mushrooms	paradajka	tomato	zemiaky	potatoes

continues overleaf . . .

A FOOD AND DRINK GLOSSARY (contd.)

FRUIT AND CHEESE

banán	banana	*hruška*	pear	*orechy*	walnuts
borievky	blueberries	*jablko*	apple	*oriezky*	peanuts
broskyňa	peach	*kompot*	stewed fruit	*pomoranč*	orange
bryndza	goat's cheese in brine	*jahody*	strawberries	*slivky*	plums
čerešňa	cherry	*maliny*	raspberries	*tvaroh*	fresh curd cheese
černica	blackberries	*mandle*	almonds	*údený syr*	smoked cheese
citrón	lemon	*marhuľa*	apricot	*urda*	soft, fresh whey
hrozienky	raisins	*niva*	semi-soft crumbly		cheese
hrozny	grapes		blue cheese		

COMMON TERMS

čerstvý	fresh	*na ražni*	grilled	*surový*	raw
domáci	home-made	*nadívaný*	stuffed	*teplý*	hot
dušený	stew/casserole	*nakladaný*	pickled	*údený*	smoked
grilovaný	roast on the spit	*(za)pečený*	baked/roast	*varený*	boiled
kôpar	dill	*plnený*	stuffed	*vyprážený*	fried in breadcrumbs
kyslý	sour	*sladký*	sweet	*znojmský*	served with gherkins
miešaný	mixed	*slaný*	salted		
na rasci	with caraway seeds	*studený*	cold		

DRINKS

biele víno	white wine	*koňak*	brandy	*suché víno*	dry wine
čaj	tea	*fľaša*	bottle	*víno*	wine
červené víno	red wine	*ľad*	ice	*nazdravie*	cheers!
destiláty	spirits	*mlieko*	milk		
káva	coffee	*pivo*	beer		

Slovak Tokaj, bordering onto the main Hungarian wine-producing region of the same name, produce a good dry white known as *Furmint*.

The most famous of the **spirits** available in Slovakia is the plum brandy *slivovice*, which originated in the western border hills but is now available just about everywhere. You'll probably come across *borovička* at some point, a popular firewater from the Slovak Spiš region, made from juniper berries; *myslivec* is another rough brandy with an ardent following.

Unlike the Czechs, the Slovaks have no great tradition of **beer** drinking, but union with the Czech Lands in 1918 gradually changed things, and since 1945, their beer consumption has increased tenfold. The Slovaks do, of course, brew their own. One of the most famous is the excellent *Zlatý bažant* (Golden Pheasant) from Hurbanovo, in the Danube basin. The central Slovak town of Martin also produces a distinctive porter, a dark, heady brew which is notoriously difficult to get hold of – try looking out for *Cassovar* instead. Other good Slovak beers include *Šariš* and *Smädný Mních*. Czech beers are also widely available, with the Bohemian *Pilsner Urquell*, *Gambrinus* and *Budvar* leading the field.

Castles, churches and museums

The Slovak countryside is dotted with castles, many of them reduced to rubble, others converted for modern use, into old people's homes, trade-union holiday retreats and even training centres for the secret police. Some have been returned to their former owners, and plenty more have been restored and opened to the public. The country's churches and monasteries have generally been better looked after than those in the Czech Republic, though many lock their doors outside worshipping hours. Museums and galleries thrived under the Communists, and those that have survived the subsequent ideological purging have little money to bring themselves up to date.

■ Castles and guided tours

Basic **opening hours** for castles and other historical buildings are usually May to September Tuesday to Sunday 9am to noon, then 1pm to 5pm; in April and October, opening times are usually restricted to weekends and holidays; the rest of the year the buildings are often closed. Access to the interior is usually only possible with a guided tour. These are usually in Slovak, occasionally in German or Hungarian, but it's always worth asking for an *anglický text*. Entrance tickets cost very little – rarely more than 50Sk – hence no prices are quoted in the text.

■ Churches and monasteries

A few of the most popular **churches** operate in much the same way as museums, occasionally even charging an entrance fee. Other churches are usually closed except for services, for which times are often posted outside the main doors, but it is worth asking around for the local *kňaz* (priest) or *kaplan* (caretaker), who will usually be only too happy to oblige with the key (*kľúč*).

In the north and east of the country, there are a small number of Orthodox (*Pravoslavný*) believers and a much larger contingent who belong to the **Greek-Catholic Church** (*Grécko-katolický*), an obscure branch of Roman Catholicism whose small wooden churches, packed with icons and Byzantine paraphernalia, appear just like Orthodox churches to the uninitiated. You'll find a much more thorough account of the Greek-Catholics and their churches in the section on Carpatho-Ruthenia in Chapter Ten. Suffice to say that the buildings are fascinating, especially their dark and poky interiors, but they are kept firmly locked with little indication of what time the next service will be held.

Slovakia once boasted a considerable Jewish population, but most fell victim to the Nazi Holocaust, helped on their way by certain members of the Slovak wartime government. Today, an estimated 2000 still live in the republic, but Bratislava is one of the few places where regular worship still takes place. Few of the country's dis-used **synagogues** have been saved from collapse, though there are some notable exceptions, such as those at Trenčín and Prešov.

■ Museums and galleries

Outside of Bratislava, Slovak **museums** have changed little since the days of communism, mostly, it has to be said, due to lack of funding. Nevertheless, you do still come across the odd gem, and most local museums boast decent collections of folk art. It's worth asking for an English commentary or *anglický text*, or else you'll normally have to make do with Slovak-only labelling. The **art galleries** of Bratislava and Košice will disappoint those hoping to find masterpieces by either Slovak or non-Slovak painters. In fact, some of the country's best indigenous art – Rusyn icons and the work of Pavol of Levoča – can only be found in the small-town galleries and churches of East Slovakia.

Opening hours for museums and galleries tend to be from 8am or 9am to 4pm or 5pm, usually without a break at lunch. Many stay open all year round or switch from a Tuesday–Sunday summer routine to Monday–Friday during the winter. Full opening hours are detailed in the guide, but ticket prices are not, since they are rarely more than 40Sk.

Public holidays, festivals and entertainment

Aside from religious celebrations and pilgrimages, the cultural calendar is dominated by arts- and music-based festivals unique to individual towns. In addition, summer is the season for village folkloric events, of which the most famous is the Východná folk festival, which takes place near

PUBLIC HOLIDAYS

January 1 (Independence Day)
January 6 (Epiphany)
Good Friday
Easter Monday
May 1
May 8 (VE Day)
July 5 (Introduction of Christianity by saints Cyril and Methodius)
August 29 (Slovak National Uprising 1944)
September 1 (Constitution Day)
September 15 (Day of the Virgin Mary)
November 1 (All Saints' Day)
December 24
December 25
December 26

Poprad. As for the arts and sport, both are only just beginning to learn to live without massive state subsidies.

■ Festivals and other annual events

Slovakia may not have a bevy of international composers to its name, but it does boast an even stronger folk tradition than the Czech Republic. The Východná Folk Festival, in late June/early July, is the biggest and most prestigious of the many annual **folk festivals**, with groups from all over Europe performing. Others worth looking out for are the one in Detva in early July, a Rusyn-based one in Svidník in mid- to late-June, and a festival with a Hungarian flavour in Gombasek every August.

The 1980s witnessed a revival of **pilgrimages** (*púť*), usually centred around the cult of the Virgin Mary. The biggest gathering is on the first weekend in July at Levoča in the Spiš region of East Slovakia, when up to 250,000 people descend on the small pilgrimage church above the town. Lesser celebrations go on in the region for the following two months.

For the Orthodox rites churches, which predominate in the east of the country, **Easter** (*Veľká noc*) is much more important than Christmas (*Vánoce*), and the often elaborate and lengthy processions and services can be well worth catching.

■ The arts

As in the Czech Republic, the **theatre** (*divadlo*) industry in Slovakia played an important part in the events of 1989, leading the way in the strikes that eventually toppled the Communist regime. In 1997, the country's theatre community found itself once more thrown into the political arena, staging what was ultimately an unsuccessful strike against the government, after they replaced several key figures in the industry with people who supported the governing HZDS party. The problem is that theatres throughout the country are still heavily subsidized by the authorities, and this allows the authorities a certain amount of leverage over appointments. Now that Vladimír Mečiar is (at least temporarily) out of the political scene, replaced by a far more Western-leaning and competent prime minister and president, some degree of independence should be restored.

For those with no knowledge of Slovak, it's best to stick to productions with less of a linguistic problem, such as opera or ballet. That said, ticket prices are cheap, and the venue and the event itself are often interesting enough to sustain you. The other genre for which language is not always a barrier is **puppetry** or *bábkové divadlo* as it's known in Slovak. Unfortunately, few traditional marionette shows are put on nowadays, with live actors taking centre stage in more and more productions, making the shows less accessible if you don't speak the language.

The **cinema** (*kino*) is cheap and generally rudimentary in Slovakia. Slovak actors have been working overtime in the dubbing studios to try and fulfil a government directive to show films with Slovak dubbing, rather than Czech, as was generally the case before independence. Most mainstream Hollywood films tend to be shown dubbed, with only the more obscure art-house films shown in their original language with subtitles (*titulky*). Beware, too, that film titles are usually translated into Slovak, so you'll need a dictionary to identify films like *Pekelná Hora* as *Dante's Peak*.

■ Sport

If there's one thing that makes Slovak sports fans really angry, it's the way that everyone assumes all the best players in the old Czechoslovak teams were Czech. In fact, many of Czechoslovakia's finest sporting moments were Slovak-inspired, most notably the European Championship-winning soccer team of 1976. Even today, the Swiss tennis star Martina Hingis is frequently referred to in the Western press as Czech, when in fact her roots are Slovak. As a result, nothing makes

Slovak sports fans happier than when they beat their former compatriots, as they have done since the split, in the country's two top sports, soccer and ice hockey. Getting tickets to watch either sport is easy (and cheap) enough on the day as matches rarely sell out. Taking part is much more difficult as there are still relatively few facilities for the general public – your best bet is likely to be to go to the plusher hotels, whose sports facilities are often open to non-guests.

The 1998 World Cup **soccer** qualifiers pitched the Slovaks against the Czechs, and, contrary to everyone's expectations, the latter came off worse. Still, the national team are clearly a long way off qualifying for either of the two major international soccer finals. Slovak club football also looks a long way off repeating Slovan Bratislava's famous victory over Barcelona in 1969 to lift the European Cup Winners' Cup (the only European title won by either a Czech or a Slovak club). Slovan remain one of the country's leading clubs, having won the first three Slovak league titles on the trot. Recently, however, they have lost ground to the likes of FC Košice and Spartak Trnava. The season runs from August to late November and from March to late June, with most matches held on Saturday afternoons.

As with football, so with **ice hockey**, the country's second most popular sport, the assumption has always been that it was Czech players who led the old Czechoslovak team to glory. Although in this case there was an element of truth in the prejudice, the Slovaks have surprised everyone with their combative spirit in recent years. Games, which can take anything up to three hours, are held in the local *zimný štadión* (winter stadium) on Sunday afternoons. The season starts at the end of September and culminates in the annual World Championships, when the fortunes of the national side are subject to close scrutiny, especially if pitched against the Czechs.

CHAPTER EIGHT

BRATISLAVA AND WEST SLOVAKIA

n many ways, the western third of Slovakia is the least typically Slovak part of the country. For a start, it's flat, fertile and fairly treeless, its only mountain range, the Small Carpathians, tame in comparison with the central mountains further east. Even the Slovak capital **Bratislava** was for centuries an Austro-Hungarian city, in which the Slovaks, like the Romanies and Jews, were a distinct minority, and far removed from the true heart of the country in the central mountain regions. The great flat plain of the **Danube**, to the east of Bratislava, is inhabited largely by Hungarian-speakers, well over half a million at the last count. The two major cities on the plain – **Trnava** and **Nitra** – although now mostly Slovak, contain some of the most important religious institutions of the old Hungarian Kingdom; and in the Váh Valley, the spa town of **Piešťany** was, in its heyday, one of the favourite watering holes of the Hungarian nobility. Further up the Váh, however, begins the Slovak mountain region and the real heartland of Slovakia, heralded by the stronghold of **Trenčín**.

Bratislava

Caught between the westernmost tip of the Carpathians and the flat plain of the Danube, with both Austria and Hungary tantalizingly close, **BRATISLAVA** has two distinct sides to it. On the one hand, there's the old town or staré mesto, a manageable, attractive, mostly pedestrianized quarter lined with Baroque palaces; on the other hand, there's the rest of the city or nové mesto, a mixture of interwar tenements and postwar high-rises typical of the former Eastern bloc. More buildings have been destroyed here since the war than were bombed out during it, not least the Jewish quarter, bulldozed to make way for the colossal new suspension bridge, most SNP, symbol of the city's upwardly mobile thrust under the Communists.

For centuries, Bratislava was known as *Pressburg* to the German-speaking world, which supplied around half its inhabitants until the 1945 expulsions, and as *Pozsony* to the Hungarians, who were forced to use it as their capital for several centuries, crowning their kings and queens in the cathedral and holding their Diet here until the Turks were finally beaten back from the Hungarian plain. At the turn of the century, the city had barely 60,000 inhabitants, most of whom were German, Hungarian and/or Jewish, with a smattering of Romanies and Slovaks. The balance shifted with the establishment of Czechoslovakia in 1918, which gave a leg-up to the Slovaks, who took over the cul-

The Bratislava area telephone code is ☎07.

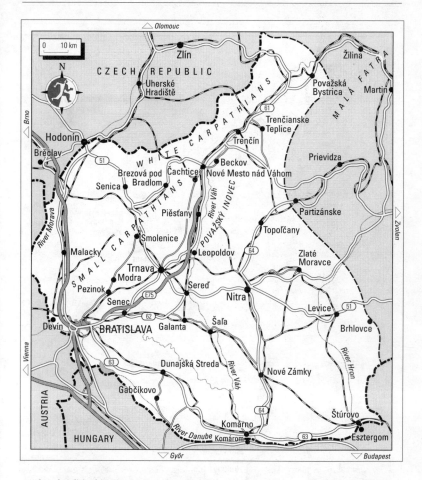

tural and political institutions and renamed the place Bratislava after Bratislav, the last Slav leader of the Great Moravian Empire.

Over the last eighty years, the population has increased more than sevenfold to 450,000, making it by far the country's largest city. However, the historical centre is surprisingly small, with most of the population living in the city's mushrooming high-rise estates. Whatever Bratislava's previous identity, it's now Slovak through and through, its youthful centre packed out with students and the new Westernized generation of Slovakia's burgeoning population. The multicultural atmosphere of the prewar days is only vaguely echoed in the city's smattering of Magyars, Romanies and day-tripping Austrians, but there's still a ring of truth to Metternich's much-quoted aphorism, "East of Vienna, the Orient begins".

You'll need a couple of days at least to soak the city in; and with none of the sightseeing crowds of Prague, the relaxed feel of the old town, and some of the best weather in the country, you'll probably want to stay longer.

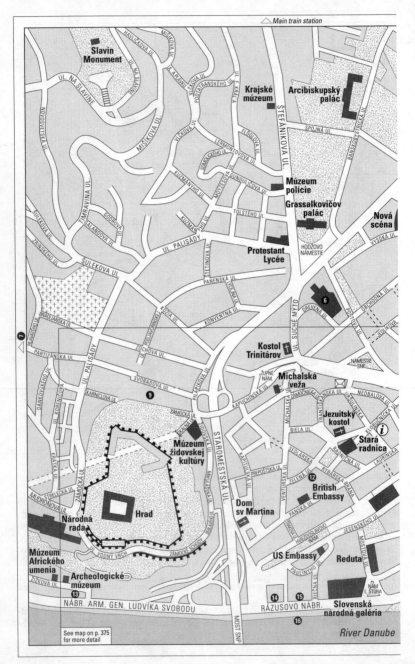

Main train station

Slavín
Monument

Krajské
múzeum

Arcibiskupský
palác

Múzeum
polície

Grassalkovičov
palác

Nová
scéna

Protestant
Lycée

Kostol
Trinitárov

Michalská
veža

Jezuitský
kostol

Stará
radnica

Múzeum
židovskej
kultúry

British
Embassy

Dom
sv Martina

Hrad

Národná
rada

US Embassy

Reduta

Múzeum
Afrického
umenia

Archeologické
múzeum

Slovenská
národná galéria

NÁBR. ARM. GEN. LUDVÍKA SVOBODU

RÁZUSOVO NÁBR.

River Danube

See map on p. 375
for more detail

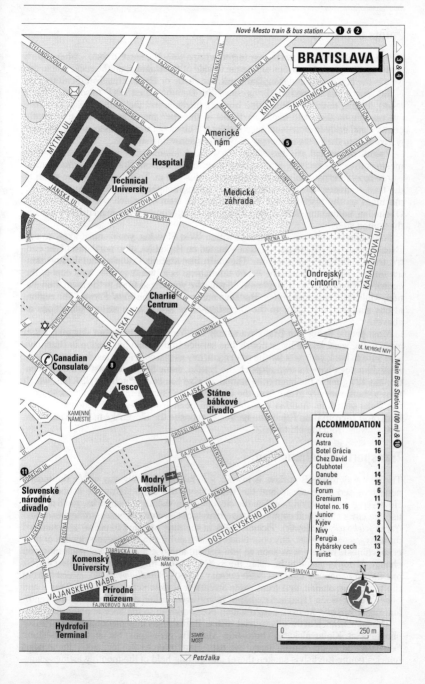

BRATISLAVA

❸ & ❹

STEFANOVICOVA UL.

FAZUĽOVA UL.

RADLINSKÉHO UL.

BLUMENTALSKÁ UL.

SKOLSKÁ UL.

MÝTNA UL.

STAROHORSKÁ UL.

KRÍŽNA UL.

ZÁHRADNÍCKA UL.

JUSTIČNÁ UL.

Americké nám

❺

CHORVÁTSKA UL.

SASINKOVA UL.

MOSKOVSKÁ UL.

Hospital

Technical University

JÁNSKA UL.

BADINSKÉHO UL.

Medická záhrada

MICKIEWICZOVA UL.

UL. 29 AUGUSTA

POČNÁ UL.

Ondrejský cintorín

KARADŽIČOVA UL.

MARIÁNSKA UL.

LAZARETSKÁ UL.

HEYDUKOVA UL.

HOLLÉHO UL.

Charlie Centrum

ČUKROVA UL.

CINTORÍNSKA UL.

UL. 29 AUGUSTA

SPITÁLSKA UL.

UL. MLYNSKÉ NIVY

✡

RAJSKÁ UL.

✆ **Canadian Consulate**

❽

KOLÁRSKA UL.

Tesco

DUNAJSKÁ UL.

Státne bábkové divadlo

LAZARETSKÁ UL.

KAMENNÉ NÁMESTIE

GRÖSSLINGOVA UL.

KLEMENSOVA UL.

GAJOVA UL.

BEZRUČOVA UL.

❶❶

STÚROVA UL.

Modrý kostolík ✚

ŠTÚROVA UL.

Slovenské národné divadlo

RÁZUSOVO NÁBR.

MEDENÁ UL.

DOBROVIČOVA UL.

TOVÁRENSKÁ UL.

DOSTOJEVSKÉHO RAD

PAČKÉHO UL.

KÚPEĽNÁ UL.

TOBRUCKÁ UL.

ŠAFÁRIKOVO NÁM.

Komenský University

PRIBINOVA UL.

Prírodné múzeum

VAJANSKÉHO NÁBR.

FAJNOROVO NÁBR.

Hydrofoil Terminal

STARÝ MOST

N

0 — 250 m

▽ Petržalka

Main Bus Station (100 m) & ❿

ACCOMMODATION

Arcus	5
Astra	10
Botel Grácia	16
Chez David	9
Clubhotel	1
Danube	14
Devín	15
Forum	6
Gremium	11
Hotel no. 16	7
Junior	3
Kyjev	8
Nivy	4
Perugia	12
Rybársky cech	13
Turist	2

Points of arrival

The geography of Bratislava is easy to get to grips with: the **staré mesto** – where you'll spend most of your time – lies on the north side of the Danube; on the rocky hill to the west is the city's most enduring landmark, the castle or **Hrad**. Equally difficult to miss is the spectacular suspension bridge over the Danube, **most SNP** (also called Nový most), leading to the vast **Petržalka** housing development that continues as far as the eye can see on the south bank. Northeast of the staré mesto are the late-nineteenth-century and early-twentieth-century residential blocks of **nové mesto**, which gradually give way to the postwar housing of the city's sprawling suburbs.

Points of arrival are less straightforward. A kilometre or so north of the staré mesto is the city's recently modernized **main train station**, Bratislava-hlavná stanica, where most international and long-distance trains pull in. To get into town, go down to the tram terminus below the station and – having bought your ticket from one of the machines on the platform (see below) – hop on tram #1, which will deposit you on Obchodná, behind the *Hotel Fórum*. Buses and trolleybuses leave from directly outside the station steps.

For trains to and from destinations within West Slovakia, you're most likely to use **Bratislava-Nové Mesto** train station, situated on Bajkalská, 4km northeast of the centre; tram #6 will take you into town. The **main bus station**, Bratislava autobusová stanica (often written as Bratislava, AS on timetables) is a twenty-minute walk east of the centre on Mlynské nivy; trolleybus #208 will take you across town to the main train station, while #217 will drop you on Hodžovo námestie near the *Hotel Fórum*. The regional bus station is next door to the Bratislava-Nové Mesto train station (directions as above).

Most people flying into Bratislava simply use Vienna's **Schwechat Airport**, 45km away to the west, linked by an hourly bus service to the main bus station in Bratislava – be sure to book your seat for the return journey as places sell out fast for some buses. Bratislava does have its own **airport**, the Ivánka, some 8km northeast of the city centre; bus #24 goes to the main train station, or else you could catch the ČSA bus, which runs a shuttle service to and from the ČSA office on Štúrova 13, timed to coincide with the flight schedule. Another possible arrival point from Vienna or Budapest is the **hydrofoil terminal** on Fajnorovo nábrežie, opposite the Slovenské národné múzeum, a short walk from the old town.

Transport and information

The best way to see Bratislava is to walk – in fact it's the only way to see the mostly pedestrianized staré mesto and the Hrad where the city's sights are concentrated. However, if you're staying outside the city centre or visiting the suburbs, you'll need to use the city's cheap and comprehensive **transport system** of buses, trolleybuses and trams (*električky* in Slovak). Tickets (10Sk at the time of going to press) are standard for all types of transport: buy your ticket beforehand (from newsagents, kiosks or ticket machines), validate it as soon as you get on, and use a fresh ticket each time you change. If you're going to be using the system a lot, it might be worth buying a 45Sk one-day (*24 hodinový lístok*) or 80Sk two-day ticket (*48 hodinový lístok*), available from the main train station, and from some streetside yellow ticket machines. Trams and buses stop between 11pm and midnight (some even earlier, especially at the weekend), and **night buses** take over, congregating every quarter to the hour at námestie SNP.

The main branch of the city **tourist office**, Bratislavská informačná služba or BIS for short, is at Klobučnícka 2 (June–Aug Mon–Fri 8am–7pm, Sat & Sun 8am–1pm; Sept–May Mon–Fri 8am–4.30pm, Sat 8am–1pm; ☎54 43 37 15), good for general queries (some English is spoken there) and getting hold of the monthly listings magazine, *Kam v Bratislave* (in Slovak but easily decipherable). They can also help with accommodation (see below) and sell you a detailed *orientačná mapa*; after working hours there is a touch-screen computer outside that can provide much of the same information. A smaller branch for information only is located in the main train station. One other excellent source of printed information is the *Slovak Spectator* travel guide, available from newsstands in the city centre and some tourist offices around the country. Although the coverage of the country focuses primarily on the main spots, the listings and off-beat advice are useful.

Accommodation

Bratislava has none of the logistical problems that plague Prague, but its status as capital, its proximity to Vienna, and the fact that it receives only a trickle of individual tourists, mean that **accommodation** is more expensive here than anywhere else in the country – inexpensive, or even medium-range hotels and pensions are few and far between, and for an old-town location, more often than not you'll pay through the nose. The cheaper hotels tend to lurk to the east and northeast of the centre, in amongst the high-rise panelák apartment blocks. While these are not the most appealing neighbourhoods, they are within easy striking distance of the centre by bus or tram. In all cases, try to reserve at least a day in advance to be sure of a room. There are relatively few accommodation agencies, but SATUR, Jesenského 3 (Mon–Fri 9am–6pm, Sat 9am–noon), and BIS, on Klobučnícka (see opposite), can book centrally located **private rooms** for around 300Sk and upwards per person (for a small fee), and the latter should have information on hostels too; at present all the city's hostels are open July and August only.

Hotels and pensions

Arcus, Moskovská 5 (☎55 57 25 22). Small pension within walking distance of the old town, just east of Americké námestie, and a rarity in Bratislava: clean, quiet, comfortable and affordable. Take any tram heading up Špitalská from Kamenné námestie. ⑤.

Astra, Prievozská 14a (☎53 41 58 16). One of the city's cheaper options, just over 2km east of the centre, with newly refurbished rooms; take trolleybus #218 from the main train station or walk from the main bus station. ④.

Botel Grácia, Rázusovo nábrežie (☎54 43 21 32). Floating hotel moored on the main embankment. Overpriced and not everyone's cup of tea, especially in summer when the mosquitoes arrive. ⑧.

Chez David, Zámocká 13 (☎54 41 38 24). Plush new kosher pension with excellent kosher restaurant attached, superbly located in the old Jewish quarter behind the castle. Less expensive and better value than many other places in this price range, but ask first if construction on a new building opposite has been completed. ⑨.

Clubhotel, Odbojárov 3 (☎44 25 63 69). Drab but clean and with a decent restaurant, this is one of the city's few really inexpensive hotels. Located 3km northeast of the centre, but easily reached by tram #2 from the main train station and #4 or #6 from Kamenné námestie. ③.

ACCOMMODATION PRICE CODES

All accommodation in this guide is graded according to the price bands listed below. Prices are for the cheapest **double room** available during high season, which usually means without private bath or shower in the less expensive places. For a **single room**, expect to pay around two-thirds the price of a double.

① Under 500Sk	④ 1000–1250Sk	⑦ 1750–2000Sk
② 500–750Sk	⑤ 1250–1500Sk	⑧ 2000–2500Sk
③ 750–1000Sk	⑥ 1500–1750Sk	⑨ 2500Sk and upwards

Danube, Rybné námestie 1 (☎59 34 08 33). This deluxe Austrian-run hotel, built in blue and grey titanium, has views of the castle, most SNP and the river, and charges over 5000Sk a double for the privilege. ⑨.

Devín, Riečna 4 (☎54 43 08 51). On the riverfront, not quite as flash as the *Fórum* (see below) but $100 a double nevertheless. ⑨.

Fórum, Hodžovo námestie 2 (☎59 34 81 11). The businessperson's hotel, on the northern edge of the staré mesto, and at around 6000Sk a double beyond the means of most solo travellers. ⑨.

Gremium, Gorkého 11 (☎ & fax 54 43 06 53). This is really the only decent, inexpensive option in the whole of the old town. Centrally located, clean, with a great café on the ground floor. ④.

Hotel no. 16, Partizánska 16a (☎54 41 16 72). Wood-panelled folksy villa, ten minutes' walk from the staré mesto. It's not cheap, but it's better value and more appealing than the big hotels. ⑨.

Junior, Drieňová 14 (☎43 33 81 11). Recently renovated hotel on the edge of a small lake 3km north-east of the city centre, with a disco, "funky bar" and erotic massage available, and a slightly dodgy clientele. Take bus #74 from the main train station or #54 from Hodžovo námestie. ⑧.

Kyjev, Rajská 2 (☎55 32 20 41). Sky-rise communist-style 1960s hotel near Kamenné námestie, with great views from the top floor. ⑧.

Nivy, Líščie Nivy 3 (☎55 41 03 89). A splash of blue amid the grey nové mesto high-rises, this new hotel is good value and has a swimming pool and weight room; take tram #8 from the main train station, #9 from Obchodná or #12 from Kamenné námestie. ④.

Perugia, Zelená 5 (☎54 43 18 18). Probably the best of the old town's plush new hotels, located right in the centre of the old town in a former palace – you're looking at around 5000Sk a double, though. ⑨.

Rybársky cech, Žižkova 1 (☎54 41 83 34). Pleasant rooms in an old fisherman's lodge by the busy road just below the Hrad, and, given its proximity to the old town, a real bargain. ③.

Turist, Ondavská 5 (☎55 57 27 89). Bargain communist-era high-rise hotel for that authentic nové mesto experience; it's located 2.5km northeast of the centre, off Trnavská cesta, bus #22, #34, #106 or #110 from the main train station. ③.

Hostels and Camping

Belojanisa, Wilsonova 6 (☎52 49 77 35). Cheapest beds in town in this converted student dormitory; tram #7 or #11 from Kamenné námestie. Open July & Aug.

Bernolák, Bernolákova (☎52 49 77 24). The liveliest hostel in the city, a block away from the Belojanisa and only a short tram ride northeast of the centre, tram #7 or #11 from Kamenné námestie. Breakfast is included, and there's a bar and regular discos and gigs. Open July & Aug.

Nešporák, Svoradova 13 (☎54 41 53 86). Another bustling, youthful hostel, centrally located just two blocks north of the castle. Open July & Aug.

Zlaté Piesky. Two fairly grim campsites, 8km northeast of the city centre, near the swimming lake of the same name; tram #2 from the main train station or #4 or #6 from town. Bungalows (③) on offer all year round; tent camping May–Sept only.

The staré mesto

Bratislava's mostly pedestrianized **staré mesto** is, without a doubt, the nicest part of the city to explore. It's been massively overhauled over the last few years, and now looks really quite stunning. The best way to approach the old town is from Obchodná – literally Shop Street – where trams #1, #5, #6, #7 and #9 all offload their passengers to walk down to Hurbanovo námestie, a busy whizzing junction on the very northern-most edge of the staré mesto.

Hurbanovo námestie and Michalská veža

On **Hurbanovo námestie** you'll find the city's biggest shoe store and, unmoved by the vulgar clamour of it all, the hefty mass of Galli da Bibiena's **kostel Trinitárov**. Inside, the single-domed nave is filled with red and grey stuccoed marble, lending the place a faded musty ambience, while the exuberant trompe l'oeil frescoes create a magnificent

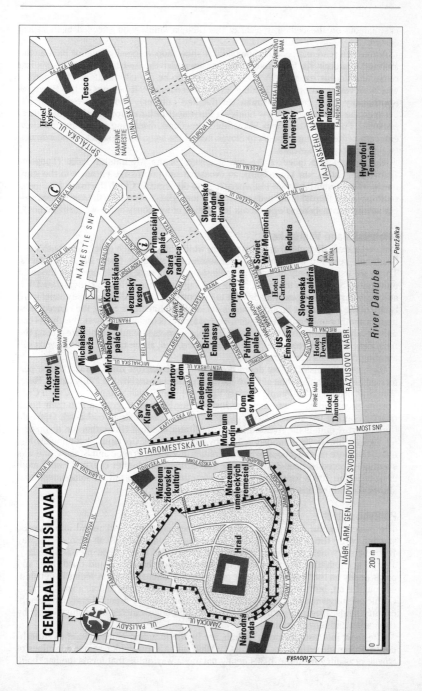

false cupola on the ceiling, typical of the Bibiena family who excelled in theatrical design.

Across the road and past the functionalist shoe shop, originally built for Baťa by the architect Vladimír Karfík, a footbridge passes under the first tower of the city's last remaining double gateway. Below, in what used to be the city moat, is a tiny garden which serves as an open-air reading area in the summer. It belongs to the **Baroque apothecary** or U červeného raka (At the Red Lobster), immediately on your left between the towers, which now houses a **Farmaceutická expozícia** (Pharmaceutical Museum; Tues–Fri 10am–5pm, Sat & Sun 11am–6pm), displaying everything from seventeenth-century drug grinders to Slovak herbal tea bags, with a series of reconstructed period interiors upstairs.

The second and taller of the two gateways is the **Michalská veža** (Tues–Fri 10am–5pm, Sat & Sun 11am–6pm), an evocative and impressive entrance to the staré mesto whose outer limits are elsewhere hard to distinguish. Climb the tower for a great rooftop view of the old town, pausing en route for a glance around to the vertical **expozícia zbraní a mestského opevnenia** (exhibition of weaponry and town fortifications).

Michalská and Ventúrska

Pedestrianized **Michalská** and **Ventúrska**, which run into each other, have both been beautifully restored and are lined with some of Bratislava's finest Baroque palaces. There are usually plenty of students milling about amongst the shoppers, as the main university library is on the right, in the building that once held the **Hungarian Diet**, and from here a passageway leads west to the **convent of sv Klara**, whose chapel spire is one of the city's most beautiful pieces of Gothic architecture. Sadly, the convent now houses another university library and, except for the occasional concert, the chapel can only be admired from its southern wall. The backstreets around sv Klara are among the most deserted (and evocative) in the staré mesto, and, at the time of writing, were still awaiting the forces of restoration.

Back on Michalská, a few doors down, is the **Mozartov dom** (Mozart once performed here as a child), one of three Baroque palaces owned by the Pálffy family. Here, Verejnosť proti násiliu (People Against Violence), the Slovak sister of the Czech Civic Forum, seconded what was then the Institute for Political Education into their headquarters during the student strike of 1989 (it's now the Austrian embassy). Opposite the Mozartov dom is the **Academia Istropolitana**, the first Hungarian (or, if you prefer, Slovak) university. Founded in 1465 by King Matthew Corvinus, it continually lost out to the more established nearby universities of Vienna, Prague and Kraków, and was eventually forced to close down in 1490. The buildings and inner courtyard were modernized in the 1960s for the faculty of performing arts, who put on some interesting shows and exhibitions in the chapel and crypt.

Pálffyho palác

The palaces of the Austro-Hungarian aristocracy continue right round into Panská, starting with the **Pálffyho palác** (Tues–Sun: June–Aug 10am–6pm; Sept–May 10am–5pm), which now serves as an art gallery for the Galéria mesta Bratislavy. Temporary exhibitions are held on the ground floor, basement and third floor, and occasionally on the first floor, too; the gallery's permanent collection seems to get shifted round a bit, but usually occupies the middle two floors. As well as a smattering of Gothic paintings and sculptures, there's a selection of pretty dreadful early-nineteenth-century landscapes and portraits, plus a few languid late-nineteenth-century works by Hungarian and Slovak artists.

The most interesting works, though, are by the founding generation of **twentieth-century Slovak artists**, such as Gustáv Mallý and Martin Benka, whose depictions of Slovak peasantry from the 1930s gently portray a way of life that forms the backbone of Slovak national identity, but has now more or less disappeared. Peasant life is also the subject of Ľudovít Fulla's paintings which deliberately recall folk tapestries. Other eye-catching canvases include Janko Alexy's wonderfully exaggerated rendering of Košice's hoary Gothic cathedral, and Miloš Bazovský's *Devil Reading a Book*.

Hlavné námestie and Františkánske námestie

Slightly further east are the tranquil twin main squares of the staré mesto: the shady **Františkánske námestie** and **Hlavné námestie**, a patch of cobbled granite focused on a Roland column, with a few acacia trees and a fountain sporting the usual cherubs seemingly peeing out of fishes' mouths; the surrounding buildings give a hint that this was once the city's main marketplace, and in summer craft stalls aimed at the tourist trade line the periphery.

On the east side of the square is the **stará radnica**, a two-storey building in a lively hotchpotch of styles with a splash of beautifully patterned roof tiles. With a Gothic core, Renaissance innards and nineteenth-century detailing, it surpasses itself in the fanciful Baroque tower and serene half-moon crenellations and fragile arcading of the inner courtyard. The building itself, with its fine Gothic vaulting and superb Baroque ceilings, is the star of any visit, but the town hall also holds several collections: the **Vinohradícke múzeum** (Tues–Fri 10am–5pm, Sat & Sun 11am–6pm) is a scholarly tribute to Bratislava's position at the centre of the country's wine industry, and the **Múzeum histórie mesta** (same times as above), a less-than-fascinating collection of historical odds and sods, saved by some winsome Art Nouveau metalwork and a torture chamber (part of the feudal justice exhibition) in the basement. Sports fans will be thrilled to see the silver sequinned suit which belonged to 1970s Slovak ice-skating champion Ondrej Nepela, and, of course, pictures from Slovan Bratislava's famous victory over Barcelona in the 1969 Cup Winners' Cup.

The Counter-Reformation, which gripped the parts of Hungary not under Turkish occupation, exudes from the **Jezuitský kostol**, nicked from the local German Protestant community – hence its lack of tower and its relatively plain facade (the gilded relief and the ornate main doors were added by the Jesuits). Inside, the nave seems to stop rather short, its best feature undoubtedly the richly decorated black and gold pulpit which is dripping with gilded tassles. Nearby, opposite the gaudy yellow Františkánov kostol, is the **Mirbachov palác** (Tues–Sun 10am–5pm), arguably the finest of Bratislava's Rococo buildings, still sporting much of its original stucco decor. The Galéria mesta Bratislavy puts on some interesting temporary exhibitions here, but the permanent collection of Baroque art and sculpture isn't up to much, save for the room of wall-to-wall miniatures set into the wood panelling. The recent addition of a few paintings by early-twentieth-century Slovak artists such as Miloš Bazovský and Mikuláš Galanda adds spice to the proceedings.

Primaciálny palác and around

Round the back of the stará radnica, with the stillness of a provincial Italian piazza during siesta, is **Primaciálne námestie**, dominated by the pastel-pink Neoclassical **Primaciálny palác** (Tues–Sun 10am–5pm). The palace's uninspiring pediment frieze, which dates from the 1950s, is topped by a 300-pound cast-iron archbishop's hat, for it was originally designed as the winter residence of the Archbishop of Esztergom. The palace's main claim to fame, however, is as the place where Napoleon and the Holy Roman emperor Francis I signed the Treaty of Pressburg in 1805, following the Battle of Austerlitz (see p.299). Fully renovated, it now houses yet more of the city's art collection, primarily portraits of the Habsburgs, but also minor works by seventeenth-century Dutch and Italian masters.

What makes the palace worth visiting, though, is the **Zrkadlová sieň** (Mirror Hall), actually several interconnecting rooms, each lined with different-coloured damask, and, of course, with mirrors. The other highlight is the set of excellently preserved **seventeenth-century English tapestries**, discovered by chance during the building's restoration in 1903. Woven in Mortlake, London, the tapestries depict the tragedy of Hero, a priestess of Venus, and Leander, the lover who swam across the Bosphorus to be with her, until one night he drowned in a storm. The gallery terminates at a small balcony from which you can view the late-Baroque chapel of sv Ladislav, completed in less than a year in 1781, and sporting a lovely oval ceiling fresco by Maulpertsch or one of his followers.

All over the staré mesto, commemorative plaques make much of Bratislava's musical connections, but apart from the reflected glory of its proximity to Vienna and Budapest – not to mention the prewar presence of a large German-speaking population who ensured a regular supply of Europe's best artistes – the city has produced only one (mildly) famous composer, **Johann Nepomuk Hummel** (1778–1837), who in any case spent much of his time in Vienna. The composer's birthplace, **Rodný dom J.N. Hummela** (Tues–Sun 1–5pm), an apricot-coloured cottage swamped by its neighbours and hidden behind a row of fashionable shops on Klobučnícka (Hat Street), is now a museum. Like Mozart, who was sufficiently impressed to give him free lessons and even put him up for a while in Vienna, Hummel was a *Wunderkind*, who began performing at the tender age of ten and was touted round Europe by his ambitious father. As a pianist in the 1820s, Hummel was one of the most celebrated performers in Europe, yet although he wrote many fine classical works, his music has been largely ignored since his death.

From the Dóm to the Hrad

On the side of the staré mesto nearest the castle, the most insensitive of Bratislava's postwar developments took place. As if the Nazis' annihilation of the city's large and visible Jewish population wasn't enough, the Communist authorities tore down virtually the whole of the **Jewish quarter** in order to build the brutal showpiece bridge most SNP (see p.381). At the same time they sliced Rybné námestie in two, leaving its central plague column looking forlorn right by the motorway bridge. And finally, the best-preserved section of the old town walls now serves simply as a kind of sound barrier, protecting the rest of the staré mesto from the noise of the traffic. At least a memorial to Bratislava's Jews has finally been set up near the underpass to most SNP, a dense iron concoction of handprints and barbed wire, with a sign commanding "Pamätaj!" (Remember!).

Dóm sv Martina

Quite apart from the devastation of the ghetto, the traffic that tears along the busy thoroughfare of Staromestská has seriously undermined the foundations of the Gothic **Dóm sv Martina** (Mon–Fri 10–11.45am & 2–4.45pm, Sat 10am–noon & 2–4.45pm, Sun 2–4.45pm), coronation church of the kings and queens of Hungary for over 250 years, whose ill-proportioned steeple is topped by a tiny gilded Hungarian crown. The new road misses the west facade by a matter of metres, engulfing the exterior in noise and fumes. The interior is disappointing, decorated mostly with neo-Gothic furnishings, the best of which are the carved animals and figures on the pews in the choir, but there are one or two outstanding Baroque features which survived the re-Gothicization. Perhaps the most striking piece is the dramatic **equestrian statue of St Martin**, executed in lead by the Baroque sculptor Georg Raphael Donner, which formed the centrepiece of the overblown main altar, erected in 1735 but removed in the nineteenth century. Far from being about to run the naked beggar through with his sword, St Martin, dressed in fashionable aristocratic garb and modelled on the donor, Count Esterházy, is depicted cutting his coat in two to share it with the supplicant. The only other slice of Baroque to have survived is the spectacular side chapel of **sv Ján Almužník** in the north aisle, once again the work of Donner, its red marble portal draped with stucco curtains and putti; unfortunately, you can only peer through the wrought-iron gates at the sarcophagus, baldachin and frescoed cupola within.

The Jewish quarter

Passing under the approach road for the new bridge, two old, thin houses stand opposite one another, both now converted into museums. The first, a yellow Rococo fancy called U dobrého pastiera (The Good Shepherd), is the **Múzeum hodín** (Clock Museum; Mon & Wed–Fri 10am–5pm, Sat & Sun 11am–6pm) with a display of – depending on your tastes – nauseatingly vulgar or brilliantly kitsch Baroque and Empire clocks; the second is the **Múzeum umeleckých remesiel** (Museum of Folk Art; hours as above), which contains a few period dining rooms and a smallish collection of national folk art objects.

Further north along Židovská, the former heart of the city's **Jewish quarter**, there's a **Múzeum Židovskej kultúry** (daily except Sat 11am–5pm) tracing the history of the Jewish community in Slovakia and the basic religious practices of Judaism. There's also a memorial to the rabbis who perished in the camps and to the Slovaks who helped save Jews from deportation.

From the folk and clock museums, **Beblavého** begins the steep climb up to the castle. For many years this was one of the city's more infamous red-light districts, serving both town and barracks from its strategic point between the two, and described evocatively by Patrick Leigh Fermor, who passed through Bratislava en route to Constantinople in 1934: "During the day, except for the polyglot murmur of invitation, it was a rather silent place. But it grew noisier after dark when shadows brought confidence and the plum brandy began to bite home. It was only lit by cigarette ends and by an indoor glow that silhouetted the girls on their thresholds. Pink lights revealed the

JEWS IN SLOVAKIA

Jews probably settled in **Bratislava** during the thirteenth century, after which they were forced to move around the city, and expelled several times, before finally finding refuge in Podhradie (literally "under the castle"), just outside the city walls, in the sixteenth century. Before World War II, Jews made up ten percent of the city's population (the vast majority Orthodox), maintaining no fewer than nineteen synagogues and prayer rooms. Bratislava was also a significant centre of Jewish **education**; here, in 1806, was founded the *yeshivah*, which became one of the most famous Orthodox institutions in Europe, a tradition carried on today by the Pressburger Yeshivah in Jerusalem. Its founder, Rabbi Hatam Sofer, died here in 1839, and his grave continues to attract Orthodox pilgrims from all over the world; it is situated in a grim mausoleum by the western exit of the tram tunnel under the castle built by the Nazis over the original cemetery. Today, Bratislava's Jewish community is very small, with only one working synagogue, on Heydukova, and a large cemetery, west of the city centre on Žižkova.

Of **Slovakia**'s considerable prewar Jewish population of 95,000, only an estimated 3000 remain. Their fate under the wartime **Tiso** regime is still a potent political issue – the suggestion made by the Czech ambassador to the US that anti-Semitism was, and still is, "endemic" in Slovakia caused anger among many Slovaks, who argue that several leading members of Tiso's government did their best to prevent the Jews from being deported. Yet since 1989, there have been several disturbing developments: a plaque commemorating Tiso has been unveiled and several Jewish cemeteries have been vandalized across the country. These incidents do not necessarily confirm the widely held Czech view of Slovakia as a hotbed of anti-Semitism, but it is particularly distasteful that anti-Semitism should continue to be a useful political tool in a place where so few Jews remain.

detail of each small interior: a hastily tidied bed, a tin basin and a jug, some lustral gear and a shelf displaying a bottle of solution, pox-foiling and gentian-hued; a couple of dresses hung on a nail." Like the Jewish cafés Leigh Fermor also hung out in (along with, though not necessarily at the same table as, the young Orthodox Jew Ludvík Hoch – better known as Robert Maxwell), all this has long since gone, but there's only a vague hint of the bohemian about the ramshackle houses now slowly being turned into swish galleries, chic bars and restaurants.

The Hrad

The **Hrad** itself (grounds open daily: April–Sept 9am–8pm; Oct–March 9am–6pm), frequently referred to as the "inverted bedstead", is an unwelcoming giant box, built in the fifteenth century by the emperor Sigismund in expectation of a Hussite attack, burned down by its own drunken Austrian soldiers in 1811, and restored under the Communists. Your first port of call should be the **Klenoty davnej minulosti Slovenska** (Tues–Sun 10am–12.30pm & 1.30–4pm), a dimly lit treasury on the left as you enter the main gate, whose most precious exhibit is in the ticket office: the *Venus of Morovany*, a tiny fertility figure said to be made from a mammoth's tusk around 22,800 BC.

The rest of the castle, housing around half of the vast collections of the **Slovenské národné múzeum** (Tues–Fri 9am–5pm, Sat & Sun 10am–6pm), is made up of two main parts. The second floor includes a long-winded exhibition of farm implements and wood- and metalworking tools; pass on through and up to the third floor until you get to the period furniture section, which ranges from heavy Renaissance wardrobes to Biedermayer dining-room sets to twentieth-century gear. The most interesting section, by far, begins with iridescent Art Nouveau glassware and bronze chandeliers, and features a whole set of bedroom furniture decorated with a peacock feather motif by Dušan Jurkovič, finishing up with a wild, Oriental-style Art Deco bed in golden-yellow. The castle's small collection of old clocks is also worth viewing, just in case you missed the museum at the bottom of Beblavého, and you also get the chance to climb to the top of the Korunná veža, one of the castle's four corner towers.

Even if you don't make it up the Korunná veža, you can get a pretty good view south across the Danube plain from outside the castle gates. From either vantage point, the panorama is nothing short of mind-blowing. Although you can gaze out over the meeting point of three countries, most of the immediate foreground is taken up with the infamous **Petržalka** estate, symbol of the new Slovak nation, dragged forcibly into the twentieth century, at great social cost. A third of the city's population – an incredible 150,000 people – live in Petržalka, whose estates retain cruelly ironic names like Háje (Woods) and Lúky (Meadows), though barely a tree remains amid this expanse of mud and high-rises; until 1989 it had the added bonus of being surrounded by the barbed wire and watchtowers of the Iron Curtain. In many respects, most notably crime and drugs, it can't compete with the worst housing estates in the West, but with the highest suicide rate in the country, it's not a place anyone would choose to live.

Around the Hrad

Before heading back down the hill, you might want to skip over to the north wall of the Hrad, which houses the **Dedičstvo hudobných nástrojov** (Museum of folk instruments; Tues–Fri 9am–5pm, Sat & Sun 9am–6pm), including some unusual and colourful wooden horns. From here, it's possible to take an alternative route back down to the staré mesto by following the path that winds down the hillside from west of the Leopoldova brána. This will bring you to a neglected couple of streets – the old fishing quarter, squeezed between the waterfront motorway and the castle hill, which harbours two little-visited minor branches of the Slovenské národné múzeum. The first is the **Archeologické múzeum** (Tues–Sun 9am–5pm), whose few notable Roman exhibits include a winsome stone lion, a sleeping marble cherub, a votive relief and a stone altar to Jupiter.

However, it's the nearby **Múzeum Afrického umenia** (Museum of African Art; times as above), housed in an attractive sixteenth-century mansion, that is the more remarkable of the two. Of all the unlikely places to find one of the most impressive collections of African sculpture outside of that continent, this has got to be one of them. Yet the range of work displayed here is staggering, from traditional masks and fetishes from the Congo to modern Zimbabwean stone sculptures. Among the most remarkable works are the "Jamaa" family tree sculptures from Tanzania, featuring miniature figures piled on top of one another, carved from a single piece of wood. Equally compelling is the final room of huge Zimbabwean ironwood busts, carved from tree trunks, sections of which are left rough to create a contrast with the polished features of the wizened chiefs. What's more, labelling is in English and Slovak, African music plays in the background, and the differentiation between the various African cultures is sensitively addressed.

Hviezdoslavovo námestie and the waterfront

Between the staré mesto and the waterfront lies the graceful, tree-lined boulevard of **Hviezdoslavovo námestie**, with restaurants and cafés along one side and, on the other, the mammoth *Hotel Carlton*, an amalgamation of three hotels finally undergoing extensive renovation for the first time since the 1920s. Pride of place in the square, and a prime spot for casual loitering, is the larger-than-life statue of Pavol Országh Hviezdoslav, "father of Slovak poetry", a minor government official in the Orava region whose poetry is still a source of great national pride.

At the square's eastern end are two magnificent late-nineteenth-century edifices: the first, fronted by the elaborate **Ganymedova fontána** depicting the Trojan prince being carried off by an eagle, and featuring some wonderful frogs, tortoises and crayfish, is now the **Slovenské národné divadlo** (Slovak National Theatre), built as a top-quality German-speaking opera house; the second, diagonally opposite, is the later, more Secessionist **Reduta**, a casino and restaurant as well as home to the Slovenská filharmónia (SF).

In between the two is a surprisingly playful **Soviet war memorial**, a complete contrast to the Slavín (see p.384), depicting a woman doing gymnastics with a laurel leaf. At the end of Mostova, which runs south along the side of Reduta, is Štúrovo námestie, its modern statue of **Ľudovít Štúr** (see p.390) and his followers – appearing to levitate – a replacement for the grandiose statue of Maria Theresa blown up by Slovak nationalists in 1919.

The Danube and the most SNP

Beyond Stúrovo námestie and the fast dual carriageway of Rázusovo nábrežie, you can stroll along the banks of the (far from blue) **River Danube** – Dunaj in Slovak. At this point the Danube is terrifyingly fast – witness the speed to which the massive double-barges are reduced when going against the current and, by contrast, the velocity of those hurtling downstream. There's a regular (and hazardous) summer-only ferry service across the river, an alternative to crossing by either of the two bridges. The larger of these is the infamous **most SNP** (Bridge of the Slovak National Uprising), for which the old Jewish Quarter was ripped up. However destructive its construction, it's difficult not to be impressed by the sheer size and audacity of this single open suspension bridge. Its one support column leans at an alarming angle, topped by a saucer-like penthouse café reminiscent of the *Starship Enterprise*. The view from the café is superlative (except after dark due to the reflection of the interior lights on the windows), but the cost of the lift and a drink puts many locals off: there's a cheaper and equally good view from the toilet. The best place from which to view the bridge is the rather forlorn funfair in the **Sad Janka Kráľa** on the opposite bank – all that's left of what Baedeker described in 1904 as "a favourite evening-promenade . . . with café and pleasant grounds" – its statue of the nineteenth-century poet Sándor Petöfi a reminder of the city's Hungarian heritage.

The Slovenská národná galéria

When the Slovaks took control of Bratislava in 1918, a town in which they had previously made little impression, they set about establishing their own cultural monuments to rival those of their predecessors, the Austrians and Hungarians. Three such buildings were put up in the waterfront district, of which the most rewarding is the **Slovenská národná galéria** (Tues–Sun 10am–6pm), housed in a converted naval barracks (*vodné kasárne*) and in the neighbouring Esterházyho palác.

The latter, with its entrance on Štúrovo námestie, now contains a collection of **thirteenth- to eighteenth-century European art** on its first and second floors, which repays merely selective viewing. Only the bizarre seventeenth-century Dutch painting of *A Frog Trial*, and two very fine portraits by the Scottish artists Henry Raeburn and David Wilkie really stand out. On the third floor, however, is a superb gallery concentrating on **twentieth-century Slovak design and architecture**, ranging from black-and-white photographs by the great Karol Plicka to zany contemporary jewellery. In between, there are some very dodgy modern ceramics and some equally dubious shaggy 1970s tapestries, but also a wonderful array of posters, from Mucha, Benka and Fulla in the 1920s to the present day, and models of the country's modern architectural masterpieces.

To reach the gallery's main building, known as the vodné kasárne, you must return to the second floor, where the two buildings are joined together, so to speak. Here, you'll usually find a couple of temporary exhibitions, as well as the gallery's collection of **Gothic art**, much of it from the German-speaking Spiš region in eastern Slovakia. The most compelling works in the **Baroque art** section are the hyperrealist "character heads", carved by the eccentric sculptor Franz Xaver Messerschmidt, each depicting a different grimace, and the icons, particularly the seventeenth-century *Last Judgement*, in which the sinful tumble into the mouth of a fish-devil. The nineteenth-century works, on the floor below, are less than inspiring, with the exception of the dark, expressionist works by Ladislav Medňanský (aka Mednyánszky) from the 1890s. For an overview of Slovak artists of the twentieth century, you need to go to the Pállfyho palác in the old town (see p.376).

The Slovenské národní múzeum and the Modrý kostolík

Further along the quayside, past the hydrofoil launch, is the **Prírodné múzeum** (Tues–Sun 9am–5pm), the unremarkable **natural history** section of the **Slovenské národní múzeum**, housed in a dark and dingy 1930s building, and only really worth visiting for its excellent temporary exhibitions and its café round the back of the building. Further east along Vajanského nábrežie stands the equally dour **Komenský University**, founded along with the Republic in 1918, whose students spill out into the nearby bars and cafés and mingle with the crowds awaiting buses in Šafárikovo námestie.

The only specific sight around here is Ödön Lechner's sky-blue Art Nouveau **Modrý kostolík** (Little Blue Church) on Bezručova, a delicious, almost edible, monument by one of Hungary's leading late-nineteenth-century architects. Decorated, inside and out, with the richness of a central European cream cake, it's dedicated to St Elizabeth, the city's one and only famous saint, who was born in Bratislava in 1207. Lechner quite clearly also designed the Gymnasium, one block north of the church, which shares the same matching bright blue paint.

Námestie SNP and the suburbs

At the northern end of Štúrova, under the shadow of the high-rise *Hotel Kyjev* and the city's gargantuan Tesco department store, is **Kamenné námestie**. It's not exactly picturesque, but this is where the whole city seems to wind up after work, to shop, grab a beer or takeaway from one of the many stand-up stalls, gossip away the early evening and, above all, catch the bus or tram home.

To the northwest, Kamenné námestie melds imperceptibly into the slightly more accommodating **námestie SNP**, with a few trees and a host of sit-down cafés with outdoor terraces. In 1989, the Slovaks gathered here in their thousands for their part in the Velvet Revolution; nowadays it's a favourite spot for political activists. At its centre is the Monument to the Slovak National Uprising, the unsuccessful antifascist coup against the Nazis in the summer of 1944 which cost the country so dear. A macho bronze partisan guards the eternal flame, while two Slovak women (heads suitably covered) maintain a respectful distance. The one building worth noting on the square is the main **post office**, on the west side, whose Art Deco atrium of coloured glass has been lovingly restored.

Hodžovo námestie and beyond

Behind námestie SNP is the brown marble and onyx abomination of the *Hotel Forum*, which looks out onto **Hodžovo námestie**, nowadays one of the city's busiest intersections, though no doubt once a princely foil for the **Grassalkovičov palác** cowering in the top corner. Seat of the president under the clerico-fascist Jozef Tiso during World War II, and later home to the Communist youth organization, the palace is now once more the official residence of the Slovak president, though its gardens, which excel in ugly modern fountains, are open to the public. Two blocks north up Banskobystrická there's another grandiose Baroque palace, once the former summer residence of the archbishop of Esztergom and, until recently, home to the Slovak Parliament, which now occupies the ugly bunker to the west of the castle.

Devotees of totalitarian architecture might also visit **námestie Slobody**, a grandiose space designed by the local Party as a monumental setting for a giant statue of Klement Gottwald, the first Communist president. Gottwald has gone, thankfully, leaving only the wickedly unappealing Fountain of Friendship and the severe concrete mass of the General Post Office building, which takes up the entire length of the east side of the square and claims to be the largest in the world. A more successful modern addition to the city is the striking inverted pyramid of the Slovak radio building, up Mýtna, northeast of the square. If you're on for a wander, head southeast two blocks or so to the **Medická záhrada** (summer 8am–9.30pm; winter 8am–6pm), a dog-free, peaceful garden marred only by the dodgy 1970s park benches and lights. Further southeast still, on the other side of Poľná lies the city's oldest cemetery, the **Ondrejský cintorín** (daily 7am–dusk), established in 1784. More park than graveyard now, the predominantly Hungarian and German graves are rarely tended these days.

To the west of Hodžovo námestie, block after block of late-nineteenth-century buildings in faded colours squat under Slavín hill. The only sight as such is the pale-blue and exceedingly plain **Protestant Lycée** on Konventná (closed to the public), outside which a tall granite column commemorates the many leading Slovak men of letters who were educated here in the nineteenth century. Surprisingly for a fervently Catholic peasant country, the Protestants produced Slovak leaders far in excess of their numerical strength, including the entire 1848 triumvirate of Štúr, Hodža and Hurban. The city's Lenin Museum used to reside in a nineteenth-century neo-Baroque palace three-quarters of the way up Štefánikova at no. 25; to make up for this irrevocable loss, there's a **Múzeum polície SR** (Tues–Sat 10am–5pm) on the corner of Gunduličova itself, with a rather comical exhibition on the heroics of the Slovak police. It features a mock-up murder scene, detailed displays of feats such as nabbing bank robbers and drug smugglers, and a machine that recognizes counterfeit notes. The highlight is a model of the communist-era border crossing at Petržalka, with a double row of electrified razor-wire fences and lookout towers for the armed guards. The old Lenin Museum is now the Dom zahraničných Slovákov (House of Slovaks Abroad) with a little-visited **Krajanské múzeum** (Compatriot's Museum; Tues–Sun 10am–6pm), Štefánikova 25, run by the *Matica slovenská* (see p.419) and focusing on Slovaks who have made it big abroad.

The Slavín Monument

Slavín hill, to the northwest of Hodžovo námestie, is crowned by the gargantuan **Slavín Monument** to the 7000 Soviet soldiers who lost their lives in the battle for Bratislava. Ceremoniously completed in 1960 to mark the fifteenth anniversary of the city's liberation, this is now one of the largest Soviet monuments still standing in the entire country, and visible from virtually every street corner in Bratislava. It's predictably militaristic, not to say phallic, a giant ribbed obelisk thrusting into the sky, topped by an anguished Soviet soldier holding the victory banner outstretched.

The villa quarter just below the monument has always been a well-to-do suburb, settled by the German middle class in the interwar period, later the exclusive territory of Party *apparatchiks*, and now something of an embassy enclave. The mild-mannered **Alexander Dubček** used to live at Mišikova 46 (Mouse Street). In 1968, he became probably the only Slovak ever to achieve world fame, a feat he accomplished by becoming the somewhat unlikely leader of a deeply divided Communist Party as it attempted to bring about *perestroika* twenty years ahead of its time. Crushed by the Soviet invasion, he spent his twenty years of internal exile here, under constant surveillance, working for the Slovak equivalent of the local forestry commission. He lived long enough to witness the happy events of 1989, appearing alongside Václav Havel to cheering crowds on Wenceslas Square and later becoming the parliamentary speaker. The circumstances of his death, in a car crash in 1992, are shrouded in controversy; his demise was a tragedy for Slovakia, which sorely lacks a politician of his international standing.

Eating

The choice of places **to eat** in Bratislava has improved enormously over the last few years, as have standards, though you're still unlikely to have the meal of a lifetime here. The most memorable aspect of the whole experience is often the ambience, and exploring the atmospheric streets of the old town by night is all part of the fun. In addition, you can also be fairly sure that, away from the places catering for those on expenses, prices remain uniformly low.

Arkádia, Zámocké schody (☎54 43 00 32). Great Slovak cuisine and a fantastic view over the Danube at this converted house halfway up the steps to the castle. Daily noon–11pm.

Chez David, Zamocká 13 (☎54 41 69 43). Strictly kosher restaurant serving fresh, beautifully prepared Jewish cuisine, but pricey for Bratislava. Mon–Thurs & Sun 11.30am–10pm, Fri 11.30am–3pm.

Corleone, Hviezdoslavovo námestie 21. The best pizza joint in the city, with a good range of moderately priced, thin-base pizzas. Daily 10am–11pm.

Klub F, Ventúrská 18. Cosy cellar offering light meals such as vegetable soup and quiche. Mon–Sat 11am–9pm.

Mali Františkanů, námestie SNP 24. Standard Slovak fare and a great atmosphere in this vaulted Gothic cellar, though you'll have to put up with the smoke and pop music. One of the only restaurants in town to stay open late. Daily 10am–6am.

Modrá hviezda, Beblavého 14. Restaurant en route to the Hrad serving decent Slovak and Hungarian specialities. Mon–Sat 11.30am–11pm.

Passage Rybárska brána, Gorkého 1. Small complex of inexpensive restaurants, including *Spaghetti & Co*, a Balkan grill, a Chinese takeaway and a pseudo-English pub.

Prašná bašta, Zámočnícka 11. Soothing interior and a lovely courtyard, perfect for the tasteful cross-cultural cuisines on offer, with Mediterranean-influenced salads and creative main dishes. Daily 11am–11pm.

Slovenská pivnica, Dunajská 18. A traditional Slovak beer hall in the unlikely setting of noisy Kamenné námestie, but its prices are low and the atmosphere is good. Mon–Sat 11.20am–11pm, Sun 11.30am–4pm.

Rybársky cech, Žižkova 1 (☎54 41 83 34). Popular and reliably good fish restaurant on the ground floor of a former fisherman's house down by the waterfront below the castle (there's a posher, more expensive version upstairs). Reservations recommended. Daily 11am–11pm.

U dežmara, Klariská 1. Tucked away in a corner of the old town off Michalská, this is a nice place to enjoy traditional Chinese cooking. Daily 11am–11pm.

Umag, Žilinská 2. Small Croat-run pizzeria on the corner of Štefanovičova near the train station, with excellent thin-base pizzas. Daily 11am–10.30pm.

Vegetarian, Laurinská 8. Plain and simple vegetarian lunch spot, with a short list of salads and soya-based main dishes. Mon–Fri 11am–3pm.

Cafés

For a relatively small city, Bratislava has an incredible number of **cafés**, ranging from coffee-and-cake pit stops for the older generation to smoky student dives. Many have tables outside in the summer, and warm snugs to sink into in the winter.

Atlantis, Štúrova 13. Coffee-and-cake student café with around thirty varieties of ice cream. Daily 10am–8pm.

Bystrica, most SNP. Sky-high café (prices as well as location) at the top of the city's main suspension bridge. Daily 10am–10pm.

Café Français, Sedlárska 7. Decent croissants and other French snacks in the Institut Français. Mon–Fri 10am–9pm.

Café Mayer, Hlavné námestie 4. A resurrected late-nineteenth-century café that tries very hard to emulate its Viennese-style ancestor – very popular with the city's older coffee-and-cake fans. Daily 10am–1am.

Drink in Gallery Andy, Beblavého 4. Convenient and convivial wine bar/art gallery decorated with a disco flavour on the street heading up to the castle. Daily 4pm–1am.

Galérie, Panská 12. Nice café in the old town that's a favourite coffee and cigarette pit stop for students and arty types. Mon–Fri 9am–midnight, Sat & Sun 4pm–midnight.

Gremium, Gorkého 11. Wonderful, smoky café/gallery in the centre, with a high ceiling and a nice balcony where you can play pool. Daily 8.30am–midnight.

Korzo, Hviezdoslavovo námestie 11. Passable shot at a Viennese-style café and a possible breakfast halt, with tables outside overlooking Rybné námestie and most SNP. Daily 9am–11pm.

Krym, Šafaríkovo námestie. Cheap, colourful pub/café with a short menu, that's also open for breakfast. Mon–Thurs 7am–10pm, Fri 1pm–11pm, Sat 9.30am–11pm, Sun 9.30am–10pm.

Kút, Zámočnícka 11. Light Mediterranean salads served in this café with burgundy walls, attached to the *Prašná bašta* restaurant. Daily 11am–11pm.

London Café, Panská 17. Tiny British Council tearoom that's famous for its quiche and salad, popular with expats and a good place to catch up on the English press. Mon–Fri 9am–9pm.

Maximilián, Hlavné námestie 5. Pleasant new café on the main square in the staré mesto, with tables spilling onto the plaza in the warm months. Daily 8am–10pm.

Múzeum, Vajanského nábrezie 2. Appealingly gloomy mustard-yellow faux-marble foyer café round the back of the Prírodné múzeum, with an Internet offshoot, *Klub Internet* in the same building. Daily 9am–9pm.

Olympia, Kollárovo námestie 20. Wonderfully tacky communist-era decor in this café above the Nová scéna theatre. Daily 11am–midnight.

Omama, Sasinkovo 19. Fun, off-beat café decorated with classic old advertisements from the interwar period. Decent menu selection too. Mon–Fri 8am–10pm.

Piano Bar, Laurinská 11. Popular little bar run by one of the stars of Slovak commercial TV, who occasionally treats his guests to an impromptu jam session. Mon–Sat 11am–midnight, Sun noon–midnight.

U anjelov, Laurinská 19. Cosy café/bar that attracts a discerning, black-clad crowd. Mon–Sat 9am–midnight, Sun 5pm–midnight.

Entertainment and nightlife

Bratislava's nightlife is still heavily biased towards high culture, with few out-and-out dance music venues or **nightclubs** to choose from. On the other hand, there are a number of bars and pubs that play loud music and stay open late, where dancing has been known to break out. For more mainstream fare, and cinema listings, pick up the monthly magazine, *Kam v Bratislave*, from BIS. In season, there are **opera and ballet** performances at the Slovenské národné divadlo and **classical concerts** at Reduta, both on Hviedoslavovo námestie, as well as a more varied programme at the modern Istropolis complex on Trnavské mýto (tram #2 from the station; tram #4 or #6 from the centre).

Bratislava hosts a couple of annual large-scale **festivals**, the most prestigious being the classical music festival in October – without the big names of Prague's, but a lot easier to get tickets for. There's also a biennial international festival of children's illustrations held in September and October in odd-numbered years, as much of interest to adults as to kids. While on the subject, if you've **kids** in tow, it's worth finding out what's on at the Bibiana children's cultural centre, which stages events, shows and exhibitions aimed at kids.

Pubs, clubs and bars

Charlie Centrum, Špitálska 4. Arts cinema complex that has a café upstairs and a spacious, loud, reasonably priced nightclub/pub downstairs. Situated behind the *Hotel Kyjev*, with its entrance on Rajská. Tues–Sat until 4am.

Dubliners, Sedlárska 6. Very popular over-the-top Irish-themed pub, complete with mock cobbled street. Daily noon–midnight.

Duna, Radlinského 11. Probably the most reliable bet for a drink and a dance after *Charlie's*, this is a predominantly student hang-out in the basement of the Technical University. Mon–Thurs & Sun 5pm–1am, Fri & Sat 5pm–4am.

Hysteria, Odbojárov 9. Worth the trek out to the Zimný štadión (tram #4 or #6 from Kamenné námestie) for this lively Tex-Mex pub, with regular pool and live music. Mon–Thurs & Sun 11am–2am, Fri & Sat 11am–5am.

Jungle Café, Obchodná 42. Wild decor to go along with your cocktails. Reggae and salsa DJ on Friday and Saturday nights. Daily 10am–midnight (often later at weekends).

KGB, Obchodná. The initials supposedly stand for *Krčma Gurmánov Bratislavy*, or "Pub of the Gourmets of Bratislava", and the dark cellar is one of the most popular pubs with the city's discerning youth. Mon–Thurs 10am–2am, Fri 10am–3.30am, Sat 3.30pm–3.30am, Sun 3.30–11pm.

Koník, Mlynské nivy 8. Lively pub near the main bus station, which attracts a young crowd. Mon–Thurs & Sat 10am–1am, Fri until 2am, Sun until midnight.

Monaco Club, Rybné námestie. Overpriced nightclub below the *Hotel Danube* popular with the usual dodgy types who like to frequent expensive hotel discos. Daily 8pm–4am.

17's Bar, Hviezdoslavovo námestie 17. Dark, lively pub with live music some nights. Mon–Fri 11.30am–2am, Sat 2pm–3am, Sun 2pm–midnight.

Smirnoff Klub, Štúrova (at the Šafárikovo námestie end). Lots of neon lights, bad DJs and dubious punters, but it can be fun if you're out late and still steaming. Daily 6pm–late.

Stará sladovňa, Cintorínska 32. The city's malthouse until 1976, *Mamut*, as it's known, is Bratislava's most famous (and largest) pub. Czech Budvar on tap, big band and country & western music Thurs–Sat, and a bingo hall and casino on site as well. Daily 10am–midnight.

U-Club, nábrežie arm. gen. L. Svobodu. Cheap, loud and slightly weird club located in an old nuclear bunker underneath the Hrad. Mon–Thurs until 2am, Fri & Sat until 4am.

Listings

Airlines Aeroflot, Laurinská 13 (☎54 43 51 92); Air France, Vazovova 1a (☎52 49 27 61); Air Slovakia, Pestovateľská 2 (☎43 42 27 44); Austrian Airlines, Rybné námestie 1 (☎54 41 16 26); British Airways, Štefaníkova 22 (☎52 49 98 01); ČSA, Štúrova 13 (☎52 96 10 73); Delta, *Hotel Kyjev* (☎52 92 09 40); KLM, Dunajská 4 (☎52 92 11 09); Lauda Air, Štúrova 4 (☎52 96 78 14); Lufthansa, Štúrova 4 (☎52 96 78 14); Slov Air, Bratislava airport (☎43 29 14 09); Swissair, Dostoyevského rad 7 (☎52 92 19 94).

Boats Slovenská plavba dunajská runs hydrofoil services from the terminal on Fajnorovo nábrežie (☎54 41 03 36) to various places along the Danube, including Budapest and Vienna (see box below for details).

Car rental Two good local firms are Recar, Svätoplukova 1 (☎55 57 64 36), and Adecar, Hybešova 36 (☎ & fax 44 88 15 72).

Cultural centres Austrian Cultural Centre, Zelená 7; British Council, Panská 17; České centrum, námestie SNP 12; Goethe Institute, Konventná 1; Institut Français, Sedlárska 7; Kultúrny inštitút Maďarskej republiky, Palisády 54; Pro Helvetia, Panská 15; Poľský inštitút, námestie SNP 27.

Embassies and consulates Austria, Ventúrska 10 (☎54 43 29 85); Britain, Panská 16 (☎54 41 96 32); Canada, Mišíkova 28D (☎52 45 21 75); Czech Republic, 29 augusta 5 (☎52 93 12 05); Hungary, Sedlárska 3 (☎54 43 05 41); Poland, Jančova 8 (☎62 80 34 18); Russia, Godrova 4 (☎54 41 34 68); Ukraine, Radvanská 35 (☎54 43 16 72); USA, Hviezdoslavovo námestie 5 (☎54 43 08 61).

Football Bratislava's premier team is Slovan Bratislava, the only Slovak club to have won a European competition. Slovan's ground is the Tehelné Pole stadium, built during World War II and also used for international games. For details of how to get there, see "Sports facilities" below.

Internet *Klub Internet*, in the *Múzeum* café at Vajanského nábrežie 2 (daily 9am–9pm), or at Heura, Laurinská 14, a bookstore/gallery with a couple of computers (Mon–Fri 8am–9pm, Sat & Sun 8am–1pm).

Left luggage Lockers at both train and bus stations.

Libraries British Council Teaching Resource Centre, Panská 17 (Tues 1–5pm, Wed 1–6.30pm, Thurs 9.30am–noon & 1–5pm, Fri 1–5pm, Sat 9.30am–noon); French Institute library (Mon–Fri 2–6pm).

Markets The best fruit-and-vegetable market in town takes place Mon–Sat in the Tržnica covered market hall on Trnavské mýto (tram #4 or #6 from Kamenné námestie). Early Saturday morning is the busiest and best time to go. The stará tržnica, at námestie SNP 25, should be reopened by the time this book appears in print, though it will likely become a more Western-style shopping mall.

Medical emergency Go to Mýtná 5 or Mickiewiczova 13.

Newspapers Interpress Slovakia, Sedlárska 2 (daily 7am–10pm); newsstand outside Slovský spiso-vateľ on the corner of Laurinská and Rybárska brána.

Post office Main post office (Hlavná pošta), námestie SNP 35 (Mon–Sat 7am–8pm, Sun 9am–2pm).

Sports facilities There are two main sports complexes, Tehelné pole and Pasienky, next to one another in the nové mesto (tram #2 from the station; tram #4 or #6 from the centre); facilities include an outdoor pool, ice-hockey stadium, cycle track and the big Slovan football stadium.

Taxis Not as bad a reputation as in Prague; try Yellow Expres (☎44 44 11 11).

Telephones International calls are best made at the 24-hour exchange at Kolárska 12.

DANUBE TRANSPORT

From mid-April to mid-October, Slovenská plavba dunajská run a variety of hydrofoil ser-vices from Bratislava: boats go as far as Vienna (1hr 30min–1hr 45min) and Budapest (4hr 10min–4hr 40min). There are also shorter domestic services to Devín, sightseeing around Bratislava itself and down to the Gabčíkovo dam (see p.397). All boats leave from the jetty on Fajnorovo nábrežie, near the Prírodovedné múzeum. For the current timetable, ask at the BIS.

Out from the city

Most people find enough in the city centre to occupy them for the average two- or three-day stay, but if you're staying around for longer, or would prefer to be among the vine-clad hills which encroach on the city's northern suburbs, there are several places where you could happily spend a lazy afternoon, all within easy reach of the city centre.

Zlaté Piesky

Out on the motorway to Piešťany, just past the city's huge chemical works, the **Zlaté Piesky** (tram #2 from the train station; tram #4 from town) is a popular destination for weekending Bratislavans. Despite its name, meaning "Golden Sands", it's a far cry from the Côte d'Azur, though on a baking hot day in August not even the stench from the nearby chemical factory can deter large numbers of sweltering Slovaks from stripping off and throwing themselves into the lake's lukewarm waters.

Kamzík

North of the main train station the city immediately gives way to the vineyards and beechwood slopes of the suburb of Vinohrady (a world apart from its vine-less namesake in Prague), perfect for a quick escape from the city. From the station you can walk for 2.5km along a yellow-marked path through the woods to the summit of **Kamzík** (440m) topped by a TV tower. If you don't fancy the walk, take bus #33 to the chairlift on the north side of the hill, or simply trolleybus #213 from Mierové námestie or námestie Slobody to the last stop and walk along the red-marked path for 1km.

Devín

Bus #29 from beneath most SNP will get you to the village of **DEVÍN** (Theben), 9km northwest of Bratislava, whose ruined **hrad** (May–Oct Tues–Sun 10am–5pm, July & Aug until 6pm), first established in the fifth century BC, perches impressively on a rocky promontory at the confluence of the Morava and the Danube. With the West just a stone's throw away across the river, border precautions used to be particularly excessive on the road to Devín – a continuous twenty-foot barbed-wire fence, punctuated at regular intervals by fifty-foot watchtowers and hidden cameras that monitored all passing vehicles. Today, though, such Cold War images seem as far removed from reality as the traditional Slovak legends that surround Devín.

In 864 and again in 871, the Slavs of the Great Moravian Empire gave the Germans two serious drubbings at Devín, the last of which is said to have left the Germans with so few prisoners with which to barter that they could only succeed in retrieving one half-dead hero named Ratbod. In the nineteenth century, Ľudovít Štúr and his fellow Slovak nationalists made Devín a potent symbol of their lost nationhood, organizing a series of publicity stunts in and around the castle in the run-up to 1848. Because of its importance in the national lore, Devín remains a symbol of Slovak strength and independence for its people, and its defining architectural feature, a lonesome round tower perched atop a spindle of rock, appears in many advertisements and political placards.

There's a good view over into Austria from the craggy ruins, as well as an **archeological museum** with objects from as far back as 1800 BC. A favourite place for weekend picnics, the castle also hosts nationalist events in July and sometimes performances in the open-air amphitheatre amongst its ruins; for details ask at BIS. If you fancy a walk, follow the red markers from just above the last stop on tram #4 or #9 for a pleasant two-hour trail through the woods to Devín. At the castle itself you can also pick up the *naučny chodník*, a 12km-long educational walking trail along the Morava river floodplain to Vysoká pri Morave.

Rusovce

In 1945, to shore up its exposed western flank, Czechoslovakia was handed a small stretch of forested marshland on the previously Hungarian right bank of the Danube. Much of this land is now taken up with the unmissable Petržalka housing estate (see p.380), but there are at least a couple more villages along the road to Györ, shortly before the Hungarian border; one of these is **RUSOVCE**, 17km southeast of Bratislava, a possible half-day trip by bus #116 which runs regularly from most SNP. Originally the Roman camp of Gerulata, it now harbours a small **Múzeum antická Gerulata** (May–Oct Tues–Sun 9am–5pm), signposted off the main road to the north, containing the results of extensive archeological excavations that have uncovered two large Roman burial sites. Nearby, a neo-Gothic **zámok** is currently being restored for the Slovenská národná galéria, though the English-style park is open at all times for picnicking and there's a series of reservoirs popular with naturists.

The Small Carpathians

From the Bratislavan suburbs to the gateway into the Váh valley, the **Small Carpathians** (Malé karpaty) form a thin abrasive strip of limestone hills altogether different from the soft, pine-clad hills of the Czech Lands. These are the modest beginnings of the great Carpathian range that sweeps round through the back door into Romania. Throughout much of the year, a thoroughly Balkan heat bounces off the sun-stroked plains of the Danube and permeates even these first foothills, whose south-facing slopes are excellent for vine-growing. There's also a smattering of castles and a whole host of hiking opportunities, all making for a welcome release from the Bratislavan smog.

The Small Carpathians force their way right into the city boundaries, making Bratislava a good starting point for **hiking** in the hills. Kamzík (440m) is the first peak (see opposite), and on a clear day the view from its television tower is difficult to beat, but if you want to do some serious trekking in unmolested countryside, continue along the red-marked path (previously known as the cesta Hrdinov SNP) that wiggles its way along the ridge of the hills all the way to Brezová, 75km away at the end of the range. There are campsites and hotels peppered along the route, and it's easy enough to drop down off the hills and grab a bed for the night.

Modra and around

If you're going in search of víno, **MODRA** (Modern), just under 30km from Bratislava and entirely surrounded by the stuff, is the most convenient place to head for. It's a typical ribbon-village with one long street lined with barn-door cottages growing fancier the nearer you get to the centre. There's an excellent little wine shop at no. 92, or you can imbibe the local wines at the co-op headquarters further down on the other side of the street. Gracing the square at its widest point is a light stone statue of Slovak nationalist **Ľudovít Štúr**, who is buried in the local cemetery (see box on next page). The nearby **Štúr Museum** (Tues–Sat 9am–4pm), in the Renaissance former town hall, is predictable enough and makes a classic Slovak school trip, though kids are generally more interested in the ice cream outlet judiciously placed next door.

The *Modra*, at no. 111 on the main street (☎0704/47 22 65; ②), is the village's chief **hotel**, though the *Club MKM* (☎0704/647 5596; ⑥) at no. 25 is much better. Alternatively, head 1km north to the Harmónia suburb, where you've a choice of pensions such as *Zita* (☎0704/47 36 64; ②), just along the road to Trnava; the nearest **campsite** (May–Sept) is 6km north at Piesok, in the hills above Modra. A good base for exploring the surrounding area, Piesok is just a five-kilometre walk from **Vysoká** (754m), quite the most rewarding peak in terms of views. For a more gen-

ĽUDOVÍT ŠTÚR

Son of a Protestant pastor, Ľudovít Štúr (1815–56) rose to become the only Slovak deputy in the Hungarian Diet prior to 1848. In the turmoil of 1848 itself, Štúr sided with the Habsburgs against the chauvinistic Magyar revolutionaries, in the hope of gaining concessions from the regime. In the end, despite aiding the Habsburgs in their modest victory, the Slovaks were offered nothing. Disappointed and disillusioned, Štúr retreated to Modra, where he lived until his premature death in 1856, the result of a gun accident. In his later years, he became convinced that Slovakia's only hope lay with Russia – now a distinctly unpopular viewpoint. Perhaps his most lasting achievement – and the reason why Slovak nationalists adore him – was the formation of what is now the official Slovak written language, based on the Central Slovak dialect he himself spoke, although even this was only achieved in the face of vehement opposition from the more Czechophile scholars who advocated either Czech or its nearest equivalent, West Slovak.

tle stroll, you could head 5km east to the hulking chateau of **Červený Kameň** (Tues–Sun 9am–4pm). Designed to put fear into enemies approaching from the plain, its defensive position and big fat bastions were created by the painter Albrecht Dürer for the unlikely sounding Fugger family. However, it was the powerful Pálffy dynasty who later transformed it into a more luxurious family residence, adding formal gardens and various other creature comforts. The castle now houses an impressive collection of period furniture, a medieval torture chamber and a seventeenth-century apothecary.

Brezová pod Bradlom and Košariská

Tucked away into a peaceful swathe of the northern Small Carpathians, the region around **BREZOVÁ POD BRADLOM** is the home of Slovak national hero Milan Rastislav Štefánik (see box below). Štefánik was born in the village of **KOŠARISKÁ**, 3km east of Brezová, in 1880, and his birthplace is now an engaging **museum** (April–Oct Tues–Sun 9am–5pm; Nov–March Mon–Fri 8am–4pm) tracing his adventur-

MILAN RASTISLAV ŠTEFÁNIK

Like so many Slovak nineteenth-century nationalists, **Milan Rastislav Štefánik** was the son of a Lutheran pastor. He got into trouble with the Hungarian authorities while still only a teenager, and later left for France to study astronomy at the Paris Observatoire. He took part in astronomical expeditions to the Sahara and the Pacific islands, and in 1914 volunteered as a pilot for the French Air Force. Along with Masaryk and Beneš, Štefánik formed the famous triumvirate which campaigned tirelessly for an independent Czechoslovak state during the war. On May 4, 1919, Štefánik died when his plane crashed just outside Bratislava, within sight of the airport. As he was the only true Slovak in the triumvirate, it was a devastating blow for Slovak aspirations, and rumours quickly spread that the plane had been deliberately shot down by the Czechs.

Under the Communists, Štefánik suffered the same posthumous fate as Masaryk: his name was expunged from the history books and his statues taken down. Again, like Masaryk, he has returned with a vengeance – many squares and streets have been renamed and his statue is now a common sight throughout Slovakia, though his pro-Czechoslovak views are not popular with all Slovaks. In addition to the new museum in Košariská and mausoleum atop Bradlo, there's a small stone pyramid commemorating his death to the east of Bratislava's Ivanka Airport.

ous life and untimely death. If you've any interest in Štefánik, you'll get a kick out of his personal photos, boyhood folk outfit, pipes, flying uniforms and personal letters from T.G. Masaryk. Much is made of his travels and diplomatic exploits, and the model and photos of the plane in which he was killed really bring to light how important his role was to the Slovak national cause.

Even more acclaim is bestowed upon Štefánik at his colossal **mausoleum** atop nearby Bradlo (543m), a short drive or steep one-hour hike up the red-marked path from Brezová. The imposing white stone really is overdone, as if you're standing at a temple, but at least the views from the hilltop are splendid. Košariská is connected by a few daily buses to Piešťany, though there are more connections in Brezová to Bratislava and Trnava. If you wish to **spend the night**, the *Penzión U Juhasa* (☎0802/94 28 07; ②) in Košariská has good rooms and a fine restaurant.

Trnava

Forty-five kilometres northeast of Bratislava, and just 35 minutes by fast train, **TRNA-VA** (Nagyszombat) is one of the few towns on the plain to have survived with its walled-in medieval character intact. The town's rich ecclesiastical history took off in 1543, when the archbishop of Esztergom and primate of Hungary moved his seat here, and reached its zenith during the Counter-Reformation, with the founding of a Jesuit university in 1635. When the Turkish threat receded, these institutions moved out, and, despite the re-establishment of Trnava's archbishopric in 1990, and the frequent references in tourist literature of the town as a "Slovak Rome" are clearly over. Nowadays, it's a sleepy place, with a pleasant old town, a couple of very fine churches and a fairly good museum – enough for an afternoon or so, but by no means an essential overnight stop.

The staré mesto

From the bus and railway **stations**, cross the new footbridge over the main ring road, Hospodárska, and head north along the leafy banks of the River Trnavka. Parallel to this runs the most impressive section of the old **town walls**, reinforced in the sixteenth century (and up to six metres thick in places) in anticipation of the marauding Turks; the only surviving gateway is the red-brick Bernolákova brána, popularly known as the Franciscan gate after the nearby church of **sv Jakub**.

Soon after the church, you come to **Trojičné námestie**, the spacious main square centred on a lively plague column, pristinely restored and dramatically lit at night. Here, Trnava's institutions old and new congregate: the **mestská veža**, dating from the beginning of the town's golden age in the sixteenth century; the Neoclassical **radnica**; the salmon-pink Empire-style **Trnavské divadlo**, the oldest theatre building in Slovakia, dating from 1831; and last, but in no way least, the **Dom kultúry**, just one of a number of spanking new buildings in Trnava that have risen up from the rubble in the old quarter.

A short walk up Šefánikova from the square is the surprisingly interesting **Jesuitský kostol**. The typically High Baroque nave is suffused with a pink light emanating from the marble pilasters; more startling though is the deliciously decorative north chapel, with bounteous vegetative motifs and floral stucco. On the east side of the chapel is a bizarre watery grotto, with a statue of Mary lit only by a dramatic shaft of light, the grotto's grille entirely surrounded by plaques and graffiti in Hungarian, Slovak and even Latin, thanking the Virgin for her various intercessions in answer to prayers.

The modern-day focus of Trnava is the newly paved main boulevard, **Hlavná**

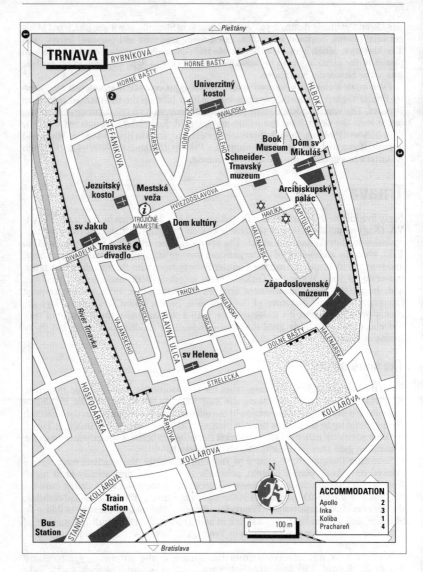

ulica, which leads south from Trojičné námestie: a pleasant window-shopping stroll. Its southern end is marked by the church of **sv Helena**, the town's oldest and most beguiling church, whose bare and miniature Gothic style is untouched by the suffocating hand of the Counter-Reformation. Next door is the town's former hospital, a Neoclassical building in an inappropriately sickly version of imperial yellow. South of sv Helena, a swathe of parkland has replaced the old fortifications, and boasts a working fountain and a new statue of Štefáník (see p.390).

The Dóm and Katedrálny chrám

East off Trojičné námestie, the **Dóm of sv Mikuláš** beckons with two rather clumsy but eye-catching Baroque steeples. Its Gothic origins are most obvious in the chancel, which boasts slender stained-glass windows and a fine set of choir stalls. It was promoted from a mere parish church following the Battle of Mohács in 1526, which caused the Hungarians to retreat behind the Danube; the royalty moved to Bratislava and the archbishop transferred his see to Trnava, setting up next door to sv Mikuláš. A century later, Trnava's position as a haven for Magyar cultural institutions seeking refuge from the Turks was further bolstered by the establishment of a university. In common with all Habsburg institutions of the time, it was under the iron grip of the Jesuits, and Trnava soon became the bastion of the Counter-Reformation east of Vienna.

The importance of religious over purely scholarly matters is most clearly illustrated by the sheer size of the **Univerzitný kostol**, down Hollého, one of the largest and most beautiful in Slovakia. The decor is mostly Italianate Rococo, with the apricot and peach pastels of the nave offset by darker stucco vegetation. The oval frescoes appear like giant lacquered miniatures, but the whole lot is upstaged by the vast wooden altarpiece, decked out in black and gold, peppered with saints, and looking more like an Orthodox iconostasis than a Catholic altar. These glory days were shortlived: with the expulsion of the Jesuit order from the Habsburg Empire and the defeat of the Turks, Trnava lost its university to Budapest, its archbishop's see to Esztergom, and consequently both its political and religious influence.

Trnava's museums

Kapitulská, the broad leafy street that sets off south from the archbishop's palace, is probably the prettiest street in town, with a cathedral-close feel about it. At its end, the plain cream mass of the seventeenth-century convent of sv Klara, now the **Západoslovenské múzeum** (Tues–Sun: June–Sept 10am–6pm; Oct–May 11am–4pm), offers a variety of exhibitions including eight rooms of folk ceramics by local potter Štefan Cyril Parrák; best of all, though, is the glimpse of the convent's former chapel, and the bits and bobs salvaged from the town's now-defunct **Jewish community**.

Trnava's Jews were actually expelled from the city in the sixteenth century, when, on the usual trumped-up charge of ritual murder, the emperor Ferdinand sent them packing through the Sereď gate, walling it up with ripped-up Jewish gravestones to bar their return. For three hundred years, Trnava was *Judenfrei*, then in 1862 the gate was removed, and the Jews began to filter back to the unofficial ghetto, located about where the main supermarket car park lies today. The disused and weed-ridden orthodox **synagogue** on Havlíka is on the brink of collapse, but the more prominent Moorish onion-domed **synagogue** (Tues–Fri & Sun 9am–noon & 1–5pm) on the other side of the street has been at least structurally restored and is used as temporary exhibition space. The reason to visit, though, is to wander about the gloomy interior, damaged by fire in the 1980s, but still retaining fragments of gorgeous frescoes and stonework. Out front, there's a large, black, tomb-like memorial to more than 2000 local Jews who were victims of the Holocaust.

The **Schneider-Trnavský museum** (June–Aug Tues–Sun 9am–5pm; Oct–May Mon–Fri 8am–4.30pm), at no. 5 ulica M. Schneidra-Trnavského, is devoted to the Slovak composer who was choirmaster at sv Mikuláš from 1909 until his death in 1958, and who clearly had very good taste in 1920s furniture. The little-visited **Book Museum** (Múzeum knižnej kultury; Mon–Fri 8am–4pm), further up the street opposite sv Mikuláš, was closed indefinitely at the time of writing, but if and when it reopens, it will focus on the many printing presses set up in Trnava by the Hungarians in the seventeenth century, and on the Slovak intellectual society here in the mid-nineteenth century.

Practicalities

The local **tourist office**, TINS (Mon–Fri 8am–6pm, July & Aug also Sat & Sun 10am–6pm; ☎0805/16186), is located in the mestská veža, and can help with **accommodation**. There should, in any case, be few problems finding a room at the swankiest option in town, the *Apollo*, Štefánikova 23 (☎0805/551 19 37; ⑥); other central options include the self-catering apartments of *Prachareň* (☎0805/551 15 22; ⑤), opposite the tourist office, and, cheapest of the lot, the pension *Inka*, VI. Clementisa 23 (☎0805/550 13 43; ②). Alternatively, you could try the *Koliba* (☎0805/533 44 59; ③), 3km west on T. Vansovej (bus #1 or #2). For **eating**, *Prachareň* has a few vegetarian dishes on the menu, and the *Pizza Corleone*, Paulínska, does decent, big pizzas (both closed Sun). In the northern part of the old town is the little restaurant *Bašta*, with good, standard Slovak fare; for beer pop into the *Pivnice nad baštem* on Hlavná ulica, while for wine, head for *U Jozefa*, an atmospheric vináreň on the same road. The billiard café on the corner of Trojičné námestie continues to be the only vaguely happening late-night place.

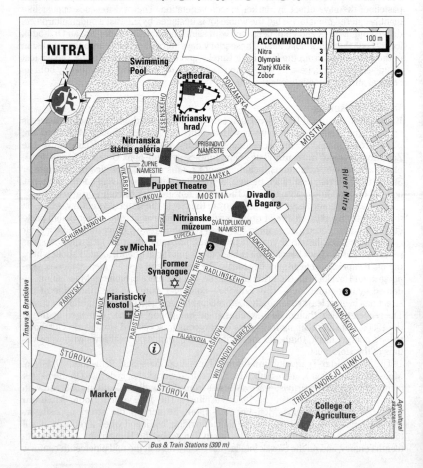

Nitra

While Trnava is stuck in the past, **NITRA** (Nyitra), 40km further east across the plain, has effectively shed its old skin and rushed headlong into the modern world. The result is a clearly divided town: on the one hand, the peaceful old quarter wrapped around the foot of the castle rock; on the other, the ungainly sprawl of modern Nitra, third largest city in the country with a population of 90,000, agricultural capital of the nation and a bustling market town. Sadly, to get to the former you must pass through the latter, since the sights are all situated in the old town, which has a certain national kudos attached to it as a centre of Slovak Catholicism, ancient and modern.

The City

The central axis of the nové mesto is the busy crossroads by the city's main **market** (*tržnica*) where the region's rich produce is sold daily. The staré mesto and the main sights are all north of here, except for the **Kalvária**, a kitsch mock-up of the Crucifixion, which crowns the summit of a small limestone hill southeast of the train station. The brutality of Nitra's modern development serves as the apocalyptic backdrop for three ugly concrete crosses, the two robbers grey and unpainted on either side of a technicolor Jesus.

Visible to the east of the market as you cross over Štúrova is the country's main **College of Agriculture**, a flying-saucer-shaped building, whose research department famously invented a strain of tree that could withstand acid rain – progress indeed. Beyond the college lies the Agrokomplex exhibition grounds, which also contain the marvellous **Slovenské Polhohospodárske Múzeum** (Slovak Agricultural Museum; Tues–Sun 9am–5pm). Though you wouldn't know it from the name or the setting – it's located at the rear of the Agrokomplex behind banks of ugly apartment blocks – this is a real gem, one of the very best museums of its kind in central Europe. In one large barracks-like building there's a display on the history of farming and commerce in Slovakia up to the Middle Ages, with an impressive array of artefacts such as 3000-year-old wheat kernels and relics from the medieval amber trade route, which passed from the Baltic Sea to Italy through Slovakia. Another concrete structure holds a fun collection of interwar tractors, including a massive red Russian combine and a wooden thresher, claimed to be the only one of its kind in the world. In the vicinity are several smaller houses with a variety of folk displays inside; an early-twentieth-century bakery, a distillery, a mill, a honeycomb pressing shop and a one-room schoolhouse with original furnishings all vie for attention. In August the whole complex comes alive as costumed guides demonstrate how the old shops work (many are still operational), and an 1885 narrow-gauge railway toots around the grounds, much to the delight of the local children. To get to the museum, take bus #8, #12, #15, #19, or #31 to the last stop at the end of Dlhá.

North of Štúrova, the main street of Štefánikova trieda has been pedestrianized and leads north past the giant neo-Renaissance **Nitrianske múzeum** (Tues–Fri 8–11.30am & noon–5pm, Sat & Sun 10am–5pm), which puts on riveting exhibitions such as "Stones today and yesterday", to the town's octagonal, Communist-designed theatre, **Divadlo A. Bagara**, on the dusty expanse of Svätoplukovo námestie. On ulica pri synagóge, west off Štefánikova, the sheer size of Nitra's Moorish **synagogue** is an indication of the strength of the town's prewar Jewish community and is now restored and used as an exhibition and concert hall. Farská, which leads you away from the chaos of the new town to the sights around the castle, is one of the most pleasant streets in the nové mesto, dotted with churches, grocery stores and snack bars.

The staré mesto

Nitra's **staré mesto** is actually very small, consisting of just a handful of streets huddled under the castle. The entrance is formed by the former Župný dom on Župné námestie, a handsome Art Nouveau building, now the **Ponitrianska galéria** (Tues–Sun 9am–4pm), which is putting on temporary exhibitions only while under restoration. The right-hand arch of the building leads to the steeply sloping old town square, **Pribinovo námestie**, a very modest affair but quite pretty and totally peaceful after the frenetic activity of the lower town. At its centre stands a very recent (and fairly ugly) statue of **Prince Pribina**, the ninth-century ruler of Nitra, who erected the first church in what is now Slovakia here in 833. Though no great believer himself, he shrewdly realized such a gesture would keep him on good terms with his German neighbours. There's also a fair amount of evidence to suggest that St Methodius, the first bishop of (Great) Moravia, was stationed at Nitra and not at Velehrad in the Morava Valley, as was once claimed by the Czechs.

Nitriansky hrad is a scruffy little hybrid, saved only by its lofty position above the river which allows a great view north over to Mount Zobor (588m), the southwesternmost tip of the central mountains. A fortress since the time of the Great Moravian Empire (of which it may have been the capital), it provided refuge for various Hungarian kings over the centuries until its destruction by the Turks in the seventeenth century. Crusty saints, a very fine plague column and two massive gateways mark the route to the remains, most of which have been turned over to the Archeological Institute and are closed to the public.

The one sight left in the complex is the **Hradná katedrála** (Mon–Fri 9am–1.30pm), an old structure which adjoins the bishop of Nitra's cosy Baroque residence. Confusingly, you enter the south door and pass through two antechambers – the first, the Pribinova kaplnka, is a Romanesque rotunda, the second is late-Gothic – before going up some more steps to the compact main church, its Baroquized marble interior in muted greys and reds. Frescoes adorn every possible space, and the modern blue stained glass in the chancel lends the whole place a magical quality. The cathedral is associated with two tenth-century Slovak saints, **Ondrej Svorad** and **Benedikt Junior**, both religious hermits who lived in the hills near Trenčín and spent most of their lives tending their gardens and vineyards. The locals, who had little time for able-bodied young men devoting their lives to spiritual contemplation, gave both of them a hard time; Ondrej Svorad escaped their wrath by diplomatically giving away a portion of his harvest, but Benedikt Junior failed to appease his enemies, who threw him off a nearby cliff and then drowned him in the River Váh.

Practicalities

If you're coming to Nitra from Bratislava, you're best off coming by **bus**, as there are no direct trains. Staff at Nitra's **tourist office**, NISYS, at Štefánikova 46 (Mon–Fri 8am–6pm, Sat 8am–1pm, July & Aug also Sun 8am–1pm; ☎087/16186), can help out with **accommodation**, though choice is limited to several (mostly ugly) large hotels. Nitra's finest hotel is the excellent *Zlatý kľúčik* (☎087/55 02 89; ⑨), with great views from its position on the slopes of Zobor to the northeast of the centre (take bus #10 or a taxi). Otherwise, you should try the *Zobor* (☎087/52 53 81; ⑥), on Štefánikova, or the dormitory-style *Olympia* (☎087/53 67 27; ③), east of the centre on trieda Andreja Hlinku – take bus #12, #13 or #23. The only time you may have problems finding a room is during the agricultural fair and the music festival, which take place in August and September respectively. The nearest **campsite**, *Jelenec* (May–Sept), is 16km northeast of Nitra in the foothills of the Tribeč, near Jelenec.

Nitra has a fair range of **eating** establishments, including the boisterous, beery *Thurzo*, on the corner of Štefánikova by the synagogue, opposite which is the

Furmanská vináreň, where you can sample *Nitria,* the local sweet white wine. Another good restaurant is the *Izba starej Matere*, at Radlinského 8, which has a nice garden and offers Slovak specialities; there's also a decent café further along the street at no. 17. *Boccaccio*, Farská 36, is a nice Italian-Slovak restaurant with a pleasant summer courtyard, and *Billich cukáren* is a swish, Italian-style, ice-cream parlour on Farská 38 and Štefánikova 39.

The Danube basin

To the east of Bratislava lies the rich agricultural region of the **Danube basin** (*Podunajsko* to the Slovaks; *Felvidék* to the Hungarians), a flat, well-watered expanse of land that benefits from some of the warmest temperatures in the country, and one of the few places in Slovakia where you can go for miles without seeing a tree. It has formed the border between Slovakia and Hungary since being handed over to Czechoslovakia in 1918, and is the traditional haunt of most of Slovakia's Hungarian-speaking minority. Sadly, this was one of the regions that suffered badly during World War II, and the subsequent rebuilding has made one place very much like another. The chief exception is **Komárno**, which, while not worth a detour in itself, has enough to make you pause en route to Hungary.

Senec

The towns of the Danube basin are probably the nearest either republic comes to seaside resorts, and in the summer the "beaches" are packed with windsurfers, canoeists and sun-seekers slobbing out along reservoirs, lakes, swimming pools and any stretch

---

THE GABČÍKOVO-NAGYMAROS DAM

The **Gabčíkovo-Nagymaros Hydroelectric Barrage** project was a megalomaniac idea dreamed up in 1977 by the Communist old guard of Hungary and Czechoslovakia, with the cynical collusion and capital of the Austrians, who were on the lookout for cheap electricity at someone else's environmental expense. However, following intense protest by the green lobby, the Hungarians unilaterally withdrew from the project in 1989 and called for an international enquiry into the environmental effects of the dam. The Czechoslovak government, however, having invested huge sums of money and desperate for an alternative source of energy to brown coal – the pollution from which is killing off the country's forests – pressed on and completed a scaled-down version of the scheme, diverting part of the Danube in 1993.

In 1997, after several years of verbal and legal sparring, the International Court in the Hague finally made a decision over the whole unhappy mess. It declared that Hungary had violated international law by reneging on the 1977 agreement. Most Slovaks rejoiced that, for once, their country had been found in the right, and that Hungarian propaganda had finally been unmasked. Unfortunately, however, the dispute is far from over. While deciding overall in Slovakia's favour, the court also ruled that the Slovaks had been wrong in diverting the Danube, which means that both sides can legitimately claim damages. Somewhat hopefully, the court ordered the two sides to come up with a joint proposal for the project (and for the damages), but this too has been stalled on account of successive years of elections in both countries. Now that both governments are at least relatively stable, talks are expected to resume. Sadly, in environmental terms, the damage has already been done, according to the WWF and ecologists on both sides of the border. You can visit the Danube barrage for yourself by boat (see p.387) or, better still, cycle along the new channel from Bratislava.

of water they can find. If you're staying in Bratislava, **SENEC** (Szenc), 26km east and just over thirty minutes by train, is the easiest place to get to and fairly indicative of the region. The Turks left one of their few monuments here, the creamy, crenellated **Turecký dom** (now the town's poshest restaurant), which, along with the large crumbling synagogue topped by a rusting Star of David, relieves the town's otherwise unprepossessing main street.

The real crowd-puller is the **Slnečné jazerá** (Sunny Lakes), a couple of reasonably warm artificial lakes southeast of town, within sight of the train station, which simply heave with visitors during the hot months, especially August. By the larger lake you'll find two campsites (mid-June to mid-Sept), bungalows and a couple of rudimentary hotels, the *Amúr* (☎07/92 40 81; ①), and *Benzinol* (☎07/92 45 07; ②). One place that doesn't draw the crowds (but should) is the extraordinary open-air **Museum of Bee-keeping** (Včelárska paseka; June–Sept Mon–Fri 9am–5pm, Sat & Sun 9am–1pm), signposted off route 62, close to the hamlet of Lučny dvor. There's honey for sale and hives of all shapes and sizes spread out in a shady glade by the bee-keeping school.

Komárno

Situated right on the confluence of the Váh and the Danube, **KOMÁRNO** (Komárom) is a Hungarian town through and through. Bilingual street and shop signs abound, and in shops you'll be greeted with *tessék* ("what do you want?") rather than the usual *prosim*. Ethnic niceties aside, however, Komárno is not going to win over many people's hearts; it's only worth a stopoff if you're passing through on the way to Budapest.

The Town
When the Czechoslovak border was dreamed up in 1919, the Hungarians of Komárom found their town split in two, with by far the most significant part – and what few sights there are – on the Slovak side. Both sides now annually reunite in late April/early May for a week of joint cultural events, known as the *Komárňanské dni/Komáromi napok*.

To get to the town centre from the **train** and **bus stations** to the northwest, take Petőfiho and you'll hit the main street, Záhradníčka, which heads south to the bridge over the river and into Hungary. The pedestrianized section of town, and the cobbled main square, **námestie gen. Klapku**, lies to the east. The latter is named after the general who fought against the Austrians in the Hungarian uprising of 1848, and whose statue is overlooked by several solid late-nineteenth-century buildings.

The **Podunajské múzeum**, with two subsidiary branches, one at Palatínova 26 (Tues–Sun May–Oct 10am–noon & 2–4pm), west of Záhradníčka, and the other just down the street east of Záhradníčka at Palatínova 13 (Tues–Sun: May–Oct 10am–5pm; Nov–April 9am–4pm), pays tribute to the town's two most illustrious and somewhat controversial sons. The first is the composer **Franz Lehár**, whose father was military bandmaster with the local garrison. Lehár enjoyed the dubious privilege of having written one of Hitler's favourite works, the operetta *Die lustige Witwe* (*The Merry Widow*), and despite the fact that his native tongue was Hungarian and his own wife Jewish, he found himself much in demand during the Third Reich. The nineteenth-century Hungarian writer **Mór Jókai**, on the other hand, was an extremely nationalistic Hungarian, who wrote a glowing account of the Hungarian aristocracy and would have had nothing good to say about Komárno's modern-day split nationality. The Palatínova 13 branch expands into greater detail about the two men's lives, while the Palatínova 26 branch is simply two small rooms containing photographs and furniture, but you won't get much from either exhibition unless you know Slovak or Hungarian.

More fascinating than either of the above is the disorientating sight of a small **Orthodox Church** (Pravoslávny kostol) in the grounds of the museum at Palatínova 26, testifying to the Serbian colonists who settled around Komárno in the early eigh-

THE HUNGARIANS OF SLOVAKIA

The creation of separate Czech and Slovak republics has brought into much sharper relief the rather more volatile relationship between the Slovaks and the 600,000 Hungarians who live along the southern border regions of Slovakia, and make up eleven percent of the country's total population. Like so many ethnic disputes in central Europe, it's an age-old conflict, one that remained fairly dormant during the communist period, but which has now returned with a vengeance.

For almost a millennium, Slovakia was an integral part of Hungary – Hungarians were the landlords, Slovaks the peasantry. Slovak language and culture was suppressed with unparalleled brutality right up until the foundation of the First Republic in 1918, when 750,000 Hungarians were left on the Slovak side of the Danube after the borders for the new republic were drawn up. Like the Germans who once lived in the border regions of the Czech Lands, Slovakia's Hungarians have never assimilated and were happy to unite with the fascist Magyar state during World War II, when Hungary was handed most of the Hungarian-speaking regions of Slovakia. Unlike their Germanic counterparts, the attempt by Beneš to expel them in 1945 was successfully blocked by the government in Budapest.

In 1989, the enforced fraternal friendship of the communist period finally came to an abrupt end with the dispute over the dam (see p.397). The rise of Slovak nationalism that took place after the Velvet Revolution has understandably worried the Hungarian community, which has itself been wooed by increasingly chauvinistic politicians, keen to score cheap political points at home. On the Slovak side, former premier Vladimír Mečiar did little to calm the fears of the Hungarian community, rejecting an EU-backed ethnic-minority law, and according to his Hungarian counterpart, even suggesting the community should be expelled. Fortunately, the June 1999 election of Rudolf Schuster – a Hungarian-speaker and advocate of governing "for all citizens" – to the presidency is expected the pave the way to more productive dialogue.

teenth century in a desperate attempt to escape the vengeful Turks. Small pockets of Orthodox believers still exist in the region, and the seventeenth- and eighteenth-century Greek and Serbian icons on display here constitute one of the best collections outside Serbia. Opposite the museum at Palatínova 13 stands the stunning twin-spired Baroque **church of sv Ondreje**, which has a cool, peach-coloured interior.

The town is also notable for its vast zigzag **fortifications** that seem much too big for the town, and its **fortress**, east of the town centre at the confluence of the Váh and the Danube, which has served as a strategic base for everyone from the Romans to the Russians, and is still in the hands of the military today. One of the town's bastions, **Bašta VI** (Tues–Sun 10am–5pm), on Okružná cesta, to the northwest of the town centre, beyond the railway lines, has been turned into a small museum (follow the signs to the *Fortezza* restaurant, see above).

Practicalities

The town **tourist office** (Mon–Fri 7.30am–4pm; ☎0819/16186) is at Zupná 5, though **accommodation** should be no problem as the town has a smattering of hotels and pensions. The *Európa*, on the main street (☎0819/73 13 49; ⑦), looks unprepossessing on the outside, but the rooms have been modernized and feature en-suite facilities and TVs, something that cannot be said for the equally central, but run-down *Danubius* on Dunajské nábrežie (☎0819/73 10 91; ①). *Ring Bar Penzión*, just off the main square at Letná 4 (☎0819/71 31 58; ④), has fairly cosy rooms above a bar. You can **camp** at the local zimný stadión (July to mid-Sept), but the riverside sites 6km west (and just 8min by train) in Nová Stráž (mid-May to mid-Sept) and 16km east in Patince (mid-May to mid-Sept) are preferable.

Basic **food** can be had at the *Litovel*, a nice pub on Dunajské nábrežie, or at the *Klapka* restaurant on námestie gen. Klapku, opposite the town hall. There are two popular Italian joints to try out: the trendy pizza parlour *Flinstonov cov*, on the main drag, and the Italian-Hungarian *Fortezza* restaurant in Bašta VI of the fortifications system to the north of the train station. The *Café Lehár*, a big turn-of-the-century building on Tržničné námestie, has potential, but the *Café Sonáta*, an old yellow mock-Gothic building near the barracks, is currently a better bet. For those who know the language, there's a Hungarian theatre, Jókaiho divadlo, halfway down Petöfiho. **Trains for Budapest** leave more frequently from the station on the Hungarian side; simply cross the bridge and the border, and turn right.

Štúrovo

"The Danube threads towns together like a string of pearls", wrote Claudio Magris, but it's doubtful he had **ŠTÚROVO** (Párkány) in mind at the time. Its major saving grace is the unbeatable view of the great domed basilica of Esztergom (*Ostrihom* to the Slovaks), on the Hungarian side of the river, to which it's been linked by a ferry service ever since the bridge was blown up by the retreating German army in 1944. Plans are afoot to construct a new bridge, though neither government is very keen on building bridges at the moment. Even the town's name is a bone of contention, with the current Slovak government insisting on keeping Štúrovo, the name given to the town by the Communists in 1948 after the Slovak nationalist (and virulent anti-Magyar) Ľudovít Štúr (see p.390), despite a local referendum which voted in favour of reverting to Párkány.

As the last town on the Slovak Danube, it's not a bad place to break your journey. Ferries over to Esztergom are frequent and you can take your car across, or you can hop on one of the international express trains that pause here en route to Budapest. The **train** and **bus stations** are actually an inconvenient 2.5km west of the town, though several local buses cover the distance. In the summer the focus of life is the town's outdoor swimming pool, fed by thermal springs, Termálne kúpalisko Vadaš, by the local **campsite** (mid-May to mid-Sept), just north of the town.

Brhlovce

The tiny village of **BRHLOVCE** nestles into the hills some 60km northeast of Štúrovo. Many of its 400-odd residents live in caves dug into the hills' soft rock faces, an oddity dating back to the sixteenth century when fears of Turkish attacks drove their ancestors into hiding. Simple holes in the short cliffs were expanded into habitable homes, and this inexpensive form of housing soon caught on. More cave homes were built in the late nineteenth and early twentieth centuries, and the troglodytes even made money by selling the rock they had hewn to local quarries. Once the living space was dug out, the walls were matted with straw and painted, and windows were carved out; in more recent years modern comforts, such as electricity and running water, have also been introduced. Although most of the cave homes are private residences, a pair of adjoining caves have been turned into a **museum** (Skalné obydlia; no regular hours but generally Mon–Fri 9am–4pm), where you can wander through the few tiny rooms. To get to Brhlovce, you'll have to rely on the infrequent buses from Levice, 10km west of Brhlovce, a fairly major bus and train stop in the region.

Piešťany and the Váh valley

Finding its source in the Tatras and carving a southwesterly course right the way to the Danube at Komárno, the **Váh** is one of the great rivers of Slovakia. Tourist office circles like to talk of the "Slovak Rhine", but despite the appearance of ruined cliff-top cas-

BOHUNICE AND MOCHOVCE

As you approach Piešťany from Bratislava, the cooling towers of the country's first nuclear power station at **Bohunice** are clearly visible on the western horizon. Built in the 1960s, but temporarily closed down in 1979 after two hushed-up accidents and only seven years of operation, Bohunice's A-1 reactor is currently being cleaned up at considerable cost to the Slovak taxpayer. The other four Soviet-designed reactors continue to function, despite being among the most dangerous in Europe, according to the US Department of Energy. The Slovaks, meanwhile, are trying to finish the second of two equally controversial Soviet-designed nuclear reactors at **Mochovce**, some 50km further east. Recent negotiations has resulted in an agreement to phase out Bohunice by 2007, as one of the two at Mochovce is now up and running, though of course protestors would rather both were shut down.

tles at every turn of the river, it lacks the magic of the Rhine valley. Heading north up the Váh from Piešťany to Trenčín, the mountains on either side keep their distance and the whole area still has the feel of the Danube basin. Beyond Trenčín, the industry, river dams and lorry-congested highway all dampen the effect of brigand hide-outs such as Vrsatec and Považský hrad. The best way to weigh up the relative merits of the region is on one of the fast and frequent **trains** from Bratislava that twist their way up the Váh valley en route to the Tatras.

Piešťany

The most convincing claim the local tourist board makes about **PIEŠŤANY**, just over an hour by train from Bratislava, is that it's the largest spa town in Slovakia, but don't expect anything akin to the late-nineteenth-century West Bohemian spas. Though the place is similarly overrun with the unhealthily rich from different parts of the German- and Russian-speaking world, the town itself is rather neglected. Instead, millions of crowns have been injected into the spa facilities, which include green spaces, clean swimming pools, and a host of other resources to which the public has access, making it a pleasant alternative to most of the "beachy" resorts further south.

The town divides conveniently into two parts: the spa island cut off from the mainland by a thin arm of the River Váh, and the rest of the town on the right bank between the main arm of the river and the **bus** and **train stations** to the west. It's a fifteen-minute walk into town down A. Hlinku and Štúrova (bus #3, #9 or #12) to **Winterova**, the main drag through the centre of town, a patchwork of muted turn-of-the-century and Secession buildings decorated with balconies and lined with cafés and trinkety shops. The main spa building at no. 29 is a typical example of Piešťany's understated architecture. Behind the bandstand in the Mestský park, there's a **Balneologické múzeum** (Spa Museum; Tues–Sun: April–Sept 9am–noon & 1–5pm; Oct–March closes 4pm) devoted to the local spa industry, but also displaying everything from a woolly mammoth's tusk to a mock-up of a Slovak folk cottage. The rest of the spa is on the opposite bank, a short stroll past **Barlolama**, the town's famous optimistic statue of a man breaking his crutches in two, and connected by the partially covered **Kolonádový most**, a graceful 1930s modernist structure, rebuilt under the Communists "for the benefit of the working class", in the words of the 1950s commemorative plaque.

One place that definitely wasn't built with the latter in mind is the vaguely Art Nouveau *Thermia Palace* hotel, which retains a hint of its bygone opulence and – if the flash cars parked outside are anything to go by – now serves the new European aristocracy. The woods and park on the **Kúpeľhý ostrov** (spa island) are decidedly verdant, with sculptures peeping out of every conceivable shrub and bush – part of the spa's annual international open-air sculpture symposium. The nearby low-lying annexes are still used for "mud wrapping and electro-treatment" to cure rheumatic illnesses (spa patients only). If you fancy a dip, the old-fashioned Eva swimming pool, 200m further north, is open to the public. From here, the sleek, ultramodern Balnea sanatorium spreads its luxurious wings the full length of the island.

Practicalities

Even if you haven't come here for treatment, you should have few problems finding **accommodation** on the left bank. *Pension Astra*, Pod Párovcami 21 (Štúrovo 0838/772 76 71; ③), is a cheerful guesthouse just a few minutes' walk north of Winterova. Other options include *Hotel Eden*, Winterova 60 (☎0838/762 47 09; ③), with a few cheap rooms in addition to more expensive ones with en-suite bath and satellite TV. Opposite is the pleasant, comfortable *City Hotel* (☎0838/772 54 54; ⑤), with a good restaurant. If these don't suffice, the **tourist office** (Mon–Fri 9am–5.30pm, Sat & Sun 8am–noon; ☎0838/16186) in the *Hotel Eden* can help. **Camping** is possible (May–Sept) at either side of the mouth of the action-packed Sĺňava lake (bus #12 or walk 1km to either), south of town. **Restaurant** prices are a little inflated, but you can get fairly cheap pizzas at *Pizzeria Orchidea*, overlooking the spa park at the end of Park pasáž, a side street off Winterova. Another popular choice with the locals is *Central*, a self-service buffet with draught beer and a patio out the back, plus a more formal restaurant. The obligatory bandstand and spanking-new **Dom umenia** (which puts on plenty of Bach, Mozart, and oom-pa-pa for the foreign guests) are laid out in the nearby Sad Andreja Kmeťa.

THE BLOOD COUNTESS OF ČACHTICE

Born in 1560, **Countess Elizabeth Báthori** was the offspring of two branches of the noble Báthori family, whose constant intermarriage may have accounted for her periodic fainting spells and fits of uncontrollable rage: other Báthoris, such as Prince "Crazy" Gábor, were similarly afflicted. As a child she was intelligent and well educated, being fluent in Latin, Hungarian and German at a time when many nobles, including the ruling prince of Transylvania, were barely literate. Brought up in the family castle at Nagyecsed, a humble town near the Hungarian-Romanian border, she absorbed from her relatives the notion that peasants were little more than cattle – to be harshly punished for any act of insubordination.

As was customary in the sixteenth century, her marriage was arranged for dynastic reasons, and an illegitimate pregnancy hushed up. Betrothed in 1571 – the same year that her cousin István became Prince of Transylvania – she was married at fifteen to twenty-one-year-old Ferenc Nádasdy. Over the next decade Ferenc was usually away fighting Turks, earning his reputation as the "Black Knight", and Elizabeth grew bored at their home in Sárvár Castle. There she began to torture serving women, an "entertainment" that gradually became an obsession. With the assistance of her maids Dorothea Szentes and Anna Darvulia (who was also her lover), Elizabeth cudgelled and stuck pins into servants to "discipline" them; even worse, she forced them to lie naked in the snowy courtyard and then doused them with cold water until they froze to death. On his return, Ferenc baulked at this (although he too enjoyed brutalizing servants), and it wasn't until after his demise in 1604 that Elizabeth started torturing and murdering without restraint. Her victims were invariably women or girls, and – most importantly – always peasants, as killing peasants could be done with impunity. Poor women could always be enticed into service at Beckov and Čachtice – Elizabeth's residences after she quit Sárvár, both then located within the borders of Transylvania – and, should word of their deaths leak out, the authorities could

Čachtice and Beckov

Halfway between Piešťany and Trenčín to the north is the industrial town of Nové Mesto nad Váhom, not a place to hang about in if you can help it, but a necessary halt if you're changing trains or buses to get to the ruined castles of Čachtice and Beckov (see below).

Of the two lofty piles of rubble perched on opposing sides of the Váh, the one at ČACHTICE, 8km southwest of Nové Mesto, has the edge on atmosphere, for it was here that the "Blood Countess" **Elizabeth Báthori** was walled in for almost four years before her death in 1614 to pay for her crimes (see below). Čachtice was her favourite castle; "she loved it for its wildness", wrote one of her posthumous biographers, "for the thick walls which muffled every sound, for its low halls, and for the fact of its gloomy aspect on the bare hillside". The prize exhibit of the village **museum** (May–Oct Tues–Sun 9.30am–4.30pm), an impassive portrait of Elizabeth herself, was stolen in 1990 and has yet to be recovered. The quickest way up to the castle is actually the stiff climb from Višňové train station (15min from Nové Mesto), rather than the two-kilo-metre haul from Čachtice village itself.

There's substantially more of a **hrad** (May–Sept Tues–Sun 9am–1pm & 2–6pm) above the village of **BECKOV**, 5km northeast of Nové Mesto and accessible only by bus. Erected in the twelfth century, this was another of Báthori's torture chambers, ruined by a fire that ripped through its apartments in 1729. The ruins are fun to explore and there's a Jewish cemetery at the base of the castle. If you're in need of refreshment, there's a *reštaurácia* just under the rock, where you can relax and watch the rock-climbers risk life and limb on the cliff below the castle, not to mention a small **folk museum** (Tues–Sun 9am–5pm).

---

hardly believe the accusations of the victims' parents against the Countess Báthori. With the assistance of Szentes, Darvulia, her son's former wet-nurse Helena Jo, and one man, the diminutive Fizcko, Elizabeth allowed her sadistic fantasies full rein. On occasion she bit chunks of flesh from servants' breasts and necks – probably the origin of the legend that she bathed in the blood of virgins to keep her own skin white and translucent.

In this fashion Elizabeth murdered over six hundred women and would probably have continued undetected had Darvulia not died. Grief-stricken, the countess formed an attachment to a local widow, Erzsi Majorová, who encouraged her to seek aristocratic girls for her victims. Enquiries by *their* parents could not be so easily ignored by the authorities, who in any case by now had their own motives for investigating *Die Blutgräfin*. Ferenc Nádasdy had loaned the Habsburg crown 17,000 gulden, which Elizabeth had persistently – and vainly – demanded back. Should she be found guilty of serious crimes this debt would be forfeited. Among Elizabeth's other adversaries were her son Paul, who had grown up apart from her at Sárvár, and one Count Thurzo, both of whom were anxious to prevent the confiscation of the Báthori estates and gathered evidence against her through-out 1610.

On December 29, Thurzo's men raided Čachtice castle, and on entry almost tripped over the corpse of a servant whom Elizabeth had just bludgeoned for stealing a pear. Thurzo secretly imprisoned the "damned woman" in her own castle immediately, so that (in his words) "the families which have won such high honours on the battlefield shall not be dis-graced . . . by the murky shadow of this bestial female". Due to his cover-up the scandal was mainly confined to court circles, although when Elizabeth died in 1614 the locals protested at her burial in Čachtice cemetery. She was later reburied at Nagyecsed in the precincts of the family vault. Due to her sex (then considered incapable of such deeds) and rank, records of her trial were hidden and mention of her name subsequently prohibited by royal command.

Trenčín and around

Despite the usual high-rise accompaniments, **TRENČÍN**, 42km north of Piešťany, is the most naturally appealing of the towns on the Váh. Its central historical core sits below by far the most impressive castle in the valley, best known as the centre of **Matúš Čák's** short-lived independent kingdom. Čák was little more than a rebellious feudal despot who set up a mock royal court, crowning himself "King of the Váh and the Tatras". He supported the young Přemyslid Václav III in his unsuccessful quest for the Hungarian crown, and had John of Luxembourg and the Hungarian King Charles Robert on the run for a number of years. Defeated only once, near Košice, he remained in control of his fief until his death in 1321, and is now happily lauded as one of the first great Slovak heroes.

The Town

Trenčiansky hrad (daily April–Sept 9am–5pm; Oct–March 9am–4pm) itself – part ruins, part reconstruction – is a fiercely defensive sprawl of vaguely connected walls and ramparts on a steeply pitched and craggy site, spectacularly lit at night. Even in its present state, it's a great place to explore, though to visit the recently restored fifteenth-century palace complex, which contains a fairly dull gallery of seals and coats-of-arms, you must sign up for a 45-minute guided tour. Slovakia's one and only **Roman inscription** of any worth was carved into the rock face below the castle (you can see it best from the back of the *Hotel Tatra*), commemorating Marcus Aurelius' victory over the German hordes in 179 AD, when the Romans had a fortified winter camp here known as Laugaritio.

Back down the cobbled lane which leads to the castle, in the elbow of the first sharp bend, is a radiant white-and-yellow **Farský kostol** on its own paved plateau – packed on Sundays, closed the rest of the week. A covered walkway leads down Hradná to the main square, **Mierové námestie**, whose young plane trees give it a Mediterranean feel. Straight ahead is the **Piaristický kostol**, ablaze with the fury of the Counter-Reformation and definitely worth checking out if it's open. Next door in the old monastery is the **Galéria M.A. Bazovského** (Tues–Sun 9am–5pm), named after the Slovak sculptor and painter who died here in 1968 and whose statues stand in the courtyard. Temporary exhibitions are held here beneath the building's surviving stucco ceilings, and on the top floor there's a permanent display of works by local artists, dominated by Bazovský's beguilingly simple depictions of peasant life from the 1930s.

One side of the square is closed by Trenčín's only remaining gateway, the **Dolná brána** – talk while you're walking beneath it and you'll never get married, according to locals. Once through it, take a sharp right and you'll discover the former **synagogue**, a grey hulk of a building – Moorism meets Modernism – completely ransacked during the war, but one of the few in Slovakia to have been fully restored. Now used as an exhibition hall, only the arcaded women's gallery and the vivid-blue painted dome give any hint of its former role.

Practicalities

The **bus** and **train stations** are located next to each other five minutes' walk east of the old town, which can be reached by crossing the park adjacent to the stations. The **tourist office** (April–Sept Mon–Fri 8am–6pm, Sat 8am–1pm; Oct–March Mon–Fri 8am–5pm, Sat 8am–noon; ☎0831/16186), at Štúrovo námestie 10, can help with most problems, and with **accommodation**, which is rather limited. Trenčín's finest **hotel** is the grandiose late-nineteenth-century *Tatra* (☎0831/50 61 11; ⑦), a pricey and plush Canadian-Slovak joint venture at the very northeastern tip of the main square. The only budget option is *Šport*

Hotel (☎0831/53 19 40; ③) on an island in the Váh, beyond the **campsite** (June to mid-Sept); pass under the railway lines and look for signposts pointing off to the right. The *Tatra* has undoubtedly the best **restaurant** in town, or else you could eat at either of the two pretty basic pubs: the *Larnius*, Mierové námestie 20, and the *Plzenská pivnica*, in the Zlatá Fatima shopping arcade off the main square. Passable pizzas can be had at *Pizzeria Venezia*, Hviezdoslavova 4, with a nice outdoor terrace, and *U Kata* on námestie Mierové, which sprawls pleasantly onto the cobbled square in the warm months.

Trenčianske Teplice

While Trenčín bakes down in the valley, **TRENČIANSKE TEPLICE**, 12km northeast, marinates in the green glades of the Teplička Valley. The nicest way to get there is on the narrow-gauge train-cum-tram that trundles up the valley from Trenčianska Teplá, less than ten minutes by train from Trenčín. Alternatively, you could follow the red-marked path 9km across the hills from Trenčín and end your walk with a dip in Bohuslav Fuchs' pool (see below).

The spa itself is little more than a collection of sanatoria, ranging from the typical nineteenth-century ochre mansion of the *Sina* to the concrete *Krym*. The town's most unusual building is the stripy *Hammam* bathhouse, whose Moorish interior is officially open only to male spa guests, though the attendants sometimes let visitors peek into this delightful Turkish bath; enter from the adjoining building around the side to the left. Architecture buffs should check out the *Mahnáč* sanatorium, a top-notch Bauhaus-style building by Jaromír Krejcar. From the same period, Brno-born Bohuslav Fuchs' swimming pool complex, **Zelená žaba** (Green Frog; Mon, Wed & Fri 11.30am–6pm, Tues, Thurs, Sat & Sun 9am–6pm), has a much wider appeal; concealed in some woods to the north of the town and cut into the curve of the hillside, it looks as good as new seventy years on, and swimming in its spring water gives the weird sensation of bathing in warm lemonade. Like all spas, the strenuous stroll is an all-important part of the cure here; so continue up the valley from the Zelená žaba, then, at the *Baračka* restaurant head up to **Heinrich's spring**, and thence on to Krájovec (557m) for the definitive view over the Teplička Valley. The whole trip should take around two hours.

To complement its resort function, Trenčianske Teplice hosts two significant cultural **events** every summer. Art Film is a small international film festival held in mid-June, which nevertheless draws the occasional big-name star; in addition, *Hudobne léto* (Musical summer), spanning mid-June to mid-August, is a series of solo and chamber music performances.

travel details

Trains
Bratislava hlavná stanica to: Brno (8 daily; 2hr); Budapest (8 daily; 3hr); Piešťany/Trenčín (1–2 hourly; 1hr/1hr 30min); Prague (8 daily; 5hr); Štúrovo (9 daily; 1hr 20min–2hr 20min); Trnava (14 daily; 35min); Vienna Südbahnhof (3 daily; 1hr 10min).

Bratislava-Nové Mesto to: Trnava (up to 15 daily; 35–50min); Komárno (6 daily; 2hr–2hr 30min).

Buses
Bratislava to: Brezová pod Bradlom (up to 8 daily; 1hr 30min–2hr 10min); Modra (every 30min–1hr; 35min–1hr); Komárno (up to 8 daily; 1hr 30min); Nitra (every 30–45min; 1hr 30min); Piešťany (hourly; 1hr); Senec (every 30min; 30min); Trnava (every 40min; 1hr); Vienna Schwechat Airport/city centre (7–9 daily; 1hr 10min/1hr 30min).

Trnava to: Nitra (hourly; 1hr–1hr 30min).

CHAPTER NINE

THE MOUNTAIN REGIONS

The great virtue of Slovakia is its mountains, particularly the **High Tatras**, which, in their short span, reach alpine heights and have a bleak, stunning beauty. By far the republic's most popular destination, they are, in fact, the least typical of Slovakia's mountains, which tend on the whole to be densely forested and round-topped limestone ranges. The **Low Tatras** and **Malá Fatra**, for example, are less monumental but also much less crowded and developed.

Geographically speaking, the region splits into two huge corridors, with the Váh valley to the north and the Hron valley to the south. **Banská Bystrica**, in the Hron valley, is one of the many towns in the region originally settled by German miners, and its old quarter is still redolent of those times. Two other medieval mining towns worth visiting are **Banská Štiavnica**, best known for its silver, and **Kremnica**, a gold-mining town set in the nearby hills. For the Slovaks, by far the most important towns historically are **Martin** and **Liptovský Mikuláš**, both situated in and around the Váh valley, centres of the nineteenth-century Slovak national revival and bastions of Slovak nationalism to this day.

In general, though, the towns in the valley have been fairly solidly industrialized and are often best used as bases for exploring the surrounding **countryside**, most easily done by a combination of hiking, cycling and taking the bus. That said, **railways**, where they do exist, make for some of the most scenic train journeys in the country. As for the region's innumerable **villages**, from which many urbanized Slovaks are but one or two generations removed, they're mostly one-street affairs seemingly unchanged since the last century.

Banská Bystrica

Lying at the very heart of Slovakia's mountain ranges, **BANSKÁ BYSTRICA** (Neusohl), is a useful introduction to the area. Connected to the outlying districts by

---

ACCOMMODATION PRICE CODES

All accommodation in this guide is graded according to the price bands listed below. Prices are for the cheapest **double room** available during high season, which usually means without private bath or shower in the less expensive places. For a **single room**, expect to pay around two-thirds the price of a double.

① Under 500Sk	④ 1000–1250Sk	⑦ 1750–2000Sk
② 500–750Sk	⑤ 1250–1500Sk	⑧ 2000–2500Sk
③ 750–1000Sk	⑥ 1500–1750Sk	⑨ 2500Sk and upwards

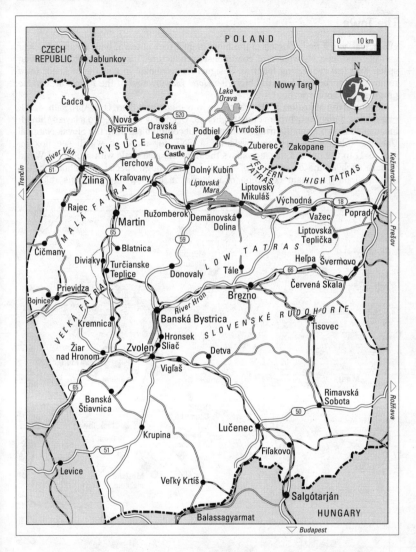

some of the country's most precipitous railways, it's a handsome historic town in its own right, once you've made it through the tangled suburbs of the burgeoning cement and logging industry. A prosperous royal free town in the Middle Ages, Banská Bystrica was the capital of the seven "Hungarian" mining towns colonized by German miners who, in this case, extracted copper from the nearby hills until the seams ran dry in the eighteenth century. Since then, the town has shaken off its Teutonic past, and is perhaps best remembered today as the centre of the 1944 Slovak National Uprising, whose history, lavishly embellished and glorified by the Communists, is now undergoing a more critical reassessment.

The Town

On arrival, you'll find yourself in the monumental part of town, built up after the war and planned as a showpiece of communist architecture. It's a thoroughly alienating space with few redeeming features, designed to culminate in a statue of Lenin (now removed), and behind him, the high-rise *Hotel Lux* (symbol of the town's inexorable progress and sophistication).

Beyond is the **Múzeum SNP** (Tues–Sun May–Sept 9am–6pm; Oct–April 9am–4pm), resembling a giant mushroom chopped in half. Originally dedicated to a lavish though insubstantial display on the triumphant march of communism from the Slovak National Uprising (Slovenské národné povstanie, or SNP, for more on which see box on pp.410–1) to the present day, nowadays the museum also deals with aspects of World War II, such as the deportation of Slovak Jews, through special exhibitions on the ground floor. The main collection of militaria on the top floor remains relatively

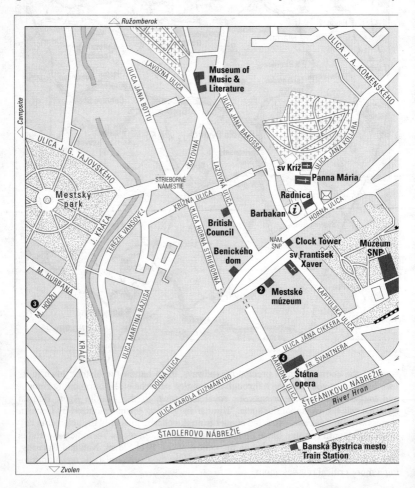

unchanged, but the two multiprojector film and slide shows (shows also in English) have been remade. The current stance is anti-Tiso, with the Communists' huge contribution to the wartime resistance now entirely ignored, though this may change in the future. Whatever the outcome, the impressive facilities create a very powerful exhibition. Outside, between the town's last two surviving medieval bastions, there's a collection of tanks and guns from the uprising.

From the giddy monumental heights of the Múzeum SNP, it's just a short step up Kapitulská to the town's recently restored centrepiece, **námestie SNP**, the old medieval marketplace and still the hub of life in Banská Bystrica. There are lots of cafés from which to soak in the scene and admire the brutal fountain, the Marian column and the charcoal-black obelisk of the Soviet war memorial, though there is talk of replacing this with the square's plague column that was moved in 1964 in preparation for a visit by Khrushchev. A new plaque at the corner of the square and Lazovná commemorates the citizens of Banská Bystrica who were imprisoned under the

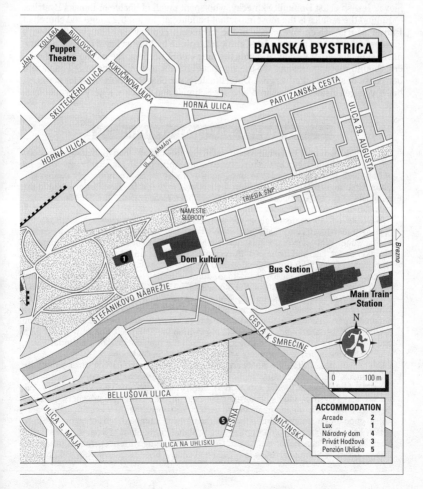

ACCOMMODATION

Arcade	2
Lux	1
Národný dom	4
Privát Hodžová	3
Penzión Uhlisko	5

Communists for their active religious beliefs. One or two of the Renaissance burgher houses bear closer inspection, particularly the so-called **Benického dom** (Venetian House), at no. 16, with a slender first-floor arcaded loggia. The sgraffitoed building opposite is now an art gallery, a few doors down from which is the most imposing building on the square, the honey-coloured Thurzo Palace, decorated like a piece of embroidery and sporting cute oval portholes on the top floor. This now houses the **Mestské múzeum** (Mon–Fri & Sun 9am–noon & 1–5pm), which contains a fair selection of folk and "high" art.

At the top end of the square, beyond the leaning Baroquified clock tower, on námestie Š. Moyzesa, is all that's left of the old castle. The first building in this interesting ensemble is the last remaining **barbakan**, curving snugly round a Baroque tower. Next door, the boxy Renaissance **radnica** (Tues–Fri 9am–5pm, Sat & Sun 10am–4pm) is now the town's main art gallery, which puts on temporary exhibitions from its extensive catalogue of twentieth-century Slovak art, including works by the Slovak Jewish artist Dominik Skutecký, who spent much of his life in Banská Bystrica.

Behind the radnica is the most important building of the lot, the rouge-red church of **Panna Mária**, which dates back to the thirteenth century and contains the town's greatest art treasure, a carved late-Gothic **altarpiece** by Master Pavol of Levoča, in the north side chapel. At its centre stands the figure of St Barbara, the patron saint of miners, though more interesting are the side-panel reliefs, including one of St Ursula and her posse of shipwrecked virgins. Unfortunately, the church is only open for services, but if you get inside, be prepared also for Schmidt and Kracker's fiery German fres-

THE SLOVAK NATIONAL UPRISING

The **Slovak National Uprising** was probably the most costly (and ultimately unsuccessful) operation undertaken by the resistance during World War II. Like the Prague Uprising of May 1945, it was portrayed in unambiguous terms by the last regime as yet another glorious (Communist-inspired) episode in the struggle to defeat fascism. But no event in the minefield of central European history has ever been clear cut, and the SNP is as controversial in its own way as the tragedy of the Warsaw Uprising.

As Hitler set about dismantling the western half of Czechoslovakia in 1938–39, the Slovaks under Jozef Tiso's Catholic People's Party established the first ever independent Slovak state. While for many this represented the fulfilment of a long-held aspiration, Slovakia under Tiso and his militia, the protofascist Hlinka Guards, was little more than a Nazi puppet state. With this realization, and the fact that, whatever the merits of independence, the country was clearly going to go down with the Nazis, Slovaks began to desert the army and join the partisans in the mountains. In December 1943, the Slovak National Council (SNR) was formed by the Communist and non-communist opposition. The London-based Czechoslovak government-in-exile refused to acknowledge the council as a national organ, maintaining that it was only a regional body, such as the 1920 constitution permitted. These arguments continued to rage within the SNR itself, and between the SNR and London- and Moscow-based exiles throughout the preparations for a **national coup**, which Moscow hoped to co-ordinate with the arrival of Soviet troops.

By the summer of 1944, the Soviet army was massed on the Polish-Ukrainian side of the Carpathians, busy parachuting in Soviet partisans and seemingly poised to liberate Slovakia. **Lieutenant-Colonel Ján Golián**, meanwhile, established a secret military centre at Banská Bystrica and began forming partisan units from escaped prisoners and army deserters. But while the mountains were perfect for concealing their activities, they were not so good for communication. In the end, the uprising stumbled into action prematurely, set off by default rather than according to any plan. On the night of August 27, 1944, the German military attaché for Bucharest, General Otto, along with his personal entourage, was captured by Slovak partisans in Martin and shot. It was the most daring and provoca-

coes, the result of heavy Baroquification in the eighteenth century. To the left of the main door, on the exterior of the church, is another Baroque addition, a wonderful 3-D tableau of the Mount of Olives, surrounded by snakes and creepy crawlies, with a premonition of Judas's betrayal in relief above the main scene.

Practicalities

Banská Bystrica's main **bus** and **train stations** are in the modern part of town, ten minutes' walk east of the centre; if you're on a slow train, you can alight at Banská Bystrica mesto train station, just five minutes' walk south of the main square. There's a **tourist office** inside the barbakan (Mon–Fri 8am–7pm, Sat 8am–3pm; ☎088/16186), which can help with **accommodation**. The finest of the **hotels** is the *Arcade* (☎088/430 21 11; ⑧), a converted Renaissance building hidden away down a passageway beside the town's museum. The fourteen-storey communist-era *Lux*, on námestie Slobody (☎088/414 41 41; ⑧), enjoys great views over the town, but is overpriced; the other central option is the late-nineteenth-century *Národný dom* (☎088/412 37 37; ③), on Národná, which has a wonderful café, but is a little dated in decor and facilities and is often full. Two other cheap options are the *Penzión Uhlisko* (☎088/414 56 12; ③), at Lesná 3, across the river from the stations, and the private rooms offered at *Privát Hodžová*, M. Hodžu 5 (☎088/415 31 19; ①; booking essential), east of the old town – walk to the end of Dolná, cross the bridge and turn right on J. Kráľa, then left on M. Hurbana. There's also a **campsite** (open all year), on Tajovského, 1km west of the main square, just by the turn-off to Tajov.

---

tive strike yet, immediately prompting Hitler to demand that Tiso invite the German army into the country, and on August 29, five SS and two Wehrmacht divisions plus sundry other troops entered Slovakia. Events could not be delayed any longer, and the uprising was officially declared by partisan radio from Banská Bystrica.

In the eyes of the Czechs at home and abroad, the Slovaks, by starting the uprising, were at last making amends for their treacherous declaration of independence in 1939, which had helped Hitler to annex the Czech Lands. Yet the majority of Slovaks who took part in the uprising (there were fewer than 500 Czechs involved) were not fighting to restore Czechoslovakia, but to help liberate Slovakia from Tiso and the Nazis. For them the SNR was the new postwar Slovak government in waiting, and when the London-based Czechoslovak government sent a delegate, the Slovaks would only recognize him as a liaison officer, and not as a superior government official. The SNR were fighting to have an equal say in negotiations after the war was over, with a view to perhaps gaining a much greater degree of autonomy, if not independence, in the new postwar arrangement with the Czechs.

Ultimately, however, the uprising failed. The Soviets flew in 2500 paratroopers, along with hundreds of tonnes of weaponry and supplies, Russian advisers, and even a dozen American OSS and British officers. Yet it was not enough, and many blamed the Soviets for not launching a full-scale offensive to relieve the uprising. To be fair, though, their supply lines were already stretched, and breaching the Carpathians was no easy task. In the end, it took the 4th Ukrainian Army over two months and some 80,000 lives to capture the Dukla Pass and reach Svidník, the first major town to be liberated. More disheartening was the Soviet refusal to allow the Allies to use Soviet air bases to drop essential equipment into Slovakia. The Slovaks kept going for almost two months before the Nazis succeeded in entering Banská Bystrica on October 28, but apart from tying down a number of German divisions, it was a costly sacrifice to make. The reprisals went on for months: whole villages were given the "Lidice treatment", and worse – women and children were no longer considered sacrosanct. All in all, well over 30,000 Slovaks lost their lives as a result of the uprising, even though by the end of the uprising, the Soviets had already begun to liberate the country.

Eating options in Banská Bystrica have improved greatly over the last few years. You can grab a freshly baked baguette sandwich at the self-service *Copaline Baguette*, námestie SNP 12, or order soups, salads and ice cream at the *Cechova*, one of many cafés nearby on námestie SNP. *EVIJO*, just down Národná from the main square, dishes out huge pizzas made before your very eyes, or for more traditional Slovak *bryndzové halušky*, head for the *Slovenská pivnica*, Lazovná 18 (closed Sun), whose atmospheric cellar is a favourite with the locals. Also of excellent quality is the *Reštauracia Hungária* at the corner of Horná and Skutečného, with upscale Hungarian/Slovak dining.

Surprisingly for provincial Slovakia, the **nightlife** scene here is fairly active. Most of the cafés on the main square stay open until midnight or beyond, and the *Zlatý bažant*, at no. 11, is a popular watering hole with, no surprise, good Zlatý bažant beer on tap. There's also a collection of beer gardens through the passage at Dolná 36. For all-night dancing, try the passable *Disco Arcade* (open till 5am), beneath the *Cechova*. Look out, too, on fly-posters for any gigs and events at the *Art Klub*, on Rudlovská, northeast of the town centre just before the railway bridge. The **Štátna opera** is the town's bastion of high culture, while the local **puppet theatre** or Bábkové divadlo, on Jána Kollára, has regular shows for adults and kids and occasional performances by foreign touring companies.

South to Zvolen

The wide valley that stretches between Zvolen and Banská Bystrica provides a perfect site for the largest air-force base in the country, used by the Soviets until recently. Zvolen itself is worth visiting for its chateau, which contains one of the finest collections of European Masters in Slovakia. If you're travelling there by train, you could also take in Hronsek and Sliač en route, and given that Banská Bystrica's attractions are fairly limited, all three destinations make for pleasant day-trips.

Hronsek

Two stops further up the track towards Banská Bystrica is the small village of **HRON-SEK**, by the banks of the River Hron. Here, on Hronsecká cesta, west off the road to Sliač, is one of Slovakia's more unusual wooden churches, erected in 1726 on what was originally an island in the river (the two giant lime trees were planted at the same time). With the Counter-Reformation still in full swing, as a Protestant church, it had to be built within a year according to strict guidelines: wood was the only material allowed, which is why there are no metal nails or plaster in the Scandinavian-style timber frame, and the belfry had to be separate. The interior, capable of squeezing in over 1000 worshippers, features seating rather like a theatre in the round. The church is normally kept locked; to get hold of the key, ask around for the local priest. If you'd rather stay out in the countryside, the local chateau, *Kaštieľ Bocian* (☎088/418 83 92; ④) has been nicely converted into a hotel.

Sliač

The nearby airstrip has made little impression on the sleepy hillside spa of **SLIAČ–KÚPELE**, 5km north of Zvolen by train. The springs were initially discovered back in the thirteenth century but were for years considered harmful rather than healing, since locals frequently came across the carcasses of birds and animals near the mouth of the source. Only in the eighteenth century was it discovered that fumes from carbonated waters, although therapeutic for humans, could, in sufficient concentration, asphyxiate small animals. A shot of the waters aside, there's nothing to do or see here as such, beyond a pleasant park, various mapped-out promenades and some far-reaching views across the valley basin. The **train station** lies between the village of Sliač and the spa, to the east, up the hill by the edge of the woods.

Zvolen

Once the effective capital of a Hungarian *župa* or regional district stretching as far as the Orava and Liptov regions, **ZVOLEN** (Altsohl), 20km and a forty-minute train ride south of Banská Bystrica, has come a long way since those halcyon days. Today, Zvolen lives off its logging industry and its key position in the country's road and rail system, and, thanks to the new bypass, Zvolen's wide main thoroughfare, námestie SNP, is now a much more pleasant place to stroll. Although small, the **Vlastivedné múzeum** (Tues–Fri & Sun 9am–5pm), on the west side of the square at no. 43, is actually better than the one at Banská Bystrica, with a good selection of folk art that includes decorated crosses from nearby Detva.

The main reason for coming here, however, is to see the town's four-cornered **zámok** (Tues–Sun 10am–5pm), which squats on a big mound of earth at the southern end of the square, with a makeshift armoured train, built in Zvolen's railway workshops to protect the Slovak National Uprising, situated beneath it. Built in the fourteenth century, the chateau fell to the exiled Czech Hussite leader Jiskra of Brandýs, who for nearly twenty years ruled over much of what is now Slovakia. Later, it became the property of the powerful Esterházy family, and, as the Turks got too close for comfort, it was transformed into the stern fighting fortress it now resembles.

Nowadays, few rooms contain any of their original decor beyond some fine Renaissance portals, though one room boasts a splendid wooden ceiling decorated with no fewer than 78 portraits of successive Holy Roman and Habsburg emperors. The rest of the apartments have been turned into an **art gallery** displaying a decent range of mostly sixteenth- to nineteenth-century European masters belonging to the Slovenská národná galéria, including works by Hogarth, Bruegel, Caravaggio and Veronese. Another section concentrates on Master Pavol of Levoča, easily the most original sculptor of the fifteenth century – a good opportunity to catch his work if you're going no further east – while the top floor hosts temporary exhibitions of Slovak art.

PRACTICALITIES

Zvolen is an easy day-trip from Banská Bystrica, but there are several places to stay, should you wish to, and a **tourist office** (Mon–Fri 8.30–4pm; ☎0855/16186) to help you, east off the main square on Trhová. Zvolen boasts several newly opened **hotels** worth trying, including the very nice *Penzión Quatro* (☎0855/532 32 56; ④) on the main square at no. 32, and the almost as good *Mestsky Hotel* (☎0855/532 51 80; ③) on the second floor of the building next door to the tourist office. A slightly cheaper possibility is *Na námestí* (☎0855/542 91 29; ③), on the west side of the square at no. 37. A short distance along route 66 to Krupina there's the *Neresnica* **campsite** (open all year), with another site by the Motová lake, a couple of kilometres east. For **food**, there's a branch of the ever-popular *Copaline Baguette*, on the east side of the main square, with a pizzeria out the back; the nearby *Jadran* is good for coffee, cakes and ice cream, while the *Victoria*, north of the main square by the main crossroads, is a good place for Zubr beer and pub food.

Banská Štiavnica

High above the Štiavnica river, on the terraced slopes of the Štiavnické vrchy, **BANSKÁ ŠTIAVNICA** (Schemitz), 25km southwest of Zvolen, couldn't wish for a more picturesque setting. An old German-speaking silver- (and gold-) mining town, its historic core has suffered from centuries of sheer neglect. The development of a modern lower town has saved the place in terms of its architecture, but turned the old town into little more than an ancient monument, as lifeless and isolated as it is beautiful. In 1993, however, the town gained UNESCO-protected status, and a concerted restoration effort is slowly taking effect.

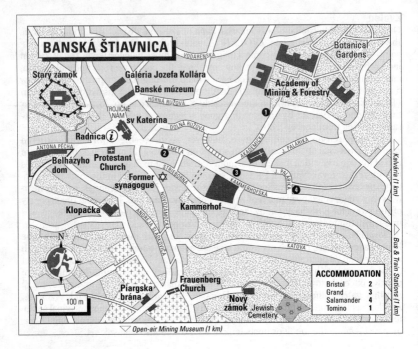

The staré mesto

Banská Štiavnica earned its medieval wealth from the silver deposits discovered here in the thirteenth century. As at Banská Bystrica, skilled German miners were brought in to work the seams, the town was granted special privileges by the Hungarian crown, and the good times rolled – as testified by the handsome burgher houses and the wonderful red marble Trinity column erected on the main square, **Trojičné námestie**. Recently restored to their former glory, their names recall their German heritage: Baumgartner, Rubigall and Hellenbach. The last served as the mining court from the fifteenth century, and now contains the geological section of the town's **Banské múzeum** (Mining Museum; May–Sept daily 8am–4pm; Oct–April Mon–Fri 7am–3pm, Sat & Sun 8am–3pm). Of more universal interest, further up the square in a beautiful sgraffitoed building, is the **Galéria Jozefa Kollára** (May–Sept daily 8am–4pm; Oct–April Mon–Fri 7am–3pm), which puts on interesting temporary exhibitions.

It's worth asking around for the key to the Gothic church of **sv Katerína**, at the bottom of the square alongside the old **radnica** whose Baroque clock tells the time anticlockwise. Lutheranism caught on fast in Slovakia during the Reformation, especially among the German communities, and opposite the radnica is one of the most impressive Lutheran churches in the country, the black-roofed bulk of the **Protestant Church**, gilded urns atop its tympanum, built shortly after the 1781 Edict of Tolerance. Up the steps from the radnica is the fifteenth-century walled **starý zámok** (old castle; May–Sept daily 8am–4pm; Oct–April Mon–Fri 7am–3pm), once the town's most important building. It was built on the same lines as Kremnica's castle (see p.416), as the town's strongbox as well as a fortified residence for the local bigwigs, and the central church-turned-fortress testifies to the panic that beset the Hungarian Kingdom during the peak of Ottoman expansion in the sixteenth century. Currently weed-ridden and undergoing slow but extensive restoration, it houses an exhibit of Baroque sculptures and medieval blacksmiths' works.

Below the castle, Sládkovičova leads past the **Belházyho dom**, a beautifully restored white Renaissance chateau, now a hospital, with an attractive arcaded loggia in the courtyard. Further up Sládkovičova is the seventeenth-century **klopačka** (May–Sept daily 8am–4pm; Oct–April Mon–Fri 7am–3pm), whose wooden "clapper" used to raise the miners from their beds at 5am (nowadays it "claps" at 10am and 2pm during the tourist season only). Inside, it's a low-ceilinged building full of character – one of its functions in the past was as city prison – and packed with displays of miners' lamps and tools. From here the road continues uphill to the red-brick **Frauenberg Church** and the portly Baroque **Piargska brána**, one of the town's former gateways that's now stranded out on the road to Levice, giving an indication of Banská Štiavnica's original size when it was the third largest town in the Hungarian Kingdom.

As further proof of this, there are no fewer than twelve cemeteries in this part of town. On a nearby hillock, the white **nový zámok** (May–Sept daily 8am–4pm; Oct–April Mon–Fri 7am–3pm) – a turreted cross between a sugar lump and a lookout tower – was yet another attempt by the town to guard against a Turkish attack. The Turkish weaponry on display is far from gripping, but there is a map showing the proximity of the Turks at the height of their power, and a viewing gallery with a fantastic panorama of the town.

By far the most interesting section of the town's mining museum is the **open-air mining skanzen** (Banské múzeum v prírode; May–Sept daily 8am–4pm; Oct–April Mon–Fri 7am–3pm), another kilometre beyond the nový zámok, along the road to Levice. Above ground, a cluster of technical exhibits charts the technological innovations of the local mining school (information in German and Slovak only), but the highlight of the museum is the trip down the Bartolomej mine shaft in hard hat and overcoat. The tour of the narrow labyrinthine tunnel network gives a good impression of the appalling conditions medieval miners must have endured, and is not recommended for claustrophobes.

For the best view of Banská Štiavnica, though, head northeast, past the imposing nineteenth-century building of the **Academy of Mining and Forestry**, whose botanical gardens (daily dawn–dusk) boast one of the finest arboretums in Slovakia, replete with Californian redwoods, woodpeckers and tree creepers, to the copper-coloured hilltop church of **Štiavnica kalvária**. The green-marked path zigzags past a succession of Baroque chapels up the hill to the lower church, then on to the summit where the climactic uppermost chapel contains a gruesome, fantastical tableau of the Crucifixion.

Practicalities

Bus connections to and from Zvolen and Banská Bystrica are fairly good, but the scenic **railway**, built by "voluntary brigades" of Communist youth workers back in the 1950s, is easily the most rewarding way of getting to Banská Štiavnica (6–7 trains daily; 1hr from Zvolen – change at Hronská Dúbrava). The station is south of the new town, with the old town a long steep hike away, but buses do a pretty good job of linking the two. Car drivers must buy a *celodenná karta* from one of the shops, restaurants or hotels in order to park (5Sk per hour). Any queries should be taken to the **tourist office** (Mon–Fri 8am–4pm, Sat 8am–2pm; ☎0859/16186), round the back of the radnica.

Banská Štiavnica is justifiably popular with German and Austrian tourists, but there should be little problem getting a **room** for the night at either of the town's two new hotels, the excellent *Salamander*, J. Palárika 1 (☎0859/691 39 92; ④), and equally good *Grand* on Kammerhofská (☎0859/691 37 82; ④). The *Bristol*, A Kmeťa 11 (☎0859/691 13 87; ②), is fine for a night, but lacks atmosphere, while *Penzión Tomino*, up

Akademická (☎0859/692 13 07; ①), has shared facilities, but is perfectly clean and a bargain for budget travellers. There are numerous other pensions and private rooms further out and in neighbouring villages, and campers have a wide choice of **campsites** southwest of the town, in amongst the many artificial lakes; originally built in the eighteenth century as part of the town's ambitious water-pumping project, they're now popular summer bathing spots. The Klinger lake is the local favourite, near the Štiavnické Bane campsite. For **food**, you can't beat the fine soups and great Slovak main dishes prepared by the *Matej*, Akademická 4. The *Salamander* also has a good dining room, and the *Banský dom* is a stylish new café, opposite the tourist office, complete with chandeliers. Other recommendations include the pizza place next door to the *Tomino* and the Asian restaurant within the *Tomino*'s courtyard. For late-night boozing, the *Klub U Červeného Kohúta* on Trojičné námestie has local flavour, while the *Marina* opposite has lots of slot machines.

Kremnica

KREMNICA (Kremnitz) isn't really what you'd expect from a wealthy gold-mining town. Perched on a semi-plateau midway up the Rudnica Valley, it's a surprisingly modest place, little more than its duo of castle and square, and certainly no match for the wealth and beauty of Banská Štiavnica, though it attracts a few more visitors thanks to its gold mint. Accommodation can be something of a problem, particularly during the Festival of Satire and Humour in early September, so it's worth considering coming on a day-trip.

Founded by the Hungarian King Charles Robert in 1320, Kremnica's gold seams were once the richest in medieval Europe, keeping the Hungarian economy buoyant and booming throughout the Middle Ages. The thick walls and bastions that still surround the town and castle were built to protect what was effectively the Bank of Hungary – the royal mint. Yet **Štefánikovo námestie**, the steeply pitched main square on which the mint stands, is now little more than a provincial village green, dotted with pollarded ornamental trees, park benches and a particularly ornate **plague column** which, topped with a flash of gold, is the only obvious reference to the town's wealth. The heavily fortified **Mestský hrad** (May–Sept Tues–Sun 9am–noon & 1–5pm) sits amid fruit orchards above the square, and has recently been restored to sparkling cleanliness. To see it, though, you're supposed to join the two-hour tour – more than enough time to view every room, painting, and statue in the small lower living quarters, plus the richly decorated church of sv Katerína, which takes up most of the upper courtyard. The atypical Gothic nave is broader than it is long, and holds five altars, all bathed in local gold, plus a stupendous 3500-pipe organ. To cap off the tour, you can climb the adjoining tower for superlative views of the grassy square below and lolling hills around. If you don't want to go on the tour, you might be able to coax the ticket-sellers into letting you wander through the grounds on your own, or you can come and hear the organ in action during Sunday Mass (9.15am).

Back on Štefánikovo námestie, there's a **Museum of Coins and Medals** (Múzeum mincí a medailí; May–Sept Tues–Sat 8.30am–5pm, Sun 9am–4pm; Oct–April Tues–Sat 8am–1pm & 1.45–4.30pm) that's been attracting visitors from all around the world since 1890. From Stalin to Churchill, they've all had anniversary Kremnitzerducats minted for them in their time. As well as some exceptionally beautiful Renaissance coins, there's a whole room of paper money, which, during the First Republic, became an art in itself, with designs by top Czech artists like Alfons Mucha and Max Švabinský. The mines still produce a small amount of gold, and the odd commemorative coin is sporadically struck at the **Štátna mincovňa** (State Mint; no admission) on the northwest corner of the square. As an unlikely accompaniment to the coin museum, the **Ski Museum** (Lyžiarske múzeum; May–Sept Tues–Sat 9am–5pm; Oct–April Mon–Fri

8am–1pm), on the west side of the square, has a collection of antique skis, tins of dubbin and a whole range of ski memorabilia.

From Banská Štiavnica, it's simplest to catch a **bus** to Kremnica, but from Zvolen you also have the choice of the **train** with its wonderful views as the track switches back and forth through the hills, climbing over 460m in just 14km before depositing you above Kremnica itself, about a kilometre southeast of the centre. If you do need to stay the night, ask at the **tourist office** (Mon–Fri 8am–noon & 12.30–4pm; mid-June to mid-Sept, also Sat & Sun 8am–noon; ☎0857/16186), in between the double gateway on the south side of the main square. The best hotel in town is the new, well-appointed *Centrál* on Dolná, just outside the double gateway (☎0857/ 674 42 10; ③), with a sauna and a bright restaurant. If this is full, try the *Veterník* (☎0857/74 27 09; ③), a few hundred metres south of the centre on Veternická.

The road to Lučenec

Heading south or east from Zvolen by train takes you through the wilds of southern Slovakia to the Hungarian border. The southbound route 66 to Šahy is the more direct if you're heading for Budapest, but the eastbound route 50 via Lučenec is more interesting. For a start, it takes you past the imposing ruined castle of **Vígľašský zámok**, 15km east of Zvolen, just beyond Zvolenská Slatina. Originally a Gothic castle, later an anti-Turk fortress, and finally an aristocratic manor house, the whole place burnt down during fighting in World War II. The ruins are a stiff, but straightforward climb up from the train station. Another 8km down the tracks is the village of **DETVA**, only really worth visiting in early July when the **folk festival** is on, reputedly one of the best in Slovakia. The traditional skills of the community lie in woodcarving, particularly the *fujara*, a cross between a flute and a bassoon, and an instrument commonly used in folk music right across central Europe.

Lučenec

Some 60km southeast of Zvolen, **LUČENEC** (Losonc) is, for the most part, a scruffy, ramshackle place typical of the border regions, with a population of Slovaks, Magyars and Romanies in roughly equal proportions. It gets few visitors, but if you're passing through it's worth checking out the two churches on the old town square, **Kubínyiho námestie**. Also worth a quick look is the **Novohradské múzeum** (Tues–Fri 9am–5pm, Sat & Sun 1–4pm), on the east side of the square, which puts on interesting temporary exhibitions. You might also take a closer look at the enormous disused **synagogue**, a few blocks south of the square beyond the also disused *Hotel Pelikán*, one of the three that used to serve the town's large prewar Jewish population.

It's a good fifteen-minute walk south along Železnicná from the **bus** and **train stations** to the town centre, but once you've hit T.G. Masaryka, the main drag through town, there are a few places to break your journey. For **food and drink**, try the (daytime only) *Pizzeria Hacienda* on Železnicná itself, or the *T&T* restaurant, T.G. Masaryka 2, which does some interesting Hungarian dishes. Due to its location right near the border, Lučenec has its fair share of **accommodation**, starting with the *Reduta* (☎0863/433 12 37; ⑤), a Best Western chain hotel round the back of the wonderful neo-Gothic shopping precinct on the south side of Kubínyiho námestie. If you're minding your pennies, there's also the *Novohrad*, Novohradská 27 (☎0863/433 12 11; ③), or the even cheaper *P7*, north of the main square at Kármána 22/A (☎0863/ 432 12 55; ②), which is kitschy but acceptable. For local and regional information, head for the **tourist office** (Mon, Tues, Thurs & Fri 8am–noon & 12.30–5pm, Wed 10am–7pm, Sat 8am–noon; ☎0863/433 1513) at T.G. Masaryka 14.

Fiľakovo and beyond

FIĽAKOVO (Fülek), a small Hungarian-speaking town just 13km southeast of Lučenec, is worth a brief stopoff, if only for the extremely photogenic ruins of **Fiľakovský hrad** (daily 9am–6pm), perched on a craggy hilltop in the Romany part of town. If you're heading south for Salgótarján in Hungary, you could also happily spend an afternoon exploring the Dolina Bukovinkého potoka, a gently wooded valley that starts 1km from the Hungarian border. Some 3km along the valley, you come to **Šomošký hrad**, another picturesque ruined castle right on the border, squatting upon vast blocks of eroded volcanic stone. Founded during the fifteenth century, its five towers survey impressive basalt formations, resembling giant organ pipes, some of which form part of a waterfall known as the *kammené vodopad*. Below the castle lies the Hungarian village of Somoskö, to which there is no access.

The Turiec valley

From Kremnica, the railway climbs another 18km or so before hitting the mill-pond flatness of the **Turiec valley**. Having climbed this far up a valley which gets progressively narrower and more dramatic, it comes as something of a surprise to find yourself in such a wide plateau: but for the cool mountain air and the Veľká and Malá Fatra in the distance, you could be back down in the Danube basin.

Turčianske Teplice

TURČIANSKE TEPLICE is the first stop on the railway as it romps across the valley floor to Martin (see opposite). A modern spa town despite its fourteenth-century origins, it boasts very hot natural springs and a striking Bedouin-blue domed nineteenth-century **bathhouse**, the Modrý kúpeľ (closed except to spa patients), with an ornate Moorish treatment. You can wander through the peaceful wooded spa park towards the **Dom Mikuláša Galanda** (Tues–Sun 10am–1pm & 2–5pm), southwest of the centre at Kollárova 74, where the influential Slovak painter Mikuláš Galanda was born in 1895. The home has been converted into a museum, with photos and personal effects of the artist

---

HIKING IN THE VEĽKÁ FATRA

To the east of the Turiec Valley lie the **Veľká Fatra**, a line of craggy mountain tops surrounded by a sea of uninhabited, undulating forest. The ridge of brittle limestone peaks from Krížná (1574m) to Ploská (1532m), via the highest of the lot, Ostredok (1592m), is the most obvious area to aim for, but the thin craggy valleys leading up to the mountains are actually much more enthralling to walk along: the two most accessible and geologically exciting are the **Gaderská dolina** and the **Blatnická dolina**. The return trip along either, including ascending at least one of the big peaks, is a full day's hike (6–7hr); it's a good idea to get hold of a *Veľká Fatra* hiking map. Both valleys begin at **BLATNICA**, one of the most idyllic villages in the Turiec Valley, with half-timbered cottages spread along both banks of the village stream. The local manor house, which features a lovely circular Neoclassical portico, is now a **museum** (Tues–Sun 9am–4pm) dedicated to the great grandfather of Slovak photography, **Karol Plicka**, whose images of the Slovak countryside are reproduced in countless coffee-table books. There are several pensions at the northern edge of the village, a *chata* colony at the entrance to the Gadierská dolina, and a **campsite** (open all year round) 1km south of Blatnica, which can be packed out in the summer season.

to complement a small but vibrant collection of his works. Galanda studied in Budapest, where his early pen-and-ink sketches included cartoons published in the Hungarian magazine *Hárman* between the wars. In the 1920s and 30s, he fell under the spell of Picasso, adopting the Spanish painter's styles in most of his subsequent works. Particularly striking among these are the gloomy Cubist *Pijani* (*Drinkers*), and the touching *Mother with Child and Poppy Flower*. Galanda won a silver medal at the Paris Exhibition in 1937, a year before he died prematurely, in Bratislava, of a stomach ailment.

The town also makes a good base for exploring the Veľká Fatra (the yellow-marked path from the station heads off into the hills), though, unfortunately, most of the town's hotels are filled with guests here for the spa. You could try *Penzión Milka* (☎0841/492 26 31; ③), a bright pink house tucked behind the radnica just off the spa's pedestrianized main street, which offers comfortable **rooms**, plus a sauna and **restaurant**. The nearest **campsite** (mid-June to mid-Sept) is a two-kilometre train journey north at Diviaky, across the river and the highway from the white seventeenth-century country house (closed to the public), but if you've got your own wheels, you'll find more appealing opportunities further north up the valley.

Martin

A town of considerable historic importance for the Slovaks, **MARTIN** and its industrial baggage occupy the last seven kilometres of the banks of the River Turiec before it joins forces with the mighty Váh. Perhaps unfairly, it's best known nowadays for its ZTS engineering works, but while this once had a monopoly on Warsaw Pact tank production, it's struggling to cope in the post-Cold War era and has had to halve its 16,000 workforce. Yet there's more to Martin than a five-minute drive through the town's confusing one-way system might suggest: for example, the country's most encyclopedic folk museum, a better-than-average Slovak art gallery and an open-air folk museum on the outskirts of the town. There's also the possibility of a day's hiking in the less visited southern range of the Malá Fatra, the Lúčanská Fatra (see box p.422).

A brief history

Established back in the fourteenth century, Martin remained the extremely unexceptional town of Turčiansky Svätý Martin until well into the nineteenth century. Then, in 1861, a group of Slovak intellectuals and clergy gathered under the linden tree in front of the Protestant Church and proclaimed the **Martin Memorandum**, which declared boldly that the Slovaks "were as much a nation as the Magyars" and asked the Viennese Parliament to establish a North Hungarian Slovak District (which would remain an integral part of Hungary) with Slovak as the official language.

Their demands caused outrage among the Magyars and were studiously ignored by the Austrians. Nevertheless, a number of important Slovak institutions were founded in the town, of which by far the most important was the **Matica slovenská**, set up to promote the embryonic national culture through education, literature and the arts. It was short-lived. The infamous Ausgleich of 1867, which effectively gave the Hungarians a free hand in their half of the empire, ensured that all Slovak institutions of higher education were closed by the mid-1870s.

During the next forty years of fanatical Magyarization, Martin remained the spiritual centre of the Slovak nation, and on May 24, 1918, Slovak nationalists of all hues gathered for the last time at Martin to sign the **Martin Declaration**, throwing in their lot with the Czechs and scuppering the Hungarians' various proposals for a "Greater Hungary". At this point Martin was still seriously under consideration as the potential Slovak capital: it was centrally located, less exposed to attack and infinitely more Slav than the Austro-Hungarian town of Pressburg (Bratislava), the other main contender, to which it eventually lost out. Since 1989, however, the Matica slovenská has re-estab-

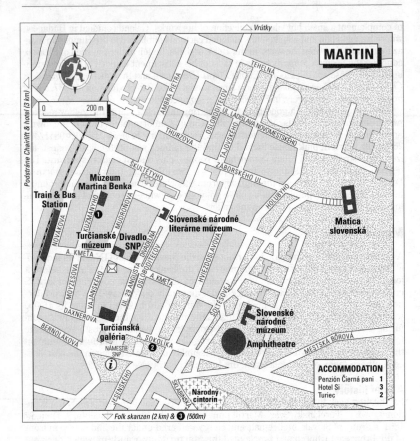

△ Vrútky

MARTIN

N

0   200 m

Podstráne Chairlift & hotel (3 km) ◁

TEHELNA

AMBRA PIETRA

UL. LADISLAVA NOVOMESTSKÉHO

THURZOVA

OSLOBODITEĽOV

TAJOVSKÉHO

ŠKULTÉTYHO

ZÁBORSKÉHO UL.

HOLUBYHO

Múzeum Martina Benku ❶

Train & Bus Station

NOVÁKOVA

KUZMANYHO

MUDRONOVA

Slovenské národné literárne múzeum

Matica slovenská

Turčianské múzeum

Divadlo SNP

A. KMEŤA

DIADEMA

HVIEZDOSLAVOVA

MOYZESOVA

VAJANSKÉHO

UL. 29 ANGUSTA

OSLOBODITEĽOV

A. KMEŤA

SOŤESOVEJ

Slovenské národné múzeum

DAXNEROVA

Turčianská galéria ❷

A. SOKOLÍKA

Amphitheatre

MESTSKÁ BÓROVÁ

BERNOLÁKOVA

NÁMESTIE SNP
ⓘ

JESENSKÉHO

SKLABINSKÁ

Národný cintorín

ACCOMMODATION

Penzión Čierná pani   1
Hotel Si   3
Turiec   2

▽ *Folk skanzen (2 km) &* ❸ *(500m)*

lished itself in the town and is earning Martin a reputation as a hotbed of Slovak nationalism, not to say chauvinism.

The Town

There's not much to choose aesthetically between what might nominally be called the old town in the south and the industrial estates to the north, but the sights are all located in the south. From the train station, Martin's modern chessboard street-plan becomes quickly apparent as you hit the first major crossroads, on which stand the **post office** and the badly managed *Hotel Slovan*, along with the **Turčianské múzeum** (April–Oct Tues–Sun 9am–5pm; Nov–March Mon–Fri 9am–5pm), named after Andrej Kmeť – paradise for your average botanist, geologist or zoologist, but of limited appeal to anyone else. Of more general interest is the **Turčianská galéria** (Tues–Fri & Sun 10am–5pm, Sat 10am–noon), one block south on Daxnerova, which houses a good range of Slovak artists in its permanent collection on the first floor. Works by Miloš Alexander Bazovský, Ľudovít Fulla and Mikuláš Galanda are all featured, while the seminal Martin Benko, who lived and worked in Martin, has a whole room devoted to him – his simple form of Expressionism became a hallmark of much of Slovak art between the world wars. The plain interwar house at Kuzmanyho 34, where Benko lived from 1958 until his death in 1971, is now the **Múzeum Martina Benko** (Tues–Fri 9am–4pm, Sat & Sun 9am–5pm), containing his archive, much of the original furniture and plenty more of his paintings.

Straight ahead, two or three blocks up tree-lined Andreja Kmeťa (which then becomes Muzeálna), is the barracks-like mass of the **Slovenské národné múzeum** (Slovak National Museum; Tues–Sun 9am–5.30pm), which commands a great view of the Malá Fatra from its steps. The museum currently houses the country's Institute of Ethnography and one of the best and most extensive and exhaustive folk collections in the country. Richly decorated costumes and folk artefacts from every region of Slovakia are on display, with Slovak and English captions explaining the exhibits.

On the other side of the open-air amphitheatre, to the south, is the **Národný cintorín**, which, like the Slavín cemetery in Prague, contains the graves of most of the leading Slovaks of the národné obrodenie. It's nothing like as impressive as the Slavín, not least because of the subdued artistry of the headstones, as demanded by Lutheranism, the religion of many of those buried here. Using the master plan near the entrance, you can find the graves of Andrej Kmeť, Janko Kráľ, Janko Jesenský, Martin Benko, Andrej Švehla, Karol Kuzmány and Svet Hurban-Vajanovský, all leading figures in the Slovak society of the nineteenth century.

Neither the old nor the new buildings of the **Matica slovenská**, founded in 1863, are anything to get excited about. The older of the two, on Osloboditeľov, has been nicely restored, and now serves as the **Slovenské národné literárne múzeum** (Slovak National Literary Museum; Tues–Fri 9am–5pm, Sat & Sun 10am–4pm). The Matica's current home, which looks rather like a giant domestic radiator, is easily spotted to the north of the Slovak National Museum.

Perhaps the most rewarding place to visit, though, is the **folk skanzen** (Múzeum slovenskej dediny; May–Oct Tues–Sun 9am–6pm, Nov–April until 5pm), 2km south of town near the Jahodnícky háj (bus #11 or #41, then follow the signs through the apartment blocks and into the woods), which gives some idea of what Martin was like during the nineteenth century. It's also one of the biggest open-air museums in the country and contains buildings from all over Slovakia, even retaining a feeling of some authenticity with a section of shops and homes laid along a road, rather than randomly strewn about.

Practicalities

Only one or two daily trains from Bratislava pass through Martin's small station; most use the train station at **Vrútky**, in a working-class suburb 7km north (numerous buses go from here to the centre of Martin), while local trains to Žilina and Zvolen use both stations. **Accommodation** is not a problem, with at least a couple of cheaper options to challenge the overpriced but comfortable *Turiec* (☎0842/22 10 17; ⑥), near the town's Catholic church on A. Sokolíka. The new *Penzión Čierna pani*, Kúzmanyho 24 (☎0842/334 85; ③), has modestly priced rooms and a popular restaurant, while *Hotel Si* (☎0842/346 59; ②), at Prieložtek 1, just off Jesenského, less than 1km south of the centre, is surprisingly nice inside despite its drab surroundings; hotel beds are cheap, and you can save even more by staying in dorm rooms for 200Sk per person. **Food** options have improved in recent years as well: all the above hotels have good restaurants, and you can get Slovak pizzas at the simply-named *Pizza* restaurant on 29 augusta. This street forms part of Martin's small but nicely restored main square, and is also home to the *Rybarská Reštauracia*, with tables on the square and a menu that goes beyond the usual to include catfish and eel. The nearest **campsite** (mid-May to mid-Sept) is in the woods west of Vrútky; if you have a car, there are two better campsites south of Martin at Jasenská dolina and at Blatnica. The Aices **tourist office** (Mon–Fri 8–11.30am & 1–4pm; ☎0842/16186), just south of the centre on námestie SNP, can help with private accommodation and *chaty*.

WALKING IN THE LÚČANSKÁ FATRA

The southern ridge of the Malá Fatra (see below), the **Lúčanská Fatra**, rises swiftly and dramatically from Martin's westernmost suburbs, making the town a suitable base for ascending the five big, bare peaks of the southern Malá Fatra. If you're staying in town, you can take a chairlift (*lanovka*) from Podstráne, 3km west of town (bus #41), which deposits you just over 1km below the highest peak, **Velká lúka** (1476m); on foot, it'll take nearly four hours. You could also stay in Podstrané at the cheap **hotel** of the same name (☎0842/389 18; ①). Ten kilometres north along the ridge are the ruins at Strečno (see p.424), about a two-hour walk. If you're camping at Vrútky, Martin's northernmost suburb, the nearest peak is the northernmost summit of **Minčol** (1364m).

The Malá Fatra

The **Malá Fatra** are the first real mountains on the road from Bratislava and are one of the most popular and accessible of the Slovak ranges. They are split in two by the sweeping meanderings of the Váh; the northern ridge is by far the more popular, boasting the highest peaks and the most spectacular valley, Vrátna dolina. The southern ridge, including the Lúčanská Fatra, is less geographically pronounced and drifts rather vaguely southwestwards, but contains a couple of non-hiking attractions. Most people use **Žilina** as a base simply because it's on the main line from Bratislava, though in fact it's too far from the mountains to be really convenient. Accommodation in the area is now much easier to come by, but if you're serious about hiking, you'll solve a lot of problems by bringing your own tent.

Žilina and around

Throughout the summer season **ŽILINA** (Sillein) is awash with coach parties, school kids and backpackers, all heading for the mountains of the nearby Malá Fatra. Few bother to venture far from the bus and train stations, though the town itself has a pleasant, compact old quarter, originating from the fourteenth century when the town was colonized by German settlers. The whole place suffered badly during the Thirty Years' War and only really began to recover with the industrial development of this century. In October 1938, the first Slovak government was formed in what became known as the Žilina Accord. It remains a bastion of Slovak nationalism, with the chief of the Slovak National Party, Ján Slota, as its mayor and with the nation's highest percentage of votes for former prime minister and local-boy Vladimír Mečiar's HZDS party.

Between the stations and the old town to the west is **námestie Andreja Hlinku**, featuring a larger-than-life statue of the cleric – *otec národa* (father of the nation) – which now thoroughly upstages the Communist mural on the Farské schody, the steps which lead up to the back end of the Trinity Church. Beyond the church is the old town's main square, **Mariánske námestie**, arcaded for the most part and dominated by the big yellow frontage of the Jesuit church. There are a couple of good cafés from which to admire the square's very Germanic, neat proportions and its fountain fringed by lofty lime trees. Next door to the church, in the old monastery, is a branch of the **Považská galéria** (Tues–Fri 9am–5pm, Sat & Sun 10am–5pm), the main part of which is on the southeast side of námestie Andreja Hlinku.

Practicalities

Few people come to Žilina to sightsee, but a lot of people end up staying here – so many in fact that it may not be easy to get a bed in high season. The local Aices **tourist office**

(Mon–Fri 8am–6pm; ☎089 16186), hidden off Mariánské námestie at Burianova Medzierko 4, can organize private **accommodation** in town or in the mountains themselves. The nicest **place to stay** is the expensive *Astoria* (☎089/62 47 11; ⑦), at the top of Národná by námestie Andreja Hlinku, followed by the new *Grand Hotel*, (☎089/64 32 65; ⑤), just off Mariánské námestie at Sladkovičova 1. The best budget option is *GMK Centrum* (☎089/62 21 36; ③), an office/restaurant/pension through a passage at Mariánske námestie 3; it's worth booking ahead for as there are only three rooms. Otherwise, try the *Penzión Majovej*, Jána Mlca 3 (☎089/62 41 52; ③), which is decent value, with en-suite showers and a location between the bus station and námestie Andreje Hlinku. For **eating out**, there are a handful of outdoor cafés and cellar wine bars on Mariánské námestie, of which the *Radničná vinareň* on the south side is probably the most likeable. The best restaurant in town is that at the *Astoria* hotel, with high ceilings, big windows overlooking the square, and a solid selection of Slovak dishes. Simpler fare and draught beer can be had from the aforementioned *GMK Centrum*, and you can pick up tasty sandwiches from the *Bagetéria* on námestie Andreje Hlinku. If you're here the night and want to eat and drink with the locals, cut a path to the cheap *Kolečko*, ul Jozefa Vuruma 13, or the basement grotto of *Klub pivnice* on Farská in the old town. You can even get online at the **Internet café** on Kálov, just off námestie Andreja Hlinku.

Budatín and Strečno

Two kilometres north of the town centre, on the right bank of the Váh (bus #22 or #24), stands the attractive chateau of **Budatín**, a characteristically hybrid Slovak affair, white-

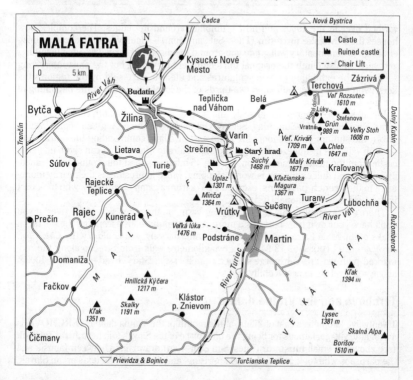

JURAJ JÁNOŠÍK

Juraj Jánošík (1688–1713) is the most famous of the many Robin Hood figures who form an integral part of the songs and folklore of the Slovak mountain regions. Most originate from the turn of the seventeenth century when the central authority of the Habsburgs was at a weak point, worn down by the threat of Turkish invasion. Like many of the rural youth of his generation, Jánošík joined up with the anti-Habsburg army of the Hungarian rebel Ferenc Rákóczi II in 1703. When they were finally defeated by the imperial forces at Trenčín in 1711, large numbers fled into the hills to continue the fight from there. Jánošík, however, opted for the priesthood and left for Kežmarok to complete his religious training. While he was away, his mother fell ill and died, and his father – who had absconded from work in order to build a coffin for her burial – was given a hundred lashes, which proved fatal for the old man. Both parents dead, Jánošík finally took to the hills and gathered round him the obligatory band of merry men, indulging in the usual deeds of wealth redistribution.

Sadly – though this, too, is typical of Slovak folklore – the crucial difference between Robin Hood and characters like Jánošík is that the latter nearly always come to a sticky end. In March 1713 Jánošík was captured by the lords of Liptov, cruelly tortured in an attempt to extract a confession, and sentenced to death in the central square of Liptovský Svätý Mikuláš, where he was hung by the ribcage. It's impossible to overestimate the importance of Jánošík to both the oral and written Slovak literary tradition. More poems, novels and plays have been inspired by his exploits than by any other episode in Slovak history – except perhaps the Slovak National Uprising (see p.410–1).

---

washed over in the 1960s and now crumbling around the edges. The complex now houses the **Považské múzeum** (Tues–Sat 9am–4pm) – a faintly hysterical communist-era English commentary will guide you around the display of carved wooden furniture, and you can also climb the original thirteenth-century tower, but the most interesting section is the exhibition of wire sculptures and utensils once sold by the region's tinkers (who made up an estimated two-thirds of the local population at the beginning of the nineteenth century).

Infinitely more impressive in scale and setting are the fourteenth-century ruins of **Hrad Strečno** (Tues–Sun: May, Sept & Oct 9am–5pm; June–Aug 9am–6pm), which crown the summit of a 200-foot cliff 11km east of Žilina, commanding the entrance to the Váh valley as it squeezes through the Malá Fatra to Martin. You can climb up to the castle from the nearby train station, but the 45-minute guided tour round the cleaned-up insides and dull exhibition is worth skipping. More interesting is the nearby monument to the **French partisans**, escaped POWs from a camp in Hungary, who took part in the 1944 Slovak National Uprising.

There's a **campsite** (July & Aug only) in Varín, on the other side of the river: if you don't have your own transport, it's a more convenient base for ascending the northern peaks of the Malá Fatra than Vrátna dolina. Alternatively, you could try the *Chata pod Suchým* hostel (☎089/69 73 94; ①), a two-kilometre walk from Strečno along the red-marked path via the Váh gorge's other ruined castle, **Starý hrad** – it's over 1000m above sea level, so expect a chilly night.

Terchová and the Vrátna dolina

Twenty-five kilometres east of Žilina, at the mouth of the Vrátna dolina, **TERCHOVÁ** is a neat little village, famous for being the birthplace of the Slovak folk hero **Juraj Jánošík** (see above). A small **museum** (Tues–Sun 8am–4pm) draws links between Jánošík and the partisans who took part in the 1944 uprising, and though all the texts are in Slovak, there's enough local folk art to keep you going, not to mention Jánošík's celebrated brass-studded belt (thought to bring good luck) and jaunty hat. On the low hill overlooking the town stands a giant futuristic aluminium statue of the man himself, one of the many mass-produced in the region. Late July and early August are good times to visit the village, during the international **folk festival** of music and dance – the valley is said to produce a higher than normal concentration of musicians. There are several **hotels** and pensions, including the central *Penzión Covera* (☎089/69 52 63; ②) above a bar, the spanking new *Hotel Terchová* behind it (☎089/69 56 25; ④), and a nice campsite (May–Sept), 3km west of the village in Nižné Kamence. For **food**, try the *Pizzeria U Adama*, just west of the centre, a typical Slovak cottage with a wood-burning oven.

The **Vrátna dolina** actually owes its winsome reputation to the gritty cliffs of **Tiesňavy**, the sharp-edged defile that acts as the gateway to the valley. A fair few buses go this way from Terchová, as well as several daily from Žilina, or it's a gentle twenty-minute walk. After such a dramatic overture, the valley itself is surprisingly sheltered and calm. The road continues a short way south through Lúky, a fairly major ski resort in winter, set against a scenic backdrop of thickly forested hilltops, and on to a smaller resort at Vratná. You can rent skis and bikes at a rental office along this road, some 2km short of Vratná. There's a wide choice of **accommodation** throughout the valley, cheapest of which is the hostel-style *Chata Vrátna* (☎089/69 57 39; ①) by the chairlift in Vratná, but you may do better in Štefanová, a small village at the end of a spur road heading east just before Lúky. Two good-value pensions here are the *Starák* (☎089/69 53 59; ②) and the *Penzión pod Skalným mestom* (☎089/69 53 63; ②), both clean and cosy, and both with **restaurants**.

Hiking around the Vrátna dolina

Most people head south for the **chairlift** at Vrátna, which takes you to Snilovské sedlo, a high saddle between **Veľký Kriváň** (1709m), the highest peak, and **Chleb** (1647m). The views are fantastic from either of the summits, but head away from the chairlift to lose the overwhelming coachloads of day-trippers; you can walk in either direction along the ridge and then head back down to Vrátna. If you're out for the whole day from Žilina, you could descend Chleb's southern face, tracking the blue-marked path that runs via the Šútovský vodopád (waterfall) to Šútovo, fifty minutes by train from Žilina. Otherwise it's over six hours across the peaks to Strečno (see oppsite).

A pleasant alternative to the above is to turn left at the Vrátna dolina fork for Štefanová (2km), in the shadow of **Veľký Rozsutec** (1610m), whose sharply pointed rocky summit is arguably the most satisfying to climb. Follow the yellow-marked path to Podžiar, where you should change to the blue path up **Horné Diery**, an idyllic wet ravine that has to be traversed using ladders and steps. The ravine ends at sedlo Medzirozsutec, the saddle between Malý and Veľký Rozsutec. The ascent takes around four hours, and the descent via sedlo Medziholie about half that.

The Kysuce region

Thirty kilometres north of Terchová, the little-known and little-visited Kysuce region, rubbing up against the Polish border and wedged in between the Malá Fatra and Orava regions to its south and east, respectively, is a tranquil area of rolling hills and small farming and logging towns. To maintain its withering folk traditions, the local authorities have established the open-air **Múzeum kysuckej dediny** (Kysuce folk museum; mid-May to Oct Tues–Sun 9am–5pm) in the hamlet of Vychylovka, near Nová Bystrica, which is well worth a visit if you're in the area. Timbered homes, barns, a functioning mill and a whitewashed church, most dating from the nineteenth and early twentieth centuries, were all rescued from imminent submergence when the nearby dam was built, and have been carefully relocated in a shady green glen. A narrow-gauge railway, originally built in the early twentieth century to carry logs out of the hills, now runs through the *skanzen* and a few kilometres into the hills around. Trains run about every hour from 9am to 3pm – try to visit at the weekend when the original steam engine pulls the single open carriage

Transport to the region is very difficult – only the occasional bus makes it here from Čadca, 25km northwest (alight at Vychylovka-Riečky) – and there is no accommodation anywhere in the vicinity. You can, however, get simple *bryndzové halušky* and cabbage soup at the Krčma z Korne, one of the folk structures. If you're driving, you can continue on to the Orava region by taking the tiny, unsealed mountain road behind the *skanzen*, skirting within 1km of Poland, before linking up with route 520 at Oravská Lesná. Route 520 is permanently closed between Nová Bystrica and Oravská Lesná, even though maps show it goes through.

South of Žilina

Just south of Žilina, along route 64 or the railway, the cement works of Lietavská Lúčka coat the valley with a grey-white dust, before a bend in the River Rajčanka brings you into the verdant wooded spa town of **RAJECKÉ TEPLICE**. For **accommodation**, plump either for the *Veľká Fatra* hotel (☎0823/49 37 27; ⑤) on Osloboditeľov, or the *Erika* pension on Pod jazierkom (☎0823/49 36 53; ②); there's also the primitive but beautifully situated *Slnečné skály* **campsite** (May–Sept), 3km back along the valley (alight at Poluvsie station), and a couple of thermal swimming pools make this a convenient base for a series of day **hikes** in the surrounding hills.

The most obvious is across the valley via the early-twentieth-century chateau of **Kunerad** (closed to the public) and up Veľká lúka (1476m), which overlooks Martin and the Turiec Valley. The blue-marked path is an alternative route back to the spa, and the whole trip is a full day's walk. A more leisurely afternoon's hike north along the green-marked path from the station takes you to the ruined castle of **Lietava**, a shade less spectacular than Strečno but still an impressive pile, some 100m above the village of the same name. The most popular destination, though, is across the hills to the **Súľovské skály** (3hr on the yellow-marked path via Zbyňov), a "rock city" made up of contorted slabs of limestone, with the ruined castle of Súľov at its centre.

Čičmany

ČIČMANY is probably one of the most hyped villages in the whole of Slovakia, and with good reason. Lying in a wide, gently undulating valley, it's a Slovak village *par excellence*: a cluster of typical wooden cottages-cum-farms haphazardly strewn about the banks of the River Rajčanka, which at this point is little more than a mountain stream. What makes Čičmany special, though, is the unique local tradition of **house-painting**, based on the patterns of the locally produced lacework. Each cottage is smothered in a simple, largely abstract, decorative mantle of white snowflakes, flowers and crisscrosses, and the only signs of modernity are electricity, telephone cables and the odd tractor. Only occasional tour groups break the spell, but even they don't stay longer than it takes to visit the small **folk museum** (Tues–Sun 8am–4pm), divided between two of the houses. The disadvantage of Čičmany's isolated position is its inaccessibility; only infrequent **buses** cover the 38km from Žilina, and though you could try hitching, the traffic is light, especially on the last 7km from route 64. Somewhat remarkably, should you make it out here, there are a few **places to stay** – try the shady, arcaded *Kaštieľ* (☎0827/921 97; ②), with its own simple restaurant.

Prievidza and Bojnice

Continuing south for another 30km along route 64 will eventually bring you to **PRIEVIDZA**, an unlovely town after the joys of Čičmany, but an essential stop for those travelling by public transport. The only reason to pause at all in the town itself is to visit the eighteenth-century Piarist church situated between the bus and train stations and the town centre, which contains a spectacular array of trompe l'oeil Baroque ceiling paintings.

Most people, though, are simply passing through en route to the very photogenic **Bojnický zámok** (Tues–Sun: May–Sept 9am–5pm; Oct–April 10am–3pm), which stands on the slopes of a woody hill to the west of Prievidza, in neighbouring **BOJNICE**. From afar, it is indeed an arresting sight, a slice of French pastiche straight out of the Loire Valley, with its conical Gothic turrets and crenellations. In actual fact, what you see now is the result of Romantic reconstructions wrought by the last aristocratic owner, Count Ján Pálffy, who inherited the family pile in 1852. Such pseudo-Gothic splendour may not be everyone's cup of tea, but it sure pulls in the crowds; with some 350,000 visitors a year, this is by far the most popular castle in Slovakia. Ghost sightings are frequent, according to the chateau's efficient PR department, but not half as exciting as the unidentified goo that's been oozing out of Count Pálffy's neo-Romanesque sarcophagus in the castle chapel's crypt over the last few years.

To get to the chateau from Prievidza bus and train stations, take bus #3 or walk the 2.5km. Since Bojnice is not really a viable day-trip from Žilina, you may find yourself spending the night here. If so, your best bet is to head for the **tourist office** (Mon–Fri 8am–6pm, Sat 8am–1pm), námestie Slobody 4, the main square in Prievidza – if you're given a choice, stay in Bojnice rather than Prievidza; *Hotel U Lipa* (☎0862/543 03 08; ②), close to the castle, is a good bet, and it comes with a restaurant. There's also a **campsite** (mid-May to Sept), with nearby swimming pool, in the woods behind the chateau; take the road to Nitrianske Rudno. Those with children may be relieved to know that Slovakia's largest and oldest **zoo** (daily: March & April 7am–5pm; May 7am–6pm; June–Aug 7am–7pm; Sept & Oct 7am–4.30pm; Nov–Feb 7am–3.30pm) is situated beside the chateau.

The Orava region

Despite its wonderful mountainous backdrop and winding river valley, the **Orava region**, northeast of the Malá Fatra and flush with the Polish border, is generally fairly bleak. For centuries it remained an impoverished rural backwater on the main road to Poland, so poor that when the Lithuanian army marched through in 1683 en route to Vienna, they burned most of the villages to the ground (including the former capital of Veličná) in disgust at the lack of provisions. Emigration to America was widespread during the late nineteenth and early twentieth centuries, and after World War II industry was hastily foisted onto the region in an attempt to save it from extinction. As a consequence, the towns are short on excitement and long on eyesores, but the artificial **lake** to the north is recommended for relatively clean swimming, and the **Western Tatras** provide a uniquely unspoilt alpine experience.

Accommodation can be a problem, so it's worth booking ahead from Dolný Kubín, the largest town in the region. Transport relies heavily on the branch line that stretches the length of the Orava valley from Kraľovany on the Váh to Trstená by the Polish border; elsewhere you're dependent on local buses or hitching.

Dolný Kubín and around

The Orava's administrative capital, **DOLNÝ KUBÍN**, is typical of the region, its faultlessly pretty hilly locale lending a kind of surreal beauty to the gleaming white high-rise *paneláky* that house most of the town's residents. Despite its unattractive suburbs, the town makes for a convenient base and stopover, and its main square, Hviezdoslavovo námestie, is pretty and inviting. Here you'll find the town's **museum** (April–Sept

Tues–Sun 8am–3.30pm; Oct–May Mon–Fri 8am–3.30pm), dedicated to the mild-mannered "father of Slovak poetry", Pavol Országh Hviezdoslav (1849–1921), who was born in neighbouring Vyšný Kubín. A few doors down, the **Oravská galéria** (Tues–Sun 10am–5pm) is a surprisingly large gallery of art from the Orava region, located in a spiffed-up Baroque palace and well worth a visit. Chronologically, the gallery starts on the second floor, with several rooms of medieval icons, statuary and some very basic portraits of local noblemen. The focus then leaps to the twentieth century, with mostly local scenes of farmers, shepherds and the Orava hills painted by, among others, Miloš Alexander Bazovský and Mikuláš Galanda. The back rooms of the gallery contain some cutting-edge sculpture – look for Jozef Jankovič's gruesome *Red Wedge* – while the avant-garde theme continues upstairs, with 1980s and '90s Slovak Pop Art predominating. Back down on the ground floor are some more gentle landscape paintings by Maria Medvecká, who hailed from nearby Tvrdošín (see p.430) and had a hand in the establishment of this gallery in 1965. Also down here are some beautiful examples of painted glass and Romantic-era folk sculpture. One other building to note on the square is the blue-and-white former **synagogue**, converted to a cinema during the 1970s, but now containing a plaque dedicated to the town's Holocaust victims.

Dolný Kubín is probably the best place **to stay** in the region, with a fine little pension, the *Marina* (☎0845/586 43 51; ②), located across from the Oravská galéria. If this is full, try the *Severan* (☎0845/586 46 67; ②), just off the main square, which is cleaner inside than its shoddy outward appearance might lead you to believe; if you require more creature comforts such as satellite TV and indoor swimming, head for the reliable *Hotel Park* (☎0845/586 41 10; ⑤), nearby. There's also a **campsite**, the *Geceľ* (mid-May to mid-Sept), with bungalows, 1km or so west along the Orava river. You can book **accommodation** for here, and for further up the valley, through the local Aices **tourist office** (Mon–Fri 8am–noon & 12.30–6pm, Sat & Sun 8am–4pm; ☎0845/16186), just off Hviezdoslavovo námestie. For **food**, the excellent restaurant underneath the *Marina* is highly recommended, and is open until midnight.

Istebné and Leštiny

The giant alloy plant and its attendant quarry at **ISTEBNÉ**, 6km west of Dolný Kubín, appear to offer little respite from the valley's depressing industry. Until a few years ago, the level of dust in the atmosphere was intolerable, regularly blackening the skies over the valley at midday. Only in the mid-1980s, when the local population threatened to move out en masse, were dust separators finally fitted onto the factory chimneys.

Miraculously, the pre-industrial settlement still exists, tucked into the hills to the north, fifteen minutes' walk from the bus and train stations. Among its few remaining wooden buildings, it boasts one of the country's four surviving **wooden Lutheran churches**, built in 1686 on slightly raised ground above the village, with the support of the Swedish king; a separate belfry was added in 1731. Inside, it's richly and prettily decorated with folk painting, especially around the pulpit and on the gallery parapet, which features naive eighteenth-century paintings of the apostles.

In the other direction in **LEŠTINY**, some 8km southeast of Dolný Kubín, there's another wooden Lutheran church, dating back to the late seventeenth century. It's a simple, barn-like structure from the outside, but the interior walls and ceiling are covered in eighteenth-century folk paintings. Once again, the gallery, and even the staircase leading to the pulpit, feature naive religious paintings from the period.

Oravský hrad

Eleven kilometres upstream from Dolný Kubín and accessible by train, **Oravský hrad** (Tues–Sun: May, Sept & Oct 8.30am–4pm; June–Aug 8.30am–5pm) is one of Slovakia's truly spectacular clifftop sights. Perched like an eyrie more than 100m above the village of Oravský Podzámok (literally "Below Orava Castle"), it's an impressive testament to the region's feudal past. Whoever occupied Orava Castle held sway over the entire region and made a fortune taxing the peasants and milking the trade into Poland. You may want to ask about the availability of English-speaking guides before signing up for a tour, as this takes over an hour. Inside, you'll be treated to hearty dollops of folk art, natural history, instruments of feudal justice and Romantic wood-panelled interiors courtesy of the last owners, the ubiquitous Pálffy family. Otherwise you can content yourself with the **mini-museum** of local artefacts in the village before heading on up the valley.

Into the Western Tatras (Západné Tatry)

PODBIEL, thirty minutes by train up the valley from Oravský Podzámok, marks the entrance to the Studená dolina, the valley leading eastwards into the Western Tatras impressively arrayed on the horizon. Many of the village's collection of traditional wooden cottages have been converted into tourist accommodation. Ask at no. 71, on the road to Zuberec, during office hours on the off chance, but it's better to try and book in advance through the Aices tourist office in Dolný Kubín or Zuberec; another alternative is the *Tatria penzion* (☎0847/83 14 23; ②), which also rents out *chaty*. In any case, the only reason to stop at Podbiel is to hitch, walk or catch one of the very few local buses going east up Studená dolina.

Fifteen kilometres east up the Studená dolina, **ZUBEREC** is only worth pausing in if you want to book accommodation through its Aices **tourist office** (Mon–Fri 8am–6pm, Sat 9am–6pm, Sun 10am–5pm). Three kilometres or so beyond lies the **Orava open-air folk museum** (Múzeum oravskej dediny; May–June, Sept & Oct Tues–Sun 8am–4pm; July & Aug daily 8am–5pm; Nov–April Mon–Fri 8am–4pm), a *skanzen* of about twenty traditional wooden buildings from the surrounding area, including a fifteenth-century **wooden Catholic church** from Zábrež, one of the few to escape the pillaging of the local Protestants. Originally built in the fifteenth century, its simple exterior gives no indication of the intricate seventeenth-century folk panel paintings inside, at their best around the main altar. There's an English-language commen-

---

HIKING IN THE WESTERN TATRAS

From **Oravice**, two main trails cover the 6km to the Polish border, of which the blue-marked one is the gentler. Once you reach the border, the blue-marked path will take you onto the ridge between the two countries and up to **Volovec** (2063m) and **Ostrý Roháč** (2084m), 1km from the border. It could easily take four hours to reach the more spectacular scenery around Volovec, making a return trip a full day's hike. If you're carrying a pack, it's possible to drop down onto the blue-marked path to the twin tarns of Jamnicke plesá and then continue for 8km to the Račková dolina **campsite** (May–Oct) or a little further to the *Esperanto* **hotel** in Pribylina; this is probably the quickest way to approach the High Tatras from the Orava region. If you do make it to Pribylina, take a turn around the *skanzen* behind the hotel.

From **Roháčska dolina**, everything happens much more quickly. As you head down the valley the brooding grey peaks begin to gather round and by the end of the road (8km from the *skanzen*; 3km from the final car park) it's only a steep 1.5-kilometre walk on the green path to the still, glacial waters of **Roháčske plesá**, hemmed in by the Tatras' steep scree-ridden slopes. A punishing 2.5km (reckon on about 2hr) along the blue path leads to the Smutne sedlo ("Sad saddle"– sad because it's the mountain's cold north face), which lies on the main Roháč ridge. Ostrý Roháč is less than an hour to the east and **Baníkov** (2178m) the same distance west, but the king of the lot is **Baranec** (2184m), a good two hours' walk to the south.

tary if you want to go round on your own, but you'll get to see more of the interior with a guide.

The Western Tatras

With the High Tatras reaching saturation point during most of the climbing season, the **Western Tatras** (Západné Tatry) are a refreshingly undeveloped alternative. They boast the same dog-tooth peaks and hand-mirror lakes, but with half the number of visitors. The best base is **ŠINDĽOVEC**, 3km beyond the folk *skanzen*, where you'll find the *Hotel Primula* (☎0847/39 50 01; ③) and the *Zverovka* and *Osobitá chaty*. Unless you've pre-booked from Dolný Kubín, however, you may have problems finding a room, though there is some private accommodation and plenty of discreet spots in which to pitch your tent. Alternatively, you could make your base further north, at Oravice, the only official **campsite** (open all year) on this side of the mountains. The main problem is getting to Oravice, which either means catching one of the few buses from Trstená (the last station on the Orava rail line) or walking 7km from the Orava folk *skanzen*. Whatever you do, don't let the logistics get you down – you'll encounter similar problems in the other parts of the Tatras. More importantly, get hold of the *Orava* or better still the *Západné Tatry–Roháče* hiking map, plus the requisite camping gear, and you'll have a smooth trip. Don't, however, undertake any mountain hiking if you've no experience, and always get a weather check before you start on a long walk that goes above 1500m. For more **information** on hiking and climbing, and important **safety hints**, see p.442.

Around Lake Orava

Back at Podbiel, the rail line continues to the village of **TVRDOŠÍN**, which boasts a wooden church containing some fantastic primitive altar paintings, all dating from the fifteenth century. The last stop on the line is **TRSTENÁ**, 6km from the Polish border, which has several accommodation options: the *Skalka* (☎0847/39 27 86; ②), is on the main square, while the ungainly *Košariská* (☎0847/39 32 51; ①) is 2km north, overlooking the lake. If you're moving on to Poland, there's enough traffic to make hitching feasible.

What was once the Orava plain became **Lake Orava** in 1954 when five villages were submerged by the damming of the river. The wooded western shore has a fair smattering of *chata* settlements and two **campsites** (mid-June to mid-Sept). One of the lost villages, **SLANICA**, was the birthplace of an early pioneer of the Slovak language, the Catholic priest Anton Bernolák (1762–1813). Hidden in the trees, on Slanícky ostrov, is the only surviving building, a twin-domed **church of sv Kríž** (June–Sept 9am–5pm) with an attractive Neoclassical loggia set into its facade, now a museum of folk art and ceramics as well as a memorial to Bernolák. To reach the island, take the hourly boat from the pier next to the Slanická osada campsite, or from Námestovo, the big new town to the far west of the lake (and thankfully out of sight from the main recreational area). Standard Slovak food can be had at the *Šalaš*, a typical pub right near the Slanická osada campsite.

The Liptov region

The **Liptov region**, to the south of the Orava region and the Western Tatras, offers a similar cocktail of traditional Slovak villages and depressed industrial towns against a backdrop of spectacular mountains. **Ružomberok**, the first town you come to, at another T-junction on the River Váh, has very little to offer except easy access to the surrounding peaks. East of Ružomberok, the Váh valley widens into a vast, partially flooded plain, whose main town, **Liptovský Mikuláš**, is similarly uninspiring, but the best placed for exploring the Low Tatras.

As in the Orava, the traditional way of life in these parts has disappeared over the last two generations. But while few mourn the demise of subsistence farming, more lament the fact that it was destroyed by forced collectivization and industrialization. Some things survive – the patchwork fields and terraces and the long timbered cottages – but give it a few more decades and the songs, dances and costumes will be of historical and folkloristic interest only.

Ružomberok and around

RUŽOMBEROK (Rosenberg), like so many big towns on the Váh, has more than its fair share of industrial suburbs and ungainly high-rise estates, not to mention a persistent smell of synthetic fabrics that's enough to put most people off. Aside from the **Ľudovít Fulla Gallery**, on Makovického (Tues–Sun 10am–5pm), devoted to Ružomberok's talented painter of the same name, the place to head for is the parish church, pleasantly aloof from the rest of town up the graffiti-filled covered stairway, the *tmavé schody*. Before the war, the local priest was **Andrej Hlinka** (see p.432), spiritual leader of Slovak separatism, *persona non grata* under the Communists but now fully rehabilitated. The church is on raised ground in the centre of town, on a square now named after him. On one corner of the square is another curiosity – a monument in honour of the Scottish academic R.W. Seton-Watson "for defending the Slovak nation", erected in 1937 and miraculously still standing. Close by there's a lovely avenue of lime trees, by far the most attractive part of town.

The **train station** is northwest of the town centre, on the other side of the River Váh (bus #1 or #8). The Aices **tourist office** (April–Sept Mon–Fri 8am–5pm, Sat & Sun 9am–noon; Oct–March Mon–Fri 8am–5pm; ☎0848/16186), at Madačova 3, can assist with finding **accommodation**, most of which is way out of the centre (no bad thing). The most central place is the good-value *Šport Penzión Blesk* (☎0848/32 17 50; ③), fifteen minutes' walk west of the centre at Vajanského 9, which has a pleasant restaurant. Other options include *Hotel Slowaps* (☎0848/32 10 34; ②), west of the centre (bus #4, #6, #7 or #10), and *Hotel Hrabovo* (☎0848/32 87 45; ③), which has a grassy banked lake in which you can swim, but is only accessible via the infrequent bus #3 or by taxi. Behind it, a four-seater cable car will take you, on the hour, to *Hotel Malina* (☎0848/32 50 70; ②), which should be reopened after renovations by the time you read this. For **food**, the best bet in the centre is probably the *Koruna*, Mostová 13, which has a courtyard and cellar dining. You can also pick up fresh *bryndza* (sheep cheese) from a stand underneath the highway, near the end of Mostová.

Around Ružomberok

One of the few redeeming features of Ružomberok is its proximity to the surrounding hills and villages. It's only a three-kilometre walk to the conic peak of **Sidorovo** (1099m) or 5km to **Malinné** (1209m), both of which are accessible via the cable car behind *Hotel Hrabovo* and guarantee extensive panoramas over the Váh and Revúca valleys. Dropping down off the fell on the south side, head for the ribbon village of **VLKOLÍNEC**, on a windy hillside to the south (and thankfully out of view) of Ružomberok. The village is accessible by bus #2 or #7 from Ružomberok to Biely Potok, but the final two-kilometre walk from the bus stop is hard work and you might be better off approaching from Sidorovo or Malinné. This is one of the best environments in which to see Liptov wooden folk architecture, though as ever there's a note of melancholy about the place. It was badly damaged by the Nazis in September 1944 in retaliation for the Slovak National Uprising, but those cottages that remain now form a protected natural *skanzen* of timber structures. One house serves as a museum

ANDREJ HLINKA

Born in the neighbouring village of Černová in 1864, **Andrej Hlinka** served most of his life as a Catholic pastor of Ružomberok. He became a national martyr in 1906 when he was arrested by the Hungarian authorities and sentenced to two years' imprisonment for "incitement against the Magyar nationality", topped up by another eighteen months for "further incitement" in his inflammatory farewell address to the local parishioners.

Although at the time still in prison, he was also viewed by the authorities as the prime mover behind the peaceful demonstration of October 27, 1907, popularly known as the **Černová Massacre**, the "Bloody Sunday" of Hungarian rule in Slovakia. When the local Slovaks protested against the consecration of their church by a strongly pro-Magyar priest, the Hungarian police opened fire on the crowd, killing fifteen people and wounding countless others.

Not long after the foundation of Czechoslovakia in 1918, he began campaigning for Slovak independence, and travelled to Paris on a false Polish passport to press the point at the Versailles Peace Conference. This earned him a spell in a Czechoslovak prison, from which he was only released after being elected leader of the newly founded **Ľudová strana** (People's Party, or HSĽS), strongly Catholic, vehemently nationalistic and the largest single party in Slovakia between the wars. From 1925 to 1928, the HSĽS's electoral clout ensured it a place in the Czechoslovak coalition government. However, the party's nationalist policies were constantly at odds with its collaboration in the Prague-based government, and eventually, in 1928, when the editor of the *HSĽS* newspaper was convicted of treason for publishing a seditious article, Hlinka withdrew from the coalition, never to return.

Hlinka's death in August 1938 was the only thing that saved him from suffering the fate of his successor in the People's Party, Jozef Tiso, who went on to become the Slovak Quisling, as leader of the Nazi puppet government, and was eventually executed as a war criminal in 1947. Nevertheless, his name lived on posthumously in the regime's elite **Hlinka Guards**, the wartime Slovak equivalent of the SS. Under the Communists, Hlinka was a clerico-fascist pure and simple, but since 1989, Slovak nationalists have conducted a concerted campaign to rehabilitate Hlinka, Tiso and company. Most Slovaks are very much in sympathy with such moves, and town councils across the republic have successfully renamed streets and squares after Hlinka. However, when a plaque in honour of Tiso was unveiled in his home town of Bánovce nad Bebravou, above the Catholic teacher-training college he founded, it provoked outrage in many quarters and was eventually removed. Undeterred, the Slovak government went ahead and chose Hlinka as one of the national figures to grace the country's new currency.

(July–Sept daily 9am–6pm), while another provides information (May–Sept Sat & Sun). With your own transport you could also explore nearby **LIPTOVSKÁ ŠTIAVNICA**, east of Ružomberok, whose whitewashed manor house was converted into the local church in 1973 and is worth a look for its shingled onion dome and conical turrets. Before you leave, be sure to appreciate the rare surviving socialist mural entitled "The Battle for Love and Truth".

Liptovský Mikuláš and around

As in Orava, the broad sweep of the main Liptov plain east of Ružomberok has been turned, for the most part, into a vast lake, whose beautiful sandy shoreline is set against the distant backdrop of the Western Tatras. Quite why it deserves the title Liptovská Mara (Liptov Sea) while the one in Orava is simply a lake remains a linguistic mystery, but a similar number of villages bit the dust in the name of "progress". On its easternmost edge sits **LIPTOVSKÝ MIKULÁŠ**, which, like Martin and Ružomberok, once played a part in the Slovak national revival or *národné obrozenie*. Nowadays, it's really only worth coming here if you're intending to explore the Low Tatras.

The Town

The first rumblings of the Slovak national revival in Liptovský Mikuláš occurred in the late 1820s when a Slovak reading room was founded, followed much later by the Tatrín literary society established by the Lutheran pastor Michal Miloslav Hodža, one of the leading lights of 1848. Hodža's house, by the Lutheran church at Tranovského 8, is now a rather uninspiring **museum** (Tues–Fri 8am–2pm), which also touches on the events of May 10, 1848, when some of Mikuláš's leading Slovaks published the "Demands of the Slovak Nation" in response to the Hungarian uprising against the Habsburgs, then quickly fled the country to avoid arrest.

Opposite the museum, in a drab grey concrete building, is the much more palatable **Galéria P.M. Bohúňa** (Tues–Fri 9am–5pm, Sat & Sun noon–5pm), whose spacious interior houses an impressive array of Slovak art. Baroque, Gothic and pre-nineteenth-century works fill the ground floor, but it's the nineteenth- and twentieth-century collection on the top floor that justifies a visit here. In addition to depictions of peasant life by the likes of Martin Benka and Gustáv Mallý, there's a whole room devoted to Bohuň's own portrait of wealthy local burghers. Bazovský and Janko Alexy weigh in with a couple of mystical, almost ghostly canvases, and there are even works by contemporary artists like Rudolf Fila.

A slightly better taste of the literary milieu of nineteenth-century Mikuláš can be had at the **Literárne a historické múzeum Janka Kráľa** (Tues–Fri 9am–4pm, Sat & Sun 10am–5pm), housed in a striking peach-coloured Baroque building on the main square, námestie Osloboditeľov. Local boy Kráľ was the foremost Slovak poet of the Romantic movement, "a lawyer who preferred the company of shepherds", or the Slovak Lord Byron as some would have it. Needless to say, he was a fervent nationalist, and only just escaped being executed for his beliefs in 1848. The museum also contains information on Jánošík, who was sentenced to death in 1713 on the square outside, which currently sports a statue of the local artist Gaspar Belopotocký.

Like many Slovak towns, Liptovský Mikuláš had a large Jewish community before World War II, established back in the early eighteenth century when Jews moved here from Holešov in Moravia. The vast majority of the 885 Jews who were transported to the camps never returned, and there is now a plaque – a hand scraping its nails down a Jewish gravestone – outside the town's huge Neoclassical **synagogue**, which has been partially restored and stands south of the main square on Hollého. Be sure to get hold of the key from the múzeum Janka Kráľa to inspect the starkly beautiful, empty interior.

At **PALÚDZA**, a kilometre west of Mikuláš town centre (bus #2 or #7 from Štúrova), is the *kaštieľ*, in whose dungeon Jánošík was tortured before his public execution on Mikuláš's main square. The largest **wooden Protestant church** in Slovakia (June–Sept daily 9am–5pm; Oct–March; phone ☎0849/559 26 22 to arrange a visit) used to stand opposite, but was transferred in the 1970s to the edge of **LAZISKO**, 5km to the southwest, beyond the village of Svätý Kríž. Built in 1774 for the local Lutheran community without a single nail being used, it's a remarkable building, with a vaguely cruciform groundplan and a weatherboarded exterior. Inside, it seats over two thousand and looks almost new, with decoration only around the pulpit, gallery and organ gallery. There are one or two buses a day from Mikuláš to Lazisko.

Practicalities

The **bus** and **train stations** are next door to each other, a ten-minute walk north of the town centre. The efficient Aices **tourist office** (mid-June to mid-Sept & mid-Dec to March Mon–Fri 8am–7pm, Sat 8am–2pm, Sun noon–6pm; April to mid-June & mid-Sept to mid-Dec Mon–Fri 9am–6pm; ☎0849/16186), on námestie mieru, can help with information and **accommodation** in the Low Tatras. The best central hotels are the comfortable *Elan*, 1 mája 35 (☎0849/551 44 14; ⑥), located east off námestie Osloboditeľov, and the *Janošík* (☎0849/552 27 21; ⑤), between the stations and centre at the corner of Janošíkovo nábrežie and Jilemnického, which is good enough if a little overpriced. If you've got your own transport or don't mind the long walk west of centre, the *Bocian* (☎0849/554 12 76; ③), near the small chateau in Palúdza, is a good choice. Cheapest beds in town are at the *Hotel Si*, 1 mája 117 (☎0849/552 29 11; ①), a twenty-minute walk east of the centre (or take bus #10) amid the apartments and office blocks. The nearest **campsite** (May–Oct) is by the lake at Liptovský Trnovec (20min by bus) on the northern shores of the Liptovská Mara, but if you're aiming to hike in the Low Tatras, you'd be better off at the *Borová Sihot* site (June to mid-Sept) near Podtureň train station, 8km east (10min by train), or the *Bystrina* site (open all year) up the Demänovská dolina (see opposite). There's a very good **restaurant**, *Liptovská izba*, on námestie Osloboditeľov, serving *guláš* and other such Slovak specialities, along with an equally good pizzeria, the *Taverna*, upstairs.

Východná and Važec

The annual **Slovak folk festival** held around late June to early July in **VÝCHODNÁ**, 15km east of Liptovský Mikuláš and thirty minutes by train, is in every way equal to Strážnice's international affair (see p.318), attracting groups from every region of Slovakia. There's no accommodation in the village (a pleasant two-kilometre hike north from the station), but during the festival there's a makeshift campsite, with many more people crashing out in the haylofts and barns of the local farmers (ask first). At any other time of the year, Východná is a modest little village, whose nondescript facades hide an array of interesting wooden buildings.

VAŽEC, one stop further on, was renowned for being one of the most beautiful villages in Slovakia and built almost entirely from wood, until it was destroyed by a catastrophic fire in 1931. However, its former reputation as a photographer's dream means that it is immortalized in many prints on display in the village **folk museum**. The purpose of most visits, though, is the **Važecká jaskyňa** (Feb to mid-May & mid-Sept to Nov Tues–Sun tours at 10 & 11am, 12.30 & 2pm; mid-May to mid-Sept hourly tours 9am–4pm), a limestone cave system discovered back in the 1920s but only recently opened to the public. To get there from the train station, walk to the other side of the village. If you need a place to stay, try the simple *Chata Greguška*, Vyšna 582 (☎0844/29 42 02; ②).

The Low Tatras (Nízke Tatry)

The rounded peaks of the **Low Tatras** (Nízke Tatry) may have less of an immediate impact than the sharp craggy outline of the High Tatras on the northern horizon, but they do constitute a more extensive range, in parts much wilder and less explored. The crudest development is on either side of the two tallest central mountains, **Chopok** and **Ďumbier**, but particularly to the east, the crowds are thin and, with the aid of a hiking map, the countryside is yours for the taking. If you're not planning anything as strenuous as hiking, you could happily spend a day or two visiting some of the **caves** in Demänovská dolina, swimming at the foot of the mountains at Tále or simply riding the chairlift to the top of Chopok and effortlessly soaking up the view.

On the practical front, **accommodation** is now no longer a problem, with plenty of private rooms available and several campsites, though still very few hotels outside the main resorts. **Transport** is also fairly good, with two rail lines serving the Váh and Hron valleys and buses taking you the rest of the way into the mountains: of course, to

HIKING AROUND CHOPOK

Most people start walking from **Chopok** (2024m), the second highest peak in the range, reached by two consecutive (and extremely popular) chairlifts from Jasná (closed May, Oct & Nov). It's about two hours across the bare fell to the top of **Dumbier** (2043m), king of the Low Tatras and the easternmost limit of this central ridge. From Ďumbier, it's six or more hours for each of the following routes: via Krupova hoľa, back down the yellow-marked path to the campsite at the bottom of Demänovská dolina; down Jánska dolina on the blue-marked path to the campsite in Podtureň, or further east to the campsite at Malužiná (turn right either at sedlo Javorie or Pred Bystrou). Westwards, it's about five hours along the ridge to the isolated hamlet of Magurka, which has a *chata* but no official campsite; otherwise it's a good ten hours' walk to the campsite and hotel at Donovaly, at the top of the pass from Banská Bystrica over to Ružomberok.

get the most out of the region, you'll need to walk – preferably armed with the map mentioned above and a stout pair of walking boots.

Demänovská dolina and the caves

Extremely overloaded buses wend their way hourly up **Demänovská dolina**, by far the most popular valley on the north side of the mountains. As soon as you enter the narrow, forested part of the valley, signs point off to the left to the **Demänovská ľadová jaskyňa** (Tues–Sun: mid-May to June & Sept tours at 9.30 & 11am, 12.30 & 2pm; July & Aug hourly tours 9am–4pm), one of Slovakia's two "ice caves". After a sweaty fifteen-minute walk up through the woods to the entrance, there's a chilly forty-minute guided tour through the cave, starting in a vast hall-like chamber of mini-stalactites and stalagmites, its walls covered in eighteenth-century graffiti testifying to the early discovery of the caves. For the final section you descend into the claustrophobic **ice chamber**, where the temperature even in summer is well below zero. Best time to visit, though, is in the spring, when the ice formations are at their best, creating huge stalactites of frozen water which drip down onto a massive frozen lake. Two kilometres further on, signs indicate the **Demänovská jaskyňa Slobody** (Tues–Sun: Jan–May, mid-Sept to mid-Nov and late Dec tours at 9 & 11am, 12.30 & 2pm; June to mid-Sept hourly tours 9am–4pm), used for storage by frostbitten partisans during World War II – hence its name, "Cave of Freedom". It's an iceless cave (though no less freezing), with a much larger and more impressive variety of rock formations than Demänovská ľadová jaskyňa.

A little further on, the road swings violently to the right and begins to climb steeply for about 1.5km until it reaches **JASNÁ**, a major ski resort for this part of the world, with sundry chair and ski lifts, as well as a smattering of **hotels** wedged into the hillsides. The nicest of the bunch is the brand-new *Grand* (☎0849/559 14 41; ⑧), complete with indoor pool, weight room and billiards. The *Liptov* (☎0849/559 15 06; ⑦) and *Junior* (☎0849/559 15 71; ③), both conveniently situated near the chair lifts, are cheaper communist-era resort hotels offering many of the same features, while the smaller and nicely renovated *Mikulášská chata* (☎0849/559 16 72; ⑤) by the lakeside is another good option. It's worth enquiring about vacancies for all the above places beforehand at the Aices tourist office in Liptovský Mikuláš. If you're trying to save money, it's reassuring to know that there are plenty of pensions and private rooms back down in the town of Demänovská dolina, just before the caves, such as the good-value *Kamenná chata* (☎0849/554 81 69; ②), which offers clean double rooms as well as more basic (and even cheaper) dorm accommodation. In fact, Demänovská dolina is generally a more congenial place to be, and the hourly bus up to Jasná makes getting to the slopes a cinch. As for **food**, practically all the hotels in Jasná have restaurants, and the one at *Mikulášská chata* stands out. In Demänovská dolina, the *Koliba* is a typically rustic Slovak pub with a fireplace in front of which to enjoy your mulled wine or a full meal. **Ski rental** is possible both in Demänovská dolina and in Jasná.

Approaching from the Hron valley

If you're coming from Banská Bystrica and the Hron valley, you'll approach the Low Tatras from the south. The Hron valley as far as **BREZNO** has been marred by industry, and the latter only has a few cheap hotels to recommend it, the best of which is the *Mestský hotel Ďumbier* (☎0867/611 26 61; ③), on the main square. There's also a useful **tourist office** (mid-June to mid-Sept Mon–Fri 9am–5pm, Sat & Sun 10am–2pm; mid-Sept to mid-June Mon–Fri 8am–5pm; ☎0867/6114221) in the central museum building on the square.

The main approach to Chopok from this side is via **Bystrá dolina**, the flipside valley of Demänovská dolina. At its southern base is **BYSTRÁ** (bus from Podbrezová station or 5km walk over the hills along the green-marked path from Brezno), a neat village riddled with private accommodation, and with a helpful **tourist office** (daily 10am–6pm). Close by is the **Bystrianska jaskyňa** (Tues–Sun: Jan to mid-May & mid-Sept to Oct tours at 9.30 & 11am, 12.30 & 2pm; mid-May to mid-Sept hourly tours 9am–4pm), the only underground cave system on offer on this side.

If you haven't booked **accommodation** in advance, scour the private rooms and pensions in Bystrá, or head 2.5km up the road to the fully equipped campsite (June to mid-Sept), in the resort known as **TÁLE**. A little further on signs point to the ageing *Hotel Partizán* (☎0867/617 00 31; ⑤), though the nearby *Stupka* (☎0867/617 00 24; ⑤) is better value, with its own swimming pool and sauna, and it can organize bike rental and other outdoor activities. There's also the cheap *Espe* along the road (☎0867/617 00 10; ②), and a wooded **campsite** along the valley road.

Buses can take you (and a whole load of others) to the very northern reaches of the valley, past the *Trangoška* (☎0867/617 00 20; ③), to the beginning of the chair lift. This rises in two stages to the top of Chopok: at the base is the *Hotel Srdiečko* (currently closed); between the two stages is *Hotel Kosodrevina* (☎0867/617 00 15; ⑤). To avoid disappointment you should **book in advance** for these hotels through the tourist office in Brezno or Bystrá. If you're walking from Tále to the main ridge, it'll take you three to four hours along the yellow-marked path to the top of **Dereše** (2003m).

The eastern peaks

East of the central Chopok ridge, the real wilderness begins. The peaks are even less pronounced and rarely raise their heads above the turbulent sea of forest where

---

RAILWAYS AROUND BREZNO

The Brezno area pulls in a fair few railway enthusiasts, not least because the line from **Brezno to Margecany** is one of the country's most scenic, including a 360-degree switchback around Telgárt. In addition, though, the line to Tisovec, to the southeast, includes what is probably the only state-owned **rack-and-pinion** railway in the world, originally built to help trains, heavily laden with iron ore, make the ascent from Pohronská Polhora to Zbojská. Last, but by no means least, there's the Čiernohronská železnica **forest railway**, built in 1896 between Hronec, 8km west of Brezno, to Čierny Balog. This last 17km-long narrow-gauge railway runs only in summer (May to mid-Sept), occasionally pulled by steam locomotives; for details enquire at the Brezno tourist office.

Slovakia's last remaining wild bears, wolves, lynx and chamois hide out. Meanwhile, the villages in the **Hron valley** are still a world of shepherds and horses and carts, with wooden houses surviving here and there among the stone, brick and cement; naturally, there's virtually nothing in the way of conventional tourist facilities. If this has whetted your appetite, the best thing to do is book your accommodation through the tourist offices in Bystrá or Brezno – or pack a tent and provisions and start walking.

The **railway** that climbs the Hron valley is one of the most scenic in the whole country (see box opposite), and if you pick the right train you can travel from Banská Bystrica through the Slovenský raj, finally coming to a halt at Košice, in three to four hours. The slower trains take significantly longer, stopping at even the most obscure villages, such as **HELPA** (1hr by slow train from Brezno), which has just one cheap hotel, *Hotel Helpa* (☎0867/618 62 35; ①). To get the magnificent view from the top of **Veľká Vápenica** (1691m), follow either the yellow- or the blue-marked tracks from the station (2–3hr), making sure the stream is on your right-hand side. One stop further on, **POHORELÁ** lies on the footpath to the next peak along, **Andrejcová** (1519m). The only campsite in the region, *Gindura* (open all year), is close by the next station along, Pohorelská Masa, but camping rough in the hills – while officially discouraged – is unlikely to cause any problems.

A lot of the slower trains pause for breath at Červená Skala, not a bad place to start one of the **best hikes** of the eastern range. Take the road to the village of **ŠUMIAC**, which sits on the broad sweep of the mountainside with a panoramic view west and south over the valley; then follow the blue-marked path up to **Kráľova holľa** (1948m), the biggest bare-topped mountain east of Ďumbier. It's another three hours to **LIPTOVSKÁ TEPLIČKA**, once one of the most isolated communities in the Slovak mountains. If you want to remain in the Hron Valley, there's a hotel and the *Penzión u Hanky* (☎0867/69 41 18; ②) in **TELGÁRT**, 4km from Kráľova holľa (get out at Švermovo-penzión zástavka), where the railway doubles back on itself before climbing to its highest point (999m) shortly before Vernár station, on the edge of the Slovenský raj (see p.458).

The High Tatras (Vysoké Tatry)

Rising like a giant granite reef above the patchwork Poprad plain, the **High Tatras** (Vysoké Tatry) are for many people the main reason for venturing this far into Slovakia. Even after all the tourist-board hype, they are still an incredible, inspirational sight – sublime, spectacular, saw-toothed and brooding. A wilderness, however, they are not. At the height of summer, visitors are shoulder to shoulder in the necklace of resorts at the foot of the mountains, and things don't necessarily improve when you take to the hills. The crux of the problem lies in the scale of the range, a mere 25km from east to west, some of which is shared with the equally eager Poles, and a lot of it out of reach to all but the most experienced climber. This is not helped by the saturation tactics of the tour operators, a logical extension of the region's overdevelopment. Yet when all's said and done, once you're above the tree line, surrounded by bare primeval scree slopes and icy blue tarns, nothing can take away the exhilarating feeling of being on top of the world.

Practicalities

Most fast trains to the Tatras arrive at the **main train station** in Poprad (known as Poprad-Tatry), which is adjacent to the **bus station**. If your budget is tight, it might be worth staying in Poprad (for which see p.439); otherwise, you may as well get straight onto one of the little red electric trains that connect all the main resorts and leave from a separate platform above the main line. There are only a few flights a day from

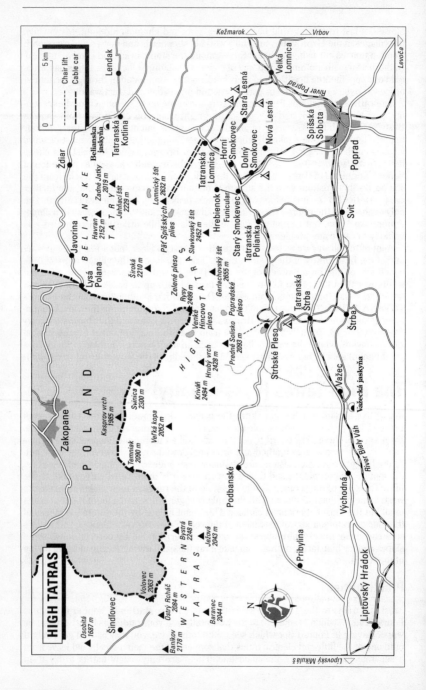

HIGH TATRAS

Chair lift
Cable car

0   5 km

Kežmarok
Vrbov
Levoča

Lendak
Ždiar
Javorina
Lysá Polana
Zakopane

POLAND

Belianska jaskyňa
Zadné Jatky 2019 m
Havran 2152 m
Jahňací štít 2229 m
Lomnický štít 2632 m

Tatranská Kotina

Stará Lesná
Velká Lomnica
Nová Lesná
Spišská Sobota
Poprad

River Poprad

BELIANSKE TATRY

Tatranská Lomnica
Horní Smokovec
Dolný Smokovec
Svit

Paľ Spišských plies
Slavkovský štít 2452 m

Hrebienok
Funicular
Starý Smokovec

Široká 2210 m
Zelené pleso
Rysy 2499 m
Venké Hincovo pleso

HIGH TATRAS

Gerlachovský štít 2655 m
Popradské pleso

Tatranská Polianka

Predné Solisko 2093 m
Strbské Pleso
Tatranská Štrba
Strba

Kasprov vrch 1985 m
Svinica 2300 m
Krivář 2494 m
Hrubý vrch 2428 m

Važec
Važecká jaskyňa

Veľká kopa 2052 m
Temniak 2090 m

River Biely Váh

Osobitá 1687 m
Šindlovec
Banikov 2178 m
Ostrý Rcháč 2084 m
Volovec 2063 m
Bystrá 2248 m
Ježová 2043 m
Baranec 2044 m

WESTERN TATRAS

Podbanské
Pribylina
Vychodná
Liptovský Hrádok

N

Liptovský Mikuláš

Poprad's tiny **airport**, west of the town (take a taxi), which means you need to book in advance to be sure of a place in summer and winter high seasons; make your reservation in Poprad at the ČSA office next door to *Hotel Gerlach*.

Accommodation in the High Tatras

In view of the region's popularity, sorting out **accommodation** should be your priority, though with so many places to stay now available, you should have few problems getting something. Whatever your budget, you should book in advance, or be prepared to take whatever's on offer (within reason); with your own transport, towns like Kežmarok are possible bases (see p.450). The PIA in Poprad (☎092/16 186 or 72 17 00), as well as the Tatranská informačná kancelária (☎0969/442 34 40), T-Ski (☎0969/442 32 00), SATUR and Slovakoturist in Starý Smokovec can all book **pensions** and **private rooms** for around 300Sk per person.

The situation with **hostels** has improved of late; Poprad now has no less than three (see p.441) to accompany the *Juniorhotel* (☎0969/442 26 61; ②) in Horný Smokovec. A fun alternative is the **mountain chaty** dotted across the range, aimed primarily at walkers and therefore often only accessible on foot; prices are around 400Sk per person, and some also serve a limited selection of food in the evening. PIA in Poprad or Slovakoturist in Starý Smokovec have the latest on availability, although to take advantage of anything they offer you'll have to be flexible about your itinerary and plan your hiking around your accommodation.

The cheapest and most reliable option (providing the weather is warm enough) is **camping**, though having said that, the big swanky international sites are among the most expensive in either republic. The best of the dear ones is the *Tatracamp pod lesom* (May–Sept) in Dolný Smokovec (get off at Pod lesom station), with bungalows, hot showers, kitchen facilities and a good restaurant. The two camps – *Eurocamp FICC* (open all year) and *Športcamp* (May–Sept) – just south of Tatranská Lomnica (get off at Tatranská Lomnica-Eurocamp FICC station) are similarly priced but without kitchen facilities, just takeaway roast trout instead. The cheapest and most basic is the *Jupela* site (May–Sept), 1km south of Stará Lesná. If you can get there with your own transport, the *Šarpanec* site (mid-May to mid-Oct), on route 67 between Spišská Bela and Tatranská Kotlina, is relatively secluded, and the *Vrbov* site (July & Aug), to the east, has hidden advantages (see p.452).

Poprad and around

While it would have been difficult a few years ago to dream up a more unprepossessing town than **POPRAD** (Deutschendorf) to accompany the Tatras' effortless natural beauty, local officials have done a good job enlivening the place in preparation for the city's long-shot 2006 Winter Olympic bid. You can't help but notice the great swathe of off-white housing that encircles the town, but much of the old town centre has been fixed up and painted in soft pastel colours to accompany the backdrop of spectacular snowcapped peaks. While it's no great joy to hang around, Poprad is refreshingly free of tour groups and a lot less pretentious than the higher resorts. It's also not a bad place to organize **accommodation** for the rest of your stay in the Tatras.

The Town

Poprad was originally one of the twenty or so Spiš towns (see p.450), though the only clue to this is the long village-like main square, **námestie Svätého Egídia**, a five-minute walk south of the train station. Here you'll find the typical Spiš burgher houses, whose two storeys are distinguished by their stone facades and wooden gables, with eaves overhanging by six feet or so. If you're planning any hiking, you can stock up on provisions at the bakery and small vegetable market on the north side of the square,

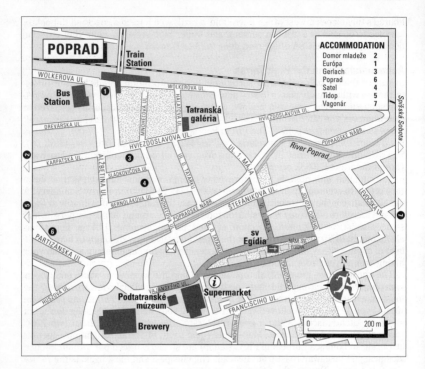

while the south side is taken up with a host of new shops, including a bookshop where you might be able to pick up relevant **maps** – look out for the invaluable *Tatranské strediská* map which contains street plans of all the major resorts (excluding Poprad, which has its own map).

If you have some time to spare, you could pop into one of the town's museums. The **Podtatranské Múzeum** (Tatra Museum; Tues–Sun 9am–4pm) on Vajanského, near the tourist office, traces the history of human settlement in the Tatras from the time of the earliest Neanderthal inhabitants. If this doesn't grab you, you could inspect either of the two branches of the **Tatranská Galéria Poprad**: the new Výstavná sieň (Mon–Fri 9am–5pm, Sat 9am–2pm) at Alžbetina 30 contains nineteenth- and twentieth-century landscape paintings of the Tatra and Spiš regions, while the Elektrarieň (May–Oct daily 10am–6pm), in a former electric plant at Hviezdoslavova 12, focuses on the area's tradition of weaving and folk dress. Otherwise, you can swim at the public pool or bake in the sauna at the public facilities on the corner of Štefáníkova and Športová.

Spišská Sobota

If you do end up staying in Poprad, the village of **SPIŠSKÁ SOBOTA** (Georgenberg), just 2km northeast (bus #2 or #4), makes for an enjoyable outing on a cloudy afternoon. Only a handful of the thousands of visitors who pass through Poprad make it here, yet it couldn't be more different from its ugly, oversized neighbour. Except during Mass on Sundays, there are few signs of life in its leafy square, and only the burgher houses hint at the fact that this was once a thriving Spiš town. At the eastern end of the square, an entire row has been recently renovated and smartly whitewashed, while in the centre huddle the old radnica, the obligatory Renaissance belfry, and the church of **sv Juraj** (St George), whose origins go back even further than its present late-Gothic appearance. Its vaulting is incredibly sophisticated for this part of the world, as are the font and a couple of the smaller chapels, but the real treat is the main **altar** carved by Pavol of Levoča in 1516, which includes a reworking of the famous *Last Supper* predella from the main church in Levoča. If the church is closed, try asking for the key from the Farský úrad (parish council) opposite. The **museum** (Tues–Sun 9am–4pm) at no. 33, on the south side of the square, is worth a look if only to see the inside of a typical town house.

Practicalities

Poprad's **tourist office**, PIA (May–Sept Mon–Fri 8am–6pm, Sat & Sun 8am–1pm; Oct–April Mon–Fri 8.30am–5pm, Sat & Sun 8.30am–1pm; ☎092/16186), at the western end of námestie sv Egídia, can organize private rooms in town and all types of **accommodation** elsewhere in the Tatras. Apart from the *Satel*, on Mnoheľova (☎092/716 11 11; ⑨), which has lots of excellent facilities, the *Poprad* on Partizánská (☎092/72 12 51; ⑦) is the best Poprad can offer in the way of hotels. The communist-era *Gerlach*, (☎092/72 19 45; ③), on Hviezdoslavovo námestie, has decent enough rooms, but a host of shady characters hanging around, and you're best off avoiding the seedy *Európa* (☎092/72 18 83; ②), with its sleazy *kaviareň* and cheap rooms with shared facilities, unless everything else is booked up. However, if you've got your own transport or don't mind taking the bus (#2 or #4), you'll get better value for money and a friendlier welcome at one of the pensions on the main square in Spišská Sobota like *U sv Juraj* (☎092/72 14 11; ②); the latter is also good for a drink or a bite to eat. Poprad's three hostels offer cheap beds and the chance to meet Slovak and Polish travellers: *Tidop* (☎092/776 73 16; ①) is located at the end of Partizánská; *Vagonár*, Rovná 7 (☎092/72 32 25; ①) is at the other end of town down Popradské brigády off the main square; and *Domov Mládeže* (☎092/634 14; ①) sits tight between the square and station on Karpatské.

Eating and drinking in Poprad has improved too. You can grab a baguette sandwich or a salad at the *Astoria*, on ulica 1 mája just off the main square, or wolf down one of the many excellent pizzas or desserts at *Pizzeria Palermo*, Štefáníkovo 4. For a proper sit-down meal, there are two popular folksy restaurants both specializing in traditional Slovak fare: the *Egidius*, opposite the *Satel* on Mnoheľova, has live music and a menu featuring soups and steaks, and the smaller *Slovenská reštaurácia* on ulica 1 mája has a typical Slovak wooden interior. If dancing's your thing, the *Surprise* disco, in the same building as the *Pizzeria Palermo*, has an animated bar as well as billiard tables.

The Tatra National Park (TANAP)

Cute, red, tram-like trains trundle between Poprad and the necklace of resorts and spas that nestle at the foot of the Tatras and lie within the **Tatra National Park** or **TANAP**. To be honest, the resorts are all much of a muchness, a mixture of half-timbered lodges from the last century and tasteless new hotels, all set in eminently civilized spa gardens and pine woods – it's the mountains to which they give access that make them worth visiting.

Hiking around Štrbské Pleso

Founded in 1873 by the local Hungarian lord József Szentiványi, **ŠTRBSKÉ PLESO**'s life as a mountain resort began in earnest some twenty years later, with the building of the rack railway that climbs 430m in just 5km from Štrba on the main line below. At 1351m, it's the highest Tatran resort. It's also the brashest, with reams of takeaway kiosks and eyesore hotel hoardings, though this has more to do with its having hosted the 1970 World Ski Championships than anything else. The ski resort part of town is

HIKING, SKIING AND CLIMBING IN THE HIGH TATRAS

It is as well to remember that the High Tatras are an alpine range and as such demand a little more respect and preparation than other Slovak mountains. Most of the trails described in the text are far from easy, and many involve the use of chains to traverse rock screes. The whole area is part of the **Tatra National Park (TANAP)**, whose often quite strict rules and regulations are designed to protect what is a valuable, fragile ecosystem – you may find that you have to pay a small fee to use some of the trails, so take some small change with you. The most important rule is to stick to the marked paths; before setting out, get hold of a *Vysoké Tatry* **map**, which shows all the marked paths in the TANAP.

In the summer months, the most popular trails and summits are literally chock-a-block with Czech, German and Slovak walkers. One of the reasons for the summer stampede is that many of the most exhilarating treks are only open from July 1 to October 30. This is primarily due to the **weather**, probably the single most important consideration when planning your trek. Rainfall is actually heaviest in June, July and August; thunderstorms and even the occasional summer snowstorm are also features of the unpredictable alpine climate. It may be scorching hot down in the valley, yet below freezing on top of Rysy.

Hiking: the golden rules
* Watch the **weather forecast** (easy enough to read even in Slovak – look for *počasie* in the paper).
* Set out **early** (the weather is always better in the morning), and tell someone when and where you're going.
* Don't leave the **tree line** (about 2000m) unless visibility is good, and when the clouds close in, start descending immediately.
* Bring with you: a pair of **sturdy boots** to combat the relentless boulders in the higher reaches; a **whistle** (for blowing six times every minute if you need help); and a **flask of water**.

Skiing
The High Tatras are as popular for **skiing** in winter as they are for hiking in summer. The first snows arrive as early as November, but the season doesn't really get going for another month. By the end of March, you can only really ski on the higher slopes reached by chair (as opposed to ski) lifts. The main ski resort is Štrbské Pleso, which hosts the occasional international as well as national event; Hrebienok (near Starý Smokovec) and Sklanaté pleso (near Tatranská Lomnica) are the other two main ski areas. Lifts generally run from sunrise to sunset, and while lift operators keep things flowing as smoothly as they can, queues for the lifts can be pretty horrendous at the busiest times – if so, head out to the quieter pistes around Ždiar or even Jezersko in the **Spišská Magura** hills.

Ski hire facilities have improved enormously over the last few years, so if you haven't brought your own equipment, gear can be rented from the likes of Crystal Ski, opposite *Hotel Fis* in Štrbské Pleso. If you've cash to spare and want to have it all planned out before you go, international branches of ČEDOK and other specialist agents organize skiing holidays to the High and Low Tatras (see pp.4 & 12).

Climbing
To go **climbing** (as opposed to hiking) in the High Tatras you need to be a member of a recognized mountain-climbing club and be able to produce a membership card. Otherwise, you are required by law to hire a guide from the Horská služba (see below), which costs a fair amount, though up to five people can share the cost of one guide. It's possible to climb throughout the year, but as with skiing, beware of avalanches. Note that *Cesta uzavretá – nebezpečenstvo lavín* means "Path Closed – Beware of Avalanches". The most popular climbs are in the vicinity of Lomnický štít, but **Gerlachovský štít**, the highest peak in the Tatras, is also high on the hit list.

For **advice** on where to and where not to climb, tips on the weather and emergency help, contact Horská služba, the **24-hour mountain rescue service** next door to SATUR in Starý Smokovec (☎0969/442 28 20 or 442 28 55).

north of the *pleso*, the second largest of the glacial lakes from which the spa gets its name; swimming in the lake is forbidden.

In summer, the only working lift is the chair lift to Solisko, from where the climb to the top of **Predné Solisko** (2093m) takes well under an hour. As with all such lifts in the Tatras, book your ride well in advance to avoid the snake-like ticket queues that have usually formed by mid-morning. If you want to explore a whole ring of mystical glacial lakes – in folk legends known as "the eyes and windows of another sea" – make the trek over **Bystré sedlo** (2314m), which skirts the jagged Solisko range; it's a round trip of around eight hours, and best done anticlockwise, heading from east to west.

A gentle one-hour walk through the forest along the red-marked path to **Popradské pleso** is all many people manage on a lightning Tatra tour. It's a beautiful spot to have a picnic, although given its popularity, by no means tranquil. Those with sufficient stamina can try the punishing hour-long climb to the **sedlo pod Ostrvou** (1959m), which gives a fantastic bird's-eye view of the lake. This red-marked path, known as the Magistrála, skirts the tree line all the way to **Zelené pleso**, 20km away in the far east of the range. If you don't have boundless enthusiasm for walking, stroll along the yellow-marked track to the **symbolický cintorín** of wooden crosses set up to commemorate the considerable number of people who've lost their lives in the mountains.

One of the most popular climbs in the Tatras is **Rysy** (2499m), on the Slovak-Polish border, which Lenin himself once climbed (from the Polish side). If you're planning on conquering Rysy, you won't have time to picnic by the lake, since it's a good six hours' return trip from Popradské pleso via *Chata pod Rysmi* (June–Oct), at 2250m the highest (and coldest) of the mountain chalets, just below the first peak of Váha (2343m). If you can find a place to sit down on the often crowded summit, it has to be one of the best views in Europe. Another possible climb from Popradské pleso is the eight-hour sweep over **Vysoké Kôprovské sedlo** (2180m) via the largest lake of the lot, **Velké Hincovo pleso**; while you're there, it's worth making the effort to take in the summit of Kôprovský (2367m) itself, less than an hour's climb.

Kriváň (2494m), the westernmost High Tatran peak (and, in comparison, relatively easy to climb), is an eight-hour return journey from Štrbské Pleso via Jaňské pleso. In 1841, Slovak nationalists Štúr and Hurban staged a patriotic march up the mountain, a tradition which is continued to this day at the end of August. Like Rysy, it's a popular route swarming with walkers at the height of summer. If that sounds like your idea of hell, try some of the trails around Podbanské or even further afield in the Western Tatras (see p.429).

Starý Smokovec

The old Saxon settlement of **STARÝ SMOKOVEC** (Altschmecks) is the most established and most central of all the spas. Along with neighbouring settlements of Noý, Horni and Dolný Smokovec, it makes up the conglomeration known as **Smokovce**. The spa's old nucleus is the stretch of lawn between the half-timbered supermarket and the sandy-yellow *Grand Hotel*, a sight in its own right. It was built in 1904 in a vaguely alpine neo-Baroque and, though the staff can be a bit snooty, it's worth having a drink in the hotel café, if only to check out the wonderful 1920s decor. There are also two **wooden churches** worth seeking out in Smokovce: the red neo-Gothic parish church behind the *Grand Hotel*, and, in Dolný Smokovec, the turn-of-the-century chapel perching on arcaded stilts.

The best place to head for help with **accommodation** is T-Ski (daily 9am–5pm), up by the cable car (they also hire out skis and bikes), or, failing that, SATUR, on the main street (Mon–Fri 8am–6pm, Sat 8am–noon). The *Grand Hotel* (☎0969/442 21 54; ⑨), with all conceivable amenities, is without doubt the finest guesthouse around, though the *Bellevue* (☎0969/442 29 41; ⑦) is less pricey and runs it a close second. To the east in Nový Smokovec, the distinctive neo-Gothic *Villa Dr Szontagh* (☎0969/442 20 61; ⑥) is a decent, cheaper alternative, as is the *Panda* (☎0969/442 26 14; ⑥) in Horný Smokovec. You can book yourself into a **mountain chata** through

Slovakoturist (Mon–Fri 8am–4pm), a couple of minutes' walk east of the main train station. The self-service **restaurant** in the Central supermarket, and the nearby *Tatra* restaurant, are both okay, and situated just a short step from the train station, though for a proper evening meal, you're better off heading for the *Grand* or the *Szontagh*.

Hikes around Starý Smokovec
If the weather's good, the most straightforward and rewarding climb is along the blue-marked path from behind the *Grand Hotel* to the summit of **Slavkovský štít** (2452m), a return journey of nine hours. Again from behind the *Grand Hotel*, a narrow-gauge funicular climbs 250m to Hrebienok (45min by foot), one of the lesser ski resorts on the edge of the pine forest proper. The smart wooden *Bilíkova chata* (☎0969/442 24 39; ⑤) is a five-minute walk from the top of the funicular. Just past the *chata*, the path continues through the wood, joining up with two others, from Tatranská Lesná and Tatranská Lomnica respectively, before passing the gushing waterfalls of the **Studenovodské vodopády**.

At the fork just past the waterfall, a whole variety of trekking possibilities open up. The right-hand fork takes you up the **Malá Studená dolina** and then zigzags above the tree line to the *Téryho chata*, set in a lunar landscape by the shores of the **Päť Spišských plies**. Following the spectacular, hair-raising trail over the Priečne sedlo to *Zbojnicka chata*, you can return via the Veľká studená dolina – an eight-hour round trip from Hrebienok. This is a one-way hiking path, so you have to do it this way round; note that it involves a 100ft rock climb on a fixed chain, and is not recommended for the faint-hearted. Alternatively, you could continue from the *Téryho chata* to Javorina, nine hours away near the Polish border, and return by bus.

Another possibility is to take the left-hand fork to the *Zbojnicka chata* and continue to Zamruznuté pleso, in the shadow of **Východná Vysoká** (2428m); only a thirty-minute hike from the lake, this dishes out the best view there is for the non-climber of **Gerlachovský štít** (2655m), the highest mountain in Slovakia. To get back down to the valley, either descend the Poľský hrebeň and return to Starý Smokovec via the *Sliezsky dom* (9hr round trip without the Východná Vysoká ascent), or continue north and track the Polish border to Lysá Poľana, the Slovak border post (10hr one-way), returning by bus to Starý Smokovec.

Tatranská Lomnica
TATRANSKÁ LOMNICA, 5km northeast of Starý Smokovec, is a smaller version of the latter. It's a pleasant place to sit out bad weather, and of course gives access to **Lomnický štít** (2632m), the second highest mountain in the Tatras, accessible by a cable car (closed Tues). It's difficult to fault the view from Lomnický štít, but purists may disapprove of the concrete steps and handrails built to prevent the crowds from pushing each other off the rocky summit. If you have problems obtaining tickets for the cable car, try the chair lift to Lomnický sedlo, the craggy saddle 500m below Lomnický štít.

Hiking options are not so good from Tatranská Lomnica, and most treks are best started from other resorts. Otherwise, cloudy days can be filled with horseracing (Sundays only), outdoor chess and the **TANAP museum** (Mon–Fri 8am–noon & 1–4.30pm, Sat & Sun 8am–noon), whose smart displays of stuffed Tatran animals and plants accompany a brief history of the region. It was only explored for the first time in the late eighteenth century when a Scotsman, Robert Townson (see p.464), who was botanizing his way round Hungary, ascended Kežmarský štít and a number of other peaks, against the advice of the local guides.

If you're looking for **accommodation**, there's a free phone by the train station with an information panel detailing your options. *Hotel Lomnica* (☎0969/446 72 51; ③) is an inexpensive, timber-clad place, with few pretensions; *Hotel Wili* (☎0969/446 77 61; ⑤) and *Renomal* (☎0969/446 79 02; ⑥) have both been modernized to a higher standard and are consequently much dearer. For **food**, the *Julia*, down from the train station, is folksy but a good bet nevertheless.

Kotlina, Ždiar and on to Poland

The overkill in the central part of the TANAP makes trekking from the relative obscurity of **TATRANSKÁ KOTLINA** an attractive alternative. Most people, however, come here not to walk, but to visit the **Belianska jaskyňa** (Tues–Sun: Jan–May, mid-Sept to mid-Nov & late Dec tours at 9.30 & 11am, 12.30 & 2pm; June to mid-Sept hourly tours 9am–4pm), fifteen minutes from the main road, whose pleasures include rock formations whimsically named the *Leaning Tower of Pisa* and *White Pagoda*, and an underground lake; another bad-weather time-filler.

The **Zelené pleso** makes a good hiking target, surrounded by a vast rocky amphitheatre of granite walled peaks including the mean-looking north face of Lomnický štít. To get there, take the blue-marked path from the southwest end of Tatranská Kotlina, and turn right onto the green trail which ends at the ruined *chata* by Biele pleso (2–3hr). From here it's half an hour to the fully functioning *Chata pri zelenom*, which sits by the green tarn itself. If you've still got time and energy on your hands, traverse the ridge to the north and mount the summit of Jahňaci štít (2–3hr round trip).

The mountains of the **Belianske Tatry**, which form the final alpine ridge in the north of the TANAP and are home to chamois, have recently reopened to the public and offer an alternative to skirting their southern slopes via the Kopské sedlo (30min on the blue trail from Biele pleso) and then on to Javorina (2–3hr).

On the other side of the Belianske Tatry, slightly off the main road to Javorina (and to Zakopane in Poland), is **ŽDIAR**, a traditional Góral community founded in the seventeenth century, which is now struggling to survive under the ever-increasing pressures of the neighbouring tourist industry. The Górale are fiercely independent mountain farmers, speaking a Polish dialect, the majority of whom live on the Polish side of the border. The village has numerous wooden cottages in varying stages of modernization, a half-timbered cinema and an unremarkable brick church. One of the houses has been converted into a modest Góral folk museum, the **Ždiarska izba** (Mon–Fri 9am–4pm, Sat & Sun 9am–noon), while numerous others, such as *Penzión Deny* (☎0969/449 82 45; ②), near the ski lifts of Bachledova dolina, will provide you with a meal and a bed.

If you're continuing your journey **into Poland**, a daily bus service will take you as far as Lysá Poľana, 12km west of Ždiar. From there you can walk across the border into Poland and catch a bus to the main Polish Tatra resort of Zakopane (see *Poland: the Rough Guide* for details).

travel details

Trains

Bratislava to: Banská Bystrica (2 daily; 3hr 10min–4hr); Liptovský Mikuláš (up to 12 daily; 3hr 30min); Martin (1–2 daily; 3hr); Ružomberok (up to 12 daily; 3hr); Poprad (up to 12 daily; 4hr–4hr 50min); Žilina (17 daily; 2hr–2hr 45min); Zvolen (6 daily; 3hr 20min).

Banská Bystrica to: Brezno (7 daily; 55min–1hr 30min); Červená Skala (4 daily; 1hr 40min–2hr 30min); Martin (4 daily; 1hr 50min); Zvolen (hourly; 20–40min).

Kraľovany to: Istebné/Dolný Kubín/Oravský Podzámok/Podbiel/Trstená (13 daily; 15min/35min/55min/1hr 30min/2hr).

Poprad (Poprad-Tatry) to: Starý Smokovec/Štrbské Pleso (hourly; 45min/1hr 40min); Tatranská Lomnica (up to 15 daily; 25min).

Žilina to: Liptovský Mikuláš (1–2 hourly; 1hr–1hr 30min); Martin (4 daily; 30min–1hr); Poprad (1–2 hourly; 2hr 10min); Rajec (9 daily; 45min); Ružomberok (20 daily; 1hr); Strečno/Šútovo (8 daily; 15min/45min); Vrútky/Kraľovany (8 daily; 30min/ 40min).

Zvolen to: Detva (9 daily; 40min); Kremnica (9 daily; 1hr); Lučenec (11 daily; 1hr–1hr 30min); Turčianske Teplice/Martin (7–10 daily; 1hr 20min–1hr 50min/1hr 40min–2hr 15min).

Buses

Banská Bystrica to: Banská Štiavnica (up to 5 daily; 1hr 30min); Martin/Žilina (up to 8 daily; 1hr

15min/2hr); Ružomberok (up to 5 daily; 1hr 20min).

Liptovský Mikuláš to: Demänovska dolina/ Jasná (hourly; 40min).

Martin to: Turčianské Teplice (hourly; 30min)

Poprad to: Zakopane (1–2 daily; 2hr 15min); Ždiar/Lysá Poľana (hourly; 1hr/1hr 30min).

Žilina to: Banská Bystrica (4–10 daily; 1hr 45min); Čičmany (up to 6 daily; 1hr 20min), Strečno/Martin (up to 12 daily; 30min/45min); Terchová/Vrátna dolina (hourly; 45min/1hr).

CHAPTER TEN

EAST SLOVAKIA

S tretching from the High Tatras east to the Ukrainian border, the countryside of **East Slovakia** (Východné Slovensko) is decidedly different from the rest of the country. The obligatory forests of pine and spruce give way gradually to acres of beech forests in the east, at their best in September and October when the hills turn into a fanfare of burnt reds and browns.

Ethnically, East Slovakia is probably the most diverse region in the country, different groups coexisting even within a single valley. The Polish-speaking **Górale** minority inhabit the Polish border regions as do the **Rusyn** minority, hill-dwelling peasants whose homeland became part of the Soviet Ukraine after 1945. While the Rusyns struggle to preserve their culture and religion in the ribbon-villages of the north and east, the southern border is home to large numbers of **Hungarians**. A third of the country's **Romanies** live here, too, mostly on the edge of Slovak villages, in ghettos of almost medieval squalor. Even the **East Slovaks** themselves are thought of as some kind of separate race by other Slovaks; indeed, before 1918 there was a movement to create a separate state for them.

A short train ride east of the High Tatras, the intriguing medieval towns of the **Spiš region** constitute East Slovakia's architectural high point, while to the south, the **Slovenský raj** offers some highly unorthodox hiking possibilities. Further south still, along the Hungarian border, the karst region of the **Slovenský kras** boasts one of the longest cave systems in the world. Along the northern border with Poland, **Carpatho-Ruthenia** – home of the country's remaining Rusyn population – is a fascinating, isolated landscape riddled with wooden churches, among the few monuments in the region to have survived the destruction of the last war. In fact, the further east you go, the more densely concentrated are the Soviet monuments of former times: retired tanks still line the highways along which they "liberated" Slovakia at the end of World War II, and the plaques and statues that were ripped down after the revolution in other parts of the two republics still stand proudly. After spending time in the rural backwaters, **Košice**, the East Slovak capital, provides a welcome, though somewhat startling, return to city life, containing enough of interest for a stopover at least before heading east towards the Ukrainian border and the deserted beech forests of the **Vihorlat**.

ACCOMMODATION PRICE CODES

All accommodation in this guide is graded according to the price bands listed below. Prices are for the cheapest **double room** available during high season, which usually means without private bath or shower in the less expensive places. For a **single room**, expect to pay around two-thirds the price of a double.

① Under 500Sk	④ 1000–1250Sk	⑦ 1750–2000Sk
② 500–750Sk	⑤ 1250–1500Sk	⑧ 2000–2500Sk
③ 750–1000Sk	⑥ 1500–1750Sk	⑨ 2500Sk and upwards

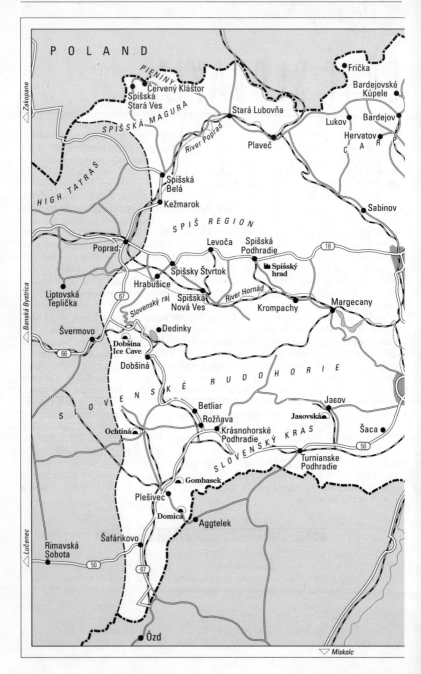

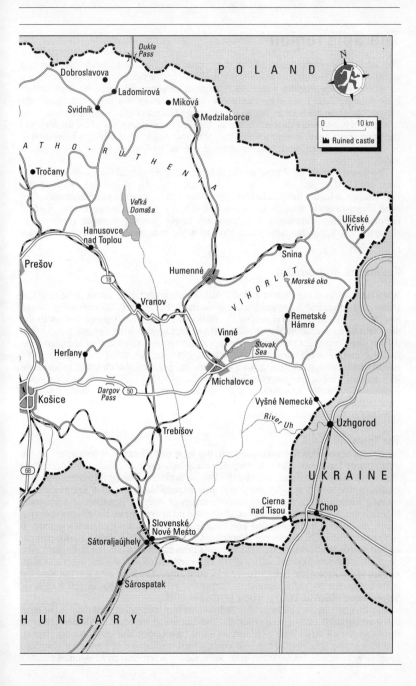

Dukla
Pass

P O L A N D

N

0   10 km

Ruined castle

Dobroslavova

Ladomirová

Miková

Svidník

Medzilaborce

A T H O -
R U T H E N I A

Tročany

Veľká
Domaša

Uličské
Krivé

Hanusovce
nad Toplou

Snina

Prešov

Humenné

V I H O R L A T

Morské oko

18

Vranov

Remetské
Hámre

Vinné

Herľany

Slovak
Sea

Michalovce

Dargov
Pass

50

Vyšné Nemecké

Košice

River Uh

Uzhgorod

Trebišov

U K R A I N E

68

Cierna
nad Tisou

Chop

Slovenské
Nové Mesto

Sátoraljaújhely

Sárospatak

H U N G A R Y

The Spiš region

The land that stretches northeast up the Poprad valley to the Polish border and east along the River Hornád towards Prešov is known as the **Spiš region**, for centuries a semi-autonomous province within the Hungarian kingdom. After a series of particularly devastating Tatar raids in the thirteenth century practically wiped out the local population, the Hungarian kings began to encourage Germans to colonize the area. With the whiff of valuable ore deposits in the air, families from Saxony (to whom the area was known as *Zips*) came in ever greater numbers, eventually establishing a federation of 24 *Zips* towns which were quickly granted special trading privileges and began to thrive.

The Saxon settlers used their wealth to build some wonderful Gothic churches, and later enriched almost every town and village with the distinctive touch of the Renaissance, a legacy that has imbued the towns with an appealing architectural coherence. Tourism aside, though, the whole of the Spiš region, including its tiny residual German-speaking community, and the much larger Romany minority, continues to share the low living standards which have been the rule throughout East Slovakia for the last century.

Kežmarok and around

Just 14km northeast of Poprad and still within view of the High Tatras, **KEŽMAROK** (Käsmark) – its name is derived from "cheese market" – is one of the easiest Spiš towns to visit. It's an odd place, combining the distinctive traits of a Teutonic town with the dozy feel of an oversized Slovak village. If you've visited nearby Spišská Sobota (see p.440), you'll recognize the familiar signs of a Spiš town: wooden gables, shingled overhanging eaves and big barn doors. Kežmarok, however, has the added attractions of a Renaissance castle, a fascinating town museum and a remarkable clutch of buildings on its southern fringe. Like the chief Spiš town, Levoča (see p.454), with which it has a long-standing rivalry, Kežmarok was a royal free town, but whereas Levoča remained loyal to the crown, Kežmarok was a consistent supporter of the rebel cause in the seventeenth and eighteenth centuries.

The Town

From whichever direction you approach, the view of Kežmarok is dominated by the giant, gaudy **Lutheran Church** (May–Oct daily 9am–noon & 2–5pm; Nov–April Tues & Fri 9am–noon & 2–4pm), built by the Danish architect Theophil Hansen, who was funded by the town's wealthy merchants and responsible for much of late-nineteenth-century Vienna. It's a seemingly random fusion of styles – Renaissance campanile, Moorish dome, Classical dimensions, all dressed up in grey-green and rouge rendering – but one of which Hansen, and presumably his patrons, were particularly fond. If you're accustomed to the intense atmosphere of the country's Roman Catholic churches, the simple whitewashed hall looks like it's been ransacked. On the right-hand side, swathed in the wreaths and sashes of the Hungarian tricolour, sits the tomb and mausoleum of the Protestant Hungarian rebel **Count Imre Thököly**, who had the Imperial army on the run for eight years or so during the anti-Habsburg Kuruc revolt of 1678, before being exiled to Turkey, where he died in 1705.

To gain entry to the Lutheran church you must buy your ticket next door in the even more remarkable, though significantly less imposing **wooden Lutheran church** (times as above), again built by a German – this time Georg Müttermann from Poprad. It abides by the strictures of the 1681 edict, which stipulated that Protestant churches could only be erected outside the town walls. Constructed entirely of wood, it couldn't be further from the Viennese cosmopolitanism of its neighbour. The interior, capable of seating almost 1500 people, is a work of great carpentry and artistry, now thoroughly restored and rendered in smooth, cream-coloured plaster.

One more building here deserves mention: the **Lutheran Lycée**, architecturally fairly nondescript but historically and culturally significant. Lutheranism, which was rife in the nether regions of the Hungarian Empire, especially those parts colonized by Germans, was also the religion of many of Slovakia's leading nineteenth-century nationalists. The Czechophile Pavol Šafárik, the poet Martin Rázus, and the writer Martin Kukučín all studied here before the Hungarians closed it down in the 1860s.

The old town itself is little more than two long, leafy streets punctuated by a mixture of plane and fir trees radiating out in a V-shaped fork from the big, boxy, Neoclassical radnica at the centre. The town's fifteenth-century Catholic church of **sv Kríž** is tucked away in the dusty back alleys between the two prongs; once surrounded by its own line of fortifications, it's now protected by an appealing Renaissance belfry, whose uppermost battlements burst into sgraffito life in the best Spiš tradition. The church itself has been recently restored, and is well worth a look inside, not least to admire the exquisite net vaulting, and the sixteenth-century main altar, which comes from the workshop of Pavol of Levoča.

The **zámok** (Tues–Sat 9am–4pm), at the end of the right-hand fork, is the main reason for the occasional Tatran tour group. For many years the property of the Thököly family, it was confiscated by the Habsburgs as punishment for their support of the aforementioned Kuruc revolt. It's impressively fortified with round towers, bulwarks, bastions and decorative Renaissance crenellations, but the museum of historical artefacts that now occupies its bare rooms doesn't really justify the hour-long guided tour. A much more interesting half hour can be spent in the nearby **Múzeum Kežmarok** (Tues–Sat 9am–noon & 1–5pm), housed in a late-seventeenth-century timber-framed house at Hradné námestie 55 (ask for the *anglický text*). The museum contains, among other things, the personal effects of Countess Hedviga Mária Szirmayova-Badányiova (1895–1973), last survivor of the aristocratic Badányi family. In among the beautiful gowns and period furniture, there's a brass samovar from Tula, and lots of luxury goods imported to the town to satisfy the tastes of the local wealthy German and Hungarian burgher families.

Finally, if you've time to spare, you could do worse than take a quick turn under the sycamore trees of the vast local **cemetery**, just off the ring road (at this point called Toporcerova, and the main road from Poprad), which gives out great views of the Tatras on a clear day. It's a fascinating testament to the diverse nationalities – Polish, Hungarian, German and Slovak – that have inhabited the region over the last century. The remaining Slovak peasantry continue to honour their dead with simple wooden crosses, while the vestigial German community, or *Karpathendeutschen* as they're known, stubbornly stick to their own language; *Ruhe Sanft!* (Rest in Peace) is to be seen on the more recent headstones, not just on the ornate, rusting, turn-of-the-century graves belonging to the now displaced German and Hungarian elite.

Practicalities

Arriving in Kežmarok by train is by far the most pleasant introduction to the town, thanks to the yellowing late-nineteenth-century station (there's also a regular bus service from Poprad). Kežmarok is near enough to the High Tatras to figure as a possible base for exploring the mountains, providing you have your own transport. Few people bother to do this, though, so **accommodation** is fairly easy to find. The **tourist office** (Mon–Fri 8.30am–noon & 1–5pm, Sat 9am–2pm), on the main square at Hlavné námestie 46, can book cheap private rooms; otherwise the best option is the excellent *Hotel Club,* on ulica MUDr Alexandra (☎0968/52 40 51; ⑤), an efficiently run, tastefully modernized place right in the old town, with an excellent restaurant on the ground floor. Cheaper options include the *Štart* (☎0968/52 29 15; ②), which lies in the woods to the north of the castle, a good twenty-minute walk from the train station.

Strážky

Just 4km northeast of Kežmarok on route 67, on the outskirts of the village of **STRÁŽKY** (Nehre), is the Slovenská národná galéria's furthest-flung outpost, the pretty little Renaissance chateau of **Kaštieľ Strážky** (Tues–Sun 10am–5pm). Unfortunately you have to go on a guided tour in order to visit the chateau (ask for the *anglický text*), which was rather brutally converted following the death of the last inhabitant, the countess Margita Czóbel. The large gallery of nineteenth-century portraits by the likes of Peter Bohúň and Dominik Skutecký is less interesting than the collection of works by **Ladislav Medyánszky** (1852–1919) – aka Medňanský – the wayward son of the local baron, who spent his youth in the bohemian Paris of the 1870s. His landscapes are reminiscent of early Impressionists like Corot, but his depictions of local peasants, gypsies and beggars are much more severe, and full of insight. The **countess Margita Czóbel** was herself something of an amateur artist, producing some winsome pen and ink drawings and watercolours in the 1920s. She was also clearly quite a character, enjoying daily swims in the local river until her death aged 81, and entertaining Alain Robbe-Grillet during the filming of *L'Homme qui ment* in the 1960s (there are photos in the chateau to prove it).

Vrbov

Five kilometres south of Kežmarok is the village of **VRBOV**. Without your own set of wheels, you'll have to rely on the infrequent bus service from Kežmarok and Poprad. The village itself is no more than a couple of grubby streets and the obligatory Romany ghetto, but continuing on the road south, the rather dubious smell of bad eggs emanates from the nearby sulphurized **natural spring swimming pool** (termálne kúpalisko; daily 8am–10pm). It's an extremely popular spot in the height of summer, when, during the evening, the pool becomes something of a floodlit social centre as the locals immerse themselves in the fizzy, steaming, therapeutic water. Should you wish to stay, there's a **campsite** (July & Aug) beyond the pool, but it's not the best of sites, not least because of the steep bank on which you have to pitch your tent.

Spišský Štvrtok

Ten kilometres south of Vrbov, and clearly visible on the road between Poprad and Levoča, is **SPIŠSKÝ ŠTVRTOK** (Donnersmark), whose splendid thirteenth-century church sits atop the village hill, its masonry tower topped by an impressive wooden spire with four corner pinnacles. The perfect French late-Gothic side chapel, built by Master Puchsbaum and tacked onto the south wall of the church, was commissioned by the Zápoľskýs in 1473 as the family mausoleum, and is, without doubt, one of the most surprising architectural sights in East Slovakia.

Stará Ľubovňa and the Pieniny

From Kežmarok, the railway draws a wide semicircle as it follows the Poprad river round to Stará Ľubovňa, a scruffy and somewhat forlorn town marginally better placed than Kežmarok for approaching the **Pieniny**, a small eruption of fissured limestone rocks that straddles the Dunajec river. As early as the 1930s, the Polish and Czechoslovak governments declared this the **Pieniny National Park**, or PIENAP, and today, despite the continuing isolation of the Zamagurie region (Zamagurie means literally "behind the Spišská Magura hills"), tourism in the Pieniny on both sides of the border is flourishing, particularly the ever-popular **raft trips** down the Dunajec (see box opposite).

RAFT TRIPS IN THE PIENINY

Raft trips are big business for the Góral folk on both sides of the Dunajec. Weather permitting, the rafting season runs from early May to late October, operating between 8.30am and 5pm from May to August, but finishing earlier in the last two months. In addition to the regular raft trips there's a canoe slalom competition on the river held over the first weekend in September, and a folk festival in mid-June.

As soon as you arrive at **ČERVENÝ KLÁŠTOR** (Unterschwaben), head for the ticket booths along the river, where various tour operators relieve you of your money (200Sk per person) and give you a departure time and ticket (the earlier you get here, the less likely it is you'll have to queue). Each *plť* (raft) is made up of five log pontoons lashed together with rope and capable of carrying up to ten passengers, plus two navigators, who are dressed up in the traditional Góral rafters' costume. Though the waters are not particularly rapid, the river winds through beautiful rocky scenery, and the guides can be a barrel of laughs. River meanderings make the whole excursion about an hour in length, but if you'd prefer to do your own thing, the trip can be made on foot by following the red-marked path 10km along the tree-lined river bank.

At the end of the gorge, you can organize for a bus to ship you back, catch a taxi or else walk 3km along the road to Lesnica, then 5km across the hills back to Červený Kláštor, where there's a **campsite** (mid-June to mid-Sept) and, nearby, a fourteenth-century **Carthusian monastery** (April & Oct Tues–Sat 10am–4pm; May–Sept Tues–Sun 9am–5pm), which contains valuable sixteenth-century murals. In the nineteenth century, the monks here compiled the first Slovak grammar and the first complete Slovak translation of the Bible. The nearest **hotel** is the *Pltník* (☎0964/25 25; ①), about 1km upriver, near which at least one other raft operator puts to water.

Stará Ľubovňa

STARÁ ĽUBOVŇA (Altlublau) itself has little to detain you, but if you've time to spare, head in the direction of the mostly ruined castle, **Ľubovniansky hrad**, which occupies a dramatic, high spur overlooking the town, 2km north of the centre. From the fifteenth to the eighteenth century, it was the main residence of the local Polish despot, who lorded it over the thirteen *Zips* towns pawned to the Polish crown by the Hungarians in the fifteenth century. Certain sections have remained intact and now serve as a **museum** (May–Sept daily 9am–5.30pm; Oct–April Mon–Sat 10am–3pm), commemorating those who were tortured in the castle by the Nazis.

Far more interesting than the above, however, is the **open-air folk museum** or **skanzen** (daily 9am–5pm), set up in the grassy meadow below the castle in the late 1970s to preserve the precious wooden architecture of the Zamagurie region, to the west of Stará Ľubovňa. In the late nineteenth century, malnutrition was the norm in rural parts of East Slovakia, and people emigrated in droves to other parts of Europe and the United States. Many of the cottages brought here from the surrounding villages were simply abandoned, and some of them now contain mementoes and personal details of the last owners (in Slovak only). It's a well-thought-out museum, and includes an early-nineteenth-century wooden Greek-Catholic church originally from Matysová, whose richly decorated interior, including an eighteenth-century iconostasis, can be viewed on request for the key.

The only real **hotel** option is the perfectly comfortable *Hotel Ľubovňa* (☎0963/32 17 51; ③), a few kilometres out of town off the road to Prešov, which has a swimming pool and gym. The restaurant here is quite good, or you could try the *pivovar* (brewery) pub on the town's main square. If you're continuing **north into Poland**, two slow trains a day crawl across the border to Muszyna (change at Plaveč on the Slovak side); the nearest border checkpoint on the roads is 15km north of Stará Ľubovňa, on route 68 at Mnísek nad Popradom.

Levoča

Twenty-five kilometres east from Poprad across the broad sweep of the Spiš country-side, the walled town of **LEVOČA** (Leutschau), positioned on a slight incline, makes a wonderfully medieval impression. Capital of one of the richest regions of Slovakia for more than four centuries, its present-day population of around 11,000 is, if anything, less than it was during its halcyon days. The town's showpiece main square is hit by the occasional tour group from the Tatras, but otherwise its dusty backstreets are yours to explore.

The first attempts at founding a town here were completely trashed by the Tatars. Then, in the thirteenth-century wave of Saxon immigration that followed, Levoča became the capital of the Spiš towns, a position it maintained until its slow but steady decline in the eighteenth and nineteenth centuries. This led to a kind of architectural mummification, and it's the fifteenth and sixteenth centuries – the golden age of Levoča – that still dominate the town today.

The old town

The Euclidian efficiency with which the old town is laid out, chessboard-style, means that wherever you breach the walls, you'll inevitably end up at the main square, **námestie Majstra Pavla**, itself a long, regular rectangle. Most of Levoča's treasures are located here, not least the threesome of the Protestant church, town hall and Catholic church, which dominate the central space. To the north, by the small park and bandstand, is possibly the least distinguished but most important building on the

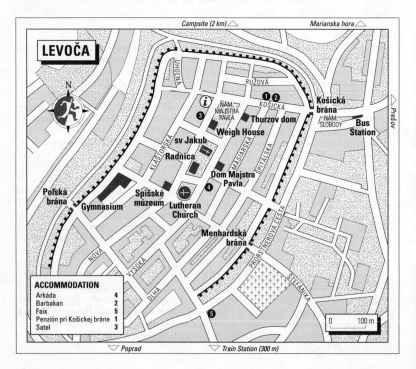

THE MARIAN PILGRIMAGE

Once a year, Levoča goes wild. As the first weekend of July approaches, up to 250,000 Catholics have been known to descend on the town to attend the biggest of Slovakia's **Marian pilgrimages**, which takes place in (and inevitably around) the church on Marianska hora, the sacred hill 2km north of the town. Families travel – in some cases on foot – for miles to arrive in time for the first Mass, which takes place around 6pm on the Saturday evening. The party goes on throughout the night, with hourly Masses in the church and singing and dancing (and drinking) outside in the fields until the grand finale of High Mass at 10am Sunday morning, generally presided over by someone fairly high up in the Church hierarchy. If you've never witnessed a Marian festival, this is the place to do it, though it only marks the beginning of a whole host of festivals which take place over the next two months in villages all over the republic. The main Greek-Catholic pilgrimage takes place some 40km northeast of Levoča, near the village of Ľutina, on the third weekend in August.

square, the former *Waaghaus* or municipal **weigh-house**, which was the financial might behind the town during its trading heyday. In 1321 King Charles Robert granted the town the Law of Storage, an unusual medieval edict which obliged every merchant passing through the region to remain in Levoča for at least fourteen days, pay various taxes and allow the locals first refusal on all their goods. In addition, Levoča merchants were later exempted from such laws when passing through other towns. Small wonder then that the town burghers were exceptionally wealthy.

Of the freestanding buildings on the main square that were paid for with these riches, it's the Roman Catholic church of **sv Jakub** (June & Sept Mon & Sun 1–4.30pm; Tues–Sat 8.30am–4.30pm; July & Aug Mon & Sun 1–6pm, Tues–Sat 9am–6pm; Oct–May Mon & Sun 1–4pm, Tues–Sat 8.30–11.30am) that contains the most valuable booty. Every nook and cranny of the building is crammed with medieval religious art, the star attraction being the early-sixteenth-century wooden altarpiece by **Master Pavol of Levoča**, topped by a forest of finials and pinnacles, which, at 18.6m in height, make it reputedly the tallest of its kind in the world. At the time, the clarity and characterization of the figures in the predella's *Last Supper* must have seemed incredible: they were modelled on the local merchants who commissioned the work (Pavol and his apprentices can also be seen behind the figure of St James in the central panel). The disciples are depicted in various animated poses – eating, caught in conversation or, in the case of St John, fast asleep across Christ's lap. Only Judas, thirty pieces of silver over his shoulder, has a look of anguish, while Christ presides with serene poise. The work took over ten years to complete, and is only one of the many Gothic altars in the church which deserve attention. The church can be visited only with a guide, and tours leave every half hour (every hour in winter) from the *kassa* opposite the main entrance.

To the south of the church is the most attractive of the central buildings, the former **radnica** (Tues–Sun 9am–5pm), built in a sturdy Renaissance style. Downstairs, the local administration still holds sway, along with a few tables and chairs for ice-cream eaters; upstairs (where you get your ticket) there's a museum on the Spiš region, and some fairly dubious contemporary art exhibitions on the top floor. Close by the southeastern corner of the town hall stands the **Klietka hanby** (Cage of Disgrace), a rather beautiful wrought-iron contraption erected by Protestants in around 1600 as a pillory for women. The third building in the centre of the square is the oddly squat **Lutheran church**, which replaced its wooden predecessor in the early nineteenth century in an uncompromisingly Neoclassical style, its bare pudding-basin interior not worth the search around for the key.

The square is otherwise lined with some fine sixteenth-century burgher houses, at their most eye-catching in the **Thurzov dom** at no. 7 – at first glance a flamboyant Renaissance structure, though in fact its most striking feature, the sgraffito decoration around the windows, dates from restoration work in 1824. Further down on the east side of the square at no. 20 is a simple two-storey building, **Dom Majstra Pavla** (Tues–Sun 9am–5pm), which historians reckon to be the house of Master Pavol. All that's known about him is what little can be gleaned from the town-hall records: he was born around 1460, sat briefly on the town council, died in 1537, and his son was murdered by a man from Kraków. Even this much is missing from the house's exhibition, which concentrates more on the Kotrba brothers who made good the woodworm of the centuries in the 1950s. Unless you're a real fan of Master Pavol's work it hardly seems worth the effort, since it contains only copies of the same work displayed in the church; however, it does allow you to get a closer look at some of the carving. If you've come this far in search of art, the **Spišské Múzeum** (Tues–Sun 9am–5pm) at no. 40 is also worth a peek for its icons, paintings and furniture culled from the Spiš region, dating as far back as the fourteenth century. Among the most important works is a beautiful Renaissance portal and accompanying frescoes, carved out from a local church.

The rest of the town's grid plan is made up of modest one-storey houses, once the exclusive abodes of Saxon craftsmen, now crumbling homes to the town's Slovaks and Romanies. You could spend an enjoyable hour wandering the streets and doing the circuit of the run-down walls: the nineteenth-century German Gymnasium in the southwest of the town has a certain curiosity value, and the sandy-coloured **Kostol minoritov** next to the Košická brána has a glorious Baroque interior.

Practicalities

If you arrive by **train** along the branch line from Spišská Nová Ves (see below), you'll find yourself a short walk southeast of the old town; the **bus station** lies close to the Košická brána in the northeast corner of town. There's a **tourist office** on the west side of the main square (Mon–Fri 10am–noon and 1–4.30pm, Sat & Sun 9.30am–1.30pm; ☎0966/16186), though outside the annual pilgrimage (see box on previous page), **accommodation** shouldn't be hard to find in one of Levoča's four hotels. The most luxurious option is the stylish *Satel* (☎0966/451 2943; ⑧), right on the main square, and with a beautiful courtyard, though the *Arkáda* (☎0966/451 2372; ⑥), also on the main square, is cheaper and no less appealing inside. The *Barbakan* (☎0966/451 4310; ⑤), on Košická, is less attractive but still comfortable, while the *Faix* (☎0966/451 2335; ②) is positively spartan. In addition, there are a couple of inexpensive pensions, the best of which is the *Penzión pri Košickej bráne* (☎0966/451 3227; ②), right next door to the *Barbakan*. There's also a **campsite** (open all year), 3km north of Levoča, in the woods by Levočská dolina.

With a fairly steady trade from locals and passing tourists, **eating** options are pretty good. Authentic Slovak pub food can be had from *U Janusa*, Kláštorská 22 (closed Sat & Sun), and from *U trí apoštolov*, above a butcher's on the east side of the main square. There's also a lunchtime-only veggie restaurant, *Vegeterián*, at Uholná 3 (closed Sat & Sun), northwest of the main square. Of the hotel restaurants the one at the *Satel*, predictably enough, rises above the others in terms of standards and price.

Spišská Nová Ves

Thirteen kilometres south of Levoča, **SPIŠSKÁ NOVÁ VES** (Neudorf) is the modern-day capital of the Spiš region, a relatively industrious town with a population of around 35,000, whose origins are as old as Levoča's, but which has borne the brunt of the changes wreaked on the region over the last century. Pawned to the Poles at the height of the Hussite Wars, along with twelve other Spiš towns, it fell to the Habsburgs when Poland was partitioned in 1772, and was immediately made the Spiš capital, a fact that played a significant part in the demise of its old rival, Levoča. As a mining town, it was virtually guaranteed to get itself on the main Košice–Bohumín railway line, built in the nineteenth century. Today, therefore, it's a good place from which to visit both the Slovenský raj and Levoča by train, but otherwise has only a few residual pleasures.

The main square is a long, broad, leafy avenue in the style of Prešov and Košice, with Zimná ulica (Winter Street) to the south, and Letná ulica (Summer Street) to the north. The central space between the two is dotted with important-looking buildings, not least the municipal theatre, **Spišské divadlo**, in grand turn-of-the-century style, worth a peek inside if only to gape at the awesome light fittings. The yellow **Rímsko-katolícky kostol** contains a couple of minor works by Master Pavol of Levoča (see opposite), and there's a small **Vlastivedné múzeum** (local musem; Tues–Fri 8–11am & noon–4.30pm, Sat 9am–1pm, Sun noon–4pm), housed in the best-looking building in town, Letná 50, which laboriously documents the mining history of the town.

Other than the above, you'll probably be most interested in the **hotels**: the high-rise *Metropol* (☎0965/42 22 41; ⑦), west of the main square on Štefánikovo námestie, has recently been refurbished, and now offers "luxury sweets" (sic); not so the *Preveza* (☎0965/42 23 71; ②), a communist-era hotel ten minutes' walk south of the main square down Kožuchova and across the river. The latter is a long walk from the **train station**, itself ten minutes' walk northwest of the main square. Decent local **food** can be had from the *Spiš* restaurant just down from the museum.

East to Spišský hrad

The road east from Levoča takes you to the edge of the Spiš territory, clearly defined by the Branisko ridge, which blocks the way to Prešov. Even if you're not planning on going any further east, you should at least take the bus as far as Spišské Podhradie for arguably the most spectacular sight in the whole country.

En route, you might spot the palatial neo-Baroque chateau at **Spišský Hrhov** peeping through its half-tamed grounds (only the latter are open to the public). There's no point in stopping off, at least until just past the village of Klčov, at which point you get your first glimpse of the **Spišský hrad** (May–Oct Tues–Sun 9am–6pm, July & Aug open daily), its chalk-white ruins strung out on a bleak, green hill in the distance – an irresistibly photogenic shot, and one that finds its way into almost every tourist brochure in the country. As a supremely strategic spot, the place was occupied from Neolithic times onwards, but the majority of what you see now dates from the thirteenth to the fifteenth century when it served as the seat of the lords of Spiš; burnt to the ground in 1781, it has been ruined ever since. It's difficult to resist the impulse to get nearer, and though the ruins are less impressive from close up, the view from the top is undeniably good. If you do wish to wander round the castle, stay on the bus until **SPIŠSKÉ PODHRADIE** (literally "below the castle") and then follow the signs to the hrad; Spišské Podhradie also has a **train station**, linked to Spišské Vlachy by a small branch line. The only nearby **accommodation** is in a couple of inexpensive pensions in Hodkovce, on the east side of the castle.

If you've time to spare, and energy to expend, take the path from Spišský hrad towards Dreveník, the limestone hill 2km southeast of the ruins, and continue another kilometre as far as the village of **ŽEHRA**. The lure here is the perky thirteenth-century church of **sv Duch**, which sports a delicately balanced shingled onion dome and matching white perimeter walls. Inside this compact little church are faded frescoes painted around 1400, and a wonderful set of richly decorative black-and-gold early Baroque altarpieces.

Spišská Kapitula

One kilometre west of Spišské Podhradie, and more rewarding than a wander round Spišský hrad, is the walled, one-street city of **SPIŠSKÁ KAPITULA** (Zipser Kapitel), once the ecclesiastical capital of the Spiš region, whose plain monastic towers are often featured in the foreground of the aforementioned photographs. From the front, the **Katedrála of sv Martin** is clearly a Romanesque church, built as a defiant outpost of Christianity shortly after the Tatar invasions. To get inside, you must first retrieve the key from the caretaker, who hangs out in the bishop's residence opposite the north door of the cathedral; he can also give you a brief guide to the church in Slovak or German. The interior was originally decorated with colourful fourteenth-century frescoes celebrating the coronation of the Hungarian king Charles Robert. Here and there these have been restored after their whitewashing by Protestants during the Reformation. The furnishings are, for the most part, neo-Gothic, but there is one altarpiece worth noting in the Zápoľský chapel south of the main nave, where a fifteenth-century depiction of the Virgin Mary clearly shows the influence of Pavol of Levoča's workshop. Outside, a couple of graceful cypress trees stand at the top of the town's single street, which is lined with canons' houses, some inhabited by people, others only by bats and rats. However, with the re-establishment of a Catholic seminary here, where the likes of Andrej Hlinka once studied, the whole place is beginning to wake from its forty-year religious slumber.

The Slovenský raj

After the upfront post-glacial splendour of the High Tatras, the low-key pine forests of the **Slovenský raj** (pronounced "rye" – meaning "paradise"), 20km or so to the southeast of Poprad, might seem more than a little anticlimactic at first glance. No hard-slog hiking or top-of-the-world views here, but, if your inclination is towards more frivolous outdoor pursuits, such as scrambling up rocky gorges and clinging onto chains and ladders beside shooting waterfalls, then the Slovenský raj may not be far from nirvana after all.

Covered in a thick coat of pine forest, the terrain – covering just twenty square kilometres – is typically karstic, with gentle limestone hills whittled away in places to form deep, hairline ravines and providing a dank, almost tropical escape from the dry summer heat of the Poprad plain. To the north, the Hornád river has made the deepest incision into the rock, forming a fast-flowing, snaking canyon flanked by towering jagged bluffs that attract some of the country's dedicated rock-climbers. The most dramatic ravines climb up to the grassy plateau of the Veľká poľana at the centre of the region. To the south, the geography becomes more conventional in the hills around Dedinky, and in winter the whole area turns into a popular ski resort.

Practicalities

It's perfectly possible to explore the area from Poprad (see p.439) by taking the **local train** to Vydrník, Letanovce or Spišské Tomášovce. However, as Poprad's not a particularly great place in which to linger, it might be more pleasant to hole up at Čingov, where you can **stay** at the friendly, family-run *Flóra* (☎0965/911 30; ⑤), which also rents outs bikes, or the *Čingov* (☎0965/336 63; ③). You could also use the village of Hrabušice as a base, as it sports a number of cheap private rooms; Dedinky (see opposite) offers up the same, or you could even stay in Spišská Nová Ves (see p.456). If you've got a tent, the Podlesok **campsite** near Hrabušice is the most convenient. The one at Čingov is more basic but less crowded at the height of summer. Both have bungalow (*chaty*) accommodation open all year.

Transport from the north to the south of the region is difficult, though there are buses from Poprad; otherwise you're best approaching from the picturesque Hron val-

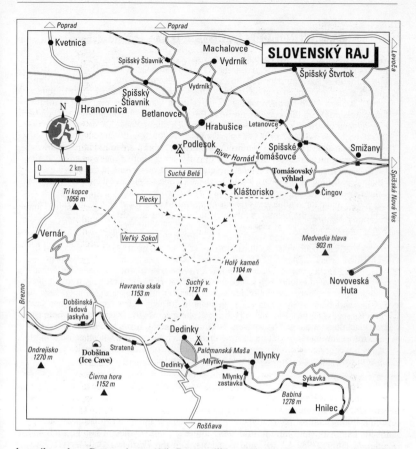

ley railway from Brezno (see p.436). Better still is to rely on your own two feet – it's not much more than 10km cross-country from Podlesok to Dedinky, but take adequate provisions with you. **Walking** is also the only way of seeing the canyons, and it's not a bad idea to try to get hold of a detailed walking map, marking all the one-way paths, before you arrive in the area. The most exhilarating tracks are those designated one-way – a strange concept to get your head round until you've been up one – and it's important to stick to the direction indicated. However much you're walking, it's best to bring a pair of sturdy boots, preferably with a good grip and at the very least splash-proof – it's extremely wet and slippery underfoot all year round. Bear in mind, too, that if you're at all scared of heights, you might encounter a few problems with some of the deeper canyons. Note that occasionally some of the one-way paths are closed off to walkers, either for repairs or to give the ravine a rest.

Dedinky and the Dobšiná ice cave

Since the creation of the nearby lake, Palcmanská Masa, **DEDINKY** has become a thriving little tourist spot all year round, and with good reason. Nestling below

HIKING ROUTES IN THE SLOVENSKÝ RAJ

With the 1:50,000 *Slovenský raj* hiking map, you can plan your own routes. If you're staying at Podlesok and follow the green markers, you immediately enter the **Suchá Belá**, one of the most exciting river beds to explore, but also one of the most accessible and therefore extremely popular at the height of the season, causing the occasional queue at crucial ladders. With so many obstacles en route, it takes nearly everyone a full two hours to stumble up this one-way ravine to the top. Similarly breathtaking stuff can be experienced up the gladed ravine of **Piecky**, which starts from 3km along the green-marked track to the Dobšinská jadová jaskyňa.

Should you need a rest after the morning's exertions, head down to **Kláštorisko**, whose sunny, sloping meadow is perfect for picnicking. If you've forgotten your packed lunch, the small *reštaurácia* at the top of the field might oblige. At the bottom of the clearing is an ongoing archeological dig where local Slavs built a monastery to give thanks for their safe deliverance from the Tatar invasions of the mid-thirteenth century.

If you continue for another half an hour along the green-marked path to the Dobšinská ľadová jaskyňa past the bottom of Piecky, you come to the deepest one-way gorge of the lot, **Veľký Sokol**, another succession of wooden ladders slung over rock pools and rapids, up the side of waterfalls and riverine gulleys. From the top, you can either walk north across the Veľká poľana plateau to Kláštorisko (1hr 30min) or head west to the top of the Malý Sokol, which swings round to join the last two-way quarter of the Veľký Sokol gorge.

The third main area to head for is the **Prielom Hornádu**, a sheer-sided breach (*prielom*) in the limestone rock forced by the Hornád river. Until recently it was impossible to enter the gorge except on ice-skates in winter or by kayak in summer. Now, in keeping with the vaguely vandalistic tendencies of the nation's trekkers, steel steps have been jammed into the rocks and rope bridges slung across the river, and the whole trip takes just three and a half hours from Podlesok to Čingov. If you're doing a round trip, take the yellow-marked path on the way back, which follows the limestone ridge high above the Hornád. The views are amazing, especially from the **Tomášovský výhlad**, a stick of exposed rock some 150m above the Prielom Hornádu.

Gačovská skala (1106m), whose spruce trees spill down to the grassy banks of the lake, it's the ideal recreational centre, with plenty of opportunities for swimming, rowing, cycling, hiking and, of course, visiting the great Dobšiná ice cave itself. Besides the lakeside campsite (mid-June to mid-Sept), there's a wide choice of hotels, such as the *Priehrada* (☎0942/982 12; ②), and pensions, like the *Pastierňa* (☎0942/981 75; ②), close to the lake. There are more options in Mlynky, 3km east of the lake, including the *Hotel Slalom* (☎0965/49 32 93; ③).

Dobšiná ice cave

The most obvious day-trip from Dedinky is the **Dobšiná ice cave** (Dobšinská ľadová jaskyňa; Tues–Sun: mid-May to late May & Sept guided tours at 9am, 11am, 12.30pm & 2pm; June–Aug guided tours hourly 9am–4pm), by far the more impressive of Slovakia's two ice caves (the other is in the Low Tatras), at its best in spring or early summer. It's basically one vast underground lake frozen to a depth of over 20m and divided into two halls, the biggest of which, the *Veľká sieň*, is over 100m across. Although the ice formations are a long way from the subtleties of your average limestone cave, it rarely fails to impress by the brute force of its size and weight.

From Podlesok, it's a three-and-a-half-hour hike, mostly through the forest. From Dedinky, simply take the train two stops in the direction of Brezno, after which it's a twenty-minute walk into the hills. It's worth bearing in mind that the caves are very popular (so get there early) and very cold (so take something warm to put on). Should you wish to **stay over**, the *Hotel Jas* (☎0942/981 72; ①) has very simple, cheap rooms, or there's the *Hotel Ruffíny* (☎0942/982 27; ③), which appears to be slipping slowly into the road.

Moving on

Dedinky lies on the wonderful Červená Skala–Margecany branch line, one of the prettiest **train journeys** in Slovakia. It's a slow run if you're going all the way to Košice (3hr 30min), but an hour less on the fast midday *rýchlik*. If you're heading south to the Slovenský kras, you may have to walk the 10km to the unprepossessing old German mining town of Dobšiná, since there's only one bus a day – if you do make it, it's a spectacular thousand-foot drop from the Palcmanská Masa. Most buses continue from Dobšiná to Rožňava, or you could take one of the seven trains a day which also cover the route.

The Slovenský kras

Like the Moravian karst region north of Brno, the **Slovenský kras** boasts some of the finest limestone caves in central Europe, the highlight of which are the Domica caves, stretching right under the border into Hungary (where they're known as the Aggtelek caves). Even now, the surrounding hills are still plundered for their ores – copper, iron and, once upon a time, gold – and the largest town in the area, Rožňava, continues to make its living from the local mines, even if the original intrepid German miners have long since gone. The towns and villages are for the most part dusty, characterless places; people are by far the dominant feature of the landscape, with large communities of Hungarians, Slovaks and Romanies living side by side.

Rožňava and around

Once the seat of a bishopric and a flourishing German mining centre, **ROŽŇAVA** (Rozsnyó) enjoys a great setting, at the meeting point of several dramatic valleys lined with rocky bluffs. Nowadays, it's a sleepy, mostly Hungarian-speaking, garrison town, though it's also an undeniably useful base when it comes to making excursions into the karst region and the nearby aristocratic haunts of Krásna Hôrka and Betliar.

The town does have a couple of redeeming features of its own: it once boasted a mint, a cathedral and an episcopal palace. Of the three, only the former **Biskupská katedrála** (now just a parish church) is worth bothering about, largely on account of its sixteenth-century altarpiece depicting the life of local miners; you'll find it just to the northwest of the expansive main square, námestie Baníkov. Also worth a look on the main square is the late-Gothic watchtower or **Strážna veža**, and the statue of the much-mourned Františka Andrássy (see overleaf), with Dionysus looking on adoringly as she comforts (someone else's) children. Lastly, there's the **Banícke múzeum** (Mining Museum; Tues–Fri 9am–4pm), set in a lovely *fin-de-siècle* block, five minutes' walk along the road to Šafárikovo – it's the second museum building you want, not the first one you come to. The museum is run by a lively retired Hungarian miner who does his best to make up for the lack of information in English. Ask to see the reconstructed (and somewhat over-clean) mine shaft tucked round the back of the building (along with an iron statue of the Hungarians' hero, Kossuth), bearing the traditional, though rather ominous, inscription *ZDAR BOH* (Good Luck).

All **transport** in the region has to pass through Rožňava at some point, although three train stations still seem a mite excessive. The one closest to the centre is Rožňava mesto, ten minutes' walk west along Štítnicka; the main one, called simply Rožňava, is a two-and-a-half-kilometre walk from town (bus #1, #2 or #6 from the station); the bus station is just southeast of the main square. **Accommodation** is fairly limited, though the **tourist office** (May–Oct Mon–Fri 8am–6pm, Sat 8am–2pm; Nov–April Mon–Fri 8am–4pm; ☎0942/732810), at no. 32 on the main square, should be able to help if you get stuck. The ugly green *Hotel Kras* (☎0942/732 4243; ④), on the corner of Štítnicka and Šafárikova, is comfortable enough inside, though if you want to splash out you'll do much better at the *Čierny orol* (☎0942/732 8186; ⑤), a lovely place on the square with all requisite mod-cons. *Penzión Fan Fan* (☎0942/732 1246; ②), southeast of the centre on route 50, is a good budget option, though the location, near the Avanti petrol station, is nothing to write home about. In addition to the fine restaurant in the *Čierny orol*, the *Átrium*, just north of the main square, does some very good Slovak dishes, or you can try the *Sabi* pizzeria on the main square.

Krásnohorské Podhradie and around

Plenty of buses run the 5km to the village of **KRÁSNOHORSKÉ PODHRADIE** (Krasznahorkaváralja), which means literally "below Krásna Hôrka castle". Dramatically situated on top of the nearby limestone col to protect the trade route between the Spiš region and Košice, the gaunt fortress of **Krásna Hôrka** (Tues–Sun: May–Oct 8am–4.30pm; Nov–April 9am–2pm) looks utterly impregnable. The original owners, the Bebeks, fell from favour when it was discovered that they had been counterfeiting money, and the castle was subsequently confiscated and handed over to the Andrássy family. Such was the wealth of the Andrássys that they were able to turn the whole place into a family museum in 1910, having a number of other places in which they actually lived. Sadly, the compulsory guided tours last an hour and twenty minutes, and are of limited general appeal.

A better bet down in the western part of the village is the original Rožňava mining museum, a fabulous Secession building from 1906, which has been recently restored and turned into the **Andrássy galéria** (Tues–Sun 9am–noon & 1–4pm). The main glass-roofed hall now contains portraits of the Andrássy family, including the two buried in the mausoleum described below, plus a large, dramatic canvas by the Hungarian painter, Ferenc Paczka, depicting the death of Attila the Hun. Look out, too, for the stork's nest on one of the building's chimneys.

Within sight of both castle and village, and without doubt the most beautiful Art Nouveau building in Slovakia, is the **Andrássy Mausoleum** (Tues–Sun: May–Oct 8am–4.30pm; Nov–April 9am–2pm), east of Krásnohorské Podhradie along route 50. It was built in 1903–04 at great expense by Count Dionysus Andrássy, in memory of his wife, the celebrated Czech opera singer Františka Hablavcová, who died in 1902. Dionysus himself was disowned by the family for marrying below his station, an action which no doubt stiffened his resolve to build an even more extravagant resting place for his lover. Set in its own carefully laid-out gardens with sombre wrought-iron gates and characteristic angelic janitors, the mausoleum itself is a simple dome structure of austere classicism. Inside, though, it bursts into an almost celebratory orgy of ornamentation: Venetian gold for the cupola, coloured marble from every corner of the globe, and as the centrepiece, two white Carrara marble sarcophagi in which both Františka and Dionysus (who died not long after the building was completed) are buried.

If you're looking for a place to stay, there's a rather grim **motel** (☎0942/732 3838; ②) right by the mausoleum, and a **campsite**, *Pod hradom* (June–Aug), to the north of the village en route to the castle.

Betliar

Though owned by the same aristocratic family, the frivolous hunting chateau at **BETLIAR**, 5km northwest of Rožňava by train, couldn't be further from the brooding intensity of Krásna Hôrka. It was adapted as late as the 1880s in an "indefinite style", as the local tourist brochures put it, to accommodate the Andrássys' popular hunting parties. The guided tour takes you past a fairly surprising array of artefacts, including some exotic arms and armour from the Far East, an Egyptian mummy, a giant elephant tusk, as well as the usual period furniture, dull portraits, and (naturally enough) rows of hunting trophies. If the tour wears you down, though, the large, well-groomed English-style park easily makes up for it, with its playful, folksy rotundas, Japanese bridge, and various mock-historic edifices.

The Gombasek, Domica and Ochtina caves

The majority of the cave systems in the Slovenský kras lie within 30km to the south and west of Rožňava, though without your own transport it's difficult to explore them in a day. As it is one of the prime tourist destinations in Slovakia, a separate pricing system has been introduced for foreigners, and it's possible that you may have to queue for the more popular caves.

Gombasecká jaskyňa

The most impressive of the cave systems, the **Gombasecká jaskyňa** (Tues–Sun: April to mid-May & mid-Sept to Oct guided tours at 9.30am, 11am, 12.30pm & 2pm; mid-May to mid-Sept tours hourly 9am–4pm), is also one of the most accessible. To reach the caves, you can catch a direct bus from Rožňava, or take the train one stop south of Rožňava to Slavec Jaskyňa station, whence it's 2km further south. There's a rudimentary **campsite** near the caves, and every June the nearby village of Gombasek (Gömbaszog) is the venue for the largest annual Hungarian folk bash in Slovakia.

The Jaskyňa Domica and Silická ľadnica

Ten kilometres due south of Gombasek, hard by the Hungarian border, are the **Jaskyňa Domica** (Tues–Sun: Feb to mid-May & mid-Sept to Dec tours at 9am, 10.30am, 12.30pm & 2pm; mid-May to mid-Sept tours at 9am, 10.30am, 12.30pm, 2pm, 3pm & 4pm): at 22km in length, this is the longest cave system in the country. The short passage from Robert Townson (see overleaf), one of the caves' earliest explorers, should give you an idea of the gushing prose they often inspire. The tours last less than an hour and include a quick boat trip on the underground river. Theoretically, it should soon be possible to continue on a longer tour over the border into Hungary, where most of the cave system lies, but so far this is possible only from the Hungarian side.

Given Domica's inaccessibility – there are around six buses a day to Plešivec (Pelsöc), 10km away, but few at weekends – perhaps the easiest and most rewarding way of getting there is to follow the yellow-marked track from Gombasek. The path climbs up onto the *planina* (see overleaf) and through the oak trees via the **Silická ľadnica** cave (1hr). The cave itself is closed to the public, but its ominous entrance is impressively encrusted with ice throughout the summer, melting to a dribble by late autumn, only to be replenished when the first cold spell of November arrives. Keep following the yellow markers east for 500m or so, then hang a right when you hit the red-marked path, whence it's a two-hour trek across the pockmarked tableland to Domica.

Ochtinská aragonitová jaskyňa

Of all the cave systems, the **Ochtinská aragonitová jaskyňa** (times as for Gombasecká) is without doubt the thinking person's cave, set apart from the others geographically and geologically. Though by no means as spectacular in scale as the other limestone caves, it has the unique and breathtakingly beautiful feature of spiky aragonite "flowers", which form like limpets on the cave side. From Plešivec, there's an infrequent train service to Ochtiná (35min), after which the cave is a three-kilometre walk uphill southwest along the blue-marked path; from Rožňava, there are even more

A JOURNEY THROUGH THE DOMICA CAVES

The following is an extract from Robert Townson's *Travels in Hungary*, published in 1793. Townson, a Scottish scientist, botanized his way around the old kingdom of Hungary, staying with a lot of good-humoured Calvinists on the way, and in the passage quoted below recounts a visit to the Domica caves, long before the days of safety barriers and electric lighting.

I descended rapidly for a short distance and then I found myself in an immense cave . . . where large stalactites, as thick as my body, hung pendant from the roof, and I was shown others where the sides were ornamented in the manner of the most curious Gothic workmanship. In some the stalactites were so thick and close together that we were in danger of losing one another if we separated but a few yards. Here aged stalactites, overloaded with their own weight, had fallen down and lay prostrate; and there an embryo stalactite was just shooting into existence.

After I had wandered about for three or four hours in this awful gloom and had reached the end of the caverns in one direction, I thought it time to come out, and I desired my guide to return. After we returned, as we thought, some way, we found no passage further; yet the guide was sure he was right. I thought I recognized the same rocks we had just left, and which had prevented our proceeding further, but the guide was positive he was in a right direction. Luckily for us I had written my name on the soft clay of the bottom of the cave, which had been the extent of our journey; on seeing this the guide was thunderstruck, and ran this way and that way and knew not where he was, nor what to do. I desired him not to be frightened, but to go calmly to work to extricate us from this labyrinth . . .

After wandering about till all our wood was nearly exhausted, we found a great stalactite from which, on account of its remarkable whiteness, I had been induced to knock off a specimen as I came by: I recollected how I stood when I struck it: this at once set us right, and after walking a little further we made ourselves heard to the other guide, from whom we got fresh torches, and we continued our route homewards without further difficulty.

So complete a labyrinth as these caverns are in some places, is not I am sure to be found in similar caverns: large open passages proved cul de sacs, whilst our road was over and under, through and amongst grotto work of the most intricate nature. I finally believe that though a man should have lights and food enough to last him a month – he would not be able to find his way out.

infrequent buses (40min). If you're travelling by car, you can reach the cave most easily from the turn-off to Hrádok on route 526 from Štítnik to Jelšava.

Zádielska dolina and the caves at Jasov

One of the more bizarre karstic features of the Slovenský kras is the forested sheets of **planina** or tableland which rise above the plains like the coastal cliffs of a lost sea. In fact, the opposite is the case, the rivers having whittled down what would otherwise be a featureless limestone plateau. Mostly, these erosions form broad sweeping valleys, but in a few cases cracks appear in the more familiar form of riverine crevices.

The most dramatic of these is the **Zádielska dolina**, a brief but breathtaking three or four kilometres of sky-scraping canyon. To get there, take the train or bus to Dvorníky, 25km east of Rožňava and 1km south of the Hungarian-speaking village Zádiel (Szádelö), at the entrance to the dolina. There's none of the Slovenský raj assault course on this hike, just a gentle yet magnificent stroll between the two bluffs. For something slightly more death-defying, return along the blue-marked track, which ascends the right-hand ridge and shadows the canyon back to Zádiel, then drops down 2.5km east of Dvorníky near the cement works of Turnianske Podhradie. For a longer hike (15km) you could follow the blue-marked path over the hills to Jasov, or take the green- then red-marked track to Pipitka (1225m), 10km away, returning to Rožňava by bus from the Úhornianske sedlo down below.

Jasov

The Premonstratensian monastery at **JASOV** (Jászó) is visible across the fields long before you reach the town. It's actually much older than its eighteenth-century Baroque appearance would suggest. The monastery church contains some superb, recently restored frescoes by the Austrian painter J.L. Kracker, who also embellished the ceiling of the library, to which you may be able to gain access. The formal gardens behind the monastery are also worth exploring. The chief reason most locals visit Jasov, though, is to see the **Jasovská jaskyňa** (times as for Gombasecká), the least-hyped caves in the karst region, which specialize in forests of "virgin stalactites" and contain some amazing graffiti scrawled on the walls by fugitive Czech Hussites in 1452. The only accommodation is the village's lively **campsite** (open all year), which also rents out *chaty*, but if you're coming from Košice, Jasov can easily enough be done as a day-trip. If you're in need of sustenance, be sure to pay a visit to the cellars of the *Zámocká pivnica*, opposite the monastery, which serves wonderful local beer, wine and food.

Carpatho-Ruthenia

Carpatho-Ruthenia* is one of those places where people hail from rather than go to. Infamous media mogul Robert Maxwell and the parents of Andy Warhol were just a few of the million or so inhabitants who left the northeastern corner of what was then the Austro-Hungarian Empire (and later Czechoslovakia) in the late nineteenth and early twentieth centuries to seek fame and fortune elsewhere, mostly in North America.

They left to escape not so much the region's unerring provinciality, but its grinding poverty and unemployment, only quite recently abated. Even in the 1950s, an estimated 41 percent of Rusyn villages were still without electricity, and by 1968 their living standards were less than half the national average. Today, the villages are still visibly poorer and more isolated than their western counterparts – until recently, few visitors had passed through since the Russians in 1945 (and again in 1968). Some things have changed, though not always for the best: the whole area took a hammering in the last war, and wooden buildings, once the norm, have gradually been replaced by concrete and brick; traditional costumes are now worn almost exclusively by the over-sixties; and the heavy industry, which was crudely implanted here by the Communists to try to stem the continuing emigration, is now struggling to survive.

From a visitor's point of view, **Prešov** and **Bardejov** are both easy to reach and immediately appealing. Further afield, transport becomes a real problem (as it is for the local inhabitants), the north–south axis of the valleys in particular hindering the generally eastbound traveller. Accommodation also peters out and declines in quality the deeper you go, so unless you have a car, you'll want to book rooms in advance. Nevertheless, it's worth persevering, if only to visit the region's most unusual sight, the Andy Warhol Museum in **Medzilaborce**.

---

*Carpatho-Ruthenia (Podkarpatská Rus in Slovak) was the name for the easternmost province of Czechoslovakia taken as war booty by the Soviet Union in 1945. Here, the term is used loosely to refer to the East Slovak districts on the border with Poland and Ukraine, where the Rusyn minority still predominate.

Prešov

Capital of the Slovak Šariš region and cultural centre for the Rusyn minority, **PREŠOV**'s present-day split personality is indicative of its long and chequered ethnic history. Over the last few years it has been treated to a wonderful facelift, and although there's not much of interest beyond its main square it's refreshingly youthful and vibrant – partly due to its university – which is unusual for a town this far east.

The Town

The lozenge-shaped main square, **Hlavná ulica**, is flanked by creamy, pastel-coloured, almost edible eighteenth-century facades, some topped by exceptionally appealing and varied gables and pediments, others, as at no. 22, embellished with frolicking cherubs, angels and even monkeys. Prešov's Catholic and Protestant churches vie with each other at the widest point of the square. Naturally enough, the fourteenth-century Roman Catholic church of **sv Mikuláš** has the edge, not least for its Gothic vaulting, its modern Moravian stained-glass windows and its highly theatrical Baroque altar-

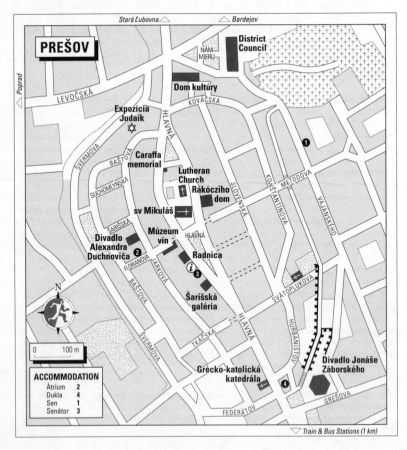

ACCOMMODATION

Átrium	2
Dukla	4
Sen	1
Senátor	3

THE RUSYNS

The **Rusyns** or Ruthenians are one of the lost peoples of central Europe. Even their name is the subject of debate, since *Rusyn* is often taken to mean Little Russian or Ukrainian, but in the Hungarian kingdom simply referred to any non-Roman Catholic Slavs. As to their political history, the picture is equally confusing. Their language is considered by scholars to be a western Lemko dialect of Ukrainian, but their homeland actually never was part of Ukraine, and the mountains in which they had settled soon became a permanent political barrier, dividing their territory between Hungary and Poland.

Meanwhile, their great cultural institution, the Orthodox Church, underwent a series of crises and schisms which resulted in the Act of Union of 1596; this established the Uniate Church as part of the Roman Catholic Church, and after 1772 it became known as the Byzantine-Catholic or **Greek-Catholic Church**. This unique religion, tied to Rome but with all the trappings of Eastern Orthodoxy, became (and still is) the carrier of the Rusyn national identity. In every other way – dress codes, mores and folklore – they were hardly distinguishable from their Magyar and Slovak neighbours. Throughout this period, they remained, as they still do to a great extent, hill-dwelling peasants with no political or economic influence.

The first national leaders to emerge in the nineteenth century were, predictably enough, Greek-Catholic priests, and – like many Slovaks at the time – fiercely Russophile and pro-tsar. They played little part in the downfall of the Habsburg Empire, and when Ruthenia became a province of the new Czechoslovak Republic in 1918, it was largely due to the campaigning efforts of a handful of Ruthenian immigrants in the USA. The Slovaks laid claim to all the land west of the River Uh (Uzh in Ukrainian), an area containing around 100,000 Rusyns; the actual province of Ruthenia, to the east, which contained not only 370,000 Rusyns but large numbers of Hungarians, Jews, Romanies and even Romanians, was annexed by the Soviet Union following "liberation" in 1945, when the Uh river became a permanent border.

On the surface, the Rusyns who remained in Czechoslovakia were treated better than any other minority since the war. Scratch this surface, however, and things begin to look much less rosy. Given a free choice (as they were between the wars and before 1948), the Rusyns tended to opt for either the local dialect or Russian as the language of instruction in their schools. After the 1948 coup, however, the Communist regime intervened and ruled that the term *Rusyn* was "an anti-progressive label" – all Rusyns became officially known as Ukrainians, and the language of instruction in Rusyn schools was changed to literary Ukrainian. The reaction of the Rusyns to the resulting pedagogical chaos was to opt for Slovak rather than Ukrainian schools. Secondly, collectivization, which disrupted all peasant communities in Eastern Europe, encouraged urbanization (and therefore Slovak assimilation). Lastly, and perhaps most cruelly of all, following the example of the Stalinist authorities, the Greek-Catholic Church was forcibly amalgamated into the Orthodox Church. Its priests and dissenting laity were, for the most part, rounded up and thrown in prison, including the Church's one and only bishop, **Pavel Gojdič**, who received a life sentence and died in Leopoldov prison in 1960.

Hardly surprising then that in the last three censuses, fewer than 40,000 declared themselves as Rusyn. No one knows the real numbers, but it's estimated that as many as 130,000 Rusyns still live in East Slovakia. Since the Velvet Revolution things have begun to look up. As in 1968, when the ban on the Church was finally lifted, the Greek-Catholics (who include large numbers of Slovaks) are busy arguing with the Orthodox community (reckoned to be as few as 30,000) who were handed control of all Church property in the 1950s. Meanwhile, **Ján Hirka**, since 1969 the unofficial head of all Greek-Catholics, was ordained as a Greek-Catholic bishop in 1990, and the martyr Pavel Gojdič was beatified. In 1991, the first World Congress of Rusyns was held in Medzilaborce, and finally, in 1995, literary Rusyn was officially codified and proclaimed before government, state and academic officials in Bratislava.

piece, flanked by barleysugar columns and complete with matching pulpit and side altars.

Behind sv Mikuláš, the much plainer **Lutheran church** (Evanjelický chrám), built in the mid-seventeenth century, bears witness to the strength of religious reformism in the outer reaches of Hungary at a time when the rest of the Habsburgs' lands were suffering the full force of the Counter-Reformation. In the 1670s, the tide turned, and a wave of religious persecution followed, culminating in the "1687 Blood Tribunal" in which 24 leading Lutherans were publicly hanged in Prešov's main square. The prime mover behind the trial was **Count Caraffa**, the papal nuncio in Vienna, whose moustached figure, flanked by a hooded executioner, stands above the grim memorial (in Hungarian) on the corner of the Protestant Lycée, next door to the church.

To the south is Prešov's **radnica**, from whose unsuitably small balcony Béla Kun's Hungarian Red Army declared the short-lived Slovak Socialist Republic in 1919. Searching desperately for a socialist tradition that simply never existed in this part of the country, the Slovak Communists made much of this brief episode in Prešov's history. In fact, it used to be the main subject of the town's Šarišské múzeum, situated in the dogtooth-gabled **Rákócziho dom** at no. 86 (Tues–Fri 9am–5pm, Sat 9am–1pm, Sun 1–5pm) – the Czechoslovak Legion's military victories that contributed to the downfall of Kun's Bolshevik government would be a more interesting replacement than the current uninspiring offering of local history and old-fashioned fire-fighting equipment.

In front of the town hall is a small garden, centred around a turn-of-the-century fountain featuring a foursome of frog, fish, crocodile and tortoise, somewhat unusually commemorating the arrival of the first Jews to Prešov in 1780. Further along on the west side of the square, the **Šarišská galéria** (Tues, Wed & Fri 9am–5pm, Thurs 9am–6pm, Sat 9am–1pm, Sun 2–6pm) puts on temporary exhibitions of Slovak art on the ground floor and in the atmospheric cellar. Finally, at the square's southern tip, is the splendid **Grécko-katolícka katedrála**, its exterior decorated with delicate Rococo stuccowork. Inside, the cathedral is filled with Orthodox furnishings, including a fabulously huge iconostasis, topped by some wonderful gilded filigree work. For the first time since the imprisonment of Pavel Gojdič (see box on previous page), the cathedral and the bishop's palace next door actually have an extant Greek-Catholic bishop and are enjoying a cultural renaissance.

Prešov may appear to be little more than the sum of its main square, but there are a couple of points of interest hidden away in the quiet backstreets. On the east side, the old town has preserved some of its ancient walls, along which you can walk, while in the northwest corner, the town's disused **synagogue** has recently been restored, and a memorial to the region's prewar Jewish community of over 6000 placed outside. The flamboyant turn-of-the-century Orthodox synagogue, which faces onto Baštova, but which you must approach from Švermova, now houses an **Expozícia Judaík** (Tues & Wed 11am–4pm, Thurs 3–6pm, Fri 10am–1pm, Sun 1–5pm), with an exhibition in the women's gallery explaining Jewish religious practices (captions are in English and Slovak). Finally, in a passage off the main square near the radnica is the **Múzeum vín** (Mon–Fri 8am–7pm, Sat 8am–noon), more a vast underground wine shop than a museum, though the proprietors do lead informative tours of the contents for visitors. Most of the stuff is Slovak, but you can also learn about (and buy) anything from French to Ukrainian tipple as well.

Practicalities

The **bus** and **train stations** are situated opposite one another about 1km south of the main square, and connected by trolleybus. There's a **tourist office** (Mon–Fri 8.30–11.30am & 12.30–5.30pm, Sat 9am–1pm; ☎091/16186) at Hlavná 67, connected to a newsagent selling a few foreign newspapers and magazines. Prešov's best **hotels** are the *Senátor* (☎091/73 11 86; ⑨), a newly done-up place above the tourist office with small self-catering apartments, or the nicely refurbished communist-era *Dukla*, south of the main square (☎091/72 27 41; ⑨). There are a few smaller **pensions** in the streets west of the square, such as the *Átrium* (☎091/73 30 25; ④), at Floriánova 4, while the cheapest option in town is the *Sen* **hostel**, Vajanského 65 (☎091/73 31 70; ①).

Away from the big hotels, **eating** possibilities are limited but improving. If it's lunch you're looking for, a freshly baked Slovak baguette from *Bagetéria*, on the main square at no. 36, is probably your best bet. A few restaurants spill out onto the square in summer, including the *Melodia* at no. 61, which has a satisfyingly long menu that doesn't overlook the needs of vegetarians. For more traditional fare, the basement *U richtára*, nearby at no. 71, is appealing; the once elegant *Hotel Savoy*, on the square, has been transformed into a bingo club, though you can still have a drink or a bite to eat there.

Prešov prides itself on its cultural traditions, with two large-scale **theatres** in town, and an annual *Hubobná jar* (Musical Spring), a cultural feast that takes place in April and May. The mainstream Divadlo Jonáša Záborského is south of the main square, while the more famous Divadlo Alexandra Duchnoviča (or DAD), is based in a theatre on Jarková, west off the square, and is home to the renowned PULS Dukla Folk Ensemble; though a Rusyn/Ukrainian theatre, plays are generally performed in Rusyn. It's also worth checking out what's on at the Čierny orol **concert hall**, down the passage beside the *Savoy*.

Bardejov and around

Over 40km north of Prešov, not far from the Polish border, **BARDEJOV** (Bartfeld) is an almost perfectly preserved walled medieval town, comfortably positioned on its own rock with the obligatory sprawl of postwar development below. Built by Saxon weavers who colonized the area in the twelfth century, it lost its German-speaking population after World War II, and nowadays, like Prešov, acts as a commercial and administrative centre for the outlying Rusyn villages, most obviously during the Saturday morning market.

The **staré mesto** (five minutes' walk southwest of the bus and train stations) remains remarkably unchanged since its Saxon days, retaining most of its Gothic fortifications, including four of the original bastions along the eastern wall. The pristine cobbled main square, **Radničné námestie**, with its characteristic triangular gables (many of which are still faced with wooden slats), is straight out of the German Middle Ages. Along the north side is the Gothic church of **sv Egídia** (Mon–Fri 9.30–5pm, Sat 10am–5pm, Sun 11.30am–3.30pm), suitably vast thanks to the burghers' wealth at the time. The interior is stuffed full of fifteenth-century carved wooden side altars – eleven in all – though only two sculptures and one painting survive from the original main altar by Pavol of Levoča; the current work is neo-Gothic. The fifteenth-century stone tabernacle is also noteworthy, as are the pew ends which feature grinning half-dog, half-monkey creatures.

The sandy-coloured building in the centre of the square is the town's Renaissance **radnica**, whose eastern facade boasts a beautiful stone staircase and oriel window, and whose gables sport sculptures of strange animals and figures. No longer a town hall, the radnica now forms part of the **Šarišské múzeum** (Tues–Sun: May–Sept 8.30–noon & 12.30–5pm; Oct–April 8.30am–noon & 12.30–4pm), housing a number of striking fifteenth-century wooden sculptures and epitaphs, as well as the original of the rather battered statue of Roland, a copy of which adorns the apex of the gable. The finest selection of exhibits is housed in another branch of the museum on the corner of Rhódyho, at the top end of the square (same times as above). Inside, there's an impressive collection of sixteenth- to nineteenth-century icons (many in need of serious restoration) and a fascinating series of models of the region's Greek-Catholic churches (see p.471).

A couple of blocks west of the old town is the former **Jewish quarter**, from which 3700 local Jews were rounded up and dispatched to the camps; a small plaque depicting two hands tearing through Hebrew script was erected on Mlýnská, ten minutes' walk west along Dlhý rad from the Republika, to mark the spot. There are now just two Jews in Bardejov, one of whom administers the cluster of buildings remaining along Mlýnská, which are undergoing slow restoration. The plaque itself is mounted on the walls of the former ritual baths, the domed building next door to what was the kosher butcher's, and behind them is the former eighteenth-century **synagogue**, which is currently rented out to a plumbing supply firm; they are only too happy to show visitors the building's rich ceiling decoration and its Polish-style four-pillared interior.

It's possible to come here on a day-trip from Prešov, though given the added attractions of the nearby spa, Bardejovské kúpele (see below), and the proximity of several wooden churches, you might prefer to stay overnight. That said, **accommodation** is something of a problem: the only functioning place at the time of writing was the *Penzión Roland* (☎0935/474 85 38; ②), with plain but comfortable rooms right on the main square. The *Republika*, just north of the old town square, is currently closed, but makes for another option if it reopens. In any case, the **tourist office** (Mon–Fri 8am–4pm; ☎093/16186), on the main square at no. 21, can be valuable in helping to arrange private rooms, or you might have to head over to Bardejovské Kúpele, where at least a couple more hotels await. Adequate **food** and beer can be had at the *U zlatej koruny* café-restaurant and snack-bar complex on the main square.

Bardejovské kúpele

Hourly buses cover the 4km from Bardejov to the spa town of **BARDEJOVSKÉ KÚPELE** (Bad Bartfeld), once a favourite playground of the Austro-Hungarian and Russian nobility. A series of devastating fires in 1910–12 destroyed most of the spa's old wooden buildings, and nowadays, aside from a few surviving nineteenth-century mansions, there's nothing much to hint at its former glory. Instead, the major attraction for non-patients is the excellent **skanzen** (Tues–Sun: April–Sept 9am–6pm; Oct–March 8am–3.30pm), on the far northwestern side of the spa, which contains a whole series of timber-framed buildings, thatched cottages and two eighteenth-century wooden Greek-Catholic churches transferred from the surrounding Rusyn villages of Mikulášová and Zboj (for more on the region's wooden churches, see opposite). The spa's only other claim to fame is its seated bronze statue of the **empress Elisabeth**, wife of the Habsburg emperor Franz-Josef I, who was a frequent visitor to the spa until her death at the hands of an Italian anarchist in 1898. A group of Hungarian admirers erected the statue in 1903, but wisely left the empress's name off the plinth, allowing her real identity to remain hidden during the ideological vicissitudes of this century. If you wish to stay, try the *Hotel Mier* (☎0935/472 45 24; ②), a spa hotel open to the general public.

Svidník and the Dukla Pass

Twenty kilometres or so due east of Bardejov and almost completely obliterated in the heavy fighting of October 1944, **SVIDNÍK** today is, not surprisingly, a characterless concrete sprawl. However, it does contain a clutch of intriguing museums and an open-air *skanzen* of Rusyn folk architecture, and hosts a Rusyn-Ukrainian folk festival each year in the middle of June. It's also by far the most convenient base from which to explore the wooden Greek-Catholic churches in the Rusyn villages, chiefly those near the Dukla Pass.

Just off the town's main street, Sovietskych hrdinov, on Centrálna, is the **Museum of Ukrainian-Rusyn Culture** (Múzeum ukrajinsko-rusínskej kultúry; Tues–Fri 8.30am–4pm, Sat & Sun 10am–4pm), containing a fine array of Rusyn folk gear and models of various Greek-Catholic churches, as well as a beautiful collection of traditional painted Easter eggs. A ten-minute walk from the museum up Centrálna past the bus station, and clearly signposted round town, is the **Galéria Dezidera Millyho**, on

THE WOODEN CHURCHES OF CARPATHO-RUTHENIA

In the villages around Bardejov, Svidník and Humenné, a remarkable number of **wooden churches** have survived to the present day. Many (but by no means all) are Greek-Catholic churches located within Rusyn villages, and most date from around the eighteenth century, when the influence of Baroque was beginning to make itself felt even among the carpenter architects of the Carpathians. A threesome of shingled onion domes, as at Dobroslava, is the telltale sign, though the humbler churches opt for simple barn-like roofs.

Without your own transport the possibility of reaching many of the churches *in situ* is limited, although there's a whole cluster within easy walking distance of the main road from Svidník to the Polish border. The easiest way of having a close look is to visit one of the **skanzens** at Bardejovské kúpele, Svidník or Humenné, each of which contains a wooden church. If, however, you do make it out to some of the villages, you'll need to ask around for the local priest (*pop*) to get hold of a key (*klúč*).

The dark and intimate interior of a Greek-Catholic/Orthodox church is divided into three sections (from west to east): the narthex or entrance porch, the main nave, and the naos or sanctuary. Even the smallest Greek-Catholic church boasts a rich iconostasis all but cutting off the sanctuary, with the familiar icons of (from left to right) St Nicholas, the Madonna and Child, Christ Pantocrator and, lastly, the saint to whom the church is dedicated. Above the central door of the iconostasis (through which only the priest may pass) is the Last Supper, while to the left are busy scenes from the great festivals of the church calendar – the Annunciation, the Assumption and so on. The top tier of icons features the Apostles (with St Paul taking the place of Judas). Typically, the Last Judgement covers the wall of the narthex, usually the most gruesome of all the depictions, with the damned being burned, boiled and decapitated with macabre abandon.

Dobroslava, 7km north of Svidník. A delightful pagoda-style Orthodox (formerly Greek-Catholic) church, with a wide cruciform ground plan, distinctive triplet of shingled onion domes and an amazing Bosch-style *Last Judgement*.

Hervatov, 8km southwest of Bardejov. This Roman Catholic church, erected in the 1490s, is the oldest in the country, and features some remarkable seventeenth-century murals depicting "wise and crazy virgins".

Ladomírová, 4km northeast of Svidník. Greek-Catholic church on the main road to the Dukla Pass, with an eccentric mishmash of pagodas, baubles and cupolas.

Lukov, 14km west of Bardejov. Orthodox, previously Greek-Catholic, church, which boasts a fantastic red-black, sixteenth-century, diagrammatical depiction of the *Last Judgement* on the iconostasis.

Miroľa, 12km east of Svidník. Eighteenth-century Greek-Catholic/Orthodox church, one of the most perfect examples of the triple Baroque cupolas descending in height from west to east.

Nižný Komárnik, 12km northeast of Svidník. An unusual Greek-Catholic church, built with a hint of Neoclassicism in 1938, not in the usual Lemko style, with the central cupola higher than the other two.

Tročany, 15km south of Bardejov. Eighteenth-century Greek-Catholic church with simple cupolas like candle extinguisher caps; renowned for its lurid, rustic icon of the *Last Judgement*.

Uličské Krivé, 35km northeast of Snina. Eighteenth-century Greek-Catholic church rich in seventeenth-century icon paintings, including one depicting the archangel Michael casually pulverizing Sodom and Gomorrah.

Partizánska (Tues–Fri 8.30am–4pm, Sat & Sun 10am–4pm), mostly given over to contemporary Rusyn artists but with a couple of retrospective rooms devoted to Milly, one of the first Rusyn artists to win acclaim for his Expressionist paintings of local peasant life. The gallery also houses some weird and wonderful sixteenth- to nineteenth-century icon paintings, among the finest in East Slovakia.

Looking something like the Slovak equivalent of New York's Guggenheim Museum, the gleaming white **Dukelské múzeum** (mid-April to Sept Tues–Thurs 8am–4pm, Fri

8am–3pm, Sat & Sun 10am–2pm; Oct to mid-April Tues–Thurs 8am–1pm, Fri 8am–3pm, Sat & Sun 10am–1pm), at the beginning of the road to Bardejov, houses a fairly standard exhibition on World War II, with plenty of military paraphernalia and a diorama of the "Valley of Death" (see "The Dukla Pass", below). About a kilometre along the Bardejov road, a gigantic **Soviet war memorial and cemetery** (vojenský cintorín) commemorates the many thousands who fell in the fighting. It's an exceptionally peaceful spot, disturbed only by the occasional coachload of Soviet war veterans, who stagger up the monumental staircase to lay wreaths to the sound of Beethoven's *Funeral March* blasting from speakers strategically hidden in the ornamental shrubbery.

On the opposite side of the road, ten minutes' walk down Festivalová, near the local football stadium, is Svidník's fairly new, **open-air folk skanzen** (Múzeum ukrajinskej dediny; May–Sept Tues–Fri 8.30am–6pm, Sat & Sun 10am–6pm). If you're not planning to visit any of the less-accessible villages, this is a great opportunity to get a close look at some thatched Rusyn cottages and a typical wooden Greek-Catholic church, transplanted from the nearby village of Nová Polianka.

Svidník really is an unpleasant place to have to stay, and the only **accommodation** is at the new eyesore on Centrálna, *Hotel Rubín* (☎ & fax 0937/242 11; ③) – if it's full, head for the **tourist office** (Mon–Fri 7.30am–3.30pm; ☎0937/16186), in the local cultural building on the corner of the main crossroads, at Sovietskych hrdinov 38. Trains don't run to Svidník, but the **bus station** is ten minutes' east of the central crossroads along Stropkova.

The Dukla Pass

The **Dukla Pass** (Dukliansky priesmyk), a fifteen-kilometre bus trip north of Svidník, was for centuries the main mountain crossing on the trade route from the Baltic to Hungary. This location has ensured a bloody history, the worst episode occurring in the last war, when over 80,000 Soviet soldiers and 6500 Czechs and Slovaks died trying to capture the valley from the Nazis. There's a giant granite memorial to the "Dukla Heroes" at the top of the pass, 1km from the Polish border, as well as an open-air museum of underground bunkers, tussling tanks and sundry armoured vehicles, strung out along the road from Višný Komárnik, the first village to be liberated in Czechoslovakia (on October 6, 1944), to Krajná Poľana.

Humenné

HUMENNÉ, like Prešov and Bardejov, is another Slovak town serving as a centre for the neighbouring Rusyn villages. It is a modern and spacious place, with more charm than you'd expect from a town based on the chemical industry; the few visitors who do make it this far (mostly American emigrés) head straight down the leafy main boulevard from the train station to Humenné's one and only sight, the stately seventeenth-century **zámok**, which is guarded by two female and two male lead lions. The **Vlastivedné múzeum** (local museum; May–Oct Tues–Fri 9am–noon & 12.30–5.30pm, Sat 9am–1pm, Sun 1–5pm), inside is not really worth visiting unless you need to escape from the rain. Instead, head northeast across the adjacent park to the **open-air folk skanzen** (May–Oct Tues–Sun 10am–5pm) round the back of the chateau gardens. Set in a pretty little meadow-cum-orchard, there's a whole series of thatched cottages and farmhouses, and a characteristic eighteenth-century wooden Greek-Catholic church from Nová Sedlica; ask for the information sheet in English (*anglický text*).

To get into town from the bus and train stations, turn right and continue along the main road, Staničná ulica, until you come to the leafy pedestrianized promenade of námestie Slobody, which leads up to the chateau. If you need to **stay**, the *Karpatia* (☎0933/775 20 38; ③) is conveniently located opposite the train station. For **food**, there's the inexpensive *Gastrocentrum* on the main square, or the *Zámocká vináreň*, in the chateau itself, which has a disco more or less every night.

Medzilaborce

Although actually closer to Svidník, **MEDZILABORCE** is best approached by train from Humenné, 42km to the south. The main reason for making the long journey out here is to visit the town's **Múzeum moderného umenia** (Museum of Modern Art; Tues–Sun 9am–noon & 12.45–5pm), one of the most surreal experiences this side of the Carpathians.

The inspiration for the museum came from local Rusyn artists and relatives of **Andy Warhol** from the US and the area around Medzilaborce, following the death of the artist in 1987. Although Warhol was born in Pittsburgh, the steel, aluminium and glass capital of the US, his real name was Andrej Varchola and his parents hailed from the Rusyn village of Miková, 8km northwest of Medzilaborce; his father was a coal-miner who, like many Rusyns, emigrated to the States shortly before World War I and was joined by the rest of the family in 1918. When fame and fortune hit in the 1960s, Warhol rarely made reference to his Slav origins, either in his work or conversation – "I come from nowhere", was his favourite enigmatic response.

Since Medzilaborce is a one-street town, it's impossible to miss the museum, a strikingly modern white building, which is unfortunately fading fast. Two giant Campbell's soup cans stand guard outside the main entrance, and the modest collection of original screen prints, on loan from the Andy Warhol Foundation in New York, are displayed upstairs in the main hall – the psychedelic *Red Lenin* and *Hammer & Sickle* are particularly appropriate choices – along with biographical details and quotes from Warhol (in Slovak, Rusyn and English) and a smattering of works by Ultra Violet. In the upper gallery, there are some derivative prints by Andy's brother, Paul, and his nephew, James, followed by a room of family portraits.

In addition to the Warhol stuff, the museum hosts temporary exhibitions, ranging from work by other Pop artists to contemporary Rusyn art, and organizes an ambitious programme of cultural events, gigs and talks. The gallery shop sells Warhol souvenirs (including tins of Campbell's soup) as well as information on Rusyn culture and language. Should you wish or need to stay over in Medzilaborce, there is one cheap, shabby **hotel**, *Laborec* (☎0939/213 07; ①), not far from the museum on ulica A. Warhola.

Košice

Rather like Bratislava, **KOŠICE** was, until relatively recently, a modest little town on the edge of the Hungarian plain. Then, in the 1950s, the Communists established a giant steel works on the outskirts of the city. Forty years on, Slovakia's second largest city has a population of over 250,000, a stunningly rejuvenated main square, a number of worthwhile museums, arguably the finest cathedral in the republic, and a lively cosmopolitanism that's reassuring after a week in the Slovak back of beyond. Just 21km north of the Hungarian border, Košice also acts as a magnet for the Hungarian community – to whom the city is known as *Kassa* – and for the terminally underemployed Romanies of the surrounding region, lending it a diversity and vibrancy absent from many provincial Slovak towns.

Arrival and accommodation

The **train** and **bus stations** are opposite each other, ten minutes' walk east of the old town, which is little more than five or six blocks across from east to west. From the sta-

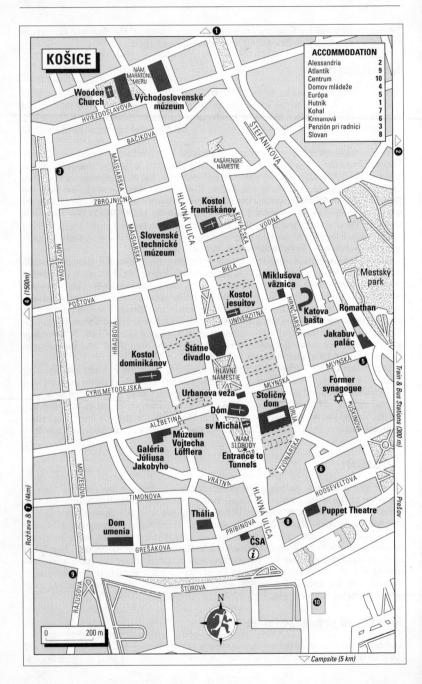

KOŠICE

ACCOMMODATION

Alessandria	2
Atlantik	9
Centrum	10
Domov mládeže	4
Európa	5
Hutník	1
Kohal	7
Krmanová	6
Penzión pri radnici	3
Slovan	8

Wooden Church

Východoslovenské múzeum

NÁM. MARATÓNU MIERU

HVIEZDOSLAVOVA

BAČIKOVA

ŠTEFÁNIKOVA

KAŠÁRENSKÉ NÁMESTIE

MAISIARSKA

ZBROJNIČNÁ

Kostol františkánov

KOVÁČSKA

VODNÁ

Slovenské technické múzeum

MOJZESOVA

MAISIARSKA

HLAVNÁ ULICA

BIELA

Mestský park

POŠTOVA

HRADBOVÁ

Kostol jesuitov

UNIVERZITNÁ

Miklušova väznica

HINČIARSKA

Katova bašta

Romathan

Jakabuv palác

Kostol dominikánov

Štátne divadlo

HLAVNÉ NÁMESTIE

MLYNSKÁ

MLYNSKÁ

Former synagogue

USKINOVA

CYRILMETODEJSKÁ

Urbanova veža

Stoličný dom

ORLIA

Dóm

sv Michál

ALŽBETINA

Galéria Júliusa Jakobyho

Múzeum Vojtecha Löfflera

NÁM. SLOBODY

Entrance to Tunnels

ZVONÁRSKA

VRÁTNA

MOJZESOVA

ROOSEVELTOVA

TIMONOVA

Thália

HLAVNÁ ULICA

Puppet Theatre

Dom umenia

PRIBINOVA

ČSA

GREŠÁKOVA

RAZUSOVA

ŠTÚROVA

N

0   200 m

△ ❶

▷ ❷

❸

◁ ❹ *(1500m)*

▷ *Train & Bus Stations (300 m)*

❺

❻

▷ *Prešov*

◁ *Rožňava & ❼ (4km)*

❽

ⓘ

❾

❿

▽ *Campsite (5 km)*

tions, head across the park to the fanciful neo-Gothic **Jakabov palác** (now the British Council), on Mlynská, built with stone left over from the renovation of the city's cathedral. The city **tourist office** (Mon–Fri 9am–6pm, Sat 9am–1pm; ☎095/16186) is at Hlavná ulica 8, at the southern end of the main square; another, equally useful information service is located in the Dargov department store at the base of the square (same hours). Given the compact nature of the city's old town, you shouldn't need to use the efficient **public transport** system, unless you're staying out in the suburbs. In any case, it's easy enough to use, just buy your ticket, which is valid for trams, buses and trolleybuses, beforehand and punch it when you get on board in the little devices to hand.

Accommodation

You might want to leave it to the city tourist office to help you book your accommodation, since they can deal with anything from hotels to small pensions and **private rooms**. With one or two exceptions, the city's hotels are overpriced communist-era places, with little to recommend them. *Domov mládeže* (☎095/643 56 88) is a year-round **hostel** on Medická, west of the centre via bus #17 or #34, or follow Poštovna to Vojenská, which becomes Ondavská, and turn left on Považská. Cheap dorm beds are also available at the *Kohal* (see below). The nearest **campsite** (mid-April to Sept) is 5km south of the city centre and also rents out bungalows; take tram #1 or #4, or bus #22 or #52, from the *Slovan* to the flyover, then get off and walk the remaining 500m west along Alejová, the road to Rožňava.

Alessandria, Jiskrova 3 (☎095/622 59 03). Košice's newly modernized top hotel, with doubles going for nearly 3000Sk, but inconveniently located ten minutes' walk northeast of the old town. ⑨.

Atlantik, Rázusova 1 (☎095/622 65 01). Small, simple, central pension that's often fully booked, so it's worth calling well in advance. ③.

Centrum, Južná trieda 2a (☎095/76 31 01). A short stroll south of the old town and, from the outside, a pretty ugly high-rise. Inside, however, it's probably the best of a bad bunch. ⑧.

Európa, Protifašistických bojovníkov 1 (☎095/622 38 97). Handily situated on the corner of Mlynská and one of the few cheapies in the city centre, but with all the worst features of communist-era hotels: unresponsive service, a seedy nightclub, and the fact that you get no en-suite facilities and no breakfast. ②.

Hutník, Tyršovo nábrežie 6 (☎095/633 77 80). Unreconstructed communist-era high-rise hotel a short walk north of the old town. Most rooms have shower, but no toilet. ⑤.

Kohal, Trieda SNP 61 (☎095/642 42 40). Large, cheap place amid the concrete high-rises, with dorm-room doubles for 320Sk and a decent restaurant. 10–15min by tram from the centre (#6 from Šturova or #9 or #R3 from námestie Maratónu mieru to Západ-Ferrocentrum). ③.

Krmanová, Krmanová 14 (☎095/623 05 65). New pension in the old town. A good alternative if the others are full, though the decor is rather sterile. ⑥.

Penzión pri radnici, Baaíkova 18 (☎095/622 78 24). Small pension with self-catering apartments, above a good restaurant in the backstreets of the old town, that offers, without a doubt, the most welcoming stay in the city for those with the dosh. ⑨.

Slovan, Hlavná ulica 1 (☎095/623 27 16). There seems little point in paying the extra at this communist-era high-rise hotel, when you can pay less for the same at the *Hutník*. ⑨.

The staré mesto

You'll find almost everything of interest on Košice's long, pedestrianized main square, which is called **Hlavná ulica** at its northern and southern extremities, **Hlavné námestie** to the north of the cathedral, and **Námestie slobody**, to the south of the cathedral. The whole area has been sensitively restored in the last few years, and, lined with a handsome parade of Baroque and Neoclassical palaces, it's really looking like the city's showpiece square nowadays, a favourite place for the local version of the evening *passeggiata*. Much of the credit for the square's wonderful revival is given to Rudolf

Schuster, Košice's mayor until 1999, when he was elected president of Slovakia. Schuster put heavy emphasis on the idea that a physically attractive city is the keystone of urban renewal, and he mobilized his finances to assure that one of the republic's most beautiful old towns would remain as such.

At the centre, dominating the scene, is the city's unorthodox – and Europe's easternmost – Gothic **Dóm**, whose charcoal-coloured stone is slowly being sandblasted back to its original honeyed hue. Begun around 1390, the cathedral was paid for by the riches of the salt trade, which reached their peak in the following century. It's dedicated to St Elizabeth (sv Alžbeta), patron saint of the cathedral, despite the fact that the city had a long and bitter row with her father, Charles of Anjou, over its monopoly of the salt trade. From the outside, it's an unusual, slightly misshapen building, with striped roof tiles like those of Vienna's Stephansdom, and a great gilded copper cupola that sits like a helmet on the main clock tower. Inside, the stellar vaulting and Gothic furnishings create quite an impression, particularly the main gilded altar which has a total of 48 panels depicting the Passion and the life of the Virgin. Also worth a closer inspection is the tall Gothic pastophory on the north side of the presbytery. One of the best features of the church is the intricate relief work above the north and west doors, their tympana respectively depicting the frantic scenes of the Last Judgement, and Christ and his sleepy disciples squeezed onto the Mount of Olives.

South of the cathedral is the similar but much smaller Gothic church of **sv Michal**, converted into a storehouse for weapons and ammunition during the sixteenth century when the threat of a Turkish invasion caused a mass exodus from the region and turned the town into little more than a military barracks. Opposite sv Michal, at no. 27 on the east side of the square, is the pale, ice-blue Baroque **Stoličný dom**, where the postwar government was declared by President Edvard Beneš on April 4, 1945, in what became known as the Košice Agreement. For the first time, the Slovaks were given equal nation status with the Czechs, but this was overshadowed by the fact that, for many, Beneš had sealed the fate of the country by handing over four key ministries to the Communists, including the Ministry of the Interior. The Communists also saw this as a turning point, and chose the house as the venue for Košice's museum of the working class; it now contains a branch of the Galéria Júliusa Jakobyho (see opposite).

Opposite the Stoličný dom is a small park in which a newly built passage leads down to a series of **tunnels** underneath the city. These tunnels were only discovered in 1996 during the installation of new utility pipes as part of the square's revitalization effort, and after archeological work had been carried out on them, they were opened to the public. Used during the Middle Ages for shelter and storage, the tunnels wiggle past sections of the old city walls, moat and alongside the foundation of the cathedral. To visit, you must wait for enough people to form a group at the tourist office at Hlavná 8 (Tues–Sun 11am–6pm), though claustrophobes might not enjoy them as they are rather dark and narrow.

On the busy north side of the cathedral, Košice's trickle of tourists dutifully admire the fourteenth-century **Urbanova veža**, the town tower which stands on its own set of mini-arcades, lined with gravestones discovered under the building during nineteenth-century renovation. Though the tower's top gallery is no longer open, the elaborate *Zvon urban* out front is a huge bell dating from 1557, which used to ring from on high. The public park and fountains at the centre of the main square are a favourite spot for hanging out and make an appropriately graceful foil for the city's grandiose **Štátne divadlo**, designed by the Austro-Hungarian firm of theatre-builders, Helmer & Fellner in 1899.

Close by, on the east side of the square, are two very fine facades dating from the same period: the one at no. 63 is the Art Nouveau *Café Slavia*, which features ceramic murals of storks and a large ceramic rondel on its central gable; no. 71, beyond the

Kostol jesuitov, sports a neo-Gothic stepped gable topped by a statue of a guy doffing his cap, and has wonderful lion brackets holding up its balcony. Further up on the same side, you might want to take a closer look at the **Kostol františkánov**, whose Baroque facade is adorned with an intricate Gothic stone relief of the Crucifixion, flanked by stucco curtains and cherubs added later on for dramatic effect; the ceiling frescoes inside the church will look great once they're restored to their former glory.

The tiny **water channel** you see running down the length of the square is another Schuster-inspired project. Centuries ago the cathedral and the small parks surrounding it stood on a small island in a stream; the stream was diverted so that Hlavná ulica could be built, but today's townsfolk wanted their stream back, so a narrow stone gulley was inlaid and the water again trickles through.

Museums and galleries

Košice's most gruesome museum is the **Miklušova väznica** (Mikluš Prison; Tues–Sat 9am–5pm, Sun 9am-1pm), down Univerzitná, whose original dimly lit dungeons and claustrophobic cells graphically transport you into the house's murky history as the city prison. Tickets for the prison must be bought from the ticket office of the geological and zoological museum in the **Katova bašta** (Hangman's bastion), through the arches diagonally opposite. If you're interested in Ferenc Rákóczi II, the museum also contains a few personal belongings and a mock-up of the rebel's house. A couple of blocks south, on Puškinova, is another grim reminder of human cruelty, the city's former **synagogue**, a pink crenellated affair built in 1927, with a memorial to the 12,000 local Jews sent to the camps during World War II. Back on the main square, opposite the Kostol františkánov, the **Slovenské technické múzeum** (Tues–Fri 8am–5pm, Sat 9am–2pm, Sun noon–5pm) holds a large and eclectic selection of "technical" exhibits, from a giant pair of seventeenth-century bellows to a Braille map of Europe. The emphasis, though, is on the wrought ironwork for which the region is famous – everything from gates to lampposts and church bells.

The city's **Galéria Júliusa Jakobyho** (June–Sept Tues–Sat 11am–7pm, Sun 11am–5pm; Oct–May Tues–Sat 10am–6pm, Sun 10am–2pm) usually puts on interesting temporary exhibitions culled from its large collection of twentieth-century Slovak, Hungarian and Austrian art: it has two branches, at Alžbetina 22, and in the **Stoličný dom** on Námestie slobody. Next door to the former is the peculiar and fascinating **Múzeum Vojtecha Löfflera** (Tues–Sat 10am–6pm, Sun 1–5pm), which features the work and private collections of Košice's most prominent Communist-sanctioned sculptor. Löffler is the man we have to thank for many of the country's most conspicuous Socialist Realist monuments of the 1960s and 1970s (a few of which litter the back courtyard), though he himself preferred working on abstract, wooden sculptures. More intriguing, though, is Löffler's collection of Slovak artists' self-portraits, which spans the entire century, and a display of local ceramics and crucifixes.

At the northern tip of the main square is námestie Maratónu mieru, named after the city's annual marathon, whose winners' names are etched into the monument at the centre of the square. On either side are the two bulky late-nineteenth-century buildings that make up the **Východoslovenské múzeum** (Tues–Sat 9am–5pm, Sun 9am–1pm). The museum building to the west is the one you want for its basement collection of extremely valuable fifteenth- to seventeenth-century **gold coins** – 2920 in all – minted at Kremnica, but stashed away by city burghers loyal to the Habsburgs when Imre Thököly's rebel force took Košice briefly in the 1670s. They were discovered by accident in 1935 by builders renovating no. 74 on the main square, appropriately enough the city's Finance Directorate. And just for good measure, if you haven't yet seen one, hidden round the back of the museum is a **wooden Greek-Catholic church**, brought here from Kožuchovce in Carpatho-Ruthenia.

Eating, drinking and entertainment

Košice's choice of places to **eat and drink** is underwhelming to say the least, though it is improving. The best places are mostly located in the streets to the east of the main square: *U vodnára*, Hrnčiarska 25, is a decent choice for a proper Slovak meal, while *Ajvega*, Orlia 10, is a popular **vegetarian** place that serves soya versions of standard Slovak dishes, washed down with fresh juices. The seafood and fish restaurant *Carabella*, just up the street at Orlia 4, does an admirable job considering its distance from the ocean. Several cafés line the west side of Hlavná ulica: *Carpano*, north of the cathedral at no. 42, aspires to be Italian and offers a limited menu of salads and light fare, while *Kleopatra Pizza Bar*, south of the cathedral at no. 24, occupies one of the finest settings of all, with outdoor tables overlooking a small park. A lively pub is the *Krivan*, two blocks west of the old town on námestie L. Novomestského; take Postová to the end, turn right up Kuzmányho, then left down Magurská. Sadly, the atmosphere at the city's most attractive **café**, the Art Nouveau *Slávia* is too snooty to be relaxing, but the soothing *Dobrá Čajovna*, Mäsiarská 42, is pleasing for its wide variety of teas.

As for **nightlife**, mainstream culture still predominates, particularly during the *Hudobná jar* (Musical Spring) festival in May. Full-scale **operas**, **ballets** and **plays** go on all year round at the wonderfully ornate Štátna divaldo (also known as the Divadlo Janka Borodáča) on the main square. Košice's philharmonic orchestra play regular **concerts** at the Dom umenia on Grešákova and occasionally inside the cathedral itself. Košice has a **Hungarian theatre**, Thália, on Mojmírova, and also boasts Slovakia's one and only **Romany theatre**, Romathan, which puts on a whole range of events from concerts to plays. You can catch **live jazz** most nights at the city's smoky *Jazz Club*, Kováčksa 39 (open daily 5pm–2am), and the occasional **folk gig** takes place at *Klub M*, Moldavská 37. The city's **nightclubs** are mostly worth avoiding, though if you're really keen to disco, head for the tacky *Jumbo Centrum*, on Masarykova, to the east of námestie Maratónu mieru, or you can club hop through the short string of places near *Kleopatra Pizza Bar* on Hlavná, south of the cathedral. To find out what's on at any of the above venues, and on the city's cinema screens, get hold of the free **listings booklet** *Kultúrny informátor* from the tourist office.

East to Michalovce and the Vihorlat

One of the most unusual sights in East Slovakia is the spectacular **Herľany geyser**, 22km northeast of Košice in the foothills of the Slanské vrchy, which shoots a jet of tepid water over thirty metres into the air for about twenty minutes or so every 32 to 34 hours. To get there, turn off route 50, up route 576 at Bidovce; Košice's tourist office will have the expected time of the next eruption, so you can plan your arrival to coincide with the geyser. East of Bidovce, route 50 plies through the **Dargov Pass** (Dargovský priesmyk), which cuts the low-lying north–south ridge of the Slanské vrchy in two. Though gentle enough to the eye, it was captured by the Soviet Army in World War II at a cost of over 22,000 men, a fact recorded by two tanks and a vast **war memorial** at the top of the pass. Coming down from the hills, you can see the hazy **Zemplín plain** below, stretching south into Hungary's Tokaj wine region and east into Ukraine.

Michalovce

Just under 60km east of Košice, and 35km west of the Ukrainian border, **MICHALOVCE** is the main point of arrival for people heading for the Slovak Sea or Zemplínska Šírava. Frequent buses run from Košice to Michalovce, but only two direct

---

HIKING IN THE VIHORLAT

The volcanic hills of the Vihorlat offer some of the most rewarding **hiking** outside the main Tatra ranges, in particular the trek up to the glacial lake of **Morské oko**. The best time to come is in late September, when the beech trees turn the hills a brilliant golden brown. The most difficult part is catching a bus further than the village of Remetské Hámre, which you'll need to do if you want to avoid walking the 9km up to the lake. In July and August, a daily bus from Michalovce to the car park just below Morské oko follows the long route along the southern shore of the Slovak Sea. The bus service that stops along the northern shore runs weekday mornings only.

From Remetské Hámre, it's a gentle two-hour hike along the pockmarked road to the lake; from the car park, it's just ten minutes. Unfortunately, it's not possible to swim in the lake since the whole area has been declared a nature reserve, but you can picnic wherever you please. Alternatively, it's an hour or so from the shores of the lake to **Sninský kameň** (1005m), a slab of sheer rock rising up above the tree line and accessible only by ladder. The view from the top is outstanding – the blue-green splodge of Morské oko, the Slovak Sea and Zemplín plain beyond are all clearly visible, and on a good day you can see over into Ukraine, just 15km to the east. If you'd prefer not to backtrack, it's less than an hour's walk north to the village of Zemplínske Hámre, from where it's a further 5km to Belá nad Cirochou (a short train ride from Michalovce).

---

trains (1hr 30min), which leave early in the morning – otherwise you'll have to change at Bánovce nad Ondravou (2hr 30min). Note, too, that the train station is a good 2km west of the town centre, whereas the bus station is just east of the main square.

Other than to change buses, there's no compelling reason to hang around in Michalovce. However, if you do find yourself with an hour to spare between departures, you could head for the **Zemplínske múzeum** (April–Oct Tues–Fri 9am–noon & 1–4pm, Sat 9am–noon, Sun 2–5pm; Nov–March Tues–Sat only), housed in the chateau behind the bus station. The elongated, pedestrianized main square, **Námestie osloboditeľov**, makes for a pleasant stroll; note the great turquoise building from 1911, now housing the *Bohéma* café, topped by a giant beehive and decorated with attractive stuccowork.

If you're **staying the night**, head for the *Hotel Družba* (☎0946/42 04 52; ⑥) by the bus station, which despite its unpromising exterior is very plush inside. For local Zemplín **cuisine**, try *Lagúna*, a block north of the main square in the park Studentov.

The Slovak Sea

A large artificial lake created in the 1960s for industrial purposes, the **Slovak Sea** (Zemplínska šírava), to the east of Michalovce, is a popular summer destination for Slovaks. Brash, cheek-by-jowl *chata* colonies make up the resorts that merge into one another along the lake's northern shores; not everyone's cup of tea, to be sure, but there are compensations – it's hotter here than anywhere else in the country, with the sun continuing to shine well into October. The water is far from crystal clear, but there are plenty of opportunities for **hiking** in the hills of the Vihorlat to the north of the lake (see box above).

VINNÉ, the first settlement you come to from Michalovce, isn't actually on the lake shore, but has its own swimming possibilities in the much cleaner mini-lake, Vinianske jazero, a short walk northeast of town, plus the ruined **Viniansky hrad** above the village (1hr 30min by foot). There is also a nice **campsite** along the lakeshore here with cheap bungalows – preferable to the sites along the Slovak Sea itself. The resorts along the sea are much of a concrete muchness, though the further east you go, the less

INTO UKRAINE

The only **road crossing** between Slovakia and Ukraine is the 24-hour one at Vyšné Nemecké; the **rail crossing** is at Čierna nad Tisou, whose railway siding was the scene of the last-ditch talks between the Soviets and Dubček's reformists shortly before the invasion of August 1968. You can obtain **Ukrainian visas** on the spot at border crossings for around £40/$60 in any hard currency, but be warned that stories of the **customs officials** at Uzhgorod (Užgorod) and Chop (Čop) on the Ukrainian side extorting cash or confiscating desirable items from travellers abound; delays of hours (even days) have been known, so a day-trip may prove impossible. The reason for this becomes apparent once you enter Trans-Carpathia; once an integral part of Czechoslovakia, it's now a forgotten corner of central Europe as poor and isolated as parts of Albania.

crowded they get. In August, **accommodation** can be a problem unless you have a tent, although many campsites have cheap bungalows to rent. The *Šírava* (☎0946/649 25 56; ④) in Kamenec has views over the sea. Of the many **campsites** along the shores, your best bet is the site just past Klokočov (mid-May to mid-Sept).

travel details

Trains

Connections with Bratislava: Čierná nad Tisou (1 daily; 8hr); Humenné (1 daily; 8hr 30min); Košice (10 daily; 5hr 10min–6hr 10min); Prešov (1 daily; 7hr); Rožňava (2 daily; 8hr).

Košice to: Čierná nad Tisou (7 daily; 1hr 10min–1hr 45min); Lučenec (3 daily; 3hr 10min); Plešivec (7 daily; 1hr 20min–1hr 50min); Rožňava (up to 7 daily; 1hr 15min–2hr).

Poprad to: Kežmarok/Stará Ľubovňa (every 1–2hr; 35min/1hr 35min); Košice (every 2hr; 1hr 30min); Prešov (2 daily; 1hr 20min); Spišská Nová Ves (up to 1 hourly; 20min).

Prešov to: Bardejov (up to 10 daily; 1hr 30min); Humenné (10 daily; 1hr 15min–2hr); Košice (up to 14 daily; 50min).

Buses

Košice to: Michalovce (1–2 hourly; 1hr 30min); Miskolc (1–2 daily; 2hr); Uzhgorod (8 daily; 4hr).

Levoča to: Poprad (up to 12 daily; 30–50min); Spišské Podhradie (up to 10 daily; 30min).

Poprad to: Prešov (up to 10 daily; 2hr); Spišské Podhradie (up to 6 daily; 45min–1hr 20min).

Prešov to: Košice (every 30min; 40min–1hr); Medzilaborce (1–2 daily; 2hr 20min); Michalovce (up to 10 daily; 1hr 45min); Uzhgorod (3 daily; 4hr).

Rožňava to: Krásnohorské Podhradie (up to 1 hourly; 10min); Ochtiná (4–5 daily; 40min); Dedinky/Poprad (up to 8 daily; 1hr/2hr).

Stará Ľubovňa to: Červený Kláštor (up to 10 daily; 40–50min); Prešov (up to 14 daily; 2hr); Bardejov (up to 12 daily; 1hr 20min); Svidník (1–2 daily; 1hr 45min).

Svidník to: Prešov (up to 9 daily; 1hr 40min); Dukla Pass (up to 4 daily; 35min); Bardejov (up to 10 daily; 1hr 5min); Medzilaborce (1 daily; 1hr 30min).

THE HISTORICAL FRAMEWORK

Czechoslovakia had been in existence for a mere 74 years when it officially split on January 1, 1993. Before that period, its constituent parts – Bohemia, Moravia and Slovakia – enjoyed quite separate histories: the first two under the sway of their German and Austrian neighbours, and Slovakia under the Hungarian crown. Only in the early days of Slav history were all three loosely linked together as the Great Moravian Empire; later, Bohemia consistently played a pivotal role in European history, prompting the famous pronouncement (attributed to Bismarck) that "he who holds Bohemia holds mid-Europe".

BEGINNINGS

According to Roman records, the area now covered by the Czech and Slovak republics was inhabited as early as 500 BC by **Celtic tribes**: the Boii, who settled in Bohemia (which bears their name), and the Cotini, who inhabited Moravia and parts of Slovakia. Very little is known about either tribe except that around 100 BC they were driven from these territories by two **Germanic tribes**: the Marcomanni, who occupied Bohemia, and the Quadi, who took over from the Cotini. These later seminomadic tribes proved awkward opponents for the Roman Empire, which wise-

ly chose the River Danube as its natural eastern border.

The disintegration of the Roman Empire in the fifth century AD corresponded with a series of raids into central Europe by eastern tribes: firstly the **Huns**, who displaced the Marcomanni and Quadi, and later the **Avars**, who replaced the Huns around the sixth century, settling a vast area including the Hungarian plains and parts of what are now the Czech and Slovak republics. About the same time, the **Slav tribes** entered Europe from east of the Carpathian mountains, and appear to have been subjugated by the Avars, at the beginning at least. Their first successful rebellion seems not to have taken place until the seventh century, under the Frankish leadership of **Samo**, though the kingdom he created died with him around 658 AD.

THE GREAT MORAVIAN EMPIRE

The next written record of the Slavs in this region isn't until the eighth century, when East Frankish (Germanic) chroniclers reported that a people known as the **Moravians** had established themselves around the River Morava, a tributary of the Danube, which now forms part of the border between the Czech and Slovak republics. It was an alliance of Moravians and Franks (under Charlemagne) that finally expelled the Avars from central Europe in 796 AD, clearing the way for the establishment of the **Great Moravian Empire**, which at its peak included Slovakia, Bohemia and parts of Hungary and Poland. Its significance in terms of Czech-Slovak relations is that this was the first and last time (until the establishment of Czechoslovakia, for which it served as a useful precedent) that Czechs and Slovaks were united under one ruler (though both sides now argue over whether the empire was more Czech or Slovak in character).

The first attested ruler of the empire, **Mojmír**, found himself at the political and religious crossroads of Europe, under pressure from two sides: from the west, where the Franks and Bavarians (both Germanic tribes) were jostling for position with the papacy; and from the east, where the patriarch of Byzantium was keen to extend his influence across eastern Europe. Mojmír's successor, **Rastislav** (850–870), plumped for Byzantium and invited the missionaries Cyril and Methodius to introduce

Christianity using the Slav liturgy and Eastern rites. Rastislav, however, was ousted by his nephew, **Svätopluk** (871–894), who allied himself instead with the Germans. After the death of Methodius in 885, the Great Moravian Empire fell decisively under the influence of the Roman Catholic Church.

Svätopluk died shortly before the **Magyar invasion** of 896, an event that heralded the end of the Great Moravian Empire and a significant break in Czech and Slovak history. The Slavs to the west of the River Morava (ie the Czechs) swore allegiance to the Frankish emperor, Arnulf; while those to the east (ie the Slovaks) found themselves under the yoke of the Magyars. This separation, which continued for the next millennium, is one of the major factors behind the distinct social, cultural and political differences between Czechs and Slovaks, which culminated in the separation of the two nations in 1993.

THE PŘEMYSLID DYNASTY

There is evidence that Bohemian dukes were forced in 806 to pay a yearly tribute of 500 pieces of silver and 120 oxen to the Carolingian Empire (a precedent the Nazis were keen to exploit as proof of German hegemony over Bohemia). These early Bohemian dukes "lived like animals, brutal and without knowledge", according to one chronicler. All that was to change when the earliest recorded Přemyslid duke **Bořivoj** (852/53–888/89) appeared on the scene. The first Christian ruler of Prague, Bořivoj was baptized in the ninth century, along with his wife Ludmila, by the Byzantine missionaries Cyril and Methodius (see above). Other than being the first to build a castle on Hradčany, nothing very certain is known about Bořivoj, nor about any of the other early Přemyslid rulers, although there are numerous legends, most famously that of **Prince Václav** (St Wenceslas), who was martyred by his pagan brother Boleslav the Cruel in 929 (see p.67).

Cut off from Byzantium by the Hungarian kingdom, Bohemia lived under the shadow of the **Holy Roman Empire** from the start. In 950, Emperor Otto I led an expedition against Bohemia, making the kingdom officially subject to the empire and its king one of the seven electors of the emperor. In 973, under Boleslav the Pious (967–999), a bishopric was founded in Prague, subordinate to the archbishopric of Mainz. Thus, by the end of the first millennium, German influence was already beginning to make itself felt in Bohemian history.

The **thirteenth century** was the high point of Přemyslid rule over Bohemia. With the Emperor Frederick II preoccupied with Mediterranean affairs and dynastic problems, and the Hungarians and Poles busy trying to repulse the Mongol invasions from 1220 onwards, the Přemyslids were able to assert their independence. In 1212, Otakar I (1198–1230) managed to extract a "**Golden Bull**" (formal edict) from the emperor, securing the royal title for himself and his descendants (who thereafter became kings of Bohemia).

The discovery of silver and gold mines throughout the Czech Lands and Slovakia heralded a big shift in the population from the countryside to the towns. Large-scale **German colonization** was generally encouraged by the Přemyslids in Bohemia and Moravia, and by the Hungarian Árpád dynasty in Slovakia. German miners and craftsmen founded whole towns in the interior of the country, where German civil rights were guaranteed them, for example Kutná Hora, Jihlava, Banská Bystrica and Levoča. At the same time, the territories of the Bohemian crown were increased to include not only Bohemia and Moravia, but also Silesia and Lusatia to the north (now divided between Germany and Poland).

The beginning of the fourteenth century saw a series of dynastic disputes – messy even by medieval standards – that started with the death of Václav II from consumption and excess in 1305. The following year, the murder of his heirless teenage son, Václav III, marked the **end of the Přemyslid dynasty** (he had four sisters, but female succession was not recognized in Bohemia). The nobles' first choice of successor, the Habsburg Albert I, was murdered by his own nephew, and when Albert's son, Rudolf I, died of dysentery not long afterwards, Bohemia was once more left without any heirs.

THE LUXEMBOURG DYNASTY

The crisis was finally solved when the Czech nobles offered the throne to **John of Luxembourg** (1310–46), who was married to Václav III's youngest sister. German by birth and educated in France, King John spent most of his reign participating in foreign wars, with Bohemia footing the bill, until his death on the field at Crécy in 1346. His son, **Charles IV** (1346–78), was wounded in the same battle but, thankfully for the Czechs, lived to tell the tale.

It was Charles who ushered in the Czech nation's **golden age**. Although born and bred in France, Charles was a Bohemian at heart (his mother was Czech and his real name was Václav): he was also extremely intelligent, speaking five languages fluently and even writing an autobiography. In 1346, he became not only king of Bohemia, but also, by election, Holy Roman emperor. Two years later he founded a university in Prague and began to promote the city as the cultural capital of central Europe, erecting rich Gothic monuments – many of which still survive – and numerous ecclesiastical institutions. As emperor, Charles issued many Golden Bull edicts that strengthened Bohemia's position, promoted Czech as the official language alongside Latin and German, and presided over a period of relative peace in central Europe, while western Europe was tearing itself apart in the Hundred Years' War.

Charles' son, **Václav IV** (1378–1419), who assumed the throne in 1378, was no match for such an inheritance. Stories that he roasted a cook alive on his own spit, shot a monk whilst hunting, and tried his own hand at lopping off people's heads with an axe, are almost certainly myths. Nevertheless, he was a legendary drinker, prone to violent outbursts, and so unpopular with the powers that be that he was imprisoned twice – once by his own nobles, and once by his brother, Sigismund. His reign was also characterized by religious divisions within the Czech Lands and Europe as a whole, beginning with the **Great Schism** (1378–1417), when rival popes held court in Rome and Avignon. This was a severe blow to Rome's centralizing power, which might otherwise have successfully rebuffed the assault on the Church that got under way in the Czech Lands towards the end of the fourteenth century.

THE CZECH REFORMATION

The attack was led by the peasant-born preacher **Jan Hus**, who gave sermons at Prague's Betlémská kaple. A follower of the English reformer John Wycliffe, Hus preached in the language of the masses (ie Czech) against the wealth, corruption and hierarchical tendencies within the Church at the time. Although a devout, mild-mannered man, he became embroiled in a dispute between the conservative clergy, led by the archbishop and backed by the pope in Rome, and the Wycliffian Czechs at the university. When the archbishop gave the order to burn the book of Wycliffe, Václav backed Hus and his followers, for political and personal reasons (Hus was, among other things, the confessor to his wife, Queen Sophie).

There can be little doubt that Václav used Hus and the Wycliffites to further his own political cause. He had been deposed as Holy Roman emperor in 1400 and, as a result, bore a grudge against the current emperor, Ruprecht of the Palatinate, and his chief backer, Pope Gregory XII in Rome. His chosen battleground was Prague's university, which was divided into four "nations" with equal voting rights: the Saxons, Poles and Bavarians, who supported Václav's enemies, and the Bohemians, who were mostly Wycliffites. In 1409 Václav issued the **Kutná Hora Decree**, which rigged the voting within the university giving the Bohemian "nation" three votes, and the rest a total of one. The other "nations", who made up the majority of the students and teachers, left Prague in protest.

Three years later the alliance between the king and the Wycliffites broke down. Widening his attacks on the Church, Hus began to preach against the sale of religious indulgences to fund the inter-papal wars, thus incurring the enmity of Václav, who received a percentage of the sales. In 1412, Hus and his followers were expelled from the university and excommunicated, and spent the next two years as itinerant preachers spreading their reformist gospel throughout Bohemia. Hus was then summoned to the **Council of Constance** to answer charges of heresy. Despite a guarantee of safe conduct from the emperor Sigismund, Hus was condemned to death and, having refused to renounce his beliefs, was burned at the stake on July 6, 1415.

Hus' martyrdom sparked off a **widespread rebellion** in Bohemia, initially uniting virtually all Bohemians – clergy and laity, peasant and noble (including many of Hus' former opponents) – against the decision of the council and, by inference, against the established Church and its conservative clergy. The Hussites immediately set about reforming Church practices, most famously by administering communion sub utraque specie ("in both kinds", ie bread and wine) to the laity, as opposed to the established practice of reserving the wine for the clergy.

THE HUSSITE WARS: 1419–34

In 1419, Václav inadvertently provoked large-scale rioting by endorsing the readmission of anti-Hussite priests to their parishes. In the ensuing violence, several Catholic councillors were thrown to their death from the windows of Prague's Novoměstská radnice, in Prague's **first defenestration** (see p.105). Václav himself was so enraged (not to say terrified) by the mob that he suffered a heart attack and died, "roaring like a lion", according to a contemporary chronicler. The pope, meanwhile, declared an international crusade against the Czech heretics, under the leadership of Václav's brother and heir, the emperor Sigismund.

Already, though, cracks were appearing in the Hussite camp. The more radical reformers, who became known as the **Táborites**, after their south Bohemian base, Tábor, broadened their attacks on the Church hierarchy to include all figures of authority and privilege. Their message found a ready audience among the oppressed classes in Prague and the Bohemian countryside, who went round eagerly destroying Church property and massacring Catholics. Such actions were deeply disturbing to the Czech nobility and their supporters, who backed the more moderate Hussites – known as the **Utraquists** (from the Latin sub utraque specie) – whose criticisms were confined to religious matters.

For the moment, however, the common Catholic enemy prevented a serious split among the Hussites, and under the inspirational military leadership of the Táborite **Jan Žižka**, the Hussites' (mostly peasant) army enjoyed some miraculous early victories over the numerically superior "crusaders", most notably at the Battle of Vítkov in Prague in 1420. The Bohemian Diet quickly drew up the **Four Articles of Prague**, which were essentially a compromise between the two Hussite camps, outlining the basic tenets on which all Hussites could agree, including communion "in both kinds". The Táborites, meanwhile, continued to burn, loot and pillage ecclesiastical institutions from Prague to the far reaches of Slovakia.

At the **Council of Basel** in 1433, Rome reached a compromise with the Utraquists over the Four Articles in return for ceasing hostilities. The peasant-based Táborites rightly saw the deal as a victory for the Bohemian nobility and the status quo, and vowed to continue the fight. However, the Utraquists, now in cahoots with the Catholic forces, easily defeated the remaining Táborites at the Battle of Lipany, outside Kolín, in 1434. The Táborites were forced to withdraw to the fortress town of Tábor. Poor old Sigismund, who had spent the best part of his life fighting the Hussites, died just three years later.

COMPROMISE

Despite the agreement of the Council of Basel, the pope refused to acknowledge the Utraquist church in Bohemia. The Utraquists nevertheless consolidated their position by electing the gifted **George of Poděbrady** as first regent and then king of Bohemia (1458–71). The first and last Hussite king, George (Jiuí to the Czechs), is remembered primarily for his commitment to promoting religious tolerance and his far-sighted efforts to establish some sort of "Peace Confederation" in Europe.

On George's death, the Bohemian Estates handed the crown over to the **Polish Jagiellonian dynasty**, who ruled in absentia and effectively relinquished the reins of power to the Czech nobility. In 1526, the last of the Jagiellonians, King Louis, was decisively defeated by the Turks at the Battle of Mohács and died fleeing the battlefield, leaving no heir to the throne. The Roman Catholic Habsburg Ferdinand I (1526–64) was elected king of Bohemia – and what was left of Hungary (mostly Upper Hungary, ie what is now Slovakia) – in order to fill the power vacuum, marking the **beginning of Habsburg rule** over what are now the Czech and Slovak republics. Ferdinand adroitly secured automatic hereditary succession over the Bohemian throne for his dynasty, in return for which he accepted the agreement laid down at the Council of Basel back in 1433. With the Turks at the gates of Vienna, he had little choice but to compromise at this stage, but in 1545, the international situation eased somewhat with the establishment of an armistice with the Turks.

In 1546, the Utraquist Bohemian nobility provocatively joined the powerful Protestant Schmalkaldic League in their (ultimately unsuccessful) war against the Holy Roman emperor Charles V. When armed conflict broke out in Bohemia, however, victory fell to Ferdinand, who tock the opportunity to extend the influence of Catholicism in the Czech Lands, executing several leading Protestant nobles, persecuting the reformist Unity of Czech Brethren who had figured prominently in the rebellion, and inviting Jesuit missionaries to establish churches and seminaries in the Czech Lands.

Like Václav IV, **Emperor Rudolf II** (1576–1611), Ferdinand's eventual successor, was moody and wayward, and by the end of his reign Bohemia was once more rushing headlong into a major international confrontation. But Rudolf also shared characteristics with Václav's father, Charles, in his genuine love of the arts, and in his passion for Prague, which he re-established as the royal seat of power, in preference to Vienna, which was once more under threat from the Turks. Czechs tend to regard Rudolfine Prague as a second golden age, but as far as the Catholic church was concerned, Rudolf's religious tolerance and indecision were a disaster. In the early 1600s, Rudolf's melancholy began to veer dangerously close to insanity, a condition he had inherited from his Spanish grandmother, Joanna the Mad. And in 1611, the heirless Rudolf was forced to abdicate by his brother **Matthias**, to save the Habsburg house from ruin. Ardently Catholic, but equally heirless, Matthias proposed his cousin **Ferdinand II** as his successor in 1617. This was the last straw for Bohemia's mostly Protestant nobility, and the following year conflict erupted again.

THE THIRTY YEARS' WAR: 1618–1648

On May 23, 1618, two Catholic nobles were thrown out of the windows of Prague Castle – the country's **second defenestration** (see p.68) – an event that's now taken as the official beginning of the complex religious and dynastic conflicts collectively known as the **Thirty Years' War**. Following the defenestration, the Bohemian Diet expelled the Jesuits and elected the youthful Protestant "winter king", Frederick of the Palatinate, to the throne. In the first decisive set-to of the war, the Protestants were utterly defeated at the **Battle of Bílá hora** (Battle of the White Mountain), which took place on November 8, 1620, on the outskirts of Prague. In the aftermath, 27 Protestant nobles were executed on Prague's Staroměstské náměstí, and the heads of ten of them displayed on the Charles Bridge.

It wasn't until the Protestant Saxons occupied Prague in 1632 that the heads were finally taken down and given a proper burial. The Catholics eventually drove the Saxons out, but for the last ten years of the war, Bohemia and Moravia became the main battleground between the new champions of the Protestant cause – the Swedes – and the imperial Catholic forces. In 1648, the final battle of the war was fought in Prague, when the Swedes seized Malá Strana, but failed to take Staré Město, thanks to the stubborn resistance of Prague's Jewish and newly Catholicized student populations on the Charles Bridge.

COUNTER-REFORMATION TO ENLIGHTENMENT

The Thirty Years' War ended with the **Peace of Westphalia**, which, for the Czechs, was as disastrous as the war itself. An estimated five-sixths of the Bohemian nobility went into exile, their properties handed over to loyal Catholic families from Austria, Spain, France and Italy. The country was devastated, towns and cities laid waste, and the total population reduced by almost two-thirds. On top of all that, the Czech Lands and Slovakia were now decisively under Catholic influence, and the full force of the **Counter-Reformation** was brought to bear on its people. All forms of Protestantism were outlawed, the education system handed over to the Jesuits and, in 1651 alone, over two hundred "witches" burned at the stake in Bohemia.

The next two centuries of Habsburg rule are known to the Czechs as the **Dark Ages**. The focus of the empire shifted back to Vienna, the Habsburgs' absolutist grip catapulted the remaining nobility into intensive Germanization, while fresh waves of German immigrants reduced Czech to a despised dialect spoken by peasants, artisans and servants. The situation was so bad that Prague and most other urban centres became practically all-German cities. By the end of the eighteenth century, the Czech language was on the verge of dying out, with government, scholarship and literature carried out exclusively in German. For the newly ensconced Germanized aristocracy, of course, the good times rolled, and the country was endowed with numerous Baroque palaces and monuments.

After a century of iron-fisted Habsburg rule, the accession of Charles VI's daughter, **Maria Theresa** (1740–80), to the throne, marked the beginning of the **Enlightenment** in the empire. The empress acknowledged the need for reform and, despite her own personal attachment to the Jesuits, followed the lead of Spain, Portugal and France in expelling the order in 1773. But it was her son, **Joseph II** (1780–90), who brought about the most radical changes to the social structure of the Habsburg lands. His 1781 Edict of Tolerance allowed a large degree of freedom of worship for the first time in over 150 years, and went a long way towards lifting the restrictions on Jews. The following year, he ordered the dissolution of the monasteries and embarked upon the abolition of serfdom. Despite all his reforms, though, Joseph was not universally popular. Catholics – by now some ninety percent of the population – viewed him with disdain. His centralization and bureaucratization placed power in the hands of the Austrian civil service, and thus helped to entrench the **Germanization** of the Czech Lands. He also offended the Czechs by breaking with tradition and not bothering to hold an official coronation ceremony in Prague.

THE SLOVAK NATIONAL REVIVAL

What the Czechs suffered in the three centuries following the Battle of Bílá hora, the Slovaks had to endure for almost a millennium under **Hungarian rule**. The territory of modern-day Slovakia was known simply as Upper Hungary, an integral part of the Hungarian Kingdom. Apart from a few German-speaking mining towns, it remained overwhelmingly rural and resolutely feudal, and those Slovaks who did rise to positions of power were swiftly "Magyarized".

The Battle of Mohács in 1526 signalled a temporary eclipse for the Hungarians as the Habsburgs assumed control of the kingdom. The eighteenth-century Enlightenment, however, boosted the **Magyar national revival**, and in 1792 Hungarian finally replaced Latin as the official state language throughout the Hungarian Kingdom. But Magyar nationalism was essentially chauvinistic, furthering the interests only of the Magyarized nobility, and the idea that non-Magyars might want to assert their own identity was regarded as highly subversive.

With a thoroughly Magyarized aristocracy, and a feudal society with virtually no Slovak middle class, the **Slovak national revival** or národné obrodenie was left to the tiny Slovak intelligentsia, comprising mostly Lutheran clergymen – passionately pro-Czech and anti-Magyar, but alienated from the majority of the devoutly Catholic Slovak peasantry on account of their religious beliefs. The leading Slovak figure throughout this period was **Ľudovít Štúr** (see p.390), son of a Lutheran pastor. Although a pan-Slavist, he was also, unlike many of his contemporaries, an ardent advocate of a separate Slovak language based on his own central Slovak dialect.

THE CZECH NATIONAL REVIVAL

The Habsburgs' enlightened rule inadvertently provided the basis for the economic prosperity and social changes of the **Industrial Revolution**, which in turn fuelled the Czech national revival of the nineteenth century. The textile, glass, coal and iron industries began to grow, drawing ever more Czechs in from the countryside and swamping the hitherto mostly Germanized towns and cities. An embryonic Czech bourgeoisie emerged and, thanks to Maria Theresa's educational reforms, new educational and economic opportunities were given to the Czech lower classes.

For the first half of the century, the **Czech national revival** or národní obrození was confined to the new Czech intelligentsia, led by philologists like Josef Dobrovský and Josef Jungmann at Prague's Charles University or Karolinum. Language disputes (in schools, universities and public offices) remained at the forefront of Czech nationalism throughout the nineteenth century, only later developing into demands for political autonomy. The leading figure of the time was the Moravian Protestant and historian **František Palacký**, who wrote the first history of the Czech nation, rehabilitating Hus and the Czech reformists in the process. He was in many ways typical of the early Czech nationalists – pan-Slavist and virulently anti-German, but not yet entirely anti-Habsburg.

1848 AND ALL THAT

The fall of the French monarchy in February 1848 prompted a crisis in the Habsburg Empire. The new bourgeoisie, both of Czech-, German- and Hungarian-speakers, began to make political demands: freedom of the press, of assembly, of religious creeds and, in the nature of the empire, more rights for its constituent nationalities. In the **Czech Lands**, liberal opinion became polarized between the Czech- and German-speakers. Palacký and his followers were against the dissolution of the empire and argued instead for a kind of multinational federation. Since the empire contained a majority of Slavs, the ethnic Germans were utterly opposed to Palacký's scheme, campaigning instead for unification with Germany to secure their interests. So when Palacký was invited to the Pan-German National Assembly in Frankfurt in May, he refused to go. Instead, he convened a **Pan-Slav Congress** the following month, which met in Prague. Meanwhile, the radicals and students (on both sides) took to the streets in protest, erecting barricades and giving the forces of reaction an excuse to declare martial law. In June, the Habsburg military commander bombarded Prague; the following morning the city capitulated – the counter-revolution in the Czech Lands had begun.

In the **Hungarian Kingdom**, the 1848 revolution successfully toppled the Habsburgs, and a liberal, constitutional government was temporarily set up in Budapest. However, Hungarian liberals like Lajos Kossuth (himself from a Magyarized Slovak family) showed themselves to be more reactionary than the Habsburgs when it came to opposing the aspirations of non-Magyars. The "Demands of the Slovak Nation", drafted by Štúr, were refused pointblank by the Hungarian Diet in May 1848. Incensed by this, Štúr and his small Slovak army went over to the Habsburgs and into battle (unsuccessfully) against Kossuth's revolutionaries. Only in August 1849 was Habsburg rule reinstated, thanks to the intervention of tsarist Russian troops on the streets of Budapest.

In both cases, the upheavals of 1848 left the absolutist Habsburg Empire shaken but fundamentally unchanged. The one great positive achievement in 1848 was the **emancipation of the peasants**. Otherwise, events only served to highlight the sharp differences between German and Czech aspirations in the Czech Lands, and between Hungarian and Slovak aspirations in the Hungarian Kingdom. The Habsburg recovery was, however, short-lived. In 1859 and again in 1866, the new emperor, Francis Joseph II, suffered humiliating defeats at the hands of the Italians and Prussians

respectively. In order to buy some more time, the compromise or Ausgleich of 1867 was drawn up, establishing the so-called **Dual Monarchy** of Austria-Hungary – two independent states united under one ruler.

DUALISM: THE CZECH LANDS

The Ausgleich came as a bitter disappointment for the Czechs, who remained second-class citizens while the Magyars became the Austrians' equals. The Czechs' failure to bend the emperor's ear was no doubt partly due to the absence of a Czech aristocracy that could bring its social weight to bear at the Viennese court. Nevertheless, the Ausgleich did mark an end to the absolutism of the immediate post-1848 period, and, compared to the Hungarians, the Austrians were positively enlightened in the wide range of civil liberties they granted, culminating in universal male suffrage in 1907.

Under Dualism, the Czech **national revival** flourished – and splintered. The liberals and conservatives known as the **Old Czechs**, backed by the new Czech industrialists, advocated working within the existing legislature to achieve their aims. By 1890, though, the more radical **Young Czechs** had gained the upper hand and instigated a policy of non-co-operation with Vienna. The most famous political figure to emerge from the ranks of the Young Czechs was the Prague university professor **Tomáš Garrigue Masaryk**, who founded his own Realist Party and began advocating the (then rather quirky) concept of closer co-operation between the Czechs and Slovaks.

DUALISM: SLOVAKIA

For the Slovaks, the Ausgleich was nothing less than a catastrophe. In the 1850s and 1860s, direct rule from Vienna had kept Magyar chauvinism at bay, allowing the Slovaks to establish various cultural and educational institutions. After 1867, the Hungarian authorities embarked on a maniacal policy of **Magyarization**, which made Hungarian (and only Hungarian) compulsory in both primary and secondary schools. Large landowners were the only ones to be given the vote (a mere six percent of the total population), while the majority of non-Magyars remained peasants. Poverty and malnutrition were commonplace throughout Upper Hungary, and by 1914, twenty percent of the Slovak population had emigrated, mostly to the USA.

Given the suffocating policies of the Magyars, it's a miracle that the Slovak national revival (and even the language itself) was able to survive. The leading Slovak political force, the Slovak National Party, was driven underground, remaining small, conservative, and for the most part Lutheran, throughout the latter part of the nineteenth century. The one notable exception was the Catholic priest **Andrej Hlinka**, whose unflinching opposition to Magyar rule earned him increasingly wide support among the Slovak people.

WORLD WAR I

At the outbreak of **World War I**, the Czechs and Slovaks showed little enthusiasm for fighting alongside their old enemies, the Austrians and Hungarians, against their Slav brothers, the Russians and Serbs. As the war progressed, large numbers defected to form the **Czechoslovak Legion**, which fought on the Eastern Front against the Austrians. Masaryk travelled to the USA to curry favour for a new Czechoslovak state, while his two deputies, the Czech Edvard Beneš and the Slovak Milan Štefánik, did the same in Britain and France.

Meanwhile, the Legion, now numbering around 100,000 men, became embroiled in the Russian revolutions of 1917 and, when the Bolsheviks made peace with Germany, found itself cut off from the homeland. The uneasy co-operation between the Reds and the Legion broke down when Trotsky demanded that they hand over their weapons before heading off on their legendary **anabasis**, or march back home, via Vladivostok. The soldiers refused and became further involved in the Civil War, for a while controlling large parts of Siberia and, most importantly, the Trans-Siberian Railway, before arriving back to a tumultuous reception in their new joint republic.

In the summer of 1918, the Allies finally recognized Masaryk's provisional government. On October 28, 1918, as the Habsburg Empire began to collapse, the first **Czechoslovak Republic** was declared in Prague. Two days later, a group of Slovaks gathered in Martin and issued the **Martin Declaration**, accepting in principle the union with the Czechs. Meanwhile, the German-speaking border regions of Bohemia and Moravia (later to become known as the Sudetenland) declared themselves autonomous provinces of the new republic of Deutsch-Öster-

reich (German-Austria), which it was hoped would eventually unite with Germany itself. The new Czechoslovak government was having none of it, but it took the intervention of Czechoslovak troops before control of the border regions was wrested from the secessionists.

In Slovakia, any qualms the Slovaks may have had about accepting rule from Prague were superseded by fear of Béla Kun's Hungarian Red Army who proceeded to occupy much of the country, and were only booted out by the Czechoslovak Legion late on in 1919. In June 1920, the **Treaty of Trianon** confirmed the controversial new Slovak-Hungarian border along the Danube, leaving some 750,000 Hungarians on Czechoslovak soil, and a correspondingly large number of Slovaks within Hungarian territory.

Last to opt in favour of the new republic was **Ruthenia** (officially known as Sub-Carpatho-Ruthenia), a rural backwater of the old Hungarian Kingdom that became officially part of Czechoslovakia in the Treaty of St Germain in September 1919. Its incorporation was largely due to the campaigning efforts of Ruthenians who had emigrated to the USA. For the new republic, the province was a strategic bonus but a huge drain on resources.

THE FIRST REPUBLIC

The new nation of Czechoslovakia began postwar life in an enviable economic position – **tenth in the world industrial league table** – having inherited seventy to eighty percent of Austria-Hungary's industry intact. Less enviable was the diverse make-up of its population – a melange of minorities that would in the end prove its downfall. Along with the six million Czechs and two million Slovaks who initially backed the republic, there were over three million Germans and 600,000 Hungarians, not to mention sundry other Ruthenians (Rusyns), Jews and Poles.

That Czechoslovakia's democracy survived as long as it did is down to the powerful political presence and skill of **Masaryk**, the country's president from 1918 to 1935, who shared executive power with the cabinet. It was his vision of social democracy that was stamped on the nation's new constitution, one of the most liberal of the time (if a little too bureaucratic and centralized), aimed at ameliorating any ethnic and class tensions within the republic by means of universal suffrage, land reform and, more specifically, the Language Law, which ensured bilinguality to any area where the minority exceeded twenty percent.

The elections of 1920 reflected the mood of the time, ushering in the left-liberal alliance of the **Pětka** ("The Five"), a coalition of five parties led by the Agrarian Antonín Yvehla, whose slogan "We have agreed that we will agree" became the keystone of the republic's consensus politics between the wars. Gradually, all the other parties (except the Fascists and Communists) – including even Hlinka's Slovak People's Party (HSMS) and most of the Sudeten German parties – began to participate in (or at least not disrupt) parliamentary proceedings. On the eve of the Wall Street Crash, the republic was enjoying an economic boom, a cultural renaissance and a temporary modus vivendi among its minorities.

THE THIRTIES

The 1929 Wall Street Crash plunged the whole country into crisis. Economic hardship was quickly followed by **political instability**. In Slovakia, the HSMS fed off the anti-Czech resentment fuelled by Prague's manic centralization, and the appointment of Czechs to positions of power throughout the region. Taking an increasingly nationalist/separatist position, the HSMS was by far the largest party in Slovakia, consistently polling around thirty percent. In Ruthenia, the elections of 1935 gave only 37 percent of the vote to parties supporting the republic, the rest going to the Communists, pro-Magyars and other autonomist groups.

But the most intractable of the minority problems was that of the Sudeten Germans. Nationalist sentiment had always run high in the Sudetenland, whose German-speakers resented being included in the new republic, but it was only after the Crash that the extremist parties began to make significant electoral gains. Encouraged by the rise of Nazism in Germany, and aided by rocketing Sudeten German unemployment, the proto-Nazi **Sudeten German Party** (SdP), led by a gym teacher named Konrad Henlein, was able to win over sixty percent of the German-speaking votes in the 1935 elections, making it the largest single party in the national parliament.

Although constantly denying any wish to secede from the republic, after 1935 Henlein and the SdP were increasingly funded and directed by Nazi Germany. To make matters worse, the Czechs suffered a severe blow to their morale with the death of Masaryk late in 1937, leaving the country in the less capable hands of his Socialist deputy, Edvard Beneš. With the Nazi annexation of Austria (the Anschluss) on March 11, 1938, Hitler was free to focus his attention on the Sudetenland, calling Henlein to Berlin on March 28 and giving him instructions to call for outright autonomy.

THE MUNICH CRISIS

On April 24, 1938, the SdP launched its final propaganda offensive in the **Karlsbad Decrees**, demanding (without defining) "complete autonomy". As this would have meant surrendering the entire Czechoslovak border defences in the western half of the country, not to mention causing economic havoc, Beneš refused to bow to the SdP's demands. Armed conflict was only narrowly avoided and, by the beginning of September, Beneš was forced reluctantly to acquiesce to some sort of autonomy. On Hitler's orders, Henlein refused Beneš's offer and called openly for the secession of the Sudetenland to the German Reich.

On September 15, as Henlein fled to Germany, the British prime minister, Neville Chamberlain, flew to Berchtesgaden on his own ill-conceived initiative, to "appease" the Führer. A week later, Chamberlain flew again to Germany, this time to Bad Godesberg, vowing to the British public that the country would not go to war (in his famous words) "because of a quarrel in a faraway country between people of whom we know nothing". Nevertheless, the French issued draft papers, the British Navy was mobilized, and the whole of Europe fully expected war.

Then in the early hours of September 30, in one of the most treacherous and self-interested acts of modern European diplomacy, prime ministers Chamberlain (for Britain) and Daladier (for France) signed the **Munich Diktat** with Mussolini and Hitler, agreeing – without consulting the Czechoslovak government – to all of Hitler's demands. The British and French public were genuinely relieved, and Chamberlain flew home to cheering crowds, waving his famous piece of paper that guaranteed "peace in our time".

THE SECOND REPUBLIC

Betrayed by his only Western allies and fearing bloodshed, Beneš capitulated, against the wishes of most Czechs. Had Beneš not given in, however, it's doubtful anything would have come of Czech armed resistance, surrounded as they were by vastly superior hostile powers. Beneš resigned on October 5 and left the country, and the one-eyed war veteran Jan Sýrový became prime minister and Emil Hácha president. Ten days later, **German troops occupied Sudetenland**, to the dismay of the forty percent of Sudeten Germans who hadn't voted for Henlein (not to mention the half a million Czechs who lived there). The Poles took the opportunity to seize a sizeable chunk of North Moravia.

Many Slovaks viewed the Munich Diktat as a blessing in disguise, since it allowed them to set up their own autonomous government, in what became known as the **Žilina Accord**. However, the "rump" **Second Republic** (officially known as Czecho-Slovakia), was not long in existence before it too collapsed. On March 15, 1939, Hitler informed Hácha of the imminent Nazi occupation of what was left of the Czech Lands, and persuaded him to demobilize the army, again against the wishes of many Czechs. The invading German army encountered no resistance (nor any response from the Second Republic's supposed guarantors, Britain and France) and swiftly set up the Nazi **Protectorate of Bohemia and Moravia**. The Hungarians effortlessly crushed Ruthenia's one-day-old independent republic, while the HSMS, in an agreement with Hitler, declared **Slovak independence**, under the leadership of the Catholic priest Jozef Tiso.

.WORLD WAR II

In the first few months of the occupation, left-wing activists were arrested and Jews placed under the infamous Nuremburg Laws, but Nazi rule in the Protectorate at that time was not as harsh as it was to become – the economy even enjoyed a mini-boom. Then in late October and November 1939, Czech students began a series of demonstrations against the Nazis, who responded by closing down all institutions of higher education. Calm was restored until 1941, when a leading SS officer, **Reinhard Heydrich**, was put in charge of the Protectorate. Arrests and deportations followed, reaching fever pitch after Heydrich was assassinated by the Czech resistance in June 1942 (see p.106). The "final solution" was

meted out on the Protectorate's remaining Jews, who were transported first to the ghetto of Terezín, and then on to the extermination camps in Poland. The rest of the Czech population was frightened into submission, and there were very few acts of active resistance in the Czech Lands until the Prague Uprising of May 1945.

In independent Slovakia, **Jozef Tiso**'s government met with widespread support, since, for the first time ever, the Slovaks were able to establish and run their own national institutions. Gradually, however, the extremist Hlinka Guards (the Slovak equivalent of the SS) got the upper hand and began the inexorable Nazification of Slovak society, eventually overseeing the deportation of Slovak Jews. The resistance movement was slow to start, but, with Nazi defeat looking more and more likely, it became strong enough by August 1944 to attempt an all-out **Slovak National Uprising** in the central mountains (see p.410-1). When the hoped-for Soviet offensive failed to materialize, the uprising was brutally suppressed and any pretence at Slovak independence abandoned for full-scale Nazi occupation.

By the end of 1944, Czechoslovak and Russian troops had begun to liberate the country, starting with Ruthenia, which Stalin decided to take as war booty despite having guaranteed to maintain Czechoslovakia's pre-Munich borders. On April 4, 1945, under Beneš's leader ship, the provisional **Národní fronta** government – a coalition of Social Democrats, Socialists and Communists – was set up in Košice. On May 5, the people of Prague finally rose up against the Nazis, many hoping to prompt an American offensive from Plzeň, recently captured by General Patton's Third Army. In the end, the Americans made the politically disastrous (but militarily wise) decision not to cross the previously agreed upon demarcation line. The Praguers held out against the Nazis until May 9, when the Russians finally entered the city.

THE THIRD REPUBLIC

Violent reprisals against suspected collaborators and the German-speaking population in general began as soon as the country was liberated. All Germans were given the same food rations as the Jews had been given during the war. Starvation, summary executions and worse resulted in the deaths of thousands of ethnic Germans. With considerable popular backing and the tacit approval of the Red Army, Beneš began to organize the **forced expulsion of the German-speaking population**, referred to euphemistically by Czechs and Slovaks as the *odsun* (transfer). Only those Germans who could prove their antifascist credentials were permitted to stay – the Czechs and Slovaks were not called on to prove the same – and by the summer of 1947, nearly 2.5 million Germans had been kicked out or had fled in fear. On this occasion, Sudeten German objections were brushed aside by the Allies, who had given Beneš the go-ahead for the *odsun* at the postwar Potsdam Conference. Attempts by Beneš to expel Slovakia's Hungarian-speaking minority in similar fashion, however, proved unsuccessful.

On October 28, 1945, in accordance with the leftist programme thrashed out at Košice, sixty percent of the country's industry was nationalized. Confiscated Sudeten German property was handed out by the largely Communist-controlled police force, and in a spirit of optimism and/or opportunism, people began to join the Communist Party (KSČ) in droves, membership more than doubling in less than a year. In the **May 1946 elections**, the Party reaped the rewards of their enthusiastic support for the *odsun*, of Stalin's vocal opposition to Munich, and of the recent Soviet liberation, emerging as the strongest single party in the Czech Lands, with up to forty percent of the vote (the largest ever for a European communist party in a multi-party election). In Slovakia, however, they achieved just thirty percent, thus failing to push the Democrats into second place. President Beneš appointed the KSČ leader, **Klement Gottwald**, prime minister of another Národní fronta coalition, with several, strategically important, cabinet portfolios going to Party members, including the ministries of the Interior, Finance, Labour and Social Affairs, Agriculture, and Information.

Gottwald assured everyone of the KSČ's commitment to parliamentary democracy and, initially at least, even agreed to participate in the Americans' Marshall Plan (the only Eastern Bloc country to do so). Stalin immediately summoned Gottwald to Moscow, and on his return the KSČ denounced the plan. By the end of 1947, the Communists were beginning to lose support as the harvest failed, the economy fal-

tered and malpractices within the Communist-controlled Ministry of the Interior were uncovered. In response, the KSČ began to up the ante, constantly warning the nation of imminent "counter-revolutionary plots", and arguing for greater nationalization and land reform as a safeguard.

Then in February 1948 – officially known as **Victorious February** – the latest in a series of scandals hit the Ministry of the Interior, prompting the twelve non-Communist cabinet ministers to resign en masse in the hope that this would force a physically weak President Beneš to dismiss Gottwald. No attempt was made, however, to rally popular support against the Communists. Beneš received over 5000 resolutions supporting the Communists and just 150 opposing them. Stalin sent word to Gottwald to take advantage of the crisis and ask for military assistance – Soviet troops began massing on the Hungarian border.

It was the one time in his life when Gottwald disobeyed Stalin; instead, by exploiting divisions within the Social Democrats, Gottwald was able to maintain his majority in parliament. The KSČ took to the streets (and the airwaves), arming "workers' militia" units to defend the country against counter-revolution, calling a general strike and finally, on February 25, organizing the country's biggest-ever demonstration in Prague. The same day, Gottwald went to an indecisive (and increasingly ill) Beneš with his new cabinet, all Party members or "fellow travellers". Beneš accepted Gottwald's nominees, and the most popular Communist coup in eastern Europe was complete, without bloodshed and without the direct intervention of the Soviets. In the aftermath of the coup, thousands of Czechs and Slovaks fled abroad.

THE PEOPLE'S REPUBLIC

Following Victorious February, the Party began to consolidate its position, a relatively easy task given its immense popular support and control of the army, police force, workers' militia and trade unions. A **new constitution** confirming the "leading role" of the Communist Party and the "dictatorship of the proletariat" was passed by parliament on May 9, 1948. President Beneš refused to sign it, resigned in favour of Gottwald, and died (of natural causes) shortly afterwards. Those political parties that were not banned or forcibly merged with the KSČ were prescribed fixed-percentage representation and subsumed within the so-called "multiparty" Národní fronta.

With the Cold War in full swing, the **Stalinization** of Czechoslovak society was quick to follow. In the Party's first Five Year Plan, ninety percent of industry was nationalized, heavy industry (and, in particular, the country's defence industry) was given a massive boost, and compulsory collectivization forced through. Party membership reached an all-time high of 2.5 million, with "class-conscious" Party cadres rewarded with positions of power. "Class enemies" (and their children), on the other hand, suffered discrimination, and it wasn't long before the Czechoslovak mining "gulags" began to fill up with the regime's political opponents – "kulaks", priests and "bourgeois oppositionists" – who numbered over 100,000 at their peak.

Having incarcerated most of its external opponents, the KSČ, with a little prompting from Stalin, embarked upon a ruthless period of internal bloodletting. As the economy nose-dived, the press was filled with calls for intensified "class struggle", rumours of impending "counter-revolution" and reports of economic sabotage by fifth columnists. An atmosphere of fear and confusion was created to justify **large-scale arrests of Party members** with an "international" background – those with a wartime connection with the West, Spanish Civil War veterans, Jews and Slovak nationalists.

In the early 1950s, the Party organized a series of Stalinist **show-trials**, the most ruthless of their kind outside the Soviet Union, including the trial of Rudolf Slánský, who had been second only to Gottwald in the KSČ before his arrest. He and thirteen other leading Party members were sentenced to death (eleven of them Jewish, including Slánský) as "Trotskyist-Titoist-Zionists". Soon afterwards, Vladimír Clementis, the former KSČ foreign minister, was executed along with other leading Slovak comrades (Gustáv Husák, the post-1968 president, was given life imprisonment).

AFTER STALIN

Gottwald died in mysterious circumstances in March 1953, nine days after attending Stalin's funeral in Moscow (some say he drank himself to death). The whole nation heaved a sigh of relief, but the regime seemed as unrepentant as ever, and the arrests and show-trials continued.

Then, on May 30, the new Communist leadership announced a drastic currency devaluation, effectively reducing wages by ten percent while raising prices. The result was a wave of isolated **workers' demonstrations** and rioting in Prague, Plzeň and the Ostrava mining region. Czechoslovak army units called in to suppress the demonstrations proved unreliable, and it was left to the heavily armed workers' militia and police to disperse the crowds and make the predictable arrests and summary executions.

So complete were the Party purges of the early 1950s, so sycophantic (and scared) the surviving leadership, that Khrushchev's 1956 thaw was virtually ignored by the KSČ. An attempted rebellion in the Writers' Congress was rebuffed, and an inquiry into the show-trials made several minor security officials scapegoats for the "malpractices". The genuine mass base of the KSČ remained blindly loyal to the Party for the most part, and the following year, the dull, unreconstructed neo-Stalinist **Antonín Novotný** – now alleged to have been a spy for the Gestapo during the war – became first secretary and president.

REFORMISM AND INVASION

The first rumblings of protest against Czechoslovakia's hardline leadership appeared in the official press in 1963. At first, the criticisms were confined to the country's worsening economic stagnation, but soon they developed into more generalized protests against the KSČ leadership. Novotný responded by ordering the belated release and rehabilitation of victims of the 1950s purges, permitting a slight cultural thaw and easing travel restrictions to the West. In effect, he was simply buying time. The half-hearted economic reforms announced in the 1965 **New Economic Model** failed to halt the recession, and the minor political reforms instigated by the KSČ only increased the pressure for greater reforms within the Party.

In 1967, Novotný attempted a pre-emptive strike against his opponents. Several leading writers were imprisoned, Slovak Party leaders were branded as "bourgeois nationalists", and the economists were called on to produce results or else forgo their reform programme. Instead of eliminating the opposition, however, Novotný unwittingly united them. Despite Novotný's plea to the Soviets, Brezhnev refused to back a leader whom he regarded as

"Khrushchev's man in Prague". On January 5, 1968, Novotný was replaced as First Secretary by the young Slovak leader **Alexander Dubček**, and on March 22 was dislodged from the presidency by the Czech war hero Ludvík Svoboda.

1968: THE PRAGUE SPRING

By inclination, Dubček was a moderate, cautious reformer, the perfect compromise candidate – but he was continually swept along by the sheer force of the reform movement. The virtual **abolition of censorship** was probably the single most significant step Dubček took. It transformed what had hitherto been an internal Party debate into a popular mass movement. Civil society, for years muffled by the paranoia and strictures of Stalinism, suddenly sprang into life in the dynamic optimism of the first few months of 1968, the so-called **"Prague Spring"**. In April, the KSČ published their Action Programme, proposing what became popularly known as "socialism with a human face" – federalization, freedom of assembly and expression, and democratization of parliament.

Throughout the spring and summer, the reform movement gathered momentum. The Social Democrat Party (forcibly merged with the KSČ after 1948) re-formed, anti-Soviet polemics appeared in the press and, most famously of all, the writer and lifelong Party member Ludvík Vaculík published his personal manifesto entitled **"Two Thousand Words"**, calling for radical de-Stalinization within the Party. Dubček and the moderates denounced the manifesto and reaffirmed the country's support for the Warsaw Pact military alliance. Meanwhile, the Soviets and their hardline allies – Gomulka in Poland and Ulbricht in the GDR – took a very grave view of the Czechoslovak developments on their doorstep, and began to call for the suppression of "counter-revolutionary elements" and the reimposition of censorship.

As the summer wore on, it became clear that the Soviets were planning military intervention. Warsaw Pact manoeuvres were held in Czechoslovakia in late June, a Warsaw Pact conference (without Czechoslovak participation) was convened in mid-July and, at the beginning of August, the Soviets and the KSČ leadership met for **emergency bilateral talks** at Čierná nad Tisou on the Czechoslovak-Soviet border. Brezhnev's hardline deputy, Alexei Kosygin,

made his less-than-subtle threat that "your border is our border", but did agree to withdraw Soviet troops (stationed in the country since the June manoeuvres) and gave the go-ahead to the KSČ's special Party Congress scheduled for September 9.

In the early hours of August 21, fearing defeat for the hardliners at the forthcoming KSČ Congress and claiming to have been invited to provide "fraternal assistance", the Soviets gave the order for the **invasion of Czechoslovakia** to be carried out by Warsaw Pact forces (only Romania refused to take part). Dubček and the KSČ reformists immediately condemned the invasion before being arrested and flown to Moscow for "negotiations". President Svoboda refused to condone the formation of a new government under the hardliner Alois Indra, and the people took to the streets in protest, employing every form of non-violent resistance in the book. Apart from individual acts of martyrdom, like the self-immolation of **Jan Palach** on Prague's Wenceslas Square (see p.100), casualties were light compared to the Hungarian uprising of 1956 – the cost in terms of the following twenty years was much greater.

NORMALIZATION

In April 1969, there were anti-Soviet riots during the celebrations of the country's double ice hockey victory over the Soviets. On this pretext, another Slovak, **Gustáv Husák**, replaced the broken Dubček as First Secretary and instigated his infamous policy of **"normalization"**. Over 150,000 fled the country before the borders closed, around 500,000 were expelled from the Party, and an estimated one million people lost their jobs or were demoted. Inexorably, the KSČ reasserted its absolute control over the state and society. The only part of the reform package to survive the invasion was **federalization**, which gave the Slovaks greater freedom from Prague (on paper at least), though even this was severely watered down in 1971. Dubček, like countless others, was forced to give up his job, working for the next twenty years as a minor official in the Slovak forestry commission.

An unwritten social contract was struck between rulers and ruled during the 1970s, whereby the country was guaranteed a tolerable standard of living (second only to that of the GDR in Eastern Europe) in return for its passive collaboration. Husák's security apparatus quashed all forms of dissent during the early 1970s, and it wasn't until the middle of the decade that an organized opposition was strong enough to show its face. In 1976, the punk rock band "The Plastic People of the Universe" was arrested and charged with the familiar "crimes against the state" clause of the penal code. The dissidents who rallied to their defence – a motley assortment of people ranging from former KSČ members to right-wing intellectuals – agreed to form **Charter 77** (*Charta 77* in Czech and Slovak), with the purpose of monitoring human rights abuses in the country (which had recently signed the Helsinki Agreement on human rights). One of the organization's prime movers and initial spokespersons was the absurdist Czech playwright **Václav Havel**. Over the next decade, Havel, along with many others, endured relentless persecution (including long prison sentences) in pursuit of its ideals. The initial gathering of 243 signatories increased to over 1000 by 1980, causing panic in the moral vacuum of the Party apparatus, but consistently failed to stir a fearful and cynical populace into action.

THE 1980S

In the late 1970s and early 1980s, the inefficiencies of the economy prevented the government from fulfilling its side of the social contract. As living standards began to fall, cynicism, alcoholism, absenteeism and outright dissent became widespread, especially among the younger (post-1968) generation. The arrest and imprisonment in the mid-1980s of the **Jazz Section** of the Musicians' Union, who disseminated "subversive" pop music (like pirate copies of "Live Aid"), highlighted the ludicrously harsh nature of the regime. Pop concerts, annual religious pilgrimages and, of course, the anniversary of the Soviet invasion all caused regular confrontations between the security forces and certain sections of the population. Yet still a mass movement like Poland's Solidarity failed to emerge.

With the advent of **Mikhail Gorbachev**, the KSČ was put in an extremely awkward position, as it tried desperately to separate perestroika from comparisons with the reforms of the Prague Spring. Husák and his cronies had prided themselves on being second only to Honecker's GDR as the most stable and orthodox of the Soviet satellites – now the font of orthodoxy, the Soviet Union, was turning

against them. In 1987, **Miloš Jakeš** – the hardliner who oversaw Husák's normalization purges – took over smoothly from Husák as general (first) secretary and introduced *puestavba* (restructuring), Czechoslovakia's lukewarm version of perestroika.

THE VELVET REVOLUTION

Everything appeared to be going swimmingly for the KSČ as it entered 1989. Under the surface, however, things were becoming increasingly strained, with divisions developing in the KSČ leadership as the country's economic performance worsened. The protest movement, meanwhile, was gathering momentum: even the Catholic Church had begun to voice dissatisfaction, compiling a staggering 500,000 signatures calling for greater freedom of worship. But the 21st anniversary of the Soviet invasion produced a demonstration of only 10,000, which was swiftly and violently dispersed by the regime.

During the summer, however, more serious cracks began to appear in Czechoslovakia's staunch hardline ally, the GDR. The trickle of East Germans fleeing to the West turned into a mass exodus, forcing Honecker to resign and, by the end of October, prompting nightly mass demonstrations on the streets of Leipzig and Dresden. The opening of the Berlin Wall on November 9 left Czechoslovakia, Romania and Albania alone on the Eastern European stage, still clinging to the old truths.

All eyes were now turned upon Czechoslovakia. Reformists within the KSČ began plotting an internal coup to overthrow Jakeš, in anticipation of a Soviet denunciation of the 1968 invasion. Their half-baked plan to foment unrest backfired, however. On Friday, **November 17**, a 50,000-strong peaceful demonstration organized by the official Communist youth organization was viciously attacked by the riot police. Over 100 arrests, 500 injuries and one death were reported – the fatality was in fact an StB (secret police) agent provocateur. Ultimately, events overtook whatever plans the KSČ reformists may have had. The demonstration became known as the *masakr* (massacre), and Prague's students immediately began an occupation strike, joined soon after by the city's actors, who together called for an end to the Communist Party's "leading role" and a general strike to be held for two hours on November 27.

CIVIC FORUM AND THE VPN

On Sunday, November 19, on Václav Havel's initiative, the established opposition groups such as Charter 77 met and agreed to form Občanské fórum or **Civic Forum**. Their demands were simple: the resignation of the present hardline leadership, including Husák and Jakeš; an inquiry into the police actions of November 17; an amnesty for all political prisoners; and support for the general strike. In Bratislava, a parallel organization, Verejnosť proti nasiliu, or **People Against Violence** (VPN), was set up to co-ordinate protest in Slovakia.

On the Monday evening, the first of the really big **nationwide demonstrations** took place – the biggest since the 1968 invasion – with more than 200,000 people pouring into Prague's Wenceslas Square. This time the police held back, and rumours of troop deployments proved false. Every night for a week people poured into the main squares in towns and cities across the country, repeating the calls for democracy, freedom and the end to the Party's monopoly of power. As the week dragged on, the Communist media tentatively began to report events, and the KSČ leadership started to splinter under the strain, with the prime minister, **Ladislav Adamec**, alone in sticking his neck out and holding talks with the opposition.

THE END OF ONE-PARTY RULE

On Friday evening, Dubček, the ousted 1968 leader, appeared alongside Havel before a crowd of over 300,000 in Prague, and in a matter of hours the entire Jakeš leadership had resigned. The weekend brought the largest demonstrations the country had ever seen – over 750,000 people in Prague alone. At the invitation of Civic Forum, Adamec addressed the crowd, only to get booed off the platform. On Monday, November 27, eighty percent of the country's workforce joined the two-hour **general strike**, including many of the Party's previously stalwart allies, the miners and engineers. The following day, the Party agreed to the end of one-party rule and the formation of a new "coalition government".

A temporary halt to the nightly demonstrations was called and the country waited expectantly for the "broad coalition" cabinet promised by Prime Minister Adamec. On December 3, another Communist-dominated line-up was announced by the Party and imme-diately denounced by Civic Forum and VPN, who called for a fresh wave of demonstrations and another general strike for December 11. Adamec promptly resigned and was replaced by the Slovak **Marián Čalfa**. On December 10, one day before the second threatened general strike, Čalfa announced his provisional **"Government of National Understanding"**, with Communists in the minority for the first time since 1948 and multiparty elections planned for June 1990. Having sworn in the new government, President Husák, architect of the post-1968 "normalization", finally threw in the towel.

By the time the new Čalfa government was announced, the students and actors had been on strike continuously for over three weeks. The pace of change had surprised everyone involved, but there was still one outstanding issue, the election of a new president. Posters shot up all round the capital urging **"HAVEL NA HRAD"** (Havel to the Castle – the seat of the presidency). The students were determined to see his election through, continuing their occupation strike until Havel was officially elected president by a unanimous vote of the Federal Assembly on December 29.

THE 1990S

Czechoslovakia started the new decade full of optimism for what the future would bring. On the surface, the country had a lot more going for it than its immediate neighbours (with the possible exception of the GDR). The Communist Party had been swept from power without bloodshed, and, unlike the rest of Eastern Europe, Czechoslovakia had a strong, interwar democratic tradition with which to identify – Masaryk's First Republic. Despite Communist economic mismanagement, the country still had a relatively high standard of living, a skilled workforce and a manageable foreign debt.

In reality, however, the situation was somewhat different. Not only was the country economically in a worse state than most people had imagined, it was environmentally devastated, and its people were suffering from what Havel described as "post-prison psychosis" – an inability to think or act for themselves. The country had to go through the painful transition "from being a big fish in a small pond to being a sickly adolescent trout in a hatchery". As a result, it came increasingly to rely on its new-found saviour, the humble playwright-president Václav Havel.

In most people's eyes, "Saint Václav" could do no wrong, though he himself was not out to woo his electorate. His call for the rapid withdrawal of Soviet troops was popular enough, but his apology for the postwar expulsion of Sudeten Germans was deeply resented, as was his generous amnesty which eased the country's overcrowded prisons. The amnesty was blamed by many for the huge **rise in crime**; in the first year of freedom, every vice in the book – from racism to homicide – raised its ugly head.

In addition, there was still plenty of talk about the possibility of "counter-revolution", given the thousands of unemployed StB at large. Inevitably, accusations of previous StB involvement rocked each political party in turn in the run-up to the first free elections. The controversial **lustrace** (literally "lustration" or "cleansing") law, which barred all those on StB files from public office for the following five years, ended the career of many a politician and public figure, on the basis of often highly unreliable StB reports.

Despite all the inevitable hiccups and the increasingly vocal Slovak nationalists, Civic Forum/VPN remained high in the opinion polls. The **June 1990 elections** produced a record-breaking 99 percent turnout. With around sixty percent of the vote, Civic Forum/VPN were clear victors (the Communists got just thirteen percent), and Havel immediately set about forming a broad "Coalition of National Sacrifice", including everyone from Christian Democrats to former Communists.

The main concern of the new government was how to transform an outdated command-system economy into a **market economy** able to compete with its EU neighbours. The argument over the speed and model of economic reform caused Civic Forum to split into two separate parties: the centre-left Občánské hnutí or Civic Movement (OH), led by the foreign minister and former dissident Jiří Dienstbier, who favoured a more gradualist approach; and Občánská democratická strana or the right-wing **Civic Democratic Party** (ODS), headed by the finance minister **Václav Klaus**, whose pronouncement that the country should "walk the tightrope to Thatcherism" sent shivers up the spines of those familiar with the UK in the 1980s.

One of the first acts of the new government was to pass a **restitution law**, handing back small businesses and property to those from whom it had been expropriated after the 1948 Communist coup. This proved to be a controversial issue, since it excluded Jewish families driven out in 1938 by the Nazis, and, of course, the millions of Sudeten Germans who were forced to flee the country after the war. A law has since been passed to cover the Jewish expropriations, but the Sudeten German issue remains a tricky one.

THE SLOVAK CRISIS

One of the most intractable issues facing post-Communist Czechoslovakia – to the surprise of many Czechs – turned out to be the **Slovak problem**. Having been the victim of Prague-inspired centralization from just about every Czech leader from Masaryk to Gottwald, the Slovaks were in no mood to suffer second-class citizenship any longer. In the aftermath of 1989, feelings were running high, and, more than once, the spectre of a "Slovak UDI" was threatened by Slovak politicians hoping to boost their popularity by appealing to voters' nationalism. Despite the tireless campaigning and negotiating by both sides, a compromise agreement failed to emerge.

The **June 1992 elections** soon became an unofficial referendum on the future of the federation. Events moved rapidly towards the break-up of the republic after the resounding victory of the Movement for a Democratic Slovakia (HZDS), under the wily, populist politician and former boxer **Vladimír Mečiar**, who, in retrospect, was quite clearly seeking Slovak independence, though he never explicitly said so during the campaign. In the Czech Lands, the right-wing ODS emerged as the largest single party, under the leadership of Václav Klaus, who – ever the economist – was clearly not going to shed tears over losing the economically backward Slovak half of the country.

Talks between the two sides got nowhere, despite the fact that opinion polls in both republics consistently showed majority support for the federation. The HZDS then blocked the re-election of Havel, who had committed himself entirely to the pro-federation cause. Havel promptly resigned, leaving the country without a president, and Klaus and Mečiar were forced to discuss the terms of what has become known as the "Velvet Divorce". On January 1, 1993, after 74 years of troubled existence, Czechoslovakia was officially divided into two countries: the Czech Republic (Česká republika) and Slovakia (Slovensko) or the Slovak Republic (Slovenská republika).

INDEPENDENT SLOVAKIA

Compared to the Czechs, the Slovaks have had a much harder time since independence in 1993. Economically, the situation is bleaker, but more worrying by far has been the country's **political instability**. Throughout his first term as Slovak prime minister, Vladimír Mečiar was plagued by allegations of corruption and charges of political interference in the media, and made inflammatory comments about the country's large Hungarian and Romany minorities. Finally in March 1994, the Slovak president, Michal Kováč – no angel himself and once an HZDS ally of Mečiar – orchestrated his removal from office and replaced him with Jozef Moravčík, another former HZDS ally of Mečiar who had recently fallen from grace.

Moravčík's attempt to put Slovakia back on the right track lasted just six months until the **September 1994 elections**, in which Mečiar's HZDS emerged once more as the largest party with 35 percent of the vote. Back at the helm, in coalition with, among others, the extreme nationalist Slovak National Party (SNS), Mečiar continued his uncompromising political style, repeating most of the gaffes of his first term of office. He conducted a relentless (but unsuccessful) campaign to remove Kováč from office – the president's son was kidnapped and later dumped, soaked in vodka, in the boot of a car abandoned in Vienna, an act he alleges was carried out by the Slovak secret service.

Perhaps the most embarrassing single episode in the country's recent history was the **national referendum**, which took place in May 1997. Along with questions on NATO membership, there was a question asking whether the president should be elected by popular vote (as Kováč and the opposition wanted) rather than by members of parliament (as Mečiar preferred). So as not to lose the vote, the interior minister removed the question from most (but not all) of the ballot papers, and the voters showed their disgust with only ten percent casting ballots. When Mečiar was asked by reporters why the question had been removed, he replied "that's none of your business". The Constitutional Court ruled that the interior minister should be prosecuted, but, not for the last time, the government ignored the Court's decision.

As a result, Slovakia was not included in the first batch of East European countries to join the EU or NATO. However, the referendum debacle ultimately proved disastrous for Mečiar. In the **September 1998 elections**, the HZDS emerged once more as the largest single party with 27 percent of the vote, but ultimately lost out to the opposition Slovak Democratic Coalition (SDK), who took 26.2 percent. The difference between the two parties was that the SDK were able to form a coalition government with three other smaller parties, including the Hungarian coalition bloc (SMK) and the former Communists (SDĽ). The new government, under premier Mikuláš Dzurinda, is intent on winning back friends in the West, and is aiming to get Slovakia back on track for EU and NATO membership. First of all, though, the coalition must get the Slovak economy back on course, which will be no easy task. Mečiar suffered a further blow in the 1999 presidential elections, when he was beaten by the former mayor of Košice, **Rudolf Schuster**. Don't write Mečiar or the HZDS off, however, as you can be sure that, if and when the anti-Mečiar alliance falls apart, they'll be waiting in the wings for another stab at power.

THE CZECH REPUBLIC

Generally speaking, the 1990s have been much kinder to the Czechs than to the Slovaks. Under Klaus, the country enjoyed a long period of **political stability**, jumped to the front of the queue for the EU and NATO, and was widely held up as a shining example to the rest of the former Eastern Bloc.

Klaus and his party, the ODS, proved themselves the most durable of all the new political forces to emerge in the former Eastern Bloc. Nevertheless, in the **May 1996 parliamentary elections**, although the ODS again emerged as the largest single party, it failed to gain an outright majority. They repeated the failure again in November 1996 during the elections for the Czech Senate, the upper house of the Czech parliament. The electorate was distinctly unenthusiastic about the whole idea of another chamber full of overpaid politicians, and a derisory thirty percent turned out to vote in the second

THE ROMANIES

Czechs and Slovaks often know as little about the lives of the half a million gypsies – or **Romanies** (Romové), as they prefer to call themselves – living in their midst as the average visiting Westerner does, relying on the prevailing media stereotypes of Romanies as black-marketeers, pimps, alcoholics or, at best, shoddy labourers. Originally a low-caste Indian tribe, the Romanies are by no means newcomers to the region, having made their way into central Europe via Persia as early as the fifteenth century. While Czech Romanies were virtually wiped out in the Holocaust, those in Slovakia survived the war. The Communists tried forcibly to integrate Romanies into Czech and Slovak society, passing laws to restrict their traditionally migratory lifestyle, and dispersing families throughout Czechoslovakia. Education in the Romany language (an ancient tongue, closely related to Sanskrit) has never been provided; instead, all Romany children are pushed as quickly as possible into schools for children with special needs, thus introducing racial segregation at an early age.

However, the treatment of the Romanies is an issue which has pushed its way to the top of the political agenda in the late 1990s. A misleading documentary shown on Czech TV in 1997 showed life for the handful of Czech Romanies who had emigrated to Canada as a proverbial bed of roses. At last, the documentary seemed to be suggesting, they had found a life free from the racism and unemployment that plague them in the Czech and Slovak republics. The programme prompted a minor exodus of up to a thousand Czech and Slovak Romanies to Canada. Another Nova documentary, this time extolling life for Czech Romanies in Britain, had a similar effect, with several hundred Romanies seeking political asylum on arrival at Dover.

Needless to say, in both cases, the Romanies were given a very cold reception. Fascists in both countries led local people in demonstrations, demanding their immediate repatriation, while the Canadians reimposed visa restrictions on all Czechs, and British Foreign Office officials made shameful appearances on Czech and Slovak TV in an attempt to try and dissuade any further applicants. While racists back in the Czech Republic gleefully plastered up "Gypsies to Canada" graffiti, the positive side effect of all this media attention has been to force Czechs to focus on the institutionalized racism of their society and the casual racism that is acceptable in almost every walk of life.

Further controversy broke out in 1999 over the planned building of a wall to separate Romanies and non-Romanies in the north Bohemian city of Ústí nad Labem (see p.232). In the end, it was pressure from the EU that forced the central government to stop construction of the wall. All this merely highlights the continued need for a concerted campaign of anti-racism in order to try and counter the prevalent prejudices of the vast majority of Czechs and Slovaks. In addition, a great deal more grass-roots social work needs to be done within Romany communities, and equal opportunities policies put in place, if Czech and Slovak Romanies are to be persuaded that staying in their country is a viable option.

round. In the end, however, it was – predictably enough – a series of corruption scandals that eventually prompted **Klaus's resignation** as prime minister in November 1997.

The **1998 elections** proved that the Czechs had grown sick and tired of Klaus's dry, rather arrogant, style of leadership. However, what really did for Klaus was that for the first time since he took power, the economy had ground to a halt. The Social Democrats (ČSSD), under Miloš Zeman, emerged as the largest single party, promising to pay more attention to social issues, though their record so far is less than impressive.

Havel, Czech President since 1993, secured another five-year term in 1998, though his health remains dodgy. The ex-playwright still commands considerable moral authority in politics, though he is by no means as popular at home as he is abroad. His marriage to the actress Dagmar Veškrnová, seventeen years his junior, in January 1997, less than a year after his first wife, Olga, died of cancer, was frowned upon by many. And his very public fall-out with his sister-in-law (also called Olga), over the family inheritance of the multimillion crown Lucerna complex in Prague, didn't do his reputation any favours either.

BOOKS

The upsurge of interest in all things Eastern European prompted a publishing frenzy in the early 1990s, but this has now fizzled out. Czech authors tend to be well represented, but Slovak fiction is still poorly served by translations.

The best place to find out about the current availability of books is on the Internet at *www.amazon.co.uk* (for the UK) or *www.amazon.com* (for the US), or one of the other Web sites set up by the large bookshops. In the list of recommended titles below, where two publishers are given, the first is the UK publisher, the second the US.

HISTORY, POLITICS AND SOCIETY

Peter Demetz *Prague in Black and Gold; Scenes from the Life of a European City* (Penguin/Hill & Wang). Demetz certainly knows his subject, both academically and at first hand, having been brought up here before World War II (where his account ends). His style can be a little dry, but he is determinedly un-partisan, and refreshingly antinationalist in his reading of history.

R.J.W. Evans *Rudolf II and His World* (Thames & Hudson, UK). First published in 1973, and still the best account there is of the alchemy-mad emperor, but not as salacious as one might hope given the subject matter.

Jan Kaplan & Krystyna Nosarzewska *Prague: The Turbulent Century* (Könemann, Prague). This is the first real attempt to cover the twentieth-century history of Prague with all its warts. The text isn't as good as it should be, but the book is worth it just for the incredible range of photographs and images from the century.

Karel Kaplan *The Short March: The Communist Takeover in Czechoslovakia, 1945–48* (C Hurst Co, UK); *Report on the Murder of the General Secretary* (I. B. Tauris/Ohio State University Press, o/p). *The Short March* is an excellent account of the electoral rise and rise of the Communists in Czechoslovakia after the war, which culminated in the bloodless coup of February 1948. *Report on the Murder of the General Secretary* is a detailed study of the most famous of the anti-Semitic Stalinist show trials, that of Rudolf Slánský, number two in the Party until his arrest.

Callum MacDonald *The Killing of SS Obergruppenführer Reinhard Heydrich* (Macmillan/Da Capo). Gripping account of the build-up to the most successful and controversial act of wartime resistance, which took place in May 1942, and prompted horrific reprisals by the Nazis on the Czechs.

Callum MacDonald & Jan Kaplan *Prague in the Shadow of the Swastika* (Quartet, UK). Excellent account of the city under Nazi occupation, with an incisive, readable text illustrated by copious black-and-white photos.

Jiří Musil (ed) *The End of Czechoslovakia* (Central European University Press). Academics from both the Czech and Slovak republics attempt to explain why Czechoslovakia split into two countries just at the point when the country looked like it had a rosy future ahead of it.

Derek Sayer *The Coast of Bohemia* (Princeton). A very readable cultural history, concentrating on Bohemia and Prague, which aims to dispel the ignorance shown by the Shakespearean quote of the title, and particularly illuminating on the subject of twentieth-century artists.

R.W. Seton-Watson *The History of the Czechs and Slovaks* (Shoe String Press in US, o/p). Seton-Watson's informed and balanced account, written during World War II, is hard to beat. The Seton-Watsons were lifelong Slavophiles but maintained a scholarly distance in their writing, rare among emigré historians.

Kieran Williams *The Prague Spring and its Aftermath: Czechoslovak Politics, 1968-70* (Cambridge University Press). This book draws on declassified archives to analyse the attempted reforms under Dubček and to take a new look at the 1968 Prague Spring.

Elizabeth Wiskemann *Czechs and Germans* (Macmillan, o/p /AMS Press, o/p). Researched and written in the build-up towards Munich, this is the most fascinating and fair treatment of the Sudeten problem. Meticulous in her detail, vast in her scope, Wiskemann manages to suffuse the weighty text with enough anecdotes to keep you gripped. Unique.

ESSAYS, MEMOIRS AND BIOGRAPHY

Margarete Buber-Neumann *Milena* (Schocken/Arcade). A moving biography of Milena Jesenská, one of interwar Prague's most beguiling characters, who befriended the author while they were both interned in Ravensbrück concentration camp.

Karel Čapek *Talks with T. G. Masaryk* (Catbird Press, UK). Čapek was a personal (and political) friend of Masaryk, and his diaries, journals, reminiscences and letters give great insights into the man who personified the First Republic.

Jana Černá *Kafka's Milena* (Souvenir Press/Northwestern University Press). Another biography of Milena Jesenská, this time written by her daughter, a Surrealist poet, whose own works were banned under the Communists.

Timothy Garton Ash *We The People: The Revolutions of 89* (Penguin/Vintage). A personal, anecdotal, eyewitness account of the Velvet Revolution (and the events in Poland, Berlin and Budapest) – by far the most compelling of all the post-1989 books. Published as *The Magic Lantern* in the US.

Patrick Leigh Fermor *A Time of Gifts* (Penguin). The first volume of Leigh Fermor's trilogy based on his epic walk along the Rhine and Danube rivers in 1933–34. In the last quarter of the book he reaches Czechoslovakia, indulging in a quick jaunt to Prague before crossing the border into Hungary. Written forty years later in dense, luscious and highly crafted prose, it's an evocative and poignant insight into the culture of Mitteleuropa between the wars.

Václav Havel *Living in Truth* (Faber); *Letters to Olga* (Faber/Holt); *Open Letters: Selected Prose; Disturbing the Peace; Summer Meditations* (all Faber/Vintage); *The Art of the Impossible: Politics as Morality in Practice* (Fromm, US). The first essay in *Living in Truth* is "Power of the

Powerless", Havel's lucid, damning indictment of the inactivity of the Czechoslovak masses in the face of "normalization". *Letters to Olga* is a collection of Havel's letters written under great duress (and heavy censorship) from prison in the early 1980s to his wife, Olga – by turns philosophizing, nagging, effusing, whingeing. *Disturbing the Peace* is probably Havel's most accessible work, a series of autobiographical questions and answers in which he talks interestingly about his childhood, the events of 1968 when he was in Liberec, and the path to Charter 77 and beyond (though not including his reactions to being thrust into the role of president). *Summer Meditations* are post-1989 essays by the playwright-president, while *The Art of the Impossible* is a collection of speeches given since he took office in 1990.

Václav Havel et al *Power of the Powerless* (M. E. Sharpe, US). A collection of essays by leading Chartists, kicking off with Havel's seminal title-piece. Other contributors range from the dissident Marxist Petr Uhl to devout Catholics like Václav Benda.

Miroslav Holub *The Dimension of the Present Moment* (Faber & Faber, UK); *Shedding Life: Disease, Politics and Other Human Conditions* (Milkweed, US). Two books of short philosophical musings/essays on life and the universe by this unusual, clever scientist-poet.

Antonín Klimek & Zbyněk Zeman *The Life of Edvard Beneš: Czechoslovakia in Peace & War* (Clarendon Press). Beneš is a fascinating figure in Czech history, revered as number two to Masaryk while the latter was alive, only to find himself held responsible first for the Munich debacle, and lastly for allowing the Communists into power in 1948.

Heda Margolius Kovaly *Prague Farewell* (Orion/Holmes & Meier). An autobiography starting in the concentration camps of World War II, and ending with the author's flight from Czechoslovakia in 1968. Married to one of the Party officials executed in the 1952 Slánský trial, she tells her story simply, and without bitterness. The best account there is on the fear and paranoia whipped up during the Stalinist terror. Published as *Under a Cruel Star* in the US.

Angelo Maria Ripellino *Magic Prague* (Picador/University of California Press). A wide-ranging look at the bizarre array of historical and literary characters who have lived in Prague, from the mad antics of the court of Rudolf II to the escapades of Jaroslav Hašek. Scholarly, rambling, richly and densely written – unique and recommended.

William Shawcross *Remember Dubček: Dubček and Czechoslovakia 1918–1990* (Hogarth Press, o/p/Simon & Schuster, o/p). Biography of the most famous figure of the 1968 Prague Spring, updated to include Dubček's role in the 1989 Velvet Revolution.

John Keane *Vaclav Havel: a political tragedy in six acts* (Bloomsbury, UK). The first book to tell both sides of the Havel story: Havel the dissident playwright and civil rights activist who played a key role in the 1989 Velvet Revolution, and Havel the ageing and increasingly ill president, who has, in many people's opinion, simply stayed on the stage too long.

Josef Škvorecký *Talkin' Moscow Blues* (Faber/Ecco Press). Without doubt the most user-friendly of Škvorecký's works, containing a collection of essays on his wartime childhood, Czech jazz, literature and contemporary politics, all told in his inimitable, irreverent and infuriating way. Published as *Head for the Blues* in the US.

Elizabeth Sommer-Lefkovits *Are You Here in This Hell Too?* (Menard Press/Central Books). Harrowing Holocaust experience told by a Slovak Jewish woman who worked as a pharmacist in Prešov until 1944.

Ludvík Vaculík *A Cup of Coffee With My Interrogator* (Readers International). A Party member until 1968, and signatory of Charter 77, Vaculík revived the feuilleton – a short political critique once much loved in central Europe. This collection dates from 1968 onwards.

Zbyněk Zeman *The Masaryks – The Making of Czechoslovakia* (I. B. Tauris, UK). Written in the 1970s while Zeman was in exile, this is a very readable, none too sentimental biography of the country's founder Tomáš Garrigue Masaryk, and his son Jan Masaryk, the postwar Foreign Minister who died in mysterious circumstances shortly after the 1948 Communist coup.

CZECH AND SLOVAK FICTION

Alexandra Buchler (ed) *Allskin and Other Tales by Contemporary Czech Women* (Women in Translation). This collection of short stories and excerpts from novels spans more than thirty years and contains a range of writing which the editor attempts to put into context.

Josef Čapek *Stories about Doggie and Pussycat* (Albatros, Prague). Josef Čapek (Karel's older brother) was a Cubist artist of some renown, and also a children's writer. These simple stories about a dog and a cat are wonderfully illustrated, and seriously postmodern.

Karel Čapek *Towards a Radical Centre* (Catbird Press, US); *The War with the Newts* (Hydra Books/Catbird Press); *Nine Fairy Tales* (Northwestern University Press in US); *Three Novels: Hordubal, Meteor, An Ordinary Life* (Catbird Press). Karel Čapek was the literary and journalistic spokesperson for Masaryk's First Republic, but he's better known in the West for his plays, some of which feature in the anthology, *Towards a Radical Centre*. Probably the best of his novel writing is contained in the trilogy, *Three Novels*, set in Czechoslovakia in the 1930s.

Ladislav Fuks *The Cremator* (Marion Boyars); *Mr Theodore Mundstock* (Four Walls Eight Windows, US). Two readable novels: the first about a man who works in a crematorium in occupied Prague, and is about to throw in his lot with the Nazis when he discovers that his wife is half-Jewish; the second set in 1942 Prague, as the city's Jews wait to be transported to Terezín.

Jaroslav Hašek *The Good Soldier Švejk* (Penguin/Viking). This classic, by Bohemia's most bohemian writer, is a rambling, picaresque tale of Czechoslovakia's famous fictional fifth columnist, Švejk, who wreaks havoc in the Austro-Hungarian army during World War I.

Václav Havel *The Memorandum* (Eyre-Methuen/Grove-Atlantic, o/p in UK and US); *Three Vaněk Plays* (Faber, o/p); *Selected Plays 1984–87* (Faber, UK). Havel's plays are not renowned for being easy to read (or watch). *The Memorandum* is one of his earliest works, a classic absurdist drama that, in many ways, sets the tone for much of his later work, of which the *Three Vaněk Plays*, featuring Ferdinand Vaněk, Havel's alter ego, are perhaps the most successful. The 1980s collection includes *Largo Desolato, Temptation* and

Redevelopment; freedom of thought, Faustian opportunism and town planning as metaphors of life under the Communists.

Bohumil Hrabal *Closely Observed Trains* (Abacus/Northwestern University Press); *I Served the King of England* (Picador/Vintage); *Too Loud a Solitude* (Deutsch/Harcourt Brace); *The Little Town Where Time Stood Still* (Abacus/Pantheon, o/p); *Dancing Lessons* (Panther/Harcourt Brace). A thoroughly mischievous writer, Hrabal's slim but superb *Closely Observed Trains* is a postwar classic, set in the last days of the war and relentlessly unheroic; it was made into an equally brilliant film by Jiří Menzl. *I Served the King of England* follows the antihero Dítě, who works at the *Hotel Paříž*, through the decade after 1938. *Too Loud a Solitude*, about a waste-paper disposer under the Communists, has also been made into a film, again by Menzl. *The Little Town Where Time Stood Still* was the last work Hrabal completed before his death in 1997. *Dancing Lessons* is a short tale from 1964, composed of a single sentence, a rambling monologue by a 70-year-old shoemaker to six sunbathing women.

Alois Jirásek *Old Czech Legends* (Forest Books/Dufour). A major figure in the nineteenth-century Czech *národní obrození*, Jirásek popularized Bohemia's legendary past. This collection includes all the classic texts, including the story of the founding of the city by the prophetess Libuše.

Franz Kafka *The Collected Novels of Franz Kafka; Letters to Felice; Diaries* (all Penguin/Vintage). A German-Jewish Praguer, Kafka has drawn the darker side of central Europe – its claustrophobia, paranoia and unfathomable bureaucracy – better than anyone else, both in a rural setting, as in *The Castle*, and in an urban one, in one of the great novels of the twentieth century, *The Trial*.

Ivan Klíma *A Summer Affair* (Penguin, UK); *My Merry Mornings* (Readers International); *My First Loves* (Penguin/Norton); *Love and Garbage* (Penguin/Vintage); *Judge on Trial* (Vintage); *My Golden Trades* (Penguin/Macmillan); *Waiting for the Dark, Waiting for the Light* (Penguin/Picador); *The Spirit of Prague* (Granta, UK); *Ultimate Intimacy* (Granta/Grove-Atlantic). A survivor of Terezín, Klíma is another writer in the Kundera mould as far as sexual politics

goes, but his stories are a lot lighter. *Judge on Trial*, written in the 1970s, is one of his best, concerning the moral dilemmas of a Communist judge. *Waiting for the Dark, Waiting for the Light* is a pessimistic novel set before, during and after the Velvet Revolution of 1989. *The Spirit of Prague* is a very readable collection of biographical and more general articles and essays on subjects ranging from Klíma's childhood experiences in Terezín to the current situation in Prague. *Ultimate Intimacy* is his latest novel, set in the cynical post-revolutionary Czech Republic.

Pavel Kohout *I am Snowing: The Confessions of a Woman of Prague* (Harcourt Trade/Harvest Books) is set in the uneasy period just after the fall of Communism amid accusations of collaboration. *The Widow Killer* (St Martin's Press, UK) is a thriller about a naive Czech detective partnered with a Gestapo agent in the last months of World War II.

Milan Kundera *Laughable Loves; The Farewell Party; The Joke; The Book of Laughter and Forgetting; The Unbearable Lightness of Being; The Art of the Novel; Immortality; Slowness; Identity; Testaments Betrayed* (all Faber/HarperCollins); *Life is Elsewhere* (Faber/Penguin). Milan Kundera is the country's most popular writer – at least with non-Czechs. His books are very obviously "political", particularly *The Book of Laughter and Forgetting*, which led the Communists to revoke Kundera's citizenship. *The Joke*, written while he was still living in Czechoslovakia and in many ways his best work, is set in the very unfunny era of the Stalinist purges. Its clear, humorous style is far removed from the carefully poised posturing of his most famous work, *The Unbearable Lightness of Being*, set in and after 1968, and successfully turned into a film some twenty years later. *Slowness* is a slim volume set in France, and his first work written in French. *Identity* is his latest novel, a series of slightly detached musings on the human condition that is typical of his later works. *Testaments Betrayed*, on the other hand, is a fascinating series of essays about a range of subjects from the formation of historical reputation to the problems of translations.

Arnošt Lustig *Diamonds of the Night; Night and Hope* (both Quartet/Northwestern University Press); *Darkness Casts No Shadow*

(Quartet/Avon, o/p); *A Prayer for Kateřina Horovitová* (Overlook Press, US); *Indecent Dreams* (Northwestern University Press, US). A Prague Jew exiled since 1968, Lustig spent World War II in Terezín, Buchenwald and Auschwitz, and his novels and short stories are consistently set in the Terezín camp.

Ladislav Mňačko *The Taste of Power* (o/p). Now living in Israel, Mňačko is one of the few Slovak writers to have been widely published abroad, most frequently this novel about the corruption of ideals that followed the Communist takeover.

Gustav Meyrink *The Golem* (Dedalus/Dover); *The Angel of the West Window* (Dedalus/Ariadne). Meyrink was another of Prague's weird and wonderful characters who started out as a bank manager, but soon became involved in cabalism, alchemy and drug experimentation. His *Golem*, based on Rabbi Löw's monster, is one of the classic versions of the tale, set in the Jewish quarter. *The Angel of the West Window* is a historical novel about John Dee, an English alchemist invited to Prague in the late sixteenth century by Rudolf II.

Jan Neruda *Prague Tales* (OUP). Not to be confused with the Chilean Pablo Neruda (who took his name from the Czech writer), these are short, bitter-sweet snapshots of life in Malá Strana at the close of the last century.

Ivan Olbracht *The Sorrowful Eyes of Hannah Karajich* (Central European University Press). A moving novel set in the vanished world of a Jewish village in sub-Carpatho-Ruthenia which shows the effects of Zionism and the terrors of Hitler.

Iva Pekarkova *Truck Stop Rainbows* (Farrar Strauss & Giroux, US). A heroine who attempts to fight, often by using sexual politics, against the grim realities of the Communist system in Czechoslovakia in the 1980s.

Peter Petro *A History of Slovak Literature* (Liverpool University Press, UK). Comprehensive overview of Slovak literature from 800 to 1990.

Karel Poláček *What Ownership's All About* (Catbird Press/Independent Publishers Group). A darkly comic novel set in a Prague tenement block, dealing with the issue of fascism and appeasement, by a Jewish-Czech Praguer who died in the camps in 1944.

Robert Pynsent (ed.) *Modern Slovak Prose* (Macmillan, UK). Literary criticism on Slovak fiction since 1954 by Slovaks and Western Slavists; hardback only.

Rainer Maria Rilke *Two Stories of Prague* (University Press of New England, US). Both tales deal with the artificiality of Prague's now defunct German-speaking community, whose claustrophobic parochialism drove the author into self-imposed exile in 1899 (for more on Rilke see Poetry, below).

Peter Sís *The Three Golden Keys* (Pavilion/Doubleday). Short, hauntingly illustrated children's book set in Prague, by Czech-born American Sís.

Martin Šimečka *The Year of the Frog* (Louisiana State Press, US). Largely autobiographical account of a young Slovak intellectual, whose father is a prominent dissident, living through the last years of Communism in Bratislava.

Josef Škvorecký *The Cowards; The Miracle Game* (both Faber/Norton); *The Swell Season; The Bass Saxophone* (both Vintage/Ecco Press); *Miss Silver's Past; Dvořák in Love* (both Vintage/Norton); *The Engineer of Human Souls* (Vintage/Dalkey Archive); *The Republic of Whores* (Faber/Ecco Press). A relentless anti-Communist, Škvorecký is typically Bohemian in his bawdy sense of humour and irreverence for all high moralizing. *The Cowards* (which briefly saw the light of day in 1958) is the tale of a group of irresponsible young men in the last days of the war, an antidote to the lofty prose from official authors at the time, but hampered by its dated Americanized translation.

Josef Škvorecký *The Mournful Demeanor of Lieutenant Boruvka; Sins for Father Knox; The Return of Lieutenant Boruvka; The End of Lieutenant Boruvka* (all Faber & Faber/Norton). Less well known (and understandably so) are Škvorecký's detective stories featuring a podgy, depressive Czech cop, which he wrote in the 1960s at a time when his more serious work was banned. The later book, *The Return of Lieutenant Boruvka*, is set in Škvorecký's new home, Canada.

Božena Slančiková-Timrava *That Alluring Land: Slovak Stories* (Pittsburgh University Press, US). Not strictly a feminist as such, Slančiková-Timrava tells her Slovak tales from a decidedly female perspective.

Zdena Tomin *Stalin's Shoe* (Dent, o/p in UK); *The Coast of Bohemia* (Dent o/p in UK). Although Czech-born, Tomin writes in English (the language of her exile since 1980); she has a style and fluency all her own. *Stalin's Shoe* is the compelling and complex story of a girl coming to terms with her Stalinist childhood, while *The Coast of Bohemia* is based on Tomin's experiences of the late 1970s dissident movement, when she was an active member of Charter 77.

Ludvík Vaculík *The Guinea Pigs* (Northwestern University Press in US). Vaculík was expelled from the Party in the midst of the 1968 Prague Spring; this novel, set in Prague, catalogues the slow dehumanization of Czech society in the aftermath of the Soviet invasion.

Michal Viewegh *Bringing up Girls in Bohemia* (Readers International, UK). A picaresque novel offering a satirical snapshot of life in post-Communist Prague.

Jiří Weil *Life With a Star* (Northwestern University Press, US); *Mendelssohn is on the Roof* (Collins, o/p in UK/Farra, Straus & Giroux). Two novels written just after the war and based on Weil's experiences as a Czech Jew in hiding in Nazi-occupied Prague.

POETRY

Jaroslav Čejka, Michal Černík and Karel Sýs *The New Czech Poetry* (Bloodaxe/Dufour). Slim but interesting volume by three Czech poets all in their late forties, all very different. Čejka is of the Holub school, and comes across simply and strongly; Černík is similarly direct; Sýs the least convincing.

Sylva Fischerová *The Tremor of Racehorses: Selected Poems* (Bloodaxe/Dufour). Poet and novelist Fischerová is one of the new generation of Czech writers, though in many ways she is continuing in the Holub tradition. Her poems are by turns powerful, obtuse and personal, as was necessary to escape censorship during the late 1980s.

Josef Hanzlík *Selected Poems* (Bloodaxe/Dufour). Refreshingly accessible collection of poems written over the last 35 years by a poet of Havel's generation.

Miroslav Holub *Supposed to Fly*; *The Jingle Bell Principle*; *Poems Before & After* (all Bloodaxe/Dufour); *Vanishing Lung Syndrome* (Faber/ Oberlin College Press). Holub is a scientist and scholar, and his poetry reflects this unique fusion of master poet and chief immunologist. Regularly banned in his own country, he is the Czech poet *par excellence* – classically trained, erudite, liberal and Westward-leaning. *Vanishing Lung Syndrome* is his most recent volume; the other two are collections.

Rainer Maria Rilke *Selected Poetry* (Picador/Vintage). Rilke's upbringing was unexceptional, except that his mother brought him up as a girl until the age of six. In his adult life, he became one of Prague's leading German-speaking authors of the interwar period.

Jaroslav Seifert *The Poetry of Jaroslav Seifert* (Catbird Press, US). Czechoslovakia's only author to win the Nobel prize for literature, Seifert was a founder-member of the Communist Party and the avant-garde arts movement *Devětsil*, later falling from grace and signing the Charter in his old age. His longevity means that his work covers some of the most turbulent times in Czechoslovak history, but his irrepressible lasciviousness has been known to irritate.

Miroslav Válek, Miroslav Cipar, Ewald Osers *The Ground Beneath Our Feet: Selected Poems* (Bloodaxe, UK). The first-ever Slovak poets to be published in Britain.

LITERATURE BY FOREIGN WRITERS

David Brierley *On Leaving a Prague Window* (Warner, UK). A very readable thriller set in postcommunist Prague which shows that past connection with dissidents can still lead to violence.

Bruce Chatwin *Utz* (Pan, UK). Chatwin is one of the "exotic" school of travel writers, hence this slim, intriguing and mostly true-to-life account of an avid crockery collector from Prague's Jewish quarter.

Lionel Davidson *The Night of Wenceslas* (Reed Consumer Books/St Martin's Press). A Cold War thriller set in pre-1968 Czechoslovakia that launched Davidson's career as a spy-writer.

Sue Gee *Letters from Prague* (Arrow, UK). The central character fell in love with a Czech student in England in 1968, but he returned home when the Russians invaded. Twenty years later, together with her ten-year old daughter, she goes in search of him.

Martha Gellhorn *A Stricken Field* (Virago, o/p /Penguin, o/p). The story of an American journalist who arrives in Prague just as the Nazis march into Sudetenland. Based on the author's own experiences, this is a fascinating, if sentimental, insight into the panic and confusion in "rump" Czecho-Slovakia after the Munich Diktat. First published in 1940.

Philip Roth *Prague Orgy* (Vintage). A novella about a world-famous Jewish novelist (ie Roth) who goes to Communist Prague to recover some unpublished Jewish stories. Prague "is the city I imagined the Jews would buy when they had accumulated enough money for a homeland", according to Roth. A coda to Roth's Zuckerman trilogy.

ART, PHOTOGRAPHY AND FILM

Czech Modernism 1900–1945 (Little Brown/Museum of Fine Arts, Houston). Wide-ranging and superbly illustrated, this American publication records the journey of the Czech modern movement through Cubism and Surrealism to Modernism and the avant-garde. The accompanying essays by leading art and film critics cover fine art, architecture, film, photography and theatre.

Devětsil – Czech Avant-Garde Art, Architecture and Design of the 1920s and 30s (Museum of Modern Art, Oxford, UK). Published to accompany the 1990 *Devětsil* exhibition at Oxford, this is the definitive account of interwar Czechoslovakia's most famous left-wing art movement, which attracted artists from every discipline.

Disorientations – Eastern Europe in Transition (Thames & Hudson, UK). A self-explanatory book of photos accompanied by Pavel Kohout's text.

Ivan Margolius *Prague – A Guide to Twentieth-Century Architecture* (Ellipsis London/ Knickerbocker). Dinky little pocket guide to all the major modern landmarks of Prague (including a black and white photo of each building), from the Art Nouveau Obecní dům, through functionalism and Cubism, to the Tančící dům.

LANGUAGE

The official language of the Czech Republic is Czech (**český**), that of the Slovakia, Slovak (**slovenský**). Both are mutually intelligible, highly complex Slav tongues. Whether they are separate languages or simply diverse dialects of a common one is still a hotly disputed issue. However, for the non-Slav, they are sufficiently distinct to cause serious problems of understanding. Unless you're here for some time, however, it's all rather academic, since you're not likely to make any great inroads into either.

That said, any attempt to speak Czech or Slovak will be heartily appreciated, though don't be discouraged if people seem not to understand, as most will be unaccustomed to hearing foreigners stumble through their language. If you know some German already, brush up on that, since, among the older generation in particular, German is the most widely spoken second language. Russian, once the compulsory second language (and therefore theoretically spoken by

There are very few **teach yourself Czech** guides available – even fewer for Slovak – and each has drawbacks. *Colloquial Czech* and *Colloquial Slovak*, both by James Naughton, are good, but a bit fast and furious for most people; *Teach Yourself Czech* is a bit dry for some. The best portable **dictionaries** are the *kapesní slovník* for Czech and the *vreckový slovník* for Slovak, most easily purchased in the Czech and Slovak republics themselves. The Rough Guides also produces a useful **Czech phrasebook**.

most of the middle-aged population), has been practically wiped off the school curriculum. English is now the foreign language most commonly taught in schools, and the number of English-speakers has been steadily increasing.

PRONUNCIATION

English-speakers often find Czech impossibly difficult to pronounce, Slovak less so. In fact, neither are half as daunting as they might first appear from the "traffic jams of consonants" that crop up on the page. Apart from a few special letters, each letter and syllable is pronounced as it's written, with virtually no letter unvoiced. The trick is always to **stress the first syllable** of a word, no matter what its length; otherwise you'll render it unintelligible.

THE ALPHABET

In the Czech and Slovak alphabets, letters that feature a **háček** (as in the č of the word itself) are considered separate letters and appear in Czech and Slovak indexes immediately after their more familiar cousins. More confusingly, the consonant combination of ch is also considered as a separate letter and appears in Czech and Slovak indexes after the letter h. In the index of this book, we use the English system, so words beginning with c, č and ch all appear under c.

SHORT AND LONG VOWELS

Czech and Slovak have both short and long vowels (the latter being denoted by a variety of accents). The trick here is to lengthen the vowel without affecting the principal stress of the word, which is invariably on the first syllable.

a like the u in c**u**p
á as in f**a**ther
ä closer to the e in l**e**t than an a
e as in p**e**t
é as in f**ai**r
ě like the y in **y**es
i or y as in p**i**t
í or ý as in s**ea**t
o as in n**o**t
ó as in d**oo**r
ô like the u in l**u**rid
u like the oo in b**oo**k
ů or ú like the oo in f**oo**l

A CZECH/SLOVAK LANGUAGE GUIDE

In many instances the **Czech** and **Slovak words** for things are the same. Where they're different, we've separated them below, giving the Czech word first and the Slovak word second.

BASIC WORDS AND PHRASES

Yes	*ano/áno* or *hej*	Tomorrow	*zítra/zajtra*
No	*ne/nie*	The day after tomorrow	*pozítra/pozajtra*
Excuse me/please/	*prosím*	Now	*hnet/teraz*
don't mention it		Later	*později/neskôr*
You're welcome	*není zač/nemáte začo*	Leave me alone	*dej mi pokoj/*
Sorry	*pardon/pardón*		*nechaj ma osamote*
Thank you	*djkuju/ďakujem*	Go away	*jdi pryč/choď preč*
OK	*dobrá/dobre*	Help!	*pomoc!*
Bon appétit	*dobrou chuť*	This one	*tento*
Bon voyage	*šťastnou cestu*	A little	*trochu*
Hello/goodbye (informal)	*ahoj*	Large–small	*velký–malý*
Goodbye (formal)	*na shledanou/*	More–less	*více–méně/*
	do videnia		*viac–menej*
Good day	*dobrý den*	Good–bad	*dobrý–zpatný*
Good morning	*dobré ráno*	Hot–cold	*horký–studený/*
Good evening	*dobrý veber*		*horúci–studený*
Good night (when leaving)	*dobrou noc*	With–without	*s–bez*
Today	*dnes*	How are you	*jak se máte/*
Yesterday	*včera*		*ako sa máte?*

GETTING AROUND

Over here	*tady/tuná*	By taxi	*taxíkem/taxíkom*
Over there	*tam*	Ticket	*jízdenka/lístok*
Left	*nalevo/naľavo*	Return ticket	*zpátečá jízdenka/*
Right	*napravo*		*spiatočný lístok*
Straight on	*rovně/priamo*	Railway station	*nádraží/železničná*
Where is . . .?	*kde je . . .?*		*stanica*
How do I get to Zvolen?	*jak se dostanu do*	Bus station	*autobusové nádraží/*
	Zvolena/ako sa		*autobusová stanica*
	dostanem do	Bus stop	*autobusová zastávka*
	Zvolena?	When's the next train	*kdy jede další vlak do*
How do I get to the	*jak se dostanu k*	to Prague?	*Prahy/kedy ide*
university?	*univerzitě/ako sa*		*najbližší*
	dostanem k uni		*vlak do Prahy?*
	verzite?	Is it going to Brno?	*jede to do Brna/*
By bus	*autobusem/*		*ide to do Brna?*
	autobusom	Do I have to change?	*musím přestupovat/*
By train	*vlakem/vlakom*		*musím prestupovat?*
By car	*autem/autom*	Do I have to have a	*musím mít místenku?*
By foot	*pěšky/pešo*	reservation?	

QUESTIONS AND ANSWERS

Do you speak English?	*mluvíte anglicky/*	Speak slowly	*mluvte pomalu/*
	hovoríte anglicky?		*hovorte pomalzie*
I don't speak German	*nemluvím německy/*	How do you say that	*jak se tohle vekne*
	nehovorím nemecky	in Czech/Slovak?	*česky/ako sa to*
I don't understand	*nerozumím/*		*povie slovenský?*
	nerozumiem	Could you write it	*mužete mí to napsat/mohli*
I understand	*rozumím/rozumiem*	down for me?	*by ste mi to napísať?*

continues overleaf . . .

QUESTIONS AND ANSWERS (contd)

What	*co/čo*	For one night	*na jednu noc*
Where	*kde*	With shower	*se sprchou/se sprchy*
When	*kdy/kedy*	Are these seats	*je tu volno/*
Why	*proč/prečo*	free?	*sú tieto miesta*
How much is it?	*kolík to stojí/koľko*		*vonná?*
	stojí?	May we (sit down)?	*můžeme/môžme?*
Are there any	*máte volné pokoje/*	The bill please	*zaplatím prosím*
rooms available?	*máte voľné izby?*	Do you have . . .?	*máte . . .?*
I want a double room	*chtěl bych dvou*	We don't have	*nemáme*
	lůžkovy pokoj/chcem	We do have	*máme*
	dvojposteľovú izbu		

SOME SIGNS

Entrance	*vchod*	Danger!	*pozor!*
Exit	*východ*	Hospital	*nemocnice/nemocnica*
Toilets	*záchod*	No smoking	*kouření zakázáno/zákaz fajčiť*
Men	*muži*	No bathing	*koupání zakázáno/ zákaz*
Women	*ženy*		*kúpania*
Gentlemen	*pánové*	No entry	*vstup zakázáno*
Ladies	*dámy*	Arrivals	*příjezd/príchod*
Open	*otevřeno/otvorené*	Departure	*odjezd/odchod*
Closed	*zavřeno/zavreté*	Police	*policie/polícia*

DAYS OF THE WEEK

Monday	*pondělí/pondelok*	Sunday	*neděle/nedeľa*
Tuesday	*úterý/utorok*	Day	*den/deň*
Wednesday	*středa/streda*	Week	*týden/týždeň*
Thursday	*čtvrtek/štvrtok*	Month	*měsíc/mesiac*
Friday	*pátek/piatok*	Year	*rok*
Saturday	*sobota*		

MONTHS OF THE YEAR

Czechs and Slovaks use completely different words to denote the **months of the year**. While the Slovaks copy the Roman calendar names, Czech uses the highly individual Slav system, in which the names of the month are descriptive nouns – sometimes beautifully apt for the month in question.

Czech

January	*leden* – ice	July	*červenec* – redder
February	*únor* – renewal	August	*srpen* – sickle
March	*březen* – birch	September	*zaří* – blazing
April	*duben* – oak	October	*říjen* – rutting
May	*květen* – blossom	November	*listopad* – leaves falling
June	*červen* – red	December	*prosinec* – slaughter of the pig

Slovak

January	*január*	July	*júl*
February	*február*	August	*august*
March	*marec*	September	*september*
April	*apríl*	October	*október*
May	*máj*	November	*november*
June	*jún*	December	*december*

NUMBERS

0	nula	14	čtrnáct/žtrnásť	90	devadesát/deväťdesiat
1	jeden	15	patnáct/pätnásť	100	sto
2	dva	16	šestnáct/šestnásť	101	sto jedna
3	tři/tri	17	sedmnáct/sedemnásť	155	sto padesát
4	čtyři/štyri	18	osmnáct/osemnásť		pět/stodpäťdesiatpäť
5	pět/päť	19	devatenáct/devätnásť	200	dvě stě/dvesto
6	šest/šesť	20	dvacet/dvadsat	300	tři sta/tristo
7	sedm/sedem	21	dvacetjedna/dvadsaťjeden	400	čtyři sta/štyristo
8	osum/osem	30	třicet/tridsať	500	pět set/päťsto
9	devět/deväť	40	čtyřicet/štyridsať	600	šest set/šesto
10	deset/desať	50	padesát/päťdesiat	700	sedm set/sedemsto
11	jedenáct/jedenásť	60	šedesát/šesťdesiat	800	osum set/osemsto
12	dvanáct/dvanásť	70	sedmdesát/sedemdesiat	900	devět set/devätsto
13	třináct/trinásť	80	osumdesát/osemdesiat	1000	tisíc

VOWEL COMBINATIONS & DIPHTHONGS

There are very few diphthongs in Czech, substantially more in Slovak. Combinations of vowels not mentioned below should be pronounced as two separate syllables.

au like the ou in f**ou**l
ie like the ye in **ye**s
ia like the ya in **ya**k
iu like the u in fl**u**te
ou like the oe in f**oe**

CONSONANTS AND ACCENTS

There are no silent consonants, but it's worth remembering that r and l can form a syllable if standing between two other consonants or at the end of a word, as in Brno (Br–no) or Vltava (Vl–ta–va). The consonants listed below are those that differ substantially from the English. Accents look daunting, but the only one that causes a lot of problems is ř (Czech only), prob-

ably the most difficult letter to say in the entire language – even Czech toddlers have to be taught how to say it.

c like the **ts** in boats
č like the **ch** in chicken
ch like the **ch** in the Scottish loch
ď like the **d** in duped
g always as in goat, never as in general
h always as in have, but more energetic
j like the **y** in yoke
kd pronounced as **gd**
l like the **lli** in colliery
mě pronounced as mnye
ň like the **n** in nuance
p softer than the English p
r as in rip, but often rolled
ř like the sound of **r** and **ž** combined
š like the **sh** in shop
ť like the **t** in tutor
ž like the **s** in pleasure; at the end of a word like the **sh** in shop

AN A–Z OF CZECH AND SLOVAK STREET NAMES

After 1989, most of the streets named after erstwhile stars of the Communist Party disappeared. This was not the first (nor the last) time that the sign writers had put their brushes to use: after World War I, the old Habsburg names were replaced by Czech and Slovak ones; then under the Nazis, the streets were named after Hitler and his cronies, only for the Czech and Slovak names to be reinstated in 1945; while under the Communists, the names were changed once (or twice) more. Since independence in 1993, the Slovaks have expunged a few Czechs and supplanted them with newly rehabilitated Slovak nationalists, and so the process continues. The following names are currently the most popular in the Czech and Slovak republics; remember that street names always appear in the genitive or adjectival form, eg Palacký street as Palackého or Hus street as Husova.

5 května (May 5). The day of the Prague Uprising against the Nazis in 1945.

17 listopadu (November 17). In fact, this street name commemorates the anti-Nazi demonstration of November 17, 1939, after which the Nazis closed down all Czech institutions of higher education. The November 17, 1989 demonstration was held to commemorate the 1939 one, but, after the attack by the police, signalled the beginning of the Velvet Revolution.

28 října (October 28). Anniversary of the foundation of Czechoslovakia in 1918.

29 August. The day the unsuccessful Slovak National Uprising against the Nazis began in 1944.

Beneš, Edvard (1884–1948). Hero to some, traitor to others, Beneš was president from 1935 until 1938, when he resigned, having refused to lead the country into bloodshed over the Munich Crisis, and again from 1945 until 1948, when he acquiesced to the Communist coup.

Bernolák, Anton (1762–1813). Slovak theologian and pioneer in the Slovak written language. Author of the first Slovak dictionary.

Bezruč, Petr (1867–1958). Pen name of the Czech poet Vladimír Vayek, who wrote about the hardships of the Ostrava mining region.

Čapek, Karel (1890–1938). Czech writer, journalist and unofficial spokesperson for the First Republic. His most famous works are *The Insect Play* and *R.U.R.*, which introduced the word robot into the English language.

Čech, Svatopluk (1846–1908). Extreme Czech nationalist and poet whose best-known work is *Songs of a Slave*.

Chelčicky, Petr (born c.1390). Extreme pacifist Hussite preacher who disapproved of the violence of Žižka and his Taborite army.

Dobrovský, Josef (1753–1829). Jesuit-taught pioneer in Czech philology. Wrote the seminal text *The History of Czech Language and Literature*.

Duklianské hrdiny (The Dukla Heroes). The name given to the soldiers who died capturing the Dukla Pass in October 1944, the first decisive battle in the liberation of the country from the Nazis.

Dvořák, Antonín (1841–1904). Perhaps the most famous of all Czech composers, whose best-known work, the *New World Symphony*, was inspired by his extensive sojourn in the USA.

Havlíček-Borovský, Karel (1821–56). Satirical poet, journalist and nationalist, exiled to the Tyrol by the Austrian authorities after 1848.

Hlinka, Andrej (1864–1938). Leader of the Slovak People's Party, which went on to form the government of the Slovak Nazi puppet state.

Hodža, Milan (1878–1944). Slovak politician who was in favour of the establishment of Czechoslovakia, led the Agrarian Party, and served as prime minister for a brief period in the 1930s.

Horáková, Milada (died 1950). Socialist deputy who was killed in the Stalinist purges.

Hurban, Jozef Miroslav (1817–88). Slovak writer and journalist who edited various pioneering Slovak-language journals.

Hus, Jan (1370–1415). Rector of Prague University and reformist preacher who was burnt at the stake as a heretic by the Council of Constance (see p.180).

Hviezdoslav, Pavol Orságh (1849–1921). The father of Slovak poetry, who lived in the Orava region working as a court official until his retirement.

Janáček, Leoš (1854–1928). Moravian-born composer, based in Brno for most of his life, whose operas in particular have become quite widely performed in the West.

Jánošík Fabled Slovak folk hero, modelled along the lines of Robin Hood, who operated in the Malá Fatra range (see p.424).

Jesenský, Janko (1874–1945). Slovak poet who accompanied the Czechoslovak Legion in its long trek across the Russia during the Bolshevik Revolution.

Jirásek, Alois (1851–1930). Writer for both children and adults who popularized Czech legends and became a key figure in the national revival.

Jiříz Poděbrad (1458–71). The only Hussite and last Czech king of Bohemia, better known to the English as George of Poděbrady.

Jungmann, Josef (1773–1847). Prolific Czech translator and author of the seminal *History of Czech Literature* and the first Czech dictionary.

Karl IV (1346–78). Luxembourgeois king of Bohemia and Holy Roman Emperor responsible for Prague's golden age in the fourteenth century. Better known to the English as Charles IV.

Kollár, Ján (1793–1852). Professor of Slav archeology in Vienna and Slovak poet who wrote in Czech and opposed the formation of a separate Slovak written language.

Komenský, Jan Amos (1592–1670). Leader of the Protestant Unity of Czech Brethren. Forced to flee the country and settle in England during the Counter-Reformation. Better known to the English as Comenius.

Kráľ Janko (1822–76). A Slovak poet who wrote folk ballads, while **Fraňo** (1903–55) is a Slovak Communist poet and no relation to the former.

Lidice. Bohemian village outside Prague which fell victim to the Nazis in June 1942 in retaliation for the murder of Reinhard Heydrich: the male inhabitants were shot, the women and children were sent to the camps and the entire place was burnt to the ground.

Mácha, Karel Hynek (1810–36). Romantic nationalist poet and great admirer of Byron and Keats, who, like them, died young. His most famous poem is *Máj*, published just months before his death.

Masaryk, Tomáš Garrigue (1850–1937). Professor of Philosophy at Prague University, President of the Republic (1918–35). His name is synonymous with the First Republic and was removed from all street signs after the 1948 coup. Now back with a vengeance.

Nálepka, Ján (1912–43). Slovak teacher and partisan in World War II who won fame through his daring antics in Nazi-occupied Ukraine, where he eventually died.

Němcová, Božena (1820–62). Highly popular writer who got involved with the nationalist movement and shocked with her unorthodox behaviour. Her most famous book is *Grandmother*.

Neruda, Jan. (1834–91). Poet and journalist for the *Národní listy*. Wrote some famous short stories describing Prague's Malá Strana.

Opletal, Jan. Czech student killed by Nazis in 1939 during anti-Nazi demonstration.

Palach, Jan (1947–69). Philosophy student who committed suicide by self-immolation in protest against the 1968 Soviet invasion.

Palacký, František (1798–1876). Nationalist historian, Czech MP in Vienna and leading figure in the events of 1848.

Pavlov, I.P. (1849–1936). Russian Nobel prize-winning scientist, famous for his experiments on dogs (hence, "Pavlov's dogs"), from which he developed the theory of conditioned reflexes.

Purkyně, Jan Evangelista (1787–1869). Czech doctor, natural scientist and pioneer in experimental physiology who became professor of physiology at Prague and then Wrocław universities.

Ressel, Josef (1793–1857). Fascinatingly enough, the Czech inventor of the screw-propeller.

Rieger, Ladislav. Nineteenth-century Czech politician and one of the leading figures in the events of 1848 and its aftermath.

Šafárik, Pavol Jozef (1795–1861). Slovak scholar and son of a Slovak Lutheran pastor whose major works were actually written in Czech and German.

Sládkovič, Andrej (1820–72). Slovak poet who lived and worked in the Detva region and whose pastoral love poem *Marína* is regarded as a classic.

Smetana, Bedřich (1824–84). Popular Czech composer and fervent nationalist whose *Má vlast* (My Homeland) traditionally opens the Prague Spring Music Festival.

SNP (Slovenské národné povstanie). The ill-fated Slovak National Uprising against the Nazis which took place in August/September 1944.

Sokol (Falcon). Physical education movement founded in 1862 and very much modelled on its German counterpart. The organization was a driving force during the Czech national revival, but was banned by the Nazis and later the Communists.

Štefánik, Milan Rastislav (died 1919). Slovak explorer and fighter pilot who fought and campaigned for Czechoslovakia during World War I.

Štúr, Ľudovít (1815–56). Slovak nationalist who led the 1848 revolt against the Hungarians and argued for a Slovak language distinct from Czech.

Šverma, Jan (died 1941). Joined the Communist Party shortly after its formation in 1921, and died fighting against the Germans.

Generally unpopular, though as a victim of the Nazis he retains a certain respect.

Svoboda, Ludvík (1895–1979). Victorious Czech general from World War II who acquiesced to the 1948 Communist coup and was Communist president during the Prague Spring in 1968 and until 1975.

Tajovský, Jozef Gregor (1874–1940). Slovak dramatist and short-story writer whose moral ethics and identification with the underdog made him a sharp social critic of the times.

Tyl, Josef Kajetán (1808–56). Czech playwright and composer of the Czech national anthem, *Where is my Home?*

Vajanský, Svetozár Hurban (1847–1916). Romantic Slovak novelist whose Russophile views were as unpopular then as now.

Wilson, Woodrow (1856–1924). US president who oversaw the peace settlement after World War I, and was therefore seen by many as one of the founders of Czechoslovakia.

Wolker, Jiří (1900–24). Czech Communist who died of TB aged 24 and whose one volume of poetry was lauded by the Communists as the first truly proletarian writing.

Žižka, Jan (died 1424). Brilliant, blind military leader of the Táborites, the radical faction of the Hussites.

A GLOSSARY OF CZECH AND SLOVAK WORDS AND TERMS

brána gate.

český Bohemian.

chata chalet-type bungalow, country cottage or mountain hut.

chrám large church.

cintorín cemetery (Slovak).

cukrárna/cukáreň pastry shop.

divadlo theatre.

dolina valley (Slovak).

dóm cathedral.

dům/dom house.

dům kultury/dom kúltury communal arts and social centre; literally "house of culture".

hrad castle.

hranice/hranica border.

hřbitov cemetery (Czech).

hora mountain.

hospoda pub.

hostinec pub.

jeskyně/jaskyňa cave.

jezero/jazero lake.

kámen/kameň rock.

kaple/kaplnka chapel.

kaštieľ manor house (Slovak).

katedrála cathedral.

kavárna/kavárieň coffee house.

klášter/kláštor monastery.

kostel/kostol church.

koupaliště/kúpalisko swimming pool.

kúpele spa (Slovak).

Labe River Elbe.

lanovka funicular or cable car.

lázně spa (Czech).

les forest.

město/mesto town; staré město – old town, nové město – new town, dolní město – lower town, horní město – upper town.

moravský Moravian.

most bridge.

nábřeží/nábrežie embankment.

nádraží train station (Czech).

náměstí/námestie square, as in náměstí svobody/námestie slobody – freedom square.

Nisa River Neisse.

Odra River Oder.

ostrov island.

paneláky prefabricated high-rise housing.

památník/pamätník memorial or monument.

pivnice/pivnica pub.

planina valley basin (Slovak).

pleso mountain lake (Slovak).

pramen natural spring.

prohlídka/prehliadka viewpoint.

radnice/radnica town hall.

řeka/rieka river.

restaurace/reštaurácia restaurant.

sad park.

sál room or hall (in a chateau or castle).

schody steps.

sedlo saddle (of a mountain).

skála/skala crag/rock.

skansen/skanzen an open-air folk museum, with reconstructed folk art and architecture.

slovenský Slovak.

stanica train station (Slovak).

staré město/staré mesto old town.

štít peak (Slovak).

svatý/svätý saint – often abbreviated to sv.

teplice spa.

třída/trieda avenue.

ulice/ulica street.

věž/veža tower.

vinárna/vináreň wine bar or cellar.

Vltava River Moldau.

vrchy hills.

vrchovina uplands.

výstava exhibition.

zahrada/záhrada gardens.

zámek/zámok chateau.

AN ARCHITECTURAL GLOSSARY

Ambulatory Passage round the back of the altar, in continuation of the aisles.

Art Nouveau Sinuous and stylized form of architecture and decorative arts. Imported from Vienna and Budapest from 1900–10 and therefore known in Czechoslovakia as the Secession rather than Jugendstil, the German term.

Baroque Expansive, exuberant architectural style of the seventeenth and mid-eighteenth centuries, characterized by ornate decoration, complex spatial arrangement and grand vistas.

Beautiful Style Also known as the Soft Style of painting. Developed in Bohemia in the fourteenth century, it became very popular in Germany.

Chancel Part of the church where the altar is placed, usually at the east end.

Empire A highly decorative Neoclassical style of architecture and decorative arts practised in the first part of the nineteenth century.

Fresco Mural painting applied to wet plaster, so that the colours immediately soak into the wall.

Functionalism Plain, boxy, modernist architectural style, prevalent in the late 1920s and 1930s in Czechoslovakia, often using plateglass curtain walls and open-plan interiors.

Gothic Architectural style prevalent from the twelfth to the sixteenth century, characterized by pointed arches and ribbed vaulting.

Loggia Covered area on the side of a building, often arcaded.

Nave Main body of a church, usually the western end.

Neoclassical Late eighteenth- and early nineteenth-century style of architecture and design returning to classical Greek and Roman models as a reaction against Baroque and Rococo excesses.

Oriel A bay window, usually projecting from an upper floor.

Predella Small panel below the main scenes of an altarpiece.

Romanesque Solid architectural style of the late tenth to thirteenth centuries, characterized by round-headed arches and geometrical precision.

Rococo Highly florid, fiddly though (occasionally) graceful style of architecture and interior design, forming the last phase of Baroque.

Secession Style of early-twentieth-century art and architecture based in Germany and Austria and a reaction against the academic establishment (see also "Art Nouveau").

Sgraffito Monochrome plaster decoration effected by means of scraping back the first white layer to reveal the black underneath.

Shingle Wooden roof tiles.

Stucco Plaster used for decorative effects.

Trompe l'oeil Painting designed to fool the onlooker into believing that it is actually three-dimensional.

Tympanum Area above doorway or within a pediment.

HISTORICAL AND POLITICAL TERMS

Czech Lands A phrase used to denote Bohemia and Moravia.

First Republic The new Czechoslovak Republic founded by Masaryk after World War II, made up of Bohemia, Moravia, Silesia, Slovakia and Ruthenia, dismantled by the Nazis in 1930–39.

Great Moravian Empire The first Slav state covering much of what is now Czechoslovakia, which ended shortly after the Magyar invasion of 896 AD.

Greek-Catholic Church Formed from various breakaways from the Eastern (Orthodox) Church in the sixteenth century, the Greek-Catholic Church retains many Orthodox practices and rituals but is affiliated to the Roman Catholic Church. Also known as the Uniate Church.

Habsburgs The most powerful royal family in central Europe, whose power base was Vienna. They held the Bohemian and Hungarian thrones from 1526 to 1918, and by marriage and diplomacy acquired territories all over Europe.

Historic Provinces Land traditionally belonging to the Bohemian crown, including Bohemia, Egerland, Moravia, Silesia and Lusatia.

Holy Roman Empire Name given to the loose confederation of German states (including for a while the Czech Lands) which lasted from 800 until 1806.

Hussites Name given to Czech religious reformers who ostensibly followed the teachings of Jan Hus (1370–1415).

Jagiellonians Polish-Lithuanian dynasty who ruled the Czech Lands from 1471 to 1526.

Magyars The people who ruled over the Hungarian Kingdom and now predominate in modern-day Hungary.

Mitteleuropa Literally German for "central Europe", but it also conveys the idea of a multi-lingual central European culture, lost after the break-up of the Habsburg Empire.

Národní fronta Literally the National Front, the dummy coalition of parties dominated by the Communists which ruled the country until December 1989.

Národní obrození/národné obrodenie Czech/Slovak "national revival" movements of the nineteenth century, which sought to rediscover the lost identities of the Czech and Slovak people, particularly their history and language.

Přemyslid The dynasty of Czech princes and kings who ruled over the Historic Lands of Bohemia from the ninth century to 1306.

Ruthenia Officially Sub-Carpatho-Ruthenia, the easternmost province of the First Republic, annexed by the Soviet Union at the end of World War II.

Sudetenland Name given to mostly German-speaking border regions of the Czech Lands, awarded to Nazi Germany in the Munich Diktat of September 1938.

Velvet Revolution The popular protests of November/December 1989 which brought an end to 41 years of Communist rule. Also known as the Gentle Revolution.

ABBREVIATIONS

CKM (Cestovní kanceláu mládeže) Youth Travel Organization.

ČEDOK Former state travel and tourist agency in Czech Republic.

ČD (České dráhy) Czech Railways.

ČSAD (Česká státní automobilová doprava) Czech state bus company.

HDĽS Andrej Hlinka's Slovak People's Party, the largest political party in Slovakia between the wars, and later the leading political force in the wartime clerico-fascist state.

HZDS Movement for a Democratic Slovakia.

KSČ (Komunistická strana Československá) The Czechoslovak Communist Party (now defunct).

KSČM Communist Party of Bohemia and Moravia.

ODS (Občanská demokratická strana) Civic Democratic Party – right-wing faction of Civic Forum.

SAD (Slovenská automobilová doprava) Slovak bus company.

SATUR Former state travel and tourist agency in Slovakia.

SdP Sudeten German Party (Sudetendeutsche Partei), the main proto-Nazi Party in Czechoslovakia in the late 1930s.

SNS (Slovenská národná strana) Slovak National Party – extremist Slovak nationalists.

StB (Státní bezpečnost) The Communist secret police (now disbanded).

ŽSR (Železnice Slovenskej republiky) Slovak Railways.

INDEX

Stay in touch with us!

ROUGH*NEWS* is Rough Guides' free newsletter. In four issues a year we give you news, travel issues, music reviews, readers' letters and the latest dispatches from authors on the road.

I would like to receive ROUGH*NEWS*: please put me on your free mailing list.

NAME . . . .

ADDRESS . . . .

Please clip or photocopy and send to: Rough Guides, 62–70 Shorts Gardens, London WC2H 9AB, England or Rough Guides, 375 Hudson Street, New York, NY 10014, USA.

IF KNOWLEDGE IS POWER, THIS ROUGH GUIDE IS A POCKET-SIZED BATTERING RAM

YOU NEED THIS BOOK!
The Times

The **Internet**
THE ROUGH GUIDE 2000
Angus J. Kennedy

THE BESTSELLING GUIDE FOR PCS AND MACS

£6.00
US$9.95

Written in plain English, with no hint of jargon, the Rough Guide to the Internet will make you an Internet guru in the shortest possible time. It cuts through the hype and makes all others look like nerdy textbooks

AT ALL BOOKSTORES • DISTRIBUTED BY PENGUIN

www.roughguides.com

Check out our Web site for unrivalled travel information on the Internet.
Plan ahead by accessing the full text of our major titles, make travel reservations and keep up to date with the latest news in the Traveller's Journal or by subscribing to our free newsletter ROUGH*NEWS* · packed with stories from Rough Guide writers.

ROUGH GUIDES: Travel

Amsterdam
Andalucia
Australia

Austria
Bali & Lombok
Barcelona
Belgium &
  Luxembourg
Belize
Berlin
Brazil
Britain
Brittany &
  Normandy
Bulgaria
California
Canada
Central America
Chile
China
Corfu & the
  Ionian Islands
Corsica
Costa Rica
Crete
Croatia
Cyprus
Czech & Slovak
  Republics
Dodecanese &
  the East Aegean

Dominican
  Republic
Ecuador
Egypt
England
Europe
Florida
France
French Hotels &
  Restaurants
  1999
Germany
Goa
Greece
Greek Islands
Guatemala
Hawaii
Holland
Hong Kong &
  Macau
Hungary
India
Indonesia
Ireland
Israel & the
  Palestinian
  Territories
Italy
Jamaica
Japan
Jordan

Kenya
Lake District
Laos
London
Los Angeles
Malaysia,
  Singapore &
  Brunei
Mallorca &
  Menorca
Maya World
Mexico
Morocco
Moscow
Nepal
New England
New York
New Zealand
Norway
Pacific
  Northwest
Paris
Peru
Poland
Portugal
Prague
Provence & the
  Côte d'Azur
The Pyrenees
Rhodes & the
  Dodecanese

Romania
St Petersburg
San Francisco
Sardinia
Scandinavia
Scotland
Scottish
  highlands and
  Islands
Sicily
Singapore
South Africa
South India
Southwest USA
Spain
Sweden
Syria

Thailand
Trinidad &
  Tobago
Tunisia
Turkey
Tuscany &
  Umbria
USA
Venice
Vienna
Vietnam
Wales
Washington DC
West Africa
Zimbabwe &
  Botswana

AVAILABLE AT ALL GOOD BOOKSHOPS

ROUGH GUIDES: Mini Guides, Travel Specials and Phrasebooks

MINI GUIDES
Antigua
Bangkok
Barbados
Big Island of
  Hawaii
Boston
Brussels
Budapest

Dublin
Edinburgh
Florence
Honolulu
Jerusalem
Lisbon
London
  Restaurants
Madrid
Maui
Melbourne
New Orleans
Rome
Seattle
St Lucia

Sydney
Tokyo
Toronto

TRAVEL SPECIALS
First-Time Asia
First-Time
  Europe
Women Travel

PHRASEBOOKS
Czech
Dutch

Egyptian Arabic
European
French
German
Greek
Hindi & Urdu
Hungarian
Indonesian
Italian
Japanese

Mandarin
  Chinese
Mexican
  Spanish
Polish
Portuguese
Russian
Spanish
Swahili
Thai
Turkish
Vietnamese

AVAILABLE AT ALL GOOD BOOKSHOPS

Est.1852

World Travel starts at Stanfords

Maps, Travel Guides, Atlases, Charts
Mountaineering Maps and Books, Travel Writing
Travel Accessories, Globes & Instruments

Stanfords
12-14 Long Acre
Covent Garden
London
WC2E 9LP

Stanfords
at Campus Travel
52 Grosvenor Gardens
London
SW1W 0AG

Stanfords
at British Airways
156 Regent Street
London
W1R 5TA

Stanfords in Bristol
29 Corn Street
Bristol
BS1 1HT

International Mail Order Service
Tel: 0171 836 1321 **Fax**: 0171 836 0189

The World's Finest Map and Travel Bookshops